To Barbara and Lyle, with many thanks for your wonderful hospitality, and with best wishes

Joe Walt
10 Febr 1996

Beneath the Whispering Maples: The History of Simpson College

Joseph W. Walt

Simpson College Press
Indianola, Iowa
1995

The Simpson College Press, Indianola 50125
© 1995 by The Simpson College Press
All rights reserved

First edition published 1995
Printed in the United States of America

First printing

ISBN (cloth) 0-9642656-0-5

Contents

Preface		vii
Prologue		xi
1	The Beginnings: 1860	1
2	The Seminary: 1860–67	13
3	Simpson Centenary College: 1867–75	31
4	Lessons in Survival: 1875–78	71
5	A College Saved: 1878–80	89
6	Out of the Ashes: 1880–86	99
7	The Builders: 1886–90	127
8	Simpson in the Nineties: 1890–99	145
9	The Shelton Years: 1899–1910	181
10	Simpson in Peace and War: 1910–19	211
11	The Good Years: Simpson in the Twenties: 1919–30	251
12	The Lean Years: 1930–36	299
13	The Prewar Years: 1936–41	327
14	Simpson in the Second World War: 1941–45	371
15	Simpson's Postwar Boom: 1945–50	391
16	Korea and Simpson's Time of Troubles: 1950–53	421
17	Simpson's Renaissance: The Kerstetter Years: 1953–63	443
18	Ralph John and the Democratization of Simpson: 1963–68	509
19	The Student Revolt: 1968–75	555
20	Collegiality and Consternation: 1975–79	605
21	From Strength to Strength: 1979–87	637
Epilogue		695
Photo Sections follow pages		94
		254
		478
		606
Bibliography		701
Notes		711
Index		823

To

*Bill and Leona Kerstetter
who took a chance on a
young historian, who led him to
appreciate—and to love—a
liberal arts college they had transformed,
and whose lasting friendship will be cherished
forever.*

Preface

This history of Simpson College has been a long time in the making. In the spring of 1984, as the College neared its 125th anniversary, I was asked by President Robert E. McBride to research and write the story of Simpson. He said he hoped the project could be completed within a year so that its publication could coincide with the College's quasquicentennial, but both of us knew that it would surely take longer than a year to produce. How much longer, neither of us could have guessed. Ten summers later, the manuscript is finally completed. I say "summers" because during the regular school year my teaching schedule and other academic obligations prevented my devoting much time to the history.

I was not the first to attempt to write the history of Simpson. In 1955, not long after I came to the College straight out of graduate school at Northwestern University, I made the acquaintance of Francis I. Moats, the grand old man of the campus and longtime head of the History Department, who had retired only two years earlier. He told me he was trying to put together a history of Simpson, but he despaired of ever finishing the research, much less writing it. The College's archives for the early years, he explained, were virtually nonexistent. A disastrous fire in 1918 had destroyed nearly everything. A conscientious historian, Moats could not find enough documentation to justify creating a manuscript, and reluctantly he abandoned the project.

In 1960, on the occasion of Simpson's centennial, President William E. Kerstetter asked Ruth Jackson, whose teaching career at the College went back to 1923, to take up Dr. Moats's project. She accepted the challenge, went to work with a will, gathering from many sources, principally alumni, reminiscences, pictures and memorabilia of all sorts, constituting an invaluable trove of information. But in an effort to produce a manuscript, she encountered the same paucity of information that had confronted Moats. She was still searching for many missing pieces when she died in 1969.

Because I was aware of the problems that had stalled the serious efforts of my two predecessors, I should have gracefully declined the honor of being named the College historian, but for reasons I still do not understand, I did not.

We did have a few sources. The board of trustees minutes had been mercifully saved from the 1918 fire because they were locked in a vault in the law office of the board president in downtown Indianola. Moats and Jackson and others had been able to assemble a collection of nearly all the College's catalogs, a virtually complete run of both the *Simpsonian* (since 1870) and the *Zenith* yearbook (since 1896), and copies of alumni publications. These were all valuable, but they did not provide an account of the day-to-day operation of the College, a glimpse of the people who ran it, who taught in it or who attended it. Too much of the story was missing.

Then, quite fortuitously, because of my involvement in the State Historical Society of Iowa, I discovered the incredibly near-complete collection of Iowa newspapers held in the library and archives of the Society, both in Des Moines and Iowa City. Could one, I wondered, find much of value in these crumbling newspapers? Did old Indianola newspapers hold the treasure that for so long had eluded us? I went to Des Moines to find out. With a mixture of hope and fear I picked up the oldest Indianola papers I could find, the *Indianola Republican* and the *Weekly Iowa Visitor* from the 1850s and 1860s. I was thunderstruck when I discovered that the story of Simpson was there, from a front page story of the school's founding in 1860 to accounts of all its struggles and triumphs.

The golden ore of history was there, but those newspapers gave up their hidden treasure only grudgingly. Only those who have searched through thousands of pages of old newspapers can know how tedious and time-consuming is the effort. There are files of twenty-two different Indianola newspapers, whose politics ranged from archconservative to radical populist and whose accounts of the College—the biggest show in town—were colored by their editors' social and political views. Often there were as many as four weekly newspapers in Indianola, all of which reported College events, the comings and goings of faculty and the ups and downs of Simpson's early and middle years. Without these newspapers, I could not have written the history of the College.

I am aware of the risks of using newspaper accounts. Written under the pressure of time and with limited access to people and events, these newspaper stories can be inaccurate, incomplete and subjective. But used judiciously, they can be enormously valuable. As Lucy Maynard Salmon has written, "The periodical press still remains the most important single source the historian has at his command for the reconstruction of the life of the past three centuries."[1] In any case, reconstructing the story of Simpson College would have been impossible without the Indianola press.

The result of my efforts is a long story, for I could not bear to leave out many details that lend substance and color to the narrative. All this is in keeping with what has become something of a tradition: there is an inverse relationship between the size of a college or university and the number of pages required to tell its story. And there is a reason for this. In the narrative of Simpson's past, we include not only the major educational developments at the College in the context of the times in which they take place; we also attempt to tell the story of people—of presidents, board members, faculty and students. For in a small college one has the luxury of caring about individuals and groups who have put the stamp of their personalities on the institution in ways seldom seen in the large university.

In compiling the record of Simpson, I have had the assistance of many colleagues, friends, students and alumni. Both Presidents Robert E. McBride and Stephen G. Jennings have lent support and encouragement—and patience—to the project chapter by chapter. Three living ex-presidents, William E. Kerstetter, Ralph C. John and Richard B. Lancaster, have provided thorough and candid written recollections of their time at Simpson. I am grateful to administrator David Crosson, archivist Gordon Hendrickson and the library staff of the State Historical Society of Iowa for their generous assistance. And through the years I have been privileged to have the help of a number of student assistants, whose efforts on behalf of this history are deeply appreciated: Tammy Bernard Rapp, Nancy Chihak Kirkendall, Sarah Minor, Tom Wright, Trish Winter, Brian Schultes, Lynn Ochiltree, James Haddox, Chad Simpson and Chris Davidson. For the copying of a large number of photographs, I should like to thank Mike Mathias, and for his general oversight of the project, I am grateful to Simpson's director of public relations, Michael Adams. For his everlasting interest and encouragement, I am indebted to Dean Melvin Henderson more than he can ever know. And the task was easier because of the support of Owen Duncan, historian and understanding colleague, who put up with my inordinate enthusiasm for digging into Simpson's past, and my old friend Terry Hoy, who kept me in good humor. And it is hard to imagine what I could have done without the unquestioning and enthusiastic assistance of Cyd Dyer, Simpson's librarian and archivist, together with Michael Wright and all the library staff. I want to thank Tom Morain of Living History Farms, who read the entire manuscript and whose comments and suggestions were helpful beyond measure. And many thanks to Simpson Alumni Director Kay Lebeda, who also read the manuscript with a keen eye. The thoroughly professional editing by Russell and Barbara Tabbert rescued me from innumerable illiteracies, misjudgments and other vain errors. For their suggestions I am deeply grateful, and for any remaining errors or inconsistencies I am alone responsible. Finally, boundless thanks are due for the careful, thoroughly competent typing of the entire manuscript by Helen Strovers, head of Simpson's Faculty Services Center, whose exacting standards and everlasting good humor were a delight. She was ably assisted by Darlene Day. When Helen Strovers retired, the finishing touches were put on by Becky Beaman and Linda Sinclair.

Prologue

Simpson College is a child of the nineteenth-century American frontier. It was born of the efforts of early settlers to blend Christian evangelism and practical needs.

It is not, and never has sought to be, a transplanted New England college. Not only were its founders not "Easterners." It was their intention to create an educational institution that met the specific needs of a particular people in a particular place. These people were recent arrivals on the frontier. They brought with them from Ohio or Indiana or Kentucky or wherever they came from a blend of sturdy individualism and egalitarianism, together with an intense, almost naive, faith in the value of education.

When the College was founded in 1860, Warren County and the town of Indianola were only eleven years old. Yet in that brief period settlers had poured in from the East. The U.S. census of 1860 counted 10,281 in Warren County and 836 in the town of Indianola, which was incorporated only three years later.[1]

As settlers started to break the sod, it was already difficult to remember that less than a score of years earlier this great, quiet, empty land had been the exclusive hunting preserve of the Indians, most recently the Sac and Mesquakie tribes. These Native Americans, whose ancestors had lived in harmony with their environment for millennia, caught fish in its streams and hunted in its woods and boundless prairies, until the inexorable advance of the white man across the continent drove them from Iowa into the marginal lands of the Kansas country and beyond.

The first white settler in what would become Warren County was a Vermonter named John D. Parmelee, who came this way in 1843 and built a sawmill on Middle River about three miles above its confluence with the Des Moines River. Only a handful of people followed, for it was only on October 11, 1845, that the U.S. treaty with the Sac and Mesquakie threw open for settlement the territory between the Red Rocks on the Des Moines River and the lands of the Sioux and the Potawatomi far to the west.

When the county was organized and the county seat selected, the site of Indianola was carefully chosen. Not far from the center of the county between South River and Middle River was a broad shelf of gently rolling, treeless land covered with deep prairie grass as far as the eye could see. Here in 1849 surveyors laid out the town around a large square on which would be erected a courthouse. Soon settlers arrived, a makeshift courthouse was put up and Indianola, named for a Texas port town, began an orderly growth.

The location of the town could hardly have been more happily chosen. One visitor from afar described its setting in early 1856: "The site of Indianola is unsurpassed in the West. When I first came within viewing distance, I was struck with the magnificence of its perspective. . . . No more grandly beautiful scope of country can be found on the green earth, in its natural shape, just as it fell from its Maker's hand, than that of which Indianola is the center."[2]

By 1860, the town square was only partly surrounded by shops and professional offices, most of them temporary, jerry-built wooden structures not unlike those familiar to later generations in Western movies. The north side of the square was still almost entirely vacant. Soon enough the rude buildings would be replaced by sturdy two- and three-story brick business blocks. Wooden one- or two-story residences of the town dwellers sprawled beyond the square for two or three blocks in all directions. Trees had been planted, and a few were beginning to provide a bit of welcome shade on hot, humid summer days. The streets, laid out on a grid and nowhere paved, were dusty in the summer, hard-frozen and rutty in the winter, and too often a mire of mud in the spring and fall. Because Indianola was not yet incorporated and provided no municipal services, few public improvements had been made. There were only a few plank boardwalks around a part of the square.

Still, it was a flourishing community, a market town for the surrounding countryside. Most business establishments and churches were located either on the square or immediately along the streets leading away from it. In 1860 one could find eleven general merchants, a hardware merchant, a druggist, five carriage and wagon makers, three millers and two grocers, one banker, one jeweler, one newspaper publisher (the *Weekly Indianola Visitor*), two printers, two livestock traders, a daguerreotype artist, a hotel keeper, an engineer, a baker and a butcher. Professionals included no fewer than twelve attorneys, the postmaster, four clergymen (three of them Methodists), four physicians and thirteen teachers in the common schools. The town's artisans were perhaps typical of a small town in the West in 1860: a gunsmith, a cooper, four cabinetmakers, fifteen carpenters, eight blacksmiths, four plasterers, a mason, a stonecutter, a tinner, a millwright, two painters, three saddlers, four shoemakers and two tailors. The town boasted only a single barber, but there were two stage drivers and two postmen. Two women were engaged in the business of making and selling women's hats, and two other women worked in their homes as seamstresses. And eight women took in laundry. One man, a certain James Bryan, reported that his occupation was that of "gentleman."

* * *

Warren County settlers had scarcely broken the prairie sod and built their first rude habitations when they started to plan for the educational needs of their children. In the earliest years of settlement in the rolling hills and broad valleys of Warren County—they liked to call it the Three Rivers Country—the new farmers and townspeople created public elementary schools both in town and in the rural areas. Called common schools, these tiny centers dispensed—usually with only one teacher—a simple primary education aimed at developing basic literacy and numeracy and inculcating the ideals of patriotism, clean living and the worthwhileness of hard work.

Soon, however, the burgeoning population of farmers and townspeople saw the need for education beyond the common school, and decided they must provide a secondary school, maybe someday even a college. The townspeople were the ones who took the lead. These were a sober, law-abiding, industrious people. A "hopeful feature about Indianola is its generally correct morals," wrote an observer during the town's early years. It was already acquiring "a reputation for being a decidedly upright, temperate and religious place."[3]

It should have been. Many of the town's leading citizens were Methodists, and Methodists in 1860 were a pious lot. The domination of Indianola by Methodists was hardly unusual in Iowa. Uniquely well suited by temperament and organization to preaching the gospel on the frontier, Methodist circuit riders had been the first clergymen to enter Iowa after the Blackhawk Purchase and in 1834 erected the first church building in Iowa, a simple log structure in Dubuque. Their experience in frontier evangelism served them well in Iowa, and in hellfire sermons Methodist preachers exhorted their charges to repent their sins. By 1860 Iowa Methodists, like their co-religionists elsewhere in America, were deeply committed to education and were establishing colleges and secondary schools in large numbers. Their enthusiasm for schools, however, was scarcely a generation old. They came late to the business. In fact, the Methodists were one of the last American denominations to embrace education as an important mission of the church. The reasons for this delay are not hard to find.

Early American Methodists, fired by evangelical zeal to win souls for Christ, were for the most part indifferent, even hostile, to higher education. Consciously antirationalistic and antiintellectual, they had a taste for passionate preaching and a rich diet of emotionalism, supernaturalism and Biblical literalism. Few of them had even a rudimentary education. Most were poor, the "unlettered, forgotten men and women of their time."[4]

When the Christmas Conference met at Baltimore in 1784 to establish the Methodist Episcopal Church in America, surely Thomas Coke was the only liberally educated man present among the founders. Even Francis Asbury, the first Methodist bishop consecrated in America, possessed only a common school education. What mattered most to him and to other Methodists was the inward experience of regeneration and preaching the gospel to the unconverted. Education could wait.

The first Methodist Discipline adopted in 1785 put it plainly: "I would rather throw by all the Libraries in the World rather than be guilty for the Loss of one Soul."[5] After all, had not John Wesley said "Gaining knowledge is a good thing, but saving souls is better"?[6] And in their eagerness to save souls, there was among these first Methodists a powerful sense of urgency.

They saved a lot of souls. As Methodist circuit riders ranged out from the Atlantic seaboard into rustic frontier communities, they reaped a harvest of converts among the rude, untutored backwoodsmen and farmers. It mattered little that the evangelists' English wasn't very good. Besides, they didn't have any books, for they could little afford them. It was a rough and dangerous life.

In the more settled region along the east coast, Methodist leaders did make one perhaps premature start in education in 1787, when they organized Cokesbury College at Abingdon, Maryland, twenty-four miles from Baltimore, the cradle of American Methodism.[7] Poor management and inadequate financial support forced the founders to close the collegiate department in 1794, and the elementary and secondary departments continued only a year more, whereupon the school building burned. Resuscitated in Baltimore, the school lasted one more year, until another fire finished it off for good. Thus ended for a time the Methodist effort to establish institutions of education. The disastrous Cokesbury fires, according to the account of M. L. Scudder, were interpreted by Bishop Asbury and the church generally "as a providential indication that God did not design that Methodists should devote their energies on behalf of education." They might support a few common schools, but many feared that "if they encouraged intellectual culture, they would find it disastrous to the spirituality and purity of the church."[8] However clear the waters in the stream of knowledge, they could erode the virgin soil of faith.

During the next four decades the church did very little to foster higher education. Rather it was caught up in its evangelizing mission. And in this enterprise the preachers of the gospel were incredibly successful. Methodist membership fairly exploded. In 1789, the year George Washington assumed the presidency, there were only 10,539 Methodists in the United States. By 1816, the year Bishop Asbury died, the number had increased to 214,235, and by 1830 it reached nearly half a million. A large share of the new members came from the frontier regions in the West, where the church continued to grow by leaps and bounds. Whether in their churches or in outdoor revival meetings, charismatic Methodist preachers proclaimed the gospel, won converts to evangelical Christianity, wrestled with the devil, whose evil power was an indubitable reality, transformed lives through the fire of the spirit, inspired the weak with visions of a blessed hereafter and condemned the wicked to an eternity of hellfire and damnation. Beyond doubt, the Methodist movement was the religious success story of the nineteenth century. By the time of the outbreak of the Civil War, it was the largest Protestant church in America.[9]

As late as 1830 there was not a single surviving Methodist college in America and only a handful of Methodist-sponsored elementary or secondary schools. Meanwhile, other churches, both Catholic and Protestant, had been seeing to the establishment of colleges and universities. In addition to the nine colonial universities that had been founded between 1636 and 1769, sixteen more were founded before 1800. Still another twenty-four permanent institutions of higher learning—seventeen of which were denominational—were created between 1800 and 1830.[10]

In all fairness, it should be pointed out that Methodists were by no means alone in their disinclination to establish colleges and universities. Much the same reluctance prevailed among Baptists, Disciples of Christ, Quakers, United Brethren and Universalists. All of them were indifferent toward higher education for the laity and positively opposed to it for the clergy. Methodists, in particular, resisted the creation of theological schools, fearing "the danger of speculation" and the intrusion of secular learning.[11]

By 1830, however, conditions were changing. The church was growing rapidly, and with that growth came an increased interest in education. Not only did the number of Methodists increase; the wealth and social position of many of its members grew. Earlier, in the eighteenth century, Methodists had attracted the poor and the uneducated; the affluent and educated were already in other churches or in no church at all. But in the mid-nineteenth century, as the church moved west with the frontier, evangelists converted men and women who either possessed wealth or would soon acquire it. With their increasing affluence, Methodists were seen to be gaining social respectability and exercising community leadership, but many in their clergy, innocent of even a modest liberal education, were ill-prepared to satisfy the needs of many of their parishioners or to compete with the educated clergy of some of the other denominations. Too often dismissed as unlettered country bumpkins, Methodist ministers found their revivalist tactics less effective than they had once been, and their congregations were sometimes frankly embarrassed. With scorn they were asked, "Do you think to teach the people, who have yourselves no knowledge?" Clergymen answered that they didn't know many books, but they knew *one* book. Still, they were stung by this opprobrium. As Lyman Beecher had pointed out some years earlier, "Religion is the last thing that should be committed to the hands of ignorant and incompetent men."[12] Or, as *Zion's Herald* complained, too many Methodists "have declaimed more and more loudly against learning, and a learned ministry, than against human depravity."[13]

Worse yet, too many Methodist youths were turning to other denominations for their education because Methodists offered them none. Many of these young people became permanently alienated from Methodism, and some of them became clergymen in other churches. The church risked losing the new generation.[14] It was clearly time for a change.

As early as 1820 a general conference of the church had recommended, after fierce debate, that Methodist conferences establish "literary institutions" as soon as practicable, and it permitted for the first time the assignment of clergymen to preside over these schools. Soon a few secondary schools were established, but no college or university, for there was still opposition to the "pretensions" of classical education. Built upon English models, colleges and universities in America taught a range of subjects based primarily on the classical languages, Greek and Latin—and a little Hebrew. With the classical languages, students could read natural and moral philosophy, mathematics, logic and rhetoric, even natural science. It was a curriculum drawn from medieval and Renaissance models, aristocratic and humanistic. It was the proper education for the professional, the arbiter of society, the gentleman. And it horrified some of the evangelical religious leaders, including a lot of Methodists. Would not such learning deflect the church from its evangelical mission?

Apparently not, decided the church's general conference in 1824, where the idea of education was well received. In 1830, the first Methodist college to survive into the twentieth century, Randolph-Macon, was established at Ashland, Virginia. The next year two eastern conferences joined forces to found Wesleyan University in Middletown, Connecticut and Wesleyan soon became a major force in validating among some suspicious Methodists the importance of liberal higher education as a proper mission of the church.[15] In 1833 and 1834 Methodists gained control of Dickinson College and Allegheny College, both founded by others in 1783 and 1815 respectively. These early colleges were so successful that most of the opposition to higher education abated rapidly.

In fact, once Methodists started founding colleges, they seemed unable to stop. It appeared as if they were making up for lost time. Between 1830 and 1861 the churches of America established 133 permanent colleges and universities. Thirty-two of these, nearly a quarter, were Methodist.[16] Among these was the first college for women in America, Wesleyan College at Macon, Georgia, originally called Georgia Female College when it was founded in 1836 and acquired by the Methodists in 1839.

During these years Methodists were also establishing dozens of academies and "seminaries" to prepare students for college-level work or for industrial pursuits.

While many of the colleges grew and flourished, not all of those established were properly managed or funded, and a number of them soon passed out of existence. An even greater number of academies and seminaries failed. Only about a quarter of those founded after 1830 were still in existence by the time of the outbreak of the Civil War. The mortality rate was appalling.

Of the thirty-four antebellum colleges established by Methodists, three were in Iowa. Iowa Wesleyan at Mount Pleasant was founded in 1842 as the Literary Institute. A secondary academy in its early years, it took the name Iowa Wesleyan in 1855 and awarded its first B.A. in 1856. Cornell College at Mount Vernon was first called the Iowa Conference Male and Female Seminary in 1853, but was raised to collegiate grade under the name of Cornell only two years later. Upper Iowa College at Fayette was chartered as early as 1850, but instruction did not commence until 1857, and the first B.A. was awarded five years after that.[17]

* * *

What happened in Methodist education and in Indianola were but pieces in the colorful mosaic of American cultural development. As the American frontier moved westward during the nineteenth century, settlers established schools for their children. The first school in Iowa opened in 1830 in a ten-by-twelve-foot log cabin in the Half-breed Tract in Lee County, three years before the Blackhawk Purchase opened eastern Iowa to white settlement. This and the other earliest schools were private, supported by the parents of the pupils. When Iowa became a territory in 1838, Governor Robert Lucas called for the creation of common schools, at least one in each county, supported by public funds. Only sixteen years later, in 1854, one could count 859 public schoolhouses in Iowa with 1,339 teachers and several thousand pupils.[18]

The rapid growth of the elementary common school in Iowa was a consequence of the new settlers' belief that education of the young served the needs of an agrarian democracy, that it confirmed and intensified national identity and that it improved society. In his 1854 address to the Iowa Senate, Governor James W. Grimes put this faith succinctly when he said, "Education is the best preventive of pauperism and crime."[19]

Meanwhile, the new state of Iowa, admitted to the Union in 1846, looked almost immediately to the establishment of a public university. Accordingly, in 1847 the University of Iowa was chartered, although it did not open to students until the spring of 1855. And when the first students arrived, it was clear that most of them were ill prepared to undertake college level academic work. Herein lay a major problem in American education. The citizenry was eager to create public common—and later graded—schools and also universities, but it long declined to fill the gap between the two.

In 1855, the year the University of Iowa opened, there existed not one public high school in the state. Hence the university created a preparatory department, for "there was no place in the public school system where a student might prepare himself to enter the University."[20] Although as early as 1849 legislation had permitted Iowa communities to organize publicly supported "union schools" which would provide instruction beyond the common schools, none had yet ventured to essay secondary education. As late as 1861, the University of Iowa counted among its 254 students only 21 of collegiate grade.[21]

In 1856, the first attempts at public high school instruction were undertaken at Tipton and Grinnell, although both seem to have been more nearly informal secondary-level work attached to the elementary program. In a few other places "instruction in the higher branches" was tacked on to graded elementary schools.[22] When people in Indianola went about the creation of their seminary in 1860, there was not one fully operative four-year public high school in the state.

Secondary education in Iowa during the mid-nineteenth century was the province of the private academy or seminary, some secular and some denominational.[23] A few struggling colleges existed, but their college-level students were few. Only Cornell, Iowa College (Grinnell), Iowa Wesleyan and the University of Iowa had granted bachelors degrees before 1860, and only a handful of these. Nearly all of the colleges were in fact first established as private secondary schools, and most of them maintained their preparatory departments well into the twentieth century. Without these prep students, few of the colleges would have survived.

L. F. Parker has called the years between 1870 and 1880 "the high school decade" in Iowa, for during that time a number of public high schools were created.[24] The Indianola high school opened in the fall of 1871. By 1875 there were forty-one high schools in the state, although only fifteen of them had "well-defined courses of study" capable of preparing students for college-level work.[25] Until the 1880s, more college entrants in Iowa still came from preparatory departments than from public high schools.

Later, as the number of high schools increased, most of the private academies declined, and one by one, most of them closed. By 1906 not more than twenty-four survived. The greatest blow to the surviving academies came in 1911 when the Iowa General Assembly passed legislation providing for state support of tuition for all students attending public schools outside their home district. Simpson's academy was among the most durable, lasting until 1925.

It is no surprise, then, that most of Iowa's present-day colleges were founded as academies or seminaries, upgrading their status to the college level as soon as the number of qualified students permitted it. Thus it is understandable why pioneer Indianola citizens, seeking to improve the level of education in their town, in 1860 undertook first to organize an academy that might, with hard work and a lot of luck, someday become a college. They really had no other choice.

I

The Beginnings 1860

For little Indianola, Iowa, it was an extraordinary gathering. A handful of the town's leading citizens, uncomfortable in their high collars and dark suits, assembled promptly at eight o'clock on a sweltering summer evening. They made their way into the sanctuary of the new Methodist Episcopal Church—the building, the only brick structure of its kind in town, had been dedicated only four years earlier—and took their seats in the sturdy oak pews up front nearest the pulpit. They were met to launch an educational enterprise they could only hope might succeed. None of them could be certain what might come of their venture, but they were determined to give it their best effort. It was Wednesday, August 1, 1860. Hardly a breath of air stirred.

The meeting was called to order by dapper Dr. Hezekiah Fisk, the respected young physician whose flourishing practice on the south side of the square was heralded in the local press with confidence-building assurances: "All diseases treated on the most Scientific Principles. Eleven years successful practice in all diseases common to the West."[1] Fisk was a pioneer; he had arrived in Indianola back in 1850 when the town was but a few months old. His interest in education had been kindled when he taught the first common school in Indianola during the winter of 1850 in a house put up by M. R. Barker. That was the same year Fisk helped found the Indianola Methodist Church. Now, almost exactly a decade later, he saw himself playing the founder's role again.

On motion, P. Gad Bryan, genial lawyer and the town's district attorney, was elected president of the yet-unnamed school. Judge Paris P. Henderson, age thirty-five, member of the Iowa Senate, and one of the county's earliest settlers, was named secretary. Both Bryan and Henderson expressed pleasure at their election, but Bryan urged that the meeting be kept mercifully brief, "lest we all expire from the heat."

Although everyone already knew why they were there, the Reverend Eli M. H. Fleming explained the purpose of the meeting. Enthusiastic about the project, he spoke at length upon the importance of establishing an institution of higher education in Indianola. "Higher education" in 1860 meant anything

1

BUSINESS CARDS.

H. FISK, M. D.,
PHYSICIAN AND SURGEON,
OFFICE AT HIS OLD STAND,
SOUTH SIDE OF PUBLIC SQUARE,
INDIANOLA, IOWA.

All Diseases treated on the most Scientific Principles.
☞ Especial attention paid to Surgery and Diseases of the Eye. ☜
Having had Eleven years successful practice in all diseases common to the West, the Doctor feels a degree of confidence in his ability to render full satisfaction in all cases entrusted to his care.

---

above the level of the common school, as the ungraded elementary school of that time was called. The need, said Fleming, was real. A serious gap existed between the common school and the college or university. Not only was the high school or academy or seminary valuable in providing preparation for college work; it was important in its own right, especially in training teachers for the common schools.

The Reverend Fleming did not have to speak very persuasively to convince his already-convinced hearers. What was important to them was the fact that the thirty-eight-year-old minister of the Indianola Methodist Episcopal Church was assuming a role of leadership in organizing a new school for the town. His cooperation was seen as vital to the success of the enterprise. "Let us call it the Indianola Male and Female Seminary," urged Fleming, who went on to suggest the opening of a subscription list. Within minutes the men present subscribed $1,800, a handsome sum in the mid-nineteenth century. And to ensure the best possible patronage for the proposed academy, president Gad Bryan appointed the Reverend Fleming, Judge Henderson and James Nicholls, a pioneer of 1849 and former county surveyor, to draw up a list of prospective trustees.

Satisfied that they had made a good beginning, they adjourned their meeting until Thursday, August 9, and solemnly strode out of the church into the sticky discomfort of the summer night.[2]

* * *

Starting up a private academy in a frontier town, a village really, of fewer than a thousand people was more than a courageous undertaking. It was an act of faith. The more so because at least three earlier attempts had sputtered and failed.

The first of these, a proprietary school established in the fall of 1855, was called the Indianola Male and Female High School, run by Charles C. Griffith.[3] At first he and R. W. Manley rented, then later purchased, the building known as the "district school house and town hall" from public school authorities, who had constructed the building in 1854 with public funds and by private subscription. Public officials had apparently decided not to use the structure for a common school.[4] Located at the corner of Main and State Streets (today Salem and Jefferson), the two-story building was tolerably commodious for a small school. At first Griffith's high school was successful. The *Indianola Republican* reported in December 1855 that fifty-two scholars were already enrolled, and more were coming. "Besides several classes in each of the primary branches, and arithmetic, geography and English grammar, classes are also formed in the higher branches, such as philosophy, algebra, chemistry, physiology, Latin, and Greek to those who desire it."[5] Though called a high school, Griffith's enterprise could accommodate nearly all youngsters. He published an advertisement announcing the opening of the second term which "will commence Monday, March 3rd, 1856," stating that "pupils of all ages will be received at any time during the session. . . . School books can be procured at school of us at Keokuk prices."[6] The school seems to have survived for about two years,[7] but it went down at least in part because of the economic depression that gripped the Midwest between 1857 and 1859. Griffith left to accept a position at Abington College and sold the school building to John T. Pressley, who conducted a school there for one year (1857–58). Pressley in turn sold the building to a man named Douthart whose attempt to run a school was successful for only about a year.[8]

Hard times did not prevent others from attempting to organize new schools. One called the Indianola Seminary opened in April 1857 with Professor C. H. G. F. Loehr and a Professor McKee as principals, together with two female assistants, one of whom was Mrs. Loehr. "It is intended," read a notice in the local newspaper, "that the Institution shall be . . . accessible to all. Its standing . . . shall be second to none. The most thorough, systematic, and practical education shall be given to its pupils, while opportunities will be afforded for every elegant accomplishment. . . . The law of kindness shall remain paramount in its government."[9] The proprietors offered instruction at all levels: primary, preparatory and collegiate. Beyond this they offered training in music and in what they called an "ornamental" department. Theirs was an ambitious undertaking, but they surely stretched the meaning of *collegiate* a bit; the four-year collegiate program embraced few courses of study that went beyond high school level.[10] Tuition charges ranged from $1.00 per month in the primary department to $3.50 for the "collegiate" senior year. Instruction on the harp or piano was $4.00 per month extra. Whatever the price, however, the Seminary offered much and produced little. It lasted only about a year.

The *Weekly Iowa Visitor* for June 3, 1858, announced that "Miss White's school for young ladies was opened at the Seminary on Monday last." The school showed early promise of success. *Visitor* editor James H. Knox urged support of the enterprise: "An able and properly conducted female academy is a necessary which the citizens of this place have long felt. Miss White comes among us highly commended for her amiability of character and educational qualifications."[11] Regrettably, the frail institution lasted only a few months, Miss White's amiability and qualifications notwithstanding. It is difficult to imagine that a girls' school might succeed where coeducational academies had failed.

A few months later there was agitation in the press for yet another attempt to open an academy in Indianola. Writing under the pseudonym "Philom," a local citizen called upon all "lovers of learning" and those who had "sons and daughters to educate" to think of the practical usefulness of such a school. "There are those in our midst," he warned

> who will remove their residences to places where they may have the privilege of just such an institution as is proposed to be built up here; and they are our best citizens, too—those who feel their duty to their children. If such facilities are not provided at home—where they would rather have them—they will find them, even if we require an expenditure of money, or a sacrifice, greater than would be their share in aiding to build such an institution as is contemplated, at Indianola. But, if success attend the efforts that are being made to build one at home, not only will such not leave us, but very many will be attracted to our country who would never have emigrated to the "Three-Rivers" country, if such an inducement had not been offered to them; and shortly our city and county would be populated with the most worthy inhabitants—intelligent, church-going, order-loving people.[12]

And that was not all. Money would flow into the town, and the value of property would be increased "because of our contiguity to the best promoter of light." He urged everyone to turn out for a meeting at the Methodist Church the next week.

Not many heeded the call, for it is recorded that the meeting was sparsely attended. Those present, however, adopted articles of incorporation for what they would call the Male and Female Academy. Local attorney Lewis Todhunter was named president of the organizing trustees and Judge Paris P. Henderson secretary. They would create a proprietary academy, but they were prepared to turn the whole thing over to the Iowa Annual Conference of the Methodist Episcopal Church if ever and whenever the church wanted to accept it.

Here they had hit upon a capital idea in more ways than one. It was doubtful that any proprietary school without institutional backing could possibly succeed in Iowa or anywhere else along the thinly populated frontier. Virtually all successful secondary schools and colleges enjoyed the patronage of the churches. It was not direct financial support that mattered so much, for there was little of it. Rather it was the benign, formal approval of the church that counted, validating these enterprises as proper Christian establishments and permitting the sponsored schools to send agents out among nearby congregations to raise money.

The idea was an excellent one, but it was one whose time had not yet come. The Iowa Conference of the Methodist Church already sponsored Iowa Wesleyan University at Mount Pleasant, the Columbus Seminary in Mills County, the Elliott Seminary in Burlington and perhaps others. And Iowa Wesleyan was ailing, $28,000 in debt and threatened with foreclosure of a mortgage on the college's buildings and grounds.[13] The conference was hardly prepared to take on more academies, however worthy. Therefore, the Indianola project languished for a season.

That same year, however, the Iowa Conference split, the western portion organized as the Western Iowa Conference, with two regular districts—Des Moines and Council Bluffs—and two mission districts—Chariton and Loudon. Then, quite fortuitously, the new conference took the decision to hold its first meeting in Indianola in the late summer of 1860. It was, then, in anticipation of this important inaugural gathering that local citizens schemed in meetings on August

1 and August 9 to lay their case for a seminary before the Methodist clergymen at the conference meeting a fortnight hence.

* * *

When the first session of the Western Iowa Conference convened at eight o'clock in the morning on August 22, 1860, twenty-nine delegates answered the roll call. One of them was Rev. Arthur Badley, Jr., who recorded in his diary that "We met at Indinola [sic], a small band scatered [sic] over all the south west quarter of the State, but we were at peace with each other. We had a good time."[14] The presiding officer was Edmund S. Janes, one of the ten American bishops of the Methodist Episcopal Church. Their six-day session occupied Indianola's First Methodist Church from morning until evening each day. Hardworking men all, they heard a long series of reports, inspirational sermons and lectures; they sat in committee meetings, sang and prayed and, in the words of one of the participants, "suffered mightily from the intolerable heat."[15]

On the fourth day of the session, a five-man education committee listened to the well-primed, carefully rehearsed Indianola citizens, including their own delegate, the Reverend E. M. H. Fleming, who presented their proposal for the seminary as well as a list of suggested board of trustees members. The committee was impressed with the sincerity and enthusiasm of the petitioners. The outcome of their discussions was just what the Indianola men wanted. In plenary session the conference adopted the committee's recommendation that

> we look with favor upon the enterprise; and we advise those engaged in it to proceed diligently, and to further the enterprise, we adopt the board of trustees appointed on the part of the people . . . with the assurance that as soon as they shall complete a suitable building worth at least $3,000, this Conference will take it under its patronage, *provided*: that the enterprise shall not be pecuniarily embarrassed, and that this Conference will not be responsible in any way, for any funds necessary for the future prosecution of the enterprise.[16]

One can surely understand the sensitivity of the Methodist Church about finances. While the church made it clear that it favored the establishment of seminaries *"wherever they are needed, and can be properly sustained,"* it sought to avoid the "pecuniary embarrassment" of "premature establishment" of such schools.[17] The fact was that far too many institutions had been founded and had failed miserably. The church was learning caution. Its experience with Iowa Wesleyan University was instructive. The oldest college in the state, the Mount Pleasant institution, only recently (1855) raised to collegiate grade, represented the acme of Methodist education in Iowa, and although it was enormously influential in the state, its finances were worse than shaky. It was primarily for this reason that the Western Iowa Conference rejected Iowa Wesleyan's request that the new conference continue its patronage of the college. It would agree only to recommend students to it.

Two more seminary proposals came before the conference session. One came from a school "now in process of erection" at Brookville, in Adams county. The conference agreed to accept it on the same basis as the one in Indianola. The other proposal came from citizens in Osceola, but because it looked less promising than the other two, the conference merely appointed a committee to look into the matter and agreed to reconsider the issue the next year.

The jubilant Indianolans were ready to proceed immediately, and they moved

MINUTES
OF THE
SESSION
OF THE

Western Iowa Annual Conference

OF THE

METHODIST EPISCOPAL CHURCH

HELD AT

INDIANOLA, AUGUST, 22D TO 27TH, 1860.

Published by Order of the Conference.

DES MOINES:
MILLS BROTHERS, PRINTERS, CALORIC BUILDING
1860.

into action in a matter of days. They rented the "old" seminary building at the corner of State and Main Streets from its new owner, John Webb, Jr. Actually the building was not very old—only five years—but it had already housed, as we have seen, a bewildering array of schools, public and private. No one, to be sure, regarded the building as a permanent home for the new school, but it was at least a place to start.

The trustees hurriedly cast about for a principal to run the seminary, and they found Elias Williamson Gray, age thirty-nine, a professor of classical languages at Iowa Wesleyan, where he had served briefly. Gray was ready for the call and rushed to Indianola to take up his duties. There wasn't much time. Less than a month elapsed between conference approval and the opening of the fall term.

The Reverend Fleming was elated when he wrote, in a letter to the editor of the *Visitor* on August 30, that the conference had surely done its part. "The responsibility," he pointed out, now "remains with the people." He called upon Indianolans to make a three-part resolution: "The first is, we can do it. The second is, we will do it. The third is, we have done it."[18]

* * *

In his essay *Self-reliance*, Ralph Waldo Emerson tells us that an institution is but "the lengthened shadow of one man." More likely it is probably a number of people, rather than one man, whose ideas and actions influence the history of an institution in such a profound way that it would be a different thing entirely had they not lived. If, then, we want to understand what kind of institution the Indianola Male and Female Seminary was, we need to take a careful look at the character of the people who founded it, for surely the little seminary at Indianola reflected the aims and aspirations, the values and prejudices, of those Iowa pioneers who brought it into being.

Seventeen men were named to the seminary's first board of trustees, and because that body included most of the persons who had striven to create the school, we shall call them the founders.

Nine were laymen; eight were clergymen. All were Methodists. Twelve were from Indianola or other locations in Warren County; the other five were from nearby Iowa towns. Most of them were relatively young, in their thirties or forties. Not one of them, of course, was a native Iowan, for hardly any mature white person living in Iowa in 1860 could possibly have been born in the state. All of them were American-born and had lived in places like Ohio or Indiana or Illinois before moving on to the prairies of Iowa in the 1840s or 1850s.

With a single exception—the Reverend E. M. H. Fleming—it was the laymen who had actively promoted the establishment of the seminary and who continued to be vigorously involved in its direction. The clergymen, for the most part, were appointed to the governing board as a symbol of the church's sponsorship. They validated the whole enterprise as properly Methodist, but, with one or two important exceptions, were far less involved in the oversight of the institution than were their lay counterparts.

Among the laymen on the board were some of the most powerful, and indeed most colorful, characters in the Three Rivers Country, as Warren County was known in those days. One of the best known was John W. Bundy of Ackworth, at forty-four the owner and operator of Bundy and Co., the most important mill in the county. Although he went about clad in the plain dress of the rustic pioneer, he had managed during his scant five years in Warren County to amass a small fortune. He was known for his straight speech and even straighter morals, and almost everyone admitted to being just a little bit afraid of him.

Associated with Bundy in his Indianola mill was founder George W. Jones, a businessman of many interests. As early as 1855 he owned a dry goods store in Indianola and also managed a grocery and queensware business.[19] Then in 1858 he joined with a man named W. T. Smith, described in the language of the day as an "Oskaloosa capitalist," to organize Indianola's first bank, the George W. Jones and Co., located on the west side of the town square in one of the first brick buildings erected in the village.[20] Thus from its first day, Simpson College and its seminary predecessor have had on their boards of trustees the premier banker of Indianola.

Bundy and Jones were the two prominent businessmen among the founders. Two others were farmers, one of whom was Albert Randolph, who owned 240 acres down in White Oak Township southwest of Indianola. Kentucky-born, he was proud of his descent from the distinguished Randolphs of Virginia. Although he was thought by some of his contemporaries to have affected the manners of a country squire, he was described by one local historian as "a man of untarnished reputation, upright and honorable in all his transactions."[21] The other local farmer was Thomas Thompson, like Randolph a native of Kentucky, who had immigrated in 1851 to Warren County, where he bought a fine piece of land, cleared it and built a house for his family, who joined him two years later. Thompson was a charter member of Indianola's Masonic Lodge and served as its first presiding officer. He won a solid reputation as a good farm manager, and would grow prosperous enough to assist in the organization of the Warren County Bank in 1870.

Two of the founders were physicians. The senior one was Dr. B. S. Noble, who in 1853 had given up a lucrative practice in Indianapolis, Indiana, to come to Indianola with his daughter and son-in-law, Dr. Mark Antony Dashiell. Dr. Noble, whose brother was governor of Indiana, established a prosperous practice in Warren County and was soon recognized as a community leader. He had helped found Indianola's Masonic Lodge in 1854 and as president of the Agricultural Society in 1856 had assisted in the purchase of twenty acres of land west of town, at sixteen dollars an acre, to be set aside for the county fairgrounds. One of Dr. Noble's juniors in the medical profession was another of the school's founders, thirty-two-year-old Dr. Charles W. Davis, who had settled in Indianola in 1856. A graduate of Wabash College in Indiana in 1848, Davis "read medicine" with a doctor in La Porte, Indiana, and then entered Rush Medical College, where he completed his professional training in 1853. He practiced medicine for three years in Indiana before pushing westward into Iowa in 1856. That there was need for him and Dr. Noble and other physicians in a frontier town and its surrounding countryside was evident from the handsome practice he built up in just a few years.

Three of the founders were attorneys. One of these was popular P. Gad Bryan, an early settler who had come to Indianola in 1850. He had gained considerable local fame when, in 1853, he fought successfully on behalf of Warren County to prevent Polk County from ripping away the whole northern tier of townships—144 square miles—called "the strip." A member of the Iowa House of Representatives in its Fourth General Assembly, he rammed the bill through that awarded the whole area, except for a few sections north of the Des Moines River, to Warren County. This victory, won by skillful oratory and some old fashioned horse trading, made Bryan an authentic local hero. He possessed other credentials as well. For one thing, he and his wife, together with the Hocketts, the Listons, the Barkers, the Adamsons and Dr. Hezekiah Fisk, had organized the Indianola Methodist Church in 1850. And because within a decade the Methodist Church was the most important institution in the county, the credit that attached to his having been among its founders earned him a rich measure of respectability, at least among the laity, if not among the clergy. Sometimes—in fact most of the time—Bryan's sense of humor got in the way of his piety. He was one of those cheerful, genial men whose often irreverent wit earned him more invitations to speak than he could accept. Whenever he rose to speak, people were ready to laugh, but because some of his humor was a bit earthy, Methodist preachers were scandalized. That bothered Bryan not the least.

Then there was another attorney, George E. Griffith, brother of Charles C. Griffith who had purchased the school building in 1855. Probably the most articulate advocate in the region in the cause of education, George Griffith was a prime mover in the organization of the Indianola Male and Female Seminary. He had helped found the Republican Party in Warren County, and at the first Republican county convention held at Indianola February 9, 1856, he delivered a stirring oration that earned him the reputation of a fire-eater. He found his real niche in the community as a trial lawyer, where his oratorical skills counted, and he soon sought public office. Although he was defeated in the race for county judge in 1859, he would later be elected to the state legislature in 1865 and would serve in the Iowa Senate from 1867 to 1871. In Des Moines, as in Warren County, he became known as an advocate of prohibition. In promoting the cause of temperance, he was not merely adhering to an article of faith of nineteenth century Methodism; he took an active role in trying to block the liquor interests at every turn.

Although Griffith's opposition to beer, wine and spirits was widely known and approved, no one in central Iowa could have been more committed to the struggle against demon rum than was the last of our trio of lawyer-founders, Lewis Todhunter. A native of Ohio, he was forty-three years old in 1860. With little formal education, he had learned a trade, traveled as a salesman, married and produced a large family. He had read law and been admitted to the Ohio bar in 1848. Two years later he took his family to Iowa and in 1854 settled in Indianola. No sooner had he opened his legal practice than he was elected county prosecuting attorney. Later he served as county recorder and treasurer and in 1857 was elected to represent Warren, Madison, Adair and Cass counties in the Iowa constitutional convention. Still later he served as Indianola's first mayor.[22] He enjoyed all his offices and seems to have served effectively. But the job he liked most was prosecuting attorney, especially when he was prosecuting people who violated Iowa's strict liquor laws. He preached the gospel of temperance— really abstinence—inside and outside the courtroom and made himself thoroughly disliked by the liquor interests. The more threatening letters he received demanding that he desist from his single-minded war against booze, the more fiery speeches he delivered damning the "purveyors of death." If one is to understand the breathtaking sobriety of Indianola and Simpson College during the late nineteenth and early twentieth centuries, one has but to understand the dedication of men like Lewis Todhunter to the cause of temperance.

All the other members of the first board of trustees were Methodist clergymen. One was a local man, Rev. J. C. Read, who served as the board's secretary for a number of years and who would hold political office as Indianola's first treasurer in 1864. Actually, Read was a shopkeeper who preached only when the spirit moved him, but the Methodist conference kept him on its roster as an act of brotherly good will. Others—all full time pastors in the conference—included Rev. Sanford Haines, the presiding elder of the Des Moines district; Rev. R. S. Robinson, the presiding elder of the Chariton mission district; Rev. Ephraim H. Winans of Des Moines; Rev. Henry H. Badley of Adel; Rev. Enoch Wood of New Virginia; and Rev. Lewis Silcott, known merely to have been a clerical member of the Western Iowa Conference.[23]

Of all the clergymen, the most important by virtue of his position was Rev. E. M. H. Fleming, who in 1860 at age thirty-eight was minister of the Indianola Methodist Church—or the First Methodist Episcopal Church, as it was formally known. He had held the post only one year, but he was expected by conference officials to serve as an important liaison between the school and the church. Fleming—his full name was Eli Maris Hurford Fleming—was selected president of the first board of trustees. Born in Chester County, Pennsylvania, in 1822, he was baptized a Presbyterian but was converted to Methodism as a young man in Ohio. Licensed to preach in Ohio in 1848, he was ordained an elder by Bishop Matthew Simpson in 1854, whereupon he moved west and became identified with the Iowa Conference. He served pastorates in Des Moines and Newton before coming to Indianola in 1859. Just a few months before he participated in the founding of the seminary, Reverend Fleming suffered the tragic loss of his wife, Sarah Jane, age thirty-five, mourned in the local press as "one of heaven's noble women."[24]

* * *

The summer of 1860, commented the editor of the Indianola newspaper, "promises to be memorable for hurricanes, hot weather, big crops, an unusual influx of Asiatic and European royalty and a super abundance of presidential candidates." National elections were only two months away. A severely split Democratic Party found its northern wing nominating Stephen A. Douglas of Illinois and its southern wing selecting Vice President John C. Breckenridge of Kentucky as its nominee. Conservative, border state old-line Whigs and Know-Nothings chose John Bell of Tennessee, while Republicans, bypassing stalwarts like William H. Seward, picked moderate Abraham Lincoln of Illinois. November, promised the Indianola editor, would see the election of Lincoln over "the most corrupt political combination ever known since the world was created."[25]

The editor's hyperbole notwithstanding, Warren County and Iowa voters made Lincoln their choice and gave him 4 of the 180 electoral votes that gained him a clear victory in the election.[26] And Lincoln's triumph at the polls hastened the irrevocable break between the North and the South. The nation was coming apart at the seams. It was not an auspicious time to start a new school.

If the issues of slavery and states' rights were not enough to discourage new ventures, the economy of the nation, and especially that of the Midwest, was depressed. The Panic of 1857 continued for at least two years, and even in 1860

PUBLIC SCHOOL BUILDING, INDIANOLA, IOWA.

prices had not yet recovered. That fall in Indianola corn brought only 20¢ a bushel, oats 16¢ to 17¢, spring wheat 75¢. In local grocery stores sugar cost 8½¢ to 17¢, butter 11¢ to 12½¢. A bushel of potatoes could be had for 15¢ to 20¢, a dozen eggs for 9¢ and a keg of molasses for $5.50.[27]

Iowa's population of 675,000 in 1860 represented an enormous increase over the 192,000 reported a decade earlier. Warren County posted more than a tenfold growth between 1850 and 1860—961 to 10,281. Although ninety-five of the state's ninety-nine counties had been organized, much of the land was still unoccupied. Even in Warren County only a modest part of the virgin soil had been broken by the plow.

Iowa's Republican governor, Samuel J. Kirkwood, whose educational attainments can only charitably be described as modest, surprised nearly everyone with his political skill and moral courage. Although his speeches could be counted on to do grave violence to the English language, his straightforward manner, not to speak of his close friendship with Lincoln, earned him the loyalty of most Iowans during the awful years of war that lay ahead.

Preoccupied with their own lives, Iowans and Indianolans in 1860 paid scant attention to events beyond the shores of America. They read in their newspapers weeks-old accounts of the exploits of Cavour and Garibaldi in the Italian *risorgimento* and were dimly aware of the Taiping rebellion in China. They did know that the pony express started speeding mail to the West that year, and they were sorrowed and angered when they read about the secession of South Carolina from the Union at year's end. Yet most of these national and world events did not touch them. It all seemed so far away.

FIRST ANNUAL

CATALOGUE

OF THE

OFFICERS AND STUDENTS

OF THE

Indianola Male and Female Seminary,

For the Year 1860-61.

WESTERN IOWA CONFERENCE.

"WE MUST EDUCATE."

DES MOINES, IOWA:
F. W. PALMER, STATE PRINTER.
1861.

Title page of the first catalog of the Indianola Male and Female Seminary in 1861.

II

The Seminary 1860–67

On August 26, 1860, the next-to-last day of the Western Iowa Conference session, the board of trustees of the Indianola Male and Female Seminary met to elect officers. The Reverend E. M. H. Fleming was chosen president, Dr. B. S. Noble vice-president, J. C. Read secretary and George W. Jones treasurer. Two weeks later the board adopted articles of incorporation for the institution.[1]

Although the board had little time to make a choice, they were, as we have seen, able to induce thirty-nine-year-old Elias W. Gray of Iowa Wesleyan University to come to Indianola to open the seminary. A native of Middletown, Ohio, Gray was educated at old Augusta College in Kentucky, where he received both his baccalaureate and master's degrees.[2] He joined the teaching staff at Iowa Wesleyan in 1853, when it was still called the Mount Pleasant Collegiate Institute.[3] The next year he was promoted to the position of professor of ancient Languages and Literature, the position he held until accepting the principalship in Indianola.

Board president Fleming put a notice in the local newspaper announcing the opening of the Indianola Male and Female Seminary's first term on September 24. The price of tuition, according to this first announcement, would range from $3.00 to $8.00 for a term of thirteen weeks, three terms a year, the cost depending on the branches studied. It was hoped that students would enroll at the beginning of the term, but they would be welcomed later too. Fleming especially invited school teachers to enter upon their normal (teacher training) studies at the seminary, promising that they would "find in this institution every facility to aid them in their noble purpose." For those who came to Indianola from out of town, board in private homes could be obtained for $1.50 to $2.00 per week.[4] A similar one-page advertisement appeared in the *Conference Minutes* for 1860, additionally calling upon "brethren in the Ministry" to advise their congregations of the existence of the seminary, "as this is the first institution put into ACTUAL OPERATION within the bounds, and under the patronage, of our noble young conference."[5]

INDIANOLA
Male and Female Seminay.

THE FIRST TERM OF THE
Indianola Male and Female Seminary

WILL COMMENCE ON THE 24TH SEPTEMBER, 1860, UNDER the superintendence of

Professor Gray,

Formerly of the Iowa Wesleyan University. The price of Tuition will range from $3 00 to $6 00, for a term of 12 weeks, according to the branches studied.

Music and Modern Languages, Extra.

For more specific terms, see the Principal.

It will be to the advantage of Students to be in attendance at the opening of the session. But in case any are hindered they will be welcomed and provided for.

TEACHERS desiring to prepare themselves better for their work, will find in this Institution, every facility necessary to aid them in their noble purpose, as special attention will be given to the subject of

Normal Instruction.

BOARDING can be had at from $1 50 to $2 00 per week.

E. M. H. Fleming,
President of the Board.

September 10, 1860.

N. B. Brethren in the Ministry will please call the attention of our people and friends to this excellent opportunity of obtaining a good education for their sons and daughters, and so much the more, as this is the first institution put in ACTUAL OPERATION, within the bounds, and under the patronage, of our noble young Conference.

E. M. H. F.

Professor Gray's first assistant was Miss Hulda C. Cowles; the second assistant was Miss S. A. Hanford. The three of them taught all the subjects in three departments: preparatory, academic and normal.

The precise curriculum of the school during its first year is not clear from the record. The first catalog, one yellowing copy of which is still extant, was published at the end of the year, and the curriculum announced in it represents what was to be taught in 1861–62. It does note, however, that during that first year "70 students were engaged in the study of Geography; 40 in Mental Arithmetic; 105 in written Arithmetic; 48 in Algebra, Elementary and Advanced; 103 in English Grammar; 12 in Fowler's English Language; 16 in Physiology; 17 in Latin, besides smaller classes in other branches." Instruction in vocal and instrumental music was planned, but it appears that Professor Gray was unable to find an instructor during that first year.[6] "The Government of the Institution," wrote Gray, "will be parental." Students were expected to remain quiet at school, and not talk to each other during classes; discipline was to rely "largely upon *private* and *moral suasion*," grounded "in the law and authority of love." It would be up to the teachers to inspire "such interest in books and study, as will insure success, and sustain a laudable ambition to make the most and the best of life."[7] Parents were advised that students needed no spending money.

"Professor Gray," wrote editor James Knox in the *Visitor*, "comes highly recommended, and we doubt not is capable of discharging his duties."[8] As Gray entered upon his duties, people's judgment about his competence seemed to be vindicated, for he took up the job with real enthusiasm. The first day of school only twenty-five scholars appeared, but by the end of the term Gray had, by dint of persuasive recruiting, pushed the number to 92. Each term after the first saw enrollment leap forward. At year's end the seminary's catalog listed by name 184 students who had studied there during at least one of three terms.[9]

In early December, at the end of the first term, Gray could give a good account of his work, pointing out that he and his board of trustees were building up a school "that would invite *immigration* and *capital*, both [of] which we need so much to develop . . . this section of the country." The seminary was, he assured those who read his report—and nearly everyone in town did read it, for it appeared in the weekly newspaper—worthy of their patronage. He concluded with a persuasive appeal for more students.[10]

While Gray was hard at work drumming for enrollment, the trustees, true to their word, were going seriously about the business of putting up a proper building. At a special board meeting on January 9, 1861, they agreed to undertake the project, but they would begin construction only after they had received contributions which exceeded the total anticipated building costs by fifteen percent. They also agreed to accept the generous donation of three-and-a-half acres of vacant land—a full city block—in a new addition to the town being platted by Jones and Windle. George W. Jones, banker and board member, was counted among Indianola's richest men, and Dr. Isaac Windle, a physician, was an entrepreneur and partner of board member Dr. B. S. Noble. The land in question lay a block or so beyond the built-up northwest corner of the town, bounded on the south by Dayton Street (now Detroit Avenue), on the west by Fremont Street (now North C Street) and on the east by Steam Street (now North B Street).[11] An undeveloped sweep of prairie, the land had not a single tree or shrub on it. Some townspeople, when they heard about the acquisition, warned that the seminary would surely fail, for no one would want to walk so far out into the country to go to school. Board members were not much persuaded by the words of the doomsayers. In fact, they decided that remoteness might prove to be an advantage. Besides, one did not look a gift horse in the mouth.

Once the site was selected, John Bundy, Lewis Todhunter and Rev. J. C. Read were constituted as a committee to "procure drafts and estimates" for the building. These men, together with a number of other board members, went out all over the county to raise the needed money for construction. "The amount of five or six thousand dollars among all the people is not too much," argued board secretary Read, who suggested that people subscribe generously and pay out their pledge in four equal installments over a twelve-month period.[12]

The response to their first fund-raising campaign was encouraging. Already by early February George E. Griffith was able to report that he had collected $350. On the sixth of that month the board adopted plans for a thirty-eight-by-forty-eight-foot two-story brick building with a pitched roof, "round head windows"—later changed to square head windows with stone caps and sills—and a full basement, the whole structure "to be finished in a neat, plain and durable style."[13]

During the next weeks the fund-raising went very well indeed, and by the end of March they had $4,350 in subscriptions. Accordingly, the board awarded the contract for the building to the firm of Carter and Woodruff of Knoxville, Iowa, and transferred to the contractor the total amount of the subscriptions, which it was the responsibility of the contractor to collect. For his part, the contractor further obligated himself to complete the building "in a good workmanlike manner."[14] Everyone hoped that construction could be completed by December 1861 in time for the opening of the second term of the 1861–62 academic year. "Let us pull together," wrote the editor of the *Visitor*, "and strengthen the hands of the builders, and the building will soon be completed, to the joy of all concerned; and a monument of the liberality and intelligence of our people."[15]

Meanwhile Professor Gray and his two assistants taught classes at the old seminary building—huge classes, sometimes numbering as many as fifty boys and girls in one room at a time. The school proved to be an instant success, and its principal shone as the brightest star in the Warren County educational firmament. Fellow teachers, somewhat in awe of his reputation, saw him assume leadership, for example, in the annual week-long Warren County Teachers' Institute, which met at the old seminary building during a snowy Christmas week in 1860. Eighty-four common school teachers, most of whom taught in one-room country schools, gave up their vacation and braved heavy snowstorms to meet five full days, Monday through Friday, from eight o'clock in the morning until nine o'clock in the evening, to listen to Gray and other school officials hold forth on a broad range of practical "how to do it" topics. It is recorded that the institute "was opened with prayer by Prof. E. W. Gray," that he lectured for two hours on geography (on the afternoon of Christmas Eve!), that on Christmas Day he was named to the committee on resolutions and spoke again for an hour on geography, that he sang in the Wednesday morning session, that he "made some very appropriate remarks respecting reading," and that on Friday, in a discussion on school government, he was "the first of many to render an opinion." He came out in favor of strict classroom discipline, hardly a controversial view during the nineteenth century. He is also recorded to have summed up his educational philosophy with the statement that "we ought to educate more and instruct less; . . . the teacher is as a guide-board at the forks of a road on a prairie. He is not to travel for the pupil but to help him at the points of specific difficulty."[16] It is clear that Gray not only had a lot to say, but also that he was listened to.[17]

One of the pupils in the Seminary was J. H. Henderson, who later would become Simpson College's longtime board secretary. On the occasion of the College's fiftieth anniversary in 1910 he recalled the school's first year and the outbreak of the Civil War:

> It is with memory vivid and clear when the news of the firing on Fort Sumpter [sic] was received, and of the intense interest and anxiety shown by every one. . . . There was an old blacksmith shop on the corner of the street diagonal from the school house carried on by Shepherd, an old Mexican soldier, and the boys of the school used to congregate at the shop and listen to the old soldier as he would talk of the war and the Union. He enlisted in the first company from Indianola. The school boys who daily visited the old blacksmith until he left for the front received lessons of patriotism never forgotten.[18]

Gray's ambition for the success of the seminary led him into more difficulty than he had bargained for. Eager to increase enrollment during the school's second term (December to March), he entered into an agreement with the subdirector of the Warren County schools, which were said to be overcrowded. He would accept into the seminary a substantial number of public school primary pupils, their seminary tuition paid by the school district. Subdirector George R. Stover justified this unorthodox arrangement on the basis of economy. To rent an appropriate room, heat it, furnish it and hire a teacher would cost the public schools more than the expense of sending the students to Professor Gray at the seminary. Stover also pointed out that the public schools, in fact, had occupied one or more rooms in the old seminary building ever since it had been built, but the new Indianola Male and Female Seminary had rented the entire building, and Gray refused to permit any students who were not in his charge to attend classes there. Consequently, Stover had permitted more than thirty "larger" (that is, advanced primary) pupils to be added to the seminary rolls.

Such an arrangement could not fail to arouse opposition among the citizens of the community, however much they might want the new seminary to succeed. In the March 7 edition of the *Visitor*, Gray, writing that "we have room at the Seminary for more pupils," expressed his appreciation for the "liberal patronage" given the school and assured townspeople that he "would labor to deserve the favor we have received." Evidently, however, at least one taxpayer was of the opinion that the seminary had received entirely too much favor, for in that same issue of the newspaper a strong letter, signed simply "Querist," posed a series of questions about the operation of the public schools, the most pointed one asking: "Is it true that the pupils who attend at the seminary, can have their tuition paid out of the public money? Does our school law contemplate that our public money shall be appropriated to the support of Sectarian Schools, at the expense of our Common Schools?" Overcrowding in the public schools, he charged, was a transparent excuse for providing financial support for the infant seminary out of public coffers. Laying the entire blame on subdirector Stover, he asserted that tax money could not legally be used to subsidize private institutions. Further, he asked "by what rule our subdirector has discriminated in favor of those children of our taxpayers whom he has sent to the seminary? Has not one child just as good a right to have his tuition paid at the Seminary as another?"[19]

These questions and charges were not trivial. Issues of this sort lay at the heart of the fundamental American principle of the separation of church and state. Subdirector Stover, ignoring the basic constitutional issue, explained in his reply published two weeks later that the common schools were indeed overcrowded, for Indianola was growing by leaps and bounds. The arrangement with the seminary was a sensible solution to the problem. "I agreed to allow [Gray] the wages per month that first class teachers charge." That was, he pointed out, the only cost to the school district. As for how scholars were selected to be sent to the seminary, Stover explained that he had asked common school teachers to make out lists of advanced scholars in arithmetic and grammar and "request them to go to Mr. Gray." The teachers made the lists, said Stover, and pupils went to the seminary only if they wanted to. "It was entirely optional [sic] with the scholars."[20]

After this the debate between Stover and the anonymous "Querist" descended into one of those wonderful verbal slugfests that enlivened the pages of the nineteenth century press before libel laws forced editors to moderate the language of their contributors. Speaking directly to Stover, the "Querist" was less than polite. Stover's explanation, he wrote, was not only inadequate; it was "covered all over with the black and fetid mucus of falsehood. . . . The fact is, sir, that you thought the Seminary could not support itself during its infancy, and that under the cover of 'necessity' you could give it some strength by giving it a little of the district *milk*; very matronly indeed." Even worse, he said, Stover, a Methodist, had hired nothing but Methodists as teachers, assistants and principals in the public schools. Charging the subdirector with maladministration, the "Querist" suggested that the best thing for him to do was to "emigrate to the Southern Confederacy, a place eminently adapted to men of your calibre and color," whereupon he concluded: "If this epistle does not have a laxitive [sic] effect upon your costive sectarian predilections, please apply for another dose and I will cheerfully give it. . . ."[21]

Infuriated by the "Querist's" hiding behind a pseudonym and stung by the charges against him, Stover let go with both barrels in the next weekly edition of the *Visitor*. Accusing his antagonist of lurking "assassin-like" in the dark, he branded his accuser "a dirty whelp, and a contemptible *knave* and *coward*; and I charge him as uttering and publishing a libelous and slanderous article."[22] Of course, the "Querist's" letters were libelous, but then so were Stover's.

There is no evidence that Stover ever did discover the identity of his antagonist, but that was not really important. What was significant was that, whatever economic advantages inhered in the public schools' arrangement with Professor Gray, the agreement blurred the line that separated church and state, and was thus unacceptable.

If any of this controversy touched Gray directly, we have no clear evidence of it. Yet it is difficult to imagine that he could have been indifferent to it. One thing is clear: he wisely kept silent during the time Stover and the "Querist" were exchanging insults.

Yet something serious happened to Gray. In the latter part of April—about three weeks into the spring term—he was noticed to be missing classes at the seminary. His assistants, unable to account for his frequent absences, tried to cover for him as best they could. Then—it must have been about the first week in May—he disappeared altogether, never to return. A number of the older students dropped out of school, but most of them remained, their courses taught by the Misses Cowles and Hanford. Editor James Knox wrote of the "sudden evaporation" of the principal, at the same time commending Miss Cowles for the praiseworthy way she carried on, right down to the day she closed the school year, as scheduled, on July 12.[23] The seminary board of trustees was in an angry mood when it charged the absent principal with dereliction in his classes, neglect of his duties and failure to give a public examination at the end of the year. They passed a unanimous vote of censure upon him for "the abrupt and unceremonious manner in which he left the school."[24]

What caused Gray to leave so suddenly? He appeared to be enjoying remarkable success during the first two terms of the year, and enrollment during the third term was excellent. Was his work compromised when he was caught in the middle of the "Querist" controversy? Was it the shattering news that hostilities had broken out between North and South? Fort Sumter was fired upon on April 12, only four days after the seminary's spring term commenced. Was it a personal matter that shall remain forever unexplained?

We do know something of Gray's later life. Whatever explanation might be found for his disappearance from Indianola, he recovered from that misstep and went on to a distinguished career. He enlisted in the army in 1862 and was mustered out at Vicksburg April 15, 1866. During the last two years of his military service he was an assistant surgeon in the fifty-eighth Mississippi Colored Regiment. Where he had learned about medicine is a mystery. In any case, in later life he served as a clergyman and wrote a book called *The New Religion*. He died January 31, 1896.[25]

* * *

Professor Gray's precipitous departure could very easily have destroyed the infant seminary, for quite naturally the confidence of the townspeople in its future was shaken. But the members of the board of trustees moved ahead, regarding the unpleasant matter as merely a temporary setback. They praised Miss Cowles for holding things together and selected her to continue as first assistant. Now they had to find a new principal. They would be able to furnish him the new building free of charge and ask him to employ his own assistants (as long as one of them was Miss Cowles) and provide his own fuel. For this he would "have all the proceeds of the School." If such an arrangement should prove unacceptable to the candidate, they should contract for his services "on the best terms they can."[26]

They could find no one who would agree to accept the principalship on an entrepreneurial basis, so they tendered the position to the Reverend Ephraim H. Winans at a salary of $500 per year, his assistant to receive $200. They hoped they could raise enough in tuition and gifts to cover these costs.[27]

Rev. Winans, at the age of thirty a popular Methodist minister in Des Moines, accepted the position in August 1861. Born in New York City April 2, 1831, Winans had entered Iowa Wesleyan University in 1855, earning the B.A. degree in the class of 1858 and a master's degree three years later.[28] A superb speaker, he was appointed pastor at Des Moines in 1860. He brought with him to Des

INDIANOLA
Male and Female Seminary.

THE SECOND TERM OF THE

INDIANOLA MALE AND FEMALE SEMINARY

WILL COMMENCE ON THE **18TH DAY OF SEPTEMBER, 1861,** UNDER THE SUPERINTENDENCE OF

PROF. E. H. WINANS,

Assisted by

MISS H. C. COWLES.

This Institution has been taken under the patronage of the Western Iowa Annual Conference of the Methodist Episcopal Church, and the Trustees design it to be a First Class Institution, second to none in Iowa.
A new two story Brick edifice will be ready for occupancy soon.

BOARDING,
AND ALL NECESSARY ACCOMMODATIONS ABUNDANT AND CHEAP.

Moines his bride of two years, Margaret (nee Wright), who gave birth to a daughter in 1861, the first of four children. Because of his good work in Des Moines and his membership on the board of trustees of the seminary, Winans was well known to the Indianola men and was a natural choice. His appointment, they reasoned, ought to go well with the Methodist conference. It did.

The 1861 session of the Western Iowa Conference confirmed Rev. Winans as principal and, because the Indianolans had met all of the requirements stipulated the year before, formally accepted the school as a conference seminary and appointed the pastors at Des Moines, Winterset and Indianola as the conference's visiting committee. Elected members of the board of trustees were seventeen men—the same number as in 1860—but only eight of them carried over from the previous year. The nine men who retired from the board included two who were preparing to enter military service and several whose record of attendance at board meetings had been unsatisfactory.

New board members included Dr. Hezekiah Fisk, who had chaired the organizational meeting of the seminary; George R. Stover, the public school subdirector who figured in the "Querist" controversy; the Hon. J. H. Gray of Des Moines, district judge since 1858 and the first judge of the new fifth judicial district (Adair, Dallas, Guthrie, Madison, Polk and Warren Counties); Rev. V. P. Fink, the pioneer clergyman who had come to Warren County in 1849 to hold meetings in the houses of the earliest settlers; G. N. Elliott and J. C. Jordan, two interested county figures; and two clergymen, Rev. U. P. Golliday, a fifty-year-old native of Indiana, who would soon serve as pastor in Indianola, and Rev. A. H. Murphy, who had served in several Warren County Methodist churches and who had been appointed solicitor for the seminary the previous January. Finally, and significantly, James Laverty, pioneer farmer, joined the board. Born in Indiana in 1822, Laverty was a graduate of Indiana Asbury University (today DePauw) and came to Iowa in 1847 with his Kentucky-born bride, Mary. He was registered as the first landholder (1848) in the eastern half of the large, seventy-two-square-mile Washington Township, where he settled on 160 acres and served for many years as a member of the county board of supervisors. Laverty was the first of his family to serve on the board of trustees of the local seminary and later of the College. His great grandson was a board member in the 1990s.

The board found it inadvisable to rent the old seminary building on Main Street for only the fall term. Construction of the new building was coming along well; they could occupy it at the beginning of the second term in December. They decided, therefore, to make do by renting several unoccupied rooms—some of them pretty awful—in a ramshackle building on the west side of the town square. It was with more hope than confidence that Rev. Winans welcomed students on the opening day of school on September 18, 1861. "We were there in dumps and heaps." he recalled later, "but we were there."[29]

In October the local newspaper proclaimed the good news: "The Seminary building will be ready for the reception of pupils on the second Monday in December [the ninth]." The announcement was, alas, an exaggeration; only the second story of the structure was finished by December; the first floor and basement would not be ready for use until the summer of 1863.

Ready or not, Winans moved the school into the building as announced, even if he could use only the upper floor. While classes met during the remainder of that academic year and the next, workmen could be heard off and on—more off than on—finishing up the rest of the building. They painted the brick exterior a lead color. Soon someone called the building "The Bluebird," and the name—later transformed to "Old Bluebird"—stuck.[30]

Although it was by no means an imposing structure, the "Bluebird Seminary" could be seen from miles away as one approached Indianola from the rolling treeless prairie that surrounded it. One early seminary instructor recalled that "to one coming from Des Moines on the stage road, it first came into view from the edge of the timber this side of Middle River," for between the river and the north edge of Indianola stretched a treeless prairie with but one farm in all that expanse.[31]

Winans remained at the helm of the seminary for two years and served also as a member of the board of trustees. During the year beginning in September 1862 he also filled the pulpit at the Methodist Church in Indianola in addition to his duties at the seminary. He stepped into the pastorate because the appointed minister, Rev. U. P. Golliday, entered the U.S. Army in mid-1862 as chaplain of the Thirty-fourth Iowa Infantry.

During his tenure at the seminary, Winans was able to arrange for graduates to be admitted by certificate to Iowa Wesleyan University at a "corresponding grade." No innovator, he put into effect the curriculum that Professor Gray had designed, including work in the preparatory, academic and normal departments. Subjects taught in the preparatory department included arithmetic, English grammar, geography, algebra and "as much of Latin and Greek as may be studied to advantage."[32]

The academic department comprised two years of study, presumably preparing pupils for college entrance. In the first year students enrolled in Latin (Caesar and Virgil), Greek (Xenophon and Homer), algebra, geometry and English language. During the second year they studied trigonometry and surveying, chemistry, physiology, ancient history, botany and natural history, astronomy and rhetoric. There were no electives. There would be additional work in German, French, drawing and painting "as soon as classes can be made sufficiently large to justify their organization." No student, said the school's catalog, would be permitted to have less than three or more than four classes at one time. It is noteworthy that no classes were offered in religion or Bible studies. Methodists were still uneasy about the deleterious effects of such instruction on one's faith. Their leaders feared that "higher criticism," whatever its academic respectability, could rob students of their faith in the inerrancy of Holy Writ. And it was through faith that the soul was nourished. At the seminary in Indianola, it was expected that students would nurture their religious lives, but not in a narrow denominational way. On Sundays "students will be required to attend religious services at some church which they may choose," and they were obliged on Sunday afternoons to meet at the seminary for a lecture by the principal or a worthy guest speaker "on some moral or religious subject."[33]

The normal department offered two classes each year in addition to the customary academic work. In pedagogy, the "methods of governing and teaching" were taught. Beyond that, prospective teachers "should be allowed to furnish a specimen of their skill in conducting and teaching a class."

In his second year, Winans was assisted by Rev. M. Richards, who replaced Miss Cowles, and the two of them appear to have worked well together. That Winans's work was satisfactory to the board of trustees was demonstrated when, in 1863, board member Rev. Enoch Wood complained that the faculty—especially Winans—had acted improperly when they expelled his son, Leander, for misconduct. After a full hearing the board voted to sustain the expulsion.[34]

In 1863 Rev. Winans was "moved up" to the position of presiding elder[35] of the Des Moines district of the church.[36] His resignation was accepted with genuine regret, for he was regarded as a first-rate speaker and a good manager. One of the qualities he possessed which endeared him to Indianola was his skill and fire as a temperance lecturer.[37]

* * *

Professor Winans's tenure as principal spanned the first two years of the Civil War, or the War of the Rebellion, as everyone in Warren County called it. Although few of the students of the seminary were old enough to march off to battle, the uncertainty of the times was reflected by a decline in enrollment during the war years.

When the war came, wrote a Warren County historian, local citizens "were startled from their dreams of the future—from undertakings half complete—and made to realize that . . . there was a dark, deep and well organized plan to destroy the government, and rend the Union in twain, and out of its ruins erect a slave oligarchy. . . . Though the drums of war sounded far away, patriotic Warren County men rallied to the Union cause, at first only a few; then, when the full fury of the war exploded in the spring of 1862, they responded in large numbers. As George Parker put it, "The blood of chivalry of Warren was sent leaping in boiling currents through veins swollen with righteous wrath, as the terrible news of Shiloh, of thousands slain and sons in Southern prisons, came to fathers, brothers and friends of those who had gone to the front."[38] P. Gad Bryan enlisted; so did Dr. Hezekiah Fisk and Judge P. P. Henderson and Lewis Todhunter and Dr. Charles W. Davis, all of them mainstays of the little seminary at Indianola.

Patriotic meetings, where citizens could vent their wrath against the "monstrous war" that the "traitorous rebels" had unleashed, were held almost weekly at the seminary. The rafters of Old Bluebird resounded to the thunder of oratory and martial song. Every time Lincoln sent out a call for more troops, Warren County responded liberally. "Patriotism thrilled, vibrated and pulsated through every heart," wrote historian Parker, to whom the events of 1862 were still fresh.[39]

The Methodists who backed the seminary at Indianola were as patriotic as the rest. "We are compelled," said the Western Iowa Conference in September 1861, "to regard all those in arms against the Government of our Country, and all those who aid and encourage them, as Traitors and Rebels." It was up to all good citizens to "suppress and crush out this unholy Rebellion." But these serious-minded, reflective men noted also that they could not "resist the conviction that the calamities now involving our Country, are a distinct manifestation of divine displeasure against us, on account of our National sins; and that we should repent and forsake them, lest they involve us in utter ruin."[40]

As the war continued, the talk at the annual Methodist conferences focused more on the wickedness of rebellion and less on God's wrath against sinners, for the clergy shared with the local citizenry the news of victories and defeats on the battlefronts, of Iowa's sons consumed in the maw of war. What everyone had hoped would be a short conflict dragged on through 1862 and 1863, and people at home heard about places like Antietam and Murfreesboro and Chancellorsville, where the fields ran red with blood. It was difficult to keep one's attention on running a school.

* * *

At dawn on Friday, September 4, 1863, the early stagecoach from Eddyville trundled into Indianola. As it reached the center of town, the driver whipped the four horses into a rapid trot around the square, finally drawing up in front of a small, wooden-fronted hotel called the Barnwell House. As the driver leaped down off his seat, out of the coach climbed two men, one well known in Indianola, the other a stranger. James Williamson, the first man to set up a law practice in Indianola, was returning home from one of his frequent journeys on business. His traveling companion, thirty-two-year-old Orlando Harrison Baker, looking dusty and tired, was arriving in town to take over the direction of the seminary.

At the hotel Baker washed up, brushed his hair and coat, and after a sturdy breakfast walked out into the street looking for somebody who knew something about the Indianola Male and Female Seminary. Already the word had gone around the square that the new principal of the school had arrived, so that he had walked no farther than the newspaper office than he ran into Lewis Todhunter, who took him over to the store of the Reverend J. C. Read and Co. The two trustees, after a bit of exploratory conversation with the newcomer, offered to take him out to the north side of town to see the almost-finished seminary building. "The lower rooms," wrote Baker years later, "had not yet been used as a school room. There had been a festival held recently in the lower room, and the temporary tables were still there; paper and the scattered remains of a feast were scattered about the floor. The festival had been held for the purpose of raising funds for the purchase of a bell." The campus was still barren of trees, "but it was surrounded by a high board fence, and the lot was planted in corn, the height and strength of which testified to the fertility of Iowa soil."[41]

Baker spent his first night as a guest in the home of Amos Barker, who was Indianola's earliest merchant and father of M. R. Barker, but it was a short night, for at four o'clock the next morning George Griffith picked him up in his carriage. The two men rode across the country to Winterset, where the annual session of the Methodist conference was meeting. They reached Winterset just in time to hear the sermon delivered by Bishop Edward R. Ames.

The new principal was also present in time to hear the claim of the Indianola seminary to conference patronage, a claim contested by a delegation, headed by Rev. Henry B. Heacock, from the three-year-old Osceola Seminary, twenty-five miles or so south of Indianola. After a heated discussion of the rival claims, the conference voted to give its blessing to both schools. Then Baker learned that Osceola was not the only other school vying for conference approval. There was one at Brookville in Adams County that had opened in 1859; by 1862 it had adopted the name of Simpson Seminary.[42] Columbus Seminary in Mills County wanted approval, too. There were rumors that still another existed at Pleasant Plains. The conference could not possibly recognize all of them, and it was clear that some of them were not strong enough to warrant approval. It was just as well that the conference ignored them, for the war was taking its toll, and only a year later the Methodist conference would hear that "of the several institutions of learning which have been proposed and placed under the care of this Conference, we find the 'Indianola Male and Female Seminary' alone, flourishing amid the pressure of the times. The rest have gone down."[43]

The Indianola school could easily have gone down too. "On the morning of the opening [of the fall term] I saw about a dozen pupils assembled, most of whom were children," recalled Professor Baker, for most of the able-bodied young men had enlisted and gone to the South. So limited were the school's funds that he had contracted with the board of trustees to run the school without salary; he would have as remuneration whatever he could make from tuition. When he saw only a handful of youngsters that first day, "it came to my mind that I had better have gone to Baker University, in Kansas as president of that institution rather than to have accepted the position at Indianola."[44]

Fortunately, Baker had brought a few hundred dollars with him from Illinois, so he remained in Indianola to make the best of it, sent for his wife and two babies and moved them into a house belonging to Jephtha Turner, a local carpenter and real estate agent. He determined to make the frail little school succeed, war or no war. There was no increase in enrollment during the fall term, but Baker's enterprising recruiting brought in a number of young women in December, doubling attendance. Still, the income of the school was not sufficient to meet expenses, in spite of what some townspeople insisted were exorbitant tuition rates—ten dollars per term. Their complaints led the board of trustees to inform Baker that they wished to regulate the fees. Baker replied that "if they wished to regulate the fees they must pay me a fixed salary, the reasonableness of which seemed evident to them, and they dropped the subject."[45]

Baker resolved to make the most possible out of the small beginning. He solaced himself with the notion that "greater credit would come to me for building up a school out of nothing, rather than to enter one that was already prosperous."[46] After all, his credentials were good. Born September 13, 1830, at Brownsville, Indiana, he earned the B.A. degree at Indiana Asbury (now DePauw) University in 1858 and received the M.A. degree there three years later. Upon graduation in 1858 he married Mary C. Ridley and accepted the headship of the Cherry Grove Seminary in Illinois, with his wife as his assistant. He remained there until 1860, when he became principal of Delaney Academy, also in Illinois, for a year. He returned to the Cherry Grove Seminary for the 1862–63 academic year before accepting the call to Indianola. At some point he had also received the call as a clergyman, for he was as often addressed as "Reverend" as he was "Professor."

Baker's house was at the northwest corner of the square, where the Indianola Banking Co. would locate in later years. "At that time," recalled Baker, "there was a diagonal path from where I lived, to the Seminary, no houses at that time between. There were no sidewalks in the town, except a board sidewalk around part of the public square—the north side of the square at that time was almost all vacant land. In muddy weather the pupils literally waded through the water and mud" to get to school.[47]

It was during the early weeks of Baker's administration that the lower floor of Old Bluebird was finally finished and a bell purchased and placed in the belfry. The southeast room on the first floor was the school's first conservatory, where music was taught by one teacher. The other seven rooms in the building accommodated all the rest of the classes in a range of subjects. Although there were times when the building was almost uninhabitable—the flues were too small to carry off the smoke properly from the stoves—Old Bluebird served the seminary well.

J. H. Henderson attended classes in the new building during its first year. There "we attended our classes, held our literary societies, prepared for the exhibitions which were always held at the close of a term in the old Methodist church then at the northeast corner of the public square." Orlando Baker and his wife taught nearly everything, climaxing each week with "Friday exercises." Henderson recalled that "one Friday there were about sixty of us and Prof. Baker gave us ten minutes in which to write on our slates an essay on 'Fashion.' . . . Another Friday some twenty-five or thirty declaimed 'A Chieftain to the highlands bound.' Some of us were compelled to commit to memory 'Thanatopsis.' "[48]

Baker lent the Seminary a measure of academic respectability. When Rev. E. H. Winans suggested Rev. Arthur Badley as successor to Rev. C. C. Mabee in the Indianola Station, as the local Methodist church was called in those days, Badley accepted the assignment "with many doubts as to my ability to fill the place. Here was our Conference Seminary. Here they need men with more litterary [sic] attainments than I had."[49]

At the close of the 1864–65 academic year Baker, now salaried, could report an enrollment of 132 in all departments, a huge increase over the previous year, the more remarkable because of the war.[50] So pleased was the Methodist annual conference of 1865 with the prosperity of the school, that they decided to designate it formally as the "Des Moines Conference Seminary."[51] The faculty, it was reported, was "efficient, doing good work in the cause of Christian education." What now was needed, responded the board of trustees, was an endowment of between $10,000 and $25,000 to give the institution permanency and "to elevate it to such a grade as the country demands."[52]

When the Civil War finally ended in 1865, the seminary enjoyed its first full year of peacetime operation. Enrollment that fall increased substantially, enough to warrant consideration of putting up another building. One of the new seminarians was Brenton Hamline Badley, son of Rev. Arthur Badley, whose new assignment in 1865 was the Indianola circuit, serving rural Warren County churches. Young Badley soon "became much interested in his studies." The elder Badley wrote at the time that "Prof. O. H. C. Baker is runing [sic] the School, he and his Wife, and they are very diligent in their work." But he also noted that "the school is feeble, a few students, and the house [Bluebird] rather poorly prepared for the business, as I conceive." Yet the next year (1866–67) he had "my children in the Simminary [sic], they boarding at home."[53] Both the conference and the board of trustees were pleased with the principal's work, and said so. Their pleasure did not, however, find expression in any tangible way. Baker could have suggested a number of ways, starting with his salary. The board, at the end of the 1865–66 school year, was happy to reelect Baker principal, but offered him the same $800 salary he had received the previous year. When he, much to their surprise, turned down the offer, they declared the principalship vacant and proceeded to elect someone else. After all, prosperity did not justify profligacy.[54]

Baker already had another offer. Perhaps it seemed to him to be a better one. He went to the Glenwood Seminary, or, as it was called in 1866, the Western Iowa Collegiate Institute, where he served as principal for two years before returning to Indianola to join the faculty of the new college.

* * *

Baker's successor at the Des Moines Conference Seminary in 1866 was the Reverend Samuel Milton Vernon, bright, ambitious and acceptably pious in spite of his "excessive" youth—he was only twenty-four.[55] He was tall, dark haired and as slim as a boy, full of catlike energy and possessed of a powerful personal magnetism. Ordained a minister in 1862, Vernon was serving as pastor of the Fifth Street Methodist Church in Des Moines when he was elected principal of the seminary. Born on a farm near Crawfordsville, Indiana, November 27, 1841, he had attended the Iowa Wesleyan Academy as a preparatory student until 1862, when he entered the University in Mount Pleasant, where he was a sometime student until he was awarded the B.A. degree in 1867. During his first year at the university, however, he was assigned by the conference to the Des Moines pastorate. That same year he married Harriet Kelly, one year his junior, who had just graduated from Iowa Wesleyan University.

Thus Vernon, though a modestly experienced pastor, had not yet earned his B.A. when he came to the seminary in Indianola. Small matter. His pastoral and administrative qualifications were thought to be more important than his academic accomplishments. Besides, the board could get him to come for $800. That amount, they promised, would be increased "whenever the finances of the School will justify it."[56] Vernon had his own reasons for taking the seminary position. A throat ailment was making his pulpit duties difficult for him. The seminary would offer an attractive change.

With an enrollment of more than a hundred pupils, the seminary opened in September 1866 with a faculty consisting of Vernon and Professor J. C. Clark, together with Mrs. A. A. Doby. In the second term they employed a Mrs. Roberts of South Bend, Indiana, and in the spring term Miss Arabella Babb, to teach music. The appointment of Miss Babb, however brief her tenure at Simpson, is worthy of special notice, for she would make history, but not in music.

In 1869, two years after her brief tenure at the seminary, Belle Babb, twenty-four years old, was the first woman admitted to the bar in the United States.[57] "You know," commented the mystified editor of the *Mt. Pleasant Journal* in a classic instance of understatement, "a female lawyer in the State of Iowa is something new." Indeed she was.[58]

Meanwhile, so successful was the little seminary at Indianola that by 1866 people were talking about raising it to the grade of a college. Members of the board of trustees had already been thinking about college level instruction. After all, the seminary was healthy, free of debt—a most unusual condition for any educational institution in those days—and enjoyed good prospects for the future. For months the board had been wrestling with the task of writing new articles of incorporation for the seminary, and it was while they were at work on that project that the idea emerged to transform the school into a college. Late in the summer—it was August 11, 1866—they hit upon a plan to effect such a transformation. It would be better to call it a scheme. It seemed to them to be a stroke of pure genius. They would call the place Ames College.[59]

Their plan was simple. They knew that the Des Moines conference session, scheduled to open at Boonsboro in just eleven days, would be presided over by Bishop Edward R. Ames of Baltimore. They would honor—they didn't say flatter—the bishop by naming their college for him, hoping to appeal to his vanity. "The Bishop was said to have a very high opinion of himself," recalled one of the trustees who was present at the conference sessions. "He was also rumored to be very well-endowed with this world's goods." They might have their college and a handsome endowment all at the the same time. Their idea of "catching the Bishop for a good round subscription"[60] was, they decided, not only eminently practical; it was in accordance with the time-honored Christian ideal of benevolence. Did not Holy Writ, after all, advise everyone, including bishops: "Lay not up for yourselves treasures upon earth, where moth and rust doth corrupt"?[61] What better treasure in heaven than a fine college dedicated to the moral and intellectual improvement of the young.

They did not know Bishop Ames. The haughty, stern-visaged paragon of virtue took one look at their proposition and rejected it with contempt, appearing to regard the perpetrators of the scheme as unwanted thieves who "break through and steal." Incorruptible and unbending—he had once turned down the presidency of Indiana Asbury University, preferring to remain in pastoral work—Bishop Ames would have nothing to do with the little band from Indianola who would do him such honor. Thus ended for a season plans for naming the college.[62]

The name could come later. For the time being they directed their attention to the erection of a new building, for without it there was no hope of having a college at all. Early in February 1867 the board began corresponding with an architect about drawing up preliminary plans for a building that would be suitable for a college. Because such a "large and substantial" structure would require additional land, George Griffith, by all odds the most generous benefactor of the school in its early days, that spring gave a piece of land adjacent to the existing grounds on the east side, enlarging the size of the campus to about six acres. By May the board decided to ask C. A. Dunham to provide finished architectural plans for the new structure. They entrusted the important matter of raising funds to Griffith and David Hallam, a man of considerable means. Hallam had organized the First National Bank of Indianola two years earlier. The two made a powerful team. To assist them the board turned to Orlando Baker over at Glenwood, who agreed to make the rounds to seek support among Methodist churches in western Iowa. Baker would prove to be moderately successful, but most of the money was raised in Warren County.[63]

While funds were being collected and plans perfected, classes at the seminary were going well. Both students and parents were especially pleased when a boardwalk was laid from the southeast corner of the campus to the entrance of Old Bluebird. The faculty were happy, too, for it meant less mud tracked into the building.

In April, Professor Vernon, still seeking his college degree, received a leave of absence to attend Northwestern University, where presumably he finished the requirements for his Iowa Wesleyan University diploma. Somehow, leaderless, the seminary completed the year successfully.

Although board of trustees minutes are uncharacteristically silent on the matter, the acquisition of collegiate status and the institution's name were major matters of concern. They would lay these matters before the next Methodist conference session.

* * *

That year the conference sessions were held at Des Moines with Bishop D. W. Clark presiding. Arthur Badley wrote that "we had the question of making a Colage of the Indinola Siminary [sic] up and debated it strongly," first in the education committee and then in plenary session.[64] The education committee was chaired by Sam Vernon, who was anything but neutral. Badley remembered that "Dr. [U. P.] Goliday [sic], Brother D. N. Smith were [the] chief opposers. [Sam] Vernon [and J. F.] Goolman and others [were] for the measure."[65] Golliday was powerful in the conference; D. N. Smith was less so, being listed in the conference minutes as one of the "superannuated and worn-out preachers."[66] Actually, the proposal had a lot of supporters. In addition to Goolman, who was presiding elder of the Des Moines district, the education committee included two clergymen known to be favorable to the proposal: J. W. Todd at Garden Grove and C. C. Mabee of Council Bluffs who had formerly served at Indianola. There were four laymen, two of whom were from Indianola: George E. Griffith and H. C. Sigler. Then there was Orlando H. Baker, former Seminary principal, who was in 1867 principal of the Glenwood Seminary in far southwest Iowa. These men buttonholed every delegate to convince them of the rightness of the seminary's cause. Opponents, who feared that the church would be morally if not legally burdened with unanticipated costs of maintaining a college, were unable to dissuade their colleagues from support for the project.[67] Badley spoke to the financial issue: the seminary's history, he wrote, "is a very pecular [sic] one. It had never so far had that financl strugle [sic] that most of our Institutions of learning have had to pass through the reason as I believe is because it has had a master financier running it in the person of Hon. George E. Griffith who has done more for the building and keeping this institution runnin [sic] than any other or I may say all others put together."[68]

On Saturday afternoon, September 21, 1867, the Des Moines Annual Conference voted "to raise the Seminary to the grade of a College, on condition that it be deeded to the Trustees appointed by the Des Moines Conference." The latter proviso was easy to accept, since the existing seminary board had on its own initiative submitted a list of seventeen names, all of which were confirmed by the conference. Further, the conference agreed to change the name of the institution to "Simpson Centenary College." It would be called "Simpson" to honor Methodism's most renowned living bishop, Matthew Simpson, and "Centenary" to commemorate the centennial of American Methodism, the celebration of which was then in progress.[69]

"Indianola has a college, and we shall make it the best in the land," said George Griffith. "It is a dream come true."[70]

CATALOGUE

OF THE

DES MOINES CONFERENCE SEMINARY,

LOCATED AT

INDIANOLA, WARREN COUNTY, IOWA.

ACADEMIC YEAR CLOSING JUNE 23D, 1865.

CALENDAR.

FALL TERM begins September 11th; ends December 15th, 1865.
WINTER TERM begins January 1st; ends March 23d, 1866.
SPRING TERM begins April 2d; ends June 22d, 1866.

DES MOINES:
PRINTED AT THE IOWA STATE REGISTER BOOK AND JOB OFFICE.
1865.

The school was called the Des Moines Conference Seminary from 1865 to 1867.

III

Simpson Centenary College 1867–75

On a sunny summer day in 1867, Sam Vernon, bone tired, drove his battered phaeton down the dusty stage road that led to Indianola from Des Moines, where he had attended the sessions of the annual Methodist conference. The meetings in the capital city had been long and demanding, sometimes inspiring and frequently boring, but Vernon had come away with the prize he had sought there. As his buggy lurched along the rutty country road, he could reflect upon his happy victory. He was pleased that after a prolonged and sometimes acrid discussion of their plan, he and the Indianola men had persuaded the conference to accept the seminary as the conference college. More to the point, he was certain that his election as the first president of the College would be a mere formality. Not bad for a young man of twenty-five. Not only had he attended the birth of the College; he had also proposed the name by which it would be known: "Simpson Centenary College."

Actually, it was not a very good name; it was too long. Never universally popular, it would last only until 1885, when it was mercifully shortened to "Simpson College." Vernon himself ultimately came around to the view that the name he had given the infant College was somehow excessive. As he wrote some years later,

> It was not entirely satisfactory to me as it was long and cumbersome, but the great Bishop's name was then a tower of strength throughout the land, and we thought that we should honor ourselves, while honoring him, in giving the college the name of Simpson. The centennial of Methodism was then the absorbing theme of thought, and it was expected to be a talisman . . . , so we put into the name a recognition of this great movement which we hoped, and not in vain, would secure its recognition in return.[1]

Although many disliked the term "Centenary"—few could even pronounce it—the name "Simpson" was universally applauded. Matthew Simpson was perhaps the best known Protestant clergyman in the North. Only Henry Ward Beecher, his Congregational contemporary, could be rated his equal. And in nineteenth-century America the great pulpit preachers were widely known and highly respected, accorded often a celebrity status. In 1867, when the College was named for him, the bishop was at the zenith of his career. His rise to eminence had been as swift as it had been unpredictable.

Matthew Simpson was born in 1811 at Cadiz, Ohio, a hamlet on what was then America's western frontier. His father, James, a Scotch-Irish immigrant from Londonderry, died of consumption when Matthew was only a few months old. The boy was reared by his mother and his uncle Matthew Simpson, whose name he bore. From Uncle Matthew the lad received most of his early education; he attended school for only two brief terms and Madison College for only two months.[2] Later he studied medicine with Dr. John McBean back in Cadiz, but in time he found himself drawn more and more to religion. In 1834, after a short eight months of practicing medicine, he joined the Pittsburgh conference of the Methodist Episcopal Church as an itinerant preacher.

Simpson's first attempts at preaching won no praise from anyone. The halting speech of his early sermons betrayed an almost debilitating self-consciousness and sense of inadequacy. It was only with constant practice, undergirded by a powerful determination to engage in a relentless battle against sin, that he grew to be an acceptable pulpit speaker. Even then, few would have made so bold as to predict that a mere two decades later his fame would rest in large part upon his astonishing oratorical skills.

After a few years in the parish ministry at Pittsburgh and Williamsport, during which time he married and worked doggedly on his preaching performance, he joined the staff of Allegheny College in Meadville, Pennsylvania as a professor in the natural sciences.[3] After only six months at the college he was named vice-president and made a member of the board of trustees. Matthew Simpson shared the conviction of leading Methodists that the church must move boldly to found colleges wherever the density of membership warranted their establishment.

One such new college was Indiana Asbury University at Greencastle. Established by Methodists as a grammar school in 1837, it opened a preparatory department the next year, and in the summer of 1839 began offering college-level classes.[4] Stung by the dominance of Presbyterians in both private and public higher education in Indiana, Methodists knew that if they were to compete, they must have a college of their own, led by an educator willing to be a pioneer in an environment hostile in more ways than one. Through the influence of Charles Elliott, the respected editor of the *Western Christian Advocate* in Cincinnati, who knew first-rate talent when he saw it, Simpson was elected president and professor of mathematics at Indiana Asbury at a salary of $1,100. At first he was disinclined to accept the position, but the challenge was tempting and the salary was good.

Simpson's nine years at Indiana Asbury saw the school develop from a decidedly frail enterprise to a solid academic institution. And president Simpson gained a reputation as one of the brightest stars in the Methodist firmament. He also became a major force in Indiana politics, assisting Democrats in overturning the entrenched power of the Whigs. Methodists voted almost to a man against the powerful Whigs, who had the massive support of the Presbyterians. Simpson savored the victory over the uppity Calvinists.

It was probably a combination of Simpson's political acumen and his reputation as an educator that won him increasing influence in the councils of the Methodist Episcopal Church. A frequent delegate to general conferences of the church, he gained the acquaintance and the respect of the leading mid-century figures in American Methodism.

In 1852, Simpson, not yet quite forty-one, was elected bishop, the office he would hold until his death in 1884. The same general conference which elected Simpson also named three other men to the episcopacy—Levi Scott of Philadelphia, Osman G. Baker of New England and Edward R. Ames of Indiana—doubling the total number of bishops in the church. These eight men, occupying the highest office in the Methodist Episcopal Church, supervised thirty-nine annual conferences, four or five each. By the time he was elected bishop, Simpson was accounted the most eloquent speaker in the church. He had converted his early weakness into his greatest strength. And soon his reputation as a brilliant ecclesiastical orator spread beyond the realm of Methodism. He was admired and envied as the friend of presidents; he knew Abraham Lincoln well, and Ulysses S. Grant and his wife attended the wedding of Simpson's second daughter, Anna. To be sure, his welcome at the White House enabled him to exercise political influence at the highest level. However, we must be careful not to exaggerate the extent of Simpson's powers of persuasion, or, for that matter, their quality, as some writers have done. The Simpson mythmakers would have him point his bony finger at President Lincoln and warn him that he must emancipate the slaves, lest the judgment of God be visited upon him. The truth is less appealing. While he believed slavery to be fundamentally wrong, Simpson did not encourage emancipation. Rather, he tried to influence Lincoln to appoint more Methodists to administrative and diplomatic posts, and occasionally he met with success.

When Lincoln was assassinated in 1865, Matthew Simpson was called upon to deliver the oration at the martyred president's funeral in Springfield. Those who listened to him that day saw the tall, spare bishop move awkwardly to the podium. He stood before them slightly stooped, his head bent down, emphasizing his low forehead. Then he began to speak, and as had happened so many times before, he seemed to spring to life, his blue eyes fairly dancing as the words tumbled out. The spellbound throng heard him eulogize Lincoln as "a good man. He was known," intoned the bishop, "as an honest, temperate, forgiving man; a just man; a man of noble heart in every way." Lincoln was surely more forgiving than was Simpson, for the bishop, while recounting the fallen president's words "with malice toward none, with charity for all," called for vengeance.

To Simpson, Lincoln epitomized America's struggle for freedom. And the struggle for freedom was, in his judgment, an inseparable part of the inevitable progress, the forward march, of civilization, a view he shared with many others during the nineteenth century. A mark of that progress was America's manifest destiny to dominate a continent, and Protestantism's destiny to dominate America and ultimately the world. He was not anti-Catholic in the way that some Americans were. Rather he believed that "Catholicism, like Islam, was the testimony of an unenlightened mind and would fall as soon as the pure Gospel had been heard."[5] God, in His providence, surely favored Protestants. "California," Simpson wrote in 1861, "while held by Papal power, hides her gold in her bosom, nor tells her hoarded wealth. She passes into the hands of a Protestant nation, and immediately she reveals her countless stores. God is in history. . . ."[6] These words would suggest that Simpson saw the identification of Protestant Christianity with the national destiny of the United States.

At heart he was no reformer. His conservatism was in harmony with the vast majority of Americans who read his tracts and thrilled to his sermons. Yet he did take a stand in favor of democratic change in the matter of accepting lay representation in general Methodist conferences. At the very time the little college in Indianola was being named for him, he was girding for a real fight on that issue, a contest which would demand much of his attention and all of his adroit political skills during the next quadrennium. He would win the battle, incidentally, and lay representatives would be seated at the general conference of 1872.

Whatever his convictions or positions on ecclesiastical or public issues, Simpson was listened to, and his words were heeded. No man in his day in America had a greater following, for he spoke for countless millions.

Such was the man for whom the college was named.[7] The founders could not have done better, and Sam Vernon could feel even a bit smug about having suggested it.

* * *

When in 1867 the Des Moines Conference confirmed the raising of the Indianola school to collegiate grade, it appointed a slate of seventeen trustees, only seven of whom were carried over from the seminary's board of the previous year.[8] The ten new members included S. R. Stone, John A. Olive, Rev. Bennett Mitchell, John Bixby, W. W. Williams, Rev. D. B. Clary, Rev. Phineas F. Bresee and H. C. Sigler, together with two men who had served on earlier seminary boards, P. Gad Bryan and Rev. J. C. Read.

The clerical contingent of the new board included Rev. Bennett Mitchell, presiding elder of the Chariton district; W. W. Williams, who would later serve at Carlisle, but who seems not to have been posted to a charge in 1867; Rev. D. B. Clary, whose assignment covered the large Indianola circuit, which comprised five scattered congregations out in the country; and Rev. Phineas F. Bresee, the charismatic pastor at Chariton, who would serve on the College's board of trustees until he left Iowa in 1883. Bresee, as we shall see, was in 1867 beginning a most remarkable career. While some of the clergymen viewed their service on the College's board as just one more irksome duty to be discharged in a perfunctory way, one more task whose rewards were unsubstantial, Bresee appeared to enjoy his relationship with the College hugely.

Of the remaining six new trustees, we have already met P. Gad Bryan and J. C. Read. Almost nothing is known about S. R. Stone, who served on the board only a year. John Bixby was a prominent Methodist layman from Quincy, a hamlet near Adel. English-born John A. Olive was well-known in Indianola. He had learned the blacksmith trade in his native land and had practiced his craft since coming to Warren County in 1852. Reputed to be Indianola's best machinist, he had been named to the town's first city council in 1864. Olive was as rough in his choice of words as he was in handling the tools of his trade. Some of the timid, somewhat sanctimonious clergymen on the board were uncomfortable around him, and said so. He did not last long on the board. On the other hand, the appointment of H. C. Sigler, the first person of several generations of that august family to work with the College, brought a powerful new voice to the board. Sigler was an Osceola landowner whose holdings were said to be something just short of baronial. The year he joined the board he opened a bank on the west side of the Indianola square in a building where Dan Peck's hardware store would stand years later. Fellow board member George Griffith seems to have had a financial interest in Sigler's bank—of course, Griffith had a financial interest in just about everything in Indianola in those days—and was the one who got Sigler interested in the College. A few years later, Sigler's bank was absorbed by the Warren County Banking Association, the broader ownership of which included Sigler as a prominent stockholder. Although he continued to reside in Osceola, his interest in and handsome contributions to Simpson Centenary College were crucial to its success during the early years.

With men like Griffith and Hallam, Bresee and Sigler and "Doc" McCleary, young Sam Vernon could look toward the future with confidence. His immediate task was to open the school for the fall term and effect the transition from seminary to college.

Classes opened in the fall of 1867 with a small group of freshmen and a handful of sophomores.[9] Most of those in attendance continued to be preparatory students in what was then called the "Academical department" and later simply the "Academy." Simpson was following the normal pattern of enrollment in nineteenth century colleges, public and private. Nearly all of them were forced to offer secondary level instruction because public high schools were not yet sufficiently widespread to prepare all those students who desired a college education. These academies, which lasted in many places until well into the twentieth century, were an integral part of the institutions in which they functioned. In places like Simpson Centenary—in fact nearly everywhere—they provided the principal source of tuition income for many decades.[10]

Vernon's faculty in 1867 numbered only four, including himself. They had to teach something like 125 students in all their courses of study, both collegiate and preparatory, with the aid only of a few student tutors and assistants. Vernon taught the classical languages and moral philosophy. He had recruited William E. Hamilton, almost twenty-two years old, a recent graduate of Iowa Wesleyan, as professor of mathematics. Hamilton, who was waiting for an appointment to the foreign mission field (which appointment never materialized) agreed to "take work in the school for a year." He taught mathematics and all the natural sciences as well. Two women served on this first College faculty, but only one of them was present when classes commenced in the fall. She was Miss M. J. McKean, who taught English literature. She came to Indianola from Northwestern Female College. The faculty, Hamilton later recalled, "consisted of a man, a woman and a boy. I was that boy."[11]

Several students served as assistants, the most promising of whom was young sophomore Brenton H. Badley, who was employed to teach three classes in the preparatory department at twenty dollars a month. Later in the year Vernon added a full-time faculty member, a Miss Barton, to teach music. She was said to be "an accomplished teacher."[12]

When the new faculty arrived for the beginning of the term in September, they found that both the college-level and preparatory classes had to be shoehorned into Old Bluebird. "The meagerness of our facilities for instruction," wrote Hamilton as he looked back on his first year at Simpson, "may be inferred when I say that I tried to teach chemistry to that class with an outfit not worth five dollars."[13] Nor was there enough room to conduct experiments had he possessed even the minimal laboratory equipment. Their new building had not progressed beyond the drawing-board stage.

Earlier that summer the board had awarded the contract for the building's construction to Jacob Reichard, in accordance with architect C. A. Dunham's plan, calling for completion of the project by October 15, 1868. The contractor, Reichard, enjoyed an admirable reputation around central Iowa. He was at work on the handsome new Warren County courthouse and had already completed the Madison County courthouse at Winterset and a major building at the state agricultural college at Ames. Because Reichard was already working in Indianola, he was in a position to submit a favorable bid at $17,500, calling for one-third to be paid when work commenced, one-third upon resumption of work in the spring of 1868, and the final third when the project was completed.

The promise of a proper college building enlivened the work of both the faculty and the students as they watched the excavation of the site and the laying of the foundation that fall. And although work in the spring got under way late, the delay could be blamed on the cold, soggy weather that beset Indianola that year. The editor of the *Visitor* was reassuring when he wrote about Reichard in May: "That which he wills, he performs, whatever the obstacles in the way to impede him. . . . [He is] alert, long experienced, [and] entitled to the confidence of the people." [14] And indeed construction moved along well as the weather improved. Soon the walls were seen to be going up on what promised to be a "magnificent edifice." In late July it was reported that window frames on the second story were being set, and just before the opening of the fall term in 1868 an admiring visitor to the campus reported that the college building was taking shape, its appearance in accordance with "the latest style of architecture, crowned with an immense tower in front, and capped with carved stone minarets at its every angle."[15] A week later the local press was confidently predicting the early completion of the building.[16] But their confidence was misplaced, for in August the laborers disappeared and work on the building stopped abruptly. Reichard, who had overextended himself in his widespread projects, had to admit to the financial failure of his firm.

What to do? Their building was only partially completed, without even a roof to protect it from the elements, and students anxiously waiting to occupy it. They had already run the college for a year without the new building. How long could they continue before disheartened students would think of abandoning Indianola and transferring to other institutions? Somehow the project must be brought to completion, and the sooner the better.

They still liked Reichard, whose affability exceeded his business acumen, so they proposed a deal: he would be paid the final one-third payment ($5,833.33) in several cash installments if he would go ahead and complete the building by June 15, 1869. Reichard, who had little choice, agreed to their proposition and went to work. By late October it could be reported that "workmen are pushing [the project] with a double rush to completion"; and at Christmastime it was noted, with some relief, that the roof would soon be on the building. And not a minute too soon, for the weather had turned exceptionally cold.[17]

Not much more could be undertaken until spring, when Reichard, whose financial position had deteriorated yet further, started work only to give up once again in a second failure. He had collected $1,500 of the final payment and had done just about that much work, but could do no more.

What had ultimately destroyed Reichard's business was a disastrous loss he sustained in building the Warren County courthouse. He had been awarded the contract for that impressive structure in 1866 in the amount of $37,500. Additions and change-orders authorized by the county board of supervisors sent the cost soaring to $89,090. Of this amount Reichard was able to collect only $50,211. He sued the county for the balance but lost in both the district court and on appeal in the state supreme court. The supreme court decision "held that the board of supervisors has no power to bind the county for the erection of a public building in excess of the amount authorized by the voters of the county." The board of supervisors was off the hook and Reichard was ruined.[18]

The double failure of the contractor stalled completion of Simpson's building for several months. No one wanted to jeopardize the legal rights of the College's board by touching the project until Reichard's revised June 15 completion date had passed. Accordingly, the board waited until its commencement-time meeting on June 9, 1869, to make arrangements to have the final work done, the board acting as its own contractor. Just possibly, they thought, the building could be ready for occupancy by the beginning of the fall term.[19]

It was. And, they noted with gratification and no small measure of relief, students had stood by the College, never doubting the successful completion of their new building. That fall they could use at least the first floor and could take a peek upstairs at the fine forty-by-eighty-foot chapel, which would be ready for use as soon as the College could afford to buy seats for it.

The formal dedication of the building, delayed until October 2, 1870, gave cause for rejoicing and "general jollification." For the occasion they welcomed Dr. E. O. Haven, president of Northwestern University, who conducted what they called a "grand rally."[20] Dr. Haven was celebrated as "one of the finest orators in the nation," and he did not disappoint them. A long poem celebrating the erection of the new building and contrasting it to the old one—"Bluebird"—was composed by Brenton H. Badley, the valedictorian of the College's first graduating class earlier that year.

> Near to a city in the prairie land
> Two temples stood. Around, the maple trees
> Were casting varied pictures on the grass
> As through their opening tops the sunlight came.
> One seemed old like the oceaned rock. . . .
>
> The other rose with beauty and with grace.
> It rested on the strong foundation stones
> And to the lofty dome that capped its height
> Betokened newness. . . .[21]

Even though some people who were present that day noticed that much remained to be done to complete the building and furnish it—for example, there was no proper lighting in the chapel until the spring of 1871—they were delighted with their graceful, elegant new College Hall.[22]

* * *

On a raw, blustery day in early November 1867, work on the new building having scarcely begun, the new College's board of trustees met with the out-

COLLEGE HALL, SIMPSON COLLEGE, INDIANOLA, IA.
1869

going trustees of the Des Moines Conference Seminary to effect the formal transition from academy to college. They adopted articles of incorporation as Simpson Centenary College and, no surprise to anybody, elected Sam Vernon president.

For all of Sam Vernon's expressed satisfaction in being named the College's first president, one cannot but wonder just how pleased he really was, for he certainly did not remain long in that office. On February 29, 1868, less than four months after his election, he submitted his resignation, effective twenty-four hours later, explaining that he had decided to enter the Drew Seminary, which had just opened that year, to pursue theological studies. The board hastily drew up a resolution of thanks to Vernon for "the influence he has exerted in the establishment of the College in this place" and for "his untiring efforts" on its behalf. The College, effused the board, had "lost its ornament and pride, the community an accomplished christian gentleman, the church a zealous and effective laborer, and all of us a warm-hearted, genial friend and brother." To these elegant words, which sounded ever so much like a funeral eulogy, they added, as a kind afterthought, their thanks for his "vigorous efforts for the promotion of temperance" in Indianola.[23] For all their words of praise, they were miffed at having been taken by surprise. They genuinely liked Vernon—it was hard not to like him—but his sudden departure forced them to scramble to manage the College in its vulnerable first year.

They asked young Professor William E. Hamilton to take the reins of leadership for the spring term while they set out to find a new president, and they offered Hamilton a salary of $360 for the term, an advance of $200 over his regular teaching salary. When Hamilton told them a few days later that he would take the job for $400 and no less, they acceded "after due consideration and finding they could do not better" to the professor's proposition.[24]

No sooner had they selected Hamilton to hold the fort for the spring than they elected Alexander Burns, vice-president of Iowa Wesleyan University, president of the College. Burns was known all over Iowa as a powerful Methodist educator. Sam Vernon had known him well, and one of the departing president's last words to the board was to recommend that they consider Burns for the presidency. In the small world of Methodist education, Burns was a natural choice. He accepted the position at a salary of $1,500, it being understood that the College would attempt to raise that figure to $2,000 the following year.

Alexander Burns was a great-hearted, bluff, smiling Irishman who, at thirty-four, was making a name for himself in higher education. His complexion was fair, his mop of hair jet black, his face almost overwhelmed by a great black beard which made him look older than he was. There was about him a kind of strength, a vitality and ebullience that made him the center of attention wherever he went. Burns never did anything by halves.

He was born in County Down in Ulster in August 1834, of Scotch-Irish parents. When he was only twelve he came with his family to Canada. Reared a Presbyterian, he was converted and joined the Wesleyan Methodist Church at Toronto in 1851. Four years later he entered Victoria University, where he was a mathematics tutor for one year and a classics tutor for two years before graduation. A superb scholar, he was awarded at graduation in 1861 the Prince of Wales gold medal as *Primus in artibus*. Although he remained at the university for a year as a classical teacher, he determined to accept the call into the work of the church. Accordingly, he entered the ministry and was ordained at Toronto in 1864. Yet he was an educator at heart and only a year later accepted the invitation of the venerable Dr. Charles Elliott to go to Iowa Wesleyan University, where he served three years as professor of mathematics and vice-president of the university. From Mount Pleasant, where he was enormously popular, his reputation spread to Indianola and far beyond.

All through the spring and early summer of 1868 the people of Indianola and the College awaited with increasing anticipation the arrival of their new president. The editor of the local newspaper, James H. Knox, had once edited the *Mount Pleasant Journal* and knew Burns well. "He is," reported Knox in March, "one of the most polished gentlemen we ever knew." Apart from his "book learning," Burns possessed a "large stock of good, practical common sense and knowledge of the world besides."[25] News of Burns very nearly crowded out the other big stories of the day: President Johnson was being impeached in Washington; Red Cloud was raising hell out in Wyoming; there was an awful epidemic of cholera in Texas; and General Grant, who would be elected to the nation's presidency that fall, was being accused for the umpteenth time of intemperance. Burns visited Indianola in early May to look things over and preached at the Methodist Church, where his oratory, delivered with a rich Irish brogue, was judged to be "earnest, plain, practical." Awed by Burns's erudition—he was reported to possess an eight-hundred-volume personal library and to be proficient in eight or ten languages—Indianola boosters were assuring themselves that with its "brilliant new president" Simpson Centenary College was "bound to be the best denominational college in the State."[26]

When Burns and his wife and child arrived in Indianola on a blistering twenty-fourth of July, just about everyone in the town was predisposed to like them.[27] They moved into a fine house Burns had purchased on a corner lot a block west of the northwest corner of the square. People said it had cost the new president a lot of money—perhaps as much as $2,000—but not nearly as much as the $5,000 William Kircher had recently spent on his mansion, the town's undoubted showplace. "Burns must surely intend to stay a while," opined one merchant on the square, "or he wouldn't have spent so much on a house."[28]

The merchant was right. Burns stayed at Simpson Centenary for a full decade and led the College with a combination of skill, good sense and enterprise during the institution's troubled youth.

* * *

Determined that he must have a strong faculty, Burns and his board recruited several first-rate scholars, among them Orlando H. Baker, the former seminary principal who had been languishing at the Glenwood Seminary for several years. Baker, delighted to return to Indianola, would instruct in classical languages while the president would teach mental and moral philosophy and foreign languages. Miss M. J. McKean, a thoroughly competent professor of English literature, was the only faculty member they kept on from the previous year, and she would stay until 1874. To replace William Hamilton, who had resigned to enter the itinerancy, they selected in mathematics and natural science twenty-seven-year-old Civil War veteran Henry F. Douthart, who had just graduated from Iowa Wesleyan in the spring of 1868. He was described as a "square faced young man, all brains, sense that runs at right angles; a man, every inch of him. . . . Like Lincoln, he can not be said to be a beauty, but then like Lincoln, he is pure mettle." And it was predicted that "he will make his mark in the world."[29] Douthart taught at Simpson Centenary two years.[30] Filling out the faculty was Florence Winkley, a Boston native hired as professor of music, the income from which position hardly matched the splendor of the title. In those days music and art teachers were given no salary at all; they had to survive from the special fees they charged their pupils. Miss Winkley could look forward to $15 per pupil for each of three terms, and although it is not recorded what she earned that first year, enrollment figures suggest that it probably did not exceed $300. Other faculty people were somewhat better paid: Burns received $1,500 that year, Baker $700, Douthart $600, and McKean $550.[31] The next year Burns would get his promised raise to $2,000; the others would receive no increase at all.

Some of the faculty did complain about their meager salaries. In June, 1870, several of them met with the board of trustees and asked for better compensation, but the board, while sympathetic, dared not offer more than it could deliver, and salary increases, if any, would have to be contingent on increased income.[32]

Income was poor. Although the College enrolled 161 students during the 1868–69 academic year, tuition income did not begin to meet expenses. If all the 30 college-level students that year had paid full tuition for all three terms—and they did not—the College would have taken in only $900. The 113 preps and 22 "specialists" (see Table 1), had they paid the full $24 tuition, would have produced

Table 1
Enrollment 1868–1880

Year	Senior	Junior	Soph.	Fresh.	Spec.	Law	Total Coll.	Prep.	Total
1868–69	0	6	7	13	22	—	48	113	161
1869–70	6	2	8	10	24	—	50	140	190
1870–71						—	37	121	158
1871–72	13	11	5	18	16	—	63	128	191
1872–73	6	15	3	37	13	—	74	163	237
1873–74	7	14	7	41	7	—	76	168	244
1874–75	5	15	9	30	39	—	98	114	212
1875–76	6	20	6	28	30	37	127	169	296
1876–77	15	16	4	46	0	28	109	92	201
1877–78	8	21	5	30	0	22	86	114	200
1878–79	6	15	4	30	0	25	80	79	159
1879–80	10	11	18	10	4	20	73	63	136

an income of $3,144. Total tuition income, therefore, could not have totalled more than $4,044 for the year. In the event, total tuition income was in fact less than half that amount—just under $2,000, and faculty salaries alone required $3,350 for the year, not to speak of the cost of assistants, the janitor, and other administrative and maintenance expenses.

In order to make ends meet, the College had to raise an endowment which it could invest, mostly in real estate mortgages, at the going rate of eight to ten percent per annum. Simpson Centenary was typical of all denominational colleges of the day; tuition charges were kept deliberately low—even though some local citizens declared they were too high—because the church believed that it had a responsibility to make a college education available to any deserving, qualified Methodist boy or girl. Furthermore, tuition charges at Methodist-affiliated institutions could not exceed substantially those set by public institutions.

That such an academic enterprise was difficult if not impossible to operate with any hope of economic success is beyond cavil. Few institutions in those days were able to accumulate an endowment sufficient to generate the kind of income necessary to make up for their low tuition charges, and for this reason, among others, tombstones of failed colleges dotted the land. The few institutions that survived did so because of exceptionally good management, generous benefactors, and lots of good luck.

Because of their reliance on endowment income for survival, colleges that were skilled at drumming up strong patronage could hope to succeed. This fact explains perhaps the urgency with which the supporters of Simpson Centenary approached their task of making the College self-supporting by raising as large an endowment as possible. The Des Moines Conference, meeting at Council Bluffs in September 1868, and chaired, incidentally, by Bishop Matthew Simpson, promised that as soon as the citizens of Indianola and Warren County had raised an endowment of $25,000 for the president's chair, the conference would pledge itself "to heartily cooperate with the [College] Trustees in completing the endowment, so that it shall be an institution worthy of our Conference."[33]

George Griffith and others took up the challenge, soliciting cash and pledges in amounts large and small. A year later they were able to announce triumphantly that the $25,000 endowment had been secured and prudently invested. Thus the 1869 Methodist conference, meeting in Indianola, where delegates could see the new college building on the verge of completion, voted to assist in the raising of an additional endowment of $20,000. The church as such would give no cash—it had none to offer—but promised "that we will welcome to our fields of labor an agent appointed by the Board of Trustees, and that we will give such agent our hearty cooperation in securing said endowment."[34] They would even preach a sermon on the subject. Beyond this, the local newspaper reported that H. C. Sigler was prepared to give $10,000 toward endowment of a third chair at the College, his offer contingent upon the success of the $20,000 fund drive in the conference.[35]

Not all the endowment was so easily raised, nor were all of the board's investments sound. But for years to come the College employed first one agent and then another to comb the conference—all of western Iowa—for subscriptions. A few of these clerical agents were quite effective and earned their ten percent commission on the money they raised; others would have done better to stay at home.

* * *

While the board of trustees gave its unremitting attention to the College's financial affairs, the president and his fellow faculty members found the development of the curriculum of study far more interesting than dollars and cents. The academic program they put together permitted college-level students to elect either the classical or the scientific course of study.

The school year, divided into three terms of twelve weeks each, opened on the first Wednesday in September and ran, with a fall vacation of two weeks and a spring vacation of one week, until the first Tuesday in June, to which was appended a full commencement week. Tuition per term in the collegiate program was ten dollars, a figure that remained constant for many years, and in the preparatory department the term tuition charge was eight dollars. Janitor's fees were two dollars per term, and music and art instruction were offered at extra cost. Boarding with private families cost from two to three dollars per week, and, as was the case in the seminary days, parents were advised not to furnish their children spending money, lest their young be drawn into profligacy.

To be admitted to the freshman class, students had to demonstrate knowledge of Latin, including Virgil's *Aeneid*, Greek, including Xenophon's *Anabasis*, algebra and geometry, English grammar and composition, American history and natural philosophy.

Once enrolled at the College, students followed a set pattern of courses, no electives permitted. In the four-year classical course, leading to the bachelor of arts degree, the first two years were given over primarily to Greek and Latin language and literature, Greek and Roman history, mathematics through calculus and the sciences (inorganic and organic chemistry, physiology, zoology and botany). During the junior and senior years students enlarged their scientific knowledge by studying physics, geology and astronomy, read classics in the original language, took up English history and literature, American literature, logic and rhetoric. And during their senior year students delved into several religious subjects, including biblical history, natural theology and evidences of Christianity, together with political economy, international law and a course they called mental philosophy. The capstone course in moral philosophy, studied for one term during the senior year, was nearly always taught by the president.

The scientific course required three years of study and led to the bachelor of science degree. Apart from its shorter duration, this course of study substituted a year each of French and German for the heavy emphasis on ancient languages and literature in the classical course.[36] In all of their three years these students studied history: one year each in the histories of Greece, Rome and England. Their courses in science paralleled those in the classical course, and their senior year was very nearly identical to that of the classical students, including all the courses in religion and the capstone course in moral philosophy.

In addition to the two bachelor's degrees, the College offered a master of arts degree, an honorary award whose achievement required no formal course of study. As was the custom of the day, Simpson Centenary conferred upon any graduate of three year's standing "whose character and occupation have been satisfactory to the Faculty" a degree at the master's level upon payment of a five-dollar fee. The granting of such an unearned degree was in accordance with precedent reaching back to the universities of medieval times.

In the preparatory department students who were not ready for college could pursue a two-year course of study, or less if their entrance examinations warranted it. These youngsters studied Greek, Latin and English grammar and literature, arithmetic, algebra, geometry, natural philosophy, U.S. history and rhetoric.

One of the principal academic features of the College was the cultivation of forensic and declamatory skills. Students were expected to demonstrate their proficiency in speaking, and to do so frequently. Class exhibitions were scheduled each year, and literary societies, which provided both oratorical and social opportunities, were organized as soon as the College was established. The Everett Society, for men, was created in the fall of 1867 and the Zetalethean, for women, that same year.[37] Membership in these societies was almost mandatory for the college-level students, participation in them strongly urged by the faculty. That the exercises sponsored by these societies, together with other exhibitions, were considered important can be measured by the lengthy critical reviews of their proceedings that appeared in the local press. Oratory not only trained students to speak; it entertained the townspeople who came to hear.

* * *

During the College's earliest years there were few specific rules of student conduct. To be sure, students were required to attend daily chapel—about twenty minutes each day—and were expected to attend the church of their choice on Sunday. Discipline was strict, but catalogs of those early years are virtually silent on the subject. Students were simply expected to conduct themselves as ladies and gentlemen. That they did not always do so is evident from the record, yet most of them did behave well nearly all of the time. It was believed that because faculty members were so young, often only a few years older than their charges, it was necessary to maintain rigorous standards of conduct. Yet President Burns disliked making a lot of rules. "There will be no ignoring of the honor of our students," he wrote in the College's catalog of 1870–71, "by an offensive parade of authority, or an extended catalogue of restrictions."[38]

No list of restrictions existed, but there were things students did not do simply because they were not done. Excessive frivolity was shunned, card playing was avoided, and dancing was never countenanced, on or off campus. Most emphatically, drinking—whether beer or wine or "ardent spirits"—was unthinkable. It was in the very nature of a Methodist college to protect the church's youth from the debilitating effects of alcohol. The president, the faculty, the entire board of trustees, not to speak of most of the townspeople, were not merely non-drinkers; they were militant prohibitionists, determined to keep the College and the town free from the evil of strong drink. They were proud that, by law, there was no saloon in Indianola. Once, during the 1870s, when a saloonkeeper, Joseph Wachenheimer, a German whose name alone suggested to townspeople a dedication to beer, opened an establishment just beyond the corporate limits east of town, the city council promptly annexed the land and closed him down.[39] After all, one of the strongest arguments in favor of locating Simpson Centenary College in Indianola was the town's reputation for hostility to demon rum. One must recall that the temperance movement in America was growing in strength during the latter half of the nineteenth century; and in Iowa Indianola shone as a beacon of hope to those who would rid the nation of the curse of booze.

It was in part because of the dedication of Republicans to the temperance cause that their party dominated Indianola—and Iowa—politics during the latter part of the nineteenth century. To be a Democrat in Indianola was to be a member of a disadvantaged minority, a rag-tag set of misfits suspected of being in favor of soft money and hard liquor. Thus, when rumors of President Grant's proclivity for strong drink were noised about town, Democrats gloated over Republican hypocrisy and Republicans damned the charge of presidential intemperance as a base canard. Grant's majorities in Warren County were huge both in 1868 and 1872, and he got the entire temperance vote.[40]

If temperance was expected as a matter of course at Simpson Centenary, sexual misconduct of any sort was not tolerated, which is not quite the same as saying that none took place. Throughout the nineteenth century on Christian college campuses students were closely chaperoned and lovingly hovered over by their elders.

The recreational activities of students were of a more innocent sort. Picnics, dinners, outings, an occasional evening at a professor's home, or the craze of the seventies, croquet, provided pleasant alternatives to studying for classes. For many students, social life centered around the literary societies and, a bit later in the decade, around the fraternities and sororities. Their social life was not extensive or very sophisticated. One of the campus editors of the day lamented the lack of "sociables" among the students.

* * *

"With Alexander Burns," wrote E. W. "Parson" Brady, editor of the *Indianola Journal*, the college "is already exerting an elevating and refining influence upon our city and county."[41] The new president preached nearly every Sunday in a Methodist church somewhere in the conference, and nearly as often he could be found on the lecture platform where his skills as a speaker enabled him to awe his audiences with brilliance and erudition or to charm and amuse them with wit and humor. And fortunately he also had a talent for organization, permitting him to make the best use of the experience he had gained at Iowa Wesleyan.

He would hear again from Mount Pleasant sooner than he expected. In January 1869, Dr. Charles Elliott, Iowa Wesleyan's former president, died. Burns

Ulysses S. Grant's victory was heralded in the Indianola *Journal*, November 5, 1868.

was invited to preach the funeral sermon. When he arrived in town, the people of Mount Pleasant welcomed back their "whole-souled, jolly, rollicking Irishman" with open arms. Among his "battalions of friends and admirers" were those who urged him to return to Mount Pleasant for good, for, they said, the president of the university, Dr. Charles A. Holmes, had just resigned to accept a pastorate.[42] Soon enough, in mid-April, Burns was invited to come to Mount Pleasant to talk with the board of trustees, and at the end of a two-day visit he was informed that he had been elected president.[43] Upon hearing of Burns's election, the editor of the *Mount Pleasant Journal* bespoke the town's excitement: "With Burns as President of our College the Institution will hum."[44]

Surely Burns was tempted to accept the offer. He loved Mount Pleasant, and the college there was older and better established than Simpson Centenary. But he was a man who took his responsibilities seriously. He could hardly abandon the Indianola school after only a few months as president. And besides, the potential for growth at Simpson Centenary was excellent, even if the Mount Pleasant paper called the college "a mere infant." Burns rather liked Parson Brady's rejoinder: Simpson Centenary College is "a mighty perfect and well-formed child," one that is growing "more beautiful and strong every day."[45]

Burns stayed. And as if to celebrate the decision he had taken, he had Jephtha Turner come over and put a wide veranda on the front of his house.

Upon the completion of the College's first successful year, Burns decided to put on a proper commencement celebration. True, there were no seniors to graduate, but that seemed to him to be a minor matter. There were several juniors. And, he reasoned, commencements in colleges in those days were a lot more than just graduation ceremonies. In an eight-day event, described in the local press as a "rich intellectual treat," students and faculty brought their school year to an end with a whole series of exercises. The Reverends A. C. Williams and Phineas F. Bresee, both of Des Moines, preached the annual sermons. Each of the literary societies held exhibitions marked by oratory and musical entertainment. The Everetts were addressed by the Hon. George G. Wright, long-time justice of the Iowa Supreme Court, who impressed his hearers so favorably that he was invited a few months later to join the Simpson Centenary board of trustees, where he would serve for more than two decades. The Zetaletheans invited P. Gad Bryan to speak to them. Bryan, the only Democrat in Iowa Parson Brady considered respectable, though misled, had just made an unsuccessful bid for the U.S. Congress from the fifth district the previous autumn.[46] Class examinations filled much of the rest of the commencement week. Most of the exercises took place at the Methodist Church, for their new College Hall was not yet ready for occupancy.[47]

Because Burns believed strongly in the importance of the natural sciences, he moved in the fall of 1869 to narrow Henry Douthart's teaching assignment to mathematics and astronomy and saw to the appointment of George C. Carpenter as professor of natural sciences. All the rest of the faculty continued from the previous year. He also instituted a lecture series and told the students that attendance was obligatory. The lecturers, listed in the College's catalog as faculty, included two lawyers, H. W. Maxwell (common law and equity) and P. Gad Bryan (constitutional law), together with two physicians, C. W. Davis and J. D. McCleary, both listed as lecturers on physiology and the "laws of life."

* * *

At eight o'clock on a late August evening in 1869 George Carpenter arrived in Indianola on the last stagecoach out of Des Moines. He was amazed to see that a few places in the town had gas lights. He somehow had expected things to be a lot more primitive out on the frontier. He climbed out of the stage, stretched his legs after the cramped ride, pulled down his luggage from its perch atop the coach, and greeted the small delegation sent to meet him. They took him forthwith to the home of Turner Harbison in the east part of town, where he would remain for the next few weeks. Because board sidewalks had not yet reached that part of town, the new professor soon became acquainted with Iowa mud. It was nearly Thanksgiving before his young wife joined him and they moved to a place nearer the College and nearer the sidewalks.

During his first year Carpenter taught not only science courses—natural science, physics and chemistry—but also two classes in classical literature for the six seniors, one in Latin and the other in Plato's *Phaedo*. Although one had to be something of a Renaissance man to do all that, Carpenter managed. In addition to his academic duties, he served the church as a local preacher, and a few years hence he would be ordained. Respectful of deity, he was awed by the world around him, full of wonder at what God had wrought in nature, be it the antics of a pocket gopher, the femur of a mastodon, a night sky ablaze with the aurora borealis, Mr. Bell's telephone, or a rainbow after a cloudburst.

Burns's appointment of George Carpenter to the teaching faculty was one of the best in the early days of the College. He remained on the faculty, with a few lapses because of ill health, until 1895. A graduate of Wesleyan University in Connecticut in 1866, he was awarded the M.A. in 1869, just prior to his coming to Simpson.

At the end of the second term of the 1869-70 year, Carpenter's colleague, mathematician Henry Douthart, resigned on account of poor health and was replaced by young William A. Lynch, who taught at the College only during the spring term of that year. The reason for his brief tenure at the College is interesting. It was 1870; the Civil War was still fresh in the memory of all Americans, and feelings were intense. It seems that on Sunday afternoons the professors, each in his or her turn, lectured in the chapel to a captive audience of students on a wide range of uplifting topics. On the Sunday it was his turn to speak, professor Lynch unburdened himself of some strongly held views on American politics. He severely criticized Reconstruction in the South and, in fact, showed some sympathy for the late Confederacy. Students were incensed and determined to show their disapproval. The next morning the professor in question was seen hanging in effigy from a railing in the belfry over the chapel. In large letters across his breast appeared the words "sic semper Copperheadis." When he saw his likeness hanging from the tower, Lynch was at first inclined to rebuke the students, whoever they were, but decided instead to laugh it off. It was recorded at the time that "no harm resulted" from the incident. Maybe not, but Lynch was not invited to rejoin the faculty the following autumn.[48]

Both the new College Hall and Old Bluebird stood on land barren in winter and planted in corn—they called it Indian corn in those days—during the growing season. Not a single tree graced the campus. Shade trees, it was said, were hard to get, but the irrepressible George Griffith, trustee and college agent at the time, and also its chief benefactor, let it be known one day in 1870 that he had planted some soft maple seeds on his place out on the west side of town. The seedlings were about the size of broom handles, he said, and the students might have them if they wished. Ever one to take advantage of an opportunity, President Burns gave the school a holiday, asking each boy to transplant one or two trees on the campus. The result was two rows of trees planted around the whole periphery of the College grounds and yet more within. Thus were planted the original "whispering maples" which became one of the College's most enduring symbols.

* * *

A few weeks after the whispering maples were planted, Simpson Centenary staged its first real commencement. Six graduates made up the first class: Brenton H. Badley, Emma M. Cary, Leonard B. Cary, Louisa Anderson, Imogene Hallam and Martha Posegate. All of them received the B.A. degree. Although few records of this important event have been preserved, we can put together a brief outline of the week's festivities, which lasted from June 2 to 8, 1870. We know that at the commencement ceremony on the eighth, Brenton Badley was the top graduate and delivered the valedictory address.[49] The salutatorian was Emma Cary, who would later teach at Simpson.[50] Both of them delivered their commencement addresses in Latin, and one cannot but wonder what the response of the audience must have been. Listening to Latin orations was not a common frontier experience. Each of the other four graduates also spoke at the commencement ceremony, mercifully in English. Each graduate was handed a fine diploma—printed in Latin—with the seal of the College embossed upon it.[51] This ceremony capped a week of intense activity which began on Thursday, the second, with annual examinations of the classes. These examinations were oral and public and would have frightened the students more, had the public shown much interest in attending. The Everetts and Zetaletheans held exhibitions on the third and fourth, respectively, and then heard addresses, the Zetaletheans on the sixth and the Everetts on the seventh. There was even an address to the X.Y.Z. Society, a group founded in 1868 which combined features of a social fraternity and a literary society. The baccalaureate sermon was delivered on Sunday, the fifth. And during the week the board of trustees met three times, mostly discussing financial matters like faculty salaries and the state of the endowment.

It was somehow appropriate that Brenton Badley received Simpson's first diploma. An outstanding young man from a noted Iowa family, he would soon marry his boyhood sweetheart and take her with him into the missionary field in India.[52]

Imogene Hallam was the daughter of Indianola banker David Hallam, an early seminary trustee. From the beginning, the College was something of a family affair.[53]

* * *

The chair of mathematics and astronomy, left vacant with the departure of "Copperhead" Lynch, was filled in the fall of 1870 by Christian M. Grumbling, a respected young professor at Mount Union College, a Methodist institution in Alliance, Ohio. He also taught German at Simpson Centenary, sharing with fellow scientist Carpenter the teaching of the modern foreign languages. It is remarkable what a range of subjects these professors were called upon to instruct, but when a college had a faculty of only five or six persons, they had to teach in a number of disciplines, for some of which they were clearly ill-prepared. Further, their daily teaching schedules commonly involved as many as six or seven hours of instruction and recitation.

"The new professor Grumbling (what an outlandish name he has)," wrote Parson Brady, "is an A No. 1 professor, besides being as pleasant as 10 o'clock on a sun-shiny May morning."[54] An effective teacher, Grumbling was popular among students and respected among townspeople. During his twelve years at Simpson Centenary, Grumbling ran to his innumerable classes, spoke frequently in chapel or in local churches, conducted summer seminars for public school teachers, worked to improve Methodist Sunday schools, and, during his spare time, looked for ways to improve the College. One such improvement was simple: during his first term on the faculty he put up window blinds in his classroom, a much-praised practical measure which surely improved the atmosphere of the place.[55] He was the only man on the faculty who could cope with the eccentricities of the stoves and flues in the building. And when he saw the need for academic assistance to students who wanted to become teachers, he organized a "normal class." One alumnus remembered him as a great raconteur. Whenever Grumbling discovered that a class was about to fail utterly in a lesson, he would close his book, smile broadly and hold forth with a seemingly inexhaustible string of anecdotes. Students, it is said, often avoided recitations by getting the professor started on his favorite stories.[56] This, of course, is a time-honored stratagem which twentieth-century students have raised to an art form.[57]

While Dr. Burns was improving the faculty by the appointment of professor Grumbling, students were enriching the quality of student life by the founding of a campus newspaper. Its inaugural issue was published on October 1, 1870. The *Simpsonian* provided students a unique opportunity to write campus news and express student opinion—polite opinion, to be sure, as editors kept a weather eye out for faculty or church sensitivity on controversial issues. Still, it was a student-run enterprise relatively free from outright censorship. It is claimed by the College's alumni, a claim supported by recent student research, that the *Simpsonian* is the oldest continuously published college newspaper in the United States.

A few days after the appearance of the first issue of the *Simpsonian*, it was heralded in the local press as a "small, neat, eight-page paper, gotten up in good style, mechanically printed upon fine book paper; and its editorial department . . . is conducted with spirit and above-average ability."[58] In his salutatory, editor William Christie Smith wrote of his inaugural edition of the *Simpsonian*, "It is now before you, for your perusal, for your patronage." And their patronage would cost subscribers a dollar a year for eighteen issues which appeared fortnightly during the academic year.[59] Smith said he was directing the newspaper not only to undergraduate readers, including Academy pupils, but also to Simpson alumni and to students of other colleges, contacted through a vigorous exchange policy with other publications.

Because its format and contents set a pattern for many years to come, the first issue of the *Simpsonian* is worthy of our close attention. Its eight pages were printed on good quality paper; the page size was $8\frac{1}{2}$ by $11\frac{1}{2}$ inches. Its front page, like all the pages set in a three-column format, featured articles concerning the College's endowment and the agents who were soliciting contributions to that fund. Though unsigned, these pieces are known to have been written by Dr. Burns,[60] and were full of expressions of gratitude for recent gifts to the endowment, as well as praise for the agent who had assisted in the enterprise. On page two were Professor Carpenter's account of a recent dazzling local display of the aurora borealis and an announcement of the dedication of College Hall set for the next day. On page three the editor spoke, his salutatory followed by several brief news items and full-column advertisement announcing the paper's subscription rates. Much of the fourth page was given over to an article entitled "Originality," signed with the pseudonym "Hons," which everyone knew was identified with their new mathematics man, Grumbling. This page was filled out with a prospectus offering, with entrepreneurial enterprise, five copies of the paper for four dollars per year, ten copies for seven dollars. Anyone getting up a club of five subscribers would receive a "fine photograph of the College" worth a dollar and suitable for framing. The fifth page offered the College directory, listing board members, faculty, and a schedule of the meetings of the literary societies, together with a couple of ads and a book review of the novel *Beulah*, by Augusta Evans. For its completion the review spilled over and used up almost all of page six, whose only other adornment was a brief announcement by the president of the next board of trustees meeting. Most of page seven was devoted to local campus and alumni news items, one of which catches the eye: William A. "Copperhead" Lynch was reported to have entered the law school at Iowa City and was running as the Democratic candidate for clerk of Henry County (Mount Pleasant). Of course, he *would* be a Democrat. The last page of the paper was filled with advertisements for local businesses. With some minor exceptions, the pattern of the first issue was repeated in subsequent editions of the *Simpsonian*.[61]

In 1870, the editor of the *Simpsonian*, William Christie Smith, was president of the men's organization called the X.Y.Z. Society, founded in 1868 as an exclusive club whose purposes were stated to be both literary and social, but which looked more like a fraternity than a literary society. Besides Smith, there were among its eight members in 1870 four more young men from the staff of the infant newspaper, and it is speculated that the idea to publish the *Simpsonian* originated in this group. "It was an English letter society," wrote student historian Christie Swain many years later, "without any real significance attached to the letters. There were never more than these original eight members. Their pass-word was 'peanuts,' and their function, as well as amusement, was eating peanuts," not an exceedingly lofty organizing principle.[62] Still, in the earliest issues of the school newspaper, the X.Y.Z. Society was listed as a literary society, meeting "every Friday evening at 7 $\frac{1}{2}$ o'clock in the Rooms of the Society at the College building."[63]

Soon enough another fraternity was organized when "an F. chapter of the I.I.I. was recently organized here and appeared with badges last Monday morning [January 20, 1871]."[64] Little is known about this organization, but from the announcement of its establishment it may have been a Latin-letter fraternity with several chapters elsewhere.[65]

In the early weeks of 1871, not to be outdone by the men, some young women met at the home of board of trustees member John Cheshire and organized the L.F.V. Sorosis. Hattie Cheshire, one of the elder Cheshire's two daughters, was

THE SIMPSONIAN.

BY PERSEVERANCE WE ONWARD MOVE.

Vol I. No. 1.   INDIANOLA, IOWA, OCTOBER 1, 1870. $1.00 A Year.

THE SIMPSONIAN
IS PUBLISHED SEMI-MONTHLY,
BY THE STUDENTS
—OF—
Simpson Centenary College,
AT INDIANOLA, IOWA.
Terms—One dollar per year in advance.

WM. CHRISTIE SMITH, Editor-in-Chief.
ASSOCIATE EDITORS:
Louie M. Dimmitt,   W. H. Berry,
H. Nell Walker,   Will A Park,
Alice M. Barker,   J. N. Reynolds,
C. K. Kennedy,   J. A. Everett.

CHAS. H. BURLEIGH, Publisher.

The College and Endowment.

That our College will be handsomely endowed and that at no very distant day admits no longer of any doubt. If there ever was a doubt regarding it, it was entirely dissipated by the action of the Des Moines Conference on the last day of its session at Montana. Methodist preachers, as a rule, are rarely hurt by a superabundance of this world's goods.— This is especially true of the noble band of pioneers, who, amid privations and toils rarely undergone by any others, have been making our beloved West rejoice and blossom as the rose. Their pioneering is almost over, and they are seeing in our rapidly advancing prosperity the legitimate results of their persevering efforts. Few of them are graduates, for the necessities of their times thrust them out into the vineyard, with such preparation as the common or graded schools afforded them. Their Conference studies, together with the school of the itinerancy did the rest. With their success the west is familiar. Rarely have we witnessed a nobler example of self-denial and liberality than that presented by these men on the 5th of September last. When the endowment of Simpson Centenary was presented by the agent we were prepared to see it disposed of by a resolution offering "Cordial Co-operation." Judge of our surprise when one-two-three-four-five—of those pioneers rose and with a clear, manly voice gave to our College $500 each. Here was the mite mighty indeed. These were followed by others subscribing $250, $200, $100, and last, though not least in our estimation, two probationers gave $50 each. The sum exceeded $6,000. Had not our excellent Bishop seen fit to urge dispatch, we have no doubt near $10,000 would have been subscribed. Now we are not of those who measure a minister's aid by the dollars and cents he subscribes. Far from it. These $6,000 tell us of the sympathy of men who have by their untiring efforts raised many a valley and overturned many a mountain. In their hearty co-operation we read the success of our College. Students will come from their various charges. Our agents will be cordially greeted and aided in their work of endowment and the hundred of the minister will be the guarantee of the thousand from the wealthy members of his charge. If the people of the Des Moines Conference catch the spirit of their preachers as we believe they will, it will be a small matter to make the Simpson Centenary a lasting power both to Church and State.

Our College Agents.

When the history of Simpson Centenary will be written, a long and grateful chapter will be required for her first agent. Simpson Centenary without Geo. E. Griffith would be 1776 without Washington, or Waterloo without Wellington. Wherever our College is mentioned; there also should it be told, that from the very conception of the idea to the completion and present endowment of the institution, Mr. Griffith has labored as no other man did, and bore responsibilities from which few would not have shrunk. If it were not for the fact that during all that time he has occupied a foremost position in every other enterprise for the development of our county, we would be tempted to believe that the College must have monopolized his thoughts by day and his dreams by night. Three years ago Simpson Centenary had no existance. To-day we see her halls filled by students from every part of the West, and her endowment fund (including Mr. Sigler's donation) about $50,000. If there is one man to whom the credit of this success is specially due that man is Senator Griffith. In saying this we are but uttering the grateful sentiment of both Trustees, Faculty, Students, and well wishers of our College everywhere.— May he long live to see the youth of our West enriched and cultured by the appliances for which he toiled so assiduously.

In addition to the $6,000 so promptly subscribed at Montana, Conference gave us the Rev. J. F. Goolman as agent.— Another of the ministers, Rev. W. F. Morrison, A. M., volunteered to canvass the northern part of the Conference.— Now if our hopes are full blame us not for we are bound by every principle of ratiocination to expect glorious success from the above appointment. Mr. G. is a man of fine abillity, pleasing address and genuine affability. Then he is a general favorite in the Conference, one of its own boys and, by the way, was one of "the boys in blue." He has had some Collegiate advantages and has learned to appreciate them. He is at home on

The first Simpsonian

a Simpson student and one of the founders of the L.F.V.[66] The letters, said the founders, stood for the motto "Lovers of Fun and Victory." The earliest record of the existence of the new group appears in an announcement in the *Simpsonian* dated February 3, 1871: "Call for meeting of L.F.V.'s at Temple de V., Saturday, 7 o'clock p.m. By order of the R.Q."[67] This cryptic statement was eagerly trans-

EXHIBITION

OF THE

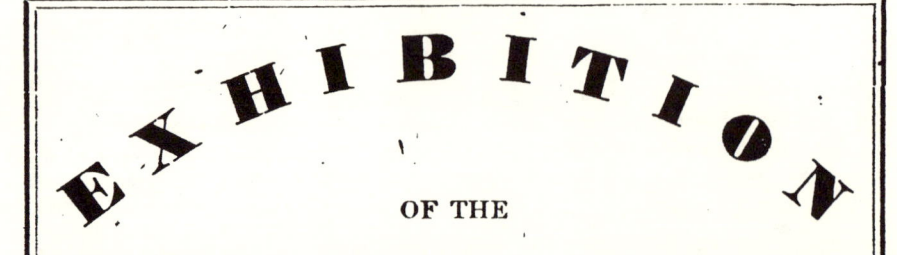

Sophomore Class!

OF

SIMPSON CENTENARY COLLEGE,

Wednesday Evening, November 30, 1870.

ORDER OF EXERCISES:

1. PRAYER—By President Burns.
2. MUSIC.
3. ORATION—*Labor*, by J. N. Reynolds.
4. DEBATE—*Should Women be allowed the right of Suffrage.* Affirmative, Hattie E. Walker; Negative, W. D. Sheetz.
5. MUSIC—*Somebody's Waiting.*
6. ESSAY—*Doubt*, by Lenea Everett.
7. ORATION—*Power of Love*, by Louie M. Dimmitt.
8. MUSIC.
9. ESSAY—*Mystery*, by Hattie Frost.
10. ESSAY—*Where shall we write our names?* by Hattie Cheshire.
11. MUSIC—*Foaming Sea.*
12. DEBATE—*Should the Constitution of the United States be so amended as to acknowledge a God and the Bible.* Affirmative, W. A. Park; Negative, W. H. Berry.
13. MUSIC.
14. ESSAY—*Art*, by A. Jewett.
15. ORATION—*Popery in the United States*, by J. A. Everett.
16. MUSIC.

LEADER PRINT, INDIANOLA, IOWA.

lated by the very nearly all-male staff of the *Simpsonian*: "Notice—There will be a meeting of the Light Footed Virgins at Temple of Virtue, Saturday, 7 o'clock p.m. By order of the Red Queen." But editor Smith and his staff could tease the I.I.I. boys too: "The Invulnerable Isolated Iron-clads will meet in their respective rooms this evening, at 7½ o'clock. By order of the Purple Rustic Chaplain."[68]

Only two years later Simpson got its first secret Greek-letter fraternity when Delta Tau Delta, founded at Bethany College, West Virginia, in 1859, planted its Xi chapter in Indianola on May 8, 1873.[69] While there may have been no connection, two of the charter members of the Delta Tau Delta chapter were William H. Berry and Clarence K. Kennedy, former members of the X.Y.Z. Society, which had died out by 1872. For reasons that are not clear, the *Simpsonian* did not note the existence of the Delta Tau Delta chapter until March 1875. Nor was the advent of another women's group noted until that same March issue of the paper.

The Lambda chapter (later called Iowa Beta) of the I.C. Sorosis was established at Simpson on October 31, 1874, through the efforts of Estella E. Walter of Mount Pleasant, Iowa, an I.C. member who transferred to Simpson. One of the Simpson I.C. founders was Ida Cheshire, the second daughter of John Cheshire, and the birth of this second Simpson sorority also took place in the Cheshire home. Founded at Monmouth College, Illinois, in 1867, the I.C. had already established chapters at six other colleges and universities before coming to Simpson.[70]

These new organizations, selective in their membership and more nearly social than literary, soon competed with the literary societies for the loyalty of their members. Although cross membership was always permitted between the social and literary societies, the popularity of these earliest social groups took an increasing share of their members' time and attention. It would not be long before more national Greek-letter fraternities would appear at Simpson.

* * *

The double failure of the contractor drove up the cost of the College's building beyond the financial resources at the disposal of the board of trustees. Not only had the debt on the building to be paid, and soon, but an endowment must be secured in order to ensure the institution's continued existence. As we have already seen, George Griffith had accepted the role of college agent and set about with a will to coax cash and pledges out of the Warren County citizenry. For him the endowment became a consuming passion. As Burns said of him, "If it were not for the fact that during all that time [Griffith was collecting the endowment] he occupied a foremost position in every other enterprise for the development of our county, we would be tempted to believe that the College must have monopolized his thoughts by day and his dreams by night."[71] By the time the Methodist conference met during the first week in September 1870, Griffith could report that the endowment had grown to almost $50,000, including Mr. Sigler's conditional donation of $10,000, but not counting a 160-acre farm, adjacent to the campus, given by Griffith to the College both for campus expansion and investment income. Burns was grateful: "Simpson Centenary without George E. Griffith would be 1776 without Washington, or Waterloo without Wellington."[72]

In an effort to meet the Sigler challenge and to help clear the building debt, the Methodist conference took up the College's cause in a meeting chaired by Bishop E. S. Jones on September 5, 1870. Burns was expecting that the clergy-

Answer to "The Latest Sensation."

DEDICATED TO THE LIGHT FOOTED VIRGINS.

AIR—*Johannes Brownus.*

The centuries are moving with a wild and breakneck pace,
And the I. I. I.'s and L. F. V.'s are joining in the race
Under Pyramid and Crescent badge the foemen take their place,
    While the world goes marching on!

  Chorus—Tempus, tempus gloriosum
          Tempus, tempus gloriosum
          Tempus, tempus gloriosum
          The world is marching on!

A group of classic maidens who have nearly passed their teens
Have decided that in future they will live behind the scenes,
And with written constitution are fulfilling their day dreams,
    And the world is marching on!!

  Chorus—

They have reached the highest zenith that humanity can find
And display the most astonishing developments of mind,
And it's evident their apron strings they're leaving far behind,
    And the world is marching on!!!

  Chorus—

Their banquet hall is covered with the wrecks of oyster shells
And plaintive sounds of French-harps murmur round these fairy Bell(e)s
While the rattle-boxes' melody the mighty chorus swells,
    And the world is marching on!!!!

  Chorus—

      "Now put me in my little bed
      And cover up my little head."

The first of Simpson's social societies were in existence by the early 1870s. The I.I.I's have some fun with the L.F.V.'s to the strains of The *Battle Hymn of the Republic.*

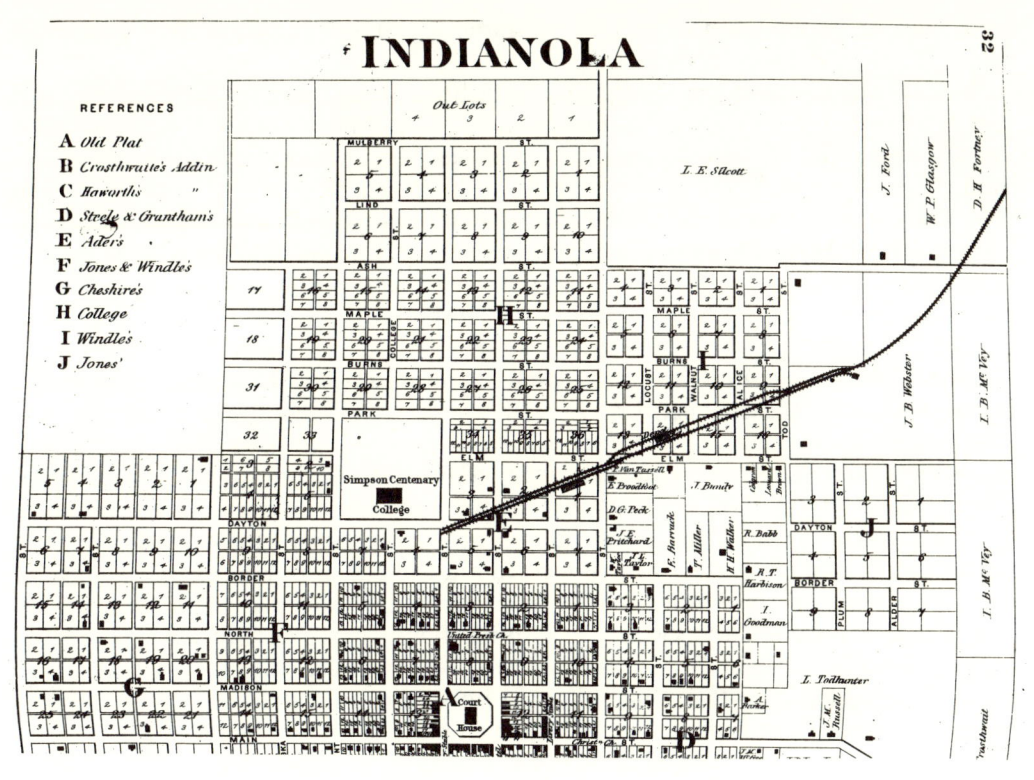

Indianola in 1872. From the *Warren County Atlas*, 1872.

men present, "none of whom is burdened by a superabundance of this world's goods," would dispose of the endowment issue in a well-meaning but empty resolution offering "cordial cooperation" to Simpson Centenary. He was flabbergasted "when one-two-three-four-five of these pioneers rose and with a clear, manly voice gave to our College $500 each. Here was the mite mighty indeed. These were followed by others subscribing $250, $200, $100, and last, though not least in our estimation, two probationers gave $50 each. The sum exceeded $6,000," every dime of which came out of the meager personal resources of these preachers.[73] It was a heartwarming display of confidence in the College and in Dr. Burns as its leader. All of the proceeds from their pledges were applied to the endowment.

Among other things, George Griffith was deeply involved in the effort to bring the railroad to Indianola. Because in 1870 rail was actually about to be laid between Des Moines and Indianola, Griffith resigned as college agent in order to devote very nearly full time to the railroad project. In his place the bishop appointed the Rev. J. F. Goolman, a Civil War veteran and former presiding elder of the Des Moines district. Burns described Goolman as a man of "fine ability, pleasing address and genuine affability."[74] He would need all the affability he could muster to raise much money in western Iowa.

He didn't raise much. A few subscriptions to the endowment were about all. By the end of the 1870–71 academic year the third floor of the college building was still not finished, and the construction debt stood at very nearly $8,000.

Even Burns's usually sunny Irish temperament yielded to gloom. The debt must be paid, and the treasury was empty.

He had not counted on George G. Wright. A man of abundant energy and powerful prestige, Wright, the former Iowa Supreme Court justice, had been elected in the fall of 1870 to the United States Senate, taking his seat in Washington on March 4, 1871. A Republican and a good Methodist, Senator Wright was already president of the College's board of trustees and an admirer of Burns.

At the baccalaureate service on the Sunday of commencement week in 1871, Burns preached an enthusiastic sermon to a packed audience, selecting for his scripture the sixteenth chapter of First Corinthians, verse 13: "Watch ye, stand fast in the faith, quit you like men, be strong." After the college choir sang, Senator Wright rose and said in his rich, baritone voice: "I have been assigned a graceless yet pleasant task; graceless, because I come begging. I want $8,000. Pleasant, because I know I shall get it." And after he practiced upon his hearers the art of persuasion for which he was renowned, the money began to flow. First of all stood the Hon. N. B. Moore. Supporting the Senator's plea, he offered to give $1,000, provided the entire debt was cleared before the benediction was pronounced. Then from the opposite corner of the platform H. C. Sigler—as if he had not already given enough—rose and pledged $1,000. Never reticent on behalf of Simpson Centenary, George E. Griffith then jumped to his feet and matched Sigler's $1,000. Captain B. C. Berry, Civil War veteran, farmer, and board of trustees member, regretted that he could not offer quite so much as the others, but gave $500.[75] Then in their turn board member George W. Jones of Des Moines and Wesley Cheshire pledged $250 each, whereupon Daniel Van Pelt and Wesley Cheshire's brother, John, joined one another in taking care of another thousand dollars. In rapid-fire order came a number of $100 offerings from people as various as local merchant M. R. Barker, P. Gad Bryan, Col. P. P. Henderson, Mrs. Thomas Hallam (David Hallam's daughter-in-law), William Taylor, Dr. Burns, postmaster J. N. Andrews, *Leader* editor M. G. Carleton, John Everett and Miss Emma Cary. Then came $100 each from the Zetaletheans and the classes of '70, '71, '72, '73 and '74. As more people caught the spirit—with evangelical urging from Senator Wright and Dr. Burns—such a shower of smaller gifts came forth that secretary J. H. Henderson had real difficulty writing them all down in his neat record book. Then came another surprise: George Griffith announced that he had two more gifts of $500 each from two absent gentlemen, Cornelius Demaree and Ireaneus Demaree. At that the audience broke into a lusty cheer. Henderson announced that they had raised $8,533. The debt was paid.[76]

It had been something like an old-fashioned revival meeting, and the College was saved, body and soul. It was almost an anticlimax when Dr. Burns, speaking a few days later at the commencement ceremony, interrupted the program to raise $1,000 to complete the third floor of the new building. He got what he wanted in a matter of minutes. "It was a virtuoso performance," commented George Griffith, who wasn't a bad performer himself. Griffith and Burns and the Senator had reason to be proud of their economic evangelism on behalf of Simpson Centenary. Their success was duly noted in the minutes of the Des Moines annual conference a few months later: "*The institution is now entirely free from debt*" and boasts an endowment of $53,000.[77]

To be president of an even temporarily debt-free college in the 1870s was destined to inspire awe and admiration among one's colleagues. The great news of

Simpson Centenary's financial solvency vaulted Dr. Burns into the role of expert on higher education. In July 1871, he addressed the Methodist state convention at Iowa City on the subject of higher education. He reassured his audience that Methodism, Iowa's largest Christian community, could surely support its four colleges,[78] but he warned that the time had not yet come for the creation of a Methodist university in Iowa. "Shall we have a Divinity School? We haven't students enough for either this or a Medical College." As for a university, "let us support our noble State University, with its strong faculty." He went on to say that colleges, for their part, "can be run relatively inexpensively with good, small faculties." Didn't Harvard and Yale grow powerful with faculties only six strong? Faculties, after all, can be put together easily: "There is no trouble in getting good men cheap. Graduates of the best colleges of the land can be procured to take a chair at $600 a year—simply for the reason that they can't get so much elsewhere." He added, with mock seriousness, "we can get good men cheap, even though we have to take women." Then, amid laughter and applause, he admitted that "as good teachers as I have seen in the school-room were women." In his ideal Methodist college he would pay professors a $1,500 annual salary each, a level of compensation that would require an endowment of $100,000 for the institution. He would keep the faculty small; there were "too many ornamental professors already."[79]

* * *

On a more distant stage great events were playing out during these months, events which were to alter the course of world history. In May 1871, the French signed a humiliating peace treaty that marked the end of the Franco-Prussian War and the ascendancy of the Germans to the hegemony of continental Europe. Three days later the new Italian government imposed on the papacy the infamous Law of Guarantes, signalling the completion of Italy's unification and the practical termination of the pope's secular power. The import of these profoundly important events was not lost upon Iowans, but their meaning was filtered through the cultural, political and religious views—one is tempted to say prejudices—that characterized a place like Indianola in the 1870s. The Prussian victory over France was characterized by a local editor as "the triumph of Teuton over the Latin, of Protestantism over Romanism, of the new civilization over the old." Similarly, in the defeat of the pope at Rome one could see that "protestantism, with its high civilization is onward to the downfall of Barbarism which is another name for popery."[80] All the more reason why a college like Simpson Centenary, in the vanguard of protestant education, must be prepared to assist in the conversion of the disadvantaged to the light of American Protestantism, as their coreligionists were doing in the Old World. Burns and his faculty took this task seriously.

The European disasters of May 1871 seemed to pale in comparison with the blow that struck Indianola and Simpson Centenary only a month later. Toward evening on Sunday, June 18, only four days after commencement, a huge storm hit Indianola with terrifying force. In fifty minutes, out of a leaden sky riven by spectacular lightning, a deluge driven by angry winds ripped through the west side of the town, twisting houses off their foundations, splitting trees apart, "huge maples split in twain."[81] A mighty gust of wind, probably not a tornado but a roaring blast, slammed into Old Bluebird, ripping away part of the roof and collapsing part of the north wall. Water and debris poured into the building, leaving it a shambles after the storm abated.

The damage to Old Bluebird was so severe that the decision was reluctantly taken to pull the building down. The new college building had been severely buffeted but remained undamaged. Within a few weeks, what was left of Old Bluebird was dismantled, people salvaging what they could of its structural parts and water-soaked contents.

When students returned to classes in the fall, they noted that Old Bluebird had "gone the way of all the earth." All that remained was a "mass of mortar and broken brick."[82] And a year later one could find only "a few foundation stones, which will soon be removed."[83] Today, a large boulder with a bronze plaque marks the location of the seminary's old structure.

The loss of Old Bluebird was serious, but it was only a minor disaster if one compared it to the great Chicago fire that came four months later. In fact, there was much in Indianola to be happy about. In 1871, in response to student demand, the first book of Simpson songs—elegantly titled *Carmina Simpsonii Collegii*—was published, selling for twenty-five cents a copy.[84] Authored by Brenton H. Badley and Clarence K. Kennedy, it was printed by Mills and Company of Des Moines.

There was yet more to sing about when the railroad came to Indianola. Only a year had passed since the transcontinental railroad had been completed out west, and Indianola pressed for a line to Des Moines to connect with the main east-west route. For several years there had been talk of building the railroad, but a lot of acrimonious debate and some intense political maneuvering between Des Moines and Indianola had stalled the project. At issue was Des Moines' unwillingness to help finance the eight miles of rail that had to be laid in Polk County. Only when the Rock Island Road came along and took the matter in hand did the project begin to move. On August 11, 1871, the first rail was laid in Warren County, and the line was completed at the end of October, the first freight being shipped from the Indianola station on the first day of November. The next evening a merry crowd of two hundred of "the best and most influential citizens of Indianola" jammed into three coaches and made the seventeen-mile trip to Des Moines in fifty minutes, accompanied all the way by the Indianola Silver Cornet Band. In the capital city they enjoyed a festive evening of dining and dancing at the Savery House. It was two o'clock in the morning before the partygoers boarded the train for the return trip.[85]

It is difficult for modern-day readers to appreciate the importance that was attached to the coming of the railroad in the rural communities of America. The presence of the railroad, or the lack of it, could spell economic life or death for a town, as many Iowa settlements would discover. And for Simpson Centenary College the railroad connection with Des Moines betokened good times for the school just as it did for Indianola. Students noticed that the Rock Island depot was located a short block east of the campus, and they concluded that it was located there for the convenience of the students.

* * *

Although Orlando H. Baker enjoyed a longer association with Simpson than any other man in his day, his career in Indianola reaching back to seminary days, he found it increasingly difficult to get along with Dr. Burns. It is not entirely

ZETALETHEAN EXHIBITION.

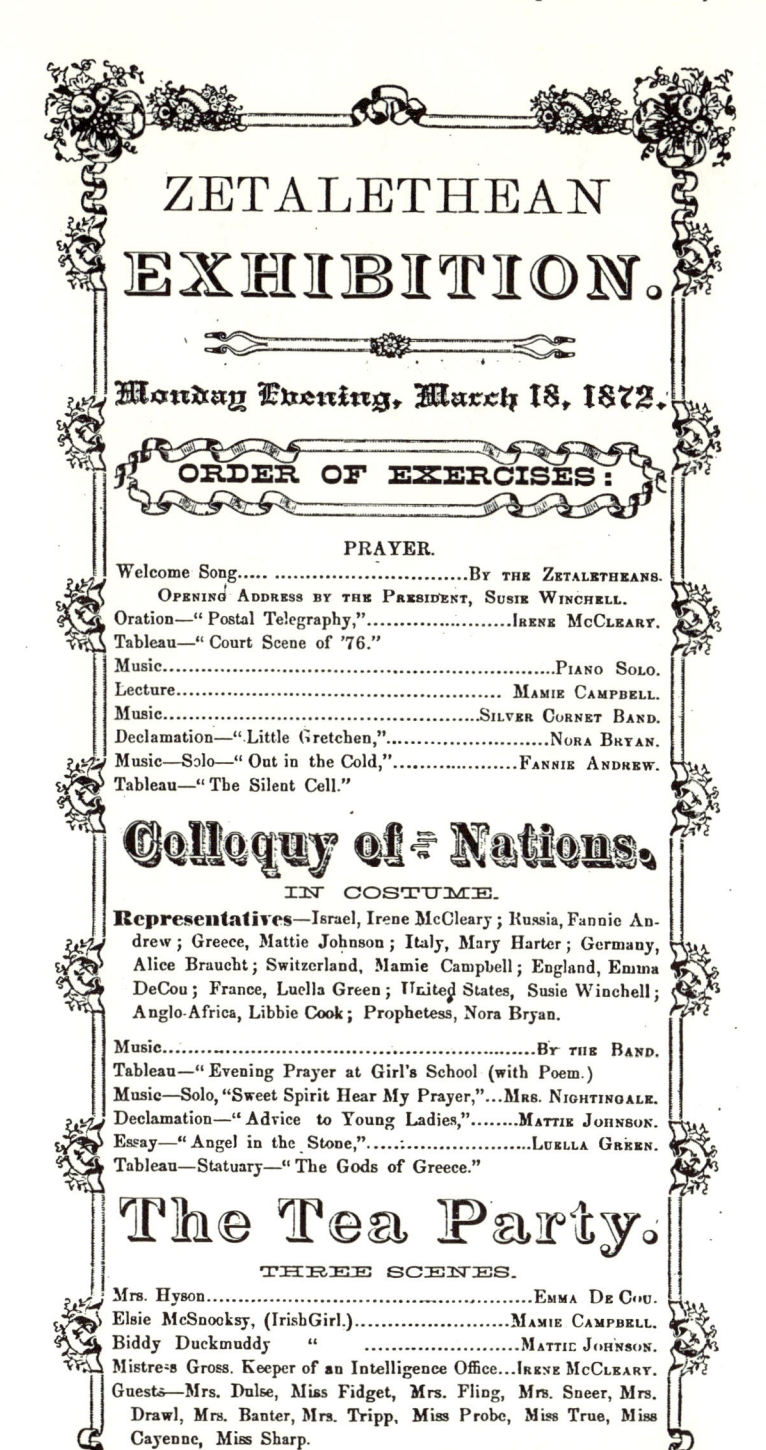

Monday Evening, March 18, 1872.

ORDER OF EXERCISES:

PRAYER.

Welcome Song.....................................By the Zetaletheans.
Opening Address by the President, Susie Winchell.
Oration—"Postal Telegraphy,".....................Irene McCleary.
Tableau—"Court Scene of '76."
Music...Piano Solo.
Lecture... Mamie Campbell.
Music..Silver Cornet Band.
Declamation—"Little Gretchen,"........................Nora Bryan.
Music—Solo—"Out in the Cold,"....................Fannie Andrew.
Tableau—"The Silent Cell."

Colloquy of Nations.

IN COSTUME.

Representatives—Israel, Irene McCleary; Russia, Fannie Andrew; Greece, Mattie Johnson; Italy, Mary Harter; Germany, Alice Braucht; Switzerland, Mamie Campbell; England, Emma DeCou; France, Luella Green; United States, Susie Winchell; Anglo-Africa, Libbie Cook; Prophetess, Nora Bryan.

Music...By the Band.
Tableau—"Evening Prayer at Girl's School (with Poem.)
Music—Solo, "Sweet Spirit Hear My Prayer,"...Mrs. Nightingale.
Declamation—"Advice to Young Ladies,".........Mattie Johnson.
Essay—"Angel in the Stone,"..........................Luella Green.
Tableau—Statuary—"The Gods of Greece."

The Tea Party.

THREE SCENES.

Mrs. Hyson...Emma De Cou.
Elsie McSnooksy, (IrishGirl.)........................Mamie Campbell.
Biddy Duckmuddy   "   ....Mattie Johnson.
Mistress Gross. Keeper of an Intelligence Office...Irene McCleary.
Guests—Mrs. Dulse, Miss Fidget, Mrs. Fling, Mrs. Sneer, Mrs. Drawl, Mrs. Banter, Mrs. Tripp, Miss Probe, Miss True, Miss Cayenne, Miss Sharp.

VALEDICTORY SONG.

Leader Print

> **CLASS DAY**
> OF CLASS '73,
> **Simpson Centenary College,**
> Wednesday Evening, June 4th, 1873.
>
> You are Cordially Invited to Attend.

clear what the problem was; one observer said it was the "radical difference of their views on questions of education and government."[86] Although the issue appears to have been an honest difference of opinion between two good—and strong-willed—men, their relationship deteriorated until they regarded each other with icy hostility. On a faculty of only five persons, such a state of affairs was intolerable. The board of trustees, hoping to avoid taking sides—they liked both men—at first urged the two of them "by mutual concession and forbearance to drop all personal differences and feelings," but they soon learned that compromise was impossible, so "without any reflection on professor Baker's work," they declared his chair vacant. Board members apparently had feelings of guilt and discomfort in their action and expressed "confidence in the integrity and fidelity of Prof. Baker and commend him to any desiring his services as a faithful and earnest teacher."[87]

Someone did desire his services. He was invited in the fall of 1871 to accept the principalship of the Algona Seminary, where he served with distinction, instrumental in having the institution raised to collegiate grade in 1873 by the Northwest Iowa Conference of the Methodist Church. He continued as president of Algona College until December 1874. And soon enough Indianola would hear of him again.[88]

In fact, Indianolans heard from him sooner than they would have liked. Shortly after his abrupt departure from Simpson Centenary in the spring of 1871, Baker printed a pamphlet, addressed to the Des Moines Conference, accusing the Simpson faculty—especially its president—of being unspiritual.[89] Whether the publication of this pamphlet was an act of petulance or an outburst of offended principle we cannot be certain. One thing is clear, however; it was really aimed at Dr. Burns who, in Baker's perhaps flawed judgment, was too entrepreneurial, too aggressive and oftentimes too secular in his management of the College.

Whatever the reasons for its publication, Baker's pamphlet aroused a furor in the conference. Nearly everyone flew to the defense of the College and Burns. The conference visitors denounced Baker's words as an "unjustifiable attack." To look further into the matter, the conference appointed a three-man committee, chaired by the Rev. C. C. Mabee of Des Moines, one of the regular conference visitors, and including trustees Rev. A. C. Williams of Indianola and Phineas F. Bresee of Council Bluffs. These men, especially Bresee, would never be accused of condoning secularism or lack of spirituality. Their report to the conference, which met at Chariton in September 1872, expressed complete confidence in the faculty and went further to commend the College for its Christian qualities:

> We hereby express our gratitude to God for the gracious revival influences which have been enjoyed by our College during the last year, resulting in bringing so many students to a knowledge of the *Love of God*. Also for the blessed fact that He has opened the hearts of so many of our wealthy laymen and friends to give liberally of their substance, until this, the youngest of Iowa's literary institutions, ranks among the foremost in financial resources.[90]

Their praise for the religious spirit of the College was surely on the mark. Simpson Centenary was indeed a "city on a hill," and both its faculty and its students were remarkably, honestly, genuinely pious. Their comments about the liberality of rich friends, however, represented at best a sanguine hope for the future.

Meanwhile, the chair of Latin and Greek languages and literature went to a new occupant in the autumn of 1871. He was Augustus Frederick Nightingale, reportedly "one of the most accomplished educators, east or west."[91] Perhaps Nightingale really did deserve the lavish praise heaped on him at Simpson, but somehow one wonders if people were trying to reassure each other that they had found someone the equal of Orlando Baker.

They hardly had a chance to find out, for Nightingale stayed only one year. One thing is certain: it would be difficult to find any other faculty member in Simpson's history who received more adulation during a mere one-year tenure. In fairness to Nightingale, however, his leaving Simpson Centenary was understandable; he was offered the superintendency of schools in Omaha at a salary of $2,400, more than double what he was earning in Indianola.

Nightingale was succeeded in classics by the Rev. C. G. Hudson, a graduate of Washington University who stayed only a year. From 1873 to 1876 that important chair was held by William A. King, a graduate of Northwestern University, after which it went to C. H. Burke, whose tenure was from 1876 to 1880.

Burke was a very able man, having studied comparative philology and Sanskrit at the University of Berlin, in those days a mecca for American scholars, and he boasted a record of seven years experience as a teacher of ancient languages in the East. Down on the Indianola square, the presence of a Sanskrit scholar in town inspired awe and a measure of mystification.

Professors Carpenter and Grumbling both remained at Simpson throughout the seventies, lending stability to the faculty. Miss McKean, professor of English literature, became discouraged with the unwillingness—or inability—of the board of trustees to increase her inadequate salary, or even pay her what she was owed, so she resigned. Her chair was taken in 1874 by Emma M. Cary, a member of the College's first graduating class and the first alumna of Simpson Centenary ever appointed to a professorship at the College. Her successors during

'78.

LICHT, MEHR LICHT.

TENTH ANNUAL

COMMENCEMENT

— OF —

SIMPSON

CENTENARY COLLEGE

Wednesday, June 12th, 1878.

— AT —

COLLEGE CHAPEL.

the decade of the seventies were Felicia C. Jones (1877–78) and Ida M. Pierce (1878–82). Other faculty positions were less stable during the decade. At least seven different people held the one music position during this period; art was taught only intermittently; and several people taught penmanship and bookkeeping, two subjects dignified after 1876 with the title "Commercial Department," under the direction of Charles L. Bare. Then there was, of all things, a program in telegraphy, taught from 1872 to 1875 by W. S. Carpenter and in 1875–76 by J. B. Fisk.

* * *

It is not widely known that Simpson is one of the oldest coeducational colleges in America. So common is coeducation today that it is difficult to imagine a time when it was not. Early American colleges, restricted to men, were imitated in the nineteenth century by the creation of a large number of women's colleges. The first truly coeducational college was Oberlin, founded in 1833. During the following decades only a few coeducational colleges were established, public or private, but among these were several sponsored by Methodists. Depending on how one calculates the order of the founding of schools—a notoriously inexact science—Simpson is among the twenty oldest coeducational colleges in the United States.

"There is perfect equality and free commingling of the sexes in all departments" of the College, noted M. G. Carleton, editor of the *Warren County Leader*.[92] Among the students, coeducation was taken for granted and was a matter of considerable pride. Student writers in the *Simpsonian* commented frequently about the failure of so many of the distinguished American colleges—especially those in the "wicked and effete East"—to adopt coeducation. When women's rights advocate Susan B. Anthony appeared in Indianola, Simpson students went almost en masse to hear her. Their enthusiastic approval of coeducation led them to approve of women's rights generally. As we shall see, attempts were made as early as 1871 to make the campus literary societies coeducational. These efforts met with at least partial success. And because the women's issue focused in those days on the struggle for the franchise, Simpson students came down solidly in favor of votes for women.

Even Dr. Burns got the gospel. Invited during his early Indianola days to address the state convention of the Iowa Woman's Suffrage Association, the president regretted that he had already accepted another speaking engagement, but in a letter to Mrs. Annie Savery, the noted Iowa suffragette who had extended the invitation, he called their logic "irrefutable, and its suggestions well worthy the attention of all who desire the complete enfranchisement of women." Assuring her that "I shall be with you," he closed his letter with the words, "I subscribe myself—One for the enfranchisement of women."[93]

While Burns and just about everyone else at Simpson favored votes for women, it would be too much to expect of them that they were prepared to see a change in the fundamental role of women in the home. They might welcome women into the workplace—Burns did to a limited degree—but they still believed that after a few years of employment the woman should settle into her true role of homemaker and mother.

A few women, rejecting the role of dutiful housewife, were ambitious enough—some would have called it brazen—to aspire to positions traditionally barred to women. One Simpson alumna went further than almost any woman dared, and in doing so she gained a measure of notoriety equalled by only a few women in nineteenth-century Iowa.

Elizabeth S. Cooke was one of five graduates in Simpson Centenary's class of 1875. An ambitious young woman, she abandoned her original intention to teach and decided to run for the office of county superintendent of common schools. True, as a woman she could not vote, but there seemed to be no law barring her from holding public office. In a spirited contest the year after her graduation from Simpson, she defeated the Democrat incumbent, Howard A. Huff, 1,531 to 1,410. But Huff contested the election, asserting that Miss Cooke was ineligible by virtue of her sex. The matter went to trial. He was 39; she was 21.

When presiding judge Sam Irwin brought down his gavel to open the trial on November 29, 1875, the courtroom was jammed to the rafters with onlookers. Although no witnesses were examined, a number of people appeared in support of either the contestant or the defendant, including an array of urbane-looking lawyers on behalf of Huff. Miss Cooke selected Dr. Burns as associate judge and was supported in court by the Hon. H. W. Maxwell, P. Gad Bryan and George W. Seevers, all of them men of solid local reputation. As the issues were debated, feelings ran high among the observers who, with little regard for the niceties of judicial procedures, were boisterously disruptive in the best frontier tradition. On December 3 the court found that Miss Cooke was legally nominated by a bona fide political party and indisputably won a majority of the votes cast. Male electors were entitled to vote for a woman if they wanted to.

Huff immediately appealed the decision to the circuit court, where in March 1876, Judge John Mitchell reversed the decision of the lower court. He also ruled, however, that Huff could not take office because he had not received the majority of the ballots cast. In this decision the judge managed to displease both Huff and Miss Cooke.

Judge Mitchell's decision was announced one day before the adjournment of the Sixteenth General Assembly of Iowa. On the last day a bill, introduced by a partisan of Miss Cooke, provided that "no person shall be deemed ineligible, by reason of sex, to any school office in the state of Iowa," and it was made retroactive to include anyone already elected. It passed. When the case was appealed to the Supreme Court of Iowa, Miss Cooke was confirmed in her right to hold the office because of the operation of this law.[94]

But women could go just so far. Dedicated as Methodists were to the cause of women's education and their enfranchisement, they did not permit women to hold leading positions in the church. To be sure, women might teach in a church-related college, but it would be unthinkable to select a woman to serve on the board of trustees, an exalted body made up of clergymen and "men of affairs." Not a single woman served on Simpson's board of trustees during the nineteenth century.

One could count eighteen men, then, and not a woman, serving on the board of trustees during the seventies. Their selection was regularized at the annual conference, six elected each year for a term of three years, their terms staggered so that it was necessary to elect only six new members at each conference. By mid-decade the composition of the board was considerably different from what it had been back in 1867. Senator George Wright was president, his position secure even though he spent most of his time in Washington, coming to Indianola only for regular meetings of the board, the most important of which came at commencement time in June. Because of his extended absences from Indianola, the senator chose not to serve as a member of the executive committee of the board, which met frequently. Instead, Dr. Burns was called upon to chair the committee, which included stalwart P. Gad Bryan together with C. C. Carpenter, governor of Iowa, the Hon. William Phillips, distinguished Des Moines attorney, and B. C. Berry. Among the other members of the board during the mid-seventies were seven clergymen in addition to Dr. Burns—one-third of the board's membership: Phineas Bresee, then pastor at Red Oak, H. H. Oneal at Chariton, R. M. Smith at Council Bluffs, J. M. Conrad at Murray, M. D. Collins, presiding elder of the Boonsboro district, and J. G. Eckles, presiding elder of the Indianola district, and, for the first time, a bishop of the church, E. G. Andrews, whose residence was in Des Moines. Lay members of the board included several old hands: H. C. Sigler, the Hon. N. B. Moore of Clarinda, the Hon. J. C. Jordan, the Hon. George W. Jones, who had been treasurer of the seminary during its first year, and a new member, L. Perkins of Des Moines.

Missing from this roster was the board's most prominent and faithful longtime member, George E. Griffith, whose fortunes had taken a turn for the worse. He had invested heavily in railroad development and had lost a fortune. Not only had he suffered personal financial reverses; he had dragged others with him who, on the strength of his recommendation, had invested as he did and lost as he did. Griffith had also seen his house burn to the ground. He soon left Indianola to try to build a new life in Missouri.[95]

* * *

Griffith was but one of the dedicated supporters of Simpson Centenary among the citizens of Indianola. These townspeople, who came to the aid of the College again and again through the years, came to feel a kind of proprietary interest in it. At the same time, they would be the first to admit, the College served them. Its presence in the community was deemed to be uplifting; it was a valued cultural resource. They found it good to have people in town whose principal occupation was intellectual and whose tastes and values could be admired, if not always emulated.

Especially important were the forensic, dramatic and musical events put on at the College and always open to townspeople, sometimes without charge. In those days before radio and television and stereophonic sound, people got their "culture" from the printed word or from live performances or not at all. Thus the importance of speakers who traveled about on the lecture circuit, of ministers who were known to be good preachers, and of homegrown talent that provided most of the entertainment and some of the edification of the masses in small-town America. By no means did the College provide all of Indianola's cultural activities, but it was responsible for a significant share of them.

The importance of these College events, especially the oratorical contests and exhibitions, can be seen in the lengthy reviews they received in the local press, full of praise for the best performances and deprecation of the worst. The critics said what they thought and spared no feelings, as was certainly the case when twenty-seven-year-old George F. Parker, editor of the *Warren County Tribune*, reviewed the college oratorical contest held at Simpson in late October 1874.[96] Most of the speakers, said Parker, "performed their parts very well, while some made ignominious failures." Fletcher Brown spoke first and did not do very well. "Standouts," said Parker, "were Misses [Elizabeth] Cooke, [Dora] Gifford and [Estella] Walter and Mr's. [J. M.] Hamilton and [R. J.] Graham, except that most were too long." He reserved his fire, however, for senior Louella Kennedy's oration, called "Is Reconstruction a Failure?" Her defense of Republican policy in the South sent Democrat Parker into a rage. Party hate and rancor, he said, had no place on the college rostrum. In a newspaper, however, it was apparently acceptable.[97]

The real trouble with most oratorical contests was that they were too long. People were more often bored than edified. The exhibitions of the literary societies and the classes, noted the critics, were shorter, but the quality of the speakers was mixed. And sometimes their speeches could be marvelously inappropriate as was the one delivered in 1872 by T. S. Everett, who expressed vehement opposition to foreign immigration. Dr. Burns, who was present, "expressed himself as being very thankful that *he* had come over before the oration was written."[98] It was, of course, difficult to achieve a uniformly high level of performance when virtually every student was expected to orate.

Without doubt the crowning oratorical event of the academic year was commencement. It commanded the attention of everyone on the campus for an entire week in early June during which they experienced a veritable orgy of lecturing, preaching, recitations and discussions. After the commencement of 1870, when the first six graduates were sent forth, the events of the week varied remarkably little from year to year. Let us select only one, the commencement of 1878, as typical of nineteenth century Simpson.

"Commencement week," exuded the *Simpsonian* reporter who recorded *in extenso* the 1878 event in the saccharin prose of the day, "brings out visitors from abroad and visitors from home, in their best holiday attire and happiest faces, and transforms the halls of the college into a fairy land filled with music, sprites and flowers." It all started on the fifth of June—it was a Wednesday—when the College "opened her hospitable doors and invited everybody to the opening feast of her tenth annual commencement." They called this inaugural event "Class-Day Exercises," the tiny printed program for which is in the College archives.

At promptly eight o'clock the eight seniors trooped into the College chapel, where a large crowd was gathered to welcome them. They were followed by the members of the junior class, who took their seats to the right. The seniors looked fresh and fit. They had returned only the day before from a three-week vacation, during which they were expected to prepare their commencement orations and for these exercises as well as for final public examinations.[99]

This first evening was not very rigorous. In a relaxed, almost playful mood these seniors could perform as a class in a sort of warm-up for the serious sessions to follow. A lusty identity with one's class marked student loyalties of nineteenth-century undergraduates in all colleges, and class-day allowed free reign to their youthful enthusiasm. Each senior got to speak.

Leading off was Mary E. "Mate" Hamilton, whose "Prologue" set the tone for the evening. Her classmate, the Rev. Albert G. Foreman, delivered what was billed as a sermon to the juniors "with melting tenderness and yearning solicitude" for that class. Bessie Guyer's "Class History" provided almost as much fun as did Ira DeLong's "Videns in Futuram," with its fanciful, preposterous prophesies. Emma Patton's "Transmission of Archives" to the juniors was responded to by Charles W. Fisk, the lone junior permitted to say anything. It was left to Susan F. Morrison, the best speaker of the lot, to deliver the only substantial oration of the evening. She chose as her topic the class motto, "Licht, Mehr Licht," and her delivery was reported to be "most excellent; her voice was clear and ringing, every word being heard distinctly in the remotest part of the chapel." Thereupon, the audience was treated to a song sung by the whole junior class, some of whom were monotones, their rendition followed by George W. Samson's "Last Will and Testament of the Class of '78." Ervilla Holmes, who delivered what was billed as the "Epilogue," made a nice speech of appreciation to Dr. Burns and presented him a handsome silver set of five pieces, the gift of the students and alumni of the College. Burns, truly surprised, blurted out a few words of unrehearsed thanks, only to be told that the gift "served him right."[100]

Examinations occupied the better part of the day on Thursday, Friday and Monday. Some of these tests were written, but others, the most important ones, were oral, and the general public was welcome to attend. Not many people accepted the invitation, but enough did to put the seniors on their mettle. While it may appear that the students were under severe pressure, it was important to them, and even more important to the faculty, that they be able to demonstrate mastery of the subjects they had studied. In a day when many people still questioned the value of a college education, it was seen as vital that Simpson display the product of its efforts.

On Friday the literary societies held their annual meetings, which were well attended. Featuring, for the most part, their younger members, the Zetaletheans met during the afternoon and the Everetts and Smithsonians in the evening. Things went smoothly enough for the women of the Zetalethean Society, but because both of the other groups met at the same hour, there was much disturbance with visitors coming and going from one meeting to the other, interrupting the speakers. Still, these crowded sessions were judged to be highly successful.

At Saturday evening's lecture before a large audience, Princeton-educated C. S. Ryman, pastor at Red Oak, held forth on "A Summer in Europe." In 1878 it was not easy to find anyone in Indianola who had ever traveled in Europe, and there was genuine fascination as Ryman put together an anecdotal account of his adventure, emphasizing the haughtiness of the English, the wit of the French and the rapacity of the Italians. Apparently neither he nor his audience was aware of the breathtaking generalizations he was making about national characteristics, and they seemed to enjoy hugely both his stories and his judgments.

It poured rain Sunday morning when Dr. Burns delivered the baccalaureate address to a relatively small audience, but that didn't dampen the spirits of the president who was reported to have presented a "brilliant, scholarly and soul-stirring" sermon. "Your teachers," he said, "desire the immortality of class '78. They have never tried to drive you, but lead you. . . . Imitate what you have found worthy in us, forget what is weak, and go forth to a life of useful, earnest work." One student who was present called Burns's address "the essence of a whole library in a single volume, the cream of a hundred sermons crowded into one." The metaphors might be mixed, but the sentiment was there.

In keeping with Simpson custom, a visiting scholar-preacher was imported for commencement week, or at least for the better part of it. For the 1878 exercises they invited the Rev. Dr. William H. H. Adams, president of Illinois Wesleyan University. Dr. Adams delivered two major addresses, the first of which was the Annual Sermon on Sunday evening. In his sermon he called on the seniors to strive for perfection in a very imperfect world. "The Doctor," wrote the *Simpsonian* reporter, "is a natural orator, perfectly easy and graceful, without affectation or attempt at the sensational." The *Weekly Indianola Herald* was somewhat less lavish in its praise, noting simply that the sermon was "highly commended by those who were present."

Dr. Adams spoke again Monday evening at the chapel to the members of all the literary societies. Because very nearly every student except the preps was a member of one of these societies and was expected to be present, the speaker had a full house. His address, entitled "Self Help," was light, anecdotal and practical, wholly in keeping with the emphasis on self-improvement so characteristic of the Victorian era.

Tuesday was commencement day for the Law Department. Organized in 1875, Simpson's Law Department was located in Des Moines, but its graduates journeyed to Indianola to receive their degree with proper ceremony. At promptly nine o'clock in the morning, seventeen of the nineteen law graduates, led by Dr. Burns, took their places at the front of the chapel. They were accompanied by Senator Wright and Bishop Edward G. Andrews of Des Moines, one of the eleven American Methodist Episcopal bishops, followed by the members of the board of trustees. Whether they knew it or not, they were in for a marathon three-hour succession of speakers, eight of them, selected from among the graduating lawyers, their addresses alternating with vigorous music by the Monroe Cornet Band. What strikes the modern-day reader about the content of these speeches is their defensive tone. Jennie Wright, for example, defended her devotion to the cause of women's rights; most of the rest of the speakers felt obliged to defend the legal profession against its critics. George A. Girard sounded the theme when he devoted most of his address to answering the question why "so much dishonesty is charged upon the profession." His answer was witty, but not very convincing: "elasticity of conscience," he said, "belongs to no trade or profession." There were, after all, doctors and even ministers whose conduct was not always above reproach, and he proceeded to name a few.

That afternoon, the law commencement reconvened to hear the last four student speakers and more band music. The valedictorian of the class, Carroll C. Wright of Des Moines, presented yet another stalwart defense of the nation's lawyers, railing against the "invidious insinuations" of the ignorant who regarded the term *lawyer* as "synonymous with dishonesty and trickery." His vindication of the profession completed, he turned the podium over to the dean of the Law Department, Judge William E. Miller, who gave an address full of sound advice for the fledgling lawyers, whereupon Dr. Burns conferred the Bachelor of Laws degree on the members of the class.

One has to admire Dr. Burns's stamina, not to speak of the members of the audience who had to sit through hours of speeches. After the all-day Law Department commencement he had to appear that evening to attend the annual oratorical contest, said to be "one of the most interesting entertainments of the week." It was a highly competitive event, the contestants having written and rehearsed their orations with infinite care. Six finalists appeared, all but one of them juniors, the Andrew Medal going to John T. McClure '79, of the Everett

Society. His subject, "The Empire of Opinion," permitted him to say almost anything, but whatever he did say was judged to have been delivered "naturally, calmly, deliberately, but forcibly . . . in clear cut, well rounded sentences, and appropriate words." Dr. Burns presented the medal to McClure, joined in a hearty cheer for all the speakers, and listened to the benediction.

Simpson commencement day exercises have always drawn surprisingly large crowds, and 1878 was no exception. "One naturally wonders," wrote John Clarey in the *Indianola Tribune*, "if there is any other college town in the world where they can seat and stand as many people on a square inch as in Indianola." By eight o'clock in the morning they were shouldering their way into the chapel, and by nine there was not even standing place remaining. Everyone was dressed to the nines, the men in somber suits and modest cravats, the well-hatted ladies in long skirts, and around the whole place there was an unmistakable scent of dusting powder and lavender. In front of the audience the rostrum was decorated with evergreens and flowers and ivy, and on the wall behind the speaker's stand a band of evergreen with the motto "Licht, Mehr Licht" in great gold letters. A lusty cheer greeted the class of eight and the dignitaries as they strode to their places, their procession accompanied by the strains of the ten-man cornet band. The five graduating women looked resplendent in their best gowns—it was said they were more frequently asked what they were going to wear than what they were going to say—and their three male classmates looked uncomfortably stiff in their just-pressed suits and well-starched collars.

After a "short, fervent" prayer by Rev. Phineas Bresee—Bresee could always be counted on to invoke a rich outpouring of the holy spirit—Dr. Burns announced the usual honors, introduced the class salutatorian, G. W. Samson, whose words of greeting put everyone at ease. Everyone, that is, except the seniors, who one by one marched up to the podium to deliver the most important oration of his or her college career. It mattered not whether the senior wanted to speak or was skilled in the craft; every graduate had to give an address at commencement, without exception.

It required the better part of two hours to hear them all. And as the parade of orators came to an end, nearly everyone present agreed that the final address, the one delivered by the valedictorian, Ira M. DeLong, was surely the best. On behalf of his class he praised the College to which they had become so attached; he asserted that the methods of instruction in the West were superior to those employed in the East; he was grateful for the mild discipline at Simpson, which he contrasted to the harsh regimen found in eastern colleges. It was not made clear how the speaker had learned about Eastern colleges, but that was probably not important. What was important was the need of nineteenth-century Iowa students for constant reassurance that their education was as good as that offered by the "leading" institutions in the East. DeLong thanked the board of trustees, the faculty and his classmates for his unforgettable four years on the campus, his sentiments expressed in words "pronounced by ablest critics to be the most eloquent and appropriate of any spoken on like occasions in the history of the College,"[101] words that "brought tears from the eyes of a great many."[102] When young DeLong sat down and the cornet band played "Sweet By-and-By," the atmosphere became almost maudlin.

The situation was rescued by Dora Gifford Honnold, representing the class of 1875, who delivered the master's oration, "Our National Fortresses," in a strong, straightforward, no-nonsense style, whereupon chairman of the board Senator Wright took over and awarded the degrees. The B.A. was conferred upon Susan Morrison, Bessie Guyer, Ira DeLong and Albert Foreman, the B.S. upon Ervilla Holmes, Emma Patton, Mate Hamilton and George Samson. Then the M.A. was awarded to Dora Honnold and the M.S. to Louella Kennedy, Elizabeth Cooke, W. S. Carpenter and Madison Cart, all of the class of '75.

If the audience thought the commencement was over, they had misjudged Senator Wright who spoke "earnestly" for one hour, after which Dr. Burns found it necessary to add a few remarks of his own about some recent College problems. When, at last, the benediction was pronounced by the Rev. S. Guyer, the tenth annual commencement of Simpson Centenary College was concluded. It was reported that everyone left the chapel in a state of euphoria. One would judge they confused euphoria with exhaustion.

Meanwhile, the board of trustees held no fewer than eight sessions, sandwiched in between the commencement events, during the course of the week. As will be seen, all those board meetings were both important and necessary.

IV
Lessons in Survival
1875–78

Alexander Burns was an ambitious man who never overlooked an opportunity to improve the fortunes of Simpson Centenary College. And he was genuinely concerned about the advancement of Methodist education in the state of Iowa. He hoped to be able to serve both of these worthy aims, but he also realized that he must curb his impatience for change.

It was during the sweltering summer of 1875, while he was out on the road raising money for the College, that he recognized the increasing difficulty of maintaining four quality Methodist colleges in Iowa, each trying to make its own way in its quarter of the state, each competing with the others in an environment which was not conducive to the success of any of them. Perhaps, he thought, they really ought to combine forces and create one really good Methodist university in Iowa.

The idea was hardly new. In fact, Burns had earlier broached the subject of uniting all the Methodist colleges in Iowa into a single Methodist university, but local supporters of each college, quite predictably, voiced sharp opposition to such a scheme. Their want of "larger vision" did not deter the energetic Indianola Irishman, however. Surely the time had come for the development of professional education for Methodist young people. True, he had opposed such a scheme earlier, but he reasoned that times had changed. He would see to the creation of a university without the support of the other colleges. He would build his great academic edifice on the "sturdy foundations" of Simpson Centenary College.

To call Simpson's foundation "sturdy" in 1875 required consummate faith and a vivid imagination. The College was running a troublesome, indeed frightening, deficit every year, losses that could only be made up either by raiding the still-inadequate endowment or by borrowing. Burns probably knew all that, but he was a risk-taker who told anyone who would listen that the best defense was a vigorous offense. Thus Burns was prepared to enlarge Simpson into a university whenever an opportunity appeared. One came along quite unexpectedly in the summer of 1875.

Burns had attended the June commencement exercises at the state university in Iowa City. As he talked with his friends and acquaintances there, he learned that Judge C. C. Cole had recently resigned his position in the law department at the university and was returning to his home in Des Moines. That wasn't all. Senator George G. Wright, chairman of the Simpson Centenary board of trustees, had also severed his connection with the state university's law school. Two very strong men. Maybe both of them would be interested in a new venture. Why not, thought Burns, organize a law school at Simpson Centenary, the first important step toward university status? He would have to have a talk with Judge Cole and Senator Wright.

No sooner had he returned from his summer fund-raising tour than he plunged into the law school project. Both Judge Cole and the Senator were enthusiastic. Burns explained that the school would be the law department of Simpson Centenary College, an arrangement that would keep total control of the school in the hands of the College's board of trustees. He recognized, of course, that the law department could not be located in Indianola, for all of his prospective faculty members, not to speak of most of the prospective students, resided in Des Moines. But Des Moines was close. It was not the first time, nor would it be the last, that the proximity of the capital city proved to be an advantage for the College.

With Senator Wright's urging, Burns moved quickly during the last weeks of the summer of 1875 to organize the law department in order that it might commence operation in September. He knew, to be sure, that he must have the approval of the entire board of trustees. Unfortunately, that body would not meet until October, but the Senator assured Burns—and the Senator could be very assuring—that the executive committee of the board, of which Wright was chairman, could take action and present the matter for approval to the full board in the fall.

Confident that the trustees would surely not take umbrage at being presented a fait accompli, Burns met with his executive committee on July 12 in one of the pleasant, plush parlors of the Savery House in Des Moines. Joining him that afternoon were B. C. Berry, P. Gad Bryan, the Hon. William Phillips, Senator Wright and the governor of Iowa, Cyrus C. Carpenter. All were delighted at the prospect of organizing the law department, and they seemed willing enough to go along with Burns's insistence that the "financial features" of the enterprise be satisfactory and that "the College should not in any way be responsible for the salary of the Law Faculty."[1] It seemed only reasonable to Burns, and the rest of those present agreed, that the law department be self supporting. More than that, the president, eyeing the College's current deficit, hoped that Simpson would benefit in rich measure from its professional department.

Encouraged by the results of the Savery House meeting and especially by the support of the governor, Burns moved ahead very quickly. Within four days, he recruited for his faculty four outstanding men. Judge Cole, former chief justice of the Iowa Supreme Court, would serve as dean and professor of commercial law. Des Moines attorney J. B. Bissell would teach pleading and practice, equity law, and in one or two other areas. Senator Wright agreed to be named to the faculty but indicated that he could not take an active role in the school until the spring of 1877. Supreme court reporter J. S. Runnells was named professor of the "law of corporations, torts, etc." Burns then persuaded all his new law faculty to sign an agreement "binding themselves to take [student] fees for their full remuneration."² Shortly thereafter Burns, with the help of Gad Bryan, selected two more men for the faculty: one was the eminent jurist, William E. Miller, who was also a former chief justice of the Iowa Supreme Court, as professor of the law of agency and partnership; the other was Des Moines attorney Galusha Parsons who was named professor of the law of bailments and insurance.

Now that he had his faculty, Burns scouted around Des Moines for appropriate quarters for the new department. He found just what he wanted in a building called the Spencer Block in downtown Des Moines on Fifth Street, within half a block of the county and federal courthouses. Here were commodious rooms for instruction, library and study use. He ordered chairs and desks and "other appurtenances" to furnish the rooms, and set about advertising the new law school throughout the state. Classes, said the announcement, would commence on September 15.³

The Iowa College of Law, "being the Law Department of Simpson Centenary College," opened as scheduled with an enrollment of twenty-five students. That first day President Burns, Judge Cole and Professor Bissell delivered addresses of welcome and instruction. Because everything had been put together in a matter of weeks, Judge Cole had not expected as many students as enrolled for the opening term. He was greatly pleased with the large number that registered, and he expressed his delight with the character and ability of the group. During the first year, a total of thirty-seven students took courses in the law department, which nearly everyone called by its formal name, the Iowa College of Law. They paid twenty dollars a term for instruction, fifty dollars for the full year.

When Simpson Centenary's full board of trustees met on October 5, 1875, Burns made a long report recounting the organization of the law department. It was a project, said Burns, "the consummation of which I considered of great importance to the institution."⁴ If any of the board members were miffed about not having been consulted in advance or if any of them had any misgivings about the future of the enterprise, they did not say so. The record shows that they expressed themselves pleased with the promising course of events and ratified everything Burns and his committee had done. The Iowa College of Law, Burns assured the board, would be operated as a department of the College, not as a separate entity. For example, it was determined that the law department commencement would be held in Indianola on the Tuesday immediately preceding the regular College commencement ceremonies.⁵

On the next day after the board of trustees meeting, Burns appeared before the Des Moines annual conference meeting that convened that day at the county courthouse in Indianola. There he won from the assembled clerics a ringing statement of approval of the idea of founding professional schools generally and of the creation of a law school at Simpson specifically. They entered, of course, the customary caveat that such expansion take place "when it can be done in harmony with the educational interests of the Des Moines Conference, and the necessary appliances can be procured without financial embarrassment to Simpson Centenary College."⁶

The new law department was without rivals in central Iowa. But its creation stirred up a storm of opposition at the state university's law school at Iowa City, whose faculty viewed the new Iowa College of Law an affront to their institution. A three-column article in the university *Reporter* declared Judge Cole's part in the establishment of an "opposition school" in Des Moines to be an act of petulance and revenge against Iowa City. There had been bad blood between the two cities for some years. It seems that eight years earlier the Des Moines-based Iowa Law School had been transferred to Iowa City after it had graduated only four classes. This move to Iowa City was widely believed around Des Moines to have been effected by powerful pressure by politicians who suggested unambiguously that the Des Moines organizers of the school, some of whom held public office, might be suspected of "using the influence given by their official position to promote their personal interest" if they opposed the transfer.[7]

The university people were probably entitled to suspect that Simpson's new Iowa College of Law was in part motivated by Des Moines local pride. But when they called its creation an act of "mendacity and adroit malevolence," they were engaging in unwarranted hyperbole. Shifting ground a bit, they lamented the fact that the new law school was the creature of a "sectarian school."[8]

Simpson Centenary's response to the attack was exceedingly mild. President Burns "regretted" the attitude of those at the university. He said that no one in Des Moines or Indianola considered the law department an assault on any school or any interest. The editor of the *Simpsonian* hoped that the university did not claim for itself "a monopoly of professional instruction" in Iowa. "We can hardly believe that the State University would deny us the privilege of sharing in her honorable toil, provided we do it well and foot our own bills," adding wryly that "it is painfully true that we do not have access to the state treasury." And because the opening of Simpson's law department did not affect adversely patronage at Iowa City, the editor suggested that, in view of a fall law enrollment of fifty-nine in Iowa City and thirty-two in Des Moines, "mutual congratulations would be appropriate."[9] The academic program of the law department enabled the student to complete the law degree in one year of three terms. The course of study was typical of American law schools in the latter part of the nineteenth century. Few law schools expected more than one year of formal study.

The method of instruction employed at Des Moines was said to be an improvement on the conventional teaching techniques found in most law schools where, because of the high cost of books, faculty were said to invite the students to "abandon the *study* of all text books and only offer instruction by *lectures*." Simpson Centenary's law department used twenty-three textbooks, some purchased by the students and some rented at low rates. These books, buttressed by lectures and recitations, covered "the entire scope of elementary law and [extended] to every topic involved in the litigation of the present day."[10]

During the five years of its existence, Simpson's law department produced ninety-five graduates with the degree of LL.B. Twenty-four of these completed their work in the first year of the school's existence, nineteen in 1877, and nineteen, twenty-one and twelve in the three successive years. Most of the students were Iowans. During the first year, for example, there were only eight out-of-state registrants, but one of these was especially noteworthy. He was Leslie M. Shaw, of Stowe, Vermont, who would be elected governor of Iowa in 1898 and would serve from 1902 to 1907 as Secretary of the Treasury in the cabinet of President Theodore Roosevelt.[11]

The relationship between the law department scholars and the Indianola students appears to have been cordial. On a Friday evening late in May 1878, for example, some of the law students journeyed to Indianola to debate a team of undergraduates from the literary department. It is clear from the *Simpsonian* account of the evening's proceedings that the debate was viewed as an intramural contest. The chapel was jammed with listeners as Carroll Wright and Howard Russell, representing the lawyers, debated George W. Samson and Ira DeLong of the literary department on the topic "Resolved, that church property should be taxed." The lawyers, who argued the affirmative, won the debate, and everyone had a fine time, including President Burns, who always enjoyed lively public speaking. The law students appear to have liked Burns. It was not unusual for him to lecture to them in Des Moines. In May 1878, for example, he read to the class in international law his well-known lecture on the "Alabama Claims" at the law students' request.

Few would have dared to question the quality of the law department faculty. Judge Cole and William E. Miller, both of whom served on the law faculty all five years, were counted among Iowa's most eminent jurists. Judge Cole served as dean during the first year, Judge Miller for the remaining four years. J. B. Bissell, Galusha Parsons and J. S. Runnells remained on the faculty only one year. In the fall of 1876 the Hon. John Mitchell, circuit judge of Iowa's fifth judicial district, joined the faculty, as did Senator Wright. Both of these served until 1880.

These faculty members, all of whom were either attorneys in private practice or members of the judiciary, took their teaching duties seriously, but none of them could have been much enriched from the fees they collected. At $50 per student yearly tuition, which amount remained constant during the five years the law department functioned, not much was collected. In an average year tuition income cannot have exceeded $1,300, and from this income the dean had to pay building rental, heat, janitorial service, instructional supplies and library books. There could not have been too much left to pay the salaries of four or five teaching faculty. True, the College in Indianola appropriated $500 for start-up costs the first year and an additional $400 in 1876–77, but Burns did want the whole enterprise to be self-sustaining as soon as possible.

It would be excessively generous to suggest that during its first year or so the law department was well managed. The teaching was good, indeed exemplary, but the law faculty members had to see to their own professional careers, and the Simpson president was unable to be in Des Moines frequently enough to ensure real continuity of management. By the fall of 1876 both Judge Cole and Judge Miller were urging the appointment of a resident law professor who would devote all his time to the classes in Des Moines. If Simpson Centenary wanted to run a first-rate law school, it should have on the ground at least one man who could be held responsible for running the program.

There was dissatisfaction in Indianola too. Members of the board could be heard muttering about not receiving financial reports from the law department. In the spring of 1877 they were urging that it either "be moved to the town of Indianola" or otherwise be "managed and connected in closer harmony" with the rest of the College.[12] Further, degrees were being routinely conferred "without any formal report or written recommendation of the faculty" and were not submitted properly to the board of trustees, which had the exclusive right to grant degrees. Regular accounting procedures, they said, must be instituted, and the finances of the law department must be kept separate from those of the

"College proper."[13] The Indianola people wanted a lot more cooperation and coordination than they had been getting.

Judge Miller responded to these complaints by offering to take full responsibility for running—and financing—the law department for a salary of $1,500 (or more if the patronage might warrant it). For this amount, he believed he could "build up the school in every way" and satisfy the understandable concerns of the Indianola people. Accordingly, on June 27, 1877, the board met with Miller at Judge Phillips' office in Des Moines, told Miller they liked his suggestion and offered him $1,200. He accepted that amount, and from that time forward the affairs of the law department continued quite satisfactorily for another three years.[14]

For reasons that had little or nothing to do with the quality or effectiveness of the law program, the board of trustees of the College backed away from the Des Moines enterprise in mid-1880. It was difficult to administer a program in Des Moines from Indianola. Faculty members, although they were successful lawyers and first-rate teachers, were unable or unwilling to give the academic enterprise the attention it deserved.

The law department did not reopen that fall. Judge Miller resigned his deanship on September 23, whereupon the Simpson board voted to discontinue the law department altogether. Lester Perkins, a board member from Des Moines, was asked "to secure the property for the benefit of the College and fully wind up the affairs of the law department.[15]

The failure of Simpson's one effort to move toward becoming a university was tied in with a financial crisis which was centered in Indianola, not Des Moines. I shall turn to that topic a bit later in this chapter.

There is an interesting sequel to the story of Simpson's onetime brush with university status. The Iowa College of Law was revived in 1881 after a lapse of only one year; this time, it was no longer Simpson's law department but a unit of Drake University, which was founded that year in Des Moines. The new affiliation was not at all surprising to those who were involved in bringing it about.

Insiders knew that one of the several persons with whom Burns had discussed his scheme of creating a university in the mid-1870s was George Thomas Carpenter, president of ailing Oskaloosa College. Carpenter wanted to transfer his college to Des Moines. Although he was thwarted in his design, he and all but one of his faculty members resigned and, together with a number of newly acquired friends of their project, including General F. M. Drake of Centerville, opened a new college in Des Moines in the fall of 1881. Carpenter had a clear field, for by this time Burns had resigned at Simpson, and neither the Methodists nor the Indianola townspeople would countenance a move to Des Moines. Committed to creating a university, Carpenter cast about to find the resources and the faculty to develop professional schools. He soon discovered the old faculty of the Iowa College of Law, still in 1881 an "unincorporated teaching group of lawyers" who could be recruited for his law school. These lawyers, of course, were "unincorporated" because the Iowa College of Law had never been an independent corporation but a department of Simpson Centenary College. For their part, the jurists and attorneys were delighted to renew their association with an academic institution. Thus the Drake University Law School of the present day has the old Simpson Law Department as its predecessor.[16]

The law department of Simpson Centenary College was the only professional school actually organized and operated by the institution. Another was planned as early as 1875 but never saw the light of day. There was a brief statement in the Methodist conference report of that year recommending the creation of a department of medicine "when such establishment can be secured on conditions equally favorable with those governing the organization of the Department of Law."[17] It was clear that Burns was especially interested in a school of medicine and, as soon as the law department was established, made it his next project. He was convinced that such a school could be set up in Des Moines with a superior faculty as soon as facilities could be secured.

On the evening of August 3, 1875, Burns met with a number of "friends of the College and of medical gentlemen" in Des Moines, with Dr. Isaac Windle, long-time friend of the College, serving as secretary. Letters pledging support were read from physicians in Dubuque, Council Bluffs, Ottumwa and other towns. The new medical school, they said, would surely become "the leading medical college in the State and the West." A resolution was unanimously adopted giving approval of "the proposal of Simpson Centenary College to establish a Medical Department at Des Moines" and urging that it go into operation "as soon as suitable buildings and outfit can be provided." Because it was clearly too late in the season to open the department that autumn, they determined to make a beginning by the fall of 1876.[18]

Burns felt confident enough of the enterprise to announce in the College's 1875–76 catalog, published in the summer of 1876, that "a Medical Department will be organized during the current year."[19] The department was never created. For one thing, the facilities and equipment required for medical instruction, however loose and flexible the teaching arrangements might be, were far beyond what the College could possibly afford. For his part, Burns thought that the lack of funds was not really such a formidable problem, and the experience of Drake University only a few years later suggests that he may have been right. And it is quite possible that Burns might have pushed the project through to completion had he remained long enough at Simpson to do so, and had the financial problems of the Indianola campus not pressed as hard as they did.[20]

It was financial problems that preoccupied Burns and the board of trustees during the latter part of the 1870s. All their energies were required just to keep the College going from year to year. None of them was more than dimly aware of the powerful economic forces that shaped their world. To be sure, they knew they were living in hard times, but they were at a loss to understand, much less to explain, the causes of the nation's economic malaise which was especially virulent in the farm belt.

There had been more than a decade of rapid deflation. Price declines since the end of the Civil War were sometimes dramatic. In 1878, for example, the *Weekly Indianola Herald* published a list of comparative prices of food and household goods between 1865, when prices were relatively high because of four years of wartime scarcity, and 1878, when they hit the bottom. A pair of boots that cost $5.50 in 1865 could be had for $3.00 in 1878. The price of calico dropped from 35¢ to 5¢ a yard, muslin from 50¢ to 8^1/$_2$¢ a yard, a pound of sugar from 20¢ to 8^1/$_2$¢, coffee from 40¢ to 20¢, a broom from 45¢ to 25¢, a pound of nails from 10¢ to 4¢, a yard of denim from 45¢ to 10¢, a good axe from $2.00 to $1.00, and a barrel of salt from $6.00 to $1.60. Farm commodity prices in 1878 were correspondingly low: corn was 16¢ a bushel, oats 15¢, wheat 82¢; cattle sold in the markets at $2.75 per hundredweight and hogs at $2.40.[21] Not a few Iowa farmers,

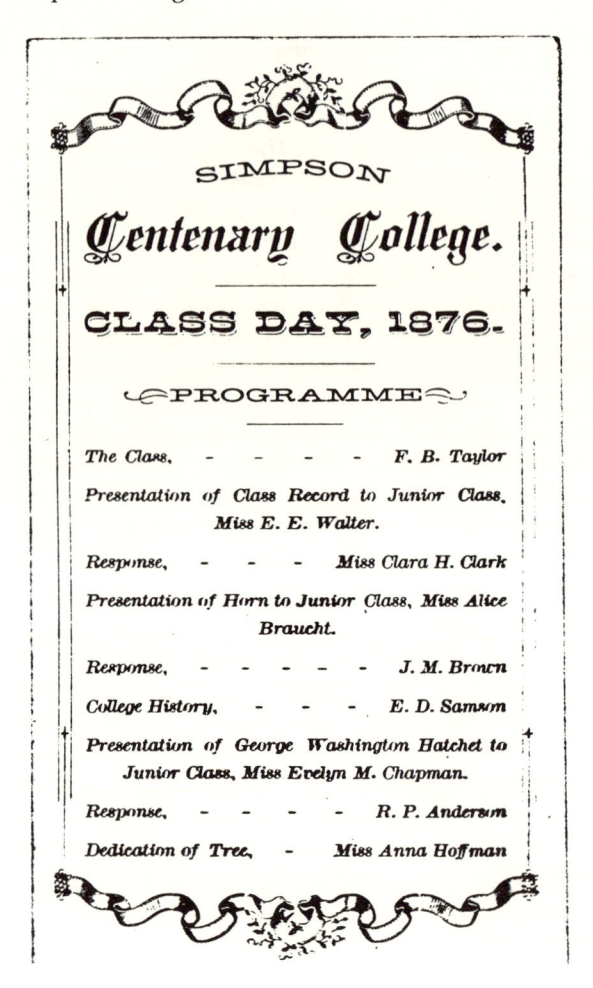

```
         SIMPSON
     Centenary College.

     CLASS DAY, 1876.

         PROGRAMME

  The Class,    -    -    -    -   F. B. Taylor
  Presentation of Class Record to Junior Class,
              Miss E. E. Walter.
  Response,    -    -    -    Miss Clara H. Clark
  Presentation of Horn to Junior Class, Miss Alice
                  Braucht.
  Response,    -    -    -    -    J. M. Brown
  College History,    -    -    -    E. D. Samson
  Presentation of George Washington Hatchet to
     Junior Class, Miss Evelyn M. Chapman.
  Response,    -    -    -    -    R. P. Anderson
  Dedication of Tree,    -    Miss Anna Hoffman
```

in desperation, were ready to take some kind of action to improve their lot by joining the National Grange (the Patrons of Husbandry) or supporting the Greenback Party, advocating cheap money.[22]

* * *

Try as he might, Burns was unable to prevent the College from slipping more and more into debt during the late 1870s. He could remember how they had totally eliminated the debt back in 1871, but he had watched deficits accumulate unremittingly since that time, the financial decline exacerbated by the depression that had been triggered by the Panic of 1873. Hard times made it more difficult than ever for all colleges to accumulate endowment funds from among their constituents. And income on endowments slowed because too many people who owed on the notes they had signed could not keep up their interest payments, much less pay the principal amount. The College could and did sometimes bring suit against defaulters, but collected little but community opposition for its effort.[23] Because colleges relied heavily on endowment income to pay their bills, the financial blow was severe; for some colleges the blow was mortal.

Simpson Centenary was hardly an exception to this frightening decline in income. As the debt mounted, so did the anxiety of the president, not to speak of the frustration of the faculty, the impatience of the townspeople and the dismay of the clergy in the conference.

By 1877, the financial plight of the College was desperate. When Burns met with his board of trustees at the close of the 1876–77 academic year, he reported honestly the dismal facts: the College's debt was completely out of hand. In the first place, there was $9,280 owed on warrants, most of which had been issued to the faculty.[24] In fact, faculty salaries were, in aggregate, more than a full year in arrears. The teaching staff, reported Burns, was suffering "great inconvenience from the inability of the treasurer to pay warrents [sic]"; these people "have been obliged to dispose of [the warrants] at discount and others are oweing [sic] embarassing [sic] amounts and very much need their money." Professor Carpenter, who was owed $1,600, needed half of that amount at once; Grumbling needed at least $500 to pay his debts and see him through the summer. Miss Cary had received nothing all year nor for the spring term of the previous year and "absolutely needs the whole amount" of the $900 owed to her. Burke had received only a small part of his salary and needed some cash. Some of the professors—especially Carpenter and Grumbling—thought they should have salary increases for the next year, but "in view of the impoverished condition of the treasury," backed away from such a request, hoping merely to get what they were clearly owed already.[25] Miss Cary gave up and resigned, but the rest of the faculty stayed on because they really didn't have anywhere else to go.

Money owed the faculty was only a part of the problem. Warrants had been issued for the College agent ($500), the law department ($319), a number of items lumped under the heading of "sundries" ($2,187) and even for the janitor's wages ($187). A little over $500 was owed in interest on these warrants. Added to this was a long-unpaid $5,000 loan from the North Western Insurance Company, another loan of $500 from the Warren County Bank and delinquent real estate taxes of $180. The total indebtedness amounted to $16,462, or approximately double the cost of running the entire College for a year.[26] And that did not take into account the nagging matter of mechanics' claims on the erection of College Hall, some of these claims going back ten years, in the amount of $2,473. Burns did not include these liens in his "official" listing of the College's debt, for the whole debt on the building was still in litigation.

The board studied the assets. The endowment stood at $65,575 on the books, but everyone knew that at least $20,000 of this was uncollectible. Interest owing the College on that portion of the endowment that they hoped was collectible was $5,500. There existed also a contingent fund of $2,917, tuition notes of $64 and, Burns noted, $101 in cash. The endowment interest was not yet paid in. Lacking ready cash, the board was tempted to raid the endowment principal, but its own rules forbade such a solution to the fiscal crisis. So board members agreed to sell the only real ready asset they had, the contingent fund notes, at a ten percent discount, to raise cash for pressing current needs. Thus they were able to pay a few bills, but were able to give almost nothing to the faculty. As a kind of act of expiation, they issued a flurry of new warrants. Everyone knew, of course, that if the local banks accepted these warrants at all, they would discount them deeply. But warrants were at least a symbol of pious good intention.[27]

All this was enough to make one wonder if the College could survive. That summer both Burns and Professor Carpenter went out into the field to raise more endowment funds—it was still not considered proper to ask church people for operating funds—and when they returned they had little to show for their efforts. Not only was the economic climate in Iowa poor; people in rural Methodist congregations were hearing rumors that Simpson was about to go under. Why throw good money after bad?

Small wonder, then, that Burns began to search for ways to restore the College to health. He still dreamed of a Methodist university, but right now he had to save a Methodist college. One solution that had some appeal was to move the College to Des Moines. Whatever the rustic charms of Indianola, the larger city could undoubtedly provide more dependable financial support. Perhaps, too, it would be easier to attract large numbers of students to a Des Moines-based institution. Besides, the law department was already located in the capital city. Moving the whole College there did make a lot of sense.

He had actually been thinking about this for several years. As early as 1875, even before the law department was organized, Burns had considered the possibility of a move to Des Moines, although at that time he had not been serious enough about it to discuss it formally with his board of trustees. Soon enough, however, rumors were flying around town to the effect that Burns and some of the faculty favored the idea. When young George Parker,[28] editor of the *Indianola Tribune*, got wind of it in a letter from Bishop Gilbert Haven, who argued strongly for the move, Parker reacted sharply. The Bishop, he wrote, "suggested that Indianola was too small a field for the giant intellects of educators and that the capital city was just the place for the college." He lashed out at Bishop Haven, calling him "an inflated, conceited blue-blood Yankee meddler," one who "knows nothing of the adaptability of our place for educational purposes." Unfortunately Simpson Centenary "looks like a little thing because Bishop Haven cannot shed the light of his genius and more especially his sensational preaching over it." It was too bad that he knew only the "scholastic shades of Beacon Street" and had no appreciation for the West.[29] The editor of the *Herald* was a bit more temperate. "Let these reports be true or false," he wrote, "it is due to the citizens of Indianola and others, who have so often lent a helping hand to this institution, to know the truth of them."[30]

Burns had not dignified these rumors by answering them. Instead, he had gone ahead in the fall of 1875 with the organization of the law school in Des Moines, permitting his critics to believe that they had misunderstood his organizing the law department to mean that the whole institution was to be moved. And there, for a season, the matter rested, although Burns, who kept his own counsel, continued to be persuaded that locating in Des Moines made sense.

The idea seemed to make even more sense when the finances of the College plunged even more into depths during the 1877–78 academic year. By the spring of 1878 the Des Moines press was reporting Simpson's problems in some detail and responding favorably to rumors of the College's possible transfer. Although no actual plans had been made, Burns did have a few private conversations with a number of leading Des Moines citizens who were interested in bringing the College there. These meetings were merely exploratory, but they could not very well have been kept secret had the participants wanted to. Yet Burns was upset when he saw the matter heralded in Des Moines newspapers, especially because he had come away from the talks with some serious misgivings about the advisability of making the move after all.

When editor John E. Clarey of the *Indianola Tribune* reported in April 1878 that "not a little discussion is taking place just now in regard to the removal of our college . . . to Des Moines," he was telling Indianolans what they already knew. He ventured the opinion that "there may be good reasons why this should be done, but we fail to see them, while we do see arguments in favor of having the college remain here." That opinion was by all odds the mildest he would utter about the College during the next few months. Within days, he was in the vanguard of an irate citizenry that saw its town betrayed and Burns as the Judas who was responsible for the deed.[31]

Never before or since has there been in Indianola such a storm of controversy centering on the president of the College. Charging that Burns had been "for the past year or two unloyal to his trust" in a number of ways, Clarey could no longer remain silent. He asserted that looking for a new location for Simpson Centenary College was not among Burns's duties, yet the president "has been devoting more energy to trying to have the college removed to Des Moines than to his legitimate work." Burns might assert the contrary, but "he has been manifesting his dissatisfaction with Indianola and toadying to a few Des Moiners. In common parlance, he imagines himself too great a light to be hid under a small bushel," so he wants to go to the capital, "where he can shine to his fullest extent."[32] Clarey was certain that Burns was deliberately making the College fail in Indianola so that the Methodist conference would be persuaded to move it to Des Moines. "In a word," wrote the editor, "he has been practicing deception."[33]

Apart from his long, ad hominem attack on Burns, Clarey summarized the arguments made by proponents of the move: (1) Des Moines was the state capital and was centrally located; (2) the law department and the general College would be located in the same place; and (3) a Des Moines location, with its large population, would help to make Simpson popular, even famous. To these arguments Clarey offered categorical refutation: (1) Indianola was certainly just as centrally located as was Des Moines; (2) if the law department could not be run separately, then one need only cut off the law school and develop the main institution, and (3) Des Moines offered the worst possible site for a college, for it contained "the corruption, the evil surroundings and evil influences" of the large city.[34] And as for making the College famous, he suggested sarcastically that people look at Callanan College, a frail institution located in Des Moines. "Its fame," he suggested, was "confined within the limits of Coon Forks, the porkhouse and brewery neighborhood and Mr. Callanan's farm."[35]

Clarey knew that there had been talk of consolidating Iowa Wesleyan University and Simpson. He had no objection to that. "Well and good," he wrote, but "let it be done here," not in Des Moines.[36]

If the editor of the *Tribune* had let well enough alone, his criticisms of Burns might have had some useful effect, but like a predator that draws blood and goes for the kill, Clarey pressed his attack too far. A week after his opening thrust, he followed up with an outburst of venom rarely witnessed even in the libelous press of the day. That Burns had "mismanaged and injured" the College were the mildest of the charges. With apparent approval Clarey quoted a local attorney who called Burns "the most consumate [sic] liar in this whole city"; he was an "unscrupulous and ambitious hypocrite" who would "stoop to any meanness." He was a "traitor to his trust" whose mismanagement of the College's finances bordered on the criminal.[37]

It is difficult to know precisely what impelled Clarey to attack Burns with such vehemence, but it would appear that apart from the threat of moving the College to Des Moines, the one issue that rankled Clarey most was Burns's objection, of all things, to a guest speaker at one of the literary society meetings that spring. The Everetts had invited Dr. C. A. Wallace, a theological liberal and United Presbyterian, to speak. Burns objected, and, according to an Everett member, "did harangue us dreadfully."[38] Burns was probably overreacting to Dr. Wallace's well-known and not-universally-admired liberalism. Burns, who had been raised a Presbyterian himself, was regarded by Methodists as a liberal, and he believed he had to bend over backwards in order not to offend his conservative Methodist brethren. Whatever the merits of this issue, he remonstrated in vain, for the Everetts defied authority and heard Wallace speak, while Burns fumed.

Within a matter of days, Burns was objecting once again, this time to the election of a nonstudent as president of the Everetts. A few of the members, angered by what they considered unacceptable presidential meddling in society affairs, left Simpson and enrolled at Monmouth College. Clarey of the *Tribune* took up the cudgel for the Everetts, accusing Burns of "lying accusations" and an "ungentlemanly onslaught" on students.[39] And no sooner had Clarey launched his campaign of vitriol against the president than A. J. Graham of the *Herald* joined in the mudslinging, publishing a statement by S. J. Graham, the aggrieved ineligible who had been stripped of his Everett presidency. He did not like Burns at all and said so in purple prose.[40]

Most of the Everetts were shocked by the rashness of these attacks in the press, and they fired off a letter defending Burns against what they called "malicious insinuations," arguing that he had treated the society with "the utmost liberality." The president, they insisted, was entitled to speak his mind to the Everetts. Declaring that they were in "full sympathy with the Doctor," they labeled the attacks of Clarey and Graham "unwarrantable poltroonery." Then, unexpectedly, one of the Everetts who had transferred to Monmouth, A. G. McCoy, whom Burns considered the prime mover in the Wallace affair, penned an angry letter to the *Tribune*, saying the editor "ought to be horsewhipped." McCoy had been angered by Burns's actions, but he believed the devil should be given his due. "I am not apologizing for Dr. Burns. I do not like him and never did," but Burns did treat the Everetts honorably and "has always done fairly by me." McCoy realized his leaving Simpson was an action taken in anger, and was sorry for it. Now he wanted to make things right by giving a positive estimate of Burns's character. And he wanted to be believed: "I do not lie, nor steal, nor commit fornication, nor bear false witness. I do smoke and swear (clerically) at editors, railroad corporations and other great companies."[41]

Predictably, the *Warren Record*, edited by young John A. Everett since 1873, flew to Burns's defense. Everett had graduated from Simpson in 1872 and admired Burns beyond measure. Was the *Tribune's* agitation against the College, he asked, a consequence of "ignorance and simpleness" or was it "pure, uncontaminated cussedness?" He concluded that it was probably both; surely it was a "contemptible and damaging" attack.[42]

Burns was stunned by the storm of controversy, for he saw the whole thing as an assault on both his judgment and his integrity. At first, trying to control his Irish temper, he remained silent, but he soon realized that his failure to answer Clarey's charges would be taken as tacit acknowledgment of their truthfulness. At the end of the commencement ceremony in June, Burns decided to speak out. Referring to "recent slanders," he deplored the "falsehoods published about me" regarding the management of the College. He had documents, he said, that would prove his critics' charges false, but he chose instead to pass them over with contempt, for they did not merit his time or attention. Obviously angry, Burns predicted that the College would live "long after its present opposers are forgotten."[43]

It remained for the Rev. Thomas Stribling Berry, the popular minister of the Indianola Methodist Church, to have the last word in the controversy, which by midsummer was growing as stale as last week's bread. In a hard-hitting letter to the editor of the *Tribune*, he sought to vindicate Burns against his enemies. Speaking on behalf of the Des Moines Conference, Berry praised Burns's "competency and fidelity as the manager of their college." He wanted to convey "sorrow and displeasure" at the treatment accorded to Burns, lamenting that "the criticisms now being made upon the school and its management are from conspicuously non-Methodist sources." Berry's suspicion that local disciples of John Knox were behind the vilification of Burns led him to discount the whole thing as an unfortunate manifestation of denominational rivalry. Burns, he said, "could not be guilty of misdirecting College funds," for it was the board of trustees that authorized every cent that was spent. Then, coming back to the issue that had stimulated the whole controversy in the first place, Berry admitted that Burns had ventured the opinion that one might consider moving the College to Des Moines, "but in fact it hasn't even come up in the Conference." If it did, wrote Berry, "the Conference would always vote almost unanimously for Indianola." But should it come up, "the most impressive reason in favor of removal would be the protracted and rather bitter assault lately made by and through your [Clarey's] paper."[44]

* * *

The harshness of the debilitating controversy over Burns's management of the College, fought out against a background of economic malaise in rural Iowa and the Midwest, can be understood better if one takes into account the radicalization of politics that was a product of hard times. Indianola—and Simpson with it—was affected by the strident words and actions of the Grange or the Greenbackers. Although the town and Warren County remained heavily Republican in politics, the disaffected farmers, supported by some townspeople, made election campaigns interesting.

Indianola even got a Greenback newspaper for a few months in 1878–79, when John A. Everett, editor of the Republican-leaning *Warren Record*, as he put it, "evolved" the politics of the paper to support the Greenback Party.[45] Alexander Burns rather liked Everett's paper. It was the only one in Indianola that supported the president and the College unqualifiedly when he was being attacked by both Republicans and Democrats. Burns, it must be pointed out, rarely if ever expressed a partisan political opinion. A Canadian, he did not participate in the political process and was delighted and relieved to have an excuse for keeping out of local party politics.

Burns might avoid politics, but faculty and students enjoyed it immensely, even though the voters of Warren County made nearly every election a lopsided contest. In the famous disputed Hayes-Tilden presidential election of 1876, the Warren County electorate handed Hayes a huge 1,024-vote margin over Tilden, and it accepted with equanimity the decision to award the victory to Hayes.[46] In any case, it will be recalled that Warren County had its own disputed local election that same year. Four years later the county went for the Republican candidate, James A. Garfield, by a majority of more than 200 over the combined vote of Democrat Winfield Scott Hancock and Greenbacker James B. Weaver, who ran a strong race in Warren County.[47] For all that, Warren County was unassailably Republican, and that party's clarion in Indianola once went so far as to note that Robert Ingersoll, the nineteenth century's most militant atheist, had damned the Democrats, associating them with secession, slavery, destruction and assassination. "It is all true," said the *Herald*. It was apparently still less offensive in Indianola to be an atheist than to espouse the Democratic creed.

Whatever their political creed, Simpsonians and townspeople alike thrilled to the printed account of the opening ceremony of the United States Centennial Exposition held at Philadelphia on May 10, 1876. Fifty thousand spectators stood in the rain at the centennial grounds as President Grant and his cabinet, members of the Supreme Court and other formally attired dignitaries moved into their places near the 150-piece orchestra and 1,000-member choir. After the playing of Wagner's "Centennial March," the opening prayer was offered by Bishop Simpson. The honor accorded the Bishop that day sealed forever in the minds of the people of Indianola and Simpson Centenary that their College had indeed been well named.

The Centennial Exposition at Philadelphia had another direct, and quite unintended, influence on the College. One of the most talked-about exhibits at the exposition, which displayed many of the products of burgeoning American industry, was Alexander Graham Bell's telephone, the instrument the inventor had patented only the previous March. Few fairgoers who gawked at the funny-looking gadget considered the invention to be of any social or economic importance, but they had fun playing with the "talking toy."

In Indianola, Professor George Carpenter asserted that Bell's invention was no toy; the telephone was an instrument of scientific significance. At least it would be useful in his classes in natural science at the College. As soon as he was able, he purchased two telephones and set up his "new talking apparatus" between his house on Madison Street and his classroom in College Hall, a distance of about a quarter of a mile. More than that, he conducted a demonstration of the new invention on January 15, 1878, before a few astonished Indianolans, including John Everett of the *Record* and John Clarey of the *Tribune*, who timorously joined the professor in singing the Doxology in chorus. "Praise God From Whom All Blessings Flow," they sang, with organ accompaniment, from Carpenter's house, while others, handing the receiver from ear to ear, listened excitedly to the tinny rendition.[48] The following Saturday Carpenter demonstrated the telephone at the College chapel; this time he charged admission. He hoped to clear fifty dollars. That would be enough to buy a telephone for the College. He was disappointed when too few were willing to pay twenty-five cents, no matter how wondrous the apparatus.

Carpenter's fame spread like a prairie fire. Soon everyone wanted to try out the telephone, free of charge if possible. People in Des Moines heard about it, and asked for a demonstration. That gave Carpenter an idea.

The professor's finest day was February 5, 1878, when he tested a telephone line hurriedly rigged between Indianola and Des Moines. He had received permission to string his telephone wires alongside the telegraph lines that followed the Des Moines-Indianola-Winterset railroad tracks. Carpenter invited nearly thirty people to join him at Rock Island Railroad superintendent Royce's private office at the depot in Des Moines, where they rang up the Indianola group—Dr. and Mrs. Burns, George Seevers and his wife, Mrs. Carpenter, Dr. Charles W. Davis and a few others—at Carpenter's house. The groups talked with each other, sang songs and played musical instruments for their mutual entertainment. For part of the evening, Carpenter had Winterset included in the connection, but the sounds were more distinct when just Des Moines and Indianola were speaking.[49]

Carpenter became something of a celebrity. The telephone was an instantaneous success, and the professor found himself, now regarded as an expert, besieged with requests to install telephones in Des Moines and Indianola. Within a few days after his first Des Moines demonstration he put in phones, the first in the capital city, between the office and residence of Dr. E. H. Carter, a prominent physician. Within a month he strung a telephone line between the Aborn House and the Governor's room at the capitol and yet another between the Aborn House and the Savery House. These hotels were the most fashionable in Des Moines in those days. Down in Indianola, Carpenter was busy installing more telephones. By mid-March 1878, Dr. Davis had a line between his office and home and had trouble keeping curiosity-seekers from playing with the fascinating instruments. A month later Burns and Carpenter had a line run between their residences. By the first day of May, W. H. Berry's office and home had been hooked up. J. H. Henderson and George Seevers, not to be outdone, had telephones installed between their offices and homes before the end of May.

On a Friday in mid-July Carpenter received a wagonload of telephones.[50] People were beginning to wonder, and so was he, if he was going to teach or go into the telephone business. Carpenter assured everyone that he intended to curtail his phone work—by now he had strung wires all over Indianola—just as soon as the new telephone company could be organized to take over the installation of new instruments and bring order out of the chaos of individual lines by fitting them into a centralized system.

Carpenter was as ready as anyone to point out that he was not the only luminary at Simpson; in fact, he always deferred to Dr. Burns, whose star was indeed bright in the local firmament. Burns's growing reputation as an outstanding educator was a source of pride to Indianolans, but it worried them that he might someday be lured away to richer fields. By the mid-1870s he was surely as well known as any college president in the state, and among Methodist academics his eminence, especially his attractiveness as a speaker, was unmatched. It should, then, have come as no surprise that when the presidency of the University of Iowa fell vacant in 1877 Burns was considered a major contender for that position. In October the local press noted that a number of newspapers in Iowa, including the Des Moines *Leader* and the Council Bluffs *Nonpareil*, were touting Burns for the job. One Indianola editor, even though he had previously been critical of Burns, wrote that "we would hate to lose him, but the Regents would do well to choose him."[51] The *Iowa State Register* observed that "the press of the State is almost unanimously recommending him as a suitable person" to head the university, and it reported that Burns, who was somewhat mystified by all the attention he was receiving, exclaimed "I never did understand the kindness of the press to me."[52]

When the board of regents the next spring selected another man, Burns was already in correspondence with friends in Canada about a college presidency in Ontario. His friends and admirers in Indianola were doubly disappointed.

Burns's resignation from Simpson was announced on July 18, 1878.

* * *

He would return to Canada to be president of the Wesleyan Female College in Hamilton, Ontario. Burns "has done much hard work" at Simpson Centenary, admitted *Indianola Tribune* editor Clarey, who had led the attack on Burns. He was "a man of wonderful natural ability, great learning, and untiring energy." The tone of the remarks was softer now, even though the editor continued to believe "a change of administration to be a necessity."[53]

Did the long controversy over the move to Des Moines cause Burns to resign his presidency of Simpson? Probably not, although he never explained why he was leaving. Surely the unceasing struggle against insolvency, which he once said had been more difficult to fight than the battle against sin, wore him down. The offer of a new opportunity in Canada, his adopted homeland, must have been attractive. Perhaps, he reasoned, in a decade a man had done as much as he could do for a college.

Burns's decision to leave could only have been strengthened by the report he had to make at the board of trustees at commencement, 1878. In almost every way, the financial health of the College had worsened. There could be scant satisfaction from the fact that the book value of the endowment was up—it stood at $70,350—because the proportion of it that had to be declared worthless was also up. The indebtedness of the College had ballooned to over $20,000. The endowment fund had been raided—somehow they had found a way to do this legally—in the amount of $1,600, a practice Burns admitted was "highly injurious to the well being of the institution," and they had to borrow an additional $1,500 at the bank for ninety days in order to meet immediate expenses. He projected a budget of $8,930 for the 1878–79 academic year, acknowledging that it was highly unlikely that revenues could come close to covering irreducible expenditures.[54]

The trustees decided to throw themselves on the mercy of the conference meeting at Atlantic in late summer. They would insist that the conference raise the money to liquidate the College's considerable debt. If the conference did not "take immediate steps to relieve the College from its financial embarrassment," then the conference had the duty, however unpleasant, "to direct that the further operation of the College be suspended until its present liabilities shall be paid and satisfied."[55]

When Burns and his family departed late that summer, a large number of friends accompanied them to the Indianola railroad station to see them off. And even those who had opposed some of Burns's policies, together with others whose hearts were burdened with the College's crushing debt, praised him beyond all measure. They were truly sorry to see him go.

A generation later, a graduate of Simpson whose college years were spent entirely during Burns's presidency remembered him vividly as "a man of genial yet commanding presence, possessing a quick sense of humor, a keen and caustic wit, boundless tact, great eloquence and scholarship."[56] Students held him in awe: "He was a court of appeal on any and all subjects." Yet they held him also in affection, for he was solicitous of their needs and concerns. "To us all," concluded the graduate, "it seems a great privilege to have been with him."[57]

Perhaps the most honest estimate of Burns's years at Simpson was written by George Carpenter when he was near the end of his long career of teaching at the College. "Dr. Burns," he wrote, "was a man of remarkable scholarship, strong in the class-room and eloquent on the platform." Nobody would have disagreed with that. But then Carpenter added these poignant words: "His ardent enthusiasm always hoped for greater things than events brought about."[58]

UNITED PRESBYTERIAN CHURCH.
Service every Sabbath at 10½ a. m. and 6½ p. m. Sabbath School immediately after forenoon service. Prayer meeting every Thursday evening at 6½ p. m.

BAPTIST CHURCH.
Rev. D. N. Mason, Pastor. Services every Sabbath at 10½ o'clock a. m. and 7½ p. m. Sabbath-school at 2½ p. m. Prayer meeting every Thursday evening.

PRESBYTERIAN CHURCH.
Rev. Silas Johnson, Pastor. Services every Sabbath at 10½ a. m. and 7½ p. m. Sabbath School at 2½ p. m. Prayer Meeting every Thursday evening.

CHRISTIAN CHURCH.
Preaching every third and fourth Sunday of each month by L. S. Brown. Social meeting every first and second Sabbaths of each month. Sabbath school at 9 a. m. Prayer meeting every Thursday evening

J. H. HENDERSON, W. H. B
HENDERSON & BERRY,
ATTORNEYS AT LAW,
INDIANOLA, IOWA

WARREN COUNTY BANK,
Buys and sells exchange, coin, government bonds, and other securities, discounts paper, makes collections on all points, and pays interest on time deposits.
DIRECTORS—John Cheshire, Wesley Cheshire, A. H. Swan, L. Todhunter, G. W. Heiny, H. C. Sigler, J. H. Whitney. John Cheshire, President; A. H. Swan, Vice-President; Burt A. Smith, Cashier; Indianola, Iowa. Correspondents—New York: Messrs. Howes & Macy; Chicago: Third National Bank.

CALL AND SEE MY
Crockery, Glass-ware,
Green, Browned and Ground Coffee.
GREEN, BLACK, & JAPAN TEA,
The best in the market. A full and complete stock of
GROCERIES AND PROVISIONS,
AT **NEW BRICK BUILDING.** West Main street, Indianola, Iowa.

MOXLEY & GRAHAM
Have just received a fine lot of
Groceries
Fancy Candies.
Tobaccos and Cigars,
Which they will sell at Bottom Prices. Keep constantly on hand
Gregory's Bread.
Opposite Warren House, Indianola, Iowa.

GO TO
Calhoun & Pelham's
FOR YOUR
Fresh Bread, Cakes, Pies, Confectronery,
ALSO
OYSTERS,
By the Dish or Can. South side Public Square, Indianola, Iowa.

If you want first class
Boots and Shoes,
Buy of A. R. Worth,
Indianola, Iowa.

M. R. BARKER & SON,
Dealers in
STAPLE AND FANCY DRY GOODS, ETC.
Take notice that we have just received our New Fall Stock of Dry Goods, which will be sold Remarkably Cheap.
Hats, Caps, and Ready Made Clothing of Various Styles.
LADIES' DRESS GOODS.
In great abundance in short, everything the people want in the Dry Goods line—and at the very lowest prices. East side Square, Indianola, Iowa.

Leading Drug Store of Warren County!
J. S. Jones & Bro.,
City Drug Store.
At D. S. Fisher's old stand are filling up with the largest stock of Drugs, Medicines, Paints, Oils, Dyes, etc., ever offered in the county.
☞ Orders Solicited. Physician's and Family Prescriptions carefully compounded. All articles Warranted as Represented, and Prices Uniform. Indianola, Iowa.

College Directory,

SIMPSON CENTENARY COLLEGE.

OFFICERS OF THE BOARD:
Hon. Geo. G. Wright, LL. D., President.
Hon. Geo. E. Griffith, Vice-President.
Hon. P. Gad Bryan, Treasurer.
J H. Henderson, Esq., Secretary.

EXECUTIVE COMMITTEE:
Rev. Alexander Burns, D. D., Chairman.
Hon. P. Gad Bryan, Secretary.
Hon. W. W. Phillips.
Hon. Geo. E. Griffith.
B. C. Berry, Esq.

TRUSTEES:
For three years—Hon. P Gad Bryan, Rev. M. D. Collins, David Hallam, Esq., B. C. Berry, Esq., Hon. Geo. W. Jones, Hon. W. W. Phillips.
For two years—Hon. Geo. G. Wright, LL. D., Rev. A. Burns, D. D., Hon. H. C. Sigler, Rev. P. F. Bresee, Hon. N. B. Moore, Rev. J. G. Dimmitt.
For one year—Hon. J. C. Jordan, Rev. A. C. Williams, Hon. C. C. Carpenter, Rev. P. P. Ingalls, Hon. Geo. E Griffith, Rev. J. M. Conrad.

FACULTY:
Rev. Alexander Burns, D. D., President, and Professor of Mental and Moral Science.
Rev. C. G. Hudson, M. A., Professor of Latin and Greek Languages and Literature.
Rev. Geo. C. Carpenter, M. A., Professor of Natural Science and Chemistry.
C. M. Grumbling, M. A., Professor of Mathematics and Astronomy.
Miss M. J. McKean, B. S., Preceptress and Professor of English Literature.
Miss Hellen Matthews, Teacher of Music.
W. S. Carpenter, Teacher of Telegraphy.
C. L. Barr, Teacher of Book-Keeping.
E. D. Samson, Teacher of Penmanship.
Mrs. Ellison, Teacher of Painting.

An early issue of the *Simpsonian*, dated February 2, 1874, carried advertisements of everything from lawyers to oysters alongside the College directory.

V

A College Saved
1878–80

Everyone loved Thomas S. Berry. No sooner was Alexander Burns's resignation announced in mid-July 1878 than Reverend Berry's admirers began to urge his election to the presidency of Simpson Centenary. At thirty-seven, he had already won for himself a reputation as a clergyman of unusual merit. He had been called to the pastorate of Indianola's Methodist Episcopal Church only the prior autumn, but in that short time, he had won a legion of devotees, some of them prominent Indianola trustees. The clergy of the Des Moines Conference were solidly in his camp. Surprisingly, all three Indianola newspaper editors, who were rarely known to agree on anything, were enthusiastic about his election. Graham and Knox, whose *Herald* broke the story of Burns's imminent departure on July 11, could scarcely hide their pleasure: "Now let Rev. Berry step into the Doctor's place. His appointment would be hailed with a hearty amen by all who know him."[1] Clarey of the *Tribune*, having led the attack on Burns for months, wrote a week later that although Burns's successor was not yet known, the citizens of Indianola were "a unit in favor of Rev. T. S. Berry." The only problem, explained Clarey, was to persuade Berry to accept the position. "He is just the man for the place." Everyone wanted the College to be a success, and "we know of no man more capable of bringing it success than Mr. Berry" who was a "man of such practical and living ideas, of such mental force, and of such moral purity and religious earnestness, that he would give the college a character and dignity that would cause it to become a power in the land."[2] Everett of the *Warren Record* truly regretted Burns's departure, but he readily agreed that Berry would be the most appropriate successor.[3] Lest the College's board of trustees not be aware of the sentiments of Indianolans on the topic, a petition was hurriedly circulated among the town's residents, and within hours ninety-one signatures were recorded in favor of Mr. Berry.

It was no contest. On July 24, eleven members of the board of trustees met in the lecture room at the Fifth Street Methodist Church in Des Moines, where they formally accepted Dr. Burns's resignation and unanimously elected Rev. Berry president. Presumably they had cleared the matter with the bishop, for a few weeks later their action was officially confirmed by the conference.

On the day following the board's action, John H. Henderson, acting on behalf of the other members, notified Berry of his election. Berry could hardly have been surprised, and although he harbored serious misgivings about taking the position, he was ready with his reply, the speed of which astonished even his most ardent supporters, for he penned his answer the day after he received Henderson's letter. In it he stated that "after serious deliberation, I do not feel at liberty to refuse the responsibility to which you have invited me, and yet I accept it with very great reluctance. The ability of the late President, Rev. Dr. Burns, has given the institution a rank hard to be maintained." Only because the College was having difficulty "securing some more experienced man," and because of "pledges of sympathy and cooperation" from the conference, he was "persuaded to give myself to a new task . . . until something better can be done."[4]

He agreed to take over the reins of the College the first week in September, allowing the conference time to find a replacement for him in the Indianola pastorate.

Berry was born at Virginia, Illinois, January 30, 1841, one of six children of Thomas S. Berry, a respected farmer who died of an apparently hereditary disease when young Thomas was only seven years old. For the next five years the youngster remained with his mother, whereupon he and his brother A. R. were taken to live with their father's brother, Benjamin C. Berry, who lived nearby. He stayed with his uncle for a number of years, working on the farm and attending public school when time permitted during the winter months. Converted to the gospel in 1856, he joined the Methodist Episcopal Church at Zion Church in what was then the Jacksonville circuit in the Illinois Conference. When he was twenty he was "licensed to exhort"—Methodists still welcomed lay preachers—and decided to acquire a college education. He entered Illinois Wesleyan University at Bloomington in the fall of 1861, but returned home sick at the end of the first term. After some weeks of convalescence he reentered college in the spring of 1862, this time at Northwestern University, but he returned home in August of that year to enlist in a company of volunteers being raised by his uncle for service in the Union army.

He was sworn in on August 15 as a lieutenant in the 114th Illinois Infantry and continued to serve in the military until the end of the Civil War. He was with General William Tecumseh Sherman in 1862 and 1863, participated in the assault on Vicksburg on May 19, 1863, and was subsequently stationed with his regiment at Memphis during the winter of 1863–64. Six months later, in June 1864, in the Battle of Guntown, about 140 miles southeast of Memphis, he was severely wounded, then taken prisoner and held for nearly a year in prisons at Macon, Mobile, notorious Andersonville and other prisons until the war's end. During his first months in prison, he suffered so from his wounds that his recovery was despaired of. He later recalled that he was so emaciated that his nurse, one of his own men captured with him, could carry him around in his arms like a small child. He did recover, however, and was released in a prisoner exchange effected in May 1865 and soon discharged.

No sooner had he returned home than he married Lou A. Van Eaton, a young woman from his home town, Virginia, Illinois, on June 29, 1865. That fall, he took his bride to Evanston, where he returned to Northwestern University. He continued his studies intermittently there and at Garrett Biblical Institute in Evanston, completing his theological studies in 1870 and his Northwestern B.A. in 1872.

Meanwhile his Uncle Benjamin, now better known as Captain B. C. Berry, had moved to Warren County in 1867. Upon completion of his work at Garrett, Thomas S. Berry sought a clerical appointment in Iowa. He was received into the Des Moines Conference on probation in 1870. His first pastorate was at Carlisle (1870–72), during which he was accepted as a full member of the conference clergy. After Carlisle came appointments to Corning (1872–74), the Fifth Street Church in Des Moines (1874–77) and Indianola (1877–78). During these years he developed remarkable preaching skills. He was no hellfire revivalist; rather he came to be known as an eloquent, logical speaker with a "rich, varied, vigorous and happy command of words" that made him the "pride and ornament" of the Des Moines Conference.[5] Yet his preaching was only one source of Berry's attractiveness. He seemed to have a genuine concern for everyone he came to know, especially those who were bereaved or suffering. He had known suffering in the dank prisons of wartime; he had lost his father when he was yet a boy; he could empathize with those who were hurting.

In order to make way for the new occupant of the Methodist parsonage, Berry purchased Alexander Burns's house west of the square and moved into it on August 30, 1878, one of the hottest days of an unusually hot summer, with his wife and two children, Hattie and Mary.[6] He greeted his successor at the church, the Rev. Felix W. Vinson, and prepared for the opening of the fall term the first week in September.

Meanwhile the College faculty drifted back into town after what had, for some of them, at least, been an eventful summer. There were six of them besides the president, and of the six only four were really full-time appointments. C. H. Burke, professor of classical languages, arrived home from vacation only a few days before classes commenced. Christian M. Grumbling, who had spent his summer holding teacher institutes nearby, was the "proud and distracted" father of a new nine-pound baby boy. George Carpenter, mainstay of the teaching staff, was back in town, but almost immediately he fell desperately ill with a recurrence of an old illness, hemorrhaging of the lungs, and had to be hurriedly replaced for the year by young John Bruce Fisk.[7] Replacing Felicia Jones, who had resigned, was the new professor of English literature, Ida M. Pierce of Sedalia, Missouri, who was a former high school teacher and graduate of the state normal school at Warrensburg, Missouri. In addition to Burke, Grumbling, Fisk and Pierce, there were William E. Andrews, principal of the commercial department, whose "salary" was drawn from whatever fees he could collect, typically five dollars per student per term, together with two tutors, sophomore Josie Baker and senior Charles W. Fisk, both of whom received free tuition for their efforts.[8]

So pleased were Indianolans with the new Berry regime that they were inclined to exaggerate the successes of the new administration in an outpouring of wishful thinking. The *Herald* reported a "considerable number" of new students that fall; the *Record* called it a "large number." The fact was that only 120 students registered, most of them preps. The total enrollment during the three terms of the 1878–79 academic year was only 159.

Berry's position was not an enviable one. Even if his well-wishers glossed over the serious difficulties of the College, he could not. As soon as classes commenced, he called into his room in College Hall the class of 1879—there were six of them—and, with a troubled heart, frankly stated the case: the College was in such dire financial straits that it might be forced to close. He offered them their credentials if they wished to transfer to another college to graduate. The students, who were aware that all was not well, held a meeting that same evening and upon consideration resolved and recorded in their class minutes that they would stand by the College "as long as there is a plank left to stand on."[9] Encouraged by this unexpected expression of student loyalty, Berry talked with the faculty. He apprised them, if they did not already know, of the gravity of the situation and urged them to stay with the College at least for this academic year.

As the unseasonable cold of late September gave way to glorious Indian summer in October, the new president threw himself into the task of putting life into a languishing academic enterprise. It was clear to him that unless the debt could be reduced substantially, Simpson would surely go under. Continuing deficits in operations were only adding to the already unbearable burden of debt. True, hard times were still plaguing Iowa and the nation, with no end in sight. Something had to be done, and quickly too.

Berry had already made what appeared to be a good beginning in September at the Des Moines Conference at Atlantic. With plenty of help from the bishop, he managed to extract from the assembled clergymen pledges of $10,400 toward payment of the College's debt, their subscriptions contingent upon the balance of the needed $15,000 being secured "otherwise" no later than by the spring of 1879.[10] "Otherwise" meant Warren County, almost the only other place to go, and the amount expected from the Indianola citizenry grew to $6,000. But the sacrifice of those Methodist ministers must not be overlooked. Some of those among them who made pledges of $50 or $100 were making no more than $450 or $500 a year in the pastorate.[11] Somehow, if the clergy could show that kind of dedication, the citizens of Warren County could be persuaded that it was in their self-interest to maintain a strong college in their community.

There is no doubt that Berry was an effective persuader. He decided that the best thing to do was to get the people together and talk openly about the College's problems. Accordingly, he held an important informational meeting at the Methodist Church on the evening of October 21. He was disappointed, but surely not surprised, when only a handful of stalwarts showed up. After all, everyone knew the College was in trouble, and most townspeople were not anxious to be asked for yet another contribution to help salvage what seemed to be a perennially crisis-ridden school. Those who were present were mostly trustees and Indianola Methodist leaders. Ed Hall, a local attorney who had once served as the town's mayor, chaired the meeting, and several trustees held forth valiantly, trying their best to put a good face on things, but on the whole their allusions to "very encouraging reports" and promises that "the College will soon be out of debt" were not very convincing. Their hearers, sprinkled about the pews in the mostly empty church, had heard such reassurances before, and they were not ready to open their thin purses, even after hearing the blandishments of President Berry.[12] His cousin, William H. Berry, put it plainly when he said: "The president asked the people of Warren County for the money. They did not give it."[13]

Reluctant townspeople were not Berry's only problem. There was an element in the board of trustees that was still in favor of abandoning Indianola and locating the College at Des Moines, and more would be heard of that scheme later in the year. But for the time being the board, with little enthusiasm and even less confidence, extended the time for soliciting Indianolans for the needed $6,000, putting off the deadline to the June 1879 board meeting. A committee was appointed by Indianola citizens to make one more valiant try to solicit the needed funds. And in spite of hard times and the pervasive fear on the part of potential donors that they were throwing good money after bad, the loyal friends of the College began to experience modest success in their efforts.

Well, they were successful until mid-May, when, to their utter dismay, a letter was circulated among all members of the Des Moines Conference urging the immediate removal of the College to Des Moines. It was signed by four clergymen: Mahlon D. Collins, presiding elder of the Des Moines district and Simpson board member, together with W. F. Harned, W. S. Hooker and C. S. Ryman, all pastors of Des Moines Methodist congregations. A valuable downtown Des Moines property, the Exposition Building, had become available, they wrote. It was priced at about $75,000. Des Moines—and presumably Warren County—citizens could buy the building and present it, clear of all encumbrance, to the conference. They urged haste, for "the offer will only be available to us for a few days," and asked for a quick response, noting that "Bishop [Edward G.] Andrews endorses the matter fully." The building, they said, was "most conveniently located" and could be "admirably adjusted for collegiate purposes." Significantly they made it clear that "this whole matter is based on the prevailing opinion that our College at Indianola will be unable to continue longer than this year."[14]

The Des Moines pastors got their response, but it was hardly what they expected. Virtually no one in the conference supported their suggestion, and in Indianola the citizens, especially the Methodists, were enraged. A reply was dictated in a letter by twelve clergymen, with President Berry in the vanguard, which was circulated throughout the conference. Their opposition to the move was cast in the form of three more or less rhetorical questions:

> First. Do you think that the Exposition Building in Des Moines, situated on one of the main streets of the city, in the very center of the business part of the city, without one foot of ground, except what is covered by the building—[is] a suitable location for our Conference College?
> Second. Is it easier for the Des Moines Conference to take another college building and organize another institution without any endowment or means of paying a faculty, other than the tuition received from students, than it would be to raise the additional ten thousand dollars necessary to put Simpson Centenary College entirely out of debt, when that college already has more than fifty thousand dollars of good, productive endowment—as reported by the finance committee of its board of trustees at their last conference meeting—with its classes of students already organized, and ten classes already graduated by its faculty?
> Third. Do you think that it is right for the Des Moines Conference to forsake Simpson Centenary College and its friends who have stood by it with their means, and its local friends who erected the building and presented it to the Conference, with twenty-five thousand dollars of an endowment fund?[15]

Their letter closed with assurances that they were making "their utmost endeavors" to raise enough money to save the College and with the request that the decision upon the question of Simpson's relocation be deferred until after the June board meeting only a few weeks away.

Meanwhile, in anticipation of that crucial meeting on which so much hinged, the finance committee of the board prepared its year-end report. It offered the worst possible news. In their fund-raising, they were still $1,200 short of their $15,000 goal. And they had to achieve it or get nothing from the conference. Further, the year's operations had produced another deficit: receipts of $5,651 and expenditures of $6,660, leaving a shortfall of $1,009. The College's total indebtedness stood at more than $21,000, and there were no viable assets to balance it off. The campus itself was covered with a past-due mortgage "equal to its entire market value." Unless the debt could be cleared away altogether—a feat no one on the finance committee dared dream of—they reluctantly concluded that the College must be closed by the end of the spring term. It was, they said, "irreligious and in utter violation of our Church polity to contract debts without some reasonable probability of paying."[16] The faculty committee of the board contributed more bad news: the faculty members were demanding cash payments—they had received nothing but warrants all year—for at least a part of their back salaries, in aggregate some $4,000. When commencement week came, not a few of the board members were ready to throw in the towel.[17]

Just prior to commencement—it was Saturday evening, June 7—the local committee soliciting the $6,000 in Warren County reported at an informal meeting of some of the College's most loyal friends that they had raised every dollar they could, and they were still $1,200 short of their goal. President Berry, who looked tired, said they should make one last attempt on the morrow at the baccalaureate service. If they were to fail this time, he said, he would be forced to agree to closing the College. Trustee Gorham Worth remembered that Saturday evening as the saddest in the history of the College: "We sat up with it all night. Nearly everybody was crying because we were going to quit it the next morning" unless God worked some kind of miracle to save the College.[18]

A packed house was a near certainty for any commencement week event, and baccalaureate Sunday, 1879, was no exception. Many of those present were saddened, however, for they feared that this would be the last baccalaureate service in Simpson Centenary's history. President Berry, whose powers of recovery seemed uncanny, was at his best on the platform, and he delivered "one of his characteristic sermons," after which Rev. Vinson, the Indianola pastor, addressed the assemblage. Surely nearly everyone present must have guessed what was coming. Rev. Vinson announced simply that $1,200 must be raised that morning among the audience present or the College would have to close. "This is the last call," he said. William H. Berry seconded Vinson's ominous prediction: unless the needed sum—the last part of the minimum of $15,000 required—was forthcoming, "those of you present here today are sitting at the bedside of dying Simpson Centenary." Thus the Macedonian cry for help was sounded.

The crowd fell into profound silence. Everyone stared forward, their eyes locked on some distant point, as if in a spell. Not a soul stirred; not even a stifled cough was heard. Berry waited, and waited yet longer as the seconds on the big wall clock ticked away. The oppressive silence seemed to stretch out endlessly. Then . . .

"Put my name down for $100," said old settler M. R. Barker from his seat down in front, his voice fairly crackling in the stillness. Then, as a rustle of relief went through the crowd, E. W. Perry and S. Strauss both offered the same amount.

Elias Williamson Gray, first Principal of the Indianola Male and Female Seminary (1860–61).

Orlando Harrison Baker, Principal of the Seminary (1863–66) and longtime member of the faculty of the College.

Samuel Milton Vernon, last Principal of the Des Moines Conference Seminary (1866–67) and first President of Simpson Centenary College (1867–68).

The Seminary building, built in 1863 and soon dubbed "Old Blue Bird," was destroyed by a windstorm in 1871.

Today a bronze plaque mounted on a large stone marks the southeast corner of "Old Blue Bird."

This rare old photograph pictures College Hall, completed in 1869, together with "Old Blue Bird," the latter destroyed only two years later. George Griffith's maple trees were still mere saplings.

Bishop Matthew Simpson.

Simpson's first graduating class numbered six: top, l. to r., Brenton Badley, L. B. Cary, Emma Cary; below, l. to r., Imogene Hallam, Martha Posegate and Louise Anderson.

The class of 1872.

Thomas S. Berry, President of the College from 1878 to 1880. He died in office at the age of 39.

Faculty member Belle Babb Mansfield in 1876. A graduate of Iowa Wesleyan College, she became the first female attorney in the United States.

An Irish-born Canadian, Alexander Burns served as Simpson's President from 1868 to 1878.

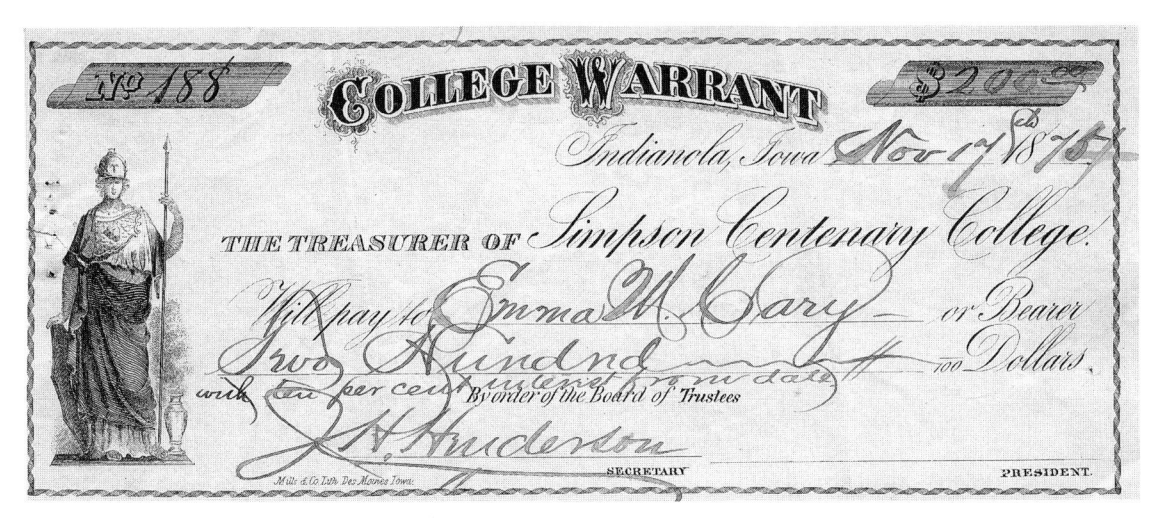

During the 1870s the College was so often short of funds that it paid faculty with warrants—promises to pay.

In the mid-1880s high-wheeled bicycles were all the rage at Simpson.

Edward Lamay Parks was President of the College from 1880 to 1886.

William E. Hamilton taught at Simpson many years between 1867 and 1911. He served as the College's President (1886–89) and came out of retirement to serve as Acting-President (1915–16).

Edmund Meek Holmes, Professor of Greek and Hebrew (1885–89) and President of the College from 1889 to 1892. He later taught Philosophy and Religion at the College (1919–33).

E. L. Miller, whose tenure at Simpson (1889–1936) was the longest of any faculty member of the College, taught Business subjects.

Simpson's authentic heroine, Kate Shelley, shown here wearing her Kappa Kappa Gamma badge.

College Hall in 1884, its sharp outlines softened by young maples.

This engraving appeared in the 1889 *Tangent*, picturing three campus buildings, although Ladies' Hall (left) was not completed until 1891.

College Hall in the 1890s.

Before they adopted coats-of-arms, Greek-letter societies used fine engraved devices rich in ritualistic symbolism.

In its early years, Simpson lent its endowment funds primarily on real estate mortgages at ten per cent interest per annum.

Fletcher Brown, Vice President of the College (1887–92) and President from 1892 to 1898.

William Buxton, Sr., first of several Buxtons who served the College for more than a century as members of its board of trustees.

Joseph Benton Harris, President of the College (1898–99).

Frank Barrows, 29 years old when this picture was taken for the 1897 *Zenith*, brought Simpson's Conservatory of Music to national prominence.

Lucien Waggener, Jr., Professor of French and German (1895–99) composed the words of the Simpson Alma Mater, "The Red and Gold."

Apart from teaching foreign languages, Professor Lucien Waggener, Jr. coached the women's golf team. He is pictured here on a brisk fall day of 1897 with four coeds: Jessie Boyd, Birdie Brown, Roxie Stuart and Laura Johnston.

Mary Condit, Instructor in Art (1896–97).

Mamie O'Flyng, Instructor in Voice and Violin (1895–97).

Martha A. Stahl, Professor of Latin from 1895 to 1904.

Professor Lucien Waggener appears here with his charges in a German play, "Unbesetzte Stühle," in the late 1890s.

Simpson's football team in the fall of 1895.

George Washington Carver was a student at Simpson in the early 1890s.

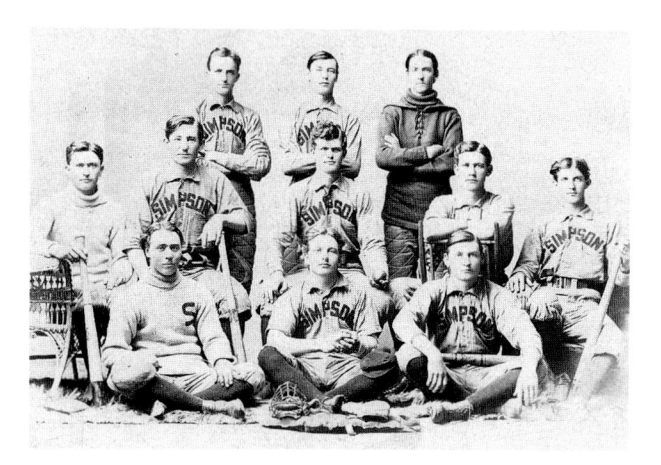

The 1896 baseball team.

Professor Hiram G. Sedgwick, who brought Engineering (very briefly) to Simpson in the mid-nineties.

Professor Hiram Sedgwick's Engineering Building (1895–96).

Students in chapel in 1899. Note the large stove against the wall to the right. The central heating plant was not built until 1901.

The 1897 track team. Its captain, long jumper and hurdler E. E. McFerrin, is pictured standing second from the left.

Ivy-covered Ladies' Hall was given the name Mary Berry Hall in 1908.

Rev. L. B. Wickersham, Field Secretary of the College at the turn of the century.

Biology Laboratory in Science Hall, 1901.

Seen in 1904 on the front porch of their recently acquired chapter house were the women of Tridelta.

All the comforts of home in Mary Berry Hall in its early days.

Regular and student staff of the dining service in Ladies' Hall at the turn of the century.

The 1902 baseball team.

Charles Eldred Shelton, president of Simpson from 1899 to 1910.

The College's first heating plant was constructed in 1901.

The Conservatory of Music building opened in 1902.

The interior of the College's Gymnasium, 1902.

John L. Tilton, Professor of Natural Sciences from 1888 to 1919.

The Administration building, constructed in 1900, burned to the ground in 1918.

Joanna Baker, Professor of Classical Languages from 1889 to 1919.

Simpson's first Gymnasium, erected in two weeks, first opened in late 1894 and was dedicated January 15, 1895.

Mary O. Hunting, Professor of Latin, 1898–1919.

A snowy winter night on campus in early 1908.

The ladies' basketball team in 1904 won the state championship.

In the fall of 1901 the Simpson Geology class picnicked at Pammel Park, Winterset.

The class of 1909 festively attired.

Women's Gymnasium class pictured in the 1905 *Zenith*.

During the Shelton years the campus was deeply shaded in a forest of maples—and a few elms.

"Prexy" Charles E. Shelton.

"Winding the Maypole." Commencement exercises in 1909.

All three of these men were local dry goods and clothing merchants down around the square. Then attorney R. B. Parrott promised $100. The Chittenden brothers gave $50, and after them came a flood of responses ranging from $50 down to $5. Many of these people had contributed generously to the College before, and the smaller amounts were reportedly pledged by "students, persons of small means, and ladies." When the last donation had been recorded, W. H. Berry announced triumphantly that $1,210 had been raised, just enough to meet the goal. "Sunday though it was," recalled one observer, "the most hearty applause followed the announcement." The people of Warren County had come through once again. But this time they had followed the College to the abyss before pulling it back.[19]

When the board of trustees met in three sessions on Tuesday, June 10, the dismal reports of the financial and faculty committees were presented, recommending the suspension of the College. Yet their reports had clearly been overtaken by events, and a majority of the board membership was prepared to move ahead. At the evening meeting that day, W. H. Berry was understandably elated when he was able announce quite ceremoniously that "there has been placed in my hands as your treasurer the full amount of fifteen thousand dollars of subscriptions made for the payment of the debt now resting against Simpson Centenary College." Of this amount, $8,800 was the amount that actually came from the September conference solicitation and $6,200 from Warren County. He was realistic enough to caution the board that "I do not wish to be understood as saying that their subscription is all good," but then one could never be sure of collecting every pledge in any college fund drive, then or later.[20]

However, a few on the board—the Des Moines recalcitrants mostly—were frankly skeptical about the College's future and made a strong case for quitting Indianola and starting over again in Des Moines. The Indianolans argued that the friends of the College had fully met the challenge to raise $15,000 and that it would be grossly unfair not to permit them to move ahead, for that was, after all, a part of the bargain. There ensued what appears to have been one of the grandest free-for-alls in the history of the Simpson board, and the issue had not been settled when they adjourned in a state of exhaustion late that night.

By the time the contestants met again the next day, the mood of the board had changed. Contention gave way to cooperation. It is not clear why the Des Moines supporters softened their stand, but no doubt informal conversations early in the day persuaded some of them to give Indianola another chance. In a thoroughly constructive session, the board members attended to the most pressing issues that confronted them: unpaid faculty salaries, the budget and the debt. After careful consideration, they agreed to pay in cash $2,200 of the faculty salaries owing and to recognize salaries as having first priority on all future tuition collections.[21] In tackling the budget they were determined to make it balance for the first time in a decade. Thus they reduced some salaries, including that of the president, and brought projected expenditures down to $5,300 for the 1879–80 academic year, a reduction of $1,360 from the prior year.[22] They determined to use the balance of the $15,000, as the pledges were paid in, to help reduce the debt. "We feel," they said, "that the heavy load of indebtedness can be removed and in time the entire debt be extinguished."[23] As a sort of parting shot, the board adopted a resolution that confirmed the victory of the Indianolans. All on the board swore their fidelity to Simpson Centenary College in Indianola, stating further that "we believe the agitation of any question looking to the establishment of any Institution of like character by this conference within the bounds of the Des Moines conference to be mischievous in its tendency, fraught with danger to this Institution and the cause of education."[24]

The next day the *Indianola Republican* trumpeted the good news in a headline employing the largest type the editor could find: "SIMPSON COLLEGE SAVED." Indianolans had met the challenge in the College's darkest hour. And, pointed out the editor, "be it remembered that this institution has made heavy drafts on our citizens before. It must be further remembered that in this township, where much of the money was raised, the people are just now paying off their $50,000 railroad tax."[25] The successful outcome, he said, must be credited to men like Gorham A. Worth, the new treasurer of the College's board, to President Berry, to John Henderson, to B. C. Berry and to W. F. Powell, the young Indianola attorney and former town mayor, a graduate of Simpson in the class of 1873. With the kind of support these men provided, "it will doubtless be a new era for Simpson Centenary."[26] The *Herald*'s account of the crisis, more subdued than its competitor's, noted that the debt still needed to be paid off, but reported that everyone in the community was pledged to support Simpson. The students were going home for the summer "fully assured that the college lives and will live, and [they] promise to return."[27] Student confidence in the College was not an unimportant consideration.

* * *

Although the College's financial plight demanded unremitting attention during Thomas S. Berry's presidency, it did not push every other concern aside. The curriculum, for instance, was strengthened in the fall of 1879 when the scientific course was increased from three to four years, leading to the bachelor of science degree, joining the four-year classical course, which led to the bachelor of arts, and a hybrid called the Latin (or Greek) and scientific course, which led to the bachelor of philosophy degree. The master of arts or science or philosophy was still routinely awarded to graduates three years after the receipt of the bachelor's degree.

Ten seniors did return in the 1879–80 year, but total student enrollment was disappointing—only 136 total, including 53 college undergraduates, 63 preps and 20 in the last class of the law department.

President Berry was much in demand as a pulpit speaker, and he found it difficult to turn down invitations to preach. For wherever he went he could talk to the parishioners about their conference College. His secular speeches were as popular as his sermons, and he lectured on an array of topics ranging from the common schools to wartime prison life. He joined other good Methodists in decrying the evils of alcohol, especially its baneful effects in Indianola, where in spite of legal prohibition of the sale of spirits except for medicinal use, "too much whiskey was being sold."[28]

Berry preferred staying on campus, where he could teach his classes, counsel with his small, congenial faculty and become better acquainted with the students. He enjoyed dropping in on Friday evenings to hear the earnest speechmaking in the literary society meetings. Random conversations with young scholars out on the campus were the highlights of his days. Sometimes, to be sure, his meetings with students provided surprises: "President Berry," reported the

Simpsonian, "is reported to have interrupted two of the students while they were applying themselves to a new study. Spades were trumps."[29]

Pleasant idylls on sunny afternoons with students were interrupted by troubling vexations. George Carpenter's serious illness worried Berry. Faculty remuneration, or the irregularity and uncertainty of it, was a never-ending, nagging problem. Then too, students were complaining about the conspicuous inadequacy of the library, containing fewer than one thousand volumes, and the lack of even a part-time librarian.[30] As we have seen, there was still pending a legal dispute about the ownership of part of the campus itself.[31] Not only that, there was still more than one mechanic's lien against the College in litigation in the courts, both in Indianola and Des Moines, growing out of the Reichardt bankruptcy a decade earlier.[32] Even the *Simpsonian* caused the president a few sleepless nights when it urged students to patronize only those merchants who advertised in the student newspaper. "It would be a good thing," stormed the editor of the *Herald*, "if [the College's] professors would bridle the smart alecks who conduct its paper." For a College that owed as much to its host town as did Simpson Centenary, stirring up such resentment around the square was a serious matter indeed.[33]

Much more serious, however, was the state of President Berry's health. Throughout his adult years he had suffered bouts of illness, all of which seemed to be related to the inherited disease that had carried away his father at a young age. The onslaught of the disease, exacerbated by work and worry in snatching the College out of the jaws of death, was unstoppable. He had always known that his life would probably be cut short by the inexorable advance of the disease, but he lived the more fully for knowing it. In January 1879, he was reported to be "very ill," but recovered enough after a week or so to hear class recitations at his residence. He was back at his room at the College a week after that. A month later, he was talking of retiring from the College presidency if he could no longer keep up the pace of the work. A few days taking the mineral waters at Colfax Springs in March seemed to help a bit, however, and he seemed to regain some of his former vigor. He managed to hold up well during the crisis-laden days of June when the fate of the College hung in the balance. He felt well enough in September to accept election by his fellow Methodist clergymen to represent the Des Moines Conference at the church's general conference scheduled to meet at Cincinnati the following January.[34]

He would never go to Cincinnati. Soon after the holidays his health failed once again. On January 17, 1880, only four days after he had attended a strenuous board of trustees meeting in Des Moines, he took to his bed, laid low by another attack of the mysterious illness. Soon his disease "assumed alarming proportions," so much so that doctors from Indianola and Des Moines were summoned to minister to him. As he clung stubbornly to life, expressions of concern poured in from all over the country. Bishop Andrews visited and relatives gathered, expecting the worst. "Mr. Berry's sickness," reported John Clarey in the *Tribune*, "has somehow taken a personal hold on almost every individual in the community." Each day people asked how he fared, and his grief-stricken family kept a vigil at his bedside. On February 5, one of those bright, crisp, sunny Iowa winter days, a calm settled over him. He prayed aloud, then cried out, "resignation."

"Resignation to what, Mr. Berry?"

A broken effort followed: "To the Divine will, whatever it may be."

He never spoke again, but lay still and peaceful, his visage as composed as a Greek sculpture, somehow at one with his fate. Still, he held out a long time. He died at two o'clock in the morning on February 10, and as the local people stirred in the frosty dawn, they learned that his battle for life had been lost. He was thirty-nine years old.[35]

The College chapel could not possibly hold the crowd of mourners who filled every seat and square inch of standing room at the funeral service two days later. Students had adorned the front of the hall with evergreens, plaiting a motto "Our President—not dead but sleepeth," beneath which was displayed a crayon likeness of Berry. As the eulogies were delivered one after another—Bishop Andrews, Senator Wright and intimates of Berry from among the conference clergy—the funeral took on the character of a memorial for a fallen hero.

That same afternoon, eleven members of the board of trustees met at Central House, a downtown Indianola hotel, where they had to determine what immediate steps to take to ensure the continuation of College work. Their first act, of course, was to express their sympathy with President Berry's family. They adopted a resolution which expressed "with profound sorrow our tribute and respect" for the late president, whose death left the College in deep mourning for "its beloved head, its devoted, cultured, upright and highly efficient instructor, its model of a Christian character and its exemplar of the highest type of Christian life and conduct."[36] The editor of the *Simpsonian*, in his tribute to Berry, spoke for his fellow students, and surely for the faculty too: "Few homes," he wrote, "are blessed even for a brief season with the presence and love of so pure, so noble and so great a man."[37]

No one wanted to lose Thomas S. Berry, but his death inspired those who cared most about the College to resolve to make a success of the enterprise, if for no other reason than to perpetuate his memory.[38]

VI

Out of the Ashes
1880–86

During the decade after 1880, Simpson Centenary College experienced an astonishing transformation. At the time of Thomas S. Berry's untimely death, the College could be accounted at best a shaky enterprise saved from extinction only by the generosity of townspeople and clergy, thought by some of their contemporaries to be perhaps more stouthearted than wise. Ten years later, Simpson glowed with resurgent vigor, solid and stable, with an air about the place of renewed confidence. This happy change did not come about all at once, nor did it come about easily.

The day President Berry was laid to rest—February 12, 1880—board members, still clad in their mourning garb, named a committee to find a new president. For the interim, they appointed George Carpenter, the senior faculty member, acting president. Carpenter, who had been on leave of absence because of ill health, had apparently recovered sufficiently to be active, and he was in town and available.

Carpenter was pleased to step into the breach, but only four days after he took over the reins of leadership, he was stricken again. It all happened very suddenly while he was on a Monday shopping trip down on the Indianola square.[1] He collapsed, his lungs hemorrhaging, and was carried into Miss McDowell's millinery store so ill that no one dared to move him for two days, when he recovered sufficiently to go home. Unfortunately, he was not able to function effectively as interim president.

The board of trustees moved quickly in its search for a new president. Senator Wright and College agent Rev. L. M. Walters took the train to Chicago late in February to talk with a bright, young pastor in that city about the position. He was Edward Lamay Parks, who had been acquainted with President Berry and who was recommended highly to the Simpson men by the "Evanston faculties"—Northwestern University and Garrett Biblical Institute. In their meeting with Parks they were so favorably impressed with the twenty-nine-year-old's grasp of the ideals and problems of Christian higher education, his piety and especially his self-confidence, that they asked him on the spot if he would permit his name to be submitted to the board "to be elected for the remaining term of the year," that is, the spring term of 1880. Only a few months earlier, Parks had accepted his "delightful Chicago pastorate" at the Ingleside Avenue Church, but the Simpson offer was intriguing. It was also urgent.

"I agreed to give a reply by the next day at noon," Parks recalled later. "Mrs. Parks and I carefully thought and prayed over the matter," consulted trusted counselors in Evanston who urged him to accept the offer, and then "replied favorably by telegram." The next evening, March 1, the executive committee of the board named Parks the new president of the College.[2]

Parks was a New Yorker by birth, a native of the little town of Dundee. He was born to George Hamlin and Julia Hollister Parks January 26, 1851. With his family he moved to Illinois where, he attended the Rochelle High School (1866) and the Jennings Seminary at nearby Aurora that same year. An able scholar, he entered the Northwestern Academy—the preparatory division of the university—in 1867 and matriculated at the university proper in 1869. At the university, he made a reputation as a superior scholar, a respected athlete and convivial member of the Phi Kappa Psi fraternity. He was also a dedicated, converted Christian. So outstanding were his academic accomplishments that during his senior year he was appointed an instructor at the university and continued in that capacity for six more years after the receipt of the B.A. in 1873.

His teaching at Northwestern did not occupy all his time, for he entered seminary studies at Garrett Biblical Institute, which shared the same campus, and earned the B.D. degree in 1878, the same year he was ordained to the Methodist Episcopal clergy.[3]

The next year, after seven years of teaching at Northwestern, Parks was ready to make a change. He decided to enter the itinerancy, and after correspondence with Thomas S. Berry at Indianola, he settled upon the Des Moines Conference as the place he wanted to go. There, he said, "I was likely to do most for Christ." No appointments were available, however, so he accepted the pastorate at Ingleside Avenue Church in Chicago in October 1879. In July he had married Isabella B. Webb of Kelley's Island, Ohio.

"Without any premonition," wrote Parks of his whirlwind long-distance courtship with Simpson Centenary, "suddenly within twenty-four hours, we were transplanted to the field first elected, but to work in a very different capacity." Notified by telegram of his election on the second of March, he and his wife "caught the first sight of Indianola on the 4th."[4]

If Parks did not know the condition of the College when he arrived, he learned about it within the first few days he was in town. He and his wife, who was expecting their first child, were put up by William H. and Alice Berry during their first week, and through them he became quickly acquainted with local board members and others on whom much of the fortune of the College depended. He was especially impressed with the strength of Gorham A. Worth "standing in the breach of an empty treasury and a ruined credit, in the college's greatest financial crisis. His assurance that the college had a financial future was the main source of my own early confidence. In those days Mr. Worth lived for the college. . . . I believe the college owed its continued existence to him."[5]

When Parks first set foot on the campus, the impression it made on him was dismal: "The appearance of the grounds and building . . . was very uninviting. There was scarcely a sound plank firm in its place on the front or inside walks."

No one had explained to him that while they were trying to save the College, the campus grounds and building had been allowed to deteriorate for lack of care. Survival was all that mattered.

At the opening of the spring term on March 10, Parks met the students, the faithful few who remained in school, in the chapel still draped with mourning for President Berry.[6] The scene was macabre. Yet he was not dismayed by his funeral reception: "I remember how profoundly these evidences of his memory impressed upon me the sacredness of the work of the college."[7]

It would appear that at no time did Parks behave as if he were only a president pro tem. He knew, and the board of trustees knew, that he must look beyond commencement day and lay plans for the future. If they liked what he did, he would stay.

The job held few allures. Everything demanded his attention at once. While he was struck with the surprisingly good quality of the faculty, he could see that they were understandably apprehensive about the College's future. The curriculum clearly needed expansion if Simpson was to live up to its academic promise. The campus building and grounds must be put into a state of reasonable repair. Student enrollment, buffeted by the winds of uncertainty during the past few years, was dangerously low. And the College was hardly out of the woods financially. The debt was still much too big. Continuing litigation of claims against the College was a running sore. Court processes were expensive both in dollars and in lost good will.

He started with the faculty. George Carpenter, of course, was ill and would go on leave at the end of the term. Burke and Pierce were salaried professors, but Burke was not well either. Lou Gregory, professor of French and music, Mary Cotton, instructor in music, and Charles A. Bunker, instructor in elocution, all in their first year at the College, were not salaried but earned their living from supplementary student lesson fees. Then there were the law department professors—Judges Miller, Cole and Mitchell and Senator Wright—in Des Moines. Parks brought with him an able young man who joined the faculty as professor of Latin, taking T. S. Berry's place. He was Charles M. Ellinwood, who had taught chemistry and physics at Northwestern.[8] He and his wife soon moved into a house on West Madison Street[9] owned by J. A. Olive, the colorful town blacksmith and former city councilman. Ellinwood would prove to be a remarkably energetic, inventive, devoted faculty member whose interest in the natural and physical sciences would thrust these subjects into the forefront of the curriculum. After only one term Ellinwood, never at home with the classics, was named professor of natural sciences and George Carpenter—whenever he could return—was assigned to teach Greek and Latin. When he was well, Carpenter could teach just about anything.

The recruitment of Ellinwood made possible an enlargement of the scientific course, and Parks also planned a considerable growth of the program in music. It was clear to him, however, that the faltering law department must be discontinued. It would have been closed had President Berry lived, and Parks merely formalized an action that was ready to be taken anyway.

There was at least one piece of good news. In what appears to be the first bequest Simpson ever received, the College was named a beneficiary in the estate of the Rev. David N. Smith, who died at Burlington, Iowa, July 24, 1879, at the age of sixty-seven. When his will was admitted to probate, it was revealed that his home and an annuity were left to his widow, and the balance of his property bequeathed to the Clifford Springs Ladies' Seminary in New York and Simpson Centenary College, the latter bequest to be used for the endowment of a chair in the natural sciences.[10]

A longtime member of the clergy, Rev. Smith had served in Iowa since 1847, but he had retired from the active clergy "because of physical disability for pulpit work." For some years, he held a responsible position with the Burlington railroad and during the latter years of his life "devoted his attention to mining interests in the West, and was at the time of his death president of the Equitable Silver Mining Company" headquartered in New York.[11] It is possible that his mining interests got him into trouble with the conference, in which he continued as a "superannuated preacher." In any case, he was charged by a member of the Methodist church in Corning, Iowa, at the conference of 1878. The charges were adjudged "very grave," and a committee was appointed to arrange a trial. Rev. Smith died before the trial could take place. It would not be the last time that a Simpson board member would get into trouble because of mining ventures that proved to be shaky. Although he was declared by the *Simpsonian* to be one of Iowa's wealthiest men, with thousands of acres of land in Iowa and Nebraska, the eventual legacy proved to be something of a disappointment, about seven hundred dollars worth of stock certificates that could scarcely be called gilt-edged.[12]

If the Smith bequest proved to be something less than hoped for—it could hardly endow one rung on a straight-backed chair in any discipline—the fundraising prowess of the new president soon established him as one of the most respected educators in the state of Iowa. Actually Parks had little training in fund-raising—most college presidents were young clergymen with limited experience—but soon enough it was noised around the conference that the new Simpson Centenary president possessed a gift for extracting a contribution from nearly everyone he talked to. Yet even the most skilled money raiser needs help, and it is apparent that two important factors enabled Parks to succeed where others had too often failed. First, the hard years of the 1870s gave way to better times in the 1880s, and people were a bit more inclined to give to the College. More significantly, the institution had passed through its crisis of confidence in the awful days of 1879, and in the new president its supporters beheld the promise of a stable future.

That same autumn the board of trustees, already catching a glimpse of Parks's influence in the conference, asked the president "to devote most of his time to the financial interests of the college"[13] and decided to dispense with the services of the Rev. L. M. Walters, the College agent. Walters was in any case ready to give up his work for Simpson, having been reported only a month earlier ill at his home in Des Moines with a "threatened attack of brain fever."[14] An amicable settlement was reached with Walters, and from that time forward Parks was on his own.[15]

The commencement of classes in the fall of 1880 saw a College full of hope. It was, in the purple prose of the local press, "like the dedication of a new institution; like the reopening of one that had been closed for a long time; like the beginning of a new life." It was, they rhapsodized, like the phoenix.[16] In view of the "negative advertising the college has had for the past few years, [the students arriving on campus represented] an encouragingly large company."[17]

Parks decided he must eliminate the College's total debt—some $22,000—in a year.[18] "The plan," he recalled some years later, "was for me to keep the general executive work of the college, being present two or three days of the week, and spend the rest of the time soliciting on the charges of the conference." With such a schedule, there was no way he could meet his classes, so teaching duties were shuffled, and his wife, Isabella Webb Parks, who held a degree from Northwestern, "where she [had been] in the front of her classes," was engaged to teach political science.[19] "It was quietly whispered . . . that they had more than filled my place," commented the President.[20] It mattered not at all that she had given birth to their first child only about a month before classes commenced that autumn.

Freed from classes, Parks went about his work. "The principal [sic] on which I proceeded was to be perfectly frank with the people." He drew up a succinct, readable summary of the debt and the assets of the College. He soon discovered that taking up a public collection in the churches was "unwise"; he got only a disappointing $85 at Corning. At Creston, the Rev. Phineas F. Bresee, board member and stalwart Simpson supporter, urged that collections be abandoned altogether and that subscriptions be solicited on a "long roll," the pledges payable only when the whole debt could be wiped out. Bresee was first on the list with $100, which amount he later more than doubled. Shortly afterwards Parks presented the list to William Buxton of Carlisle, who put his name down for $1,000. "When I reported [this pledge] to Mr. Worth, he remarked, 'Mr. Buxton will yet give the college $10,000.' "[21] Then board member Henry C. Sigler gave $5,000, and with these large sums "the snow-ball began to grow rapidly." In the spring of 1881, Sigler added $2,000 to his pledge on condition that the entire debt be paid by September when the Des Moines Conference was scheduled to meet in Indianola. At commencement in 1881 Sigler's subscription was announced, as was that of his brother, David S. Sigler of Corning for another $5,000. At the conference in Indianola, the Rev. W. C. Martin was immensely helpful in overcoming "decided opposition among the ministers," as was the presiding bishop, Dr. W. X. Ninde, who subscribed $100 himself. With only a fraction of the total amount remaining to be raised, Judge Wright came through with $500 and Parks himself pledged to "stand good for $1,000." Such a gift, amounting to the better part of a year's salary, was seen as an act of heroism on the part of the thirty-year-old president. For his part, he "sat down behind the platform with his head in his hands to weep tears of joy."[22]

He wept for joy too soon. One can imagine his surprise the following spring when treasurer Worth informed him that "other claims which the college had to pay besides those on the warrant book" had first claim on Simpson's resources. Even with all the subscriptions, they were still $2,500 short. Not only that, but $1,500 of the existing pledges were still unpaid. What was to be done? The debt must be paid in full or the Sigler pledges would not be collectible. Lest they not reach their goal, Parks advanced the entire $4,000—"much more than I was worth"—and assumed the risk of collecting outstanding pledges and raising the balance in new gifts. The debt was thus paid off by the spring of 1882. Three years later, the $4,000 Parks had advanced was repaid, and he could breathe easily once again. "But when the notes were repaid," he recalled, "I remarked to Mr. Worth: I would never do the like again."[23]

While the president was out raising money, he canvassed the territory in search of students. In this endeavor he was highly successful. During the six-plus years

Table 2
Enrollment 1880–1890

Year	Senior	Junior	Soph.	Fresh.	Spec.	Total Coll.	Prep.	C.M.A.*	Total**
1880–81	4	11	13	30	4	62	114	16	184
1881–82	8	7	20	31	1	67	133	34	216
1882–83	6	13	24	33	8	84	150	94	268
1883–84	11	14	14	22	17	78	134	168	270
1884–85	10	11	13	22	22	78	116	139	249
1885–86	10	9	15	26	25	85	93	238	301
1886–87	6	10	19	41	34	110	113	125	332
1887–88	7	13	18	45	3	86	81	71	238
1888–89	11	13	25	32	19	100	116	121	303
1889–90	12	9	18	28	27	94	131	144	302

*C.M.A.: Commercial, Music and Art special students, nearly all of whom were of common school or high school age.
**Excludes duplicates.[24]

of his administration, student enrollment increased from 136 (1879–80) to 301 (1885–86).

Not only did student enrollment grow; the faculty was enlarged as well. When the law department was discontinued in the spring of 1880, nine faculty members remained, including the president. Two of the six salaried professors, Burke and Carpenter, did not return that autumn. Burke resigned as professor of Greek in late June to pursue a career in law. His place was taken by Byron C. Mathews, a recent graduate of Syracuse University, who was also named librarian, not a very onerous assignment in those days.[25] Mathews came with the "highest testimonials" and was accompanied by his wife, who was said to be "an accomplished musician and a fine German student."[26] George Carpenter was on leave for the entire year, as he would be for the following two years until his health improved sufficiently to enable him to take up his teaching duties again. To round out the faculty and to meet the demand for "practical" courses of instruction, the board of trustees appointed William H. Jordan to instruct in bookkeeping and penmanship and Joseph B. Harris to teach telegraphy.[27] Grumbling, Pierce, Ellinwood, Gregory and Bunker continued in their teaching positions.

During the Parks administration, two strong professors resigned, one of them under a cloud. Christian M. Grumbling was a veteran faculty member in mathematics whose teaching had been regarded as exemplary from the first day he came to the College in 1870. In all his twelve years, he got on especially well with the students; Simpsonian editors always wrote about him with respect and affection. They enjoyed his company, whether he was helping to "sod the triangle in front of the east college building"[28] or putting on an oyster feed for some of them at his home on Madison Street.[29] They mourned with him when his youngest child died[30] and said of him after many years of teaching: "His eye is not dim nor his natural force abated."[31]

Students and colleagues were shocked, then, when, at the close of the 1881–82 academic year, Grumbling resigned. What surprised them even more was the reason. He had offended a member of the board of trustees, it was charged, by engaging in partisan politics. Major John Kern, a well known Warren County farmer from Norwalk, lost an election and blamed Grumbling for his defeat. Kern was a powerful man, not accustomed to losing. He had served in the Ninth Iowa General Assembly in 1862, had enlisted at the close of that session in the army and rose to the rank of major in the Thirty-fourth Iowa Infantry. He had helped organize the Norwalk Methodist Church, was a former member of the county board of supervisors and two-term treasurer of the county, and ran for reelection to that latter post in the fall of 1881.[32] Grumbling, who had gained a wide reputation as a Chautauqua speaker, summer teachers' conference leader and potential candidate for state superintendent of public instruction,[33] was said to have spoken out against the candidacy of Major Kern and may indeed have been at least partly responsible for his defeat. Clarey of the *Tribune* certainly blamed Grumbling, calling his actions during the election campaign the "dirtiest kind of dirty manipulating." Simpson, he insisted, should not keep such a charlatan on its staff. "Mr. Grumbling's conduct wasn't simply indiscreet," he wrote. "It was indecent and insulting to every honest voter in the county."[34] That Grumbling was a Republican and the major a Democrat should have put the professor on the side of the angels, but Kern was not forgiving.

In the months that followed, most people were inclined to forget what seemed to be, after all, a minor political skirmish, but some of Kern's supporters were not. While it is not entirely clear precisely what happened, Grumbling's position was declared vacant at the end of the academic year and he departed the scene with acute signs of political assassination. That board of trustees members were embarrassed about what they had done is manifest, for they were reticent about naming a successor to Grumbling, who had strong and vocal support. Not only were students upset about his leaving, but also Bishop John F. Hurst, a board member from Des Moines, was known to be angry about the precipitous dismissal. The Corning district in conference passed a resolution in support of Grumbling, and "leading members" of the Des Moines Conference were insisting on a review of the matter.[35] The board of trustees stalled most of the summer, but because of the pressure had to call a special full board meeting on August 15 to settle the issue. Even then they could not resolve the problem and threw the decision to the executive committee of the board, which was forced to take action the next day, for the opening of the fall term was only weeks away.

They elected Arthur H. Giles to the chair of mathematics and astronomy at a salary of nine hundred dollars, but Giles turned them down,[36] whereupon they offered the post to Eudelmer Fitch Cuykendall, M.S., who at the last minute accepted their invitation. Grumbling, who had a right to be furious about the blatantly political forced resignation, accepted it with remarkably good grace.[37] Cuykendall remained at the College only one year. When he departed, the trustees persuaded Rev. William E. Hamilton, who had taught at the College back in 1867–68 and who had been fifteen years in the itinerancy in the Des Moines Conference, to return to academe.[38]

Ida May Pierce resigned her post at Simpson in February 1882 and traveled to San Antonio, Texas, in the company of her father, the Rev. J. N. Pierce, to join her terminally ill fiancé and former colleague Charles H. Burke, who had resigned from Simpson in 1880. There she married Burke on February 28. He died the following day. The *Simpsonian* noted, with appropriate delicacy, that she was called away "by the dangerous sickness of a friend to whom she feels that she owes attention."[39]

When the young widow returned to Iowa, she sought to regain her position at the College. The board of trustees, however, had already offered the chair to

Kate Baker only forty-eight hours earlier.[40] Although Mrs. Burke was disappointed, she secured a teaching position at the Indianola High School.[41] Young Charles W. Fisk had taught Mrs. Burke's classes temporarily at the close of the winter term, whereupon Miss Baker took over the position for the balance of the academic year,[42] and remained on the faculty until 1885.

Parks's faculty appointments were on the whole good, and during his last year at the College the number grew to fifteen, including three in music and one in art. It was his special good fortune in 1885 to bring the young, handsome Rev. Edmund M. Holmes, a Simpson Centenary graduate in the class of '80, to Indianola to accept the chair in Greek and Hebrew. In Holmes and Hamilton he had two future Simpson presidents on the faculty roster.

The president was pleased with the improved academic strength of the faculty, but he was equally gratified to see what he perceived to be the "spiritual work of the college" take on new vitality. In spite of the difficulty of getting faculty members to be regular in their attendance at chapel—which of course was required of students and faculty alike—"the tide of spiritual life," wrote Parks of those years, "usually rose gradually from the opening of the year, and the day of prayer for colleges was observed as a great spiritual feast at which the more marked ingathering of souls commenced. It was usually followed by special revival meetings every night for two or three weeks, till the unconverted material which it seemed possible to reach was exhausted."[43] For their part, the students were reasonably pious and accepted evangelization by their mentors with patience. But their real enthusiasm was demonstrated at literary society elections or Kappa Alpha Theta receptions or baseball games against the town boys, or evening "bums," where the attractions were seldom spiritual.

Yet one religious experience stood out in everyone's mind as the crowning event of the Parks years. It happened at commencement in 1882, when Bishop Matthew Simpson visited for the first and only time the college that bore his name. Although he was seventy-one years old and not strong, the Bishop journeyed to Indianola for the College's commencement.

The *Herald* had been heralding his visit for two months,[44] and excitement was building to a fever pitch among students and townspeople. When Frances Willard, founder of the Women's Christian Temperance Union and powerful orator against the evils of strong drink, spoke in town on June 8, she sensed the powerful undercurrent of expectancy among the people she met. It is difficult for us a century later, sated with the febrile emanations of the electronic and print media, to appreciate the fervor aroused in small-town nineteenth-century Iowa by the appearance of an eminent speaker. Nor can we comprehend the respect accorded in those days to the ecclesiastical celebrity. And Matthew Simpson was, even at his advanced age, a certifiable celebrity.

In anticipation of the huge crowd that would surely attend the bishop's sermon and address to the societies, the *Simpsonian* editor reported in May that "a large tabernacle tent has been procured in which the services during Commencement will be held." It was Mr. Sigler's "camp meeting tent," larger it was said than Barnum's show tent, and it could accommodate 1,500 people.[45]

When Matthew Simpson addressed a throng on Sunday morning, June 18, the crowd filled every seat in the tent in spite of leaden skies and intermittent heavy rainfall. It is fortunate that among those present was Frank B. Taylor, editor of the local *Advocate-Tribune*, for his is the only surviving account of what the Bishop said that day.[46]

As the visitors hurried into the tent from the rain-swept campus, they found the bishop, the faculty and nearly every member of the board of trustees seated on the rostrum. The choir, sitting on the right and apparently oblivious to the oppressive humidity, opened the exercises by singing the rousing anthem of rejoicing, "Lift up your heads, ye golden gates, and let the King of Glory in." During the prayer and psalm singing that followed, Frank Taylor, who was seated near the front of the tent, was watching Matthew Simpson. He observed the old gentleman closely and jotted down his thoughts:

> The Bishop's face brightened up till it was not difficult to imagine that you could see a growing inspiration almost shining from it. By watching this change, which was very marked, one could learn something of the source of his wonderful power. He seems to live upon the sounds and sights of the sanctuary. They are food and drink, and even wine to him; for they seem to fairly intoxicate. He has thrown his great soul into this great work of the ministry, and the two have mingled inseparably and both grown greater together. He is white with age, and shows signs of feebleness; but his eyes are clear and have a peculiar sparkle and takes possession of our eyes as his words do of our ears.[47]

Simpson spoke without a note, and his voice was strong and clear, his words heard distinctly at the very back of the tent. He selected for his text the last words of the prophet Malachi: "And he shall turn the heart of the fathers to the children, and the heart of the children to their fathers, lest I come and smite the earth with a curse" (Malachi 4:6). It was a sermon of triumph, full of the marvelous confidence of the nineteenth century American in the inevitability of progress, a grand forward thrust made possible by bringing individuals and nations to Christianity: "We have the promise that the day is coming when this world shall be given wholly to Christ; when wars shall be done away with; when great national sins shall no more exist. This time is far away. I shall not see it. But it is sure to come."

Signs of this progress were everywhere. "God gave man this world to possess and to rule. . . . It is ours to improve and glorify. We are to make this earth some day as on the very verge of heaven. Better times are in store for humanity, times when wars and strife shall cease, when covetousness shall no more rule. We have the promise of a new heaven and a new earth. Righteousness shall rule. . . . The majority shall be on the right side."

That was, of course, the side of Christianity, the sort of Christianity that is marked by children who care lovingly for their parents and parents who educate their children and who together destroy evil after evil, just as the people of Iowa were doing at that very time, "vigorously attacking a great enemy of the young race and the hinderer of Christian progress." He followed this obligatory reference to the temperance movement by a summary of his paean to progress in which he underscored the Christian and American contributions to the advent of a heaven on earth.

On the progress of women: "Christianity has taken woman by the hand and lifted her to her place by the side of man."

On language: At Babel God scattered man, and today Christianity reduces the number of languages spoken so that people may understand each other better. This brings "growing harmony among nations," when, as in the prophecy of the Revelator, the nations, like the beasts, shall live peaceably together: "The day is coming when men shall all come together and be one people."

On history: It is history that records and demonstrates human progress. Hence, "the teaching of history is one of the great civilizers." Yet "outside of Christianity there is but a page of history, and the church preserved even that."

On America: A Christian nation, it has been blessed above all, a realm where "the poorest mother in the land may look with love and pride upon her boy and know that he may become president."

But, Simpson warned, there are forces that oppose and impede the march of progress. There is paganism and the "misdirected" religions in the non-Christian world. There is Darwinism: "The scientist laughs at us for saying that man has been on the earth but about six thousand years. And if he has been here longer, where is his record?" Worst of all, there are the great cities where vice and corruption lead to ruin. "Jefferson," he pointed out, "the clearest thinker among American statesmen, except on the one subject of Christianity, called cities putrefying sores on the body politic. Is it not the cities of Iowa that you fear in your present [prohibition] contest?" Yet he held out some hope for great urban centers: "The vice of cities is now being tempered by righteousness." Progress will prevail.

The bishop closed with a tribute to the College that bore his name, associating it with the progress he had extolled: "I am glad to meet you, friends, on this ground today. This college tells me that the hearts of Iowa fathers have been turned toward the children. You have builded for eternity. . . . I am glad to live in such a day as this. I look almost with amazement upon its spirit and its works. What may be before us I cannot tell; but as a citizen of America I rest my hope for its future on the religious education of its youth. Christianity is the only . . . influence to build up and save the earth from sin."[48]

In his lecture to the societies the next evening, Simpson picked up on his idea of progress, noting that without leaders, little progress was possible or likely. He laid before his youthful listeners a view of the great vistas of service open to them and spoke of the qualities of leadership. He closed, wrote a reporter who was present, "with the fullest, richest burst of eloquence that has ever greeted ears in our college, picturing in a sentence the glorious future before the youth of this day, and exhorting them to be a part [of] the great company of workers who are transforming this into a new earth."

Frank Taylor spoke for all of Simpson's hearers when he summed up his impressions of the bishop's visit, which he termed a "benediction": "Thousands will remember the white-haired, broad heavy-browed man of the glowing heart and burning tongue, standing on life's western verge, as the brightest vision of their lives. He is considerably stooped, and when he straightens with the utterance of a great thought, his broad shoulders rise, and seem to lift his whole audience one notch higher in the scale of thinking, feeling and living."[49]

Students and faculty, townspeople and visitors from near and far basked in the bright light of Matthew Simpson's presence, inclement weather notwithstanding.[50] The same storm that dampened the proceedings at Indianola brought a devastating tornado to Grinnell, where both the town and the college, called Iowa College in those days, were almost totally destroyed. On the evening of Bishop Simpson's lecture, a collection was taken up, providing something more

SIMPSON CENTENARY COLLEGE,

DESIRES TO CALL SPECIAL ATTENTION TO

The Advantages Offered

TO THOSE DESIRING TO START IN SCHOOL

AT OPENING OF THE WINTER TERM

THOSE DESIRING TO PURSUE COMMON ENGLISH BRANCHES will find classes of various grades in English, Grammar, and Arithmetic, and classes in Physiology, Elocution, etc., in all of which special attention is given to thorough drill in the elements.

THOSE DESIRING A THOROUGH BUSINESS COURSE will find excellent instruction in book-keeping in all its forms, Business Penmanship, Business Correspondence, Business Ethics, Detection of Counterfeit Money, Business and Legal Forms, Commercial Law, etc.

THOSE DESIRING TO PREPARE TO TEACH will find classes in the elementary or advanced branches well suited to their needs.

THOSE DESIRING TO TAKE A REGULAR PREPARATORY OR COLLEGE COURSE will find classes beginning Latin, Greek, and Geometry and other elementary and advanced classes so that they cannot fail to find suitable work. The class beginning Latin is a special class designed to overtake the classes beginning last fall.

THOSE DESIRING TO PURSUE SELECTED STUDIES will find either elementary or advanced classes which will certainly give them profitable work.

THOSE DESIRING TO STUDY PIANO OR VOICE CULTURE will find instruction which is not surpassed in the Northwest.

EXPENSES VERY LOW.

The Next Term Opens Wednesday Dec. 31.

For catalogue and full information, address the President,

E. L. PARKS, INDIANOLA, IOWA.

Drumming up new students for the 1884–85 winter term. *Simpsonian*, December 1884.

than $200 "for the benefit of sufferers at Grinnell." Board president Rev. Bresee and John Henderson were asked to "forward the collection and express our sympathies to Iowa College."[51]

Not only were Simpsonians proud of their institution in the reflected brightness of the bishop's visit. It was announced at commencement that the College had operated in 1881–82 with an unheard-of surplus of $180, and better yet, the debt fund showed an equally incredible surplus of $983. Simpson Centenary had not merely survived. Under Parks's unexpectedly vigorous leadership, and after only two years, the College was debt-free.

* * *

In the fall of 1882, Simpson enrolled 210 students, including both undergraduates and preps. Of these, 209 were relatively unknown. One of them, however, was known all over America. She was Kate Shelley and she was a true heroine.

Only a year earlier, not far from Boone, Iowa, young Kate, then only fifteen years old, had risked her life to warn a station agent that a passenger train, hurtling through the night in the midst of a great storm, was destined for disaster, for the railroad bridge had collapsed. The train was halted in the nick of time, and many lives were saved.

The story of Kate Shelley's heroism was told again and again until it became a part of the legend of nineteenth-century America. The Iowa General Assembly awarded her a gold medal for bravery and two hundred dollars in cash. The school children of Dubuque presented her a medal. The *Chicago Tribune* raised a fund to help the impoverished Shelley family get out of debt. The railroads showered her with gifts. She became one of the most famous women of her time. The press heralded her heroism in sensational—and often apocryphal—stories and editorials. Dramatic readings were produced, poems composed.

The colorful tale of Kate Shelley, printed in dramatic detail in the Chicago newspapers, caught the eye of the indomitable Frances Willard, who persuaded the Women's Christian Temperance Union to give twenty-five dollars toward a fund to send Kate Shelley to college. She then wrote to her good friend Isabella Parks at Simpson, whose unshakable devotion to the cause of temperance endeared her to Miss Willard. Mrs. Parks set about raising the money to pay for a year of schooling at Simpson for young Kate.

Kate Shelley entered Simpson Centenary in the fall of 1882. Because she had not yet completed high school, however, she was required to spend a year as a preparatory student in the academy. Whatever her scholastic status, however, when she arrived in Indianola she was the object of everyone's affection. Rushed by all four of the sororities, she was within a few weeks initiated into Kappa Kappa Gamma.[52] With Kate Shelley on the campus, declared the *Simpsonian*, the College "is bound to become famous."

Shelley completed her preparatory work in the spring of 1883 and returned for the 1883–84 academic year,[53] when she was listed in the catalog as an unclassified student in the common English course. She completed that course, earning at the same time a certificate in teaching. After several years of teaching and lecturing,[54] she was appointed stationmaster by a grateful North Western Railroad at Moingona (1903), where she served until her untimely death in 1912.[55] She never married.

Today a great bridge spans the Des Moines River on the main line of the North

Western Railroad between Ogden and Boone. A spectacular span, one of the longest and highest of its kind, it is called the Kate Shelley Bridge.

* * *

President Parks hurried back to Indianola from conference sessions at Clarinda in order to be ready for the opening of the fall term on September 19, 1883. His report to his fellow clergy at conference had been a positive one. Things were going exceedingly well at the College, and he could take no small measure of satisfaction in Simpson's prosperity, much of which he ascribed to the strong, immensely helpful board of trustees.

Nine new members were elected each year to three-year terms on the College's twenty-seven-man board. In the fall of 1883 the eighteen carryover members included seven clergymen: Mahlon D. Collins of Corning, who had figured as one of the "villains" in the attempt to transfer the College to Des Moines; Benjamin Franklin Wilson Crozier of Clarinda; William Spearing Hooker of Shenandoah, the presiding elder of the Council Bluffs district; Thomas McKendree Stuart of Chariton; William David Bennett of Bedford; Charles Strickland Ryman, the presiding elder of the Des Moines district; and Felix W. Vinson of Colfax. The eleven continuing laymen included Judge William W. Phillips of Des Moines, who had assisted in the creation of the law department nearly a decade earlier; Benjamin Franklin Kauffman, a Des Moines attorney and prominent Methodist layman; Capt. Benjamin C. Berry of Indianola, the senior board member with fifteen years of service; Elias Watson Perry, a Virginia-born Indianola merchant who had served during the Civil War in the Thirty-fourth Iowa Infantry; three out-of-towners whose service to the board was necessarily limited: Judge Platt Wicks of Harlan, Lew Ellsworth Darrow of Corning and Stephen Rice Page of Boone. An important member of the Warren County board contingent was John Hancock Henderson, the popular young Indianola attorney, son of Paris P. Henderson, the county's organizing sheriff. Young Henderson, the first white male child born in the county, had been a member of the Simpson board since 1869, the year after his marriage to Nancy Spray, and would remain secretary of the board for the rest of his life. His uninterrupted service on the board set a record that is unlikely ever to be matched—seventy years, until his death at ninety in 1939. Another powerful Warren Countian was fifty-three-year-old William Buxton, Sr. of Carlisle, who had been on the board since 1876 and who was already a major benefactor of the College. Born in Derbyshire, England, Buxton had come to the United States when he was twenty-one, settled briefly in Indiana and rode from there to Warren County on horseback in 1852. Six years later, he married Massachusetts native Betsy Bramhall. They had one son and four daughters. In the county, Buxton was a prominent stock raiser whose nearly two thousand acres qualified him in the minds of most locals as landed gentry, if not nobility. He also owned a woollen mill at Palmyra, one of the oldest in central Iowa. In the fall of 1883, he had just organized the Warren County Bank in Indianola. He would continue on the Simpson board until 1917, and his son, grandson and great-grandson would serve after him. Between 1876 and 1985, the College's 125th anniversary, a Buxton served on the board of trustees without interruption.[56] The other local man was Gorham A. Worth, longtime cashier at the First National Bank and treasurer of the College. An Indiana native, Worth had earlier served as postmaster in Indianola (1862–68), was surely one of the most trusted businessmen in the community, and was active in any number of organizations from the Methodist Church to the Masonic Lodge. He was probably more responsible than anyone for saving the College from extinction in 1879.

Nine new members of the board were elected at the Clarinda conference. Six of these had served previously. Among these was Senator George G. Wright, probably the board's best-known member among the Iowa public and a veteran of fourteen years of service. Another was attorney Edward Hall of Indianola, of the firm of Hall and Carruthers, two gentlemen engaged in the practice of law but also billing themselves as "real estate agents and money lenders." A forty-five-year-old native of Ireland and Civil War veteran, Hall, a Presbyterian, had lived in Indianola intermittently since 1866 and was married to Mattie T. Noble, daughter of Dr. B. S. Noble, who had helped organize the Indianola Male and Female Seminary back in 1860. Also serving were John C. Mitchell of Nevada, Judge Benjamin Franklin Clayton of Macedonia, Rev. Emerson Kinne Young, a New York native who was pastor of the First Church in Des Moines, and Dr. Parks, president of the College. The three new members were O. A. Bartholomew, a graduate of Indiana Asbury University who lived at Chariton, and two clergymen, Rev. William C. Martin, the presiding elder of the Atlantic district, and Rev. William C. Smith of Woodbine, a graduate of Simpson Centenary in the class of 1871.

While the board was a good one, it was missing one of its oldest, most prominent, and surely one of its most active members. Phineas F. Bresee had quite suddenly departed from the conference and moved to California. It was strange not to find Bresee, with his ebullient personality, his infectious enthusiasm, his mind overflowing with new ideas, holding forth at board meetings, encouraging the timid, scolding the lazy, praying with a peculiar and almost palpable fire for the blessings of the Almighty upon their little College. He had joined the board in 1867, the year their Des Moines Conference Seminary was upgraded to collegiate status, an action which he strongly favored and helped to bring to pass. During the years that followed he supported the College with unflagging energy. Whenever it needed an advocate in the conference, he was there. While he did not participate in the day-to-day management of the College—that was not the job of a board member then or now—he did contribute time and money and exerted his very considerable influence in the conference on its behalf. Carl Bangs has written of Simpson College that "during the first 16 years of its existence, its spirit and growth were due more to the efforts of P. F. Bresee than to any other one person."[57] While Bangs's assessment of Bresee's influence is extravagant, it is true that of all the conference clergymen who worked with the College during its early years, Bresee was by all odds the most effective. And because the church loomed large in the life of Simpson in those days, clergymen on the board of trustees were shown great deference.

It was, then, particularly distressing that Bresee departed the scene so suddenly. The reason was that he got caught up in a fraudulent silver mining scheme that so injured his reputation that he found it no longer possible to stay in Iowa. He was surely no criminal. But he seems to have been a not-too-reluctant dupe, not unlike many of his clerical colleagues and lay friends, all of whom should probably have known better.

In an effort to supplement his meager clergyman's income, he looked for investments that promised a handsome return. From another Methodist minister he learned of a "sure thing," a silver mine in Mexico that was purported to be a virtual Eldorado. Bresee invested heavily, encouraged other Methodist ministers to buy stock in the mine, sold stock to his own parishioners and urged his clerical colleagues to do the same. Thus, when the whole mining scheme turned out to be an elaborate fraud, Bresee was humiliated.

It would appear that the embarrassment—seeing people lose the homes and farms they had mortgaged to invest in the mines—was too much for him. He simply could not face all those people who had believed in him. "Hence," he said later, "I deemed it best to take a transfer to some distant Conference."[58] Dead broke, with a wife and six children, he moved to Los Angeles in August 1883.[59]

Bresee prospered in California, where he served a number of growing congregations. But he and his family lived in accordance with a spartan regimen and punishing frugality. Quietly, systematically, he repaid everyone in Iowa to whom he had ever sold mining stock—many thousands of dollars.[60]

During his years in the Southern California Conference—he served there as presiding elder in 1891-92—he emphasized more and more in his preaching and teaching the doctrine of personal holiness, a concern shared by those in the Pentecostal movement. He began to work more and more with the urban poor. His evangelical work among those who were down and out led to his forced withdrawal from the Methodist conference in 1894, after thirty-seven years as a minister.

The next year Bresee organized the Church of the Nazarene, which met the needs of the people with whom he was working. These people, he noted, were too frequently ignored by the stylish downtown congregations of churches in the so-called mainstream of protestantism. The first service of his new church was held October 6, 1895, at his tabernacle on South Main Street. He lived twenty years more, long enough to see the church he founded grow and spread through the United States and Canada and, through missionary enterprise, to the world beyond America.

Less than a month after Bresee's departure from Iowa, the Des Moines conference at Clarinda expressed regret at the "loss sustained in the removal of Rev. P. F. Bresee, President of the Board, who has for so many years been a faithful friend of the College and an efficient member of the Board."[61] At its 1884 commencement Simpson awarded Bresee, *in absentia*, the honorary D.D. degree. That was the least the College could do. He would be missed.

* * *

When President Parks came to Simpson Centenary in early 1880, the campus was in very poor condition, a victim of "deferred maintenance." The single building was in a sorry state of disrepair, and the grounds looked like an ill-kept hayfield in a grove of half-grown maple trees. The new president, brushing aside arguments about what the College could not afford, moved ahead with a few of the most-needed improvements. New sidewalks were constructed that spring, a boon in muddy weather, and the chapel was papered freshly in time for commencement.[62] But he could move only so fast. It was reported the following spring that the College baseball players had burned off the prairie grass on five campus acres for a ball field. "It would improve the looks of the grounds if more of the campus had been included in the fire," quipped the editor of *The People's Advocate*.[63] The board slowed things down by ordering no further repairs "in view of financial exigency" while Parks was still out raising the money to pay off the debt.[64] After that burden was lifted, the board was more willing to permit the president to make more campus improvements. The building was repaired and repainted and a fine new board fence erected around the front of the campus.[65] A new organ was purchased for the chapel, and the whole College rejoiced "in the hope of steam heaters."[66] In 1884, in order to provide a better exit for the chapel, a covered external stairway was built, cascading down from the rear of the College Hall. When it was completed it was declared, somewhat defensively, that it did not mar the appearance of the building "to any considerable extent," but in the years to come it came to be regarded as an unimaginably ugly appendage, called by students and faculty alike, and not altogether with affection, the "hog chute."[67] To compensate for this visual atrocity, President Parks, in one of his last acts as president in 1886, authorized the purchase of a lawn mower. It cost twelve dollars.[68]

The burgeoning enrollments of the mid-1880s meant serious overcrowding in the College's single building. Both undergraduate and preparatory classes competed for what little space there was. It became clear to President Parks that more room must be found somehow. As a stopgap measure, he rented some rooms in nearby private houses for a few classes—especially music and art—and reminded everyone who would listen to him that the only permanent solution was a new classroom building.[69] As soon as he heard the report of the death of Bishop Simpson in the early summer of 1884, he persuaded the board of trustees to make plans for building a new Simpson Memorial Hall, and he asked former president Sam Vernon, who returned to speak at the College's commencement that year, to assist in raising funds in the East for the project.[70] To be sure, Parks conceded that what was needed even more was a women's boarding hall. At that time, the young men who attended the College could be boarded in private homes and boarding houses of quite varying quality, but women students, most of whom resided in private homes where they were not always adequately protected, seemed to be inappropriately cared for. Board of trustees members and the faculty believed that the College bore the responsibility for the physical and moral well-being of Simpson's women students. They must be kept out of harm's way.

While plans for a dormitory were being studied, it was announced in mid-1885 that a private boarding hall for women was being built by Elias Proudfoot and that it would be presided over by Prof. Hamilton and his wife.[71] Such a building was helpful, but the College needed its own ladies' boarding hall, and the next year President Parks was out raising money for it. Solicitation of funds went slowly, however, and it would be 1889 before construction actually commenced on Ladies' Hall. Meanwhile, students could take their meals together in men's or women's boarding clubs for about two dollars per week.

When Parks first came to Simpson, the College still published no specific rules of student conduct. The 1879–80 catalog continued the policy of Alexander Burns, saying as little as possible about the subject. It merely noted that Indianola "*prohibits the license of the sale of intoxicating liquors* and is free from those allurements to vice and those unworthy attractions which are found in big cities."[72] The catalog supported the idea of student self-government, required "good conduct and faithful work" and relied on "the honor and moral sense of the students to secure those ends." In 1886, alarmed by reports of "licentious misconduct" of some students and disgusted by the growing use of tobacco, the faculty produced "a set of iron-clad rules."[73] They were published for the first time in the 1885-86 catalog: "The improprieties of deportment of which the Faculty take account include all immoral conduct; the use of ardent spirits and tobacco; card-playing, theater-going and dancing; rude or ungentlemanly or unladylike conduct in or about the College building, on the streets, or at boarding places; absence from chapel, recitation or church without excuse; absence from rooms after 10 P.M., except in cases of necessity or attendance on such public entertainments as may have been approved by the Faculty."[74] Further, students were reminded that they were "residents of the city and . . . subject to state and city laws."[75]

It should not be assumed that the sharp contrast between the statements about student conduct in the 1880 and 1886 catalogs represented any sort of revolutionary change, however different the language. The unspoken was simply expressed explicitly. What appears to have brought it on was the faculty's objection to smoking, which seemed to have been epidemic among the young men on the campus. It is, then, puzzling to note that two months after the new rules had been promulgated, there appeared in the *Simpsonian* a display advertisement for "Richmond Straight-Cut (No. 1) Cigarettes."[76]

Students' reaction to the new rules was exceedingly mild, perhaps because in their view not much had changed. The *Simpsonian* did note "some rebellious sentiment" on campus, especially regarding the ban on theater-going. Surely the faculty would not object to Shakespeare. They didn't, of course, and students were happy to accept the faculty "clarification" that this was, after all, an honor code; the rules were "merely requests, and that non-compliance with them will meet with the disapprobation of the faculty." How such disapprobation would take form was left indefinite.[77]

In any event, discipline cases were few and far between. There were none at all in most years. In 1884, "it became necessary to request several young men students not to return to College next year owing to their bad influence in the school by reason of habits of dissipation and other irregularities."[78] "Dissipation" was usually the code word for consuming "ardent spirits," and it was not tolerated, especially in view of the fact that undergraduate tippling would set a bad example for prep students, some of whom were no more than fifteen years old.

It probably wasn't dissipation that caused energetic, mischievous John Fitch Conrad to leave Simpson Centenary in the middle of his junior year. From a farm in Lucas County, Conrad had entered the College in the fall of 1879 as a first year prep student and enrolled in the freshman class two years later. He left Simpson in March 1884, enthusiastically urged to do so by President Parks. Conrad later recalled the last of his many conversations with the president, who, like all presidents of his day, was responsible for student discipline. Parks "told me that if I applied myself I would surely become a leader among men; and, he added, he had never seen a boy who could keep more students from studying than I, and with so little seeming effort. His talk was very earnest."[79]

It is no doubt true that Conrad's heart was not in his studies. He remembered vividly "that first day in college, when the faculty were trying to organize us into classes, . . . W. T. [his friend William Townsend Thompson of Fennimore,

Richmond Straight Cut No 1.

CIGARETTES!

CIGARETTE SMOKERS who are willing to pay a little more than the price charged for the ORDINARY TRADE Cigarettes, will find THIS BRAND superior to all others.

The Richmond Straight Cut No. 1 Cigarettes are made from the brightest, most delicately flavored and highest cost *Gold Leaf* grown in Virginia. This is the *Old and Original Brand of Straight Cut* Cigarettes, and was brought out by us in the year 1875.

BEWARE OF IMITATIONS, and observe that the firm name as below is on every package

The Allen & Ginter Branch of the American Tobacco Co.,

MANUFACTURERS,

Richmond, - Virginia

Although the College issued a prohibition of tobacco use as early as 1886, this advertisement appeared regularly in the *Simpsonian* as late as the 1890–91 academic year.

Wisconsin] asked me what I was going to take up. I told him if it did not clash with penmanship or one or two other studies my heart was set on, I would like to take astronomy. My notion was that astronomy taught only the names of the stars and gave general directions how to find them, then quit. This struck me as being a nice, clean study." His studies, clean or otherwise, seem never to have gotten in the way of late night scuffles or exquisitely premeditated pranks, for which he became well known. Yet he fancied himself a good writer.

In his freshman year he wrote an essay for Ida May Pierce's class in English composition. "I had written a powerful theme on 'money,'" he recalled. "It made John Stuart Mill and Henry Clews seem like amateurs. Besides being powerful, it was flowery and figurative. . . . I had written it with a Spencerian pen, with many shades and flourishes. It was only human nature to let my pride stalk a bit." He fastened the pages of his "masterpiece" together with a baby blue ribbon and handed it to the professor—he called her the "preceptress." Then thunder struck. "How a gentle, refined creature like Miss Pierce could be so heartless and cruel is a mystery to me still. But she took that theme, and with a big, blunt, blue lead pencil she practiced her cruelties on it. . . . Whenever she added a comma she made a stroke that looked like one of Swift's hams. If I had overlooked a letter she added it—and the rest of the word was obscured." She made proofreader-like strokes, indicating that the desecration was continued on the margin, and when she would transpose a phrase she made that sentence look like four hills of potatoes that the hogs had been at. . . . It was awful!" Such experiences, he averred, led him away from academic endeavor and into devilment.[80]

Perhaps part of J. F. Conrad's problem at Simpson was that he was a Democrat in a nest of Republicans. He and his friend Olin A. Kennedy from Milo, a year ahead of Conrad at Simpson, were members of the same independent eating club. They called it Eta Pi. Kennedy remembered the time Conrad, still a prep student, created a sensation at a meeting of the Everett Society when "Fitch blurted out in the heat of debate that the soldiers of the South were as sincere in what they did as were the soldiers of the North."[81] Kennedy and Ed[mund] Holmes had to talk fast to keep some of the more "rabid adherents of Republicanism" from throwing Conrad into South River.[82] As Kennedy put it, Conrad "brought with him such a cantankerous brand of Democracy that some of the professors regarded him as anything but safe and sane." One of them called him an "insurgent," and he probably was just that.[83] Yet they were probably not really alarmed by Conrad's predictable outbursts, for they were convinced that colorful Iowa politician Jonathan P. Dolliver—later Senator Dolliver—was right when he proclaimed that "Iowa will go Democratic when Hell goes Methodist."

Whether the issue was politics or social issues or academics, students gave vent to their opinions and expressed their enthusiasms in the pages of the *Simpsonian*. Although it was, like the College, perennially in financial difficulty, the campus newspaper, published monthly in magazine format, carried everything from serious articles about national and world issues to trivial campus gossip. It could voice fierce opposition to Russian nihilist terrorism or Mormon polygamy in Utah. It mourned the assassination of President Garfield and the death of Matthew Simpson.[84] Its huge commencement edition each year contained most or all of the addresses made during the week, including the senior orations.[85] Most of the monthly outpouring of the *Simpsonian*'s reporters, however, chronicled campus events: reflections—usually complaints—about classes and examinations, comments about the faculty—usually compliments—or the comings and goings of students.

It is the lives of the students, their problems and their activities, that quite properly the *Simpsonian* chronicled most diligently. It is striking, for example, how much serious illness plagued the students, necessitating their dropping out of school for a week or a term. And every year one or more students or young alumni died of some malady, known or little understood. So limited were students' financial resources that a large number of them left school during the spring term, sometimes to teach in the common schools, to earn enough to return the following fall. Summers were given over to farm employment or door-to-door selling—peddling stereopticon slides was a favorite—by the men. Women had considerable difficulty finding summer employment at all.

Student activities burgeoned during the 1880s. While the literary societies, with their emphasis on oratory and debate, remained important, the Greek-letter societies were increasing in popularity, affording to their members intimate friendships in organizations without faculty regulation or oversight. Until 1878 women could join the L.F.V. or the national I.C. Sorosis. Early that year a third women's secret society was founded, called Theta Gamma Chi. The *Simpsonian* soon got wind of it and in its March 1878 issue reported the "rumor of a new secret society, but no one willing to acknowledge membership in it."[86] More than a year later it was reported that "Theta Gamma Chi Sorosis had a banquet at the home of Miss Lillie Jacoby."[87] Meanwhile, Bertha C. Morrison, one of the members, read in a college publication of a young woman in Greencastle, Indiana, receiving a Theta badge for Christmas. Morrison wrote to her, saying "I am a Theta too and would like to know about the Theta organization in Greencastle." Kappa Alpha Theta had been founded in 1870 at Indiana Asbury (now DePauw University) in Greencastle. In 1879 it had seven chapters, all located in the Midwest. After some correspondence, Morrison and her Simpson sisters noted "to our great delight we were nationalized and still remain Thetas as before."[88] Iowa seemed to be a long way from Indiana, so the chapter, called Theta of Kappa Alpha Theta, was chartered and installed in early 1880 entirely by correspondence.

Only weeks later, on April 10, 1880, Kappa Kappa Gamma, founded in 1870 at Monmouth College, chartered its Omicron chapter at Simpson Centenary. There were seven charter members.[89] The June issue of the *Simpsonian* heralded the presence of the new group: "We notice several of the young ladies of Simpson College have succeeded in obtaining keys of—we were going to say heaven, but suppose Kappa Kappa Gamma will do as well."[90]

During the early eighties two more national Greek-letter fraternities for men appeared to provide rivalry for Delta Tau Delta. One was Phi Kappa Psi, formally chartered in 1882, but recognizing de jure a fraternity that had actually been on the campus for nearly three years. Back in 1876 Cassius Coe from Norwalk, Iowa, wrote to the Grand Chapter of Phi Kappa Psi seeking a charter for Simpson. Coe was a sometime student at Simpson. He attended as a freshman in 1874–75 and as a junior in 1878–79, but was not listed as a student during any of the three intervening years. In any case, his petition received no response. Phi Kappa Psi's chapter at the State University of Iowa had died out in 1876, and the fraternity was not interested in any Iowa college. Unaware of Coe's efforts, however, a group of Simpson students sent a second petition to Phi Kappa Psi in April 1878. This request was vetoed by one Phi Psi chapter, as was a third petition by yet another single vote.

Then, in 1879, the Phi Kappa Psi chapter at Monmouth College, threatened with destruction when the college abolished fraternities, undertook to transfer its charter to Simpson. A group of Monmouth Phi Psis came to Indianola and initiated the petitioners. Although they had no badges, the initiates reportedly donned "pieces of blue and white cloth with 'Phi Kappa Psi' printed on them" and wore them "instead of pins on commencement day, 1879."[91] Reaction in Phi Kappa Psi chapters ranged from hearty support for to adamant opposition to the unchartered "chapter." One Phi Psi alumnus official was sympathetic and wrote to one of his colleagues that while he was "emphatically opposed" to organizing chapters "contrary to the Constitution," the deed had been done, "and the Indianola boys are not to blame."[92]

In 1881 the Simpson men, unsure of their status, made one more try. This time they had a powerful ally. "The president of Simpson College," they wrote, "is a Phi Kappa Psi, E. L. Parks of Evanston (Illinois) University." When the petition went out to the Phi Psi chapters for a vote on November 30, 1881, it was accompanied by a letter of recommendation from President Parks. They got their charter, and the chapter was formally installed June 16, 1882. They called the chapter Iowa Delta.[93]

In 1880, while the Phi Kappa Psi situation was at its worst, a group of Simpson undergraduates organized a new fraternity and called it Rho Alpha. Their group found instant acceptance on the campus. In the fall of 1882, Rho Alpha pledged five very strong men, four of whom spearheaded the drive to secure a charter of a national fraternity. They soon entered negotiations with Alpha Tau Omega. In a way, theirs was an unusual choice, for ATO was founded in the South in 1865, and nearly all the growth of the fraternity had been in the South and the East. Although the fraternity had established two chapters in the West (Arkansas and Oregon State), both had died out in 1882. Thus when ATO chartered the Rho Alpha group at Simpson, the new chapter was the only one in the fraternity west of the Mississippi. One of the charter members of their new Iowa Beta Alpha chapter was William Buxton, Jr., whose father was on the College's board of trustees. All the arrangements for chartering and installation were conducted by mail. The charter members were initiated March 16, 1885.[94] The creation of this new chapter was, both for Rho Alpha and ATO, a good match.

In the 1880s fraternity and sorority chapters were small, rarely counting more than fifteen or twenty undergraduate members.[95] The names of these groups, if not their activities, derived from the emphasis on classical languages and literature that characterized nineteenth-century American colleges. Hence their members referred to themselves as Greeks and to all non-Greek students as "barbarians." The "barbs," reported one pro-Greek editor of the *Simpsonian*, were combining—always a dire threat to the Greeks—and "laboring very earnestly to advance the cause of barbarism."[96]

It was the Greek societies that were responsible for the publication of the College's first yearbook. "A scheme to publish an annual is afoot," reported the *Simpsonian* in late 1883.[97] Issued at commencement time in 1884, the *Tangent*, selling for fifty cents a copy, was a production of the six Greek chapters on the campus at that time.[98] Said to be the first yearbook published in the West, the *Tangent* reportedly contained an account of each secret society. In addition, "considerable space is given to each college class in turn, and to various organizations and clubs." In its pages, complete with steel-engraved illustrations, "some curious statistics are compiled, and the record of the year is certainly truthful and will be valuable for reference for matters of vital importance."[99] Intended to be an annual, this much-praised publication did not appear again until 1889, when its second—and last—issue was produced. Each year the Greek societies hoped to publish their college yearbook, but its production costs more often than not foiled their plans.[100]

If they could not afford to publish a regular yearbook, the Greek-letter society members did set the fashions on campus. During the eighties, it was straw hats and canes for the men and calicos for the women. Calicos, indeed, were attractive but hardly elegant; a local merchant down on the square advertised the material at twenty-five yards for a dollar.[101] More expensive, and surely more exciting, was the bicycle, the high front-wheeled kind or the new rear-drive "safety" machine, ridden by young daredevils who risked their lives pedaling on Indianola's mostly unpaved streets. Townspeople were fascinated with "this novel method of travel," but concluded that most of the bicyclists were almost certainly demented.[102] And if male students tired of bicycling, they could join the new Athletic Association, organized April 14, 1883, with "football, baseball as the principal games, with possibly lawn tennis and cricket [sic]."[103] Soon enough, women clamored to be admitted to the club, and the men gave in without a struggle, nonetheless haughtily suggesting that "milder games be secured for their benefit."[104] Baseball was the only men's sport that was widely played. And some of its student practitioners were good. While he was at Simpson, Winfield Scott Kelly, who entered as a freshman in 1884, "pitched baseball and had the reputation of being the first man in southwest Iowa to throw a curved ball.[105]

It was not only students who organized groups for work and play. During the eighties, the Alumnal Association, originally established during the last year of Alexander Burns's presidency, came into its own.[106] The first mention of a College Ladies' Aid Society can be traced to early 1880.[107] It would appear that their first "good work" for Simpson was "calcimining and painting the halls and the library" of the College building, for which they received the formal thanks of the board of trustees.[108] That same year the Berry Memorial Association, organized to raise funds to honor the late Thomas S. Berry, completed its first modest drive for memorial gifts.

Berry was not the only person mourned at Simpson during the eighties. When President Garfield died in September 1881 from a gunshot wound suffered at the hand of an assassin, the College chapel was draped in black and displayed a large picture of Garfield surrounded by black and white crepe paper, the rostrum overhung with the stars and stripes. At the year's opening convocation, President Parks asked the students to sing "Nearer My God to Thee" to honor the fallen president.[109] The next year, no one at Simpson mourned the death of Charles Darwin. A marvelously equivocal notice of his passing appeared in the *Simpsonian*, the writers somewhat uncertain what to say about the man whose controversial writings threatened somehow their comfortable cosmology.[110] Simpsonians were, however, genuinely grieved to hear of the death of pioneer trustee George Griffith, who died at Warrensburg, Missouri, May 21, 1885. He had been the College's most stalwart supporter during the first fifteen years of its existence.[111] No prominent person's death struck the College more, however, than that of Matthew Simpson in mid-1884, just before commencement time. At a solemn memorial service on June 22, President Parks was joined by Professor William E. Hamilton, William H. Berry, ex-President Sam Vernon and several leading conference clergymen, all of them eulogizing this most eminent Methodist bishop of his day.[112]

It is quite possible that the death of Matthew Simpson led to the decision of the board of trustees to shorten the name of the College by dropping the word *centenary*. In any case, there was only a two-month interval between the time of the campus memorial service and the first mention of the board's intention to make the change.[113] After much discussion, especially among conference clergy, the final decision to call the institution simply "Simpson College" was taken June 23, 1885.[114]

A tangible memorial to Bishop Simpson was received quite unexpectedly in June 1886, when Dr. T. B. Neely, a clergyman in Pottsville, Pennsylvania, sent a gilt bas-relief of the bishop as a gift to the College. Done in the late years of Simpson's life, the relief was encased in a heavy carved oak frame. In the sturdy shipping crate was a letter from Dr. Neely. "The relief," he wrote, "represents the Bishop in advanced years but in good health and brings out every characteristic of his expressive countenance even to the smallest detail."[115] Commissioned by Philadelphia art dealer Christian Faser, the relief sent to the College was a copy, the only copy, of the original.[116]

In the judgment of the president of the College, the presentation of the bas-relief of Bishop Simpson was a pleasant distraction in an otherwise troublesome spring. Although he had cleared the College's debt during his first year on campus, Parks saw deficits in operations in 1883 and 1885, and he anticipated a serious shortfall in the 1885–86 academic year, which in the event amounted to more than $3,000.[117] Part of the problem, quite clearly, was that the men's boarding hall, a rented off-campus facility, was losing money.[118] As with tuition, the College never charged enough for its services to meet expenses. And if financial woes were not enough, Parks felt obliged, as spring days awakened student passions, to remind them in chapel of the sinfulness of some of their iniquitous behavior, singling out especially their proclivity for "theater-and concert-going."

It was concert-going that provided President Parks, students and faculty the greatest excitement of the year, leaving town-gown relationships the worse for the experience. It all started one day in May 1886, when a small army of students trooped down to Frank Miller's bookstore on the square to purchase opera house tickets for the Mendelssohn Quintet Club concert. When they learned that the best seats had already been sold to townspeople, they were angered, charging discrimination against students in favor of Frank Miller's town cronies. Burning with indignation, the students returned en masse to the College chapel, where they held a noisy meeting. Sixty-eight of them signed a resolution urging their fellow students to boycott Miller's bookstore and buy their books "directly from the publishers." Moreover, they would withhold their patronage of the "student-haters" in the town, several of whom they mentioned by name in the heat of the moment. They fired off a copy of their written resolution to the *State Register*, in order to give it the widest possible circulation. The *State Register* published their resolution, commenting that there was much ill feeling in Indianola "over a trivial matter," and charged that in their boycott, the students were adopting the tactics of strikers.[119]

The reaction of the Des Moines press was not exactly what the students had in mind when they sent in their resolution. Now they were angry at both the Indianola businessmen and the *Register* as well. In Indianola, the editor of the *Advocate-Tribune* could hardly feel sorry for the students. "It was," he wrote, "the students themselves, by choosing the course of anarchists, who have brought disgrace on the fair name of Simpson. Not content with adopting the methods of anarchists, they deliberately resolved to publish their infamy to the world, and chose the *Register* . . . [to convey] to the world the story of there [sic] own folly and wickedness. . . . All the friends of the College," concluded the editor, "will exert themselves to mark the evil tree and labor to have it destroyed root and branch, before it is too late." The editor, moreover, could not refrain from noting that some of the "anarchists" were students preparing for the ministry. "The true character of some of our pretended preachers," he wrote, "was revealed in a startling manner. . . . They are the men who are to preach 'Thou shalt forgive thy brother seventy-times seven.' "[120]

What was unfortunate in this episode, the cause of which was indeed trivial, was that it exposed a measure of displeasure, if not bitterness, in the community regarding the College. Indianolans had created Simpson, nurtured it, and more than once had saved it from extinction. "Ever since the College was commenced the citizens of Indianola have been bled for its support," said one angry townsman. And the business community was not benefitted by the College as much as some of its supporters claimed. Student spending in Indianola was, they said, consistently exaggerated. The town was hardly dependent on the College for its survival or prosperity. "We can not say that Simpson's students are any worse than those of other colleges," conceded the *Advocate-Tribune*, but they were pretty bad. They "caroused at night, disturbing the sleep of citizens," they walked "three or four abreast on a four or six foot sidewalk . . . crowding men women and children whom they meet, off the walk." A whole range of student excesses and peccadillos were paraded in the local press, and the ill feeling died down only slowly.[121]

Ambivalence toward the role of Simpson in Indianola would affect some of the citizenry from time to time, but for the most part the relationship between town and gown, especially the more responsible elements of both, was amiable enough, and such outbreaks of hostility as exploded in the spring of 1886 were relatively rare.

Even in that difficult spring, deficit or no deficit, the College was flourishing. Although enrollment dropped that year (1886) from 233 in the winter to 195 in the spring term, the decrease was less than expected, and such a falloff was an annual occurrence in most Midwestern colleges. The *Simpsonian* noted matter-of-factly that students were dropping out "to earn enough to return."[122] Actually, enrollment was not really bad at all. In fact, Simpson's one building could not possibly hold all the students in all the classes of both College and Academy. Rented rooms in town for business and music classes were inadequate at best. The time had come, everyone agreed, for the College to take a major step forward by putting up at least one new academic building. To that end A. H. Swan of Indianola made an unconditional gift of $2,000, and President Parks, immensely encouraged by this generous contribution, declared that he hoped to raise $15,000 by the fall of 1887.[123] In his fund-raising efforts he was joined during April and May 1886 by Bishop W. X. Ninde who was known to be as persuasive in extracting cash from Methodists as any man in the land.[124] In a few weeks they raised $1,000 in Des Moines and $250 in Norwalk, and more was coming in from other nearby towns.[125] The president and the bishop were a great team. They shared much: devotion to the mission of the church, a passion for education, and a love of people; and they laughed that they had even been fraternity brothers in college.[126] The bishop accepted an invitation to deliver the annual sermon at commencement, where he hoped to bring in a few more dollars for Simpson.

On May 4, 1886, President Parks was able to report at morning chapel that he and the bishop had already raised $2,500 toward the building fund. In that same chapel service, however, he stunned his audience with the announcement that he was resigning the presidency of Simpson to accept a position as professor of systematic theology at the Gammon School of Theology in Atlanta, Georgia. He explained that he had been called "to a position that greatly enlarged his sphere of usefulness, a position the duties of which accorded with his own tastes." The call, said Parks, was "a providential one" and it was "his duty to accept it." His resignation would be effective at the end of the academic year. His eyes, wrote the *Simpsonian* reporter, "filled with tears, and the emotion almost overcame him." The whole assembly was cast into gloom. After a perfunctory benediction, students and faculty filed slowly out of the chapel.[127]

Because the Gammon School of Theology accepted all qualified students regardless of race, and because of powerful racial segregation in the South, Parks said that he expected his work there to be "confined almost entirely to the education of colored students for the ministry . . . for the elevation of this unfortunate people." He saw in his new assignment a broad opportunity for service to his fellow man. The church had called him. He could not but accept the call with rejoicing.

Lest one conclude that Parks was somehow such a paragon of virtue as to be unreal, one need only examine closely what the man said and what he did. Exemplifying a Christian piety that was utterly without hypocrisy, he expected much of himself and of those who were engaged in the cause of Christian education. "The faculty," he said, "should collectively and individually regularly plan for and engage in work for the salvation of their students and their advancement in the Christian life. The work should be both official and non-official, regular and irregular, pre-arranged and spontaneous." He expected the trustees to select a faculty, "every member of which is not only an earnest Christian, but a man or woman whose Christian character and influence in the community are marked . . . and who feels a profound conviction that he is called to be a Christian teacher."[128] And a Christian teacher he was, whose unconditional affection for his fellow man led him to make good on his public statements and commit his life to the education of black students in an age when such a venture required courage. He remained at Gammon for eighteen years and, after a two-year pastorate at a Methodist church in Arkansas, returned to the realm of black higher education in 1907 at Howard University, a premier black institution in Washington, D.C., where, in addition to teaching in economics, he served as treasurer and registrar (1909–19) and subsequently as dean of men (1919–26).

In his distinguished career as an educator, Parks never abandoned his belief in Christian education, whether lecturing in Bible schools or on the Chautauqua circuit. He authored a number of studies in systematic theology, on the Christian life and on books of the Bible. Fifty years after leaving Simpson, he died at Washington May 24, 1936. During the last days of his life he recalled to a visitor the "halcyon days at old Simpson," when both he and the College were young. He never forgot his struggle to make a frail little school strong. He did not forget either that he largely succeeded in that enterprise. And Simpson did not forget him.

As early as June 9, 1886, the board of trustees met to elect a successor to Parks. A leading contender for the post was the Rev. Thomas J. Bassett, principal of the preparatory department at DePauw University. But because several ballots resulted in a deadlock between Bassett and other candidates, no election was possible. At one point, the board asked Parks to reconsider his resignation, but their effort was in vain. In mid-June two faculty members were sent to Greencastle to meet Rev. Bassett and returned with a negative recommendation.[129] Unsure of where to turn next, the board elected professor William E. Hamilton vice-president of the College and asked him to serve as acting president for the time being.[130] Then, a few weeks later, a notice appeared in the Indianola press that the Rev. H. A. Gobin, D.D., professor of Greek at DePauw, "who has lately been elected President of Simpson College, arrived in the city last evening." If Gobin did indeed arrive, it was surely not to accept the presidency of the College."[131] Hamilton continued to serve as acting president until April 27, 1887, when he was formally elected president by the board.[132]

* * *

Commencement in June 1886, well attended as usual, was "peculiarly interesting," for President Parks's imminent departure was on everyone's mind, and those who attended crowded around him, each seeking to say the right words of farewell. Featured speakers, apart from Parks himself, included Rev. Dr. J. H. Vincent, a leading clergyman, and Dr. John T. McFarland, President of Iowa Wesleyan University, who was a Simpson graduate in the class of 1872. Reported extensively in the Indianola press and exhaustively in a sixty-four-page issue of the *Simpsonian*, the eight-day series of events, with the exception of the almost embarrassing adulation heaped upon the departing president, received mixed reviews. Addresses by the guest clergymen were praised, as were the appearances of President Parks, especially his baccalaureate sermon in which he laid stress on his deeply held conviction that "intellectuality alone is dangerous if morality be neglected." Student orations, whether delivered as part of the literary society exhibitions or the Park or Badley or Buxton contests, were not received with uniform approbation. For example, Kate Meek's speech on the character and influence of John Brown was praised because "the delivery was almost faultless"; Flora Isinger, a prep student, delivered an oration adjudged well written but "monotonous in delivery." Oscar Shaw, a senior prep student, who held forth on "Mormonism," did not fare so well. "The history and evils of this sect were set forth in very good shape, but the delivery was bad." There were, alas, too many Oscar Shaws whose orations had to be borne with patience and fortitude. Worse was the commencement concert, a superb performance by students from the conservatory of music, marred by "a crowd of uncivilized heathen in the back part of the chapel [who] persisted in making disorder during the whole of the program."[133]

Although student rhetoric and valedictories occupied center stage during commencement week, it was the unannounced remarks of George Carpenter, longtime Simpson professor, that riveted the attention of his hearers. It was at the last chapel service, the second day of commencement week, that Carpenter rose and asked to be permitted to make a "few remarks" about his religious beliefs. He was visibly disturbed and clearly on the defensive. His religious views, he said, had been "willfully misunderstood" in the past, and reports going around Simpson, slanders actually, needed to be laid to rest. What had brought Carpenter's Christian faith into question was his modest advocacy of the Darwinian theory of evolution, which as a scientist he found not only fascinating but also eminently reasonable.[134] Methodists of his day, to be sure, were as shocked by Darwin as were most Christians of their generation, and the professor's flirtation with the notion that life forms on earth were a consequence of natural selection was more than most of his acquaintances could bear. He argued that in spite of his attraction to Darwinism he was a "true and earnest Christian." Remarkably, he convinced his hearers that he was no apostate. They seemed to forgive his lapse of faith in the Biblical account of creation, and the local press declared him to be acceptable to the church, "though at times he is somewhat eccentric."[135]

Carpenter never repudiated Protestant Christianity. He never repudiated Darwin either.

ment in the selection of proper questsons for the society to discuss.

June 3d. Vice President Reese in chair. Literary productions were splendid. Among those worthy of mention are the performances by the Misses Condit, Morris and Stanley. Discussion in regard to entertainment to be given in the near future.

June 10th. Society adjourned without the usual order of business.

EVERETT SOCIETY.

May 27.—A good session and an excellent program presented. Archer, Elrod, Fegtly, Thornbrue, were each fined 25 cents for absence, being on a picnic at Summerset, setting a queer precedent.

June 3.—A warm evening but a large and attentive audience filled the hall. Program good. Music excellent. Considerable business transacted. A tax of 60 cents per member levied to complete payment on hall repairs.

June 10th. A fine evening, consequently the audience was large. The program was good. Sam Fegtly favored the audience with a good declamation. A committee was appointed to challenge the Smiths to a tug of war on Field Day. The challenge was accepted, so look out for fun.

JUNIOR CONCERT.

The members of class '88 were greeted by a large audience at their concert given in the M. E. church, on the evening of May 24th. After prayer by Prof. Holmes, the program was presented as follows:

PART FIRST.

Orchestral (4 pianos) "Soldiers' Chorus," Schubert, Junior class.
Ins. Solo, "The Spectre Chase," Perillo, Miss Flora Dunlap.
Vocal Quartette, "Blow on, Ye Winds," White.
Ins. Solo, "Friska," Giacomo Gade, Miss Frankie Bay.
Orchestral (4 pianos) "Bohemian Rhapsodie," Loew, Junior class.
Vocal Quartette, "Summer Time," Webster.

PART SECOND.

Ins. Duett, Overture to "Poet and Peasant," Brunner, Miss Gertrude and Flora Dunlap.
Vocal Solo, "Sunset," Dudley Buck, Miss Susie Henderson.
Ins. Solo, "Valse Brilliante," Moskowski, Miss Hattie Berry.
Vocal Quartette, "Native Land," White.
Orchestral (4 pianos) "Grand March de Consert," Berg, Junior class.

Misses Mary Hall, Mable Jamison and Ada Baker, members of the class whose names did not appear on the program, took part in the orchestral pieces. Misses Todd and Henderson and Messrs. Trimble and Aylesworth composed the vocal quartette. The entertainment throughout was thoroughly meritorious and much appreciated by all present.

AGENTS WANTED,

TO CANVASS FOR THE CELEBRATED B. W. KILBURN

Stereoscopes and Stereoscopic Views,

Goods attractive and easy to sell. Ordinary agents can make from $60 to $125 per month above all expenses. Address JAS. M. DAVIS, Gen. Manager & U. S. Agent for Kilburn Goods. 207 Dollman St., St. Louis, Mo.

EMPLOYMENT

FOR THE SUMMER VACATION.

PLEASANT AND PROFITABLE.

Establishing and Replenishing **LIBRARIES** under an entirely new system. We want about five men from Simpson, preferably those who have had experience canvassing, and will pay

✠ GOOD WAGES ✠

Write at once, if interested. Address   H. PARMELEE LIBRARY CO., Des Moines, Ia.

The June 1887 *Simpsonian* carried advertisements for summer student employment.

VII

The Builders
1886–90

When he accepted the acting presidency of Simpson in the fall of 1886, William Ennis Hamilton was already a veteran. He had first joined the faculty back in 1867, the year college-level work commenced and a month before his twenty-second birthday. He remained on the faculty, teaching mathematics and all the sciences, for only a year, whereupon he accepted a pastorate at Onawa. He served in the itinerancy for the next fifteen years, during which time he moved to a new congregation on the average of once every two years.[1] In this constant moving about he was no different from other Methodist clergymen of his day, but it still seemed to him to be a real Iowa pastoral merry-go-round. In 1883, "just when I was feeling the need of a rest from the care and toil of the pastorate," he was notified of his election to the chair of mathematics at Simpson Centenary. He is known to have regarded this appointment as "providential," for it changed markedly the direction of his career.

After three years at the College, Hamilton was ready once again to return to the pastorate and would have done so had it not been for the resignation of President Parks. The board of trustees, he recalled in later years, "thought it necessary that I should take charge of the school until a president could be secured."[2] Actually, the board had looked at a number of candidates for the presidency but could not agree on a choice, and so turned to Hamilton to fill in until they could find their man. Frustrated in their intention to act either quickly or decisively, board members came to the early conviction that Hamilton was managing the College well. It is quite evident that within a few months they were not looking very hard to find another man at all, and the following April they confirmed their satisfaction by electing Hamilton president without qualification.[3]

A native of rural New Richmond, Ohio, Hamilton was born October 9, 1845, the son of William Lyon Hamilton, farmer, school teacher and sometime lay Methodist minister, and Eliza Ann Duncan, daughter of a veteran of the War of 1812. Hamilton was the eldest of seven children, only four of whom survived to their twenty-first birthday.[4] In 1856, the family moved to Henry County, Iowa, where the elder Hamilton purchased a tract of land, engaged in a number of successful business enterprises and became known around Mount Pleasant as a dedicated churchman and rock-ribbed Republican. Young William was reared as a fairly typical farm lad and attended country common schools. Because he showed exceptional academic promise, he prepared for college at Mount Pleasant High School and, at seventeen, entered Iowa Wesleyan University. That was in the fall of 1863, in the midst of the Civil War. Unable to resist long the call to arms, he volunteered for military service the following May, enlisting at Mount Pleasant as a member of Company H, Forty-fifth Iowa Volunteer Infantry. After a brief five months of military service, he was mustered out at Keokuk.[5]

Satisfied that he had done his duty in the cause of the Union, Hamilton returned to Iowa Wesleyan and in 1867 completed his B.A. degree in the classical course. Meanwhile, he married Isabella Anderson of New London, Iowa, in February of 1866. When his appointment to the Simpson faculty brought him to Indianola in the fall of 1867, his first child, William O., had just been born, but did not survive. Later three more children were born to the Hamiltons while he was serving in the pastorate: Ida B. (1872), Theodosia E. (1878) and Florence M. (1881).

In taking the helm of the relatively sturdy Simpson craft in 1886, Hamilton at forty possessed the advantage of experience—four years of widely separated teaching at the College and fifteen years in the itinerancy. He was able to understand how far the College had come in those years. He had learned to deal with people, to cope both with the adolescents in his charge and with their parents. In the conference, he enjoyed a wide acquaintance with clergy and laymen whose good will was crucial to Simpson's success. On campus his role was more complex: students saw him as both judge and mentor, at one moment stern-visaged and a trifle sanctimonious, at another fatherly and open-hearted. Sometimes he appeared quite prepared, like Zeus, to hurl from his academic Olympus thunderbolts at mere mortals who would defy or ignore his omnipotence; at other times he fairly glowed with parental affection, ever concerned about "the intellectual and moral progress of those among whom his lot [was] cast."[6] He understood that although the students were for the most part dutiful, even deferential, "I should not like to try to hold two or three hundred students *if* they were disposed to the contrary. I remember at the close of the first year that I had not, during that time, received a disrespectful word from a single student."[7]

Nor did he have any serious problems with the faculty. During his first year all the leading professors from the previous year stayed on. There was Carpenter in Latin, Minnie Jay in literature and history, Ellinwood in natural sciences, Holmes in Greek and Hebrew, Cromer in German and French, and Milton E. Phillips, who taught mathematics and headed the normal school and business school. Cornelia Saleno in art, Fannie Patterson in piano, and William Mercer in mathematics, Theo Manning, a pianist who was principal of the school of music, and Ernest H. Thornbrue, academy instructor in penmanship, rounded out the roster of the returning faculty. Five new people joined the faculty that autumn: M. L. Bartlett in voice culture, Bertha Todd in piano, Fannie H. McPherrin in rhetoric, J. B. Mather in elocution and Elmer E. Evans in shorthand.

In addition to the regular faculty, there were a number of part-time people teaching things like music, art, rhetoric, elocution or penmanship. For the most part, these instructors were assigned to teaching in the academy or, in the case of music and art, to working with primary pupils. Few of them held college degrees, and a good number of them were college, or even preparatory, students who were provided tuition and a modest stipend for each term of teaching. Today we might call them student interns who added a bit of teaching to their own undergraduate studies. For example, in President Hamilton's first year, six of those listed in the College catalog as faculty were in fact student assistants.[8] Because of the custom of appointing undergraduates to academy and fine arts teaching and because even the "permanent" faculty in these ancillary areas were expected to exist from whatever they could collect in special fees, turnover in these areas was rapid, and the quality of these programs suffered accordingly.

Although the membership of the twenty-seven-man board of trustees changed appreciably during the three years of Hamilton's tenure as president, the executive committee was stable enough. With a single exception, the same five men served as members of that group where most of the decisions were made. Hamilton served ex officio as chairman. The other four were old stalwarts: Gorham Worth, John Henderson, the perennial secretary, Ed Hall and the Rev. William S. Hooker, pastor of the Indianola Methodists.[9] When Hooker was transferred to Creston in 1888, his place on the executive committee was taken by William H. Berry, an old hand on the board. "The general public," wrote Hamilton of the services of these men, "has but little idea of the sacrifice of time and convenience made from year to year for the sake of the cause of education, by the members of the Executive Committee."[10]

These strong men did yeoman service during Hamilton's three-year tenure as president. "There were difficulties in those days," recalled Hamilton of his presidency, but he took charge of a much stronger College than had President Parks six years earlier.

However strong the College was, any new president faced the perennial problem of money. Although President Parks had cleared the College's debt early in his administration, each subsequent year saw a struggle to stay even, and in some years there was a deficit. In 1885–86 it was $3,195.[11] Hamilton learned soon enough, if he did not already know, that raising money in the conference was an onerous and thankless task. In spite of his optimism about Simpson, he was troubled by "the poverty of our territory [and] the indifference of many who should have been friends of the school."[12]

But neither Hamilton nor the board of trustees was discouraged. In fact, they looked forward to a major expansion of the College's facilities. It was difficult to decide which had priority, a new classroom building, especially adapted for use of the sciences, or a women's boarding hall. In light of increasing enrollment and the inadequacy of both College Hall and existing off-campus boarding arrangements for women, both new buildings were urgently needed. They decided to put up both buildings at once.

To hammer away at the debt problem and to raise money for their ambitious construction program, they determined to bring into the faculty the best fund-raiser they could find. They chanced upon their man after a year-long search and formally elected him to the vice-presidency of the College and to the chair of mathematics, the latter position something of a formality, for it was intended from the outset that he should devote nearly all his time to the formidable task of raising money. Thus began the long, successful career of Fletcher Brown with Simpson College.[13]

Thirty-seven years old, Brown was a native of Ohio. At the age of fourteen he had come to Jasper County, Iowa, with his family. He studied two years as a preparatory student at nearby Central College at Pella and enrolled at Simpson as a freshman in 1873. After he graduated in 1877 with a B.A. in the classical course, he entered Drew Theological Seminary in Madison, New Jersey, where he earned the B.D. after two years of study. Simpson awarded him the M.A. in 1880—as usual, unearned. Meanwhile he entered the parish ministry and served with marked success charges in Carlisle, Dunlap and Carson prior to returning to Simpson in 1887 as vice-president.[14]

No sooner had Brown moved his family to Indianola—he had married Ervilla Holmes, who graduated from Simpson in 1878—than he plunged into the task of shaking dollars out of the Methodist tree. It was not easy, but Brown was more than equal to the task. His personality and appearance helped. Gregarious and ebullient, he charmed nearly everyone he met. His blue eyes fairly flashed when he spoke. Some said that with his fair hair, light complexion and luxuriant moustache, he looked ever so much like a young Mark Twain.[15] Around the Methodist conference he was accounted a fine speaker, almost as good as his Simpson colleague, Edmund Holmes, whose erudition was legendary. The board's bold plan was to raise $50,000, most to be used for two new buildings. They hoped to raise $25,000 the first year and $12,500 during each of the two successive years.[16]

Brown had scarcely been a few weeks out among the Methodist congregations than he was able to report real success.[17] To the $2,500 already raised by Parks in 1886, Brown added $700 at Macedonia and similar amounts at Creston, Shenandoah, Carson, Oakland, Hancock and Avoca. One by one the churches responded to Brown's persuasive plea for help. By the following spring he had raised $16,246, of which $14,633 was designated for the building fund, $1,513 for an endowed "alumnal chair" professorship, and the balance of $100 for "apparatus."[18] By the time of the conference meeting at Creston in September 1888, Brown reported that he had raised "nearly $20,000."[19] And by mid-1889 the board of trustees learned that the figure had passed $30,000.

At first, the people in Indianola balked when asked for yet another subscription. When an article appeared in the *Advocate-Tribune* announcing a meeting at the courthouse the evening of October 31, 1887, townspeople were assured that "it is not the intention at this meeting to ask for any money."[20] But most Indianolans had heard such promises before and remained at home. College supporters were surprised and disappointed. "The matter was thoroughly advertised," lamented the editor of the *Advocate-Tribune*, "and yet there were not over five or six dozen at the meeting."[21]

The atmosphere at the courthouse that evening was gloomy. Complaints were heard on every side. For one thing, the continuing deficit was described as a "running sore" that seemed to refuse to heal. The College never seemed to be able to meet its expenses. Even though President Hamilton had pared the deficit to $1,915 during the 1886–87 academic year, few had confidence that Simpson could ever operate in the black. Trustee Gorham A. Worth was frankly pessimistic: the College was falling more deeply into debt and would die, he feared, if not rescued. The only way to save it was "to put our hands into our pockets and raise the money," but he wondered aloud if many would respond to the call. William H. Berry was more positive: Indianola had always supported the

College. True, "people ask when will all this end? Why, goodness gracious, it will never end." The local supporters of the College would have to come up with several thousand dollars every year for operating expenses, and Indianolans should probably give half of the $20,000 needed for new buildings. Fletcher Brown, who had been "industriously canvassing" for aid for the College out in the conference, reported that he was being told that "the people here are not sufficiently enterprising." He was going to raise not $20,000, but $50,000 in three years, and "Indianola must raise a large portion of this." If those present were not discouraged when they entered the meeting held at Indianola on October 31, 1887, they were certainly not much encouraged by what they heard there. When, late in the evening, chairman Captain Berry asked Lewis Todhunter to speak, the usually voluble Todhunter made no response at all, and "after a painful silence the meeting adjourned."[22]

The dismal reaction of Indianola Methodists was understandable and should have been anticipated. They had just erected a new church building at a cost of nearly $15,000, and few had yet paid in their pledges toward its construction. They said they were simply not ready to consider yet another draft on their tautly-stretched resources.[23]

Hamilton and Brown could have been discouraged, but they were not. They went out and enlisted the support of some of the best speakers in the conference, called another meeting, their invitation containing the ritual assurance that this was "not a meeting for collection." This one was held December 15, 1887, at the church, and in a sort of revival atmosphere the Simpson men inspired the many people present to renew their faith in the College and its future. Somehow the people of Indianola would find the money to help with the buildings.[24] And slowly, but surely, the money came in.

* * *

The trustees planned to call their new academic building the Scientific and Normal Hall, and they hoped that it would not cost more than $10,000.[25] The decision to build it, "pending the successful collection of subscriptions," was made in the fall of 1886, but it was not until the spring of 1888 that they selected Willis Proudfoot of Wichita, Kansas, as architect.[26]

Whatever design and specifications Proudfoot would come up with, the College already had the brick for construction. On the strength of the board's decision to go ahead with the project, Indianola manufacturer J. H. Carruthers, owner of the Warren County Coal, Brick and Tile Co., made an offer the board could hardly refuse. In return for "the use of" $3,000 of endowment money for one year—he could, of course, provide security for this—he would give the College 500,000 "merchantable brick" and provide more brick if needed at cost, in any case not more than $4 per thousand.[27] He would deliver the brick before May 1, 1887. The contract was signed a fortnight after the offer was made.[28]

The *Simpsonian* reported in its March 1888 issue that the architect "spent a few days here recently." In that visit, the location of the new structure was determined: it would stand on the old baseball ground, midway between the main building and the eastern limit of the campus, set back a few feet to the north, fronting toward the south, as did College Hall.

Proudfoot's blueprints for the building, completed in just a few weeks, showed a forty-by-eighty-foot three-story structure of what the *Advocate-Tribune* called "pressed brick," rather tall and boxy, but presenting a "handsome classical facade." The design of the building was said to be "the latest," not at all unlike other public buildings of that day, with large, airy rooms and huge windows, "not exactly Gothic, but approaching that style." Actually, it did not really approach much of any style at all; one could call it a sort of nineteenth-century eclectic. The roof was steeply pitched, giving room for a "well arranged and capacious attic," lighted by a huge skylight.

The interior of the building contained a number of rooms, large and small, for a variety of purposes. On the ground floor, there was a large room for the College museum together with two music rooms, the location of which "will be more desirable for ladies than one in an upper story," to be "nicely furnished" and supplied with pianos. In the northwest corner was the boiler room, equipped to provide steam heat for both the new building and for College Hall. On the second floor was a large laboratory "for the experimental sciences," and adjoining it was a smaller "private laboratory" and storage area. To the west of these rooms was a science recitation classroom, and beyond it, west of the staircase, was a room for the College library, which would "dispense with the necessity of using the library for a class room." All the rooms on the main floor had high, fourteen-foot ceilings, lending an air of spaciousness.

Upstairs were rooms arranged much as on the main floor, including a large study hall, a cloak room, two ample classrooms and one additional room, twenty-one feet square, whose use was not yet designated. The attic was one huge "apartment" with an open ceiling under the great pitched roof, lighted from above, and given over to instruction in art. It would be difficult to imagine a more attractive art studio.[29] Nothing was said about women having to climb to the top floor. Perhaps art students were thought to be more hardy than the musicians.

When the executive committee of the board looked at Proudfoot's plans on April 19, 1888, they were delighted and decided to advertise at once for bids from local contractors, with a deadline of May 1. In spite of the board's allowing less than two weeks to receive bids, two were submitted on time, one from Elias E. Proudfoot and another from E. W. Fortney and Son, both of them prominent Indianola builders. The general contract was let the next day to Elias Proudfoot for $10,300, signed and formally approved by the board on May 7.[30]

Ten days later it was reported that "excavation and work on the new building is beginning," and as soon as the stone arrived, the foundations could be put in. By the time of commencement in mid-June, people could see that construction was moving forward rapidly, campus visitors eyeing with approval the rising brick walls. During the summer and early fall the actual construction was completed, and on November 16 the board awarded Elias Proudfoot the contract for furnishing the interior of the building at the figure of $3,645, payable by May 1, 1889. To the local firm Davis and Hamilton, they gave a contract to paint the roof for $55, bringing the total contract cost of the science hall to exactly $14,000.[31]

Right after Christmas, on December 29, the board noted that the work had been completed "to our great satisfaction" and accepted the building. They paid Proudfoot the final $2,700 due on the general contract and decided that it would be a good idea to buy insurance on the building.[32] During the winter and the spring the building was painted, and most of the furnishings, equipment and apparatus were installed. "The building is high," said one enthusiastic observer. "Much of Warren County can be seen" from the top of it.[33]

At three o'clock on the afternoon of June 26, 1889, the building was dedicated in a simple ceremony. For that event a platform was erected in front of the new structure. The Rev. F. M. Bristol of Chicago spoke on the rather broad topic of "Christian Civilization," at the conclusion of which William H. Berry took it upon himself to take up a collection "to defray the expenses of commencement." He got about a hundred dollars, which, he allowed, was probably enough. President Hamilton spoke briefly, recounting the highlights of the history of Simpson, after which he ceremonially tendered the new building to the board of trustees, accepted on their behalf by Berry. The dedicatory prayer was offered by the Rev. William S. Hooker.[34]

Pleased as they were with their new Science Hall, its construction was not accomplished without incident. Tragedy struck when on Saturday, December 22, the first day of the Christmas vacation in 1888, twenty-year-old Santaro Miyada, a Japanese student preparing for the ministry, who was exploring the nearly-completed building, stepped on a loose plank in the second story of the building. The board gave way, he fell a good twelve feet and the board followed, striking him on the head. He was taken by friends to his room at the home of Orlando H. Baker, one-time seminary principal and Simpson professor, where Miyada languished for days. He died the following Saturday.[35]

The resignation of Charles Ellinwood in June 1888 was a disappointment to everyone who knew him. It seemed somehow wrong that he should leave the faculty just when the new science building was being erected. During his eight years in the faculty he had advanced the cause of the natural sciences at Simpson as had no other. Much of the equipment and apparatus the College possessed was a consequence of his enterprise and perseverance, and he paid for much of it out of his own pocket. When he announced his departure, the board knew it must replace him with a strong man, especially in view of the construction of the new building. They selected John L. Tilton, a graduate of Wesleyan University in the class of 1885, who held a recently awarded M.A. In choosing Tilton, the board did better than they knew. He remained on the faculty for thirty-two years, a mainstay of Simpson natural science, as well known among his professional colleagues around the nation as he was on the streets of Indianola.[36]

* * *

If the building of Science Hall advanced the academic thrust of the College, the construction of "Ladies' Hall" celebrated the first step in Simpson's emergence as a residential liberal arts institution. Impelled to action by marathon deficits in the operation of off-campus boarding houses, the board of trustees resolved in early 1887 to build "at once" what they called "Ladies' Boarding Hall" for "not less than $15,000." Considered "an absolute necessity," the building would be erected as soon as $10,000 had been pledged. They would ask Willis Proudfoot to draw up preliminary plans.[37] Fletcher Brown would raise the money.

One of Brown's schemes involved naming the sleeping rooms in the hall for donors who contributed as much as $250. It required two years of constant and inventive hustling, but by mid-1889 Brown could announce that M. C. G. Burns, a farmer near Milo, had endowed the thirty-second and last room in the building.[38]

Proudfoot submitted preliminary drawings in the fall of 1888, and they were accepted with only minor alterations. In excited anticipation of breaking ground the following spring "as soon as the frost is out of the ground," Fletcher Brown bought 90,000 bricks at a bargain price, "to be delivered at once."

"Where do you want all this brick?" asked the deliveryman.

"Up on the northwest corner of the College grounds," replied Brown. Until that moment, no one had determined with any certainty where the new residence hall would be located. The board confirmed Brown's decision at the end of October. And there the bricks sat all winter long as an earnest of the board's intent.[39]

Everyone seemed to be happy with the location of Ladies' Hall except the baseball players whose field was on the building site, having been moved to that part of the campus when their old field had been taken by the new science building. "The committee that located the new dormitory," lamented a writer in the *Simpsonian*, "spoiled our base ball ground so badly as to cause our athletes to look for a new one."[40]

When Proudfoot presented his final plans for the new building, everyone noted that its style was very similar to that of the science building: heavy, ponderous, solid, massive, a fortress meant to keep the right people in and the wrong people out. Its ground floor contained a large dining hall that would serve for decades as the College's only campus refectory. On the main floor was an attractive lounge, the only room in which young ladies were permitted to entertain young gentleman callers, a matron's suite and a number of sleeping rooms. On the top floor (not counting a great storage attic beneath the pitched roof) were the rest of the sleeping rooms. Just outside the building was a small structure containing separate "water closets, modern in every respect," not to be confused with bathrooms, of which there were none.

When bids were opened April 2, 1889, the contract was won by E. W. Fortney and Son, whose $15,215 figure for the base contract was only $268 under that firm's nearest competitor, Elias Proudfoot, who was finishing the science building. Construction did not begin at once, however, because Brown insisted that not enough money was actually in hand. President Hamilton agreed; he would not start until he knew the project could be finished without incurring more debt.[41]

It was not until late autumn that excavations began and the foundations were laid. During the winter, no outside construction was possible because of the cold. Only in April 1890 could the *Simpsonian* report that "work has commenced on the Ladies' Boarding Hall" and that the brick walls would go up as soon as the lime for the mortar arrived. During the balance of the spring the building took shape. So rapid was the construction that the board had to borrow $5,000— against pledges—to pay Fortney on schedule. Hamilton didn't like that a bit, but they had really no choice.[42] By commencement time, the building was coming along very well.[43]

When Ladies' Hall opened to students on a wintry January day in 1891, the residents paid $2.50 per week, including meals. Technically their room rent was free, for each room had been endowed, but within a few years, it was clear that the endowments were insufficient, and modest room rental was charged. Rooms in the hall were provided with carpets and such heavy furniture as bedsteads, mattresses, tables, chairs, wash stands and "crockery."

Thus began the long career of the College's first residence hall. It was operated only with those regulations "deemed necessary to secure conditions of real culture and development of womanly character."[44] It became known soon enough as the "home of the seven o'clock rule" as the matron hovered over the girls like a Victorian mother concerned about the purity of her daughters.

From the beginning, Ladies' Hall was a success. It housed sixty-four young women and one matron in comfort and security. It continued to serve in whole or in part as a residence hall until 1967, when the building was given over entirely to instruction and faculty offices.

* * *

In anticipation of the completion of the new construction, the board ordered from the Western Engraving Company a fine steel engraving picturing the three campus buildings. The illustration was first printed in the June 1889 issue of the *Simpsonian* and appeared on the back cover of the 1888–89 College catalog which appeared later that summer. For many years that illustration decorated nearly every piece of literature sent out by the College to its constituents.[45]

The new buildings were every bit as attractive—inside and outside—as they appeared in print. One reason was that at the same time the two new buildings were constructed, College Hall was refurbished so as not to appear diminished by its new neighbors. It was amazing, said those who worked on it, what a little scrubbing, papering and painting could do. It didn't cost much, and the students contributed a fair share of the funds to do the job.[46] "Since its renovation," commented the *Advocate-Tribune*, "the chapel presents a splendid appearance . . . and with its seating capacity [nearly 400] it makes a fine hall indeed. . . . The old building, with a few hundred dollars expended upon it could scarcely be recognized."[47]

If the buildings looked attractive, the campus grounds did not. A quarter of the College's twelve acres was fenced off as a cow pasture. The rest of it, the stretch of land surrounding the three buildings set in a grove of maples, was messy, uneven and cluttered, with wagon tracks cut into the black soil, the grass unmowed, tree branches littering the landscape. "The College can't afford to clean it up," lamented the *Simpsonian*. Too much had been spent on buildings. "It is proposed that the students devote a little less time to base-ball and croquet and that each able bodied male student be required to work . . . with axe, hoe, shovel and wheelbarrow. By this way, if no other, the ground can be cleaned and leveled up and made presentable for Commencement time."[48] A few weeks later, the *Simpsonian* editor noted approvingly that "the student bee on the College campus prior to the opening exercises [of commencement] was highly beneficial."[49]

The undergraduate curriculum remained much the same as it had been since the 1870s, although the number of course substitutions or electives a student could take grew slightly. Still, most of a student's work, whether in the classical, philosophic or scientific course, was clearly prescribed. By 1889, for example, the student in the classical course was permitted only one elective in each term of the sophomore year (mathematics, French or German) and two electives in the senior year (biology, Greek, didactics or the Greek New Testament). Because the rigor of any of these electives was about the same, no one found an easy way to get through.

The requirements for admission to the freshman class were stiff: twenty courses, including five in Latin, three in Greek, three in mathematics, including algebra and plane and solid geometry, three in English, including rhetoric, grammar and composition, one in American history, four in natural and physical science, including both physics and chemistry, and one in art. Some Iowa high schools could provide this preparation; some could not. In some small towns and rural areas, there was no high school at all. Hence, the continuing popularity of the Simpson preparatory school, as well as the preparatory departments of other colleges or the independent private, usually church-related academies like the very good one at Ackworth, just five miles east of Indianola. President Hamilton believed that the Simpson preparatory department could be improved by extending the course from two to three years, a reform which he accomplished in the fall of 1888.[50]

In Hamilton's day, Simpson offered a bewildering array of degrees and diplomas. There was something for everyone. For example, in 1888–89, undergraduates could earn the bachelor of arts degree by pursuing the classical course, the bachelor of philosophy in the philosophical course and the bachelor of science in the scientific course. In each of these, a master's degree was also provided for those "who have been engaged for three years in pursuing a Professional Course" such as law, medicine or theology, or who "have pursued advanced Literary or Scientific studies," or "a prescribed course of postgraduate study, which will be furnished on consultation with the Faculty." The more or less honorary M.A. degree continued too, but its days were numbered. In music, one could study for the bachelor of music and, after two more years of prescribed study, could receive the master of music degree. For those who wanted to combine normal, or pedagogical, training with regular undergraduate study, there was a three-term course in didactics, taken in the senior year, which qualified students to teach in the public schools. The regular four-year normal course offered a diploma, not a degree, but if the holder of the diploma wanted to stay on one more year, he or she could earn a degree called the bachelor of didactics. In the school of art and the commercial school one could earn a "handsome diploma."

Undergraduates divided fairly evenly among the three regular baccalaureate degree programs. In the 1888–89 academic year, for example, twenty-seven were enrolled in the classical course, twenty-four in the philosophical and thirty in the scientific. If there was any trend to observe, it would be that as time went on fewer students opted for the classical course, very likely because they sought to avoid the rigors of Greek. Very few took degrees in music. Most of Simpson's music enrollment was part time, and many of the pupils were children taking voice or piano lessons.

Music, to be sure, was a part of the curriculum from the first day the seminary opened, but it was not until 1882 that it was organized, together with art, in a Department of Music and Fine Arts. The next year it was separated from art and called the Musical Department—there seems to have been no art instruction at all that year—and in 1885, it took its place next to the School of Art and School of Business as the School of Music. As early as 1881, a Summer Music School was held, a session of nearly four weeks' duration which continued quite successfully for several years. In the fine arts, Simpson tended from the beginning to emphasize music over art, a pattern which has continued down to the present time. For many years music offered a degree program while art did not.

Nor did business courses rate a degree program, at Simpson or elsewhere. Variously denominated the Commercial Course, the Commercial Department, the School of Business or Commercial School, the program rarely offered work beyond bookkeeping, commercial law and what they called "Business Practice." It would be another generation before business administration would flower as a part of the regular undergraduate curriculum.

Similarly, teacher preparation was for the most part accomplished without a degree program. In those days, a high school education qualified one to teach in the common schools, and most normal training was at the high school, or preparatory department, level. If one wanted to teach in a high school, a bachelor's degree was expected, with a three-term course in didactics taken as an elective during the senior year. In 1888, Hamilton planned the creation of a normal school, featuring a four-year course leading to a diploma, followed, on election, by one additional year leading to the bachelor of didactics degree. To run the new program he looked for a strong man and found him in the person of Milton E. Phillips. Phillips, who would also teach mathematics, unfortunately had already signed a contract to serve as principal of Panora High School in Guthrie County, but he was released from his obligation in July and was able to start at Simpson in September 1888 at $1,200 a year.[51] Phillips spent the next academic year planning the curriculum of the normal school, which opened in September 1889.

The first mention of night classes at Simpson was heard at the beginning of Hamilton's first year as president. Business subjects were taught in the commercial rooms downtown over Whitney's store.[52] The College required a minimum enrollment of twenty persons in each evening class. It appears that some of these courses did materialize. Three autumns later the *Herald* announced that Simpson's night school would open "next Monday evening."[53]

Whether in evening classes or regular college courses, Hamilton agreed in early 1889 to excuse from the final course examination those students who had an average of ninety or better in the course.[54] This new policy gained instant popularity, for students found examinations as distasteful then as they do today.

Students not only complained about final examinations. Some courses, they averred, were exceedingly demanding, requiring them to study so hard that their health could be endangered and their psyches undermined. Sophomores, who judged themselves to be the most aggrieved in this respect, were especially exercised about the rigors of the course in general history. Unfortunately their protest found little support in the faculty. Even the student editor of the *Simpsonian*, evidently a conscientious student, belittled their lamentations.[55]

For the most part, students were dutiful enough about attending their classes, even if they didn't like the heavy reading assignments and the searching recitations that repeatedly exposed their lack of preparation. And they attended daily chapel because they were required to do so. Some of them observed from time to time that the faculty seemed not to like chapel any more than the students did: "On December 10 [1888] only two of the faculty were present at chapel exercises."[56] When students suggested a faculty roll call, attendance of their mentors reportedly improved.

Students showed considerable enthusiasm, on the other hand, for violating some of the rules they didn't like, especially the ten o'clock curfew which, according to the local press, was "repeatedly and systematically violated." Students were seen "parading the streets" or "loafing at the rooms of their friends."[57] Worse than that, some of the boys were known to smoke cigarettes. "Some twenty students took a smoke over the prohibition of tobacco" when it was first announced in 1886.[58] And some of the boys continued to smoke surreptitiously even though they were told that their souls, not to speak of their bodies, were endangered. "Cigarettes," declared the non-smoking *Simpsonian* editor, "will blight the religious tendencies in a man's heart quicker than benzine will kill a cockroach."[59]

Because fraternities were widely suspected of harboring the most hardened smokers and of fostering a cavalier disregard for faculty rules in general, President Hamilton was frequently at pains to point out their putative derelictions. At the end of his term as president, he expressed his pleasure in learning that "there is an increasing disposition among the best students in the school to ignore the associations of Greek letter fraternities."[60]

Some of the best students did indeed ignore fraternities and sororities, but more of them did not. During the late 1880s the Greeks flourished as never before, counting among their members nearly seventy percent of the undergraduates and even a few preps. In May 1889, the last year of Hamilton's presidency, two national Greek-letter societies installed chapters at Simpson.

Actually Delta Delta Delta, which granted a charter to the eighteen-year-old L.F.V. Sorosis at Simpson, was not yet a national sorority at all, but a local society for women, founded Thanksgiving evening, 1888, at Boston University. Why a New England sorority would plant its second chapter way out in Iowa is explained by the remarkable career of an unusual young woman, Etta May Budd. She was a graduate of Iowa Agricultural College in Ames (1882), where she had founded a society which she hoped would establish chapters in other colleges. She had corresponded with a number of local societies, including the L.F.V. at Simpson, but her project languished while she went off to study painting at the Boston Museum of Art. While resident there during the 1888–89 academic year, she encountered one of the freshman initiates of the months-old Delta Delta Delta, who introduced her to the Tridelta founders. Soon it was agreed that Budd's Ames local group and the L.F.V. would join Tridelta, and as an earnest of their intention, the Boston Tridelts initiated Budd in early March 1889.

Although the plan was to initiate the Iowa Agricultural College group first and the L.F.V. a little later, the Indianola women, facing three strong rivals in rush, urged the early chartering of their chapter. Accordingly, the Simpson charter was granted on April 27, 1889, and a fortnight later the chapter was installed as Delta Deuteron (later simply Delta).[61] Thus the Simpson chapter made Tridelta a national sorority. The Ames group, because of anti-fraternity sentiment, was not installed until 1890. The Simpson chapter flourished, especially when Etta May Budd joined the faculty of the College in the fall of 1890.

Only fifteen days after the installation of the Tridelts, the Sigma Alpha Epsilon fraternity initiated its Iowa Sigma chapter. The leading spirit behind the birth of SAE at Simpson was John Pearl Morley, who had entered the College in 1887 as a prep student. In 1888, Morley and a few of his prep friends, imitating the three collegiate Greek-letter societies on the campus, decided to create a fraternity of their own in the preparatory department. On March 3, 1888, they founded a local society called Phi Lambda Mu. At twenty, Morley was older than most of the preps, and he was a natural leader.

When, during the 1888–89 school year, their organization grew in size and closeness, these preps wanted to avoid splitting up and joining one or another of the existing Simpson fraternities. In order, then, to perpetuate their bond, they undertook to seek a charter from a good national fraternity. They turned first to Sigma Chi, which had a strong chapter in Iowa City, but when the Sigma Chis investigated, they understandably declined to grant a charter to prep students. Much the same thing happened when the Phi Lambda Mus sought charters from Phi Delta Theta and Phi Gamma Delta, for neither would countenance chartering a group of prep students. Disappointed but not deterred from their goal, Morley and his cohorts now changed their tactics. They approached Sigma Alpha Epsilon and took care not to mention that they were sub-freshmen. The SAEs, like the ATOs, were predominantly a Southern fraternity, founded at the University of Alabama in 1856. Its oldest chapter in the North was scarcely six years old. But the SAEs were interested in spreading northward, and showed interest. After much correspondence and a vote of its chapters, SAE sent a senior from Mount Union College, Edwin L. McMillen, to Indianola to install the chapter. Only upon his arrival in town did he learn that most of the Simpson boys were preparatory students, and it was too late to back off. So he installed the chapter on May 25, 1889. Morley did point out to the SAEs that by the following fall nearly all of the Iowa Sigma members would be college undergraduates.

President Hamilton deplored the growth of the Greeks, but there was little he could do to prevent it. On the other hand, he did like the Y.W.C.A. which had been established on the campus in February 1884 and which joined the national Y.W.C.A. in 1887.[62] The theater was another matter. Hamilton liked dramatics even less than Greek-letter societies, and he roared his disapproval when students were seen entering the opera house down on the square: "I'd rather see them enter a bordello!" And he was supported by the faculty. Yet they encouraged students to produce a play at the College. What made plays off campus objectionable and those on campus acceptable was never made clear.[63]

At least Hamilton did not object to athletics. He was indifferent to them, but he recognized that many of the students, including many of the women, were passionately addicted to games like baseball and croquet. And during his administration a new sport made its appearance, a game they had been hearing about, and even experimenting with, for a few years. "Why not organize a foot ball team?" asked the *Simpsonian* rhetorically as early as 1887. The game, which originated in the East, was still evolving in the 1880s, lodged somewhere between rugby and modern-day football, and it was taking the country by storm. In 1888, several teams were organized at Simpson. That autumn there were no fewer than two games a week for six weeks, played with lots of enthusiasm and no uniforms and no protective gear of any sort. Some matches were intramural; others were played with informal teams from the town. At first there were no coaches and few rules. A year later it was suggested that the College organize an official "eleven" and challenge Drake to a game.[64] Professor John Tilton was taking a special interest in the new sport, and its introduction at Simpson owes much to his interest and enterprise.

Tilton was not only interested in football; he helped also to bring military training to Simpson. Many years earlier there had been talk of organizing a military unit, but nothing had come of it.[65] In the spring of 1889, however, Tilton recruited enough young men—about twenty-five of them—to form a military company and secured the services of Richard J. Gaines, a preparatory student with military experience, as drill master.[66] The next fall the unit created a sensation when "the cadets filed into the chapel with their new gray uniforms" that had cost $16.30 apiece.[67] Military drill would remain, with occasional interruption, a feature of Simpson undergraduate life for three decades, until the end of the First World War.

It is not entirely clear precisely when Simpson first adopted school colors. As late as 1886 there were neither colors nor a school yell,[68] but by mid-1889 the colors red and gold had been chosen. The colors were first announced in the second edition of the *Tangent*, published by the eight Greek-letter societies in 1889 under the co-editorship of H. A. Youtz, E. H. Thornbrue and Lester W. Haworth. Well gotten up, handsomely bound and happily informative, the book contained 114 pages of text plus 10 pages of advertising, including, *horribile dictu*, a cigarette advertisement, which only confirmed President Hamilton's judgment about the obduracy of wayward youth. But the students loved the *Tangent*. The *Simpsonian* called it a "howling success,"[69] and it cost only fifty cents a copy.

The school year that witnessed the second volume of the *Tangent* also saw the organization of Simpson's first student council. It was called the Student Senate and consisted of ten members—four seniors, three juniors, two sophomores and one freshman—elected by the entire student body.[70] The first election took place in May 1889.[71] One of the seniors chaired meetings, but no one was yet designated student body president.

* * *

At the College's commencement in 1887, an honorary degree was awarded to Brenton H. Badley, valedictorian of Simpson's first graduating class in 1870. A missionary of extraordinary dedication in India, he had founded in northern India the Lucknow Christian College, still flourishing today. When he received the handsome diploma—awarded in absentia—he wrote to his wife Mary, who was summering in Pauri in the northern Indian mountains. Expressing his amazement at the honor accorded him, he wrote, "I wonder what the trustees were thinking about! It is a great surprise to me. At home many preachers work hard to get the degree and pull a great many strings therefore [sic], I, as you know, have never pulled one. I had thought that perhaps by 50 I might *possibly* be thus honored, but this at 38. . . . As it is I am like the Irishman, 'not dead but spacheless.' "[72] His wife replied that it was "eminently fitting" that he should receive the doctorate. "I think you deserve to be the first one honored, for not one of the other students has been so thoughtful of the College as you have since you graduated."[73] Perhaps some of those other graduates might have taken issue with Mary's assertion, but none would have disagreed that Badley was worthy of the honor. As it turned out, it was indeed fitting that the College awarded him the degree when it did, for only four years later he succumbed to tuberculosis. He died at Lucknow November 20, 1891. He was forty-two.[74]

* * *

The years of William Hamilton's presidency witnessed a remarkable growth in the stability and prosperity of Simpson, with two new buildings, a healthy enrollment and an able faculty. Although in their curriculum they probably tried to do too many things in an effort to provide something for everyone, the core undergraduate college courses of study were strong, equivalent, they liked to say, to the best colleges in the Midwest. The prospects for the success of the College had never looked brighter. Both Indianola and Iowa Methodists could look on Simpson with justifiable pride.

It was, then, with dismay and no little anger that they had to endure once again the threat of the removal of the College from Indianola to Des Moines, an idea they thought had long since been laid to rest. The scheme to create a large, multipurpose Methodist university would not die, however, and in the late 1880s, its proponents breathed new life into it.

The College and the town and, for that matter, the Methodists had already rejected out of hand a proposal, said to have been hatched in Iowa City, to merge all thirteen of the colleges and universities that were members of the Iowa Collegiate Association into one huge state university, locating that institution at Iowa City.[75] The idea was dismissed as preposterous. It was attacked by all the church-related colleges, whose very reasons for existence were profoundly different from those of the public universities. At Simpson the most strongly voiced objection, quite aside from the impracticability of it all, had to do with the quality of student life: "Indeed the state universities are proverbially at fault in the too gentle restrictions which they place upon vice and immorality," wrote President Hamilton, and he surely spoke for the entire faculty.

Far more serious was the threat that came from inside the church, especially its Des Moines constituency. Why support four Methodist colleges (Cornell, Simpson, Iowa Wesleyan and Upper Iowa University) meagerly when the church could support one university liberally? A university could provide professional and graduate education, perhaps even a theological seminary.

But the colleges would have none of it, and most Methodists in Iowa backed them, except for a fair number in Des Moines who stood to gain if the university, as certainly it must, were to be located there. The Rev. Emory Miller, pastor of the Indianola Methodist church, said that insofar as Simpson was concerned, "Indianola holds the key to the situation, and no power can take it from her. Indianola can voluntarily surrender the position and give up the key, but the Conference cannot honorably and will not try to take it by force."[76] The conference, in fact, did support the college and in its September 1888 annual session at Creston, rejected a plan that would create a central university that would be of a "higher graduation [sic] than that of our existing colleges" and that would "not come in conflict with or be a rival to them." Regarding such a proposition foolhardy, conference delegates adopted the following resolution by a large majority:

> WHEREAS, we believe that one college within the bounds and under the patronage of this Conference is all the Conference is able to sustain, and
> WHEREAS, we are now making an effort to raise money for the purpose of making Simpson College more effective, and
> WHEREAS, to undertake to raise funds for another institution as contemplated by the propositions presented would greatly embarass [sic] the work being done for Simpson College, therefore
> RESOLVED, that we cannot accept the propositions made for the establishment of a University at Des Moines.[77]

That should have settled the matter, but it did not. The proposal cropped up again the next year, when nineteen members of a forty-two-man "Des Moines Conference Commission" met at the capital city and voted eleven to eight to "receive propositions" for creating a central Methodist university "in or contiguous to Des Moines."[78] This resolution, observed the editor of the *Herald*, had "but one effect, and that is to aggravate the friends of Simpson College." It was, he said, "uncalled for and unnecessary."[79] And when the 1890 conference was held on Simpson's home ground at Indianola, no further action was taken. The proposition was not even discussed, the commission's report relegated to the last page of the conference minutes for that year. There, for a season, the matter rested.

When William Hamilton resigned as president of the College on June 17, 1889, during commencement week, it appears that the board of trustees was taken by surprise. They had just fixed his presidential salary at $1,400 for the coming year, when Hamilton, without explanation, announced that he "severed his connection with this Board of Trustees." He fully expected to be assigned to a pastorate in the Des Moines conference, but agreed after some discussion to continue on the Simpson faculty. Board members were pleased that "he remains with us as a member of this body that we may avail ourselves of his experience and wise counsel."[80] That same day they elected Edmund M. Holmes president of the College. Holmes was a brilliant scholar, erudite and articulate, regarded by everyone as the natural choice for the job. Hamilton did return to the faculty where he served for another quarter of a century.

* * *

Probably no one ever stepped into the presidency of Simpson with greater ease than did Edmund Meek Holmes. As an alumnus of the College and an active member of the teaching faculty, Holmes was seen by some people to be a convenient choice, a man who was handy and available, one whose presence spared the board of trustees a long search for a new administrator. He was safe, clerically acceptable, admirably scholarly, a man whose knowledge of Simpson exceeded that of any other candidate for the position. They would soon discover, if they had ever doubted it, that in Holmes they had given the College a truly gifted leader.

Holmes's family was of English origin. He was born in Hardin County, Ohio, the fifth of six children of a Methodist pastor, the Rev. Jacob M. Holmes, and Margaret Bradford Holmes, born in Ohio in 1823 of Ulster Irish parents. When Edmund Holmes was ten years old his father brought the family to Iowa, accepting a call to the Methodist Church in Altoona in the Des Moines Conference. That was the first of many charges that took the Holmes family from one town to another in western Iowa.

Young Holmes attended Clarinda High School before entering Simpson as a preparatory student in 1875. After one year in the academy, he continued as a freshman in the classical course. During his undergraduate years he was known as a superior student, an active member of the Everett Literary Society, of which he was president during his junior year, and a loyal member of Delta Tau Delta fraternity. But he was surely best remembered as a brilliant speaker, eloquent, persuasive, held somewhat in awe by his fellow students. Licensed to preach immediately upon his graduation from Simpson with the B.A. degree in 1880, he served for a summer as a junior preacher in the south Indianola circuit, whereupon he was accepted as a full-fledged member of the conference and appointed for a year to the pastorate at Casey.

In the autumn of 1881 Holmes entered the Garrett Biblical Institute at Evanston, Illinois, where he graduated in 1883. He returned to the Des Moines conference, assigned to the pastorate at Carroll, a town where Methodists were a tiny minority "in a sea of papists." After a trying two years there, he was quite ready to accept election to the chair of Greek at Simpson. He would recall, however, that the bright spot in his "sentence" at Carroll was his marriage in 1884 to college classmate Carrie Merrill Page of Boone, Iowa. They had four sons and a daughter, most of whom attended Simpson in later years.[81]

Holmes's election to the presidency of Simpson in 1889 was apparently well accepted by the students.[82] His years as professor of Greek, noted the editor of the *Simpsonian*, had "won for him an enviable place in the affections of the students and patrons of the College."[83] It appears that the faculty members were pleased too, for he was one of their own.

It was not only the elevation of Holmes that found favor with the faculty. They also praised the appointment of Joanna Baker as Holmes's successor in the chair of Greek. Miss Baker, daughter of Orlando H. Baker, succeeded to the position that her father had held seventeen years earlier. A child prodigy, Miss Baker, at the urging of her scholarly parents, had begun studying Greek and Latin at the age of four. By the time she was eight she had read Xenophon's *Anabasis* and at fourteen compiled a lexicon of Sophocles' *Oedipus Tyrannus*. Two years later, when her girlfriends were struggling with Julius Caesar's *Gallic Wars*, she was a tutor in Greek at Simpson. She earned her B.A. degree at Cornell College and completed the M.A. at DePauw University in 1888, a year before she joined the Simpson faculty. Around Indianola her appointment to what was considered the premier chair at Simpson was regarded as wholly appropriate. Elsewhere the elevation of a woman to a position of academic leadership in a coeducational college, especially in the conservative Midwest, was sensational news. *Harper's Bazaar* told the women of America that Joanna Baker's appointment was truly significant, "showing the progress of woman since it was first permitted to her to acquire the alphabet."[84] Baker remained on the Simpson faculty for thirty years, watching the fortunes of women improve and the fortunes of Greek, her first love, decline as the classical curriculum of the nineteenth century gave way to the practical, vocationally-oriented curriculum of the twentieth. Nevertheless, her enthusiasm for the classics never flagged, and she never lost the assured confidence that a knowledge of Attic Greek lay at the heart of the education of the civilized human being.[85]

THE RED AND GOLD.

Words by Lucian Waggoner. Air:—"Eton Boating Song."

1. Come we will sing to-geth-er...... Once more the ring-ing song,...... A strain that the com-ing class-es,...... Un-ceas-ing-ly shall pro-long...... The prais-es of our Al-ma Ma-ter,...... Dear Simp-son thy sons so bold......... Will cher-ish thy rec-ol-lec-tions...... And swear by the Red and Gold......

2. Fade-less still the lau-rels...... Won by the foot-ball team;...... Here's to the Knights of the dia-mond,...... Bright-ly their vic-t'ries gleam,......... No fear,...... for to-mor-row's strug-gle...... Shall ev-er new tri-umphs hold,......... While the stur-dy sons of Simp-son......... Press on with the Red and Gold......

3. Though in years be-fore us,...... Life's skies grow dull and gray,...... The friends of our youth...... are scat-tered,...... We jour-ney our lone-ly way;............ Sweet mem-o-ries oft will lin-ger...... Of those...... dear days of old,............ When be-neath...... the whis'-pring ma-ples,......... We flaunt-ed the Red and Gold......

Copyright, 1902, by Hinds & Noble.

(3)

Even if it spelled the composer's name incorrectly, the College's 1939 songbook carried the words and music of Simpson's Alma Mater, composed in the 1890s.

VIII

Simpson in the Nineties
1890–99

On a sunny Tuesday morning in September 1890 what looked for all the world like a small army of students descended on the College to register for fall classes. They crossed the dusty road that fronted the campus and clambered over the stile that provided the only access to the College grounds, for the campus in those days was surrounded by a high board fence. As they joined the long line that had formed in front of College Hall, they could admire off to the right the new Science Hall, still a trifle barren in its newness, and to the left, up on the corner of the campus, the brand new Ladies' Hall, reportedly nearing completion. George Griffith's maple trees were fully grown now and provided welcome shade from the hot summer sun.

Returning students greeted each other cheerfully as they waited to sign up with the registrar, who had set up his desk on the rostrum of the chapel upstairs, his faculty colleagues fluttering around the place trying to be helpful and greeting students as they sat down before the registrar. The process was relatively simple, for there were few choices in the curriculum, whether academy or college, but it required the better part of the day to finish.

For old students, registration day was one great joyous reunion, and they walked about the campus with that easy confidence that comes from knowing their way around. New students, on the other hand, appeared to be a bit less at ease, apprehensive about what awaited them here. Some of them felt terribly alone.

One of them was especially anxious, for he had arrived on campus that day utterly without introduction to or prior communication with the College. As he finally reached the head of the line, he stood silently and expectantly, ramrod straight, every muscle in his body tense. The registrar looked up at him with an expression of astonishment mingled with mystification, for he beheld a tall, black, gangly young man whose countenance reflected the fear in his heart. He was George Washington Carver, he announced in a high-pitched voice, and he had come to enroll at Simpson. He presented his credentials, waited for a few frightening moments as the registrar and President Holmes examined his high school record. He could scarcely believe what he heard when Dr. Holmes broke into a hearty smile, reached out to shake his hand and said "Welcome to Simpson!"[1]

Acceptance at Simpson was for Carver the realization of a dream. Born a slave on a Missouri farm in the early 1860s, he had come a long way for a young man of his race in the nineteenth century.[2] His was a life of adventure—and misadventure. He was the second son of Mary "Carver." His father was unknown, probably a black farm hand. When he was a baby, George and his mother were carried off in a bushwhacking raid, and their white owner, Moses Carver, a German immigrant, is said to have sold a fine horse to raise the ransom money to buy them back. Young George was recovered, but his mother had disappeared and was never seen again. He and his brother, Jim, were reared by the Carvers.[3] George was frail and sickly as a youth, but he showed remarkable promise as a student. The Carvers decided he must be given an opportunity for more education than was available in a country school, so they sent him off to Neosho, Missouri, where he attended school for several years, completing most of his high school course. He even dreamed of going on to college some day. For a time, however, he had to put his education aside and make a little money. He operated a small laundry in Minneapolis, Kansas, and a few years later moved to Kansas City. There he learned of a small Presbyterian college at a place called Highland, in northeastern Kansas, where, it was said, he might be permitted to study. He applied for admission and was thrilled to receive a letter of acceptance, signed by President Duncan Brown of Highland University. In September, 1885, Carver took the train to Highland. Few young blacks, he reflected, were being afforded such an opportunity as was he, and he realized how fortunate indeed he was. It seemed almost too good to be true.

It was too good to be true. When he presented himself before Dr. Brown, he was refused admission because he was black. The school would accept Indians, but not Negroes. There was, to be sure, the letter of acceptance, but Carver had not indicated his race on the application. An unfortunate mistake had been made, explained the president.[4] Disappointed, Carver gave up trying to go to college. He stayed around Highland, working in the nearby fruit orchards for more than a year, then followed his white friend Frank Beeler out to Ness county in western Kansas where he homesteaded 160 acres of land. The land was poor, the weather brutal, but he persevered until he received title to the land in June 1888. And soon enough, driven by a desire to get on with his life, he mortgaged the farm and headed eastward through Kansas, ultimately making his way up into Iowa.

At Winterset, Iowa, he got a job in a local hotel and a bit later opened a laundry. At the Baptist Church he met Dr. and Mrs. Milholland, leading citizens of the town, who befriended him. They were impressed with his artistic ability. He could paint really very well. Although he had only limited training, he seemed to possess natural talent with a palette and brush. He also sang tenor in the Baptist church choir and learned to play the piano tolerably well. But what the Milhollands noticed especially was Carver's astonishing ability with living plants, particularly flowers. He could not only paint them; he could make them grow and flourish whenever he set his hand to it. If he had so much promise, whether as an artist or as a horticulturist, reasoned the Milhollands, he should certainly be afforded an opportunity to further his education. They urged him to reconsider going to college. Why not enter Simpson, a Methodist college only twenty-five miles away? Carver recalled in later years that the Milhollands were pleased with themselves that they had been broadminded enough to recommend a Methodist college to a Baptist youth.

In September 1890 Carver packed his few belongings, including some cactus plants he had raised, into a bundle and set out for Indianola on foot, in order to save train fare. He carried with him barely enough money to pay for one term at Simpson.

Because he had not earned a full high school diploma, Carver was enrolled as a "select preparatory student," taking courses in grammar, arithmetic, essay writing and etymology. He paid his twelve dollars tuition for the fall term, and, by his own recollection, had only ten cents left on which to live until he could find some means of earning his way. With his ten cents he went to the local butcher shop and bought five cents' worth of suet, then to a grocery store down on the square where he spent his remaining five cents on cornmeal. These purchases would keep him alive for a week.[5] Meanwhile he opened a laundry. Dr. Holmes promised that he would urge the students to bring him their soiled clothes.

Holmes also saw to it that Carver was given the use of a small shack not far from the campus. At the local dump he found a cookstove; from local merchants he got a boiler, wash tubs, a washboard and some soap and starch on credit; and he scrounged a few wooden crates for furniture. On one of the boxes, in a place of honor, he placed the precious cactus he had carried all the way from Winterset. He was ready for school and for business.

At first no one came with his laundry, and the suet and cornmeal were running low. Unfortunately, Dr. Holmes had forgotten to announce Carver's enterprise at daily chapel. When the president was reminded by one of Carver's instructors, he made up for his omission by making an elaborate plea to the students to avail themselves of this helpful service. Students, especially the boys, who hated to wash clothes, were soon coming with their laundry, and many of them tarried to talk with Carver on all manner of topics. "I may have been the first to take him my laundry," recalled John P. Morley, who was a sophomore the year Carver entered Simpson. "And I may have been a help in advertising his laundry in my boarding club. I made it a point to visit with him when I took him my shirts and when I went after them." Carver seemed to enjoy these conversations while, as one of Morley's classmates put it, "he took on the job of keeping clean a bunch of dirty roughnecks."[6]

Morley's reaction to Carver was probably fairly typical of the students. "I am sure," he wrote, "the entire College community accepted him in full equality." Some may have ignored him, but if they shied away from intimate association, it was perhaps as much the difference in age as in race. Carver was in his mid-twenties, while most of the students were in their teens. That he was black was not a novelty at Simpson. He was not the first black student to enroll at the College.[7] That there was some level of racism on the campus is undeniable, but it was never openly expressed. For one thing, it would never do for a college named for an abolitionist as prominent as Bishop Simpson to discriminate against a student because of his color. Besides, there were a number of black families in Indianola, most of whom had fled Missouri before or during the Civil War, and these families were liked and respected in town. Their African Methodist Episcopal Church, just a few blocks from the campus, brought their black community together. Carver, then, was surely no curiosity at Simpson on account of his race. As Morley put it, "As I came to know him, I saw much beyond the color, so that I soon ceased to sense the color at all."[8]

Carver applied himself assiduously to his academic work, but from the first day on campus what he really wanted to study was art. He had read in the College catalogue of the new Science Building where there was "an elegant art room immediately under the sky-light,"[9] and although he had been told at registration that art study was out of the question, he ventured up to the huge studio to make his desire known directly to Etta Mae Budd, the young art teacher who had joined the faculty only that year. She was not inclined to permit him to enter the class, but something about Carver struck her, and she said he could attend an art class on a trial basis for two weeks, after which she would let him know if his talent warranted his continuing.

The next two weeks were sheer agony for Carver. For Etta Budd the two weeks provided time to observe his work and to get to know the remarkable man who, she noted, was but a few years younger than she. When he summoned the courage at the end of the trial period to ask her if he might remain in the class, she replied that indeed he could. From that day forward, Etta Budd became not only his teacher but his friend. Under her tutelage his talent blossomed, for she was soon content to let him paint what he liked most: flowers and plants. Some of his work done in her studio was later exhibited, and one of his paintings won an honorable mention award at the Columbian Exposition in Chicago in 1893. Today twenty-seven of the paintings Carver did while he studied art with Etta Budd at Simpson hang in the Carver Museum at Tuskegee.

In order to pay the extra tuition for art instruction, Carver split firewood for Miss Budd. For her part, she rallied college students and townspeople to help him, but advised them to do so unobtrusively, for he wanted no charity. John Morley recalled that when the college boys saw how poorly Carver was situated they took up a collection and "one day when he was at class they took in furniture to make him comfortable." Now he had a proper bedstead and even dishes and cutlery. He suspected who was responsible for his good fortune, but "all denied having a hand in it."[10]

Meanwhile, Miss Budd called on her friend, Mrs. Arthur Liston, up on Howard Street, asking her to help this "very promising young man." Mrs. Liston and her husband ran the local bookstore down on the square, the one where college students bought their textbooks, and she was known to do all manner of kindnesses for the youngsters who patronized their establishment. She responded at once to Etta Budd's plea. Mrs. Liston went straightway to Carver's humble dwelling, but as she thought about what to say to him, it seemed at the moment more appropriate to ask for assistance than to offer it. She was trying to paint a picture of her flower garden, she said rather lamely to Carver, and seemed not to be getting it right. Perhaps he could help.

He could. And he not only improved her painting; he improved the flower garden as well, until it became one of the showplaces of Indianola. Nearly every day Carver could be seen turning in at the Liston place, where he might study for hours sitting in the big square bay window, and with each day his friendship with Mrs. Liston deepened. He was soon accepted as an unofficial member of the family. In the years that followed they never lost touch with each other, carrying on a lively correspondence as long as she lived. She always signed herself "your mother."

In the meantime Carver studied evenings at his shack by the light of an oil lamp, and on weekend afternoons he walked in the woods with his new young friends, explaining to them the plant life, the wildflowers or mushrooms along the way. Some of the younger ones called him "Mr. Carver" out of respect for his age and mature, serious bearing. Others invited him to join their literary society—it is not recorded which one he chose—and persuaded him to play on the College baseball team. He was not a very good athlete, but he loved the easygoing camaraderie on the ball field. He enjoyed especially the campus Y.M.C.A., for its members strove to combine Christian concerns with academic enterprise. His Y friends were so taken with Carver's unabashed, natural piety and his impressive maturity that they selected him as one of their representatives at a regional convention of the organization. That four-man Simpson delegation consisted of two Japanese students, Carver and one white American.

In the spring, Carver wrote to Mrs. Milholland:

> You will doubtless be surprised to learn that I am taking both vocal and instrumental music [piano] this term. I don't have to pay any direct money for my music, but pay for it in paintings. They are very kind and take especial pains with me. I can sing up to high D and three octaves below. My health is very good with the exception of a bad cold I contracted yesterday by working in the studio when there was a draft blowing through. However, I will take some quinine tonight and hope to feel better in the morning. I have trebled the work I had last term and it keeps me very busy.[11]

On the whole his academic work was excellent. In the thirteen courses he took in the three terms of the 1890–91 school year he was graded 90 or above in ten of them. His weak subject was arithmetic, in which he dropped from 92 to 78 in the second term and got no grade at all in the spring term.[12]

His heart was in art, not mathematics. When he persuaded Etta Budd to permit him to paint still life, especially flowers, he was truly happy. "He could not copy," writes one of his biographers; "he was very poor at that, but he made his compositions from memory. He could bring to life again any flower he had once seen, from bud to full bloom, and started at once on the yucca of the plains which he remembered from his desert days [in western Kansas]."[13]

Miss Budd was delighted with Carver's progress in art. He was surely her best student, for, as she put it, "painting is in him."[14] Yet she was troubled. What future could there be for Carver as a painter? Could a black man make a living as an artist? The more she thought about it, the more she noticed that Carver was fascinated not only with painting plants and flowers; he loved them and nurtured them in their natural state. Why should he not perhaps study botany? Or agriculture? He could still paint as an avocation, but he could do much more for himself—and his race—in science. Therefore she urged Carver to leave Simpson, to transfer to Iowa State, the agricultural college at Ames, where her father, Dr. Joseph Lancaster Budd, was professor of horticulture.

Her logic was persuasive, and Carver did leave Simpson in 1891 to study agricultural science at Ames, but the parting was difficult. It would have been much easier to remain in the comfortable security and warmth of Simpson. "That college was Paradise for me," he said many years later. He arranged to finish up his spring courses ahead of time, for the school year at Iowa State began in the spring of the year. He packed up his few belongings and prepared once again to face an uncertain, but potentially promising, future.

That the students in Indianola expected Carver to come back is evident from an entry in the June 1891 *Simpsonian*: "Our friend, Mr. Carver, who won many compliments on his work in the Art department this term, will return next fall and enter Junior classical. He will graduate both in Art and Collegiate departments in '93."[15] But that was not to be.

At Iowa State, Carver was accorded a "less than warm" reception by the students, but the faculty people were cordial and helpful. In time he adjusted to a life without art, for he vowed not to paint while he was at Ames.[16] No sooner, however, had the school year concluded in November,[17] than he returned to Indianola to attend Miss Budd's art classes during the winter term. There he painted to his heart's content, waiting until the last minute to return to Ames for the opening of school in the spring. The next winter he intended to come back to Simpson once again, but he was dissuaded from doing so by his mentors at Ames, who wanted him to stick to agriculture, not "fritter away" his time painting. He did visit Simpson during that winter of 1893: "G. W. Carver," wrote the editor of the *Simpsonian*, "a former student, but now of the Iowa Agricultural College, came in Jan. 24, and remained for several days visiting old friends."[18] True, the College catalog for 1892–93 lists him as enrolled in art during the winter term, but the listing is surely an error, mistaking the intent for the deed.[19]

Simpson students did not forget their remarkable black friend, and when he graduated at Iowa State in November 1894 some of them "sent him a handsome bouquet as a token of remembrance."[20]

Carver was Iowa State's first black graduate, and he stayed on for two years to study for his master's degree and to teach as an assistant in botany. In 1896, he accepted the offer of Booker T. Washington to come to Tuskegee Institute to take charge of the agricultural department. There Carver could experience true self-fulfillment and serve his people at the same time. His practical contributions to experimental and applied science, together with his assistance in the fundamental transformation of agriculture in the South, earned him the reputation as the greatest living black man in America. And, as time permitted, he even painted a little.

Carver studied at Simpson only a fraction more than a year. Yet, he would remember "those halcyon days at Simpson" as among the best in his life, "for there are so many sacred memories clustered in and around those beautiful, historic grounds."[21] It was true, he said, that "I owe to Simpson College my real beginning in life."[22]

It was appropriate that the first college to award Carver the honorary doctorate was Simpson in 1928. And thirteen years later, at the 1941 commencement, Carver delivered the baccalaureate address to an audience of more than two thousand. Though the weight of years bore down upon him, he told of the times when the people of Simpson welcomed a poor black man and gave him hope.

Just a year before Carver's stunning baccalaureate address, Dr. John O. Gross, who had been Simpson's president from 1938 to 1941, visited Carver at Tuskegee. At that time the aged scientist said to him, "Everything here is the result of a vision I had while attending Simpson."

"Just what was the vision?" asked Gross.

"At Simpson College," replied Carver, "the kind of people there made me believe I was a human being."[23]

* * *

During the three years of Edmund Holmes's presidency the quality of the College's academic instruction improved markedly. Perhaps the new thrust had to do with the way Holmes exercised leadership. It was not so much a matter of changing the courses of study: the academy (preparatory) program was strengthened by adding a fourth year, but the undergraduate baccalaureate program remained unchanged. Rather it was Holmes's success in maintaining a stable faculty, keeping able people in the half dozen most important chairs.

There was George Carpenter in Latin. Classical languages were not Carpenter's first love, but he was willing to teach where he was needed, and he certainly knew Latin as well as anyone. He was, of course, a mainstay of the faculty, already having spent twenty years in the service of Simpson, but Holmes worried about the professor's failing health. Catherine Cromer taught German and French, but she resigned in 1891. Her successor was Eleanor M. Stark, who soon made her mark at Simpson. "Miss Nell Stark," purred the editor of the *Simpsonian*, "has completely won the hearts of the students. . . . The Dutch verbs may have been a little odious at times, but the pleasant smile and hearty manner of the *Mademoiselle* [sic] as she is affectionately called—have sufficed to sweeten the harsh gutteral of the most desplicable [sic] of all languages."[24]

J. L. Tilton continued in natural science, his reputation growing by the year. Joanna Baker's Greek classes were brilliantly taught and demanding. Some students who respected Miss Baker and honored ancient Greek preferred to do so at a distance and so avoided taking the classical course where Greek was required. For those students who did enroll in her classes, she organized a Greek club where conversational Attic Greek was encouraged. She also offered extension work—Greek by correspondence—with people, mainly clergymen, who wanted to be able to read the New Testament in the original. Helen M. Andrews occupied the chair of English and history, having joined the faculty in the fall of 1889.[25] Milton E. Phillips taught mathematics and headed the Normal School, but in 1890 he resigned to accept the presidency of Southwest Kansas College in Winfield, Kansas. "It is much to be regretted," commented the *Advocate-Tribune*, "that the college could not see its way clear to pay him a salary that would keep him here."[26] In fact, in the 1889–90 school year Phillips received the highest salary of any of the teaching faculty—$1,200—and his successor, William T. Noss, was hired the next fall at a salary of $1,000.[27]

The situation in music was not so stable, and it had not been so for a number of years. Bertha Todd, who came to head the School of Music in 1888, departed two years later, succeeded by C. W. Bricker, whose wife joined him on the faculty teaching piano.[28] Lilly Jacoby had also come to Simpson in 1888 as an assistant instructor in piano. President Holmes was not at all certain why the College needed three instructors in piano, even if there was not much cost involved. The College possessed only two or three old, battered pianos that no one could seem to keep in tune. He decided that music needed some attention, and he took action in 1891. All four of the faculty people in music—the Brickers, Todd and Jacoby—departed in June of that year, and Holmes determined to build the whole program from ground up. He looked around with great care to find just the right person for the job. After a several-month search he found Frank Eliot Barrows, a recent graduate of the Oberlin Conservatory, one of the best in America. Holmes told everyone that this young man was a pianist of outstanding talent and that he showed real promise.

Holmes was right, and the real history of music at Simpson begins with Frank Barrows's arrival on campus. Born at Hudson, Ohio, on February 13, 1867, Barrows began his music studies at the age of seven with his mother, who was a pianist. At seventeen he began his formal music education, studying two years at the Cleveland Conservatory of Music and four years at Oberlin, where he graduated in 1890. He studied the next year in New York under Albert Ross Parsons, William Mason and Mrs. A. K. Virgil. When he came to Simpson, he was prepared to build a conservatory of real quality, and Holmes was delighted to cooperate in the enterprise. In his first year they brought in only one additional faculty person, E. C. Conser, a recent graduate of Knox College, to teach voice and violin.

One of Barrows's first acts was to find at least one new piano. He went to the president with a plea for new instruments. He wanted to do a good job, he said to Holmes, for after all "a workman is known by his tools."

"I have always heard that as 'a workman is known by his chips,'" countered Holmes.

"Give me the tools and I will make the chips."

Holmes liked that. He called the executive committee of the board together so that he and Barrows could lay their plans before them. The board agreed to permit Barrows to go ahead and buy one new piano, but they pointed out that unfortunately the College exchequer could not bear the cost. The very next day Barrows went to Des Moines to look over new pianos, and "on the evening of the Senior Reception of that year the chapel was graced by the appearance of a new Knabe Grande piano."[29] He had bought the piano out of his own funds and presented concerts and recitals all year long to help pay for it. Fifteen cent admission fees did not accumulate funds very fast, but he worked at it, and so did Mrs. Conser.

There were still other faculty members under President Holmes worthy of note. One was Edward L. Miller, instructor in commercial subjects and head of the School of Business and a recent graduate of Tri-State Normal College at Angola, Indiana. Miller, age twenty-two when Holmes brought him to Simpson in the fall of 1889, remained for nearly five decades, setting a record for tenure in a single position. Assisting Miller in his first year was Royal A. McClure and after that Estella Trueblood, both of whom taught typing and shorthand. They were student assistants who taught part-time in return for tuition remission and a small stipend. After completion of her commercial course at the College, Trueblood, a member of one of Warren County's most prominent families over at Ackworth, remained on the staff as a full-time faculty member for a number of years.

At the end of the 1889–90 school year Cornelia Saleno, instructor in art, resigned quite suddenly. President Holmes and the board of trustees scurried to find an acceptable replacement. They were lucky when they found Etta Mae Budd, an 1882 graduate of Iowa Agricultural College, who had studied painting at the Boston Art Museum. Etta Budd was no stranger to Simpson. A year earlier—in the spring of 1889—she had been instrumental in the chartering by Delta Delta Delta of Simpson's local L.F.V. sorority. When she arrived in Indianola to

Table 3
Enrollment 1890–1900

Year	Senior	Junior	Soph.	Fresh.	Spec.	Total Coll.	Prep.	C.M. A.N.*	Total**
1890–91	7	10	21	30	15	83	145	253	354
1891–92	10	14	26	20	22	92	205	179	416
1892–93	8	26	15	27	14	90	202	216	454
1893–94	25	4	9	25	20	83	163	245	447
1894–95	7								398
1895–96	6	15	12	33	0	66	129	298	480
1896–97	10	8	20	52	0	90	117	405	532
1897–98	9	13	24	53	0	99	130	396	545
1898–99	10	15	24	53	0	102	124	282	432
1899–00	14	15	32	51	0	112	152	415	558

*Commercial (Business, Shorthand and Typing), Music, Art and Normal.
**Excludes duplicates.

take up her duties in art, she was delighted with the huge, airy studio under the skylight in Science Hall.

If the faculty was reasonably strong, the board of trustees was excellent, even though drawn entirely from southwest Iowa. This geographical limitation reflected the Methodist Church's sponsorship of several colleges in the state, each of which institutions claimed a part of Iowa and informally agreed to refrain from recruiting students or board members in the territories of its Methodist sister institutions.[30] In 1890 Simpson's board included twenty-seven members, sixteen laymen and eleven clergymen. Seven were from Warren County and two from Des Moines. Virtually all were Methodists, hardly a surprise in view of the stipulation in the College's charter that required approval of the board's membership by the annual session of the Des Moines Conference.[31]

Throughout the nineties, board members continued to be elected for three-year terms, nine new members each year. Many, to be sure, were reelected at the close of their term, giving the board marked stability. In 1900, twenty of the twenty-seven members had been serving in 1890. One of the seven who had left the board was William E. Hamilton, who returned to the faculty in 1892. Even more stable was the executive committee of the board, the membership of which included the president of the College as chairman,[32] John H. Henderson as its perennial secretary, together with Gorham A. Worth and William H. Berry, both of whom served throughout the decade. The only addition during the nineties was William Buxton, who moved from Carlisle to Indianola in 1893 and was named to the executive committee in 1894. Most of the board of trustees' work was accomplished by the executive committee. These men monitored the policies of the College, hired new professors and set faculty and staff salaries, approved all expenditures and managed the endowment. In those days it was much more involved in the day-to-day management of the College than it would be in later years as the administrative staff expanded.

The board of trustees could be pleased with the growth of enrollments (see table 3). During the decade total enrollment swelled from 354 to 558, more than a fifty-seven percent increase. However, most of this improvement took place in nondegree enrollments in business, music, art and teacher training, areas of instruction in which the student count went from 253 to 415, a growth of nearly two-thirds. Regular undergraduate enrollment in the arts and sciences grew from

83 to 112 during the decade, a little better than one-third, while preparatory student attendance remained static, growing from 145 to only 152.

Simpson's enrollments were little affected by the hard times of the 1890s,[33] in large part because the agricultural Midwest suffered relatively less than the industrial urban areas. The financial panic of 1893—in June alone 128 banks failed—plunged the United States into the worst depression in the nation's history, and the devastated economy was agonizingly slow in making a recovery. In 1893 it was not the panic that attracted the attention of the people down on the town square or out at the College; it was the huge, colorful Columbian Exposition at Chicago. Everyone wanted to go that summer, and many did, joining the twenty-seven million fairgoers who walked along the Midway.

* * *

Edmund Holmes served three years—1889–92—as Simpson's president, during which time the College continued to progress satisfactorily. He was an able academic leader, but his heart was with the pastoral calling, and he returned to the itinerancy in 1892 and thereafter served several charges, among them Indianola (1907–12). All he asked of the bishop was that he not be sent back to Carroll. He wasn't.

The board of trustees had tried to persuade Holmes to stay on at Simpson, for his academic and spiritual leadership, together with the solid financial management of Vice-President Fletcher Brown, had moved the College forward in a most gratifying manner.[34] Rev. W. S. Hooker and veteran board member William H. Berry pleaded with Holmes to continue in the presidency, at least for the 1892–93 year, but Holmes was adamant. Disappointed, the board turned to their vice-president, the strongest man they knew, and announced on June 15 that because Holmes "cannot accede to the request made of him by the Board of Trustees this morning," Fletcher Brown would take over the office "until such time" as a new president was selected.[35] After a few months, the board stopped looking for a new president, for in Brown they had a strong leader whose knowledge of Simpson and its needs was unparalleled. Brown was a good fund-raiser, but his skill was tested during the next few years, for during the 1890s finding generous donors was indeed a challenging task. His six-year presidency was more successful than might have been expected in hard times, but money continued to be a problem.

* * *

Robust enrollment figures were regrettably not reflected in the College's financial ledgers. It was not that Simpson's financial well-being deteriorated; rather its dismal annual reports did not improve, leading the College's friends to despair of its ever coming even close to breaking even. Deficits in operations continued to pile up year after year: $1,720 in 1891, $2,480 in 1896, $1,711 in 1899. Only in 1898 were board members stunned when the treasurer reported an unheard-of surplus of $79.86.[36] Although today these deficits in nine out of ten years in the nineties may not seem large, they represented in most years more than ten percent of the total cost of running the College. The result was a persistent, nagging burden of debt, a financial albatross that included unpaid warrants—mostly arrears in faculty salaries—together with mortgages and "borrowing" from scarce endowment capital. At the end of Holmes's presidency in 1892, the aggregate debt stood at $29,219, including $13,650 owing the College's endowment. The next year under President Brown there was not enough income to meet current expenses, not to speak of paying off some of the debt, so the board of trustees quietly wrote off the troublesome endowment debt, reducing the corpus of the endowment by a good twenty-five percent as they did so. In 1897, in an act of despair, the board discussed a proposal to borrow $25,000 to pay off all their obligations, if necessary mortgaging the whole campus. But because the College's credit standing with lending institutions was dubious, the matter was dropped.[37]

Unless the endowment—good, productive endowment—could be increased to, say, $100,000, the College was doomed to struggle with annual shortfalls in revenue. The philosophy of the board, the faculty and the church had not changed: tuition was kept deliberately low to enable any poor Methodist youngster to have the opportunity for an education. It was, moreover, clearly a matter of pricing the College in line with its competition. Fletcher Brown pointed out that in order to break even, Simpson would have to charge each of its 350 students $75 per year. "But state colleges, and endowed schools all around us are offering tuition almost free, and the college which wishes to attract and hold students must offer as good facilities as others, and at low rates."[38] Tuition in 1890 for a three-term, thirty-seven week academic year in the undergraduate liberal arts courses was $37, and by 1900 that figure was dropped to $32 for a thirty-eight week year, although a $2 per term "incidental fee" brought the total up to $38, still only a dollar a week.[39] The aggregate tuition collected in a year did not even pay faculty salaries, not to speak of the rest of the College's expenses. In 1896, for example, students paid a total of $8,393 in tuition; faculty salaries were $11,562. Small wonder there was a serious deficit, which led to further raids on the precious endowment, which in turn reduced the return on what little capital the College possessed.

Even before Fletcher Brown succeeded Holmes as president in 1892, he persuaded the board of trustees that the endowment must be increased to $100,000. Everyone agreed that such an amount would surely guarantee a deficit-free future, but few believed such a goal to be attainable. Still, if anyone could do it, it was Brown, whose irrepressible enthusiasm encouraged others to take heart. He would have a talk with some of the board members.

In the fall of 1891, one board member responded. William Buxton of Carlisle, by all odds Simpson's most generous benefactor in the nineteenth century, offered $10,000, contingent upon others in the church in southwest Iowa giving at least $20,000 before February 1, 1893. Brown went to work. Fifteen months later, just before the deadline, the campaign went over the top with $21,896 in pledges ranging from Gorham A. Worth's $1,005 to the 50 cents given by H. C. Morgan of Tingley, the latter gift matched by a number of Simpson students.[40] Once again, it was Indianola that came through with the largest share of the gifts. On the afternoon of Sunday, January 29, 1893, at an emotion-charged meeting at the Methodist Church, W. E. Hamilton and William H. Berry presented the challenge to the members. As the editor of the local *Times* reported it:

> The President, Rev. Fletcher Brown, had charge of the collection, and with his colored chalk and little squares charmed the people. So deep was the interest, that out of a large congregation only seven persons left the church, all others remaining until 2 o'clock, when the last square on the black board was filled,

then came that peculiar sensation that is not describable that sometimes runs through a great congregation when a crisis is past, when all the people rise up as one and sing out their pent up feelings in a doxology of praise. It was one of the never-to-be-forgotten events in a life time, and those who were present received a hundred fold more, in that one moment of excessive joy, than all the sacrifice and effort cost. Thus closed a service, the effects of which will reach down the years, and after Simpson has its thousands of students, and thousands of money the beginning of its later growth and development will be traced to the collection of $11,750.00 on Sunday, Jan. 29, 1893, which saved the $30,000.00 which goes into its permanent fund.[41]

By the end of the 1892–93 academic year the total endowment, including old (good) notes, the new subscriptions and cash, was $47,473, still a long way from $100,000. But a year later the board received a modest bequest from the estate of the Rev. Dr. Uri P. Golliday, who had died in 1890, and a gift from Mrs. Carrie Southard.[42] Then, to everyone's surprise, the College received a handsome gift, something over 200 acres of farm land west of Des Moines in Dallas County, from the Rev. Edward P. Vail, age seventy-one, a retired pastor in Des Moines whose wife had died the previous May.[43] Vail put the land into the hands of the College in return for a lifetime annuity. So pleased was Vail with the regular income he received that two years later he deeded an additional 240 acres of "very valuable land . . . worth $12,000." Fletcher Brown was delighted, and he hoped Vail would set a good example. "When we think of how much he has done," he wrote, "we also remember that there are possibly hundreds of our laymen—men and women—who could give in a similar way to the cause of Christ."[44]

Encouraged by the growth of the endowment, which reached $67,282 by mid-1895, President Brown abandoned his $100,000 goal as too fainthearted and started campaigning for a $500,000 figure. At six percent interest—the going rate at the time—the College, he reasoned, would receive $30,000 per year income, enough to "meet the legitimate expenses of the school." After all, if John D. Rockefeller could give $1,000,000 to the University of Chicago in one year, couldn't all the Methodists in southwest Iowa come up with half that sum?[45] Meanwhile, Simpson, for all of Brown's dreams, was still running deficits.

Part of the problem was the inability—or unwillingness—of Simpson's Methodist constituents, at least those outside of Indianola, to come up with an annual $3,000 "Simpson collection" endorsed each year routinely by the annual conference session. The results were always disappointing: usually less than half of the amount requested. "This failure from year to year," lamented the board of trustees, "to loyally and conscientiously bring up the amount apportioned to the various charges . . . lies at the foundation of the embarrassment we are compelled to face from year to year consequent upon our inability to meet current expenses."[46] It was difficult for the Simpson people to understand, or to acknowledge, the fact that no matter how dedicated in the abstract Methodists were to the cause of Christian education, their enthusiasm for throwing a dollar into the collection plate on "Simpson Sunday" flagged.

In their appeals to church people, Simpson's leaders faced something of a dilemma. If they pleaded poverty too much, few would give. Why donate money to a losing cause? If, on the other hand, they were tempted to proclaim their successes, many would conclude that there was no need to contribute at all. Fletcher Brown had to confront this perplexity every time he got out a new issue of *The Educator*. This publication, written and edited by Brown and Orlando H. Baker and printed by Brown on an old printing press he installed on the ground floor of the new science building, proclaimed the virtues of Simpson while urging its readers to support the College, preferably with cash. Brown established this propaganda paper, neatly gotten up in six bimonthly issues of sixteen to twenty pages, in early 1889, during his second year as vice-president of the College. To get it out he enlisted the aid of Orlando H. Baker as coeditor. Baker readily fell in with the project, and his remarkable verbal gifts showed in the quality of the articles that graced the pages of their little periodical. Baker stayed on as coeditor until 1892, when President Benjamin Harrison appointed him U.S. consul at Copenhagen.[47] That same year Brown was elevated to the presidency of Simpson, but he continued publishing *The Educator* single-handedly, writing copy, soliciting advertising, setting type, printing and mailing 4,000 copies. Only when he resigned as president of the College did Brown discontinue *The Educator* after nearly a decade of continuous publication. And, as he said in his final issue in 1898, "It has never cost the college a penny."[48]

The Educator was not without its critics. A few of the faculty people thought Brown spent too much of his time on it. More serious were the complaints of W. H. Schooley, the colorful editor of the *Advocate-Tribune*, who did not like it for two reasons: it drained advertising and printing revenues from the weekly newspapers—during the mid-nineties there were four of them—and it engaged in what Schooley thought was misleading propaganda. He exploded when he saw a cut of College Hall labeled the "Business College" where Brown was touting the Business School. That, fumed Schooley, was a "deliberate misrepresentation," and so it was.[49] Nor did any of the editors like it when the entrepreneurial Brown decided the College could do job printing in its shop when the press was otherwise idle.[50] Understandably townspeople were alert to any attempt of the College to engage in any enterprise that competed with their own business establishments, especially during a time of severe depression. Brown, they concluded, was a businessman at heart and had to be watched. Even the *Simpsonian* disliked *The Educator*, its editor snarling that it merited "the contempt of persons of ordinary intelligence," an outburst occasioned by Brown's having announced one day in chapel that *"The Educator* is our college paper."[51]

President Brown might lavish much attention on his publishing venture, but the College certainly did not lavish much money on new buildings in the nineties. The new science building and the Ladies' Boarding Hall had required a major capital outlay, and a mortgage remained on the dormitory for several years. And even though the College began to experience severe overcrowding because of burgeoning enrollments, the board of trustees determined to forego new construction while attempting to increase the endowment. Nevertheless, circumstances dictated the construction of two modest structures, one in 1893 and the other in 1895.

Very modest indeed was the new gymnasium, dedicated on January 15, 1894. There had been talk about such a building for several years. A gymnasium had been proposed as early as 1889 by the Y.M.C.A., and an exercise room was fitted up early that year with makeshift apparatus in the basement of the science building. "For a long time," wrote a student, "this feature of our training here has been conspicuous for its absence."[52] Most of Simpson's students came from the farm where they were accustomed to vigorous physical exertion, and the neglect of their need for exercise, apart from those who participated in organized sports, endangered their health. In keeping with a growing national awareness of the importance of regular physical conditioning, Simpson did the best it could with severely limited resources, promising to do better soon. What they had in one cramped room wasn't much, and soon enough the pressure of high student enrollments reduced the space for the gym to next to nothing. Responding at last to persistent student clamor, however, the board decided to build a thirty-three-by-fifty-foot building "for physical culture." Workmen started construction on January 2, 1894, and completed it in less than two weeks—surely a record time. It was dedicated on January 15. A simple one-story structure situated northeast of the Ladies' Boarding Hall, it was built of barn lumber left rough, with a wood plank floor inside. Six square curtained windows on each side admitted light, and the one-room building was heated by two cast-iron stoves, one at each end of the room. It was furnished with benches, basketball hoops, wall pegs, tumbling pins, hanging rings and other equipment for both men's and women's sports. It was hardly a showplace, having cost only $1,000.[53]

If the gymnasium was something less than impressive, at least it represented the College's recognition of the growing importance of physical education. Not much grander a structure was the Mechanical and Electrical Engineering Building, erected in 1895 at a cost of approximately $2,000 after Brown and the board decided to offer its students an opportunity to study the latest thing in modern technology. Quite apart from the question of the appropriateness of engineering in a liberal arts college, the brief flirtation of Simpson with that branch of learning provides one of the colorful chapters in the history of the College's early years.

The story began when Fletcher Brown, ever alert to the possibility of extending Simpson's attractiveness to students, met Hiram G. Sedgwick, engineer, inventor, minister of the gospel and entrepreneur. Bluff, big-hearted and supremely self-confident, Sedgwick was certifiably brilliant, and he had a real knack for self-promotion. Brown had first met him during the mid-eighties when Sedgwick was making a name for himself as a Bible-toting, hellfire-and-damnation preacher in the Upper Iowa Conference. He knew Sedgwick to have an education, or at least wide experience, in engineering, so he was not surprised when the pastor gave up his ministry in 1887 and opened a department of mechanical and electrical engineering at Griswold College in Davenport, Iowa.

Two years later, Sedgwick decided to pull up stakes and head south. Brown tried to persuade him to come to Simpson instead, but Sedgwick declined the offer. At Nashville, Tennessee, he organized an engineering department at Central Tennessee College under the auspices of the Methodist Church and in the interests of the Freedman's Aid Society. He took with him a whole shop full of machinery and equipment said to be worth some $30,000, and soon his school was said to be gaining "a most enviable reputation."[54] He remained five years at Central Tennessee, his career there coming abruptly to a close when in November 1894 his shop and all its machinery were destroyed in a fire.

Sedgwick returned to Iowa in early 1895, "open to another engagement." President Brown immediately took up correspondence with him, and within a few weeks Simpson's board of trustees entered into a contract with him to start a School of Mechanical and Electrical Engineering. It was scheduled to open on January 1, 1896. By the terms of their ten-year contract, Sedgwick would provide instruction and all the necessary machinery and equipment. How he managed to acquire $30,000 worth of new machinery is not recorded. Perhaps his Tennessee loss was insured. Simpson would provide Sedgwick a building and agreed to pay his salary monthly in cash.[55]

The building was exceedingly simple, a rectangular one-story barn-like wooden structure forty-eight by ninety-six feet, with a pitched roof supported down the middle by sturdy poles. It was large enough for Professor Sedgwick's machine shop and electrical laboratory, and it cost the College $2,000 to put it up. Sedgwick, dubbed by the local press as "dean" of the new department, arrived in Indianola on the Tuesday before Thanksgiving and started putting up the engines and machinery. Completed on time, the building was ready for classes on January 1, 1896, as scheduled.

The announcement of the new program took up four pages in the College's 1895–96 catalog, promising "to teach not only Science (to know), but Art (to do)," and it would accomplish these ends in a four-year program in either mechanical or electrical engineering leading to the bachelor of engineering degree. Beyond that a three year [graduate] course "will be planned" for which "the degree of Master of Engineering will be conferred." This was surely to be no trade school; rather its purpose was "to teach the underlying principles of all methods along their respective lines," a statement of intent that was not a model of clarity. It does appear that despite its impressive name and the claims of its promoters, the engineering program looked ever so much like high school machine shop, to which were added a few decorative liberal arts courses. The tuition for three terms of thirty-eight weeks was fifty-seven dollars.[56]

When Sedgwick met his classes for the first time on a wintry January day, enrollment was disappointingly thin, but it was unrealistic to expect many to respond to a program that commenced in mid-year. Nevertheless, those who enrolled liked the classes, and for a time all went well with the new enterprise. When Warren County clerk of court A. V. Proudfoot visited the department at the end of February, he was awed by the complexity of the equipment and the variety of operations performed there, permitting the students to "turn out any kind of an instrument from a common screw bolt to the finest dynamos and most delicate and powerful microscopes and telescopes."[57] The building was even equipped with a long-distance telephone.[58]

And in early March, Sedgwick, ever on the political alert, presented student-manufactured paperweights to state officials in Des Moines, including the Governor Francis M. Drake and his lieutenant governor, the speaker of the house and assorted members of the senate and house of representatives in the general assembly. In the columns of Indianola's *Times* Sedgwick was praised for "making quite a success of the mechanical department of Simpson."[59] Everyone seemed to approve of this new academic thrust. This was serious, practical, no-nonsense education, all the more praiseworthy for its emphasis on applied science. In an age of expansive industrialization, nothing could be more central to America's needs. In Indianola's part of America, Hiram Sedgwick was the man of the hour.

Soon enough, however, there was a problem, and the problem was money. The board of trustees had contracted to pay Sedgwick's salary in cash and did not do so. This, they argued, would discriminate against other faculty members who were routinely paid with warrants. Besides, "the College is now unable to so pay," and, even if Sedgwick's contract called for separate treatment, such a procedure "doesn't seem fair" to the rest of the faculty. What the board desired was to put engineering "on a self-supporting basis"—like music—so that the proceeds would pay Sedgwick's salary and remit the balance to the College treasury.[60] Sedgwick responded quite rightly that a contract was a contract, and he wanted cash.

Nothing would move the board to give Sedgwick what he wanted, and it was clear to everyone that the College had violated the contract. So in June 1896 Sedgwick went to the law, employing one of Indianola's premier attorneys, O. C. Brown, to represent him. Brown arranged an out-of-court settlement with the College providing that Sedgwick's resignation be accepted, that the ten-year contract be legally cancelled and that his warrants be paid. He should be allowed thirty days to move his equipment.[61]

Sedgwick did not need thirty days. Within ten days after he reached the settlement with the College, representatives from half a dozen schools were after him, among them Highland Park College in Des Moines, which had just come under new management. Lest Sedgwick contract with some other college, the anxious Highland Park people "came to Indianola, reaching here at midnight by carriage, routed Prof. Sedgwick out of bed, held a consultation at the machinery hall, looked over the plant," and arranged then and there to bring his whole operation to Des Moines.[62]

President Brown received considerable criticism for losing Sedgwick and the engineering program, and it is easy to understand the community's distress, particularly in light of Brown's having trumpeted the merits of the program only months earlier. For his part, Sedgwick bore no grudge against the College. He continued to reside in Indianola with his family for a year or so before moving to Des Moines. And in 1899, to show that there were no hard feelings, he made the College the gift of a telescope mounting "and apparatus connected therewith."[63] By that time it was being noised about town that Sedgwick had given up his academic career altogether and was embarking on "bigger things." Meanwhile he and his Indianola attorney, O. C. Brown, had become fast friends and spent a lot of time together.[64]

It was a good thing, too, that he had O. C. Brown for a friend, for if anyone needed a good lawyer in the years to come, it was Sedgwick. As O. C. Brown's granddaughter, Dorothy Daniel, recalled in her delightful book *Circle 'Round the Square*,

> Professor Sedgwick was probably the handiest kind of friend a lawyer could have. No matter what else came along in the world of litigation, Grandfather always had Sedgwick to defend, not only in court against the Masons of Davenport and Sedgwick's own kith, kin, wife, and partners—to name a few—but at board meetings and by mail, phone and telegraph. Between crises, Grandfather still had Sedgwick to advise, admonish, and cuss out. No wonder Grandfather adored Sedgwick to the bitter end. He was practically indispensable.[65]

Fortunately for Simpson, Fletcher Brown's other appointments to the faculty brought in people who were considerably less controversial—Brown would have said "colorful"—than was Professor Sedgwick. Six of the key faculty chairs were occupied by the same people throughout Brown's presidency (1892–98), providing stability: John Tilton in science, Joanna Baker in Greek, Frank Barrows in the conservatory, E. L. Miller in the commercial program, Estella Trueblood in shorthand and typing and William E. Hamilton, returning to Simpson in 1892 to teach moral and intellectual philosophy, replacing departing President Holmes.

In other faculty positions there were changes from time to time. In art, Bertha S. Stacy, an 1891 graduate of Cornell College who had studied an additional year at the Cowles Art School in Boston, replaced Etta Mae Budd who went to work for the Melrose Art Studios in Des Moines.[66] Only twenty-two years of age when she came to Simpson in the fall of 1892, Stacy remained four years, struggling with a department that attracted only a few students and which was never given the kind of attention lavished upon music.[67] When she left in 1896, she was replaced for a year by Mary Condit, who headed what was generously called the "School of Art." The next year (1897–98) no one seems to have taught art at Simpson at all, and when instruction was resumed in the autumn of 1898, art attracted only a few students.

If art brought discouragement, foreign language engendered real enthusiasm. When popular linguist Eleanor Stark resigned in 1893, the College board elected a graduating senior, Joseph O. Watson, to the chair of German and French.[68] The son of Judge Joseph C. Watson, who had come to Warren County from [West] Virginia in 1854, young Watson was a brilliant, well-liked youngster who had his heart set on a career in the law, but liked the opportunity to teach the languages in which he had been such an apt student. Two years later he left Simpson to enter the law school at the State University of Iowa, where he graduated in 1897. By the time Fletcher Brown left Simpson, young Watson was already back in Indianola starting his legal practice.[69]

On the Simpson faculty Watson was succeeded by handsome Lucien Waggener, a native Kentuckian and Princeton University graduate (B.A. 1887 and M.A. 1890), who had subsequently studied at the University of Jena in Germany and at the Sorbonne in Paris. At thirty, Waggener was quite unlike anyone who had been seen on the Simpson faculty: aristocratic, debonair, courtly, devastatingly attractive to the young women who flocked to his classes and probably the only man in Iowa who spoke German and French with a soft Kentucky accent. Talented in more ways than one, he composed the words of the College's "Alma Mater," called simply the "Red and Gold," set to the music of the traditional "Eton Boating Song."

> Come we will sing together
> Once more the ringing song,
> A strain that the coming classes
> Unceasingly shall prolong;
> The praise of our Alma Mater,
> Dear Simpson, thy sons so bold
> Will cherish thy recollections
> And swear by the Red and Gold.
> Though in the years before us
> Life's skies grow dull and gray;
> The friends of our youth are scattered,
> We journey our lonely way;
> Sweet memories oft will linger
> Of those dear days of old,
> When beneath the whisp'ring maples
> We flaunted the Red and Gold.

Waggener also loved golf and soon organized an all-female golf team. They didn't have any golf clubs, but that did not dampen the ardor of the young women who kept their eye more on Waggener than on the ball.[70]

Young Waggener's success was matched by that of John Tilton whose science classes and laboratories were filled to overflowing. President Brown agreed that Tilton needed help and persuaded the board to elect Lewis A. Youtz associate professor of science. Youtz, age twenty-nine when he joined the faculty in the fall of 1893, was a Simpson graduate in the class of 1890. He had entered the College in 1884, but was financially unable to complete his course of study in four years, dropping out of his classes twice to teach school. During the three years after his graduation, he taught science in Iowa public schools and in the summer of 1893 studied organic chemistry at Harvard. During the six years he remained on the Simpson faculty, Youtz taught a good share of the classes in chemistry and biology, permitting Tilton to concentrate on physics and his first love, geology. He always deferred to Tilton, referring to him as his "much senior" colleague, although in fact Tilton was not more than eighteen months older than Youtz.[71]

George Carpenter, of course, could have taught science courses, but he was needed in Latin. In the fall of 1894, however, having suffered for years from ill health, he finally felt compelled to resign from the faculty. At fifty-four, he was the senior member of the faculty, having served twenty-five years, longer than any other up to that time. Somehow he sensed that his work was done, for in a matter of a scant four weeks—it was Monday, October 1—he died.[72] Memorials published in the local press were extravagant in their praise of Carpenter as a man and a teacher. His funeral drew an enormous crowd of college friends and townspeople. Both President Brown and William Hamilton spoke eulogies. One of the local editors recalled Carpenter as "a quiet, unassuming man spotless in character; kind and affectionate to his family, beloved by all who knew him."[73] The board of trustees remembered him a little differently: "[He] was a Christian; with a temperament not at all demonstrative and with a bent of mind toward speculations which in many men would have been dangerous. . . ."[74] They could not forget that he had always rather admired Charles Darwin.

To fill the breach, the board asked Orlando H. Baker to teach Latin for the 1894–95 year, and fortunately Baker, whose political fortunes with the U.S. State Department were at the nadir during the Cleveland years, graciously accepted the invitation.[75] Thus permitted time to seek a permanent replacement in Latin, the board, after a careful search, elected to the position another of their own graduates, Martha Stahl, age thirty-three, who had completed her undergraduate studies in 1889. Upon leaving Simpson, she had taught in high schools for five years and was doing graduate work in Latin at the University of Chicago when she learned of her new position. She remained at the College for many years.

In mathematics—actually they called it "mathematics and didactics"—William T. Noss continued to serve under President Brown from 1892 to 1895. He had originally joined the faculty under Holmes in 1890, and was on the whole well-liked and respected. One occasion, however, in early 1891 caused an uproar both on campus and in town. Noss was speaking in chapel about national unity, and he urged the necessity of forgiveness between North and South, of healing the wounds of war, of reconciliation and Christian charity. He thought it was a rather good speech. However, the local press and some of his colleagues and students didn't like his speech at all. "Prof. Noss," editorialized the *Herald*, "has been taking delight of late, in eulogizing the name of Robt. E. Lee and other rebel

Generals, which we want to say here, is entirely out of place." After all, "Gen's. Lee and Jackson were traitors and most notorious ones; they were parties to the systematic starvation of our soldiers." Noss should be silenced, for "no teacher in Simpson College should be allowed to impress on the minds of the young that these men were Christian gentlemen." Too many young lives had been lost in the cause of the North "to tolerate the doctrine he would teach in our schools."[76]

Noss could scarcely believe the vituperous outcry against what he thought was a sensible plea for understanding. But what he did not understand was that, although the war had been over for nearly thirty years, too much bitterness, indeed vindictiveness, festered in the hearts of Iowans to permit them to countenance the least measure of forgiveness of rebels. Perhaps Noss did not suffer the opprobrium heaped upon young William "Copperhead" Lynch a generation earlier, but he learned quickly enough to select the topics of his chapel addresses with great care. And in time people forgave him even if they did not forgive the rebels, ascribing his single dereliction to the fact that, after all, he was a Baptist.

Noss received his doctorate in mathematics from Allegheny College in Meadville, Pennsylvania, toward the end of 1892,[77] and thus became the first Simpson faculty member to hold an earned doctorate. At that time few faculty people anywhere in America had received the Ph.D. from an American university, for the first graduate programs leading to that degree were offered in 1885 at Bryn Mawr and Johns Hopkins, influenced by the pattern set in the German universities, admired in the late nineteenth century as the best in the world.

For all his superior academic preparation, Noss seems to have been unable to avoid alienating a number of the members of the board of trustees, and in the spring of 1894 they noted in their minutes simply that "the chair of mathematics and didactics remains to be filled." They relented, however, because they could not find anybody acceptable to replace Noss and kept him on another year, and kept looking.[78] The next January a number of students, with whom Noss was popular, circulated a petition "to have a certain member of the faculty retained." These youngsters, members of the Alpian [Literary] Society and some lower classmen, were seen by the editor of the *Advocate-Tribune* to be misled: "They know most certainly that a change in the management and instruction of the school is demanded by all true friends of the college."[79]

Noss's successor was Perry Wilson Jenkins, age twenty-eight, a native of Indiana who had completed both his preparatory and undergraduate education at Miami University in Oxford, Ohio. After a semester of law school at Cincinnati he joined the faculty of Sweetwater College in Tennessee, moving in 1892 from there to Amity College in College Springs, Iowa.[80] Amity was an exceedingly frail institution, and upon the abrupt departure of its president, Jenkins was called upon to step into the breach, "which he did in a very creditable manner."[81] He decided to leave Amity as soon as an opportunity came along and was happy to come to Simpson. He stayed on the faculty as Simpson's professor of mathematics and astronomy for the remainder of the decade.

Even though Noss had departed the scene, Simpson was not without a Ph.D. on the faculty, for in the fall of 1895 Emma Kate Corkhill, a graduate of Iowa Wesleyan, who had earned the doctorate in English history and literature from Boston University in 1893, was appointed to the chair of English and history, replacing Helen Andrews. She continued to teach at Simpson through the rest of the nineties.

In keeping with the new emphasis on physical education, the board appointed Lillian A. Newland, a graduate of the Columbia School of Oratory, instructor in "oratory and physical culture." A large woman, she was accustomed to dress in the latest fashion, with huge puffed sleeves, her blouse festooned with ribbons matching the shiny ribbon perched on the top of her blond tresses. "She teaches physical culture after the Emerson system," reported the *Simpsonian* with evident pride.[82] Her pioneer physical education classes were popular during her two years at Simpson. When she departed in 1896 she was succeeded by Agnes J. Wilson, who was educated at the Cumnock School of Oratory and who remained at the College until 1899. She was employed as instructor of elocution and physical culture. The change in title is instructive; oratory was thought to be insufficiently broad a term to describe what Wilson was called upon to teach.

It is difficult to keep up with the changes of the teaching staff in the conservatory. Apart from a remarkable record of permanence in its leadership—Frank Barrows headed it for thirty-three years—the tenure of most of the other faculty members was usually exceedingly short.[83] In part this was due to the fact that staff selection was entirely in the hands of the director,[84] who was seeking ever-better musicians and was hard to please. Probably far more important was the fact that none of the music faculty was paid a salary. All of them had to exist on what they could collect in tuition and lesson fees, and soon enough they tired of living in penury. From the day he came to Simpson, Barrows employed a number of assistants as he built the conservatory: E. C. Conser in voice (1891–95); Lucy M. Haywood in piano (1894–96); Mamie O'Flyng, a Simpson graduate in 1894, who had studied an additional year at the Oberlin Conservatory of Music, in voice and violin (1895–97); Henry R. Boyden, another Oberlin Conservatory graduate, in piano (1896–98); Elizabeth Michener, another Oberlin product, in violin, harmony and musical history (1896–99); and Ethel Cooledge, yet another Oberlin graduate, in voice (1897–99). And during a two-year absence of Barrows from the campus (1894–96), Carrie L. Willard of Oberlin took charge of the conservatory.[85] One thing was certain: Barrows had good connections at Oberlin.

Simpson's faculty during the Brown administration, never more than seventeen strong, including the president, had to staff seven or eight academic programs: the College of Liberal Arts, offering three baccalaureate degrees; the Normal School, a four-year degree course for teachers; the Simpson College Academy, the preparatory school for the liberal arts; the School of Business, a nondegree program in commercial studies; the School of Shorthand and Typewriting, providing training in stenography; the Conservatory of Music, a four-year course which did not begin to offer the bachelor of music degree until 1900; and the School of Art. The 1895–96 catalog listed as an eighth program Mechanical and Electrical Engineering, and when that department abruptly closed in mid-1896, another eighth "school" was created, this one called the School of Oratory and Physical Culture, in which oratory was a two-year program and physical culture a one-year course of study.

That all of these programs were far more than a seventeen-person faculty could possibly teach should have been obvious to almost everyone. But Fletcher Brown was nothing if not a salesman, and one has only to peruse some of his full-page advertisements in *The Educator* to appreciate that Simpson in the nineties was offering a great deal more than it could deliver.[86]

But what the College did provide, especially for its regular undergraduates in the liberal arts and sciences, was a solid classical education, first-rate instruction for the most part, and a salubrious, intimate environment in which real learning could take place. And if some of the programs were hardly college grade, they probably met the academic and vocational needs of the students about as well as those in other similar colleges of the Midwest, for Simpson, though far from the centers of scholastic innovation and reform, did not exist in a bucolic Iowa vacuum.

In fact, especially in the 1890s, Simpson began to become consciously aware of its place in American higher education. The president of Simpson started attending regularly the gatherings of the presidents of all the Methodist colleges when he went in November 1893 to Syracuse, New York.[87] Beyond that, faculty members took leaves of absence to further their graduate education. Tilton spent the 1894–95 year at Harvard; Frank Barrows took a two-year leave of absence to study music in Berlin;[88] and the year Brown retired from his presidency Joanna Baker was preparing to take the next academic year off to study toward her doctorate at the University of Chicago. New faculty, recruited in what amounted to a national market, brought with them new enthusiasm from their experiences in a score of other church-related colleges and public universities. While it is true that Midwestern colleges were not in the vanguard of educational change, it was difficult for them to lag far behind.

If Simpson was not lacking in ideas, it certainly did fall behind in the physical maintenance of its buildings and grounds. In spite of what their faithful janitor, Silas Van Liew, could accomplish in keeping classrooms and hallways clean, campus buildings began to show wear, the more so as serious overcrowding put a strain on all the facilities. Telltale signs of poor maintenance were everywhere: falling plaster, leaking roofs, loose boards, peeling wallpaper and balky stoves, not to speak of the scrawls of student graffiti on the walls and pocket knife carvings on the furniture.

The grounds were yet worse. Except for the one-day campus cleanup each spring, not much was done to protect the grounds from the ravages of severe weather and careless students or stray animals. When the board fence that fronted the campus fell down—or was it pushed down?—in 1892, everyone agreed that the place probably looked better without it.[89] Besides, if the grounds were not securely fenced, perhaps Fletcher Brown would not permit his hogs to root around among the campus trees and shrubs. One would have thought Brown had learned his lesson a year earlier when the senior students had rounded up his pigs and turned them loose in College Hall.[90] He averred, however, that his pigs ate everything in sight and thus kept the grounds clean. He called them his "sanitation department." It is true that in 1894 board of trustees members were thanking the Rev. A. D. Field for trying to beautify the campus with flowers and shrubs, but the next year they were grumbling that things were "a mess," largely the consequence of abuse by nonstudents who drove carts and buggies onto the grounds, tied their horses to trees during ball games and trampled down shrubs. The janitor, they said, needed to prevent such trespass. They did not suggest how he should accomplish that worthy aim.[91]

A few campus improvements were completed, but progress seemed to be glacial. It required three years of planning before a screened walkway was put up between the new boarding hall and the "ladies' retreat," as their outdoor facilities were called by these decorous Victorians. Meanwhile, they were willing to build a "closet" for young men, so long as it did not cost more than one hundred dollars.[92] College Hall needed extensive repairs, but little was done until late in the decade when a meeting of the big, annual State Oratorical Contest on the campus forced the board to do something, lest the College be embarrassed. Corrugated iron ceilings—to prevent falling plaster—were installed, walls and floors repaired and painted, the rostrum in the chapel rearranged and the old chandeliers in the chapel replaced by electric lights.[93] They had been talking about electric lights for nearly a decade.[94]

The reluctance of the board of trustees to spend money on campus maintenance or improvements made it react with ambivalence to the proposal of the campus Y.M.C.A. and Y.W.C.A. to erect a fifteen thousand dollar building for their needs. Such a structure would include "at least one gymnasium, two parlors, separate bath rooms, and assembly and committee rooms." While no objection was raised to the project—the executive committee of the board gave its "hearty approval"—it was made clear that the Y could expect no financial support from the College nor would President Brown have enough time to raise money for it out in the conference.[95]

Not at all discouraged, the Y people organized a fund-raising campaign of their own. In chapel on February 6, 1894, they publicly announced their project. Faculty and students responded enthusiastically, and "in less than one and one-half hours, $6,000 were subscribed . . . [and] an additional $1,000 were raised by the students before the sun set in the western horizon." It was an impressive performance. "It was God's answer to our prayers," exulted senior Takeshi Ukai.[96]

Their prayers notwithstanding, the Y students never got their building. It proved impossible to raise enough additional funds. However, they were partially satisfied when after the departure of Hiram Sedgwick and his engineering program it was decided to convert the vacant building into a gymnasium with bathing facilities. Even this rather simple transformation required several years to achieve, for as late as mid-1898 the board was still talking about "how the Industrial Building can be utilized."[97] That fall the conversion was accomplished, the total cost only five hundred dollars for materials and labor, with students doing most of the work.[98] It was finally ready for use in the spring of 1899.[99]

* * *

No matter how unpretentious their new gymnasium was, Simpson students were grateful that their elders were responding to a long-held concern for the physical well-being of undergraduates. They were beginning to realize what students already knew: athletic activities, whether formal or informal, intramural or intercollegiate, were rapidly gaining a position of major importance on the campus. It is almost incredible to watch the growth of organized sports during the 1890s.

At the beginning of the decade a few young men played in a few sports irregularly, wherever they could find an open space to mark off for a field or a track. By 1900 far more students participated, both male and female, in a larger number of sports: baseball, croquet, lawn tennis, track and field, football, basketball, golf and a limited amount of gymnastics. And they were provided reasonably adequate playing fields.

Football, the *dernier cri* of the nineties, is a case in point. The first college football game west of the Mississippi was played only in the fall of 1889 when Grinnell defeated the University of Iowa 24-0. Football was new and exciting. And it was rough. It wasn't until 1886 that the rules had been changed to prohibit hacking, throttling, butting or slugging, and it was hard to persuade players that helmets were not "unmanly."

Football found its way to Indianola as early as 1888 when Simpson fielded its first team—or teams—and played a few games with town boys. In 1890 the purchase of a new football was considered sufficiently newsworthy to rate an article in the Indianola press.[100] It was not until 1892 that Simpson's first football score was reported in print, a loss to Des Moines University, 14 to 6.[101]

The next year was Simpson's *annus mirabilis* in football, a five-game season in which the team, piling up 174 points, was unbeaten, untied and unscored-upon. The Simpson eleven scored victories over Des Moines University (28-0) and twice over Drake (6-0 and 64-0!). Captained by Fletcher Homan, the team had no real coach, but its student manager, senior Charles B. Cheney, goes down in the record book as Simpson's first football mentor. In the century since the great team's romp through the 1893 season, no Simpson team has come even close to matching its record.

Three years later, the College's 1896 yearbook for the first time published a photograph of the 1895 football team, picturing fifteen uniformed men—eleven regulars, three substitutes and an umpire—with their manager and coach, mathematics professor Perry W. Jenkins. And "we have the best foot-ball field of any college our size in the state," boasted the editor.[102]

In the fall of 1895 players began to wear protective gear—"football armor" was the term sometimes used—to protect themselves from injury. However strange the equipment looked, most people approved of its adoption. The *Advocate-Tribune* editor, however, thought the concern for safety exaggerated: "An aspiring athlete," he quipped, "clad in all these extraneous adjuncts to the football player's outfit would be safe from injury by anything short of a railroad collision."[103] Still, to be cautious was to be wise, and players donned the protective equipment, at least some of it. By 1898, participants and a growing number of spectators were taking the game seriously. Sometimes emotions got out of control, as they did at a game against William Penn in October of that year when Simpson fans, charging that the referee had "robbed Simpson of the victory" in its 5-0 defeat, chased him all the way to the railroad depot as he dodged "brickbats, clubs and tin cans."[104] That same year rumors flew around Indianola that Drake University had lured away two football stalwarts, senior Elvin McFerrin and freshman Joe Kies, with promises of free tuition.[105] An investigation neither confirmed nor destroyed the rumor, but both remained at Drake and played football, while Indianola seethed with indignation. Nor did the Simpsonians get much help from the national Amateur Athletic Union, whose purpose was to regulate such infractions. Paradoxically, that organization—like its later counterpart, the National Collegiate Athletic Association—professionalized amateurism.

Simpson's teams were indeed amateur, but there is no doubt that in attracting student interest, athletics began in the nineties to outrank all other college activities. Baseball continued to reign as the premier sport, and the Simpson nine was remarkably successful. In the 1894-95 school year, for example, the team won eight out of nine games.[106] Tennis was immensely popular among men and women students alike, so much so that by 1894 there were four grass courts on the campus, barely enough to meet the demand when the weather was pleasant.[107] Track and field events attracted a fair number of competitors, especially at the annual Field Day held during commencement week in June, although a proper track was not completed until the spring of 1898.[108]

The first record of basketball at the College appeared in the *Simpsonian* in the late winter of 1895: "Miss [Lillian] Newland [the new professor of physical culture] is organizing a club for Basket Ball. This is an excellent game and one that has become very popular in many colleges. We shall be glad to see it introduced at Simpson."[109] Both men and women took up the new sport with relish, the women at first more successfully than the men. It seems that the women's game was reasonably decorous, while the men's competition, before the rules made the game more civilized, was said to be "a rough and tumble fight and a noise not unlike that heard at a stock shipping station." Next to basketball, observed one critic, "foot-ball is mere child's play."[110] Until the men could moderate their tendency toward mayhem, it was the women who played the game for Simpson. By 1897 the first women's teams were organized, one of which wanted to represent the College in an "external" game with the west-side high school in Des Moines.[111] The men did not engage in intercollegiate competition until 1902.

Despite the growing popularity of sports among the majority of the students, the faculty and board of trustees were at best ambivalent about activities that did not nourish the intellect or the eternal soul. A few faculty members—for example, Jenkins and Tilton—delighted in the new trend, while some of their colleagues were hostile. Hamilton was the most outspoken of those who disliked all extracurricular activities, except those of a religious nature, calling them a waste of time. In 1894 he delivered a paper on athletics at the Iowa State Education Association meeting, where he opposed "match games between colleges," and he made his unpopular views known on campus.[112] A few years later he spoke out against the selling of season tickets to athletic events.[113] In 1897 the board of trustees, alarmed at the somewhat chaotic development of one sport after another, determined "that the athletic sports of the students be placed under the control and supervision of the faculty."[114] While their action was intended to regulate, indeed to slow, the unchecked boom in athletics, student enthusiasm, not to say that of the public, did not abate.

No athletic event could be properly celebrated without organized cheering and flaunting the school colors. Every group had a yell—classes, fraternities, literary societies—and it seemed only appropriate that Simpson have one too. In early 1891 such a yell was adopted with enthusiasm, "precipitated upon the unsuspecting citizens [of Indianola] in such torrents as to call forth the indignation of the police."[115] Whatever its merits, this yell was replaced by another, selected "because of its capacity to carry enthusiasm:

"Rickety, rickety, biff, boom, bah!
Simpson, Simpson, rah, rah, rah!"[116]

* * *

It is perhaps not surprising that on American college campuses in the 1890s interest in the military grew, reflecting the expansive nationalism of the era. At Simpson John Tilton's volunteer company, organized in 1889, attracted the interest of a growing number of students, but it was not until two years later that an official military unit was established on the campus.[117]

During May 1891 students circulated a petition to create such a unit, citing the nation's need for reserve troops, the value of physical exercise, the inculcation of sound discipline and the desirability of offering the kind of training afforded by the "best colleges."[118] Approved without hesitation by the faculty and the board of trustees, the Simpson College Battalion was created in September 1891 with John Tilton as commandant. Thus Simpson joined the nation's agricultural colleges and nearly a hundred other colleges and universities authorized by Congress to provide "training in the art of war" to their undergraduates. Students in the battalion were expected to drill between three and five hours per week under instructors and with equipment provided by the government.

Obtaining equipment—especially rifles—was not easy, but Tilton and Judge John H. Henderson persuaded the Iowa legislature to enact a law permitting the issuance of National Guard equipment to college battalions. That same legislation also provided for an annual inspection of college battalions by an officer of the Iowa National Guard.[119]

Bearing their rifles and wearing their new uniforms, the battalion first drilled on October 2, 1891. The uniform included a collared blouse-like coat with bone rather than brass buttons, matching trousers and an ordinary military-style hat, the entire outfit of steel gray wool, "neat, durable and cheap," worn with white gloves.[120] It could be purchased down on the square at Kittleman and Buxton's, who did a land-office business supplying sixty men their uniforms. Democrat W. H. Schooley, the clever curmudgeon who ran the *Advocate-Tribune*, couldn't resist a political sartorial comment: "As the college faculty are strongly Republican, we suppose Republican papers [there were two of them in town] will not charge that this uniform is in bad taste because rebel soldiers once wore the gray."[121]

Each autumn Tilton appointed the new cadet officers on the basis of examinations he administered to the whole corps, and enthusiasm remained high. Those students who rose to top cadet posts might be commissioned officers in the U.S. Army by the battalion. By 1899 twenty men had passed the examinations that qualified them for such commissions.

Enlistment in the battalion was voluntary through the 1890s, but after the turn of the century two years of drill became obligatory for all male students. Whether anyone questioned the propriety of the College's maintaining a military unit—even a volunteer one—is not known. If there were any who opposed, they kept silent, or their voices were drowned in the patriotic chorus that accompanied the lead singers praising "Imperial America."

No sooner had the Simpson Battalion been established than women students clamored for a drill team of their own, and almost immediately their demand was met. "A Ladies' Drill Corps has been organized," noted the *Advocate-Tribune* in November 1891 "and will be under the supervision of Mrs. Conser [Frank Barrows's only voice instructor]."[122] A few months later President Holmes, on behalf of "the Ladies' Military Companies," presented the men's battalion a handsome flag with a few well-chosen words. John Tilton responded for the men.[123]

Tilton commanded the Simpson Battalion throughout the decade, but in 1894 the board of trustees transferred the property of the unit from Tilton to the College,[124] an action urged by military authorities and thoroughly acceptable to Tilton, whose dedication to the battalion never waned. Tilton was if anything a patriot, and when war came a few years later he was prepared, if necessary, to lead Simpson troops into battle.

The drums of war against the Spanish began sounding all over America after the U.S.S. *Maine* was blown up in Havana Harbor on February 15, 1898. Echoing the yellow journalism of the Hearst and Pulitzer press in the East, Indianola editors voiced their indignation at Spain's treatment of Cuba, calling the Spanish a "treacherous, cruel and bloodthirsty people."[125] With praise for President McKinley, Simpson students too supported the war when hostilities began in April. But the *Simpsonian* sounded a note of conservative caution and denounced the reckless jingoism of the nation's public press that "seeks only to feed the depraved mind of the sensationalist," and called for sober reflection and the avoidance of popular demonstrations. "Patriotism," wrote junior student Samuel M. Holladay, "does not consist in resolutions and noise, blunder and bravado," and he asserted that there was "as much pure and undefiled patriotism to the square inch found in Simpson College and in Indianola as any other equal area in the United States." In keeping with that spirit, Tilton went quietly to Des Moines to confer with Governor Leslie M. Shaw (an alumnus of Simpson's law school) about the impending war crisis.[126]

By month's end several Simpson students, following the lead of Tommie Neill of Indianola, had acted upon their patriotic impulse by going home to prepare for war. Others were writing for parental consent, and an estimated forty young men said they were willing to go to Cuba to help fight what U.S. Secretary of State John Hay called a "splendid little war."[127]

The war was short and it was, on the whole, immensely popular. In June, Simpson was hearing from its sons scattered over the globe from Cuba to the Philippines.[128] But most of the students stayed in school for the balance of the academic year, and by the time the fall semester commenced, the war was over. A year later Simpson hosted a big veterans' reunion, especially honoring the Iowa Fifty-first Regiment, in which nine Simpsonians had served. The ex-soldiers, some of them still just boys, reminisced and joked like seasoned veterans, and at the end of the evening the strains of "America" blended with college yells, all those present thanking God that not one Simpson boy had lost his life in the war.[129]

* * *

The attention of Simpson people to the military and to physical fitness seems unfortunately not to have had a salutary effect on the health of students. In spite of advances in medicine and sanitation, Americans suffered mightily from disease and frequent epidemics, and college students were among the most vulnerable. When one reads the *Simpsonian*s of the 1890s, one is struck by the appalling health problems that beset the students, striking them down as seriously as they had at any time since the College's founding. One epidemic after another raged among the students: diphtheria in 1890, scarlet fever in 1891, measles in 1893, pinkeye in 1895, the grippe and measles again in 1896, and so on and on. Nearly every month brought reports of students forced to drop out of school because of illness, or worse news that a young alumnus had died of tuberculosis, or worse yet a report like the matter-of-fact story about Archie Fleming who went berserk, tried to choke his roommate and had to be corralled down at the depot and sent home.[130] In the face of these calamities, the faculty felt helpless and could not but ponder the transitoriness of life and the inscrutability of fate.

* * *

For most Simpsonians in the nineties, classes commenced at seven-thirty in the morning, students complaining that such an early hour was uncivilized and faculty maintaining that one should not waste one's forenoons. In mid-morning, chapel met for half an hour, and attendance was, of course, compulsory for all students, a requirement that was threatened when soaring enrollments made it extremely difficult to shoehorn the whole student body into the chapel at one time. Few students liked the chapel services, not so much because the services were religious in format, but simply because they didn't like being forced to go.

Class recitations were compulsory too, but students accepted the strict regimen of class attendance as a necessary, if onerous, part of their education. Some subjects and some professors were more demanding than others. One heard more complaints about history and foreign language recitations than about other classes. It was said of the forty-two students who enrolled in Catherine Cromer's German class in 1891–92, only nineteen survived the year. Kate Corkhill's history classes instilled in her charges a fear that drove them to uncommon industry. Final examinations—for those whose performance did not exempt them from these exercises—were an "injustice" awaited with dread. Conjugating Greek verbs bordered on cruel and inhuman punishment. Wasn't it true that a student at the University of Michigan had gone insane from too much study?[131] Small wonder students were ill so much of the time; they were academically overstrained.

The faculty endured these complaints with patience and a fair sense of humor. Actually, most classes were not excessively demanding, but students could be expected to mutter objections to those they perceived to be difficult. And because there were still few electives in the curriculum, some students felt academically confined and regimented. In the regular undergraduate curriculum, only a few new courses were introduced in the nineties.

One of these was the study of the Bible. The course was first taught at Simpson in the fall of 1894, and the decision to introduce it was controversial. That few church-related colleges taught Bible courses in the nineteenth century might seem odd to those who would expect the Christian scriptures to be at the center of their teaching. But such was the fear of "higher criticism," of studying the Bible as history or literature or poetry in a way that might challenge the inerrancy of holy writ, that it had not been brought into the classroom as a subject of academic inquiry or instruction.

Toward the end of the century, however, the wisdom of not teaching undergraduates the Bible was called into question. At Simpson the Y.M.C.A. and Y.W.C.A. were calling for study of the scriptures. It was preministerial student A. E. Slothower who got to the heart of the matter when he wrote in the *Simpsonian* in 1892:

> There is need of Bible study in college at the time when science is being studied, for at this point in some institutions, especially, the Christian student finds himself faced with many questions which seem at first thought to set the Bible and science at varience [sic], and the skeptical student finds food for his theory in wrongly appropriating scientific truths.

Scientific truth had to be confronted with scriptural truth, for, as Slothower pointed out, "a student who graduates from a Christian college without giving his heart to God is one of the most difficult cases to reach in the evangelization of the world."[132] It was precisely this concern that led the churches and college faculties to relax their opposition to Bible study.

When Simpson introduced Bible study as a freshman requirement in the fall of 1894, it became the seventh of twenty-three Iowa colleges and universities to do so. "The Bible," explained the College's catalog, "is studied as a text-book." That such a study was necessary was soon evident to everyone, including the *Simpsonian* editor who observed that in their Bible recitation "several of the present [freshman] class searched about 15 minutes for the book of Hezekiah."[133] They soon realized, if they did not already know, that in student homes the Bible was universally possessed, commonly displayed and little read.

* * *

Students voiced their approval or dislike of everything from classes to national politics in the *Simpsonian*, which continued to be published monthly through the nineties. The quality of this campus news organ varied from excellent to poor, depending on the competence of its editorial staff. Because the editor was elected each year by the literary societies and because elections too often became contests between Greeks and "barbarians," students were more lucky than wise when they selected a qualified person to run the paper. The Indianola press, in a mood of uncommon unanimity, was dismayed by the quality of the *Simpsonian*, judging it "below standard" or "poor" or "a disgrace to college journalism."[134] It is possible that the attitude of these editors was influenced by the fact that Fletcher Brown was printing the *Simpsonian* on his campus printing press, at least during the early part of the decade. In any case, the *Simpsonian* did have its good years and its bad years, with 1896–97 being probably the worst. Still the paper was read, and it represents the best barometer of student opinion available to the historian.

The nineties witnessed the demise of one Simpson publication and the birth of another. The *Tangent*, the yearbook published by the Greek-letter societies in 1884 and 1889, was scheduled for a third volume in 1891. But it never appeared.[135] For one thing, there were fewer fraternities and sororities than there had been only two years earlier, and the cost seemed prohibitive to those that remained. In June the local *Herald* feared the sands were running out: "We are waiting with bated breath to hear something of the *Tangent*. Judging from the awful silence concerning it, we conclude it is defunct. . . ."[136]

It was defunct, and five years elapsed before a new yearbook called the *Zenith* appeared, published by the senior class in the spring of 1896. Well gotten up, it was a 148-page, soft-bound volume in horizontal format, something like a miniature photo album, fully illustrated and containing sections devoted to faculty, the classes, Greek-letter societies, literary societies and athletics, together with a brief history of the College and a listing of its graduates. Broader based and better financed than its predecessor, the *Zenith* was well received. During the nineties two more editions appeared, one in 1897 and the other in 1899, both edited by the junior class and both similar in content and appearance to the 1896 edition, except that they were—fortunately—cloth bound. So pleased was the board of trustees with the new yearbook that it appropriated ten dollars in 1896 and twenty-five dollars in 1897 toward its publication cost.[137]

As early as 1890 a student committee considered the advisability of issuing a new songbook, but was soon reported to be "stuck on account of lack of funds."[138]

It was only in 1898, after several false starts, that the new songbook appeared, containing all the College and class songs and yells, the volume "neatly clothed in the college colors."[139] It proved to be as useful as was the *Student's Hand Book*, edited by Ambrose E. Talley, which appeared in the fall of 1894 and which was followed by a new edition in the spring of 1897.[140]

The College's student publications chronicled important or frivolous events with equal zest. And the Indianola papers rarely missed an opportunity to take note of student doings, with an emphasis on the frivolous, even outrageous, behavior of the more inventive souls in the student body. Their pranks were mostly harmless: hanging the College's skeleton on the flagpole (more than once), sprinkling cayenne pepper around just before chapel services, ringing the College bell at two o'clock in the morning, painting the chapel stoves and the ornamental cannons—the ones installed in front of College Hall right after the Spanish American War—bright red, turning loose a rooster in chapel, or frightening the girls in Ladies' Hall with ghostly apparitions. Their violations of College rules were selective: they were careful to observe most of the rules most of the time, except, say, the ten o'clock curfew, which they found unduly restrictive. A few of them were known to gamble at cards or were seen at the theater in town. A few were suspected of getting drunk in Des Moines and were severely disciplined.[141] An exasperated *Simpsonian* writer, after reporting some of the more egregious escapades of the month, concluded that some Simpson students were "the best arguments for the theory of evolution."[142]

Most of the students behaved quite acceptably, and the faculty frequently took note of that happy fact. They even admitted at one point that some of the rules in Ladies' Hall were probably too strict, like the one forbidding women to speak to men after leaving the table. Townspeople had taken to calling the place a "nunnery" and urged relaxation of the more odious regulations.[143] The faculty responded positively, in part because faculty members were among the most consistent violators of the dining hall rules. The faculty also noted with pleasure that male students were smoking less, abandoning mustaches and bathing more.

Benjamin F. Clayton, chairman of the board of trustees, whose son had only recently graduated from Simpson, observed student behavior in the early nineties:

> The character and mental caliber of the Simpson student, we presume, will compare favorably with those of like institutions. They are no better, probably no worse. There are about as many schemes to evade college discipline; as much "tick-tacking the town" and as many hazing parties; as much sharp practice on the college authorities and the verdant "new student"; as much moonlight rambling; as many fabrications in the form of pledges of eternal fidelity between the sexes; as many happy unions and as many disappointments as the result of college courtship; as many drones and as many bright students as may be found in the average college.[144]

But mostly the students "bummed." *Bum* was a term used from about 1880 to the mid-1920s to describe any informal outing. Oftentimes the bum was an outdoor affair, but it could be within doors as well. Sometimes a bum required days or weeks of preparation; sometimes it was put together on the spur of the moment. Any group—a class, a literary society, a fraternity or sorority—could participate. In November 1891, the Everett Literary Society held its annual bum at its hall, entertaining the Zetaletheans. At ten o'clock in the evening the entire group adjourned to Jacoby and Anneberg's Restaurant, where "oysters were eaten and crackers were thrown for an hour or more."[145] Or one could read in 1892 that "the Sigs (SAEs) have entered into possession of their new quarters, and in celebration of the occasion they held a notable bum."[146] On Halloween, 1897, the Pi Phis bummed at the home of Effie Busselle. The next month the Alpians held their fall bum at the Todhunter House, and after "whirling away a few hours in merriment," they banqueted at Hoyt's. And a few weeks later the sophomores bummed at the home of Wesley Honnold. So common was the term, that "bum" came to be used as a transitive verb: "I move that we *bum* the fair damsels on Saturday evening." Or as an adjective: "Refreshments were served by the bum committee." Not only used in various parts of speech, the bum was applied to a bewildering array of social events. As Ruth Jackson, longtime professor of English at the College, wrote as she recalled that era: "There were bums and bums. The delicate line of distinction between a picnic and an outdoor bum, or between an informal indoor social affair and an indoor bum, is a line that apparently was easily recognized by both student and faculty member during the approximately four decades that the bum flourished."[147]

Student socializing was for the most part easygoing, centering on conversation and eating. By all odds their favorite food was oysters, taken raw only by the practiced veteran and eaten by most everyone else cooked or in a buttery stew. Hardly a native product, oysters seemed exotic, and they were imported into Indianola, it seemed, by the carload. Every banquet and every bum featured oysters. And if their printed banquet menus are to be believed, the feasts were Lucullan, oysters and all.

The groups that "bummed" earned the loyalty of their members: class loyalty, society loyalty, fraternity loyalty. Loyalty to one's class at Simpson was more nearly possible in the nineteenth century when no graduating class ever numbered more than twenty-five. We learn that in 1897 the senior class of nine had six officers, a yell, colors (white and blue) and an extravagant sense of tradition: "The tribes of Simpson," wrote their historian, "combined in arms against the '97's and fain would have trampled the beloved white and blue in the dust, but the '97's gathered themselves together as one man and defended the flag, even with their life blood."[148] This sort of class loyalty could lead to hazing of freshmen, although it only rarely got out of hand. The stalwarts of the sophomore class of 1894, in an excess of zeal, carved a huge '94 into the stone entrance of the Science Building, an act the faculty described as vandalism and which led to the suspension of nine sophomores and the disciplining of a freshman who said he knew who did the deed but would not reveal his name. The president of the College hired a stone mason to efface the offending numbers, paid him $5.40 for his day's labor and billed both the freshman and sophomores for it. W. H. Schooley called the brouhaha "a pleasant oasis in the desertous monotony of school life."[149]

Literary societies in the nineties continued to enroll nearly every Simpson full-time student, undergraduate and prep alike, and membership in them was much encouraged, in effect required, by the faculty. At the beginning of the decade there were four of them. The Zetaletheans (1867) for women, the Everetts (1868) for men and two coeducational societies, the Smithsonians (1876), named for their patron, the late Reverend D. N. Smith, and the Philomatheans (1882). All of them met either on Friday or Saturday in their well-appointed rooms in College Hall. "Their work," stated the College's catalog, "affords excellent facilities for acquiring self-possession, originality, power of expression, and a knowledge of the topics of the day."[150] At the beginning of the decade, all the societies accepted prep students into membership. Their meetings were sometimes exciting, sometimes dull, usually instructive, and their annual exhibitions were well attended.

A number of changes came during the nineties. The Philomathean Society disbanded at the end of 1891, replaced by the Lowell Lyceum.[151] At the same time the societies all passed rules excluding preps. Accordingly, the Alpian Society was organized in September, 1892. "The membership is confined to Preparatory and Normal students."[152] And the January 1894 *Simpsonian* announced the organization of the Gradatim Society, whose membership similarly was made up exclusively of prep students. A year later, the Everetts and Smithsonians merged to become the Smith-Everett Society, retaining the Everett male-only membership policy.[153] At the end of the decade there were, then, five societies, three for undergraduates and two for preps: Zetalethean, Smith-Everett, Lowell Lyceum, Alpian and Gradatim. Among student leaders, five societies were thought to be too many. Cursing the ghost of Adam Smith, senior Edward N. Calhoun deplored "unlimited and unrestricted competition." Too many societies—there were six at one point in the mid-nineties, vitiated the quality of all of them, even the oldest. "When the old institutions of a school begin to decline and meet with disappointment at every hand," something needed to be done.[154] He was referring, of course, to the deterioration of the once-distinguished Everetts, the victim of too much internecine society rivalry in too small a college.

The societies were not even doing a good job of honing the oratorical skills of their members, an enterprise supposedly central to their purpose. Oratory continued to be an activity of major importance, but it was the College's Oratorical Association that organized and promoted it most effectively. State oratorical contests generated more excitement than major athletic events, and winning orators were accorded the honors of heroes. Students like John P. Morley and George Clammer, both accomplished orators at the state and national level, earned unending praise from students, faculty and townspeople, their orations printed in full in the local press. Meanwhile, speechmaking in the literary societies simply did not measure up to the standard of quality they had once known.

Still, the societies held the steadfast loyalty of their members. So did the Greek-letter fraternities, each of them competing with the others and all of them making common cause against the "barbarians." The attractiveness of the Greek societies rested upon their selectivity, their active, intimate social program, and the fact that they were the only groups left on the campus that were still totally student-run. It was of course this last-named characteristic that made them particularly unpopular with the faculty. Among nonfraternity students, on the other hand, it was the observed clannishness, the uncontrolled tribalism of the Greeks that seemed to create divisiveness where it was unnecessary and uncalled for, and which led to "barb" solidarity against the "frats."

Probably the best year for the Greeks was 1888–89, when they were responsible for the publication of the second *Tangent* yearbook. Four national men's groups existed: Delta Tau Delta (1873), Phi Kappa Psi (1882), Alpha Tau Omega (1885), and Sigma Alpha Epsilon (1889). For the women there were Pi Beta Phi (1874), Kappa Alpha Theta (1879), Kappa Kappa Gamma (1880) and Delta Delta

Delta (1889).[155] After 1889, however, the fortunes of the Greeks deteriorated until, by the turn of the century only two sororities survived—Pi Phi and Tridelta—and all the fraternities had perished.[156]

In a way the fraternities brought their troubles on themselves. Their competitiveness, their exclusivity, their tendency to gang up on the "barbs," led to an inevitable reaction. As one after another Greek society died out, the remaining ones fought to retain their slipping campus prestige. Literary society elections—especially in the Everetts—became Greek-"barb" contests, as did elections to the student council or to the top editorial positions on the *Simpsonian* and the *Zenith*. And as time went on, the outnumbered Greeks lost nearly every contest.

Yet they still might have survived—for their purposes did meet important student needs—had it not been for one additional factor that was crucial: in the nineties, Simpson students experienced a powerful onslaught of religious revivalism never seen before or since on the campus. It is difficult to know exactly how it all started, but it is clear that the growth of Christian piety paralleled the growing importance of the Y.M.C.A. and Y.W.C.A. on the campus. The Inter-Collegiate Y.M.C.A., in a period of phenomenal growth, had organized at Simpson in 1881 and the Y.W.C.A. three years later. We have already noted the efforts of the Y to erect a building on the campus, and although that effort failed, the power and prestige of the organization continued to grow. "The Y.M.C.A. is mightily influencing the spiritual life of the college," wrote one of its members in 1896, and he was right. By 1894 a whole section of each issue of the *Simpsonian* was given over to Y news. Two years later the Y.M.C.A. was organizing Bible classes "with splendid enrollment," meant to supplement the required freshman Bible course and far less likely than the faculty-taught course to compromise spirituality with "higher criticism."[157] Prayer meetings attracted a growing number of students. The Y.M. and Y.W. organized an annual uplifting lecture series which sometimes drew as many as three hundred persons. With earnest endeavor, the Y sought to bring students to the point of Christian conversion and to foster right living among the converted.

When the twenty-five Iowa college Y.M.C.A.s, representing 1,900 members, held their annual convention at Oskaloosa in 1895, they noted that only 2,700 of 5,100 Iowa college men were Christians, but that conversions were increasing rapidly. Their work was cut out for them, for they estimated that it required seven men a full year to effect one conversion. And for the converted, they urged continuing vigilance with respect to the seven deadly "temptations and perils" that surrounded the Christian college man: (1) bad associates, (2) worldly ambition, (3) intemperance—especially the use of "ardent spirits," (4) gambling—which included any kind of card playing, (5) secret sin—the nineteenth-century euphemism for masturbation, (6) dishonesty in class—and presumably dishonesty anywhere, and—perhaps the most dangerous of all—(7) skepticism. Recommended to their members were faith, secret and public prayer, Bible study, evangelism and organized revival work. If they carried on with these commendable efforts, they might match in the next twelve months the 178 conversions effected during the last.[158]

In their endeavors the Y had a host of allies. The Methodist Episcopal Church held regular revival services, and rarely were Simpson students missing from among those converted. The Simpson Ministerial Association was organized among the preministerial students—about twenty percent of the male under-

> **DRINK COCO COLA**
>
> It is a Delicious Beverage and has good medicinal properties.
>
> **Try it for Headache, Nervousness, Exhaustion.**
>
> **The Osborne Pharmacy**

Simpsonian October 1897

graduates—and worked to recruit others for full-time Christian service. The Mission Band, organized in 1891 and twelve strong in 1896, was preparing to carry the gospel to foreign lands, and its members met every Thursday evening.[159] All-College prayer meetings routinely drew more than a hundred participants. And a "temperance alliance," which first met in 1892, sought to reassure students in their mass meetings that abstinence from alcohol was fundamental to Christian living and urged general prohibition. And that wasn't all. More people were talking about the "poisoning influence that tobacco has on the intellect."[160]

The antitobacco drive won the support of the *Simpsonian*, which stopped carrying cigarette advertisements in the early nineties. A few years later, however, an advertisement invited students to come down to the soda fountain at the Osborne Pharmacy and "Drink Coco Cola [*sic*]. It is a Delicious Beverage and has good medicinal properties. Try it for Headache, Nervousness, Exhaustion."[161] Its "medicinal properties" reportedly consisted of caffeine, extracts of the African kola nut and coca leaves, the latter also used in the production of cocaine. It was hard to keep ahead of sin.

Most of the manifestations of the religious revival were wholesome, constructive and well-intentioned. Yet as in any such movement, there lurked the risk of a descent into a kind of parochial self-righteousness, a narrow sectarianism that bespoke a failure of Christian charity. And some very intemperate utterances as well. It started innocently enough in 1891 with a report in the *Simpsonian* by a Simpson alumnus, M. R. Harnard, who had recently visited Italy and Egypt. In Rome he recalled finding a theological school educating foreigners to do missionary work. Among these were "between six and seven hundred young men taken from our homes in America to be drilled and become skilled in the delusions of Roman Catholicism." And at al-Azhar University in Cairo he found seven thousand students with "dark brown faces and black heads," whose "peculiar drone or sing-song noise" seemed to have little to do with serious study. He found these places a stark contrast to "our beautiful and magnificent Simpson in the Center of the Garden of the World."[162]

Harnard's observations, of course, could be dismissed as harmless provincialism or, at worst, racism or xenophobia. But a few months later Ed Hatfield, editor of the *Simpsonian*, let loose a blast of abusive rhetoric aimed at the *Niagara Index*, the student organ at Catholic Niagara University in New York, which had criticized some "doggerel poetry" that had appeared in the *Simpsonian*. Asserting that "popery and Irish blarney are at a serious discount at present," he laid out an insulting challenge: "Just place a deposit with your priest sufficient to get your soul prayed out of purgatory, come out across the Mississippi and we will take your greasy pontifical paraphenalia [sic], twist it into a rope and with it hang you to a telephone pole." Lest he be misunderstood, he added, "The coyotes will hold a wake over your carcass while your little soul goes flitting down to Limbo."[163] One would have thought young Hatfield had been somehow offended.

That Hatfield would harbor such outrageous thoughts might be ascribed to the widespread prejudice of protestants against Catholics in that day, but that he should feel free to print them—and not be taken to task for doing so—can best be understood as a reflection of the prevailing revivalist climate at Simpson. When the stunned Niagara editor labeled Hatfield's article "the most vituperative, insulting venomous article that has appeared in any college paper this year"—and he was probably right—Hatfield simply returned to the attack: "We know of nothing more rediculous [sic] than a ridiculous religion and nothing more contemptible than a contemptible creed."[164]

One could abuse Catholics at a distance—there was, after all, not one Catholic at Simpson during the entire decade—but any excess of religious zeal could find the zealots prepared to label people and institutions not sharing their enthusiasm to be utterly lost, if not evil. And at Simpson the Greek societies, especially the men's groups, were a—perhaps unintended—victim of revivalist piety, for their fraternal tribalism seemed but a parody of Christian brotherhood, their secularism appeared to border on the hedonistic, and their secret rituals, handshakes and pagan oaths had all the earmarks of idolatry. And so by decade's end all four of Simpson's fraternities sank in a sea of righteousness.

Athletics might have been a victim, too, but seemed capable of reform. The Y.M.C.A. declared itself willing to "cooperate with the athletic boys of the school and establish a higher grade and more perfect system of Athletic sport."[165] The Athletic Association was understandably wary about such an offer of cooperation, fearing a takeover.

In any case, there is little doubt that the late nineties marked the zenith of overt Christian piety among students at Simpson. There were those who called the College a "tower of sanctity, a bright light emanating from the city on a hill." Small wonder traveling salesmen started calling Indianola "the Holy City."

Fletcher Brown could not have selected a better time to resign his presidency and return to the itinerancy than 1898, for the religious revival was at its height, the College was reasonably solvent, enrollment was good, and the nation was in the midst of a popular war. The board of trustees, apparently taken by surprise by Brown's sudden announcement, tried valiantly to dissuade him from his decision, but to no avail. He said simply that it was time for him to move on.[166]

Brown left Simpson a hero. He had come to the College eleven years earlier, recalled the Andersons in the *Herald*, "when the college was practically stranded," as its vice-president for finance. Five years later he took charge of the institution as president, vice-president, financial agent and treasurer, carrying it through the next six years, "five of which were characterized by unusual [national] financial depression." Although his critics had been severe, "Fletcher Brown has done a work for Simpson College that will live as a monument to his name more lasting than marble or brass."[167]

* * *

When the Rev. Joseph Benson Harris was selected Simpson's eighth president, he had been serving three years as pastor in the Methodist Church in Indianola and thus was well known to College people. He was born July 14, 1859, in Belmont County, Ohio, the son of a Methodist minister who died when young Joseph was but five years old. He came with his widowed mother, sister and two brothers to Iowa at the age of ten. Three years later, he began work as a messenger boy for the Western Union Telegraph Company. When he was but fourteen he took charge of the telegraph office of the Chicago, Burlington and Quincy Railroad, and by the time he was seventeen he was employed as a train dispatcher and was managing the Western Union telegraph office in Creston, Iowa.

It was after his conversion to Christianity and affiliation with the Methodist Episcopal Church in 1878 that he began thinking about his education. He decided to attend Simpson to study for the ministry, but because he had not attended high school he was required to complete two years in the preparatory program, even though he was already twenty-one when he entered. He attended to his studies diligently, joined the Phi Kappa Psi fraternity, but soon felt compelled to attend to his religious life. In his second year at Simpson he dropped out to take charge of what was called "the New York circuit." New York, it must be pointed out, was a rural hamlet down in Wayne County, southeast of Indianola. The following autumn (1882) he reentered Simpson, this time as an "unclassified" student, and soon he was admitted "on trial" to the Des Moines Conference and in 1885 to full membership, although he had not earned a degree from Simpson. But his possessing neither an undergraduate nor a seminary degree was no impediment to the rapid advancement of his clerical career.[168] It was, of course, his successful pastorate in Indianola that drew him to the attention of Simpson's board of trustees when the presidency fell vacant in 1898.

Harris responded to Simpson's emergency, but he preferred the pastorate and said so, promising to serve at the College no longer than a year, time enough to permit the board to search for a new president. It was not his intention to change anything at the College, and he did not.

Yet, he made a powerful impression on the College during the one short year he stood at the helm. Students would never forget the tall, gaunt, almost cadaverously thin man who stood before them in daily chapel, his blue eyes illuminating his countenance as he spoke in measured tones. His preaching was remembered as didactic rather than oratorical, his sermons laced with wit and down-home humor. Students liked him because they sensed that he genuinely liked them. His relations with everyone at the College, from proud and sensitive William Hamilton to amicable Van Liew the janitor, from the most self-confident senior to the greenest prep, proceeded from instinctive good will that lent warm vigor to his hearty Methodist handshake and zest to his utterances.

Everyone was sorry to see Harris leave at the end of the year to take the pastorate at Denison, Iowa.[169] Members of the board of trustees expressed their disappointment, and a few of the laymen among their number were so bold as to suggest what had heretofore been unthinkable: why not seek a layman as president of the College, one for whom the office was not merely a stopover between pastorates? It was an idea whose time had come.

IX

The Shelton Years 1899–1910

The election in 1899 of Charles Eldred Shelton as the ninth president of the College represented a real departure from the tradition of clerical leadership that had marked Simpson and nearly all other denominational schools of the nineteenth and early twentieth centuries. Shelton was not a clergyman, nor was he seminary trained. At the time of his election he was the highly successful superintendent of schools in Burlington, Iowa, and was sought out for the Simpson presidency because of his undoubted managerial talents.

All of this is not to say, however, that Shelton was not a dedicated and active Methodist layman. He was a product of the Methodist parsonage; his father, the Reverend Orville Clarkson Shelton, was for more than fifty years a prominent clergyman in the Iowa Conference. To be sure, not every child of the parsonage could be counted on to brim with Christian piety, but young Charles did seem to share the powerful religious convictions of his parents and acted upon those convictions.

Born in Mount Pleasant, Iowa, June 16, 1859, Shelton was reared in first one town and then another as his father moved from congregation to congregation in the itinerancy. When he was sixteen years old he entered Iowa Wesleyan University, where he graduated in 1879. The next year he was admitted to the bar and essayed a career in the law. After only eighteen months in practice, however, he became dissatisfied with the life of an attorney and determined to become an educator.

In the fall of 1880 he married Julia Woodward, an alumna of Iowa Wesleyan, and immediately embarked with his bride upon a difficult and distant assignment in educational work under Bishop William Taylor's system of missions in Brazil. Upon their arrival in that country he and Julia set to work, and for the better part of two years they organized schools in Pernambuco and Bahia.

It was as a schoolman that Shelton "found his forte."[1] Upon his return from Brazil in 1882 he served as principal of schools in Agency (1882–84) and DeWitt, Iowa (1885–89). His administrative ability was matched by his teaching skills, especially in history, which was his first love. Most of all, he wanted to teach teachers how to teach history. In 1889 he joined the faculty at Western Normal College in Shenandoah, Iowa, where he remained three years, after which he taught a year at Lincoln Normal University, in Lincoln, Nebraska. Soon enough, however, his administrative gift led him to be invited to take the position of superintendent of public schools in Burlington, Iowa. He served in that role for six years, until his election to the presidency of Simpson in 1899.[2]

When the board of trustees began to cast about to find a new president for the College, they sought someone with demonstrated skills in managing an educational enterprise. He should be able to teach, too, for it was expected that the president would assume an instructional role alongside the rest of the faculty. One can find no evidence that anyone complained—at least publicly—that they did not choose a clergyman. That he was a good Methodist layman was cachet enough for Shelton when he was selected. The board approved his election at its June meeting at commencement time in 1899.[3]

It was soon evident that the Board had acted wisely in selecting Shelton. For one thing, the new president was aware of what he was getting into: a reasonably healthy church-related college that could be made considerably stronger by the application of sound management principles and a cautious but determined effort to improve and modernize the curriculum. He not only seemed to understand Simpson's most pressing needs; he possessed the courage and intelligence, together with a fair measure of tact and good will, to translate ideas into reality.

Shelton's eleven years at Simpson, which closed with the College's Golden Jubilee, were a time of unprecedented growth and change. In some ways the shifts were subtle, in other ways profound. It is true, of course, that not all the transformation of Simpson was the work of its president, but it very likely would not have happened without him. By all odds he was the strongest leader of the College during its first half century.

"He was a man of truly imposing appearance," recalled Alma Robbins White, a student during Shelton's early years at Simpson. "He was a big, hearty man, handsome and dynamic. He dominated the scene wherever he was. In the classroom he made history come alive, and when he walked around the campus, one had the impression that he knew what was going on. We called him 'Prexie,' and I think he liked it."[4]

The president's office, located at that time on the ground floor of College Hall, consisted of an anteroom and a classroom. Every weekday morning Shelton reserved an hour for students to come in and talk to him about any kind of problem, scholastic or personal. Sometimes, to be sure, they were called in to discuss their academic progress or some breach of conduct. Such interviews were brief, Shelton signaling the conclusion of the session with a sharp rap of his gavel. "He knew how to mete out discipline, all right, but though he was strict, he was always fair."[5]

* * *

The men who were most responsible for bringing Shelton to Simpson were several hard-working Indianola trustees who continued to guide the work of the board throughout the Shelton years. Their leader was Benjamin F. Clayton, Indianola's redoubtable mayor. Clayton was a native of Kentucky who had come to Iowa in 1873 and to Warren County in 1891. A powerful businessman, he owned rich farmland in western Iowa and other properties as far west as California and British Columbia. He was president of a string of banks in towns scattered along the Union Pacific Railroad in Nebraska and Colorado. Apart from his business and farming interests, Clayton was widely known in Republican politics, having served in three sessions of the Iowa General Assembly and four years as mayor of Indianola. In the mid-nineties he took over the presidency of Simpson's board of trustees. Both his son and daughter were graduates of the College. It was Clayton as much as anyone who saw the need for a more businesslike administration of the College than it had heretofore enjoyed. Preachers, he said, were almost as impractical as professors.

He found ready allies in William Buxton, Simpson's most generous benefactor and chairman of the executive committee of the board, and both banker Gorham A. Worth and attorney William H. Berry, together with Berry's partner, John H. Henderson. They were supported by a board of trustees that was disposed to leave to the Indianola men the task of working on a day-to-day basis with the new president.

During the first decade of the twentieth century, Simpson's board of trustees had a fairly stable membership. Of twenty-three laymen who served during the Shelton era, twenty served the entire eleven years and two for ten years. The clerical members tended to serve shorter terms; only four of them—including William Hamilton who was a faculty member—served the entire eleven years.[6] It is hardly surprising that the terms of the clergymen were relatively brief in view of their peripatetic pastorates around the conference. At any one time there were twenty-seven trustees, nine elected annually by the Des Moines Conference for three-year terms. All were from southwest Iowa. It was fairly typical that of twenty-seven trustees, seventeen were laymen and ten were pastors. Then, as now, the executive committee and officers of the board watched after the day-to-day affairs of the College while the larger board, meeting customarily only once or twice a year, tended to validate or serve as a check on the work of the executive committee.

Had circumstances permitted, Shelton would have come to Simpson a year earlier than he did. When Fletcher Brown retired as president in 1898, the board's "committee on faculty" urged the election of Shelton, but "his absence in Europe at that time and his contract with the Burlington school board, both prevented."[7] Thereupon the board elected Reverend Harris, who accepted their invitation with the understanding that he would remain only one year. The following spring the board "immediately sent a sub-committee to see [Shelton who] gave them a favorable answer." A month before he was formally elected, the local press was already announcing that "the position will be offered him and he will accept it."[8]

When Shelton arrived in Indianola with his wife Julia and their only son, Whitford, a lad of fourteen, he found at the College a faculty of sixteen, not counting four assistants, three of whom were undergraduates and one a recent graduate. In the full-time faculty still only one, Emma Kate Corkhill, professor of English, held a Ph.D., and she was on leave during Shelton's first year.

The sixteen faculty members—nine men and seven women—included seven stalwarts who remained at the College throughout Shelton's administration. Their leader was William E. Hamilton, the old man of the faculty, who held the College's only endowed professorship, the William Buxton Chair of Moral Sciences.

His courses were required, but the students did not protest. Studying with Reverend Hamilton was "one of the things you had to do," reflected Alma Robbins White. "He was a gentle, dear old man, loved, respected and very religious, but he was really not an excellent speaker."[9] John L. Tilton in natural sciences taught an array of classes, none more happily than geology, and supported energetically both the military corps and intercollegiate athletics. Determined to work toward a doctorate, he took a leave of absence in 1902–03 to do graduate study at the University of Chicago. Two years later he was elected vice-president of the Iowa Academy of Science, and subsequently its president.[10] Joanna Baker continued to teach Attic Greek to students who seemed to be growing increasingly indifferent to the beauty of the Hellenic tongue. Then there was William B. "Billy" Read, whose mathematics classes produced terror in his students in their classroom recitations. E. L. Miller, both principal and chief instructor in Simpson's school of business, was starting his second decade of teaching at the College. Frank Barrows was the highly successful director of the Simpson Conservatory of Music, which he had built from a small, undistinguished program to a school of eminent reputation in the state and region. Also among the long-term faculty people was Estella Trueblood, who taught almost entirely in the business school and in the academy.

There were other faculty persons whose tenures were shorter, like Martha Stahl. The students called her "Aunt Martha," but never to her face. Strict, dynamic and a superior Latin teacher, she was thought to be a permanent fixture at the College, but resigned in 1904, owing to her forthcoming marriage to a businessman in Mount Ayr, Iowa. Her successor was Mary O. Hunting, a graduate of Alma College, who had earned her M.A. at the University of Michigan and who was already known at Simpson, where she had filled in for a year for Joanna Baker when she was on a leave of absence to do graduate study. In English literature there was Kate Corkhill, who returned from a year abroad in the fall of 1900 and continued teaching with great success until she resigned in 1902 to accept a position at Lawrence University in Wisconsin. Her replacement was Elisabeth C. Bentley, who had earned her B.A. at Missouri Wesleyan and had completed two years of graduate study at Boston University. She came to Simpson from Baker University in Kansas.[11] Cultured and dainty—she was said to come from a "very civilized" family—she was described as always impeccably dressed and perfectly coiffed. She was in her thirties when she came to Simpson and never married. Hence she was an ideal selection as "resident chaperone" for the Tridelta sorority when they acquired their first house on the north side of the campus from Mrs. Liston in the fall of 1904. Never severe, Miss Bentley enjoyed the easy informal relationship with the girls as much as she did the rigors of daily recitation in the classroom. As one of the Tridelts put it, "No one would do anything to harm or embarrass her."[12] She remained at Simpson six years. When she resigned in 1908 to go to her hometown, St. Joseph, Missouri, to teach English, the *Simpsonian* noted that she was "without doubt the most universally liked of any at Simpson." The day she departed the College scheduled breakfast at 6:45 A.M. so that the students could go to the train to bid her farewell.[13] Her place at Simpson was taken by A. W. Goodenough, a product of Oberlin College who had done graduate work at Yale. Goodenough proved to be an engaging teacher whose strong background in oratory served him well in the classroom.[14]

It appears that the most difficult chair to keep filled was that of German and French. During the Shelton years no fewer than five people held down that position: Louise A. Vail (1899–1900), Rebecca C. Shepherd (1900–02), Ida B. Steyer (1902–07), Marcia B. Lutz (1907–09) and Hildegarde Jend (1909–10). While a number of explanations may be offered for the rapid turnover, it is certainly true that this position was not highly paid. The seven hundred dollar annual salary in 1899 increased not at all in eleven years, while the best-paid faculty were earning twice that amount. And the position, one can note, was always held by a woman.

Tilton was, of course, the mainstay in the sciences, but there was relatively rapid turnover among his colleagues, too. In the associate professorship in natural science one could count five men during the Shelton years: J. G. Goodwin (1899–1903), A. N. Martin (1903–05), B. A. Place (1905–06), Floyd Bartell (1906–07) and Edwin A. Jenner (1907–10). Then in 1907 a new position was created in chemistry, the first appointee being C. J. Holmes, who remained only a year. In the fall of 1908 Holmes was succeeded by Jesse Allen Baker of Lafayette, Oregon, a graduate of McMinnville College, who had earned his M.A. at Denison University. Shelton could not have known how well he had chosen his new man in chemistry. Baker would remain at Simpson for nearly five decades, providing continuity of excellent teaching in the natural and physical sciences.

When President Shelton arrived at Simpson, the College's work in the School of Oratory and Physical Culture, a two-year nondegree program, was relatively limited, but it grew as the College's faculty perceived the need for formal instruction in speech. The popularity of public speaking, long regarded as an indispensable component of undergraduate experience, continued to be demonstrated in the weekly well-attended meetings of the literary societies and the almost frenzied outpouring of excitement that accompanied the annual local and statewide oratorical contests. Little by little the work of these student-run enterprises was being absorbed into the College's curriculum.

In 1896 Simpson had created its School of Oratory and Physical Culture. At first glance the combination of instruction in public speaking and "physical culture" may seem strange, but it was intended that those who learned to speak well should also learn to develop and control their physical movements with grace and ease. The teaching of physical culture was even accorded sacred endorsement: "Know ye that your body is the temple of the Holy Ghost . . . ; therefore glorify God in your body."[15] By 1899 Simpson's combined program enrolled thirty-five students—some of them crossover enrollees from other departments—taught by a faculty member whose five hundred dollar salary was low even for Simpson, but who was expected to supplement that meager stipend by teaching private individual lessons at seventy-five cents an hour or class lessons at three dollars per term. Of the four people who taught oratory during the Shelton years, three were products of the prestigious Columbia School of Oratory in Chicago: Jennie W. Newman (1899–1902), Charles A. Marsh (1902–05) and Adin C. Krebs (1906–08). Newman left after three lackluster years to take a position in North Dakota. Marsh, who had taught elocution at Iowa Wesleyan and at Oberlin, was considerably more effective, but he departed quite suddenly in November 1905, leaving to his assistant the task of completing the fall term. Krebs arrived the following January and remained until the spring of 1908. That next autumn the position went to young John Dunn Martin, who had joined the Simpson faculty in 1904. Martin was a product of the Cumnock School of Oratory, connected with Northwestern University, where he completed his two-year course in 1900. Before coming to Simpson he had taught three years at the Denison (Iowa) Normal College, even though he did not yet hold the B.A. degree. He was brought to Simpson to teach as a student assistant in oratory and in the Normal School and to serve as the College's registrar, all the time working toward his undergraduate degree. His graduation in June 1908 coincided with Adin Krebs' departure, so he was promoted to the directorship of what was by then called the School of Oratory. Apart from his teaching duties, he directed plays and served as faculty secretary.

While the College's work in oratory improved markedly during Shelton's administration, it was the Conservatory of Music that vaulted ahead by leaps and bounds. Under Frank Barrows's leadership the program was regarded as one of the strongest in the West. When he had come in 1891, Barrows and one assistant taught all the music classes in two cramped rooms in Science Hall, with 40 students enrolled. By 1910 the conservatory had a building of its own, and Barrows counted six colleagues in a strong program with an enrollment of 335.

Shelton liked music and he respected Barrows, who ran the conservatory independently. As director, Barrows financed most of its needs through student fees, kept almost no accounts that were decipherable and seemed always to finish the academic year in the black. Shelton and the board of trustees were frequently, and understandably, anxious about the inscrutable nature of the conservatory's finances, but Barrows could be extraordinarily reassuring about such things. Besides, the music was magnificent, whether it was a well-rehearsed student recital or a full-scale performance of a Haydn oratorio. For the most part, Shelton let Barrows run his own show.

In the decade no fewer than twenty-two faculty taught music classes or provided private instruction or both. It may well have been more, for most old College catalogs cannot be depended upon to contain complete listings of all the part-time people who taught lessons in mandolin or flute or whatever. Thus we can mention only the best known of the music people, the ones who were talked about whenever the growing reputation of the Simpson Conservatory was the topic of conversation. In voice there was Alexander Emslie, a Scot who had come to the United States in 1888 and whose work with large choral groups was outstanding. Upon Emslie's resignation in 1905 Barrows selected Joseph W. Leach, educated in London, Paris and Milan, who served for three years. He was succeeded in 1908 by John M. Henderson of New York City, a mature musician with a "superb bass voice." Barrows boasted that Henderson was "one of the strongest additions to the Conservatory faculty that has ever been made."[16]

Barrows was a pianist, and although he performed only rarely, he was regarded as a superior teacher who accepted nothing less than the best possible work from his students. He was able to recruit his very best piano student, Everett "Tip" Olive of Scranton, Iowa, as his assistant. Then after Olive's graduation in 1900, Barrows urged him to stay on at Simpson in full-time teaching. The gifted young pianist remained at Simpson for twenty years. He is the composer of many of the College's best-known traditional songs. Barrows upgraded the level of instruction in the conservatory by the introduction of a full Bachelor of Music program.

"Tip" Olive was one of the first five Simpson undergraduates to earn the bachelor of music degree, all conferred in 1900.[17] Two other talented members of that same class were similarly recruited by Barrows, first as student assistants during their senior year and then, upon receiving their degree, as full-time instructors. One of them was Barrows's sister, Mary Alice—always called Alice—a talented pianist whose soft-spoken, easy-going camaraderie with her colleagues belied a gritty determination to achieve something like perfection in her playing and that of her students. She remained at Simpson throughout Shelton's tenure. The other member of the 1900 trio was John J. Landsbury, an able young man from tiny Pender, Nebraska, who taught harmony, counterpoint and analysis. His music theory classes, he conceded, were not among students' favorite ways to spend time, rather something to be endured. Always impeccably dressed, Landsbury hid his youth behind pince-nez glasses and a schoolmasterish precision in speech. His manner of presentation changed little during his seven or eight years on the music faculty.[18]

Although instrumental music received less attention than piano or voice, several capable people, all of them violinists, taught in the conservatory. Frank Sloan, who taught violin and music theory, served from 1899 to 1901. Oberlin-trained Elizabeth Michener followed, combining violin and piano in her single year on the faculty. After Winfred M. Colton taught violin and orchestral instruments for three years (1902–05), young Daniel H. Bonus, like Colton a product of the Chicago Musical College, instructed in violin and orchestral instruments during the remainder of the Shelton era.

If any musician at Simpson of those years achieved national fame it had to be Arthur Middleton, whose magnificent bass voice brought him to Simpson as a student, kept him on briefly (1900–02) as a faculty member and sent him forth to the world as a teacher and leading vocalist with major orchestras, touring opera companies and, during the early years of the First World War, the Metropolitan Opera in New York City. Many years later Barrows recalled his first encounter with Middleton back in 1897 or so. He had heard that there was a remarkable young singer out in western Iowa who ought to come to Simpson and wrote to him at his home in Missouri Valley that he would come out to see him while on vacation that next summer. Middleton replied that he would be in a small place in Nebraska and could meet Barrows there as he was passing through.

"I got word to him," said Barrows, "that I would be at the station on a certain freight train and asked him to meet me. We met and we talked over the possibility of him coming to Simpson.

"There was nothing in the town except a station, a corn crib and rolling prairie as far as the eye could see." With an audience of the stationmaster and a couple of awestruck passengers, he asked "Mid" to sing, "of course without accompaniment."

"I doubt if there was a piano within ten miles. So, while the freight train was backing and switching in the leisurely way such trains have of doing, Mid sang and I knew he was all right. He came to school in the fall."

At Simpson Middleton studied voice with Alexander Emslie, and ever afterwards he regarded the dour Scotsman as his mentor. When Middleton returned to Indianola for a triumphal concert in 1923, he was sorry his teacher could not be present, for "I can't begin to estimate what I owe to Alexander Emslie and Simpson College."[19]

Simpson's dedication to the fine arts has always been selective, at least from the time Barrows arrived in the early nineties to push music into the forefront. Theater continued to be an amateur affair, performed fairly regularly with student casts under faculty direction. The situation in art was only marginally better. When Shelton assumed the presidency in 1899, Simpson's School of Art, a fragile enterprise at best, had been suspended entirely for two years. Shelton made no attempt at first to revive the art program. Although his 1899–1900 faculty listed Edith Riggs, who had attended the School of Art before its discontinuance, as an instructor in drawing, there was little for her to do. The next year the president turned over art instruction entirely to Charles A. Cumming, "a pupil of Boulanger and Lefevre, Paris," whose proprietary art school in Des Moines assumed control of the program.[20] Thus the College that year advertised its Academy of Art, announcing that Mr. Cumming "comes once a month to talk on art and composition" and that the program on campus "is under the immediate charge of Mr. Fred N. Keith."[21] For the next few years both Cumming and Keith were listed in the College's catalogs, even if Cumming's role was largely supervisory. Then, in 1904, the College discontinued the connection with Cumming and employed Eunora Maxson, a Simpson undergraduate in her sophomore year who had studied at the Chicago Art Institute, to handle the program. Doubling as student and teacher, in her four years she almost tripled the number of students in art, but their number was slight when compared with the huge attendance in music.[22]

When Maxson earned her B.Ph., the direction of Simpson's School of Art was turned over to a senior student, Avery Craven.[23] Shelton was in fact looking for a way to continue the art program, at least in name, without spending much on it. To be sure, in young Craven he found a competent, indeed gifted artist, said to have "large natural ability."[24] Craven had studied at the Cumming School in Des Moines, where his drawings and watercolors were deemed first-rate. Quite apart from his talent in art, Craven was a superior student president of the Kallonian Literary Society and an accomplished public speaker. His oration entitled "Count Tolstoi" won him "first place honors at the State Oratorical Contest during his senior year.[25] He was also an all-round athlete who performed exceedingly well in football, basketball, track and field. His record-winning time in 120-yard high hurdles stood for a number of years as Simpson's best. He won the state championship in pole vaulting and served as president of the Simpson Athletic Association. How he managed that first year to do his senior courses, serve as sergeant-major on the staff of the Simpson Military Academy, orate, play football and basketball, run track *and* direct the School of Art has never been entirely clear, but then Avery Craven was if anything versatile.

After his graduation in the class of 1908 Craven continued to direct the School of Art for two more years, teaching also history and civics in the Simpson Academy and, in his spare time, coaching the College's track team. It was in history that Craven really found himself. And after he left Simpson and completed the doctorate in history, he taught in several institutions before settling as chairman of the Department of History at the University of Chicago where his teaching and revisionist publications earned him a reputation as one of America's leading historians.[26]

Meanwhile, art at Simpson languished.

* * *

When Shelton took up his duties at Simpson, he was pleased to see that his faculty, with support of the board of trustees, had already embraced, however tentatively, the elective principle in degree programs. For decades the College had clung to a prescribed curriculum, one for each baccalaureate degree, permitting virtually no election at all, except perhaps for the substitution of French for German in the junior or senior year. All other academic programs, including the Academy, specified each and every course to be studied, and fixed precisely the order in which each would be undertaken. All this was in the best tradition of American higher education.

In the 1890s the winds of curricular change began to blow, however softly. During most of that decade, the Simpson student had two elective choices (out of approximately thirty courses) in the classical or philosophical programs, and no choice at all in the scientific. Then, in 1899, the concept of term hours was introduced, a term hour defined as "one exercise per week requiring on an average two hours for preparation and recitation."[27] Students were required to complete 232 term hours for graduation, or an average of nineteen or twenty credit hours per term. At the same time—this was just before Shelton arrived on the scene—the elective principle was clearly adopted. All students in the liberal arts had to complete ninety-two hours of required core courses and between sixty and eighty-four in additional specified subjects, the number of hours depending on the degree sought. Thus there remained between fifty-six and eighty term hours of elective courses, representing a major shift in the direction of free choice.[28]

In the nine years that followed, the curricular programs remained essentially the same as they were when Shelton arrived, yet one could note a tendency to expand slightly the required segments of the several courses, so that by 1908 students had between fifty-four and sixty-eight hours of electives.

The idea of elective courses in the curriculum was perhaps the most hotly debated issue in higher education in the latter part of the nineteenth century. Proponents saw it as a call for freedom and a frank admission that in its prescribed courses no college could teach a student all that was worth knowing. The explosion of knowledge, especially in the natural sciences, was making specialization necessary. Opponents, however, saw the adoption of electives an act of abandonment of tradition, a kind of academic anarchy that at best could lead to dilettantism and at worst to anti-intellectualism. Frederick Rudolph has called the elective idea "one of the most creative, and also one of the most destructive, educational developments of the post-Civil War years."[29]

The father of the elective idea in American education was Charles William Eliot, whose forty-year tenure as president of Harvard saw the transformation of an excellent regional college to a great national university. And what Harvard did many others imitated. Within three years after his coming to Harvard in 1869, Eliot began to introduce the elective principle gradually, and by 1897 the only required course in the curriculum was one year of freshman rhetoric. His adversaries were legion, including probably most of the Harvard faculty, and decades later even Harvard historian Samuel Eliot Morison would lament "It is hard saying, but Mr. Eliot, more than any other man, is responsible for the greatest educational crime of the century against American youth—depriving him of his classical heritage."[30]

Still, the elective principle was an idea whose time had come. Eliot was utterly unapologetic: "Direct revelation from on high would be the only satisfactory basis for a uniform prescribed curriculum."[31] His commitment to science and freedom, his insistence that, in education, process was more important than subject and his practical assertion that election would improve the motivation of students who were increasingly indifferent, or even hostile, to the classical tradition persuaded an increasing number of colleges to consider discarding their rigid curricula in favor of election. In spite of the outburst of President James McCosh of Princeton who said "Freedom is the catch-word of this new departure. . . . It is a bid for popularity,"[32] one college after another relented and adopted the elective idea in one way or another.

The idea moved westward very quickly. After 1890 places like DePauw and Illinois College were introducing electives, and soon enough the movement found its way into the Trans-Mississippi West, especially in the state universities. Two conditions might inhibit the adoption of the elective principle: narrow sectarianism and poverty. Simpson was denominational, to be sure, but it was not and never had been narrowly sectarian. It *was* poor, however, and the introduction of electives clearly necessitated a broader curriculum, more courses and more teachers. These things cost money, and in Warren County money was scarce.

Yet Simpson went ahead with its curricular change, partly because it seemed to be the right thing to do. Also the College was emboldened to take this step because its enrollment was increasing fast enough to justify the expense. For better or worse, election was here to stay, and at Simpson any number of further characteristics of the twentieth century curriculum were an inevitable result of this daring step: majors and minors, concentration and distribution of subjects and a host of other innovations.

Within a few years after the reforms of credit hours and electives had been adopted, Shelton and the faculty perceived a real problem with the three-term calendar of the College. For one thing, the terms were of unequal length. The fall term lasted fifteen weeks, the winter term twelve and the spring term eleven. It was extremely difficult to assign proper credit hour values to courses of unequal duration. Far more serious, however, was the dropout problem. The winter term nearly always saw a reduction, and spring term a calamitous attrition, in student enrollment. By adopting a two-semester calendar the College could solve the problem of uneven terms and provide students one less chance each year to drop out of school.

When the College adopted the semester calendar in the fall of 1908, the new system was popular among faculty and students alike. Actually, at first each semester was divided into two terms of equal length, but all courses were calculated and evaluated by the semester.[33]

During the Shelton years the areas in which the College offered instruction remained quite stable. For example, in his last year at Simpson (1909–10), the catalog announced nine "departments" of instruction:

    I. College of Liberal Arts
   II. Academy
  III. School of Education and Special Courses
  IV. School of Business
   V. School of Shorthand and Typewriting
  VI. Conservatory of Music
 VII. School of Oratory

Table 4
Enrollment 1900–1910[34]

	Senior	Junior	Soph.	Fresh.	Special	Total
1900–01	16	17	46	55	0	134
1901–02	21	27	34	88	0	170
1902–03	35	17	45	82	0	179
1903–04	16	25	55	71	0	167
1904–05	26	19	45	116	0	206
1905–06	41	25	27	138	4	235
1906–07	34	23	21	139	4	221
1907–08	31	24	28	132	12	227
1908–09	28	34	61	125	0	248
1909–10	20	38	95	129	3	285

	Prep.	Business etc.	Music	Art	Normal	Unclass.	Net Total*
1900–01	112	162	214	5	106	10	629
1901–02	148	201	196	6	102	15	836
1902–03	114	197	222	5	74	9	772
1903–04	139	176	225	8	87	10	777
1904–05	135	183	236	10	75	12	792
1905–06	160	190	300	6	87	0	851
1906–07	186	169	333	20	82	0	854
1907–08	177	181	203	—	65	0	853
1908–09	204	134	233	—	62	0	881
1909–10	175	106	224	—	47	0	837

*Excludes duplicates.

VIII. School of Art
IX. Military Academy

While it was probably not intended to be, the listing of such a broad array of offerings was misleading. For one thing, instruction in some areas, like art and oratory, was exceedingly thin. Further, only the College of Liberal Arts—and perhaps the Military Academy—was entirely made up of college-level undergraduates. The others were either partly or, in the case of the Academy, entirely made up of children or secondary level pupils or part-time adults. Beyond the College of Liberal Arts, only in the Conservatory of Music was a baccalaureate degree offered. One could also earn a master's degree in a number of fields. No longer awarded almost automatically three years after graduation, the M.A. could be earned in one year of resident or three years of nonresident study.

Generally, however, the level of instruction improved as the College's enrollment burgeoned during the first decade of the new century.

Enrollment of regular undergraduates more than doubled during the decade while the academy enrollment, quite surprisingly, grew by a healthy fifty percent. The conservatory saw a bulge of enrollment in the middle of the decade, but lost more than a hundred pupils in the 1907–08 year.[35] The numbers in business dropped as did those in the normal school, the latter unexpected in view of Shelton's interest in teacher preparation. Still, the College's total enrollment showed a healthy gain throughout the decade, a tribute to Shelton's leadership and the growing reputation of Simpson. It was, to be sure, a relatively provincial place. In 1910, for example, fully ninety per cent of the students came either from Indianola or the rest of southwest Iowa—inside the Des Moines Conference—while only four students were residents of other Iowa localities. Twenty-two came from out-of-state and five from foreign countries. It was a comfortably homogeneous campus with its own character. No serious effort was made to recruit students from outside the conference. Male and female in almost even numbers, most were Methodist; a few were Presbyterians or Baptists or other protestants. It is doubtful if a single student was Catholic.

* * *

As more students flocked to the College, overcrowding became a formidable problem. Classes were too large; there were too many of them vying for acutely limited space; students were tumbling out all over the place. On the one hand, it was a pleasant problem to have; on the other, it caused Shelton and his board of trustees a mighty collective headache as they scrambled to raise the funds to build new structures to house their jam-packed classes.[36] "We need," said Shelton soon after his arrival, "one or more buildings to meet the present necessities of the institution," whereupon the board resolved formally to raise $20,000 for construction.[37] By June 1900, William H. Berry was able to report that "we have approved plans of architects Proudfoot and Bird for two buildings: the Conservatory of Music and Administration Building." Bids were already in, the lowest being a total of $12,798 for both buildings.[38] He indicated a further pressing need for a central heating plant and "water closets" inside Ladies' Hall.

Construction of the administration building occupied the rest of the summer and the fall. Of brick veneer, it was a compact (fifty-four by thirty-two feet) three-story attractive but no-nonsense building located midway between College Hall and Ladies' Hall, its entrance facing the south.[39] By late October the brick work was completed and in December the building was ready for occupancy.[40] On the ground floor were two large rooms and one small space which were intended for the College library. On the second floor were one large recitation room for history and two small rooms for the president. On the top floor were two large rooms, one for the Autokallonian Literary Society and the other for recitation, and a small room whose use was as yet undesignated.

"The new administration building is a real beauty inside and out," proclaimed the *Indianola Herald* in a burst of community pride. Shelton was delighted with the new building, but he was forced to defer moving the library into the building because of the intense pressure from Frank Barrows's conservatory, which found itself virtually homeless. The year prior to Shelton's arrival at Simpson, the music people had been moved from their inadequate rooms in Science Hall and were shoehorned into even less space in College Hall. Overcrowding in the latter building, together with the substantial growth in music enrollment, made their situation untenable. Therefore, it was decided to find quarters in town for the music school, at least for the time being. Barrows rented a house on North B Street for the 1899–1900 academic year, but it proved unsatisfactory. So the following fall he rented rooms over the Osborne Pharmacy on the southeast corner of the Indianola square, where the conservatory somehow functioned until the administration building was completed.[41] With no great enthusiasm, Shelton agreed to permit the music school to occupy the entire building, except for his own three-room kingdom on the second floor—his office, anteroom and history recitation room—until a proper conservatory building could be erected. Shelton liked music, but he enjoyed a rehearsed performance, not the rehearsal itself. The walls of the new building were thin, and the cacophony of instruments and voices was well-nigh unendurable. As one student put it, "Here our long-suffering president sat in his office, or heard his classes day by day with the air filled with the murderous clang of pianos, violins and voice all about him, and there he was held prisoner."[42] It is small wonder, then, that Shelton redoubled his efforts to erect the conservatory building and saw to it that it was located in the extreme northeast corner of the campus, as far from the president's office as possible.

Although Rev. L. B. Wickersham, the College's field secretary, found it an exhausting task, even with Shelton's help, to raise money among conference congregations, enough funds were on hand by the end of the summer of 1901 to justify moving ahead with construction of the conservatory. Wickersham could be pleased that at Creston he had come up with $1,681, that amount ensuring the success of the fund drive.

The contract for the conservatory was awarded to Elias Proudfoot in the amount of $9,175 and construction commenced in May 1902.[43] By October it was nearing completion, and it was ready for occupancy by Thanksgiving time.[44] The new three-story building was described as "a substantial structure of pressed brick" with "an elaborate system of deadening [that] prevents the practice in one room from interfering with that of another."[45] It contained lecture and practice rooms, a recital hall seating 150 persons, a club room, offices, waiting room and a library. Like the Administration Building, it was equipped with electric lighting and was heated by steam. Its proudest feature was the only elevator on campus, in fact the only one in Indianola. Intended to hoist pianos from one floor to another, it was apparently not properly designed for the use it got and soon fell out of service. Especially attractive were the stained glass windows that graced the landing and recital room—later known as Edgerton Hall.[46]

Shelton was brimming with good will when he and Barrows hosted a lavish social at the new conservatory on the evening of December 10, 1902, only a fortnight after the musicians had moved in. He combined the formal opening of the new building with a reception for 250 invited guests and state dignitaries, in which enterprise he and Mrs. Shelton were assisted by Richard C. Barrett, the State Superintendent of Public Instruction,[47] in order that these friends of Simpson "might meet and greet each other and be entertained by music" performed by students. Everyone seemed to enjoy the evening's festivities, even William H. Berry, who was recovering from a broken arm he suffered when inspecting the partly-finished conservatory.[48]

Much less dramatic than either a new administration or conservatory building, the College erected a much-needed central heating plant in 1901. Recognizing the persistent annoyance, not to speak of danger, of the recalcitrant and mostly unreliable stoves or jumbled building heating systems, the faculty, for many of whom getting heat into their frigid classrooms went quite beyond their professional expertise, pleaded for relief. Shelton agreed, and although a central boiler that would service all the campus buildings was expensive, it was clearly necessary, and the matter was urgent.[49]

Proudfoot and Bird designed the building and its radiating tunnels that would carry heat to all the buildings, with capacity to service future additional structures. Located next to the women's gymnasium and north of College Hall, it was constructed during the summer and fall of 1901 at a cost of $11,600.[50] As radiators were being installed in all the buildings, the eighty-five-foot chimney was topped out and the boilers hooked up.[51] The November *Simpsonian* announced that "within a week it will be in operation."[52] The school paper also observed that the new plant "will add greatly to the appearance of the college grounds," an opinion shared by almost no one, then or now.[53]

During the first days of the new century the most exciting talk was about a new auditorium or gymnasium, or combination of the two. This would be a major project, the largest ever undertaken by the College, but overcrowding, especially in chapel, was becoming intolerable. When the addition of chairs in the chapel did not solve the problem, Shelton was obliged to experiment, and during the winter term of 1902 he divided the student body into three groups for daily chapel, one contingent meeting in the Administration Building, a second in the commercial room and the third in the chapel proper, everyone meeting together on Fridays at the Methodist Church.[54] The experiment was a failure, for it was a little like trying to run a three-ring circus, and the Methodist Church, which would seat eighteen hundred, was said to be too dark for daytime meetings, although why it was too dark on Fridays and bright enough on a Sabbath morning was not made clear. In any case, the next fall Shelton squeezed everyone back into the chapel by means of some judicious reseating, putting all the seniors on the platform with the faculty, a solution approved by everyone except the seniors.[55] Simpson still needed an auditorium.

The 1901 *Zenith*, published in May of that year, featured a drawing of what would be called the "Epworth Auditorium," so named in the hope that the Epworth Leagues of the conference would contribute handsomely toward its construction. It is a stroke of good fortune that the College could not afford to build it, for it was egregiously ugly. Besides, its design accommodated only an auditorium, not a gymnasium at all. Of course, the board of trustees wanted an auditorium while the students and coaches wanted a gymnasium, each conceding that the other had a reasonable claim to second place.[56]

As the years passed and promises of an auditorium-gymnasium came and went, plans for the structure underwent a metamorphosis. Increasingly, the need for an auditorium seemed less urgent and the need for a gymnasium more pressing. Also demanding attention were the Christian associations. Thus, by 1909 a new set of plans was drawn up which emphasized a gymnasium, but with ample space for seating upwards of three thousand persons and rooms for the Y.M.C.A. and Y.W.C.A. and even a swimming pool, which would, said Shelton, "contribute infinite profit and pleasure not only to the school but to town." The building would enable Simpson to bring "the greatest speakers and greatest musicians of the land" to Indianola or to conduct "great gatherings for religious purposes" in a huge gymnasium-auditorium "unsurpassed even by the extravagant expenditure possible to our state institutions." The building, he said, with furnishings would cost a good forty thousand dollars.[57] To Shelton's enthusiastic description Frank Henderson, writing in the *Herald*, added a powerful moral justification for the building, pointing out that the gym would be open to young people, attracting especially the young boys of the city. It would be "the means of keeping them off the street associating with evil companions." While some of his readers might wonder where a boy could find an evil companion in untainted Indianola, he insisted that "the curse of the day is in the harmful amusements that are indulged in by the young," lamenting that "our churches make no effort along the line of amusements."[58]

The arguments in favor of the building, whether practical, commercial or moral, were all persuasive, but for too many years the money was not there. To call the campaign among the Epworth Leagues disappointing would be far too rosy a judgment; the league was simply not interested. As was so often the case with Simpson, it was the Indianola people who came through. Working with Shelton on the project were board members Carl Sigler and Harry E. Hopper '93, both powerful local businessmen, and the three of them were able to announce in early 1910 that three-quarters of the funds were either pledged or in hand. They recommended to the board that construction should proceed at the earliest possible date.[59] But only six days earlier Shelton had announced his resignation,[60] and the board postponed action on the new building until a new president could take office. While it was a disappointment to Shelton that he could not see through the construction of his gymnasium-auditorium, he could depart with a reasonable assurance that it would finally be built.

Meanwhile the College built a library.

When the musicians moved into their new building in late 1902, the library was relocated to the ground floor of the Administration Building.[61] Libraries were, Shelton noted with relief, a lot quieter than pianists or sopranos. Apart from that, the tiny library was growing, especially since Lucy Silliman of Nevada, Iowa, donated one thousand dollars to establish "a working reference library" at Simpson.[62] More than 1,000 books were added by late 1904, bringing the book collection to 4,203 volumes, still pathetically meager but much improved over its former state. Meanwhile the city of Indianola was building a fine public library with a generous gift from Andrew Carnegie.[63] If Mr. Carnegie could build a library for Indianola, why not one for Simpson College as well, reasoned Shelton. Although some townspeople were quite certain the great philanthropist would surely not consider two projects in the same small Iowa town,[64] Shelton and his board persevered, and, with the willing assistance of Senator Jonathan P. Dolliver, fired off a request to Carnegie and received an unexpectedly rapid response. Carnegie would grant Simpson ten thousand dollars toward its new library.[65]

Shelton was jubilant. "Bully!" he exclaimed when he heard the news, and the local press rejoiced with him and for him: "Too much praise cannot be awarded Dr. Shelton for his splendid success in acquiring this fine gift to the college."[66] To no one's surprise the architectural plans were drawn up by Proudfoot and Bird and the contract awarded to Elias Proudfoot in mid-1906.[67] Construction was soon under way and proceeded rapidly. By the time school started in the fall the building was entirely enclosed, and the finishing work was commencing on the inside. At the beginning of the winter term in January, books were transferred into shelving in the new structure, which everyone could see was much larger than Simpson's modest book collection required. Therefore, both the psychology and philosophy departments were moved into the building.[68] They, together with the School of Oratory, the Y.M.C.A., Y.W.C.A. and registrar, occupied the entire ground floor. The library, "a thing of beauty, light and well arranged," was comfortably housed upstairs in a large room with bookcases all round and a fine vaulted ceiling.[69] Although the exterior of the building would never win any architectural prizes, the well-appointed rooms inside were attractive and serviceable.

On a lovely June afternoon in 1907 the Carnegie Library was dedicated in the midst of a busy commencement week. The principal speaker, Harvey Ingham, legendary editor of the *Des Moines Register and Leader* and one of the best-known

Iowans, held forth quite appropriately on the virtues and advantages of the small college, calling upon upward-striving Simpson students to avail themselves of the splendid opportunities that awaited them. The Reverend Fletcher Homan, on behalf of the board of trustees, presented the library to the College, whereupon Raymond Baird, speaking for the graduating seniors, presented eight handsome oak tables to be placed in the reading room of the library, and his presentation was followed by a series of acceptances and music by a faculty-student string quartet. At the close of these exercises the audience was escorted to the new building "to behold the object of the afternoon's celebration."[70] Shelton enjoyed the tour so much that three days later he conducted one himself for the entire board of trustees.[71]

In his brief remarks at the dedication ceremony, Shelton predicted that "the time will never come when we will need the whole building" for the book collection. Yet little more than a decade later the library occupied the entire building, and the staff was complaining of overcrowding. Shelton was surely a fine historian; he was a poor prophet.[72]

The four new buildings erected between 1900 and 1907, and very nearly a fifth, if the near-realization of the gymnasium-auditorium is taken into account, would endure as a lasting monument to the enterprise of Shelton and the generosity of Indianolans and church people around the conference. It is true that so much construction activity strained the finances of the College, but few could gainsay either the need or the worth of these new facilities in a time of rapid growth. It is true that four score years later only one of Shelton's buildings, the library, now known as the Art Center, is still standing, and even that one no longer serves the purpose for which it was originally intended; still each of these structures served generations of students and served them well.

To these major projects one may add a number of modest undertakings—things beyond ordinary maintenance—that improved the appearance of the campus and the safety and operation of the College's programs. New brick or cement walks were laid, joining one building to the others; a well was dug to provide the college its own water supply; the two thoroughly inadequate gymnasiums were spruced up to serve until a real one could be built; athletic fields were moved and moved again as new buildings encroached upon or totally overran their grounds; and electric lights were installed in all the buildings. The College was beginning to fill up its parklike campus, and it soon became evident that in the not-too-distant future more land would be needed to keep up with Simpson's growth. Accordingly, when two full city blocks just north of the campus were offered for sale early in the decade, Shelton and most of his board favored acquiring them,[73] but hesitated because of the press of new construction. A few years later they considered the purchase again, but by this time the price had risen to five thousand dollars,[74] and even though the *Simpsonian* urged them to proceed,[75] they could not see their way clear to act.

Soon enough the problem was solved for them. William Buxton purchased the land from E. W. Hartman and deeded it to the city of Indianola to be used as a park, the town's first. He then asked the city to vacate the street that separated the park land from the College.[76] In this transaction Buxton had the best interests of both the College and the city at heart. On the one hand it provided Indianola a public garden and arboretum that soon became a source of community pride, named Buxton Park by grateful city fathers. On the other hand it edged the

Simpson campus on the north, providing, with its wide swards of lawn, decorative flower beds and graceful trees, a lovely approach to the College. Moreover, by placing that land into a sort of arboreal mortmain, it protected Simpson from the almost irresistible temptation to put up buildings on it. Thus today it retains its pristine beauty, undefaced and unbuilt upon.

* * *

Shelton would be remembered more for the buildings he put up than the budgets he balanced, but in fact the finances of the College during the first decade of the twentieth century were less troublesome than they had been during the nineties. Actually the word *budget* is inappropriate, for it was only in the middle of the decade that the board of trustees could be persuaded that making estimates of anticipated income and expenses would be somehow useful. In any case, in the eleven years of his administration, only one year showed a serious deficit, and a few were marked by modest surpluses.[77] At the same time Simpson's endowment, small by any measure, grew from $42,000 to $81,000 and with it the College's income from its investments, derived mostly from mortgage loans.

Fund-raising drives followed each other with little or no interval. The Twentieth Century Fund, started in the late nineties, never did do very well and limped into the first year of the new century without signal result. Shelton began talking with the board as early as 1904 about a Jubilee Campaign to commence in 1905 and run through the College's golden anniversary in 1910.[78] When the fund drive got under way, one of the most attractive features of it was a scheme whereby a donor could, for a gift of $1,000, set up a full-tuition scholarship in perpetuity.[79] In a day when no one considered the possibility of inflation of prices, such a plan seemed eminently reasonable. Years later the College would encounter problems when donors insisted that their $1,000, which earned between $30 and $50 per year, pay full tuition of their nominee regardless of the amount of the College's annual charges.

The Jubilee Campaign went well, especially because the College secured the services of the Reverend Fletcher Homan as field secretary in the fall of 1905. He was surely the best fund-raiser Simpson had encountered in its history.[80] The goal was ambitious: raise the College's endowment to $100,000 by 1910.

The biggest boost to Simpson's finances came when Shelton and Homan made a trip to New York City and came home with a challenge from Andrew Carnegie: raise $80,000 for the endowment and Carnegie would match it with $20,000.[81] Shelton and Homan went to work, making the tedious rounds of conference congregations. "I hate begging for money," said Shelton, who found fund-raising the least attractive part of his work. Homan, on the other hand, seemed to enjoy these financial forays hugely. Shelton was glad he did, and when their efforts began to pay off, the whole enterprise seemed to be worth it. It was back in Indianola, however, that things went best.

The day really wasn't auspicious at all, a dreary, frigid Sunday in January 1907, most of the large congregation of the Methodist Episcopal Church not having been alerted to what awaited them as they filed into the sanctuary. Promptly at 10:30 A.M. Fletcher Homan opened the service, put up a big chalkboard, and started asking for $1,000 contributions to Simpson's endowment. His skill at working up an audience to a fever pitch of excitement never served him better. Shelton recalled that he gave a performance he would place "somewhere between that of a cattle auctioneer and a Pentecostal evangelist." One after another of the most prominent townspeople, caught up in the spirit of the event, responded to the call and pledged $1,000, until $13,000 had been promised, after which yet another $2,000 was pledged in smaller amounts. It was hard to turn Homan down, especially when Homan himself made the first $1,000 commitment. The Doxology was sung, the meeting was over, and Shelton, radiant with the glow of success, fairly shouted "Bully! Bully for Simpson!" It was, its gloomy weather notwithstanding, a "red letter day in the life of Simpson College."[82] So pleased were Homan and Shelton with their achievement that they went out and raised another $7,000 in Indianola in a matter of days. The match for the Carnegie offer was going to be met.

When Homan left Simpson eighteen months later to accept the presidency of Willamette University in Oregon, Shelton was truly sorry to see him go. Homan would not be the last man to be selected for a college presidency because of his fund-raising ability.

Homan and Shelton had done their work well. When the president received a telegram in January, 1910, from Carnegie that his check for $20,000 would reach him in a few days, the College bells rang for half an hour.[83]

Much of what they raised in those days went to pay for new buildings, but at the end of the decade Simpson's productive endowment, as we have seen, had very nearly doubled. And although the College's debt also increased—from $15,400 in 1899 to $25,900 in 1910—it seemed to be more manageable as time went on.

Meanwhile, tuition income increased sharply because of enrollment gains and because Shelton was able to raise tuition charges from $32.00 per year in 1899, first to $39.50 in 1902, then to $41.00 in 1904 and $56.00 ($46.00 tuition and a $5.00 per semester "registration fee") in 1909. He would have raised it yet more, but he had to watch what other schools were charging—especially Drake and the other Iowa Methodist colleges—and what the conference would find acceptable.

* * *

President Shelton enjoyed a powerful reputation as an educator in Iowa. His experience in public education and his wide acquaintance in school circles in the state served him well. Always active in the Iowa State Teachers' Association, he was elected its president at the end of 1901 for the 1902 year.[84] Later that summer he was appointed a curator of the State Historical Society.[85] Soon enough he was regarded a spokesman both for public education and history. At the close of his term as head of the teachers' association his presidential address combined a knowledge of both. To say the least, his remarks were controversial. "Something must be done for our country schools," declared Shelton. "Three-fourths of the teaching of the rural schools of Iowa is absolutely worthless," and a large portion of youngsters "come to manhood practically untaught." Apart from a few exceptionally bright children, most rural children "can hardly read, can cipher but little, and can use the English sentence not at all with accuracy."[86] The fault, he said, lay not with the teachers or superintendents; both were "underpaid, and overburdened." Rather the problem was the people's "unawareness of the problems of rural education."[87] Too many of the ungraded country schools were of poor quality, and in too many rural areas high schools were nonexistent. Small wonder Simpson, like other colleges in Iowa, maintained a strong preparatory department.

Shelton's indictment of the state of rural education caused a storm of controversy and a lot of defensive rhetoric on the merits of the one-room school. His purpose, of course, was to provoke state officials and politicians to take action to remedy the sorry condition of the struggling country schools.

The president's interest in education and history, together with his love of travel, led him to take his family abroad as often as he could. Usually, through connections with one or more professional tour groups, he led tours to various parts of Europe. In those days not many Americans, except missionaries or a few business people, had either the means or the desire to travel long distances, but Shelton was not an ordinary American. During his years at Simpson he took his family abroad three times, twice for a summer and once for the better part of a year. For the latter journey he was granted a leave of absence beginning in June 1906 to study the schools of Great Britain, returning in late March of the next year, arriving home in ample time to dedicate the College's new Carnegie Library. While he was away, old reliable William E. Hamilton served as acting president. Shelton returned to Europe for the entire summer of 1908, this time to Greece and then to the Near East for the entire summer of 1908, where he "has been studying history, in which he has been specializing for years."[88] This time he managed to get back to Indianola only two days before school opened in the fall. He was planning yet another trip abroad when he resigned in 1910.

Shelton was not the only one to travel abroad. The language professors and especially the music people went to Europe, especially France and Germany, for further training. In fact, few musicians considered themselves truly prepared in their art without study with European masters. Between 1901 and 1910 Barrows went to Europe no fewer than six times, twice (1903–04 and 1905–06) for a full year. The highlight of his travels was surely a year of study with Camille Saint Saens and Gabriel Faure in Paris. Winfred Colton spent two years in Germany, Olive a year in Berlin, Leach fifteen months in Italy and Emslie a summer in London. In literature and foreign language several people studied summers in Europe, notably Elizabeth Bentley in literature, Ida B. Steyer in German, together with Martha Stahl and Mary O. Hunting in Latin. Joanna Baker traveled the farthest, visiting her father in the U.S. Consulate in Australia before making her way around the world. It would be difficult to label the faculty of Simpson provincial.

With all that coming and going, it was sometimes difficult for the College's officers to keep track of the conservatory. Music, we can recall, was managed separately from the rest of the College, yet was a part of it. Its building was constructed and maintained with College funds; much of its most expensive equipment, like pianos, was charged to the Simpson general account, but all music student tuitions and faculty salaries were collected and disbursed by the director. And Barrows, as we have already noted, had little head for business, or at least for keeping accounts that anyone else could make out. When board members discovered, for example, that the College still owed twenty-six hundred dollars for more than twenty new pianos and an organ that Barrows had charged to the College, which derived no income from the conservatory, they made it clear to the director that he might charge no more equipment to the College.

They lamented that they did not know whether the conservatory's accounts were in surplus or deficit. Barrows didn't know either, and the matter was dropped.

The conservatory's impenetrable finances were only a part of the problem. No one was quite certain, but when Arthur Emslie suddenly resigned at the end of the academic year in 1906, people noticed that tension had developed between him and the director in spite of their long-standing friendship. Had Emslie gone off to another college in another state, there likely would have been no problem. But he did not. He remained in Indianola and that summer organized with considerable fanfare what he called the "Independent Conservatory of Music," in direct competition with Simpson's music school.[89]

Barrows was surprised and angered, but he was too much of a gentleman to say anything. But then Emslie was a gentleman too, and he never was heard to say an unkind word about Frank Barrows. It was a sort of Warren County standoff, neither of the two men willing to cut the other one down. To say the least, Indianola was not large enough to support two conservatories, however worthy, and both Barrows and Emslie knew it. Their contest was fascinating, the talk of the town: genteel, cultured, well-mannered and absolutely deadly.

Each would outperform the other. Emslie, whose forte was vocal music, was extraordinarily effective with large vocal ensembles or operatic companies. Barrows could draw upon the talents of his thoroughly competent faculty, fortified by the appointment of Emslie's successor, Joseph Leach, on whose shoulders would fall the principal task of overmatching their rival.

So confident was Barrows at first that Emslie's conservatory would fail that he went ahead with plans for a leave of absence for himself and for two of his young colleagues, Olive and Colton. All three of them spent the entire next year in Germany.

Meanwhile, Emslie rented temporarily rooms in the Indianola Bank Block and on September 11, 1905, opened his Independent Conservatory of Music and hired a staff, consisting of his wife and Effie Silliman.[90] He advertised for students, a considerable number of whom came to him because of the excellent reputation he had earned during his Simpson years. All this seemed, however, to have no visible effect on the College conservatory, where enrollment actually increased from 304 to 333 in the 1905–06 academic year. When Leach, to no one's surprise, replaced Emslie as director of the choir at the Methodist Church,[91] Emslie simply transferred his allegiance and took over the Presbyterian choir, reasoning that this was certainly an appropriate move for a Scotsman. At the same time, he opened a class in Winterset, expanding his musical outreach, but that enterprise lasted only a few months.[92] More successful was a fine sixteen-voice madrigal choir which drew more than 600 listeners to one of its concerts.[93] The following spring he pulled together enough singers and instrumentalists to put on two performances at Spray's Opera House of Verdi's *Il Trovatore*, a successful effort, declared Emslie, in spite of his being the "butt of ridicule and laughter" for attempting such an ambitious production. People were saying that he could not do more than "a few scraps" of the opera, he wrote in a letter to the *Advocate-Tribune*, but he did the whole thing, and all with local talent.[94]

When Emslie reopened his school in the fall of 1906 and Barrows had returned from his year abroad and Leach from a summer in Milan studying with Signor Leoni, the rivalry intensified and came to a dramatic climax when both Barrows and Emslie resolved to perform Haydn's oratorio *The Creation* at holiday time.

Both men went to work to assemble a huge chorus, soloists, accompanists and orchestral talent, each vowing to outdo the other. Each advertised widely in the local press, drumming up interest in what was becoming a mighty contest of talents and wills. The press kept score: Emslie would use a chorus of sixty voices (September 13); at Simpson 150 showed up for rehearsal (September 27); Emslie's performance promised to be the best since he did it back in 1899 (October 11); Emslie's chorus was now 80 (October 18); Barrows and Leach were pushing their singers hard while Emslie started rehearsing twice a week (November 1); Arthur Middleton would sing in Emslie's oratorio (November 8); Simpson's version would perform at the Methodist Church, Emslie's at the Presbyterian Church (November 15).[95] Then, a few days before his November 21 performance, Emslie declared "we are ready to show a fair minded public that we can deliver the goods as advertised." He added that "we are the only school in Indianola to give the oratorio complete; all we want is a fair field and no favor. . . . The time for talk is over. We just let the people judge."[96]

Emslie's *Creation was* good, presented to a packed house and earning hearty applause. But the Simpson performance was better. "The grandest production of 'The Creation' ever witnessed in Indianola," proclaimed the *Advocate-Tribune*, "was that presented by the Simpson conservatory of music at the Methodist Church last Wednesday [December 12]." A "magnificent" 135-voice chorus was matched by the conservatory orchestra, "undoubtedly the best orchestra in the West." And in an oblique reference to Emslie's production the critic added "To the conservatory is due the credit of having presented, we believe for the first time in Indianola, 'The Creation' without having to send away for one or more soloists." And Barrows at the pipe organ played "in his usual masterly style."

Barrows and Leach had won. About the best Emslie could do after that was advertise his school as one that operated with "no graft," whatever that meant.[97] His school went downhill from that time on, and soon enough he was looking for something better. Fortunately he was invited to direct the school of music at Colorado Agricultural College (now Colorado State University) at Fort Collins, a position he held for many years. Before he left Indianola that summer, he put on one last opera festival, which earned lavish praise in the press.[98] And, as the years went on, it appears that neither Emslie nor Barrows bore a grudge. Two gentlemen had struggled in clean rivalry; one had been driven from the field, but he survived to play another day on another field.

* * *

In many ways Alexander Emslie's rival music school had the ultimate effect of strengthening Simpson's, and President Shelton who had been happy to have an excuse not to intervene or even give advice during the two-year contest, was of course pleased that the conservatory emerged the victor. On another field of play, however, he was forced to take an active role in a dispute he would have preferred to avoid, for it had nothing to do with the curriculum or the academic mission of the College. The problem was football.

As the reader will recall, Simpson had first organized a football team in 1892 and played an intercollegiate schedule only since 1893, but by the time Shelton came to Simpson, the sport was well established and very popular among the students. Coached by recent young Simpson graduates who had played well or by equally young instructors who had distinguished themselves in the game, usually at the State University of Iowa, Simpson teams performed very well through the fantastic 1903 season—in their first five games that year they scored 216 points to their opponents 0—only to falter in 1904 and 1905. It was in 1904 that the Simpson eleven received their worst drubbing in history, an 87–0 loss to Iowa Agricultural College at Ames. They could take some small comfort that on that same day Grinnell lost to the University of Minnesota 126–0 and Wisconsin walloped Drake 81–0. It was a bad day for Iowa football.[99] But win or lose, football grew more acclaimed. And rougher.

"Football is rough," admitted a *Simpsonian* writer in 1900. "It is rather too rough for girls, as it is a little more vigorous and taxing than croquet. Boys . . . of slender physique . . . should not be allowed to play."[100] But the writer would agree that although there was a fine line between "clever tactics and foul play," football should not be condemned merely because it was rough. He would agree with the sentiment uttered later by President Theodore Roosevelt, deploring the idea that any college "turn out mollycoddles instead of vigorous men."[101] Still, football was a dangerous game, especially so because players were afforded little protection, either by their uniforms and helmets or by the rules of the game. In 1905 alone, eighteen young Americans died playing football. That year John Tilton, who loved the game, conceded in an article in the *Des Moines Register and Leader* that football was too rough and suggested substituting a sort of outdoor basketball played on a 100-yard field, a suggestion that found no favorable response.[102] Joe Trigg, writing in the *Iowa State Register*, said "reform in football is as impossible as it is in cussedness."[103] Many college administrations agreed, and, following Harvard's lead in early 1906, abolished intercollegiate football. Columbia, California, Stanford and others gave up football for a decade. Others either suspended or completely eliminated it. Grinnell and the state normal school at Cedar Falls responded to the trend and abolished football. At Simpson the game's roughness was the chief source of opposition, but the faculty was also concerned about rowdiness at the games and reports of widespread gambling, not to speak of what they considered unethical recruitment. Had not coach Amos Alonzo Stagg at the University of Chicago once tried to lure standout player and team captain Bert Kennedy away from Simpson?[104] The College's board members, dismayed by the "physical and moral" dangers of the game and baffled by its popularity with students, voted in the spring of 1906 to abolish intercollegiate football. Students reacted with disappointment, but accepted the decision handed down from on high.

For two seasons Simpson played no intercollegiate football.[105] A fairly elaborate intramural program kept interest in the sport alive while not really lessening the dangers of the game.[106] In 1907 and again in 1908 the board received petitions seeking the reinstatement of the sport.[107] And, persuaded that safer uniforms—especially helmets—and appropriate rule changes were forthcoming, the board, by a narrow vote of twelve to ten, restored football in June 1908, effective in the coming fall season.[108] The students rejoiced. Shelton, who accepted the roughness of football so long as it was clean, fair and reasonably safe, breathed a sigh of presidential relief.

Football was not the only part of the extracurriculum that demanded the president's attention. During the course of his administration the "fraternity question" continued to occupy more of his time, and that of the faculty and board, than it should have. For part of the problem Shelton was himself responsible.When he arrived in 1899, there existed only two sororities—Pi Beta Phi and Tridelta—and no fraternities, the others for the most part driven out by the spirit of religious revivalism that had characterized student life in much of the nineties. It was soon evident to everyone that while Shelton was a good Methodist, he was not much of a revivalist, and did not encourage or find to his taste the kind of spiritual emotionalism he found on the campus. Then, perhaps, the revivalist crusade had simply run its course, and with its disappearance one could sense a decline of opposition to "secret" organizations. The mood of the campus changed.

Thus, when a group of sixteen young men organized a local fraternity in the fall of 1902, neither Shelton nor the faculty nor the students voiced any opposition to it.[109] At least not immediately. For two reasons Shelton was inclined to favor the new Kappa Theta Psi group. He had been a member of Beta Theta Pi when he was a student at Iowa Wesleyan and had enjoyed his fraternity experience. Perhaps more important, however, was the fact that his own seventeen-year old sophomore son, Whitford, was a charter member of the new fraternity. In any case, neither he nor most of the faculty bore any animosity toward Greek-letter societies, so long as they behaved themselves, and the new Kappa Theta Psi found an atmosphere of acceptance on campus. Less than two months later a second men's group appeared, at first calling itself Alpha Phi and later Alpha Iota Phi.[110] "The new fraternal life," declared the *Simpsonian*, "is the result of the growing condition of the school."[111] Indeed it was, but it would have been unthinkable without Shelton.

Soon Kappa Theta Psi sought a charter from Sigma Alpha Epsilon and Alpha Iota Phi from Alpha Tau Omega, two national fraternities from earlier days. Kappa Theta Psi's petition failed, and the boys decided to remain a local society; Alpha Iota Phi was chartered by the ATOs and reinstated toward the end of the 1904–05 academic year.[112] That same year a new local sorority was established, calling itself Alpha Alpha Gamma. Two years later it was chartered as the Mu chapter of Alpha Chi Omega. And yet another men's group appeared in 1905, called Phi Delta Kappa. After an unsuccessful attempt to gain a national charter, however, the group died out after a little more than three years' existence.

It was perhaps inevitable that this flurry of activity among the Greeks should arouse opposition among those students who found them to be elitist, clannish and, worst of all, secret. Between 1905 and 1910 a small group of students repeatedly petitioned the president, the faculty and the board of trustees to abolish Greek-letter societies. Because their antifraternity views were vigorously supported by many among the clerical contingent on the board and by a few faculty led by respected veteran William Hamilton, Shelton, in spite of his personal views, saw to it that they received a respectful hearing. The leaders of the antifraternity forces included the College's leading prohibition orator, together with a young woman headed for missionary service in India and a member of the leading men's literary society, a serious group indeed.[113] The board of trustees was inclined to leave the control of fraternities to the faculty; the faculty preferred not to deal with the matter at all. Frustrated, the antifraternity forces took their case to the Methodist conference which met at Osceola in September 1905, but the conference properly judged that it was an internal Simpson matter and referred it back to the board of trustees.

Undaunted, the dissatisfied petitioners presented their case several more times to the conference, each time receiving the same response as before. At length the board of trustees, hoping to clarify its own position in the controversy, resolved that since "fraternities now exist among the students, and have existed for a long time, therefore . . . we do not now deem it wise to take any action whatsoever on the petition referred to us [again] by the annual conference which looks to the interference with existing conditions, but the supervision of fraternities be left as far as practicable to the governing body of the institution."[114] But such was the persistence of the anti-Greeks that they, supported by the "barb" editor of the *Simpsonian*, persuaded the faculty to call for an investigation by the board and faculty together of "the relation of the fraternities and soroses to the college." To this the board was agreeable and in 1910 appointed three trustees to "look into the matter."

While the Greek-letter societies were disliked by some, they were popular with most of the students. Their rivalry was for the most part healthy, and their presence was surely not as divisive as, say, class competition. Students' identification with their graduating class, complete with class colors, yells and songs was powerful. And sometimes the rivalry got out of hand, as it did in the spring of 1905 when a spirited competition between classes erupted into disorder and what some called "criminality," necessitating the intervention of the local Indianola gendarmerie. An embarrassed board of trustees deplored such "lawlessness and hoodlumism" and called for stiff penalties against the offenders.[115] The following fall Shelton delivered a stern lecture on rowdyism,[116] but he was of the growing conviction that students must take responsibility for their own behavior, individually and collectively. A patriarchal system might safely give way to a more nearly democratic one.

A few months later he created the College Council, the membership of which included three from each of the four undergraduate classes, one each from the academy and the conservatory, two faculty people (one a professor and the other an instructor) selected by their colleagues, and the president of the college ex officio. The council was empowered to deal with "any alleged offense of any student against good morals, good manners, or the order and discipline of the school," but did not "in any manner release the faculty from ultimate responsibility" for governing the College.[117] The College Council was an instant success, and a year later was seen to "promise much good," whether dealing with class rivalry, chapel disorder, or some breach of the rules like card playing or smoking cigarettes. More significantly, it was able to revise the "entrance pledge" which had required each student to agree to a long list of prohibitions printed in the current catalog. The new agreement, adopted in 1907, simply stated that no student would be permitted to remain at Simpson "whose connection with it is injurious to others or unprofitable to himself."[118] There was more here than just a change in wording; it was a bold step in democratizing the campus and changing the attitude of students toward themselves and their relationships with others. The importance of Shelton's contribution to this process cannot be overemphasized.

Some observers insisted that the improvement in student behavior—at least that of the boys—could be accounted for by the rigors of military discipline in the Simpson Battalion. In 1901 the formerly voluntary military drill was made compulsory for freshmen men and for all male academy, normal, business and shorthand students. Six years later the obligation was extended to two full years for undergraduates. Drill was held normally twice a week, later increased to three times per week in fall and spring. During the nineties the battalion had been managed by a faculty member, usually John Tilton, on a part-time basis, but in 1900 the U.S. Army posted retired Captain (later Major) Daniel Robinson to Simpson as instructor in military science and tactics. A disciplinarian he was, but the students liked this crusty old warrior—he must have been nearly seventy—who had fought Seminoles, Apaches, Navajos, Utes and Mormons, not to speak of rebels in the Civil War while serving in New Mexico and with the Army of the Potomac.

Shelton thoroughly enjoyed the old soldier's presence on campus and with him conceived the idea of sending the whole battalion to the St. Louis World's Fair in 1904.[119] Soon enough a formal invitation was received and the entire contingent, lacking only a few young farm boys whose help was required at home, left Indianola on June 8 and enjoyed a ten-day holiday, including the great "Iowa Day" at the fair, when they drilled smartly before a huge crowd of onlookers. The commandant was immensely proud of his boys' performance that day.

Robinson stayed at Simpson five years, and there is little doubt that his battalion regimentation helped shape up a lot of small town and farm boys. His successor, Lt. Emory S. West, age thirty, a veteran of four years of warfare in the Philippine Islands, came in 1905 and for nearly three years seems to have served well. Ill health forced his being relieved in late 1908 by Lt. R. M. Nolan, First U.S. Cavalry.

* * *

There is no doubt that throughout the Shelton years Simpson continued to be a denominational college and that participation in religious activities and church attendance was expected of students and faculty alike. Yet during the course of the decade the expression of religion gradually became less and less marked by emotional revivalism. Early in the decade one could hear that "seventeen boys were converted" at one Y meeting or that "thirty-two students became Christians at Rev. Wickersham's revival," but only a few years later such conversion experiences were not mentioned at all.[120] That is not to say that students lost their faith, but many did begin to take up harmless secular interests. A few of their leaders, to be sure, would continue to inveigh against dancing—a favorite antidancing tract was entitled "Dancing with Satan"—or take to the lecture platform to condemn strong drink. But most Simpson undergraduates, not to speak of the academy youngsters, were interested in social good times and sports and all the wondrous gadgetry that America was producing in abundance, from phonographs to automobiles. Toward the end of the decade the student editor of the *Simpsonian* observed ruefully that attendance at the College's voluntary spiritual meetings "could have been improved upon."[121]

Although they were increasingly attracted to the many manifestations of secular culture, they harbored stern prejudice against the urban world from which that culture emanated. Simpson's enviable "balance of soul and body," wrote one student, was due to the fact that "our students are rural bred," which allowed them to be "in touch with [the] practicality of agriculture and the exhilerating [sic] freshness of natural scenes. Very few of our number are purely city bred or tainted with the foul breath of urban corruption."[122] Their lovely college, in its bucolic setting, provided them with the best of all worlds. Whether such views represented charming naivete or insufferable provincialism probably remained in the eye of the beholder.

Whatever the appeal of the rural Midwest, the prevalence of illness was as serious in Indianola as it was in the big city, and death was a common visitor. We read often of faculty and students struck down by grave illness. Mathematician Billy Read had to resign after eleven years to go to Colorado to try to survive tuberculosis. Old William Hamilton was ill for weeks at a time. Ida Steyer was out for a full term suffering from an "unknown malady." J. Allen Baker nearly died of typhoid fever the first summer he was in Indianola. President Shelton's wife, Julia, suffered ill health for years and died a few years after she and her husband left Simpson. Students were no more protected from illness than were their elders. In one year alone—1901–02—three students died, Bobbie Brown of tuberculosis, Grace Erickson of acute appendicitis and, in January 1902, Mary Berry of both a congenital disease and complications from surgery.

The death of Mary Berry struck the campus with grief, for she was one of Simpson's most loved and respected undergraduates. She was the daughter of former President Thomas S. Berry. When she was only three years old he died in office and within months her mother died as well. Reared by her uncle and aunt, Captain and Mrs. B. C. Berry, until she was ten, she was sent to live with the William H. Berrys, who gave her a home until just a year before her death when she returned to live with Mrs. B. C. Berry. Suffering from the same congenital disease that had struck down her father and his father before that, she developed appendicitis on top of that, and after surgery died on January 28, 1902. A member of Delta Delta Delta, she was popular with her classmates, one of whom wrote "Christian duty was well defined in her mind and in her quiet sweet manner she did an inestimable good to those about her."[123]

Mary Berry left half of her modest estate to Simpson as an endowment "for the purchase of scientific equipment." Her sister, Hattie Berry Morley '93, cooperated in the establishment of the fund, in the amount of $3,622.12, which was incorporated into the College's endowment.[124]

Her estate was not the only thing that would keep alive the memory of this extraordinary young woman. Several years later the decision was taken to rename the Ladies Boarding Hall Mary Berry Hall. The remodeled building was formally dedicated November 6, 1908, at an elegant reception in the "beautiful new parlors" of the building. The guest of honor for the occasion was Hattie Berry Morley, whose husband, the Reverend John P. Morley '93, was a recent addition to the College's board of trustees.[125]

The reception that dedicated Mary Berry Hall was fairly typical of the social events that highlighted the school year at Simpson. Class picnics, "bums," daring rides in Professor Miller's new automobile, fraternity and sorority open houses and banquets of all sorts relieved the routine of classes. It is incredible how elaborate many of the banquets were. When, for example, Mayor Clayton of Indianola hosted a dinner for the 1901 winning football team, their Sunday repast at the Todhunter Hotel included veal broth, roast beef with brown gravy, roast pork, baked chicken with dressing, giblets with celery sauce, raisin fritters with lemon sauce, escalloped oysters, mashed potatoes, stewed tomatoes, corn, coleslaw, pickles and other condiments, gooseberry, cherry and mince pie and lemon pudding.[126]

Then there were sports events in their season, literary society speeches and debates, lectures by nationally known figures. All these provided the students with a relatively rich fare of cultural edification, entertainment and diversion in a day when colleges and small towns had to make their own way in such things.

One of the major events of the year was Founders and Benefactors Day, typically scheduled as near Washington's birthday as possible, when Simpson people, old and young, could celebrate their past with a good dinner and lots of speechmaking. Another was the State Oratorical Association's annual contest, where the College's very best public speakers competed for top honors. The winner came home a conquering hero, properly accorded celebrity status. When, for example, Melvin Roy Talley '03 won the state contest with an oration delivered before two thousand people at the Oskaloosa Opera House on February 27, 1903, the news was flashed back to Indianola late in the evening and the town whistle blown to herald the victory. The following Monday was a day of jubilation. At a rousing 9:00 A.M. chapel, the seniors were attired in caps and gowns, board members beamed and a hoarse President delivered an "inspiring address" followed by yells and songs. Then five hundred cheering students and the College band "marched triumphantly down to the city and massing in the court house yard gave vent to further demonstration." Classes were dismissed for the day. Talley, who later became a clergyman, was the man of the hour, for he brought to his alma mater the highest recognition that could come to an Iowa college in those years. Later few would recall that his oration entitled "Anglo-Saxon Supremacy" was an incredibly ethnocentric exercise in self-congratulation that, had it been delivered today, would be labeled blatantly racist.[127]

Simpson students, like their elders, might have been ethnocentric, hardly a surprise in a day when American leaders talked of doing good unto "our little brown brothers" or "carrying big sticks," in the afterglow of the Spanish-American War, but they were not opposed to women's rights.[128] The issue of women's suffrage was put to a vote of the student body in 1900, and the women did not suffer, 219 voting in their favor, 159 against. It would appear, declared the *Zenith*, that "co-education undoubtedly fosters co-suffrage."[129]

* * *

In the winter of 1910 President Shelton informed his board of trustees that he would resign at the end of the academic year.[130] Much as he loved Simpson, he said, the time seemed right for him to make a change. A number of things impelled him to take this action, he explained, one of which was his wife's continuing ill health. She needed "a more congenial climate."[131] His presidential duties required him to spend too much of the time away from her and from home. Besides, he really disliked fund-raising, and the last couple of years he had been doing a much greater share of the development work than heretofore. The healthy Golden Jubilee Fund, to be sure, was a monument to the success he enjoyed in an enterprise he found distasteful. But the Golden Jubilee itself seemed to mark the end of an era in Simpson's history. Above all Shelton believed that he had done all he could do for Simpson and that the College needed fresh leadership.[132]

When the board could not persuade Shelton to reconsider his action, they asked former President Edmund M. Holmes to head a seven-man committee to find a new president. Holmes set to work at once to make a nationwide search, and as soon as he located a few strong prospects, sent William Berry and Ben

Clayton east in the spring to take a look at them. Upon their return, Berry and Clayton recommended strongly the selection of Francis L. Strickland of Northport, Long Island, a well-known Methodist clergyman of "pleasing and strong personality" who was said to be "at the zenith of his powers."[133]

Strickland was interested, and as soon as it was clear that he was the nominee, set out for Indianola. He was in fact elected by the board on June 3 and pulled in to Indianola on the train the next day with his written acceptance in his pocket.[134] His participation in the Golden Jubilee celebration smoothed the transition from one administration to the other. It was good to see one much-loved man almost literally pass the torch of leadership to his successor, full of promise.

* * *

Of all events of the school year, commencement was still by far the most important. It was homecoming time for alumni, a chance for the literary societies to demonstrate their skills, an opportunity to hear any number of uplifting sermons, and it still lasted a good eight days. The people of Simpson and Indianola seemed to be tireless, flocking to the main events, especially the commencement ceremony itself, in huge numbers. The graduating classes were larger now, and because of that fact, all seniors were no longer required to deliver commencement orations. That seemed to be a relief to everyone, especially to the seniors. For many years honorary degrees had been awarded and conferring them was becoming an increasingly important part of the commencement exercises.

* * *

The event of the decade, to be sure, was the Golden Jubilee celebration of 1910. The great anniversary was commemorated as a part of commencement that year. All the living past presidents were there: Vernon, Parks, Hamilton, Holmes, and Brown.

Three bishops participated, a new president of the College was elected, and ground was broken—more as a promise than a reality—for the new gymnasium. There were speeches and sermons aplenty, dramatic performances, a songfest that featured the publication of a new Simpson song book and even a "very pretty winding of the maypole."[135] The conservatory outdid itself with a huge production of *Aida* at the Methodist Church. At one of the sessions a grateful College presented John H. Henderson a fine gold-headed cane in recognition of his forty-one years of service as secretary of the Board. "There has never been a meeting of the Board," said Shelton, "at which he was not present."[136]

In spite of rain and mud, 510 people paid their fifty cents and showed up for the three-course Golden Jubilee luncheon held in the old gymnasium on June 8. Sam Vernon, at sixty-eight, then residing in Philadelphia, still looked marvelously fit as he spoke, reminiscing warmly about the early days of Simpson. Turning to a timely topic that was on his mind, he could not resist speaking out, to little avail, against intercollegiate football. Parks's address was mostly a tribute to President Thomas S. Berry, whom he succeeded. And newly elected President Francis Strickland spoke discreetly and briefly, realizing perhaps that he was the new man on the scene, well advised not to say too much. John Horsley '09 led the cheering. More than 120 graduates of the College, representing nearly every class since 1871, were present.

At the commencement exercises the next day, as twenty-three seniors received their diplomas, former president Edmund M. Holmes electrified the audience with the announcement that the College had just received a gift of twenty-five thousand dollars from Harry Hopper to endow a chair in Latin in honor of Dr. George Carpenter, whose daughter Hopper had married. Harry Hopper was at that moment considered Indianola's most successful citizen.[137]

Indeed, when it was all over the Golden Jubilee could be accounted one of Simpson's most memorable events ever. And of all the speeches and songs and high drama of the week, no one would be able to forget President Shelton's farewell address. Perhaps more a sermon than a speech, his words were spoken softly, in a fatherly tone that students had come to expect from "Prexie." He talked of love, of not "imputing sinister motives" to the actions of others, ninety-nine out of a hundred of whom "are trying to do the right thing." He urged his students to "make this life count for something which reaches beyond the present."[138] "It was perhaps the most touching speech I have ever heard," said one of the graduating seniors. He was leaving Simpson, he said, because it was time to leave. He would miss it terribly.[139] And he would be missed, too.

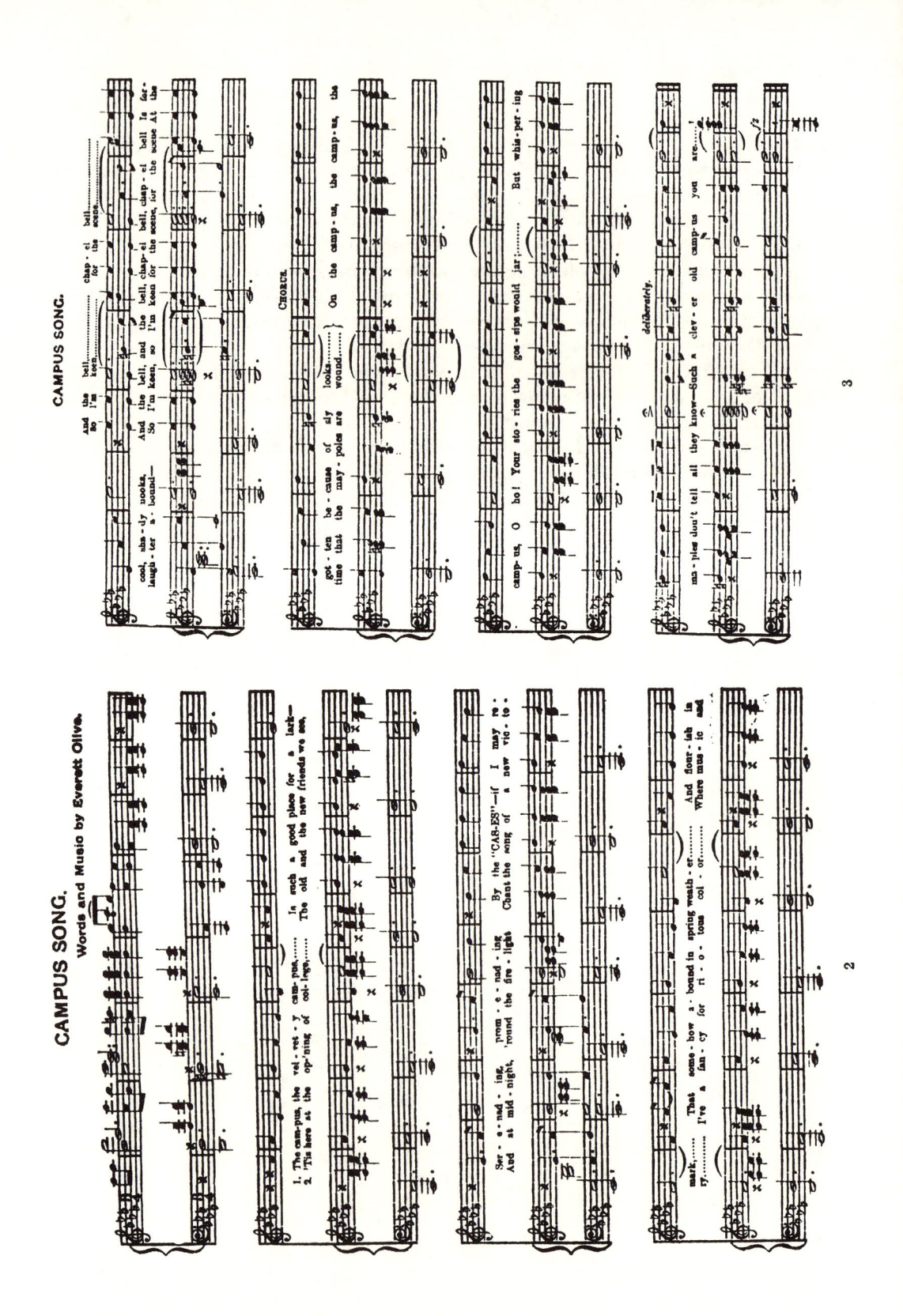

"The campus, the velvety campus . . ." one of Everett "Tip" Olive's many catchy College songs, became a Simpson favorite after the turn of the century.

X

Simpson in Peace and War 1910–19

Anyone who takes a close look at the administrative record of Charles Eldred Shelton's two successors, Francis Strickland and James Campbell, is likely to be struck by an affirmative spirit of continuity that marked their management of the College. They built upon Shelton's success. They put up buildings, hustled for money, prodded the faculty, and looked after the students with increasing intensity, but they did not, nor did they intend to, change the direction of Simpson's growth.

Francis Strickland's five years at Simpson were by any measure quite successful, but as he often reminded his admirers, much of what he was able to accomplish he owed to the quiet competence of his immediate predecessor. James Campbell, although he spoke of it less frequently, recognized his debt to both Shelton and Strickland, and indeed his debt to others, for a president alone does not a college make. Without trustees like William Buxton and Carl Sigler, or faculty giants like William Hamilton, John Tilton or Clyde Emmons, or the good Methodists of Indianola who rallied to the College's aid again and again, even the best president would have been severely handicapped.

When Simpson's trustees selected Francis Lorette Strickland the tenth president of the College, they balanced the fact that he was a New Yorker born and bred against the more weighty consideration that he was a distinguished Methodist minister who sprang from a long line of followers of Wesley. For his part Strickland, age thirty-nine, was ready to strike out and try something new after a decade of pastoral life conducted almost within shouting distance of his birthplace. A college presidency in faraway Iowa seemed to offer the challenge of adventure and the opportunity to explore a new avenue of service.[1]

Strickland was born in Brooklyn, New York, May 8, 1871, to Frank L. and Emily Clauney Strickland, and was reared in the shadow of the Nostrand Avenue Methodist Episcopal Church, where he attended Sunday school from the time he could remember. He joined the church at the age of twelve, flourished in the faith and by the time he was twenty-one was licensed as a local preacher. Meanwhile he graduated from Brooklyn Polytechnic Institute, a secondary school with an eminent reputation, and entered New York University, where he was a brilliant scholar and a popular member of the elite Psi Upsilon fraternity. After his graduation from N.Y.U., he entered Boston University, where he studied theology, earning his Bachelor of Sacred Theology in 1896. He remained for a few months at Boston as a student in philosophy under Borden P. Bowne, whom he revered as the "great intellectual awakener." Awarded the Jacob Sleeper Fellowship by Boston University, Strickland went to Germany later that year to study first at the University of Jena and then at the University of Berlin, in those days a kind of academic mecca for young American scholars.

Upon his return from abroad, Strickland entered his home conference, the New York East, serving pastorates in Flushing, New York (1899–1902), Bay Shore (1902–06) and Northport (1906–10) on Long Island. Meanwhile he completed the Ph.D. in philosophy at Boston in 1903, the same year he married Antoinette Louise Brown, a graduate of Syracuse University.[2] In his pastoral work, Strickland enjoyed great local success, especially as a speaker and organizer, and after a decade in the pulpit it was said of him that he had "won the recognition in the group of scholarly young ministers in their vicinity."[3]

When the New York *Christian Advocate* learned of Strickland's election to Simpson's presidency, it was lavish in its praise, confident that "he will address himself to the college work with a full knowledge of the requirements and with high educational ideals."[4] Equally impressed was an Indianola editor who called him "scholarly, refined, and devoted."[5] He was after all, an urbane, almost elegant man with sophisticated tastes, and one who, Indianolans soon learned, did not suffer fools gladly. He would have a real adjustment to make in small-town Iowa among the culturally unwashed. And local people, if they were to get along with the new president, would have to curb their almost innate propensity to suspect that anyone who came from the fleshpots of the East, even a Methodist parson, must be somehow stained with evil.

When he first arrived on campus to accept the presidency, Strickland impressed everyone he met with his magisterial bearing, for he spoke with almost painful care in clear, well-crafted sentences. He was a small man, dwarfed by Shelton when they stood together to be photographed. Hair the color of ebony crowned his full face, set off by intense black eyes, aquiline nose, and well-trimmed moustache. He seemed somehow utterly unconscious of his appearance, but Indianola people noticed that he was always well-turned-out, his neat if not elegant dress matching the precision of his discourse.

For their part, the Indianola trustees liked Strickland, and, as soon as they got to know him, so did the students and faculty. Once townspeople discovered that he was no stuffed shirt and could be personable and witty, they came to accept him too. Out in the conference, however, many of the pastors, not to speak of their flocks, found him to be too "modern" for their tastes. Many thought his intellectualism cold and his sermons, delivered with an alien New York accent, strangely unspiritual. Most of all, they feared that he might relax the vigilance he was expected to maintain in monitoring the behavior of the students in his charge.

They needn't have worried. He was as strict in his enforcement of College rules as had been any of his predecessors, and he had ample occasion to do so with students who seemed to be increasingly disposed to test the moral resolve of their mentors.[6] At the same time, he sought to emphasize the positive side of his relationships: at Simpson, he promised, "my ambition will be to be considered the personal friend of every young man and woman who enters her doors."[7] He also reminded students of a truth he understood better than they: "We make some of the finest friendships in life in college, unalloyed by considerations of commercial or political advantage—a dross which too often tarnishes the social relations of later life."[8]

Strickland believed that the most important relationship of all on a college campus was that between students and faculty. "Splendid buildings are good," he wrote, "but splendid teachers are better—men and women of high character, broad scholarship, big ideals and sympathies."[9] He was favorably impressed by the faculty people he found at the college, both because of their quality and their stability. A few of them were working on advanced degrees at important universities in the United States and abroad.[10] With the recruitment of John P. Morley in 1911 and Samuel Weir in 1914 he added two more Ph.D.-holders to the faculty. John Morley had graduated from Simpson in 1893 and earned the doctorate from Boston University in 1902. While in the pastorate he had served several years on the College's board of trustees. He was considered a worthy replacement for beloved William E. Hamilton, who retired in the spring of 1911, accorded the designation "emeritus," the first Simpson professor to be thus honored.[11] Weir, who remained four years at Indianola, took the place of Allen M. Ruggles, whose college-level teaching in education had been considerably less effective than his presiding over the academy. Strickland was not displeased to see him go to Wisconsin to do civil service extension work.

William E. Hamilton's retirement—he planned to go live out his days in Arkansas—seemed to mark the end of an era for Simpson, where the grand old man had enjoyed an association since 1867. Although he genuinely eschewed any sort of attention to mark his leaving, one after another of his former students and faculty colleagues could not forego the pleasure of honoring him, and so came forth with encomiums and reminiscences that did him justice. Martha Stahl Beall, '87, former student and colleague, recalled that during her student days his recitations always "led up to a climax. . . . With kindling eye, buttoning his coat as he arose, the Doctor would advance toward us a few steps and with thundering voice proclaim the eternal verities of God as revealed in his doings with men." Students were, she said, "lifted out of themselves, . . . exhilarated." He was "a very mountain of integrity, a Gibraltar of moral strength." Dr. Tom Throckmorton '07, of Chariton, could remember that when he was in some sort of trouble with Dr. Shelton he went to Hamilton and received good, fatherly advice: "Never," said Hamilton with a chuckle, "flaunt a red flag in an angry bull's face." It is perhaps difficult to think of Shelton as an angry bull, but the advice led young Throckmorton to make his peace with "Prexie." Others, remembering Hamilton's love of truth and love of people, joined Kate Corkhill in calling him "my ideal of an educator."[12] His place would be difficult to fill, but John Morley could handle the job if anyone could.

In keeping with his belief in "splendid teachers," Strickland was extremely careful in replacing departing faculty members. For example, when young John Dunn Martin departed in 1912 after eight years at Simpson—four as a student and four as professor of oratory, registrar and secretary of the faculty—Strickland picked as Martin's replacement an Iowa native, Levi P. Goodwin, a 1910 graduate of Albion College, who had recently been engaged in teaching and the ministry.[13] Goodwin taught both public speaking and English and enjoyed "great success" in forensics, especially debate, during his three-year tenure at the College.[14] Then, when Samuel H. Dodson, Simpson's "open and fearless" historian,[15] resigned in 1913 to go on the lecture circuit in the East, Strickland traveled twenty-five hundred miles and interviewed three men before selecting A. Conn Klinger, an experienced teacher who had just completed two years of graduate study in history at the University of Wisconsin. Klinger, whose specialty was modern European history, remained six years at Simpson.

When Dudley D. Griffith took a leave of absence in 1913 to continue graduate work at the University of Chicago, Strickland persuaded Aubrey W. Goodenough to return to Simpson to teach English literature. Goodenough, whose B.A. was from Oberlin in 1906, held an M.A. from Yale and had taught at Simpson from 1908 to 1910. From Simpson he had gone to Whitman College in Walla Walla, Washington, where he taught for a year, and for the next two years he worked on his Ph.D. at the University of Wisconsin. He remained at Simpson for five more years, during which time his course in contemporary literature attracted as many as sixty students at a time, proving to be the most popular elective course in the College's curriculum.[16]

Actually Strickland's administration was blessed with striking stability in the faculty, especially among the full professors who anchored the teaching staff. He could count on people like Tilton, Joanna Baker, Hunting, Jend, Jenner, J. Allen Baker, Hayward, Emmons and Miller, not to speak of Grace Beam and Carrie Van Gilder in the academy and Frank Barrows in the conservatory.

He was inclined to leave the management of the conservatory to Barrows, whose staff numbered between five and seven during these years. Notable among the new musicians was Herbert A. Harvey, who joined the faculty in the fall of 1911. He was a graduate of the Cincinnati School of Music and taught violin and conducted the orchestra. A talented musician and well-liked teacher, Harvey became a fixture at Simpson, and after Barrows's death in 1924 he took over the leadership of the conservatory, a position he held until his retirement in 1940.

An exception to the gratifying stability of Simpson's faculty was the position in French, which Strickland noted had about as much reliability as the premiership in the French Republic. During Strickland's first year, what French there was was taught by Hildegarde Jend, whose classes in German would have kept her quite busy without the additional burden of a second language. In 1911 Katherine MacLaggan joined the faculty full-time in French. Well-prepared, MacLaggan was a graduate of Bucknell University and had taught two years at Crandan Hall in Rome before continuing her studies at the University of Grenoble. She came to Simpson directly from a year-long teaching stint at Beaver College in Pennsylvania. But she remained only two years, replaced by Louise Wellwood from Kansas, whose broad experience included teaching French in America, English in France and both English and French in Santo Domingo. Wellwood lasted only a year at Simpson, whereupon she went off to Central America to teach. Her successor was Florence Hier, whose tenure at Simpson was only two years. She held an M.A. from the University of Cincinnati and had studied in France.[17]

Hildegarde Jend in German made a fateful decision in 1914 to take a year off to go to Berlin for additional study, and Strickland engaged as her replacement Blanche A. Roe, a Bryn Mawr Ph.D. who had studied at Jena, Berlin and Leipzig. Jend sailed to Germany early in the summer. When the First World War broke out, however, she decided to return to the United States. For the rest of that school year she resided with her mother in Detroit until she could return to Simpson, full of tales about a world gone mad.[18]

Simpson's faculty consisted in those days of two groups, one of older people whose teaching careers had commenced before the doctorate was typically expected for a professorship, even in the best small colleges, and another of young, upward-striving teacher-scholars for whom Simpson College was a stopping-off place on the way to a doctorate and a life of teaching and research in a large university. There were, of course, exceptions: J. Allen Baker later earned the doctorate and, like fellow scientist Tilton, stayed on at Simpson throughout his teaching career. Then there were remarkable women like Joanna Baker, Mary Hunting and Hildegarde Jend, all of whom were respected teachers and accomplished scholars. Still, Strickland would have liked to attract more Ph.D.s to the faculty.

One reason for Simpson's failure to bring in more Ph.D.s was its relatively low salary scale. In the academy, for example, Grace Beam was paid only $700 per year—$50 less than the custodian in the gymnasium—as late as 1915, while Mary Hunting and Joanna Baker earned $1,000 each, and neither had a salary increase during the entire decade after 1910. Even John Tilton, at the top of the salary scale, received only $1,700 per annum. Strickland himself was hardly overpaid; he received $3,000 annually, and he saw no raise during his five-year tenure at Simpson. The College's finances, more often in deficit than not, could afford no more.

Strickland believed the College must do better, reporting to his trustees in 1912: "We cannot afford to retain inferior teachers simply because they will stay for small salaries. Nor can we afford to employ inexperienced teachers, allowing them to pass on to other institutions as soon as their effectiveness has been increased by experience."[19] But then one could never expect to make much money teaching in a church-related college. Serving as a faculty member was a commitment, a dedication of one's life to the betterment of humankind, like preaching or nursing or taking the gospel to the heathen. One must not presume to profit in the service of the Lord.

*   *   *

Piety was surely not confined only to the faculty. A fair number of students, especially those who saw themselves as postulates looking toward a lifetime of Christian service, were genuinely, unabashedly devout. And, as one might expect, most members of the board of trustees, whether clergymen or laymen, saw their work for Simpson as a matter of acting out their religious commitment.

With exceptions. One board member, in spite of his sturdy Methodist credentials, was known to be profusely profane. Gorham Worth was different from the ordinary person who swears because he is too ignorant of the English language to express himself without profanity. His cursing was deliberate, purposeful, and exceedingly colorful. And because Worth was the perennial treasurer of the board—he had served uninterruptedly since 1879, almost as long as the elder William Buxton—he was present at all the meetings, where his unashamed language shocked his colleagues, especially the clergymen. But his reputation as a banker and his hard work on behalf of Simpson through the years led almost everyone to make allowances for his predictable blasphemy.

Once, however, Worth seemed to go too far. During a commencement week an esteemed bishop of the Methodist Church was the guest of the College, and one day it was his luck to walk down the street with Gorham Worth. True to character, Worth displayed his proficient profanity until the bishop could stand it no more. He protested, "Brother Worth, it pains me greatly to hear you profane the name of my Lord. I must ask you not to do so in my presence."

Worth stopped in his tracks, turned to the bishop and replied, "Well, who do you think you are, anyway? That's the way I talk before Jesus Christ. Do you think you are better than He?"

The bishop's reply is not recorded, but a few years later Worth experienced a sort of linguistic conversion and gave up profanity altogether, "apparently convinced that his example was not a good one for the young people in whom he was greatly interested."[20]

Worth was one of several dedicated trustees, local men all of them, who, as members of the executive committee, continued to watch over the affairs of the College. As Simpson grew and the work of the board became more complex, the size of the executive committee increased from five in 1910–11 to seven from 1911 to 1916, and for the three years after that it varied from eight to ten. The full board of trustees continued to number twenty-seven, nine new members elected each year for a three year term. The selection of new members was theoretically the province of the annual meeting of the Des Moines Conference of the church, but in practice the board was a self-perpetuating body. In the entire history of Simpson College, there is not one instance in which the conference delegates did not approve viva voce the list of candidates submitted by the College's board. To be sure, the strongest influence in the recruitment and election of the new trustees was increasingly the president of the College himself.

When Francis Strickland came to Simpson, the board's membership consisted of eighteen laymen and nine clergymen, together with seven ex officio churchmen selected by the conference. Throughout his five-year presidency, the lay-clerical balance did not change much. In 1914–15 the laymen numbered nineteen and the clergymen seven plus six ex officio.[21]

One member of the board in 1910 was the Rev. William M. Dudley, a seasoned minister in the itinerancy who had been first elected to Simpson's board in 1905. One of President Strickland's first acts upon arriving in Indianola was to employ Dudley as vice-president and financial agent. Dudley, a graduate of Iowa State College, had earned his S.T.B. at Garrett Biblical Institute in Evanston in 1886,[22] and through the years had emerged as one of the most prominent and respected Methodist clergymen in Iowa. Strickland hoped that the glow of Dudley's popularity in the conference would somehow reflect on Simpson and open the minds and hearts and pocketbooks—not necessarily in that order—of southwest Iowa Methodists in enthusiastic support of the College.

While Dudley went to work out in the field, Strickland focused his attention on the academic curriculum. He was pleased that Shelton had opened up the courses of study to permit a modest number of elective classes. He approved of the semester calendar and the term-hours concept of academic accounting. But he recognized the need for some degree of specialization for all students. In the old days, he wrote, colleges "gave their students allopathic doses of Greek, Latin and mathematics, put a sheepskin diploma written in Latin into their hands and sent them forth to be ministers, doctors or lawyers." But the emergence of the natural and social sciences, together with the democratization of American higher education, demanded change. "It's all different now," said Strickland. "A college education is not a luxury enjoyed by the few but a necessary training for life needed by the many."[23]

During the 1910–11 academic year, Strickland and the faculty wrestled with the development of a new curriculum to match the needs of the new era.[24] To achieve that end, the faculty created what they called the "Group System," something very like majors, except for somewhat less concentration in a single discipline than is the case today. During the freshman and sophomore years students took mostly required courses, a broad-based liberal arts program including forty-nine required semester hours, plus four hours of "physical culture." During the junior and senior year, students elected one of twelve "groups": (1) English, (2) history and political science, (3) mathematics, (4) philosophy, (5) Latin, (6) Greek, (7) French, (8) German, (9) chemistry, (10) biology, (11) earth science or (12) physics and pre-engineering.[25] These groups varied considerably in the number of hours required, ranging from sixty-one in philosophy to 112 in physics and pre-engineering. For example, the Greek group included thirty-four semester hours of Greek language, four hours of Bible, ten hours of history (of which six hours were specified in Greek and Roman history), three hours of mathematics, eight hours of modern language, six hours of psychology, two hours of public speaking, eight hours of science, a two-hour course in philosophy called "Theory of Thought and Knowledge," and four hours of physical culture. Because the Bible, mathematics, modern language, public speaking, science, philosophy and physical culture overlapped with the general all-College degree requirements to the extent of thirty-one hours, the net required segment of the curriculum, including the Greek group, was 103 hours, permitting the student twenty-five hours of electives to make up the 128 hours required for graduation.

To implement their new curriculum and provide many more courses, the teaching obligation of instructors was increased. In 1910–11 sixteen full-time teaching faculty (not counting those in music, physical culture, military science or in the academy) were responsible for 111 different one-semester courses ranging from one to four hours' credit. While some of these courses were taught only in alternate years, there were extra sections of heavily enrolled courses. Five years later seventeen full-time people were expected to teach 172 courses, more than a fifty percent increase in offerings with only one additional faculty member to do the job. Even with most of the professors teaching five or six courses or sections per semester, it was virtually impossible to deliver instruction in all the courses listed in an ambitious college catalog. That faculty members were overworked was a matter of dismay and embarrassment to Strickland and the board of trustees, who tried to ameliorate the situation by providing student assistants to help with grading papers and the like. Still, it was clear that the academic ore of the College's teaching staff was in danger of being mined out.

During his penultimate year at Simpson, Shelton had eliminated the undergraduate bachelor of philosophy and bachelor of science degrees, neither of which was really relevant any more in light of the abandonment of the rigid curricular requirements. Only the undergraduate degrees in arts and music remained. Then, soon after his coming to Simpson, Dr. Strickland secured the consent of a willing faculty to drop the master of arts degree, which had been rarely conferred during the years after its acquisition was no longer a pro forma honor.

* * *

The introduction of physical education into the required curriculum exposed the lack of facilities and staff for "physical culture" for women. When the board of trustees looked into the matter, they found that "the equipment is entirely inadequate"—not to speak of the building that passed for a women's gymnasium—and deferred the requirement for women until a new gymnasium could be built.[26] Accordingly, when the new facility became a reality, they employed June Hamilton Rhodes, a graduate of the Burnham School of Physical Training in Milwaukee, as Simpson's "woman physical director" to take charge of women's gym classes.[27] She also coordinated the coaching of the women's athletic teams.

A few years later women had more to cheer them. In the fall of 1915 Simpson began instruction in home economics, which, given the social patterns of the day, appealed exclusively to women.

Bringing home economics—some called it "domestic science"—to Simpson was a consequence of the unremitting hard work and never-say-die spirit of a remarkable woman, Sara Sigler, whose husband was a prominent local member of the College's board of trustees. Mrs. Sigler, whose homemaking skills were admired and whose garden made the Sigler home a showplace in Indianola, took note of the fact that too many young women who wanted to go to Simpson instead went to Iowa State, where they could study home economics. Because she loved Simpson and believed that, properly taught, "domestic Science was a lot more than cooking or sewing learned at home from mother," she determined that something must be done. Therefore, one fine spring day in 1915 she marched up to the campus and called on Dr. Strickland. Why, she asked, was it not possible to offer home economics in the college curriculum? The president agreed with her proposition that it should be taught, but there was no place on campus to teach it. Nor did the College have the proper equipment for such a course or the money to buy it. If a building, properly equipped, were available, then perhaps a faculty member might be found to teach the proper courses.

Undismayed, Sara Sigler and a whole bevy of Indianola matrons descended on the campus a few days later, "exploring every possible nook from the attic of Mary Berry to the basement of Science Hall," but could find no suitable quarters.[28] They were just about to give up when it occurred to Mrs. Sigler that the old women's gymnasium, though not much of a building, had been simply used for storage since new quarters had been found for women's physical education. The building could be remodeled at very little cost, and equipment could be found somehow.

Encouraged by Sara Sigler's determination, President Strickland, whose chief attraction to home economics was the undeniable fact that "we lose to other colleges" by not offering it, urged the board of trustees to "fix up the Ladies' gymnasium" and find some way to equip it. He guessed it could be done for $1,500.[29] He already had $100 from Mrs. Sigler, an equal amount from the senior class, and $200 from the Indianola Women's Club. Dr. Dudley, he said, could raise the rest.[30]

Dudley raised some money, to be sure, but Sara Sigler raised even more, and together they had enough to complete the task. True to his promise, the president engaged the services of the College's first home economics professor, Mary

M. Nordstrum, who had earned her bachelor of science degree from Iowa State only in 1914.[31] She took up her duties in September 1915. A few weeks later it was reported that "the next few days will see the completion of the work on the building,"[32] described by one writer as a "neat little stucco bungalow," all painted white.[33] It even contained electric stoves. Mrs. Sigler had seen to that. More importantly the home economics curriculum, properly installed as a "group" in the College catalog, required, beyond the obligatory courses in domestic science, twenty-nine semester hours of laboratory science in addition to the College's general liberal arts program. Nearly everyone agreed that, apart from elementary sewing and cooking, the women in home economics encountered a respectably demanding course of study. Sara Sigler, understandably proud of her accomplishment, was delighted to know that next autumn "Home Economics at Simpson will be no longer an impossible dream but an established fact."[34]

If the women were delighted by the introduction of home economics into the curriculum, the men of Simpson had mixed emotions about the discontinuance of required military training in the Simpson College Battalion. It all came as something of a surprise in 1911. When Lt. R.M. Nolan, who had served as commandant of the College's military unit, departed late in 1910, the War Department posted Major Edward H. Catlin "for duty as military professor." A fifty-two-year-old graduate of West Point, Major Catlin was a Spanish-American War veteran who had once served as a professor of military science at Norwich University, a military college in Vermont.[35] He served well enough at Simpson during the months he was on the campus—December to May—but the Battalion was not especially popular with undergraduates. Most of them dropped out after their obligatory two years of drill, and many managed to get exemptions even from the minimum requirement. Hence during the 1910–11 school year, only two companies and a small band remained, some eighty-eight men, only a handful of whom could be considered enthusiastic about drill. Their number having fallen beneath the government's minimum of one hundred participants, the War Department ordered the battalion shut down.[36] The College's cache of arms was returned. Some of the undergraduate battalion officers were disappointed, but among the faculty only John Tilton voiced any opposition to the removal of the military presence on campus.

A matter of far greater importance to students was the system of grading in the classroom. Up to this time the College had followed the widespread practice of evaluating student academic performance on the basis of zero to hundred percent. To be sure, such a system made for very fine distinctions; some felt the distinctions were too fine. The suggestion was made by students that the College adopt a simpler system of letter grades: E for excellent (the top 3 to 4 percent in a class), S for superior (75 to 96 percent), M for medium (50 to 75 percent), I for inferior (25 to 50 percent) and F for failure (0 to 25 percent).[37] After considerable discussion and some controversy—Clyde Emmons animadverted upon the difficulty of selecting honor students with such an imprecise measure—the faculty adopted the new grading scale in the spring of 1913. The students were pleased with the new order of academic accounting; the faculty managed to get used to it; the board of trustees took no notice of it.

* * *

During the decade 1910–20 the College's total enrollment continued to be quite stable. (See table 5.) But while the undergraduate numbers increased—from 232

Table 5
Enrollment 1910–1920

	Senior	Junior	Soph.	Fresh.	Special	Total
1910–11	28	49	68	87	0	232
1911–12	50	47	52	83	4	236
1912–13	41	41	54	113	0	249
1913–14	41	40	68	123	0	272
1914–15	41	47	83	128	0	299
1915–16	51	73	88	120	0	332
1916–17	46	65	73	177	3*	364
1917–18	46	39	100	154	2	341
1918–19	28	44	69	165	3	309
1919–20	47	53	75	194	0	369

	Academy	Business	Music	Normal	Net Total**
1910–11	92	54	136	10	544
1911–12	74	61	154	17	533
1912–13	66	78	149	0	535
1913–14	80	68	193	13***	546
1914–15	69	78	195	45	
1915–16	83	74	194	41	639
1916–17	98	69	177	3	645
1917–18	54	71	126	3	577
1918–19	38	117	82	0	528
1919–20	66	106	153	1	578

*After 1916 the figures in this column represent post-graduate enrollment.
**Excludes duplicates.
***After 1913 the figures in this column represent special, non-college-level enrollment.

in 1910–11 to 369 in 1919–20—academy attendance dropped by almost a third—from 92 to 66.[38]

The balance between males and females in the student body was remarkably even in both the College and the academy, while the business program drew more men than women and the conservatory far more women than men. For example, in 1915–16 there were 164 undergraduate men and 168 women; in the academy were forty-one men and forty-two women; in the school of business fifty-three men and twenty-one women; and in the conservatory women outnumbered the men 135 to 59. The 1915 summer school, which attracted a fair number of school teachers as usual, enrolled 253 women and 162 men. The net total for the entire College was 276 men and 363 women. Nearly all of the students came from southwest Iowa. In that respect not much had changed; the student body remained comfortably homogeneous.

Apart from curricular change and a stable enrollment, Simpson experienced during the Strickland years dramatic growth of the campus, the endowment and the library. New land and a handsome new gymnasium were the consequence of the stunning generosity of one man, and the tripling of both the endowment and the library book collection were stimulated by the external demands of the major accrediting bodies, the North Central Association and the Iowa State Board of Educational Examiners, not to speak of Simpson's hope of influencing philanthropic organizations like Carnegie and the General Education Board of the Rockefeller Foundation.

As we have seen, Simpson people had been talking about an auditorium or gymnasium, or both, for some years, and there were those who despaired of seeing either one of them materialize. Only about twenty thousand dollars had been raised toward construction, far short of the goal of some fifty thousand dollars.

The students wanted a gymnasium, for the buildings then being used for athletics were pathetically inadequate. Because of this, the basketball team was experiencing difficulty putting together a schedule of games. No one wanted to play on Simpson's cramped basketball court, with its uneven floor, low ceiling and iron posts down the center of the playing area. Colliding with the posts had knocked more than one basketball player senseless. Strickland and the board had to agree that a gymnasium probably took priority over an auditorium, much as they personally preferred the latter.

The matter was settled decisively when, in a chapel address April 14, 1911, Senator William H. Berry electrified the whole student body by announcing that Harry Hopper had firmly decided to build and present to the College a new gymnasium. "It will be built," he said, "entirely at the expense of Mr. Hopper."[39] And it was.

Scarcely two months later Hopper gave the College a four-and-a-half acre tract of land he had recently purchased for forty-five hundred dollars from Calvin Haworth.[40] The land would be used for an athletic field. It was probably this second gift, coming along so soon after the gymnasium announcement, that led the *Des Moines Register and Leader* to comment editorially:

> [Harry Hopper] gives with a heart full of generosity out of a purse full of riches. He gives as though he considered his wealth as a trust to be used not for himself or his family alone, but for the good of others, also. He gives to an institution maintained to help young men and women, with a remembrance of his own boyhood days when he struggled hard to get an education and a start in life and overcome the handicaps of poverty. Such rich men make themselves a blessing to the world.
> Harry E. Hopper, this new philanthropist, is winning everlasting gratitude for himself from the thousands who know of his benevolences to Simpson College.[41]

The editorial writer's praise for Simpson's benefactor was matched by an outpouring of good will among people in Indianola. Most of them knew that Hopper had indeed come up the hard way. Born in 1862 into a family of longtime Methodists in Henderson County, Illinois, about twelve miles southeast of Burlington, Iowa, he was the son of John Wesley Hopper, a prosperous businessman and Caroline Elliott Hopper. His father died when Harry was only eight years old, and therewith died the family's income. The boy soon found himself responsible for his mother and three surviving sisters. He was able to complete a common school education, but could only dream of secondary school or college. After herding cattle for a time on the open range in Pottawattamie County, Iowa, he persuaded his mother in 1880 to pull up stakes and bring the family to live on a western Iowa farm he had purchased "subject to heavy encumbrance" near Emerson in Mills County.[42] There he farmed and engaged in stock dealing. He was so successful that within eight years the farm was paid for, and he decided to enter Simpson as a preparatory student in the fall of 1888.

Hardly a typical prep, Hopper was a twenty-six-year-old on a campus mostly full of teenagers, and unlike many of those lively youngsters, he was an unusually serious student, completing the academy course in only one year. The next year, his mother and unmarried sisters moved to Indianola while Hopper matriculated at the College as an undergraduate in the scientific course. Such a move from the farm to the town was not at all uncommon in those days. The farm could be left in the hands of a trusted tenant while the family followed their student to a college town where a house could be leased or even purchased on fairly easy terms. Thus the cost of college attendance was reduced, especially if one could accommodate a few boarders. And it kept the family together.

At Indianola, Hopper ran to classes and studied diligently, but he had little time for college activities. Rather, he devoted his spare time to more nearly entrepreneurial enterprises. A good judge of horses, he bought colts, broke them and sold them at a profit. He also bought and sold butcher cattle, driving them across country to the Des Moines packers and markets. Then, in the spring of 1893, during his senior year in what Don Berry later called "the dull times of the second Cleveland administration,"[43] Hopper bought and platted forty acres of land in the northwest part of Indianola. From the sale of these building lots he made a handsome profit, launching himself into the local real estate business.

For several years Hopper bought and sold Warren County land successfully, especially after the return of good times in 1897. Soon, however, dissatisfied with the limited opportunities afforded in settled central Iowa and enamored of the possibilities of wheat-growing in Canada, he staked his fortune on huge tracts of virgin land in Saskatchewan, and he won in grand style. From 1902 to 1907 he operated out of Milestone, in southern Saskatchewan, handling hundreds of thousands of acres in huge blocks, land grants held by the Canadian Pacific Railway. Meanwhile, in 1895 he had married Edith Carpenter, the second daughter of Professor George Carpenter. While Hopper spent weeks at a time in Canada, his wife remained in Indianola.[44]

Canada was a new frontier, and in time Hopper was running excursions for potential land buyers and making huge transactions, "often buying and selling whole townships with the nonchalance [with which] a grocery clerk would hand over a can of baking powder."[45] One of his last deals would become legendary: he traded an entire township of Saskatchewan land with C. W. Williams, of Galesburg, Illinois, for two famous old trotting stallions, Allerton and Expedition, and a string of mares to go with them, for his horse farm in Warren County. Hopper truly loved horses, and Allerton was one of the best in the country.

When the railroad declined to sell land in huge parcels to speculators any more, Hopper decided he could do better by dealing in British Columbia standing timber, which could still be handled in huge quantities. Large profits from timber made Hopper Indianola's first millionaire.

But Hopper never lived like a millionaire. Rather, he gave money away almost as fast as he made it. Don Berry, who worked with and for Hopper for a number of years, has written that "he had a pervading ambition to do something really worthwhile for Simpson College, and to make Indianola a better city."[46] Before 1910 he had made a number of modest donations to the College in its perennial fund drives, but it was at the Golden Jubilee celebration that he gave twenty-five thousand dollars to establish an endowed chair in Latin in honor of his father-in-law, the late Professor Carpenter. And it was only ten months later that he announced his decision to build the new gymnasium. He had never had time for athletics when he was in college, but he wanted others to have that opportunity.

Proudfoot and Bird, who by this time had become Simpson's official architectural firm, designed the building, by far the largest built at Simpson and at the time surely the most modern, capacious gymnasium in the state. Hopper, serving as his own contractor, watched over the principal features of the building's planning and construction. His secretary, Carl F. Brown '03, handled the details and paid the bills. Construction began in June 1911 and required thirteen months to complete.

Considered a massive structure at the time, the new gymnasium was 120 by 106 feet and stood three stories tall. Its great central basketball court was roofed by a huge steel truss ceiling with a seventy-foot central skylight. The exterior was faced with a golden tone brick trimmed with Bedford limestone. Two fine entrances stood at the north and south of the building, each ornamented with stone and fluted columns. The basketball court, 117 by 70 feet, was floored with polished hard maple and contained a suspended running track of heavy cork, allowing for indoor use, eighteen laps to the mile. The skylights were thirty-two feet above the gym floor. Included in the building were offices, exercise and training rooms, and locker rooms for both men and women. In part of the basement was an excavated area designed for a future swimming pool.[47]

In the fall of 1911, during the time the building was going up, Hopper fell seriously ill while on a business trip to Chicago. He was diagnosed with stomach ulcers and was so sick that he remained for several weeks at the Congress Hotel before he could safely be moved. He then arranged to go to California, where it was hoped the climate would assist his recovery. For that journey of recuperation he was accompanied by Don Berry as his private secretary. Meanwhile at Indianola, Carl Brown paid the bills as long as he could, but finally he had to inform his bedridden boss that the ready money had given out. Hopper hesitated not a minute, "sold some precious stocks he had laid away for a nest egg," and the building was completed.

When Hopper returned to Indianola that next summer, Brown entered Hopper's office one day and laid a paper on his desk. Suspecting what it was, Hopper laid his hand across the paper to hide its contents and asked "what is this paper, Carl?"

"That is a complete summary of the cost of the gymnasium."

"All I want to know is, is it all paid for?"

"Yes," replied Brown, "every item is paid."

"Then, please take this report and tear it up, and never tell me what it cost. Then if anyone ever asks me what it cost, I can honestly say that I do not know."[48]

From that day forward things went downhill for Hopper. His health problems prevented his giving the attention his far-flung business enterprises demanded. But the most serious blow came in 1914 with the outbreak of the First World War, which virtually shut down all dealings in Canadian timber, "but did not stop the payments that were due on what he had already purchased."[49] The Hopper empire came tumbling down, and he never hit his financial stride again. Years later he and Edith retired to California, where both his son and daughter and their families lived, there to reside in a little house, behind his daughter's home in San Gabriel, watched after by his children. When he died at eighty-two on September 29, 1944, he was penniless.[50]

But he was never happier than he was the evening they dedicated Hopper Gymnasium, October 9, 1912. It was a festive program. After the orchestra played and the ladies glee club sang, Charles Enos, the superintendent of construction, presented the building to Hopper, who in turn presented it to the College in a moving address. Responses were delivered by William H. Berry for the board of trustees, by his old classmate John P. Morley for the faculty, and by Joseph Wayte, president of the senior class, Charles E. Bentley '04 in behalf of the alumni, J. F. Samson,'86, for the city of Indianola, Charles R. Brenton for the state board of education and the Reverend Charles R. Bair '03 for the Des Moines Conference. The fifteen hundred people who were present included nearly every Simpson student, the seniors clad in caps and gowns, together with Indianolans and visitors, all of whom were truly impressed as they swarmed over the building after the formal exercises were concluded.

There is an important sequel to the story of Harry Hopper and his gymnasium. When the time for turning the building over to the College was approaching, President Strickland suggested that they hire some college boys to take care of the janitorial work. Hopper demurred, pointing out that the building, especially its fine floors, deserved the attention of a trained custodian. In a matter of weeks he found in Chicago a recent immigrant, a young Scotsman from Dundee by the name of Peter Ross, who was an experienced maintenance man. Hopper hired Ross on the spot, brought him to Iowa and paid his first year's salary of $750.[51] Ross arrived in Indianola in the fall of 1912, brought his wife and child over from Scotland, and stayed. Loved by everyone for his competence, his rich Scottish burr and his unfailing good humor, Peter Ross watched after and hovered over Hopper Gymnasium for thirty-eight years, retiring in 1950.

Many years later, after Hopper had lost nearly everything of his own, a friend asked him if he regretted having made that huge gift to Simpson College. "No," replied Hopper, "that is the one investment I still have left."[52]

How much did the gymnasium cost? At the time it was under construction, everyone talked of a "$50,000 building." Delays and upgrading of the quality of materials drove the price up, some guessed, to as much as $75,000. Later people were saying that it might have cost more than $100,000. We shall never know. Carl Brown, who paid all the bills, never divulged the final figure, even to his wife, and when he died in 1969, his secret died with him.[53]

* * *

Though Simpson could celebrate its good luck in seeing a new gymnasium placed in its lap by a single generous benefactor, it found the amassing of vitally needed endowment funds an exceedingly difficult challenge. Yet in the Strickland years the College met with considerable financial success, even if that success did come in fits and starts.

No one doubted that endowment funds were desperately needed. When Dr. Shelton left the presidency, the productive endowment stood at about $110,000, counting the recent Carnegie gift of $20,000. That autumn, the board of trustees adopted a plan to raise the endowment to $400,000 and secure an additional $100,000 for construction of an auditorium or, as they were now calling it, a "Central Building." The incentive to press ahead with this ambitious program was provided by at least two forces, one a carrot and the other a stick. On the one hand, the College hoped to attract substantial gifts, perhaps as much as $50,000 each, from the Rockefeller General Education Board and the Carnegie Foundation, both of which expected academic institutions under consideration to have "productive endowment of at least $250,000." On the other hand, the

State Board of Educational Examiners had issued an ultimatum to Iowa colleges: to be rated a "first class" college, an institution had to have, no later than January 1, 1912, a productive endowment of $200,000 or more. Denial of the top "first class" rating could deliver a devastating blow to Simpson.[54]

As if chased by demons, Vice-President William M. Dudley went to work with a will. Fortunately he could count Harry Hopper's $25,000 for the Carpenter endowed chair, and after a strenuous campaign was able to report just before Christmas 1911 that Simpson had met the goal demanded by the state board. The endowment had now passed the $200,000 mark, ten whole days ahead of the deadline.[55]

The endowment minimum was only one of the demands set by the state board. Most of the other requirements the College could and did meet easily, but one which set a minimum of at least 7,500 volumes in the College's library, exclusive of pamphlets and government documents, proved difficult.[56] The librarian's count showed only 5,500 volumes in mid-1911, a terrible showing reflecting years of neglect. When the College's budget was in deficit—and it usually was—the purchase of library books was the easiest thing to cut. Now they had to make good years of deficiency in a matter of weeks. In a special fund drive nearly $2,000 was raised to purchase the needed books. In late November, Strickland announced that an order for 1,300 books had been placed, but that more funds were needed to pay for them. A two-dollar gift, he pointed out, would underwrite the cost of a new book. A week later the Indianola Women's Club came through with a gift of $500 and beyond that organized what they called "dime thimble parties," bringing together ten women who would bring their dimes and sewing to a social. Then each of these ten would invite ten of their friends to a similar party, and so on and on, all their dimes to buy books for Simpson. It is doubtful if these events raised much money, but as a touching demonstration of Indianola's everlasting support of the College it deserves being recorded.[57]

But still more books were needed. Finally, in mid-December 1911, the Macedonian cry went up in Indianola, imploring Warren County residents to donate a thousand books—good books, they hoped—within the next two weeks.[58]

As usual, the local citizens came through as boxes of books were delivered to the library in buggies, automobiles and children's wagons, and if the quality or condition of some of the volumes left something to be desired, the goal was met, breathtakingly close to the New Year's deadline. At a board of trustees meeting in January, the president could boast that 3,000 volumes had been added in a matter of weeks, roughly 2,000 bought and 1,000 donated.[59] One could almost hear a collective sigh of relief.

Simpson, said Strickland, must stop living so dangerously, lurching from crisis to crisis. Somehow it had to get ahead and stay ahead. The College's financial history read something like the *Perils of Pauline*, and that must stop. He proposed that the endowment be increased to $400,000 by January 1, 1917, and that $100,000 of that amount be requested of the Rockefeller Fund. Beyond the endowment goal, Simpson should of course raise $100,000 to build the Central Building. Meanwhile Strickland was happy to note that the College operated in the black— by nearly $2,000—in 1911–12, and that $25,000 had been left to Simpson in the estate of James B. Tiffin.[60] That was at least a good start.

While Dudley moved around the conference raising endowment funds, the College adjusted to the luxury of owning the state's finest athletic center. Soon enough they tore down the little white building that had served as a men's gymnasium, selling the scrap lumber from it for $681.50. It would "soon be a verdant part of the campus," rejoiced the editor of the *Simpsonian*.[61] Moreover, everyone liked the handsome new gate to the campus, a gift of the class of 1912.[62] Made of "pressed brick trimmed with Bedford stone," it was constructed during the fall of 1912. The next year saw a new fireplace in Mary Berry Hall and the cleaning, papering and painting of all the buildings. But many were still complaining about the appearance of the campus. So many trees had been planted that parts of the campus were beginning to look like an "impenetrable forest," and although there were walks on the campus, almost no one used them. Professor Jenner tried to make things look better by planting some flower beds, but his commendable attempt at beautification was declared to be only moderately successful.[63]

Campus appearance was deemed important but not vital. Strickland's first priority was raising enough short-term funds to keep the College going while seeking major gifts for long-term needs. Still there were disappointments in both categories, and short-term deficits piled up with unremitting regularity.[64] A request to Carnegie for funds to enlarge the library met with a curt rebuff. Carnegie's private secretary wrote, "Mr. Carnegie directs me to say to you that he no longer sees his way clear to assist any colleges whose boards of trustees are elected by denominational bodies." Strickland's follow-up letter to Carnegie received no response.[65] Dispirited, the president believed that he could not successfully turn to the College's alumni, who in his judgment possessed "a lamentable lack of loyalty and almost total absence of a sense of responsibility" to Simpson.[66]

Dudley was as effective in the field as anyone could be, and the president made the gratifying discovery that John Morley had an uncommon knack of coaxing money out of reluctant prospects and thus used him more and more, especially in the churches. Their requests for support from the Des Moines Conference were hardly excessive. In 1913, for example, they asked for an average of twenty-five cents per member. At that time there were approximately 54,000 members (not counting children) in 84 churches. A goal of $13,500 seemed reasonable. They would have been quite satisfied with $10,000. What they got that year was $2,052, a sorry fraction of their asking.[67]

The conference was only marginally more receptive when the College undertook a major fund drive in the fall of 1915. As the effort got underway, the *Simpsonian* complained harshly: "Be it to their shame to have it said, Methodist churches have actually discouraged and hampered the campaign. Individuals have deliberately prejudiced communities" against Simpson's agents.[68] Yet, for all the students' somewhat overwrought outcry, the churches did respond to Simpson's distress, although their generosity broke no records. In fairness to the churches, they were not wealthy by any means; many of them suffered from underfunding and competing demands on their slender resources. Simpson was rarely high on their list of priority expenditures.

The new campaign was urgently needed, and it was mercifully brief. It was necessary because the College's perennial deficits—$10,697 in the 1915–16 academic year—its debt and higher costs, not to speak of the external pressures of accrediting bodies and philanthropic institutions, forced Simpson's leaders to revise their fund-raising goals sharply upward. It was brief, beginning at the end of September and concluding its work at the end of December 1915. During that period they sought to raise $300,000 for the endowment and—one more time—$100,000 for the "Central Building."[69]

The campaign got off to an encouraging start when they brought in Bishop Frank M. Bristol from Omaha on October 17 to speak at the Methodist Church. Heartened by their initial success, the faculty pledged $6,000 and the students an amazing $7,178.50, nearly $26.75 each. By the end of the first week in December, their endowment goal was half met. But, with only seven days left, they still had $100,000 to go. Finally, on Tuesday evening, December 21, over five hundred people gathered at the Indianola Methodist Church to participate in the final act of the drama. Three telephones were installed in the choir loft, and what was surely Simpson's first "phonathon" got underway at seven P.M. sharp. Every new gift occasioned a cheer from the audience. One ninety-year-old man gave a dollar. Others gave more, much more. By the evening's end they had met their goal. The *Indianola Herald* announced their triumph: $307,133 for the endowment, bringing the total to more than a half million dollars. And the building fund, while not yet $100,000, looked promising.[70] When the board of trustees met the following June, President Hamilton reported that the endowment stood at $596,698.[71]

Simpson's fund-raising success in 1915 appears not to have been influenced adversely either by the proposed merger earlier that year of the Iowa and Des Moines Conferences of the church or by a proposed merger of colleges. The first of these would have placed Simpson and Iowa Wesleyan College into the same conference. "Two colleges," noted the Simpson Board of Trustees, "of the same character doing the same work and appealing to the same clientele, both for students and financial support, would present a situation fraught with embarrassment and possibilities of evil."[72] William H. Berry reported that he had written to Hugh A. Cole, president of the Iowa Wesleyan Board of Trustees, in January asking Cole's thoughts about the conference merger and suggested a meeting to talk it over. Receiving no response, he wrote again in March, and this time Cole replied that he thought "it would be a mistake to make the consolidation (of the two colleges) you speak of." Berry was perplexed, for he had referred to the consolidation of the conferences, not the colleges.

Cole was probably unduly sensitive. He had reason to be, for he had recently learned that the University Senate of the Methodist Church had ruled that its related colleges, to be ranked as "standard," must have a productive endowment of $200,000 by January 1, 1916. "Under this pressure," wrote an Iowa Wesleyan College historian, "for Iowa Wesleyan could not comply with the requirements, the Trustees and friends of the institution began to cast around for some way out of the difficulty."[73] Because Simpson did meet the church's requirements, a merger with Iowa Wesleyan College was a possibility, but no one at Simpson is known to have suggested such a move. A different sort of merger was proposed, however, by Parsons, a Presbyterian college that was having its own problems. Its proposition was presented at the Methodists' annual Iowa Conference meeting held in Centerville in September 1915:[74] Parsons, Iowa Wesleyan and Simpson should merge under the name "Iowa Union College," the school "to be located at either Mt. Pleasant, Fairfield or Indianola as deemed most advisable." The Iowa Conference appointed a five-man committee to study the matter, and so did the Iowa Presbyterian Synod. But Simpson would hear none of it, and the Des Moines Conference subsequently refused even to appoint a committee. That ended for a time talk of any kind of a merger for Simpson.[75] Nor did the conferences merge, so the question of a union of Simpson and Iowa Wesleyan was rendered moot.

Certainly no one at Simpson was keen for union with another college, and the matter was little discussed on the campus, which is not to say that Strickland and the board members were not preoccupied too much of the time with the state of the College's financial health. It was not that Simpson suffered from any dread fiscal disease; it was more nearly a matter of chronic malnutrition.

They did raise tuition, but not much. During Strickland's first year, the annual rate was $46 in the School of Liberal Arts; in the 1914–15 year, it was $52. Academy tuition increased not at all, nor did the cost of the Normal Course. The Business School went from $50 to $60 and Shorthand and Typing from $62 to $70. In 1910–11 they tacked on a $10 "registration fee" that included admission to the Lecture Course and all athletic events for the year. During the next few years it was called a "semester fee" ($10 or $12), to which was added a "gymnasium fee" of a dollar per semester. Then, as now, the College was wary about pricing its tuition too high. It watched with great care what other colleges were doing and acted accordingly.

A serious problem was the fact that fully a quarter of Simpson's students came with either full scholarships or reduced tuition. The full scholarships provided some real problems. For one thing, as tuition increased, the income from a typical $1,000 endowed scholarship no longer earned enough annually to pay the full amount. Further—and this was a serious source of irritation to the College people—some donors, permitted to name *any* student as the recipient of their "perpetual scholarships," were using their $1,000 gifts as an investment and were charging the recipients for them. Such an abuse could not be countenanced, but for the moment not much could be done about it.[76] A promise was a promise.

Estimates for the total cost of attending Simpson in 1910–11 ranged from $150 to $225 for the year, depending on the course of study, private lessons or laboratory fees, or whether one resided on campus or in private lodgings in town. By 1914–15, those figures had risen to a range of $214 to $249. It is quite possible that these calculations, which were published in the College's catalogs, were deliberately modest, in order not to frighten off any prospective students.

It appears to have come as a complete surprise at the College when Francis Strickland announced in the spring of 1915 that he was resigning his office to take a teaching position as head of the Department of Philosophy at West Virginia University.[77] His action caught the board of trustees off-guard too. Unwilling to act with undue haste in their recruitment of a new president, the board decided to name an interim president for a year, and to no one's surprise turned to their only emeritus professor, doughty William E. Hamilton, who was enjoying his retirement down in Arkansas. The old man, of course, consented to come back. "If Simpson needs me, I'll be there," he said. It was the fifth time he had served either as Simpson's president or its acting president.[78]

Hamilton returned to Indianola that summer and assumed his duties on August 15. He accepted a salary of a mere $166.67 per month.[79] Perhaps he expected his own modest compensation to serve as a model for the whole faculty. He held the line on faculty pay, saying, "I have not seen any necessary incongruity of plain living with high thinking." What mattered, he said, was the quality of instruction: "If the class room work is good," he declared, "the school is a success though its buildings fall into decay and an under-paid faculty [be] clothed in rags." Yet he knew, and so did the board, that Simpson must compete in the marketplace with other colleges for faculty, and he was deeply hurt when one local businessman contemptuously insisted that "if the teachers in Simpson College were worth more they would be getting more."[80] Still, only two faculty members received salary increases for the next year—$100 each—and several were replaced with people who accepted lower compensation than their predecessors had received.

Hamilton did believe, however, that the College should start providing some kind of retirement benefit, predicting that if nothing was done, "the condition of them may be pitiable in the extreme." He suggested an amount that was hardly excessive: ten dollars per year for each year of service. But the board, with its eye on the College's perennial deficit, passed over Hamilton's sensible suggestion. It would be many years before the College offered any kind of retirement compensation. And, one must recall, this was long before the days of social security.

As we have already noted, it was during Hamilton's brief administration that the College's most successful fund drive up to that time was completed, adding more than $300,000 to the endowment. While surely Dr. Dudley was primarily responsible for this signal success, the mere presence of the "grand old man of Simpson" was widely believed to have a profound influence on the willingness of donors, especially those in Indianola, to be generous.

Encouraged by the doubling of Simpson's endowment, a group of thirty Indianola business and professional men, some of whom were trustees of the College, organized in April 1916 what they called the Simpson Extension Association, the purpose of which was to purchase and hold a tract of land for the use of the College at some future time. With what turned out to be remarkable foresight, they began to acquire, piece by piece, two blocks south of the campus and the full block west of that, together with the half block south of Hopper Gymnasium.[81] One by one the residences on this land would be removed, some of them many years later, as the College needed the space for construction.

The board of trustees deliberately held off their search for a new president until the success of their endowment campaign was assured. That done, a four-man search committee was selected. They got plenty of advice, most of it unsolicited. No sooner had Dr. Strickland resigned than Joanna Baker wrote a letter signed by fourteen other faculty members, urging the board to find a president "who will be academically oriented, who will work well with the faculty," someone who would be "not just concerned with endowment campaigns and buildings."[82] In March 1916 board chairman William H. Berry and Dr. R. E. Shaw went to the eastern seaboard while Harry Hopper and Dr. E. M. Holmes went to Chicago.[83] Armed with a list of nine criteria on which to make their selection—number nine was "a wife"—they looked at five candidates. One they liked turned them down. Then, while in Boston to look at one candidate, they learned of yet another in that area. More by accident than design they met the Reverend James Watson Campbell, a Methodist minister in Newtonville, Massachusetts. They interviewed him, heard him preach in his own church, liked him instantly, and after conferring with the other members of the board, offered him the presidency.

Campbell was characterized in glowing terms: "affable, approachable and popular but dignified though democratic."[84] With that description, he had a lot to live up to, probably more than anyone had a right to expect.

Urged to come to Indianola to look the College over, Campbell accepted the invitation on the condition that neither the faculty nor the students be told who he was. He wanted to see them as they really were. Later the students remembered his spring appearance on campus: "A middle aged gentleman visited many of our college classes," wrote one of them in the *Simpsonian*, and they wondered who he was. Some speculated that he was a "railroad president who was going to run an interurban between Des Moines and Indianola"; others thought he was a "state inspector" or a "manager of some factory." Everyone agreed that he was "a fine looking man, tall and broad shouldered, with a clean cut face, and a clear, honest eye." They were truly surprised when the "admired stranger" turned out to be their new president.[85]

Board secretary John H. Henderson informed Campbell of his election and the financial terms of his contract. He would receive $3,500 per year and $4,000 the next year "if the state of the College's finances allow."[86] Campbell replied on May 4: "I accept this position on the terms you indicate. . . . I shall continue to pray that the splendid history of the College with its noble spirit and fine traditions may begin another chapter even better than anything that has gone before."[87] Campbell had a way with words.

And he moved very quickly, arriving in Indianola in time to take up his duties on May 15, 1916. At a reception in his honor at Hopper Gymnasium on May 20, the new president, like his immediate predecessor, felt the necessity to apologize for his eastern origin. Surely, there were those who preferred a western man for president, but they were going to have to learn to live with another Yankee. Though "bred and buttered in the East," he protested that it was no way his fault.[88]

Campbell was a Pennsylvanian by birth and rearing. The son of George W. and Mary D. Campbell, he was born at Warren, Pennsylvania, September 14, 1872. He proved to be an exceptional student and earned a whole series of degrees: the B.A. from Allegheny College (1893), where he was a member of Phi Beta Kappa, the B.D. from Drew Theological Seminary (1899), the M.A. from Harvard (1908) and the Ph.D. from Boston University (1909). Later his undergraduate alma mater awarded him the honorary D.D. (1912). Ordained to the Methodist Episcopal ministry in 1895, he served in three Pennsylvania charges before accepting the call to the pastorate in Newtonville, Massachusetts, where he served eight years (1908–16) before accepting the presidency of Simpson. He married Edith M. Payne of Cherry Creek, New York, in 1898. Two years prior to his marriage he had traveled extensively in Egypt and Palestine.

Dr. Campbell's inauguration on Tuesday, October 10, 1916, was a festive occasion, with representatives from more than a score of colleges, the faculty in full plumage, students, townspeople, and probably the greatest aggregation of college and university presidents in Simpson's history. At the morning inaugural ceremony, presided over by ex-president Hamilton at the packed Methodist Church, the people joined the sixty-five-voice choir and orchestra in a powerful rendition of "Faith of Our Fathers," after which the board president presented the keys and the charter of the College to its new president, reminding him eloquently of "halls and temples which metal key cannot unlock." Campbell's address, "Some Christian Ideals," set forth his philosophy of education combining the ideals of enlightenment, spirituality and patriotism, after which Dr. Elbert Robb Zaring, editor of the *Northwestern Christian Advocate* in Chicago, invoked the blessings of deity upon the people, the College and its new leader. At a luncheon for 268 guests at Hopper Gymnasium, the governor of Iowa, G. W. Clarke, and one college president after another responded to the words of toastmaster Dr. Charles Wesley Flint of Cornell College. Especially pleasing to Campbell was the response of Dr. William H. Crawford, president of Allegheny College, who had also delivered an informative lecture on Savonarola the previous evening.[89] At yet another major speaking event that afternoon, Governor Clarke presided and the major address of the day, "The Finished Product of the Christian College," was delivered by Dr. James A. Beebe, president of the Iliff School of Theology in Denver. A Simpson graduate in the class of 1903, Dr. Beebe proved that he deserved his reputation as a powerful orator. That evening at eight o'clock, if the participants still had the strength for it, a huge public reception was held for the new president and all the honored guests.

As brilliant as was the induction of their new president, nothing touched the hearts of Simpson people quite as profoundly as did the "greeting" of their beloved retiring president, William E. Hamilton. Looking back on a long lifetime, he recalled as a member of the "passing generation" that

> Fifty years ago some of us thought that the world was "waiting for us." There were many things to be done, and we *thought we* could do them. The years have fled and we have had two surprises: first, we have not been able to swing this old world as we expected. We are surprised that we have not been able to accomplish more at the tasks at which we set ourselves. Second, we are astonished at the number of really good things done in the world, in the doing of which we have had no share.
>
> Simpsonians, may a better fortune attend you. May you have a part in every good work. May you accomplish the things we are obliged to leave undone. May you *realize*, in fullest measure, the fulfillment of your fondest hopes of efficient service and at the last hear the Master's "Well done."
>
> *Morituri, salutamus.* We who are about to die, salute you.[90]

* * *

Dr. Campbell, whose tenure at Simpson from 1916 to 1919 was relatively brief, presided over the College during troubled times. The war that seemed far away in 1914 was convulsing Europe with its unprecedented carnage, and by late 1916 seemed to be drawing the United States into its vortex. Although President Woodrow Wilson was reelected that autumn because "he kept us out of war" and antiwar sentiment was powerful, Americans found themselves increasingly sympathetic to the cause of the Entente powers. Even in Iowa, where more of its population was descended from German ancestry than from any other, isolationists, and pro-Germans were heard from less and less as the war exacted its brutal toll.

Campbell left no doubt as to where he stood. "I believe every college ought to be a school of patriotism," he said.[91] And his unabashed loyalty to the nation was expressed more and more in terms of opposition to the Germans and support of American military preparedness. Coincidentally, within days after Campbell's arrival on the campus in the spring of 1916, Lt. Ray C. Baird, a Simpson alumnus, wrote urging the restoration of military drill. He called upon the new president to "help build the wall to protect the principles you teach. Reinstate military training in some form and develop a body of men from whom the official personnel of the nation's military forces can be drawn in case of need."[92] Campbell supported such a move, but the idea received a decidedly cool reception among faculty and students alike.

Although students, in response to an eloquent plea, raised twelve hundred dollars in the fall of 1916 for college men in prisoner-of-war-camps in Europe, many of them were decidedly dedicated to American neutrality. Young Fletcher Brown '18, son of Simpson's former president, wrote at the time the United States broke diplomatic relations with Germany in February 1917, that "we had barely finished thoroughly whipping Villa, restoring peace and order in Mexico, recalling our standing guards from the border . . . when along comes this break with the Kaiser." The crisis, he insisted, was "silly." The United States should "keep neutral."[93] A few days later, on February 12, 1917, an editorial in the *Simpsonian* carried the same message. The United States was "absolutely unprepared" for war. And surely President Wilson was "neither so bloodthirsty nor so foolhardy as to attempt to cross the ocean and combat a powerful foe." Therefore, Americans needed "to keep our heads, stay at home."[94]

In chapel the next week Campbell, in a strident—some called it jingoistic—call to arms, characterized the world conflict as one of good and evil. "Patience is a virtue," he said, "but our patience is rotting into cowardice." It is time for us "to rise in our might" to protect our weaker brother. "No state will send nobler men than Iowa. I am willing to shed the last drop of my blood in the hour of my country's need."[95] But not all the students were quite so ready to be called: If we join the war, editorialized the *Simpsonian* on February 19, "instead of protecting our people, we lead them to slaughter. Inspired by false patriotism and emotion, we rush madly to destruction."[96] Now the president announced the resumption of military drill at Simpson; that same day John L. Chew, a bright young freshman orator, won second place in the State Peace Contest with an eloquent speech condemning militarism.[97] A few weeks later, Campbell declared himself in favor of universal military training.[98] That was April 2.

Four days later the United States declared war on the Central Powers, and no one talked of peace any more. One week later a "monstrous assembly" of three thousand shouting students and townspeople filled Hopper Gymnasium to the rafters, waving flags and shouting their support for the war in a great patriotic rally. Up on the bunting bedecked platform sat the bearded veterans of the G.A.R. The Indianola High School Chorus sang the "Marseillaise" in passable French; John Tilton pleaded for more Simpson men to drill; and President Campbell exulted: "If there ever was a holy war, this is it," whereupon everyone sang "America." That same day, military recruiting started in Indianola, and the first two Simpson men enlisted: Russell Jackson and Morrill Clarke volunteered in the Navy and left the following Monday.[99]

By late April, military drill was being conducted regularly under College auspices. Simpson undergraduates, townspeople, even high schoolers, armed with hoe handles in place of rifles, made up the 117 members of the "battalion," which, to be sure, was not an official military unit, but rather an impulsive patriotic response to a crisis.[100] A few weeks later the *Simpsonian* reported that already thirty-eight Simpson alumni and undergraduates had enlisted, including young alumni like Clayton Lane, Bill May and Hurford Stone. By summer's end, most of the volunteer battalion had enlisted. Confronted by a serious loss of male enrollment, the College attempted to persuade the War Department to put a military training unit on the Simpson campus, but to no avail. There was, regrettably, "a shortage of officers in the service of the army."[101]

Stung by the army's rebuff but heartened by an unexpectedly healthy enrollment in the fall of 1917, Campbell gave another rousing anti-German speech at the opening convocation, in which oration he simplified the nature of the World War as "right and justice and truth" on one side and "might makes right" on the other, for this war, he said, was "born out of criminal ambition and false philosophy."[102] His sentiments, however, were relatively mild when compared to the vitriolic pieces that appeared in the College and city press, stories of German atrocities, the wickedness of Bismarck for creating the German nation in the first place, and hatred for the Hun. Commenting in the *Simpsonian* on a news story about the Kaiser and the Turkish Sultan having exchanged decorations, an undergraduate wrote "The honors are even—the hero of the Belgian and *Lusitania* murders honors and is honored by the hero of the Armenian massacres."[103] Some were even inspired to write poems, like the one that appeared in the November 26 *Simpsonian*: "I didn't raise my boy to be a slacker." And if students wanted to, they could go down to the local movie house to see *The Kaiser, the Beast of Berlin*.[104]

Simpsonians weren't burning German books, but some people in Iowa were. Everything German was to be rejected. One no longer ate hamburgers or sauerkraut, but rather "liberty sandwiches" or "liberty cabbage." The Indianola schools discontinued the teaching of German language in the middle of the 1917–18 school year, and the local commercial club, with the support of the *Indianola Herald*, urged the College to do likewise: "No language is worthy of our admiration or study whose people have the ideals and principles shown by the Huns during the four years the world has been drenched with bloodshed."[105] Less than a fortnight later, at its annual commencement week meeting, the board of trustees voted that German would be taught in 1918–19 "only on demand" and "if enough students want it." Without ceremony, they dropped Hildegarde Jend from the faculty.[106]

Indeed, no German was taught at Simpson in 1918–19, but the War Department, in a change of heart, promised in June 1918 to establish a Students Army Training Corps on the campus in the fall.[107] Campbell and the board were elated, for the S.A.T.C. would keep men in school and, further, "We can save the $1,600 which we now spend on athletics." Enlistment in the S.A.T.C. should be "entirely voluntary."[108]

A contract was signed with the War Department in August and the S.A.T.C. unit was organized October 1, 1918, when seventy-nine undergraduate men were sworn into the service. Lieutenants Gerald Frey and Carleton B. Pierce were in command of the unit, and while their conduct did not always please College officials—they smoked and drank and used "colorful" language—they seem to have worked effectively with the student soldiers. Lieutenant Harry Gardner was their rifle instructor. At first, the boys had neither uniforms nor rifles, but they were supplied within a few weeks. Meanwhile the board authorized leasing a large residence on Detroit Street, the former home of Aubrey Goodenough and his family, to be equipped and used as an infirmary, while the College, in order to comply with the needs of the military, employed a local dentist, Dr. Dale Weeks, as a "Department of Sanitation and Hygiene" for the corps.[109] The S.A.T.C. boys were housed in Mary Berry Hall, and the girls thus displaced were assisted in finding alternative housing in town.[110] The Baker residence across the street from the campus was hastily fitted out as a small women's dormitory. Somehow the girls managed, on short notice, to find accommodations.

The life of the S.A.T.C. at Simpson was short. Only weeks after its establishment the war was over. It was demobilized December 4, 1918.[111] The boys would miss their pay. The College, on the other hand, profited quite handsomely from the army's brief sojourn on the campus. When compensation was made, the government paid the College $10,467, described by Dr. Campbell as a "fair settlement." Indeed it was.

While the S.A.T.C. and the war overseas made the managing of the College difficult, it was the epidemic of influenza that made a shambles of the 1918–19 academic year. It was bad enough that preparations for the establishment of the S.A.T.C. caused a two-week delay of the opening of the College's fall semester—classes did not start until a rainy October 1—but far worse was the outbreak of "Spanish influenza," which struck Iowa with terrifying force as it swept across the country.[112] In October the College, indeed the entire community, was quarantined, and all the girls and a few of the non-S.A.T.C. boys went home between October 10 and 29. When the quarantine was partially lifted on October 26, they returned to the College and remained on campus, although they did not attend regular classes, substituting a modified system of "correspondence courses."[113] The S.A.T.C. boys stayed on campus throughout, attending classes by themselves, and, of course, the faculty continued to teach.[114]

It was during the November lull in the flu epidemic that the war ended. When word of the armistice reached Indianola at three o'clock in the morning on Monday, November 11, students were "awakened by shouts and roaring automobiles." They piled out of their beds and quickly joined improvised parades. Amidst all the cheering, bonfires were lit and effigies of the Kaiser and his crown prince were burned. The S.A.T.C. marched downtown to the square. Classes were cancelled and the S.A.T.C. boys were given one day of liberty. That evening everyone enjoyed an impromptu entertainment at Hopper Gymnasium.[115]

The war was over but the influenza was not. Another, even more virulent, assault of the disease late in November brought another quarantine of Simpson and all of Indianola. Classes were again curtailed, the S.A.T.C. boys attending but wearing flu masks over their noses and mouths. Leland Cox died of the flu on November 23. Forty-eight hours later, Dr. Campbell first suspended chapel meetings for the balance of the semester and then forbade all meetings of any sort. The Wednesday after Thanksgiving Gladys Kelly died. The next morning, the president and faculty closed the College down and on December 7 the S.A.T.C. demobilized.[116] The campus was empty. A few days later they learned that Florine Beckhart had died.[117]

After the New Year, the worst of the influenza epidemic seemed to have passed. So much time had been lost that when students returned to the campus on January 6, 1919, the faculty had to improvise in order to complete a year's academic work in a year's time. They concluded the first semester at the end of January, by which time they estimated that they had completed about one-third of the instruction for the year. Then they divided the balance of the year into two terms, one commencing February 3 and ending April 21, and a second session beginning on April 24 and concluding on June 25. Classes would be longer each day, and some Saturday sessions would be held. Students accepted the intensified schedule because they could see that the College was trying "to give them their money's worth," and they were almost ecstatic to hear that on account of the new schedule chapel would be omitted for the rest of the year.[118]

When the class of 1920 published its *Zenith* in the spring of 1919, it contained a list, certainly incomplete, of 250 Simpson alumni who had served in the armed forces during the war, together with the names of the seventy-nine members of the campus S.A.T.C. unit. Some of the alumni had distinguished themselves and were much decorated for bravery. Not one Simpson man died in battle, although it was learned in early 1919 that Dr. E. B. Rogers, '03, had died in France on New Year's Day. He appears to have been the only wartime service fatality.[119]

* * *

The faculty remained quite stable during Campbell's three years at Simpson. There were, to be sure, a few changes. When John Morley took a leave of absence to go to Los Angeles during the 1917–18 academic year,[120] Benjamin D. Scott was brought in to teach philosophy, Bible and psychology. Scott, a clergyman, had earned his B.A. at the University of Southern California, his S.T.B. at Boston, and had completed most of his Ph.D. at Boston by 1917. Although not as personable as Morley, Scott continued at Simpson in the 1918–19 year while Morley came home and took over the position of vice-president or executive secretary, assuming the leading role in the College's fund-raising efforts. In English, Aubrey Goodenough decided to return to the University of Iowa for further study; his replacement, Leroy B. Greenfield, a 1903 graduate of the University of Oklahoma who had earned his master's degree at Chicago, remained only one year at Simpson. When Samuel Weir departed unexpectedly in 1918, the College hired Dr. Robert A. Cummins as professor of education and sociology. Like Greenfield, Cummins stayed only one year. Nearly all of the rest of the faculty members, including most of the faculty in the conservatory, stayed on through the entire Campbell administration.

But not all of them. J. Allen Baker, with nearly a decade of service on the faculty behind him, was invited by the U.S. government at the end of 1917 to take a sensitive position at the Atlas Powder Works, a huge munitions plant at Lake Hopatcong, New Jersey. Baker considered this wartime duty a call to service of his country, and went.[121] He promised to return to teaching after the war, "because he prefers to work with boys and girls rather than ammonium nitrate."[122] After a bit of scrambling the College found Harold L. Maxwell, a recent graduate of Cornell College, to fill in for Baker, but before the spring semester ended, he was drafted into the army.[123] As soon as possible, he was in his turn replaced by Harry Aiman Geauque, who had earned his M.S. in Chemistry at the University of Kansas in 1914.[124] It was a bad year for chemistry at Simpson.

President Campbell, in accordance with his advocacy of career-oriented education, took the lead in establishing a college-level department of economics and business administration. He believed that Simpson's Business School could continue its usefulness, but it was not a college-level degree program and never would be.[125] Simpson, he believed, must join other wide-awake colleges in upgrading its preparation of young men and women to enter the world of business. His resolve to do so was strengthened by the experience of two young Simpson alumni, J. Hugh Jackson '12, and Howard Noble '14, who graduated first and second, respectively, in their classes at the graduate school of business administration at Harvard in 1919. So striking was their academic success that the dean of the school wrote to Dr. Campbell that he was putting Simpson "on our list of accredited colleges."[126]

Campbell had suggested the new department in his first report to the board of trustees, looking toward offering instruction in the fall of 1917, and an able economist was recruited.[127] He was Jesse H. Bond, who held a B.A. and M.A. from the University of Oregon and a Ph.D. from the University of Wisconsin (1915) and who had been teaching for two years at the University of Idaho. Bond, however, was another casualty of war, for he left in mid-year "to do statistical work in Washington, D. C.," and he was not replaced.[128] The board of trustees deferred the development of the new department until after the war.[129] In early 1919 Campbell found an alumnus of his alma mater, Allegheny College, Jessie Squibb Robinson, to take this important position. Robinson, who had completed his Ph.D. at Johns Hopkins in 1917, was serving with the Federal Board for Vocational Education when Campbell signed him up to come to Simpson. He would begin his duties in September 1919.

For the most part, faculty compensation remained quite steady during the better part of Campbell's administration, with a few increases of $50 or $100. Then, as the war sent living costs skyrocketing, the board responded by increasing salaries substantially for the 1919–20 year, some for as much as $300, representing a raise of twenty to thirty percent in some cases. Although it enabled faculty only just to keep up with inflation, the action of the board met with gratitude and relief.

Campbell's problems with the faculty were actually few, but he worried about the board of trustees, for it seemed that its long-time leadership was slipping away. Gorham A. Worth, the Indianola pioneer whose colorful language had been cleaned up before Campbell came to town, died on October 22, 1916. He was remembered as "the man who saved Simpson College" back in 1879.[130] A few months later Campbell was stunned when William H. Berry, the mainstay of the board for fifty years and in 1917 still its president, resigned. "Fifty years is long enough," Berry is reported to have said. The following spring William Buxton, Sr. died at the age of eighty-nine.[131] A forty-two-year board veteran, he had been Simpson's most consistent benefactor. And although his son, William Buxton, Jr., remained on the board, Campbell knew somehow that it would not ever be the same. Attorney A. V. (Aaron Van Scoy) Proudfoot, age fifty-six, became president of the board in 1918 and Clyde Proudfoot, part owner of the Worth Savings Bank—there were a lot of Proudfoots in Warren County—was the new treasurer.[132]

Campbell was worrying about the board's leadership and trying to run a college during wartime when disaster struck in the night of February 12, 1918. Just before midnight Junia Todd,[133] the dean of women, looked out from her room at Mary Berry Hall and saw a bright light in the nearby administration building. At first she guessed that it was a janitor doing his work late, for Simpson had played a basketball game with Drake University earlier that evening. But the light had a peculiar color, so she sent a boy over to see what was causing it. He came running back, crying "There's a fire, and it's all over the place." Todd turned in the alarm, but by that time the flames had rushed up the central stairway and apparently had engulfed the whole interior of the building. As the cry went out over the campus, a large crowd gathered in the cold night, but could do nothing to save the building except to form a bucket brigade and "thoroughly drench" the nearby Home Economics Building. The firemen who arrived on the scene minutes later could do little but watch the building being consumed in flames. By one o'clock it was all over. The building was a total loss. Firemen and students pulled down what remained of the tottering south wall lest it collapse on passers-by. They did pull two safes out of the smoldering ruins the next morning, but most of their contents were charred beyond recognition.

The loss of the building was bad enough, but the destruction of the contents was far worse. Aubrey Goodenough's books and all the notes he had taken at Yale and Chicago and Oberlin were gone. Earle Ross, who had come to Simpson only that year in history, lost three hundred books and all his papers. Mary Hunting, Joanna Baker and Thomas E. Wiggins, assistant professor of English, saw years of work and research notes go up in flames. These were wrenching personal losses. But well-nigh ruinous for the College was the loss of many of its records. Its archives of reports and correspondence and most student records were gone. The board of trustees minute books remained, but that was only because they lay in the safety of secretary John H. Henderson's office. It would require years of painstaking effort to reconstruct student academic records, and during succeeding generations, people despaired of ever putting together a history of the College with nearly all of the original sources gone up in smoke.[134]

What had caused the fire was a mystery. It surely was not the heating system, for the building was heated from the central plant. Wild rumors flew around Indianola: maybe it was spontaneous combustion. Several reported having heard an explosion just a few minutes before the fire was discovered; maybe it was German bombs. And some said it was probably some irate Drake student bent on revenge. Hadn't Simpson just walloped Drake in basketball that very evening by a lopsided score of 53 to 8?[135]

It was never discovered what had caused the fire. And the four thousand dollar insurance payment represented scant compensation for the loss. Meanwhile they needed to find recitation rooms for the faculty, furnishings and offices for administrators. In order to give the president and his secretary, the treasurer and the registrar someplace to work, the College rented a house, referred to as the "Slocum property," for twenty-five dollars per month from William Buxton, Jr. The house was not much, but somehow they would make do.

The burning of the Administration Building made the need of the new "Central Building" even more pressing. If, however, they were to construct the new building, the money for it—still about $11,000 short—would have to be raised. That would not be easy in wartime.[136] Besides, the College's $10,644 deficit in 1917–18 forced the board to borrow money to pay faculty salary warrants. The College's debt had soared to more than $85,000.

A few months later, things had changed. The war was over, students were crowding into colleges everywhere, and Simpson returned somehow to normal. Higher income from tuition promised to erase the deficit, and the College's fund-raising could make a new beginning. As early as July 1918, the board selected an old firm with a new name, Proudfoot, Bird and Rawson, to design the Central Building.[137] The style, they said, would be "Collegiate Gothic," quite a departure from the design of earlier campus structures.[138] The building, arranged along a central hallway, would contain seven large classrooms and as many faculty offices on the ground floor. A large staircase in the center of the structure would lead to the second floor with a suite of administrative offices, commodious meeting rooms for the Y.M.C.A. and Y.W.C.A., and two large paneled meeting rooms with great cathedral ceilings, one at each end of the building, for the literary societies. On the third floor was yet another literary society meeting hall.

Because of the building's large size, it was going to be difficult to locate it on the existing campus without severe crowding. But they would try. They would position their new building on an east-west axis, approximately 150 feet long and 50 feet wide, directly in front of College Hall, the south face of the building running along the north side of Detroit Street, reaching within a few feet of the street itself. The campus gates would have to be moved. Most of the two blocks south of the campus had already been purchased, and it was clear that the College should buy the remaining properties in order to open up some space south of the new Central Building. The campus gates could be moved down to Clinton Street.[139]

The board of trustees were acquiring the needed properties as quickly as circumstances would allow. They picked up the Ivyl McCoy property for $2,100;[140] then the Beymer residence just to the south of it for $4,000;[141] then the Louck property;[142] and then, in a major deal with D. C. Bingaman, they traded some Saskatchewan land they had received from Harry Hopper for an entire city block, "except for the right-of-way of the railroad running through it."[143] Now, with the entire two blocks—between Buxton and C Streets and between Detroit and Clinton Streets—in its possession, the College petitioned the city council of Indianola to abandon two streets—Detroit between Buxton and C and B Street between Clinton and Detroit, to which the city fathers acceded with good grace.[144] One by one the houses on the properties were either sold and moved off or torn down.

Not everyone was happy with the College's new land acquisitions. An unidentified Indianola citizen, signing himself the "Observer," echoed in the local press the sentiments of a number of local people who questioned the wisdom of enlarging the campus. "Simpson College," he wrote, "has probably made its growth, and the addition of two blocks to the campus will likely be futile." Invoking the shades of Mark Hopkins and the log or Dr. Arnold and Rugby, he pointed out the obvious: a college's "usefulness" is measured more by the faculty's teaching and the students' learning than by the size of its buildings. "There is so much need of funds," he wrote, "for the current work of the church in educational, evangelistic and missionary fields that it seems a waste of sacred money to purchase two blocks of valuable residences to make a lounging place for additional students that Simpson will probably never have."[145]

Undeterred by such complaints, the College went ahead with its development plans. Dissatisfied with the projected location of the new building which would stand almost on top of College Hall, the Board decided wisely to move it to the new part of the campus, roughly on the northeast corner of B Street and Detroit, both streets then being torn up and handed over to the College.[146] The new orientation of the building would be north and south, with its main entrance on the east side, a solution the architect found to be felicitous. Soon the plans were completed, approved, and put out for bids.

Eleven bids were opened on May 20, 1919, at the College's temporary office "crowded with men, old and young, short and tall, happy and despondent."[147] The successful bidder for the general contract was the Arthur H. Newman Company of Des Moines; the Carstens Brothers of Ackley, Iowa, won the contract for plumbing, sheeting and wiring. The total cost was $119,568, somewhat more than the original $100,000 estimate. Although not all the money was yet in hand, or even pledged—they still needed $30,000—the project went ahead.[148] A festive crowd gathered as President Campbell broke ground on the site of the old Baker house on June 11 during commencement week.[149] Construction began soon, and although the builder at first experienced difficulties finding materials made scarce by the war, the building was finished very nearly on schedule.

Breaking ground for what they would now call the "Administration Building" was very nearly Dr. Campbell's last official act at Simpson. Two days later he announced his resignation, effective August 31, in a chapel address. Just about everyone was taken by surprise. Students found it difficult to understand "why he lays down the reins when all looks so bright."[150] Others were equally puzzled by what seemed to be a precipitous act on the part of the president. A few days later, however, he provided a clue to the grounds for his action when he talked to the board about the "need of a new spirit" at Simpson. He lamented an "absence of loyalty among alumni" and "a spirit of undisguised hostility to the College" among some of the ministers in the Des Moines Conference, and a "lack of enthusiasm" among others (presumably the faculty). But most dismaying, he said, there existed "among too many of the Trustees . . . an inability to rise above personal feelings, personal interests and personal ambitions in their relations to the school. . . . Petty, narrow and selfish views should give way to high ideals."[151] Thunderstruck, the board accepted his resignation and undertook the recruitment of a new leader for Simpson.

* * *

During the years from 1910 to 1919, through the administration of three presidents, the lives of students, their attitudes and enthusiasms, their academic aims and personal behavior changed at an accelerating rate, especially after the First World War began to awaken in them an awareness of a world outside Warren County.

These youngsters lived in an era of growing democratization in which the bonds of long-accepted authority were being increasingly challenged. We can see this, for example, in the changing patterns of student governance. Simpson's College Council, created by Dr. Shelton to give the students a voice in their own affairs, soon enough came to be overawed by the faculty people in its membership.[152] Certainly in the abstract the faculty believed in cooperative, collegial management of college life, but in practice they could not resist functioning *in loco parentis*, or, as one irreverent student put it, *in loco imperatoris*. In their deliberations, the students seemed always to defer to faculty wishes. Attendance at meetings lagged, and sometimes their sessions were months apart. A laconic comment in the *Simpsonian* noted that "the College Council had its first meeting this year" in mid-November.[153] During the year that William E. Hamilton served as interim president, students were calling the Council "useless."[154] During the Campbell years the College Council was a dead letter, and a Student Council, with no serious decision-making power whatever, was substituted. Students called it "a standing joke."[155] Interestingly, the week Campbell resigned, a student-proposed re-creation of the Collegiate Council was approved by the faculty. Its new constitution provided for nineteen members, including the president of the College (ex officio), three faculty members appointed by the president, three each from the four college classes and one each from the Conservatory, the School of Business and the Academy. The structure of this new group was not much of an improvement on the one created by Shelton, but students hoped it would function more democratically.

The popularity of the literary societies was deeply affected by the changes in student attitudes. The faculty gave them unstinting support; in fact it was difficult for either undergraduates or academy students to escape election to one or another of them. "Each student is advised to connect himself with one of these societies," stated the College catalogs of these years. Their doings were followed in detail by the student publications, and there is no question but that their members profited from the debates and orations and discussions of timely topics carried on in weekly meetings.[156] Three women's societies, the Zetalethean, the Alpian and the Crescent, the last-named organized in 1911, and two men's societies, the Everett and Kallonian (popularly called the "Kiyis") served the undergraduates and the Lowell and Pierian Societies, which consolidated in 1913, the students in the Academy, the Business School and the Conservatory, both male and female.

Because the work of the societies required study in preparation for their exercises, some students hit upon the idea that their work should earn academic credit. The faculty rejected the notion out of hand, and many members of the societies themselves opposed the idea for quite a different reason: If credit were given, the faculty would "perforce have to supervise the societies," and "ultimately rob the societies of all the spirit of independence and personal responsibility" they possessed. The critics were probably right, but the request for credit suggests that society membership was being regarded as an obligation as much as it was an opportunity.[157] Further damaging to their popularity was the involvement of the societies—especially the Everetts—in college politics, either in league with or opposition to the Greek-letter fraternities. They began also to notice a falloff in attendance at their weekly meetings and blamed competing social and athletic attractions on and off campus. Some students were finding it more fun to go to the local motion picture palace than to attend a society debate.[158] In comparison to the blandishments of the silver screen, literary societies were "boring."[159] During the influenza epidemic all society meetings were forbidden, and some students said openly that they were happy not to have to go. And not long after the war, the idea of college credit for society was once again broached: "*something* needs to be done to revive the literary societies," agonized the *Simpsonian*.[160] Nobody seemed to notice the one thing that, more than anything else, had led to the decline of the societies. The College's faculty, recognizing the value of essay writing, speech and debate, had incorporated these activities into the curriculum. Unintentionally and without planning, the societies' main raison d'etre had been quietly taken over by the adult establishment.

In a way, much the same thing happened in athletics. Once run as a student enterprise, college sports were now managed and coached by adult professionals. The result, however, of the "takeover" of athletics by their elders in no way diminished the popularity of sports among the students. Nothing could draw a crowd like an organized sports event. The boom in college athletics at Simpson was but a reflection of a national phenomenon. In all parts of the country college teams offered the athletes the thrill of competition and the community a medium of healthy entertainment. The revival in 1896 of the Olympic Games, with their emphasis on the performance of the gifted amateur, provided just the impetus that would transform casual boys' games into structured, well-ordered contests where excellence mattered more than recreation.

Especially popular were the team sports which offered the greatest crowd appeal: football in the autumn, basketball in the winter and baseball in the spring. A sport like track and field competition, emphasizing individual performance, although it rarely drew large crowds of onlookers, was valued highly by the participating athletes and honored as the competition that boasted a great tradition. Although nearly everyone would have agreed with Simpson's June Hamilton Rhodes who insisted that "athletics for women are just as important as for men,"[161] sports among females enjoyed little public appeal. At Simpson all women's athletics, although they attracted considerable participation, remained strictly at the intramural level until the 1920s.[162]

Football was already the most popular team sport nearly everywhere, and it was certainly so at Simpson, coached by young, for the most part relatively inexperienced, recent graduates of larger universities where they had excelled as players. Such a man was Carroll N. "Chick" Kirk, a 1908 graduate of the University of Iowa, where he had been captain of the football team. But he, like his successors at Simpson, remained only a short time before moving on. After Kirk's two-year tenure (1909–11), Harold J. Iddings (1911–14) coached for two seasons,[163] Arthur Aston (1914–15) only one stormy year, Archie "Bunt" Kirk, "Chick" Kirk's younger brother (1915–16) also only a year, Chester C. Dillon (1916–18) two years, and Nile "Soup" Graves until 1921.

These coaches, whose brief tenure in some cases can be explained by the miserable salaries they were paid, had to take what they got in the way of talent. Rarely was any boy recruited to play sports at Simpson, and no one received an athletic scholarship.[164] Sometimes the coaches were lucky; most of the time they were not. The forward pass, for example, seemed to mystify Simpson players and their coaches for a few years. During the nine-year period from 1910 to 1919, Simpson won only 23 games against 35 losses. The worst season was 1911, when they won no games at all, but 1917 was almost as bad. That year they had no wins but managed to tie Drake 7–7 in the last contest of the season. Surely the best record was chalked up the very next year when, in spite of losses to Iowa State, Drake and Grinnell, Simpson scored five wins and 176 points in eight games, one of which was a forfeit by Coe because the whole Coe team contracted ptomaine poisoning in Iowa City and could not play. Included in Simpson's victories that year was a 76–0 shellacking of Des Moines College. Simpson's team captain, Arthur Sells, was called "one of the greatest players of the year" in Iowa by the Des Moines press, and standout graduating players were Rex Dunn, William "Obie" Hamilton and Ira Collins, the player the women thought was the most handsome young man on campus.[165]

Basketball wasn't much better, although the 1913 team was excellent. In the first contest of that year, the Simpson men defeated the University of Iowa 25–14 in the first game ever played in their new Hopper Gymnasium. They went on to win every game except one, and that one was forfeited to Grinnell when, in a hot debate with the game's officiating, Coach Iddings pulled his players out of the game and went home.[166] In retaliation, Grinnell severed all athletic relations with Simpson for a year. Although in some other years Simpson's record was so bad that the *Simpsonian* called basketball "a farce," later in the decade Simpson men had a very good year when G. Arthur "Chick" Grant captained a team that scored ten victories and 426 points to its opponents' 323 in sixteen games.[167] In 1919 Clare Hendrickson, who was almost as good at basketball as he was at track, was named to the all-conference team.[168]

For the most part, Simpson's basketball teams during these years ranged from just above average to poor. They held their own during the Strickland and Hamilton years, but in 1917 won no games at all. In 1918 all games were cancelled on account of the war, and in 1919 Simpson played only three games, losing two of those.

Only toward the end of the decade did Simpson do really well in track, in large part because of team captain Clare Hendrickson, whose performance captured honors in high jump, pole vault, 120-yard high hurdles and just about everything else that involved running or jumping. Praised as "easily the outstanding man of the season" in 1918, he was surely one of Simpson's greatest athletes ever.

After the completion of Hopper Gymnasium and laying out the new football field and track, Simpson could boast athletic facilities as good as any small college in Iowa. The new football field, the land for it a gift of Harry Hopper, was oriented on an east-west axis just north of the campus, running from C Street east to the grounds of the conservatory building, with Buxton Park bordering it to the north. President Strickland pronounced himself pleased with "Simpson's peerless athletic grounds" and wholesome sports program.

Old Reverend Hamilton begged to differ. In his presidential report to the board of trustees in the spring of 1916, he expressed his disapproval of organized sports. "The only virtue of intercollegiate athletics," he said, "is that they are popular."[169] Sometimes the faculty agreed with him, and from time to time cracked down on athletes who in their judgment were spending too much time in sports and too little on their classes.[170] They worried about the risk of injury, especially in football.[171] They were shocked when they heard once that on the train home from a game in Cedar Rapids, some players reportedly played cards and smoked cigarettes.[172] They were not pleased to note one year that only 72 of 172 men in the College were involved in athletics, while the rest received no physical training at all.[173] Yet a number of them enjoyed attending the games. Professor Emmons served in 1916–17 as president of the Iowa Intercollegiate Athletic Conference and John Tilton made no secret of his enthusiastic endorsement of any and all sports. He was, for example, delighted when the inveterate Scotsman, Peter Ross, introduced soccer to the campus and served as volunteer coach. "Soccer is a coming game as well as a keen one," said Ross.[174] His statement was perhaps a trifle premature; soccer at Simpson was an idea whose time had not yet come.

Students supported athletics individually and collectively. The Joshua Club, organized in 1909, came into its own as a support group, calling itself a "student organization for the manufacture of 'pepper.' "[175] Then there were the Meccawees, a lively club created to support women's sports.

* * *

In those days there was plenty of social security. Simpson, like the community of Indianola, had clubs and societies for just about everything. Of these, by all odds the most popular among a majority of the students were the Greek-letter fraternities and sororities. They were also the most controversial among the faculty and a substantial minority of the students.

The reader will recall that in 1910 Dr. Shelton and the board, bowing to alumni antifraternity sentiment, had appointed a committee to look at the "fraternity question" and "settle the problem once and for all." The investigation was to focus on fraternity scholarship, said to be dismal, loyalty to the literary societies, suspected to be shaky, and attitude toward religious organizations, thought to be less than amiable.[176] After months of somewhat desultory discussions in which more heat than light was generated, the committee found, to no one's surprise really, that sorority scholarship was excellent and fraternity scholarship poor, but the "barb" men were even worse.[177] The Greeks dominated the literary societies, probably for political reasons rather than for dedication to scholarship, and the boys were indeed guilty of ignoring the Y.M.C.A., which they regarded as a "preachers' club." Further, they were found to foster a nondemocratic spirit and believed to monopolize the loyalty of their members. Therefore the committee persuaded the faculty to adopt rules to "regulate and control" the Greek societies, allowing them to exist one more year on probation to the College's leadership. The faculty voted to take "absolute control" over all the groups in order "to protect the social life and college loyalty of the students of our institution" and forbade the rushing or pledging of any prep student or College freshman, activities said to be "inimical to the growth of a proper class spirit during the Freshman year and also the cultivation of a strong college loyalty."[178] To ensure the enforcement of their purpose, they created the College Women's League "to supervise suitable social life for all the women of Simpson."[179] It would "control all women's activities." But because its membership included no sorority women at all, the league's pronouncements had little credibility, and within a year or two nothing more was heard of it. Why no one thought of such a committee to control men's activities is not clear.

The fraternities survived, and were declared in 1912 to be temporarily "under control and restraint,"[180] but soon enough they were once again in trouble with the faculty. It was discovered that one by one they were renting or buying properties in town to be used as chapter houses, providing room and sometimes board to their members.[181] Because the College, after all, provided only limited housing for women and none at all for men, it should have been hardly surprising to anyone, but the faculty and board worried about proper supervision of any housing not under their direct control. They shuddered to think what kind of improprieties could take place in these dwellings. The best they could do was insist that they employ housemothers to provide minimal oversight, insisting that the Greek houses employ married women for the job.[182]

Actually, the faculty was divided on the fraternity question. Most of them were inclined to follow the lead of old Reverend Hamilton who called them the College's "greatest evil" because, he said, "the segregation of such a number of good men into an exclusive society works a cultural injury to those who from choice or necessity are left out."[183] Some faculty, on the other hand, found the fraternities quite acceptable, even attractive. Some were Greek alumni themselves or had been elected while members of the faculty. In 1912, for example, four faculty people—Olive, Harvey, Griffith and Ellis Rhodes—were members of ATO; two were Tridelts—Katherine MacLaggan and Persis Heaton—and Mrs. Strickland was the sorority's "patroness"; Effie Silliman, June Hamilton Rhodes and Nell Harris were Alpha Chis; and John Morley in philosophy had been the principal founder of SAE's one-time chapter at Simpson. That the faculty could never speak with one voice about the Greek societies weakened the effort of the most militant among them to get rid of the "frats."

But they kept trying. In 1918, William Hamilton, goaded by rumors that students, emboldened by the "loose behavior" engendered by wartime conditions, were "dancing in the sorority houses," chaired a committee to investigate this outrageous breach of Methodist morality. Few confessed dancers could be found, but his investigation concluded that the fraternities were by their very nature "antithetical to a high type of Christian development," and recommended that they be ultimately eliminated. But "in view of the unusual conditions that we now have" no action should be taken until after the war.[184] And there the matter rested.

Meanwhile three new Greek societies appeared on campus, one of which survived only a year. In May 1917 a fourth sorority was founded with ten charter members. Called Theta Lambda Rho, it managed to pledge four more undergraduates, but by the end of the following school year it had disappeared without a trace.[185] More fortunate were two societies established at very nearly the same time in the conservatory. For the men there was the Pi chapter of Phi Mu Alpha Sinfonia, installed on March 2, 1917, with sixteen charter members—four faculty members and twelve undergraduates. The national organization, founded in 1898 at the New England Conservatory of Music, functioned as a professional society, open to all male students interested in music, whether members of the social fraternities or not.[186] The following fall, the Mu Alpha chapter of Mu Phi Epsilon for women was established. It was installed early in November 1917 with seventeen charter members.[187] Its national organization, founded in 1903 at Cincinnati's Metropolitan School of Music, was likewise a professional society, but at first the Simpson chapter attempted to rent a chapter house and exclude all sorority girls and rush in competition with them. Soon enough the national organization had to threaten to revoke the charter of the Simpson chapter if it did not open its membership to all undergraduate women, irrespective of their affiliation. Offered no choice, the chapter complied.[188]

* * *

Fraternities and sororities and literary societies held meetings once a week. Chapel was every day. And it was compulsory, its format essentially unchanged for more than a generation. Students trooped into the large second-story assembly room in College Hall for thirty minutes of prayer, hymn singing, announcements and preaching. Often the program was secular, featuring student orators, and not infrequently it took the form of a pep rally complete with class and college yells and some of the bouncy Simpson songs that "Tip" Olive had composed. Still, because attendance was required, most students didn't like it and said so. Their ingenious excuses for missing chapel demonstrated a real capacity for creativity, but they knew that penalties for absence were relatively light and only selectively enforced. The president might call upon the faculty to exercise "gentle compulsion," but attendance still lagged.[189] A 1914 *Simpsonian* "scientific" survey revealed that only about six out of ten students were at chapel on any given day. Surprisingly men edged out women and Greeks bested the "barbs" four to three (the Kappa Theta Psi were pretty bad). Y.M.C.A. and Y.W.C.A. members were not particularly outstanding, while the faculty fared worst of all, with fewer than a third of them present.[190]

During wartime, students' attitudes toward chapel hardened, leading one student to sound the clarion call for revolution: "Compulsory chapel and compulsory church! Does that not sound just a little like the things from which our forefathers tried to escape in England?"[191] The revolution, however, was averted when the influenza epidemic forced a cancellation of chapel for two months, after which the president, in response to a student petition, tried making chapel voluntary.[192] Attendance promptly plummeted to an all-time low.

The unpopularity of chapel was not really a measure of undergraduate religiosity. Lest anyone doubt that Simpson was a Christian college, students were required to attend the church of their choice on Sundays. No statistics were kept, but probably a good number did go down to hear Reverend Willis preach at the Methodist Church. A few Presbyterians, accounted in those days to be comparative liberals, attended one of the two churches of that denomination. A sprinkling of students might go to other churches. There were no Catholics, and indeed no Catholic Church in Indianola existed. But that didn't matter. Everyone knew that Catholics were all going to hell anyway. After church one might go for a walk or read uplifting literature or look at stereopticon slides. One was not to go to a party or play games or go to the movies or ride in an automobile. Or even study, the one prohibition students found praiseworthy and observed to the letter.

Revivals were held less frequently than ever before. That is not to say, however, that they were unimportant in the community. In 1915, a week of fevered evangelism saw over 250 people converted. At other times still more souls were saved, but it is doubtful that many of these were college students.[193]

Although they eschewed revivalism, students were proud of Simpson's alumni serving as ministers or missionaries. At least 140 graduates were serving pastorates, ninety of them in the Des Moines Conference. One issue of the *Simpsonian* listed no less than forty Simpson-educated missionaries in the field, the vast majority of them in China and India. Their stories of dedicated service were lovingly recorded in the College's publications. Students could read that "Miss [Lydia A.] Wilkinson [of the class of '92] was in Foochow," where she had been "working among the heathen for twenty-one years,"[194] or thrill to the story of Lulu Golisch, who had left Simpson to go to China back in 1905 and found herself caught up in the revolution against the Manchus in 1911.[195] Closer to home, they learned that Fern Smith was teaching in a mission school in Utah, "saving Mormon youngsters for Christianity."[196] And Indianola Methodists and Simpson students were providing financial support for young Chris Soelberg in Rangoon, Burma.[197]

They were respectably religious, and they were sincere about it. Was not Indianola still called, after all, the "Holy City"? All this is not to say that they did not enjoy an active social life. In addition to sporting events there were fraternity parties and serenades (the ATOs, it was said, always sang in tune, because they had "Tip" Olive to help them; the Kappas, who tried to sing in tune, were said to sound like twenty-five hungry tomcats on a fence). Students could look forward to the annual "Fete des Fous" carnival or Campus Day, with its happy combination of work and play. Performances at the conservatory were usually excellent and offered a rich variety of musical fare, ranging from trumpet recitals to symphony concerts or a fully staged rendering of *The Pirates of Penzance*. Informal get-togethers were common, but they were being called "bums" less frequently now.

The favorite colloquial term of the day was "case," describing almost any romantic boy-girl relationship.[198] And if contemporary student publications, not to speak of long-remembered anecdotes of alumni, are to be believed, romance flourished beneath the whispering maples. The sentiment was captured in one of "Tip" Olive's unforgettable melodies:

> The campus, the velvety campus
> Is such a good place for a lark—
> Serenading, promenading
> By the "CASES" if I may remark. . . .[199]

Whether students had a "case" or not, their amusements were mostly quite innocent. They could always go down to the Indianola square and visit some of their favorite haunts. They could stop by Mr. Zondervan's bakery for a doughnut. His were "full-bodied, sturdy, indestructible, unsinkable, indigestible. And they cost a penny apiece."[200] They could browse at Liston's bookstore or indulge themselves with fudge or peanut brittle, anise drops or angelica at the Candy Kitchen, or look at the display pictures at Zarley's photography salon, or even take in a movie at the Empress.[201] What they could not do was to go to a saloon or a pool hall, for there were none in Indianola. Nor could they buy cigarettes. No one sold cigarettes in Indianola; it was against the law.[202]

It was not against the law to dance, but it was against the gospel according to John Wesley, and the Simpson president and faculty were charged with the task of seeing to it that the ban was enforced. Today it seems incredible that the board of trustees and faculty spent so much time on this issue, but participating in the struggle against dancing became the litmus test of one's devotion to Methodist moral rectitude. It is true that dancing may have seemed dangerously seductive to board members, who even complained about "seating young men and young women indiscriminately in classrooms."[203] Their views were shared by people out in the Des Moines Conference, typified by the resolution of one of the districts calling upon Simpson to stop teaching "folk lore dances" because it violated the Methodist discipline.[204] The College complied readily.

Even the nine o'clock curfew for women, whether they lived at Mary Berry or in dwellings off-campus, seemed insufficient defense against dancing, especially after the war began to have a liberating effect on student behavior. The president suspected—and he was probably right—that terpsichorean sin was rampant in places like sorority houses *before* nine o'clock.[205]

Curiously, picnics, unlike dancing, were thought by nearly everyone to be harmless outings, where the focus was on good food and nonalcoholic drink.[206] The boys, of course, knew better. As Dorothy Daniel remembered, "There is nothing that can be done at a dance—any dance—that approaches the opportunities of even the first maneuver on a blanket at a picnic. In a way it might be said that whatever the things were that John Wesley tried to discourage by frowning on dancing could be done quicker and (according to your point of view) better at a picnic."[207] One suspects the girls knew this too. The faculty never caught on.

* * *

The use of alcohol was another matter. So powerful and pervasive was the proscription of strong drink at Simpson that one would have searched in vain to find a student who indulged in it. They might call the last nightly train back from Des Moines "The Boozer," but they returned to campus sober. In their rejection of alcohol, students were reflecting a growing public sentiment all over the nation that favored prohibition. Indeed, drinking was a serious social evil. Led by the preministerial students, the College sponsored a local branch of a national student prohibition organization. They were proud that Fred Ingvolstad won the State Prohibition Oratorical Contest in 1913 and that Claude Martin repeated that performance the next year. Then Ingvolstad won again in 1916, going on to win the Midwest Sectional Contest and to place fourth in the nation. Said to be able to mesmerize his audience, the young Simpson orator combined the skills of a revivalist preacher and snake oil salesman. He was jubilant, as was just about everyone in Indianola, when the Eighteenth Amendment to the U.S. Constitution was ratified early in 1919 and the Volstead Act passed the following October. The "death of the Honorable Jno. Barleycorn" was hailed as a moral victory in Methodist Indianola, where citizens were proud that nothing much would change. Righteousness had triumphed.

The temperance cause was only one of the large public issues that intruded into the provincial placidity of Warren County and Simpson. People had always taken their politics seriously, but Republican Indianola was shaken when in 1912 the Wilson landslide buried Teddy Roosevelt and the Bull Moose, the Republican President William Howard Taft coming in a poor third. A straw vote that fall at Simpson treated poor President Taft even more shabbily; it gave Wilson 109 votes, Roosevelt 99 and Taft only 29.[208] And it is worth mentioning that the student poll included women, as did every vote Simpsonians ever conducted, for among them support for women's suffrage was an article of faith. When the war was over they only intensified their work for women's votes. They also favored, almost without dissent, the Wilsonian dream of a League of Nations and cheered enthusiastically when ex-president Taft spoke on campus as he barnstormed the nation stumping for the league and internationalism. They were disappointed, if not angered, when the U.S. Senate "irreconcilables" dumped the league.

Somewhat more controversial, or at least ambivalent, was Simpson's response to the rise of socialism on America's college campuses. The *Simpsonian* noted in 1911 that there were already twenty-nine chapters of the six-year-old Intercollegiate Socialist Society in colleges across the country—none yet in Iowa—and that popular writer Jack London was a member. When, a few years later, members of the English Club were reading London's *Revolution and Other Essays*, they were both shocked and fascinated.[209] One of them wrote, "Mr. London's thinking is clear, incisive . . . arrests attention, and carries conviction." One of his classmates countered with, "I would rather risk my happiness and prosperity in the hands of the grasping capitalists of the present because they have the brains."[210] To be sure, the brains of the Simpson scrutiny of socialist ideas was English professor Audrey Goodenough, who was surely no socialist but who believed that his students should examine important ideas, even controversial ones. Lest his less venturesome colleagues be put off, he related socialism to Christian tradition, leading one of his students to assert that "socialism is Christianity applied to present social problems, and true Christians are acquainted with the problems of the day, and are in hearty sympathy with the basic principles of modern socialism."[211] So successful were these discussions that a class in modern socialism was organized.[212] Both Goodenough and education department head Samuel Weir, who lectured to the class on "The Misconceptions of Socialism," conducted the program carefully. Socialism, Weir assured his fellow faculty, "shows growing opposition to the saloon;" it is today "the largest international political movement in history," and everyone knows that "the present competitive system is completely un-Christian."[213] They insisted that they were making no attempt to convert students to socialism; rather they believed simply that students needed to become well informed about such an important international movement.

Campus opposition, among both students and faculty, was not long in coming. "Socialists advocate free love," asserted one preministerial student. "Socialism and anarchy are about the same thing," said another.[214] For the next few months the discussion was intense, but the war and the Communist revolution in Russia soon confirmed the widely held view that all socialists were just a bunch of bearded, bomb-throwing Bolsheviks.

Whether the subject was socialism or war or domestic politics, the *Simpsonian* brought something of the world to its readers. Published each week during the academic year, it was for the most part competently edited and professionally printed.[215] Of course most of its contents were devoted to campus issues: the announcement of the next promising chapel address and a follow-up praising its uplifting message; blow-by-blow accounts of football and basketball games—with maddening omissions of often depressing final scores—and other events, news of the fraternities and literary societies, undergraduate and alumni personals and editorials whose quality ranged from the thoughtful to the banal.

The *Zenith*'s quality ranged from acceptable to excellent. The one published by the Class of 1912 was a work of art, and it lost money.[216] Some of the contents of this and other editions of the yearbook, especially the illustrations and photographs, are valued artifacts, but carelessness in proofreading, chiefly of people's names, can be disconcerting. Because these early yearbooks were published by the junior class, the edition published by the class of 1911, although labeled the 1911 *Zenith*, actually recorded the events of the 1909–10 school year, and so on, providing an unending source of confusion to anyone unfamiliar with this arcane practice.

It is surprising that the College's student publications were as good as they were, for their editors and business managers were elected by the student body, and like every other political contest on the campus, these elections were commonly Greek–"barb" encounters. Everyone could vote for the staff of the *Simpsonian*, but only sophomores for that of the *Zenith*. Either way, the Greeks battled the independents, who were convinced that only they voted for people on the basis of merit. One year neither the sororities nor the "barbs" managed to put up candidates, so the Kappas and the ATOs split the *Simpsonian* pie between them, electing Douglas Naylor (KOY) editor and Harold Pote (ATO) business manager.[217] Actually, to everyone's surprise both of them did a good job.

The *Zenith* was supported in part by a modest subsidy from the College treasury, but the *Simpsonian* people had to exist from subscription revenue, and sometimes their income was exceedingly poor. "The editor will soon be working on a rock pile," if subscriptions were not paid up, wrote one distraught journalist.[218]

Their entrepreneurial spirit was perhaps not as keen as was that of the undergraduate manager of the college bookstore, which occupied a small frame building on Buxton Street south of the science building. Running the bookstore was the most remunerative enterprise on campus, its manager selected by no vote at all. It was a private business, a convenience to the College that operated freely with the blessing of the Simpson president.

Freely, that is, until James Watson Campbell arrived. It was May 1916, and the student manager for the next year, Irl Marshall, a junior with a keen instinct for profit, prepared the pro forma contract with the College and presented it to the president. Campbell, who had more than an inkling of the potential financial advantage of all this to young Marshall, decided that the College should take all the profits and pay the manager a modest salary for his work. It was not fair, said Campbell, for one student to get rich at the expense of his fellow students. Marshall, who knew an obdurate adversary when he saw one, argued that what he was doing was only what he had been taught in the Simpson classroom, and after calling the president a number of unkind names, transferred to Drake.[219]

* * *

One of the changes at Simpson, little noticed at the time, was the gradual replacement of some of the long-time stalwarts who had either directed the affairs of the College or had taught in its faculty or counted themselves among the best-known of her alumni. We have already noted the deaths of Gorham Worth and William Buxton, Sr. Still others were lost—people like Orlando Baker, whose long Simpson career as seminary principal and professor had been followed by an equally distinguished one in journalism and the U.S. consular service. Baker died at the age of eighty-three while on a ship coming home from his last post in Sandakan, North Borneo.[220] Reverend William S. Hooker, whose fund-raising efforts for the College were crucial, died in 1912 after several years of failing health. That same year ex-president Fletcher Brown was killed in an accident in South Dakota. People could remember that he was "an encyclopedia of information in regard to [Simpson] history." Earlier prominent faculty members Christian M. Grumbling, Kate Corkhill and the improbable Hiram Sedgwick all died within a few months of each other in 1913 and 1914. "Billy" Read, who had served eleven years in mathematics, lost his battle against tuberculosis in December 1918. And no one would forget when Simpson's authentic heroine, Kate Shelley, met an untimely death in 1912 up in Moingona.

The Simpsonian

Volume 49   MONDAY, NOVEMBER 25, 1918.   Number 2

SIMPSON PUTS UP SPLENDID FIGHT

Slippery Field Prevents Red and Gold Warriors from Carrying off Long End of Score

GAME AT DRAKE STADIUM

In the annual contest with our ancient rivals, Simpson outplayed and outfought Drake, but a slow start in the first quarter, cost our team the victory. Two touch downs and a goal in the first five minutes proved too great a handicap for the Red and Gold warriors, although they easily outplayed the Bulldogs three of the four periods, and only a slippery field prevented the score from being in our favor.

With only one minute left to play and the ball in Simpson's possession on its own five yard line, a forward pass was called for. A beautiful pass from Hartsell sailed straight into the waiting arms of Piffer The latter raced down the field, dodged the last Drake tackler and with a clear field before him slipped and fell and was downed by a Drake tackler from behind. If it is not been for the excessively slippery field, there is no doubt but that our fleet-footed end would have scored the second touchdown for Simpson and tied the score. Drake received the kickoff and worked the ball down the field on plays around the ends and through the line. A forward pass was attempted over the goal line but it failed. Simpson then punted out of danger and on the first play Drake scored a touch down on a forward pass. The second Drake touchdown was made a few minutes later and was the result of a long pass. The ball was worked under the shadows of the goal line on a forward

Erection of New Central Building Now a Certainty

Coming of Peace Makes Beginning of Construction in Near Future Highly Probable

ARCHITECT'S PLANS SUBMITTED

Simpson college will really have a new central building in the near future. Plans now propose to commence it as soon as war conditions permit the obtaining of the necessary building materials. The estimated cost is $100,000 of which $60,000 in cash and pledges has already been secured.

At the close of college in the spring the expectation was to start the new building in June and have it well under way by the opening of college this fall. But when Simpson students returned in September their hopes and ambitions were prostrated for they found no stately edifice with pinnacles looming to the sky. The building committee decided that more than half of the needed sum should be in sight before the building be commenced. When a satisfactory amount was secured, the present situation of labor and manufacturing enterprises made it impossible to get the needed labor and materials for construction.

The new structure is to occupy a position south of the present chapel building. After the new building is constructed it is planned to remove the old chapel and replace it with a new one.

All of the administrative offices and seven large class recitation rooms, three literary society halls and rooms for the Y. W. and Y. M are included in the architects' plan of the new building. The style of architecture is that known as the Collegiate-Gothic. The main entrance will be at the south side of the building.

The two blocks south of the present campus belong to the college. These will be cleared and a beautiful campus laid out with a wide wall extending from the central building south to Clinton avenue where the campus gates will be placed.

COLLEGE CLASSES HOLD ELECTIONS

Freshmen Take Much Time for Deliberation Before Casting Ballots; Upper Classmen Act Quickly

ZENITH STAFF COMPLETED

On Monday night, the eleventh of November, occurred the annual class elections. According to a time honored custom, the freshmen met in Oratory hall, the sophomores held down the chapel room, the juniors were packed in chapel 6, better known as the old German room, while the seniors held forth in the philosophy room.

The freshman, as usual, were a long time coming to a decision, and were just casting a second ballot for president as the other classes adjourned. They made up in pep however, what they lacked in speed.

The other classes, blase and indifferent from long practice in such affairs, elected their officers with what is commonly known as neatness and dispatch. They found time, however, to look around over their depleted ranks and wonder where all their former members had gone.

The senior class can boast but twenty-two members. The junior roll holds but fifty names, an appalling contrast to its even hundred names of last year. The sophomore class has sixty-four members, while the freshmen head the list with one hundred and ten members. The freshmen enrollment only is average, which is no doubt due in part to the advantages offered boys who are high school graduates by the S. A. T. C. unit.

It was also necessary at this time for the junior class to fill some vacancies on the Zenith staff. As Lucile Porter, elected last spring for girl's

The construction of the new administration building, later called Hillman Hall, was assured by late 1918.

XI

The Good Years: Simpson in the Twenties 1919–30

When John Linnaeus Hillman came to Simpson in the fall of 1919, he was fifty-four years old and at the height of his powers. He was a native of Ohio, born in Licking County July 8, 1865. He grew up in his native state and attended Ohio Wesleyan University, where he graduated in 1886, having been honored by election to Phi Beta Kappa. Three years later he completed the Bachelor of Sacred Theology at Boston University's School of Theology, and by the time he came to Simpson had already earned honorary doctorates from Baldwin-Wallace College (1900) and his alma mater, Ohio Wesleyan (1911).[1] A few months after he finished his work at Boston University he married Lizzie L. Howes at Dennis, Massachusetts.[2] They had three daughters, Gertrude, Alice Mary and Helen Frances, and two sons, Paul M. and John W.

Hillman's two decades as a pastor brought him to ever larger churches as his reputation as an effective preacher, counselor and manager grew.[3] All but one of these pastorates were in Ohio or Pennsylvania; for five years, beginning in 1912, he served at First Church in Des Moines, where he and his family became comfortable with central Iowa and familiar with the conference college down at Indianola. In fact, in 1914 he was elected to a three-year term as a member of Simpson's Board of Trustees and thus was able to become fully acquainted with the College, both with its strengths and its problems.

Committed still to a career in the itinerancy, Hillman accepted a call to the prestigious St. Paul's Church in Toledo, Ohio, in 1917. Two years later, however, he accepted the invitation to the presidency of Simpson. Surely he was no academician, and he had thoroughly enjoyed his pastorates. But he saw in Simpson's invitation a real challenge. He knew he could manage a church; maybe he could manage a college.

Hillman had never stayed in one pastorate more than five years. He would remain at Simpson seventeen years, the longest tenure of any of the College's presidents up to the present time.

Like Charles Shelton, Hillman was a big, full-fleshed man who was rarely seen in any garb other than a well-fitting dark suit, complete with the proper matching waistcoat, accoutered with a fine chain of gold from which his gleaming Phi Beta Kappa key dangled. When he presided on the rostrum in chapel or at a faculty meeting or at a weekly prayer service, or if he sat at his desk in the Administration Building, there was no doubt whatever in anyone's mind about who was in charge. He could intimidate misbehaving or indolent students with Jovian majesty, and even a few of the faculty were a bit afraid of him. "He was almost too dignified," recalled one of them. Others found him for the most part warm and caring, and rarely was there a faculty- or student-sponsored event where he was not present. When Campus Day came in the spring, he appeared in his three-piece suit, Phi Beta Kappa key and all, but he also had a rake and worked with the rest of them, then attended the mock chapel he knew would parody his mannerisms of voice and movement unmercifully. And he seemed to enjoy it. Harold Watson said it best: "I developed a deep affection for the Old Man, as he sometimes called himself, found him easy of access, wise in counsel, tolerant of honest mistakes, affable on most occasions."[4]

If it is true that Presidents Shelton and Strickland and Campbell attended Simpson during its adolescent years of awkward growth, then surely it was John Hillman who presided over the rites of passage that signaled the entrance of the College into maturity; for in the 1920s Simpson came of age. The outward signs were there to see: solid membership in the North Central Association of Schools and Colleges, approval by the American Association of Universities and the American Association of University Women, receipt of a major grant from the General Education Board of the Rockefeller Foundation, not to speak of ready acceptance of Simpson graduates into all the leading professional and graduate schools across the nation. To Simpson and its loyal Warren County supporters this recognition was seen as validation of Simpson's growing academic reputation in Iowa and the Midwest.

More important, however, were changes, many of them subtle, some of them wrenching, and almost none of them planned, which made Simpson a very different place than it had earlier understood itself to be. These changes were hardly unique to Simpson. But they affected Simpson in its own way and in accordance with its own history.

There was, for example, a powerful and for the most part unanticipated democratization of American higher education after the First World War. Undergraduate enrollment in colleges and universities had already nearly quadrupled between 1900 and the end of the war, and few expected it to continue to grow significantly. But between 1920 and 1930 it doubled again, passing the million mark.[5] Simpson, like most other colleges in Iowa, also experienced marked growth during the postwar period. (See table 6.) Total full-time enrollment (not counting summer school students) jumped from 497 in 1919–20 to 824 in 1925–26, an increase of nearly sixty-six percent, and while hard times in the agricultural Midwest forced a falloff in the latter part of the decade, Simpson's 1929–30 enrollment stood at 699, still a healthy forty-one percent gain for the decade. The figures are even more impressive if one looks at the liberal arts enrollment, excluding academy, business school and conservatory students, which increased from 369 in 1919–20 to 698 in 1925–26, a striking gain of eighty-nine percent in just six years, and with an enrollment of 650 in 1929–30, a still handsome gain of seventy-six percent for all the 1920s.

"Our colleges have been invaded by the whole populace," wrote Dean Max

Table 6
Enrollment 1920–1936

	Senior	Junior	Soph.	Fresh.	Total College
1920–21	47	56	97	166	366
1921–22	53	68	87	224	432
1922–23	56	67	184	265	572
1923–24	67	131	161	322	681
1924–25	111	80	205	301	697
1925–26	72	135	194	297	698
1926–27	110	115	185	229	639
1927–28	116	118	187	262	683
1928–29	106	130	179	249	664
1929–30	95	127	190	238	650
1930–31	92	107	181	209	591
1931–32	103	106	186	205	606
1932–33	96	97	148	165	506
1933–34	81	92	120	190	483
1934–35	88	60	142	194	484
1935–36	72	81	151	218	518

	Academy	Special. & PG & Uncl.	Business	Conservatory	Net Total*
1920–21	54	2	84	156	495
1921–22	41	9	68	143	528
1922–23	46	6	98	162	654
1923–24	42	11	96	187	780
1924–25	26	12	79	234	817
1925–26	18	23	97	243	824
1926–27	3	10	—	197	734
1927–28	—	3	52	139	720
1928–29	—	11	52	192	721
1929–30	—	—	51	218	699
1930–31	—	2	56	158	632
1931–32	—	—	—	132	638
1932–33	—	23	—	69	529
1933–34				71	499
1934–35	—	—	—	100	518
1935–36	—	1	—	92	538

*Excludes duplicates.

McConn of Lehigh University in 1928.[6] And few would deny that more and more of the nation's parents had by now convinced themselves that a high school education would no longer do. A college degree would open the door to the traditional professions or, more importantly, to a career in business. Learning was not an end in itself; the purpose of an education was to prepare for a career.

At many universities and colleges, the hordes of new students included a much broader spectrum of society than these schools had ever seen. In classrooms across the nation, the sons and daughters of blue-collar workers rubbed shoulders with those of privileged families. At Simpson, however, there was really little discernible broadening of the class of people from whom the students came. It was more nearly a matter of making room for many more of the middle-class farm and small-town youngsters Simpson had always attracted. They were still a homogeneous population. In the spring of 1925, for instance, eighty percent were Methodists, only 45 of 697 liberal arts undergraduates were from out of state, and few if any of them could be counted in the underclass.[7]

More of the same, but it *was* more, and the College benefited substantially from the burgeoning enrollments of the early twenties. Fortunately, it had room for them. The new Central Building—they would soon call it the "Administration Building"—was almost ready for occupancy in the fall of 1920. For the first weeks of the semester both faculty and students had to scramble to find adequate quarters for class meetings, but on October 6 they were able to move into the commodious classrooms and offices that occupied the entire ground floor of the building. Two months later the president and his administrative staff moved in as the second and third floors of the building were opened.[8]

Meanwhile, in an effort to make room for growing numbers of students, the board of trustees decided to reconstruct College Hall, or "Old Chapel," as they were now calling it. It was a decision not easily arrived at. After fifty years of heavy use and too many seasons of deferred maintenance, Old Chapel was regarded by some people—especially President Campbell—to be beyond repair, ready for the wrecker's ball. It would be best, agreed some of the members of the board, to pull it down, for with its unsteady, leaning tower, its dilapidated classrooms, its tawdry society halls and chapel space already far too small for a growing student body, it would serve no useful purpose once the new administration building was in use. On the other hand, an upsurge of nostalgia and sentiment among alumni, the older faculty and even some of the students sought to save the historic structure from the demolition gang. Led by the College's financial secretary, irrepressible John P. Morley, the traditionalists took advantage of Campbell's departure from the scene and determined to bring the new president over to their cause. No sooner had he arrived on the campus than he was taken aside by Morley and allowed to share the latter's technicolor vision of a "rejuvenated edifice in the midst of the whispering maples." Hillman was charmed. "It was awfully hard to say 'no' to John Morley," said the president.

When experts were called in to look at the structure, they declared the foundation sound, the walls safe, the roof solid.[9] But the tower, dangerously out of plumb, must go; the soft home-made brick on the building's exterior must be faced with something more durable; the hideous "hog chute" at the rear of the building should be replaced by a modern fire escape.

Morley was not a fund-raiser in vain, and he went to work organizing the College's alumni to "translate the gold of sentiment into the clinking silver of dollars." Together with O. E. Smith and Ethel Shaw, officers of the alumni association, he drummed up support for the project. The *Simpsonian* provided moral support, declaring that while "the Old Chapel cannot be accused of being beautiful," it should be remodeled and modernized.[10] Then Morley invited more than a hundred unsuspecting alumni to a free dinner at Mary Berry Hall, where Hillman, now a true believer in Morley's project, issued the challenge. "It is a crime from the standpoint of the college," he said, "and an outrage on the community of Indianola to bring strangers to the chapel of Simpson College." Its condition is "a disgrace." But, he assured them, with their help it could be magnificently redone. The whole building would be refaced with a deep red flint brick, the awkward front entrance entirely rebuilt, changing the windows and doors "to coincide with the latest style of architecture," and the inside floors, walls and woodwork refinished. The chapel on the second floor would be transformed into an auditorium, seating 475 persons on a sloped floor "with opera chairs in tobacco brown" and the platform rebuilt in the west end of the room. Morley fairly bubbled as he delivered his after-dinner speech in which he said of the building,

Carroll N. Kirk became Director of Athletics in 1909 and served until 1911.

During the early years of the twentieth century, the military played an important role at Simpson.

Francis L. Strickland served as President of Simpson from 1910 to 1915.

"The Old and the New." President Shelton greets incoming President Strickland in 1910.

Dedicated on a beautiful June day in 1907, the College's new library was a gift of Andrew Carnegie.

The Trideltas hold a reunion in 1910.

Simpson's track team in 1911.

The Class of 1914 sweeps and rakes the campus in the spring of 1911. Variously called "Clean-up Day," "Flunk Day," or "Campus Day," it is one of Simpson's hoary traditions.

The "Bachelor's Retreat," located on North Buxton Street across from the Conservatory of Music, 1911.

It was men and horses that built Hopper Gymnasium. These photos were made at the construction site in the summer of 1911.

Hopper Gymnasium, completed in 1912, was in its day the finest structure of its kind in the state of Iowa.

Major Edward H. Catlin, Instructor in Military Science and Tactics, 1910–11.

Simpson's state championship basketball team in 1912–13. In the first game ever played in Hopper Gymnasium, Simpson defeated the University of Iowa 25–14. Pictured are, top row: Coach Harold Iddings, players Graves, Saur, Corbin, Wilson and Piffer; bottom row: Cuthbertson, Sells, Jackson, Slocum and Dyke.

Completed in the fall of 1913, the campus gate was presented to the College by the Class of 1912.

Harry Hopper, the Simpson alumnus whose benefactions made possible the building of Hopper Gymnasium.

The *Simpsonian* staff admires its own product in 1913.

Ladies' Glee Club, 1913. They were state champions.

Coach Chester C. Dillon served as Director of Athletics from 1916 to 1918.

The student-owned and operated College Book Store in 1914.

Levi P. Goodwin taught English and Public Speaking from 1913 to 1916.

Lilah Edna Pote '15 (in white blouse) and her roommate at Mary Berry Hall.

Frank Perrin Henderson '99, served on Simpson's board of trustees from 1919 to 1954.

Campus scene showing College Hall (left), the Library and Hopper Gymnasium in the background, together with Mary Berry Hall and the Home Economics building (right).

Alpha Tau Omega (lower left) and Kappa Theta Psi (lower right) maintained fine houses for their members. For years they were the only men's housing on campus.

The College's Heating Plant, view from the north with tennis courts in the foreground.

Interior of Hopper Gymnasium.

Sara Sigler's triumph at Simpson was the transformation of the old Women's Gymnasium into a Home Economics building, opened in 1915.

College Hall was outfitted with a covered fire escape (right) which the students soon called the "hog chute."

James Watson Camppbell, President of the College (1916–19).

The president's house at the time John L. Hillman took up his duties at Simpson.

Everett "Tip" Olive, who taught at Simpson from 1900 to 1920, wrote many of the College's favorite songs.

Leslie M. Shaw, of the Class of 1876 in Law, was Governor of Iowa (1898–1902) and Secretary of the Treasury of the United States in the cabinet of President Theodore Roosevelt.

Niles "Soup" Graves, Director of Physical Education for Men (1918–21).

President Hillman at his desk, 1922.

President Hillman was a familiar figure in chapel—nearly every day. Here he appears in 1922.

President John Linnaeus Hillman (1919–36).

The Madrigal Singers set out in a hearse-like bus for their 1926 tour.

Delta Delta Delta    Alpha Chi Omega    Zeta Tau Delta 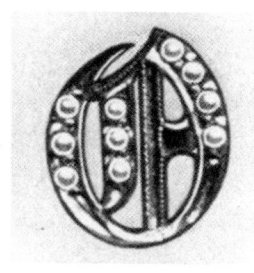   Omicron

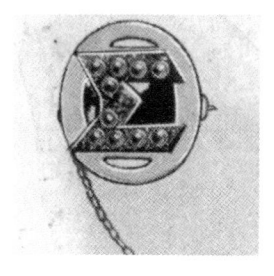

Beta Sigma Omicron 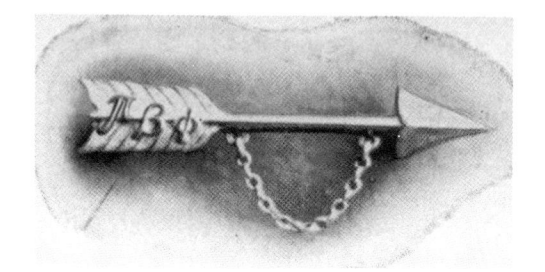   Pi Beta Phi 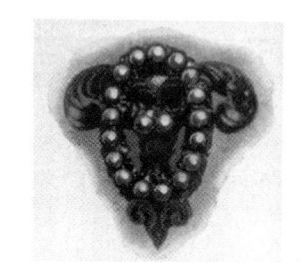   Theta Upsilon

During the 1920s Greek-letter societies abounded at Simpson. Their badges (sororities above and fraternities below) make a colorful display.

Alpha Tau Omega 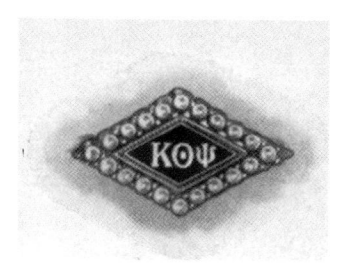   Kappa Theta Psi    Theta Kappa Nu

Gamma Kappa Delta    Alpha Delta Alpha

Sigma Delta Chi

Rae L. Dean, Treasurer and Business Manager of the College (1919–45).

Four Simpson presidents attended the College's Commencement in 1923. L. to r.: Charles Eldred Shelton (1899–1910), John Linnaeus Hillman (1919–36), Edmund Meek Holmes (1889–92) and William E. Hamilton (1886–89).

Clyde W. Emmons, Professor of Mathematics and College Registrar (1910–45).

During the early 1920s the College Council, composed of both faculty and students, was a powerful and effective body.

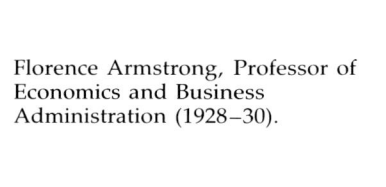

Florence Armstrong, Professor of Economics and Business Administration (1928–30).

C. Noel Workman was Director of Physical Education for Men (1923–26).

During the 1920s Simpson's football teams drew enthusiastic crowds to the College field, located where Barker, Pfeiffer and Kresge halls now stand.

Cecil Cushman, Director of Athletics from 1921 to 1924.

In 1925 Simpson boasted a fine new cinder track.

One of Simpson's all-time greatest football teams.

Kenneth "Moco" Mercer was one of Simpson's football greats.

Francis L. Moats, Professor of History and Political Science and sometime Dean of the College (1921–53).

Jesse Allen Baker, whose tenure at Simpson was one of the longest ever, served as Professor of Chemistry from 1908 to 1954.

Ruth M. Jackson, Professor of English (1923–26; 1936–68), who also served as Dean of Women from 1936 to 1947.

English Professor Harold Francis Watson was a mainstay of the Simpson faculty from his arrival in 1924 to his retirement in 1960.

Hiram Smoots Doty, first a Professor of Biology and later Professor of Geology, taught at Simpson from 1919 to 1963.

William Charles Hilmer, Professor of Classical Languages (1920–41) and Vice President of the College (1933–41).

Josiah B. Heckert, Professor of Economics and Business Administration, 1920–25.

Herbert A. Harvey, Instructor in Violin (1911–24) and Dean of the Conservatory of Music (1924–40).

Peter Ross, brought from his native Scotland to Simpson by Harry Hopper in 1912, superintended the College's athletic facilities for four decades.

Simpson's women's soccer team was a powerful aggregation in 1924–25.

Senator A. V. Proudfoot '85, Chairman of the Board of Trustees of the College, 1918–37.

For more than half a century the great smokestack of the Central Heating Plant stood sentinel over the campus.

Marjorie Earl Camblin '29, a Simpson beauty who was the first Drake Relays Queen.

Earl Enyeart Harper was President of Simpson from 1936 to 1938.

John Owen Gross, President of Simpson from 1938 to 1941.

G. Christie Swain '35, whose history of Simpson, published in the 1935 *Zenith*, served the College for more than a generation.

The Lane sisters, Leota '25 and Lola '27, were the toast of Hollywood in the late 1920s and the thirties.

The Theta Kappa Nus built a fine house in 1932. Seven years later, Theta Kappa Nu merged with Lambda Chi Alpha under the name of the latter.

Alpha Chi Omega was the first–and only–sorority to build its own chapter house.

Campus buildings seem dwarfed by the "whispering maples."

The Delta Delta Delta house on North C Street, opposite Buxton Park.

"It will be enduring and beautiful as new."[11] It will require only a "few thousand dollars" to complete the work. By this time everyone knew that their free dinner wasn't free.

Construction began on June 1, 1920. Several months and thirty-seven thousand dollars later the work was completed, and everyone declared that it was money well spent. Although they missed the old belfry and the swarm of bees that went with it, the fresh yet traditional appearance of the building would continue to grace the campus for years to come.[12]

Upon the completion of the new administration building and the restoration of Old Chapel, a joint dedication and rededication was held January 20–21, 1921. In a banquet and two ceremonial sessions, a parade of clerics and local celebrities, people like Harvey Ingham of the *Register* and Bishop Homer C. Stuntz from Omaha, judged that Simpson's fine new buildings would obviate the need to construct anything more for many years to come. When William E. Hamilton intoned the prayer of dedication, perhaps only a few who were there recalled that Hamilton's association with the College went back to the very year when he watched them break ground for Old Chapel the first time.[13]

Another old building, one that no one would have described as an impressive edifice, disappeared from the campus during the summer of 1920. The old, white frame bookstore on the east edge of the campus was "gently raised, tenderly placed on trucks and hauled away."[14] As a symbol of student entrepreneurial spirit, it would be missed.

The little bookstore was not the only thing on campus in need of removal. The soft maple trees planted fifty years earlier were showing signs of advanced age. "The whispering maples won't whisper much longer unless we save the ones we still have and plant some new ones," commented the *Simpsonian*, echoing what everyone had been saying for a long time.[15] Complaints about the trees were almost as strident as the objections to the cow-paths that crisscrossed the campus in the absence of adequate walkways. The new president did order the trees trimmed, and some well-intentioned young people even planted some new trees, which unfortunately were elms.

* * *

The opening of the Administration Building and remodeling of Old Chapel allowed Simpson by the fall of 1920 to provide adequate space for its growing student body. In order to cope with growing numbers of students and an expanding curriculum, the College's leaders added a number of faculty during the early twenties. When John Hillman arrived in 1919, the faculty numbered thirty, including the president (nineteen in the liberal arts college, three in the academy, two in the business school and six in the conservatory). A decade later there were thirty-three in the college, two in business and ten in the conservatory, for a total of forty-five, an increase of exactly fifty percent.

Administration of the entire College was handled either by faculty members or by a handful of officers, assisted by a small secretarial staff. In addition to the president, one could find in 1919 John P. Morley as financial secretary, Rae Lancaster Dean, a Simpson graduate in the class of 1902, taking up his duties as the College's first full-time treasurer and business manager and Junia Luella Todd '98, functioning as dean of women and matron of Mary Berry Hall.[16] Gertrude Sidney Bean and two part-time assistants handled the library, and a small janitorial staff under the watchful eye of Peter Ross kept the buildings clean and in a reasonable state of repair when there was a reasonable amount of money available to get the job done. During the decade, only one major administrative post was added. In 1921 Hillman was persuaded by the alumni to hire Loren C. Talbot '03, as alumni secretary. All other administrative tasks were handled by the faculty in addition to their teaching duties. For example, Clyde Emmons took on the job of registrar in 1921, for which he received no supplementary salary until 1929. He must have liked the job, for he continued in it until his retirement in 1945. Charles N. Burrows, Simpson's first professor of sociology, who joined the faculty in 1923, took on a new position as dean of men in 1925 in addition to his teaching obligation and held that administrative role for fourteen years.

The appointment of Rae Dean, whose tenure as senior financial officer of the College would last until the end of the Second World War, recognized the fact that the business affairs of a growing college needed full-time professional management. Thus when in the fall of 1918 Clyde Proudfoot resigned as treasurer of the board of trustees, the opportunity existed to make a change gracefully and bring Rae Dean, who was already serving a three-year term as a member of the board, into full-time service.[17] Dean never brought about an increase in the College's always-sagging revenues, but he certainly managed what revenues there were with skill and tact.

"As I look back," wrote Harold Watson many years later in his copious memoirs of the College during those years, "the outstanding characteristic of the early administrative system was its simplicity. It was carried on with a minimum of red tape and considerable flexibility in behalf of the individual student, by a group most of whom had worked together long enough to be a team."[18] One thing is certain: the cast of administrative and support staff was minimal, and it was effective. And as one looks back on those years, the figure of the College's president looms very large indeed.

* * *

Hillman quickly earned the respect of everyone at the College, and of no one more than the members of the board of trustees, especially its president from Indianola, A. V. Proudfoot, whose leadership of the board continued throughout the new president's administration. Proudfoot never wavered in his support of Hillman, nor did the other Indianola members, nine of whom in 1919 included Harry Hopper; William Buxton, Jr., president of the brand new Peoples Trust and Savings Bank; Judge John A. Storey, associated with the Warren County Bank; old John H. Henderson, member of the board since 1869; F. Carl Sigler, who with his wife were among Simpson's most generous benefactors; young Frank P. Henderson, John's son, in legal practice with his father;[19] S. M. Holladay and the Rev. J. W. Campbell. Among the rest of twenty-seven trustees were several outstanding public figures: Charles R. Brenton of Dallas Center was a rising star in the Iowa banking world; E. T. Meredith, former U.S. Secretary of Agriculture under President Wilson, was Des Moines's leading publisher and printer; and Gardner Cowles was making the *Des Moines Register* into one of America's premier newspapers. Only five of the twenty-seven, apart from Hillman, were clergymen, but one had to take into account seven additional ex officio pastors, including old William E. Hamilton and the remarkably popular Fred N. Willis of Indianola, all of whom participated in general board meetings.

Ten years later the board membership still numbered twenty-seven, but its membership had changed profoundly. Without exception, the regular members were laymen and not all of them came from southwest Iowa. The board first broke with geographical tradition in 1920, when it elected Charles E. Bentley, a Simpson graduate of 1904, of Chicago to a three-year term. The next year saw the election of Mark R. Tennant '12 of Sioux City, the first Iowa resident from outside the old conference boundaries. A yet more powerful tradition was set at naught in 1924 when Martha Stahl Beall of Mount Ayr was named to the board, the first woman ever. "Aunt Martha," the reader will recall, was an 1888 graduate of Simpson and had taught Latin at the College during the late nineties and early part of the new century, serving as librarian during part of that time. After her departure from the College in 1904, she had married and settled into the easy comfort of small town Iowa life, where she became a community leader and church stalwart. Her election to the Simpson board recognized not only her estimable reputation in southwest Iowa but also the fact that women, having won the vote, were now entitled to participate in the governance of the nation's many institutions. To some people it was, in fact, surprising that Simpson, with its history of coeducation and support for women's rights, had not acted earlier to bring women into the board of trustees, but among the all-male groups that actually proposed and elected new members, the idea had probably never been broached. It was not until Simpson sought recognition by the American Association of University Women in the twenties that the board's dereliction with respect to women came to light, whereupon the men, trying to look as guiltless as possible, acted with dispatch.

There was nothing particularly ominous about the disappearance of clergymen from the roster of regular trustees, for throughout the twenties there were a half dozen or so ex officio members, pastors all, whose number included the minister of the Indianola Methodist Church, the district superintendents in the Des Moines Conference and, of course, President Hillman himself. Not only were these pastors voting members of the board; they also were entitled to vote separately as a body on any issue that came before the board, possessing in effect a veto on anything passed by regular board members. Honored more in the breach than the observance, this voting provision in the College's by-laws was in effect a dead letter, but the board was sobered by the mere threat that the clergy might nullify a decision in their role as guardians of morality and keepers of the keys to the Kingdom.

Though the board experienced real change during the twenties, the faculty of the College became increasingly and gratifyingly stable. After the revolving-door years of wartime and the immediate post-war settling out, Hillman was able to appoint a number of people who would decide to make their careers at Simpson. He started with a few who were already on board and who would remain throughout his seventeen-year administration. Clyde Emmons, efficient and quiet, already a veteran of nine years at Simpson, held the chair of mathematics. Principal of the academy was Grace Beam, who had by this time become a Simpson legend. And principal of the School of Business (still a non-degree program) was Edward L. Miller, "a practical spoke in Simpson's wheel,"[20] in the middle of his teaching career at Simpson which spanned a record-breaking forty-seven years (1889–1936).

In the fall of 1919 Hillman brought several new people into the faculty. One of them was biologist Hiram Smoots Doty, who held an M.A. from Iowa State College (1915) and had done additional graduate study at the University of Chicago. At thirty he was Simpson's most eligible bachelor, and he would remain eligible the rest of his life. Edmund Meek Holmes, Simpson's dignified former president, returned from the itinerancy to take up the post in philosophy and Bible created by the departure of President Campbell. A man of unaffected piety, Holmes was a committed Christian, a trifle unbending, a "firm believer in the right"[21] who seemed somehow to be living out his life in the wrong century. Coming to the academy to teach English was Nina Hohanshelt Brown, whose enthusiasm was as infectious as Holmes's placidity was calming. The valedictorian of Simpson's class of 1903, she was the wife of Carl Brown, whom the reader will remember as the man who assisted Harry Hopper in the construction of the gymnasium.

At the end of Hillman's first year, the faculty suffered two severe losses. One of these was Joanna Baker, for thirty years Simpson's true classicist. She resigned to take a teaching position at Erie College at Painesville, Ohio. Perhaps at a women's college she would find more Greek and Latin language students than at Simpson, where, since the abandonment of the old curriculum, enrollment in the classical languages had plummeted. As she departed, she sold off the old Baker home to make room for the new administration building. To replace Baker, Hillman hired Carroll H. May, a product of his alma mater, Ohio Wesleyan, where May had been a member of Phi Beta Kappa. With a Harvard Ph.D. he seemed to be the perfect choice, but the students complained that he was even more demanding than Baker, indeed unreasonable. "He thinks that the average student should study an average of two hours for each class," exploded an outraged writer in the 1920 *Zenith*. May's classes very nearly melted away, and by the end of the school year he decided to find other employment. His successor in the fall of 1920 was William Charles Hilmer, former vice-president of Morningside College, who had completed his doctorate a decade earlier at the University of Illinois and could teach not only classical languages but most of the modern Western European ones as well. If need be, he could be the whole foreign language department, and in fact as enrollments in languages declined, he was just about that. Hilmer's flexibility enabled him to remain at Simpson until 1941.

Joanna Baker's resignation was sad, because she and her father had attended to Simpson from its infancy, but even more surprising, and disturbing, was the loss of John L. Tilton, the College's senior faculty member, who resigned after thirty-two years to accept a position as chairman of the Department of Geology at West Virginia University. Though stunned by his departure, Simpson people had to realize that Tilton had earned a national reputation as a geologist and could go just about anywhere he pleased. West Virginia was a challenge: the very Appalachian landscape that predisposed that state to poverty was also a veritable textbook of geology. Besides, Tilton had heard good things about the university from Francis Strickland. Hillman found Tilton a hard man to replace. First he found an Indiana University Ph.D. named Eula McEwan to take the post. Students found her scholarly but not very approachable. A mystified sophomore student declared that the professor was interested in "scientific things that are well-nigh unspellable."[22] McEwan remained only a year and a half, resigning in mid-year. Fortunately Hillman found a replacement in young William

F. Leicht, a state geologist in Wisconsin. Leicht was still working intermittently on his M.A. degree, and seemed acceptable enough, but when more than three years later he had not completed the work on his degree, Hillman decided the time had come to find a new geologist. His search was highly successful when he found Louise Fillman, who had only recently completed her doctorate at the State University of Iowa. She would remain at Simpson until 1941.

J. Allen Baker returned in 1920 to teach chemistry at Simpson after his two years of wartime service with the munitions industry and a subsequent brief flirtation with Iowa Wesleyan. He completed his doctorate in 1926 and remained at the College for the rest of his career. Short, square, slightly balding, with a round, cherubic face, he alternately charmed and coerced students to do their best, all too often with woefully inadequate equipment. The year 1920 also saw the appointment of Eva F. Stahl as assistant professor of English. A Simpson graduate in the class of 1901, she had earned an M.A. at Michigan a decade later and had done a bit more graduate work at the University of Chicago. In the nineteen years that followed her joining the English faculty at Simpson, she taught composition and literature classes.

As Iowa and the nation worked their way out of a short, severe economic depression in 1921, Simpson saw the arrival of its first full-time professor of physics, Arthur Blaine Carr. A graduate of Albion college, where he had known Clyde Emmons, who seems to have suggested his coming to Simpson, Carr had completed the M.A. in physics at the University of Michigan in 1916 and had been studying for three more years at Northwestern University. Small and wiry, he seemed to be all muscle and brain. His exploits as a featherweight wrestler were known far and wide. When he came to Simpson he was agonizingly close to the completion of his Ph.D. and expected to finish it "within a year or so," but as happened too frequently with young professors in private colleges, a heavy teaching load together with marriage and small children to care for made it fatally easy for him to postpone the research and writing of a dissertation. Although he taught with apparently real success at Simpson for twenty-five years, producing physics students whose accomplishments in graduate studies attested to the quality of their preparation, he never completed the doctorate. Unfortunately, for many years this same story was repeated again and again at Simpson, certainly to the detriment of faculty morale if not to the excellence of classroom performance.

Although he could not have guessed it at the time, Hillman's appointment of Francis I. Moats to the chair of history in 1921 was either a stroke of genius or an incredible piece of good luck. Moats was already known to everyone in Indianola; when still a boy he had attended the academy for two years (1907–09). As an undergraduate at Simpson he had cut a wide swath. Known as "Felix" in those days, he was reputed to be the political boss of the campus. After graduating in 1913, he went on to Northwestern University, where he completed the M.A. in history with distinction and was awarded a university fellowship for an additional year of study. After three halcyon years at Evanston he decided to become gainfully employed, accepting a position at Montana Wesleyan College, where he learned to enjoy the expansive life of the West. After two years there, however, he accepted a commission in the U.S. Army and embarked on an adventurous, if brief, military career as a first lieutenant in the 9,000-man American Expeditionary Force that landed in Vladivostok in 1918 in an effort to support the White Russian forces against the Bolsheviks and to prevent the Japanese from permanently occupying strategic areas of the Asian mainland. When he returned to the States in 1919, Moats went back to his teaching duties at Montana Wesleyan for a year, whereupon he accepted a teaching post at Illinois College in Jacksonville, where he taught for only a year before coming to Simpson.

When Moats and his wife Fanny arrived in Indianola, he took up his teaching duties with vigor. Precise in speech, military in bearing, he stood ramrod straight in the classroom, his glasses and balding pate—his colleagues started calling him "Curly"—making him look older than his thirty-six years.[23] Although he was an expert on church history, especially Methodist history, his broad-based teaching of both history and political science won a host of admiring students, and his classes were always crowded. Because of Moats, an unusual number of undergraduates decided to major in history. He completed his doctorate at the State University of Iowa in 1926 and remained on the faculty, later serving as dean of the College, until his retirement in 1953.[24]

As Moats and his wife settled in, soon building a family consisting of two sons, Robert and William, and a wondrous cow named Esmeralda, life at Simpson quickened. And at the same time the academy was strengthened by the addition of Edith Belle Whitaker, a quiet, hardworking young 1920 Simpson graduate. Although it is probable that her appointment was intended to be short-term, she remained on the staff for eighteen years, the first few years in the academy and later in the College proper.

If Simpson was going to be up to date, reasoned Hillman, it should establish a chair in sociology. Though courses in that field had been taught for years, it was regarded as a sort of stepchild of history or of education, and there were those who thought it should stay that way. A fair number of faculty people were ardently opposed to sociology's elevation to full department status. Wary lest a kind of academic Gresham's Law would apply, to the detriment of the humanities, conservatives warned of a diminution of academic rigor, of a loss of the pure waters of knowledge in the sands of counterfeit scientism. Hillman, unperturbed and even a bit amused by the passion of faculty discussion, went ahead and appointed Charles N. Burrows to the chair of sociology in the fall of 1923. A graduate of Missouri Wesleyan College who had earned his S.T.B. at Boston University, Burrows was judged to be acceptably pious, especially because he was a protege of Simpson's own Dr. James A. Beebe '03, dean of the Boston School of Theology, who vouched for him, and he was well trained in sociology. No sooner did Burrows arrive on the campus than any opposition to sociology melted away, for he was a thoroughly well-informed scholar and likable teacher, and two years later he was given additional responsibility as dean of men, a position he would hold for fourteen years. "In a day of some formality," recalled Harold Watson, "he called most of his fellow professors and the students in his classes by their first names."[25] One probably had to expect that sort of thing from sociologists.

In the fall of 1924 the chair of English fell vacant. For the previous five years under Hillman, two people had held that important post. The first was Simpson alumnus Frank Luther Mott '07, who was already an accomplished writer and journalist. Mott had edited both the *Simpsonian* and the *Zenith* as an undergraduate and had nearly completed the Ph.D. at Columbia. After two happy and successful years teaching at Simpson, Mott went on to a distinguished career in journalism and a Pulitzer Prize, ultimately making the University of Missouri's School of Journalism one of the premier graduate programs in that field in the nation. When Mott left Simpson in 1921, he was replaced by Henry Broadus Jones, who came to the College from eight years of teaching in North Carolina. After three years in Indianola, however, he decided to go on to the University of Chicago to complete his doctorate.[26]

Hillman's choice fell on Harold Francis Watson, a young assistant professor of English at the University of Maine. A Pennsylvanian by birth, Watson had attended public schools in New York State and received both his B.A. (1918) and M.A. (1920) degrees from New York University. While working on the M.A. he was an instructor at N.Y.U., then moved to Hedding College in Illinois for two years before taking the position at Maine. He was attracted to Simpson by the opportunity to head the Department of English and shape its program, something he could not do in a larger university at such a young age.

He was certainly not prepared to be charmed by Indianola and Simpson, but both the town and the College impressed him favorably when he arrived in the late summer of 1924. We have from Watson a delightful account of his coming to Simpson.

> As soon as my bus crossed the Warren County line and rushed along the spacious gravel road,[27] I was enthralled by every wooded hill, every pasture dotted with grazing cattle, every hedgerow dancing in the good Iowa breeze.... This was a beautiful land, a gracious land, a land smiling with promise. As we topped a rise, there in the distance was my first quick view of Indianola, the houses almost concealed by the greenery of elms and maples. The bus dipped down again, and then climbed a long hill to turn right—west—into town.
>
> The nearer impression of Indianola was as delightful as the distant one. At the northeast corner of the community, the Jefferson Way was not built up, and the bus turned abruptly from what seemed a country road, into the quiet shaded street I was later to know so well as Kentucky Avenue, and then south down Buxton to give me my first panorama of Simpson College. Our destination was Lem Swartslander's restaurant on the south side of the Square. This was just across from the Victorian Court House with its hitching posts still standing on the west side—and still occasionally used by farmers living on impossibly muddy roads, who came in on horseback Saturday afternoons....
>
> In my first days, aside from Hopper Gymnasium crowded in among the dwellings on North C Street, the Simpson campus extended two blocks east from C Street to Buxton and roughly three blocks south from Franklin to Clinton. Buxton Park—then at its loveliest—even the Victorian bandstand looked freshly painted!—was north across Franklin. Just south of it was the old athletic field with its weather-beaten bleachers.... Then came Mary Berry and the rather unattractive heating plant, whose magnificent chimney was the only rival of the [town's] old water tower, later replaced, and of the grain elevator, later burned. Sandwiched between was a temporary building—in use not more than thirty-five years—at that time devoted to Home Economics. The Conservatory of Music, not yet designated Barrows Hall, although the fame of the late Professor Barrows illuminated the modest building, stood east of the athletic field with a delightful shaded walk leading to it. The old Library, old Chapel, and old Science Hall still performed their appropriate functions, but the old pump beside the Library did not. Near by, a slight ridge in the Campus was said to indicate where the first building, nicknamed Old Bluebird from the color of the brick, had stood before it blew down.
>
> The Administration Building, comparatively new and spic and span, stood in lonely grandeur south of the Chapel Gate. The whispering maples planted about

1870 were near the end of their life cycle but were most impressive. A grassy expanse stretched east to Buxton Street, unbroken by Carver Hall or the present Chapel, but marred by a railroad siding. I was told that a few years earlier student resentment of the eyesore had resulted in a track-raising and the necessity for disciplinary action. An ancient rent-house defaced the corner of Buxton and Clinton. And just north of this on Buxton was another old relic housing the College Bookstore. South of the Ad Building, part of B Street entered the Campus far enough to provide frontage for two more antique domiciles. On the C Street side of the Ad Building, there was parking space for eight or ten cars, never to my recollection fully occupied. In 1924–25 not more than three or four faculty members had cars, and even those plutocrats ordinarily walked to work. A widespread belief obtained, borne out in practice, that every place in Indianola, from the Post Office in the Harlan Building to what was then called the Horse Park, could be reached from every other place on foot. If any students aside from the young preachers had cars, I was not aware of it.[28]

It is doubtful if either Hillman or Eastern-bred Watson thought the latter's stay at Simpson would be long, but Watson truly liked Indianola and proved it by staying on until his retirement in 1960. Even before he taught his first class, he married his fiancee Martha Hoyt Tucker, asking John Hillman to perform the ceremony, a happy moment that created a lasting bond between the young couple and "Prexy."

With the appointment of Watson we have introduced what he liked to call the "Old Guard" of the Hillman era—those people who either antedated Hillman or who were appointed by him and who remained throughout his incumbency. "They were a goodly company," wrote Watson, "and just rehearsing the names is nostalgic."[29] It was people like Baker, Moats, Doty, Emmons, Hilmer, Holmes, Carr, Brown, Burrows, Stahl, Whitaker, Beam and Miller, who gave Simpson its character, and it was these dedicated professors who, together with their president, brought Simpson to a position of eminence in Iowa and in the church that it had not enjoyed before.

When one speaks of the "Old Guard," surely one might add to their number Herbert Archibald Harvey, who took over the leadership of the conservatory upon the death of Frank Barrows in April 1924. Barrows would be remembered as the man who took over a modest music program and brought it to eminence in the region during his remarkable thirty-three years at Simpson. Harvey, who had joined the music faculty in 1911, carried on in Barrows's place after a brief interlude during which Alice Barrows, Frank's sister, completed the work of the 1923–24 school year. Harvey would continue as dean of the conservatory until his retirement in 1940. Yet another stalwart comes to mind: James Henry Inman accepted the chair in education in 1929, coming to Simpson from Illinois Wesleyan University, where he had taught for two years. Inman's doctorate was from the University of Illinois, and he joined the Simpson faculty in an important position that had not been one of Simpson's strengths since Nelson L. Bossing had resigned in 1927.

Another long-time faculty member was Nina V. Mitchell who came to Simpson in the Department of Education in 1928, only two years after her graduation from old Des Moines University, and the same year she completed the M.A. at the State University of Iowa. She, too, would spend the better part of her career at Simpson, remaining until 1952.

Of course there were many other less permanent members of the faculty, but we dare mention only a few whose influence was more profound than their tenure at Simpson would suggest. One was Berthemia McCarthy, who taught modern foreign languages between 1922 and 1932. Her teaching was said to be really very good, but even though she struggled with graduate studies at the State University of Iowa for seven summers, she failed to complete the M.A. degree, and when faculty cutbacks were necessary when the depression of the thirties came, she was one of the first to go.

Wilbur C. Dennis, who had come to Simpson in 1916, continued on the faculty during the early Hillman years, first as a professor of English and public speaking, later concentrating his effort in speech. It was his resignation in 1925 that brought Edith Whitaker to Simpson. That same year saw the departure of Helen L. Pohle, who had taught mostly Spanish for five years after 1920, but did not continue because, like her colleague Berthemia McCarthy, she did not complete the work for her M.A. In English Ruth Jackson, sister of J. Hugh Jackson, who was nearly everyone's favorite Simpson alumnus, joined the faculty in 1922 and taught for four years. A graduate of Simpson, she had completed her M.A. at the University of Chicago, and returned there in 1926 to continue work on the doctorate.[30] Because she would return to Simpson in 1936 and remain until her honorable retirement in 1968, she would find herself included by brevet in Harold Watson's "Old Guard."

At this point in my account I must make a point of personal privilege and mention a man whose tenure at Simpson was brief but without whom this story of Simpson would not have been written at all. He was Franklin Daniel Scott, who joined the faculty as an assistant professor of history in 1925 and remained until 1928, when he went off to Harvard and a Guggenheim Fellowship to complete his doctorate. A gifted European historian who had earned both his B.A. and M.A. at the University of Chicago, Scott brought along his bride of a few months, Helen Giddings Scott, to Indianola. Both of them found the place agreeable, Professor Scott's secret pipe smoking notwithstanding. One semester—it was the spring of 1927—while the dean of women was off doing graduate work, the Scotts were asked to substitute as house parents in Mary Berry Hall, where they were to watch over the young ladies with due vigilance. Helen Scott was designated matron and dean of women, surely the youngest in the history of the College,[31] while her husband, in addition to his teaching duties, superintended the staff of the building, including the boys who tended the furnace. It was in the boiler room, a basement cubicle they lovingly called "Poker Flats," where the boys who tended the furnace lived, that Scott found his true refuge, for there he could read and smoke a pipe to his heart's content, confident that his vice would remain undetected. After three happy years at Simpson, they departed as had others who needed to take that next big step to the doctorate. Ten years later Scott joined the history department at Northwestern University, where he remained for the rest of his distinguished career. It was at Northwestern in the early 1950s that he served as my adviser and mentor, suggesting to me in 1955 that I might like to consider looking at a position at Simpson, a "very good little college in Iowa."

* * *

No matter how isolated Simpson and Indianola were in those days, neither could remain unaffected by the powerful forces that swept across America. Some of these forces were trivial; others were very serious indeed.[32]

There was, for example, the Red Scare. The success of the Bolshevik Revolution in 1917 and the creation of the Communist Third International in 1919 aroused fears of a huge radical conspiracy against the government and people of the United States. Millions, including some Iowans, expected the imminent outbreak of the Red revolution. Their fighting blood was still up after the war, and their hatred of Germans, echoed in the sort of vituperative comments for which President Campbell had been infamous, was quickly and easily transferred to hatred of the Bolsheviks. In 1920 the nation witnessed the excesses of the Palmer raids and the arrest of Sacco and Vanzetti. Even if by the end of the year the Red Scare subsided as quickly as it had begun, it left a legacy of hatred that was to plague the country for several years. Repression of blacks, Jews and labor, not to speak of the phenomenal growth of the Ku Klux Klan in the early twenties, bore testimony to the intensity of feeling against any persons or groups suspected of being infected by the Reds.

The reverberations of the Red Scare were felt at Simpson. Suddenly as if some hidden hand of the censor had come down on their college paper, students read not a word about socialism, a topic that had enlivened the columns of the *Simpsonian* for a number of years. Now they could read instead in the local press about the fulminations of the Ku Klux Klan down on the town square.

The Reverend Thomas L. Roberts of Sheffield, Iowa, organizer of the Klan, billing himself as a past chaplain of the American Legion, addressed a crowd of onlookers in the courthouse yard on Saturday evening September 8, 1923. Reportedly a good speaker, Roberts asserted unapologetically that the basic tenets of the Ku Klux Klan rested on "anti-Catholic and anti-negro sentiment."[33] Only a few months later, a riotous meeting was held "within the sacred walls of the Warren County Courthouse," addressed by Dr. N. C. Carpenter of the Capitol Hill Christian Church of Des Moines and attended largely by "people from Des Moines with a few citizens of Indianola and curious college students." After the customary damning of Catholics, who "want to destroy our public schools," Jews, who wouldn't accept Christ's divinity, immigrants, who harbored alien ideas and were probably Catholics or Jews anyway, not to speak of public officials, who spent "hundreds of dollars . . . each year for the education of the 'niggers,'" he led the crowd out to the edge of town, "just north of the Kappa Theta Psi house, where a large twelve foot cross blazed in the darkness of the night."[34] A year later a huge Klan rally on the fourth of July at the Warren County Fairgrounds was an all-day affair with ball games and picnics and oratory, all of it capped by a "mammoth Klan pageant, requiring more than five hundred robed Klansmen and Klanswomen," with a parade and fireworks and the obligatory cross burning. They hoped for fifty thousand spectators. To the everlasting credit of Indianola and central Iowa, not many came.

The local press opposed the Klan from the beginning. "A Catholic, a negro or a Jew," editorialized the *Indianola Herald*, "can be as good an American as anyone. The Klan seeks to stir up racial and religious hatred when our country was founded on principles of religious and personal freedom."[35] Don L. Berry of the *Record* was furious: "Any race," he wrote, "that expects to maintain its own place in the sun by the continued subjection of other races is kicking against the pricks of all history. . . . If any man joins the Klan thinking there is any shortcut to preserving Americanism, he is only making himself think he hears a noise. . . ."[36]

How did Simpson people respond to the phenomenon of the Klan, with its message of hate? Mostly they simply ignored it, except for that evening when the hooded Klansmen burned the huge cross out behind the Kappa Theta Psi house, something it was impossible to ignore. One boy, standing inside the house looking out the window at the spectacle later remembered how he felt that night: "It was in a way beautiful; it was exciting, it was somehow wonderfully, attractively sinister. But the awful feeling came over me that I was looking into the face of evil."[37]

* * *

Although the prosperity of the 1920s was muted in Iowa, owing to the stubborn agricultural depression that persisted through most of the decade, Iowans shared in the growing abundance of material goods which became available after a period of relative scarcity. After the First World War, the United States achieved the highest standard of living of any people in history. By 1929 per capita income reached $681, the result of an enormous increase in efficiency of production and consequent rise in physical output of American industry. Construction boomed, road building—in Iowa they called it getting Iowa out of the mud—poured public money into the economy. Millions basked in the sunlight of the new wealth.

"Dazzled by the prosperity of the time," writes William Leuchtenburg, "and by the endless stream of new gadgets, the American people raised business in the 1920s into a national religion and paid respectful homage to the businessman as the prophet of heaven on earth."[38] A group of college students voted Henry Ford as the third greatest man of all time, "surpassed only by Napoleon and Christ."[39] Lavish praise of business was the order of the day, and Edward Purinton was about as lavish as one could get when he wrote, in 1921: "What is the finest game? Business. The soundest science? Business. The truest art? Business. The fullest education? Business. The fairest opportunity? Business. The cleanest philanthropy? Business. The sanest religion? Business."[40] A few years later President Calvin Coolidge was saying, "The business of America is business."

The nation responded to the new faith. The great universities rushed to open or expand colleges of business administration or commerce. At Stanford University one could soon earn a "full fledged, solid gold, fourteen-carat" Ph.D. in business,[41] joining Harvard, Wharton and Northwestern in the vanguard of business education as that science ascended from the level of the trade school to the Olympian heights of the graduate school seminar.

Simpson found itself powerfully affected by the new respectability of business education. For decades, to be sure, Simpson had conducted a School of Business, and its principal, Edward L. Miller, was the College's senior faculty member after John Tilton left. But no one had many illusions about Miller's program, and while some credits earned in the School of Business could be applied toward the B.A., certainly little thought had been given to making it a full degree course. Its purposes were more modest and its accomplishments more limited than that.

Toward the end of the First World War, Simpson began to hear more and more about the virtues of business education. The profound success of young alumni like J. Hugh Jackson and Howard Noble at Harvard's graduate program in business, not to speak of their specific urging, led President Campbell to propose in 1918 the creation of a Department of Economics and Business Administration, offering courses leading to the B.A. degree. The war forced a postponement of the plan for a year, but before he resigned, Campbell appointed John Squibb Robinson to the chair of the new department, it being understood that the old School of Business would continue as a nondegree program as heretofore.[42] Robinson, billed (by Campbell at least) as the prophet of the new order, did indeed organize the department, but it seemed that he no sooner moved in than he moved out, accepting a position at Carleton College at the close of that first postwar academic year.

Under Robinson the new department was organized but not truly founded. That happy duty fell to a most remarkable young man, Josiah B. Heckert, whose relatively short tenure at Simpson, just five years, not only placed the department on a sound footing but exercised an influence that elevated business to a place of respect in the curriculum. Far more importantly, Heckert developed lifelong personal relationships with his students in a way that was unique in Simpson's history.

Heckert was a graduate of Kansas Wesleyan and had completed an M.A. in economics at the University of Kansas. During the First World War, he served as an army officer, including a year in France, afterwards returning to college teaching and part-time reporting for the *Kansas City Star* and *Topeka Daily Capitol*. When Simpson discovered him in 1920 he was teaching at Dakota Wesleyan College.

Heckert preached the gospel of business with uncommon enthusiasm. "How to make money," he explained, "that is the subject with which business administration deals." In short, it meant "securing profits," which accorded with the aims of an era when materialism became almost a religion, the moguls of big business serving as the high priests of the new prosperity.[43] But until their message could penetrate Iowa and Warren County, Heckert in fact taught more economics than business administration courses. Simpson students were a trifle slower than some to accept the new ways. Meanwhile Heckert organized a first-rate lecture series, inviting leading Midwestern businessmen to share their stories of success with his students, whom he required to attend. He worked very hard every day, rarely climbing into his Ford car to drive home until after six o'clock in the evening. He expected as much of his students. "He makes his students work—and think—but every one of them would fight for him," was a comment in the 1924 *Zenith*. Believing that it pays to advertise, he persuaded Harvard's graduate school of business to place ads regularly in the *Simpsonian*.[44] Immensely popular, Heckert was invited to address groups on and off campus. Hardly surprisingly, he was invited to be a charter member of Indianola's Rotary Club in 1922 and later served as its president.

Among the organizations that clamored to hear the new guru of capitalism speak was the college Y.W.C.A. He obliged them—it was in May 1922—by explaining to these young women, whose sophistication he judged to be primitive, what men expect of the women they marry. "College men," he said, "desire girls who are attractive in appearance." It is therefore "irreligious [remember, he was talking to the Y.W.C.A.] for a girl to fail to cultivate physical charm and beauty." As he warmed to his topic he emphasized that "it is a part of your Christian duty as college girls to develop qualities of physical charm and attractiveness, to dress neatly and tastefully." Further, "college men desire the athletic type of girl, girls who are active and vivacious," and although a man wants "intellectual companionship," he doesn't expect his wife to know anything about his profession or job. Rather she should cultivate the arts "which add much to the charm of the home," show "sympathy for [her husband's] ambitions," providing their lives with "spiritual qualities" and love. This recipe for marital bliss seems to have gone down well with his eager listeners, for it was printed *in extenso* and without comment in the next edition of the *Simpsonian*.[45] Heckert, not unlike most men of his generation, while supporting votes for women and dedicated to the principle of coeducation and finding it easy enough even to accept women in the workplace, at least temporarily, could not conceive of them in management roles. It is reported that some years later he changed his mind.

Because the Bachelor of Arts degree by its very nature continued to be grounded in the humanities and natural sciences, Heckert in 1923 persuaded the faculty to adopt a new degree, the Bachelor of Science in Business Administration, which deemphasized the liberal arts, especially troublesome things like foreign language, and tilted its program toward a concentration on professional studies.[46] In Heckert's department, then, one could choose either the B.S.B.A. or the B.A. in Economics. By the latter part of the twenties, more students were enrolled as majors in these two programs than in any other department of the College. Such was the attraction of career-oriented education and the popularity of its persuasive salesman at Simpson, reinforced by the undoubted early success of its graduates in the business world, that Heckert was quickly conceded to be the rising star of the Simpson faculty.

His star shone brightly enough to be seen elsewhere, and soon enough he began receiving offers to go to other colleges to teach. In August 1922 he asked the board to release him from his contract so that he could accept a position at the University of Chicago, but with the opening of classes only weeks away, President Hillman insisted that the contract be honored. Heckert stayed, but the board raised his salary to $3,000, the highest of any on the faculty, even more than they paid the football coach.[47] They also agreed to hire young J. Raymond Smith as a full-time assistant in the department.[48] Once again—this time in August 1924—Heckert asked to be released from his contract and returned only after Hillman chased him down in Chicago and persuaded him to come back— at a handsome raise in salary to $3,500. When the same scenario was replayed a year later, scarcely three weeks prior to the opening of the school year, neither Hillman nor the board had the means or the heart to carry on the battle to keep Heckert, so they released both him and his wife so that Heckert could accept a professorship at Ohio State University.[49]

In their three bouts with Heckert, Hillman and the board learned a hard lesson. If the College wanted to keep top-flight faculty in new, high-flying fields where qualified teachers were scarce, it was going to have to pay for them, and pay dearly, for in the case of a discipline like business administration, it was in competition for talent not only with other colleges and universities but with American business and industry as well.

Josiah B. Heckert went on to a distinguished career at Ohio State, but he never forgot Simpson or the young people whose lives he had touched during his years in Indianola. He kept track of the seventy or so students who had majored in his department, writing to all of them each year, compiling their replies for the information and edification of the whole group. His letters advised, encouraged, congratulated and so delighted these bright, success-oriented Simpson alumni that they were in time referring to themselves as the "Heckert group." Fifty, indeed sixty years later, Heckert, long after his retirement as head of the department at Ohio State, was still writing to that very special band of people he had come to know when all of them were still young.[50]

* * *

Taylor C. Miller, recommended highly by the departing Heckert, was employed at the last possible minute before classes commenced in the fall of 1925. With an M.A. from Washington University and further work at the University of Chicago, together with three years of teaching experience, Miller was a fortunate choice to head the department. What was unfortunate was that he stayed only two years, succeeded by his assistant, Harry Kunze, a 1922 Simpson graduate, who then held the departmental chairmanship only one year. His successor was yet another Simpson graduate, Florence A. Armstrong '06, who had earned her M.A. from Radcliffe in 1916 and her doctorate in economics eight years later. An experienced teacher, she was clearly dedicated to economics more than to business administration, which seems to have diminished the popularity of the latter not the least. One cannot help but wonder if Josiah Heckert was surprised to hear that a woman now sat in the chair he had occupied at Simpson.

Though Dr. Armstrong was eminently qualified in her field of teaching, her time at Simpson was short, for she departed after only two years. Clearly the department could not flourish without some continuity of management. Accordingly Hillman exercised great care in choosing Armstrong's successor, and in order to make the position attractive, conceived a combination of department chairmanship and dean of academic administration, the latter a part-time post that would relieve the president of some of his more onerous on-campus duties. After a considerable search, Hillman and the board selected Winfred E. Payne, chairman of the economics department at Battle Creek College,[51] who, they reported, was "interested in the application of Christianity to the business world."[52] They had found their man, and Payne stayed.

Beginning in 1927 the chairman of the department was designated the "William Buxton Professor of Economics and Business Administration," holding Simpson's third endowed chair, created by the gifts of the two William Buxtons, senior and junior.[53] And only two years later, in the fall of 1929, the scion of the Buxtons, William III, was named assistant professor in the department.[54] Young Buxton, a superior scholar and student leader when he was an undergraduate at Simpson, had completed his degree at mid-year in 1928 and had engaged in graduate study at both the University of Chicago and Northwestern.[55] He remained a part-time member of the faculty for a number of years while working at his father's highly successful bank down on the square. Though he labored under the burden of being the heir of Indianola's most prominent family, among students and colleagues, even the professors old enough to be his parents, Buxton was immensely popular, demonstrating competence and an easygoing democratic camaraderie combined with an infectious sense of humor. One of his friends said of him that his secret to success lay in never taking himself too seriously. The friend may have been right.

There is at Simpson a nostalgic footnote to the growing vocational orientation of American higher education in the 1920s. In an aspect of mourning, the editor of the *Simpsonian* animadverted upon the demise of the classics in all of their manifestations. Although Simpson's baccalaureate diplomas, he pointed out, had abandoned Latin and had been worded in English since 1907, honorary doctorates continued to carry the Latin text. "It is well known," lamented the writer, "that not more than fifty people in Iowa can read Latin," for ever fewer students wrestled with it either in high school or college. "The use of Latin on diplomas carries with it a memory of a time when college students were animated by intellectual curiosity rather than by a desire to increase their earning power."[56]

For all the growing popularity of business, Simpson continued in the 1920s to produce more elementary and secondary teachers than it did businessmen and during that decade took two important steps that underscored its commitment to the teaching profession. Teaching shared with business the assurance of reasonably certain employment upon graduation, although the teachers almost certainly faced a life of genteel poverty. In early 1928 the faculty approved a new degree, the Bachelor of Science in Education, like the B.S.B.A. and the Bachelor of Science in Home Economics (introduced in 1917) cutting out some of the liberal arts requirements in order to accommodate more courses in pedagogical technique. At the same time they adopted a new two-year college-level program for training primary teachers, and the College hired Nina V. Mitchell[57] to teach the appropriate elementary courses. It will be recalled that prior to this time "normal training" did not necessarily include any post-secondary academic work, so the adoption of the two-year college program represented a significant step forward in teacher preparation. In its inaugural year at Simpson (1928-29) it enrolled twenty-seven freshmen and twenty-four sophomores and continued to be popular at the College for many years afterwards.[58]

The introduction of the three bachelor of science degrees, together with the two-year elementary teaching program, inevitably altered the balance of fields of study in which students were majoring at Simpson. In 1920, for example, the year J. B. Heckert arrived on the scene, only seven upperclassmen (juniors and seniors), out of 113, were majoring in business administration and nine in economics. In 1929, nearly a decade later, with nearly twice the upperclassmen (221), only six were majoring in economics while the number in business administration had shot up to twenty-nine. Only music, with thirty-seven, could count more majors than business administration. English held its own in numbers with 26 majors both in 1920 and 1929, but its share of upperclassmen was halved. By 1929 the number of upperclassmen in those fields Harold Watson liked to call the "Inhumanities" ballooned from 16 to 71. Still, more than two-thirds of Simpson students were graduating in the traditional liberal arts fields, including music (Simpsonians were frequently reminded that music was one of the traditional seven liberal arts). The more menacing onslaught of the "Inhumanities" was yet to come.[59]

During the 1920s those students who chose to complete the requirements for the B.A. degree were expected to meet a thoroughly respectable set of general liberal arts and science requirements that remained very much the same throughout the decade, including the completion of two years each in natural science, English and a foreign language. In addition students selected a major—they stopped calling them "groups" after 1920—in one of approximately twenty fields. In order to encourage them not to postpone their attack on the general requirements, all entering students were enrolled in a Freshman Studies Program, which included four courses: English, foreign language (German, French, Spanish, Greek or Latin), science and one additional course from a fairly restricted list of solid liberal arts offerings. Most B.A. programs required 121 hours of academic work plus three years (two semester hours) of physical education. Harold Watson recalled that Simpson's requirements, "compared with the conventional offerings of the universities I had attended or taught in . . . were about standard." There was, of course, a Bible requirement, "which seemed to me legitimate in a church-related college." And Watson was happy with the way Bible was taught. "Had the material presented," he wrote, "been couched in the faulty archaism and cacophonous redundancy of most contemporary so-called translations by scholars with no pretensions to literary ability, I should have resented having to expose my majors to clerical gobbledegook, but in those days a strong flavor of King James permeated the quotations."[60]

As enrollments in the college-level departments soared, attendance in the academy dropped precipitously, for by 1920 nearly every town of any consequence in Iowa boasted a high school, effectively eliminating the need for the academies that had so long been a mainstay of secondary education.[61] As academy attendance dwindled, the few who were left included mostly older students, some of them in their twenties, who had missed out on a high school education for one reason or another and who seemed to feel more comfortable in a college setting. It was true of some of them that "their desire for an education," as President Hillman remembered it, "was the result of a religious awakening which had come in the late teens or early twenties. Some of these were very promising students, but their number was declining each year."[62] Though it was perhaps useful to serve these academic stragglers, it was no longer practical to do so. Sentiment and tradition spoke for retaining the academy, but good sense dictated that it be laid mercifully to rest. Moreover, accrediting agencies were beginning to require complete separation of an academy from the college, and Simpson had neither the means nor the desire to do that. Accordingly, the board of trustees decreed early in 1923 a phasing out of the academy, offering only the last two years of its program in 1923–24 and the final year in 1924–25.[63] As one looks at the record of its last days, one searches in vain for an appreciation of the historical importance of the academy to Simpson or of its contribution to the education of thousands of young Iowans. Out of stern necessity it was allowed to die, and no one clamored to bring it back. Yet it is perhaps not too late even now to say a word of praise for its esteemed role in the life of Simpson College.

* * *

During the 1920s the conservatory was probably the best-known part of Simpson College beyond Indianola and Warren County. Frank Barrows continued to provide stimulating leadership and to recruit able faculty and a fair contingent of gifted students. Comfortable with the way things had always been done, Barrows made few changes either in the curriculum or the physical arrangements of his domain in the northeast corner of the campus. For example, long after the College had adopted the semester system, the conservatory continued to run on the old three-term year, and the academic accounting of courses and credit hours was consequently unique to that school within the institution. Barrows's program was thoroughly professional, his regular undergraduate students enrolled in music courses for roughly two-thirds of their college work. For the Bachelor of Music degree forty semester hours in the College of Liberal Arts were required, including English (six hours), psychology (six hours) and twenty-eight hours of electives, including three years of physical training.

The conservatory program offered a wide range of musical studies. Music theory, including harmony, counterpoint and analysis, was required of all candidates for a degree, as was music history. Instruction in voice, piano, violin and cello and pipe organ permitted students to specialize in accordance with their talent and interest. Because many graduates would go into teaching, Barrows saw to it that the requisite courses in public school music for state certification were offered, although he told anybody who would listen that he thought they were a waste of time.

Because performance was expected of all music students, the academic year was peppered with individual recitals and punctuated by performances of a whole array of ensembles: Herbert Harvey's Conservatory Orchestra or the Men's or Ladies' Glee Club, the Madrigal Singers or the College Band. Barrows demanded a high level of performance and he nearly always got it, whether it was a production of *The Pirates of Penzance* or a Christmastime performance of *The Messiah*. The best of the ensemble groups toured Iowa annually, providing first-rate performances of great music both in the cities and in rural communities starved for culture.

Barrows was disappointed in 1920 to lose "Tip" Olive, who like so many in those years, was captivated by the lure of the West, but he had people like Persis Heaton in piano, Ira Pratt and then Bernhardt Henry Bronson in voice or Herbert Harvey in violin. Heaton, a product of Simpson, had been on the faculty since 1910 and remained until the time of her marriage in 1926. Ira Pratt, whose voice teaching was exceptional, left Simpson in 1921 to accept the deanship of the School of Music at Kansas State at Manhattan. Privately trained Bernhardt Bronson proved to be a worthy successor to Pratt. For his part, Harvey was good at just about everything from theory and orchestration to violin and cello and was clearly emerging as Barrows's chief confederate in the conservatory. The Simpson orchestra which he conducted was reputed to be the best in the state.

"Prof" Barrows continued to run the conservatory as a private enterprise. He collected the tuition, paid the faculty, assigned teaching duties and kept the profits, paying the College only for the maintenance of the building. Hillman never asked him what the profits were, and Barrows never volunteered to tell him, relying on his somewhat sniffy Victorian conviction that a gentleman did not talk about money, ever. The fact is that Barrows's earnings were exceedingly modest. The president needn't have worried.

What did indeed worry Hillman and quite a few others was the state of Barrows's health. At the end of the 1923 school year Barrows confided to a friend that he felt "worn out," but he stayed on and worked through the summer session. After a month of vacation he felt a bit better, but by mid-year he was complaining of dizziness and finding his teaching duties increasingly difficult. By mid-March, at the end of the conservatory's second term, he was so ill that he suspended his classes entirely and two weeks later took to his bed with a severe throat infection. Nothing would avail, and he died on April 17, 1924, not yet fifty-seven years old.[64]

For the conservatory the death of Frank Barrows marked the end of an era, a memorable thirty-three years of impressive growth and undeniable success. As his three sisters and two brothers gathered at Indianola to mourn Barrows's untimely death, one of them, Alice, agreed to stay on and conduct the affairs of the conservatory for the balance of the school year. She had taught at Simpson years before and knew its ways.

Of all the tributes that poured in from people who knew and respected Barrows, Don Berry of the *Record* said it best:

> Prof. Barrows was a rare performer on the piano, but his modest disposition did not seek laurels on the concert platform. He preferred to develop in others the skill which would be the proof of the merit of his school. His willingness always to allow to others the credit for their work, the plaudits and the encores and the public recognition, gained from those associated with him the confidence that here was a man who was not trying to rise on the shoulders of others, and one to whom friendship meant more than gain.[65]

Soon enough they would name the conservatory's building "Barrows Hall," for no one had been more intimately involved with it than the professor.[66]

It was fortunate that Herbert A. Harvey, who had taught in the conservatory for thirteen years, was able and willing to accept the leadership of Simpson's music school. So well prepared was Harvey to make this move that the program continued smoothly and without the slightest interruption. By the end of the decade a faculty of seven had grown to eleven. Notable among the new people was George Weiler, a talented pianist who came in the fall of 1924 to take Barrows's old students; he remained for sixteen years. Paula Postel taught piano, organ and harmony for three years after 1926. That same year Myrtle Bussey replaced Persis Heaton in piano and Lester E. Spring joined the faculty to teach voice. Spring's work with choral ensembles was exceptional, keeping him at Simpson for fifteen years. There were others, many others, people of superior talent, but in most cases their time at Simpson was relatively brief.

The conservatory during the 1920s will be remembered as a Simpson success story. The library, on the other hand, will not. Chronic malnutrition was its chief source of weakness. Never high on the priority list of the College's administration, it was very nearly always the last to be funded and the first to be cut. And because the operation of Simpson was perennially in deficit, the library seemed always to lose out. Interestingly, the library book budget, minuscule at best, was the one line item in the budget for which the president had to obtain specific, separate board approval. One would think he would be embarrassed to ask for so little for something so important, so utterly central to the life of the College. For example, in June 1924 he asked for $1,000. In 1926–27 the budget was $870, and in spite of repeated comments by outside agencies about "breathtaking deficiencies," the 1928 allocation was only $1,250.[67] How poor were these amounts? When one puts together the cost of staff, building maintenance and books and periodicals, the library's share of the budget was less than two per cent, a sorry showing at best.[68] Their underpaid, untrained librarians, usually serving without an assistant or adequate student help, did the best they could with slender resources. But their cataloging was later noticed as being "startlingly original," and valuable first editions were allowed to circulate. A few rarities were even set aside for discard until rescued by knowledgeable faculty members.

The Good Years: Simpson in the Twenties   273

During the eleven years between 1919 and 1930 four women served valiantly as librarians: genial Gertrude Sidney Bean (1919–21), who left after two years to take over a boys' school in Penang in the Straits Settlements; Ellen Creek (1921–28), who tried to learn her craft as she went along; Erma Bingham (1928–29), whose year can only be described as discouraging; and Inis Smith, Simpson's first truly professional librarian, graduate of a school of library science, who came in 1929 and "brought order out of chaos."[69]

Whatever the deficiencies of the library, students made excellent use of what material there was. The book collection, numbering approximately 12,000 volumes in 1919, grew to 21,000 volumes by 1930 and in that latter year was receiving about 100 current periodicals. Circulation figures were indeed remarkably high, and the library was crowded with undergraduate patrons. Faculty members were exceedingly careful with their tiny book budgets. The history department, for example, never had more than $75 dollars to spend on library books in any one year, but they seem to have made good use of that pittance, for their students just about read the books to death.

* * *

"A flashing, red-haired youngster, running and dodging with the speed of a deer, gave 67,000 spectators jammed into the new $1,700,000 Illinois Memorial Stadium the thrill of their lives today, when Illinois vanquished Michigan, 39–14. . . ."[70] Red Grange, the Galloping Ghost, phenomenon of the gridiron—they called him the "Wheaton iceman"—ran ninety-five yards with the opening kickoff and scored a touchdown before the game was ten seconds old. He scored three more touchdowns in the next twelve minutes before Coach Bob Zuppke took him out of the lineup. Frenzied spectators were witnessing college football's greatest individual performance of all time.[71] It was October 18, 1924.

That same month Army played Notre Dame in New York City, and after the game Grantland Rice wrote: "Outlined against the blue-gray October sky, the Four Horsemen rode again. In dramatic lore they were known as famine, pestilence, destruction, and death. These are only aliases. Their real names are Stuhldreher, Miller, Crowley and Layden."[72] Knute Rockne and the Four Horsemen won Notre Dame its first national football championship in 1924 and won for themselves immortality in the Valhalla of American sports.

Big-time college football, a phenomenon that exploded in the 1920s, captured the imagination of the public and spawned imitation in nearly all the schools and colleges of America. True, small colleges like Simpson had been playing football for many years, but never before was the game regarded with such importance or played with such intensity. The pages of the *Simpsonian* were filled with reports and splashed with photographs of Simpson's team members, captains and individual performing stars. Long articles provided blow-by-blow accounts of every contest, and the popularity of football rubbed off on other sports, especially basketball and track. Yet for all the attention given to intercollegiate athletics at Simpson, the day when the College's teams could compete with the state universities of Iowa or Nebraska or Missouri was now long past, at least in the major team sports. The gridiron performances of Yale or Illinois might take place in stadia seating tens of thousands; Simpson's home games were played before a few hundred souls seated in rickety bleachers out behind the heating plant, and too often the gate receipts—tickets cost fifty cents each for those few who were asked to buy them—were insufficient to pay the afternoon's officials.[73] Things were better in basketball; at least Simpson could claim to have as fine a gymnasium as any, but its teams could compete only with those of other small colleges or middle-size places like Drake.

Simpson's football teams performed for the most part poorly in the first years after the First World War. A lackluster season in 1919 was followed by a disaster in 1920 when the team suffered losses to Drake (66–0), Morningside (52–0) and Grinnell (81–0) and seems not to have won any games at all.[74] Students were disappointed, Coach "Soup" Graves was mortified and alumni were on the warpath. In fact, no one had seen Simpson's alumni, at least the male contingent, so upset about anything before, and soon enough, their dismay found voice.

On the evening of April 9, 1921, a number of these men gathered in Des Moines, discussed the abysmal state of Simpson's athletics—they meant football—and determined to do something about it.[75] Their plan was simple: they would take over Simpson's athletics and run the program right. Eight days later they presented a three-point plan to the executive committee of the board of trustees which would "reorganize" Simpson intercollegiate athletics: (1) Simpson would delegate to "a committee of the Alumnal Association"[76] the "complete control of athletics" for three years, including selection of the athletic director; (2) the matter of player eligibility would remain exclusively in the hands of the faculty; and (3) President Hillman would possess veto power on the selection of the athletic director. Pending the acceptance of this scheme, they asked that "several alumni members" be added to the College's committee to select a new athletic director for 1921–22, pointing out that it was urgent to reach a decision because the selection of the new coach "must necessarily be made at once." The promoters reminded the board members of the importance of alumni support, which "the school does not at present enjoy," warned of "wide-spread alumnal indifference" to an anticipated fund-raising campaign, and contended that athletics could rally alumni support and enthusiasm. After minimal discussion the board accepted their proposition.[77]

Heartened by their success, thirty-four eager alumni met on Saturday, April 25, at the Fort Des Moines Hotel in the capital city,[78] where they agreed to underwrite the new coach's salary beyond what the College was willing to pay in 1921–22 and to pick up the entire salary the following year, providing the entire Alumnal Association would give its assent at its upcoming annual meeting in June. How much should the salary be? "If Simpson athletics were to flourish," they said, "the salary of a coach must be made sufficiently attractive to get the best man in the business," and they already had a man in mind.

The much-advertised alumni meeting on June 6 endorsed the plans of the committee as a part of what they were calling the "Greater Simpson" movement, which would be managed by a full-time alumni secretary.[79] The three hundred alumni and students who crowded into the chapel that evening greeted with enthusiasm the nostrum that "the successful college of today must conduct itself as a good business firm."[80] And apparently one way to achieve that admirable goal was to get a winning football team. The sport was accepted; games had to be won. After all, these Iowans, like all Americans, lacked a psychology for failure. As Mark Tennant, one of the alumni spokesmen put it, "We are aiming first at improved athletics. . . . We cannot have a winning school without winning athletic teams." Visible, successful sports will attract young people; the publicity given a winning school will bring more endowment; more endowment will in turn "lead to an improved student body, an improved faculty, and a stronger course of study."[81] Tennant seems to have stated here for the first time what came to be called the "athletics formula" for propelling Simpson on to greatness. It would be repeated many times in the future, but never again with quite the unquestioning acceptance accorded it at that moment.[82]

The alumni did indeed organize, establishing clubs all over Iowa and the nation. The *Simpson College Bulletin*, adopting a newspaper format, kept alumni and friends informed of the College's progress, and the association hired Loren Talbot, a Simpson graduate in the outstanding class of 1903, as alumni secretary. "Tabby" Talbot had worked for Don Berry downtown on the *Record*.[83] Installed in an upstairs office in the Administration Building, Talbot composed Simpson propaganda by the yard while marching like a gate-keeping sentry to and fro in his office, all the time chewing on a toothpick.

After a longer search than they had anticipated, the new sports moguls selected Cecil A. Cushman as athletic director and coach of almost everything. Cushman, a Texan and protege of Centre College's C. B. Moran, the man who led the "Praying Colonels" to a 6–0 victory over Harvard that fall, did not have much to work with when he walked on to Simpson's football field, but no one expected miracles.[84]

There were no miracles. The 1921 football season was disappointing, producing only two modest wins (over Parsons and Penn), one tie with Iowa Wesleyan and a string of losses, including a 70–0 drubbing by Coe and a 56–0 thrashing by Cornell. But after the debacle of the 1920 season anything looked good, and students and alumni alike were hopeful for the future. Meanwhile that same autumn the College dropped out of the Iowa Conference, which forbade freshman participation in varsity sports; too many of its nonconference foes were playing freshmen, putting Simpson at a distinct disadvantage. After Simpson quit only three schools—Coe, Cornell and Dubuque—remained in the old conference.[85] The very next year, however, the Iowa Conference was reconstituted with uniform regulations, and Simpson happily rejoined.[86] Organized in May 1922 at Cedar Falls, the new conference included eight (later twelve) charter members, and Clyde Emmons of Simpson's faculty was elected president. At its first full-scale meeting at the Randolph Hotel in Des Moines on December 8, 1922, with all twelve schools present, Emmons was reelected president and served successfully for two years. First called the Iowa Intercollegiate Athletic Association, the name was changed slightly in 1927, substituting the word *conference* for *association*. By 1930 the conference's membership was fourteen.[87]

Cushman's second year was much better. Playing with its freshmen, Simpson won half of its gridiron matches and outscored its foes 87 to 55. But apparently Cushman did not do well enough, for toward the end of the basketball season in 1923 the College announced the appointment of a new athletic director, C. Noel "Dopey" Workman, a former star quarterback for Ohio State, who had also played college basketball and baseball. Twenty-six years old, five feet eight inches tall and weighing only 167 pounds, Workman was proof that one didn't have to be the size of a gorilla to play big-time football. As for poor Cushman, the *Simpsonian* reported laconically that his plans were "not as yet definitely decided upon."[88]

Workman made the miracle happen. Giving due credit to his predecessor, he took a good small college team and made it into a great one. In 1923 Simpson suffered only one defeat—to Iowa State—in nine games, outscoring its opponents 289 to 37 points, and during the following season the team went undefeated, its perfect record marred only by a tie in the game with arch-rival Parsons. In both 1923 and 1924 Simpson was the undisputed champion in the Iowa Conference. Its football players were local heroes, boys like team captain and all-conference tackle Joe Meek, Kenneth "Moco" Mercer and John Shultz in 1923; or the next year captain Kenneth Karr, Mercer, Walter Officer and Leslie Holladay, who was an all-conference tackle in 1924–25–26. Then there were two Simpsonians, Barney McCoy in 1924–25 and Charles "Chic" McCoy in 1927–28 who were selected all-conference in both football and basketball in the same year.

Mercer was one of Simpson's all-time greatest athletes. He came to Indianola as a freshman from Albia, and during his undergraduate career earned fifteen letters in football, basketball, wrestling and track. In football he became a legend, scoring 348 points in his four years, being selected all-conference halfback three years in a row (1923–24–25).[89] After graduation from Simpson he played professional football for Philadelphia in the National Football League before returning to Simpson as an assistant coach in the 1930s. Meanwhile, in Indianola football was king.

Workman's 1925 team posted a very respectable 6–2–1 record, sharing the conference crown with Upper Iowa. Workman's reputation for success was by now so great that at the end of the 1925 season Iowa State made a successful bid for his services as coach. It was an offer Workman could not refuse.

College officials asked the departing coach if he had a suggestion about a replacement, and after conferring with Andrew G. Reid of Waterloo, president of the College's alumni association, President Hillman and Rae Dean selected Harry "Hoge" Workman, Noel's brother, who was head coach at the University of Redlands in California. Harry had been an All-American quarterback in his 1923 senior year at Ohio State and had coached at Redlands only a year, but was regarded by many to be the equal of his brother. And Noel helped persuade him to accept Simpson's offer. For their part, Hillman and Dean hoped devoutly that Noel Workman's talent for winning would rub off on his younger brother.

Harry Workman was a good coach, compiling a satisfactory 22–18–3 record during his five years as football coach between 1926 and 1930, posting only one losing season. But his teams, alas, never acquired quite the luster that attached to the great 1923 and 1924 elevens.[90]

While football received more attention than all other athletics combined, basketball was the great winter sport, and Simpson's record was quite respectable throughout the twenties, ranging from an outright conference championship in 1920 under "Soup" Graves through six winning and five losing seasons, the worst of which were 1921 and 1930. In all these years the football coach also coached basketball, and because athletic directors were invariably chosen for their football prowess, it can be regarded as a happy accident that they achieved a good record in basketball as well.

Because it had such a fine gymnasium, Simpson hosted a big invitational regional basketball tournament in the early spring each year, when as many as three hundred boys from thirty or so high schools descended on the campus to play for what came to be touted as a state championship, largely because it included the big Des Moines high schools. Each year the event drew large crowds of cheering spectators, and each game received wide press coverage. Locally, the *Simpsonian* not only reported the whole tournament in detail, but also, with an eye to student recruitment, filled its pages with pictures and articles promoting the virtues of Simpson, especially its athletics. In time, the tournament became a victim of its own thirteen years of success, and in 1926 the Iowa High School Athletic Association, which at that time opposed post-season play-offs, requested Simpson to discontinue its tournament, and the College reluctantly complied.

During this era, track replaced baseball as the most popular spring sport, and Simpson's teams were very good, ranking in the top three in the conference most years, but winning the Iowa Conference Track Meet only once, in 1926. That was the year Dr. H. L. Johnson, the team's trainer, coached the boys only because Noel Workman had already taken up his duties in Ames. Baseball, the oldest sport at Simpson, languished during the twenties, and it nearly died out for lack of interest, suffering in part probably because of the notorious 1920 White Sox scandal that festered for months on end, tarnishing the reputation of the all-American sport. Simpson played only four games that year, a few in 1921 and only one other season (1923) during the entire decade. What baseball there was at Simpson was intramural, with either the ATOs or the Kappas as the customary winners.

During these years tennis became very popular, both as an intercollegiate and recreational sport.[91] Simpson organized its first wrestling team in 1923 and early in 1924 met Iowa State Teachers College in its first intercollegiate wrestling meet.[92] Wrestling "has already gained an immense following" in Iowa, stated the *Simpsonian* the next year as it gleefully recorded the College's first win in that sport, a 21–0 defeat of Des Moines University.[93] Golf was first reported in the *Simpsonian* when the Simpson team lost to Drake and Des Moines University in May 1927.[94]

For the most part Simpson's athletic relationships with other colleges were cordial, but in 1926 an ugly brawl at a basketball game with Iowa State Teachers College in Cedar Falls led to a total suspension for several years of athletic relationships between the two schools. Simpson charged "unsportsmanlike conduct on the part of Teachers players which caused a near riot" following the game, but did admit that the Simpsonians "may have been a little too aggressive in their actions." Both coaches tried to quell the free-for-all, but Noel Workman, fiercely angry because he was attacked by spectators, immediately notified the I.S.T.C. athletic director that "all athletic contests now scheduled are cancelled and no more will be scheduled."[95] The feud lasted until the fall of 1929, when everyone decided to forget the past and resume relationships.

The faculty, concerned that the mania for athletics threatened to have a deleterious effect on scholarship, introduced strong rules relating to academic eligibility for participation, and these rules were enforced, often to the anger and dismay of the players themselves or their local Simpson fans. Determined to maintain academic integrity, the faculty held their ground, although few of them would have gone as far as the *Des Moines Register* when it denounced college athletics "which are out of hand," suggesting that all professional coaches be fired and unpaid student coaches be installed.[96] The *Register*'s complaint was but a cry in the wilderness, for college athletics were powerfully entrenched, wildly popular and probably less debauching than gambling or smoking cigarettes.

Sports, to be sure, were enjoyed by athletes and spectators alike. As the crowds of fans grew at Simpson, one could be deafened by organized cheers in Hopper Gym led by "the Joshua," as the head cheerleader was first called, his name derived from the pep club of earlier years. But what to call the team? What was a proper name to match the "Bulldogs" or the "Trojans" or the "Hawkeyes"? "Simpsonians" or "Simpsonites" had been used for a time during the earliest days, but both sounded awful. Near the turn of the century Joanna Baker, relentlessly dedicated to civilizing her students in Greek suggested the name "Achaeans," pointing out that, after all, the tough Achaeans had defeated the Trojans with both strength and guile. Yet although her logic was impeccable and the name had a nice ring to it, she had to admit that most Iowans couldn't pronounce "Achaeans." When the Des Moines press began to call Simpson teams "Methodists," people from Iowa Wesleyan complained that they had a prior claim to the name, and moreover they insisted that they were more devoutly Methodist than Simpson, if that was possible. For a while the *Simpsonian*, in an apparent effort to evoke the sentiment that derived from the College's arboreal tradition, called the teams the "Maple Leafs," but that sounded too much like a Canadian hockey team. During the two decades after 1910 the name most prominently used in the College's publications was simply the "Red and Gold" for the school's colors, but this nickname was never entirely satisfactory because it could refer only rather abstractly in the singular to an athletic team as a whole, not to the players individually or as a group.

In an effort to settle this weighty matter, alumnus John Horsley, no mean cheerleader himself in his day, proposed in a *Simpsonian* article late in 1930 that Simpson adopt the name "Redmen." He wrote that "it gives opportunity for all the Indian lore and traditions, picturesque vocabulary, and is easy to say. The Simpson colors lend themselves easily to the title, and no other team in the conference at least has used or is using it."[97] "Redmen" it was; "Redmen" it would remain for many years.

* * *

It seems that few of the men around Indianola thought much about the "Redwomen." Women's athletics continued to be conducted entirely on an intramural basis, but that is not to say that they were unimportant. In fact, very nearly as many women as men were involved in one sport or another. The entire program was managed by the Women's Athletic Association, with active teams in soccer, field hockey, volleyball, basketball, tennis and baseball (yes, baseball, not softball), and competition in all of these sports was keen.[98]

The strength of the Women's Athletic Association grew in spite of the relatively brief tenure of the women designated director of physical education for women. No fewer than seven women held that post during the eleven years between 1919 and 1930.[99] Actually, it wasn't a very attractive position, hovering somewhere down near the bottom of the salary scale. And although a number of recent college graduates took the position and conducted a lively program, they stayed at most two or three years, attracted elsewhere by better remuneration and, perhaps, by more visible appreciation of their work. They knew that when the alumni talked about great athletics making a great college, they did not have women's sports in mind. The idea of supplementing the salary of a women's coach would have sounded absurd. At least it seems not to have occurred to the College's administrators. And although the salaries of female faculty in academic fields were improving when compared with those of their male counterparts, such was hardly the case in athletics. In 1928, for example, Harry Workman was paid $3,500 ($2,500 from the College and $1,000 from the alumni association), while Helen Westfall, coaching the women, received $1,600. This disparity, reflecting the perceived relative importance of men's and women's athletics, was hardly peculiar to Simpson. This same primitive state of affairs existed in all of Iowa and all the nation.

* * *

The passion for college athletics underscored the fact that American higher education, even in places like Simpson, was being called upon to adjust to a student constituency no longer homogeneous and to offer education to two very different types of students: "a minority, who are intellectually gifted and carry on the old collegiate tradition . . . toward intellectual and spiritual goals; and a large majority who are avowedly non-intellectual."[100] The new majority, contrary to expectations, did not loaf or turn to vice. They did study, albeit in a perfunctory way, but for the most part they turned their attention to extracurricular activities. In doing so, however, they were intelligent and perceptive enough to create in the extracurriculum significant instruments of self-education. Many of them, as we have already observed, admired and sought to emulate those qualities of character which they believed would surely lead to practical success in the business and professional world. They invested their prodigious energies in the sort of activities which put a premium on such qualities as fighting spirit, the will to win, initiative, planning and organizing. It was, after all, these qualities that would help them get jobs and promotions. The extracurriculum boomed.

Alongside athletics, the Greek-letter societies were the most obvious manifestation of the new spirit. During the 1920s they reached the zenith of their power and influence on the campus, in part because they were organized, entrenched in popularity and self-governed. They became "the stronghold and chief agency of the new majority education."[101] Never before or since has Simpson harbored so many Greek-letter groups as it did during the twenties. Whatever one's view toward such groups, they appeared to serve a practical purpose. "Certainly during the Hillman administration," writes Harold Watson, "the lack of adequate housing and cafeteria facilities at the College and in the community rendered the services of the fraternity and sorority houses absolutely essential." Beyond this, recalls Watson, "my own observation at Simpson was that the Greeks provided pleasant living conditions,[102] companionship, some measure of social training, practice in cooperation, opportunities for leadership, and in some cases at least the inculcation of systematic study habits."[103]

Among the fraternities Alpha Tau Omega and Kappa Theta Psi attracted most of the student leaders, but they could not accommodate all who desired membership. Thus during Hillman's first year at Simpson, a new fraternity by the name of Sigma Delta Chi was organized by fourteen prominent undergraduates.[104] An immediate success, the new fraternity rented a chapter house and grew in numbers and prestige to match its older campus rivals. In 1923 it sent a delegation to Ames to a province convention of Sigma Alpha Epsilon, seeking a charter to reestablish the old Simpson chapter of that national fraternity, but the SAEs turned a deaf ear to their entreaty. Disappointed, the local Sigma Delta Chi group, led by J. Raymond Smith '23 and Ward H. Rockey '26, a year later joined with old established locals in ten other colleges and created a new national fraternity, Theta Kappa Nu, which grew and prospered, chartering more than fifty chapters before it amalgamated in 1939 with Lambda Chi Alpha.[105] Only a year later, in the spring of 1925, yet another fraternity was established, this one called Gamma Kappa Delta, which three years later accepted a charter as the fifth chapter of Alpha Delta Alpha a "national" fraternity confined entirely to Iowa colleges. Although considerably less successful than Theta Kappa Nu, the new fraternity initiated Daniel Seaton, who in future years would serve as a distinguished director of admissions of the College.

Meanwhile, not to be outdone, the independent men—the Greeks had mercifully ceased calling them "barbarians"—decided to organize, creating the Commons Club, modeled on the plan of the famous Denison University Commons Club. Assisted by professors Holmes, Hilmer and Dennis, they conceived of an open society with "brotherhood to all, a non-exclusive democracy, and an unswerving loyalty and devotion to Simpson College."[106] Founded January 5, 1922, it attracted forty independent men, and thanks to its open membership and because of (or in spite of) broad faculty support, it was highly successful, moving into a house and within months accepting a charter of the American Association of Commons Clubs.[107] Some years later, yet another rather amorphous group of independent men organized, calling themselves the "Outlaws," but did little except participate in intramural sports for a few seasons. A few men—only about twenty—remained obdurately independent, not affiliated with any fraternity or quasifraternity like the A.C.C. They were widely regarded as either admirably self-possessed or quaintly misanthropic.

The women were as caught up in the headlong plunge into organized groups as were the men. To the three well-established national sororities were added two new women's groups. Beta Xi, founded in the fall of 1922, was absorbed two years later into a small national sorority called Theta Upsilon, which surprised everyone by competing very well indeed with its older rivals. Zeta Tau Delta, founded as a local in January 1925, was chartered as the Alpha Omicron chapter of Beta Sigma Omicron, an old national sorority which had experienced a rather checkered past. And like the men, independent women, perceiving the need to organize, created in the spring of 1926 a nonselective group called Omicron, the stated purpose of which was to provide "opportunity for adequate social life to all women students in Simpson College not affiliated with any other social organization." The following fall, with a membership of ninety-three, it was far and away the largest organized group at Simpson.[108]

Because the social fraternities and sororities provided their members bed and board, a broad social program, and a powerful sense of belonging, they captured the primary loyalty of their members. Other campus organizations possessed somewhat less appeal, but in their various realms of specialty they were, if well led and clearly defined, of considerable importance. We have already noted the establishment of Phi Mu Alpha and Mu Phi Epsilon for the music students and Pi Kappa Delta, the national forensics fraternity which developed a first-rate program of intercollegiate debates and oratorical contests. In 1922 the local Pi Kappa Delta chapter hosted the society's national convention in Indianola. Of course both the Y.M.C.A. and Y.W.C.A. continued to attract a broad spectrum of students who found their worthy programs attractive and spiritually fulfilling. The president of the Y.W.C.A., recalled Harold Watson, "was unquestionably the First Lady of the Campus." The Y.M.C.A. was less prominent, but "its presidency was important enough to be fought over by the Greek-letter fraternities."[109]

During the 1920s a number of specialized societies appeared, each seeking to bring together students with similar academic interests. The Blackfriars (1923) was a dramatic club which assisted in college play production. Harold Watson saw to the chartering of the Kappa Alpha chapter of Sigma Tau Delta (1925), the English departmental society, which was in time assigned the supervision of some of the College's publications. Pi Gamma Mu, a prominent honor society in the social sciences, was brought to Simpson in 1928 by history professors Francis Moats and Franklin D. Scott. In dramatics and the arts Phi Mu Gamma (1925) enjoyed a brief career. That same year saw the founding of the Beta chapter of Beta Beta Beta, a recognition society in biology. In 1921 the preachers—preministerial students were usually thus designated—organized a local group called the Homiletics Club and another—with broader membership—called the Oxford Club, which in 1927 came to be known as Delta Epsilon, a coeducational evangelistic group which declared itself to be "a vital force for righteousness on the campus."[110] And it was clearly the view of the ministerial students and their crowd that righteousness was in short supply at Simpson. The Cosmopolitan Club, affiliating itself with a similar organization founded at the University of Wisconsin, sought to fight provincialism and to create world citizens.

"Simpson College is probably over-organized," wrote editor Wendell Tutt in what is surely a masterpiece of understatement.[111] One thing was certain: at Simpson it was your own fault if you couldn't find an organization to join.

The founding of Epsilon Sigma in May 1924 provided the College's outstanding students an honor society with the same requirements which prevailed for election to Phi Beta Kappa. The impetus for its establishment as Simpson's premier scholarship honorary was the hope, indeed expectation, that the faculty would pursue successfully the chartering of a Phi Beta Kappa chapter. In 1923 both Cornell College and Drake University had received charters. Simpson had also submitted a petition that year, but lost out in what was described as a "toss-up" decision to Cornell. Three charters in Iowa in one year were too many. Simpson should try again. Disappointed but hopeful, the Simpson people prepared to submit another petition "as soon as the College was in a position to meet the society's increasingly stringent requirements." It was believed that Simpson would be ready to try again "in a few years."[112] Meanwhile they would elect to Epsilon Sigma up to ten percent of the senior class, a handful of exceptional juniors and a specified number of alumni (fifteen years after their graduation) whose scholarly or professional achievements merited recognition. Watched over at first by Clyde Emmons and in later years by Ruth Jackson, Epsilon Sigma continues down to the present day as the most important academic honor Simpson bestows upon its most competent undergraduates.

The literary societies continued to decline but refused to die. In so many ways they were relics of an earlier age, social dinosaurs in a world where the climate had changed. Unable to compete with the social life provided by the fraternities or with the entertainment provided by the movies and radio, they saw their chief function, debate and oratory, taken over by the faculty in speech courses or by specialized, almost professional, groups like Pi Kappa Delta. They were perceived to be in trouble early in the decade. Speaking of an attempt to pump new life into the societies, the *Simpsonian* despaired: "Alas, 'twas only a dream, the cold winds of indifference blew; the dews turned to frost and the societies, now shorn of any protection, are slowly succumbing to exposure." They are "on the verge of self-extermination."[113]

Such predictions of imminent death were a trifle premature. Still, although membership held up, attendance at meetings was poor, especially among the men's societies. "Since the campaign last fall for the recreation of the literary societies was staged," lamented one observer, "a few heartsick members have strayed forth on Monday nights to the literary halls to foster a vague tradition that there once were literary societies which flourished, with much the same feeling [with which] a laboratory historian visits the scenes of excavated cities to imbibe the spirit of a long gone civilization."[114]

Amid cries that "something should be done to revive the declining interest" in the societies, the Kallonians gave up the ghost in the spring of 1922 and the Everetts accepted a charter of a national Greek-letter literary society called Kappa Phi Sigma in 1925 in the hope that the Greek designation would somehow make it more popular. It didn't.

The women, more dutiful about attendance, continued to support their societies, although attendance lagged. Surprisingly, a fourth women's society, the Clionian, was organized in 1923 and managed to survive almost a decade. The Alpian, Crescent and the ancient Zetalethean limped through the decade and were still standing in 1930. The Lowell Pierean succumbed with the disappearance of the Academy.

Although literary societies, emphasizing the spoken word, continued their decline, student publications, emphasizing the written word, flourished. Edited and for the most part financed by undergraduates and aimed at a student readership, these publications were accorded considerable independence by the faculty, and their editors went about their tasks responsibly. The oversight of all student journalism was in the hands of an administration-faculty-student publications board. During the twenties the board's membership included President Hillman, Eva Stahl of the English Department, one other faculty member, current and former editors and business managers, the entire board chaired by the student council president. This committee established broad policy for all publications, but its principal function was to select the editor and business manager for each publication.

Without exception the publications were still what might be called concessions. The College took little or no financial responsibility for them. The students had to make their own way, and usually they did so quite handsomely. Like the manager of the bookstore, the business managers of the *Simpsonian* and the *Zenith*, not to speak of the salaried or profit-sharing editors, were envied as authentic campus capitalists, quite apart from their roles as undergraduate opinion-makers.[115]

Because the *Zenith* was still published by the junior class, only members of that class were eligible for election to staff positions. Though the yearbook continued to be denominated by the year of the class that published it, creating confusion then and now, there was some logic in allowing juniors to take the responsibility, for it provided an extra year to pay the bills. Usually the *Simpsonian* was edited by a senior, but in the spring of 1925 a bright freshman named Wendell Tutt was elected to serve as editor for the following year, and he was subsequently twice reelected. His three-year tenure set an all-time record for any Simpson publication. Harold Watson, who was serving on the publications board at that time, called Tutt "one of the best editors of my time."[116] For one thing, in his belief that his readers could reflect intelligently on events beyond the walls of their alma mater, Tutt honored the *Simpsonian* tradition of speaking out on national and international issues. In that same spirit, his successor, Marjorie Earl, took issue with the editor of the Coe College *Cosmos*, who argued that college papers should not bother with editorials on national issues except those associated with education. Like Tutt, she continued to present lively editorials on everything from race prejudice in American society to German dirigibles on the Atlantic and Herbert Hoover in the White House.

The *Simpsonian* mirrored student—and often faculty—opinion just as Indianola's *Record* or *Herald* reflected community views and standards. And some of these views do not always support the stereotypical judgment that easily dismissed Iowa as a bastion of conservatism. For example, John Hillman, who nobody ever accused of being a liberal, was heart and soul in favor of an international peacekeeping organization, a lifelong Republican who admitted that he would "rather take [his] chances on a League of Nations with Harding than with Cox." He rejected the stubbornness of the irreconcilables who fought the League,[117] and his position was echoed by chapel speakers and student editorials.[118] More than once he made disarmament the topic of his Thursday evening prayer meeting talks.[119] Students and faculty alike gave vigorous support to the entry of the United States into the World Court; in a national student poll, only 30 out of 546 Simpson votes were cast against it, far below the national average.[120] They raised questions about sending American Marines into Central America and in 1927 supported the Kellogg-Briand Pact that outlawed war as an instrument of national policy. In fact, the *Simpsonian*'s constant stand in favor of peace drew the fire of an irritated local American Legion member who would have been a lot angrier had he read the favorable review given to Sherwood Eddy's chapel sermon that lauded the Bolsheviks. Said Eddy, "Far greater good will come out of Russia since their revolution in 1917 than came out of France following her revolution."[121] Regarding the famous Teapot Dome scandal, editor Tutt stood firmly on the side of the angels: Harry Sinclair might go free, he wrote, but "in the eyes of the American people, he stands convicted. The slime is whitewashed, but the odor remains."[122]

Rarely did the *Simpsonian* encounter student opposition to editorial stands that in some places would be regarded as controversial. Rather the editor had to endure student apathy and lethargy. Discouraged by student inattention to world events, he wrote that "the indifference of the average student is appalling."[123] For their part, students were comforted by the knowledge that their editors were keeping track of what was happening in the world out there, for most of them were too busy to notice.

As one peruses the *Zenith*s and *Simpsonian*s of the twenties, one cannot help but be impressed with the consistently high quality of these student publications. With rare exceptions they were informative, attractive and tasteful, for the most part conscientiously and meticulously edited.

In the spring of 1920, a promising new student publication was launched under the inspiration of Frank Luther Mott, who had joined the faculty only that year. The *Simpson Literary Quarterly*, a well-printed thirty-six-page periodical appeared at the beginning of the second semester, featuring carefully selected samples of the best undergraduate writing at the College. One would have to go far to find something of higher quality than, for example, Alice L. Wheeler's "One Block in the Structure" in that first edition.[124] As long as Mott stayed at Simpson the *Quarterly* was competently edited, although hardly surprisingly its financial base was never really adequate. After Mott moved on, and as the bills mounted, the publication, however worthy, could not survive and was forced to cease publication in 1922. After the Sigma Tau Delta chapter was installed in 1925, Simpson students found an outlet for their literary compositions in *The Rectangle*, the honor society's semiannual publication. In 1924 a new Simpson songbook was printed, the first since 1910. It sold for fifty cents, and it sold well.[125]

* * *

Although the acquisition of a Phi Beta Kappa charter continued to elude them, the Simpson faculty and administration could take comfort in the fact that the College's North Central Association accreditation was never really in any danger. In accordance with the practice of the time, universities with graduate programs rated baccalaureate colleges whose graduates sought to undertake advanced studies. The University of Illinois had raised Simpson's status in 1920 from Class C to Class A; Harvard was actively recruiting Simpson graduates; Columbia University accorded Simpson full recognition in 1923; a number of other leading universities followed suit, including Yale, Princeton, Chicago, Michigan and Wisconsin.

The most important accreditation of all came late in 1924, when the American Association of Universities placed Simpson on its approved list. Earlier that fall a careful investigation had been undertaken by Dr. David A. Robertson, a dean from the University of Chicago and assistant director of the American Council on Education. Hillman later recalled that when he heard that the inspector was coming, he was attending the Methodist conference sessions in Clarinda and hurried home to be on hand for the inspector's arrival.

> I returned that evening to Indianola and as I entered the chapel the next morning I saw Professor J. Hugh Jackson, one of our most outstanding younger alumni, sitting in the visitors' row. I said to him, "Professor, I do not know of anyone I would rather see than you this morning. The inspector for the Association of American Universities is coming today and you are exhibit A." Jackson was at that time a member of the faculty of the Graduate School of Business Administration at Harvard University. The inspector was the Dean of Chicago University who afterward became the president of Goucher College. He was acquainted with Professor Jackson through some teaching Jackson had done in the summer school at Chicago University.[126]

Robertson inspected the Carnegie library, classrooms and laboratories and talked with President Hillman and the heads of all academic departments. "At the end of his visit," recalled Hillman, "he volunteered to say that his impressions were very favorable."[127] Some weeks later Hillman received a letter from Adam Leroy Jones of Columbia University, chairman of the Committee on Classification of the association: "I take pleasure in informing you that at its annual meeting

November 1 the American Association of Universities voted to add Simpson College to its list of approved institutions." He declared that they were especially impressed with the success of Simpson graduates in the great universities.[128] A.A.U. recognition meant that Simpson students could transfer their courses to any other institution without question and that graduates could enter any graduate school for which they were academically qualified.

Further recognition came in 1927 when the American Association of University Women accepted Simpson alumnae into membership. Approval by the A.A.U.W. took seven years and a lot of work to achieve. Before Simpson could even make application, a number of changes in the College's practices needed to be effected. Women had to be given places on the board of trustees. The dean of women had to have at least an M.A. and full membership in the faculty. There had to be some women with the Ph.D. who were heads of departments, and there had been no discrimination against women in faculty salaries. Another obstacle, recalled Hillman, was that "the chairman of the committee to pass on our application was the head of the department of history at Goucher College. She had formerly been a member of the faculty at Grinnell College and had to be convinced that Simpson had improved from the Simpson at the time she was at Grinnell."[129] Apparently she was persuaded, because Simpson did receive her recommendation and hearty welcome. Since that time Simpson graduates have been welcomed into A.A.U.W. chapters everywhere, and an active chapter of A.A.U.W. continues to flourish in Indianola.[130]

With A.A.U. and A.A.U.W. membership, Simpson's standing seemed to be deservedly secure. "Even the University of Iowa," writes Harold Watson, "seemed no more condescending to us than Harvard was to Iowa."[131]

* * *

The remarkably improved standing of the College was gratifying, but everyone knew that it could be damaged seriously if the endowment was not increased and greater financial stability achieved. Even if no expensive new buildings were erected throughout the remaining years of Hillman's administration, a growing faculty and expanding student body, together with the services, equipment and supplies they needed to carry out their tasks, required an ever-larger budget. Tuition income was not meeting much more than a third of what it cost to run the College. The rest had to come from gifts and endowment income. And Simpson's estimate of what constituted an adequate endowment seemed to grow much faster than its ability to raise funds.

Hillman started by making a list of the things Simpson needed most: dormitories, a chapel, a power plant, reconstruction of the science building, athletic fields, expansion of the campus itself and, of course, paying off the College's debt and acquiring an adequate endowment. This last-named was indeed the most pressing concern, for without successful fund-raising the other needs would be more difficult to meet.[132] But the total cost of their wish-list added up to more than three million dollars, far more than they could dream of raising. Hillman and the board of trustees undertook to trim their list, but could not get it down below two million dollars. They decided to try to raise that amount. And to start their venture they would call on the General Education Board—the corporate name for the Rockefeller Foundation—in New York City. Winning a major grant from the foundation was a long shot, but it was worth the attempt.

Hillman and board chairman A. V. Proudfoot took the train to New York in mid-1922 to lay their case before the foundation. "The securing of this subscription was not easy," recalled Hillman in later years. "Already the Foundation had made commitments to two Methodist colleges in Iowa [Morningside and Cornell] and their policy was not to contribute to more than one college of a particular denomination in any one state. That was emphatically stated to me on my first visit to the Foundation."[133] Yet they were hopeful, for they had been assured that their application would at least get a hearing. It did.

In April 1923 two urbane representatives of the foundation journeyed to Indianola and spent two busy days on the campus. They talked with faculty and staff, scrutinized the College's financial records and examined business management practices. If they liked what they saw, their manner and demeanor did not reveal it, and as they departed it seemed ever so much as if they were anxious to quit the squalid hinterlands and return to civilization. Therefore it was with considerable surprise that Hillman received a letter a month later informing him that the foundation had considered Simpson's application favorably. If Simpson would pay off all its debts "they would give us one dollar for every two we added to our endowment until they had given us $200,000."[134] At that time the College's endowment stood at about $550,000. Unfortunately its debt, occasioned mostly by recurring annual operating deficits, had ballooned to more than $215,000. Thus, to ensure receipt of the total Rockefeller challenge, Simpson would have to raise at least $615,000 in cash—not pledges—to pay its indebtedness and provide $400,000 in matching funds.[135] The Simpson people were delighted that with the Rockefeller gift they had put into place the linchpin that would make fast the wheel of their fund-raising drive.

Meanwhile, during the cold winter of 1923 Hillman and the board had begun laying plans for Simpson's greatest-ever financial campaign. They had already determined to use professional help for such a major undertaking. With conference approval they brought in Dr. John W. Hancher, counselor in finance with the Board of Education of the Methodist Church, who arrived in Indianola late in January. Widely reputed to be a wizard of finance in Methodist circles, Hancher would advise how to plan the campaign and would assume overall direction of its execution. In Indianola he was joined by Bishop Homer C. Stuntz from Omaha and Dr. James A. Beebe, who came all the way from Boston.

It was a full weekend. Bishop Stuntz spoke on world affairs at chapel on campus on Friday morning, at the Rotary Club at noon and to a "spellbound" audience of several hundred that evening at the Methodist Church.[136] At the Indianola Hotel the following day he and Dr. Hancher met with board members A. V. Proudfoot and William Buxton, Jr., together with Dr. E. M. Evans, district superintendent of the church's Des Moines district, Rae Dean and the Reverend L. A. Bradford, the Ames pastor who was head of the Wesley Foundation at Iowa State College.[137] These were the men who would help direct the campaign which they decided to call the "Simpson-Wesley Development," with an ambitious goal of $2,000,000 for Simpson and $125,000 for the Wesley Foundation at Iowa State College. Hancher selected Dr. W. H. Cable, Simpson's vice-president, and Dr. Albertus Perry "from the staff office" of the Methodist Board of Higher Education codirectors of the campaign. Assisted by a secretarial staff, they would handle the details of the fund drive, headquartered in the College Administration Building.[138]

It was intended that the campaign be a brief one, to be launched on April 28 and concluded on June 10. Declaring that "this campaign cannot fail," Bishop Stuntz formally proclaimed the opening of the fund drive from the pulpit of Indianola's Methodist Church on the morning of April 29, and because the bishop was known to shun failing ventures, his words were believed. Simultaneously the campaign was announced to every congregation in the Des Moines Conference.

Never before had Simpson alumni and the Methodists of southwest Iowa seen anything like the high-powered whirlwind crusade for dollars that soon swept over them. Agents fanned out all over the territory to persuade them to "open their hearts and their pocketbooks," whether it be the banker's largess or the widow's mite. To reach beyond a million dollars in cash contributions they used an arsenal of instruments—things like five-year pledges in cash, annuities, insurance, and estate notes—most of which were utterly beyond the comprehension of many of the potential givers.

Back on campus, the campaign announced in late May that the faculty and staff had signed up one hundred percent as had the junior and senior classes and the entire conservatory, faculty and students alike. Altogether, students pledged an amazing $42,000, and the faculty's equally impressive gifts brought the total campus subscription to more than $75,000.[139] At this point the Reverend W. M. Dudley, former vice-president of the College, joined the campaign staff.

As usual, Warren County people came through generously. Board of trustees members led the way. A committee of women raised $50,000 in Indianola alone. But in Des Moines and the rest of Simpson's "territory" the campaign lagged. And some hoped-for major gifts were still pending when the fund drive came down to its last few days.

On Saturday morning, June 16, only four days away from their self-imposed deadline, the fund-raisers could count only $1,125,000 in cash and pledges, less than sixty percent of their goal. Dr. Hancher arrived that day to "put the drive over the top," but it required all his self-confident ebullience to put a good face on things. There was much to do and precious little time to do it.

Dr. Hancher went to work with a will. His faith in the venture, his certitude about its success was infectious. He directed some of his lieutenants to make personal calls on nearby hold-outs. He kept the telephone lines abuzz with pleas to some of the bigger prospects on their donor list. On Sunday—they called it inappropriately "Gleaning Sunday"—the campaign netted only $40,000 more. By Monday afternoon the big chalkboard in the Administration Building showed the total at a disappointing $1,370,000. Monday was surely the gloomiest day of the campaign.

Then a bolt of lighting struck. Late that evening Dr. Hancher announced a $100,000 gift "from an alumnus," then several more substantial contributions. By day's end the total stood at $1,564,639. Tuesday was better, as a number of major pledges were chalked up—more than $200,000—bringing the total to $1,787,191. Wednesday, the last day of the drive, saw them still short of their goal by nearly a quarter of a million dollars. Still more calls went out. At noon they had $1,817,519 and by suppertime perhaps a few thousand more than that.

Keen suspense marked the closing hours of the campaign. As the evening wore on, the figures inched up ever so slowly. At 11:07 P.M. the total reached $1,844,953. A few minutes later, while a large group of alumni waited expectantly as they watched the bulletin board, the board of trustees went into session and discussed plans to underwrite personally any shortage. At 11:57 Dr. Hancher, whose dignity rarely permitted him to make any show of emotion, was heard to let out a whoop when another $100,000 pledge came in. Then another call pledging that same amount came through two minutes later and put them over the top with $2,065,556. Word of their success raced through the streets of town, reaching a huge crowd down on the square of students and townspeople who were waiting for a chance to celebrate. As the chapel bell rang, the demonstration, complete with skyrockets and Roman candles, illumined the night sky and sounded the cry of victory.[140] By the next morning board chairman A. V. Proudfoot announced that the total had reached $2,074,410. Exultantly the board notified the General Education Board that with "bonafied [sic] pledges" in hand for more than two million dollars, "the conditions of the subscription contracts are met."[141]

When the giddiness of the blazing night gave way to the cold reality of the morrow, the campaign leaders realized that although they had indeed raised more than two million dollars, very little of it was in cash. Most of it was in estate pledges, life endowments, annuities and scholarships. A few months later they were forced to admit that the pledges showed "an abnormal amount of paper with indefinite terminal dating."[142] Too many gifts amounted to IOUs that could be too easily forgotten.

Probably most of the donors intended to meet their obligation to the endowment campaign, but they were, in the words of Vice-President W. H. Cable, "so shackled by lifetime habits of conservatism and procrastination that they wait until robed in a shroud, and then it is too late."[143] Cable knew what he was talking about, for a number of significant donations were lost because the donors died, having failed to specify properly the bequest in their wills. Simpson's two million dollars suffered substantial shrinkage. A year after the conclusion of the campaign, Hillman reported that they had collected $256,613 in cash or marketable property, but that amount was woefully short of what was needed to match the Rockefeller grant. The College's debt had meanwhile grown to $216,575, and after meeting part of the campaign expenses only $25,145 had gone into the endowment.[144] Moreover, there was a hot dispute raging between Simpson and the Wesley Foundation with respect to division of the paid-up pledges. Although the disagreement was settled by arbitration, feelings were bruised.

It required altogether seven years to meet the Rockefeller challenge. The General Education Board was remarkably patient, extending again and again the deadline for satisfying the conditions of its challenge, finally setting December 31, 1930, as the absolute terminal date. In October 1928, the G.E.B. set aside $49,306.50 for Simpson, proportional to the amount the College had raised toward its full commitment, and added another $64,736.77 in February, 1929.[145] A year later, still $200,000 short of the amount needed for Simpson's match, Hillman sent out an appeal to alumni. "Not to secure all of this money will be little short of calamitous," he wrote. "There are many claims upon you but what one is more sacred?"[146]

This time the alumni did respond, and Simpson could announce to the G.E.B.— in the nick of time—that it had paid the entire College debt, had met all the costs of the protracted campaign and had more than $400,000 of new productive endowment. True to its bargain, the G.E.B. completed its payment with a check for $90,981.52.[147] The Simpsonians were ecstatic, for now their endowment exceeded a million dollars.

The long, grinding endowment campaign so monopolized the attention of Simpson's leadership that not one new building was begun during the entire Hillman era. And that is not to say that no new buildings were needed. Like a chapel. The president, dismayed by the impossible task of crowding more than a fraction of the students into morning chapel, dreamed of an adequate structure for worship and convocations. Housing for students was overcrowded, and rooming in local Indianola residences had reached a saturation point. A dormitory for men was desirable; another dormitory for women was an imperative. The College could afford neither.

Then, quite fortuitously in early 1923, a recently constructed apartment house right across the street from the conservatory was for sale at the right price. Upon investigation Hillman found that it would accommodate fifty-four girls and a matron, with six girls occupying each of nine apartments. Rae Dean concluded the purchase deal with local realtors Browne and Schrier, whereby the College traded a 200-acre farm near Denison and assumed a $20,000 mortgage on the apartment house.[148] Named Lorraine Hall, the building would serve for many years as a comfortable residence hall for women.

Fund-raising and careful economics notwithstanding, the College saw one annual deficit follow another as certain as winter follows fall. Depending on a growing endowment to provide the difference between profitability and loss, Hillman and his board kept tuition charges low, well below the average for Iowa private colleges. Between 1920 and 1930 the charge for tuition remained an unvarying $100 per year, while the "semester fee" rose from $18 per year to $60.[149] Had Simpson charged the same tuition and fees as, say, Cornell College ($150 per year), the deficit could have been eliminated. But Hillman, backed especially by the clergy in the conference, was determined to keep the cost of attending Simpson within the range of any Methodist youngster's family income. The estimated total cost for a year at Simpson rose very slowly, from $404 in 1920 to $475 in 1930.[150]

* * *

If John Hillman and the board of trustees had been able to effect their purpose, Simpson students would have been protected from the hedonism that characterized the roaring twenties, all of them kept safe and secure in the arcadian innocence of rural Iowa. They were pleased to announce in the College's catalog that Indianola was "peculiarly free from vice and intemperance" and assured parents that "unwholesome amusements are not tolerated by either the city or the College."[151] And while the catalog did not spell out which amusements were forbidden, everyone knew that Simpsonians were still expected to abstain from alcohol, card playing, theater-going and dancing, not to speak of "moral misconduct."

To put the matter positively, the College was unabashedly Christian. "We believe," declared the catalog, "that the education is partial which ignores the moral and spiritual nature, and that religion has a definite place in the development of character." To that worthy end, therefore, Simpson would seek "to surround its students with helpful Christian influences, and to do its work in a wholesome Christian atmosphere,"[152] providing daily chapel services, the Y.M.C.A. and Y.W.C.A. and urging weekly church attendance in town.

All students were required to complete one semester of Bible study for graduation in any major. It was the only academic requirement in religion, much lighter actually than that imposed by many other denominational colleges. In addition students were expected to attend chapel four days a week. Hillman would have preferred daily attendance, but the chapel was so crowded that some relief was necessary. The young men were seated on one side of the aisle and the young women on the other, all by class, the seniors in the front and the freshmen in the rear. The faculty—those who attended at all—were seated on a long platform in front facing the students. The program remained much the same as it had been for decades: prayer, perhaps a hymn, a short sermon or lecture, a college song and announcements. Traditionally the president spoke on Monday, and Hillman was remembered as "a master of the fifteen-minute address."[153] Sometimes faculty members spoke, and not infrequently bishops and other distinguished visitors held forth on timely and uplifting topics. Harold Watson recalled that Simpson chapels in those days were "unusually good."[154] Most of the students would probably have disagreed with him.

Thursday prayer meetings were not compulsory, but they were usually well attended. Dr. Hillman presided whenever he was in town, and students suspected that attendance was boosted by Hillman's habit of counting members present from each organization, leading the fraternities and sororities to require their freshmen to attend as a pledge duty. Nearly all the students did attend church on Sunday with some regularity, and they were even known to have attended evangelistic services at the Methodist Church, probably because of peer group pressure as much as religious conviction.

Smoking was prohibited on campus, and the ban seems to have been observed except for the handful of renegades who were rumored to light up down in the furnace room at Mary Berry Hall. There was a fire danger in most of the campus buildings. Cigarettes were not sold anywhere in Indianola, which made it at least inconvenient to indulge. Probably a few of the boys, if they smoked at all, did so on the upper floors of the fraternity houses. And the women seem to have rejected entirely the advertiser's invitation to "reach for a Lucky instead of a sweet."

Still, the tobacco companies earnestly sought to enlist college students into the ranks of regular smokers. In 1927 Simpson officials and Indianola townspeople alike were enraged by a report that the American Tobacco Company had obtained a list of all college students in Indianola and was planning to mail a sample package of cigarettes to every man at the College. True, by city ordinance the company was forbidden to sell cigarettes in Indianola, but nothing prevented their giving them away. Worse yet, John Piffer, a local farmer, applied for a license to sell cigarettes just outside the city limits. The license was refused by the county board of supervisors "on the grounds that it would be contrary to the interests of Simpson College and would circumvent the regulations of the city council."[155] Faced with a solid wall of resistance, both Piffer and the company backed off.

Smoking was one thing, but drinking was quite another. Virtually all of the students supported prohibition and did not drink. Undergraduate opinion at Simpson, bolstered by the threat of punishment, kept things in line. Few even indulged in legal "near beer," which contained no more than one-half of one percent of alcohol by volume. One would have to drink a keg of it to get drunk, and even college boys in places like Des Moines and Chicago did not possess such a colossal capacity, much less those in Indianola. For all the huge popularity of fraternities and sororities at Simpson, the Greeks were no more likely to fall prey to "demon rum" than were independent students, and they were truly shocked when authorities raided the Sigma Chi house up at Ames, discovering an alky cooker and a cache of bottles of "a particularly corrosive product of the amateur still."[156] In 1928 Simpson students, not surprisingly, supported Herbert Hoover against the "wet" Al Smith. "Prohibition," wrote editor Wendell Tutt, "is of too great importance to the security and prosperity of this nation."[157]

Dancing was another matter. President Hillman was even more opposed to any kind of dancing than were his predecessors, if that is possible. He "made no secret of his conviction that this recreation was a snare of Satan."[158] Students were equally persuaded that it was an innocent and thoroughly enjoyable pastime. Hillman managed to hold the line throughout the twenties, although it must have required a herculean effort to do so, and there is little doubt that he wasted an incredible amount of time and energy to effect his purpose. He must have known that students were dancing at parties and at public halls in Des Moines. He must at least have suspected that behind shaded windows in the fraternity houses members and their dates were doing something more than singing "Yes, We Have No Bananas" or playing mah-jongg. At one point, Dr. Hillman tried to make a distinction between "dancing" and "promiscuous dancing," but since he would have designated the minuet and the gavotte, not to speak of old-fashioned square dancing, as "promiscuous," the distinction was not particularly helpful.[159]

Simpson was probably not the last college bastion of Methodist morality, but it was surely one of the last, at least as far as the public record goes. Not many students seem to have violated the rigid canons of sexual behavior, in part because the opportunities to transgress were relatively few. Some, of course, did, but the canons of behavior dictated that they feel guilty for their transgressions. And there was indeed pressure, especially on the women, to conform to conservative Christian principles. The story is told about a Simpson coed who was discovered to be pregnant. As Harold Watson remembered it, "A self-constituted committee of student leaders grilled the putative father, found that he was without funds, took up a quiet collection, warned him to marry his sweetheart or else, and after the ceremony saw them off to a distant state."[160]

The moral behavior of the students was a good deal more straight-laced than was their dress. Take, for example, women's skirts, which very nearly reached the ankles in 1920, only to rise resolutely until they scarcely covered the knees a decade later, a phenomenon viewed by the dean of women as a sign of the ineluctable barbarization of womankind. Equally shocking was the fashion of bobbed hair among young flappers whose "irresponsible enthusiasm" threatened to take them beyond redemption.[161] "Nearly all the girls are doing it now," reported the *Simpsonian* with evident approval.[162] What the boys were doing was wearing knickers and greasing their hair with the latest fragrant pomade. "The Simpson College bookstore," declared a notice in the *Simpsonian* in early December 1924, "has received 360 sample bottles of 'Glo-Co' hair tonic," and they were offered free to all Simpson men, first come first served. It is not reported how many takers there were.[163]

Their dress and their grooming were not the only aspects of popular culture that found their way to Indianola. Radio was taking the country by storm and would become a permanent fixture of American life. Radio broadcasting, which began with the airing of the Harding-Cox election returns in November 1920 on station 8ZZ, later KDKA, in Pittsburgh, mushroomed into the fastest growing industry in the country. It seemed that nearly everyone was adjusting headphones to a simple crystal set or listening to music and news filtered through the crackling static of the radio receiver. Simpson faculty and students were captivated. Physics professor A. B. Carr let it be known in 1922 that Simpson was "badly in need of a complete radio outfit which will not only receive but send."[164] Until that came along students learned to build their own rudimentary sets. The first radio "event" at Simpson allowed students to listen to the inauguration of President Calvin Coolidge on March 4, 1925, their radio hookup at the chapel provided by the Hansell Garage in Indianola. "What a marvel, almost a miracle it is," exulted the editor of the *Simpsonian*.[165] Four years later Francis Moats saw to the installation of a radio and huge loudspeaker to hear the inaugural of President Herbert Hoover.[166] But surely it was the broadcast of the College's popular—and bloodthirsty—"Scalp Song" from New York City that truly dazzled Indianolans.[167] Radio was here to stay, and they loved it.

If students tired of radio they could go to the movies and thrill to the exploits of the great film idols in the heyday of the silent "flickers." While Simpson coeds swooned at the showings of *The Sheikh*, starring swarthy Rudolph Valentino, the boys could enjoy the feminine attributes of Clara Bow as the "It" girl. Down at the Empress they could see Lon Chaney in *The Hunchback of Notre Dame* or laugh at Harold Lloyd in *The Freshman* for thirty-five cents, but when Cecil B. DeMille's extravaganza *King of Kings* came to town in 1929, the price of a ticket went up to fifty cents. Although it turned out to be an exercise in poor timing, the tinny piano at the Empress was finally replaced by a fine pipe organ in 1928, the year the first all-talking picture came along to make theater organs obsolete. Two years later the Empress was advertising sound movies and kept the organ too.

Among the earliest singing stars were the Lane sisters, Leota and Lola, and what makes them important to our story is that both of them were products of Indianola and Simpson. They were the daughters of Dr. Len and Cora B. Mullican. Mullican was a local dentist and a crusading Democrat in a day when Democrats in Indianola were an endangered species. He and Cora B. had five daughters, all of them remarkably talented, of whom four ultimately entered show business. The oldest was beautiful Leota, a spectacular blonde. Next was Martha, whose interests were academic rather than musical and who therefore never went near the stage. Dorothy, on the other hand, could sing like an angel and pounded the piano at the Empress for extra money. The two younger girls, Rosemary and Priscilla, still schoolgirls during the 1920s, would follow their two sisters into the movies some years later.

Leota was a soprano. She studied at Simpson, where she sang in just about everything and played leading dramatic roles on the stage, culminating in a creditable performance as Juliet in *Romeo and Juliet* directed by Professor Wilbur C. Dennis.[168] She earned her B.M. in 1925. Meanwhile Dorothy entered the conservatory to study voice. Blonde like her sister, she sang with a compelling contralto voice. More than that, she had a stunning figure, a flawless complexion and "that invitingly exciting look of sin you wouldn't be sorry for."[169] Both Leota

Iowa Girls Reach Broadway And Can't Believe It's True

Starring in New York Was Beyond Fondest Dreams of Leota and Lola Lane, "Close Harmony" Sisters to Open Here.

(From the New York Telegraph)

Whatever Leota and Lola Lane, (stage names of Leota and Dorothy Mullican) may have dreamed of fame and fortune, their imaginations bore them no farther along that gilded highway than to Des Moines, a distance of twenty miles from their home town of Indianola, Iowa.

Starring on Broadway would have struck them as exceedingly funny three weeks ago. Singing close harmony, with their bright curls nodding a cheery hello to a sophisticated New York theatre audience would have shocked their sense of fitness of things—before Gus Edwards "listened in" on a concert given by the Des Moines Rotary Club and decided then and there the sisters should warble in the "Greenwich Village Follies" if he had to spirit them away to accomplish it.

"We came," said Leota as she beckoned frantically to her sister to come back-stage and help her out with the interview, "but we honestly didn't think for a minute Mr. Edwards intended to give us parts in a big production right off the bat—er, ah, well, you know what I mean; we thought it was stock or something just to give us a start."

"We did not," interrupted Lola, almost upsetting her sister in her rush into the conversation. "You know perfectly well we were sure he would not have us after he found out we'd never even seen a musical comedy or revue, much less sing in one. We were scared to death, but we thought it would be fun to be able to say we had been in New York. The folks back home"—and Lola's voice became confidential—"have the idea you have to be absolutely wonderful to do anything in New York."

Leota began to giggle.

"They'll burn up when we send them clippings and things. Not mother and dad," she added hastily.

Elderly Sister Attitude

Leota, slender, with pale gold hair wrapped in bands above finely chiseled features, has an elderly sister attitude toward Lola, younger by one year and almost exploding with exuberance. Lola described the folks back home with a grimace, pulling her mouth down in the corners and swishing her curls behind her ears in a lightning-like gesture. She finished the pantomine with a few steps of the Charleston, then settled herself to the serious business of answering questions.

"It's the first time in all our lives anybody ever wanted to hear about us. I'm afraid we'll forget something terribly important. We're graduates of Simpson college in Indianola," she said profoundly. "We have three younger sisters and"—

"Lola!" The name was like a long wail from Leota. "I can't find my clippings to show! What if I've lost them?"

Leota snapped open the inner clasp of her purse while Lola waited in dread anticipation, then both girls fell gingerly on a wad of newspaper in among the change.

"It's safe," breathed Leota, and handed over for inspection excerpts from the society columns of the Indianola papers. The girls had been extensively entertained by Indianola's elite on the eve of their departure. Mother had forwarded the notices.

"New York is so marvelous we can't be a bit homesick," Lola explained, "only it's awfully nice to hear what they do. I wish we had so much money we could send for the whole town to come and see us when we open Monday night in the show.

Think of Folk at Home

"Can you imagine Mr. and Mrs. Dunning seeing the Follies?" Both girls went into gales of laughter. "Mrs. Dunning told us you couldn't

The Lane sisters became film sensations in the twenties. This article appeared in the *New York Telegraph* in 1926.

and Dorothy were members of Theta Upsilon and active in student life, but their real interest was in the performing arts.

Thus, when Gus Edwards, the Broadway producer, brought his troupe to Des Moines toward the end of 1925, both girls contrived to get an audition with him. Their ploy worked, and after a few anxious weeks they received a telegram from Edwards offering them a contract with his show on Broadway at more money than either of them had ever dreamed of. Edwards, who was quite sure the name "Mullican" would never do on the Great White Way and who loved the liquid sound of *l*, renamed them Leota and Lola Lane.

From the Broadway stage both of the newly-christened Lane sisters went on to Hollywood and fame in the movies. In the spring of 1929 Simpson students migrated in droves to the Orpheum in Des Moines to see Lola Lane star in *Speakeasy*. Her voice "charmed the audience."[170] The next fall she "shrugged her sultry way" through *The Girl From Havana*, that modest triumph followed by one after another film production. None of these films ever won an Academy Award, but to people in Warren County that didn't matter. "After all," remembered one of them, "there isn't anything much more exciting than seeing somebody you went to school with burst forth from the screen."[171] And when both of the sisters visited their old alma mater in 1930, they were returning in state, accorded the attention they deserved as honest-to-goodness celebrities.

"Within a decade," wrote a historian of the period, "the radio and the movies nationalized American popular culture."[172] This was especially true among college students who provided a large share of those who listened and viewed. Never before had youngsters in the hinterlands of Iowa been so connected to the centers from which that culture emanated. Their language, for example, especially their slang, reflected the homogenization of much of America. Everyone wanted to have "pep" so that one could enjoy "making whoopie." And the universal approval of anything was "swell."[173] In music the jazz craze, too, was universal, even though everyone at Simpson knew that they could listen to it but not dance to it.

If they could not dance, they could find compensations in a plethora of organized activities and events that could more than fill the time of the most dedicated refugee from academics. One could, for example, be elected to the College Council, the undergraduate governing body that was still hunting for some balance between the faculty preference for perfect order and the student preference for amiable chaos. Determined not to repeat "the farcical performances of previous councils," the College Council in 1921 was slightly restructured, but it still seemed to be overawed by President Hillman and several faculty members who sat with the fifteen students (three freshmen and four from each of the other classes) in their deliberations.[174]

The council had a particularly difficult time monitoring the College's honor system, which among other things required students to certify that they had neither given nor received assistance on each examination. Throughout the decade the council heard of violations but was helpless to do much about them because students were reluctant to accuse fellow students of cheating, even in the most blatant cases. Knowing this, some faculty monitored their examinations, effectively nullifying the honor system in their classes. By the latter part of the 1920s the system was being called "a dead letter." Said the *Simpsonian*, "Anyone who would live up to all its obligations would be widely regarded as a prig."[175] Cheating became so troublesome that the faculty began talking of draconian measures, a sure sign that their legal code was hard to administer.[176] By the end of the twenties the honor system was being called a farce, but those who called for its discontinuance could not find much support. Few wanted to admit that Simpson could not make an honor system work.[177]

The Interfraternity Council was more fun than was student government, but probably not much more effective. The women had organized a Panhellenic Council some years earlier, but the men were slower to get together. It was Wendell Tutt who called for the creation of an I.F.C., for he knew that such organizations were working well elsewhere. Disappointed that the fraternities were dealing with each other "at arm's length," Tutt urged cooperation and friendly rivalry. He hoped, too, that fraternities would stop seeing the faculty as their "natural enemy."[178] The I.F.C. was formed, and it became a permanent feature of the Simpson scene. Yet in those first years, aside from a couple of interfraternity banquets where the imported speakers produced terminal boredom, the I.F.C. remained a pleasant but relatively ineffective instrument of student governance.

Much more memorable were the events, most of them student generated, which enriched the school year. Freshman Week, an orientation period for new students, was introduced in 1925, bringing freshmen to the campus a week before the commencement of fall classes. It sought to ease the transition from high school to college, to place the students properly in classes and to inform the new arrivals of what Simpson expected of them and what they might expect from Simpson. Avoiding excessive placement testing or adolescent socialization games, the Simpson program was uncomplicated and constructive. The Y.M.C.A. printed a "freshman bible," a handbook of useful information.

During the weeks that followed, upperclass students took it upon themselves to orient the freshmen a bit more. Their hazing activity, never condoned by the faculty, was minimal, confined usually to requiring the newcomers to wear green caps until Homecoming Weekend. Even that modest requirement was resisted from time to time, never more vigorously than when six freshmen, in an act of retribution, kidnaped Raoul Calkins, the head of the green cap committee, from the Commons house and drove him to the woods five miles out of town, where they left him to find his way home. The faculty was not amused, and the six, together with two female accomplices, were denied the right to participate in athletics or other activities and the freshman class president, one of the conspirators, lost his position.[179]

By the 1920s it had become a tradition for the Greek-letter organizations to hold their formal pledging ceremonies on the same evening in the early fall. After the ceremony, each fraternity paraded its new recruits before each sorority house and was routinely invited in for refreshments while the sorority introduced its pledges. The fraternity neophytes were expected to make dates with the freshmen girls for the evening.

Homecoming developed rapidly from relatively modest beginnings in 1921, the year the alumni took control of the College's athletic program.[180] So successful was Homecoming that it became the principal event of the fall semester, complete with house decorations, a parade with floats and the college band marching behind its strutting drum major, a big football game and *apres* receptions for alumni. Everyone would remember the 1927 celebration as a standout.

On a gorgeous Indian summer day, 2,500 spectators crowded into the "stadium" to watch Simpson defeat Parsons 13–12 in a hard-fought football game, after which a thousand of them feasted on roast buffalo.

After its inception in 1924, a skit night called "Miniature Orpheum," soon shortened to "Mini-Orph," was hugely popular. Inspired by the Orpheum Theater in Des Moines, where vaudeville was performed, student groups produced a program of short dramatic and sometimes musical acts parodying national and local issues and personalities or burlesquing campus problems. The quality of these skits varied widely, and some of them required the blue pencil of a judicious faculty censor, especially the annual efforts of one of the fraternities noted for its barnyard humor.

In some ways the biggest event of the college year was Campus Day—some still called it "Flunk Day"—when everyone, faculty and students alike, pitched in to help clean up the campus. And in those days before the College was able to afford an efficient maintenance staff, the campus was much in need of its annual face-lift. The selection of the day was a closely guarded secret, known only to the student body president who signalled the beginning of the event by ringing the chapel bell at seven o'clock in the morning. Everyone piled out in work clothes to a prearranged assembly point. Then, rake in hand, they were directed to assigned work areas on the campus. About nine o'clock the bell called everyone to "mock chapel," where students were totally in charge, wreaking good-natured dramatic revenge on faculty and administrators. Harold Watson, who was a victim of student hilarity as often as anyone, remembered wryly that "the take-offs on faculty idiosyncrasies were frequently effective and sometimes even corrective."[181] Chastened faculty and satisfied students then scattered all over the county for picnics, usually the first of the season.

Mostly Simpson people made their own entertainment, provided their own instruction and inspiration. Once in a while, however, they were privileged to welcome to the campus speakers of national or even international repute. They listened to the great Methodist missionaries, men like E. Stanley Jones, who tried to inspire them, and Bishop Brenton T. Badley, who did inspire them.[182] In 1928 they heard Norman Thomas, running for the U.S. presidency on the Socialist ticket, declare that "one of the blackest pages in human history is the advent of machinery. . . . We have slums and poverty instead of emancipation."[183] They rather liked Thomas, even though most of them loved machines and didn't know a slum from a cow barn. They liked gentle, powerful Carl Sandburg even more, charming them as he recited his poetry.[184] And if they really liked speakers, there was plenty of home-grown talent, young silver-tongued orators like Walter Dillon '26, the gifted freshman who won the state oratorical contest in 1923 or Horton Talley '27, who won four years later.[185]

Oratory was of course still a principal feature of commencement, but attendance lagged after the advent of Homecoming, with its active athletic and social agenda. Although the commencement program continued to offer a rich menu of orators and preachers, its participants were now confined to faculty, graduates and their families, and a few hardy townspeople. Even the stoutest supporters of old-fashioned leisurely commencements were suggesting that perhaps the event could be shortened by a day or two. Or three.

The pace of life was faster. There seemed to be too little time any more. But the twenties had been good to Simpson. Under John Hillman the College prospered as never before. "Some argument might be made," wrote Harold Watson, "that the College reached a height in 1924–25 not again to be attained for decades." He remembered the time after 1924 as the "Seven Good Years."[186]

Miss Mildred Edwards visited Thurs-
ay and Friday of Easter vacation in
es Moines with Miss Margaret
riffith.

Mrs. R. E. Brooker of Grinnell,
rmerly Miss Hazel Perley, spent
veral days last week in Indianola at
e home of her parents.

Watch This

Space

for

Announcement

Next

Week

College Book

Store

Student operated

atement of the ownership, management, circulation, etc., of the Simpsonian published weekly at Indianola, Iowa, required by the act of
congress of August 24, 1912.
Publisher, Clint L. Price, Indianola,
wa.
Editor, Allan J. Stanley, Indianola,
wa.
Business manager, John H. Noble,
dianola, Iowa.
 John H. Noble, business manager.
Sworn to and subscribed before me
is 10th day of April, 1921.
    Mrs. C. L. Price,
        Notary Public.

ROWE'S BARBER SHOP
is everybody's barber shop.
We **specialize** in everything in barber work.
East Salem Avenue

Postoffice Barber Shop.

Harvard Graduate School of Business

A two-year course in business, open to college graduates, leading to the degree of Master of Business Administration.

The School aims to give its students a basis of facts and principles which the beginner who is looking forward to executive work cannot readily obtain in his early business experience.

The case method of the School provides training in analyzing actual business problems.

The various courses are correlated in the following study groups: Accounting, Banking, Business Statistics, Foreign Trade, Industrial Management, Lumbering, Marketing, Transportation.

Registration for 1922-23 is limited. For further information and formal application blanks, write to

Dean W. B. Donham, University 22
Harvard Graduate School of Business Administration
Cambridge, Massachusetts

SABIN'S EDUCATIONAL EXCHANGE

Founded 1893 Shops Building, Des Moines, Iowa. Known all over the Middle West and West for
Prompt, Efficient and Reliable Service
to School Boards, Superintendents and Teachers. Enroll now for positions for 1922-23. ENROLLMENT FREE.

E. T. Housh, manager   Anna Allee, assistant manager

So successful were Simpson's graduates at the Harvard Graduate School of Business that the Cambridge people began advertising regularly in the *Simpsonian* in the 1920s.

XII

The Lean Years
1930–36

As Tuesday, September 3, 1929, dawned in Indianola, it promised to be one of those hot, sticky dog days of late summer. By early afternoon the air was thick as the temperature soared into the mid-nineties. Townspeople took to their front porches seeking refuge from the brutal heat. Few seemed to have the strength even to fan themselves as they looked out at the shimmering heat rising from the walkways. Up at the College the energy level was not much higher as the faculty pushed themselves to be ready for the new batch of freshmen who would arrive on Friday. One thing was certain; the single topic of conversation all over town was the heat.

Tuesday, September 3, 1929, was hot across most of America, but nowhere was activity more feverish than in New York at the stock exchange where the Big Bull Market soared to record heights. Stock prices that day reached their peak in the great boom of the twenties. After that day, stock prices sputtered, dropped a little, rallied and dropped again.

New York was a long way from Iowa. In Indianola, where few knew or cared about the wild speculation that fueled the big stock boom, playing the stock market was looked upon as something akin to riverboat gambling or carnival huckstering. It was something nice people didn't do. Therefore most people in Indianola, even the bankers and the business professors up at Simpson, took only passing notice of the gyrations of the stock market as it began to fall during the next few weeks.

Then on October 24 a panic of selling deluged the market, and in spite of attempts by the big New York bankers to rescue the market during the days that followed, the bottom fell out on the twenty-ninth. The next morning the story was on the first page of the *New York Times*: "Stock prices virtually collapsed yesterday, swept downward with gigantic losses in the most disastrous trading day in the stock market's history. Billions of dollars in open market values were wiped out as prices crumbled under the pressure of liquidation of securities which had to be sold at any price."[1]

People in Indianola read about the late October financial debacle in their morning *Des Moines Register* in much the same way they would skim over the news of a South American revolution. The really big event that week was Simpson's festive Homecoming, where more than two thousand fans watched Harry Workman's football eleven roll up 714 yards on offense, smashing Parsons 40–0. There might be chaos on Wall Street, where many a financier had been cleaned out, but no one in Iowa was throwing himself out of a window in despair.

Of course no one could have known then that the crash of the New York stock market portended the coming of a terrible economic depression. For one thing, the market's collapse did not cause the bust, but it did signal the beginning of a downward slide that seemed to have no end.

Iowans had reason to be insensitive to the beginning of the Great Depression. The Midwest had seen a collapse of farm prices back in 1921, and the region had never really recovered, had never really shared in the good times that marked the 1920s.[2] As Joseph Frazier Wall has so aptly put it, "The rural Midwest was a rudderless boat floundering in a trough of depression on the high seas of American prosperity."[3] Because they had not much shared in the nation's good times, Iowans could perhaps be excused for not noticing hard times when they first came upon the whole country.

In the 1920s Iowa's farms and the small towns that depended on them were in deep trouble. Farmlands that had sold at wildly inflated prices in the war years—prices that bore no relationship to the productivity of the soil—dropped precipitously in value. Banks that had lent money on these lands, often on second and third mortgages, found themselves hard pressed when falling commodity prices forced farmers to the wall, unable to repay their loans. All five banks in Indianola were hard hit. One of them, the Indianola Banking Company, failed in 1926, undermining confidence in the stability of the banks that remained. Virtually all of Simpson's endowment funds, invested in farm and town real estate mortgages at 5 or $5^1/_2$ percent interest, were endangered as borrowers too often found themselves unable to pay. We have already noticed, too, how difficult it was for Simpson to raise the funds to match the Rockefeller challenge grant, for too many of the donors, faced with the continuing agricultural depression, found themselves unable to honor their commitments. This was surely the primary reason why Simpson's two-month 1923 financial campaign dragged on for seven agonizing years.

All of this is not to overlook the fact that Simpson made great strides under President Hillman during the 1920s, boasting an enlarged student population, growing faculty, a million dollar endowment, strengthened curriculum and a sharply improved standing in the educational world. But try as it might, the College could not shake itself free from persistent deficits, low salaries and a deliberately low tuition rate.

Because neither Simpson nor Indianola was a stranger to financial stringency, the worsening economy of the nation after 1929 entered only gradually into their consciousness. But soon the disease that struck the main arteries of the nation's production and commerce spread inexorably into the Indianolas of America, and everyone could feel the whole body sicken, its forward motion arrested, its limbs withering, its nerve ends exposed.

At Simpson it took a while. The 1929–30 academic year seemed to be quite normal. Enrollment was down a bit, but not enough to be worrisome. Faculty went about their tasks, students studied and played much as before, and Dr.

Hillman spent more time thinking about the dance question than the nation's ailing economy. The next year was not so good. In September 1930 two more banks failed in Indianola, the Worth Savings Bank and the Warren County State Bank, affecting the deposits of hundreds of Indianolans, among them some of the Simpson people.[4] More ominous was a drop of very nearly ten percent in the College's enrollment. Everyone began to feel the ripples of uncertainty that spread through the Midwest. They were hearing more about the need for retrenchment and economizing; and they felt the nagging fear of unemployment.

The depression deepened in the winter of 1931-32, the whole nation locked in a state of economic paralysis. Unemployment soared, commodity prices plummeted—the market price of corn eventually bottoming at ten cents a bushel—and deflation triggered salary cuts for those who were employed. It seemed that everyone tightened their belts, hunkered down and prayed that things would get no worse.

As the nation sank into the economic abyss, Simpson could not escape the effects of hard times. Sagging enrollment, falling tuition receipts, a drop in endowment income and a catastrophic decline in church beneficence thrust Simpson into the bread line of American colleges. That it was a long line was not particularly comforting.

Enrollment dropped nearly thirty percent between 1929 and 1933, from 699 to 499, but it could have been worse.[5] Because jobs were hard to find and because parents kept their faith in the importance of a good education if young people were going to compete for what jobs there were, they sacrificed to send their children to college. Still, enrollment was down. And because tuition and semester fees—$160 per year—did not change at all in the decade after 1928, the College's income was severely affected. Rae Dean also soon discovered that as the depression worsened, charging tuition was one thing and collecting it was another. Students usually paid up, but collections were slow. "We must wait for our corn-hog contract to be paid," was a common student plea.

Simpson's tuition had rarely met more than a third of the annual budget. Endowment income was expected to provide much of the balance, but after 1930 one after another of Simpson's real estate investments got into trouble. People couldn't pay their debts, and Simpson couldn't afford to foreclose on mortgages either on moral or financial grounds. Only the addition of the Rockefeller grant in 1930 prevented endowment income from suffering serious decline. The Methodist conference was hard put to assist the College, for it was suffering too. Back in 1922 Simpson received $22,000 from the "conference sustenation fund"; in 1932 the amount was less than $1,000.[6] If the conference in the 1930s had given Simpson annually as much as 25 cents per member, the College would have received nearly $15,000. The merger of the Iowa and Des Moines Conferences, brought about at the church's general conference at Atlantic City in 1932, did not substantially affect Simpson's financial base of church support, for Iowa Wesleyan would of course share in any future conference beneficence.[7] Gifts from the Methodist Board of Education declined and eventually very nearly dried up altogether.[8]

Meanwhile, pledges made during the great endowment campaign (1923-30) became exceedingly difficult to collect. As early as February 1931, Vice-President Willis H. Cable reported that "the many bank failures and the general depression" were affecting the payment of pledges and making virtually impossible the raising of new money.[9] His report the next year was even more gloomy: "With disheartening uniformity we are told of inability to pay. Pressure is of little avail as most of the people do not have the money with which to pay and cannot get it. To crowd unduly would turn friendship and good will into dislike and enmity." He had real empathy with those who could not meet their pledges. For many of them, he said, "hope is abandoned as riches have made for themselves wings and have flown away, leaving our friends possessed of sad memories and empty purses."[10]

Declining income meant even greater deficits than usual. The 1930–31 year saw a shortfall of nearly $10,000. But it was the next year that brought disaster; the deficit soared to over $45,000. Thus, less than eighteen months after being declared debt-free, Simpson was back in debt more than $50,000.

Retrenchment was the order of the day. Administrative costs were pared. In 1932 the office of the dean of administration, created only in 1930, was dropped, reducing W. E. Payne's salary by $700. He returned to full-time teaching.[11] The next year the position of vice-president was discontinued, and Willis Cable was retired with thanks. His duties were to be absorbed by alumni secretary John Horsley "without additional salary."[12] Administrative travel was reduced sharply, although there really was not much there to cut. The *Simpson College Bulletin*, the alumni publication, was reduced in 1932 from four to two issues a year.

Because it seemed important somehow to have a vice-president, the board appointed language Professor William C. Hilmer to that post "without additional compensation."[13] Before he came to Simpson in 1920 he had served as an academic dean at Morningside College, so it was assumed that he knew what vice-presidents were supposed to do.

Cutbacks in faculty and staff were inevitable. Perhaps these were needed anyhow, for a study by the Methodist Board of Education in 1930 pointed out that Simpson's faculty was larger than needed for its student population.[14] And as enrollment slid downward, the need to downsize the faculty became an imperative. In 1931 two positions were dropped, the assistant professors of chemistry and English. The next year when psychology professor Byron E. Horn took a leave of absence to work on his doctorate at the University of Southern California, his sister, Vera E. Horn, was employed as a substitute for the 1932–33 year.[15] When Byron Horn did not return the following fall, his position was consolidated with the chair in education. Three more positions were dropped in 1932, as Berthemia McCarthy in foreign language, Mary Smith who taught typing and shorthand, and the College nurse Abbie M. Taber were let go.[16] McCarthy's classes were picked up by her colleagues Anna Belle Wilson and Dr. Hilmer. Typing and shorthand instruction was taken on by Florence H. Cox, the president's secretary.[17] The College's health services were "practically dismantled." Its dispensary closed and nursing duties were handed over to home economics instructor Elizabeth A. Stewart.[18] Ethel G. Inman in education was cut to half time, while Katharine Renich in history and Doris Engelking in speech saw their positions reduced to two-thirds time.[19]

The fall of 1933 saw still more cutbacks. Anna Belle Wilson was dropped from the faculty, leaving only Dr. Hilmer, with the help of Eva Stahl in Latin, to handle all the foreign language instruction.[20] We have already noted that Byron Horn did not return that year, and by eliminating the Bachelor of Science in Home Economics—at least for the time being—the second full-time position in that field could be cut, causing assistant professor Alice M. Sundt to leave the faculty. Veteran professor Edmund Holmes, who was suffering from poor health, retired and was not replaced, President Hillman himself picking up his duties.[21] Finally, dean of women Edna Stuntz agreed to teach typing and stenography at no extra salary. Thus five faculty positions were eliminated. "We part with these faculty members," said Hillman, "with a feeling of genuine and deep regret."[22]

Faculty cutbacks were only the beginning. Departmental equipment budgets were slashed; the purchase of books for the library very nearly ceased; faculty travel was discouraged, building maintenance deferred. Things like new uniforms for the football team, new furnishings for Mary Berry Hall or new costumes for a theater production would have to wait.

Retrenchment forced curricular changes, some of which in retrospect seem quite positive. One of these innovations was "co-op ed." In order to help students combine employment with full-time study, the College adopted in 1931 a cooperative education program that enabled students to alternate semesters of employment and study, permitting typically two students to alternate in the same job year round. While not many students availed themselves of this opportunity, it served well those who did, and the program probably attracted some young people to Simpson.[23] Co-op students could expect to graduate in four years by attending summer school each year. The problem with the program was its administration, which demanded far more time than the College could afford to give it.[24] It faded out after a few years and was revived only a generation later.

More promising but even less popular with students was the introduction of comprehensive examinations in all major fields of study. Drawing upon British and European models, Dean W. E. Payne suggested the adoption of such examinations, calling upon students to integrate the knowledge gained from the courses in their chosen field of study as the capstone of a Simpson education. Adopted by the faculty in the spring of 1932,[25] these three-hour comprehensives (oral or written) were held first in 1933, about four weeks before the end of the school year.[26] Students hated comprehensive exams, and, if the truth is to be known, some faculty found their administration to be a much bigger chore than they had envisioned it to be.[27] Consequently, as the years passed, one department after another either "restructured" or dropped comprehensives altogether. Twenty years later only the English Department, led by indomitable Harold Watson, still conducted these exams, and students were still complaining about the injustice of it all.

In 1932 the College, following the lead of others, altered its grading system to simple letter grades of A, B, C, D, and F, together with P for pass, I for incomplete, E for conditional (i.e., the student needs to do more work to earn a passing grade), Q for dropped unofficially, and similar rankings still essentially in use today. This replaced the old system that had been in use since 1913.[28]

Already in 1930 the old School of Business was being merged with the Department of Economics and Business Administration. Although the catalog for the 1930–31 school year still listed Edward L. Miller—then in his forty-second year at Simpson—as principal of the School of Business, the course listings were integrated with those of the Economics Department. In the 1931–32 catalog Miller was listed as "Associate Professor of Economics and Business Administration." The effective dropping of the nondegree program in business was a distinct step forward. Yet it is worth remembering that many of the young people who had earned diplomas from Simpson's business school held important positions all over the country, "a tribute to the quiet little man who taught them."[29]

Other curricular changes during the depression years seem to have been impelled by three powerful forces. One, of course, was the need to retrench, to cut back, to provide the best education at the least cost. The second was a powerful continuation of the drive for career-oriented, practical training in everything from accounting to pedagogy. The third was the popular educational ideal of adapting the curriculum to the needs and abilities of the individual child. For Simpson, although no one wanted to admit it, another equally unmistakable pressure was at work: the overall academic quality of the students was down. While the best students were still excellent, the College's sagging admission standards were permitting youngsters to enter who could not successfully meet existing graduation requirements.

Accordingly, the faculty (by no means unanimously) accepted a set of curricular changes that responded to these pressures. These included(1) an expansion of "professional study" in business and "social service," (2) a broadened—and less demanding—year-long freshman survey course combining history, sociology and economics, and (3) an "individualization experiment." By "individualization" the curriculum would indeed be adjusted to meet the needs of the child. As Dean W. E. Payne, still in his first year at Simpson, put it, "Students are different in ways not comprehended by 'degree of scholarship' or 'natural ability.' In consequence of this realization, registration next year [1931–32] will be a matter dependent upon the needs of the individual students." While requirements for graduation would not be altered, a special committee would be empowered to make exceptions for any degree candidate. "For instance," explained Payne, "if John Jones has had particular difficulty in high school science, it will be the duty of the committee to discover the difficulty, and the privilege of the committee to exempt John Jones from the science requirement." Any and all other adjustments might be allowed, especially for those less-than-articulate underclassmen in whom foreign language induced terror. All of this was intended to avoid "forcing the individual into the cast or the mold."[30] Rather it would enable the student "to have the advice of the faculty members in selecting the courses best adapted to fitting him for the work he wishes to do in life," while the freshman survey course would "furnish the new student a foundation for choosing his courses and in determining his life work." It would appear that all these curricular changes were predicated on the notion that vocational training was central in the life of the Simpson student.[31]

Two years later, the decline in enrollment and reduction of teaching staff necessitated further contraction of the College's curricular offerings. The long-standing requirement of two years of foreign language for the B.A. degree was dropped, and instruction in Spanish ceased altogether. With the retirement of Dr. Holmes, the Bible requirement was reduced from six to four hours. The psychology major was discontinued, but a physical education minor was restored, presumably as a consequence of student demand.[32]

* * *

As painful as faculty and curricular cutbacks were, they were not drastic enough to compensate for the decline in the College's income. Sterner measures would have to be taken, especially after the sickening deficit of $45,000 in 1931–32. If really deep cuts were to be made in the budget, they would have to look at faculty salaries.

Hillman and the board were loath to reduce the already low salaries they were paying the faculty. They had been stung by the criticism leveled in the report of the Methodist Board of Education's 1930 survey which stated that "Simpson College has one of the lowest faculty salary scales ever found by members of the survey staff in an accredited institution." Even allowing for Indianola's low living costs, the survey committee was appalled by what it found, although it had the impression "that the faculty is much stronger than would be expected in view of the salaries paid."[33]

Low salaries notwithstanding, something had to be done. Accordingly, when contracts for the next academic year were sent out in the spring of 1932, each faculty member was asked to sign the following agreement: "I accept the position in the Simpson College Faculty to which I have been re-elected for the year beginning September, 1932 and ending June, 1933, at a salary of $ _____ payable in twelve monthly installments with the understanding that this salary is basic and is subject to reduction made necessary in order that the college may live within the income of the year, such reduction to be made on a percentage basis applicable alike to all members of the Faculty." Hillman agonized over having to take this drastic step. "This [agreement] will likely lead to serious dissatisfaction in faculty ranks and a lowering of college morale," he said to board members.[34] He was right.

When classes resumed in the fall of 1932, enrollment was down by more than a hundred, even worse than either Hillman or Rae Dean had feared. "Everyone was pessimistic," wrote Harold Watson as he recalled the events of those early fall days. "The cut was going to be drastic. We were to hear the bad news, whatever it was, at the first faculty meeting," scheduled to meet a fortnight later. "Prexy was more discouraged than I had ever seen him, and I suddenly realized that he was no longer young." Watson tried to be cheerful, even reassuring. "I hope you're right," replied Hillman in a voice that carried no conviction. "Rae Dean," continued Watson, "was even more brusque than usual. He too was worried, and seemed to have aged in the few weeks."[35]

It was an especially solemn faculty gathering. They met in the usual place, the southeast corner classroom on the ground floor of the Administration Building. In those days it was still known as "Dr. Holmes' room." They were all expecting the worst. The president entered, looking tired. He adjusted his glasses, unbuttoned his jacket, nervously fingered his Phi Beta Kappa key, rocked back on his heels and opened the meeting. He omitted the usual words of welcome and came to the point. Salaries, he announced, would be frozen as they stood, and for the 1932–33 year fifty percent would be paid, although no one would receive less than $720 for the year. Other than that minimum, there would be no exceptions. That meant that President Hillman and Rae Dean would take their reduction along with everyone else.

The faculty people were stunned. They had expected cuts, maybe as much as twenty-five percent, but not this. "The shock was so great," wrote Watson, "that the whole group was quiet for a few minutes, and then one or two of the women wept silently, and some of the men asked questions in voices that sounded strange." The meeting adjourned quickly. The dazed faculty people drifted away wordlessly, all of them wondering what exactly to do next. Watson remembered that "I hurried home to report to my wife Martha that I was now a $1,425-a-year man. Her characteristic comment was that others would starve before we did!"[36]

* * *

No one starved. No one actually went without food. No one at Simpson lived very high, but things could have been worse. Most of the faculty still had their jobs, and few further staff cuts would have to be made. They could take some comfort in the knowledge that the same deflation that ruined Iowa's farm economy also brought substantial reductions in the price of goods and services.[37] Lower prices, then, compensated for at least a portion of the otherwise devastating salary loss. Just how devastating that loss was can be seen in the faded pages of the College ledger book for that year. The average faculty salary (including supplements for those who shared administrative duties) for the 1932–33 year was nominally $2,270, but the amount actually paid averaged only $1,148, with no one receiving less than $720. The average faculty salary in American colleges and universities that year was $2,700.

In many ways 1932 was the cruelest year of the depression. Across the nation thirteen million people joined the ranks of the unemployed, and millions more were underemployed. People in the great cities, in the countryside and in small towns like Indianola lived from day to day, using up their savings, borrowing on their life insurance, refinancing mortgages, and if they were desperate, selling possessions or swallowing their pride and borrowing from relatives. They did what they could, but they could not but encounter everywhere a sickening sense of helplessness in the face of unexplainable, impersonal forces.

No one knew how long hard times would last. "Perhaps the worst feature [of the Depression] was the dreary year after year of constant uneasiness as to what might happen next," wrote Harold Watson. "But once one had adjusted to never buying new clothes, never subscribing to feed the starving Ruritanians, never paying dues to anything, and always staying home, life was at worst simplified."[38]

For the faculty, not much improved during the next few years. In the 1933–34 year salaries, still frozen, were still paid at fifty percent, and the 1934–35 year saw no improvement until the end of the year, when there was enough left in the treasury to give each faculty member about a four percent "bonus." For 1935–36 the amount paid was increased to two-thirds of the frozen salaries, and it was the same the next year. In 1937–38 most people received seventy-five percent, plus a modest bonus, in 1938–39 about ninety-five percent. In 1939–40 the frozen salaries were abandoned, and a few people even received a modest raise. For most people, however, they were barely able in 1940 to match what they had been making in 1927 or 1928.

It was perhaps inevitable that Simpson's financial embarrassment would lead to a decline in the effectiveness of the faculty. Those who might have spent their summers in graduate study instead taught in the College's uninspiring ten-week summer session in order to eke out their salaries by two hundred or so dollars. Few attended meetings of learned societies because of the expense. When the College sought to remedy the situation by helping with dues and travel cost, the lowest paid faculty "protested that they needed the money for groceries."[39] And because of the inaccessibility of a large research library, few faculty were

Trustees Laud Cooperation of Simpson Faculty in Crisis

The following letter of appreciation was recently transmitted to C. W. Emmons, secretary of the faculty, by a special committee of the Board of Trustees:

To the President, Members of the Faculty and Employees of Simpson College:

The Board of Trustees of Simpson college in semi-annual session today, have heard with especial satisfaction concerning the spirit and morale of the college faculty. We realize that you are meeting real difficulties and experiencing anxiety and severe trials in the adjustment of your financial obligations. It is a matter of deep regret to us that the college funds are in such condition that we are unable to pay salaries in full.

We think you will realize the wisdom of the policy that we are following in not paying more largely than our income will warrant, but at the same time, we are deeply sorry for the distress which is caused you who are dependent upon these funds for your living. But in spite of this, we are cheered by the knowledge that your spirit and attitude are such that the work of the college is not impaired, but is being carried on on a high level of efficiency.

We assure you, as we have previously done, that whensoever conditions change so as to warrant it, it is our full intention to restore you to your basic salaries as rapidly and as fully as possible. We are heartily in sympathy with the policy of the business management whereby no current income is being devoted to old debts but all income is being used for current claims, thus making it possible for you to receive a larger proportion of your salaries than would otherwise be the case.

Again, we thank you for your kindness, your patience, your cooperation and loyalty. We have not wished to remain in silence and let you assume what our feelings are, but have wished in a very definite way to convey to you our sentiments.

Special Committee of Board of Trustees.
R. M. Shipman
Mearl A. Gable
W. L. Fleck

The alumnae and actives of Pi Beta Phi entertained at a buffet supper at the house in honor of Mrs. Merle Potter of St. Paul, Minn. Mrs. Potter is the vice president of this province of Pi Beta Phi and came to confer with Mrs. William Buxton III, who is president of the province.

Beta Sigma Omicron entertained the Commons Club at an informal party at the home of Mr. and Mrs. A. M. Kelley Friday evening, March 10.

Patronize Simpsonian Advertisers

Simpsonian, March 3, 1933.

writing books and journal articles or preparing scholarly papers. On the one hand the faculty felt itself humiliated, its pride broken, imagining itself to be some sort of persecuted minority. It was, of course, nothing of the sort. Others in the community suffered as much or more. On the other hand their sense of mutual deprivation promoted a sense of community, a powerful camaraderie.

It goes without saying that the faculty remained quite stable during the Great Depression. Twenty of the thirty-four regular 1930 faculty, together with five of the eleven conservatory teachers, were still there in 1936.[40] And of course in 1936 there were only twenty-six regular faculty and nine in the conservatory. It was, to be sure, stability born of unforgiving necessity. There was, after all, no place else to go. Because almost no openings were available anywhere, professors everywhere hung on to their teaching positions for dear life.

Sometimes the older ones hung on much longer than they wanted to, but they could not afford to retire. Old William E. Hamilton had last taught at Simpson at the age of seventy-two and did not retire from the itinerancy until three years later. Dr. Holmes stayed on until his health broke, forcing his retirement at seventy-four. When illness would finally force E. L. Miller to retire in 1936, he was in his seventies.

Simpson had no pension plan at all. Beyond their meager salaries, faculty and staff members received no financial benefits whatever—no retirement plan, no health and accident insurance, none of the perquisites that seem so common and so necessary today that it is difficult to imagine that they did not always exist. People met the living costs of retirement through personal savings, individual insurance and annuity schemes or by moving in with their children. As the Great Depression wore on, the retirement issue at Simpson was exacerbated by salaries so low that hardly anyone could afford to squirrel away even a few dollars in savings. Some kind of a pension system was not just desirable; it was urgent.

Board chairman A. V. Proudfoot, moved by the plight of the faculty, in late 1934 initiated discussions with them about adoption of some kind of a pension plan.[41] The faculty, led by Clyde Emmons and Harold Watson, undertook a careful investigation of current practices in other private colleges. They learned that of eighteen colleges they surveyed—seventeen replied—all had pension plans in place. In those schools, faculty who retired at the age of sixty-five or seventy, typically contributed five percent of their income each month, matched by five percent from the college, toward their retirement pension. Some schools participated in the Teachers Insurance and Annuity Association (TIAA); others operated their own plans. Emmons and Watson recommended that Simpson run its own system, require retirement by the age of seventy, keep retirement benefits equitable with existing pensions of Methodist clergymen, and permit faculty members who leave Simpson prior to retirement to retrieve their own contribution at the time of departure. Emmons and Watson insisted, however, that a system of faculty tenure must be instituted before putting into place a pension plan of any sort.[42]

Discussion of pensions laid bare a sore spot in Simpson's faculty. Clerical members of the faculty—people like Hilmer and Burrows, not to speak of President Hillman himself—did receive pensions while lay members of the faculty did not. And because the "preachers" had no obligations to the College which the professors did not have, their preferential treatment was resented. The matter became explosive when the Iowa-Des Moines Conference in the fall of 1934 voted to charge pension fund assessments for Simpson's clerical contingent against the faculty budget. Harold Watson remembers that this action was taken "despite Prexy's heated protest that they were thus taxing the lay members of the faculty to pay [the assessments]! Prexy is going to compel Hilmer, Burrows, etc., including himself, to pay them out of their own salaries. I have never seen such lay hostility to the clergy. But three cheers for Prex!"[43]

The board of trustees backed Hillman in his refusal to accede to the conference decision, questioning its legality and constitutionality.[44] Unfortunately, this dispute deflected their attention from the matter of retirement benefits for the entire faculty, and by the time Hillman retired in the spring of 1936, nothing had been done. Pensions would have to wait.

President Hillman suffered as much as did the faculty. It was not just a matter of the halved salary; in fact, that seemed to be the least of his concerns. Rather it was the sense of responsibility he bore for the faculty and students in his charge, for the standing of the College, for the quality of the education it was providing and for the supportive Christian atmosphere he sought to ensure. It was in his nature to try to emphasize the positive, and when events made that difficult to do, he tended to say nothing. With sadness people noticed that when he could no longer report a healthy gain in enrollment at fall convocation, he cancelled fall convocations. He was spending more time in his spartan office, decorated only with a no-nonsense calendar advertising the Atlas Portland Cement Company on the wall behind him and a large map of Iowa on which someone had marked the home towns of that year's Simpson undergraduates. This is not to say that he was reclusive, only that he felt the weight of his burdens and sought to avoid distractions. He was also a good churchman and thoroughly enjoyed the frequent visits to nearby Methodist congregations or the infrequent journeys to visit general conference or meetings of the Methodist Book Concern, of which he was a prominent member. In what spare time he had he loved to read and, when the spirit moved him, to play golf.

A. V. Proudfoot remained chairman of the board of trustees throughout these trying years, lending his support to Hillman and the faculty and persuading other members of the board to do likewise. These men were no faceless, remote overlords. They were people one saw down on the square, in the grocery store or in the next pew at church. Some of them were experiencing severe financial problems of their own, and they did understand the hardships that fell upon the College faculty and staff. After a particularly wrenching semiannual board meeting in early 1933, in which they determined that they must continue to pay only half-salaries, they wrote a thoughtful letter explaining their decision and commending the faculty for its remarkably good spirit and morale: "We realize that you are meeting real difficulties and experiencing anxiety and severe trials in the adjustment of your financial obligations." The board was "deeply sorry for the distress" of the staff but expressed itself "cheered by the knowledge that your spirit and attitude are such that the work of the college is not impaired."[45] Of course the work of the College *was* impaired, but not for want of faculty spirit. And no one on the campus was heard to blame the board of trustees for the hardship which they all shared.

Meanwhile, in order to attract students, the College offered extensive scholarship aid to those who would come, and it seemed that almost all the students were hard up. In order to spread out limited funds to the best advantage, the College rarely awarded more than half tuition to any one student. This converted the problem of the old $1,000 endowed scholarships, heretofore a serious annoyance, into a full-fledged crisis. Donors were demanding full scholarships for the students they named as recipients. Tuition in 1929–30 was $100 per year, while the scholarship endowment was earning between $50 and $55. Because the College felt morally bound to honor these scholarships, it experienced an unsustainable drain on its slender resources. The semester fee—in 1929–30 it amounted to $60—could of course be assessed on the students' bills, because it was technically not tuition. In order to protect the College, Rae Dean suggested in 1931 that the College lower its tuition charge to $60 and increase the semester fee to $100 for the year. That way the College would lose no more than five to ten dollars on each endowed scholarship awarded. "It is in the interest of equity and justice to all that the change is made," declared Dr. Hillman as he announced the reversal of fees on March 7, 1931.[46] To be sure, donors grumbled, but nearly everyone else found the decision eminently fair. This fee schedule remained in place for the balance of Dr. Hillman's administration.

Tuition and fees were of course only a part of students' college costs. Yearly board and room charges consumed more than half of their budget. In 1929–30 a room in Mary Berry Hall cost $72 per year ($2 per week) and board was $216 ($5 per week), but in 1933 these charges were reduced to $54 ($1.50 per week) and $126 ($3.50 per week) respectively.[47] The fraternities and sororities charged considerably less, as their members pooled their resources and lived cooperatively, often supplementing their meager provisions by fetching farm produce from home. At the Theta Kappa Nu house the boys were doing all their own work except for cooking, hoping to cover all costs for $10 per month per man. One cooperative group that did all its own work reportedly managed, with the help of parents who from time to time supplied some of the food, to keep their board costs to 77 cents per week per person.[48] In Lorraine Hall, where women lived in light housekeeping apartments for $1.50 a week with no charge for cooking, cooperative living was the order of the day, although College officials worried that inadequate nutrition might cause health problems.[49]

To meet the cost of tuition and board and room, students now depended more than ever on help from home, for part-time jobs were increasingly difficult to find. Not only were there fewer work opportunities, but the jobs that existed were taken by otherwise unemployed older adults who were supporting families. While it is no doubt true that few Simpson students had ever literally worked their way through college the way Harry Hopper did, still part-time employment had supplemented scholarships and whatever parents could afford to pay. But as the depression deepened in 1932, student jobs evaporated like water on a summer sidewalk.

Little remedy for student unemployment was had until the middle of the 1933–34 academic year when the federal government instituted what was called the Student Relief Employment Program, a part of President Franklin D. Roosevelt's New Deal.[50] Under this scheme students could be employed by the College at 30¢ an hour for up to fifty hours per month to assist with school costs. For its part, the College had to agree to reduce by $25 the annual tuition of students who participated. Simpson employed more than thirty students in the spring semester of 1934 to do janitorial, library and research jobs on the campus, and the next year could hire up to twenty-one men and twenty-one women.[51] No doubt the S.R.E. program kept some students in school who otherwise might have dropped out. Nationwide the S.R.E. was a great success. Secretary of Labor Frances Perkins and Interior Secretary Harold Ickes were especially enthusiastic about it. Rae Dean was enthusiastic too, for he estimated that the College's tuition income would be improved by at least $1,800 per year. S.R.E. did not solve the problem of meeting the cost of a college education for Simpsonians, but it helped.[52]

* * *

The worse the economy behaved, the more Americans were trying to understand it. Often they could make no sense of it at all, and in the Midwest some disillusioned and bewildered farmers struck out in blind rage against the impersonal forces that were ruining them. In Iowa there was violence up around

Sioux City in 1932, when Milo Reno's Farmers' Union tried to lead a statewide farmers' strike. In other parts of the state angry farmers crowded into farm foreclosure sales, intimidated potential serious bidders, bought farms for one dollar apiece and gave them back to their grateful former owners.

Most Midwesterners had no taste for violence, but they sought to explain the Depression or to devise ways to bring the nation out of it. Soon some of them were talking about technocracy, a movement conceived by amateur economist Howard Scott and based on the doctrines of Frederick Soddy and Thorstein Veblen. Technocracy would put the management of society into the hands of scientists and engineers. The popularity of the movement peaked in the winter of 1932–33. In January, Francis Moats, briefly attracted to the gospel, sought to explain to a somewhat mystified Simpson audience technocracy's application of the principles of engineering to the prevalent American social and economic system.[53] Moats's hearers found the whole thing too abstruse, too far removed from the practical problems they faced, and when the New Deal arrived a few months later, technocracy was all but forgotten.

If technocracy failed to catch hold at Simpson, socialism did. Viewing the onset of the depression as evidence of the imminent collapse of capitalism, socialists believed that their day had come, and no one welcomed the new day more than Dr. Winfred Payne, Simpson's dean (until 1932) and economics head. Payne was a Marxist, but he was no crimson communist. His was a much tamer brand of what might be called democratic Christian socialism. Never devious, always forthright, he made no apologies for his views, which he asserted to be rooted firmly in Christian tradition. Speaking to the Y.M.C.A. in early 1931, he stated: "Elimination of the profit motive and compensation based upon the needs of the individual" must occur before true democracy can be achieved. To be sure, "the elimination of . . . profit presupposes the elimination of private property," and "while such an act might be called socialism, it might also be called Christianity."[54] A few months later, declaring that "nearly all agree that socialism is the only satisfactory way out of the economic crisis," Payne urged students to organize a local unit of the League for Industrial Democracy, a national liberal student movement.[55] When its Simpson chapter was founded a year later with about twenty members, the L.I.D. declared that by the exercise of "thought, deadly and dangerous," it would direct its efforts toward "a more equitable social order."[56] At their first meeting, held at the Theta Kappa Nu house, the L.I.D. members discussed, of all things, technocracy, deciding after they talked it out that socialism, not technocracy, was America's hope. The ATOs were relieved that the meeting was not held at *their* house.

Hiram Weld headed Simpson's L.I.D. group, but the main force in it was a fellow junior from Whittier, California, Gerald Binkerd, whose motto was "Take on new thoughts, throw off old habits." Between them they directed the efforts of the group with the benign inspiration of Dr. Payne. Most Simpson students remained predominantly conservative. In the 1932 presidential election a student poll gave Hoover an overwhelming 275 votes to 70 for Roosevelt and 55 for Norman Thomas. Among those who could actually vote, Thomas beat F.D.R. by two votes.[57] But things can change. Two years later the students voted their approval of Roosevelt's New Deal policies 222 to 158.[58] However, when it came to war and disarmament, more than a third of them declared themselves pacifists, refusing to bear arms under any circumstances. "War under any condition is unexcusable," declared an editorial in the *Simpsonian*.[59] This sentiment was consistent with earlier support for disarmament.[60]

* * *

At its mid-year meeting on February 15, 1933, the board of trustees reelected John Hillman president of the College for a three-year term. In a time of drastic retrenchment, no one wanted to make a change in Simpson's leadership. Hillman would have preferred to retire—he was nearly sixty-eight years old—but he realized that 1933 was no time to abandon an ailing college.[61]

Simpson was indeed ailing, but was trying to live within its budget. Unfortunately, not everyone was confident about the College's future. Around town there were widespread rumors that the school "would suspend operation or close next fall." Board chairman A. V. Proudfoot, who knew every detail of Simpson's financial status, branded the rumors "utterly false and silly,"[62] but despite his positive reassurance, the rumors would not stop. One report had it that Simpson was being sold to the Catholic Church, and no matter how far-fetched the notion that Indianola would soon be "chained to the pontiff at Rome," there were those who believed it, and it may have cost Simpson some enrollment for a year or two.[63]

The faculty, reported Hillman in 1934, was bearing up under hardship "with admirable spirit," but could not be expected to remain long at the College if other opportunities came along. "I speak of a peril that is even now imminent," he warned the board. There was also the risk of jeopardizing Simpson's standing with the North Central Association and the American Association of Universities. Somehow the College must increase its revenues. Maybe, he said with more hope than conviction, the worst of the depression was over.[64]

The depression wasn't over. The summer of 1934 brought searing drought and the chinch bugs that devastated the crops of Iowa and the Midwest. In a mid-July heat wave the thermometer rose to an average of 106 degrees, and on August 8 hit an all-time peak of 113 degrees. Crop losses in Warren County alone topped two million dollars. The corn crop was the lowest since 1894.

In view of all this bad news, Simpson expected yet another serious drop in enrollment. But to everyone's surprise, the 1934 registration reached 440 by September 12, and another 44 were added during the next few days.[65] When it was all sorted out, enrollment in the College (not counting the conservatory) was up by only one student, but with that one student Simpson seemed to have turned the corner. And when a year later enrollment in the liberal arts college increased by thirty-four, it was clear that the College was indeed on the mend. Better yet, Hillman could report that of 218 freshmen, more than thirty percent had been members of the National Honor Society in high school.[66]

* * *

People driving into Indianola would scarcely have seen a community that looked like it was in the grip of a depression. Rather they would have been struck with how normal everything looked: well-kept homes along streets shaded by great arching trees and the town square surrounded by neat shops and stores that looked out on the town's centerpiece, the great brick courthouse with its ancient tower and sandstone trim. Nothing in town looked more normal than the College, with its green swards of lawn, its forest of maples and elms, its gracefully aging buildings. Nor was there anything unusual about the appearance of the students who strode the walkways of the campus, who crowded into the classrooms or disported themselves on the playing fields. Certainly few of them appeared to be brooding about the nation's economic malaise. Nor were they.

Unlike most of their elders, students adjusted with remarkable resilience to the rigors of life in the Depression. This is not to say that they were unaware of the immense problems confronted by their elders. But they learned quickly to do with less, to have a good time for little or no cost, to be innovative in finding ways to meet college expenses, to act as if everything was normal even if it was not.

Most students did put their academic work first, for they believed that successful performance in the classroom should translate into a good job four years hence. Given the poor economy of those years, it is hardly surprising that they preferred to major in "practical" fields like business administration or teacher preparation which provided the surest, most direct path to employment. As the *Simpsonian* observed in the spring of 1933, if it weren't for teaching jobs in the public schools, few graduates of Simpson would have any job at all that next fall.[67] While that was not literally true, it is surprising how many did enter teaching, even if only for a few years.

Outside the classroom, student enthusiasm for sports, organized social life and other manifestations of popular culture continued unabated. Athletics, especially football, occupied an inordinate amount of students' time and attention, not to speak of that of their elders. A home football game attracted a larger crowd than a major platform speaker or even the annual performance of *The Messiah*. Basketball games were far more popular than the best oratorical performances or theater productions.

The director of athletics was thought by many to be second in importance only to President Hillman. Thus when Harry Workman resigned in the spring of 1931 after a generally successful five years at Simpson, the search for his successor engendered more interest than any other campus issue.[68] People were delighted when the choice fell upon Lloyd C. "Judd" Dean, who seemed able to coach everything.[69] Dean, a 1926 graduate of Cornell College, had been head basketball and track coach and assistant football coach at his alma mater. He was described variously as "the smartest football player Cornell ever had," or "a gentleman both in victory and defeat." Cornell's Latin professor said that "it is hard for me to avoid superlatives when I talk about Mr. Dean."[70] Dean must have been special.

There was no depression in Simpson football. Although Harry Workman's 1930 team did poorly, Judd Dean's four years at Simpson were triumphs. The 1931 and 1933 teams took the conference championship and the 1932 team placed second. The major reason for the success of the 1931 eleven was the stellar play of another Simpson football great, Elvin "Kink" Richards, who had a tremendous year. Apart from three losses that year to big schools—Drake, Iowa State and Ohio University—Simpson won its games and went 6–0–0 in the Iowa Conference, mostly due to Richards's exceptional play at fullback. That year Richards was named to the all-state team, which included players from Drake and Iowa and Iowa State, and then was picked for the all-Midwestern first team alongside players from Notre Dame and the Big Ten. Richards had come to Simpson from Des Moines University when it closed. He was one of few Simpson players to succeed in professional football, signing a contract with the New York Giants in the summer of 1933.[71] During his first season with the Giants he gained the most yardage of any player in the national professional football league, 277 yards in six games, while Simpson basked in the reflected glory of it all.[72]

Back in Indianola, fans were delighted that four of the five 1933 home games would be played in the evening. Installation of twenty-two 1,500-watt Benjamin floodlights mounted on five poles on each side of the football field was completed in time for the opening of the season. Although Rae Dean was known to be favorable to sports, no one was quite sure how he persuaded the Indianola City Council to contract for the lights, even though he did promise that they would be paid for out of gate receipts from the games.[73]

In 1934 it seemed impossible to declare a conference football champion. The difficulty stemmed from the adoption in 1930 of a complicated rating system devised by E. G. Stanley of William Penn College and Rae Dean of Simpson.[74] Appropriately designated the "Stanley-Dean System," it rated teams on the basis of the strength of the opposition met by each team, not by percentage of wins. Most of the time the system worked well, but in 1934, although St. Ambrose boasted a perfect 5–0–0 record against lackluster competition, Upper Iowa's 5–0–0 record against tough opponents should have made the choice an easy one. But Upper Iowa had used ineligible players and was forced to forfeit two games, dropping it to 3–2–0. This moved Simpson, with a mediocre 3–2–1 record, to the top under the Stanley-Dean system, even ahead of St. Ambrose. Complicating the matter further was the unfortunate fact that St. Ambrose had defeated Simpson 7–6 that season. Because of these circumstances, writes "Buck" Turnbull in his history of the Iowa Conference, "the conference did not officially recognize a champion." However, since the league had adopted the Stanley-Dean system for better or worse, Simpson is listed as the 1934 football winner."[75] A year later the Stanley-Dean system was dropped.

During Judd Dean's successful years as coach, the Simpson basketball teams were a bit better than mediocre, their best performance coming in 1934, when the team ranked sixth of fourteen in the conference, winning twelve of its nineteen games overall (seven of eleven in the conference). The track teams were always good, never ranking below fifth in the conference; in 1933 they took a close second place behind Iowa State Teachers College with 42½ points to the Teachers' 44. Baseball returned to Simpson in the spring of 1933. Simpson defeated Parsons 9–8 in the first conference game on its home field, following up with five more conference victories and no losses for the year.[76]

Judd Dean's success at Simpson led Cornell College to offer him the head coaching position there in 1935. Simpson people understood Dean's decision to return to his alma mater, but they were truly disappointed to lose a man who had served as a respected model for undergraduate athletes. From a field of about forty candidates Simpson found a worthy successor in Frank Casey, who had been serving as athletic director and coach at Buena Vista College for the past eight years. Casey, whose appointment was announced February 27, 1935, would remain at Simpson for twenty-five years.[77] Probably no man would have a greater impact on Simpson athletics than this tall, slim, gentlemanly newcomer, strikingly effective both on and off the field.

The results of Casey's first year at Simpson were mixed: a terrible football season with only one win, a good basketball season—the best in years—finishing fourth in the twelve-school Iowa Conference and a championship in track. All in all, he was not displeased, nor were the rest of the people at Simpson. And he was happy when the conference that year dropped the complicated Stanley-Dean rating system.

* * *

During the Lean Years the Greek-letter societies continued to be the only college activity that could compete for popularity with organized athletics. For better or worse, much of Simpson's undergraduate social life was centered around these living units.

All six of the women's groups survived the hard times of the 1930–36 era, ending up stronger perhaps than they had ever been. Among the men's groups, on the other hand, there was a shakeout that saw five groups reduced to three. The two older fraternities, Alpha Tau Omega and Kappa Theta Psi, continued to be very strong. Each had a fine house and a healthy membership. The younger Theta Kappa Nu and A.C.C. were experiencing problems. By 1935 Theta Nu's membership had fallen to about fifteen. Meanwhile, dissatisfied with its national affiliation, the A.C.C.s withdrew from the national A.C.C. and initiated negotiations for merger with their next-door neighbor, Theta Nu. Faculty advisers of both groups approved the move, and on March 23, 1935, twenty-five members of A.C.C. were initiated into Theta Kappa Nu. The combined fraternity, with a membership of forty, emerged as a formidable competitor on campus.[78] Not so fortunate was Alpha Delta Alpha which was able to pledge only two men in 1931 and gave up the ghost in the awful summer of 1932. The demise of some Greek-letter chapters and the merger of others was not an uncommon phenomenon on American campuses, where chapter houses, whether owned or rented, were lost as memberships declined along with the enrollments of their host institutions.

Every fraternity or sorority wanted a chapter house, and on many campuses these groups provided an important component of student housing. At Simpson the houses provided about a third of the women's and *all* the men's housing apart from individual private accommodations in homes or a few temporary small independent cooperative groups.

It is something of a paradox that as the depression tightened its hold on the country, in 1930 and 1931 Simpson's Greeks, having for the most part occupied rented facilities, decided now to buy or build their own houses. At that time only two fraternities owned their own homes—Kappa Theta Psi in "Old Brick," a fine structure on East Franklin, and the ATOs in their huge frame house on Jefferson Way. In 1927 the Pi Beta Phis, led by Sara Sigler (whom we have already encountered bringing home economics to Simpson), had bought the John Schee home at 406 North Buxton for $13,000, the first Simpson sorority to own its own home. Three years later the Tridelts bought a lot for $1,000 next to Harry Weinmann's home on North Buxton, several blocks from the campus, only to discover that they needed the College's permission to locate and to build a house. When they presented architect's plans for their house, together with the plan to finance the project, the board of trustees, after several months of study, approved the plans but disapproved the location. They thought it too far from the campus.[79] If Simpson's young women were to be properly protected, they needed to live close by. Sororities, they decided, could buy or build houses only on streets directly bordering the campus or Buxton Park: on North C Street, Girard Avenue or North Buxton Street. But because the entire area was built up, it meant sororities would have to buy an existing residence and either remodel it or remove it in order to build. The Tridelts were frustrated and dismayed.

Then, fortuitously, the handsome residence of Judge John A. Storey on North C Street was offered to the Tridelts for $15,000, and the judge agreed to take their lot on North Buxton as part of the down payment.[80] The sorority occupied the house the following fall.

No sooner had the Tridelts bought their house than the Theta Kappa Nus, still inadequately housed, determined to build their own fraternity house, even if it meant removing an existing structure to do so. They looked at the college-owned house formerly occupied by Professor J. Allen Baker on North C Street, just north of Hopper Gymnasium, and struck a deal whereby Professor Baker would purchase and remove the house and the Theta Nus would buy the lot for $3,500 and build a new house on it.[81] The College agreed to finance the $17,000 cost of the new house out of endowment funds, for it looked like a very good—and indeed controllable—investment.[82] The plans for the house were identical to the Theta Kappa Nu chapter house at Baldwin-Wallace College in Berea, Ohio.[83] Built by the Harlan Lumber Company of Indianola, the building went up during the summer of 1931 and was ready for occupancy in the latter part of October. An attractive Tidewater colonial three-story structure of light buff brick with a great pitched roof pierced by large dormer windows, it was the first fraternity house at Simpson built for that purpose.

Alas, for the Theta Kappa Nus building a house was one thing and keeping it was another. It would be difficult to imagine a more inauspicious time to build a new fraternity house or, for that matter, any other student housing as college enrollments began to decline. Only a few months after the Theta Nus occupied their fine new home they found that with declining membership they could not fill all the beds in the house, and they were having difficulty collecting room and board from those who remained. The College agreed in 1932 to collect only interest on its loan, deferring principal payments "until conditions improve." But as the depression ground on, the Theta Nus could not meet even the interest payments, forcing the College in 1934 to take over the ownership of the building and rent it back to the fraternity.[84]

Meanwhile the Alpha Chi Omegas wanted to build a house on a property known around Indianola as the old Briggs place on North B Street, just off Girard, apparently close enough to the "approved zone" for sorority dwellings to earn board of trustees approval. Their new house, explained members of the Alpha Chi house corporation, could be constructed for $15,000. The board readily approved the building plans, but balked when the Alpha Chi house corporation president, Thelma Talbot Sprague, requested that Simpson lend $5,000 toward the new house.[85] They informed her that "the by-laws of the College would not permit a loan for this class of property," a puzzling assertion in view of their having made a loan to the Theta Nus only a few months earlier.[86] Disappointed but undismayed, the Alpha Chis went ahead and built their tidy, red brick chapter house with private financing. Contracts were let in June 1932, and the house, accommodating twenty women and a housemother, was completed a few months later.[87]

In the fall of 1930 the College remodeled Park Hall, an older building opposite the northeast corner of Buxton Park, so that it could be occupied by the Beta Sigma Omicron sorority.[88] A year later the Theta Upsilons moved into a big College-owned house at 512 North Buxton after it was extensively remodeled and enlarged for them at a cost of something over $6,000.[89]

The flurry of house building and remodeling in the early 1930s, although it came at an inopportune time from the standpoint of financing, did substantially improve Simpson's student housing. The new dwellings were considerably more comfortable, and more importantly, they were safer. There had been serious fires in nearly all of the old rented houses, none of them occasioning a loss of life, but frightening nonetheless. All the new fraternity and sorority houses were equipped with improved electric wiring and proper fire escapes.

Although membership in some of the men's groups declined during the Depression, on the whole numbers remained fairly stable in the Greek organizations until 1934 when the freshmen joining dropped precipitously consequent to a decision by the board of trustees to deny College or government S.R.E. aid to any student member of any social fraternity or sorority. The College, reasoned the board, could ill afford during hard times to subsidize social expenses in organizations that could be seen as "purveyors of frivolity." That these same fraternities and sororities were providing bed and board for a substantial number of Simpson students, consistently at less cost than that charged by the College, seems to have been of little moment. Thus many students, confronted with a choice of a scholarship without a fraternity or no scholarship with one, were compelled to accept the former. It is astonishing that the Greek groups survived at all.[90] Only twenty-two men pledged fraternities in the fall of 1934, that small number surely a factor in the decision of A.C.C. to merge with Theta Kappa Nu that same year. Probably it was not the intention of the board or the faculty to threaten the existence of the Greek groups, for the College depended on them for housing. When the faculty removed the odious restriction in the spring of 1936, membership in the social groups returned quickly to normal.[91]

The Greek-letter societies consistently turned in a better academic performance than did their independent counterparts, with the egregious exception of one or two fraternities that consistently competed for last place. The Alpha Chis and Tridelts vied nearly every year for top honors, while the Kappa Theta Psis were at the bottom so often that it became for them almost a perverse point of pride. All this led faculty administrators, educationists and sociologists to seek rational explanations for the constant, almost wearying, poor academic accomplishments of the men in comparison with the fine work of the coeds, as if the phenomenon were unique to Simpson.[92] Clear-cut answers eluded them, but if one asked the women undergraduates, they would point out that women simply studied more than men. They weren't sure why. The young men were quite sure they knew why, but all of their explanations would today sound irredeemably sexist.

Of course, the designated keepers of the undergraduate academic fire were the literary societies, and during the 1930s the flame very nearly went out. These groups probably would have done poorly even if there had been no depression, but they declined even more rapidly than anyone, including their last die-hard members, could have anticipated. In 1930 four women's societies—the Zetaletheans, Alpians, Crescents and Clionians—functioned alongside the lone surviving men's society, the Kappa Phi Sigmas. At the depth of the depression in October 1932, three of the women's societies—the Alpian, Crescent and Clionian—merged, creating one organization, called Sigma Gamma Rho, which would compete with the ancient Zetalethean for the limited number of women still attracted to their programs. Kappa Phi Sigma, the Greek-named inheritor of the grand old Everett Literary Society, carried on feebly until the end of the 1931–32 school year, but did not reorganize the following fall. To some of the older faculty it was a matter of deep regret that they were called upon to witness the passing of Simpson's oldest literary society after sixty-five years, for in days gone by when it was at its best, the Everett was a formidable instrument of education for its members.

If the literary societies were moribund, Pi Kappa Delta and the oratorical and debate teams flourished.[93] Especially successful was the team that placed first at a state forensics meet in 1932,[94] and three years later Simpson's debaters met with signal success.

Publications suffered as it became more difficult for students to afford the subscription price of the *Simpsonian* or the purchase price of the *Zenith*. The editorial quality of the newspaper remained high, but coverage was severely reduced. Shaky finances forced the staff to reduce the *Simpsonian* to a single sheet in 1933, and soon thereafter it started to appear only biweekly.[95] Whatever its size and frequency, the paper was put together by a number of able editors, none more controversial than Ray Shipman, who had the temerity to criticize the fraternities for their everlasting politicking and intramural bickering. Calling the Greeks "a disgrace to the College," he concluded that "Simpson would be better off without such organizations, but of course we're just a misanthropic grouch."[96] The Greeks agreed that he was certainly that and probably a socialist too.

The *Zenith* during the Depression suffered even more than the *Simpsonian*. Everyone wanted a yearbook but few wanted to pay for it. Finally, in the desperate fall of 1933 the situation was so bleak that editor Daryl Benson despaired of publishing it at all, and it was Christmastime before it seemed worth taking the risk. The whole venture depended on students' willingness to pay $1.50 for a copy. With a skeleton staff Benson put together an abbreviated paper-cover version of the yearbook, including only the essentials. Because the staff couldn't afford the price of as many engravings as they desired, they decided to expand the advertising section in the back of the book by including a short history of Simpson College, because setting type was cheaper than paying for engravings. Besides, it seemed appropriate to include a history, for after all this was the 1935 *Zenith*, commemorating the College's seventy-fifth anniversary. To compose this history they looked around and found Christie Swain, a junior who was willing and able to do the job on short notice. It is doubtful that Swain could imagine that the history he penned—about twelve pages of actual printed text—would serve as the only history of Simpson College for more than half a century.[97]

Christie Swain was not a typical Simpson undergraduate. When he entered Simpson he was already pastor of the Methodist Church at Sheldahl, Iowa, and he continued to serve that little church all the time he was a student at the College. He was also supporting a wife and two children on the salary of a rural parson. A superior scholar, at Simpson he did just about everything. He was a gifted speaker and writer; he was vice-president of Pi Kappa Delta and a member of Sigma Delta Tau; he was president of the Pi Gamma Mu social science society and president of A.C.C. at the time of its merger with Theta Kappa Nu; he sang in the madrigal choir, worked for a number of worthy causes on campus and edited the *Simpsonian* during his senior year. He was elected to Epsilon Sigma and named a "representative man" of the College. It was a remarkable record, but it would probably surprise Christie Swain to learn that fifty years later he would be remembered at Simpson as "the man who wrote the College's history."

As early as 1931 there was talk of celebrating the College's diamond anniversary in 1935.[98] How to mark that important milestone? They might put up a new chapel building, or raise another $250,000 for the endowment, or increase enrollment to, say, 700; and surely they could put on a pageant and even commission a full-length history of the College "from the time it was 'Old Bluebird' until the present."[99] But these worthy aims were overtaken by events as the depression covered the land. Each year after 1931 there seemed to be less and less to celebrate. By 1934 it was clear that the College could not even afford the cost of a modest commemorative program. Accordingly in early 1935 the board decided that they must regretfully postpone the event at least until 1936, perhaps even to 1942, the seventy-fifth anniversary of Simpson's becoming a four-year college.[100]

Students were not deeply moved by the cancellation. They were far more interested in pursuing their academic work as quickly and efficiently as possible in order to prepare themselves for the job market—if there was one—and to have more time meanwhile for extracurricular activities.

Some of the student activities appear not to have changed much. A comment in the *Simpsonian* in 1932 that a recent student council meeting "was, for once, businesslike," suggests that most of the time they were not.[101] Many students, including the Greeks, were ready to admit that fraternity manipulation of elections was at the root of the trouble with student government; too many of the representatives were elected for their popularity, not for their competence.[102]

Student government, for all its failures, was far more popular than was the honor system, by now flawed beyond redemption. In spite of the publication of all of the nineteen elevating principles of the code each fall, students observed it less and less.[103] It came to an ignominious end one day in 1933 when President Hillman discovered "widespread cheating" in his Bible class. He went back to his office, sat down and issued a presidential edict discarding the honor system once and for all.[104] Students and faculty concurred readily with the president's action, all of them relieved to be free from a system that unfortunately did not succeed at Simpson.

It appears that during the depression years only one new organization was founded on the campus. It was Alpha Psi Omega, a national coeducational recognition society in drama, chartered at Simpson April 24, 1935. The existing Blackfriars organization was retained as a society for theater underclassmen.[105]

* * *

On the whole Simpson students were a well-behaved lot, acceptably respectful of their elders and not given to intentional discourtesy or disorderly conduct. This is not to say that they accepted all the College rules unquestioningly or that they were somehow unable to think for themselves, for they were inescapably affected by the powerful, mostly secular, influences that were liberating—some would say corrupting—young Americans as they threw off the restraints of tradition. And it was clear that at Simpson, as elsewhere, the student agenda only infrequently matched that of the faculty or the board of trustees. Students put a high priority on classroom education as preparation for a career, valued the peer group interaction they found in activities outside the classroom and tended to be impatient with, if not hostile to, the behavioral expectations of the old-time religion. For example, one student noted that during four years at Simpson the average student spent 198 hours in chapel.[106] Somehow that fact was supposed to speak for itself.

In the faculty, as usual, there was division. Some were willing purveyors of career education; others were not. Some sympathized with students who showed their discontent with the old ways, the old expectations of behavior, the old restrictions; others viewed the new secular culture with suspicion or distaste, fearing that it would lead to immorality and hedonism. At yet another level was the board of trustees, stalwart defenders of the faith who were prepared to do battle against the worldly forces of Babylon that threatened to drag civilization into the abyss.

If one examines the written records of Simpson in the 1930s or hears the accounts of student life from the alumni of that era, the one issue that dwarfed all others, that spelled liberation to the students and descent into the abyss to the board of trustees was dancing. Today it seems unimaginable that dancing could have been found so important that it led, for the the first time in Simpson's history, to a head-to-head confrontation between the students on one side and most of the faculty and the board of trustees on the other. Never before had students at Simpson declared a revolution against authority. This time they did.

It started in early 1931. As we have seen, the College rule against dancing was clear, unequivocal, universally known, and widely disobeyed secretly. But the students were tired of secrecy, saw no reason whatever for continuing the ban on dancing, and determined to petition the faculty and board to relent and abandon the no-dancing rule. They signed petitions, but they perceived that their entreaties were either refused or ignored. The president and board, however, later stated that they had received no petitions at all, even though students insisted they had turned them in. Nevertheless, petitions or no petitions, President Hillman declared that the authorities could and would draw the line: there would be no dancing, their decision made clear in a ringing declaration issued by the board in 1931.[107]

The controversy soon took on the character of a classic political contest between the governed demanding participatory democracy and the governors insisting on recognition of duly constituted authority. John Swisher, a senior history major and active ATO, in a *Simpsonian* guest editorial entitled "Autocracy vs. Democracy," asked "If we contribute to the support of [society's] institutions should we not be permitted to share in determining our own destiny?"[108]

At the end of the fall semester of 1931 a group of members of the S Club, the campus athletic lettermen, decided to challenge the no-dancing rule and hold an off-campus dance in town. Led by senior Thomas M. Anderson, all-conference end in football and basketball and track star, former president of the student council and a Theta Kappa Nu member from Chariton, the S Club scheduled their dance at Indianola's Modern Woodmen Lodge Hall for Wednesday, December 16, after a College basketball game, the night before school was to be dismissed for the Christmas holidays. They engaged an orchestra and printed tickets to what was labeled an "all-college concert," which fooled no one, including President Hillman.[109]

At chapel on Monday, two days before the scheduled event, Hillman read a carefully prepared speech in which he called upon students to use their reason, not their emotions, in dealing with the dance issue. Warning them of the potentially devastating withdrawal of financial support from Simpson should dancing take place, he added, "May I not ask if the present procedure is not most uncalled for? [It is] in defiance of properly constituted authority," which he labeled as "criminal."[110]

That afternoon the students held a mass meeting at the chapel where 256 of them signed a petition requesting the Wednesday dance be approved and that dancing be permitted for the rest of the academic year. That same evening a delegation delivered the petition to board chairman A. V. Proudfoot, who pointed out that no action could possibly be taken until the next annual meeting of the board the following June. He suggested they present their petition to Dr. Hillman.

Tuesday morning Hillman spoke again before a packed chapel meeting and Proudfoot reinforced what the president said. The students responded with another mass meeting Wednesday noon.[111]

The dance did not take place. The lodge, bowing to administrative pressure, withdrew the offer of its facilities. The whole plan collapsed, and Anderson announced at the conclusion of the Wednesday basketball game that the dance was called off "due to threat of arrest."[112]

Down at the *Record* Don Berry, who was no friend to what he called the "Don Quixotes of the Silver Slipper" up at Simpson, cheered for the victory of Hillman and the forces of rectitude:

> Like a Central American revolution the threatened terpsichorean rebellion in Simpson College has apparently collapsed. General Tommie Anderson has retired to the hills of Lucas county to check up on his fortunes. No airplanes are being used to locate him. It is understood that no decision has been reached as to the extent or method of his discipline when he returns from exile after the holiday vacation. Discipline will be administered, it is said, not as severe as facing a firing squad, but severe enough that the object of it will know that leading revolutions against properly constituted authority is not what it is cracked up to be.[113]

Tom Anderson did not return to Simpson that year. The administration had won a clear victory, but the war was still on. The agitation for dancing continued. Several polls were conducted on campus, on at least one of which students were asked to sign their names. The board solicited opinion from the conference clergy and laity. Hillman canvassed the College's alumni.[114] At its June meeting in 1932, the board voted overwhelmingly to retain the no-dancing rule, in spite of the results of their own polls which in aggregate showed 870 votes favoring change to 572 opposed.[115] Why, asked the board, should they "accommodate rule-breakers" whose "poverty of social ingenuity" leads them "toward extravagance and unnecessary expenditure"? They were clearly annoyed at having to deal with this issue when they were dealing with larger, more important matters like slashing faculty salaries, hardly a pleasant duty.[116]

For some months the dancing controversy died down, only to erupt again at a St. Patrick's Day party the following March 1933, at the College chapel. About ten o'clock, with students, faculty and administrators present, the lights suddenly went off, the orchestra continued playing, and it was believed that about ten couples danced in the dark. Dr. Hillman told the orchestra to stop playing, someone found the light switch and restored illumination, and the party was over. Later "Prexy" averred that no dancing had taken place, "despite the statement by a number of students who said they witnessed the dancing by couples whose names they would not reveal."[117]

That was only the beginning of the end. The following Friday dancing by students was reported at the Indianola Country Club, and seven culprits were called in to meet with Dr. Hillman and A. V. Proudfoot "to show why they should not be suspended for violation of College rules." Their suspension would be cancelled if they promised "not to violate or encourage the violation of college rules, especially the rule against dancing."[118] Six refused to sign at that time, but later reconsidered and were reinstated. When students heard of the threatened suspensions, they were up in arms, their anger directed against the administration and even more against the "meddlesome and autocratic" board of trustees.

The climax of the dancing revolution came on Friday morning, March 24, 1933, when John Horsley introduced Senator Proudfoot, who went before the student body in chapel to review the actions taken by the board and to announce in stentorian tones that it was the consensus among the trustees that the ban on dancing be continued. "It is better," he declared, "to close the doors of the institution than to have rules violated and abrogated."[119] The students were ready for him, and his words were greeted with a chorus of boos, and as soon as the faculty left the platform, he became the target of a hail of oranges and eggs "and other missiles" thrown by a number of boys—Proudfoot thought there were about twenty-five or thirty of them. "I sat there still as a stone wall," said Proudfoot. Their aim was good. "Numbers turned their heads around to see how I was taking the bombardment."[120] Someone even fired blanks from a pistol. And none of them was apprehended then or later.

It is to Senator Proudfoot's credit that he had the courage to go before a hostile student body and tell them what they did not want to hear. And after the violent confrontation that fateful morning in chapel, his only comment was "Well, at least the eggs were fresh!"

That afternoon a hurried meeting of the board of trustees heard Proudfoot's report of the morning violence and decided emergency action must be taken at once. A telegram went out to all board members: "MEETING OF THE TRUSTEES OF SIMPSON COLLEGE CALLED MARCH 25, 1933 AT 2:00 P.M. IMPORTANT MEETING. WIRE ANSWER."[121]

Eighteen members were on hand—a nineteenth arrived late—for the first emergency meeting of the board in Simpson's history. The minutes of the meeting, all of which was held in executive session, are the most detailed of any recorded up to that time. Proudfoot put it to the board. "I have no reason to assume but that this outbreak was mob spirit that had boiled over and could not be restrained." What happened was, he said, a flagrant violation of the rules and regulations of the College. But it was precisely one of the rules that was the subject of controversy. One trustee volunteered the observation that "perhaps we can work out some way to enforce it, but I don't see how unless we fire the faculty and the student body." It was J. O. Watson, the board's token liberal, who was the realist: Students, he said, "are dissatisfied with the rule," stating of course the obvious. They are "sufficiently intelligent that to read the riot act to them would do no good." He suggested that the board ask the students to observe the ban for the balance of the school year with a promise that "regulated dancing" would be permitted the following fall.

A student delegation led by spokesman Cloice Myers was thereupon admitted to the meeting. Myers apologized for the student body and the riotous conduct at chapel, but was eloquent in his urging that the ban on dancing be lifted. Indianola alumnus Seth Shenton—not a board member—appeared too, advising the board members to go beyond the dancing issue and try to understand students better. "Young America," he said, "is a pretty hard house to handle. You can guide, but not drive."[122] Those present listened, and when prominent ministers as well as lay members of the board supported liberalization, the "sentiment turned toward compromise," and they voted eighteen to one to accept J. O. Watson's resolution, in spite of the warning of one that this was "an unconditional surrender" to the students.[123] Proudfoot voted with the majority, probably with some relief.

In June the board made good on its promise to permit dancing the next year, but felt constrained to insert into its statement the relevant passage from the Methodist Discipline which spoke of "improper amusements and excessive indulgence in innocent amusements" as being "the first easy steps to the total loss of character." One of these amusements was dancing. Further, they absolutely forbade dancing on campus, the one place where that amusement could be kept relatively innocent.[124]

The first authorized, fully chaperoned, fraternity dance was held by the ATOs in the ballroom of the Masonic Temple on November 10, 1933, and the next January students held their first prom, complaining that the event had to be staged off campus. It would seem, said the students, that the board has announced that "we wash our hands of the affair, Dance; but if you go to Hell, remember 'we told you so.'"[125]

Risking the fires of Hell, the students danced, and within a few years dances were held even in Hopper Gymnasium. In her report to the board of trustees in the spring of 1934, straight-laced Edna Stuntz, dean of women, acknowledged that dancing "has gone over much better than I dared hope it would." She was receiving "good reports from chaperones," and was convinced that "campus morale is better." The dances were "well conducted, nice affairs," with attention to those who preferred not to dance. "I will admit, however, that as I had never been to a dance before last fall, I am not a very expert critic in the comparative merits of its execution. Perhaps I should include that in my summer education."[126]

John Hillman still urged the students to forswear dancing. Most did not.

* * *

Defeated on dancing, the board of trustees and Hillman transferred their energies to fighting another ugly manifestation of sin. With the repeal of the Eighteenth Amendment in 1933, the people of Indianola faced a new adversary, and if John Hillman hated dancing, he hated the liquor traffic even more. He had been eight years president of the Iowa Anti-Saloon League and was known as a forceful prohibition lecturer.[127] Therefore when word reached them that the state of Iowa, which now controlled both the wholesaling and retailing of alcohol, was considering establishment of a state liquor store in Indianola, the board passed a resolution "unalterably opposed" to such a store and fired it off to the authorities in Des Moines.[128] By return mail Hillman received a letter assuring him that Simpson's resolution "will be taken under advisement."[129] Many others were equally opposed to selling liquor in Indianola—had not Indianola voted three to one against repeal?—and the store was not opened. The city remained saloon-free for many more years.

While there was not much talk about it, a few Simpson students experimented with strong drink, even before the repeal of prohibition, and among some of the undergraduate men beer became popular after it became legal. But whatever student tippling took place was kept quiet, and no one really expected College authorities to condone alcohol under any circumstances. Most students still abstained, for there was little to tempt them in Indianola. And besides, money was in short supply.

Activities they had in rich number, the depression notwithstanding. The big events of the year continued—freshman week, pledge night, homecoming, Miniature Orpheum, campus day and commencement. And in 1934 the Phi Mu Alpha music fraternity added an important new event, the Interfraternity Council Sing, in which the fraternities competed with well-rehearsed choruses. Some years later this event became the All-College Sing, involving also the sororities and independent residence halls. Apart from organized events, students could go to the movies in town or picnic out at Lake Ahquabi, the new state park built by Roosevelt's Civilian Conservation Corps. Or in that last vestige of class hazing, they could spend time making sure the freshmen wore their caps, green in some years and red in others.

During the worst years of the Depression the College was ill able to afford speakers or entertainments of any sort, but by early 1934 things had improved enough to bring in two well-known lecturers, Countess Alexandra Tolstoy and W. E. B. DuBois. It would be difficult to find two people more nearly worlds apart. DuBois was especially provocative in a college that rarely saw an African-American, the George Washington Carver tradition notwithstanding. The next year they heard Edwin Markham read his own poetry.

During these years the Simpson community was saddened by the death of a number of people who had figured prominently in the affairs of the College. In late 1929 their beloved old William E. Hamilton, twice a widower, died from a paralytic stroke in Indianola. In 1930 they learned that former president Edwin Lamay Parks (1880–86) died in Washington, D.C., and were shocked to hear that John L. Tilton, one of Simpson's long-time great faculty members, dropped dead while lecturing in his classroom at West Virginia University one morning in the late fall. Noted alumnus and banker Leslie Shaw, former governor of Iowa and U.S. Secretary of the Treasury under Theodore Roosevelt, died in March 1932. Closer to home, in the last days of 1933 everyone was struck by the death of Edmund Holmes, who had retired only the previous spring.[130]

Important as they were, none of these deaths would be remembered by more people for years to come than the tragic 1935 accident on campus involving twenty-two-year-old freshman Mildred Hedges. One morning after a class which met on the third floor of Old Chapel, she joined a number of students who crowded into the great open stairwell that graced the entrance hall of the building. Just as she started to descend the stairs, she stumbled on a step, pitched over the ornate wooden bannister and fell eighteen feet to the floor below, striking her head on a table with a sickening thud. Four-and-a-half hours later she died at the Methodist Hospital in Des Moines. John L. Hillman assisted at her funeral in Scranton, Iowa, and about twenty-five of her college friends were present.[131]

Soon a kind of mythology began to grow up around this tragic incident. Some years later people were hearing reports that on late nights—moonless nights to be sure—the sounds of a ghost could be heard in the ancient building. Thus was created the legend of the ghost of Old Chapel, still believed in by those who want to believe. One cannot escape the feeling that somehow poor Mildred Hedges deserved a quieter, more decorous immortality.[132]

* * *

In May 1920, when the Methodist General Conference met in Des Moines, President Hillman, just then concluding his first year as president of Simpson, had met the daughters of Bishop Matthew Simpson. There were three of them: Mrs. Ella Buoy and her maiden sisters, Ida and Sarah Elizabeth Simpson. "When I asked them if they would care to visit the College that bore their father's name," wrote Hillman later, "they said they would be pleased to do so. One morning I took them in my automobile and drove to Indianola." They lunched at Mary Berry Hall, said they enjoyed their visit and each of them handed Hillman a check for $250 for the College. "I had not been a college president long enough to know how to receive such unexpected gifts, and I felt as if I had been robbing orphans." This was only the first of several gifts. They contributed $5,000 to the big 1923 endowment campaign and sent another substantial gift later. When the one married sister died, she bequeathed a trust fund to a niece, after whose death $10,000 would come to the College.

When Hillman and his wife attended the Methodist Conference at Kansas City in 1928, they expressed their gratitude to the two maiden sisters for Mrs. Buoy's generosity. One of the sisters said, "We might as well tell you now, that there is more, much more, coming to the College." They explained that they owned a piece of property in downtown Pittsburgh which "will come to Simpson when we are gone." After the Hillmans visited them at their home in 1932, one of the two sisters, Ida, did not long survive, dying on November 12, 1933. Then in early 1936 Hillman received word of the death of Elizabeth. The value of the Pittsburgh property, together with part of the residuary estate, amounted to approximately $280,000, the largest single gift the College had ever received.[133]

Hillman had come to have real affection for the quaint, old-fashioned Simpson sisters, and their handsome gifts provided a happy and indeed very substantial capstone to his efforts to enrich Simpson through the years. It will be recalled that Hillman had been reelected by the board in 1933 for a three-year term, and he insisted that it be his last. In 1936 he would celebrate his seventy-first birthday, and it was time to rest. Accordingly, in the fall of 1935 a committee of the board of trustees undertook a careful search for Hillman's successor and found their man in a matter of months. Because there seemed no point in waiting, the board invited the new president to take up his duties at the beginning of the spring semester in 1936. Hillman agreed to stay on and teach Bible for the balance of the school year, whereupon he would enter an honorable retirement.

Hillman had loved the work at Simpson, for he believed in Christian education. He was successful at the College because he understood that in a place like central Iowa a college must provide preparation for both the world of work and the world of the mind, even if he did believe that the world of the mind was where most people would find happiness and fulfillment. He believed that "if his boy were to be nothing but a driver of mules, he would want him to go to college because he would want to put as much distance between the boy and the mule as possible."[134]

XIII
The Prewar Years 1936–41

The Seven Lean Years, inaugurated in 1932 with Biblical precision, had not yet run their ruinous course when John Hillman retired in early 1936. The Great Depression still held the nation in its grip, although one could discern a few hopeful signs that the worst of it was over. Whether it was Roosevelt's New Deal or simply the inscrutable movement of the classic economic cycle, things seemed to be a trifle better now. At least they weren't getting any worse.

Except for the weather. In Indianola, like the rest of the Midwest, people in early 1936 shivered through the worst winter in recent memory. Numbing below-zero cold and terrifying blizzards that swept snow into mountainous drifts devastated the heartland of America. Many towns and hamlets and the farmsteads that surrounded them found themselves hopelessly isolated, cut off from sources of food and fuel on which they depended.

At Simpson, where the heating plant used a small mountain of coal during a normal winter, supplies were consumed at an alarming rate as local temperatures plunged below zero and stayed there. For a few weeks there was talk of closing the College down, but to avoid an interruption of classes everyone bundled up and endured half-heated classrooms and cold sleeping quarters. "Unless unforeseen developments arise," said Rae Dean in mid-February, "the College will be kept open in spite of the cold and coal shortage," reassuring people that a carload of coal should be delivered "by next Tuesday."[1] It was, and the College somehow saw the winter through.

It was in the midst of that bone-chilling winter that Simpson welcomed a new president. And the weather notwithstanding, Earl Enyeart Harper got a warm reception.

Aware that Dr. Hillman was determined to resign no later than 1936, the board of trustees had for some time been conducting a careful search for a successor.[2] After consulting the faculty on the matter, they focused on one man whose reputation they already knew and admired.[3] Earl Harper was president of Evansville College in Indiana, a small Methodist school of about three hundred students down on the Ohio River where Harper had enjoyed a successful nine-year administration. More than that, he was known to be a stalwart churchman, an accomplished orator and talented musician. He had been brought to the attention of the Simpson committee by a number of people who admired his leadership. Dean Long '24, a Simpson alumnus who was professor of economics at Evansville College, recommended him highly as did another Simpson alumnus, Robert Guy McCutchan '04, dean of the DePauw University Conservatory of Music, who had come to know Harper as a fellow member of the commission for the Methodist hymnal. Simpson's dean of men Charles Burrows had been a classmate of Harper when they both studied at the Boston University School of Theology in the early twenties. All were enthusiastic about this man whose dynamic personality, they promised, would sweep Simpson people off their feet.

At the invitation of the board, Harper visited Indianola briefly just before the Christmas holidays in 1935, spoke at chapel, talked with faculty, board members and a handful of townspeople, "looking us over," as A. V. Proudfoot put it.[4] They looked Harper over too. While he may not have swept them off their feet, he did make a very good impression. Two days before Christmas Proudfoot wrote to the candidate asking him on what conditions he would accept the presidency of Simpson.

Harper replied in a long letter on the twenty-seventh that he would come to Simpson for a salary of $5,280 plus house and automobile, together with the cost of moving to Iowa. Further, he would not want to do any teaching as Hillman had done for sixteen years. Would Hillman consent to teach the Bible classes for the balance of the school year? If this set of conditions "places too high a premium upon my services for Simpson College to ask me to come, I am happily situated here and can go on indefinitely," with a "palatial" home and the assurance that the Evansville board of trustees "will pay $5,500 or even $6,000 if I remain and ask them to do so."[5]

Harper drove a hard bargain. Hillman's base salary that year was only $3,500, and along with the rest of the faculty he was receiving only two-thirds of that.[6] But Harper's confidence in himself was shared by the Simpson people, who wanted him enough to meet his demands. The board agreed to his conditions and the deal was done. As soon as Dr. Hillman was apprised of the selection of the new president, he sent in his letter of resignation, and did so with a sense of relief. "As you know," he wrote, "I have desired release from the responsibilities of my position for some time."[7] He would be happy to continue his Bible instruction until the end of the spring semester. Two days after receiving Hillman's letter the board formally elected Earl E. Harper president with the understanding that he would take up his duties by January 27, the first day of the new semester. They also honored Dr. Hillman by electing him president emeritus of the College.

When Harper and his family arrived in Indianola on a frigid day in late January, two months before his forty-first birthday, Simpsonians and townspeople alike were curious about the new president, and they were prepared to like him. Who was this bright, spirited young man who was to serve as the College's fourteenth president?

A native of Missouri, he was born a child of the parsonage in the little town of Coffey, March 28, 1895, the son of the Rev. William Craig and Linna May Enyeart Harper.[8] He grew up in Nebraska, where his earliest talent seemed to be in music. His singing won plaudits during his high school years. When he was but a youngster of nineteen he "responded to the call of the spirit" and entered the pastorate in rural Nebraska churches. Innocent of any ministerial training, he preached on Sundays while attending Nebraska Wesleyan College during the week. After graduation in 1918 he went on to study at the Boston School of Theology, where he earned the S.T.B. degree in 1921.[9] He continued his studies at Harvard and the University of Chicago. For the next few years he was a pastor in the New England Conference, sharing his time between preaching and teaching choral and orchestral music at the college level. Before he was thirty he had published a book entitled *Church Music and Worship* (1924). His remarkable ability as a speaker, musician and college teacher brought him to the attention of Methodist educators across the nation, and in 1927, when he was only thirty-two, he was elected president of Evansville College. At that time he was the youngest college president in America.

Meanwhile he married Clara Fern Lieber of Papillion, Nebraska, in 1916. A graduate of Nebraska Wesleyan's Conservatory of Music, she was an accomplished musician, a vocal soloist and director of children's choirs. By the time they were asked to come to Simpson, the Harpers had three children, Hugh Philip, 16, Shirley Ann, 10 and Craig Thayer, 8.[10]

Not only was Harper a popular lecturer and an effective platform speaker with a sense of the dramatic; he was also a skilled organizer, the first Simpson president who valued and understood the power of public relations. His inauguration, held three months after he arrived on campus, provided the first convincing demonstration of his skill at putting on a good show.

* * *

On the eve of Dr. Harper's formal inauguration, the College, under the leadership of Vice-President Hilmer, recognized the retiring Dr. Hillman at a special program in his honor at the Methodist Church. Tributes, some formal and others unabashedly sentimental, followed one upon the other from people as varied as President D. W. Morehouse of Drake University, Don Berry of the *Indianola Record* and Martha Katherine Riggs, a missionary's undergraduate daughter from Rangoon, Burma. The *Simpsonian* probably said it best: "Whatever he does and wherever he goes, the heart of Simpson will go with him."[11]

Inauguration day, April 20, 1936, was packed with activity. At ten o'clock that morning an "educational conference" drew a large crowd at the Methodist Church. Addressing the participants were a number of prominent speakers, including Simpson's own J. Hugh Jackson, dean of the graduate school of business administration at Stanford; Agnes Samuelson, Iowa's state superintendent of public instruction, who had only recently been elected president of the National Education Association; and President Eugene A. Gilmore of the University of Iowa. At the festive luncheon where tables were set for 360 people in the spacious parish hall of the church, President Emeritus Hillman presided with wit and grace, introducing first the governor of Iowa, Clyde L. Herring, and then one after another educational dignitary, each of whom spoke words of congratulation and felicitation to the new president. Echoing their sentiments were spokesmen for the faculty, trustees, students and alumni of the College.

After a rousing concert by the Fort Des Moines Army Post Band on the campus, the great processional formed, the faculty garbed in medieval academic splendor. Led by the band, the dignitaries, followed by the choir and the whole student body, marched in solemn formation to the church sanctuary, lavishly decorated for the ceremony now to take place.

Most accounts of the exercises of the afternoon called the event an inauguration, but most of the people who were present were as likely to remember it as a coronation. Never had Indianola seen so much pomp and ceremony, all of it filmed for posterity and broadcast live by radio over stations KRNT in Des Moines and WMT in Cedar Rapids. Marshal of the day was Vice-President Hilmer. The charge to the new president was presented by Bishop Frederick D. Leete with fitting solemnity, whereupon Dr. Harper delivered an address entitled "The Liberal College: Agent of Culture and Civilization." In his speech the new president set forth not only his educational philosophy but also some unveiled hints about the way he intended to preside over the fortunes of the College.

Asserting that "the liberal college is the supreme institutional servant of man in his striving to know the meaning and value of life and . . . to live significantly," he saw the college's task to be "assisting men and women in achieving culture and civilization." While the college must be practical and its training sound, it "vindicates itself practically as well as ideally through the service it renders to the individual in his struggle toward culture . . . in its efforts to achieve civilization." If the liberal college is to be "the incarnation of its ideals," it cannot tolerate balancing its budget on the backs of an underpaid faculty or foregoing purchases of needed equipment. Nor can it serve twentieth-century American youth by "enforcing outmoded modes of recreation and diversion" which would "certainly result in unhappiness and frustration for all concerned." Having thus laid the dancing issue to rest forever, whereby he earned instant popularity with nearly all the students present, he went on to call for the elimination of "artificial barriers of creed, color, religious faith, political conviction, or social background" in society. There must be open discussion and debate at Simpson, but "no partisan propaganda of any type or description should be tolerated on the campus or in the classrooms," a comment which many interpreted as a not-very-subtle warning to Winfred E. Payne, the College's resident socialist. And lest anyone confuse free speech with democratic college governance, he pointed out that "no liberal college in its administration and teaching function can be effectively governed by the process of political referendum" or "a majority vote of the constituents." In his mind these constituents included students as well as alumni and church members in the conference, most especially the last-named. Though "education without religion is incomplete education," the liberal college is often accused by parents and clergy of shaking the beliefs of youngsters coming out of the Sunday schools of their childhood. "Perhaps it does," admitted Harper. "But perhaps the reason is that, spiritually speaking, these young people have been taught, or at least permitted, to believe that two and two are five. The moral responsibility of the college is to assure them that the sum is four."[12] It was clear to anyone who was even halfway attentive that their new president would make changes at Simpson, and probably sooner, rather than later.

At the conclusion of Harper's address several honorary degrees were awarded, as much to underscore the ceremonial grandeur of the proceedings as to recognize the merits of the recipients.[13] When the closing prayer was spoken by retiring John Hillman, there were those present who saw it as a benediction on a whole era at Simpson.

* * *

Never before had Simpson seen an easier, more pleasant passing of the torch of leadership than it enjoyed during the spring of 1936. Formally John Hillman resigned January 4, and within forty-eight hours the board elected Earl Harper president, but informally the transition of administration was considerably less abrupt, facilitated by the new president's respect for his predecessor and the old president's graciousness as he let go of the reins he had held for seventeen years.[14] Hillman's remaining on campus to teach Bible during Harper's first semester proved to be immensely helpful.

In late January, for example, before classes commenced for the new term, Hillman accompanied Harper on a visit to Elizabeth Simpson at her home in Philadelphia, permitting her to become acquainted comfortably with Simpson's new leader. She showed her gratitude for their visit by presenting them an original letter of John Wesley, written in 1776. "This is for the College," she said simply.[15]

* * *

During his first semester at Simpson Harper laid plans for fundamental administrative and curricular reform, but not without doing his homework first. Even before he arrived on the campus he reviewed with care the exhaustive study of Simpson conducted by the Methodist Board of Education in 1930, noting that few of the pointed suggestions for improvement had been acted upon. To be sure, a number of the recommendations, however appropriate, cost more than the College could afford in depression years, which had led Dr. Hillman to postpone making any change at all. Harper believed that a number of important steps could be taken at little or no cost. For weeks after his arrival in Indianola he discussed these reforms with board members, faculty, alumni, churchmen and students. He studied the academic structure of other colleges and universities, and by the time of the June board meeting was prepared to present for approval several far-reaching measures.

Most important was the reorganization of the whole structure of the academic program and the faculty. He proposed eliminating the position of vice-president and restoring the office of academic dean, suggesting the appointment of veteran historian Francis Moats to that office.[16] He would eliminate all of the seventeen academic departments—there had been as many as twenty of them back in 1930—and organize the curriculum into five divisions, each led by a chairman appointed by the president:

Division I: Language, Literature and Fine Arts
Division II: Social Science
Division III: Natural Science and Mathematics
Division IV: Education and Philosophy
Division V: Health and Physical Education[17]

The divisional model was hardly an original idea in the world of higher education, but its success elsewhere made it attractive to Harper and quite acceptable to the faculty. The elimination of departments would mean the dropping of all the traditional majors, substituting for them what Harper called "fields of concentration."

Because very nearly every department head—almost sixty percent of the faculty—held the rank of professor regardless of degree status or experience, the teaching force was incredibly top-heavy. Harper corrected this disparity by replacing retiring or departing professors with teachers of a lower rank or by gently demoting a few whose preparation or time in service did not warrant a full professorship. He proposed that in 1936–37 there should be eleven full professors (a reduction of six), three assistant professors and twelve instructors in the full-time faculty. It is a tribute to his powers of persuasion that he already had faculty approval of this reorganization before he took it to the board.

Not content with restructuring the curriculum, Harper also altered the way Simpson handled the extracurriculum. He proposed the creation of what he called "the Student-Faculty Federation," a series of five committees with six members each—three faculty members appointed by the president and three undergraduates appointed by the student council. There were committees for religious life, public occasions, fine arts, publications and social life. The whole federation would be directed by an administrative board chaired by the president and including in its membership the academic dean, the deans of men and women and three officers of the student council. And "on this board," pointed out the *Simpsonian* without comment, "there is an exception to the rule of every [member of a] committee having an equal vote; Dr. Harper reserves the right of veto."[18] Apart from the fact of joint student-faculty participation, this new structure was by no means a restoration of the old College Council, which had busied itself almost exclusively with student behavior. Nor was there any danger of the intrusion of democracy into the College's governance. The president would remain firmly in control.[19]

Both the reorganization of the curriculum and the Student-Faculty Federation were accepted enthusiastically by the board in June 1936 and went into effect the following autumn. There is little doubt that these changes were the most important contribution of Dr. Harper to Simpson College during his administration.

The new president's concept of college administration understood the role of the board of trustees to be policymaking, raising money, oversight of the administration and the budget and selection of the chief administrative officers of the institution. It should permit the administration to do its job without interference and should avoid even the appearance of managing the College. Nor should the administrators "pass the buck" to the board whenever confronted by a difficult situation. Harper pointed out, for example, that "a mistaken policy has prevailed at Simpson in so far as the board of trustees has undertaken by legislative action to direct the social life of the college campus." The board, he asserted, must trust the administration to deal correctly and sensitively with social life. And even though the administration "cannot please everyone," it will make "crystal clear" why its rulings and procedures are adopted. The same principle should hold in all areas of the College's governance. With Harper, there was to be no doubt about who was in charge.[20]

The new president had further recommendations that *would* cost money, and he insisted that he and the board would have to find the funds to underwrite that expense. At the top of the list was, of course, the matter of faculty salaries. He proposed that for 1936–37 full professors be paid an average of $2,810 per year, assistant professors $2,462 and instructors $1,855. While these were far below the national or even Iowa levels, for Simpson they would represent a great vault forward.[21] Moreover, the College must pay salaries in full. Reporting salaries at par to the various accrediting agencies and then paying only a fraction of them was clearly deceptive, a practice John Hillman had deplored and which Harper said would not be continued, no matter what the consequences. And to pay the proposed salaries in full would cost thousands.

That wasn't all. The library, Harper said, needed either to be enlarged or replaced. The book collection was inadequate as were facilities for study, especially the interior lighting of the building. The librarian should be contracted for the entire year, not just nine months, and she needed further professional training. The conservatory was likewise in considerable disarray, especially its building, which needed major repairs too long deferred because of hard times.

How much would all of this cost? Harper proposed, with Rae Dean's assistance, a budget which would spend $154,444 while taking in $114,250, producing an expected deficit of $40,194. The board's job, he explained to his stunned listeners, was to fund that deficit. "No subtraction from the proposed expenditures can be conscientiously recommended." Most board members looked nervously at the floor, each somehow expecting a draft on his personal savings, no one wishing to speak. Harper went on. He had a plan. "Let's ask faculty to contribute 15% of their income."[22] That would generate $9,000. The administrators would come up with $5,000 in gifts from Simpson's Des Moines alumni and Methodist church people out in the conference. He would expect the board members to underwrite personally $20,000. All this amounted to $34,000. "We can add $6,000 to our [$90,000] indebtedness. You may think I have asked too much," he said, "but other Boards of Trustees have done as much. If you don't do these things," he warned, "we must cut programs *and* faculty, and that is very dangerous."[23]

The board did indeed think it was too much, insisting that faculty salaries remain exactly what they had been the previous year and that only two-thirds be paid.[24] Even so, they adopted a budget that projected a huge deficit, part of which would be met by additional borrowing, increasing the College's debt to $100,000, the entire amount refinanced during the 1936–37 academic year.[25]

President of the board, Senator A. V. Proudfoot, was conspicuously absent at this crucial June 1936 board meeting, for he lay gravely ill in a Des Moines hospital. Three days later he died, having served Simpson for twenty years as a board member, all but one year as president.[26] It would be months before the board could bring itself to elect a new president. Meanwhile the students, in an effort somehow to make up for their outrageous behavior toward the old man during the dancing controversy, the next year dedicated the *Zenith* to the senator's memory, quoting the words of Don Berry: "He looked upon the local, educational, and evangelistic program of the church as a man-size job worthy of all his best thought and effort. . . . He faced unpleasant realities without resentment and performed unpleasant tasks without bitterness."[27]

* * *

When John Hillman retired once and for all in the spring of 1936, Dr. Harper replaced him in the classroom with a full-time veteran professor, Howard Fifield Legg, who had chaired the Department of Bible and Philosophy at Evansville College for eleven years. Harper, who was able to talk almost anybody into doing just about anything, persuaded the fifty-five-year-old Legg to follow him to Indianola, where indeed he found a home, remaining at Simpson until his retirement in 1946. Legg was an able scholar. A graduate of Wesleyan University in philosophy and psychology in 1904, he had earned his B.D. from Drew University in 1907 and two master's degrees from Boston University. After fifteen years in the pastorate he took up college teaching. When he and his wife came to Indianola they had three sons, one of whom, Sherwood Fifield, a twelve-year old, was still at home.[28]

Legg was certainly the most widely heralded of the new faculty in the fall of 1936. Another who came was William Paul Carter, who for the year replaced sociologist Charles Burrows, who took a leave of absence to lecture for a government agency called the Adult Forum.[29] In speech, replacing Julie Fossum, was young Virginia Jane Miller, a 1930 Phi Beta Kappa graduate of Allegheny College, who had completed two years of graduate work at Yale University's noted School of Dramatics.

In English Ruth Jackson returned after completing several years of graduate work at the University of Chicago. She had taught at Simpson during the twenties. Her appointment combined teaching with her new role as dean of women, replacing Edna Stuntz, who retired to her Colorado home after fifteen successful years at Simpson.[30]

In home economics it was exceedingly difficult to maintain any continuity of management. Between 1936 and 1941 there were no fewer than four instructors who attempted to run the one-woman department, but none of them found much success in the enterprise.

In business administration it was only marginally better. In the fall of 1936 Gilbert Maynard, a fresh Simpson graduate, came to assist Dr. Payne in the department. He replaced—just for a year—venerable E. L. Miller, who retired after a record forty-seven years on Simpson's faculty. Maynard's appointment bore testimony to the difficulty of finding an experienced teacher in a competitive field at a price Simpson could afford to pay. The next year, two new people came in business administration. One was Herbert E. Miller of DeWitt, Iowa, who recently had completed his M.A. at the University of Iowa and who, like Maynard, remained only a year at Simpson. The other was Hortense Bement, who taught chiefly commercial subjects.

By far the most important, and certainly the most enduring, appointment Harper made during his tenure at Simpson brought an exceptional young woman into the faculty in the fall of 1937 as instructor in biology and chemistry. She was Margaret "Peg" Liebe of Cleveland, Ohio, a Phi Beta Kappa graduate of Wooster College, who had earned both her M.A. and Ph.D. at the University of Michigan. Later she recalled that Dr. Harper admitted hiring her over another because "I can't afford to hire a first-class man, so I am hiring a first-class woman."[31] She was not sure whether she had been complimented or not. Her $1,800 salary notwithstanding, she stayed on to become a valued member of the science faculty. During the fall of her second year at the College, already promoted to an assistant professorship, she announced her engagement to Vinton C. Watson, a popular young local alumnus, and they were married in December. She continued teaching until 1941, when she took an extended leave-of-absence—fourteen years—to rear three children.

* * *

The fall of 1936 saw President Harper much in demand as a lecturer, for he had spent two months that summer in the Soviet Union, where he studied political and economic conditions. Although he returned home with no illusions about the nature of Stalin's totalitarianism, he did express his admiration for the democratic rights proclaimed in the new Soviet constitution of 1936 and the obvious rise in living standards throughout the country. His lectures, illustrated by motion pictures, were said to be informative and entertaining.[32] After all, few experts on the U.S.S.R. were to be found in Iowa in those days, permitting most of Dr. Harper's observations to be accepted as gospel.

By going to Russia Harper had been lucky. He missed the worst of the summer weather that seared Iowa and destroyed most of the state's crops. After the bitter cold of the past winter, the summer heat broke nearly every record. In July the mercury soared past 100 degrees and stayed that way for days on end. On the fifteenth it hit 108 degrees down on the square in Indianola.

At Simpson it was expected that the blistering summer weather, the severe drought and dismal crop forecasts would hurt fall enrollment, but to everyone's surprise more than 530 students registered in September, nearly a hundred more than anticipated, an increase of sixteen percent over the previous year.[33] On the one hand the bonus of new students eased the budget problem; on the other hand it meant severe overcrowding in lower division class sections and very nearly intolerable teaching loads for some of the faculty.

As students returned to their classes in the fall of 1936, they found a new set of degree requirements already in place, but upon examination they discovered that the changes were more cosmetic than substantial, responding to the reorganization of the curriculum that had created the five academic divisions while eliminating departments of instruction. Although Harper wanted to use the term "field of concentration," the tradition of selecting departmental majors continued both formally and informally. Only four courses were specified for all degrees: English 101–102 (freshman composition) together with Old Testament and New Testament. All students were required to complete two years (two semester hours) of physical education activity. Beyond this, all students were to complete ten hours in each of Divisions I, II, III and IV in addition to a "major" of "not less than twenty hours," and take a comprehensive examination in the "major department" during the last semester before graduation.[34]

Because of its lack of specificity, this curriculum permitted students who were so inclined to elect courses—and instructors—whose requirements were at best minimal. It could, of course, be argued that such courses, described only charitably as invitations to indolence, should not have been tolerated, but it is well known that even the most vigilant presidents and deans and curriculum committees could not induce all faculty members to provide reasonable academic rigor in all of their classes. The students, of course, knew exactly which classes imposed only leisurely demands; the fraternities kept lists of them.[35] What is perhaps surprising is that many students, with the encouragement of their faculty advisers, selected substantial courses for the right reasons.

Simpson, said President Harper, was offering too many degrees. It would be best to offer only two—the B.A. and B.M.—and to drop the B.S. in Home Economics, the B.S. in Education and the B.S. in Business Administration. During his first year he was able, primarily because of financial urgency, to persuade the faculty to drop the separate home economics degree, but he made little headway against the B.S.Ed. and B.S.B.A.[36]

* * *

"Harper was a real showman," recalled Marcelyn Taggart Orr, who was a sophomore the year the new president arrived on campus. If his grand inauguration did not convince people of his skill, his platform performances, whether preaching in a Des Moines church or delivering baccalaureate or commencement addresses at high schools near and far, persuaded everyone that Simpson had found a powerful, very shrewd spokesman.[37] He seemed never to stop. Aware of the value of the media, he worked with the conservatory to develop an entertaining and informative radio show and persuaded station WOI at Ames to air it. First broadcast in early 1937, the program became a regular offering at four o'clock each Tuesday afternoon, directed and narrated by voice professor Lester E. Spring, who worked many hours every week putting the show together.[38] Harper was also convinced that good public relations began at home. Soon after his arrival in Indianola, he began inviting groups of twenty or so students and a few faculty into his home, where he and his wife entertained with unaffected ease and good humor. He called these get-togethers "talkies," encouraging a free exchange of ideas in a pleasant, informal setting. No subject was taboo. To be sure, some students attended only out of a sense of duty, but most of them enjoyed these occasions immensely.[39]

Harper's flair for the dramatic was never better demonstrated than it was the day Chet Nolte graduated. M. Chester Nolte, who combined marriage and teaching in a Civilian Conservation Corps camp at Indianola with Simpson studies, completed his academic work in the fall semester of 1936. It was rare for any student to graduate in January, and no ceremony was planned for this class of one. After the last day of examinations on January 29, Nolte received word that his diploma was signed and awaiting him at the College office if he wanted to come in and pick it up. As he has recalled:

> It was one of those winters you read about—snow deep upon the ground, temperature well below zero, roads drifted shut. My parents could not be on hand to see me graduate, and Brother Glen was stuck in a snowdrift delivering papers on his route. My bride of six months was recovering from surgery in [Des Moines] Methodist Hospital. . . . I'll just go in and pick up [the diploma] and be on my way. I needed a lift—maybe this would be it. But I failed to reckon with the kindness of those who knew my plight, and who wanted to show they cared. What followed might have been one of those passing moments in life, but instead it turned out to be an event one can never forget. The new President's secretary, Florence Cox, was cordial and invited me to take a seat while she completed "some arrangements." What she did was scurry up and down the halls rounding up an audience—there was Harriet Neades from the Treasurer's office, Wilma Hardin, secretary to the Registrar, John Horsley, Alumni secretary, Dean Burrows, and several others including my major professor, Dr. Francis I. Moats. In a few minutes we were quite a group, all waiting expectantly for Dr. Harper to make his appearance. Being new, he could not be counted on to follow earlier patterns, and expectations ran high. Finally in came Dr. Harper, resplendent in morning coat, grey striped trousers, Ascot tie and wing collar, carrying what appeared to be my degree. A hush fell over the little group, and Dr. Harper, true to Methodist tradition, opened the saddlebags and let us have the full load, from Genesis, through Exodus, Psalms and the Prophets pausing along the way to include his audience along with myself in the address. I sur-

mised that since I was to be his first graduating senior, he had decided to spare no effort in making me realize he would not thrust me out into a cruel world utterly without supporting doctrine or friendly advice even though I was the lone maverick in the herd.[40]

Dr. Harper obviously enjoyed Chet Nolte's one-man commencement, an agreeable rehearsal for the big one the following June when the "herd" of seventy-plus in the class of '37 would graduate. Determined that the June ceremony would be a "feast of the spirit," Harper as spiritual chef delivered the baccalaureate sermon himself and invited the Reverend Dr. Ralph Sockman, pastor of Christ Methodist Episcopal Church in New York City and one of America's most celebrated clergymen, to speak at commencement.[41] Measured by the quality of the orators, Simpson's graduates were indeed feasted. But even more important in Harper's eyes was the wide publicity that heralded Dr. Sockman's pilgrimage to Indianola and Simpson.

Harper never let an opportunity slip by that would bring Simpson to public attention. In the spring of 1938, for example, he persuaded the United States Post Office Department to authorize a special cancellation of all letters sent by airmail from Indianola throughout the week of May 15 to 21. The device would picture the Simpson administration building. In anticipation of this special event, which coincided with "National Air Mail Week," but which commemorated nothing at Simpson that anyone could think of, the Indianola Chamber of Commerce and the College sent out five thousand letters to former Simpson students, urging them to buy lots of six-cent airmail stamps, affix them to envelopes, address them to all their friends and acquaintances and have their letters posted in Indianola during that magic week in May. "Put Simpson on the map by sending your letters airmail."[42] People responded in droves. According to postmaster Luther Williams, Indianola processed a record volume of mail as stamped envelopes poured in by the thousands to be mailed with the special cancellation. Williams kept his employees up nights to handle the mountain of mail that carried the imprimatur of Indianola and Simpson to the waiting world. "Mr. Williams," asked one of the exhausted postal workers, "how do we send an airmail letter from here to Milo?"[43]

Meanwhile Dr. Harper maintained a fast-paced speaking schedule in his relentless campaign to make Simpson better known across the land. When he conducted religious services in conference churches, he took with him the College choir, garbed in satiny red and gold gowns he had selected. "These meetings," writes Gilbert Caldwell, "were carried on with a great deal of pomp and ceremony which was a typical characteristic of the president."[44] Yet while some Iowa Methodists were enchanted by the Harperian theatrics, "others resented it tremendously."[45] Still, they liked his preaching.

The peripatetic president did more than preach. On the lecture platform he was accounted an expert on education and especially on international affairs. He continued to hold forth on the Soviet Union, for he was one of few Americans who had ever been there. Alarmed by the rise of Hitler, he urged Americans to prepare for war, should it come. "America can keep out of war. Morally she should. Honestly, I don't think she will," he said in an Armistice Day speech as early as 1936.[46] His address to the Des Moines Daughters of the American Revolution about military preparedness was so popular that he repeated it before a national D.A.R. conclave in Washington, D.C. In other quarters, however, isolationists found his statements offensive. When he predicted in 1937 that the United States would be at war against the totalitarians within five years, his critics were legion. Even the *Simpsonian* disagreed with him, not because of isolationist sentiment but because it thought Harper's tirades against the Nazis were misdirected. He had picked the wrong enemy: If war comes, said the *Simpsonian* in the spring of 1936 when Hitler occupied the Rhineland, "it will come not because of German aggression, but because of the blundering of French statesmanship." Germany wanted equality in Europe, not war. "Distasteful as it may be to praise Hitler, we believe in his dramatic Rhineland exploit, he has proved himself a statesman of the first order. . . . He has dramatized the entire case against the unspeakable Versailles Treaty."[47]

Of course most Americans would not have agreed with either Dr. Harper or the *Simpsonian*, but both continued to speak out as a matter of conviction, and at least Harper was increasingly sought out as a speaker by churches, secular organizations and schools far and wide. In fact he was so much in demand that he contracted with a booking agency in Chicago to handle his speaking engagements. This move was clearly a tactical error; it just didn't seem right for a Simpson College president to merchandise his speechmaking, no matter how exceptional his talent. Hiring an agency suggested that Harper no longer regarded public speaking as a part of his presidential responsibility; it had become a source of personal financial gain.[48]

* * *

Dissatisfaction with Harper's oratorical marketing off campus was really a minor matter compared to the massive problems that lurked on campus. Most of these were things about which Harper or his faculty could do very little. Freezing winters, blistering summers, drought, chinch bugs, a yet-unstable economy—all played their role in the economic malaise that continued to grip the Midwest and Simpson with it. At Simpson the deficits continued, in fact worsened in the train of the changes Harper and the board agreed to effect in the spring of 1936. And in spite of their best intentions, the board could authorize no raises for faculty and paid only two-thirds of contract salaries during the 1936–37 year. Dr. Harper's personal magnetism and unique personality, together with his boundless enthusiasm helped to restore faculty morale. He gave them hope, but no financial reward. Although enrollment unexpectedly increased in the fall of 1936, a phenomenon that "can be attributed to no one except Dr. Harper," it declined a year later, forcing postponement once again of a number of much-needed improvements.

Several money-saving schemes were adopted in the 1936–37 academic year. In accordance with Harper's modernist predilections, it was decided, for example, that all scholarships reserved for children of clergymen be discontinued. Usually "preachers' kids" had received an automatic tuition reduction of fifty percent. Harper believed that all students should compete equally for a share of the College's scanty scholarship funds, and the board backed him up. But such was the hue and cry among conference clergy that the College hastily backtracked a year later, restoring the scholarships. Harper was dismayed but realistic: "Some of the things which are right are not expedient. I have been driven to the conclusion that there is more misunderstanding and unhappiness involved in this move than is justified by the results."[49] Henceforth all ministers' children would receive a flat thirty dollar per semester reduction in tuition, but Harper had his sweet revenge: these scholarships would be no longer limited to Methodist clergy. The children of ministers of "any and all faiths" could participate.

Other equally ineffective attempts to reduce costs were essayed; the only one that worked was the continued underpayment of faculty salaries. As late as June 1938, although he deplored the "fictitious salary basis" in effect since 1932, Harper could recommend to the board that only two-thirds salary be guaranteed. He hoped, of course, that "we may be able to pay three-quarters" for 1938-39, but it was unlikely that such a goal could be reached. Still, he felt he must say to the board that "Simpson College must under no circumstances continue to attempt to adjust its income by means of cutting salaries," the very thing he had just admitted it must do. "This," he said, "is what threatens loss of national accreditment."[50]

Indeed it did. The American Association of Universities notified the College as early as the spring of 1937 that it would make a thorough investigation of Simpson. The following November Dean Lutz of Stanford University, a man predisposed to like Simpson because of his friendship with J. Hugh Jackson, made an on-campus inspection. Dismayed by the state of the College, he was forced to recommend that the A.A.U. suspend Simpson for two years, pointing out that if no improvement was forthcoming, the College would be dropped entirely from the list of approved institutions.

Two matters stood out in the A.A.U. report. First, the deceptive practice of "publishing and reporting" faculty salaries at one level and actually paying them at another was unconscionable. Even at par the salaries were awful; at one-half or two-thirds or even three-quarters they ranked among the worst anywhere. Secondly, the library was wholly inadequate, something that should have surprised no one. The building was too small, poorly lighted and ill-equipped. Its librarian evoked sympathy but little admiration; she needed considerably more training to become truly effective. Worst of all, the book collection was far too small for a college of Simpson's size. All of these problems must be addressed—and corrected—before Simpson could be restored to A.A.U.'s approved list.[51]

The A.A.U. blow fell hard upon Simpson; yet worse was the egregious failure of a major fund-raising campaign that followed. Raising money, to be sure, was a major obligation of the president and the board. Ascertaining needs was not very difficult. There were so many of them. If tuition was to be kept low—an article of faith at Simpson—the College had to have much more endowment money, enough to bring the total endowment to two million dollars. Apart from the obvious deficiencies of the library, there were physical campus improvements that had to be considered as well. As early as 1936 Harper engaged the services of a landscape architect from Iowa State College to make a campus development plan. The resulting study called for a chapel, a modernized heating plant, a president's home, an annex to Hopper Gymnasium for women's physical education. To these were added subsequently library improvements and landscaping.[52] During the following year plans for the campaign were refined, and in the spring of 1937 the board decided to raise $600,000 in a brief hard-hitting period of solicitation among alumni, church people and local citizenry.[53] They engaged the professional services of the firm of Tamblyn and Tamblyn of New York City to help direct the endeavor. None of them had any illusions about an easy campaign. Said Harper, "Great inertia must be overcome, and numerous criticisms must be anticipated" which should be dealt with "patiently, tolerantly, but intelligently."[54] The plan was to concentrate their efforts first in Iowa, then move to other areas where numbers of Simpson alumni resided.[55]

Simpson's well-laid campaign strategy went awry when it was discovered that the Methodist Hospital in Des Moines, whose list of potential donors matched much of Simpson's, had decided "at the last minute" to increase its $100,000 quest for funds to $500,000 and was conducting its campaign almost simultaneously with Simpson's.[56] The Des Moines Conference clearly should have regulated the matter of conflicting fund drives but did not. The hospital's campaign "drove us out of Iowa," lamented Harper. Therefore the decision was taken to shift the emphasis of Simpson's fund drive from Iowa to California where lived the greatest concentration of Simpson alumni outside of Iowa. Dr. and Mrs. Harper spent two months in California—from November 1937 to January 1938—where they saw an outpouring of enthusiasm in excellent attendance at alumni dinners. The president performed in vintage Harper style in public relations for Simpson, but apart from the gift of one $70,000 trust fund, found that "outright pledges . . . were few in number and slight in amount." The dream of a $600,000 campaign turned to dross. When he returned home barely more than empty-handed, he reported that "I have never known so great effort and expense expertly directed, apparently acceptable, to result in so great failure on the part of a constituency to cooperate either in undertaking to raise money or in making actual contributions." It was, he concluded, an "extraordinary and tragic development."[57]

What had happened? What was to be done? In a long letter to Harper, the Tamblyn and Tamblyn people suggested that the California campaign failed for three reasons: the alumni, too many of them teachers and preachers, were "not well situated financially; California *is* a long way from Iowa"; and "the [1938] recession has been at its height" during Simpson's appeal; one could see that "temporarily giving has practically ceased."[58] Tamblyn was as disappointed as were the Simpson people; he agreed to a very fair settlement with the College, reducing his firm's fee to a fraction of the amount originally agreed upon.[59]

Simpson still needed money, and needed it fast. When the board heard in February 1938 the bad news of the campaign's failure, Bishop G. Bromley Oxnam, having been elected to the board only the previous summer, volunteered the view (with his usual hyperbole) that "something . . . heroic in nature has to be done to save the school. Big money," he said confidently, "often comes after many failures."[60] But Simpson was neither on the verge of collapse nor could it expect an infusion of "big money." Its immediate, insistent need was enough ready cash to operate the College for the rest of the year, to treat if not cure its case of acute "financial anemia." They would call in Dr. John L. Seaton to look over the College's local fund-raising potential. Seaton, regarded as an oracle in the world of fund-raising, was president of the University Senate of the Methodist Episcopal Church, president of the Association of American Colleges, president of Albion College and one of the chief surveyors for the North Central Association, whose recent report on Simpson "did not make pleasant reading." Seaton agreed that the College should undertake a modest fund-raising campaign in central Iowa to generate funds for current expenses, enough to cover most of the year's deficit.[61]

The campaign for $25,000—$10,000 would come from Warren County alone— was carried on during the week of March 14, 1938, to secure a "living endowment," the equivalent of income on $800,000 of new endowment.[62] By April 1 the Indianola drive had secured just over $10,000, an accomplishment Dr. Harper said somewhat extravagantly "may prove to be a turning point in the history of the institution."[63] The next phase reached out to Des Moines and southwest Iowa, where solicitation continued through the spring months, reaching its $15,000 goal by the time the semester closed. This maintenance fund would tide the College over, but Harper faced the unpleasant probability that he would have to repeat the disagreeable business of playing the mendicant year after year. Somehow it seemed humiliating to be little more than an academic panhandler. "In study and thought upon the situation now forced upon us at Simpson College," he had said to the board in February, "I have found and still find myself engaged in a severe spiritual struggle."[64]

* * *

Of all the problems Dr. Harper faced at Simpson, none was more wrenching, more perplexing than was the dismissal of Winfred E. Payne from the faculty. So freighted with emotion, so controversial in tone, so challenging to the College's very reasons for existence, the "Payne Case" tended to rivet the attention of everyone, to blot out all other issues or events during the eventful spring weeks of 1938. Professor Payne, it will be recalled, had joined the Simpson faculty in the fall of 1930, succeeding Florence Armstrong. His appointment combined the professorship of economics and business administration with the newly-created post of dean of (academic) administration. When the depression forced cutbacks, however, the deanship was abolished. Payne stayed on as a full-time professor in the teaching faculty with somewhat reduced salary.[65] During the years that followed he authored two books, *Iron Laws or Bubbles* and *Behavior of Conflicting Economic Groups*.

It was not long before President Hillman began hearing complaints about Payne's classroom performance, not to speak of his formal and informal appearances off campus. He was reportedly highly critical of American capitalism, and, as we have seen, became increasingly open about his socialist predilections. In conservative Indianola an avowed socialist was unlikely to get a sympathetic hearing. At the College most of the students found him a stimulating lecturer and open-minded scholar. Some of them, as we have seen, influenced by Dr. Payne's liberal economic views, had organized a chapter of the League of Industrial Democracy as early as 1932, and a few of them became disciples of either socialism or Dr. Payne or both. President Hillman did not consider Payne particularly harmful. He later wrote, "I thought he was more of a propagandist for a particular viewpoint in economics rather than seek[ing] to win the students to discipleship of a particular viewpoint." Hillman did, however, complain that Payne "insisted on running his department according to his own mind regardless of faculty and administration regulations." At the same time, like nearly all who knew the man, Hillman "always had a very high regard for the personal and Christian character of Dr. Payne."[66]

When Dr. Harper succeeded President Hillman in 1936, he found that opposition to Payne had by no means diminished. "Before one year had passed," recalled Harper, "I became convinced that Professor Payne was not a satisfactory member of the faculty nor of the administration."[67] But under the pressure of immediate financial and curricular problems he postponed dealing with the matter. Then during the dark spring of 1938, in the midst of the A.A.U. suspension and the fund-raising fiasco, the Payne case came to a head. Harper could no longer avoid the issue, for this time his hand was forced by the board of trustees. When the board met at its midwinter session on February 9, 1938, Harper submitted the names of all faculty for the 1938–39 academic year for approval, the list normally endorsed routinely by the board without discussion. A majority of board members present, however, this time refused to approve Dr. Payne's reappointment, voting to postpone a decision pending a revised recommendation from Dr. Harper and action by the executive committee of the board of trustees.

On March 10, just a month after the board meeting, Dr. Harper, after a thorough discussion of the matter with Dr. Payne, recommended to the Executive Committee that Payne "be asked to resign from the instructional staff of the College." The reasons for this were set forth as follows:

1. During tenure of eight years Doctor Payne has failed to win the confidence of the Board of Trustees and the administration of Simpson College with reference to his efficiency as a member of the college faculty.
2. Doctor Payne is characteristically so prolix in speech and writing, indirect in reasoning, and uncertain in his conclusions as to incapacitate him for effective service in educational and administrative councils.
3. Many complaints have been lodged with the educational administration of the college that Doctor Payne does not make effective use of his opportunity as a teacher of the subjects assigned to him.
4. Doctor Payne's theories and convictions with reference to social, economic and political matters, while subject to no rightful challenge per se, apparently result in frequent misdirection of his course and distortion of his emphases as an instructor in his field of instruction.[68]

At the same time Dr. Harper advised Payne "that his own personal interests would be best served by quietly resigning and seeking placement elsewhere."[69] But Payne had no intention of resigning. As was his right, he demanded a hearing before the board of trustees. His request for the hearing was politely worded: "It would please me much indeed if our procedure could be of such a nature as to prevent the slightest suspicion that Simpson College—a liberal arts institution—prevents its professors from discussing modern economic and business problems in a realistic and honest manner."[70] A staunch member of the American Association of University Professors, he sought the advice and support of that organization. By some the A.A.U.P. was respected as a thoroughly professional association; others disdained it as a "professors' labor union." The A.A.U.P. proceeded cautiously, and while it examined the case, Payne's hearing was scheduled for March 31 and April 1 with the board's five-member Faculty Committee, all of whom could be described as moderate to conservative in their views, but probably not ultraconservative.

While Payne's case was pending, Harper invited Dr. John L. Seaton of Albion College to, as we have already noted, make a survey of Simpson with an eye to the college's fund-raising potential. After two days in Indianola, Seaton submitted his report, an eight-page, single-spaced document which contained trenchant, sometimes severely critical, observations and thoughtful suggestions for the improvement of Simpson. One paragraph of his survey, however, was deleted in the mimeographed copies that were distributed to the faculty. "I come now," Seaton wrote,

> to a matter which is extremely painful. In my opinion, it is necessary not to renew the appointment of the Professor of Economics and Business Administration.
>   There is no doubt that he is very well informed and stimulating to many students. On the whole, however, the judgments of his work are adverse even from students who are personally attached to him. Some of them said to me that while they disliked to see him go they believed it was for the common good. The same unfortunate qualities noted at Simpson College were also in evidence when he served in Battle Creek College, which is only twenty-five miles from Albion. While the change may involve some immediate difficulty, postponement will do no good. There are other teachers who in the near future should be discontinued, but there is little use of mentioning them now. I think that they are fairly well known to the authorities. The change here suggested would permit, I think, of the consolidation of Economics and Business Administration, a consolidation much to be desired in a college of liberal arts.[71]

Although Seaton's recommendation was unknown to faculty or students, news of Payne's "imminent dismissal" soon became known all over the campus during the gray weeks of March. The *Des Moines Register* of March 27 carried the news to the whole state of Iowa. Attempted student demonstrations for and against Payne were quickly stifled. The leaders of these movements were informed that any sort of protest action "would injure Professor Payne, especially in securing another position."[72] Still, students favoring Payne's retention signed petitions to the board of trustees. Supporters constructed a strong letter to Simpson alumni in an effort to "stir them into action favorable to [Payne's] cause."[73]

During these weeks, first one and then another student, nearly all of them favorable to Payne's cause, sought out the president in his office and talked with him "at great length" about the matter. "These have been thoroughly representative young men and women," wrote Harper, "and they have indicated that they represent student opinion generally. I have questioned all these young people very thoroughly, perhaps even severely."[74] What he heard disturbed him. A fair man, he came to believe that some, but not all, of the charges against Payne were prejudicial and overblown, and he reported his findings to the faculty committee of the board. Before Payne's hearing, the trustee committee adopted a resolution to the effect that

> this committee unanimously agree before beginning this hearing that Dr. Payne's personal views as to economics or politics are not under attack. This committee feels that Dr. Payne or any other person or member of the Simpson faculty is entitled to the privilege or independence of thought and freedom of expression. The issue of academic freedom is not involved.[75]

The hearing was conducted with solemnity and apparent good will. A complete transcript of the proceedings was prepared by a court reporter in shorthand but not transcribed.[76] A week later the trustee committee submitted its report, the salient portions of which stated:

> Evidence was introduced showing that Doctor Payne's teaching ability in the field of Economics has been underestimated. It was shown that his instruction is provocative of thought and acts as a mental stimulant to his students, especially to the more thoughtful group and the upper classmen. There is no doubt of Doctor Payne's mastery of the economic field. His books, more particularly his last one, have called forth many commendatory remarks. He enjoys good

standing among his colleagues in the field of Economics. He has excited the interest of men in our Conference who take advanced social viewpoints, and of persons whom he has met as a lecturer, even though they may not always agree with his point of view. Graduate students in the field of Economics who have come from his department have excelled in post-graduate work. It has been evidenced that certain students come to Simpson College due to Doctor Payne's presence on the faulty, and there are students who have expressed themselves as not desiring to be in our school if he were not there.

On the other hand, it has been clearly brought forth that Doctor Payne is lacking in administrative ability, and that he is not a competent teacher in certain fields of his department, especially in that of Business Administration. It has further been clearly shown that Doctor Payne was a definite problem to the previous and present administrations. Tension has existed as to administrative details involving the president, the dean, the registrar, and regulations generally agreed upon. There is evidence of definite failure to cooperate with the administration, irregularity in administrative procedure, repeated misunderstanding and misinterpretation of friendly criticism, a false defensive attitude unwarranted by circumstances, and an attitude of mind which may not incorrectly be described as a martyr complex. There is evidence as to halting, indirect and inconclusive speech. However, it should be noted that there is apparently a marked difference between Doctor Payne's expressions in speech and those which he employs in his books. Definite complaints have been lodged against the Business Administration department, and there are some complaints which have been made against the instruction in the field of Economics, both by students and by parents.[77]

The committee did not, on balance, believe that the facts warranted the "immediate, direct dismissal of Doctor Payne," but believed that he should be relieved of all administrative responsibilities, including both his position as head of the Division of Political and Social Science and the chairmanship of the Department of Economics and Business Administration. He would continue to hold the endowed William Buxton, Jr., Chair of Economics and Business Administration in a reorganized Department of Sociology and Economics headed by Charles Burrows. If these changes were acceptable to Payne, he would be accorded a regular reappointment. But "in the event [such] an arrangement cannot be worked out amicably, or if it is found that Dr. Payne is unwilling to adjust himself to such a recommendation, and the conditions complained of continue, the Committee recommends that his relations with the college be terminated at the end of the first semester of the school year 1938–39."[78]

Payne at first resolutely refused any such humiliating "demotion," but under protest accepted a contract containing most of the objectionable features, reasoning that a flawed contract was better than no contract at all. There, for a season, the matter rested.

* * *

Not long after he found respite from the Payne case and even before the modest maintenance fund drive was concluded, Harper made a decision. At nine-thirty in the morning of May 3 he went before the faculty and announced his resignation, effective June 30, 1938, "in order to accept a very unique post and opportunity at our own state university."[79] He had decided, he said, to accept the position of director of the School of Fine Arts and director of the Memorial Union at the State University of Iowa. At one o'clock that same afternoon he met with the executive committee of the board of trustees where he formally submitted his letter of resignation.[80] Everyone was "shocked at the suddenness of the move."[81] To board members the announcement came "like thunder out of a clear sky."[82]

It shouldn't have. All through the spring of 1938 they could read the signs of disappointment, indeed despair, in their president's countenance as he wrestled with the demons of disaccreditation and insolvency. They could surely see that he was the kind of man on whom persistent financial instability, leading to scarlet pecuniary embarrassment, was taking its toll. The university offered him a way out. More than that, it promised him liberation from the onerous, lonely responsibility for a struggling college and allowed him to flourish in those enterprises most suited to his talents and personality. He loved music; so did his wife, a gifted singer. He loved shows and programs and public speaking. The opportunity to do all of these beckoned when he received the call from the university's president, Eugene A. Gilmore.

Harper's opportunity was Simpson's loss. To some people at the College it looked like a catastrophe. Frances Moats, who of all Simpson people perhaps knew Harper best, was thunderstruck. "I'm weak at my stomach," he said. "The job here is difficult. He has labored hard on our financial problem." John Horsley felt that Harper's departure boded ill for Simpson: "The whole situation here is a question mark."[83] Down at the *Record* office, editor—and Simpson trustee—Don Berry disagreed. Seeking to dispel the gloom, the awful sense of deprivation that had settled over Indianola, he wrote, "No institution ever suffered by the service of a strong man. Even though his service is cut off just when it seems that his great work is only begun, the college has profited by his presence."[84]

Indeed it had. Dr. Harper gave Simpson a boost in morale that even unremitting poor salaries and failed fund-raising could not efface. His reorganization of the curriculum and restructuring of the faculty were reforms that endured. Moreover, he taught his colleagues the value of public relations as a means of revealing the substance of the Simpson academic experience. Simpson was the better for its having come to know Earl Harper. That Harper's decision to go the state university was a good one is evidenced by the fact that he enjoyed great success there, remaining until his retirement in 1963. And in his periodic visits to Indianola, he rejoiced in Simpson's later successes.

* * *

The same day Earl Harper resigned, board president William T. Hamilton named a committee of five chaired by Bishop G. Bromley Oxnam of Omaha to look for a new president for Simpson.[85] At the same time a faculty committee was constituted as a consultative group, chaired by Dean Francis Moats.[86] Bishop Oxnam, unable to attend meetings or to participate effectively in the search for a new leader, turned over his duties as chairman to Frank Henderson, who pursued the matter with vigor. While many candidates were nominated, especially by leading Methodist academicians and administrators, the choice of the committee fell unanimously upon a genial Kentuckian, John Owen Gross.

Gross was not looking for a job. He was happily situated as president of Union College, a small Methodist school in Barbourville, Kentucky. In fact, when he passed through Chicago on his way "to look over the situation" at Simpson late in July, he told the secretary of the Methodist Board of Education "that he hardly knew why he was going out to Indianola, that he had no desire to leave Union College, but was going at the invitation of the committee and felt that he owed them that courtesy." But after seeing Simpson and talking with the search committee on July 26, Gross was "greatly impressed" with the opportunities at Simpson.[87] For all its problems, Simpson was a stronger institution than was the one in which he was serving. During his nine years at Union he had taken a tiny two-year college, improved its academic standards, instituted a four-year curriculum, gained regional accreditation and increased the size of the student body. But Union in 1938 was an academic toddler compared to the more mature Simpson. And Simpson's endowment, seen from the hills of Kentucky, looked impressive. If Gross could do for Simpson as much as he had done for Union, the College would surely flourish. Agreeing to a salary of $4,200 plus a car and the president's home, together with moving expenses, Gross accepted the presidency of Simpson when notified of his election.[88]

John Gross was born at Folsom, Grant County, Kentucky, July 9, 1894, the son of William and Anna Chrisman Gross, and grew up in Covington, just across the Ohio River from Cincinnati. He also grew up in the northern branch of Methodism, as did many in divided Kentucky. Always a proud Kentuckian, he "doted on writers like Jesse Stuart, and admired Lincoln as a native Kentuckian."[89] He attended little Asbury College at Wilmore, Kentucky, where he graduated in 1918.[90] It was at Asbury that he felt the call to enter the ministry. From there he went to the Lane Seminary in Cincinnati for a year and studied briefly at the University of Kentucky, then entered Boston University School of Theology, where he earned his S.T.B. in 1921. While still a seminarian, he wed Harriet Lucretia Bletzer. They had three children: George Albert, John Birney and Harriet Lucille. Upon his graduation from theological school Gross's first appointment was to the pastorate of the Methodist Church in Barbourville. Four successful years there readied him for appointment as superintendent of the Barbourville district; and four years later, in 1929, he was elected president of Union College. He was an active Mason and had served a year as chaplain of the Kentucky Royal Arch Masons and of the Kentucky Grand Council of Royal and Select Masters.[91]

Because Gross believed he must not leave Union College without giving its trustees time to look for a successor, he preferred that he not take up his duties at Simpson before November 1, 1938, although he did agree to attend the Des Moines Conference sessions in Fairfield in September and to preach at the Indianola Methodist Church on September 18. The Gross family actually arrived in Indianola during the second week in November.[92]

Meanwhile an administrative committee consisting of Francis Moats, Clyde Emmons and Rae Dean had managed the affairs of the College through the summer and the better part of the fall semester. Enrollment that autumn was 451, down from 490 the first semester the previous year.[93]

* * *

The new president's inaugural, in accordance with Simpson tradition which allowed time for careful planning, was held the following spring. The two-day event brought a number of dignitaries to the campus on the weekend of April 22 and 23, 1939. Among the guests were seventeen college presidents and a raft of educators, churchmen and officeholders.

On Saturday morning at 9:30, after a brief College band concert, the colorful processional formed—the band, the choir, the presidential party, the college presidents, the Simpson board of trustees, 113 delegates from colleges and universities together with representatives of eight learned societies, then the faculty and the senior class, all under the direction of marshal William C. Hilmer. From the campus, the procession moved at a stately pace to the Methodist Church, where every seat was taken by a huge assemblage. Presiding was W. T. Hamilton, chairman of the Simpson board. In a program enriched by choral and instrumental music, Dr. Daniel L. Marsh, president of Boston University and a friend of the new Simpson president, delivered the charge. Gross responded with his inaugural address entitled "The Unchanging Fundamentals of Simpson College," from which his hearers could take comfort that the frenzied pace of change set in motion by Earl Harper would slacken somewhat.

At a complimentary luncheon, formal congratulations were extended to Gross by Iowa Governor George A. Wilson, Drake president D. W. Morehouse and other pillars of the state's educational establishment. A reception for the public followed at three o'clock that afternoon.

The following morning the inaugural service at the church featured Bishop H. Lester Smith of Cincinnati, Ohio, a last minute replacement for another bishop who was unable to come.[94] That afternoon Bishop G. Bromley Oxnam of Omaha led what was called the "consecration service." His address, "The Christian College," an acceptably bland offering from a man who could be expected to say almost anything, was broadcast nationwide.[95]

* * *

Even before his inauguration, Gross was immediately confronted with the thorniest problems left by the Harper administration. The ones he singled out for immediate attention were the restoration of American Association of Universities membership, improvement of student recruitment, financial recovery to avoid deficits and to pay full faculty salaries, rejuvenation of the conservatory and reduction of the size of the faculty.

Scaling down the size of the faculty could begin with Winfred E. Payne. For his part, Payne hoped that the resignation of Harper and the coming of a new president would lead to reconsideration of the termination of his services.[96] When it became clear that Gross preferred not to deal with this academic hot potato, Payne sought to rally supporters to force the issue, on more than one occasion invoking the name of revered Dean Hugh Jackson of Stanford in support of his cause. Jackson, however, protested the use of his name and wrote to Payne:

> I must repeat that I think it unfortunate that the point of view of the man in charge [of an Economics department in a small college] should be either that of a reactionary or that which tends towards socialism or perhaps even further to the left. Yours, I have been informed on various occasions, had been the latter point of view, and to the extent that that is true, I repeat that I think it unfortunate for the Department of Economics and Business Administration and for the College as a whole.[97]

Hugh Jackson was not the only one moved to revive the protest against Payne's incumbency. A number of board members renewed their attacks on his teaching. And townspeople too. It seems that at a meeting of the Quarter Century Club, a local Indianola essay group of which he was a member, Payne delivered a paper in which he excoriated the banking system worldwide, buttressing his views by quotations from a prominent London newspaper. Challenged by several townspeople, he was forced to admit to deliberate misquotation of his sources, amounting to outright falsification, a breach of academic integrity considered unforgivable by his fellow club members.[98]

Hard-pressed by a veritable storm of opposition that grew through the wearying months of early 1939, Payne wrote to the A.A.U.P. on April 27 requesting an investigation of his dismissal. Ralph E. Himstead, General Secretary of A.A.U.P., agreed to Payne's request and wrote to Gross, asking him "if he would receive a visiting committee to inquire further into the facts of Professor Payne's dismissal."[99] Gross replied that he would like to have time first to prepare a report for the A.A.U.P., which request was granted. The report was not sent to Himstead until October 14, 1939, by which time Payne had already departed from Simpson. After studying the Simpson statement, the A.A.U.P. decided that an on-campus investigation was indeed warranted.

It was not until March 14–16, 1940, that a two-man Investigating Committee came to Indianola. They were D. R. Scott, professor of accounting and statistics and William L. Bradshaw, associate professor of political science, both of the faculty of the University of Missouri. At Simpson they conducted three days of interviews with President Gross, members of the board of trustees and the faculty, a number of clergymen—not members of the board—and others. At the conclusion of their investigation, Scott and Bradshaw concluded that there was no record of incompetence in teaching business administration and that Payne's classroom performance in economics was admirable. They were shocked by the intensity of local opposition to Payne "indicated by the way in which trivial incidents in the meetings of a private discussion club were seized upon and presented as proving conclusively his lack of intellectual honesty."[100] Payne, they noted, "says that he is neither a socialist nor a communist," and they found no evidence to the contrary. They countered Hugh Jackson's views on Payne's acceptability. "It would be unfortunate," they wrote, "if our colleges should select their faculties only from middle-of-the-road individuals and give that qualification priority over intellectual capacity and teaching ability, for by so doing they would handicap themselves as centers of free intellectual inquiry."[101] Although Simpson people asserted throughout that the issue centered "not on *what* he taught or tried to teach, but on *how* he attempted to teach and administer," the visiting committee was equally certain that this was not the case and that "most of the criticisms of Dr. Payne were trivial and irrelevant as regards his worth as a teacher."[102] In fact, an adjustment which at one time appeared possible was subverted by the "uncompromising attitude" of Dr. Harper and the board.

Their final statement was surprisingly mild, concluding simply that "tenure conditions at Simpson College are not in accord with generally accepted principles of good academic practice and that the dismissal of Dr. W. E. Payne was a specific departure from acceptable standards of academic tenure."[103]

The A.A.U.P. did not censure Simpson College, to the relief of nearly everybody except Payne. Although the *Des Moines Register* editorialized carelessly, reporting that Simpson had "been put on the 'blacklist' of the American Association of University Professors," the College was subject to neither sanctions nor penalties.[104] This was confirmed in a letter to President Gross from Dr. Himstead, who wrote, "It was concluded that the administration of Simpson College should not be placed on the list of censured administrations at present, but that developments at the College as regards academic freedom and tenure and faculty-administration relationships should be kept under careful observation."[105]

In his reply to the general secretary, Gross asked simply, "If Simpson College is not on the censored [sic] list, will you write to the *Des Moines Register* and correct the statement?"[106] There was no correction.

When one examines this controversy that gripped Simpson for three years, it becomes obvious that, their protestations to the contrary, Simpson officials dismissed W. E. Payne for his political, social and economic views strongly held and freely expressed, not for incompetence, a charge for which they could never make a convincing case. At the same time, the A.A.U.P. report erred in asserting that Payne was no socialist. Of course he was a socialist, however Christian, and he trumpeted that fact proudly and frequently to anyone who would listen. As young alumnus Eugene R. Melson put it, "The basis of [the criticism] has never been Dr. Payne's adequacy as a teacher; it has ever been his liberal beliefs in the field of economics."[107] Margaret "Peg" Watson, a young biology instructor during those turbulent years, later recalled that "Simpson really wasn't ready for Dr. Payne."[108]

Simpson could probably have tolerated a Christian socialist had Payne not been the only professor of economics on the campus, sending forth his charges into an irretrievably capitalist world. As Gilbert Caldwell put it, "If Simpson were a large institution and could have numerous professors in each field with a variety of convictions, the situation would have been different."[109]

Payne's replacement was acceptably middle-of-the-road, and it was rumored that he was required daily to damn Karl Marx and the robber barons with equal vigor. Meanwhile, Payne found it exceedingly difficult to find another teaching position and soon gave up the search. In 1941 the Simpson *Alumni News Bulletin* reported that "Dr. and Mrs. W. E. Payne have moved to Laredo, Texas, where he is representing the National Farm Machinery Cooperative and selling in Mexico and the southern states."

* * *

Although the Payne case convulsed Simpson's administration and faculty during the 1938–39 academic year and distracted them for more than another year as the A.A.U.P. investigation dragged on, Gross determined not to permit the controversy to monopolize his time and attention. He had no illusions about Simpson's manifest weaknesses. He surveyed the College's attendance since the last "normal" year in 1927, noting that the record was one of almost steady decline until 1936, when it stabilized somewhat. Simpson shared with other Midwestern colleges the problem of attracting students, and once having attracted them, keeping them. In a report to the board of trustees toward the end of his first full semester on campus, he attempted to pin down the reasons for enrollment losses, concluding that they surely included the A.A.U. suspension, serious student attrition, poor student housing, the deterioration of the conservatory and generally flagging morale. "We cannot deny that the institution is sick," said Gross, "[but] the illness is not malignant."[110]

Perhaps not, but the problem of student attrition was especially troublesome. Too many freshmen did not return the following year, and the dropoff at the end of the sophomore year was calamitous. Of the freshman class of 1934, fewer than 29 percent graduated in 1938. The average for the prewar years (1936 to 1941) was somewhat better, 46 percent, but still discouraging.[111] "The fact that our student persistence record," said Gross in a report to the board of trustees

Table 7
Enrollment 1936–1941

	Senior	Junior	Soph.	Fresh.	Spec.	Total	Cons. Reg.*	Cons. P.S.S.*	Net Total**
1936–37	85	98	175	209	1	568	48	11	579
1937–38	84	105	158	158	2	507	49	38	545
1938–39	102	83	119	161	0	465	47	43	508
1939–40	80	75	135	207	0	497	52	40	537
1940–41	69	83	176	171	1	500	—	50	550

*Reg. = Regular, P.S.S. = Public School and Special
**Excludes duplicates.

in 1940, "is not very much different from that of other colleges should not make us indifferent to the possibility of decided improvement."[112]

It was not just a matter of "student persistence" to graduation. Nor was it a lack of financial aid for students through scholarships, grants-in-aid, loans, work or National Youth Administration employment. Simpson's student aid budget, revealed a study of six similar liberal arts colleges in 1940, was far and away the highest—$53,000 annually against an average of only $30,000—and its tuition charges were twenty percent below average—$200 versus an average of $252. The College could not afford the aid it was awarding. Nor was it getting its money's worth. During the five years before 1940, Simpson's entering freshman fell into the lowest quartile among the two hundred colleges using the American Council of Education psychological tests. "Surely," concluded Gross, "if the use of scholarships does not bring students who are average or above, they are not aiding in building a strong institution."[113] Small wonder, then, that the faculty, dismayed by the generally poor performance of their charges, tended to give relatively low grades. The best students, they would hasten to admit, were as good as they had ever been. It was just that there were so few of them. That this kind of faculty distress was shared by nearly every other Iowa college was not particularly comforting.

Nevertheless, there were real strengths at Simpson. The endowment was among the best of any Iowa colleges, the core faculty was very strong, the campus attractive and most of its physical plant adequate; church relations were excellent and town-gown links were as good as they had ever been. These were some of the attractive qualities that had brought Gross to Simpson in the first place.

But if the hemorrhage in enrollment was to be stanched, the College had to move and move quickly to deal decisively with its most compelling problems. Simpson, asserted Gross, must regain American Association of Universities accreditation, strengthen campus morale and banish a "spirit of defeatism," work much harder on student recruitment, especially in *selecting* freshmen, upgrade the conservatory and energize the College's work in career placement.[114]

The restoration of A.A.U. approval was an imperative, "a crisis that must not be ignored." Actually, only a handful of Iowa colleges were on the A.A.U.'s list of recognized institutions,[115] but Simpson's having been on the list and having been suspended was widely misunderstood as a total loss of accreditation and was severely harmful to student recruitment and retention. The A.A.U. suspension had singled out two problems which had to be addressed if Simpson was to regain approval: faculty salaries and the library.

Salaries, frozen since 1932 and paid only partially, were pegged at seventy-five percent of par during Harper's second year (1937–38), and a small bonus was paid at the end of the year. Because President Gross did not arrive on campus until well into the 1938–39 academic year, salaries were already set at seventy-five percent of par, but he saw to it that by year's end everyone received a ten percent bonus. For 1939–40 Gross insisted, and the board concurred, that frozen salaries be abandoned and that all salaries be paid in full. For that year, remembered Harold Watson, "as a division head I was guaranteed and paid $2,725.00—$25.00 a year more than I had started with at Simpson fifteen years before."[116] In any case, guaranteeing and paying salaries in full met the principal objection of the A.A.U. Besides, it was the right thing to do.

At the same time, President Gross maintained that the faculty, in view of the serious enrollment decline, was too large. The Seaton report only underscored the advice he was receiving from others: a modest and selective reduction in the teaching staff would enable the College to pay the salaries of those who remained. Too many people were teaching too many small classes.[117] Surely three or four or five people could be let go. Accordingly, Eva Stahl was retired in the spring of 1939 after nineteen years on the English faculty—she also had taught Latin, which was dropped altogether—and the departments of English and speech were combined. Katharine Renich, a veteran of ten years in history and art, was dropped from the faculty while academic dean Francis Moats returned to full-time teaching in history. What few courses there were in art were transferred to the Department of Education, which was in its turn combined with the Department of Psychology, permitting the elimination of the position held by James W. Layman, who had joined the faculty only in 1937. The employment of Forrest D. Brown as professor of education and psychology, dean of the College and dean of men covered the teaching duties of Layman, strengthened the staff in education and of course replaced Moats and Burrows in the two deanships. Thus at least two full-time positions were eliminated.[118]

Forrest D. Brown came to Simpson in 1939 from two years as head of the Department of Education at Mary Baldwin College. A native Kansan, he was a graduate of Fort Hays State College in Kansas, where he had also completed the M.S. degree. He earned his Ph.D. at the University of Cincinnati in 1933. When he came to Simpson he was thirty-two, married, with one daughter. Praised for his "personalized instruction" in the classroom, Brown seemed to wear his many hats with considerable ease and was known for "sure and unfaltering" discipline among the students and for his "tireless efforts" among the faculty.[119]

Staff reductions, together with the replacement of Dr. Payne by Percy L. Guyton as the new William Buxton, Jr., Associate Professor of Economics and Business Administration in the new combined department headed by Burrows, eased the financial strain on the budget and seemed not to weaken instruction.[120] Then, in the fall of 1938, Robert J. Samson, a Simpson graduate who had just completed his M.B.A. at Harvard, joined the faculty in business administration and stayed on for two years, during which time he not only performed well in the classroom but also strove valiantly to assist with placement of graduates in the corporate world. Soon enough, however, he himself joined that corporate world, where the remuneration for his undoubted talents was considerably more generous than he could hope for at Simpson. In his place the College hired Texan Casey W. Kunkel. With a Chicago M.A., experience at the Haskins and Sells accounting firm and a year of teaching at the Citadel, Kunkel proved to be a well-qualified successor to Samson.

When in the spring of 1939 Edith Whitaker left Simpson after eighteen years to marry R. J. Gunn and live in Anchorage, Alaska, she was replaced in speech by Nelda C. Kurtz, a 1937 graduate of Albion College, who had earned her M.A. from the University of Minnesota. Otherwise, with few exceptions, during the Gross years the faculty remained quite stable.

In the spring of 1941 William C. Hilmer retired after a distinguished forty-two-year teaching career, twenty-one of those years at Simpson. It was his pride that he had never in his entire career missed a day of class on account of illness. Looking back on his years of college instruction, Hilmer wrote in the 1941 *Zenith*, "Teaching as a life work is one of the finest opportunities. The association with young people, getting their views, and aiding them in their efforts to prepare for life is great work." But in some ways it had been frustrating work, for over the years Hilmer had watched the foreign languages, especially the classical languages, shoved out to the periphery of the curriculum or out of it completely by depression, vocationalism and what he and Harold Watson labeled the onslaught of the "Inhumanities."

Yet the College was not prepared to abandon the foreign languages altogether and looked for a generalist who could teach enough different foreign languages to justify one full-time position in order to teach the few hardy students who still wanted to study French or German or even Spanish. Gross was fortunate to find Roberta Riegel, a faculty member at Anderson College in Indiana, who seemed to be able to teach any and all foreign tongues. A Missouri native, Riegel was a graduate of Central Methodist College at Fayette, Missouri, and had earned her M.A. in French and German at the University of Chicago. After that she studied Spanish for a year at the University of Arizona, and then completed her Ph.D. at the University of Illinois in French and Spanish. She studied one summer at the Alliance Francaise program in Paris and the summer of 1941 in Mexico. Prior to her joining the faculty at Anderson College she had taught at Heidelberg, Albion and Evansville Colleges. Roberta Riegel was a rare find for Simpson. She taught at the College until her retirement twenty years later, and during many of those years she carried the banner of foreign language proudly and alone.

In his effort to address the most serious deficiencies of the College, Gross next attacked the problem of the library. Every study of Simpson had criticized it as inadequate, and Gross determined to do something about it. To put the building into good shape would cost an estimated $15,000 for an addition on the west side of the building with steel shelving for 45,000 volumes, for new lighting, seating and an upgraded ventilation system. Because the cost was moderate and the need great, the board decided to go ahead with the project. Plans were prepared by Keffer and Jones of Des Moines and the construction contract awarded to L. V. Seibert, a local Indianola builder. The metal shelving and fireproof flooring for the three-story stack room was custom installed by the Remington-Rand Company.[121] Construction was under way in mid-summer and completed in the late autumn of 1939. When visitors were able to view the remodeled building at an open house the first week in January, they found the main reading room on the second floor airy, well-lighted and commodious, and much of the old clutter of book shelving moved into the new addition. The circulation desk was now downstairs, the stack area closed off and the old wooden stacks removed. There was even a comfortable librarian's office. The best news was that the project had cost only $9,330.[122]

To help pay for renovation and long-deferred maintenance of campus buildings, the board sought to improve its earnings from the College's endowment. The Chicago investment firm of Montcreiff and Tittle, employed by Earl Harper only in 1938 to manage the investment portfolio, was not performing as they had hoped and tended to charge more for its service than did the trust departments of reputable banks. Young William Buxton III therefore led the move to retain the First National Bank of Chicago with an eye to broadening Simpson's investments beyond the traditional real estate mortgages into bonds and equities.

The College's farms were another matter. In 1939 Simpson owned twenty-five farms, 3,442 acres of Iowa land modestly valued at $264,585, or about $77 per acre. But income from this land was only about two and a half percent, an amount that could be improved with better farm management. The employment of Everett R. Brewer as farm manager was surely a step in the right direction,[123] but even more important was a change in farm policy from one of exploitation to one of conservation and improvement of the soil. Gross, who had seen the heartbreaking results of abuse of the land in his native Kentucky, contended that if renters on Simpson's farms continued to "mine" the soil and if the College continued to ignore their depredations, even the wealth of the rich farms of Iowa could be squandered needlessly and very quickly. And properly maintained farms should in time produce abundant crops and increased income.

Gross attempted no major fund raising campaign. Indeed he knew that such a fund drive was needed—he talked at one time of the need for $500,000, at another for $1,000,000—but in each of the three years he was at the helm he attempted to raise no more than a modest maintenance fund sufficient to keep the College out of the red.[124] Although these efforts provided no capital funds for much needed student housing or a new chapel, they did halt the wearisome deficits that had plagued the College for years.

Dr. Gross's efforts with faculty, the library and the budget were crowned with success when the president received word on November 21, 1940, that Simpson had been fully restored to accreditation by the American Association of Universities.[125] As the news flashed across the campus and down to the square, it was as if the ravages of drought and depression had been healed. Simpson's self-esteem, battered during the Lean Years of bleak inexpectation, was reclaimed. Graduates could be confident their academic credits would be accepted at professional and graduate schools. For all its problems—and its tribulations were hardly unique—Simpson could once again hold its head high among its fellow colleges, its worth validated at an important moment in its life. And John O. Gross was that moment's hero.

* * *

In an act probably no one would have called heroic, John Gross united the College of Liberal Arts with the Conservatory of Music and thus brought to fruition a design that none of his predecessors would have dreamed possible. He took the matter up with the board of trustees at their mid-year meeting in March 1940, successfully persuading them that such a merger was timely, indeed overdue. For many years the relationship of the conservatory with the rest of the College had been awkward. Simpson's president, not to speak of the board, watched the conservatory pursue its own course, recruit its own faculty and students, manage—or mismanage—its own finances and conduct a thoroughly professional program. Under Frank Barrows, the conservatory had flourished, and music at Simpson was so strong that everyone worked to smooth out the occasional rough spots that appeared. The president might possess only a vague impression of the work of the music faculty and have not even a clue as to the state of the imponderable finances of the conservatory, but he knew Barrows somehow did understand all those things, and he was content to leave well enough alone. With Herbert Harvey, after Barrow's death in 1924, it was different. Harvey was an accomplished violinist and able conductor, but he was a far better musician than manager, and the depression years only underscored that fact. President Hillman, in the paralysis of hard times, decided not to take action, and Earl Harper, who was keenly aware of the deficiencies in music, found his attention diverted toward more urgent needs than reorganization of the conservatory.

When John L. Seaton visited the campus in 1938, he recommended merging the conservatory with the school of liberal arts, and early the next year Gross was talking about a reorganization of music "in order to meet accreditation requirements."[126] A few months later, noting a disastrous decline in conservatory enrollment, he could not but conclude that "perhaps a separate Conservatory with pseudo-official relationship to the college has served its day."[127] Harvey reluctantly agreed and decided that it would be best to clear the way for President Gross to appoint a new head of music, now incorporated as the Division of Music in the regular academic structure of the College. "We hope," said Gross, "the new division will be founded on an academic basis and seek to create a healthy, normal love of music with less emphasis on the professional aspects."[128] Harvey asked for and was accorded a one-year leave of absence. He remained with his wife and younger son in Indianola and attempted to collect something more than $20,000 owed him by former students. At the close of the 1940–41 year Harvey's relationship with Simpson ceased.[129] The new appointee would assist President Gross in selecting new music faculty.

It would be a major task to integrate personnel, to provide budget, assume debts on equipment and maintain Barrows Hall. For that reason the plan to create a department of art in the new division was postponed. In any case, the new division head would be a musician.

Indeed he was. From a large number of applicants Dr. Gross selected Sven Victor Lekberg, a forty-year-old brilliant pianist and composer. A native of Chicago, Lekberg graduated from Northwestern University with a B.M. degree in 1923. Upon completion of his undergraduate work, he entered the Schola Cantorum, where he studied under Vincent D'Indy and Paul Braud. Later he studied at Paris's Ecole Normale (1930–31) with Paul Dukas, Alfred Cortot and Lucien Wurmser, and in 1939 completed his Master of Music degree at the Eastman School of Music. In addition, Lekberg's professional career provided broad experience in teaching and administration. For three years he was director of music at Western Union College (later Westmar and Teikyo-Westmar) at LeMars, Iowa; three years as head of the piano department at Ohio University in Athens; five years as dean of the school of music at Augustana College at Rock Island, Illinois, where he was called upon to effect the same kind of reorganization that Simpson was contemplating; and for three years he was connected with Kansas Wesleyan College at Salina, the president of which "released Mr. Lekberg reluctantly in order that he might come to Simpson."[130] Eastman director Howard Hanson praised Lekberg as "an excellent musician with a splendid background, an able composer and theorist, and a pianist and organist as well. He is a man of the highest type of character with a splendid personality."[131] He might have added that Lekberg was an incurable Swedish-American and a Lutheran. He was also an inveterate pipe smoker. He was hardly the stereotypical Simpson faculty appointee.

"Is it all right if I smoke my pipe in the privacy of my office?" asked Lekberg as he met with President Gross the first time after he arrived on the campus.

"We don't smoke on the Simpson campus," replied Gross plainly, but somehow Lekberg sensed that the assertion was made without conviction.

"Do you mean to say that I can't smoke my pipe in my office?"

"We don't smoke on the Simpson campus," repeated Gross officially and with even less conviction.

"Do I understand you to be saying that you don't give a damn if I smoke my pipe in my office?"

"Let's talk about music," suggested the president.[132] From that day forward, during thirty-plus years at Simpson, Lekberg smoked his pipe daily in his office, with smug contentment and utterly without guilt. No one else on the faculty dared follow suit. But Gross's willingness to make an exception to the Methodist discipline endeared him to Lekberg.

No sooner had Lekberg arrived in Indianola than he married Mildred Anderson, a talented musician he had come to know as a colleague at Augustana. With this marriage came two daughters of Mildred's by a former marriage, Barbara and Jane. Mildred Lekberg, a native of the state of Washington and Swedish too, held a B.M. and M.M. from the University of Washington. Within two years she joined the Simpson music faculty. For the next twenty-six years Sven and Mildred Lekberg taught and cared for generation after generation of Simpson undergraduate musicians, whom they frequently entertained in their home on North Buxton Street in the delightful clutter of Swedish bric-a-brac, French art and Sven's immense library that reflected his eclectic tastes. In short, the Lekbergs soon became a Simpson institution.

Lekberg's first task was to recruit a suitable faculty. In the spring and summer of 1940 he interviewed and auditioned what seemed like an army of talented musicians, and one by one he put together his staff. First there was Edmund J. Marty, who taught instrumental music and public school music and conducted the College band. A graduate of Lawrence College in Appleton, Wisconsin, Marty had earned a master's degree at Northwestern University.[133] The only member of the conservatory faculty Lekberg selected to stay on was Lester E. Spring, a fourteen-year veteran voice instructor who remained on the faculty only one more year. In stringed instruments, replacing Harvey, Lekberg found a remarkable young man named Paul Reisman, a native of Budapest and graduate of the Royal Hungarian Academy of Music who had headed the violin department under Imre Waldbauer at the Gimes Institute of Music at Budapest. Reisman also was first chair violinist in the Budapest Symphony Orchestra under conductors like Bruno Walter, Otto Klemperer and Eugene Ormandy. In 1938 he left Budapest on the last train to leave Hungary in the political crisis of that year and came to the United States on an exchange scholarship, attending the Westminster Choir College at Princeton, New Jersey, and playing first chair violin in the Trenton Symphony. When he arrived in the United States he spoke only Magyar and German. By the time he came to Indianola he had acquired a fair English vocabulary, but his pronunciation was truly awful. Most Indianolans found it quaint.[134]

When the Division of Music—it was designated Division V as Health and Physical Education were absorbed into Division IV—commenced operation in the fall of 1940, Lekberg and the entire music staff were employed directly by and were under the direct supervision of the College. Soon three hours of required work in fine arts was added to graduation requirements of all students. At the same time the Bachelor of Music degree was retained alongside the Bachelor of Arts in music.

* * *

It did not escape the attention of President Gross that 1940 marked the fiftieth anniversary of George Washington Carver's enrollment at Simpson. Manifestly the College's most distinguished alumnus, Carver was living out his days at the Tuskegee Institute in Alabama, where he had had an incredibly fruitful career in research and teaching since Booker T. Washington had brought him there in the 1890s. Deeply religious, shy, almost reclusive, Carver continued doggedly to pursue yet new practical ways to free the southern black from agricultural serfdom. Though frighteningly frail, he clung to his work like a man possessed, led always, he said, by the spirit and inspiration of God.

President Hillman had hoped to welcome Carver "home" to Simpson when the scientist was awarded an honorary degree in 1928. But a serious injury—he was knocked down and gored by a bull—prevented Carver's making the long journey to Iowa. The degree was awarded in absentia. Now Gross wanted to invite Carver to preach the baccalaureate sermon at the 1941 commencement, and he wanted to deliver the invitation personally.

In July 1940, President and Mrs. Gross, and their daughter Lucille, accompanied by the president's secretary, Florence Cox, made a trip by automobile to visit Dr. Carver at Tuskegee.[135] On the seventeenth the members of the party made their way to the campus and were led to the great scientist's laboratory, where they were introduced to the old gentleman, slim as a reed. They found him working on a yucca plant, not unlike one he had painted half a century earlier at Simpson. He welcomed them graciously, responded warmly to their questions, seemed at times caught up in a sort of reverie as he recalled his Simpson days. But he apologized for seeming to be preoccupied, for he "had just had an inspiration in connection with the yucca."[136] As if the flash of insight, an evanescent thing, might flee his consciousness, he worked on the plant most of the time during the interview.

From the interview two important images stand out. First and foremost was Carver's unhesitating conviction that he was merely an instrument in God's hands. "My laboratory," he said, "is God's little workshop." He would have it known of himself that "here's a scientist who believes that science depends on God. Science is truth. God is truth." It was also clear that Simpson had a special, almost legendary place in Carver's own story. "What I am doing is through Him who makes it possible through the vision received through going to Simpson." He remembered "those blessed people," Etta Budd, Mrs. Liston, Dr. Holmes. "I just love to hear their names." God, he believed, had brought him to Simpson, and "Simpson was the beginning. . . . There is where I got my inspiration."[137] There his life was changed.

Carver interpreted his own history, the history of America and contemporary world events as the working out of the will of the Creator. "Why," he said, "the reason for the war in Europe and the terrible condition today, I believe, . . . is God's method of purifying the world. Isaiah in the Book of Prophecy said God took [the] scourge of Babylon to purify the world. We are not in a much better condition now than Sodom and Gomorrah were. Now it has to be purged."

President Gross agreed: "Don't you think that the defeat of France was not by the armies of Hitler, but by the fact that its people were dissipated in sin? We all know the reputation of the morals of France."

"As ye sow, so shall ye reap," nodded Carver.

Having thus disposed of the French, the president repeated his invitation to Carver to come to Indianola the following spring. "Through the providence of the Almighty," said the old man, his voice cracking with emotion, I may get back there. . . . I would love to come back. . . . Physically, I am not so well, but I believe that I am going to be permitted to go."[138]

Although he was indeed infirm, Carver made the difficult journey to Iowa. Introduced as "Simpson's most distinguished son," he spoke to a crowd of more than 2,000 persons at Simpson's baccalaureate service on June 1, 1941. A loud speaker carried the proceedings to hundreds outside who were unable to get seats in the packed Methodist Church.

"A frail, wrinkled and aging Negro," wrote the *Des Moines Register*'s Donald Grant, "stood behind the pulpit at the Methodist Church in Indianola Sunday morning and talked to God." Carver said the conversation started simply enough: "Mr. Creator, I would like to know something about the peanut."

And God said, "Take some peanuts apart and find out for yourself."

Although none of the rapt listeners recorded the words spoken that morning, they watched with love and admiration the aged, thin, stooped black man with a high-pitched voice talk about talking with God.[139]

Carver thoroughly enjoyed his brief stay in Indianola and the warm hospitality of his Simpson hosts. Protected by his young assistant, Austin W. Curtis, from engaging in too much activity, Carver returned as quickly as possible to his Tuskegee lab, where he and Curtis were trying to develop a cheap paint made of clay and used crankcase oil, the better to help southern blacks paint their shacks.

* * *

Because of the difficulty of raising capital funds of any consequence, the College saw no major construction during the Harper and Gross years. After Gross had familiarized himself with the physical plant, however, he did make some modest changes. Lorraine Hall, for example, discontinued as a women's dormitory after seventeen years, was refurbished and converted into eleven apartments rented out to faculty or townspeople. The Omicron, Theta Upsilon and Beta Sigma Omicron houses were given over to cooperative women's housing. Theta Upsilon secured the former president's house on North Buxton, while Omicron passed out of existence and struggling Beta Sigma Omicron's tiny membership would have to do without housing at all.[140] Because the old president's house at 710 North Buxton had been deemed inadequate for Dr. Gross's family, the board sought a more commodious dwelling. Fortunately in the summer of 1939 such a house became available, and the College traded Swan Farm in White Oak Township and a small amount of cash for it. Located at the corner of Girard Avenue and North B Street, facing Buxton Park, the house required only minimal refurbishing and served most satisfactorily as the president's home for many years.[141]

The College bookstore, having relocated from an old house to another on campus, was cramped and ill-equipped. Rae Dean recommended during the summer of 1941 that the building be removed "the cheapest way" and that the bookstore be moved to more spacious and well-appointed quarters.[142] By the opening of the fall semester that year students were pleasantly surprised to find their bookstore located in Room 14 of Old Chapel under the management of Frank Chisman.[143]

Since its earliest days home economics had been shoehorned into the squat little old building east of Mary Berry Hall. It would have required a gift for euphemism to call the building plain. Almost any new accommodations would have been an improvement. Hence when the Fred Pemble residence on North C Street—just north of Hopper Gymnasium—went up for sale in 1940, the College was interested, for even though far from ideal, it would provide more room for home economics for a nominal investment.[144] And perhaps later the house could be redone and enlarged. After nearly a year of negotiations, the board authorized the purchase of the Pemble property "for $5,500 or less."[145] It required another year to complete the purchase of the house and to renovate it sufficiently to accommodate home economics as a practice house and for classes in textiles and sewing. The old building continued for the time being to house nutrition and foods classes. A major "addition to the [new] building will come as soon as possible," announced the *Simpsonian*.[146]

Dr. Gross realized that these and other minor campus improvements[147] were indeed helpful, but the great needs were student housing and a chapel that could seat the entire student body. It was his view, supported by many, that part of Simpson's failure to attract students was its lack of adequate housing. A new dormitory for women was a pressing need. "One for men should be considered also," he reported to the board in 1941. "The inability of the College to keep its students together under competent guidance is a weakness that constantly militates against the effectiveness of the institution." And, he pointed out that, once built, residence halls could be expected to be self-supporting. Perhaps the College could even invest some of its permanent funds to provide these new buildings.[148]

* * *

The College's undergraduate publications continued to be informative and reflective of student opinions and values. If the overall quality of the students was suspect, the talents of the editors of the *Simpsonian* and *Zenith* were not, their journalistic efforts being thoroughly creditable.[149] In the fall of 1940 the student directory, published as usual by the Y.M.C.A., got a new name, the *Password*. The name proved to be enduring and the quality of the directory excellent. The same can be said of the *Simpson College Bulletin*, published quarterly by the College's office of public relations for the 7,500 alumni of record. Well-written and balanced in its presentations, it was immensely popular with its readers. The name was changed to *Alumni News Bulletin* in mid-1940, but resumed its old appellation in 1946. In the fall of 1939 a new edition of the *Simpson College Songbook* was published at fifty cents a copy. Sales were good.

A few new student organizations appeared during the prewar years. In 1936 student ministers organized a group called Kappa Chi, the "Preachers of Christ," with sixteen charter members and took into their membership the ordained people on campus—Harper, Hilmer, Burrows and Legg—together with President Emeritus Hillman.[150] Successful among the future preachers, Kappa Chi would be remembered for its group photograph in the 1938 (the *second* 1938) *Zenith*, striking a pose that looked something like an overpopulated Last Supper. In the first days of 1939 the Beta Beta Beta biology honorary reorganized after several years of inactivity and has continued to this day as a strong society with ardent faculty support, and in early 1942 the Blackfriars, the freshman-sophomore theater society, was revived after lying dormant a few years.[151] Sigma Gamma Rho and Zetalethean, the last vestiges of the old literary societies, gave up the ghost in the spring of 1940. Neither reorganized that following fall, and no literary society has existed at Simpson since that time. On the other hand, Pi Kappa Delta, heir to the oratorical enthusiasm of the old literary societies, thrived, its principal public speakers and debaters continuing to win honors for Simpson. The 1941 *Zenith* noted the founding that year of an organization for independent women called Off-Campus Coeds.

The Greek-letter societies for the most part continued to be successful, although the number of students choosing to join them varied widely from year to year. In 1936, 121 pledged; in 1938, only 60 joined during rush week (13 more pledged a few weeks later); and two years later the number was up to 67. The three fraternities were healthy, but only three of the six women's groups maintained a strong membership. Theta Upsilon, Beta Sigma Omicron and the nonselective local Omicron suffered from declining numbers. Omicron died in 1940 and Beta Sigma Omicron, after two years of fruitless struggle, was closed the following spring. Theta Upsilon, on the other hand, revived and built its membership to a respectable level. It was quite evident that Simpson could not support more than four sororities.

Two of the women's societies perennially led the campus in scholarship rankings. In ten semesters during the prewar years Pi Beta Phi won the grade cup six times and Tridelta four. The ATOs led the men's groups most of the time, with Theta Kappa Nu usually the runner-up, and both turned in quite respectable performances. Kappa Theta Psi, consistent with its hallowed tradition, remained in the academic cellar—except once, in the spring of 1938, when a modern miracle occurred: the Kappas won the men's grade cup, not so much because they did so well as because the competition did so poorly.[152] Embarrassed by their sudden scholarly notoriety, they made up for their unexpected success by doing particularly poorly the next semester.

If the Kappas—or KOYs—were not noted for their academic achievements, they succeeded signally in other ways, especially in Homecoming competition. They won the famed Tomahawk the first time it was awarded in 1939. Selected as a symbol of Simpson's Indian traditions that had developed through the years and offered to that group judged to perform best at the fall Homecoming in float, house decoration and "Simpson Spirit" competition, the Tomahawk was a duplicate of an original belonging to the father of Simpson's new economics professor, Percy L. Guyton. The original tomahawk was found in Mississippi many years earlier and evidently had been "wielded by a brave who was a member of a tribe from outside the state." The duplicate, fashioned by the J. W. Lundy marble works, was bound to its hardwood handle with rawhide "in typical Indian fashion."[153] At that same 1939 Homecoming, at a huge bonfire the night before the game, Dorothy Spence, who was appropriately of partial Mohawk descent, reigned as the first Princess and voice professor Lester E. Spring, who really looked the part, as the first Big Chief. And just to prove that it wasn't all a fluke, the KOYs won the Tomahawk the next year as well.[154]

In the fall of 1939 the Theta Kappa Nu national fraternity merged with another national fraternity in one of the largest amalgamations ever accomplished in the Greek-letter world. Brought together were the larger Lambda Chi Alpha, founded in 1909 with 78 chapters and 21,000 members, and Theta Kappa Nu, founded in 1924 with 37 active chapters and approximately 7,000 members. Both were relatively young fraternities which had grown rapidly, but which duplicated chapters on only nine campuses. Simpson's Theta Kappa Nu chapter, as we have seen, was one of the founding chapters of its national organization and was very strong at the time of the merger with the larger fraternity. With the incorporation of the Theta Nus, Lambda Chi Alpha could count 105 chapters, the fourth largest in the nation. All alumni of Theta Kappa Nu were classified as full members of Lambda Chi. The formal installation and celebration of the union took place on October 11, 1939, with Clyde Emmons, the respected adviser of the Simpson chapter, presiding at a festive banquet attended by Lambda Chi dignitaries and a lot of jubilant young men.[155]

* * *

Under the direction of Frank Casey, intercollegiate men's athletics during the prewar years continued to be frustratingly uneven. In basketball and track, thanks largely to Casey's inspired coaching, Simpson compiled an enviable record. In other sports—tennis, golf, wrestling and baseball—the Simpson record was at best mediocre.

The big disappointment was football. After winning the conference championship three times under Judd Dean, the team had an ignominious 1–8 season in 1935. During the following six years (1936–41) Simpson compiled an abysmal 9–43–2 record. The 1936 season wasn't so bad. Tommy Anderson—the one who had been rusticated for leading the troops who wanted to dance—returned to complete his college work, and he helped coach the football team to a 3–6 record.[156] After that nothing seemed to help. The coaches applied their finest skills. Students and townspeople flocked to the games, hoping for a win. The worst seasons were 1937, 1938 and 1939, with no wins in 1937 and one each in 1938 and 1939 against an accumulated 25 losses. Yet even in defeat the Simpson men could evoke admiration. In 1938 they suffered an awful drubbing at the hands of Washington University in St. Louis, 58–6. But a sportswriter for the *St. Louis Globe-Democrat* praised the Redmen. He recalled that after the half-time intermission, with the score 51–0, "Simpson returned to the field a beaten team. They were leg-weary, tired from opposing a bigger team, powerless to stop a smooth-running offense. They were beaten in everything but courage." In the second half—without Washington U's first team for a while, but with seven of their eleven regulars at the end of the game—Simpson held their opponent to a 7–6 advantage. David had certainly not defeated Goliath, but he came away from the fray with honor.[157]

In the wake of all the gridiron humiliation, the College's alumni once again bestirred themselves. With some urging, the S Club organized in November 1940 an "alumni division," dedicated to the improvement of Simpson's athletics, by which they meant Simpson football.[158] Only a few weeks later a "Quarterback Club" was founded by a number of interested alumni led by Vinton C. Watson, Carl W. Johnson and Casey Williams. Appropriately they elected banker William Buxton III as treasurer and stated that their purpose was the "recruitment of athletes."[159] Among other things they urged scholarships or grants-in-aid to provide for the subsidization of players. What they seemed not to notice was that nearly everyone at Simpson, athletes included, was already being subsidized more handsomely than the College could afford. The problem for Simpson was how to reduce student aid, not increase it. Besides, several years earlier Simpson had joined other Iowa colleges in cracking down on recruitment and subsidizing of athletes, which was clearly going on in some schools. The Iowa College Presidents' Association condemned "the granting of scholarships, grants-in-aid or rebates to anyone on account of athletic prowess."[160]

Meanwhile, recognizing that Frank Casey could not be expected to coach three major sports with equal effectiveness, John Gross and the board decided to find a full-time football coach at a price they could afford to pay. That meant finding an able but inexperienced young man, probably straight out of school, who showed real promise, and taking a chance on him. In the spring they found a candidate who appeared to be ideal. He was Robert J. Waldorf, a 1940 graduate of the University of Missouri, a three-year veteran guard on Missouri's highly successful team and picked during his senior year to most of the all-conference teams of the Big Six. A major in history and economics with high grades, he was a member of the SAE fraternity and good all-round athlete. He was also impressively connected; his father was Methodist Bishop Ernest Lynn Waldorf of the Chicago area; one brother, Lynn Waldorf, was the head football coach at Northwestern University and another brother, Paul, coach at Fort Hays College in Kansas.[161] When he arrived in Indianola to take up his duties on September 4, Waldorf brought with him his bride of five weeks, Martha Frances, a graduate of Missouri, where she was affiliated with Kappa Kappa Gamma.[162]

It did not require much time for Waldorf to discover that three disastrous seasons had taken their toll. He didn't have much to work with. His rag-tag team had a lot of spirit and very limited playing skills. He was afraid they would play poorly, and they did. Even so, with a win-loss record of 1–7–1, that season was the best in four years, their scoring the best in six years. And the following year, with a football camp behind him, a lot of prayer and with ten returning lettermen, the team improved markedly. They didn't win any prizes, but they scored three wins against five losses and one tie, with stellar line play by senior Ken Tannatt.

Waldorf was called upon to do a lot more than coach football. He handled all the men's physical education classes, taught a coaching class, and if Peter Ross is to be believed, was the best intramural director the College ever employed. And he seemed to enjoy all of it. But after two years he accepted a position as line coach at Marquette University. "I have enjoyed working with everybody at Simpson," he said, "especially with the boys on the football squad. They tried hard and did a good job for us."[163]

Even though football was the most visible sport at Simpson, it was certainly not the only popular one. Basketball aroused as much passion among spectators as ever, and Simpson still boasted the best gymnasium and the best coach in the Iowa Conference. Frank Casey took a very good basketball team and made it better. During those prewar years—the seasons of 1937 through 1941—Casey's teams ranked never below fourth in a field of thirteen conference schools. They were runner-up three years and conference champion in 1940 with a team that went 14–2 in the conference and 20–4 overall. Standout players included forward Tom Sharples, who took all-conference honors in 1937, right after having been named to the all-conference football eleven the previous fall. Center Glenn "Bodge" Bowles was the conference top scorer with 177 points and was an all-conference pick in 1938. The next year Bowles and Clarence "Cowboy" Cline were among the five top conference scorers as Simpson's team came in second behind a powerful St. Ambrose aggregation.[164] Then came 1940, a season Casey had predicted would be a rebuilding year after losing Bowles and other strong seniors. He hadn't counted on sophomore Wayne Burns or freshman Evo Sjeklocha, who, with Cline, junior Eugene Braught, and sophomore Mike Reed, led the team to the conference championship, the first ever for Simpson. Sjeklocha—no one could pronounce his last name so they just called him "Ee-voh"—and Burns were named to the 1940 all-conference team.[165] And Frank Casey was on top of the world.

Casey was a great basketball coach. He was an even better track coach. He loved track and field, for no other sport, he averred, balanced individual and team efforts more perfectly. He could take a group of young men of above average talent and mold them into star performers. In his very first year at Simpson in 1936, his track team won the first of five consecutive conference championships, slipping only in 1941 to third place behind "Moco" Mercer's Dubuque team and St. Ambrose. Casey had good talent to work with: runners like Claude Alexander, Al Major[166] and Andy Rabuck, pole vaulter Burt Frey, hurdler Bob Moats, Chuck Evans throwing the javelin and William Lounsbury the discus—all conference winners in one or more years. Beginning in 1936 Simpson's mile-relay team won nine consecutive conference victories. For any college, it was an enviable record.

In other sports—baseball, wrestling, golf and tennis—Simpson fielded teams, although many conference schools did not. Some of the Redmen teams were successful, especially those in baseball acquitting themselves very well against nines from colleges large and small.

Women's athletics continued to be exclusively intramural, but they could sometimes release as much energy and excitement as did the men's sports. In late 1941, recognizing the broadening of recreational opportunities for women, the Women's Athletic Association was restructured and renamed the Women's Recreational Association.[167] Just a year earlier Ruth Lautenbach, director of physical education for women, resigned at midyear to accept a position at Oregon State Teachers College at Monmouth. Fortunately, within a fortnight Simpson found a replacement, Alice Elizabeth Roose of Iowa City, who capably filled in for the spring semester of 1940.[168] The following year young Ruth Estelle Fussner, who had earned her B.S. in Education at Miami University in 1937 and her M.A. from New York University, took over women's physical education, but she remained only a year, succeeded in the fall of 1941 by Pauline Stimson, whose experience included four years at Buena Vista College and whose M.A. in health and physical education came from Columbia University. Stimson served three years at Simpson, and under her direction women's athletics thrived.

* * *

Apart from sports and social organizations, students had available for their enjoyment a reasonably rich selection of activities and cultural presentations, not to speak of the traditional events that punctuated the school year, providing a pleasant counterpoint to the fixed pattern of classes. During the Harper and Gross years, Homecoming continued to attract large crowds, its festive ceremonies embellished after 1939 by colorful Indian "royalty"—the princess, brave and "big chief" selected from students and faculty—and the awarding of the tomahawk. Most years the *Messiah* was regular Christmas fare, followed in March by Miniature Orpheum, which was proving to be a running contest of wits between faculty censors bent on excising vulgarities and deliberate indiscretions from the skits and the fraternity boys equally determined to retain them. Usually the fraternities managed to outwit the faculty, and the audiences loved every minute of it.[169] Campus Day continued to be hugely popular, but of course any event that brought the cancellation of classes for a full day was certain to win student approval. Then there was commencement, still an impressive event but one whose character was changing. The days of endless student orations, public examinations and field days were far in the past. John Gross decided to shorten the event to three days, and few complained. Baccalaureate and commencement speakers continued to be chosen with care. We have seen already that George Washington Carver delivered the baccalaureate address in 1941. The next day the commencement speaker was the honorable Alfred M. Landon, the great friend of Indianola publisher Don Berry and 1936 presidential candidate who had been buried in the Roosevelt landslide.

There were dances too. As soon as Earl Harper arrived at Simpson, the ban against on-campus dances was lifted, and within a very short time the annual Beauty Ball, recognizing the most beautiful damsels and handsome swains at Simpson, became the social event of the year. To select the beauty queen and her attendants students turned to some "objective" outside source for judgment. In 1939, for example, the *Simpsonian* announced that the judge that year would be Ronald "Dutch" Reagan, former Des Moines sportscaster who was making good in Hollywood at Warner Brothers.[170]

Because of Simpson's musical tradition, the school year was crowded with concerts and recitals, many of them of remarkably high quality, as were the theater productions. And during these years students could meet and listen to a number of well-known speakers, people like writer Emil Ludwig or America's first female ambassador, Ruth Bryan Owen, daughter of William Jennings Bryan, or philosopher-historian Will Durant, who followed up his visit to Simpson by sending the library a copy of *The Life of Greece*, the first volume of his monumental work on western civilization. Author Lloyd Douglas came in 1939, and Simpson alumna Leota Lane returned in triumph to present a concert late that same year. Simpsonians also could expect each year, around Homecoming time, to hear Fred Waring and his Pennsylvanians sing Tip Olive's "Scalp Song" over the national airwaves, to the joy of all those who didn't mind the bloodthirsty lyrics.

Religious life was healthy, with students reasonably diligent about attending local church services and listening to religious speakers ranging from the "Red" Bishop G. Bromley Oxnam to the missionary-evangelist E. Stanley Jones. Students still did not like compulsory chapel, but they disliked it less after Dr. Harper reduced the number of chapel services to three times per week.[171]

During the prewar years the undergraduate student council came to be seen as less and less representative of natural student constituencies. For example, no longer were students conscious of being, say, a member of the class of '41; rather they tended to identify with their living groups—fraternities, sororities, dormitories or co-op houses. Accordingly, in early 1941, at the suggestion of student body president Jim Angell, students prepared the draft of a new constitution under which the governing body, to be called the "Student Congress," represented primarily living groups, the number of representatives from each dependent on the size of the organization. Presented to the Student Council February 7, the new constitution was accepted in a student referendum two weeks later.[172] When the Student Congress first met on March 20, it counted delegates from Alpha Chi Omega, Alpha Tau Omega, Campus Cottage, Center House, Delta Delta Delta, Independent Men, Kappa Theta Psi, Lambda Chi Alpha, Mary Berry Hall, Off-Campus Coeds, Park Hall, Pi Beta Phi and Theta Upsilon. With minor variations, this form of undergraduate governance continued for many years.

Student behavior was on the whole very good, although once in a while complaints were heard about hazing of freshmen, either in the S Club or out on campus, where self-appointed guardians of tradition enforced the wearing of green freshman caps.[173] Earl Harper tolerated the hazing so long as it didn't get out of hand. At the same time, during his first year at Simpson he issued a new set of social regulations, announcing that (1) permission must be had to join any campus organization, (2) social functions were limited to Friday and Saturday evenings, (3) women's hours were fixed at ten o'clock on weeknights and midnight on weekends, (4) all events were to be scheduled and properly chaperoned, (5) Thursday evenings were reserved for the College prayer meeting and (6) unacceptable improprieties would include immoral conduct, consumption of intoxicating liquor and all rude, ungentlemanly or unladylike conduct.[174] There were, of course, things the regulations did *not* cover, like table manners. The mealtime behavior of the men was reportedly so bad at Mary Berry Hall that "the dining room is in an uproar continually."[175] Sometimes it was almost as bad in chapel, inspiring the faculty to distribute to all students a document entitled "Chapel Etiquette." Suggestion number five captured the spirit of the thing: "If you do not like the hymn, prayer, music or address, that fact is most probably a reflection on you, personally, rather than upon the chapel activity. It follows that it would behoove you to camouflage this inner cultural deficiency by assuming an attentive and appreciative exterior."[176]

* * *

In a survey of 758 of the 834 Simpson graduates of the 1930s, the popular notion that the College produced nothing but teachers and preachers was proved to be untrue, but a substantial forty-two percent did fall into those combined categories (thirty-seven percent in teaching and five percent in Christian service). Teaching and the ministry were conceded to be admirable, indeed noble occupations in the service of mankind, but they were also known to provide their practitioners meager incomes that denied these people surplus funds with which to endow such worthy recipients as their alma mater. Only 11 of the alumni of the thirties were lawyers; 7 were physicians and 8 farmers, but fortunately 111—14 of them women—or fifteen percent were in business. True, of the women, 177 were homemakers, but 190 were either in graduate school or in the work force.[177] It was surmised that a study of earlier graduates would have yielded similar results.

Speaking of earlier graduates, during these prewar years some of them were making names for themselves. Merrill J. Holmes '08, son of past president and professor Edmund Meek Holmes, who in mid-career had devoted twelve years to the education of black people, was now elected vice-president of Illinois Wesleyan University. Hurford Stone '16 was named assistant dean of undergraduate affairs at U.C.L.A., joining stalwarts like Howard Noble and Max Dunn at that university before moving on in 1940 to become vice-president and dean of students at the University of California at Berkeley. And Fred Smith '09 in 1936 left Harvard to become vice-president and dean of deans at the University of Tennessee at Knoxville, just a year after he had received the honorary LL.D. degree from Simpson.[178]

It was good, too, to read about the blazing success of Harriet Henders (Harriet Henderson when she was in her hometown, where she was known as Judge J. H. Henderson's granddaughter) in the opera world. Selected by Arturo Toscanini to sing the lead role in Beethoven's *Fidelio* at the Salzburg Festival, she sang in Europe a number of years before returning to New York to make her debut at the Metropolitan Opera in *Der Rosenkavalier* December 29, 1939.[179] It was also in 1939 that Frank Luther Mott, director of the School of Journalism at the University of Iowa and both a Simpson alumnus and former faculty member, won a Pulitzer Prize for his three-volume work entitled *A History of American Magazines*, published by the Harvard University Press. Indianola's Don Berry, no mean journalist himself, rejoiced in Mott's award. "There is nothing," wrote Berry, "of the popular, cheap sensationalism in Dr. Mott's writings. They have, rather, the charm of better music."[180]

* * *

Although Fred Smith loved to return to Indianola, he made the journey twice with a heavy heart when first his mother and then his father died within months of each other in 1939. The death of his father, William Christie Smith, on October 2 at the age of ninety-three, was not only a deep personal loss for Fred Smith; it took from Simpson a close tie to its earliest days. We remember the elder Smith as a graduate in the class of 1871, the first editor of the *Simpsonian* and a longtime Methodist clergyman. The spry old gentleman—he was the subject of Ripley's "Believe It or Not" when he walked a tightrope at the age of eighty—had outlived nearly all his friends and contemporaries, but continued active and interested in the world around him until the end.[181] John Horsley remembered him as a man "keen of intellect, strong in his convictions about right and wrong and a tireless worker against evil." He might also have mentioned that he possessed a marvelous sense of humor that contributed as much as anything to his long and joyous life.[182]

Harriet Henders, like all Indianolans, mourned the death of her grandfather, Judge John H. Henderson, at his home in Santa Ana, California, September 30, 1940. The Judge had served an astounding seventy years as a member of Simpson's board of trustees, a record never even approached by any other person. For fifty of those years he had been secretary of the board, signing during those years every diploma Simpson awarded, until he turned the position over to his son Frank who in 1940 was still holding the job. The board lost two other members: emeritus trustee E. D. Samson of Des Moines in 1938 and F. Carl Sigler, a remarkably effective trustee for thirty-three years, who died March 31, 1941.[183]

* * *

Except for the time when students permitted a Halloween frolic to turn into a riot, landing forty-three of them in Mayor N. D. Gordon's court, relations between the College undergraduates and the townspeople were good, indeed at times cordial.[184] Gordon, serving his sixth term as mayor, had been having his own problems and was inclined to leave the discipline of college students to the College.[185] For their part, students were pleased to see a number of local improvements. They liked the new Empress Theater (on the site of the old one on the square). Two more developments they noticed could be credited to Roosevelt's New Deal. Lake Ahquabi, a fine recreational state park a few miles south of town, completed by the C.C.C. in the hot summer of 1936, soon became a favorite site for picnics and outings. Three years later when students circled round the square they would find a new courthouse, perhaps not as impressive as the old one, but solid. The old graceful brick and stone courthouse with its fine tower—it had been built by the same Reichard who built College Hall seventy years earlier—had decayed beyond repair. The new building, starkly plain and clad in buff brick, was built by the W.P.A. and looked it, but everyone was grateful that this and other recovery projects had provided jobs for unemployed Iowans. At the dedication of the new building, Dr. Gross was the principal speaker.[186]

Providing jobs for unemployed Iowans could cost Simpson money. When streets adjacent to the college were paved, the tax assessment was staggering, or at least it seemed to be in those days of scarcity. Faculty people were upset because they saw the paving assessments coming out of their meager fractional salaries. As late as 1937 Simpson still owed the city more than $1,500 in delinquent paving taxes. They were paid grudgingly.[187]

Townspeople, overwhelmingly Republicans, were given to animadverting on the indolence and unreliability of youth when they learned that sixty percent of Simpson's students favored Roosevelt's seeking a third presidential term, but praised their intelligence when a campus poll in November 1940 gave Wendell Willkie 207 votes to 119 for F.D.R.[188]

* * *

Preoccupied with their own economic and social problems, Simpson people, not unlike most Americans, became only gradually aware of the threat of war coming out of Europe and Asia in the late thirties. But in time they could not ignore it. The Italian invasion of Ethiopia, the rise of Nazism in Germany—they could listen through the static of the airwaves to the speeches of Adolf Hitler on their radios—and the outbreak of civil war in Spain in 1936 stimulated lively debate in the heartland about America's proper response to momentous world events. In Indianola one could encounter pacifists, isolationists, internationalists and interventionists, and as Europe raced headlong toward war, the tone of the local debate became more strident. Scarcely a month after Hitler's *Anschluss*, the takeover of Austria, Simpson students voted almost unanimously to write to their congressmen to oppose war, even defensive war. The editor of the *Simpsonian*, no interventionist himself, nevertheless took issue with his fellow students. War should be condemned, he said, but a war to protect one's homeland was surely just. Any people, he said, will fight when attacked, and should.[189]

No matter what their views about war, everyone listened to young Alan DuVal, a Simpson senior and prominent Theta Kappa Nu, who spent the entire summer of 1938 studying in Germany. DuVal was the only person for miles around who had seen the Nazis at first hand, and after his return he was much in demand as a speaker. People were captivated by his observations and stories.

Because of the immediacy of DuVal's experiences, Simpson people paid closer attention than they might have otherwise that fall when the Sudeten crisis ensured the collapse of Czechoslovakia and the November horror of *Kristallnacht* signalled the beginning of the end for German Jewry. The Indianola public library even ordered a copy of *Mein Kampf*.[190]

Most students who thought about international affairs were horrified by the prospect of a European conflict that could drag America into the abyss and supported one peace movement or another. The *Simpsonian* announced a special assembly scheduled for Thursday, April 20, 1939, the purpose of which was to support the national Students Protest Against War. And even after war broke out in Europe the following September, a local poll found students overwhelmingly opposed to war, only twenty of them willing to go to war to stop aggression. They were comforted when President Roosevelt proclaimed United States neutrality.

Neutral or not, the whole nation was concerned about preparedness. In the fall of 1939 the Civil Aeronautics Authority selected Simpson as one of many colleges to participate in a student pilot training program. The course of study, Dr. Gross assured a nervous board of trustees, was "in no way related to military organization or military training," an explanation that was not entirely convincing. Included in the training was a four-hour course in the principles of aeronautics and seventy-two hours of ground schooling taught by Simpson's own Professor Carr and fifty hours of flight training by a government-certified pilot at the Des Moines airport.[191] Nine men and one woman completed the entire course of training during the 1939–40 academic year, and thirty-five more enrolled the following year. It was an excellent program, even though many suspected that the tense international situation bore more than a casual relationship to it. It was in any case short-lived, for overcrowding at the Des Moines airport caused its termination in the summer of 1941.[192]

The debacle at Dunkirk and the fall of France in June 1940, leaving Britain and the Commonwealth to face the Axis powers alone, were sobering. Former Simpson president Earl Harper, speaking before a packed audience at the College chapel a few weeks later, warned that "like a juggernaut [Germany] has crushed nation after nation until its driver stands today the undisputed master of continental Europe." America, he cried, must "arm, organize, drill, in a word prepare for war."[193] But in angry response to the international firebrand Harper, Don Berry of the *Record*, the voice of Indianola's isolationists, warned that the United States must not allow itself to be drawn into the maelstrom of Europe's war.[194]

"Fifty-eight Simpson students and seven professors registered for the draft last Wednesday," announced the *Simpsonian* on October 21, 1940. Clearly America was following the course supported by Dr. Harper and other advocates of massive rearmament and vigilant preparedness. Already Simpson could report its first enlistee, Merle Boeck '40, who had joined the Army Air Corps soon after his graduation.[195] Soon more would follow.

If the United States was girding itself for war, editorialized the *Simpsonian* in May 1941, we need more than military superiority over "the bloodthirsty schemer of Germany, the Sphinx of Russia, and the pussy footed Latin Lion. We need ideological superiority, a triumph of the *ideas* of democracy."[196] And the following November, as the massive German invasion of the Soviet Union was beginning to stall and less than a month before Pearl Harbor, seventy-nine percent of Simpson students voted that the U.S. should stay out of the war but supply the Allies. *Simpsonian* editor Frieda Axthelm was livid, accusing her fellow students of immaturity and ignorance of international affairs. "We must wake up!" she wrote. "We must realize that the impending international crisis is vital and cannot be controlled by wishful thinking at this point, but will soon call for action in order to protect our democracy."[197]

In mid-November, while the Iowa Collegiate Peace Association was planning a statewide meeting and oratorical contest scheduled to meet at Simpson December 5, a remarkable speaker appeared on campus, an old friend of Dr. Moats. He was Dr. H. F. McNair, professor of Far Eastern history at the University of Chicago, and he asked Simpson students to turn their attention for a moment away from Hitler's war in Europe and focus on the volatile conflict in Asia. His address was entitled "What Japan Wants in the Far East."[198] Three weeks later the Japanese attacked Pearl Harbor and changed the life of every American.

* * *

Earlier, on May 8, 1941, less than four weeks before George Washington Carver was scheduled to arrive for commencement, John Gross went before the faculty and students in chapel and announced his resignation, explaining that he had accepted the invitation to head the Department of Institutions, General, in the Division of Educational Institutions of the Board of Education of the Methodist Church. His headquarters would be in Nashville, Tennessee. In his new capacity he would supervise the church's interests with the 120 institutions affiliated with the Methodist Church, including 9 universities, 9 theological seminaries and 61 senior colleges like Simpson. The offer from the church had come "entirely unexpectedly," he said. It presented him "an opportunity in . . . Christian education" and marked a distinct advantage for him.[199]

In part Dr. Gross's departure from Simpson was a consequence of the unification in 1939 of three Methodist bodies: the Methodist Episcopal Church, the Methodist Episcopal Church, South, and the Methodist Protestant Church. "A series of events following the unification," reported Gross, "and particularly the death of the late Dr. W. M. Alexander of the Board of Education, like a stream, have carried me into a new setting."[200] He said he would not forget Simpson or its interests. Meanwhile, he promised to remain at Simpson "until a successor is chosen."[201] He almost kept his word.

The Simpsonian

SINCE 1870

VOLUME XXXXII — INDIANOLA, IOWA, MONDAY, NOVEMBER 25, 1940 — NO. 10

A.A.U. REINSTATES SIMPSON

TEACHER'S POWER TOO MUCH FOR REDMEN, 52-7

Subs Count Simpson Marker

Iowa State Teacher's powerhouse proved entirely too much for the Redmen last Saturday as they mauled the vistors by a score of 52-7. It was the last game of the season for both teams.

Averaging two touchdowns a quarter the Tutors simply outran their heavier opponents to pile up a total of 500 yards gained from scrimmage. The Redmen, depending principally upon Byer Farnham, were able to annex only 50 yards through the fast charging Teacher's line.

Touchdown

Two subs accounted for the only Simpson touchdown in the final quarter when John Moore connected with a long pass to Bob Means who outdistanced the opposition secondary to cross the goal. This touchdown play went 70 yards starting on the Simpson 30.

Roy Jessen and "Tiny" Beasley, four-year veterans, saw plenty of action in this their last game for the Red and Gold.

A 10-second dash man, Claude Santee, led the Teacher's attack by personally accounting for four touchdowns.

Vacation Begins Wednesday; Double Cut Rule In Effect

Thanksgiving vacation for Simpson students begins next Wednesday, Nov. 27, at 12:15 o'clock p. m. Classes will be conducted on a shortened schedule Wednesday morning.

It has been announced by the Dean's office that double cuts will be charged against students missing classes either immediately preceding or immediately following the vacation—that is either Wednesday, Nov. 27, or Monday, Dec. 2.

No excuses other than those acceptable for any other class cut will be satisfactory for those two days. Specifically students living at considerable distance from Indianola, will not be given additional vacation time.

SIMPSON TO PRESENT VESPER SERVICE

On December 15, Simpson college will present a Vesper service under the direction of the Music Hall. The Madrigal choir will sing a group of several sacred songs and Christmas melodies. Mr. Reisman is planning to have the orchestra make its second public appearance at this time.

This service is to take the place of the annual presentation of the "Messiah" by the entire Simpson student body.

DEBATE CREIGHTON

Two Simpson debate teams last Thursday met teams representing Creighton University of Omaha, Neb. Representing Simpson were Alice Sayre, Mary Jane McClure, Harley Heerema and Bob Flint.

Both debates were non-decision.

Bulletin Board Rules Established

Because of the large quantity of various types of notices which are placed on the bulletin board in the main entrance of the Administration building, causing the students to ponder unnecessarily long to decipher the main news topics, the student council has taken a step toward organizing the bulletin board system on the Simpson campus.

Don Osborn, chairman, Bob Chenoweth and Eddie Pittman were appointed to draw up some rules and regulations. These rules which will go into effect immediately after Thanksgiving vacation are as follows:

1. All notices should not be larger than 8x10 inches. They should be double-spaced typewritten. Small notices should not have excess margin. At least two tacks should be used to hold the notices in place. For the notices on the outdoor boards at least three tacks should be used.
2. Notices should be dated and signed.
3. Signs for social affairs etc. should be approved by one of the committee.
4. Notices that do not comply with the above rules will be subject to removal.
5. Notices should be removed when they are out of date.
6. Location of Notices: Administration Building—All vital temporary notices are to be placed on the main bulletin board. Administration Building, North Entrance—"Long term" and permanent notices are to be placed on the two boards. Chapel—This bulletin board should contain duplicates of main bulletin board notices which concern the majority of the student body.
7. No notices are to be placed on trees.

Mrs. Overton, Guest of Last Week, Found Simpson Students Not "Puritanish"

Denver . . . Dallas . . . Des Moines—she takes them all in her stride, and speaks offhandly of 60,000 miles of travel by air. This energetic personage is none other than the lecturer and author, Mrs. Grace Sloan Overton, who last week conferred with Simpson college students on youth problems.

Mrs. Overton has an overwhelming fund of knowledge from contact with hundreds of university men and women, and while answering their questions, is constantly adding to her data on youth.

She has traveled extensively and closed a six months' tour of Europe a month before Hitler came into power. "The young people in Russia and Germany have always been led," she said, explaining the support given Hitler by the German youth. Mrs. Overton felt that the so-called radical tendencies of American youth have been grossly over-exaggerated. "The American Youth Congress is not the powerful organization that we have been led to believe. It has only a membership of 3,000 and how can 3,000 young people disrupt an entire country? Our real danger lies in our faulty economic system." Concern was expressed over the two Thanksgiving dates in the United States and she pointed out that in Europe the argument over the dates was regarded as a sign of internal dissension.

Loss of Freedom

Mrs. Overton said when she couldn't make up her mind about the draft question. However, when asked about the loss of freedom through the draft, she emphatically "would rather lose freedom to preserve Democracy than to lose freedom to establish Dictatorship . . . It's worth giving a year to keep Democracy." She did express fear of the demoralizing effects which are to be encountered when 800,000 men enter military training over a five year period.

Turning the conversation to women, Mrs. Overton scoffed at the belief that modern women have lost their femininity. "They haven't lost their femininity. They've just changed type. In fact, I believe they are even more charming than formerly. Clothing has finer and simpler lines and a greater interest is shown in the care of hands and nails."

Admiration

Mrs. Overton did not find the students on the Simpson campus at all "Puritanish" and felt that they brought the same problems to her that were bothering youth all over the country. She expressed admiration for their cooperation and friendliness during her visit.

This week Mrs. Overton will be in Youngstown, Ohio, and then will attend a meeting of Illinois Deans in Chicago. Following this conference she will go to her home Adams, New York, when her nine weeks lecture tour draws to an end this Sunday. If conditions permit, Mrs. Overton will lecture next year in the South American universities.

Coach Speaks at Colo

Coach Casey, at present busy grooming the Redmen for a busy basketball schedule, took time out last week to make a talk at a Colo athletic banquet. Coach's subject was, "Where Are You Going?"

Tomorrow night, Coach makes another talk, this one at a varsity rally in Orient where Frankie Berlin, 1940 Simpson graduate, has just completed a successful football season as coach.

Coach Casey has several further speaking appearances scheduled for after Thanksgiving vacation.

MOVES SCHOOL INTO TOP BRACKET

Suspended Since 1937

President Gross last Thursday received word that Simpson college has been restored to the list of fully accredited colleges by the Association of American Universities. Effect of this reinstatement is that Simpson is moved up into the higher bracket of highest educational accreditation. In Iowa only six other colleges, Coe, Cornell, Drake, Grinnell, Loras and Iowa State have been recognized with a similar distinction. Iowa University is a member of the accrediting association.

To Simpson students this latest achievement means that upon graduation they are eligible to admission to any graduate school in the country. This accreditment also enhances their chances of obtaining teaching fellowships in the universities that are members of this association.

Requirements

The requirements for approval of any college are strict and not emphasis upon the essentials of college education. The opening paragraph of the "Memoranda of Approved Procedure" published by the association reads as follows: "The Association of American Universities is primarily an association of graduate schools. Its reason for having an approved list grows out of its interest in the preparation of students for graduate work. It regards as the chief ground for the inclusion of a college in its approved list evidence that the college is successful in a high degree in stimulating scholarly interest in its students and in preparing them for more advanced scholarly endeavor."

Certain other matters are taken into account in studying the fitness of any college for this recognition. They include: "The character and quality of the student body; the faculty and the conditions under which it works; the administration of the institution; its

Continued on page two

TO MEET CENTRAL

Tomorrow, Tuesday, six Simpson debaters travel to Pella to debate teams of Central University on the national Pi Kappa Delta question: "Resolved, that the nations of the Western Hemisphere should enter into a permanent union." Making the trip will be Frances Heerema, Elizabeth Henderson, Persis George, Alice Sayre, Bob Flint and Harley Heerema.

Freshmen Outscore Creston J. C. 39-23

Twelve Redmen frosh last Friday night served notice to last year's conference championship team veterans that there is going to be a hot scramble for varsity positions on the basketball court this season, by overwhelming a good Creston Junior college quintet 39-23.

Eddie Freese and Harry "Peter" Noblitt, led the attack with plenty of assistance from Roy Jorgenson, Ron McConnelee, Merrill Ewing, Park Jackson, "Buzz" Shanklin, Keith Martin, Jim Vlassis, Bob Rogers, Sumner Morris, and Arnold Nelson.

Orval Double and Roy MacDonald paced the losers.

The College's regaining full accreditation by the Association of American Universities in 1940 rated a headline in the *Simpsonian*.

XIV
Simpson in the Second World War 1941–45

It was President Gross's intention to remain on campus until his successor was chosen. As early as June 1941, a presidential selection committee, led by Bishop J. Ralph Magee, went to work on the matter, examining a number of candidates, most of whom were put forward by a sort of Methodist "old boy" network of prominent clergymen, church bureaucrats and seminary academicians. By the end of the summer, however, the committee was no nearer a decision than it had been in June. Gross decided he could wait no longer before reporting to his new job in Nashville. "Today," reported the *Indianola Record* on August 29, "is Dr. Gross' last official day as Simpson's president."[1] The Grosses departed for their new home in Tennessee the following week, although their elder son George returned within days to Simpson to begin his sophomore year.

Still far from finding the right man, the board named an interim committee to administer the College until the new president's arrival. Chaired by Dean Forrest Brown, it included business manager and treasurer Rae Dean and registrar Clyde Emmons.[2] Everyone hoped the administrative trio would have to preside only a few weeks. It turned out to be months.

Finally the presidential sleuths found their candidate, and not far away, either. He was Edwin Edgar Voigt, pastor of the First Methodist Church in Iowa City and director of the Wesley Foundation serving students at the University of Iowa. After board chairman William Hamilton drove over to Iowa City in the autumn with Frank Henderson and Henry Sampson to meet with Dr. Voigt, they were persuaded that he was by far the strongest candidate for the Simpson presidency and recommended enthusiastically his election. So certain were they of success that they invited Dr. and Mrs. Voigt to come to the campus on December 15, the day the election was scheduled. As expected, the vote was unanimous, whereupon the Voigts were invited in and introduced to the twenty board members present.[3] Although Voigt preferred to wait until the first of March to take up his duties, the board persuaded him to come at the beginning of the second semester. Several months of government by committee, quite apart from the war emergency, made the matter of taking charge urgent.

Voigt was delighted to take over the reins of leadership at Simpson, "an excellent small college with a real place in Iowa." In the face of widespread predictions that the small, church-related liberal arts colleges of America were really a thing of the past, an educational relic whose extinction would be hastened by the war, Voigt asserted that although "I have no blue prints, I have a conviction that the liberal arts college has to survive and make a contribution to American life on the basis of what it does to the moral and spiritual life and the character of the young men and women who go out from its halls." He was confident, but he also expressed concern about the future. At a recent meeting of church dignitaries in Nashville, he recalled, "I came away feeling that as a church we did not have a very definite idea as to what we ought to do in our church colleges."[4]

As a churchman and educator, the new president was eminently qualified to lead Simpson through the war years that lay immediately ahead. He was just under fifty years old, at the height of his powers. Born on a farm in Kankakee County, Illinois, February 13, 1892, he was the son of Theodore G. and Dorothy Kukuck Voigt and grew up in the solid rural and small town Midwest. Soon after he completed his B.A. at Northwestern University, where he had been a preministerial student and member of Beta Theta Pi, he enlisted in the United States Army as a second lieutenant during the First World War. After the war he returned to Northwestern, where he earned an M.A. degree while also teaching classes for a year in Biblical literature at the university and completing his Bachelor of Divinity Degree at Garrett Biblical Institute. That year he married Eleanor Hemsted Dodge, a graduate of Mills College in California. They had two children—Paul Stuart, who was thirteen when the Voigts came to Indianola, and Nancy, twelve. In 1921, while still completing his work for the M.A., Voigt was named Thayer Fellow at the American School of Oriental Research, an impressive appointment for a young scholar. He completed his formal education at Yale, where he earned the Ph.D. in 1924. A Hebrew scholar, his accomplishments in his special field of Biblical literature brought him a faculty position at Garrett, where he taught Old Testament interpretation for eight years before accepting the associate pastor's position at the First Methodist Church of Evanston under Dr. Ernest F. Tittle.

The years in Evanston were productive and pleasant, but Voigt wanted his own church. Accordingly, he found attractive the opportunity to go to Iowa City to be pastor of the First Methodist Church and also director of the Wesley Foundation at the university, permitting him to combine his clerical and academic interests. Iowa City liked Dr. Voigt and he liked Iowa City. The church flourished, and at the Wesley Foundation he was able to serve the religious needs of students in a secular institution. Dr. Harper came to know him, and so did President Virgil M. Hancher, both of whom recommended him to Simpson without qualification.

When he took up his duties at Simpson on January 26, 1942, Voigt was confronted with challenges that demanded immediate action. To be sure, there was no hysteria or panic on campus following the outbreak of war. But the College

Table 8
Enrollment 1941–1953

	Senior	Junior	Soph.	Fresh.	Special	Total	PSM & Spec.*	Total
1941–42	59	77	111	158	2	407	19	426
1942–43	50	61	106	159	0	376	37	413
1943–44	26	20	48	111	4	209	60	269
1944–45	22	26	76	131	5	260	65	325
1945–46	42	53	97	166	7	365	76	441
1946–47	82	91	168	305	7	653	91	744
1947–48	132	139	204	301	5	781	75	856
1948–49	108	148	237	314	8	815	53	868
1949–50	141	138	208	224	15	726	75	801
1950–51	125	117	157	189	9	597	—	597
1951–52	89	79	106	156	10	440	—	440
1952–53	80	66	108	139	6	399	—	399

*Public School Music and Special.

already had suffered a serious drop in enrollment and was forced to make adjustments that could not be postponed.

After five years of relatively stable attendance—ranging between 508 and 579—Simpson's enrollment plummeted to 426 in the fall of 1941, a loss of 124 students from the previous year. (See table 8.) Thirty-one of these could be accounted for by a sharp but not very significant decline in public school music students (from 50 to 19), but the drop of 93 regular liberal arts students (59 men and 34 women) was puzzling. It would be easy to suggest that the nation's rearmament program and the enactment of the first United States peacetime military draft, requiring all men between the ages of twenty and thirty-six to register, kept young male high school graduates out of college, but those factors could not explain why women's enrollment fell by more than twelve percent. Harold Watson believed that it was a matter of instability at the top, "the short, conflicting, tumultuous administrations" of Harper and Gross, submitting the College to four different presidents in the difficult decade that concluded with the end of the Second World War.[5] Whatever lay behind the enrollment problem, Voigt had to wrestle with it from the day he arrived on campus, and it would not go away. During his ten years at Simpson, the college seemed to be on a sort of enrollment roller coaster, with either too few or too many students. The College was controlled by its enrollment, not in control of it.[6]

Simpson's board of trustees, sensitive to the problems of wartime but not equipped to do much about them, was supportive of the administration and the faculty. Board membership through the years had become increasingly secular. Only three of its regular twenty-seven members were clergymen.[7] Local people made up one-third of the board.[8] Six more were residents of Des Moines.[9] Only three were from out of state, and the rest were mostly from small towns in Iowa.[10] In addition to the twenty-seven, six clergymen, including President Voigt, served ex officio.[11] The executive committee was important, those board members who met frequently, who were most familiar with day-to-day events at the College, and hence who wielded the most power. Indianola men all, they were President William T. Hamilton, grocer; Vice-President William Buxton, Jr., bank president; Secretary Frank P. Henderson, attorney; and Treasurer of the College and the board, Rae L. Dean.

Was the management of the College, lodged entirely in Indianola, too provincial? It required Bishop Magee to say what Voigt was thinking: Simpson must go beyond Warren County for its executive committee, recruiting people "able to represent the wider reaches." Don Berry agreed, "You know, this has been in the back of my head for a long time."[12] But a board committee charged with recommending either the replacement or enlargement of the executive committee, recognizing the sensitivity of this issue, did nothing. There the matter rested for another decade.

On the other hand, the idea of enlarging the size of the entire board from twenty-seven to thirty-six, which required amending the College's charter and by-laws, was warmly received and put into effect in 1943.[13] And alongside the increase in numbers came a restatement of administrators' duties and a thorough restructuring of many of the board committees. Some of the clergymen were convinced, for example, that the investments committee, made up only of bankers and businessmen, should be enlarged so as to include clergymen who would represent "the moral interests of the college."[14]

Meanwhile, Dr. Voigt took a close look at the faculty he had inherited from his predecessors. Literally, he went from classroom to classroom, usually unannounced, to see the instructors at work. What he found hardly surprised him. Among the "old guard" he found some of the best teaching anywhere by people whose teaching styles differed as much as the disciplines in which they instructed. J. Allen Baker, still a powerful presence in the lecture hall or in the laboratory, labored with his chemistry students, setting standards barely within their grasp, evaluating their work severely. For those who withstood the rigor of his classes, medical school or graduate study held no terror. Baker's good friend Hiram Doty taught classes that struck no fear in anyone. Inordinately popular, he set modest demands, graded papers generously and gave almost anyone a C grade just for showing up in class. An undomesticated bachelor, he refused to cook for himself, taking his meals over at the Kappa Theta Psi house—he said the food at Mary Berry was not fit to eat—but people guessed he enjoyed the easygoing, rough and tumble camaraderie at the Kappa house, and the food was tolerable. He became a kind of godfather to the KOY boys, many of whom were far more interested in football and girls than in biology, but as the years went on he managed to win over a fair number of youngsters to a serious interest in the sciences. Few faculty could match the number of students Hiram Doty placed in graduate programs in biology or later in geology.

No one accused Francis Moats, once again back in the classroom after retiring as dean in 1939, of lenient treatment of students. Bald and bespectacled, as precise in language as he was correct in behavior, Moats was known to be a great lecturer, a storyteller, a historian who clung to the old-fashioned notion that good history was good narrative. His doctoral dissertation on the history of the Methodists in higher education before 1860 led him to an interest in Simpson's history, an enthusiasm he shared with Ruth Jackson, whose English classes were models of correctness in a way that Harold Watson's were not.

If one were to select Simpson's all-time greatest teacher, Harold Watson would surely rank at or near the top. Among the better students, his classes, always demanding, never boring, were perhaps the most popular on campus. He had the skill to make even English composition interesting, and he consistently assigned himself sections that included the least proficient freshmen. But it was his literature classes that filled every seat in his commodious classroom on the west side of the Administration Building. There is about some of his best-known lectures an aura of legend. It is said that when word got out on campus that he was going to deliver his famous lecture on "The Theme of the Dragon in English Literature," students would crowd into his classroom, the overflow visitors seated on the floor or standing along the walls as they listened spellbound to an urbane, thoughtful, witty, thoroughly entertaining and informative ramble through some of Britain's classics. If anyone was inclined to question the effectiveness of lecturing as a pedagogical technique, he or she had but to sit at the feet of Harold Watson, one of the great practitioners of the art.

Clyde Emmons's teaching was hardly the stuff of legend, but he was a serious, competent mathematician whose classes, like his dreaded five-credit course in differential calculus, had a way of separating academic sheep from goats. Tolerating no nonsense in the classroom, he struggled with a heavy load of classes while performing the duties of registrar of the College. Charles Burrows, an able sociologist, had experienced the same problem as he combined teaching with the office of dean of men until his retirement from the latter in 1940, only to take on the duties of dean of the college in 1943 when the holder of that position was called into military service.

Dr. Voigt would find others whose teaching was exceptionally good. Howard Legg's classes in Bible and religion attracted many students; James Inman, whose classes dealt much with the nuts and bolts of teacher training, helped Simpson produce a large and for the most part competent corps of educators. Roberta Riegel's multilingual talents helped her to succeed with an unremitting schedule requiring her to juggle instruction in three languages. In order to teach all the classes called for in the College's catalog, she was expected to schedule as many as nine courses each semester, a twenty-seven-hour per week teaching obligation. Always kind, sweet-tempered and absolutely unflappable, Dr. Riegel was never heard to complain. In elementary education Nina Brown, starting her twenty-third year of teaching at Simpson—she and Hiram Doty had come the same year—was much loved. Sven Lekberg in music, back on campus to start his second year, had successfully reorganized the Music Department and was prepared to bring the program up to a very high standard.

A few other faculty members, noted President Voigt, were frankly mediocre; a few more were young, able enough but inexperienced. But once he had surveyed the academic scene, he was little short of astonished that Simpson, for all of the vicissitudes it had experienced, was able to benefit from the undiminished vigor of a solid core of dedicated teachers who had demonstrated their loyalty to the College again and again.

* * *

Shorn of its academic pomp, Voigt's inauguration was conducted the morning of May 25, 1942, in austere fashion in services that combined the plain inaugural ceremony with commencement.[15] The new president's eloquent inaugural speech was also the commencement address for the sixty-seven graduates. Responding to the charge intoned by Virgil M. Hancher, president of the University of Iowa, Voigt spoke briefly about his vision of Simpson. "Our college will be judged," he said, "by the kind of citizens it produces and by the kind of life they foster in their respective communities. If they can contribute to the betterment of mankind and the welfare of society, their Alma Mater will have fulfilled its highest function." He saw the church as the ally of the College in "the creation of communities where free men have a right to their freedom because they are wise and disciplined and competent and good."[16] But mostly Voigt directed his remarks to the sober graduating seniors who faced an uncertain, possibly precarious future.

Master of ceremonies at a well-attended luncheon was Frank Luther Mott, who introduced an array of speakers including the governor of Iowa, George A. Wilson, Presidents Charles E. Friley of Iowa State College, Samuel N. Stevens of Grinnell College and Nelson P. Horn of Baker University, all of whom spoke impressively. But the luncheon guests seemed to come alive when student body president Glen Lamb and retiring President John O. Gross welcomed the new president cordially.[17]

That was it. Other commencement week activities, including the crowning of the May queen and the winding of the Maypole, were cancelled.

Indianola people liked the new president. What they saw was a mild-mannered man, soft spoken and gentlemanly, never thrusting himself forward, easy to meet and regarded by nearly everyone as "very human." One student remembered him as a "friendly man, an exceptionally good mixer" with an infectious smile that won a legion of admirers. He was at the same time a "suave diplomat" who ably maintained the dignity of his position.[18] But his genial and sometimes self-effacing behavior masked a powerful internal drive, an aggressiveness that directed his personal and professional life. He knew where he wanted to go and was determined to get there. Simpson was an important step in the journey.

* * *

The morning after Pearl Harbor, *Simpsonian* editor Frieda Axthelm commented soberly that "we have to be realists. . . . All this has come to us as a terrible shock. We didn't think such things could happen in our generation."[19] A few days later the College brought in two high-ranking military officers to talk to a large gathering of students, most of them bewildered by the emergency, not certain what to do, many of them thinking of volunteering in an outburst of patriotism. Urging the students repeatedly to stay in school as long as possible, General Charles H. Grahl reminded them that "obviously, a man who has the most schooling is going to be the most valuable to his country when he is called."[20] Students could surely expect to be deferred until the end of the semester, perhaps longer.

At semester's end in January 1942, a few men dropped out to enter the service, but the College's decline of 43—23 men and 20 women—in enrollment was actually fairly normal for midyear. Still, it was evident that unless the College could attract a military training unit, enrollment would drop severely. To be sure, some of the clergymen opposed any military presence on campus as contradictory to the Christian principles on which Simpson was built. But this was, indeed, a time for realism, and their voices were drowned out in a patriotic, college-saving chorus. A few months later the College received word that it was approved by the Navy for its V-1 officers training program, a four-semester schedule of math, science and language preparatory to officer candidate school, and the Army indicated that such a program might be acceptable for its trainees. "Our course of study," announced Voigt to the board in May, "has been shaped so as to meet the requirements of our armed forces." If Simpson could not attract a military or naval program, the College, said Dr. Voigt, "will have only women and a few 17-year old boys."[21]

Alas, the V-1 program did not materialize at Simpson, and no military unit was secured during the war. Enrollment declined at Simpson as it did in most Iowa colleges. There was a mild drop in 1942–43 to 414—Voigt hoped it would not fall below 400—and a precipitous decline to 269 in 1943–44, then a modest recovery the next year to 325.

Few institutions did obtain military units. Some of the small colleges like Simpson possessed reasonably adequate instructional staff and facilities, but few had sufficient housing for even a fraction of the 400 or more students who would be enrolled in each of the Navy's V-1 or V-12 programs. Dr. Voigt traveled to Washington, D.C., in early 1943 to make one last effort to obtain some kind of a military unit, but there was no hope, and he came home empty handed.[22] The rejection pointed up Simpson's greatest need: housing, both for women and men. The president put the construction of new men's and women's dormitories at the top of his list of imperative campus improvements.

Many young Simpson men, impelled by patriotism, enlisted in one service or another; others transferred to larger universities with military programs, while some simply waited until they were drafted. The big call-up of reserves came in the spring of 1943. By midyear the campus, noted one of them, was beginning to look like a convent.

A number of faculty people reported for military or other public service as well, most of them in the spring of 1943. The first to leave was James Inman, who left in mid-December 1942 to serve for a few months as an instructor at the U.S. War Training School at Des Moines. His wife substituted for him until he returned in the fall of 1943. Dean of the College Forrest Brown was ordered into the Navy as a lieutenant (j.g.), reporting for a training program at New York City preparatory to taking command of a Navy V-12 unit.[23] Appointed to fill in as dean until Brown returned was Charles Burrows. Young Morris S. McKeehan, who had joined the faculty in biology only in the fall of 1942, was commissioned an ensign in the U.S. Naval Reserve in April and departed May 1 for Harvard University for a training program before seeing service in the South Pacific.[24] In mid-April Percy Guyton, who held the William Buxton, Jr., Chair in Economics and Business Administration, accepted a position as assistant state price officer in the Mississippi office of the federal Office of Price Administration at Jackson.[25] Nelda Kurtz, who had been teaching speech and English at Simpson since 1939, accepted an appointment in the Red Cross and was sent overseas. And Dr. Baker, who had taken employment in a war industry during the First World War, followed his patriotic instincts and worked for a summer, then took the entire 1943–44 academic year to teach first in an Army Student Training Program unit at the University of Iowa and later in a military training unit at the State School of Science at Wahpeton, North Dakota.[26] Physical education instructor Pauline Stimson, like Nelda Kurtz, joined the Red Cross in 1944.

For the most part the College made do as nearly as possible without employing new teachers. It was hardly necessary in any case, for enrollment could scarcely justify retaining the faculty that remained on the job.

As Simpson students and graduates answered the call to arms, the greatest number entering the armed forces in 1943, they marched off to Army training camps, Air Corps bases, Navy and Marine training centers and college V-5 and V-12 units; and from there hundreds of them were sent across the country and overseas into battle. In 1944 the *Zenith* managed to gather pictures of 144 of them, 13 of them women, and recorded their exploits in the service of their country: Larry Bounds '43 was a Navy ensign "somewhere in the South Pacific" as was Howard Myers '46 in the Army Signal Corps; Myron Criswell '43 was on LST 243 in the Southwest Pacific; Frieda Axthelm Earl (later Yakish) '42 was a Navy personnel officer in Norfolk, Virginia; Dick Barker '43 was an Army officer flying over the hump from India to China; Charles Abrahams '40 was a flyer "recently transferred to the Marine Air Corps"; Bernard Mick '45 was in Navy V-12 training at Wellesley College; Dick Hillis '41, taken captive by the Germans when his plane was shot down over Tunisia, was a prisoner of war in Stalag Luft III, "where he writes he has been well treated"; Marilyn George '45 was recruiting for the WAVES in Cincinnati; Bob Means '44 flew his first mission as a tail gunner on a B-17 in January 1944 and was "recently reported missing in action"; Leland McGraw '46 was scheduled to receive his ensign's commission in July; Bob Maynard '44 was a gunner with an airborne reconstruction crew in the Pacific; Lucinda Graves '37, a lieutenant in the Army Nurses Corps had moved with the Allied invasions of North Africa and Sicily and was reported to be somewhere in Italy; Warren Simpkins was awarded the Silver Star for gallantry in North Africa; Herschell Abbott '39 was awarded the Distinguished Flying Cross; Kenneth Takehara '46 was in Army intelligence; George Barnett '43 had served in Australia and New Guinea and was known to be somewhere in the South Pacific; Dick Hobbs '48, was serving as a gunner on "one of the newer battleships in the South Pacific."[27]

And this was but a sampling of the admirable war record of Simpson people who never once questioned the necessity or rightness of the cause for which they fought and died. In 1944 three young men were known to have paid the supreme sacrifice. They were Byron Kern '41, a Naval Air Corps flyer, who was missing in action after an airplane accident in November 1943 while on duty in the Caribbean; James Vlassic '44 of Indianola, who was killed in a flight training midair collision in October 1943; and Private First Class Bert Robinson '46, a "red headed freshie" from Boone when he was called up in 1943, who was killed in action in France July 17, 1944.[28] These were but the first reported war dead. The casualty lists grew long as the war reached its climax with the destruction of Hitler's Third Reich and the massive assault on the Japanese Empire. In mid-1945, by the best count the College could make, there were 884 Simpson people in the service—more than ten percent of the total living alumni body of the College—and 18 gold stars on the Simpson service flag hanging in the Student Union. Nine men were missing in action.

* * *

Back on campus in Indianola, the faculty and students—ever fewer of both—went about their appointed tasks. Everyone seemed more serious now, the faculty with their obligation to prepare their charges for an uncertain future, the students with the realization that their changed world demanded of them an accelerated maturing. Anticipating this new spirit of resolution, the faculty in the spring of 1941 adopted a strengthened set of requirements for the Bachelor of Arts degree. It redistributed the fifty-two credit hours of work required in the four divisions—no required course yet existed in the new Division V in music—but more importantly provided much greater specificity within those fifty-two hours, including four to six hours in English literature, four hours in Bible as heretofore, a year course in the Origin and Development of Western Culture, at least eight hours in one or more of the laboratory sciences and three hours in philosophy. In addition the student was to complete a major of at least twenty hours and take a comprehensive examination in that major field of study. These graduation requirements remained unchanged throughout the wartime emergency and were regarded as a decided step forward toward academic excellence.

Yet to Harold Watson's dismay—and that of some others as well—the College seemed to take a step backwards when in 1944 the faculty approved, after a verbal free-for-all a full major in physical education.[29] Watson was never able to reconcile himself either to the expense of the program or to the "academic prostitution" of the "football major" that he regarded the most egregious intrusion of the "inhumanities" ever permitted at Simpson. He was quite certain that illiterate oafs whose only talent lay in their ability to knock the brains out of other oafs on the playing field would be able to go through Simpson as though they were frolicking on a jungle gym.

Watson needn't have worried. What he failed to see, or perhaps found distasteful, was the fact that the greatest stimulus to adopting the major in physical education was the expressed concern of the military services about the sometimes appalling lack of physical fitness among draftees and the need for physical training instructors to remedy the deficiency. No one, after all, denied the value of physical education for America's youngsters, and only with the major could Simpson help to prepare teachers in that field. More significantly, the number of young men choosing the major was relatively few, and most of them were acceptably literate. Yet more significantly, at the same time the faculty adopted a physical education major for women, and not even Harold Watson complained.

Only two new courses were adopted as a consequence of the war. Professor Burrows developed a course called War and Social Welfare and Pauline Stimson started offering work in first aid.[30]

Because some small Iowa high schools did not offer all the courses the military services deemed necessary to prepare youngsters for their training programs, the armed services asked colleges to accept "students who have reached the classification of high school seniors" into course work including English, U.S. history, the laboratory sciences, mathematics and French or German languages, provided these students possessed "a proper level of intellectual, social and emotional maturity" and ranked in the top half of their class. With some reluctance the Simpson faculty approved the program, but no recruiting efforts were made and few high schoolers came.[31]

* * *

A month before John Gross left Simpson, Rae Dean was delighted to announce to board members that because of a healthy enrollment and stringent economies the College's exchequer showed a surplus of nearly $3,000 for the 1940–41 academic year.[32] Perhaps, said one astonished clergyman, the College was entering a new era of financial prosperity. It was a short-lived era, for two months later autumn enrollment slid sickeningly downward, and in December the war changed everything. People were talking once again about retrenchment.

There was no talk of cutting faculty salaries, which were low enough already. But as faculty and staff were called into wartime service, the College hired no replacements, simply spreading the work among the people who remained. To be sure, there were fewer classes, but there were also fewer students.[33] They would make do.

Still there were deficits during each of the war years, in spite of careful control of expenses and management of resources.[34] The endowment was performing well, providing nearly half of the College's annual income. Tuition income was down with enrollment loss, and scholarship awards in proportion to tuition were far higher than any college in Iowa or any of fourteen colleges nationwide with which Simpson chose to compare itself. Simpson's two hundred dollar annual tuition fee was among the lowest in the region.

Unless the College could increase its tuition income, a highly unlikely prospect given wartime enrollments, the only road to solvency was through fund-raising. While launching a fund drive in wartime might seem to be an act of futility, jobs were plentiful and for the first time in many years people had money to spend. President Voigt, convinced that a major campaign would be successful, started laying plans for it as early as the spring of 1942 and received conference approval for it within weeks.[35] They would call it the "Forward Simpson" campaign and go for one million dollars.[36] Bishop J. Ralph Magee gave the effort his "hearty approval," especially when the College retained the services of Dr. J. Wesley Miller, counselor and director of institutional financing with the Methodist Church, reputed to be one of the best fund-raisers in the Wesleyan world.[37]

The following November the nine-month campaign began in earnest. Dr. Miller and his secretary set up an office in North Hall in the administration Building as they set out to solicit 20,000 people—10,000 Simpson alumni and 10,000 members of the Iowa-Des Moines Conference. There really weren't 10,000 Simpson alumni, unless one counted the academy students of old and all the children—now presumably grown—who had taken music lessons at the conservatory, but that seems not to have deterred them.[38]

Don Berry down at the *Record* glowed with approval of the campaign. The College, he said in a long editorial, could have reduced itself to a skeleton organization and hunkered down to await the coming of peace. But "the management of the college has not adopted any such timid, defeatist course. It has not even chosen the middle course of drifting along on the level. It has chosen, thank God, to attack."[39]

Although lack of volunteer workers and gasoline rationing threatened to hobble their efforts, Miller and his people—Frank Henderson headed the Indianola committee—conducted a businesslike solicitation effort. By the end of May they reported having contacted 8,615 people and having received 2,216 pledges in the amount of $114,135. They believed they could complete the campaign by the end of July and would probably raise $150,000, woefully short of the million dollar goal.[40] Warren County had supplied more than $40,000 and could be expected to go to $50,000, but among alumni the campaign was disappointing and among conference Methodists disastrous.[41]

Some said the failure could be explained by Simpson's recent unfortunate blunders in public relations. When Earl Harper had said he would make Simpson the best College in the West, "he had delusions of grandeur." Then John Gross came along and said Simpson was "in a critical plight," so why should one give to a losing cause? Now Simpson comes again with a mixed message of fiscal crisis on the one hand and postwar promises on the other.[42] It was evident, said Voigt, that "we have been hiding our light under a bushel; we have been permitting the uninformed or the malicious to detract from our record of service." Wasn't it true, for example, that since 1936 twenty-one of forty-seven new ministers entering the Iowa-Des Moines Conference were Simpson graduates? Wasn't it true that, in a recently published list of fifty-nine Methodist colleges, Simpson ranked easily in the top third?[43] Perhaps Robert A. McBain '10 said it best in a letter to the president: "Dr. Voigt, it's not a question as to whether or not Simpson has a place in the future, but more a question as to those who direct its affairs being convinced of that fact."[44]

Whatever the causes of the failure of the campaign, one thing should have been clear, but apparently was not. Simpson was playing to the wrong audience. That fact was underscored a year later when the Gardner Cowles Foundation announced a $100,000 gift to Simpson to be used toward the erection of a George Washington Carver Hall of Science in memory of Simpson's most distinguished son, who had died at Tuskegee January 5, 1943. In consideration of the Cowles gift, President Voigt agreed to undertake a special campaign to raise $30,000 to provide equipment for the new building.[45] "We have much confidence in the future of Simpson," said Gardner Cowles, "and we hope this new building will be an inspiration to the alumni and other friends of the college."[46]

In winning the support and confidence of Gardner Cowles, Simpson made a quantum leap forward. A recognized force in Des Moines and the entire Midwest, Cowles had come to Des Moines in 1903 and purchased control of the *Des Moines Register and Leader* with Harvey Ingham as editor. With Cowles and Ingham the *Register* became a newspaper of national prominence. A few years later Cowles bought the *Tribune* and created the Register and Tribune Company. He also published the *Minneapolis Star-Journal* and *Tribune*, as well as *Look* magazine, printed in Des Moines. Beyond this, the Cowles enterprises included radio station KRNT in Des Moines and stations in New York, Jersey City, Boston, Sioux City, Yankton and Washington, D.C.

The Cowles gift, exceeding the total net amount realized from the several-month fund raising drive, buoyed the whole Simpson community. Sven Lekberg, a man not given to emotional frenzy, was inspired to compose a rousing song called "Forward Simpson" to honor the occasion.[47]

Scarcely a month later Dr. Voigt confided to his board confidants that he had received an assurance of $100,000 from an anonymous donor toward a new dormitory, contingent upon the College's raising funds to ensure the completion of the project.[48] And he was happy to note that the Methodist Board of Education sent Simpson $1,000 for "library enrichment," tangible evidence that Dr. Gross continued, as he had promised, to look after the College's interests. The library had earlier been the recipient of a generous gift of $1,000 from William Buxton, Jr., to be used to establish a fine arts book collection.[49]

Construction of the science building and the new dormitories would be possible only as soon as the war-imposed limitation of $5,000 for civilian building projects was lifted.[50] Meanwhile the College could use for current expenses the interest derived from the cash received in the Forward Simpson campaign. It did not eliminate the deficit, but it surely helped.

Because of wartime restrictions no major construction projects were undertaken, but a number of modest improvements were made, several of them really a matter of maintenance too long deferred. Barrows Hall, for example, was terribly run down. It seemed an irony for students to be studying fine arts in a building "where there is scarcely any semblance of beauty."[51] The appearance of the conservatory was considerably improved during the summer of 1943, all of the rooms being refloored, redecorated and painted.[52] A few months later, in a project conceived by Professor Stanley Martin and under the leadership of Naoma Perrin '46 and the Religious Life Council, a fund drive was launched to construct a "Little Chapel" in a small room off the large assembly hall on the second floor of Old Chapel.[53] Over $1,000 was raised on campus, supplemented by a gift from the educational fund of Indianola's Methodist Church. The lovely little sanctuary, with its hand-carved walnut altar, cross and candlesticks, its fine polished pews, its large pulpit Bible given by the Student Congress and Christian flag presented by the Women's Society for Christian Service, was made the more opulent by the red velvet curtain behind the altar, the rich blue carpet and simulated stained glass window. Following its dedication May 23, 1944, by Bishop J. Ralph Magee, attended by a number of faculty, students and townspeople, Kazuo Wesley Mukoyama, the infant son of Simpson alumna Helen Takehara Mukoyama, was baptized by Dr. Burrows, assisted by President Voigt and Bishop Magee.

From the student point of view, the most important construction project was the new student union. The name suggested rather more than the reality—a modest recreational area on the ground floor of Old Chapel—but the students were delighted with what they realized was the promise of things to come. It was a long time coming. As early as 1939 the old student council had a little extra money and conceived the idea of using it as a nest egg for a student union. Nothing much happened, however, until December 1940, when Frieda Axthelm, who was an energetic activist, laid out a plan for a student center and persuaded the student council to part with $100 toward the project. Maybe, she said, it could be combined with the bookstore, now located in Old Chapel. It is "to be a point of attraction for future students, to eliminate commotions in the library, to supply a social center for students—and to furnish light reading material."[54] Students responded enthusiastically, but the administration at first did not, because it was not certain where to find the funds or what to do with the classes that would be displaced in Old Chapel.

The matter was brought to fruition by the unremitting effort of Student Congress president Glen Lamb, who chaired a student committee which went before the full board of trustees in early 1942 to plead for approval of the project. Lamb, a fiercely independent, popular preministerial student, won the day. One trustee later confessed that he and his colleagues supported the scheme "because Glen Lamb was behind it."[55] Work on the project began that spring and continued through the summer. When classes commenced in the autumn, students pitched in to finish the work, painting, scrubbing, bringing in old furniture, putting up curtains and selecting rugs.[56] They installed a fountain and booths from a downtown cafe that had closed. All was in readiness on Homecoming morning, October 25, 1942 when, with fitting ceremony, Professor Percy Guyton, head of the Social Life Committee, presented Dr. Voigt who presented Mrs. Sigler who, in her turn representing the board, handed over the keys to the new union to Student Congress president Byer Farnham. Farnham cut the ribbon and proclaimed the opening to be official. The students soon were calling the snack bar the "Wigwam." This "hangout," provided at minimal cost, did much for student morale. It also turned a profit, which did much for administrative morale.[57]

Although the College could construct no buildings during wartime, nothing prevented making a postwar campus plan. President Voigt proposed to the board in 1943 that they retain an architect to draw up a comprehensive campus plan. He would design several buildings, preferably in a style that would be compatible with the Administration Building. A plan of sorts, said Voigt, was put together while Earl Harper was at Simpson, "but it was done hurriedly." Voigt had learned about a remarkably good planning process undertaken by Dr. Wick Sharp, a Simpson alumnus who was president of Pfeiffer Junior College in North Carolina. Until we have a plan, said Voigt, "we can't even plant a tree in the right place."[58]

That fall the board met and contracted with Odis Clay Poundstone, of Atlanta, Georgia, the architectural firm that had done the admirable Pfeiffer plan.[59] Within days Dr. Voigt received preliminary sketches of a campus plan, calling for the demolition of Science Hall and the erection of a number of new buildings, including two new dormitories, the Carver Science Hall and perhaps a chapel on the site of the old science building, enlargement of the library, construction of a swimming pool on the west side of Hopper Gymnasium and rebuilding of the Pemble house for home economics. Campus landscaping, suggested Poundstone, could begin at once.[60] Because some of the new construction, most likely the two new dormitories, would be built on the existing football field, the College needed land for a new field. Accordingly Rae Dean saw to the purchase of all the land remaining in the block south of Hopper Gymnasium. Cleared and leveled, this full city block and a half would provide ample space for a new football field, comfortably adjacent to Hopper.[61]

Meanwhile the College would have to wait until the end of the war to begin fulfilling its exciting plan.

* * *

By all odds the most constructive action affecting Simpson taken during wartime was the organization in midsummer 1944 of Simpson Guild. Led by Cora Dean and Anna Buxton, twenty women met on July 13 at the home of Daisy Henderson and formally founded the group they had been planning for several months.The guild, said its creators, would aim to bring to Indianola women the intellectual and cultural resources of the College and coordinate the interests of all women working for the welfare and general development of the College. Elected the guild's first president was Eleanor Voigt. "We felt," she said, "that now, with Simpson's future looking so constructive in the light of the Cowles Foundation gift, is a fine time to culminate our plans in a working guild." Elected vice-president was Ruth Schooler Felton '39; Mildred Lekberg would serve as recording secretary; Margaret Watson, at thirty-two already a retired veteran of the Simpson faculty, would be corresponding secretary and Ruth Greenwalt Parsons '35, treasurer. Their first open meeting, to which all women interested in Simpson were cordially invited, followed in October, and the group met quarterly thereafter.[62] Anyone who signed up during the first quarter was listed as a charter member, and by January more than a hundred had paid their membership fees.[63]

It would not be long before the College community would hear from Simpson Guild. Their first "good work" involved an expenditure of two hundred dollars to brighten up the lounge and hallway of aging Mary Berry Hall, the project undertaken at the close of the school year in 1945.[64] And that was but the first of dozens of helpful and timely improvements these loyal and thoroughly practical women made all across the campus. The College would be ever in their debt.

* * *

In the spring of 1945, as the Allies closed in on Hitler's Reich, it seemed the end of the war was in sight. But on the eve of victory in Europe, the nation was stunned by the death of President Franklin D. Roosevelt. In Indianola Don Berry, who for twelve years had attacked Roosevelt and the New Deal with unremitting ferocity as a sort of Christian duty, wrote a tribute to the fallen leader, words perhaps not as eloquent as those of his Kansas colleague, William Allen White, but generous nonetheless: "All must admit that he had the qualities of leadership to a degree attained by few men of this or any other time. . . . He will not be forgotten in history. His personality was too forceful and his career too unique to permit his name to be played low in future appraisals of the events of this century."[65]

As the College shared both the mourning and the euphoria, it seemed that this was a time for endings as well as new beginnings. Clyde Emmons, age sixty-four, a fixture on the faculty since 1910 and a first-rate mathematician who had served more than two decades as Simpson's registrar, asked to be relieved of his administrative duties the first of March and retired from the classroom at the end of the spring semester for reasons of ill health. His associate in the office, Maxine Keyes Kimer '40, stepped in as "acting registrar for the emergency."[66] A few months later Voigt announced the appointment of Edna Dean Miller, a 1930 Simpson graduate, as acting registrar in what turned out to be more than just a temporary position, for she "acted" as registrar for a year and a half.[67] During the war Emmons had been a member of the Warren County Selective Service Board, a responsible and difficult assignment.[68] He had served under seven Simpson presidents, almost as many as his colleague J. Allen Baker.

John Horsley, Simpson's director of public relations and admissions since 1929, resigned in October 1944 to accept employment in the auditing department of the Lockheed Vega Aircraft Company in Burbank, California. He hated to leave Simpson, but the princely salary tendered by Lockheed was an offer he could not refuse. Meanwhile, employed in early 1944 to replace Horsley in both public relations and student recruitment was Ralph E. Whipple, assistant director of public relations at Allegheny College. Whipple, a graduate of Missouri Wesleyan College, held a M.Ed. degree from the University of Missouri. He had served as a school superintendent in Illinois and was director of public relations at Carthage College for a year.[69]

The retirement in the spring of 1945 of Rae L. Dean as Simpson's conscientious treasurer and business manager brought to a close the career of one of the College's most able servants. On the staff since the spring of 1919, the beginning of John Hillman's administration, Dean had superintended the College's finances through good times and bad. Nothing had delighted him more during the darkest years than to be able to effect economies that enabled him to squirrel away enough money to provide a five percent or ten percent bonus to the underpaid faculty and staff. At sixty-five Dean, after twenty-six years of "sterling service to his alma mater" was ready to retire: "I notice I am a little more weary when night comes than I used to be," he said.[70] Dean's place was taken by another Simpson graduate, Wendell Tutt '28, whose successful career in business, launched by an M.B.A. from Harvard, had brought him to managership of the Des Moines office of the Fox Chemical Company.[71] Tutt had joined the College's board of trustees in 1942 and at the time of his appointment as treasurer and business manager was a member of the executive committee.

In addition to these key administrative changes, all of them taking place within a matter of months, several other people left the Simpson scene during the war. Casey Kunkel, after only two years teaching economics and business, earned his C.P.A. in early 1942 and resigned at the end of that same semester to enter business.[72] The man who replaced him, Edward I. Crawford, educated at the University of Washington and the University of Southern California, remained only two years, leaving in 1944 days before the beginning of fall classes to go to Rollins College in Florida. Two years later Simpson librarian Inis Smith resigned to accept a position at William Penn College,[73] whereupon Beryl E. Hoyt, Simpson '36, was asked to return to her alma mater. Hoyt had earned a masters degree in library science at the University of Illinois in 1937, after which she served for three years as librarian at Indiana Central College. She attended Northwestern University for two years, earning the M.A. in 1942 prior to joining the staff of Dakota Wesleyan as librarian, where Simpson found her once again.[74] Another disappointing loss was that of Paul Reisman, who resigned in the summer of 1945 to become head of the violin department at the University of Illinois.[75]

The loss of faculty during the latter years of the war worked no serious problem because enrollments were so low. But the primary reason for faculty attrition was economic; Simpson's salaries were noncompetitive. Although modest increases had been voted by the board in 1942 to compensate for sharply rising prices of everything, salaries remained too low.[76] Voigt realized that if faculty remained underpaid, only mediocre people would stay long. Good people would come for only a few years before moving on. That would mean "broken continuity in the educational program and resultant deterioration in quality." The 1945 salary scale at Simpson started instructors at $1,800 and paid experienced full professors only $3,000, still far below the national average. If compensation levels were not improved, warned Voigt, "I fear that we cannot get quality young men to come here even for a short time." But to remedy the situation would create costs "far above that which we can expect to receive from added tuition." Therefore, increasing the endowment was the only viable solution for the problem.[77] The fact is, however, that tuition had *not* increased in several years and remained among the lowest in Iowa. What is striking is that neither Voigt nor the board seem to have discussed the desirability of increasing tuition or of acting seriously to reduce the inordinate amount of scholarships and grants awarded to students. Yet there were longtime faculty people at Simpson who were fully committed and would remain in spite of poor salaries. What they could see, after all, was that what they were paid in 1945 was an improvement on 1939 levels.

During the 1944–45 academic year an important change was made in faculty organization. In order to make the five instructional divisions of the College more effective, the president and the board, with faculty encouragement, created what they called the "Faculty Council," which included in its membership the president, registrar Emmons, the five division chairmen—Watson, Burrows, Baker, Casey and Lekberg—and the (acting) academic dean, in this case Burrows until Dean Forrest Brown returned from the Navy. In structure this was not much different from the council Earl Harper had created in 1936, but its administrative functions and broad policy-making authority were far greater than those foreseen by Harper, and in the new Faculty Council the president possessed one vote and, at least theoretically, no veto power.

* * *

Only eighteen months after a frail George Washington Carver had delivered the baccalaureate address at Simpson, he died at Tuskegee where he had earned his reputation as one of America's great scientists. Already the United States government had made plans to buy the site of Carver's birthplace in Diamond, Missouri, in the southwest corner of the state.[78] Simpson people were quite aware that for them there was an irony in Carver's passing. They mourned and celebrated a legend, an anomaly in Simpson's history. Unable to count a single black in the student body of the College whose most famous alumnus had been born a slave, they could not but reflect upon the record of a half century during which the rate of progress toward racial justice had been glacial. Some felt a twinge of responsibility, even guilt.

Simpson lost others, perhaps less eminent than Carver, but well remembered. There was classicist Mary O. Hunting, whose death at an advanced age in 1943 at Maywood, Illinois, reminded older alumni of her forceful, almost enjoyable Latin classes.[79] More immediate was the unexpected death of Rachel Page '30, President Voigt's secretary, who died February 17, 1945, of extremely high blood pressure. A service at the chapel February 19, conducted by Dr. Voigt, and a full page dedicated to her memory in the 1945 *Zenith* attested to her popularity. A poem by librarian Beryl Hoyt ended with these lines:

> She walked with beauty in her loving heart,
> And now lives on in beauty's land apart.[80]

To its faculty member of longest standing Simpson said farewell when E. L. Miller died March 1, 1945, after nine years in retirement.[81] Earlier, Simpson people learned that Moy Sing Bo, the spare Chinese whose laundry down on the square had kept clean generations of Simpson students and Indianolans, died in Des Moines at an undetermined age, still plying his trade down to the last tub.[82]

* * *

If one considers the ruinous drop in wartime male enrollment, it is surprising that Simpson was able to field teams in nearly all intercollegiate men's sports throughout the war. As we have seen, between 1941 and 1943 the number of undergraduate men declined only about fifteen or twenty percent, not enough to cripple the athletic program, but in the fall of 1943 three out of four of the men were gone. At its wartime enrollment nadir, Simpson could count only thirty-four male undergraduates in all. Based on such numbers, what Coach Frank Casey was able to do seems little short of heroic.

Simpson managed to put a football team on the field every year, and only Central among its conference rivals was able to do the same.[83] The 1941 and 1942 seasons, in spite of the absence of a military unit on the campus, were relatively normal. The 1941 team went 2–4 in the conference and 3–5–1 overall, not a very impressive showing, but better than the previous season. The bright spot that year was Byer Farnham's fourth place scoring honor in the conference. The 1942 season was better, Simpson's eleven tying for third in the thirteen-school conference with four wins and one loss, scoring 105 points to their opponents' 39. This time Byer Farnham was third in conference scoring, and both he and guard Robert Piffer were named to the all-conference team.

In the fall of 1943, after the big spring military call-up, Simpson enrolled exactly forty-six men. Frank Casey looked at his football prospects and didn't know whether to laugh or cry. He had one returning veteran, sophomore Walter LaFollette, and he was the shortest boy at Simpson. Of nineteen others who could be persuaded to turn out for practice, eleven had never donned a football uniform before. Elwyn Jacobs, from Klemme, Iowa, had never even seen a football game until he came to Simpson, but he was big. He would do. Most of the rest of them weighed in at less than 175 pounds. Freshman Jim Weinman weighed 140; James Hashimoto, fresh from a Japanese-American internment camp, weighed 135 as did Robert Day. Then there was Herman Strom, who tipped the scales at a mere 118. Small wonder the Des Moines newspapers called them "Coach Casey's kindergarten." And before their first game, two of the twenty dropped out.

The eighteen-man squad played four games, two with Central and two with Cornell.[84] Because both of those schools did have Navy units, which permitted their trainees to play college sports, their teams were big and relatively experienced. The Simpson boys played bravely, splitting with Cornell but losing both contests with Central. They would not soon forget their 13–0 Homecoming victory over Cornell, especially the electrifying moment when Donald "Red" Sager ran an interception ninety-three yards for a touchdown, the second of two scores he tallied for the day. His first touchdown came on a pass from freshman Philip Sturm, the boy who that same day got off a breathtaking seventy-five-yard punt.[85]

The three losses that season were predictable, but the "kindergartners" played with courage. "Last Friday night," wrote Dot Schlick in the *Simpsonian*, "Simpson lost a football game to Central of Pella; we lost it by a touchdown and a safety. But we won that game in spirit, a hundred times over." Against a Central squad composed of Navy boys from California and New Jersey and Mississippi, Simpson could be proud of "the spirit that a student minister showed when he was so knocked out he couldn't walk" or "of a boy who will play football with a broken bone in his foot. We are proud of the spirit that makes boys who have never played football before go out to practice and get sore, aching muscles, bruises, sprains, concussions . . . and still think the game is wonderful."[86]

The 1944 season was considerably more wonderful than the one that preceded it. Twenty-four of the sixty-one men on campus went out for football that fall, played six games (two each with Central, Wartburg and Cornell Navy), of which they won three, tied two and lost only one. Of the four conference games Simpson won three and tied one, winning an unofficial conference championship with its all-civilian team. Standouts that year were halfback Jim Hoyman, who caught a pass and ran fifty-five yards for a touchdown against Cornell, together with two freshmen who had never played football before—Bob Williams, whose three touchdown passes won the Homecoming game against Central, one of them set up by Marvel "Marty" Clarke, who ran an intercepted pass to Central's ten-yard line.

Casey's basketball teams, with one exception, did well. His 1942 squad won the conference championship with a 12–2 record and placed two men, center Wayne Burns and guard Mike Reed, on the all-conference team.[87] The 1943 team placed second in the conference behind Luther. Evo Sjeklocha was the league's top scorer with 243 points and Les Deaton was fifth with 173 points. In 1944 things were as bad in basketball as they were in football, with only a handful of men from which to choose. Half the team was made up of football players who were no more experienced in the one sport than they were in the other. Simpson played an eighteen-game schedule—ten in the conference—against such teams as the Iowa Seahawks, the Ottumwa Naval Air Base and conference foes St. Ambrose, Loras and Central, all of which were aided by Navy units. Although the Simpson men won only five of their games, Elwyn Jacobs ranked fifth in conference scoring with 142 points. Casey's team improved sharply in 1945, ranking fourth in the conference, with forward Chuck Kuchan one of the scoring leaders.

Coach Casey's great record in track held up as Simpson took the conference championship in both 1942 and 1943. But in 1944 the coach was able to take only four men to the conference meet at Dubuque, where they took a disappointing fourth place. Loras and Dubuque, with Navy V-12 units, ran away with the meet. In 1945 Simpson was a bit better, but Moco Mercer's Dubuque squad, powered by its Navy V-12 personnel, dominated nearly every event. Simpson's lone blue ribbon was Robert Dykstra's 115' 4" discus throw.

During wartime, Iowa Conference baseball was not sufficiently developed to warrant keeping records. In 1942, for example, Simpson played six games, only one with a conference opponent. It lost twice to Iowa State, but won two against Drake and one each against Parsons and Iowa State Teachers. The 1943 season was something of a repeat: six games with two losses to Iowa State, two victories over Parsons and a split with Iowa State Naval Training. Simpson won half its games in 1944 and in 1945 fared poorly, winning only one game.

Everyone loved Frank Casey and demonstrated their affection in mid-1943 when a hundred people gathered for a surprise recognition dinner at Burkey's club rooms honoring the coach's eight-year career at Simpson. Rae Dean spent half a day compiling Casey's winning statistics, and they were impressive: 135 wins in basketball against 30 losses; seven conference championships in track in eight years with never a dual meet lost; and an even fifty percent win-loss record in baseball. Casey liked the fine wrist watch he was presented, but he liked even more the unstinting support shown by colleagues and townspeople for his teams.[88]

Nor was Mona Casey to be forgotten. Her interest in women's physical education and athletics was evident, and when Pauline Stimson resigned in 1944 to go into Red Cross service, Mona Casey was employed as acting instructor of physical education, a title she would hold for nine years before a future president decided she had been "acting" long enough and made her a full instructor. Women's athletics, under the direction of the physical education faculty and the Women's Recreational Association, continued to be strong, featuring a first-rate intramural program in a number of sports.

* * *

Simpson's four sororities continued to be healthy and active during the war years, attracting an even greater proportion of undergraduate women than before. Each maintained a house; of the four, only Theta Upsilon did not own the building it occupied. Membership of Alpha Chi Omega, Tridelta and Pi Phi was almost equal with between thirty-five and forty women each, while that of Theta Upsilon was considerably smaller. There existed also a strong Independent Women's Organization which in February 1945 merged with the Off Campus Coeds to become what they called the S.I.S. Club, or Strictly Independent Simpsonettes. It would have been difficult to find a more trivial or banal title for an organization; the name alone would have condemned it to an early demise, and in the event seems to have helped.[89]

The fraternities continued a fairly normal existence until the spring of 1943, when very nearly all the men on campus went to war. In the autumn, with virtually no members remaining on campus, all three of them were declared inactive "for the duration." The men were gone, but what was to be done with their houses? Because the Lambda Chi Alpha house was adjacent to the campus, the College took it over and used it as a dormitory for the few men who were in school, agreeing to return it to the Lambda Chis after the war. The matter was more complicated for ATO and Kappa Theta Psi. The ATOs retained their house for some months, in February 1944 entering into a four-month contract with the Indianola Recreational Association for use of the first floor of the building as a recreation center for young people.[90] Within the year, however, the decision was taken to sell the house, for the fraternity planned to erect a fine new house as soon as peace and its members returned. Reluctantly Kappa Theta Psi sold Old Brick—they had been in it since 1908—for there was little use for the house during wartime, and no one had a clue as to how long the war would last. Both fraternities were in any case urged by College officials to locate their chapter houses closer to the campus. Maybe that would be possible after the war.

Meanwhile, as students and faculty adjusted to rationing of everything from sugar to shoes, they learned to make do with less, especially gasoline, which was severely rationed. Those whose employment did not justify more were allocated only two gallons per week with an A coupon book. It took too much gas to go anywhere outside of Indianola, so people learned to stay on campus.

During the latter two years of the war, those young men who were still in school—seventeen-year-olds, preministerial students, and those classified 4-F in the draft (physically unfit for service)—found the campus a male paradise. By the spring of 1944 when women outnumbered men four to one, a man who couldn't find a date on Friday evening was truly to be pitied. Some women took matters into their own hands. The *Simpsonian* noticed, for example, that Marilyn Scheib, a vivacious Tridelta from Perry, "spends hours in the library pondering over the intricacies of philosophy. We wondered why until we found 'Philosophy' wears long pants and a tan jacket."[91] Some of the women did act ingeniously by importing healthy males from other colleges, an act considered by Simpson men to be despicable and probably treasonous. Somehow they all survived.

Traditional campus events continued, albeit in curtailed form. Homecoming was never omitted, even if the football eleven showed little promise. The *Messiah* was not presented in 1943 and 1944 for lack of tenors and basses. Miniature Orpheum was mostly a women's show, with the faculty pitching in to make up for the loss of fraternity skits. Everyone remarked that even Bishop Magee would find the skits wholesome, their language worthy of Campfire Girls. Beauty Ball was dutifully scheduled, but the crowds were not as big as usual. Campus Day was less fun because there were fewer picnics because there were fewer boys. Baccalaureate and commencement were compressed into one day in order to save everyone's precious gasoline ration.

After the spring of 1942, when Cornelia Otis Skinner appeared on campus, speakers and special programs were scarce, victims of travel restrictions and budgetary constraints. But the few that did come to campus were well attended. Andre Maurois, the brilliant French author, was the best in 1944. The next year witnessed the celebrated Dr. Ernest Tittle at Religious Emphasis Week, WHO radio war correspondent Jack Shelley speaking in chapel, and Dean William J. Faulkner of Fisk University, a leader in the movement for racial justice, in vespers one evening.

In the 1943–44 school year Simpson enrolled six Japanese-American students. Most of them were like Jimmy Hashimoto of El Monte, California, whom we have already encountered on the football team and who had spent a year and a half at Camp Manzanar, the huge Japanese relocation center for ten thousand Niseis in the central California desert. Later he had worked eight-hour days for sixteen dollars a month in the beet fields of Idaho. He was happy to enroll at Simpson, taking a full schedule of classes while working part-time at Mary Berry Hall. Simpson was happy to have him, and the others.[92] To their friends back in the western relocation camp, they wrote in 1944: "We certainly welcome the change from those two years of hostile and rugged camp life . . . to the happy circumstances in which we now find ourselves." Having gone from deprivation into freedom, they had found themselves: "You do not know how wonderful it is to be accepted into a community again without any regard to our ancestral background. Here at Simpson College, through our daily associations, we have found everything that is American in spirit."[93]

Simpson also provided assistance to a number of Latin American students, five from Panama and one from Cuba. The Panamanian students held scholarships from their own government in cooperation with Simpson. They were the first of a considerable number of Panamanians who would study at Simpson during the following decades.[94]

* * *

The defeat of the Germans in May 1945 permitted the United States and the Allies to bring their overwhelming might against Japan, the Soviets promising to join the battle as soon as they could transfer forces from west to east. At commencement that year baccalaureate speaker Dr. Fletcher Homan and commencement speaker Dr. Avery O. Craven, both distinguished Simpson alumni, delivered addresses full of hope. And by the time classes opened in the fall, Hiroshima and Nagasaki, heralding a new age of nuclear power, had helped to bring the war against Japan to a swift and decisive conclusion. Amidst all the euphoria of victory, as everyone looked forward to the uncertain future, Simpson's leaders asked two important questions about their own future: With the war's end, would the veterans returning to college come to Simpson? Where in the world will we put them if they do?

XV
Simpson's Postwar Boom 1945–50

The war veterans came, and in large numbers. Some of them would have returned to college in any case, but their number was profoundly increased by the generosity of the federal government. Anticipating the war's end, President Franklin D. Roosevelt had signed into law in June 1944 the Serviceman's Readjustment Act, soon referred to as the "GI Bill of Rights," providing generous educational benefits to men and women who had completed as little as ninety days of service in the armed forces. It was a way of extending the thanks of a grateful nation to all those whose young lives had been interrupted by the war. It proved to be a popular and therefore expensive benefit, but never in the history of the American republic was money more wisely spent as an investment in the nation's future. Millions of men and women would most likely have been unable to afford the cost of higher education had it not been for the GI Bill.

But would the GIs come to Simpson, either those whose educations had been suspended or those who would enter college for the first time? The conventional wisdom at the time predicted that few would elect to enter the "fresh water colleges out at the crossroads of rural America"; rather they would flock to the big universities, especially those whose comprehensive offerings included practical business and professional programs that would most certainly ensure employment in the workplace. The Simpsons of America would choke on the dust of those running past them.

As is so often the case with prophecy in American education, the prophets were wrong. The GIs went everywhere, and a fair number of them chose to reenter the colleges they had left behind. Simpson soon realized that it had better brace itself for what—on small-college terms—could be a student onslaught. Almost overnight, President Voigt and his faculty were forced to shift their concern and attention from how to manage war-induced austerity to facing the challenge of burgeoning enrollments. In the fall of 1945 classes began on September 13, only eleven days after the Japanese signed the formal document of surrender ending the war, but already there was a noticeable, and gratifying, increase in enrollment. Women's enrollment held steady while the number of men increased from 53 the previous spring to 97. Total enrollment was still a dismal 276, but the days were full of promise.[1] And they were not long in coming. The second semester, which commenced January 21, 1946, saw men's undergraduate enrollment increase to 151, and the number of women even increased by 9 to 188, making a total of 339. It was hardly an onslaught, but it was a beginning.

The fall of 1946, it happened. All over America the GIs virtually stormed the nation's colleges, and Simpson, like its sister institutions, found itself delightfully, frustratingly overrun. Male enrollment soared to 367 and female numbers rose to 225. In precisely one year the College's enrollment had more than doubled. Now the question was how to instruct and see to the housing and feeding and recreational activities of what looked like a horde. To be sure, after years of enrollment drought, it looked ever so much like a golden horde.

* * *

Few changes and no additions to the teaching staff had been needed in the fall of 1945, for enrollment had not justified any, but within a year the pressure to find new faculty was intense, as colleges the country over scrambled to find the best people available. Fortunately, Voigt and the board had anticipated the 1946 enrollment increase by hiring a number of new faculty people to teach the courses needed, especially in freshman and sophomore classes.[2] On the whole the new faculty members were young and inexperienced; some were found to be less able than their credentials would suggest, but a few were exceptionally good and proved to be valuable additions to the staff.

In the fall of 1946 returning students were astonished to find relatively few faculty on hand from the previous year. Only seventeen of last year's twenty-six were among the thirty-six full-time people on the teaching staff. And of the twenty new people only one appointment was to a full professorship. Replacing retiring James H. Inman[3] in education was Glaydon Robbins, asked to serve as chairman of Division IV and head of the College's educational placement bureau. Robbins had done all his academic work at the University of Minnesota. Although he did not yet hold a doctorate, he had served as a school principal and as superintendent of schools in Stillwater, Minnesota, and had been assistant director of the University of Minnesota's model high school. When Howard Legg in religion retired and went off to California to live,[4] Dr. Voigt appointed to that position Livingston N. Witten, a young Missouri preacher who had been educated at Central College at Fayette, Missouri, had earned his B.D. at Southern Methodist University, and had completed a considerable amount of graduate study at the University of Chicago.

By all odds the most troubling faculty loss in the fall of 1946 was the resignation in sociology of Charles Burrows, who had been serving as acting dean during Forrest Brown's absence in the Navy. When Brown returned to the campus at the beginning of the spring semester in 1946, Burrows was granted a leave of absence—by no means his first one—to teach sociology at Trinity University in San Antonio, Texas. He liked Texas and the next summer severed his connection with Simpson after twenty-three years to remain at Trinity. Dr. Voigt decided that permitting faculty to take leaves of absence to teach elsewhere was probably not a very good idea.[5]

In business administration Robert Samson, fresh from more than two years in the Navy, returned to Simpson to head the department.[6] To assist him, the president appointed Chester Morgan, a high school principal who had taught several years in economics and accounting at Mount Pleasant High School. Both Samson and Morgan held the rank of associate professor. Other appointments at the assistant professor level included elderly Grover Hawk in biology, young, scholarly Robert W. Twyman in history, an earnest young Korean by the name of Kwang-Won Kim in Bible and religion, Gerard Schultz in sociology, and Ethel D. Anderson in home economics. The latter two of these would come to be widely known among College people and the Warren County citizenry, Schultz because of a series of important sociological surveys in Indianola and his coauthoring the history of the county with publisher Don Berry, and Ethel D. Anderson because she brought stability and distinction to Simpson's program in home economics. "Ethel D" became something of an institution of her own right during her fifteen years at Simpson, for she extended the meaning and effect of home economics far beyond its customary limits. Believing that what the College's students and faculty, indeed the whole community, needed was proper social education, she set forth to provide the rudiments of civilized living that Emily Post, not to speak of Matthew Simpson, would have admired. Genteel etiquette was not only taught; it was practiced, or she would know the reason why. So powerful was the force of her personality that her well-planned, suitably staged receptions, teas, dinners and even simulated wedding ceremonies induced well-nigh model behavior, at least in her presence, in everyone on campus from young football toughs to aging faculty curmudgeons.

Of the nine appointments made that fall of 1946 at the instructor level, one was truly memorable. Elizabeth White, a Simpson graduate in the class of 1931, taught English and speech for the next fourteen years, serving additionally as dean of women for the decade between 1950 and 1960. A talented woman of charm and wit, she contributed to the life of the College in a measure far beyond the requirements of her teaching responsibilities or her administrative office.[7]

During the next three years, when the crush of students was most acute, the faculty—or much of it, at least—seemed to be in a state of constant change as people, uprooted by the war and appearing to be constantly on their way to something else, came and went with bewildering rapidity. Of eighteen new appointments in the fall of 1947, only four lasted longer than four years, most of them only one or two. Among those new people who remained for a long term was Myron L. Sorden, whose M.A. from the University of Iowa was complemented by work with government agencies. "Mike" did yeoman service in accounting for twenty-nine years and built an enviable record of placing Simpson graduates in some of the nation's leading accounting firms. He was known to comment with a sigh that the entering salaries of last spring's graduating seniors were higher than those being paid to Simpson's veteran professors.

Stuart Peterson, a 1934 Simpson graduate who returned with a Ph.D. from the University of Iowa, taught psychology, chaired several academic divisions and functioned ably in guidance and personnel services until his untimely death in 1961. In music Ben Vandervelde, an extraordinary violinist, whose favorite pastime was hunting pheasants or rabbits in Warren County's fields and woods, remained for twelve years until lured away by a college in South Dakota, where the hunting was said to be even better. Then there was irrepressible R. G. "Hap" Miller, the Keokuk High School football coach and former mentor at Indianola

High School, whose eleven-year tenure as instructor in physical education and forceful football coaching were memorable.[8] Of the others, Beulah Altman, the rather dignified maiden lady whose B.A. dated from 1905, taught French, stayed until 1951 and would probably have remained at Simpson a few years longer had not her position been terminated due to the enrollment slump that came after 1950. Some of the new faculty were bright young people on their way up, like historians Delber McKee or L. Gene Lavengood, who would later become a formidable presence at Northwestern University.[9] John H. Cooper came in physical education and remained three years.

No one would forget Nina Hohanshelt Brown, who retired in 1947 after twenty-eight years of teaching in the academy and College education classes. She was a member of Simpson's remarkable class of 1903 and had joined the faculty in 1919, the year Hiram Doty came to Indianola. President Voigt said of her, "Simpson College has never had a more loyal and faithful member of the staff than Nina Brown."[10] She was replaced by a Kentuckian named Uberto Price, a man with college teaching experience in North Carolina and Kentucky.

New appointments in 1948, the year the College's enrollment hit a postwar peak, were actually relatively few. Of six new people that year, one, Clifford Lott, who shared his time between teaching Bible and serving as director of religious activities, remained on the staff for eight years. All the rest enjoyed relatively brief stays at Simpson.[11] The next year, owing to a number of resignations, the turnover was greater. Nine new people came, three of them in new positions and six as replacements. Veteran professor Hiram Doty, evoking the tradition of John L. Tilton, revived the Department of Geology, which created an opening in biology. Charles W. Kern accepted the new position but stayed only a year, at which time he was succeeded by an extremely able young man, an Army Air Corps veteran named David Mobberley, part biologist and part philosopher, one of the most perceptive and stimulating teachers of science ever to grace the Simpson faculty. Paul A. Merkle joined the chemistry faculty in 1949 and continued seven years, but Dorothy E. Gill, who came to assist Ethel D. Anderson in home economics, stayed only one year. And the College had a stroke of good luck when Leslie Bechter came to Simpson in 1949, replacing Virginia Frank. During his fifteen year tenure he taught English and served as registrar for a number of years, dean of academic affairs for one year and dean of men for three. John D. Potter replaced Herbert Markle in business administration and stayed on for seven years, while Robert C. Farb took Gene Lavengood's place and remained for six, resigning in 1955 to study for the ministry. In physics, when Roy L. Horn resigned, Alvin L. Lugn, Jr., took his place and remained three years, while Henry M. Furst who succeeded Glaydon Robbins in education, stayed only one. Furst's successor in the fall of 1950 was plainspoken, forthright John E. Dahl, whose tenure at Simpson constituted an eleven-year demonstration of how an old-fashioned schoolmaster could make his charges toe the line. In mathematics Ervan S. Dornbos replaced Victor Gunn, the first of a long line of short-term mathematicians. Simpson had been spoiled by thirty-five years of Clyde Emmons. Now good mathematicians, ones who could communicate their sometimes arcane science to students in whom things like calculus induced terror, continued to be exceedingly hard to find.

If you are exhausted by this long account of the comings and goings of Simpson's faculty, indeed an iteration of names as wearisome as the begats of Holy

Writ, then I have succeeded in conveying the instability, the frustrating task of maintaining a curriculum with its many majors with numbers of new people who provided welcome freshness but little continuity. Moreover, as late as 1949 there were only six Ph.D.s on the entire faculty, testifying to the difficulty of finding an experienced, well-educated teaching staff.

This unsettled state of affairs, nonetheless, was more apparent than real, for although literally dozens of teachers, young and old, passed quickly through Simpson's halls, there was at the heart of the faculty a corps of stalwarts, Harold Watson's "old guard," who managed rather adroitly to provide the College a sense of direction, indeed of mission. For it was people like Moats, Doty, Baker, Riegel, Watson, Ruth Jackson and Frank Casey, all of them unreservedly committed to Simpson through years of service in good times and bad, who provided the College its rudder in stormy weather. One is tempted to ask if Simpson deserved them, but then of course they *were* Simpson.

* * *

These longtime faculty members not only went about their appointed tasks in the classroom or the laboratory or on the playing field; they also gave unstinting support to the administrators who were wrestling with uncommonly difficult financial and logistical problems, all of them running to keep up with a world that seemed to be racing out of control. President Voigt was as genuinely popular among those who worked with him on the campus as he was among townspeople and alumni. Few presidents of Simpson have been regarded with such affection. And fortunately for him, Wendell Tutt, his quietly competent treasurer and business manager, who was proving himself a worthy successor to Rae Dean, stayed at his side throughout his presidency. "Wendell always knew where we kept everything," recalled Voigt years later, "and he seemed always to be able to find a way to dig up money to pay for things when the rest of us despaired."[12]

In July 1947 seventy-four faculty and staff members attended a picnic to bid farewell to Dean Forrest Brown, who was departing to accept a deanship at Fresno State College in California. He had stayed on at Simpson only three semesters after his Navy discharge. New deans were hard to find, but Voigt had, as he put it, more luck than he deserved when he found Oliver H. Bimson, a highly recommended man in mid-career who enjoyed a fine reputation in professional education. Bimson had served as superintendent of schools in Lincoln, Nebraska, had worked more recently for the United States Office of Education as chief of the division of surplus property utilization for Nebraska and Wyoming, and was a widely-known and respected officer of the National Education Association. A graduate of Nebraska Wesleyan, he had completed his doctorate at the University of Nebraska. In his fifties, Bimson was a gentlemanly, deliberate, sober, soft-spoken administrator who knew how to cut through a problem to make a sound decision. He was also known to be a devout Methodist and militant Rotarian whose well-ordered life evoked admiration among Simpson faculty and students alike. He spent the rest of his career as Simpson's dean.

Some of the administrative positions were far less stable than the academic deanship. When, for example, Ruth Jackson asked to return to full-time teaching, the president had difficulty finding a dean of women who would take on that not altogether attractive position for any length of time. First he employed Edna Caroline Miller, who agreed reluctantly to combine the deanship with teaching in education, but she resigned at the end of the 1947–48 academic year because of ill health. Her successor was Emily Philpott, who had served three years as an officer in the WAVES—Voigt guessed she understood something about discipline—and who stayed on at Simpson only two years. In 1950 he had better luck when Elizabeth White, who knew Simpson if anyone did, accepted the position on condition that she be permitted to continue teaching in English and speech. Continuity in the registrar's office or in the office of public relations was poor and turnover rapid—four people in each position during the eight years after the end of the war. It was far better in the library, where Beryl Hoyt remained reassuringly at her post.

* * *

Although their number was barely adequate to provide the number of classes required in the curriculum, the faculty strove valiantly to do a difficult job well, and for the most part they succeeded. Working in their favor was the stability of the curriculum. During the fourteen years between 1940 and 1954 there were no substantial changes in the requirements for any of Simpson's three degree programs. While there may well have been some doubt as to whether Simpson's unvarying curriculum represented stability or ossification, it was at least reassuring to most that *something* remained stable in a world being transformed.

Even comprehensive exams survived, in spite of a student petition submitted nearly every year to abolish them. When no petition was forthcoming in 1948, *Simpsonian* editor Harold Hall, who counted himself among the minority favoring comprehensives, observed that "last year's crusade died out before it really got started. . . . If a person can't pass a comprehensive examination, he has been carrying on a good bluff about long enough."[13]

If the faculty and curriculum, including comprehensives, did meet the challenge, housing most certainly did not. "Our housing accommodations," said Dr. Voigt, "make us blush with embarrassment."[14] The College's single proper dormitory, Mary Berry Hall, housed only fifty-five women. College-owned Park Hall, a converted private house serving as a cooperative residence for women, housed a few, but the building had seen better days. There was virtually no on-campus housing for men at all. Although Simpson's 1946–47 catalog stated that "the college provides three good resident dormitories on or immediately adjacent to the campus," all three were old residences holding a small number of men each in something less than regal accommodations. To call them "good" was to invent a new level of euphemism. Really, the only adequate men's housing was in the Lambda Chi Alpha fraternity house with accommodations for thirty-two. Toward the end of the war both the ATOs and the KOYs had sold their unoccupied houses and were now looking for something to rent.

Too long the College had relied on the fraternities and the good citizens of Indianola to house its male students. Now only one fraternity house remained—the College had used it as an independent men's residence hall during the war—and it was difficult to find private accommodations for men in town. Women's housing was better, especially when one includes the four sorority houses. But the College's continuing conscientiousness about acting *in loco parentis* required that most of the women be lodged in College-supervised housing, and there was not enough of it.

During the 1945–46 academic year, as men's enrollment began to climb, business manager Wendell Tutt surveyed the availability of housing in Indianola. He could find only about a dozen rooms in private homes for single men and no apartments at all for married veterans. The problem was hardly unique, for all across America colleges were scrambling to find accommodations for their expanding enrollments. But the problem *was* unique in Simpson's history, for never before had more than a handful of married students enrolled at any one time. Now the College was confronted with the immediate need of housing not only for single men, but especially apartments for married veterans who wanted to bring their wives and children with them to school. In those days, Indianola, like most small towns in the Midwest, boasted few apartments of any sort.

Just when the search seemed hopeless, Tutt learned that the Federal Housing Authority was making available to colleges surplus buildings—either barracks-style dormitories for single men or apartment-style units for family housing—from war centers around the country. Such war surplus buildings seemed to be exactly what Simpson needed for temporary housing, so Tutt made application for units that would accommodate a total of 100 single men and 50 married veterans and their families.[15] If approved, the buildings would be moved by the government to Indianola and erected on or adjacent to the campus. The College had to decide—and quickly—where to locate the buildings, and finding labor to put them up would be a problem.[16] Meanwhile the College fitted out Campus House, a big white house on the southeast corner of the campus, for single men; next door to the north—they called it Campus House Number Two—they created two apartments for married veterans; and at 400 West Ashland three apartments were carved out of a large College-owned family dwelling. More help came when the purchaser of the Kappa's "Old Brick" housed twelve men there.[17]

Soon enough Tutt received word that Simpson was approved by the F.H.A. and allotted five wooden "panelized buildings" containing twenty family housing units, the first of a number of such buildings Simpson received in the next months. To make room for the first family units, two houses on D Street were sold and moved off an area southwest of Hopper Gymnasium.[18] The land was graded and the units installed during the summer of 1946, and the first families moved into Hopper Terrace on September 29.[19] Meanwhile, in May the F.H.A. authorized three buildings providing units for eight more married couples and sixteen single men, wooden army barracks from the prisoner-of-war camp in Clarinda, and two months later provided yet three more. Five of these buildings were placed north of Science Hall—it was called Tilton Court—and one for single men down on the south edge of the campus on Clinton Street.[20] By the end of October all the units were occupied, to the delight of the students and the relief of the administration.[21]

The barracks were a godsend, especially after enrollments of veterans, both married and single, skyrocketed in the fall of 1946. Though crowded and sometimes drafty, these less-than-ideal accommodations, painted gray or institutional green, filled a fair part of the housing gap until permanent residence halls could be built and the crush of returning veterans abated. Because the barracks were all serviced by city utilities and enjoyed fire and police protection, the College undertook on its own volition to pay an annual sum in lieu of taxes, a "contribution to local governments," a good-will gesture to Warren County and the city of Indianola.[22]

Married students paid twenty-eight dollars a month plus gas and electricity for an apartment, single students the same rate that prevailed in Mary Berry Hall. These costs, together with tuition fees, fell within the allotment the veterans received under the GI Bill. And good news for Wendell Tutt: the barracks housing turned a profit.[23] Yet better news was the government's decision in 1948 to permit Simpson to acquire complete ownership and control of the barracks without cost to the College.[24]

The barracks helped immensely, but during the period of the GI invasion there were never enough of them, especially for the married students. Some of the veterans, discouraged, either went elsewhere or waited for the scarce accommodations, but former Sergeant Roland Horn of Pleasantville conceived a unique solution to the problem. When told that he would have to provide his own housing for himself and his wife when he enrolled at Simpson in the fall of 1946, Horn transported his house from Pleasantville to Indianola and put it down onto a makeshift foundation at Vanderpool's cabin court on North Jefferson.[25]

* * *

No one expected the barracks housing to do anything more than tide the College over until it could erect permanent housing. As we have already noted, the Forward Movement campaign had listed as top priorities both a women's and men's dormitory, and as soon as the war was over College officials were talking about what to build, where to build it, and when to start construction. Soon enough, however, two major obstacles appeared: construction costs, like the price of almost everything in postwar America, already up thirty to thirty-five percent, were spiraling upward, and building materials were still scarce. Nevertheless, plans could be made in order to be able to move ahead as early as possible. "While temporary housing for students is important," said Tutt, "we have not forgotten the need for permanent housing."[26]

Accordingly, at the same time the College applied for F.H.A. barracks housing, it invited Odis C. Poundstone and his associate to come up from Atlanta, bring his preliminary residence hall plans and have a talk. When the architect—his firm was called Poundstone, Ayers and Goodwin—arrived January 15 with drawings for two dormitories, board members liked what they saw and asked Poundstone to design also a commons building with a dining hall, together with the Carver Science Hall and the Sigler Home Economics Building as well. The courtly Georgian agreed to their request and went to work.[27] Altogether it was a huge building program, and Simpson was in a race against an economic inflationary spiral. Poundstone, with unaccustomed enterprise, said he would hurry.

He did not have to hurry much, because Poundstone soon divined that the Simpson people were not really clear what they wanted, and it was evident that although the College had raised a substantial sum of money, construction costs were increasing faster than money to pay for them could be collected. Meanwhile, said Dr. Voigt, "the college is losing more by the lack of proper dormitory facilities than it can possibly save by awaiting lower building costs."[28]

A year went by before Poundstone presented his drawings to the board, locating the two dormitories and student union on the existing athletic field on the north side of the campus. To his dismay, he found that "some [board members] were not in complete agreement with the architect's recommendations," for they opposed the athletic field site.[29] A month later they were telling themselves that "they *must* make a decision on the location of buildings with Mr.

Poundstone."[30] In May the architect presented an alternate plan that would place the buildings on land to be purchased east of Buxton Street, whereupon the board "approved Mr. Poundstone's plan with the exception of a definite location for the athletic field," leaving Mr. Poundstone the most perplexed, frustrated Georgian in Iowa.[31] After another year went by he expressed his consternation in a letter to President Voigt, pointing out that "this matter has been up, and presumably settled, so many times that I feel somewhat embarrassed about going through the discussion again." It was his view that it was simply wrong to move the site of the proposed buildings "just to save a totally inadequate athletic field."[32] There is little doubt that the acrimonious debate on locating the dormitory complex was exceedingly harmful, for every month of delay portended increasing construction costs.

Finally it was agreed to build the dormitories on the old athletic field, the decision no doubt prompted by a gift of $10,000 from LeRoy Neal Neff of Madrid, Iowa, to help construct a new football field south of Hopper Gymnasium.[33] When Poundstone's drawings were accordingly sent out for bids in May, board members were stunned when the lowest bid for two buildings was over $600,000; for one building (the women's dormitory) the bid was a disheartening $327,500. The figures seemed astronomical. Two buildings were out of the question. They would be able to build only the women's dormitory, and even that only after they had negotiated a fixed fee contract with Wildes Construction Company of Waterloo in the amount of $297,941 (later raised to an even $300,000).[34] The College met the cost with $181,000 available funds in hand or in pledges and $119,000 from endowment funds.

The new women's dormitory was the first major construction project at Simpson in twenty-nine years. An attractive brick "collegiate gothic" style building with a high pitched slate roof, it would hold sixty-eight women, and its unfinished third floor would accommodate twenty-five more when completed. Its appearance, in keeping with the Administration Building across campus, was indeed impressive. All of Poundstone's planned Simpson buildings were of identical style, what one critic labeled "Cornfield Gothic." No one was ever heard to call them daring.

Construction of the women's dormitory required more than a year, but it was remarkably well done. Women first moved into the building October 6, 1949.[35] Meanwhile the men holed up in the temporary barracks or in relatively cramped quarters in college-owned independent residences or fraternity houses.

The problem of men's housing proved to be more obdurate than women's, and it was men who abounded. On the face of it, it would seem to have made more sense to build a dormitory for men than for women, but three considerations led the board to determine that if they could not do both, they would favor new housing for women. First, the barracks did relieve the worst pressure for men's accommodations. They were certainly adequate for returning vets, whose views on housekeeping might be cavalier but who could be expected to enjoy the camaraderie afforded in these primitive digs. Women, quite frankly, needed something nicer. Further, the College continued to be protective of the young women entrusted to its care, insisting that all unmarried women who did not reside at home be housed in College-supervised residences. If that policy was to continue, for enrollment of women increased too in the immediate postwar years, a new dormitory was urgently needed. And finally and most critically, the funding for two dormitories was not there; cost estimates had doubled in less than five years. Men's housing would have to wait.

* * *

Housing students was one thing. Feeding them was another. The dining facilities in the basement of Mary Berry Hall were strained during normal times; the anticipated arrival in the fall of 1946 of several hundred additional students, most of them hungry boys, precipitated a culinary crisis. More dining space had to be found, and found fast.

The solution to the problem lay near at hand. Diagonally across the street from the southeast corner of the campus was Indianola's large Masonic Hall, and the friendly Masons agreed during the summer of 1946 to permit Simpson to equip the basement of the building for a second dining hall. Dubbed the Chieftain when it opened in the fall, it could hold more than a hundred men, about as many students as typically took their meals at Mary Berry Hall.[36]

The Chieftain operated successfully for a year and a half, but it was relatively expensive for the College to operate two separate dining halls.[37] An economy of scale could be realized if the two were consolidated. Accordingly, Mary Berry Hall was remodeled to provide efficient cafeteria-style service, considerably less homelike than in earlier times, but much more economical to operate.[38] In January 1948, at the end of the first semester, the Masonic Lodge operation was shut down with many thanks to Warren County Lodge No. 53 and a new Chieftain opened at Mary Berry.[39] Under the direction of Lochie Hornaday, the cafeteria was soon serving upwards of two hundred students lunch and dinner every day. The consolidation, Wendell Tutt was pleased to announce, helped to forestall an increase in student board charges.[40]

* * *

Once the College had met the urgent needs for housing and feeding its students, its leaders examined the only slightly less pressing problem of classroom space. Although the major undertaking, erecting the Carver Science Hall, had to await adequate funding, less ambitious projects could be taken on to relieve serious overcrowding. What took place during the next few years, however, seems to have been far less thought through and prioritized than it was simply a rapid response to immediate pressures and providential happenstance.

It is, for example, doubtful that the Music Annex would have been built had not the same public authorities that had made available the barracks housing offered Simpson in mid-1947 additional structures that could, with good luck, imagination and very little cash, be converted to classroom uses.[41] Within a month the board was looking at architect's drawings for a Music Annex. Sven Lekberg made a persuasive plea for more space, especially for a large room for ensembles like band and orchestra and a few smaller spaces for practice rooms and offices. The buildings offered by the Federal Works Agency seemed ideally suited to these uses, so plans were completed by local architect L. C. Langdon, the new facility to be located immediately south of Barrows Hall along Buxton Street.

In July construction of the foundations began, and soon parts of several dismantled frame buildings were lifted onto them to create an L-shaped building, the main part sixty by thirty feet and a wing measuring thirty by thirty feet, providing approximately 2,700 square feet of floor space. Included in the building was also a room for a small radio station together with a control booth, plus workspace for the *Zenith* and an office for superintendent of buildings and grounds Don Drury.[42] Because the outside of the building was severely plain, the decision was taken to face it with a veneer of red brick, a relatively inexpensive measure which considerably improved its appearance.[43] It was dedicated January 16, 1949, in a ceremony featuring the College choir, an address by Methodist district superintendent Dr. Raoul C. Calkins of Des Moines, presentation of the building by Wendell Tutt to board president William T. Hamilton, and a tea served by members of Mu Phi Epsilon.[44]

As soon as the musicians moved into their new annex, the scientists, likewise cramped into limited quarters, took over the old, often leaky, building that had temporarily housed the musicians "until the new Carver Science Hall will be erected." They would have a seven-year wait.

More students at Simpson meant more administration, and soon enough the offices on the second floor of the Administration Building, confined to a row of rooms on the east side, were crammed with new people performing new functions, like managing veterans' affairs, and others bearing up under an increasing work load. To gain needed space the treasurer's office took over all of South Hall, where the College's theater was located, permitting other officers to occupy the treasurer's vacated space.[45]

The theater, temporarily homeless, was moved into the second floor chapel, or assembly hall, in Old Chapel. It was now impossible to accommodate more than a fraction of the student body in the old hall, and weekly chapel, as we have seen, had already moved to the First Methodist Church two blocks south of the campus. Remodeling of the hall for a theater was accomplished during early 1949 at a cost of approximately $7,000.[46] Included was a twenty-by-thirty-foot stage with proper theater curtain, lighting equipment, and a sloped floor with seats for 220 persons, twice as many as the capacity of South Hall.[47] Speech and drama classes met on the third floor of Old Chapel, sending business administration classes downstairs.

To make room for business classes, the Student Union lounge—not the Wigwam—was reduced by sixty percent to make way for a classroom, the remaining space remodeled attractively. The "redecorated Union" reopened in late February.[48] "In the not too distant future," promised the *Zenith* later that spring, "Simpson's building program will construct an entire new Student Union that will indeed be the envy of colleges throughout the middle west."[49] Theirs was more a fond wish than a promise, but although it took twenty years to be realized, it did come true.

Probably the most controversial project of the postwar years pitted the athletic traditionalists against the "progressives" who wanted to build a new athletic field. As we have seen, the debate dragged on for two or three years before the decision was made to build the new dormitory complex on the old field and to create the new field south of Hopper Gymnasium. The traditionalists readily agreed to build what they hoped would be a second field. Thus as early as 1946 preparations were underway, calling for the removal of three dwellings from the area between Hopper Gym and Clinton Street a block and a half to the south.[50] The College had recently purchased Detroit Street and the alleys that ran through the area from the city.[51]

Earlier the board of trustees, equivocating, agreed to grade some of the area south of Hopper Gym "for a field or for a building."[52] In the late fall of 1946 workmen felled a huge elm as a first step in clearing the land in accordance with a plan drawn up by J. S. Dodds, an Ames civil engineer. The graded area, stretching all the way to Clinton Street, could settle over the winter.[53] Not certain whether creating the new field meant giving up the old one, the *Simpsonian* asked the following spring if Indianola really needed two football fields.[54] Dr. Voigt seemed to answer by pointing out the "urgency" of action on a new field, in order to have it ready for at least partial use "when the dormitories go under construction in the spring" of 1948.[55] In the president's mind, there was no question about where the dormitory complex should go. We should, he said, proceed that fall with the removal of stumps, trees, brush and other debris in order to make the uneven field ready for final grading the following spring.[56]

Earthmoving equipment handled some 15,000 cubic yards of earth as the large area was smoothed over. It was called Neff Field because of the $10,000 contribution of L. N. Neff toward the project.[57] Once the earth settled properly, a good cinder eight-lane track was laid down.[58] An aerial view of the campus published in the 1949 *Zenith* showed off the new field, track and all, but no grandstands. To make good on some sort of seating, the Simpson College Alumni Association, led by Herrold Mann '31, raised $15,000 to build all-steel stands seating 1,200, 120 feet long and 28 feet deep with fifteen rows of seats.[59] Completed in the early autumn of 1950, the grandstand and Neff Field itself were dedicated during the half-time intermission at the Homecoming game with the University of Dubuque October 24, the first game played on the new field. The total cost of the project was $37,000.[60] For a while, however, all games would have to be played during daylight hours until electric lighting could be installed.[61] It was not until 1953 that Simpson struck a deal with the Indianola schools, whereby the city put in proper lighting for the privilege of using the field for its home football and track events.[62]

It took even longer to build the Sigler Home Economics Center than it did the athletic field. What started out to be a modest remodeling of the old Pemble house on North C Street turned out to be one of those projects that grows in the doing. As early as 1945 Sara Sigler told Dr. Voigt that she would provide sufficient funds—some $40,000—to remodel the Pemble house and add on laboratory and food preparation areas to the rear of the building. Odis Poundstone, ever the obliging architect, prepared preliminary drawings, looking toward construction the next year. "Mrs. Sigler's lifetime concern in beautifying the American home and its surroundings," said President Voigt, "gives her a natural interest in providing an adequate home economics center for Simpson."[63]

The departure of Helen Schooley and arrival of Ethel D. Anderson to take over the Home Economics Department caused an inevitable, and probably fortuitous, delay in getting the project underway. Ethel D. was full of ideas for improvement of the project, all of which Mrs. Sigler supported enthusiastically but which increased costs and required repeated new renderings by the patient Poundstone. Then, suddenly and utterly without warning, Sara Sigler died May 21, 1947, and with her passing the project, of necessity, was suspended. It was not just a matter of financing the building, for which Mrs. Sigler had provided in her will. Rather it would somehow appear unseemly to move ahead without observing a proper period of respectful mourning.[64]

Soon it was discovered that Mrs. Sigler had left the College a 320-acre farm as part of her pledge to pay for the home economics building. The land would be sold to provide cash for the project.[65] It was nearly three years, however, before it was possible to proceed. And instead of using the Poundstone plans, the board engaged the services of Roland G. Harrison of the firm of Wetherell and Harrison of Des Moines, who redesigned the building, combining "modern, regency and southern colonial trends."[66] Of course, meanwhile the cost of the construction had increased, leading the board to a local builder, Harold Threlkeld, one of the last of the true craftsmen in central Iowa. He agreed to put up the building at cost plus ten percent.[67]

Threlkeld went to work in February 1951 and labored through the spring and summer. Completed in September, the building was dedicated October 2 in an impressive afternoon ceremony featuring an address by Bishop Charles W. Brashares and attended by students, alumni, townspeople and no fewer than 275 Methodist pastors who happened to be at a meeting on the campus from four Iowa districts. Never before or since has a structure dedicated to the physical nourishment and raiment of humankind been given such an extravagant spiritual send-off, accompanied by anthems of heavenly praise sung by the Simpson choir. To be sure, President Voigt did express earthly praise for Sara Sigler's humanitarian generosity. "This is a dream which has come true," he said. "A dream by a great woman who commenced to dream of this house 40 years ago."[68] It was a dream shared by Ethel D. Anderson, and no one would ever doubt that, from that day forward, it was Ethel D.'s house.

That same fall William Buxton III, new president of the Peoples Trust and Savings Bank and member of the executive committee of the board of trustees, donated funds to build three fine new asphalt-surfaced tennis courts on the southwest corner of the campus, a stone's throw from the Administration Building. When completed in early 1952, the new courts represented an attractive and appreciated addition to the campus.[69]

* * *

"One could wish that he had clairvoyant powers with which to predict the future," said President Voigt in the spring of 1946, just a few months before the veterans overran the campus, "but educators, like statisticians, are notoriously without prophetic powers." Already 1,687,000 veterans were enrolled in America's colleges, and Simpson was going to get its share of the massive numbers yet to come. "We must be alert," warned Voigt, "so as to take advantage of every fortuitous circumstance that may arise."[70] Upon analysis he concluded that Simpson's academic offerings had "special excellence" in five programs, and that these programs deserved the lion's share of financial and faculty support. It was a matter, he said, of going with one's strengths.

The five areas he singled out were strikingly varied. The first was preministerial education for students bound for the seminary. Simpson's church-relatedness, expressed in the College's long tradition of supplying the largest contingent of Methodist clergymen in Iowa, demanded careful nurturing of a lively, low-cost program in a supportive Christian environment. Secondly, there was teacher training, a long-standing program now invested with a sense of urgency because of a huge shortage of teachers in the postwar world. Simpson, said Dr. Voigt, should return to its fifth place rank (behind the three state universities and Drake) in teacher preparation. Beyond educating "teachers and preachers,"

Simpson offered outstanding work in business administration, music and physical education. "The world needs to be fed, housed and clothed by men and women we choose to call business people," he told the board of trustees, and with young Robert Samson to head the Department of Business Administration, Simpson could attract a large contingent of students eager to join the ranks of corporate America. Music was another major source of strength. After some years of "eclipse," music at Simpson "has redeemed itself," Voigt reported. It was "drawing students in a way that recalled the days of Barrows." Earlier that year Simpson had been accepted as an associate member of the National Association of Schools of Music, and by January of 1948 would be accorded full membership status.[71] Finally there was physical education, training high school coaches, a wildly popular program that reportedly needed more equipment and field space to make it truly effective. "Every encouragement to this program is urgently recommended."[72] One could hear audible groans from Harold Watson and Francis Moats, deploring the upsurge of the "football major" at the expense of the liberal arts. Their objections were but cries in the wilderness, unheard in the rush to the goalposts. By 1947 physical education, with ninety majors, was, according to Frank Casey, the second most popular program at Simpson after business administration.[73] And it was the most expensive department in the College.[74]

In 1946, when young Gene Carter joined the faculty to teach sociology, the College became part of an interesting and highly successful experiment. They called it the Warren County Group Ministry. Age thirty, the Reverend Carter, a recent graduate of Garrett Biblical Institute, came to Simpson for the express purpose of organizing and directing the new program.[75] The Warren County Group Ministry responded to a real problem in rural America. The United States, in a demographic revolution impelled first by hard times and later by the war and new agricultural technology, witnessed in the thirties and forties an acceleration of the flight from the farm to the city, where economic opportunity beckoned. Even though Iowa possessed some of the finest land in the world, it too experienced the depopulation of the countryside, attended by wrenching change in the institutions that had long been the glue that had held rural society together. Among the most prominent of these institutions was the church. Rural clergymen could only watch with dismay the loss of membership in their churches, their congregations ebbing away until the little rural churches were no longer viable. The handful of parishioners left in a small church faced a difficult choice: they could either close the church and consolidate the congregation with another nearby or find some way of conducting the program of the church at much lower cost, appropriate to their low numbers. In Warren County in 1940 there were no fewer than twenty-one Methodist churches serving a population of 17,000. By 1946, however, eight of the churches had already closed, and the remaining thirteen were served by three full-time ministers and "supply preachers."

People at Simpson hit upon an idea. Why not use preministerial students to fill the pulpits of these churches, relieving the tiny congregation of the cost of a clergyman's salary? Maybe a "circuit-riding" full-time minister could continue to serve a number of rural churches with these student pastors as assistants. Or perhaps the student ministers could do the job unaided. Thus was born the Warren County Group Ministry. The idea soon caught on, and Rev. Carter directed the program, inaugurated in the fall of 1946 with a three thousand dollar grant from the Methodist Church general board, which was intrigued by the possibilities of the program.[76] At the same time Carter also taught two college courses in rural sociology.

The Group Ministry was an instant success. Within two months Carter had put together a team of seventeen young men, twelve of them ex-GIs, and thirteen young women, most of them Simpson undergraduates, who preached on Sundays, organized community activities, visited the sick and comforted the bereaved in village and country churches. Attendance in the student-served parishes improved as farm families responded to the youthful enthusiasm of the Simpson students. It was good for the church too, explained Carter. "When I was a student, 42 percent dropped out of the ministry because of the strain of doing a job without any help or supervision. These young people learn more in a month under supervision than we learned in three years by trial and error."[77] In October 1947, after a full year of operation, Carter was using a twenty-five-passenger bus for the "250 mile journey each Sunday to take student ministers to their various churches."[78] So popular and effective was the program that it was written up in *Time* magazine and drew attention of church leaders all over the United States who were wrestling with the problem of how to serve their declining congregations out in the countryside.

To be sure, the program had its critics. There were those who thought there were far too many rural Methodist churches. Carter argued that there were too few ministers, not too many churches. Further, some traditionalists grumbled about "lady preachers," but for the most part the young women who participated were well received. They were indeed in the vanguard of women who would assume an honored place in the parish clergy. Carter's little band of young Methodists, rocked in the cradle of Iowa self-sufficiency and Christian openness, showed the way.

In another program of experimentation, Simpson was selected in late 1946 by the Northwestern University School of Dentistry as one of three colleges where it would conduct a two-year research program in prevention of tooth decay, testing the effectiveness of dentifrices containing fluoride.[79] Although the results confirmed the value of fluoride in promoting dental health, the Northwestern people seem not to have known that Indianola water was already fluoride-rich, a factor which may have influenced substantially their findings.

* * *

The flood of GIs was the major reason why in the fall of 1946 Simpson was besieged by applicants for admission, but it was not the only reason. The Second World War, like other great conflicts, brought with it an accelerating democratization of American society, leading more students than ever to seek a college education. The College could not possibly accommodate all those who wanted to enter. For the first time in its history, Simpson was forced to adopt some serious criteria of selection for its student body. Some of the standards were uneven and were surely discriminatory—as are all admissions standards—but they reflected Simpson's traditions as well as its hopes for the future. Simpson would limit its enrollment to (1) former students, (2) children of Simpson alumni, (3) children of ministers of the gospel, (4) applicants ranking in the upper quarter of their high school graduating class, (5) those who had no housing needs or (6) those who fell below the top quarter category who showed "outstanding ability."[80] To Harold Watson and other guardians of the academic fire, the last-named category, which did not stipulate what kind of "outstanding ability" to be recognized, probably ensured the recruitment of football and basketball players whose "outstanding ability" was hitting the line or the hoop.

For the next three years the academic quality of entering students did improve, and a larger proportion of Simpson's student population was persisting to graduation.[81] In both 1948 and 1949 the freshman class was limited to 250.[82] Faculty people were pleased; morale was noticeably better than it had been. Simpson seemed to be on the move.

Recognition was not long coming. After a thorough investigation, the National Vocational Guidance Association gave its approval to Simpson's guidance services.[83] Then, in 1950, the College received what looked like the *Good Housekeeping* seal of approval when that magazine described Simpson as one of approximately one hundred "colleges of merit" in the United States. Of the four Iowa schools listed—they included Coe, Cornell and Loras—Simpson was reported to have "the lowest overall cost per year."[84]

Simpson's modest cost was widely thought to be a virtue, but in fact it was a serious problem. In keeping with the College's long tradition of rock-bottom tuition, board and room charges, Voigt and the board were reluctant to raise student fees unless and until the College's finances seemed to be at the point of desperation. At the end of the war Simpson's tuition was still only $200 per year, but as prices skyrocketed with the removal of war time price controls, the board was forced to consider an increase. In 1946 they pushed it up to $220, but this was only a fraction of what was needed. During the following semesters they permitted it to rise to $300, but feared to go higher lest they price the College out of the market. It required months of agonizing, for example, before taking the decision to raise room charges at Mary Berry Hall from $2.50 to $3.00 per week.[85] Influenced profoundly by the clerical members of the board, who sincerely believed that Simpson must still be affordable to any qualified Methodist youngster, Voigt fought to keep the College's charges as near those of the state universities as possible. "Contrary to rumor," said the president in 1949, "there will be no change in tuition rates at Simpson College in the coming academic year."[86] He repeated this formula the next year: "Rumors that a tuition raise will be made next fall are entirely unfounded." Simpson, he said, would be "in line" with other colleges.[87] The fact was that while most of Simpson's competitors among church-related and independent colleges raised their tuition fees substantially, Simpson did not. To be sure, during the immediate postwar years, large enrollments masked the problem, but after 1950 the low-cost policy would wreak havoc with the College's budget.

Meanwhile, income was sufficient to meet expenses, in part because of impressive summer school enrollments. Understandably the returning GIs wanted to accelerate their education as much as possible by attending school throughout the year. During the summers of 1947 and 1948, for example, summer enrollments were the highest in the history of the College.[88] Two summer sessions of five weeks each permitted students to earn as much or more academic credit than during a regular semester. And at $75—later $80—the summer school tuition was a bargain. In 1947 the College for the first time scheduled formal August commencement ceremonies for those students who completed their work during the summer.

Not only were tuition charges at Simpson low; scholarship costs were relatively high. And many scholarships were awarded to students whose academic promise was at best dubious. To bring some order into the procedure, it was determined that scholarships would be awarded only to "those who are scholarly minded." Aid to athletes or musicians or to those whose academic gifts were limited would be henceforth called "grants-in-aid." It was surmised that fewer students would qualify for assistance, reducing the outlay for what amounted to heavily discounted tuition fees. Indeed the cost of scholarships declined, but grants-in-aid increased dramatically. At the same time, the College imposed a $25 application fee for entering students, together with a $10 dormitory room reservation fee.[89]

Recruitment of new students was complicated by the fact that both Simpson and Iowa Wesleyan College were in the same Methodist conference, each college agreeing not to recruit in the other's "territory." Generally it was agreed that Simpson could recruit no farther east than Knoxville, but such self-limiting restrictions were becoming increasingly artificial and difficult to enforce. A related issue was the division of conference beneficence between the two colleges. The practice of dividing the largess on the basis of enrollment worked to the advantage of Simpson, and in accordance with this formula by 1949 Iowa Wesleyan was receiving only forty-two percent, Simpson fifty-eight percent. A conference committee, with representation from both colleges, ruled that after June 1, 1949, the funds would be divided on a fifty-fifty basis. The amount thus lost to Simpson was not great, however, and relations between the two colleges remained cordial. In time, too, the question of who might recruit where disappeared as all colleges engaged in an annual recruiting free-for-all.[90]

* * *

Although in those few years of high enrollment Simpson's operating budget was adequate, the College's endowment was inching upward only glacially. Capital needs were still unmet, the new women's dormitory being the only major permanent installation in years. President Voigt was keenly aware of Simpson's long-term problems and determined to help his board of trustees see the choices it must make. Simpson, the president told his board at its winter meeting in February, 1947, was at a fork in the road. One alternative, following A.A.U. suggestions, called for Simpson to compete strongly with the five other A.A.U.-approved colleges in Iowa, urgently requiring better facilities in science, adequate housing for all resident students, a library triple the size of the existing one, and "a larger and better trained faculty." For all this the College would have to raise $5 million by 1960—$2 million for construction and $3 million for endowment. "These are the standards," he said, "if we want to play in that league; that is what we must require of ourselves." The other alternative is to drop down and operate on a different level, becoming "the outstanding coeducational junior college west of the Mississippi." Most importantly, he said, "I ask urgently that we not drift into some middle-of-the-road mediocrity, but that we courageously and boldly choose one course or the other."[91] The mere mention of the term "junior college" was enough to arouse the board to action. Simpson would become a "five million dollar institution."

Five million dollars would be slow coming. The Forward Movement campaign had been conspicuously unavailing, but its failure could be ascribed to the uncertainties and vicissitudes of war. The board in 1948 decided to undertake a new capital campaign. Although they were tempted to save money by running their own campaign without professional assistance, Voigt persuaded them to hire expert counsel.[92] Accordingly, they retained the services of A. Ivan Pelter Associates of Ludington, Michigan, to conduct the campaign for $550,000, primarily in the Methodist conference and among Simpson alumni. Active solicitation was scheduled to begin in the fall of 1949, but was delayed nearly a year.[93]

Even before the beginning of the fund drive, a number of significant gifts and estates augmented the College's endowment. While no one of these was exceptionally large, the total amount of nearly $100,000 was gratifying.[94] These gifts were, of course, in addition to the Sigler, Cowles and Pfeiffer contributions toward the building fund. By the end of the 1950–51 academic year, the endowment stood at just over $1,500,000.[95]

Quite apart from raising money for endowment and capital needs, the College's administrative officers gave attention to the welfare of the faculty. Faculty salaries, for years among the lowest in Iowa, did not improve as fast as the cost of living shot upward, but some efforts were made to bridge the income gap. The standard salary for division heads was increased in 1946 from $3,000 to $3,300, and the next year everyone on the staff received an across-the-board five percent "cost of living" bonus.[96] For 1947–48 there was another bonus of five percent on half of everyone's salary or wages. But when the board voted to raise President Voigt's salary to $7,200, he declined with thanks to accept "such an extravagant increase," urging that his salary be no more than $6,600.[97] Young faculty members, on the other hand, asked for a reconsideration of salaries in the spring of 1948, complaining that a married person with a family could not live on what was being paid. The board responded as best it could by setting the minimum salary for a married man (women were not mentioned) at $2,800, for a married man with a wife and child, at $3,000.[98]

One way of compensating faculty was providing inexpensive housing to many of the younger people who could ill afford to purchase a house in Indianola. Rental properties were virtually nonexistent except at Lorraine Apartments, and few new faculty wanted to make the sort of commitment required in house ownership. Through the years, looking toward campus expansion, the College had bought up a number of modest houses and rented them to incoming faculty at bargain rates. When, for example, a large number of new people came to teach in the fall of 1946, the College undertook to provide housing for fifteen of them, in a few cases by buying up properties near the campus.[99] Nonfaculty residents in Lorraine Apartments were tendered cash offers to move and make room for new instructors.[100] Once established, some of the faculty members bought the houses they were occupying from the College.[101]

If faculty salaries were generally poor, the College's pension system was worse. College teachers were still denied coverage under federal social security and at Simpson were dependent on the pittance they received under the College's retirement plan in addition to their own savings. In 1946 a retiring professor received $15 per year for each year of service, an associate professor $12, an assistant professor $10 and an instructor $7.50. Thus, for example, when Howard Legg retired that year, he was entitled to an annual pension of $150.[102] When administrator John Horsley retired two years later, he received $12.25 per month.[103] Something had to be done.

In the summer of 1947 the College contracted with the Bankers Life Insurance Company, setting up a significantly improved pension plan, calling for a five percent contribution from the faculty member, matched by five percent from the College. Although the plan did not provide a handsome return, a retiring professor's pension would exceed federal social security benefits. At the request of the faculty, all persons who were employed prior to 1942 were continued under the College's old plan while new people would be enrolled in the Bankers Life plan from the time of their initial employment at Simpson.[104] The next year the board adopted a tenure and retirement policy, formalizing practices that had become enshrined in custom.

Tenure would be normally granted with the seventh annual contract. Although no specific academic degree requirement would be imposed until many years later, evidence of good teaching was expected. The retirement age was set at sixty-five.[105] But in carrying out its new policies the College once again found that it was called upon to pay into the Methodist Church pension fund 13.5 percent of the salaries of the five clerical members of the faculty—Carter, Witten, Peterson, Garrett and Voigt. The church insisted on payment, and the faculty was equally adamant in opposing it. For months it was an issue that strained relations with the conference, and it required patient negotiation before the church was willing to back down with grace.[106]

To summarize its policies on faculty tenure, retirement and pensions, the College issued in 1948 a comprehensive statement which included a strongly-worded declaration regarding academic freedom in keeping with the principles laid down in 1940 by the American Association of University Professors. In the years to come, to be sure, Simpson presidents would be confronted from time to time with the unfortunate and frustrating necessity of dismissing a faculty member for cause, but they unfailingly took pains to adhere scrupulously to the principle of academic freedom, not merely as an act of penance for the clumsy handling of the Payne case, but simply because it was the right thing to do.[107]

* * *

After the Second World War it was difficult to count Simpson among the "defender of the faith" Christian colleges in America. As America became more secular, so did Simpson and dozens of other colleges like it. This move away from a religious orientation was by no means planned, in no way deliberate, nor did it mean a sharp break with the College's past. Some things changed faster than others; other things changed hardly at all. It was, however, inevitable that with the rush of GIs returning to school, Simpson encountered a new and different student population, many of whom were older, more experienced and worldly-wise than the typical eighteen-year-old freshman from Seymour, Iowa. It proved to be increasingly difficult to tell a veteran who had been flying B-24 bombers that he must not drink a beer at a Des Moines tavern or smoke a cigarette on campus. It was even more difficult to persuade him to come to chapel once a week, no matter how uplifting the message. It was dismaying to learn that few men or women were choosing to enter Simpson simply because it was a church-related college. They came to Simpson for its secular education, not its religious environment. These students were by no means hostile to the church. It was just that they had other things on their minds, and many of them rationalized their behavior by pointing out that the principle of freedom of religion could also mean freedom *from* religion—at least for a while.

Take smoking, for example. A remarkably large number of young men had taken up cigarette smoking during the war, and some of them found it difficult to cut down on, much less quit, the habit. For a while they observed the Simpson no-smoking-on-campus rule by standing across the street to light up, but in their annoyance they began to see the regulation as an infringement on their personal rights, an arbitrary limitation of their freedom. Finally they determined to put an end to it. The *Simpsonian* helped. In September 1946, editor Jo Hunter Liggett laid down the challenge: "We must recognize smoking as a national habit, and not brand it as a social evil. . . . We are no longer children, in fact many of us are veterans and family men who rebel at being treated as children. . . . 'No smoking on campus' is a Simpson tradition, but even tradition must yield to the dictates of modern society."[108] A week later, the students took action.

It was the custom in those years for the faculty to walk in a group to weekly chapel at the Methodist Church two blocks away. One sunny morning, as the professors marched out the east door of the Administration Building, moving through the portico where the words "Ye shall know the truth and the truth will make you free" were etched convincingly into the wall, and led by Dr. Voigt, they were greeted by dozens of young men on both sides of the walk, each one silently, confidently, even jauntily holding a lighted cigarette, their ranks forming a smoky gauntlet through which the astonished faculty was forced to pass. Not a word was said by anyone. And afterwards, no notice was taken of their act of defiance. No rules were changed. But from that day forward smoking on the campus—not in the buildings, to be sure—was commonplace, at least among the men. Women students for the most part did not smoke, and those coeds who did were known to gather secretly in sorority house basements, where their confinement produced an atmosphere that must have been very nearly lethal.

Smoking was not their only vice. They wanted to dance too, and not on campus. Some of the returning GIs were led by William K. Billingsley of Newton. Both his father, Dr. John W. Billingsley, and his mother, Mabel Smith Billingsley, were Simpson alumni in the class of 1910, and the senior Billingsley had served in the Iowa legislature. Young Billingsley and his confederates proposed to build a roadhouse just north of the city limits on the highway to Des Moines. "We think we can swing the deal and it is no fly-by-night affair," Billingsley told the Indianola City Council. There would be meals and dancing but no slot machines, liquor or beer.[109] But since the roadhouse would be constructed outside the corporate limits of the city (to avoid city fees), Billingsley was referred to Lincoln Township trustees, and there the matter rested. Dr. Voigt was relieved when the GIs abandoned the project because of cost.

As student behavior was increasingly difficult to control, College authorities had to be prepared for anything. Still, they were shocked when in the spring of 1948 a coed charged that she had been raped by an Indianola man, the first reported act of such violence in the College's history.[110]

President Voigt was deeply concerned, as were others, by the profound and disturbing changes wrought by the GIs, who looked at the College's administration as if they were army brass. It required patience and determination to convince the ex-soldiers and sailors that Simpson was not an army encampment. There was, lamented Voigt, too heterogeneous a faculty and student body during those difficult years. There was too little cohesiveness. "There was no king in Israel and each man did what was right in his own eyes." Simpson students had to be brought back to Christian ways, he said.[111]

"Our greatest and most urgent staff need," said Dr. Voigt in 1948, was a strong leader in religious life who would "project the values of religion into the entire life of the campus."[112] And a year later he was saying that "without apology, the Methodist institution [like Simpson] must seek to win its students to the Christ."[113] Yet students seemed not in the mood to be won over to anything, especially weekly chapel services. "This year," complained the *Simpsonian* editor, chapel is "compulsory at ten a.m. Tuesdays," and "you have to sit in church (!!) on the most uncompromising wooden benches in southern Iowa."[114]

* * *

Students did, however, sit for hours on equally uncompromising steel benches to watch athletic events. Sports revived after the lean wartime years, and Simpson's teams acquitted themselves well. In football the revival was slow. The curtailed schedule of wartime was extended through the fall of 1945 as Simpson played two games each with Central, Cornell and Doane and one game with Wartburg in a disappointing season of five losses and only two wins. The next year, with Coach Ken Tannatt helping Casey, the sixty-man team posted a slightly improved 3–5–1 record, winning but two conference games. The 1947 season was only marginally better, with three wins, four losses and two ties, but Kermit Tannatt of Greenfield was named an all-conference end and Simpson's 6–6 Homecoming tie with Central snapped a fifteen-game Dutch winning streak. When Ken Tannatt accepted the head coaching position at Indianola High School in 1948, former Simpson player John Cooper returned to take over assistant football coaching duties under Hap Miller.[115] Cooper's amiability notwithstanding, the season was very nearly a disaster with only two wins in nine games.

In view of Simpson's lackluster record on the gridiron, no one was prepared for the 1949 season when the team won the Iowa Conference crown with a perfect 6–0 record in the conference and eight wins overall against a single loss to Coe College early in the season. Backfield ace John Mills, tackle Bob Miller and fullback Jim Wright were picked for the all-conference eleven. Hap Miller was clearly Simpson's man of the year.

That same year William Penn College was ousted from the Iowa Conference for playing ineligible transfer men, but in all fairness it must be pointed out that the Statesmen awarded no athletic grants-in-aid and had lost twenty-nine straight conference games between 1941 and 1949. Earlier, in the fall of 1948, conference officials had decided to divide the thirteen-college league into a northern and southern division in order that teams could play a reasonably representative schedule. In football, basketball and baseball, there would be playoffs between the winners in each division, beginning in the basketball season of 1950.[116]

Athletic grants-in-aid were a problem. Of the twelve colleges remaining in the Iowa Conference, only Iowa Wesleyan did not make such awards. Simpson had always granted scholarships on the basis of both scholastic merit and financial need, not to speak of "performance" talent, as in music. But as we have seen, a clear distinction was made between scholarships and other forms of aid, and most aid to athletes fell under the rubric of grants-in-aid for "performance." While many, indeed most, athletes did not receive such financial assistance, the trend was toward "paying for playing." Given the high proportion of Simpson men participating in sports, such a policy would become predictably expensive. Once started, it was difficult to stop.

Although football could boast one conference championship, basketball under Coach Casey was more consistently successful during the first five postwar seasons, with four winning seasons and only one poor year when the team went 11 and 17 (7 and 8 in the conference). During those years Simpson placed forward Chuck Kuchan on the all-conference team in 1946 and Jack Blake in 1949. Conference scoring leaders included Kuchan and Daryl Seley in 1946, Kuchan again at the top with 216 points, together with Les Deaton in 1947, Jack Blake in 1948 and Chuck Kerr in 1950. Of all the basketball games during these years, none was more memorable than the last game of the 1948 season, played at home against Upper Iowa and dedicated to Simpson's beloved Peter Ross, whose years of service in Hopper Gymnasium had endeared him to generations of Simpson athletes. The seventy-two-year-old Scotsman, crippled with rheumatism, was there to raise the huge flag of his adopted country at the game's opening. They played that one for Ross, humbling the Peacocks 73–59.[117]

Frank Casey continued his winning ways in track, the team taking the conference championship in both 1946 and 1947, but during the three following years lost out to a powerful Loras aggregation. Still, Frank Casey's record of nine championships in twelve years represented a remarkable performance.

Simpson's baseball fortunes were not bad at all during the postwar years. Twice the team defeated Central by huge scores: 26–9 in 1946 and 25–14 in 1950. Their 1946 season was excellent; in 1948 under Hap Miller they lost only one game in the Iowa Conference. And in 1949, with the superb pitching of Keith Bishop, they were declared co-champions in the Iowa loop with similarly unbeaten Buena Vista.

* * *

Returning GIs, strong, mature, more worldly-wise than the eighteen-year-old youngsters who came to Simpson full of wide-eyed wonder, were expected to find many of the activities and enthusiasm of their younger schoolmates much too adolescent. The conventional wisdom predicted that these veterans would find skit nights, songfests, homecoming hi-jinks and fraternities intolerably frivolous. The conventional wisdom was wrong. A substantial number of ex-GIs flocked to the fraternities and their traditional activities, and in doing so changed both the groups and some of their traditions. For some, those who had been members before going off to war, fraternity was part of coming home. For others who had never been in college before, the Greek-letter groups offered an easygoing camaraderie not unlike the closeness they had experienced with wartime buddies in the service. For still others, the fraternities provided opportunities for participation and leadership in organizations that were refreshingly voluntary.

All three of Simpson's fraternities revived after the war, but their formal reactivation was delayed until enough returning members were present to effect a proper organization of the groups.[118] There was opposition to permitting the return of the fraternities, the objectors protesting that the Greek-letter groups were exclusive and therefore undemocratic.[119] But the power of tradition, strengthened by the seduction of sentiment and the expectations of the potential proselytes themselves, ensured the return of the Greeks. Formal rushing was permitted in April 1946, and although their numbers were few and they had no houses yet, within a fortnight fifty-eight men—most of them returning GIs—were pledged to the three fraternities.[120]

Pledging new men was easy. Finding housing for all of them was not. Kappa Theta Psi had sold its house toward the end of the war, and ATO soon after.[121] Neither had been able to generate much income from the buildings during wartime, and in any case both looked toward the possibility of building fine new houses as soon as postwar membership warranted.[122] The College-owned Lambda Chi house was occupied by freshmen boys, but was returned to the fraternity in the fall of 1946. At the same time the other two groups were housed "temporarily" in two College-owned houses, the ATOs at Park Hall at 800 North Buxton and the KOYs at 400 West Ashland.[123] Neither house was adequate, but both fraternities hoped their stay would be brief. Their hopes for new houses, however, were dashed as building costs soared beyond their means. The ATOs occupied Park Hall for a frustrating seventeen years, watching the building become yearly more dilapidated. The Kappas lived at their assigned house for a few years before moving across the street to the east into a slightly larger dwelling to live out an equally discouraging seventeen years.

Meanwhile, in the fall of 1946 rushing of new freshmen was deferred a semester; fraternities were restricted to pledging sophomores or upperclassmen, with a limit of ten per fraternity.[124] Freshmen pledging in the spring was enormously successful, with Lambda Chi pledging a record thirty-seven freshmen, ATO fifteen and Kappa seven.[125] By this time fraternity membership was as large as it had ever been at Simpson, with a mix of roughly half ex-GIs and half new undergraduates. With seventy-three pledge and active members, Lambda Chi Alpha counted ten percent of the entire student body.

Across the nation fraternities changed as the veterans joined in regimental numbers. In most schools unfettered hazing, long an evil wherever it prevailed, was either curbed or disappeared entirely, principally because the ex-GIs would not put up with it. But at Simpson where hazing had been relatively harmless, the veterans seemed to find it amusing and generally not likely to endanger life and limb. In some ways the persistence of freshman caps and the silliness that enlivened that phenomenon was probably as intimidating as was fraternity hazing. Perhaps the greater problem was a measurable increase in consumption of alcohol by returning servicemen, who had learned to drink in the military. While virtually none of them took a drink on campus, plenty of them did so off campus, to the consternation of the College's administrators. By no means was drinking confined to the fraternities, but it was perhaps more evident there. Fraternities were very adept at organization, and they were seen to be especially skilled at organizing sin. When Indianola about that same time opened its first real tavern, Don Berry at the *Record-Herald*, that veteran fighter against demon rum, was certain that Indianola and Simpson and all of Warren County had gone to hell in a handbasket.

Drunk or sober, the fraternities continued to be extremely popular. By 1949, with Simpson's enrollment pushing eight hundred, a group of young men organized a fourth fraternity. Led by athlete John Sawyer of Shenandoah and Robert "Deac" Trevethan, editor of the *Simpsonian* from Atlantic, twenty-one young men organized the Gamma Sigma Rho fraternity. Sawyer and Trevethan had conceived the idea in December 1948 and had put together the group by early

March 1949, at which time they received faculty and Interfraternity Council approval. They selected as their adviser physics instructor Roy L. Horn.[126] During the following months they sought out a national fraternity with which to affiliate. Coincidentally, that same year the Pi Kappa Phi national fraternity chartered a chapter at Drake University, and through this expansion became aware of the Simpson Gamma Sigma Rhos. In the late fall, now housed in Campus House number 4 on the corner of Buxton and Clinton, the Simpson boys decided to petition Pi Kappa Phi for a charter, and "after many phone calls and letters" were accepted within a matter of weeks.[127] Initiated on February 12, 1950, by national president Howard D. Leake and the Drake chapter, the new chapter gathered after the ceremony at Shannon's Cafe down on the square for a banquet. Representatives of Pi Kappa Phi's two other Iowa chapters, together with other fraternity officials, joined in the festivities.[128] Denominated the Beta Zeta chapter, the Simpson group was the forty-fifth chapter, the third in Iowa, of Pi Kappa Phi, which had been founded at the College of Charleston in 1904.[129]

It would have been difficult to find a more enthusiastic group than the young Pi Kappa Phis. Their fervor, however, did not extend to scholarship, and they soon took their place at the bottom of the heap, much to the relief of the Kappa Theta Psis.[130] Poor academic performance and rowdy behavior, together with something less than conscientious financial responsibility, not to speak of Simpson's lower enrollment, weakened the Pi Kapps during the following semesters.

Far away from Simpson, a fraternity at Dartmouth College caused a national furor by initiating an African-American student. When one considers that most American institutions, including the armed services throughout the Second World War, were still rigidly segregated by race, that Jackie Robinson had only recently broken the color line in baseball, and that Brown vs. Board of Education, the Selma sit-ins, federal troops at Little Rock and the Civil Rights Act all lay in the future, the Dartmouth initiation was a courageous, forward-looking act. *Simpsonian* editor Robert Trevethan probably reflected the attitude of much of the Simpson community when he wrote to defend fraternities which were, he said, admittedly "based on a principle of exclusion, a principle which perhaps in an ideal educational set-up would not be operative." But he went on to say that "we must admit that we were somewhat pleased at the action of the Dartmouth group. It shows that some of the arbitrary and unjust standards that some groups have set up are under attack by more farseeing individuals."[131]

Meanwhile the four Simpson sororities, relatively unaffected by wartime want or postwar plenty, maintained a steady course, although the membership of the Theta Upsilons remained quite small. The Trideltas and Pi Phis battled for scholastic honors, the former winning top honors in 1945 and 1946 and the latter from then onward. Leading the Pi Phi contingent was Indianola French major Genelle Grant, who seemed to make 4.00 averages effortlessly. During her senior year she and her Lambda Chi boyfriend Claude Morain, a history major from Perry, made the only 4.00 averages in the student body. When they later married, their friends, awed by this intellectual merger, speculated that any future Morain children would be indeed brilliantly endowed.

It was not only the Greek-letter societies that led some to observe that Simpson seemed to be overorganized. Independent organizations abounded. Early in 1945 the Off-Campus Coeds and the Independent Women had merged to form the S.I.S. (Strictly Independent Simpsonettes) with a large membership.[132] In the fall of 1946 the men organized the Simpson College Independent Men's Organization which participated eagerly in a wide range of College activities. More durable than earlier independent organizations, it affiliated in 1950 with the National Independent Student Association, which counted four Iowa chapters among eighty-six nationwide.[133] Alongside these fairly typical independent groups was one called the Simpson Dames, established in 1946 by wives of returning GIs.[134] Two problems continued to plague the various independent groups. First, many of their members seemed to be more conscious of what they were not rather than what they were. They were not Greek, yet in their organization and activities they appeared more often than not to imitate the Greek-letter societies. Secondly, they were unable to attract as members those students who liked to call themselves "independent independents," that is those who spurned membership in any group, pointing out the obvious, that when people join any organization they must give up some measure of freedom.

Honorary and recognition societies continued to stimulate interest in those areas or studies to which they were dedicated. Epsilon Sigma recognized the College's best scholars, but it was far less visible than it should have been, primarily because it elected most of its members only at the very end of their college career. Pi Kappa Delta in forensics, Alpha Psi Omega and Blackfriars in theater, Mu Phi Epsilon and Phi Mu Alpha in music, Pi Gamma Mu in social studies, Sigma Tau Delta in English, and Future Teachers of America in education all flourished. A Home Economics Club and International Relations Club served students with interest in these fields. Beta Beta Beta was reorganized with sixteen members in December 1949 in one of its periodic resurrections.[135]

Two important new student groups were created in these postwar years. One was the Bizad Club; the other was Alpha Phi Omega. The former, organized "to promote the interest of students in the business world and to serve as a medium of contact for alumni in business and students," was the brainchild of professors Robert J. Samson in business administration and Chester A. Morgan in economics, two energetic, hard-headed, talented teachers whose practical experience in the business field convinced them of the importance of bringing students and businessmen together.[136] To that end they put together the Bizad Club early in the fall of 1946. At the first meeting on September 23 a large number of students turned out, some out of genuine enthusiasm and others because they enjoyed being on the good side of their professors.[137] Soon enough undergraduates flocked to the well-planned programs of the club, one of which was a well-attended homecoming luncheon addressed by Colonel Kenneth Karr, a 1925 Simpson alumnus who was legal counsel for the huge Crane Company of Chicago, manufacturers of valves, pipe fittings and plumbing supplies, who discussed management-labor relations.[138] The following February their guest speaker was sports legend Joe Meek, executive secretary and manager of the Illinois Federation of Retail Associations, whose conservative views caused Dr. Moats to shake his head in dismay, wondering where he had gone wrong years ago when Joe Meek was his student. By year's end the Bizad Club counted a healthy membership of fifty-one undergraduates.[139]

The Simpson chapter of Alpha Phi Omega, a national service fraternity dedicated to promoting the high ideals of Scouting among college men who were former members of the Cub Scout or Boy Scout movement, was first conceived in the spring of 1948 by Jack Keeton, a sophomore sociology major from Albia, who had become acquainted with the fraternity through his work with Scouting.[140] As soon as Simpson was notified by Alpha Phi Omega the following fall that it was on its approved list of institutions, former Scouts were invited to meet to discuss organizing a chapter.[141] Soon after their organization was perfected, the group was notified that their application for charter was approved. Installed on December 16, 1948, the twenty-third anniversary of the founding of Alpha Phi Omega at Lafayette College, the new Eta Beta chapter was launched with thirty-four undergraduate members and six faculty advisers.[142] It was an immediate success, for it seemed to do almost everything. One after another campus service project was initiated and carried through by the Alpha Phi Omega members, the most ambitious of which was their effort to raise $750—to be matched by the College—to purchase a lighted athletic scoreboard.[143] During their first full year of operation they sponsored as a fund-raiser a barbershop quartet contest which proved to be almost as popular as All-College Sing.[144]

The postwar student body, larger and more diverse than it had ever been, tended to ignore the Christian organizations which had attracted their members from the entire student population, not just those who were preparing for full-time Christian service. Thus the Y.W.C.A. was weakened and the Y.M.C.A., after one year of postwar activity, disbanded in the spring of 1947. Two years later a representative of the Y, Clarence Elliott, came to the campus to attempt to interest students in reviving the organization, citing among its benefits "lighting the spark of religion which transforms an informed onlooker into a responsible participant in our common life." When he did not find much response, the *Simpsonian* noted simply that there was "some question as to its potential viability here now."[145] Although attempts were made periodically afterwards to revive the Y, they proved futile. Some faculty and many alumni were saddened to see the Y.M.C.A. depart the Simpson scene where it had stood as a beacon of morality and right conduct for so many decades.

In contrast to the decline of the Christian organizations, Simpson's student publications continued to enjoy robust health, even though their finances were frail. In 1948 the *Zenith*, owing to a last-minute change in publishers, was two hundred dollars in the red, but the Student Congress obligingly bailed the yearbook out by pledging the profits from that year's Miniature Orpheum event.[146] While the makeup of the *Zenith*s of those years was hardly inspired, the annual editions were informative and for the most part well written. Similarly, the *Simpsonian* continued to present campus news and opinion competently, while graphically it remained very conservative indeed.

The best development on campus, however, was the revival of a Simpson literary journal. With profound pleasure Harold Watson was able to announce that the English Department and Sigma Tau Delta, the English honor society, would publish a literary journal again.[147] They did not want to use the old name, but it required months before an appropriate new one was selected. It was only in May 1949 that the first edition of the *Sequel* appeared, containing an attractive selection of the best student prose and poetry of the 1948–49 academic year.[148] It cost twenty-five cents a copy, and it was sufficiently popular to warrant continuing publication down to the present time.

Traditional campus events continued or were revived during the postwar years. Because the wartime male exodus had curtailed Homecoming, the Tomahawk was not awarded again until 1946.[149] The *Messiah* continued to be sung at Christmastime, with Simpson professor Hadley Crawford directing a chorus of 150.[150] The Interfraternity Sing, renamed All-College Sing and sponsored by Phi Mu Alpha, was revived in 1948 after seven years.[151] Miniature Orpheum, a relatively innocent production during wartime, when only women's groups competed, once again challenged the vigilance of the censors when the fraternities reentered the competition with skits that in their unedited form could make a sailor blush. In 1948 the *Simpsonian*, hardly a guardian of prudery, admitted that there were "too many smutty jokes" in "an adolescent and immature" Miniature Orpheum, but reported the next year that the show "went well. It was clean fun."[152] The fraternities grumbled about the curtailment of free speech. In the spring, Campus Day saw the detritus of winter cleared away and picnics organized, while May Day saw the crowning of a queen only a matter of days before commencement.

It is surprising that during these turbulent postwar years Simpson provided only a limited number of featured speakers on the lecture platform, and of these only a handful were memorable: Congressman Karl Mundt of South Dakota speaking on "what to do about Russia"; Southern news commentator John Temple Groves asking Northerners not to give advice to Southerners, who would "give the colored man anything so long as segregation is retained"; foreign correspondent Robert St. John, who tried to make sense out of events in Europe; or former Chancellor of Austria Kurt von Schuschnigg, who had languished seven years in a Nazi concentration camp, talking about the resistance of his homeland to Hitler.

* * *

It was inevitable that a Simpson filled to overflowing with ex-GIs would be sensitive to world affairs. Now that wartime collaboration with the Russians had given way to competition for the "hearts and minds" of the world's peoples, not to speak of a numbing fear among countless Americans of an expanding red tide of Communism, Simpson students might have been expected to share the national mood. But they rejected the jingoism of many of the country's leaders. Instead they listened respectfully when John Strohm, former managing editor of *Prairie Farmer*, came to Simpson and made a highly favorable report of life in the Soviet Union as he observed it during a two-month visit there.[153] A short time later the editor of the *Simpsonian*, Dick McMullin, deplored the Communist witch hunt in the United States: "This same thing happened about twenty-five years ago, and it proved only that there weren't enough honest to goodness Communists in the country to provide a good lynching . . . but that a lot of good citizens have to be beaten up and jailed to make a purge worth while."[154] They had no illusions about Communism and its threat, but expressed their concerns with moderation and restraint.[155] At the same time they were ambivalent about peacetime military conscription,[156] and in 1948 in a campus poll on the eve of the presidential election gave Thomas E. Dewey a huge majority of 367 to President Harry S. Truman's 150.[157] After all, this was still Iowa. And when Truman was victorious, the *Simpsonian* put the same question others were asking: "What Hoppened [sic]?"[158]

Politics aside, Simpson students, whose interests and enthusiasms only occasionally matched those of their faculty mentors, were predictably caught up in most of the fads and fashions of their own era, from popular music played by the big bands on the radio to hair styles that required men to keep trim and the women to wear their tresses at almost shoulder length. The *Simpsonian* expressed mild disapproval of jeans for school wear, opposition to women wearing any sort of trousers and apoplectic condemnation of long skirts. "During the summer [of 1947]," wrote editor Harold Hall, "a fashion trend came up from the dim past and skirts are going down as a result." And women, he lamented, were gullible, slavishly following the latest fashion trends. He recalled nostalgically "the time when skirts were raised to the point where legs were seen in all their glory. Now this is to be discarded and men will again be in the dark."[159] Other (male) students joined the chorus of disapprobation for reasons ranging from comfort to unpatriotic waste of material, expressing sympathy for girls forced to buy a new wardrobe for college.[160] To their delight and amazement their views were echoed by no less than the Methodist Bishop Charles Brashares, who in a chapel address at Simpson stated from the pulpit that "the longer skirts women are now wearing . . . are very wasteful of cloth which is sorely needed in many foreign countries."[161] Having received this clerical imprimatur, Simpson men continued their campaign of remonstrance, utterly without effect. For their part, women enjoyed no success either in their attempts to persuade the men to forswear wearing white socks as an accompaniment to everything from gym shorts to a three-piece suit.

There were people who found this sartorial discord to be intolerably trivial. But then it all happened the same year the first flying saucer over Warren County was sighted over at Hartford one dark July night.[162] There was said to be nothing trivial about reports of visitors from outer space.

There were also people who were convinced that there had to be a connection between flying saucers and the punishing weather Indianolans suffered during 1947. In early June the county was hit by torrential rain—4.47 inches fell in two hours on June 4—which caused the worst local floods in history.[163] All the rivers were out of their banks, all roads were closed, and Indianola was four weeks without railroad service. Newspapers were flown to Indianola from Des Moines. Damage to crops, bridges and buildings was estimated to exceed two million dollars.[164] Two months later the whole county was sweltering, and what corn was left from the floods was wilting in the scorching sun. The heat wave persisted into Simpson's new school year, climaxing with a record 104 degrees on September 8, the highest temperature in the state.[165] It had to be the flying saucers.

The weather did improve during the following years. And it is comforting to know that a 1950 poll confirmed that most Simpson students didn't believe in flying saucers.[166]

When Indianola celebrated its centennial in August 1949, some faculty participated, but students for the most part missed the exciting event, which took place while they were still home for the summer. In preparation for the centennial, Central Construction Company of Indianola had repaved the town square.[167] The town was growing. The 1950 U.S. census reported that Indianola's population had grown to 5,146.[168]

* * *

Simpson alumni, especially those who had graduated during the twenties and thirties, were beginning to make their mark in the world. The College's publications during the postwar years heralded their successes and shared their pride of accomplishment. There were educators like Howard Noble, Max Dunn and Earl Miller at U.C.L.A.; Hurford Stone, dean of students at the University of California at Berkeley; J. Hugh Jackson[169] and Barrett McFadden at Stanford's prestigious graduate school of business administration; Merrill Holmes, elected president at Illinois Wesleyan in 1946; Malcolm Love, appointed dean at Denver University in 1948; Avery Craven, who was honored by an invitation to teach at the University of Sydney in Australia while on leave from the University of Chicago; and Paul Giddens, who was writing a history of the Standard Oil Company of Indiana, his fifth book. Recognition was accorded a number of rising stars in the corporate world, people like Dean Prather, the new president of A. C. Nielson of Canada, Ltd. in Toronto, or Ivan Willis, appointed vice-president in charge of industrial relations at International Harvester in Chicago. Simpsonians were intrigued to learn not only of Harry Bullis's move from president to chairman of the board of General Mills but also of his marriage in 1948 to an exotic Polish countess.[170] Other alumni were posted abroad in the U.S. Foreign Service, people like veteran diplomat Clayton Lane, who had spent many years in India before his return to the States to take the post of executive secretary of the American Institute of Pacific Relations; Eugenie Moore Anderson, appointed ambassador to Denmark by President Harry Truman in 1949; Loris Craig, who was appointed a vice-consul in the Republic of China (Taiwan); and Alice Sayre, whose remarkable career with the State Department's intelligence service took her first to Cyprus for two years on a mission she was not at liberty to discuss. Harold Pote moved up to the position of personnel director of the Boy Scouts of America, while Ruth Sayre was elected president of the Associated Country Women of the World. Many others, surely equally worthy of mention, were moving into careers that were a credit to themselves and their alma mater.

In these years Simpsonians expressed special concern about the handful of alumni of Japanese nationality with whom the College had lost touch during the war. Soon enough they learned that although these alumni had fortunately survived, they were suffering real privation. As soon as possible, Simpson students gathered a whole library of books and some household articles and shipped them to the Reverend Takeshi Ukai, whose home had been destroyed.[171] Later they heard from Yasu Iwasaki, who survived the nuclear blast at Nagasaki. She had suffered severe burns on her right hand and arm even though she was in a school building two miles away from the center of the blast. "I really know what war means," she said to her Simpson friends when she attended a reunion in Indianola in 1950. "When I was in an air raid shelter, I said that if I got through alive, I'd devote myself more aggressively to peace and Christian principles."[172] While one could understand the nation's depersonalization of the "Jap" enemy during wartime, it was difficult to think of these gentle Christian souls as the foe.

Another gentle Christian, George Washington Carver, was appropriately remembered when a U.S. postage stamp was issued in his honor on January 5, 1948, only the second stamp ever to commemorate the memory of a black man in America.[173] The following autumn several representatives of the George Washington Carver Foundation at Tuskegee were on campus gathering information about the great scientist's life in Indianola at Simpson.[174]

* * *

The death of William Buxton, Jr., on November 19, 1945, while not wholly unexpected, was nonetheless a blow to the entire Simpson community. He was seventy-eight. No man had been more consistently active on behalf of the College than had he during nearly sixty years since he completed his studies at Simpson in 1888. His gifts of time and substance were reckoned beyond measure, and a professorship named in his honor was indeed but modest recognition of his unmatched services to the College. His place on the board of trustees was taken by his son, William Buxton III.[175]

Still remembered by some of the older faculty and townspeople was former President James Watson Campbell, who died at seventy-seven in Erie, Pennsylvania, late in 1949. Dr. Campbell's presidency was recalled as a strong one and the president himself remembered as a "true patriot" who guided the College on a firm course during the First World War.[176]

* * *

Probably no alumnus of Simpson was more loyal to his alma mater than was Don Berry, whose newspapers attracted an astonishing number of subscribers with Indianola connections from all over the nation, all of them interested in what was going on in Indianola and at the College. Whenever Berry heard a good story that sounded the praises of Iowa or extolled local people, he was delighted to retell it in the pages of his papers. One such story found its way to Indianola all the way from California, and he recorded it with ineffable pride:

> They undertook to razz George Barnett ['46] on the campus of Stanford University one morning and here is how far they got with it:
> A group of students in the graduate school of business administration were assembled on the campus looking over their lesson before going in to class. As they were about to break up one man said:
> "From where do you fellows all come? I'm from Harvard myself."
> "I'm from Indiana U.," said the other.
> "And I'm from Northwestern," said the third. "Where do you hail from, Barnett?"
> "I'm from Simpson," replied George.
> "Where's that?" queried one.
> "Simpson College, never heard of it," said another.
> "Well, now," said George, "you know this McFadden who teaches this class where we are going."
> "Yes, sure we know him."
> "Well, he's from Simpson. And look on the title page of your textbook. You see it was written by Howard Noble?"
> "Yes, Howard Noble."
> "Well," grinned George, "he's from Simpson, too. And you've heard of Dr. J. Hugh Jackson, dean of this whole graduate school?"
> "Yes, sure."
> "Well, he's from Simpson. Where did you say you guys are from?"

Berry's piece was reprinted in more than fifty Iowa newspapers, for there was surely no local sport more popular than poking fun at big city dudes, arrogant urban sophisticates who looked upon the Simpsons of the world as hopelessly hayseed.[177] There was, of course, in Berry's story a broad streak of old-fashioned Midwestern agrarian populism that revealed its own brand of arrogance, but Iowans loved it.

XVI

Korea and Simpson's Time of Troubles 1950–53

The GIs who crowded onto American campuses during the postwar years brought record enrollments to Simpson and most other colleges. When the number at Simpson reached 781 full-time students in the 1947–48 academic year, veterans accounted for an impressive thirty-eight percent.[1] The following fall when student numbers reached an all-time high, the proportion of ex-GIs dropped only a single percentage point. By the spring of 1950, however, the graduation of many of the veterans reduced Simpson's enrollment to 668, less than twenty-five percent of whom were ex-GIs. Clearly, the GI flood was ebbing rapidly and the College could expect to return to a "normal" enrollment of 500 to 550. But three things conspired to cause an alarming exodus during the next three years.

The first was the predictable decline in veteran's enrollment. By 1953 it was down to 30. The second blow was more serious. On June 25, 1950, Communist North Korea launched an invasion across the thirty-eighth parallel into South Korea. The Security Council of the United Nations, in an unwonted and coincidental act of unanimity, two days later adopted a U.S. resolution for armed intervention. That same day President Harry Truman ordered American forces to help South Korea repel the invasion.

Although only three weeks before the outbreak of the Korean War President Voigt had predicted that Simpson's enrollment would remain steady, it most certainly did not.[2] The College's fall 1950 enrollment, down seventeen percent from the previous year, reflected the enlistment during the summer of a number of students in the military, together with a further loss of veterans. Even the 597 students who enrolled that fall could not be sure they would be able to remain in school. Many decided to drop out during the course of the semester in order to avoid being drafted into a service they did not like.[3] "There are arguments pro and con upon whether to enlist or not," editorialized the *Simpsonian* in January 1951. "The men enlisting, now, base their arguments on the present law which states that once you receive your orders to report for your physical you can enlist into any branch of the armed forces. Therefore they are enlisting before they take their selective service physical. Practically all college students were reclassified over the holidays from IIA to IA. In this way they must report for their physical when their number comes up."[4] Other students, willing to take their chances, reasoned that the more education they received the better off they would be in the Army, and chose to remain in school.

To counteract "the panic that has swept through college men since re-classification," Dr. Voigt, Stuart Peterson and David Mobberley met with more than 200 undergraduate men in early January to discuss the draft situation, urging the students to remain in college at least until the end of the school year.[5] "Simpson," explained Dr. Voigt, "is in constant contact with government offices which make surveys of colleges for this purpose." Their explanations and encouragements had a calming influence on the men, at least for a few months.

Meanwhile, Voigt and a few board members determined that they had to consider the possibility of organizing some sort of a military unit on Simpson's campus. They knew, of course, that such an endeavor would surely encounter stiff opposition among many of the clerical members of the board, but they believed that failure to attract either a Navy or Air Force program would mean an unsustainable loss of enrollment. Their best chance, it appeared, was to approach the Army Air Force, which operated 125 college Air Force R.O.T.C. units and had just announced that it would increase that number by 62 at the beginning of the 1951 academic year. Accordingly, when the Army Air Force surveyed ten Iowa colleges, investigating the facilities on each campus, Simpson was included. In mid-February 1951, Colonel George A. Bosch of the State University of Iowa and Colonel Woodrow B. Wilmot of Bradley University arrived in Indianola and in a day completed their inspection.[6] It required another month before a deeply-divided Simpson board of trustees could decide—in a close vote by ballot—even to apply for an Army Air Force R.O.T.C. unit.[7] Opponents held out the hope that a rumored Federal Manpower Commission plan to establish "special non-military government training units . . . for college campuses" would materialize.[8] It never did.

Simpson was notified early that it would not be considered for an A.F.R.O.T.C. unit because of its "inadequate" housing for male students. Inadequate indeed. Simpson's first dormitory for men was still in the planning stage.

A year later, in the spring of 1952, Voigt acknowledged to the board of trustees that Simpson's failure to offer R.O.T.C. to entering freshmen was hurting enrollment, lamenting that "large numbers of boys are yielding to the blandishments of R.O.T.C. schools." Even more disappointing was the report of Des Moines attorney and board member Allen Whitfield, who had attended the recent General Conference of the Methodist Church, where delegates took a strong position in opposition to R.O.T.C. The church's declaration stated that "Methodists have always held to the separation of church and state. The installation of R.O.T.C. units in church colleges is in violation of this principle." The church seeks "an attitude toward government of patriotic loyalty joined with intelligent criticism." A military unit on a college campus "frequently inhibits freedom of individual thought and action." At the same time the church recognized the financial problems of Methodist schools. "We urge adequate support of them by the entire church." Whitfield's attempts to modify the severe language of the church's statement were voted down overwhelmingly. It was clear, he said to his fellow board members, that the General Conference was critical of any Methodist institution with R.O.T.C. or one "which considers the possibility of applying for such a unit." Dr. Voigt fairly exploded with indignation and dismay. "If our church," he cried, "believes that R.O.T.C. is not conducive to the spirit of a Methodist college campus, then, of course, the statement [about adequate support of colleges by the entire church] needs implementation beyond pious words." Only recently the church had favored the idea of fifty cents per member for Methodist institutions, but had "done really absolutely nothing about it."[9] Few of his colleagues had ever seen President Voigt quite so angry. Those board members who upheld the General Conference declaration kept their counsel and remained silent.

Only the previous fall, following Congress's vote in June 1951 to extend selective service and lower the draft age to eighteen and a half, Simpson's enrollment had slid to 440. By the time the Korean armistice was signed at Panmunjom in July 1953, student numbers dropped to an alarming low of 377.

There is little doubt that the inexorable drop in veterans enrollment, together with the attrition of young men caused by the Korean War, accounted for much of the devastating contraction of the College's student population. But there was a third factor, perhaps not noticed at the time and certainly never publicly commented upon. The enrollment of women shrank from 256 in 1948 to a low of 147 in the spring of 1953, a drop of forty-three percent. Yet one could count on the fingers of one hand the number of women who had entered the armed forces. Surely something besides the war was responsible for the fact that fewer women were choosing to enter Simpson.

One is tempted a generation later to suggest some possible explanations beyond those offered at the time for Simpson's frightening enrollment losses. For one thing, nearly all private colleges in the Midwest were affected by the growth of the public institutions, which seemed to be less touched by the Korean War than were the independent schools. Further, the tendency, especially during these years of emergency, for an increasing number of young women to enter the workplace straight out of high school depressed the number of potential freshmen students at some colleges. More significantly, it is evident that Simpson's Methodist affiliation was far less decisive than it had once been in influencing students to select the College. This is not to say that Simpson's church relationship was in any way harmful; it is simply that it was no longer an important positive factor in attracting students. It is equally clear, however, that the Simpson board of trustees and administrators saw the College as an extension of the church in its educational mission, even though Simpson's students—and potential students—did not. The College was still recruiting students almost entirely within the boundaries of the Methodist conference that stretched across southwest Iowa, a region unrelentingly dependent on the fortuity of agricultural production.[10] Area farm income probably influenced Simpson's welfare, as it always had, more than anyone realized at the time. And during these years farm prices were rising incrementally while farmers' costs seemed to be rising exponentially. In such times farmers did what farmers had always done; they hunkered down and waited for better times, and while they waited, Simpson and other colleges like it suffered a student drought.

Of course, Simpson was not the only college in Iowa to experience a serious downturn after the outbreak of hostilities in Korea in 1950. Nearly every independent or church school was adversely affected. Even Grinnell College, surely the strongest liberal arts college in Iowa, experienced a time of financial stringency. Simpson's decline, while not unique, was profound.[11] Yet amidst this sickening downhill slide, Voigt, ever the optimist, believed he could see better times ahead. After a hoped-for successful conclusion to the Korean War, and barring "an international cataclysm, colleges may expect to be overrun again by 1956."[12]

Meanwhile, in the face of impending deficits, Simpson was compelled once again to retrench. Because they had already received contracts for the 1950–51 academic year, faculty people were kept on or hired as replacements in spite of the enrollment loss. Most of the new people in 1950, to be sure, were replacements. In biology David G. Mobberley, who had just completed his M.S. at the University of Michigan, took the place of Charles W. Kern. Robert Haney Scott, whose B.A. and M.A. degrees had been earned at the University of Kansas, temporarily took over for Chester A. Morgan in economics and business administration. Morgan was working on his doctorate at the University of Iowa. In history Howard S. Greenlee, who had just completed his Ph.D. at the University of Chicago, followed Delber McKee, who resigned to pursue graduate study at Stanford University. McKee had filled in during the 1949–50 year for Gene Lavengood, who had taken a leave of absence but did not return to Simpson. In home economics Virginia E. Bice replaced Dorothy E. Gill, who left Simpson to pursue graduate work, and Myra Safley, who had earned a masters degree in music at Indiana University, took the place of Elizabeth Stone in piano. There was only one new full-time position that year: Dr. Voigt hired Willard B. Frick in psychology. Frick held his B.A. from Lincoln Memorial University and had done graduate work at the University of New Mexico and Peabody College.

It was at the end of the 1950–51 year that the faculty axe fell, slicing nine positions and reportedly causing "cries of woe."[13] People who were either dropped from the faculty or who, seeing the handwriting on the wall, found positions elsewhere, included Beulah Altman in foreign languages, Elva Bramhall in English and speech, John Cooper in physical education, Ervan Dornbos in mathematics, Willard Frick in psychology, Grover Hawk in biology, M. Rae Lugn, a part-time instructor in art, John D. Potter in business administration, Uberto Price in education, Gerard Schultz in sociology, Robert H. Scott in economics and business administration and Virgilia Wade in dramatic art. Because Nina Mitchell Goltry in education received a leave of absence for the 1951–52 academic year, two new people were employed, replacing her and Uberto Price. One was Katherine Keyhoe, a graduate of Iowa Wesleyan (1923), who had served for a number of years as superintendent of an elementary school in India and most recently as a teacher in Ottumwa. The other was Luella Specht, a graduate of Iowa State Teachers College (1935), who had earned her M.A. at the State University of Iowa. Miss Specht, who had at one time taught at a state teachers college in South Dakota, was the county supervisor in elementary education for O'Brien County before coming to Simpson. The only other addition to the faculty that fall was Jane M. Merkle, employed as a part-time instructor in advanced speech and play production. With a B.A. from Carthage College (1937) and an M.A.

from Iowa, she joined her husband, Paul, who had come to Simpson in chemistry two years earlier.

Little more reduction could be made in 1952–53, although Voigt admitted to the board that "we have faculty now [36 plus two on leave of absence] that can handle a hundred more students than [the 391] we have." But he found it "hard to trim it much more."[14] There was an irreducible minimum below which he dared not go, lest the College's academic programs be endangered.

For that fall Voigt found replacements in a wide variety of academic fields. Reverend Donald H. Koontz took over Gene Carter's courses in sociology and ably assumed directorship of the Town and Country Church, as Carter's Warren County Group Ministry was now being called. Koontz, who was a graduate of Asbury College and Garrett Biblical Institute and who had done work in "world sociology" at Northwestern University, became a fixture at Simpson, teaching classes, conducting sociological surveys in the community and running institutes on what he called aerospace sociology. A dour, soft-spoken native of Indiana, Koontz surprised faculty and students alike with his keen organizational abilities, masked by gentle, almost phlegmatic mannerisms. He stayed on at Simpson until his retirement in 1980.

Joining the faculty that same fall in mathematics was Lloyd O. Ritland, who came to Simpson after teaching at Grand View College in Des Moines for two years. Replacing Alvin L. Lugn, Ritland had also taught at a number of other secondary and collegiate institutions, including an appointment at his alma mater, Luther College. Having earned his M.S. at the University of Iowa, he had completed additional work at Iowa, Iowa State and the University of Southern California. Replacing Chester A. Morgan in economics was Everett L. Refior, who was completing his doctorate at the University of Iowa after teaching at Iowa Wesleyan for three years. Refior's education included a year at the University of Glasgow and another year at the University of Chicago.

Other new faculty in the fall of 1952 included Margaret E. Harvey in music, replacing Myra Safley. A gifted pianist, she was a graduate of MacMurray College for Women, held a masters degree from Northwestern and had studied for a summer at Julliard. Prior to coming to Simpson, Harvey had taught at Mary Hardin-Baylor College in Texas. Her low salary—she started at only $2,800 per year—was a bargain for Simpson, attesting to both the College's impoverished exchequer and the scarcity of teaching positions for even the best musicians. Mary R. Bronner, a graduate of Iowa State College, replaced Virginia E. Bice in home economics. Because she was completing a term of graduate study at Cedar Falls, Bronner was unable to take up her duties until December, but the College was fortunate to secure the temporary service of Ruth Ann Sayre during the better part of the fall semester.

Two new faculty people were employed as one-year replacements for Livingston Witten in religion and philosophy and David Mobberley in biology, both of whom received a leave of absence to pursue graduate studies. Standing in for Witten was Harry W. Beardsley, an Oklahoma City University graduate who had completed the course work for his Ph.D. at Boston University. He had taught at Texas State College for Women and had conducted extension classes at the University of Alabama. Because Witten did not return to Simpson, Beardsley continued as a member of the faculty until 1956. Replacing Mobberley for one year was Dixon L. Riggs, who had served two years as a graduate research assistant in the Institute of Human Biology at the University of Michigan after earning his B.A. at Marietta College and his M.S. at Michigan. Employed part-time in English and journalism was David E. Pullman, who held an M.A. in journalism from the University of Iowa and who came to Simpson primarily to work as the College's director of publicity.

Not everything was dark during those days of decline. In 1950 employees of nonprofit institutions were made eligible to participate in the federal Social Security program on a voluntary basis. Within a short time eighty-nine of Simpson's ninety-nine employees indicated their desire to take part in the program. And because it required only six quarters of income to qualify for Social Security benefits, Simpson undertook to ensure employment to about-to-retire staff members, including veteran faculty people Francis Moats and J. Allen Baker, together with staff members Bert Gose, Clarence C. Litzenberg, longtime keeper of the fire in the heating plant, Peter Ross, John Main and R. I. Faucett, in order to permit them to qualify.[15] At the same time, the College continued to rent houses to faculty at artificially low rates in a time of sharply rising prices.[16]

Not only was there sharp reduction and rapid turnover in the faculty during the Korean war years; the administration of the College underwent change as well. President Voigt could depend on Bimson as dean, Tutt as treasurer and business manager, Merrill Ewing as assistant business manager, Beryl Hoyt in the library and Paul Borthwick, who had joined the staff in 1948 as superintendent of building and grounds. Other positions were less stable. When Emily Philpott resigned in 1950 to return to graduate studies, Voigt asked Elizabeth White to take on the duties of dean of women in addition to her instructional work in English composition. In the process he saved one salary. In the registrar's position, turmoil reigned. When Ralph Whipple resigned in early 1950, Voigt appointed Matilda Womer, a graduate of Ohio Wesleyan who held an M.A. from Syracuse, to that position. When she in turn resigned in October after only nine months of service to marry Marvin Wilkinson of Indianola, Voigt decided to leave the office vacant. "For the time being," he said, the Registrar's chores could be handled by the secretarial staff. Much the same thing happened when E. S. Newton, who had served as director of public relations for only a year, resigned in 1950. The position was left vacant for two years. Only in the fall of 1952 did President Voigt appoint David E. Pullman, a 1950 graduate of Simpson who had just completed his M.A. in journalism at the University of Iowa, to handle Simpson's publicity, to advise the *Simpsonian* and *Zenith* and to head the office of public relations.

The temporary reduction of these several administrative positions enabled the president in the fall of 1951 to name a new vice-president, the first in nineteen years. He was Gilbert G. Stout, a Methodist clergyman from Keokuk. A graduate of the University of Wichita who did his seminary work at Garrett Biblical Institute, Stout had come to Iowa in 1943 and had served as minister at Dallas Center for five years prior to going to Trinity Church at Keokuk. "The Rev. Mr. Stout," observed Don Berry in the *Record-Herald*, "will generally have charge of the promotion of the College interests with the public as regards to finance, student admissions and alumni relations."[17] Of course, what Dr. Voigt wanted Stout to do was to move about the conference raising funds, and Stout was reputed to be a good fund-raiser.

* * *

In spite of heroic efforts to reduce costs, President Voigt could not keep them below the College's plummeting revenue. Each year after the outbreak of the Korean War the deficits accumulated: $21,017 in 1950–51, $12,157 in 1951–52, and something over $12,000 in 1952–53.[18]

To be sure, part of the financial problem was the reluctance of both the board and the president to increase tuition or board and room charges sufficiently to keep abreast of the nation's galloping inflation. The College's tuition charge of $350 in 1948–49 was raised not at all during the next two years. In 1951 tuition was increased modestly by $35 to $385 and the following year by a timid $15 to $400. No increase was made for 1953–54. Board charges were increased from $308 to $360 per year and room fees were not raised at all. The cost of attending Simpson remained among the lowest of the Iowa independent colleges. It would appear that Simpson administrators believed that pushing up the cost would make a bad enrollment situation yet worse.

Spurred by the difficulties of attempting to run a college during a time of national emergency, Simpson people began to look for an association with other similar colleges in its region. In early January 1951 ten college presidents who were attending the Association of American Colleges meeting at Atlantic City, New Jersey, decided to form a college association "to strengthen the cause of modern liberal arts Christian education within the member colleges and to promote this cause before the public who are too often ignorant of this aspect of the colleges."[19] Nine of the colleges were approved by the Association of American Universities; the tenth was a Canadian school outside the realm of A.A.U.'s purview.[20] A subsequent meeting on March 26 approved a constitution for the new conference and elected officers.[21] The organization, dubbed "the Midland Conference," would meet annually, immediately before the conclave of the North Central Association of Colleges. Few associations started off with such promise. Unfortunately, after only a couple of years of desultory exploration to find a reason for its existence, the conference passed away, never to be heard of again.[22]

Far more successful was the Iowa College Foundation, of which Simpson was a charter member when it was created in 1952.[23] Organized for the purpose of doing collectively what many of the colleges were unable to do individually, the foundation set out to seek funds from corporate donors who might be persuaded to contribute to a consortium of independent Iowa colleges what they might be reluctant to give to any one of them. For Simpson, the Iowa College Foundation opened up an entirely new, if modest, source of funding. More significantly, it led Simpson trustees and administrators to consider for almost the first time potential contributors outside the ranks of its own alumni or its conference congregations. Although Simpson's share of the funds collected in any year was never large, the aggregate amount of the gifts in time has been substantial.

* * *

When Simpson was founded in 1860, its stated purpose was "to encourage and promote the cause of Christian education generally and to extend the influence of science, art and Christian culture."[24] At that time, and in each generation thereafter, the College's curriculum represented the current expression of Simpson's mission as that generation understood it. During the Voigt administration, spanning a decade that witnessed two wars separated by a turbulent interlude that seemed to be dominated by the shock troops of secularism, the curriculum remained fairly stable. Even when the College was forced to retrench during the Korean War, the requirements for the B.A. and B.S.B.A. degrees were not seriously compromised, although the range of choice in the required general education courses was considerably narrowed. To earn a degree students were still required to earn fifty-two semester hours of credit in general studies. These included sixteen hours in Division I (with ten hours in specified English courses and at least three hours in speech or foreign language), twelve hours each in Divisions II, III and IV, where most of the courses were specified precisely, allowing very limited election. Critics of the program conceded that if the purpose of the general studies segment of the curriculum was simply to ensure a distribution of a significant part of the student's academic program across the curriculum, it was surely successful. Yet they pointed out that, like so many college general studies programs, it somehow lacked any real focus or direction, no sequencing or deliberate connection of one course to another, no considered design or rationale. Harold Watson, one of the critics, put his finger on the required curriculum's chief deficiency. It was, he said, cobbled together by a fragmented and frightened faculty, some of whom were unwilling to permit a requirement in one department without a quid pro quo in their own. Thus in order to inject some rigor into the curriculum by including some strong courses in the requirements, the faculty permitted the inclusion of a number of courses of questionable merit.[25] Beyond the College's general studies program, degree requirements included the completion of a major and passing a comprehensive examination in the major field. A C grade average was required for all work offered for the degree.

The Bachelor of Music and Bachelor of Music Education degrees, both of which required 79 semester hours of work in the major, could accommodate only 32 hours of course work in general education. Accordingly, music students took no work in science, no history or social sciences. In order to include the additional 18 hours of state-mandated professional education courses in the B.M.Ed. program, students had to complete 138 hours (compared to 124 hours for the B.A.), an exceedingly difficult regimen if they wanted to graduate in four years. For all their protestations of devotion to liberal arts education, the music faculty was determined to maintain a thoroughly professional, conservatory-style education. No one questioned the excellence of the music program or the quality of musicianship. And no matter how much the historians or biologists groused about "semiliterate singers" or "half-educated pianists," music was the queen of the sciences at Simpson, and everybody knew it.

Music customarily enrolled less than ten percent of the students as majors. In a 1952 survey, 36 of 391 students declaring majors listed music as their preference. Business administration claimed the largest number—65—followed by primary education tied with physical education at 42 each, home economics with 25, intermediate education and ministry with 22 each, chemistry with 19 and history with 15, trailed by a scattering in a wide range of traditional majors. Although some of the most popular studies were in the career-oriented fields, a good half of Simpson students planned to graduate in the liberal arts.[26]

Although Voigt frequently spoke out in favor of the liberal arts, he was willing to consider any number of vocational programs if they promised to slow the decline in student enrollment. He was ready to start a nurses training program with the Iowa Methodist Hospital in Des Moines and was disappointed when it did not materialize.[27] When student numbers continued their decline in 1952, he and many board members were prepared to jettison junior and senior level liberal arts courses with low enrollments—except those that served preministerial students—while retaining upper division courses in education and home economics.[28]

Still, for all the threats to the health of the humanities and the sciences, the liberal arts endured. More than that, in many a classroom they flourished, as dedicated faculty fought a rear guard action to prevent cutbacks. One had but to walk down the hall of the Administration Building to hear Harold Watson or Ruth Jackson holding forth, to peek into a chemistry laboratory in the old science building to see J. Allen Baker, aged and still charismatic, teaching with the same enthusiasm he had demonstrated a generation earlier, or to listen to Francis Moats deliver a well-crafted lecture and know that his students were sitting at the feet of a master. In short, the old guard, together with a few of their young disciples, people like Dave Mobberley and Howard Greenlee, were holding high the liberal arts tradition of Simpson. When Moats retired in 1952 and Baker a year later, each could look back on a remarkably successful life in teaching.

And who could forget that morning on a raw March day in 1951 when Harold Watson enlisted the talents of Peter Ross, central Iowa's most literate retired custodian, to speak to his eleven o'clock literature class? They would remember the old gentleman, white haired and bent with age, reciting in his clipped Scottish dialect the poems of Robert Burns, singing in a sweet tenor voice the lovely strains of "Flow Gently, Sweet Afton," and providing an "enthusiastic description of the trials of Tam O'Shanter."[29] This was one of Ross's annual recitations that had become a classic on the Simpson campus.

Ross's 1951 performance was his last. The Simpson community was saddened when the energetic little Scotsman died the next summer. Editor Scott Krane said what was in the hearts of all when he wrote in the *Simpsonian* about a man who

> through his own personality made himself a beloved institution. . . . He was a friend to more Simpson students than any other single person. Peter will never be forgotten by those who have heard him recite the poetry of Robert Burns or by those he helped in the numerous little problems which arose around the gym. And who could fail to be stirred by the sight of Peter slowly and proudly raising the flag of his adopted country before a Simpson basketball game.
>
> To those who knew him Peter will never be forgotten.[30]

* * *

During the first summer months of the "police action" in Korea in 1950, before Simpson's enrollment began to fall precipitously, the board of trustees continued to look at the College's construction needs. Available capital funds, consisting primarily of a $100,000 Annie Merner Pfeiffer pledge and the Gardner Cowles $125,000 gift (raised from $100,000), would meet only a fraction of the estimated cost of the three buildings the board of trustees proposed to erect. Still needed was $125,000 to complete the student union building, $150,000 more for the George Washington Carver Science Hall and $275,000 for the dormitory for men, making a total of $550,000 required to fulfill the entire building program.

The amount of money needed was indeed daunting, but the board set about to raise the whole amount in what they hoped would be a rapid, effective campaign. There was an air of urgency in their planning meetings, for the terms of the provisional Pfeiffer gift stipulated that to secure the $100,000 the College must let the contract for the student union and dormitory by January 8, 1951. Fortunately the board had already received almost a year earlier the endorsement of the Iowa-Des Moines Conference of the church for their fund drive, now designated the "Forward Movement Campaign."[31] General chairman of the drive was Bishop Charles W. Brashares, whose name was expected to open the hearts and pocketbooks of Iowa Methodists. Regrettably, it did not.

Although the campaign, carefully planned by professional counsel A. Ivan Pelter, was kicked off at the Methodist Church in Creston September 4, 1950, it never really got going. By the following February, at a time the campaign was supposed to be hitting its stride, Dr. Voigt could report only $121,169 pledged, of which $41,136 was in cash. The most Simpson could expect to get from conference churches was about $250,000, said Voigt with more hope than confidence. The whole fund drive, he lamented, was "disappointing." Somehow "we have not adequately 'sold' Simpson College to our church constituency, in spite of zealous efforts to do so over the period of the last seven years." The campaign in the Des Moines district netted only a modest return.[32]

In Warren County, to be sure, things went better, but then local people had always come through for Simpson. The Indianola drive, launched in April, was given impetus by the offer by the General Board of Education of the Methodist Church—through the good offices of John O. Gross—of $10,000 if Indianola would come up with $90,000. "All this outside money," said Board of Trustees Chairman William T. Hamilton to any Indianolan who would listen, "is coming to Indianola and will be spent here." These "outside givers," he pointed out, "have made their contributions to Simpson College because they believe in Christian education, and they have made these gifts with no thought of financial return." Thus "the citizens of Indianola should welcome an opportunity to make this undertaking a success and thereby make Simpson College strong."[33]

Still, when Voigt reported the general campaign results to the board at its June meeting that year, the figures were not encouraging. A total of $212,816 had been pledged, of which $69,237 was in cash. To do follow-up solicitation the board employed Simpson alumnus Dr. Guy Fansher '06, who had served eleven years as Methodist minister at Red Oak.[34] Less than a fortnight later the campaign total stood at $245,351. But the cost of the fund drive was $58,282, leaving a net—in pledges and cash—of $187,069, roughly one-third of their goal. The only really good news was that the Pfeiffer trustees had told Dr. Gross in Nashville that they would extend the deadline for their gift to January 1, 1953, but that there would be "absolutely no further extensions."[35]

Dr. Fansher stayed on as a fund-raiser for Simpson, his assignment to continue working with conference congregations, a relatively thankless task. In early 1952 the Forward Movement campaign was renamed "the Century Fund," looking to Simpson's centennial in 1960.[36]

Once again, Simpson was looking for capital funds in most of the wrong places. While some of the alumni were indeed good prospects, the churches and their congregations clearly were not. Conference congregations had never supported Simpson liberally, and there was little reason to believe that their attitude toward the College or their ability to give would change substantially. It appears that Simpson people either did not understand or refused to accept the fact that for any conference pastor, even those who were Simpson alumni, collecting money for Simpson represented a serious conflict of interest. Most of them were having enough difficulty making ends meet in their own churches, and they tended to see a dollar collected for Simpson to be a dollar lost from their lean church budgets. Small wonder, then, that many of them expressed their love for and admiration of Simpson but did little to further its interests locally.

At the same time the College did receive a few fortunate windfalls that nearly matched its financial campaign efforts. From the estate of Eliza R. Bailey of Greeley, Colorado, the College received $33,973.[37] From the estate of Dr. Elmer E. Kelly came $70,000, which was immediately allocated to the building fund.[38] Then in 1953 the Stanton Anthony Riker estate brought $5,000 to Simpson "to aid junior and senior students majoring in the study of the Bible."[39] Something of a surprise was $3,000 from Elizabeth M. Williams, the widow of the Reverend J. M. Williams of Des Moines, in settlement of an old unpaid pledge from the 1923 fund-raising campaign.[40]

Meanwhile, during the time the campaign for capital funds was meeting with discouraging results, the operating budget of the College could not be kept under control. Falling tuition income and rising costs led to a crisis situation by the fall of 1951. To alleviate the problem the board of trustees agreed to borrow $100,000 from the Equitable Life Insurance Company of Iowa, putting up the valuable Pittsburgh property as collateral. The loan would enable the College to pay off a $40,000 loan owing the Iowa State Bank and to "provide $60,000 working capital [i.e., operating funds] for the current emergency period."[41]

By the spring of 1952 Dr. Voigt could report that $300,000 in cash was available for construction projects, far short of the $800,000 needed.[42] By that time it was evident to the board that there was no way Simpson could raise that kind of money without borrowing at least part of the needed funds. Board members had been aware for nearly two years that government loan funds were being made available to colleges and universities on a limited basis for dormitory construction.[43] After gradually overcoming their inhibitions about going to the federal government for help—they had feared government aid might mean government interference and a blurring of church-state separation—they decided that the terms of the loans were so attractive that Simpson would be foolish to pass up the opportunity. It was only in 1952, however, that the loan program was funded sufficiently to give the College a reasonable chance for success with its application.

Wendell Tutt was appropriately designated as Simpson's man to negotiate with officials of what was now called the "Federal College Housing Loan Program."[44] It was decided that Simpson should apply for a forty-year loan of $225,000 for construction of the men's dormitory, at 3.01% interest.[45] The terms of the loan were indeed exceedingly generous. When the board agreed to seek the loan in November 1952, it was understood that it would require three to six months to process Simpson's application.[46] Because no construction contract could be awarded until the loan was approved, the College would not be able to meet the "final" Pfeiffer deadline. Thus while architects Poundstone, Ayers and Godwin were preparing final working plans and specifications for both the dormitory and the student union, the College asked the Pfeiffer trustees for yet one more extension. This time, because it was clear that the College was on the verge of commencing construction, the Pfeiffer trustees notified John O. Gross that Simpson could have three more months to award the contract.[47] Already the College had been authorized by the National Production Authority to commence construction and had been granted an allotment of critical materials for the two buildings.[48]

Simpson received word in April that the $225,000 loan had been approved. The College's negotiating officer was invited to appear in Washington, D.C., at 8:30 A.M. on April 28, 1952, to execute the loan agreement.[49] Wendell Tutt and William T. Hamilton were selected to go to Washington, but Hamilton suggested that Frank P. Henderson go in his place. Frank, after all, was an attorney and could deal with any legal issues that might arise. Tutt and Henderson made the trip, and the dormitory was thus assured. But they still needed an estimated $118,000 to complete the cost of the student union. Until that amount was somehow forthcoming, no contract could be let. Once again they went back to the General Board of Education of the Methodist Church for another extension on the Pfeiffer gift. The general board, authorized to act on behalf of the Pfeiffer interests, replied that Simpson would be granted the extension until January 1955, "with the understanding that no further extension would be given."[50] And it would be an agonizing several months more until a contract could be awarded for construction of the two buildings. By that time Dr. Voigt had resigned and a new president was in office.

* * *

The struggle to make the men's dormitory and student union a reality so monopolized the attention of Simpson people that it eclipsed other campus improvements that must not be overlooked. For example, with the construction of dormitory housing on the old football field next to Buxton Park, the College would have no practice field, and surely one was needed. The board's choice fell upon a tract of land along E Street south of Franklin Avenue and north of Detroit Avenue. In order to make enough space, the College bought some property from O. N. Lafollette of Indianola and another small parcel from V. C. Loring of Mason City.[51] After these purchases were completed, the College requested the Indianola City Council to close Euclid Avenue between D Street and E Street. This, said Wendell Tutt, would make possible locating a full-size practice field. The council cheerfully obliged.[52] In the fall of 1951 and the following winter the land was graded and seeded.[53] A little later that year the dusty parking lot behind the Administration Building, described as "a disaster" in view of the increasing number of automobiles crowding into limited space, was enlarged and surfaced with rock and oil.[54]

During the years of planning for the men's dormitory, the fraternities, unhappy with their inadequate old houses but unable to afford the cost of constructing modern dwellings, made any number of proposals to the College for fraternity housing. Administrative officials were fully aware of the sorry state of fraternity housing and concerned about the fraternities' plight, but were in no position to offer more than reassuring sounds of friendly sympathy.[55]

* * *

Meanwhile, only Lambda Chi Alpha among the four fraternities could be said to be adequately housed. No doubt its attractive dwelling was a major factor in Lambda Chi's reputation as the strongest fraternity on the campus. It certainly was the largest, and its lopsided success in pledging new men each year led to the abandonment in the fall of 1952 of deferred pledging—which had required freshman men to wait a semester before joining a fraternity—and limiting any one fraternity to a total membership of fifty-eight (twenty-five percent of the College's total male enrollment).[56] Even at that, Lambda Chi's roster totaled fifty-four during the 1952–53 school year—thirty-five initiated members and nineteen pledges. Among the pledges that fall was Robert Larsen, a freshman music major from Walnut, Iowa, who had come to Simpson in order to study piano with Sven Lekberg. When Larsen was initiated the following February, he was the five-hundredth member of the Theta Lambda Chapter of Lambda Chi Alpha.[57] Not only would he later join the Simpson music faculty soon after his graduation in 1956 and succeed Sven Lekberg as chairman of the department in 1965, but also his fellow initiate Ross Leeper would return to Simpson many years later in instrumental music and as director of the College band.

Although neither ATO nor KOY were as large or as prominent as Lambda Chi, their chapters flourished in spite of their dilapidated housing. The ATOs even wrested the scholarship trophy from Lambda Chi once in the spring of 1952. The Kappas continued their hallowed tradition of poor scholarship, even managing to rank below the Pi Kappa Phis, whose scholarship was abysmal, and scored their all-time worst in the fall of 1952 with a 1.588 average (on a 4.00 scale). Even Hiram Doty, who regularly took his meals at the Kappa house, was dismayed, suggesting to the boys that a modest amount of studying might improve their standing.[58] That same fall the KOYs celebrated their fiftieth anniversary, and although none of the charter members was able to attend, a large body of alumni did, including Simpson's board of trustees president William T. Hamilton, who was happy to point out any number of his Kappa alumni brothers whose mediocre scholarship record did not seem to stand in the way of great success in life. That was not the kind of thing President Voigt or Dean Bimson or most of the faculty wanted to hear.[59]

If the three old fraternities functioned well, the young Pi Kappa Phi did not. While it no doubt suffered from the College's falling enrollment, it encountered other problems as well. With little direction from alumni and minimal assistance from its national office, the chapter dwindled in size and effectiveness. When national Pi Kapp visitation officer Ramon F. Sanchez came to the campus during the fall of 1952, he found the condition of the chapter beyond redemption. In early February 1953, Dean Oliver Bimson announced that he had received word from the national office of Pi Kappa Phi "that the operation of the Simpson chapter will be discontinued by removal of the chapter."[60]

Three of the four sororities were strong and healthy, but the Theta Upsilons, who celebrated their twenty-fifth anniversary at Simpson in 1950, declined in numbers until there were only four pictured with their housemother, Belva Crosswait, in the 1952 *Zenith*. President Voigt found it necessary to quell the rumor that the national sorority was about to withdraw the chapter's charter. "Theta Upsilon will remain at Simpson," he said, "and is welcome to do so."[61] When the Theta Upsilon field secretary visited in early 1953, many feared that she would recommend closing the chapter, but she was heartened to find a small but intensely loyal, enthusiastic group of young women.[62] Although their chapter was tiny by any standard, its members participated with zest and considerable courage in every College event and competition. They surely made up in closeness what they lacked in size. The other sororities, to be sure, with their larger numbers, walked away with most of the prizes and trophies. The Alpha Chis finally successfully challenged the Pi Phis' four-year scholarship dominance, winning the trophy five of six semesters between 1950 and 1953, and the Tridelts won the Tomahawk at Homecoming in 1951.

* * *

Simpson's enrollment decline after 1950 was reflected on the playing field as it was in the classroom. After winning the conference championship in 1949, the football team saw its fortunes take a bad turn. Reviews of the three seasons beginning in 1950 speak of "bad breaks and lack of reserves" of a team that played "good, clean football" (1950), a team "jinxed by [military] service and graduation" (1951) and "the only conference team to score on [Iowa] Wesleyan, the Iowa Conference champs" (1952), as the Redmen compiled a dismal record of eight wins and eighteen losses.[63] Still, some individual standout players won all-conference honors: guard Everett Hidlebaugh in 1950, tackle Al Benson and back Jim Mathew the next year, and tackle Bob Moore and back Ed Weeks in 1952. Weeks was also the leading conference scoring ace in 1952, and Howard Justice tied for second place that same year.

The powerhouse teams of the conference in 1950 and 1951 were St. Ambrose and Loras, each compiling a 5-0 record in the conference before meeting in the play-off, won by St. Ambrose both times. Football was surely king at St. Ambrose, whose 1950 team, playing a thirteen-game schedule, won its first four games in thirteen days. After both Loras and St. Ambrose utterly dominated the conference again in 1951, the other league members voted to drop both schools from conference football competition after the 1951-52 year. At the other end of the athletic power spectrum was William Penn, which dropped out of the conference in 1950 after twenty-nine straight football losses.[64]

Frank Casey's basketball teams won about one-third of their games during the 1950-53 era, compiling a 24-50 record. In spite of their disappointing record, these teams produced several top players, including all-conference forward Roger Cleven in 1952 and Ed Weeks, whose basketball prowess matched his skill in football, in 1953. Had scoring records been kept in 1952, Cleven's 370 points would have put him among the conference leaders. The team's strength was bolstered in the 1953 season when Chuck Kerr returned to Simpson after his second hitch in the Navy.

Coach Casey's track teams performed well, placing third in the conference in 1951, second in 1952 and third in 1953, well behind conference leader Dubuque, coached by Simpson alumnus Moco Mercer. During these same years Hap Miller's baseball teams performed very well indeed. In 1951 they lost to Iowa Wesleyan for the southern division championship; in 1952 they shared the conference crown with Loras behind the superior pitching of Clair "Skip" Eason. Unfortunately no suitable date could be found for a play-off. The 1953 season, highlighted once again by Eason's pitching, saw the Redmen win the southern division and lose to Buena Vista in the play-off for the championship 2-1.

During these years there was a concerted attempt in the conference to curb overemphasis on athletics, especially football, and to regularize recruiting and awarding of athletic grants-in-aid to players. In the fall of 1951, for example, the decision was taken to eliminate spring football practice. Simpson was unaffected because it never had held spring practice, but St. Ambrose was defiant, providing good reason for the conference's dropping St. Ambrose from membership.[65] The following February the presidents of member colleges met at Waverly to deal with the growing burden of athletic scholarships and recruitment practices. Their meeting, however, produced little more than a pious declaration that Iowa Conference schools should follow N.C.A.A. guidelines and stiffen eligibility rules for athletes. Simpson was at this time a member of N.A.I.A., which Frank Casey had helped found in 1940. The N.A.I.A. sought valiantly to make athletics a part of a student's academic experience and to eschew the professionalism of big, money-making programs. But N.A.I.A. too permitted grants-in-aid to athletes under sufficiently liberal guidelines as to invite abuse, and abuses there were.

For its part, the North Central Association, the academic agency on whose accreditation Simpson depended, deplored the growth of athletic scholarships. In a 1952 statement the association made its position clear: "Special efforts to recruit students of athletic prowess for the primary purpose of developing winning athletic teams are unworthy of an institution of higher education." Further, "students should not be subsidized for athletics nor should athletic ability be taken into consideration in granting student aid." Nor should outside groups contribute either to the athlete or to the college's athletic aid budget.[66]

President Voigt was convinced that the hard-line North Central Association stand would lead to subterfuge, for "any institution will find appropriate financial need for every athlete of quality and ability." He concluded that "N.C.A. means what it says, but will not be able to enforce it." He was candid in admitting that "we compete for students" and give athletes scholarships. But, with just a trace of self-righteousness, he proclaimed "we never give more than half scholarships, while other colleges are giving up to full tuition."[67]

The problem of athletic scholarships would continue to plague Simpson and its fellow Iowa colleges until the advent of Division III in the N.C.A.A., forbidding athletic scholarships altogether.

* * *

Simpson's undergraduate publications, like its intercollegiate athletics, suffered from the loss both of students and funding after 1950. The editor of the 1952 *Zenith*, Jerry Howlett, apologized for the quality of the yearbook, citing "increased cost of production in publishing and the decrease of the budget." Actually, the volume he and his staff produced was really quite attractive and informative, graphically a considerable improvement over the much larger *Zenith* of the previous year. The *Simpsonian*'s revenues declined as enrollment fell, and it is remarkable—and admirable—that the quality of the newspaper was sustained. In the fall of 1951 it was reduced from thirty to twenty-four issues per year in order to stay within its reduced budget. The Homecoming edition, scheduled for October 8, was said "to be late or not at all."[68] If it was published, no copy of it seems to have survived. The *Sequel*, though reduced in size, continued to showcase the best undergraduate writing at Simpson.[69]

Whatever the quality of the College's student publications, their staffs never had enough space or the facilities to do their work, and their pleas for improved working conditions fell on deaf ears. Yet during those difficult years one important step forward was taken when it was determined to create a publications board to select editors and business managers of the *Zenith* and *Simpsonian*, previously named by the Student Congress, a procedure that had been sometimes swayed by independent-fraternity politicking.[70]

That campus politics was for the most part dominated by the Greek houses should be no surprise, for in 1950 almost forty-seven percent of the undergraduates were affiliated and by 1953 the percentage had climbed to fifty-seven percent.[71] Yet the Greeks turned out a substantial, crucial vote for nonaffiliated Perry Wilkins, one of only three black men in the student body, who was elected Student Congress president for 1953–1954 by a lopsided 167 votes to 90 for his nearest rival.

* * *

President Voigt, distressed by the bewildering, indeed frightening, changes in student mores and behavior, troubled by the powerful forces of secularism that swept over the campus, sought to counsel undergraduates to accept a Christian way of life at Simpson. "To be civilized human beings," he said at the first college chapel of the year in the fall of 1951, "means to accept the folkways of the group and while in Rome to act as the Romans do." But he went on to say: "Obviously, too, the opposite is true. To accept without protest everything that takes place or is offered us is an indication of weakness. A student who has been reared to observe certain niceties and respect certain sanctities and then turns collegeate [sic] or worldly, makes himself ridiculous." He pleaded for student understanding of Simpson's determination to uphold Christian standards. Although "a certain campus democracy is part of the place and . . . is part of us," he said, "we know equally well that [students at] an educational institution, affiliated as we are, with a church, simply don't have a bar, a bingo game and a Bohemian indifference to the clock or personal decencies." He counseled students "to avoid future discomfitures, not to indulge in small peccadillos which may be found out next semester or next year."[72]

Religious activity on the campus was intermittent and church events for the most part poorly attended. When popular alumnus Glen Lamb spoke at Religious Emphasis Week in 1951, he drew a large crowd, but the name of the event itself underscored the fact that religion was not emphasized most of the time. Interest in religious matters "kind of comes and goes" at the College, commented the *Simpsonian*. How could it be made more integral to Simpson life? How about competition? "Would it be right to have competition on something of a religious nature in order to sell it?"[73] Maybe they could offer a trophy for the campus organization that scored the highest average attendance at Sunday school or at vespers. Maybe the sororities could assign their pledges to earn points by going to church en masse. Small wonder Voigt was depressed.

To counteract the slide into secularism and to reassure conference clergy that Simpson was still dedicated to the cause of evangelical religion, Voigt invited the Methodist ministers from the entire state to hold their Iowa Pastors School at Indianola, as nearly centrally located as any place in the state. The 1953 school, for example, drew 300 pastors during late January between Simpson's fall and spring semesters. Most were housed in Mary Berry and the "new" women's dormitory; 24 of them slept on cots in the men's locker room in Hopper Gymnasium. Although none of them met any vacationing Simpson students except by accident, they returned home reassured about the College's role as promoter of Christian virtue and its students as an acceptably Christian lot.[74] The pastors school became an annual week-long event at Simpson, helping to cement the relationship between the College and the church.

Religious or not, students were on the whole well behaved. True, some young women were "campused" (i.e., confined to the campus and not permitted to engage in organized social activities) for a weekend because of violating the residence hall curfew; some young men (those few who were caught) were put on "social probation" for indiscreet beer drinking or other assorted mischief, but most students either obeyed the rules or were extraordinarily skilled in circumventing them.

Students during these years enjoyed "picnics and parties" most of all, and these events were usually well chaperoned by faculty members. Writing on "Social Life on the Simpson Campus" in the 1953 *History of Warren County, Iowa*, young biology professor David Mobberley, who had his finger on the student pulse better than anyone besides the dean of women, reviewed the major traditional activities of the school year. One gets the distinct impression that Mobberley knew more than he was telling when summarizing the social events of the 1951–52 year. He praised Miniature Orpheum, noting that "in recent years the skits have been of excellent quality and the competition has been especially keen,"[75] despite the fact that the *Simpsonian* had exploded with indignation the prior spring, charging that "the work of good men and the reputation of Simpson College are undermined by the filthy jokes at Miniature Orpheum."[76] Recalling "mock chapel," a feature of Campus Day in the spring of the year, Mobberley acknowledged approvingly that "students avail themselves of the opportunity for presenting caricatures which depict the mannerisms exhibited by many of the professors on campus." He found it "the most hilarious occasion of the whole college year," a judgment not shared by some professors whose mannerisms had been lampooned only too skillfully. At the end of this account, Mobberley tried to put the College's social life into perspective: "It should be remembered that, while the major emphasis in going to college should be directed toward the accumulation of knowledge and skills, the whole process of becoming adjusted to adult living in the twentieth century must take into account the meeting of social needs and the learning of social graces. The entire social life program of the college is directed toward that end."[77]

It is understandable why the students elected Mobberley "Big Chief" at Homecoming that year. Few professors were as popular as he, despite the fact that his classes in biology were rigorous in the extreme. And Ethel D. Anderson, unremittingly dedicated in her home economics classes and informal activities to the cultivation of the social graces among the students, some of whom were known to have rough edges that needed smoothing, took up her civilizing mission with the zeal of an evangelist.

* * *

When President Voigt went to the West Coast late in 1950 to visit alumni, he called on Ella Dowler Duncan, at ninety-one the College's oldest alumna, at her home in Beverly Hills. Although she had enrolled in the class of 1876, she attended Simpson only two years from 1872 to 1874. An original member of Simpson's I. C. Chapter, founded in 1874, she was in 1950 the oldest living member of Pi Beta Phi in the United States.[78] Proud of her antiquity, she welcomed Dr. Voigt in an acceptably grandmotherly way. The activities of other alumni of more recent vintage were reported in the College's publications. Avery Craven '08, chairman of the history department at the University of Chicago, reported from England his appointment as visiting Pitt professor of American history at Cambridge University.[79] On a journey from India, James McEldowney '28 visited the Simpson campus, expressing the hope that his children might be able one day to attend Simpson.[80] They did. Nearer home, three alumni served in the Iowa General Assembly in 1951: Helen Rohrer Crabb '40 and L. Dee Mallonee '12 in the House of Representatives, and Jay Colburn '16 in the Senate.[81]

The 1950–51 edition of *Who's Who in America* contained the names of twenty-eight Simpson graduates, representing 9.4 entries per 1,000 graduates. Among the thirteen Iowa colleges and universities, both public and private, whose graduates were listed in a survey of the *Who's Who* biographies, Simpson ranked third behind Grinnell and Cornell.[82]

Among Simpson's distinguished alumni was Dr. Paul Giddens '24, whose career in academic and public history had led him to the post of curator of the Drake Museum at Titusville, Pennsylvania. In early 1953 he accepted the post of president of Hamline University in St. Paul, replacing Hurst R. Anderson, who had been called in June 1952 to the presidency of American University in Washington, D.C. As Giddens walked in the door of his new school in January, he ran into the chairman of the philosophy department, who had just been elected president of Simpson and was on his way to Indianola within a matter of days.

The College mourned the loss of a number of alumni during these last Voigt years. Chief among them was Dr. Edward H. Todd '88, president of the College of Puget Sound from 1913 to 1942, who died at his home at Tacoma, Wash. on May 19, 1951, just nine weeks after the death of his wife, Florence Moore Todd, also a Simpson graduate.[83] Anna McLaughlin Buxton '90, the widow of William Buxton, Jr., and mother of William III, died August 25, 1950.[84]

* * *

Indianola was still a Republican stronghold during the early fifties, and to a degree Simpson students reflected the political coloring of the local community and the other southwest Iowa rural counties from which most of them came. In the general elections in 1952 Warren County contributed to the Eisenhower landslide. The four Indianola wards gave Eisenhower nearly a 3 to 1 majority over Adlai Stevenson and came through for Republican incumbent Governor William S. Beardsley of New Virginia by almost the same margin over Democrat Herschel Loveless.[85] Down at the *Record-Herald* Don Berry savored the victory as a farmer welcomes a rain after a long drought. "We sympathize," he wrote, "with those Democrats who feel this morning that the life of the nation is threatened. We have felt that way for the past five presidential elections. We are still alive. We believe the Democrats will find that the sun will still rise and the government at Washington still lives. For the time being our heart goes out to them until their legs become steady again."[86]

Because the Simpson political poll a week before the election had given Eisenhower almost exactly the same margin—2 to 1—that prevailed in Warren County, there was no marked political tension between the College and the local community. Simpson was as welcome in Indianola as it had ever been, especially when a survey conducted in 1950 showed that the College's faculty, staff and students spent an aggregate $359,000 per year with Indianola businesses, exclusive of what the College itself actually bought locally.[87]

Further cementing good town-gown relationships, Dr. Voigt announced in 1951 the creation by the College of a Community Service Award "to give recognition and appreciation to the person who has rendered outstanding leadership and service to the civic betterment of the Indianola community with particular emphasis on voluntary service rather than that which comes through a profession or through line of duty."[88] The first award, for 1951, honored outstanding Indianola high school teacher Arthur Eady primarily for his service as chairman of the board of the Warren County Group Center.[89] From that time forward the award came to symbolize the mutual good will that marked the relations between the College and the community.

* * *

For Dr. Voigt, the celebration in January 1952 of his tenth anniversary as president of Simpson was a bittersweet event. On the one hand he could enjoy immensely the surprise party staged at the Y.W.C.A. room by the faculty and staff and attended by local members of the board of trustees.[90] On the other hand, the College was only days away from another semester of record low postwar enrollment, and prospects for improving admissions were dismal.

During the months that followed, Dr. Voigt prepared himself for a change. A combination of weariness in the Simpson presidency and a longing to do what he had long dreamed of doing led him to consider taking action sooner rather than later. Through the years he had attended Methodist general conferences and meetings of the church's college presidents and had become well known among the nation's Methodist leaders. A role in church leadership attracted him. The opportunity for such a role was afforded him at the church's nine-state, northcentral jurisdictional conference at Milwaukee, Wisconsin, where he was elected one of three new bishops on the fourteenth ballot on July 11, 1952. He was assigned to a new episcopal district that included North and South Dakota, headquartered at Aberdeen, South Dakota.[91] Duly inducted into his new post on Sunday the thirteenth, he submitted his resignation at Simpson forthwith.[92]

The following Tuesday the executive committee learned to their dismay that Dr. Voigt would need to take up his new duties in South Dakota in no more than three weeks.[93] That same evening faculty and board members and their wives and husbands honored the new bishop and his wife with an informal reception at the new women's dormitory. Wendell Tutt, who introduced Dr. and Mrs. Voigt in a brief program, lavished great praise on the president and his wife, reviewing the major accomplishments of the Voigt administration, capped by the "two new buildings which we hope will be started before the snow flies." The president responded appreciatively, beaming in anticipation of the challenge of his new calling: "We could not have hoped for the honor we received," he said.[94] Still, to those who attended this pleasant event Dr. Voigt's imminent departure was troubling.

The board of trustees moved immediately to name an executive committee to run the College until a new president could take office, selecting Oliver H. Bimson, dean of the College as chairman, together with treasurer Wendell Tutt and vice-president Gilbert S. Stout. The committee would take up its work on the effective date of Dr. Voigt's resignation, August 9.[95]

At the same time, they selected the first members of a search committee to look for a new president. Board president William T. Hamilton chaired the group which included board secretary Frank P. Henderson and William Buxton III, president of the Peoples Trust and Savings Bank. Chairman Hamilton, however, sensing that the time was right to turn over the reins to another, resigned from the board altogether at the time of Voigt's departure. His place on the search committee fell to Don L. Berry, vice-president of the board.[96] In an unusual departure from normal practice, Dr. Voigt was named to the search committee, but his role was minimal, for he left Indianola in late August to take up his episcopal duties in South Dakota.[97] Upon Voigt's departure the board brought in fellow board member Raoul C. Calkins, superintendent of the church's Des Moines district, who was immediately chosen to replace Hamilton as chair of the search committee. Thus there was on the committee an appropriate official to represent church interests in the selection process. And by mid-September the committee had been further enlarged by adding Agnes Samuelson, assistant director of public education at the National Education Association's national headquarters in Washington, D.C., and N. D. McCombs, superintendent of schools in Des Moines, both Simpson board members. When Gerald Ensley was installed as Bishop of the Iowa-Des Moines Conference's 280,000 Methodists September 18, 1952, he was included in the search committee by brevet. Then, apparently as something of an afterthought, the board asked three faculty members to join the committee: J. Allen Baker, Howard S. Greenlee and Sven Lekberg.[98]

Starting its work in August, the expanding search committee sought and received a large number of nominations for the presidency of Simpson. Don Berry observed that their quest might be a long one. "It could take several months," he guessed. It did.

* * *

At a festive farewell reception for the Voigts at the parish hall of the Methodist Church in early August, two hundred and fifty friends and well wishers joined to pay tribute to the work of this popular president and wife. Yet for all the kind words and expressions of admiration for Dr. Voigt, a few of those present—especially those who knew the College best—were concerned, even fearful about Simpson's future. It was late summer now, and fall enrollment did not look good. They were on the verge of building the long-needed men's dormitory and student union, but the whole process had dragged on for too many wrenching years. The faculty, much reduced in members, was in turmoil still. Only six of them had been at Simpson a decade earlier, their small number damaging continuity. The College leadership seemed to have no agreed-upon vision of what Simpson's mission was or ought to be. Simpson seemed to be stumbling along, taking one year at a time, its course uncharted, its curriculum unfocused, its faculty undercompensated, its students unmoved.

In his letter of resignation, Dr. Voigt seemed to sense the malaise that held Simpson in its grip: "I have hoped, and I do hope for great things for Simpson," he wrote, "and I am saddened by the knowledge that more progress has not been made during the ten years I was privileged to hold this office of high trust." Surely, he said, "new leadership will be advantageous."[99]

Some years later, when he was serving, in his second episcopal appointment, in the Illinois conference, Dr. Voigt, recalling his years at Simpson, spoke nostalgically about the good times and the bad. Asked to evaluate his contributions to the College, he said "I don't think I did anything that was wrong when I was at Simpson, but I know now that there were a lot of things that I did *not* do that were right." Probably, he said, the College should have reached out beyond the Methodist conference for support; perhaps "we should have not been so fearful about raising tuition charges"; and it was clear that the board of trustees needed restructuring. "We were comfortable in our warm little Indianola cocoon, perhaps too oblivious of the world beyond us, but I know too that there was a beautiful butterfly in that cocoon, just waiting to emerge. It did, and I am so happy to see the new Simpson spreading its wings."[100]

THE SIMPS

DEVOTED TO THE NEWS AND VIEWS OF SIM

VOLUME LXXXII   INDIANOLA, IOWA, MONDAY, SEPTEMBE

RELIGIOUS EMPHASIS WEE

SORORITY RUSH ENDS, 22 COEDS PLEDGED TUESDAY

Rush Week Activities Listed

Twenty-two Simpson coeds have taken the first step to becoming part of the Greek sorority world. Pledging was preceded by a "rush week" that fully lived up to its name.

Activities got under way with the Pan-hellenic tea held for sorority women and girls out for rushing at the Pi Beta Phi house Tuesday, September 16. Wednesday and Thursday rushees attended one hour parties at each of the four sorority houses, Alpha Chi Omega, Delta Delta Delta, Pi Beta Phi, and Theta Upsilon.

Two hour invitational parties were held at the sorority houses Friday and Saturday. Preference dinners Monday night were followed by after-hours candlelight serenades.

Pledging ceremonies were held Tuesday evening for the following girls:

Alpha Chi Omega—Lu Ann Groteluschen, Audubon; Joyce Hamilton, St. Joseph, Mo.; Joanne Heidman, Granger; Helen Jensen, Harlan; Barbara Launspach, Indianola; Carol Shearer, Peru; Marie Vickroy, Indianola; Lee Ellen Vieth, Oakland; Mary Kay Wires, Des Moines.

Delta Delta Delta—Jackie Beaman, Mount Ayr; Allegra Bryan, Indianola; Loreta Gilliland, Indianola; Jeanne Peterson, Indianola; Keralyn Phillips, Griswold; Karin Quick, Des Moines; Cheryl Randleman, Carlisle.

Pi Beta Phi—Barbara Anderson, Madrid; Cynthia Jones, Oskaloosa; Myrna Kirkham, Norwalk; Doris Kitzman, Beaman; Eleanor Miller, Knoxville; Darlene Stout, Parsons, Kansas.

All are freshman girls with the exception of Miss Stout who is a transfer student.

Miss Elizabeth White, dean of women, directed the activities.

Shirley Gardner assisted by Bev Labertew was in charge of Alpha Chi rush plans. A circus theme complete with Audrey the trained bear was used for their one hour parties. Tri Delts with Kathryn Smith as rush Chairman staged a style show at their first parties. Bluebeard and his seven wives appeared at the Pi Phi house during the one hour parties. Coleen Daulton and assistant Gloria Metcalf headed Pi Phi rush activities.

Enrollment Reaches 400 Mark Last Week

As of Wednesday there were 400 students enrolled for the first semester at Simpson college, according to the Registrar's office.

The student body is composed of 237 men and 163 women. A breakdown by classes shows 79 seniors, 67 juniors, 108 sophomores, 139 freshmen, and seven specials. The difference of 40 students between last fall and the present enrollment is almost the same as the decrease in veterans of World War II enrolled at Simpson. In 1951-52 there were 58 vets compared to 20 this semester. However nine students from the Korean campaign are now registered for classes. Last year there were no students in this classification.

Five Students' 4.00 Averages Top Honor Roll

Five students topped the honor roll for the second semester of last year with 4.00 (straight A) averages. They were Earl Boltinghouse, Anna Channel, Ralph Keller, William McCutcheon, and George Paterson.

Boltinghouse was a freshman, Miss Channel a junior, and the remaining three were seniors.

HONOR ROLL

4.00—Earl Boltinghouse, Anna Channel, Ralph Keller, William McCutcheon, George Paterson.
3.82—Robert Wiley.
3.74—Roger Witke.
3.73—Marilyn Hull.
3.62—Robert Embree.
3.60—Shirley Broderson, Beverly Labertew.
3.57—Theora Snethen, Janet Wilson.
3.53—Martha Dinwiddie, Shirley Zaiger.
3.50—James Nelson.
3.47—Jo Ann Guthrie, Carmen Vasquez.
3.44—Eugene Young.
3.42—Betty Budd, Joyce Fulton.
3.41—Keith Swanson.
3.40—Kathryn Smith.
3.38—Mary Faith Hays.
3.36—Bernadine Hodges.
3.33—Jean Blouse, Earl Henry, David Ward Young.
3.31—Charlotte Clark.
3.29—Glen Johnson.
3.27—Barbara Compton.
3.25—Albert Benson, Nelson Crow.
3.24—Shirley Kapple, Scott Krane, James Reed, Jo Ann Stark.
3.21—Kermit Cook, Amy Myers.
3.18—Darlene Miller.
3.17—Madalyn Clark.
3.14—Virginia Baxendale, Samuel Lundhigh, Roberta Swigart.

Dr. Voigt Resigns To Become Bishop

Dr. Edwin E. Voigt is a newly-elected bishop of the Methodist church. Election came at the North Central Jurisdictional conference of the church, at Milwaukee, July 7-13.

Dr. Voigt's assignment is the newly created episcopal district including North and South Dakota. The Voigt family left Indianola the last of August and will make their home in Aberdeen.

An administrative committee, appointed by the board of trustees to handle the college vacancy until a president is chosen, is composed of Dean Bimson, chairman, Business manager Tutt and vice president Stout.

A selection committee of the board of trustees has been appointed to nominate a new president. Upon nomination by this special committee the board of trustees vote on the candidate. This selection committee is composed of chairman Raoul C. Calkins, minister, superintendent, Des Moines district, Methodist church, Des Moines; William Buxton III, President, Peoples Trust & Savings bank, Indianola; Don Berry, vice president of board of trustees, Indianola; F. P. Henderson, attorney, Indianola; Agnes Samuelson, Assistant director of public education, National Education Association, Washington, D. C.; and N. D. McCombs, superintendent of schools, Des Moines. The committee has been meeting candidates but is far from a selection according to Mr. Berry.

ALPHA CHI OMEGA HAS TOP GRADES FOR LAST TERM

ATO Leads All Men's Groups

Alpha Chi Omega won the top honors for the second semester last year, according to the figures released by the Registrar's office. The Alpha Chi's grade point average was 2.687.

Second honors went to Pi Beta Phi with an average of 2.593.

The average for "organized women" the second semester last year was 2.572. This was .028 over that of the "All women" average.

Alpha Tau Omega won top honor's in the men's organization, with an average of 2.292. They also made the greatest improvement in grade point average. Their average the second semester was 2.292 compared to 2.115 the first semester. This moved the Taus from 14th to 12th.

The grade point average for the "entire student body" dropped from 2.332 to 2.310. The figures for organized women, all women and all men were lower, but the organized men's average went up .037 points.

SUMMARY OF SCHOLASTIC RATINGS

Second Semester—1951-52

Alpha Chi Omega	2.687
Pi Beta Phi	2.593
Organized Women	2.572
All Women	2.544
Delta Deltao Delta	2.537
Mary Berry	2.529
Women's Dormitory	2.434
Center House	2.432
Theta Upsilon	2.401
All Nat'l Org.	2.328
Entire Student Body	2.310
Alpha Tau Omega	2.292
Lambda Chi Alpha	2.244
All Men	2.146
Organized Men	2.129
Pi Kappa Phi	1.880
Kappa Theta Psi	1.844

Administrative Rule Changes Announced

With the beginning of the school year getting into full swing, some changes have been made since last year.

One of the changes is the ten minute period between classes, differing from the five minute period last year. The administration felt that this was a very beneficial change since it will aid both the student and the instructor.

For the student it will permit him to get to his next class without having to rush so much. This way he is enabled to be in his seat at the beginning of the class hour instead of coming in late. As far as the instructor is concerned, he should definitely be able to start his class five minutes after the hour without any interruption. The student body should not abuse this plan by staying for an extra cup of coffee, nor should the professor by keeping his students after the bell has rung.

Another major change is the fact that class attendance is not turned in every day to the Dean. This plan differs from last year's when each instructor's report was turned in daily to the Dean of the college. Students are therefore responsible to the instructor of classes they

continued on page 3

In September 1952 the *Simpsonian* announced the beginning of Religious Emphasis Week, the departure of President E. E. Voigt who was elevated to a Methodist bishopric, declining enrollment, sorority rush and academic grade rankings of campus individuals and groups. Note that only 16 students earned a grade point average of 3.50 or higher.

XVII

Simpson's Renaissance: The Kerstetter Years 1953–63

The search for a new president, undertaken as soon as Ed Voigt announced his resignation in July 1952, should have been easy, for there were candidates aplenty. It seemed that nearly every Methodist bishop or seminary head, not to speak of local conference clergy, submitted nominations. Any number of hopefuls sent in their own applications, some of their thick dossiers crammed with impressive documentation and enthusiastic letters of recommendation. If the number of candidates was any measure, it should have been easier to find a new president than it was to hire a new instructor in sociology, but it was not. The search committee soon discovered that some of the strongest nominees were either uninterested or were already committed elsewhere. Others were interested enough, but upon examination of the condition of the College, found the challenge too formidable. Only a handful emerged who were clearly promising. Still fewer were interviewed intensively, and of these only one or two seemed right for the job. Then the best of these withdrew from consideration. After months of work, the search committee came up frustratingly empty-handed.

What was to be done? It would have been embarrassing to reopen the search formally, and there was the risk that if they turned to their usual sources of information, they would get more of the same sort of nominees. Perhaps, just perhaps, suggested Don Berry, they were looking in the wrong places. William Buxton was inclined to agree. Bishop Gerald Ensley, whose ex officio membership on the search committee was thought by some to be primarily ornamental, and who had consequently been disinclined to take a lead in the process, now responded thoughtfully to Berry's suggestion. They had not really thought to look beyond the active parish clergy for a new president. Why not, he said, consider people from the realm of Methodist higher education. If the suggestion to look beyond the clergy for candidates had the support of a bishop, reasoned the search committee, it must be all right. Perhaps unconsciously they had neglected to seek out candidates from other colleges. The only earlier Simpson leaders who had come from other academic institutions were presidents Harper and Gross, and although both had come from former college presidencies, they stayed at Simpson only two and three years respectively, hardly long enough to satisfy the College's needs.

"I know a remarkable young man," said Bishop Ensley, "who just might be interested in coming to Simpson." He was Dr. William Edward Kerstetter, head of the Department of Philosophy and Religion at Hamline University in St. Paul, Minnesota. True, he was only thirty-nine, and he possessed neither experience in college administration nor a record as a full-time minister in a church. But, said Ensley reassuringly, Kerstetter was a good Methodist, an ordained clergyman who had served as a chaplain in the Army, held an earned doctorate in philosophy, was a happily married father of two children, but above all was reputed to be a strong man with a vision of what a college of liberal arts and sciences ought to be. If there was anything Simpson needed in 1952, it was a dedicated leader who not only knew where he wanted the College to go but who also possessed the practical skills of statesmanship to translate his vision into reality. Everyone agreed to have a close look at Kerstetter. It was a long shot, but at the moment Kerstetter was their only target. Bishop Ensley would give him a call.

* * *

William Edward Kerstetter was born April 25, 1913, at Lykens, a village on a tributary of the Susquehanna River called Wiconisco Creek in the upper reaches of Dauphin County, a few hills away from the state capital at Harrisburg. He was the son of Pennsylvania Dutch coal miner William Kerstetter and Susan Rudisill Kerstetter. The boy's earliest years were lived in an atmosphere of simple piety and hard work. Life in the isolated mining communities was never easy, and for the Kerstetters it became incalculably more difficult when the elder Kerstetter perished in the great influenza epidemic in 1919 at the age of thirty-one, leaving his wife and four children—young Bill had two older sisters and a brother younger by two years—to fend for themselves.

The widow Susan secured employment as an unskilled clerk at the state capitol in Harrisburg but was hard put to make ends meet for her family. How to rear and see to the education of four children seemed to be an almost insurmountable task until she learned about Girard College, a prestigious preparatory boarding school in Philadelphia. Founded in 1848 with a handsome bequest from the great banker and financier Stephen Girard (1750–1831), the school was established to make available a free elementary and secondary education to poor orphaned or fatherless boys. Young Bill Kerstetter, nine years old and ready for the fourth grade, entered Girard College in the fall of 1922. A good student, he met and exceeded the high academic standards for which the school was known. And the next year his brother, age eight, entered Girard as well.[1] They lived at the school nine months a year and spent their summers at home with their mother and sisters.

At Girard, Kerstetter grew accustomed to the boys' school atmosphere, conformed to the discipline of the headmasters and excelled in soccer, baseball and basketball. In the classroom, on the playing field and in the residence hall, he learned to relate to boys from varied ethnic and religious backgrounds. "At Girard," recalled Kerstetter later, "I learned compassion for those who suffered prejudice."[2] He also demonstrated remarkable academic ability, graduating as salutatorian in his 1930 class and recipient of the coveted Key Man Prize, a fine watch awarded annually to that senior student judged to have the outstanding overall achievement in scholarship, athletics, citizenship and leadership.

Upon graduation Kerstetter worked for two years at the Bell Telephone Company of Pennsylvania in its plant accounting office, joined the Methodist Church with which his family had already affiliated and decided to study for the Christian ministry. In the depth of the depression he entered Dickinson College, one of Methodism's oldest academic bastions, at Carlisle, Pennsylvania. There he majored in English literature and took a minor in philosophy, continuing the pattern of academic excellence that had earned him a scholarship at the College. He proved also to be a remarkably versatile athlete, lettering in soccer, basketball and track. Later he was captain of one team, co-captain of another, and coached one sport during his senior year, when he was also selected as the most valuable basketball player.

Kerstetter was initiated into the Phi Kappa Sigma fraternity and resided in the chapter house after his freshman year in a residence hall. Around the house he was regarded with some awe as an intellectual, a preministerial nondrinker whom they nicknamed "Bishop." The name is an interesting commentary on the way his fraternity brothers saw Kerstetter. They could have called him "Parson" or "Preacher," but this young man was too dignified, too reserved for anything less than "Bishop." True, some of the boys called him the "Dancing Deacon," presumably out of respect for his athletic or even terpsichorean skills.

From Dickinson Kerstetter entered Boston University's School of Theology in 1936 to study for the ministry. There he worked under some of the brightest stars in the Methodist constellation, but best by far was Edgar S. Brightman, whose brilliant teaching in philosophy persuaded Kerstetter to seek a Ph.D. in that discipline. After graduating magna cum laude in theology in 1939, Kerstetter was awarded the Jacob Sleeper Fellowship for study in Europe, but Hitler's attack on Poland prevented overseas study of any kind. Instead he continued his studies with the aid of prestigious fellowships and summer employment at Boston University's graduate school, receiving the Ph.D. in philosophy in 1943. His work with Brightman was supplemented by study with Ralph Barton Perry and William Ernest Hocking at Harvard and personal acquaintance with Alfred Martin Whitehead. With wide interests in philosophy, Kerstetter concerned himself with social philosophy, philosophy of religion, theory of knowledge and philosophy of science, all of which would lead him ultimately to a special interest in the philosophy of education. His doctoral dissertation, a study of democracy, was entitled "John Locke's Conception of Freedom." His research for the dissertation, he has said, "enriched my life and thought."

His life was meanwhile also enriched by his marriage on Christmas day, 1941, to Leona Frances Bateman, whom he met while he was serving part-time as an assistant to the Rev. F. Gerald Ensley at a church in Norwood, Massachusetts. She was a Norwood girl, daughter of the owner of the Norwood Dairy, and she was, at the time she met Kerstetter, studying at the New England Conservatory of Music. They had two children, William Edward, Jr., born in 1944 and Laura Lamson, born four years later.

Upon completion of the Ph.D., Kerstetter entered military service. From 1943 to 1946 he served with the Army Air Force as a chaplain with the rank of first lieutenant and then captain. For fifteen months he sweltered at the Yuma Army Air Base in Arizona, moving in 1945 for a few months to a post in Salt Lake City. Soon after the conclusion of hostilities in August 1945, he was transferred briefly to Tokyo and then to the Philippines for the better part of a year.

No sooner was he discharged from the military than he started his teaching career at Methodist-affiliated Baldwin-Wallace College in Berea, Ohio. At Baldwin-Wallace, where he remained five years, he served as head of the Department of Philosophy.

In 1951 Kerstetter was invited by Hurst Anderson, president of Hamline University at St. Paul, Minnesota, to accept the chairmanship of the Philosophy and Religion Department there. Impressed with Anderson, who was by then a leading figure in Methodist higher education, Kerstetter accepted the Hamline appointment. He was disappointed when Hurst Anderson left Hamline at the end of the 1951–52 academic year to assume the presidency of American University, but he liked Hamline and the students in his classes.

Then one evening late in the autumn of 1952 the telephone rang at the Kerstetter home. It was F. Gerald Ensley calling from Iowa. Ensley, whom Kerstetter had come to know and admire back at Norwood, had combined the pastorate with a position as professor of systematic theology at Boston University. In the summer of 1952 he was consecrated bishop and assigned to Iowa. Now he wanted to talk with Bill Kerstetter about Simpson College.

* * *

"I was, of course, greatly taken by surprise" by the Bishop's call, recalled Kerstetter. He was beginning only his second year at Hamline and was certainly not looking for a new position.[3] In fact he was at first reluctant to talk with the Simpson people at all, for it might be regarded unseemly for him to abandon his teaching position so soon after accepting it. Still, it might not do any harm to see what Simpson had to offer. And, to be sure, it was gratifying even to be considered for a college presidency. He would go to Indianola and have a look.

When he visited Simpson, Kerstetter was hosted by a search committee that was hopeful that at last it had found the right man. For his part, Kerstetter was intrigued with the possibility of putting his vision of a liberal arts college education to the test. Years later, he still remembered vividly his first visit to the campus:

> The [search] committee was made up of trustees, faculty and administrators. We discussed everything that anyone could think of. One of these things I remember still is that I was asked several times what, if I came to Simpson as President, might my program be? I told them repeatedly that it is impossible to say at this point, since I really don't know enough about the College. In our rather thorough conversation, however, I had said enough to give them a general impression of my major concerns and enthusiasms about liberal arts education. Some of this was puzzling to the committee, but they nevertheless asked whether, if they invited me to come to Simpson as President of the College, I would be interested in such an invitation. I said that if such an invitation came I would of course have to think about it very carefully and talk it over thoroughly with my wife, but that our meeting today did make such a possibility seem challenging.[4]

Predictably, Kerstetter came away with mixed impressions. What he saw at Simpson both troubled and intrigued him. The search committee members were refreshingly honest in admitting the College's weaknesses and proud to point out its strengths. That Simpson was reeling from the blow of lost enrollment was evident at every hand. The downturn was evident simply by looking at the place. Dr. Kerstetter's first impression of the College's tree-shaded campus was that it looked seedy and ill-kept. Most of the buildings seemed to be run down, victims of too many years of maintenance deferred.

The College's board of trustees, led by a tight group of dedicated Indianolans who constituted the important executive committee, seemed to be helpless, or at least stymied, by the inexorable forces of war and inflation that marked the late Truman years. Their loyalty to Simpson was rock-solid, but for many of them the demands of making policy for a college in an increasingly complex, urbanized, cosmopolitan world were greater than they had ever known, and the demands on their personal wealth—increasingly board members everywhere were being asked to come up with unaccustomed large gifts from their own resources—were daunting.

Further, the morale of Simpson's largely underprepared and generally underpaid faculty was low. By 1952 cutbacks made necessary by the frightening drop in enrollment left a teaching staff of uneven quality. There were, to be sure, the old stalwarts, some of whom, like Baker and Moats, were at the point of retirement. By virtue of ability and commitment, these old-timers performed splendidly in the classroom, and by virtue of long tenure they were reasonably well paid. But the younger faculty contained too many whose academic preparation was inadequate—only one held a Ph.D.—or who were frankly left behind when their postwar colleagues either went on to advanced degrees or to teach elsewhere. Kerstetter would find that too many in Simpson's faculty were either old and good or young and mediocre.

Reflecting the mixed strength of the faculty, academic course offerings at Simpson in 1952 varied widely in quality. In some areas, notably English, history, chemistry, biology and of course music, instruction was superior. But fewer students were enrolled as majors in these strong fields, in part because they were seen to be difficult and partly because of the student demand for practical, vocationally-oriented education. Enrollments in business administration grew apace, even with an ever-changing, for the most part indifferent faculty, while those in English sagged. Education—elementary and secondary—drew a large number of majors while chemistry and especially mathematics attracted few. Men's physical education, preparing primarily high school coaches, was the most popular single major on campus, and no one ever accused it of making excessive academic demands on anyone. And besides, everyone liked Coach Casey. But even the best of Simpson's long-time faculty found themselves struggling with a decimated curriculum that seemed to have neither focus nor direction.

If Kerstetter could see these serious failings—low enrollment, besieged trustees, uneven faculty and curriculum—he could also find real underlying strengths on which to build. First and foremost, Simpson's endowment was one of the best among colleges of Iowa. Rising land and security prices, in addition to the modest bequests added during Voigt's years, pushed the total endowment above $1,500,000, and the income from it helped to prevent recent enrollment declines from being as devastating as they might have been. Although the College's low operating income reflected poor enrollment and deliberately low tuition charges, Simpson was reasonably sound economically. And if the campus was not very attractive, its appearance could be improved with a limited outlay of funds. The much-needed men's dormitory, the student dining hall and the Carver Science Building, for none of which there was quite enough money, could be constructed with even a limited improvement in the College's finances. The funds already collected for them, including Annie Merner Pfeiffer's $100,000 toward the dining hall and the Cowles Foundation's $125,000 toward the Carver project, could now be augmented, in the case of the dormitory at least, with government loans.

There was more. Kerstetter recognized that there was a strong core of faculty members whom he could hope to enlist to improve the curriculum, people who should be ready to reassert the primacy of the liberal arts. And on the board of trustees were people who were clearly ready to support fundamental curricular and structural change. Further, there was evidence of solid support in the Indianola community, as there had always been. He was also gratified to discover that the College had a number of truly distinguished alumni who were uncommonly devoted to Simpson.

When he returned to St. Paul, Kerstetter was interested in the Simpson presidency, and at length he decided to accept it if it was offered him. The offer came soon.

It was a blustery, cold day late in December when the executive committee of Simpson's board huddled with the presidential search committee and a few other local board members at the Savery Hotel in downtown Des Moines. After an animated discussion, the Reverend Raoul C. Calkins, the serious, dignified chairman of the search committee, presented the candidate and his wife to the assembled group, whereupon William E. Kerstetter was unanimously elected president of the College.[5] Naming the new president was merely a formality, for the candidate had been informed prior to his departure from St. Paul that his election was assured. But it was nevertheless a pleasant formality, and a reassuring one at that. The next morning board members met with the new president "to discuss urgent college problems, particularly student recruitment and fund-raising."[6]

Recognizing the immediacy of Simpson's serious concerns, Kerstetter was anxious to move his family to Indianola as soon as possible. Of course, he had to complete his first-semester teaching duties at Hamline, but he was able to make the move in mid-January, 1953. The acting president of Hamline was "extremely cooperative," proud no doubt that one of his faculty members had been tapped for a college presidency.

In some ways Dr. Kerstetter knew more about Simpson than Simpson knew about him when he came to Indianola that winter. Had the College people been more well-informed about him, they might have had at least an inkling of what the next decade would bring, for they would have found him to be a powerful, sensitive man, sometimes aggressive and at other times hesitant, unforgiving and forgiving, authoritarian and democratic, tough-minded and gentle. In short, William E. Kerstetter was a very complex man. And he would transform Simpson College.

* * *

Resourceful and rarely daunted, Kerstetter attacked Simpson's problems on several fronts, starting with the board of trustees. Its forty-one members included a number of outstanding people, some of whom were alumni of the College. Most of them lived in Iowa; only six were from out of state. Of the thirty-five Iowans, ten were from Warren County and fifteen were from Des Moines—a heavy concentration of local people. Only two were women, former Superintendent of Public Instruction Agnes Samuelson and alumna Amy Robertson, the remarkable self-made woman from Promise City, Iowa, the latter elected by the alumni. Ten were clergymen in addition to the president of the College.[7]

The problem was not quality. Rather it was the composition of the board's officers and executive committee, which oversaw the day-to-day operations of the College. The president of the board, Indianola grocer William T. Hamilton, had only recently resigned his position after nineteen years on the board and fifteen years as its president. Because of the search for a new president, the board chairmanship was left vacant until his arrival. Vice-President Don L. Berry, Secretary Frank P. Henderson and College Treasurer Wendell M. Tutt, Indianola men all, served alongside an eleven-man executive committee, a majority of whom were Warren Countians.

It was Kerstetter's judgment that if Simpson was to move ahead, it must recruit leaders whose breadth of vision transcended the bounds of Warren County and central Iowa. He was not persuaded that the officers of the board, however dedicated and loyal their service, possessed the cosmopolitanism he had in mind. Seizing the opportunity to effect change quickly, he initiated action that led to the election of A. Paul Thompson of Des Moines as president of the board.

Thompson's election, as fortuitous as it was decisive, immediately brought new vitality to the board. Age forty-three, he was at that time vice-president and chief financial officer—later president—of Iowa Power and Light Company, Iowa's leading utility corporation. A graduate of Ohio Wesleyan University, he was a lawyer and expert in financial matters. More than that, Thompson combined solid, down-home virtues—working with the Y.M.C.A. and the Boy Scouts and teaching a Sunday school class at the Methodist Church—with an elegance of bearing and sophistication that made him at home in a larger world.[8]

Kerstetter went beyond the installation of Thompson. He persuaded the board to restructure its leadership, enlarging the number of officers from four to seven, and to reconstitute or eliminate entirely some of its committees.[9] Three new vice-presidents were selected, replacing outgoing Vice-President Don Berry: Kenneth MacDonald, vice-president and executive editor of the *Des Moines Register and Tribune*, a man of awe-inspiring intellect and impeccable taste; Simpson alumnus Ivan L. Willis, genial, sharp-witted vice-president of International Harvester Company in Chicago, who brought to the board real executive talent and a breadth of experience unmatched by many of the College's graduates; and the Rev. Walter M. Scheuermann, minister of the Central Methodist Church at Oskaloosa, whose presence in the board's leadership recognized the importance of Simpson's church relationship. Representing the continuing presence of the "old guard" in the board's leadership were William Buxton III, who served as chairman of the executive committee, Frank P. Henderson, secretary of the board since 1919 and College Treasurer Wendell Tutt.

The reaction of some of the Indianola trustees to vaulting Thompson, who had never served on the board, into its leadership was less than enthusiastic.

More than that, there was resentment that two of the vice-presidents—MacDonald and Willis—had been members of the board for barely two years. Some of the townspeople never forgave Kerstetter for wrenching the control of Simpson out of the hands of the community that had loyally supported it for nearly a century, people who had time and again pulled it back from the abyss. Yet others were supportive, not the least of whom was Don Berry, whose voice in Warren County counted for much and whose unflinching advocacy of Simpson's growth and progress recognized the imperative of fundamental change.

During the years that followed, Kerstetter influenced powerfully the strengthening of the board of trustees, recruiting people like California industrialist Judson Perkins, Chicago executive Harold W. Dotts, Cleveland manufacturer Harold N. Graves and President James W. Wallace of Pioneer Hi-Bred Corn Company, Iowa's most powerful agribusiness. But what would prove to be the most significant new board appointment was attorney Luther L. Hill, Jr., scion of a distinguished Des Moines family. Educated at Williams College and Harvard Law School, Hill had only recently returned to Des Moines after serving during 1950–51 as law clerk to Justice Hugo L. Black of the United States Supreme Court. Admitted to the Iowa bar, he entered legal practice with the firm of Henry and Henry and became a member of the legal staff of the Equitable Life Insurance Company of Iowa. A World War II Army veteran, he married Sara Sigler Carpenter in 1950. She had powerful Indianola connections, for Simpson benefactress Sara Sigler was her maternal grandmother, and her father and mother, George and Helen Carpenter (Dartmouth and Swarthmore respectively), occupied the family's impressive home on West Ashland in Indianola.

Luther Hill was only thirty-one years old when he was elected to Simpson's board of trustees, and any number of resident critics animadverted upon the questionable wisdom of electing such a "youngster" to Simpson's governing body. But Dr. Kerstetter's judgment was vindicated many times over, for Luther Hill would became a mainstay of the College's trustees. More than that, in a sense he made Simpson a consuming hobby, almost an obsession, lavishing on it time, money and attention and, above all, wisdom that combined a happy mixture of visionary passion and sober judgment. Years later Kerstetter recalled Hill's election to the board as one of the most gratifying and productive actions of his entire administration.[10] The restructuring and strengthening of the board of trustees, said Kerstetter, was clearly "the most fruitful long-term contribution" he was able to make at Simpson. "Immediately," he recalled, "this policy brought enhanced prestige, increased wisdom, and enlarged circles of financial support" to the College.[11] And after a brief period of adjustment, even the most sedulous critics of the new regime were forced to admit that the board's broader-based leadership afforded considerably more support for Simpson than could have been provided by Indianola and Warren County alone.

* * *

Long before he came to Simpson, Kerstetter had formulated a philosophy of liberal arts education that he longed to see attempted in some college somewhere. Modern college and university curricula, he observed, failed utterly to provide a "unified insight into the structure, the meaning, the purposes of human life" or even to help the student discover "a point of view, a world view, arising out of all vitally relevant information drawn from the many fields of learning and from general human experience." Rather most curricula delivered "miscellaneous information, scattered and divided data, chaos, incoherence," not even suggesting "the ideal of unified insight."[12] Even those colleges that required survey courses in the major divisions of the curriculum were giving "only bigger pieces," and those that provided a senior "unifying" seminar were making only "a late stab at truth." What was needed, reasoned Kerstetter, was a four-year, integrated, focused search for a unified world view through liberal arts studies "whose ideal is reconceived and redirected." The goal was "a mind which stands, in imagination, *at the center*, outside or above all separate fields and their inadequate exclusive categories, and seeks impartially to interpret the unified, overall meaning of the varied claims of fields and disciplines of knowledge."[13]

Kerstetter believed, with Jacques Barzun, that scholars in the House of Intellect all too frequently locked themselves into separate rooms, refusing to talk with each other. Not only would Kerstetter open the doors that shut historians off from physicists or philosophers from psychologists; he would invite them into the great, central, open family room where they could seek integration, unity and sustained focus.

How could one translate the need for unified insight into a specific series of courses of study? Kerstetter had already made a beginning during the time he was at Baldwin-Wallace, where he converted his introduction to philosophy course to one he called "Introduction to the Liberal Arts," because he had observed that most students who came to college "didn't know what the hell they were doing there."[14] When he went to Hamline he took that course with him, convinced that students there, too, needed to see the connections and relationships and purposes of the liberal arts if their education was to have real integrity, real wholeness.

As much as anything else, it was probably the alluring prospect of an opportunity to create a new curriculum that proved to be Kerstetter's prime motive for making the move to Simpson. As he debated the pros and cons of accepting the Simpson presidency, his wife, Leona, was the one who put the challenge to him. "Bill," she said, "you're always talking about this [curriculum] problem. Let's go to Simpson and see if you can do anything about it."[15]

So pressing were the immediate, urgent problems of finances, student recruitment and board of trustees reorganization that Kerstetter was unable to attack the curriculum until the fall of 1953. When he did, he discovered how difficult it was to persuade the faculty to make any major change. He was quite aware that in curricular matters the faculty was sovereign and jealously guarded its prerogatives. He was also aware that Simpson's liberal arts requirements for the B.A. and B.S.B.A. degrees were already thought by some people to be too heavy, and few faculty members showed an inclination to reduce any of the existing requirements. Harold Watson, whose long tenure at the College earned for him a rich measure of respect, observed frequently that Simpson's "general education" requirements were far too extensive, but that such an overload was the price of ensuring the inclusion of the humanities and the natural sciences. Kerstetter soon realized that the new courses he sought to introduce would for the most part have to be added on to the already-bloated requirements, for nearly every faculty member sought to defend his or her department's turf.

Kerstetter was not easily discouraged; rather he proceeded with a combination of unfaltering determination and deferential diplomacy. And soon some of the faculty, especially people like Watson, Sven Lekberg, Roberta Riegel and David Mobberley, caught the vision the president outlined for Simpson.

They called it the "Vital Center" program, for it would provide the "center" courses through which students could "integrate and bring focus to their studies," what Kerstetter called "a vital, creative center at the heart of a liberal arts curriculum."[16] Further, these courses would cluster primarily in the sophomore and junior years, at the center of the students' academic career. "The expectation," said Kerstetter, "is that when [students] finish four years of study with these courses at the center, they will graduate decidedly superior, in their maturity and competence for citizenship, to groups who normally graduate from colleges today."[17]

After a good deal of fervid discussion and academic horse-trading, the faculty adopted the Vital Center program at its last meeting before the Christmas holidays in December 1953. It accepted also the creation of a number of new courses that would complement the core of the Vital Center.

The Vital Center program consisted of four three-hour courses. The first two would be taken in the sophomore year, the third in the junior year and the fourth by seniors. When students returned to school after Christmas in January 1954, they read that the faculty had "heartily endorsed" the new curriculum that would commence the following autumn. The *Simpsonian* described the four new Vital Center courses:

1. **Introduction to the Liberal Arts.** Here the great questions of mankind will be offered as the key to selection and integration of significant knowledge into creative wisdom. Here the fruitful methods of pursuing understanding (and the illuminating assumptions of these methods) will be clarified and practiced.
2. **Religious and Philosophical Backgrounds of Western Civilization.** This second course will deal with the religious and philosophical backgrounds of Western civilization. Students will seek to clarify, more fully, great questions and challenging answers to them by wrestling with the great alternatives suggested by Western thought.
3. **Meeting of the East and West.** In this course the intention will be to bring students into the same vital contact with the great civilization-shaping ideas of the East, with similar essential values resulting in this context as in the second course. At the close of this third course, special attention will be given to the further imperative question as to what it is that the East and West have in common. The course will concern the vital points at which East and West differ, and the possible circumstances and conditions under which, out of differing civilizations, there might arise what one prominent American so well designated as "one world."
4. **Individual Study.** This fourth course will be devoted to individual study, carefully supervised by faculty members, in which students will read great literature they have not yet touched in their various courses. This will be for the purpose of rounding out and uniting their current reading with the whole range of study provided by their college courses, stimulated by the principles and motivations of the courses of the Vital Center. On the basis of such reflection, students will then write a paper entitled "My Present Philosophy of Life."[18]

The first two courses in the Vital Center program would be introduced in the 1954–55 academic year, the Meeting of the East and West the following year and "Individual Study" in 1956–57.

There was more to this new academic program than the introduction of the four Vital Center courses. A number of existing courses were totally restructured and several new courses were introduced to complement the Vital Center series.

A new, condensed Introduction to the Bible course reduced the religion requirement from four semester hours to two. A new Introduction to Science course was introduced for freshmen, its purpose to acquaint students with the purposes and techniques of science, to familiarize them "with the scope, possibilities and limitations of science" and to acquaint them "with the role of science in modern civilization."[19] These two new courses would typically be taken in the freshman year, together with a semester each of psychology and speech, a full year each of freshman composition and Western civilization, plus one elective course each semester.

Western civilization was seen as an appropriate and necessary background for the two Vital Center courses studied in the sophomore year alongside a year each of English literature and one of the natural sciences. During the sophomore year one also typically completed a six-hour sequence in one of the social sciences (economics, U.S. history, political science or sociology), together with an elective each semester. In addition, during each of the four lower-division semesters, students were to complete a one-credit-hour physical education "conditioning activities" requirement.

Having examined the history and ideas of the West, the students enrolled in the Meeting of the East and West course during one semester in the junior year in order to take a look at the civilizations of the East. In this forward-looking experiment in multiculturalism, Simpson placed itself in the vanguard of those academic institutions seeking to provide at least the beginning of global education for its students. It was thus in the mid-fifties one of few colleges, or perhaps the only college in America that specifically required every student to study the East as a prerequisite to graduation.

For juniors still another new course was created, Simpson's first-ever all-college requirement in the fine arts, Introduction to Music. Reflecting the College's strong program in music, the course was well taught and graciously received. It was a pity, however, that a similar course in art was not introduced at the same time. That deficiency reflected another reality: Simpson had never given even a fraction of the attention to art that it had to music. Apart from some manifestly feeble arts and crafts courses in elementary teacher training, no art was taught at Simpson at all when Kerstetter arrived. He determined to remedy that egregious omission in the College's curriculum, but he would have to wait.

The price of the inclusion of the Vital Center in Simpson's curriculum was high. The total required segment of the students' 124-hour program was fixed at 57 hours, to which was added a major field of concentration of approximately 30 to 36 semester hours. There was little room in most students' schedules to accommodate elective courses, especially among the fairly large number of people who were meeting state certification requirements in teacher education. Yet, however much some faculty and many students complained about the burden of all-college graduation requirements, everyone was forced to agree that at Simpson no student would be deprived of a solid liberal arts education. More than that, no student could escape coming to terms with what the liberal arts were about, indeed "why in hell they were in college anyway."[20]

* * *

Creating the new Vital Center curriculum was one thing. Finding faculty to teach it was quite another. As soon as the faculty adopted the new program,

Kerstetter set about finding just the right scholar to teach the two sophomore Vital Center courses. The other lower division courses, including the condensed one in Bible and the new Introduction to Science could be taught by existing staff, Clifford Lott and Harry Beardsley in Bible and David Mobberley in science. Mobberley was by training and inclination admirably qualified to deal with a philosophical approach to science. Kerstetter had come to know him when he was a student at Baldwin-Wallace. Since Mobberley had come to Simpson, he had gained the respect of his colleagues and a real following among the students. He was precisely the kind of scholar-teacher Kerstetter hoped to find for every classroom and laboratory at Simpson. The Western civilization courses would be ably taught by Robert Farb and Howard Greenlee, while English composition and literature were provided for by veterans Harold Watson, Ruth Jackson and Les Bechter.

Kerstetter knew that the search for the new Vital Center instructor was crucial to the success of the program. He proceeded most cautiously during the spring of 1954 to find just the right person, one who was comfortable both in philosophy and religion, one whose Methodist credentials would validate his presence among Simpson's clerical contingent but who would be without a hint of the sectarian in his or her approach to the liberal arts, one whose breadth of interest would ensure the sort of academic integration Kerstetter expected to make the key to the new curriculum. After examining any number of candidates, the president selected Phillips Moulton, then serving as pastor of the Park Slope Methodist Church in Brooklyn, New York, and a lecturer at Union Theological Seminary. Moulton was a 1931 graduate of Ohio Wesleyan, where he had been president of the student body and a member of Phi Beta Kappa. Immediately after his graduation he studied at the University of Marburg in Germany for a year. Later he did graduate work at Princeton and Boston Universities and completed his bachelor of divinity degree at Yale in 1942 and a Yale Ph.D. in 1949. Prior to accepting the Brooklyn pastorate, Moulton had taught in Danforth programs at Boston University and Garrett Biblical Institute. At the age of forty-four, Moulton was old enough to have acquired solid experience in his field and young enough to relate comfortably with students. His reputed classroom demeanor and broad-based interests seemed to make him stand out among his fellow applicants.[21]

So concerned that the first Introduction to the Liberal Arts course be taught just as he envisaged it, Kerstetter decided to handle the large Monday and Wednesday nine o'clock lectures himself during the inaugural year. It would be exceedingly difficult to combine teaching with his many other duties, but he was determined that as the curtain went up on the Vital Center drama all the lines would be spoken right. Moulton, who was singularly impressed with the content and approach of the course, fell in with the plan. He handled four one-hour discussion groups, numbering about thirty students each, three of which met on Saturday mornings. To no one's surprise, Kerstetter taught the course only once. For one thing, Moulton did so well that the president was comfortable permitting him to carry on unaided with both the lectures and discussions. For another, Kerstetter soon discovered that combining teaching, even one course, with the duties of the presidency was very nearly an impossibility.

When both Clifford Lott and Harry Beardsley resigned in the spring of 1954, Kerstetter was unable to replace them at once, so he asked Phillips Moulton to assume responsibility for the two-hour Introduction to the Bible course as a part of his teaching duties. He taught the Bible course successfully for three years, until growing enrollment permitted the appointment of a new person in religion. James L. Christian, who completed his Ph.D. in religion at Boston University in mid-1957, came that fall to teach Bible and other courses in religion, remaining at Simpson two years.

During the 1954-55 academic year Kerstetter learned that if it had been difficult to find an instructor for the first two Vital Center courses, it was going to be even more difficult to find a teacher who could combine a familiarity with the philosophies and religions of the Middle East, South Asia, China and Japan with a solid grounding in the history and politics of all Asia. Any number of specialists in one or another discipline or geographical area could be found, but Kerstetter wanted a generalist, one who preferably knew Asia at first hand.

He was lucky. While visiting on the East Coast he learned about the remarkable, almost improbable Clayton Lane, who was at the time teaching at St. John's College at Annapolis, Maryland. St. John's, he knew, was a unique institution, where the entire curriculum was built around a fundamental examination of the "Great Books." Lane, whose marvelous command of the classics of Asian religion and literature had attracted him to St. John's, had been teaching there only a matter of months, having joined the faculty in 1954 not long after taking early retirement from the Foreign Service at the age of fifty-nine.

Lane, a native of Guthrie Center, Iowa, had attended Simpson in the years just before the First World War, (1914-16). He had served in the Navy two years, attended Stanford and then completed his B.A. at the University of California at Berkeley in economics in 1921. After two years of graduate study at Berkeley, during which time he taught economics and international relations at St. Mary's College in nearby Oakland, he served for three years with the U.S. Department of Commerce in Washington while lecturing on Europe and Asia at Georgetown University. He was a U.S. trade commissioner in Berlin and Vienna in 1927-28, after which he entered the U.S. Foreign Service as commercial attache in places like Warsaw and Johannesburg. During the Second World War he served as American consul in Calcutta and as director of War Economic Operations in the American diplomatic mission at New Delhi. After the war and his years in India, he was briefly U.S. commercial attache at Beirut and Damascus, then served in a number of agencies, ending his public service as deputy assistant director for the Far East in the Mutual Security Agency (1952-53). A lifelong Democrat, he found government service no longer to his liking with the advent of the Eisenhower administration. After a year of work in area studies with a Baltimore foundation, he accepted the teaching position at St. John's.

It is not entirely clear how Kerstetter managed to entice Lane and his artist wife Bent, nee Dorothy Bent, to come to Indianola, but it is clear that Lane, although he would never admit it, reserved a place in his heart for the land of his birth and for Simpson even though he had often referred to Iowa, not in jest, as the "cultural desert of America."[22] In any case he listened to Simpson's new president.

When they met at the Statler Hotel in Washington, D.C., on April 29, 1955, Kerstetter's entreaties were beguiling, his description of the Vital Center intriguing. He described enthusiastically the thirsty minds of young Iowans, minds that were vessels into which the well-traveled diplomat and Asian scholar could pour the wealth of his knowledge. Lane was flattered and at the same time genuinely impressed with Kerstetter's academic philosophy. Although he had no use for missionaries, it is tempting to think that he saw himself as a cosmopolitan cultural agent whose noble task it was to embark on a *mission civilisatrice* in the cornfields of the Midwest. His wife came to share his enthusiasm for the venture, especially when Kerstetter asked her to serve as Simpson's artist-in-residence.[23] Offered a contract in May, the Lanes visited the campus toward the end of that month and signed the contract.[24]

While Bent Lane readied her studio in the old Wigwam in College Hall, Clayton made his final preparations for his teaching duties. During the fall semester of 1955 he taught the Meeting of the East and West and Thought and Culture of the Middle East courses in the Philosophy Department. Bent taught a creative painting workshop, the first proper art course offered at Simpson in many years.

During the next five years the Lanes made an extraordinary contribution to Simpson. Indianolans were impressed with their civilized conversation, their sophisticated, almost courtly, behavior, their cosmopolitan outlook, their warm good will that made them the center of much of campus life. Clayton's classes bowled the students over, and he lured them into reading the Qur'an, the Bhagavad-Gita and introduced them to Lao-Tzu's Taoism as soon as they grew accustomed to his rich British accent, an eccentricity he acquired quite unconsciously during his many years among the English expatriates in India and the Middle East. Students soon learned they could drop into his office on the ground floor of the Administration Building, where they would enjoy stimulating conversation and a nice cup of hot tea.

Clayton Lane made no compromises with Iowa provincialism as he labored to make Simpson and Indianola better known as an oasis of civilization. He and Bent conducted their lives very much as they would have in Annapolis or Beirut or Bombay. Sometimes Indianolans were not quite ready for Clayton's unconscious flouting of local convention. Although on campus he was always impeccably attired in pin-striped suit and tie, his thick handlebar mustache trimmed, his eagle-bald pate glistening, Lane could be seen on a Saturday morning taking his constitutional, striding determinedly and obliviously down North Buxton Street in khaki shirt and walking shorts, shod in sandals and wearing a pith helmet.

Bent was a trifle more conventional, her soft, friendly visage crowned by meticulously coiffed jet black hair. Her art classes were well attended, and her evening lectures, at which she held forth on such contemporary topics as impressionism or dadaism, entertained admiring if somewhat mystified local audiences. She had no truck with traditionalism, her own abstract paintings and mosaics reflecting her taste for the most contemporary styles. It is safe to say that in Indianola her work was much admired and little understood. She was not always successful in her campaign to improve the level of appreciation in art on the campus. One of the stratagems she employed was lending her paintings to residence halls and sorority and fraternity houses. She would never forget, however, hanging one in a prominent place in the living room of one of the fraternity houses. Entitled "Painted Desert," the oil was an abstract piece with predominantly yellow and red hues. The boys in the house, puzzled by the description, soon renamed it "I Had Eggs with Catsup for Breakfast." Bent Lane did not think that was funny, and as she retrieved the insulted painting, she muttered something about adolescent barbarism.

* * *

After the Vital Center program and its new faculty had been in place for two years, the president invited a selected group of faculty people to participate in a study of the program, its philosophy, purposes and presentation. From the Board of Education of the Methodist Church the College received a four thousand dollar grant to pay the expenses of a ten-day seminar for eighteen people, including the president and Dean Bimson, librarian Mary Marquis and fifteen faculty members.[25] In late August 1956, just prior to the opening of the fall semester, faculty spent three and one-half hours each day in class lecture and discussion and the balance of their time reading many of the materials used in the Vital Center courses.[26] In discussing everything from Plato to the Bhagavad-Gita, faculty people agreed that while the dominant perspective at Simpson was to be the Christian liberal arts, "the emphasis in this program is on the intrinsic importance . . . of the great *questions*, not on providing dogmatic answers . . . , and not on indoctrinating students with conclusions."[27] Faculty participants profited immensely from their study. One of them, in reporting their workshop to the faculty that fall, summed it up well: "We are not proposing to graduate students possessed of rare wisdom and maturity—but only students who have begun a quest." Another said "I no longer feel on the periphery of the Vital Center, but part of it."[28]

The purposes of the Vital Center, together with an account of the summer workshop, were summarized in a book authored by Kerstetter and Moulton and issued in 1957 as a volume in the Studies in Christian Higher Education series published by the Board of Education of the Methodist Church. Entitled *An Experiment in General Education: Development and Evaluation*, their study proved to be a valuable contribution to the literature on general education in institutions of higher learning.

* * *

Even before the Vital Center program was in place, Kerstetter undertook an ambitious project, one whose purpose it was to bring a number of outstanding speakers of national and international repute to Simpson for one weekend during the academic year. The address of each speaker was to relate to a central theme selected for the event, which he called the "Christian Liberal Arts Festival." It was important, he believed, to expose Simpson students to some of the best minds and to provide Simpson exposure in Iowa and the nation. Kerstetter persuaded the board of trustees to postpone his inauguration and to combine it with the first Christian Liberal Arts Festival (soon known by the acronym CLAF). And putting together such a program would require time. If anyone had misgivings about it in the beginning, the stunning success of the event converted even the most cynical observers into believers. As students, townspeople and visitors crowded, on May 7–8, 1954, into Hopper Gymnasium, where every seat was taken for each session, they heard a series of speeches around the central topic "Definition, World Significance and Academic Pattern of Christian Liberal Arts," as Kerstetter called it, "a special *celebration* of the whole idea of the liberal arts."[29] Of course, it also laid the groundwork for public appreciation of Simpson's brand new Vital Center program. For the keynote speaker the president chose an old and admired acquaintance, Dr. Charles Malik, at the time foreign minister of Lebanon and ambassador to the United States and the United Nations. Surely the best known Christian from the volatile Arab world, Malik was a brilliant speaker. Just a short time before he was to appear at the CLAF, he was elected president of the General Assembly of the United Nations.

Although Dr. Malik, owing to a delayed flight, had to be rushed under police escort from the Des Moines Airport to Indianola, he was able to present his address at the inaugural ceremony on Saturday on time to an enthusiastic overflow crowd, including 180 colorfully robed representatives of colleges and universities and learned societies. Other speakers during the weekend included Simpson alumna Eugenie Moore Anderson, former U.S. ambassador to Denmark; former Simpson president John O. Gross, executive secretary of the Division of Educational Institutions of the Methodist Church; Arnold Nash, professor of the history of religion at the University of North Carolina; and Warren County-born Elton Trueblood, professor of philosophy at Earlham College in Indiana. At the inaugural ceremony Saturday afternoon, Bishop F. Gerald Ensley read the charge to the new president. Dr. Kerstetter responded by outlining, in a speech entitled "A Pattern for Christian Liberal Arts," the principal purpose of Simpson's new curriculum.

The first Christian Liberal Arts Festival was a rousing success. It achieved precisely what Dr. Kerstetter had hoped for it: an unabashed, spirited salute to the liberal arts, an almost palpable lift in student and faculty morale, a sense that the College was making direct connection with the larger world beyond the verdant fields of Warren County, and, importantly, renewed attention to Simpson in the press, radio and in that new medium of communication, television, in 1954 still in its infancy in Iowa. It was, said Kerstetter, "a very great weekend in the life of Simpson College." In fact, he recalled years later, "the Festival was so stimulating and so admired that it was immediately clear to me that we ought to do this again."[30] Accordingly, no sooner had the first festival concluded than he was laying plans for the second.

Delayed until the fall of 1955—nearly everyone agreed that the best time for such an event was during the fall months—the second CLAF featured Gardner Cowles, president of the *Des Moines Register* and editor of *Look*, and Simpson alumnus J. Hugh Jackson, dean of the graduate school of business at Stanford. They shared the podium with Earlham College Professor Elton Trueblood, whom Kerstetter admired so much that he listed him in the catalog as Simpson's "Educational Consultant." In a thumping address extolling the devotion of a few students to the liberal arts, Trueblood deplored the dedication of too many students to the frills of campus life, things like social organizations and athletics. He declared Simpson's 52–0 defeat of Central College of Missouri in football that same October afternoon "immoral," a judgment not calculated to endear him to undergraduates or, for that matter, to the coaching staff.[31]

During the years that followed, the Christian Liberal Arts Festivals attracted a truly remarkable array of outstanding speakers whose messages, some uplifting and others sharply critical, brought to Simpson audiences a level of sophistication, of cosmopolitanism, of humane reflection that was enviable. Among those who participated during the remaining years of the Kerstetter era were Ralph J. Bunche, Under-Secretary of the United Nations; former U.S. Vice President Henry A. Wallace, whose wife Ilo was a Simpson alumna; Stanley S. Kresge of the Kresge Foundation, an institution whose continuing generosity to Simpson was to grow into a powerful and gratifying relationship; journalist Carl T. Rowan; U Win, ambassador of Burma to the United States and a leading Buddhist scholar; Bishop Ivan Lee Holt of the Methodist Church; former chancellor of the University of Chicago Robert M. Hutchins; Arthur S. Flemming, U.S. Secretary of Health, Education and Welfare; Cuthbert A. Simpson, Dean of Christ Church, the Oxford College at which John Wesley had studied; and Sir Hugh Foot, ambassador of the United Kingdom to the United States.

The address of Dean Simpson at the ninth CLAF in 1962 marked the realization of another Kerstetter initiative, the Oxford Exchange Program, which came about as much by luck as by design. Kerstetter was selected by the Board of Education of the Methodist Church to join a group of eleven other Methodist college presidents in a six-week journey abroad in the fall of 1960. The trip included visits to universities all over Europe, from Moscow and Leningrad in the east to Cambridge and Edinburgh and Oxford in the United Kingdom.[32] The last part of their lengthy tour took them to Oxford University and especially to Lincoln and Christ Church, the colleges where John Wesley had studied. As he stood in the magnificent dining hall at Christ Church—this was the very hall in which the royalist parliament of Charles II had met during England's seventeenth-century civil war—Kerstetter studied the portraits of the Christ Church greats, worthies and prime ministers and the likes of John Locke and John Wesley. A thought occurred to him. Would it not be possible to create a relationship between Christ Church and Simpson, for was not Wesley the spiritual founder of Simpson as he was of the church from which the founders of Simpson sprang?

He said nothing of this when he and the other presidents were introduced to Christ Church Dean Cuthbert A. Simpson, but after his return home he pondered the question and decided to act. "I . . . got in touch with [Dean Simpson]," recalled Kerstetter, "by writing him a very brief letter saying that I would welcome the opportunity to meet with him again to discuss what for me was a very exciting idea. He warmly acknowledged my letter and invited me to come." Kerstetter returned to Oxford the next summer, determined to accomplish his purpose. Dean Simpson, a Canadian by birth, listened to Kerstetter's proposal for an exchange. Simpson College would send a student to Christ Church every other year to study there for two years and Christ Church would send a faculty member to teach at Simpson during the fall semester each year. "I think that we could do that," said Dean Simpson. "But I think it would be more significant in every respect if I made this recommendation to the chapter of Christ Church, and thus have it endorsed and supported by *their* authority."[33] And it was done. In the fall of 1962 J. Steven Watson, senior censor of Christ Church, taught at Simpson for a semester, occupying with his wife Heba the "Oxford apartment" tastefully done up in Lorraine Hall. And in the fall of 1963 Simpson's first Oxford student entered Christ Church for a two-year program leading to the Oxford B.A. He was Ronald Mathias, a Simpson graduate from Indianola, whose academic accomplishments and rare promise made him the ideal choice for this honor. Mathias completed his Oxford degree in 1965.

There would be a very tangible symbol of the Christ Church and Simpson relationship. While he was inspecting the magnificent precincts of Christ Church with Dean Simpson, Kerstetter noticed the scaffolding and stone work where the College library was being restored. On the ground in front of the building's facade lay a number of stones from the old building that the Dean explained would not be used in the reconstruction work. Immediately an idea struck Kerstetter. "Would it be possible," he asked, "if one of those fine stones could be sent to Indianola, bearing an inscription that would commemorate the relationship of Wesley to Christ Church and Simpson? Of course it could, and some months later the stone arrived. It would be installed in a prominent place in the new College chapel that Kerstetter hoped to build soon. Carved into the face of the limestone block were the words:

> THIS STONE FROM THE COLLEGE LIBRARY HAS BEEN PRESENTED BY THE DEAN AND THE CHAPTER OF THE CATHEDRAL CHURCH OF CHRIST IN OXFORD OF THE FOUNDATION OF KING HENRY VIII TO SIMPSON COLLEGE AS A MEMORIAL TO JOHN WESLEY, A COMMONER OF CHRIST CHURCH 1720–1724.

* * *

As we have already noted, less than a month after Dr. Kerstetter arrived on the campus in the winter of 1953, only 377 students returned for the second semester, a decline of 22 from the fall semester. It was the most dismal enrollment count since the worst year of the Second World War. Clearly, something had to be done about recruiting new students and retaining old ones, for the College's health, indeed its survival, depended upon a student body large enough to support an adequate educational program and the faculty to teach it. In many ways, then, the College's admissions operation, long the province of the academic dean and one or two traveling counselors, needed strengthening, for its efforts were vital in attracting good students to come to Simpson. Accordingly, Kerstetter asked Dean Oliver Bimson to devote more attention to admissions, to produce more attractive recruitment publications and to provide more direction for the College's two admissions counselors. Ever aware of the almost incalculable value of good public relations in marketing the College to high school graduates, Kerstetter emphasized with his staff the importance of informing Simpson's many publics about the new curriculum, the new forward thrust of the College.

Results did not come at once. Enrollment in the fall of 1953 was a disappointing 385. However, the Korean War came to an end during the summer of 1953, as President Dwight D. Eisenhower's new Republican administration took over in a nation enjoying unprecedented prosperity. The advent of peace was an event of happy portent for all American colleges, including Simpson. It is also true that the number of students graduating from Midwestern secondary schools was rising sharply, providing a growing pool of potential applicants. More significantly, a growing proportion of high school graduates were electing to enter college, enabled to do so by good times and influenced to do so by the promise of improved employment opportunities.

Thus Simpson's attractive new programs found an increasing response from young people and their parents. The turnaround came in the spring semester of 1954, when enrollment grew from 385 to 394. It was well-nigh unheard of for enrollment to increase between first and second semesters. Then, in the fall of 1954, coincidental with the advent of the Vital Center program, enrollment jumped to 511, thanks to a much larger freshman class and remarkable retention of sophomores who would be the first to experiment with the new general studies courses. Kerstetter was ecstatic; so was everyone else at Simpson.

Simpson's Renaissance: The Kerstetter Years   461

Table 9
Fall Enrollment 1953–1962

	Senior	Junior	Soph.	Fresh.	Special	P. T.	Total
1953–54	61	62	105	154	0	3	385
1954–55	69	78	149	211	0	4	511
1955–56	83	117	146	232	0	5	583
1956–57	102	122	172	218	0	4	618
1957–58	115	134	185	229	4	14	667
1958–59	125	130	176	189	11	22	631
1959–60	116	124	171	252	9		672
1960–61	102	132	198	241	10		683
1961–62	124	143	195	267	2	13	744
1962–63	148	163	212	199	4	16	742

After 1954, enrollment continued to climb.[34] (See table 9.) In early 1958 Kerstetter removed the responsibility for student recruitment from the office of the academic dean and appointed as his first director of admissions young history professor Joseph W. Walt, who agreed alongside his teaching duties to take on the task of setting up an independent office of admissions. The next year, Walt chose to return to full time teaching, and the director's position went to Daniel G. Seaton, Simpson alumnus in the class of 1932.[35]

Not only did enrollments continue to grow, but also the academic quality of the College's new students increased markedly as measured by scores on Scholastic Aptitude Test results and high school class rank of applicants for admission.

* * *

We have already seen that Kerstetter recruited an able faculty to teach the several courses in the new Vital Center program. Phillips Moulton, who remained on the faculty four years, refined splendidly the two sophomore Vital Center courses. When he resigned in the summer of 1958 to accept the presidency of Wesley College and deanship of the school of religion at the University of North Dakota in Grand Forks, Kerstetter was truly sorry to see him go, praising his "high competence, loyalty and devotion."[36] Fortunately the College was able to replace Dr. Moulton temporarily while searching for his successor. Luike J. Hemmes, a "master teacher" who had retired in the spring of 1958 after a successful thirty-two-year career at Kalamazoo College, came to Simpson as a John Hay Whitney Foundation Distinguished Visiting Professor in Philosophy.[37] A native of Germany, Hemmes had come to the United States in 1905 and earned the M.A. and B.D. degrees from the University of Rochester Theological Seminary and the Ph.D. from the University of Chicago. As a part of his schedule, Hemmes taught one of four sections of the sophomore Vital Center courses; one section was taught by James L. Christian of the Philosophy and Religion Department and the other two sections by Simpson's new academic dean, M. Francis Christie.

Christie succeeded Dean Oliver H. Bimson, who retired at the end of July 1957, moving with his wife, Essel, to Boulder, Colorado.[38] Christie, very much his own man, would develop a leadership style, in relationship both to the president and the faculty, which set him apart from others. At thirty-four, Christie had earned an enviable reputation as a biblical scholar and Methodist clergyman. A graduate of Hendrix College (1944), he completed his M.A. at Southern Methodist University (1947) and the Ph.D. at Vanderbilt University (1952). Since 1951 he had been a faculty member at Birmingham-Southern College. One national Methodist leader reportedly called Christie "the best teacher in religion he has found in his direct contacts with Methodist colleges."[39] He combined teaching the two sections of Vital Center with his duties as dean of academic affairs for that first year.

In the fall of 1959 the Vital Center program, not to speak of the Department of Philosophy and Religion, was strengthened immensely by the addition of three full-time instructors. The new chairman of the department and coordinator of the Vital Center program was Jack Padgett, a superior teacher who had taught philosophy several years at Juniata College in Pennsylvania and also at Tufts University and Boston University. A 1950 graduate of Juniata, Padgett had earned the S.T.B. from Boston University's School of Theology in 1953 and had just completed the Ph.D. at Boston University before coming to Simpson. Alongside Padgett came Edward C. Cell, an energetic young graduate of Boston University (1956), who held the B.D. from Andover-Newton Theological School (1956) and the M.A. from Princeton. He was at work on his Ph.D. at Princeton when he joined the Simpson faculty and would complete it in 1963. The third of the new trio was young Richard W. Hostetler, whose academic preparation included a B.A. from Ohio State University, the B.D. from Garrett Biblical Institute, the M.A. from Northwestern University and a just-completed Ph.D. from the University of Iowa. The faculty for the Vital Center courses and for the Department of Philosophy and Religion was as strong as it would ever be, in spite of Clayton Lane's grumbling about Simpson's being "overrun by a pack of Methodist parsons." When Lane retired at sixty-five the following year, he was not at all sanguine about the future of his "Meeting of the East and West" course. Would it fall into the hands of those who did not share his enthusiasm for and appreciation of Asian thought and culture? He need not have worried, for his immediate successor—for one year—was young historian James M. McCutcheon, just returned from a Fulbright Scholarship in London. McCutcheon, a University of Wisconsin Ph.D., was eminently qualified to teach the course. He remained at Simpson only a year (1960–61), when he accepted a tempting offer to work in the East-West Center at the University of Hawaii, where he would stay for many years. After McCutcheon's departure the course was taught by Dr. Hostetler.

Sometimes Clayton Lane's forthrightness, not to speak of his colorful views about the role of Christianity in the non-Christian third world, immersed him in simmering controversy. No one, for example, could forget his address to the Indianola Rotarians one Friday noon in March of 1957. As he held forth on the failures of American foreign policy, he couldn't help focusing on what he considered the sins of Christian missionaries, especially in China. "Missionaries," he avowed, "are revolutionaries, subversive persons who are always meddling with people's fixed ideas." They "made no attempt to understand the Chinese people but tried to mold them to western standards." Hence the Chinese "regard us as barbaric, uncivilized people who sent ignorant people to them, the oldest, richest civilization in the world."[40] Whatever the merits of Lane's animadversion, nearly everyone at Simpson and in Indianola had a cousin or aunt or uncle who was or had once been a Methodist missionary somewhere, and nearly all of them took grave offense at what they considered the intemperate tone of Lane's remarks.

Although he was astonished by the sensitivity of local people, he was not prepared to abandon his views. Nevertheless, he attempted in a letter to the *Record Herald* to round off the sharpness of his attack, admitting that "our mission boards, universities and foundations tried with high purpose to be helpful in both personal and national relations. Yet," he pointed out, "the results disclosed astonishing failures and a bitter reaction against us." He concluded, "I know very well that a great many Americans overseas have done their utmost to serve God, to seek truth and to achieve human brotherhood. Most have learned that good East-West relations require a two-way street."[41]

The explanation didn't help much. "How can a man," asked his critics—and they were legion—"hold such opinions and teach at a Christian college?" Kerstetter, whose own brother labored in the mission field in Africa, tried valiantly to calm the storm of protest, but because he believed that all faculty people had a right to express freely their own social and political views, even, or especially, if he disagreed with them, he was unable to placate the critics. It required the editorial wisdom of Don Berry, whose credentials as an Indianolan and Methodist were unassailable, to bring the whole matter into focus. Admitting that Lane had "stirred up a bunch of Kilkenny cats" with his Rotary speech, he dismissed as nonsense the question of whether such a man should be permitted to teach at Simpson. "If Mr. Lane is correct, the churches need to do some serious searching of the personnel of their missionary programs." On the other hand, "If Mr. Lane has drawn incorrect conclusions, then the question of his fitness to teach in a Christian college is not based on his attitude toward missionaries, but on the inaccuracy of his thinking. . . . If Mr. Lane's critics want to make their objections stick, they must show that Lane didn't know what he was talking about. . . . With the utmost reluctance can we believe that Mr. Lane is right in his statements regarding missionaries. But if he is, do we hide our heads in the sand or do we face the facts?"[42] Fortunately for Kerstetter, not all faculty members were as outspoken or controversial as was Clayton Lane.

* * *

Among the thirty-seven full-time faculty members at Simpson when Kerstetter arrived in early 1953, eight remained for the entire decade of his presidency: Hiram Doty in geology, Les Bechter and Ruth Jackson in English, Don Koontz in sociology, Luella Specht in education, Sven and Mildred Lekberg and Helen Malone in music. Mike Sorden returned to the teaching staff in business administration in the fall of 1953 and remained throughout the rest of the Kerstetter years and beyond.

The remaining twenty-eight faculty people in the spring of 1953 included Dixon Lee Riggs in biology, filling in for David Mobberley, who was on leave for the academic year; J. Allen Baker in chemistry, completing the last of his years at Simpson that had begun in 1908; Paul Merkle in chemistry; Lloyd O. Ritland in physics and mathematics; veteran Harold Watson in English together with David E. Pullman, who divided his time between his duties as director of publicity and instructor in English and journalism; Elizabeth White in English and speech; Roberta Riegel, who taught five sections of three languages in the College's undernourished Foreign Language Department; Clifford Lott, Livingston Witten and Harry W. Beardsley in philosophy and religion. Beardsley, who held a Boston University M.A., was in his first year at Simpson. In history were Howard

Greenlee and Robert Farb, while old-timer Francis Moats was helping out on a part-time basis. In economics, Everett L. Refior had joined the Simpson faculty in the fall of 1952. There was John D. Potter in business administration; Stuart Peterson, who served as professor of psychology and director of student personnel services; John Dahl and Katherine Keyhoe in education; Ethel D. Anderson and Mary Bronner in home economics. In physical education were Frank and Mona Casey and football coach R. G. "Hap" Miller. And in music were Hadley Crawford in voice, Ben Vandervelde in violin, Margaret Harvey in piano and Carlton Chaffee, teaching his last year at Simpson in instrumental music. Also in her last year at the College was Beryl Hoyt, librarian.

As Kerstetter, armed with the new curriculum, set forth on the task of improving the quality of the faculty and of increasing salaries and benefits, he sought out mostly young people either with a Ph.D. or within dissertation's length of one, preferably with "Phi Beta Kappa standing or its equivalent," and above all with "healthy, creative personalities."[43] In this endeavor he soon discovered that he had ample latitude, for the 1950s were years of volatility and rapid turnover in college faculties everywhere, and Simpson was no exception. During his ten years at the College, Kerstetter was able to make no fewer than eighty-four appointments of full-time faculty, roughly half of which were still in place when he departed. Simpson did see a remarkable increase in the number of people holding doctorates from seven in 1953 to twenty in 1962–63. And in that same period of time the number of Phi Beta Kappas on the faculty rose from zero to seven.

To be sure, some members of the board of trustees were not unhesitatingly impressed with all these new Ph.D.s and Phi Beta Kappas. "The important thing I'd like to know," said Ivan Willis, "is whether these people with fancy credentials can teach." Kerstetter stated, somewhat defensively, that "while we have added several men [sic] with Ph.D.s and members of Phi Beta Kappa to our faculty, they have been selected with primary thought also to their ability as teachers."[44]

"Hmph," hmphed Willis, who allowed as how he'd have to see how they performed in the classroom.

In those same years, faculty salaries rose from an average of $3,050 to $6,850 per year. Even allowing for inflation, the increase was impressive.

Noteworthy among the new faculty were a number of people who remained at the College long enough to become a part of its tradition and to have an impact on its growth. Perhaps it is arbitrary to do so, but we shall select for mention those Kerstetter appointees who remained at Simpson at least five years—a college generation plus one.

Jane Merkle, who had taught English and speech on a part-time basis for two years, was given a full-time contract in the fall of 1953. Her husband Paul had been a member of the faculty in chemistry for several years. A talented teacher and director, she would be remembered for her sensitive productions during the next seven years of first-rate drama. Few would forget Robert Larsen or Leland Kearney in *Cyrano de Bergerac* or Gwen Groomes in *St. Joan*, all the more remarkable for the severe physical limitations of the ill-equipped theater in the Old Chapel of College Hall.

Robert R. Bruner (1953–59), a graduate of Central College at Fayette, Missouri, who had earned his M.A. at the University of Iowa, replaced Carlton Chaffee, who had accepted a position at the University of South Dakota. Bruner superintended Simpson's music education program and directed the College's band.

It was Simpson's good fortune that Margaret L. Watson agreed to return in 1955 to the faculty in biology after a fourteen-year absence. For the next twenty-two years (1955-77) she would combine teaching and research and did real justice to both.

While undoubtedly the shining star among the new faculty in 1955 was Clayton Lane, the new youngster at Simpson was Joseph W. Walt in History. With a B.A. and M.A. from the University of Tennessee and the near-completion of the Ph.D. at Northwestern University, he replaced both Howard Greenlee and Robert Farb. Not at all certain he would want to stay at a small college, he intended to get a couple of years experience at Simpson, then go on to the "big leagues." But, by his own admission, he "fell in love with Simpson" and stayed on. Whatever else could be said of him, he was durable, and in later years was persuaded to undertake the writing of this volume of Simpson history.

Among the seven new additions to the faculty in 1957 were Clifford L. Meints, Harold A. Heckart and Gladys M. Moore. During the four years since the retirement of Dr. Baker, it had been difficult to find a chemist who wanted to make a career at Simpson, but with Meints, Kerstetter had found his man. With a B.S. from Purdue and the M.S. from Ohio University, Meints was completing his work on the doctorate at the University of Oklahoma. He soon assumed a role of leadership in the sciences at Simpson. In his many years at the College—he is still teaching as this history is being written—he kept himself and the sciences at Simpson abreast of the knowledge explosion. For example, although he was a religious conservative and traditionalist who might be expected to be cautious about newfangled devices, he embraced the computer revolution, understood its complexities and in a series of well-conceived workshops, taught his colleagues, some of whom were innocent of even the most rudimentary knowledge of the field, to learn not only how to operate a computer but to understand what the new technology was doing. Harold Heckart (1957-62), a fresh Ph.D. from Iowa State, taught both physics and mathematics. He must have taught well, for an alumnus who holds a doctorate in mathematics said only recently, "I learned more math from Dr. Heckart than I ever did from anyone else, before or since." Gladys Moore's (1957-77) two decades at Simpson saw hundreds of young men and women prepare for teaching in the elementary schools. Her instruction was low-key and effective, her sense of humor infectious, and her loyalty to the College unconditional.

When veteran Hiram Doty suffered a series of heart attacks in the spring of 1960, the College was fortunate to find as a "temporary" replacement an experienced geologist who happened to be in Ames visiting family members at the time.[45] His name was Herbert Alberding, an ebullient, improbable extrovert who was, if anything, the opposite of the taciturn, almost dour, rockbound Doty. The older man had won over dozens of students to the study of geology by patient indirection; Alberding would bowl them over by frontal attack. Alberding had earned his B.S. from Northwestern and the Ph.D. from the University of Arizona in 1938. Degree in hand, he took his new bride Martha May to the Philippines, where he worked for several years as a mining geologist. During World War II he continued his work in the United States, whereupon he accepted a position as a petroleum geologist in Venezuela and Colombia until his visit to Iowa in 1960. Not only did Alberding soon enough make a place for himself in the classroom and laboratory, but everyone noticed the quickening of the social life among the faculty. President Kerstetter chose to ignore reports of the delightful entertainments in the Alberdings' Swiss chalet home out on Scott Felton Road, where the genial hostess served Lucullan repasts and the host mixed and served colleagues and friends what were surely the strongest drinks this side of Lynchburg, Tennessee, while reveling in the latest campus gossip. Alberding, not to speak of Martha May, made himself an indispensable part of the Simpson scene, and when the beloved Hiram Doty died at seventy-four in the winter of 1963, he took over all the teaching duties in geology, continuing until his retirement in 1976.[46]

In the fall of 1960 several strong new faculty members joined the staff. Upon the retirement earlier that year of Harold Watson after thirty-six years as one of the all-time most successful teachers in the history of Simpson, Kerstetter determined that Simpson must recruit a strong, experienced person as English Department head. He remembered an especially effective, mature professor from his Baldwin-Wallace days, Donald A. Koch, whom he persuaded to come to Simpson after serving ten years on the Baldwin-Wallace faculty. Koch was a graduate of Baldwin-Wallace (1942) and had earned the Ph.D. from Western Reserve University in 1954. Just before he came to Simpson, Koch had taught at the University of Sao Paulo in Brazil as a Fulbright lecturer. With his wife Ruth and two sons Don and Dan, both of whom would later graduate from Simpson, he came to Indianola in the summer of 1960 and immediately made himself a part of the College and the community. A scholar as well as superb classroom lecturer, Koch edited a new edition of Timothy Shay Arthur's *Ten Nights in a Bar-room* published by the Harvard University Press in 1964, Mary Jane Holmes's *Tempest and Sunshine* and Susanna Cummins's *The Lamplighter* (1968) and a Festschrift in honor of his mentor at Western Reserve, Lyon N. Richardson (1972). It required a strong person to assume the mantle of a Harold Watson, and fortunately for Simpson, Kerstetter had found the right person. Koch would serve ably until his retirement in 1980.

Another newcomer in 1960 was Terry Hoy, the first person ever appointed at Simpson exclusively in the field of political science. A South Dakota native, he had earned his doctorate at the University of California, Berkeley, in 1956. A quiet and sometimes shy man—unless he was discussing political theory or philosophy—surprisingly he had been during World War II a member of the famed Merrill's Marauders, engaged in fierce guerrilla-style warfare in the Burma-India-China theater of operation. Not only a war hero, he was an experienced teacher, having served as a member of the faculty in the University of Maryland's overseas program in Iceland and Korea. Hoy became the mainstay of Simpson's political science program, and continued teaching until his retirement in 1986.

As Don Koch undertook the strengthening of the English Department, he sought out an experienced teacher and scholar. After examining a number of candidates, he was able to persuade Joseph E. Brewer, whose special field was British literature, to join the faculty. Brewer was a graduate of the University of Akron and held an M.A. from the University of Cincinnati and the Ph.D. from Western Reserve (1954). Koch had known Brewer when they both taught at Baldwin-Wallace. Brewer had moved to Long Beach State College in 1958, and it required all of Koch's charm and magnetism plus the offer of full professorship to bring

Brewer to Iowa. His classes were popular and well taught, but soon people were calling Joe Brewer "unconventional," a term that understated his myriad, yet beloved eccentricities that ranged from sartorial nonconformity—purple ties with green shirts—to a fondness for slivovitz, a fiery Yugoslavian plum brandy with absolutely lethal properties. As Terry Hoy recalls Brewer's years at Indianola, "Joe could be expected routinely to shatter the decorum of any group he encountered." He remained happily at Indianola with his wife and three young sons until, in 1967, he heard the siren call to return to California as a dean at Stanislaus State College. The day the Brewers left town dozens of well wishers came to see them head west in what looked ever so much like a Gypsy caravan.

Once the implementation of the Vital Center curriculum was complete and the students had adjusted to the College's new reaffirmation of the centrality of the liberal arts, Kerstetter dared to put one more important piece into place as the edifice of the Simpson curriculum. With the encouragement of any number of faculty, led by Harold Watson, Joe Walt, Les Bechter and of course Roberta Riegel, the faculty in the spring of 1960 adopted a twelve-hour requirement in foreign language. It took persuasion and compromise to get the measure through the faculty—for example the Western civilization requirement was reduced from two semesters to one—but Kerstetter's leadership was crucial to its adoption.[47] As he reported this action to the board of trustees in early June that year, he was prepared for possible dissent from among board proponents of career education. He said with conviction that "any tendency to settle for narrowly scientific, technical training or purely and barrenly intellectual preparation would not only devastate the historic and essential nature of Simpson, but its unique individuality and ground of distinction would be lost and its power and its worth reduced. We must keep this at the center of all our thought."[48] Harold Watson wrote of the restored foreign language requirement that it was a "triumph for righteousness over the forces of Sheol. . . . At least I was again willing to send our catalog to my friends—something I had refrained from doing for some years."[49]

In the fall of 1960 freshmen could enroll in one of the traditional modern languages plus a new one, Russian, offered for the first time ever. Roberta Riegel, enjoying her final year of preretirement, was assisted by Les Bechter in Spanish and Joe Walt in German. Employed to teach a section of German and two sections of elementary Russian was Viola Lecis, a graduate of the Institute of English in Riga, Latvia, part of whose education had been in the Soviet Union.

As enrollments grew the next year, new part-time help was added in order to staff the fourteen sections of elementary and intermediate classes. Two superior secondary school teachers were "borrowed" from Roosevelt High School in Des Moines: Floyd Pace[50] in Spanish and Glenn E. Buhr in German. Pace taught at Simpson for only one year, but Glenn Buhr became a longtime member of the faculty. He was a graduate of the University of Northern Iowa (1952) and later earned the M.A. at Middlebury College (1966). Remarkably skilled and splendidly fluent in German, Buhr soon made a place for himself at Simpson. It is doubtful that any faculty member in the history of the College ever contributed more than did Buhr to the development of a program in international studies. An early advocate of language study—under Simpson auspices—abroad, Buhr put together a semester program at Schorndorf in Baden-Württemberg that later became a respected model for language study overseas.

When Roberta Riegel retired, Josephine DeBoer, a dignified lady of seventy-five who had retired three years earlier at the University of California at Berkeley after a teaching career that spanned forty-two years, accepted a one-year appointment to handle all the instruction in French.[51] The following fall she was asked to return to teach Spanish for a year. Meanwhile, in 1962 the College selected as its new chairman in foreign languages Jay W. Gossner, whose degrees were all earned at Syracuse University (Ph.D. 1951) and who had studied at the Ecole des Hautes Etudes, Sorbonne (1948–49). Gossner provided powerful leadership in the burgeoning language program. With the demeanor of a French baron, impeccably attired in a pin stripe suit, he, together with his wife Evelyn, brought to the faculty a formality and elegance it had rarely seen. Apart from his formidable knowledge of French literature, Gossner's mastery of the intricacies of wine vintages, French cheeses and gourmet French cuisine rivaled that of Julia Child. Under Gossner (1962–66) the languages at Simpson flourished. During his first year at the College, for example, he saw to the installation of Simpson's first language laboratory.

Recruited in 1961 to teach part-time in the Department of History, Gary Valen, a Simpson graduate (1960) who had gone on to earn his M.A. at the University of Iowa, was asked the following year to teach German together with Buhr and Walt, alongside his classes in history. Although Valen assisted in German for a few years, he gradually moved entirely into history, remaining on the faculty until 1974, when he took over as director of the Brenton Student Center for a year, whereupon he would be appointed dean of students, a post he held for nine years (1975–84). Valen, whose teaching style was relaxed, comfortable and uniquely effective, and who was consequently immensely popular among students, took time to work on his doctorate at Syracuse University, but did not complete the degree, partly because of his growing interest in student development as an area of professional growth.

When Jim McCutcheon left Simpson in 1961 after only a year, the Department of History looked for a new American historian and found one in the person of R. William Helfrich, a graduate of Capitol University, who was about to receive the Ph.D. from Indiana University. Young, bright, nattily attired, almost punctilious, he soon became known as one of Simpson's most able—and most demanding—classroom teachers. The best students found his classes exciting and provocative; less able students avoided his classes altogether. As time went on, his teaching methods and materials became less conventional, his dress considerably more informal, his social views more nonconformist, his political stance farther to the left. But his academic standards never wavered, his classroom demands never flagged, and his attractiveness to students who were willing to meet those demands never abated. He retired in 1988, not long after his latest triumph, a *Simpsonian* poll that voted him the toughest professor at Simpson.

In the fall of 1962—Kerstetter's last year at Simpson—six new people joined the faculty. In biology there was Donald G. DeLisle, who had completed his doctorate at Iowa State only that summer. In physics and mathematics came Waldo Curtis, whose Ph.D. had been earned at the University of Washington in 1951. For a much-needed post in economics Richard D. McClintic, who held an M.S. from the University of Illinois, was recruited. In home economics Dolores Gade replaced Ethel J. Horner, who had taught full-time only one year. Gade's M.S. was from the University of Nebraska (1961). Richard deLaubenfels, whose career had included a number of years of highly successful teaching and theater directing at Yankton College, was invited to handle classes in speech and to direct the College plays. Since Jane Merkle's departure the work in drama had been supervised by Marla Del Wright (1959–61), and Emma Sue Phelps (1961–62), who stayed on part-time for another year. DeLaubenfels's endeavors at Simpson during eleven years—he retired in 1973—confirmed the good judgment of those who brought him into the faculty.

With the appointment of Waller B. Wiser as dean of the chapel and assistant professor of psychology in the fall of 1962, Simpson people were able to make the acquaintance of a remarkable man with a colorful history. A native of Maryland, he grew up in his home state and attended high school where he could be described as an indifferent student. He remembered that he graduated dead last in his class. Even before his graduation he enlisted in the Army Air Corps—he was too young to enlist but fibbed about his age—and served four years as a combat pilot in China during World War II. Those four years changed him. When he was finally discharged from the service he sought to enter college and to become a minister to the gospel in the Methodist Church. In spite of his abysmal academic record, Western Maryland College took a chance on him. There he proved himself, graduated with honors in 1951, went on to Drew University, where he earned the B.D. and S.T.M. degrees, and from there moved to Boston University, where he completed the Ph.D. in pastoral psychology in 1962. Kerstetter had become aware of Wiser through friends at Boston University and recalled that Wiser's wife, nee Elaine Smith, had graduated from Baldwin-Wallace while Kerstetter was teaching there. Although Wiser was assigned teaching duties in psychology and religion, he proved his worth many times over as an administrator during the years to come.[52]

* * *

When Dean Francis Christie left Simpson at mid-year in early 1959 to accept a position as head of the Philosophy and Religion Department at Mount Union College in Ohio, Kerstetter appointed Leslie Bechter as acting dean.[53] Bechter served ably and dutifully during the year-long search for a new dean. In March 1960, Kerstetter announced the appointment of Byron C. Lambert, chairman of the Division of Humanities at Milligan College, Johnson City, Tennessee. Lambert was a graduate of the University of Buffalo, where he also earned an M.A. in English. Afterwards he graduated with classical honors from the Butler University School of Theology. From there he went on to the University of Chicago, where he earned the doctorate in American cultural history in 1957. With his wife Phyllis, he came to Indianola to take up his duties in July 1960.[54] Even-tempered, gentlemanly, soft-spoken, Lambert worked well with Kerstetter and gained the confidence of the faculty. It was, then, disappointing that after only two years his wife's ill health forced him to resign.[55] Les Bechter took over once again, this time as dean in his own right, and remained in that position through the balance of Kerstetter's administration.[56]

When he was not filling in as dean of the College, Bechter served as registrar (1954–59), replacing Barbara Tunnicliff, who had held the post for a year, or as dean of men (1959–62) in addition to his teaching duties. If there was ever a workhorse on the faculty, Les Bechter was surely it, and one never heard a breath of complaint from him about the heavy load he carried year after year. After his retirement as registrar, the position was taken over by Mary Grassfield, the efficient, hard-working sister of Edith Feyerharm. Students found Grassfield a sympathetic and helpful official who did a lot more than merely record grades and issue transcripts. She put a human face on an otherwise impersonal function.

In 1960, after Joe Walt had completed his doctorate at Northwestern, Kerstetter appointed him assistant to the president for student development, with special attention to student recruitment and retention.[57]

In the business office of the College and in the development function, Robert W. Feyerharm, who joined the staff in 1955, continued to focus his attention on internal finance. An assistant business manager, Edwin R. McKee, had been employed in February 1954, replacing Merrill Ewing, and remained until 1956,[58] whereupon Feyerharm, with Kerstetter's ready assent, hired a promising, recent graduate of Simpson, Doyle Woods '56, who would become a mainstay of the College's business office for many years to come.[59] Three years later Woods was promoted to business manager.[60]

Feyerharm's assistants in the important development effort included Claude Smith—until 1956—and for a few months in 1956 Le Roi Dixon, soon replaced by George Hladky (1956–59). From Simpson, Hladky went on into business in Indianola, later publishing a newspaper, the *Reminder*, managing a cable television station, and serving as perhaps Indianola's most colorful mayor in all time. Hladky was succeeded in Simpson's development office by Gerald "Skip" Farley, a Simpson alumnus in the class of 1953.

When the New Century Fund was launched by the College at the time of the centennial, Marvin Ashlock received the title of vice-president for development, a position that has been continued to this day. Ashlock's successor, appointed in 1962, was Jess S. Mullin, lauded in the local press as "a senior director of national professional counselling firms for eleven years."[61] Although his years at Simpson were few, he formed lasting ties in Indianola, the most important of which was his marriage to Helen Malone of the music faculty.

An important part of the College's development program was the cultivation of Simpson's remarkably loyal alumni. In order to give Simpson's graduates more attention, Kerstetter appointed the College's first alumni secretary in many years. He was Charles H. Kayton, a fresh 1958 Simpson graduate hired immediately upon completion of his B.A. degree. Young Kayton continued as alumni secretary throughout Kerstetter's administration, meanwhile cementing relations with the faculty by marrying home economics instructor Marilyn Houghton in 1961.

* * *

Probably no president of Simpson has placed as great an emphasis on public relations and publicity as did William Kerstetter. It was not enough to be good; the College must be *seen* to be good, or success would elude it. He was careful about what was written or said in the name of the College, and determined to make Simpson known throughout the Midwest and the nation. He was delighted when a very positive article entitled "Surprising Simpson" appeared in 1956 in *The Iowan* magazine, and shared the campus pride when Simpson was named by *Time* magazine in 1961 as an up-and-coming college with a strong program in general studies. He was more likely than others to judge the work of the public relations people with a critical eye. His exacting demands and high expectations probably made life difficult for several who held the post—David

E. Pullman (1952–55), Daniel Thornburgh (1955–57), Bill Peters (1957–59), and J. Robert Walker (1959–62).

Not wholly satisfied with Simpson's public outreach, Kerstetter cast about for someone to take over public relations while keeping Bob Walker on in publications. Joe Walt suggested the name of a young friend who had recently completed his Master of Science in journalism at Northwestern University. He was Robert Goodloe, a bright, urbane, energetic youngster who grew up in Scarsdale, New York, and who was well trained for the Simpson position. But since he had recently discovered that he had a remarkable singing voice, Goodloe wanted to take a job where he could continue voice study and perhaps perform. Simpson seemed right for that. When Goodloe came to the campus a few weeks later for interviews, he asked to be able to sing for Sven Lekberg as a kind of audition. Lekberg, more out of courtesy to colleague Walt than from real interest, agreed to hear Goodloe sing in Edgerton Hall, with Robert Larsen accompanying, but he didn't expect much. No sooner had Goodloe sung one song, however, than Lekberg, amazed at the natural quality of Goodloe's rich baritone voice, rounded up all the faculty and students he could find to hear the rest of the singer's "audition."

Goodloe got the job, and started to work in February, 1961.[62] His work in public relations and publications was very good indeed, and his singing was even better.[63] He would go on to win the Metropolitan Opera regional auditions in 1963, the national auditions a year later and receive a Metropolitan Opera contract, launching an impressive singing career.[64]

* * *

Turning from public to internal relations, Simpson embraced the idea of a dean of students only very late. The old pattern of a dean of men and dean of women had served the College well, and these functions could be handled by people who divided their time between deaning and teaching. Serving as dean of men were Donald Barnhart (1953–56), George Montagno (1956–58), Benjamin Vandervelde (1958–59) and Les Bechter (1960–62). Then, in 1962, Kerstetter decided to appoint as dean of students Frank A. Beu. Beu would teach psychology alongside his administrative duties; being a dean of students at Simpson would not require *that* much time. And Kerstetter kept on as dean of women Helen Malone, who had succeeded Elizabeth White in 1959.[65]

* * *

Under Sven Lekberg the Department of Music flourished, scarcely suffering the enrollment downturn that affected the rest of Simpson during the later years of the Voigt administration. The department handled most of its own faculty and student recruitment and, within reasonable constraints, set its own agenda. During the early Kerstetter years the department was exceedingly stable. Apart from Robert Bruner's replacing Carlton Chaffee in the fall of 1953, no changes occurred during the next four years. Then in 1957 Margaret Harvey resigned to accept a position at Luther College at a salary considerably greater than she was receiving at Simpson. Her departure enabled Sven Lekberg to bring back to the College Robert Larsen, a 1956 Simpson graduate in music who had very nearly completed the Mus.M. degree at the University of Michigan.[66] Lekberg considered Larsen the most gifted piano student he had known during his entire career and was delighted to welcome him to the staff.

An all-around musician, Larsen would teach at Simpson from that day to this, taking time out only during one academic year to work on his doctorate at Indiana University. No sooner had he come to Simpson than his chief interest turned from piano to voice, especially to opera. In mid-February 1958, Larsen directed the first opera ever at Simpson, *The Consul* by Gian-Carlo Menotti, a modern production which had premiered only in 1950.[67] Given the limitations of Simpson's "Little Theater," the production was excellent. The following year when Larsen directed *Die Fledermaus*, Johann Strauss's nineteenth-century romp, with Larsen accompanying on the piano, opera had come to Simpson to stay. To be sure, *Die Fledermaus* was technically an operetta, but it was one that had long since been legitimized in the repertory of the New York Met, so Larsen was on firm ground.[68] He knew it would be popular, and it was, especially so because it was sung in English, a practice that soon became a Larsen trademark. Larsen, still in his early twenties, believed opera was for the people, and the first requisite of popular understanding was that listeners be enabled to follow the story line by knowing what was said as well as sung. Despite criticism from some opera purists, Larsen never wavered in his insistence on the use of English. Meanwhile he organized anew the Madrigal Singers, a remarkably effective and popular small group that performed primarily Renaissance music.

His passion for opera led Larsen to go to Indiana University, widely regarded as one of the best opera programs in the nation, to earn the doctorate. The student operas became larger, more elaborate, more successful, leading to the founding of the Des Moines Metro Opera in 1972.

While Larsen continued to teach piano, his consuming interest in opera shifted somewhat the focus of the department toward voice, altering the role of Hadley Crawford, who had been the mainstay of voice instruction at Simpson since 1945 and whose choirs were highly praised. Because the climate in the department had changed, Crawford resigned in 1959. During the next five turbulent years, three men held the chair in voice: John T. Campbell (1959–60), Donald W. Nelson (1960–62) and David Nott (1962–64). Such a turnover deprived the department of the stability it needed in voice.

The departure of Robert Bruner that same year brought into the faculty Bruce N. Degen, a graduate of what is today S.U.N.Y.-Potsdam (1954), who had just completed his Mus.M. degree at the prestigious Eastman School of Music. A talented bassoonist, Degen handled Simpson's wind instrument program and provided instruction in music education for the many majors who planned to teach in public schools. For many years he was lead bassoonist in the Des Moines Symphony Orchestra. In 1971 he completed his doctorate at the University of Rochester and in 1974 was promoted to a full professorship in music. He remains at Simpson as this history is being written. In his corner of the music program, there was indeed stability.

Another musician resigned in 1959. Ben Vandervelde, who had taught violin at Simpson for twelve years, accepted a post at Northern State Teachers College at Aberdeen, South Dakota. Replacing him was Samuel Minasian, a graduate of Cornell College who had earned his Mus.M. at Eastman School of Music in 1952. During his five years at Simpson, Minasian taught stringed instruments and resurrected the College's orchestra, which he called the "Simpson-Indianola Symphony." Robert Larsen was especially pleased with the new orchestra, for he saw the possibility of doing opera with full orchestral accompaniment. A further bonus with the appointment of Minasian was his wife, Mary Joyce, an accomplished musician in her own right, who taught preparatory piano on a part-time basis.

During the Kerstetter decade, as had been true during earlier decades, people in the Simpson community could enjoy the world's greatest music. Sometimes the theater or auditorium was less than adequate, but the music was glorious and varied. There was something for almost every taste: a jazz ensemble, All-College Sing, student and faculty recitals, band and orchestra concerts, choral music and opera. Scarcely a week went by during the school year that did not offer the whole college community—and the townspeople—something thoroughly worthwhile. One has only to reside for a time in a community that does not offer this cultural program to appreciate what music at Simpson provided to those who came and were enriched for doing so.

* * *

Music at Simpson was unapologetically a professional program, setting major course requirements for the B.M. degree far in excess of any discipline for the B.A. degree. There was a B.A. in Music offered, with a thirty-six hour major requirement, but students were frankly urged by the music faculty to avoid it, and nearly everyone did. The musicians in the faculty tended to react to all proposals for curricular change with an attitude that ranged from caution to fierce opposition, especially if any such change might mean an increase in liberal arts requirements at the expense of courses in music.[69] Accordingly, changes in all-College requirements were usually adjusted downward for the B.M. after patient negotiation with Sven Lekberg and his faculty. Still, so great was the mutual respect which Dr. Kerstetter and Professor Lekberg held for each other that the Kerstetter commitment to elevating the liberal arts at Simpson was neither opposed nor challenged. Besides, noted Lekberg with a long draw on his ever-present pipe, wasn't music one of the seven liberal arts?

Apart from the introduction of the Vital Center and the foreign language requirement, other curricular changes during the 1953–63 decade were accomplished with relative ease. Within three months after Kerstetter's arrival at Simpson in the first days of 1953, Simpson received notification that it was accepted for participation in the Washington Semester Program, which permitted as many as four junior or senior Simpson students to study government and politics in the nation's capital. By the College's agreement with American University, which administered the program, Simpson students paying their regular tuition at the College would receive full credit for their academic work. This highly successful program, still in place in the 1990s, was the first of several similar, external study opportunities the College made available to students during the years that followed.[70]

In keeping with the College's rising standards, the faculty adopted late in 1957 new regulations for academic probation, suspension and dismissal. Freshmen would be required to achieve a cumulative 1.65 gradepoint average (4.00 = A) in order to continue, sophomores a 1.80 average and juniors and seniors a 2.00 average.[71]

Although no one had said anything about it, faculty people were noticed to be scheduling fewer Saturday morning classes each year. Students, of course, hated Saturday classes, especially for their dampening effect on Friday evening social activities, but faculty didn't like them either. Besides, all of America seemed to be moving to the five-day week. By the spring of 1960 only seven classes or sections were left, taught by five intrepid faculty members who liked morning hours. The whole faculty finally took notice of the matter and voted on May 26, 1960, to go to a five-day week. The new schedule still permitted a free hour between 9:30 and 10:30 on Tuesday and Thursday in order to accommodate the required Tuesday chapel services.[72] "Officials pointed out," reported the *Record-Herald*, "that the Saturday mornings may then be used for faculty conferences, lab-research and extended library use," a statement that surely must have been made tongue-in-cheek.[73] A suggestion to return to 7:30 A.M. classes, abandoned in 1947, was met by a combination of horror and contempt.

That same spring the faculty, concerned that the requirement in freshman composition was not adequately ensuring student writing competence, voted to require the writing of an English proficiency examination in the junior year. Hardly a panacea for the problem of inadequate student writing, the requirement did nevertheless bring attention to the need for monitoring composition throughout the faculty.[74]

The following year Don Koch and Joe Walt, in the interest of academic integration and outreach, proposed the creation of a summer American studies program and received for it a $10,000 grant from the William Robertson Coe Foundation. Twenty-five outstanding Iowa high school teachers were invited to come to the campus for a five-week intensive study with five nationally known scholars, including Simpson alumnus and Civil War scholar Avery O. Craven from the University of Chicago, Carl Bode, specialist in popular American culture, from the University of Maryland, literary historian Robert Spiller of the University of Pennsylvania, Arthur Link, the Woodrow Wilson scholar from Princeton and Clarence L. Ver Steeg, American colonial historian from Northwestern University. Don Koch and Jim McCutcheon taught in the program as well, and Joe Walt took care of administration. Enormously successful, the program received funding for four more years, bringing to the campus another hundred secondary school teachers from the Midwest, together with a splendid array of scholars in American history, literature and intellectual and cultural studies.[75] After McCutcheon's departure, Bill Helfrich stepped in to assist in the program. Most of the participants loved it.

In a further effort to emphasize Simpson's liberal arts commitment, the faculty authorized in 1962 the abandonment of the Bachelor of Science in Business Administration degree. All majors in Business Administration would henceforth receive the B.A. The change was thoroughly noncontroversial, for the requirements for the B.S.B.A. and B.A. had been identical for years.[76]

In addition to these improvements in the College's curriculum and academic practices, the faculty during the latter years of Dr. Kerstetter's administration wrestled with three serious issues, two of them of nationwide concern and the other strictly a Simpson matter. The first involved the numerous loyalty oaths and other tests that had been imposed on public school teachers during the years since the passage of the McCarran Internal Security Act of 1950, which was followed by the relentless search for Communists and "fellow-travelers" during the McCarthy days and after. Later the U.S. government had included in the application for student loans under the National Defense Education Act a loyalty oath from students, together with a disclaimer certifying that the applicant was not and never had been a member of any organization dedicated to the overthrow of the government. For the faculty, the issue, had it been considered purely on philosophical grounds, was simple. They almost unanimously opposed both oaths and disclaimers. But should we protest and urge our students, who were also objecting to the rules, to refuse to sign, thereby very likely jeopardizing their eligibility for needed loans? The faculty did just about all it could do; it protested the oath and the disclaimer affidavit but left to students the decision as to whether to sign. Most did sign. They needed the money.[77]

In a further move to democratize Simpson, both students and faculty adopted in 1963 a strong policy that banned discrimination on the basis of race, color, creed or national origin in the College or in any of its campus activities, teams or organizations.[78] Principally directed toward the College's Greek-letter organizations, some of which had been known to have discriminatory—especially racial and religious—clauses in their national constitutions, the faculty legislation represented a strong, if somewhat belated, response to a major national issue. Every national Greek-letter group at Simpson, with one possible exception, had long since removed any discriminatory regulations from their constitutions and national laws. Still, the civil rights movement represented a major force in the country to which Simpson people found it important to speak.

The third issue was an intramural matter. It seems that a number of faculty people were known to be a little restless because of what they regarded a paternalistic—a few suggested dictatorial—style of leadership on the part of the president. No one, to be sure, would disagree that in 1953 the College had needed a strong hand to make necessary changes, nor could any deny the almost unbelievable gains the College—and indeed the faculty—had made in a decade. However, the faculty and some administrators sought to create at Simpson a more nearly collegial form of governance. This is not to say that Dr. Kerstetter ruled by fiat—even though faculty often jokingly referred to him as "Kaiser Bill." He ruled by the strength of his powerful personality. So persuasive, so forceful and directed was his leadership that other voices were stilled, other opinions unexamined. Perhaps he had done his job too well. The Simpson family was large, robust and well-developed. And it was maturing.

In the winter of 1962–63, the last months of Kerstetter's administration, a group of young faculty, anxious to change all things, decided to organize a chapter of the American Association of University Professors. Like-minded faculty joined happily, while others, some of whom were identified as standing closer to the center of Kerstettian power, signed up in order to exert a moderating influence on the group. Though not formally chartered until a few weeks after Dr. Kerstetter left Simpson, the inception of A.A.U.P. can be seen in part as a reaction to the centripetal force of the president's control.[79] The president himself was a member of the A.A.U.P., having joined the organization when he was teaching full time, and was not opposed professionally to its being organized at Simpson.

Even the most restive among the faculty, however, were quite ready to praise Kerstetter's generous personnel policies. Faculty salaries had more than doubled in a decade. The size of the faculty had grown from thirty-seven in early 1953 to fifty-two full-time in 1962–63. The total salary budget had increased from $115,000 to $373,000, even in a time of inflation an impressive gain. After 1961 faculty and staff received tuition grants ranging up to full tuition for their children who enrolled as full-time students.[80] That same year the College dropped its ban on married couples being employed full-time.[81] In a further development, faculty and staff benefits were markedly improved.[82] These constructive changes, signaling the College's robust health, tended to make it extremely difficult for faculty to find fault with Kerstetter's leadership, try as some of them might.

Any concerns about administrative practices were customarily expressed with delicacy and circumspection. Faculty people were considerably less inhibited, however, if they fell into disagreement with each other. Few would forget the row in the mid-fifties over the advisability of seeking an Air Force R.O.T.C. unit for Simpson. Hardly a new idea, the matter had emerged in the past and nothing had come of it. This time the faculty debated endlessly on the topic, the proponents of pacifism led by Phillips Moulton and the "militarists" by David Mobberley. When the debate exhausted the faculty, the two gentlemen took their fight to the local newspaper, their letters to the editor entertaining the local community for weeks. When a particularly shrill attack by Moulton was published, Mobberly commented to the author of this history, "I never knew anyone more ready than Moulton to fight at the drop of a hat for pacifism." Soon enough the tempest abated. Simpson never did get an A.F.R.O.T.C. unit.

Occasionally Cliff Meints's religious conservatism elicited spirited response from his colleagues. In the fall of 1960, for example, Meints presented in a chapel address a powerful and persuasive defense of what would come to be called "creationism," a rejection of Darwin's theory of evolution and natural selection. His words brought forth a rejoinder from science colleague Jack L. Carter in a letter to the *Simpsonian*. Pointing out that Meints was a chemist, not a biologist—as if that somehow mattered—Carter assured one and all that Meints's views "are not the views of the biology department." Flatly he stated that "the theory of organic evolution is an underlying principle in all fields of biology." One could hardly find a basic text in biology that was not based on the theme of organic evolution, he wrote. "The same is true of historical geology, paleobotany, paleontology." Finally, "I believe the theory of organic evolution will be around and going strong long after Dr. Meints and I are gone."[83] Their exchange hardly ended the evolution-creationism debate at Simpson.

Not so much a disagreement with colleagues, but instead a fear for the future of the Vital Center program led Clayton Lane in 1960 to take a parting shot on behalf of civilization, which he seemed to find in short supply at Indianola. As he and his wife were preparing to retire, he noted a *Simpsonian* editorial penned by editor Paul Brown praising Lane's work at the College. It was important, said Brown, that Lane be replaced with someone equally competent in Asian Studies. He did not sound hopeful.[84] In response to Brown's compliment and concern, Lane expressed his thanks, pointing out at the same time, "For me Simpson has been another post in the under-developed areas," but that the results of his efforts had proved to be more than he expected. He praised Kerstetter's vision and specific planning of the entire Vital Center, noting "his vision and breadth of view attracted me here [and] kept me here longer than my personal inclination impelled." He hoped too that the course would not be changed, although "many critics would like to see it abandoned and Simpson restored to its pre-Kerstetter eminence as the best Methodist college in Warren County."[85]

Meanwhile, in a thoroughly noncontroversial mood, two Simpson faculty members were awarded honorary doctorates, both in 1957. Illinois Wesleyan University conferred upon Sven Lekberg the Doctor of Humanities at its Founders Day Convocation in February. The following autumn Simpson honored senior professor Hiram Doty with the degree of Doctor of Science as a part of the fourth Christian Liberal Arts Festival.[86] Doty was visibly as nervous as a schoolboy when Dr. Kerstetter read the citation praising his contributions to Simpson:

> The essence of his genius is difficult to discern. Yet something of that greatness we can see. You are one of the great teachers of America.
> Your colleagues say, "When the rest of us give a student up as hopeless, or are powerless to help him, Doty persists with a genius that saves him." . . .
> A legend among alumni, singular among your colleagues, you have been singled out by them, after 39 years of service at Simpson, to receive what is only the second honorary degree voted for a colleague by the Simpson College faculty in a century of time.[87]

* * *

While curriculum and faculty development occupied a considerable amount of his time and attention, Kerstetter, together with a cooperative board of trustees, set about early on to improve the College's finances. The best of plans, no matter how well-laid, would come to fruition only if there was money to pay for them. And to call Simpson impoverished in 1953 scarcely describes its state; in terms of ready funds, it was surely an academic pauper.

Kerstetter, with the enthusiastic support of his reformed board, moved quickly on two fronts. First, because the College was heavily dependent on tuition income, he worked to increase student numbers and tuition charges. As we have seen, within a year enrollments began to move upward and continued to do so. His efforts to raise tuition were slowed by the board's caution, lest the College raise its tuition too fast and too much. Their reasoning was that if students did not elect to come to Simpson with its low tuition, would even fewer come if tuition were raised? Kerstetter's philosophy was that people value what they pay for. Simpson's job was to charge enough tuition and provide an education that justified the price.

Tuition was not increased at all until the fall of 1956, when it rose to $480 per year, up $80. Meanwhile, however, Kerstetter had persuaded the board to accept in the fall of 1954 a $65 annual "general fee" to cover the cost of an array of student activities together with testing, counseling, health, registration and other administrative services.[88] The increase, which the board found acceptable if it was not called "tuition," was helpful and was met with only an expected amount of student grousing. In the years that followed, Kerstetter continued to push for tuition increases in an attempt to make Simpson's charges comparable with similar Iowa institutions. In 1958 tuition rose to $580, in 1960 to $650, in 1961 to $720, and in 1962 to $800, exactly double what it had been in 1953. The general fee rose from $65 to $80 in 1958, and to $100 in 1960. And during the decade room charges were hiked from an annual average of $150 in 1953 to $280 a decade later. Board, on the other hand, only went up very modestly, from $378 to $420.

The College's budget produced surpluses every year Kerstetter was at Simpson, permitting the gradual liquidation of the debt and the application of funds to ongoing capital projects.

The other economic front was, of course, fund-raising, and that meant careful cultivation of corporations, foundations, the church, alumni and other selected individuals. Here the president knew he had his work cut out for him. Only minimal efforts had been made with corporations and foundations. And although Simpson's alumni were loyal, their giving had been, with a few notable exceptions, disappointing, totaling only $16,000 in 1953–54. Small wonder the College was grateful for the Methodist conference's $31,000 that same year.[89]

Within months the board and the president put together a major fund-raising program. They called it the "Centennial Fulfillment Program." Toting up the College's immediate needs—for buildings, operations and endowment—the board came up with a figure of $2,565,000, soon increased to $2,870,000 but later scaled back to what they hoped would be more realistic $1,800,000.[90] Ivan Willis was named chairman of the drive and Ralph McGee of Osceola, vice-chairman.[91] Although it was well organized and well carried out, the drive sputtered, partly because the professional counsel selected was both costly and ineffective.[92] By the end of 1954 only $272,000 had been raised, and by mid-1955 the date set for the conclusion of the active campaign, but $332,000.[93] It was a thoroughly disappointing effort.

Undaunted, Kerstetter decided to do most of the fund raising himself. He relied during his first two years primarily on Wendell Tutt, the College's business manager, whose duties had been confined to internal finance and who had performed remarkably well in view of the College's limited resources. Without Wendell Tutt, the College's condition would have been far worse than it was. Kerstetter was looking for someone, however, who would supervise and coordinate "those duties normally discharged by a college treasurer and business manager as well as the total financial development of the college, including fund-raising operations."[94] When Tutt resigned in October 1954,[95] Kerstetter moved ahead with the search for a new financial vice-president. He found his man at Carleton College in Minnesota. He was Robert W. Feyerharm, at fifty-one a widely experienced professional in college finance who had served in a number of capacities for twenty years at Yankton College in South Dakota, before going to Carleton. A devoted and active Episcopalian layman, he took up his duties at Simpson on April 1, 1955.[96]

Feyerharm and Kerstetter worked admirably together throughout the years they shared at the College, and the growing success of Simpson's fund-raising efforts—after the Centennial Fulfillment Fund disaster—was largely due to their combined efforts.

Alumni giving moved along gratifyingly, as did corporate and foundation grants, notably $93,500 from the Ford Foundation and a $100,000 challenge grant from the Kresge Foundation, both in 1956.[97] The Kresge gift, which the College did match, established and endowed the George Washington Carver chair in science.[98] Clifford Meints was the first appointed to the Carver Chair and has been its sole occupant down to the present time.[99] Both Meints and Margaret Watson received handsome National Science Foundation research grants during those years.[100]

As Simpson approached its centennial year, the board of trustees decided, in view of the College's recent success and the opportunity to commemorate its founding in 1860, to undertake another major fund-raising campaign. Accordingly, in early 1960 the Centennial Fulfillment Program was laid to rest, its hardworking but disappointed executive committee replaced by a new Simpson Development Council.[101]

President Edwin E. Voigt, 1941–52.

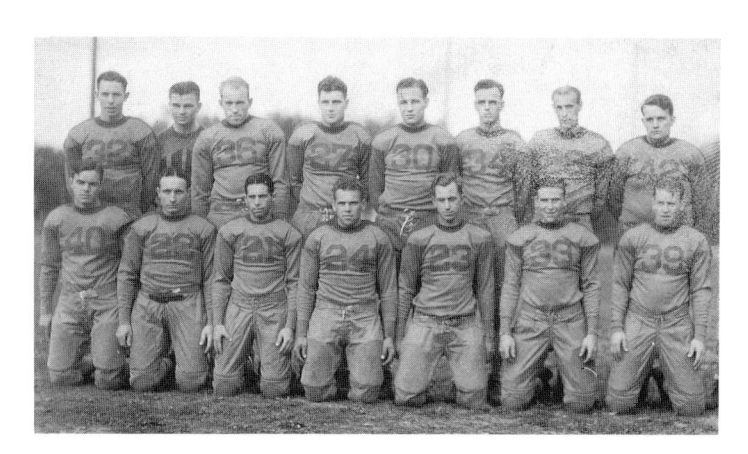

Fifteen lettermen from the 1934 football team.

W. E. Payne, Professor of Economics and Business Administration, 1930–39.

Edmond J. Marty, Instructor in Band Instruments, leads the College band at Homecoming time, 1940.

President Edwin E. Voigt.

George Washington Carver delivers the Baccalaureate Address at Simpson, 1941.

President John O. Gross visits George Washington Carver at the Carver Museum in Tuskegee, Alabama in 1940.

George Washington Carver delivers the Baccalaureate Address at Simpson's 1941 commencement. Dr. Gross (left), Carver (center) and Walter M. Scheuermann (right).

Japanese American students at Simpson in 1943–44: Standing: Arthur T. Sugino, James Hashimoto, Stanley T. Aoyagi; Seated: Sumiko Hashimoto; Inserts: Marion Konishi, Karen Toda.

The 1944 *Zenith* staff, like all of Simpson, was mostly female. Standing: Marjorie Martin, Katherine Lofgren, Wendell Lawhead, Cheryl Bressler; Seated: Bernadine Frame and Editor Adrianne Shaw.

Simpson's 1943 football team, dubbed the "Kindergartners," won one game and lost three. Top row: Ash, Ball, Butler, Day, Hashimoto; Middle row: Hatton, Hoffman, Jacobs, LaFollette, Lamb, Lawhead; Bottom row: Miles, Sager, Strom, Sturm, Tucker, Weinman.

One of the earliest Simpson students to serve in the Second World War was H. Frieda Axthelm (Yakish), an Ensign in the WAVES.

Among those who served in the armed forces during WWII include: Berttene Jenkens, Marine Corp.; Jack Harvey, Navy; Gene Brucker, Army Air Corps; Loraine Davis, Naval Air Corps; Charles Flesher, Army; Jerry Hammand, Army Air Corps; Leland McGraw, Navy; John Moore, Army; Paul Kirby, Army; Bernard Brennan, Navy; Bob Rogers, Army; Chad Boltz, Army Air Corps; Ray Moore, Army Air Corps.

An aerial view of the campus (from the south) locates—among other things—the barracks buildings moved onto the campus after World War II.

Bob Woodcock sets an Iowa Conference pole vault record in 1950.

With three wins, two ties and only one loss, Simpson's football team was declared conference champions in 1944.

The Redmen won the conference championship in football in 1949. Here Larry Parr makes a short gain against Iowa Wesleyan.

In 1949 students could enjoy their new lounge in Old Chapel (College Hall).

Some classes were less stimulating then others (1949).

Football players find their field has shrunk as builders arrive to construct the new women's dormitory (October 1948).

Coach Frank Casey, whose career at Simpson stretched from 1936 to 1960, makes a point to basketballer Gene Braught, 1941.

The "New" women's dormitory opened in 1949. This view is from the east.

The check-out desk at the Carnegie Library served students until the new Dunn Library was opened in 1964.

R. G. "Hap" Miller was football coach at Simpson from 1947 to 1958.

Standing in the Wigwam, Hack Kim reads the bad news of the attack of North Korea on South Korea in 1950.

The dedication of Sigler Home Economics building in 1951.

The Music Annex, completed in 1950, provided a large practice room for instrumental music.

To accommodate growing postwar enrollments, the College "imported" some wartime barracks and placed them at three locations on campus.

Home of the College's president from the 1950s to the 1970s, located at Girard and B Street.

Entrance to Hillman Hall.

Freshmen in the 1950s were subjected to a battery of tests as soon as they arrived on campus.

A new, if short-lived, fraternity was Pi Kappa Phi, chartered in 1950.

The Theta U's occupied this trim house at the corner of Buxton and Girard.

The ATO's occupied this house from war's end in 1945 to 1963.

William E. Kerstetter, President of Simpson from 1953 to 1963.

President Kerstetter presents a citation to Charles Malik, Secretary General of the United Nations, at a Christian Liberal Arts Festival on campus.

Perry Wilkins, student body president in 1953–54.

Student body president "Mac" McFarland rings the old chapel bell to signal the beginning of campus day.

Artist-in-Residence Bent Lane brought Art instruction back to Simpson after a number of years. (1955–60).

The Iowa Association of Colored Women presented Simpson a gift of $5,000 toward the construction of the George Washington Carver Hall of Science in 1956.

A memorial plaque was placed in the George Washington Carver Hall of Science when the building was dedicated in 1956.

The Lambda Chi Alphas were perennial winners of All College Sing.

Clayton Lane joined the Simpson faculty in 1955 after a distinguished career in the U.S. Foreign Service.

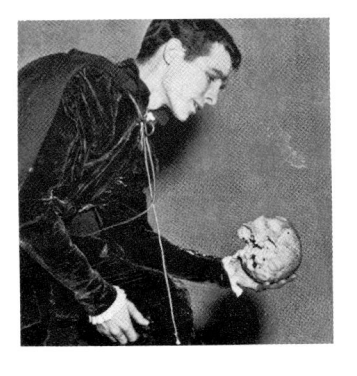

Leland Kearney as Hamlet. (1958).

When football star Bill Graves graduated in 1958, he received a commission in the U.S. Marine Corps.

By the 1950's dancing on campus was a common experience for Simpson students. Before the mid-30's dancing was absolutely forbidden.

Sitting 'round the fire at the Lambda Chi house (1953).

At Homecoming time each year, Simpson social groups competed—with floats, house and window decorations—for the Tomahawk, the coveted symbol of the "Spirit of Simpson."

"S" Club members loved to haze freshmen (1957).

1959 Homecoming Royalty: Princess, Lida Shoemaker; Big Chief, Myron Sorden; Brave, Gary Valen.

The Trideltas selected an oriental theme for their 1958 homecoming float.

Everyone remembers the day that classes were dismissed because of snow (1959).

Stuart C. Peterson taught in the Department of Psychology from 1947 until the time of his death in 1961.

Visiting Oxford University Professor J. Steven Watson taught at Simpson during the fall semester of 1962. He was later president of St. Andrews University in Scotland.

Homecoming Royalty, Fall 1961.

Robert Feyerharm, Vice President for Finance, 1954–69.

Football mentors in 1962 were Assistant Coach Bill Hulen, Head Coach Ken Heizer, and Assistant Coach Larry Johnson.

In 1963 the women's dormitory—henceforth known as Kresge Hall—was enlarged to more than twice its former size.

Acting President Hurford I. Stone, 1963. He graduated from Simpson in 1916 and had served as Dean of students at the University of California at Berkeley.

Architect Richard Neutra who designed Dunn Library and three fraternity houses at Simpson.

Administrator Waller B. Wiser came to Simpson in 1962 as Dean of the Chapel. Then served as Dean of Students (1964–68) and Dean of Academic Affairs (1968–73).

Ralph C. John, president of the College from 1963 to 1972.

The Pi Phis entertain Dean Cuthbert A. Simpson of Christ Church, Oxford University.

Don L. Berry '03, publisher of the Indianola newspaper for nearly fifty years, town patriarch and longtime member of the Simpson board of trustees.

Professors Donald A. Koch, Terry Hoy and Herbert Alberding at the 1965 Commencement.

Tom Hensley and Ron Miller '65, receive the Barborka Trophy from Dr. Clifford Barborka at Commencement, 1965.

Freshman registration, 1965.

Fans shivered through the Homecoming game of 1966.

"Can't you say that in Canadian?" Coach Ken Heizer confers on the sidelines with Jim Henderson, wide receiver from Toronto, Ontario.

From Simpson, Robert Goodloe (center), went on to a successful career at the Metropolitan Opera.

John L. Sullivan coached the Redmen football team from 1966 to 1971. His assistant (right) was Richard Starr.

As is customary at Simpson commencements, the whole faculty is decked out in full plumage in its procession to the ceremony.

Simpson Alumnus (1960) Donald D. Gibson, instructor of History (1967–68) helped organize the Iowa presidential election campaign for Sen. Eugene McCarthy in 1968.

Ethel D. Anderson, Professor of Home Economics, 1946–61.

Margaret L. "Peg" Watson, Professor of Biology, 1937–41 and 1955–77.

Public relations man Gordon Brown shares a light moment with Lu Jean Cole, Director of the Brenton Student Center.

Smith Chapel was dedicated in the fall of 1968.

The Smiths of Smith Chapel, David and his sister Alida.

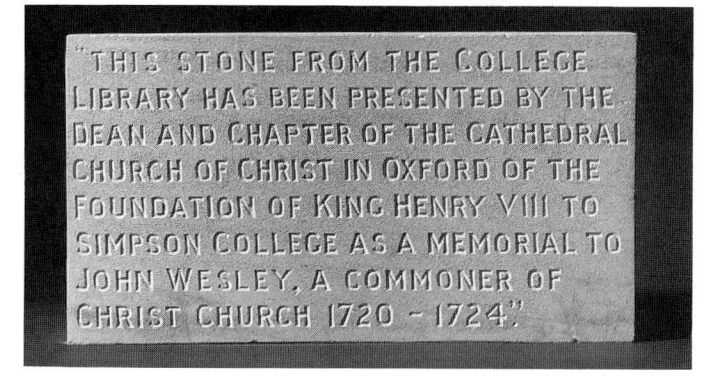

The "Oxford Stone" from the Library at Christ Church, Oxford University, presented to Simpson in 1967.

Tom Ackerman, the man who brought balloons to Simpson and Indianola.

The fall 1972 football team was coached by Al Paone (second from right), assisted by Richard Clogg, Richard Starr and Larry Johnson.

Up-and-coming music star John Denver performed at Simpson for a full week in 1969.

With the Centennial year already underway, the board created what it called the "New Century Fund," a campaign expected to require as many as ten to twelve years to complete. To administer the program it employed the services of the John Price Jones Co. of New York, whose representatives met with the full board at its annual meeting in June. Although the board hoped to mount an $8,000,000 campaign, the John Price Jones people urged that the goal be reduced to $5,000,000 and that the duration of the drive be shortened substantially. That fall John Price Jones sent to campus an energetic, hard-driving, experienced fund-raiser, Dr. Marvin Ashlock, to put the campaign together and run it.[102] Ashlock was designated "special assistant to the president for development," while Bob Feyerharm was assigned management of the College's business affairs. By now both Kerstetter and Feyerharm had learned that one man could not handle the internal finances of a growing college and also run a major development campaign.[103] Ashlock arrived on the campus with the grace of a baby elephant, trumpeted the aims of the campaign and set to work with more enthusiasm than finesse. Ashlock was rough, but his methods worked.

It was a good time to start, for once again the College's exchequer had rung up a budget surplus—this time more than $27,000. And the board had adopted Simpson's first million dollar-plus annual budget in the College's history.[104] Moreover, Simpson had just received word that alumnus Clare Barker '17, for years a leading figure in Indiana University's School of Commerce, had died, leaving his entire estate to Simpson, representing the largest single bequest—something more than $227,000—the College had ever received.[105] Then there was the gratifying and largely unexpected decision of the South Iowa Conference of the Methodist Church just a year earlier to raise its annual giving to Simpson to $100,000 per year for the next decade.[106] In view of the conference's generous pledge, the decision was taken not to attempt any direct church solicitation in this campaign.

The New Century Fund sought to raise $875,000 for a new library, $500,000 for a chapel, $100,000 for an addition to the women's dormitory and $3,525,000 for the endowment. The first phase would, not surprisingly, try to raise money for the new buildings. The endowment could come later.

By the time the campaign was announced publicly in April 1961, a considerable sum had already been raised. Alumnus and trustee Judson Perkins of La Jolla, California, headed a huge Development Council—the College's catalog published in 1961 listed 114 members—consisting of board members, outstanding alumni, parents and friends.[107] Ashlock's first report to the board of trustees indicated striking success. A faculty-staff campaign had brought in nearly $34,000. Students had contributed $678, trustees $104,285 (their goal was $100,000), and Des Moines alumni so far $6,373. Des Moines and Indianola businesses were yet to be contacted. More importantly, large gifts could be counted a part of the drive: a pledge toward the chapel from David O. and Alida Smith ($200,000), the net amount of the Clare Barker estate of $197,000,[108] a grant from the Gardner and Florence Call Cowles Foundation ($200,000), $300,000 of the pledge of the Methodist Church, another Kresge Foundation grant of $25,000 and miscellaneous collections of $11,819, for a total in gifts and pledges of $1,078,959, representing a major portion of the amount needed to erect the needed facilities, and a considerable percentage of the $1,685,000 first phase goal.

The campaign continued until the end of Kerstetter's presidency, with considerable success. Major gifts and estates included modest grants from U.S. Steel, Maytag, Iowa Power and International Harvester, an additional Kresge Foundation gift of $75,000 toward the new library, a Kellogg Foundation award of $100,000 for library books, $50,000 from the J. Hugh Jackson estate, $20,000 from alumna Olive Pearl Clark's estate, and, most notably, $225,000 from alumnus Rex A. Dunn '13 of Compton, California.[109] By Kerstetter's own reckoning, "We raised considerable money for various projects, approximately $6,000,000 [in] cash, pledges and wills, some of which had been developed by our predecessors."[110] And in 1963, $6,000,000 was indeed a very large sum of money.

* * *

Much of Simpson's fund raising during the 1953–63 decade was directed toward an extensive and much needed building program. During more than three decades since the erection of the Administration Building, only two major building projects had been completed, Sigler Hall and the women's dormitory. Of greater concern was the sorry condition of most of the existing buildings, some of which needed substantial repair and refurbishing. Two construction projects, both intolerably delayed, were agonizingly close to being realized, yet the funds for their completion were only partially in hand. The new men's dormitory was ready to go, but the student union was not.[111] Still, in order to reduce costs, the board of trustees wanted to advertise for bids for both buildings simultaneously. Bids for both were accordingly solicited in late summer, 1953.

When bids were opened on September 4, the lowest totalled $594,257—$324,310 for the men's dormitory and $269,947 for the student union.[112] Architects' fees, furniture, equipment and extras raised the total cost to $713,011 ($377,142 for the dormitory and $335,869 for the student union). The winning bidder on the general contract was W. A. Klinger Company of Sioux City, Iowa.

While the resources were present to go ahead with the dormitory, the College could count only $120,000 toward the student union, a woeful $215,869 short of the building's cost. Because the board did not dare go ahead with more than one building, it negotiated with Klinger and the subcontractors, revised the project downward and awarded the contracts for the men's dormitory on September 15,[113] and "before a week had passed, a bulldozer had taken over for plunging fullbacks" on the old football field.[114]

The dormitory accommodated 123 men. Solidly built of steel, concrete and brick, with a great pitched slate roof, it matched the "collegiate Gothic" architectural style of the four-year-old women's dormitory.[115] Completed on time for the opening of classes in September 1954, it was filled to capacity, Simpson's first college-owned men's housing in a structure built for the purpose. Dedication of the building was delayed until the student union could be completed.[116] Meanwhile a housemother was employed for the 1954–55 academic year, an arrangement that proved to be not entirely satisfactory. Desiring to provide for the residence hall more of a living-learning experience, Kerstetter persuaded new history teacher Joe Walt in the fall of 1955 to reside in the "housemother's" suite and serve as an academic counselor for dormitory residents. Walt managed to survive the experience, even to enjoy it, until his increasing duties at the College led him in 1959 happily to turn the job over to another. In 1963, the building was named "Barker Hall," honoring the loyalty and generosity of Clare Barker to Simpson.[117]

It was board member Ken Brown who pointed out that one problem with the student union project was that the building was too big. Could it not be redesigned and reduced in its function to the most-needed uses.[118] Kerstetter reluctantly agreed that it was realistic to go ahead with a pared-down plan, and within a few months the architects provided what was needed.[119] At the same time the board voted "to take $262,000 in invested funds and make them available for immediate projects," allocating $92,000 for debt retirement and the balance for several construction projects and campus improvements.[120] While it was dangerous to spend a portion of the College's endowment, both the board and Kerstetter saw it as a matter of investing in Simpson's future.

They renegotiated the contract with Klinger and the subcontractors, arriving at a $258,000 price tag for the scaled-down student union, which they called "Annie Merner Pfeiffer Hall." Although available funds totaled only $224,000, they voted to go ahead, hoping that they could raise $34,000 in the next nine months.[121] The contract was signed in early August 1954, and construction commenced within days.[122] The building included a large dining hall, seating up to 450 persons, and kitchen, together with a small snack bar on the first floor. The second floor was almost totally given over to a large concert hall, soon called "Great Hall," seating upwards of 650, and a sun deck on the south side over the kitchen and overlooking the campus.[123] Although construction proceeded ahead of schedule, the cost of equipment and furnishings, together with the default of the electrical contractor, raised the total cost of the building to $318,254 (later reduced to $291,967), which put the College into a temporary financial bind.[124] Nevertheless the building opened on time, and residence hall students took their meals there, Mary Berry's hallowed dining hall having been closed down. Everyone agreed that the new dining hall was very pleasant indeed.[125]

Students, however, were expecting more than a dining hall. Long promised a "student union," they found only a tiny snack bar and no recreational area at all. Where were the facilities that "were supposed to stock this extravaganza?" they asked in the *Simpsonian*. Could students group around an old upright piano there and harmonize? Could they have a spirited game of table tennis or shuffleboard among the chairs and tables? Clearly, a student union it was not. But the dining hall was needed, and the Great Hall proved to possess superb acoustics. "Almost everyone" wrote Don Berry in the local newspaper, "is taken by the grandeur and gracefulness of the huge hall. The massive wooden beams, strikingly matching chandeliers and large windows at each end . . . make the room particularly distinctive."[126] Students soon adjusted. A real student union could come later.

No sooner was Pfeiffer Hall under construction than the College turned its attention to the long-awaited Carver Hall of Science. Here again plans for the building had to be scaled down if there was to be any hope of meeting the ever-rising costs of construction. The architects, the firm of Tinsley, Higgins, Lighter & Lyon, of Des Moines, were most cooperative, cutting out of the building an entire third floor with its pitched roof and reducing hallways by judicious relocation of interior walls. The new plans called for 264,000 cubic feet of space, including laboratories and lecture rooms for physics, chemistry and biology, plus a drafting room, photographic darkroom, a science library, seminar room, offices for staff members and a small attached greenhouse. At the entrance to the building was a fine foyer with a marble memorial inscription and bronze relief plaque honoring George Washington Carver. In the basement was a 250-seat sloped-floor lecture hall. The building would be located along the south side of the campus, along West Clinton Street.[127]

Low bidder was Fane F. Vawter Company, Des Moines, whose base bid was $215,840. The subcontracts, plus equipment and furnishings, brought the total cost of the building above $350,000. Construction continued throughout the next academic year.

The building was dedicated in an impressive ceremony at the third Christian Liberal Arts Festival in October 1956.[128] Present for the event and participating in the program was Ralph J. Bunche, Undersecretary of the United Nations. Just before coming to Simpson he had received the Nobel Peace Prize. While Bunche had no illusions about the difficulties that confronted the American Negro—the nation was at that moment in the midst of the school integration crisis—he recalled that Carver "in his life and time . . . helped to open new doors of opportunity and [gave] hope to Negro Americans; he inspired them to a new confidence in themselves." Another who personally knew and admired Carver when he was a boy growing up in Ames, wandering through fields with the older scientist studying flowers and plants, was former Vice President of the United States, Henry A. Wallace. Happy that Carver had been introduced to the liberal arts before he went to Ames, Wallace warned: "A civilization based exclusively on technology is certain to be warped." Gardner Cowles, whose handsome $175,000 gift made the new science hall possible, praised "the new spirit and faith in future growth now evident at Simpson." Bishop F. Gerald Ensley sounded a word of caution: "Science," he said, "reigned supreme for a time and threatened to become all-encompassing. . . . Science can be employed for evil as well as good, for wonder drugs as well as wonder narcotics." But on a happier note, he concluded that "Science blasts the entire idea of racism and will destroy the myth that one race is better than another."[129]

Of all the people who attended the Carver dedication, none were more welcome than the delegation of the Iowa Association of Colored Women, headed by Miss Jessie Walker of Des Moines, whose $5,000 gift toward the construction of the building was surely among the most notable. No individual or group made a more sacrificial contribution to the building, nor were any more esteemed for what was surely a gift of love.[130]

As the new buildings went up, it became increasingly clear to Kerstetter and the board that the campus would soon be overbuilt if more land was not acquired. The president mentioned the matter as early as the summer of 1954.[131] That fall he pointed out that an eighteen-acre parcel of land, "the only vacant ground adjoining the campus in any direction," owned by R. E. McAninch, was available for purchase and urged its acquisition.[132] The board agreed, but negotiations over price dragged on for many months. Only in mid-1956 did the board agree to buy 4.3 acres of the parcel, Kerstetter still arguing for acquiring the entire eighteen acres, lest the opportunity slip through their fingers. The board remained cautious, however, and only the smaller parcel was purchased, located across E Street to the west of the practice football field.[133] "As soon as sufficient funds are available," reported the *Simpsonian*, the land "will be leveled off and converted into a recreational area for field hockey and intramural football and baseball."[134]

Still anxious to enlarge the size of the campus, Kerstetter learned in late 1957 that 8.3 acres of land, bounded by E Street on the east and on the north by Iowa Avenue, and owned by Leo and Pearl Frazier, was available for $18,900. The board authorized the president to go ahead, also "to negotiate for options on adjoining tracts."[135] Kerstetter needed little prodding and negotiated for several tracts at one time.[136] The Frazier parcel was purchased in January for $15,000.[137] A tract just west of the Frazier property, located along West Iowa and belonging to Carroll Wood was purchased for $3,500.[138] Another parcel owned by Paul Bishop was added, at a price of $5,000, and in a matter of weeks the College acquired an eight-acre tract, just south of the Frazier land, from Fred Glascock for $26,000.[139]

These land purchases doubled the size of the campus from approximately twenty-four acres to fifty acres. Twenty-two of the acres had been added in one month.[140] It is true that some of the College's resident critics growled about the College "taking over" too much of Indianola's west side, but these additions to the campus would prove to be one of the more forward-looking accomplishments of the Kerstetter administration. The president himself explained why he was deeply concerned about campus expansion. "Historically," he wrote, "throughout our nation, most colleges have either lacked the vision . . . or have lacked the courage to pay the cost in their own generation, in a sense, letting the future take care of it—at which time it was tragically too late."[141] And that was not all. The College continued to buy individual properties adjacent to the campus—especially those lying between the "main campus" and the new land west of E Street—as they became available. The wisdom of these purchases would become evident within a very few years.[142]

Meanwhile, Kerstetter made the improvement of the appearance of the campus a priority. There was plenty to do. There were things like cleaning up around Mary Berry Hall, where a hideous parking area west of the building was closed and a lawn planted, not to speak of fencing in an unsightly garbage area behind the dormitory. The area around the barracks buildings was cluttered and messy and needed a major cleanup. An attractive sign, fourteen feet long and five feet high, was erected along North Buxton Street, announcing "Simpson College, Founded in 1860."[143]

Beautification of the campus was dealt a serious blow within months after Kerstetter's arrival in Indianola. On the evening of June 17, 1953, the worst windstorm—some people were sure it was a tornado—in recent history swept through Indianola, accompanied by a deluge of rainfall. Electrical power was out for up to forty-eight hours and one thousand telephones were out of order. The north part of town was hardest hit. "Simpson College's whispering maples," reported the local newspaper, "took a terrific beating during the storm, and the campus was littered by fallen branches. Several windows in the library building were broken." More frightening was the near-injury of the infant daughter of Charles and Roberta Kerr, who lived on campus in the Tilton Court barracks. Plaster fell on the baby as a tree limb crashed through the roof of their apartment.[144] Dozens of the College's maples and many elms were either plucked entirely out of the ground or lost huge branches. As the campus cleaned up, tree surgeons declared many of the trees unsalvageable. And the cost of the rehabilitation of the campus was something the College could ill afford. Not until several years later would an organized replanting take place.

In an effort to remove some of the clutter that marred the north part of the campus, Kerstetter in 1957 ordered the demolition of the ancient structure, just west of the heating plant, most recently used as a storage shed. Built by President Fletcher Brown in the 1890s at a cost of about $1,000, it had served variously as the ladies' gymnasium and military armory until 1912, as a storage building from 1912 to 1915 and as the home economics building until the completion of Sigler Hall.[145]

* * *

Increasing enrollment exerted pressure on the College's residence halls, especially for women students, and if Simpson was to continue as a residential college, more housing was needed. To this end the third floor of the new women's dormitory was finished off during the summer of 1959, providing room for an additional forty-two women.[146] It was "almost" completed when the women arrived in the fall. But even without curtains or door knobs, coeds were happy to be housed on campus.[147]

The third floor completion was only a temporary remedy. Much more was needed as women's enrollment shot up from 147 in the spring of 1953 to 308 in the fall of 1962. A large new women's residence hall, or an equally large addition to the existing one, was needed. Although the cost would be great, government loans were available at attractive rates of interest for revenue-producing campus facilities.

The project would have moved ahead quickly, but was stalled by an unfortunate controversy about architectural style. It all started innocently enough. Looking toward the erection of a chapel and a new library, the board of trustees agreed in 1958 to seek out a new architectural firm.[148] Sensing the expansive vision of the "new" Simpson, and tired of Simpson's recent "cornfield Gothic" architecture, several board members, led by engineer Kenneth Brown, together with a few faculty people with Clayton Lane in the vanguard, recommended that the College seek out a firm with an international reputation. One of the best, they agreed, was Vienna-born Richard Neutra, a world-famous architect of the firm Neutra and Alexander in Los Angeles. Neutra's designs, consciously seeking to relate buildings to the natural world surrounding them, were spectacularly modern. Clayton Lane remembered his stunning U.S. Embassy building at Karachi; Ken Brown had marveled at some of Neutra's home designs. Trustee Luther Hill was enthusiastic about Neutra, as was Des Moines newspaper executive David Kruidenier, for whom Neutra had designed a house. Not only was Neutra selected to make plans for the library and chapel; he was named "campus architect" and went to work.[149]

There were few problems with plans for the library, certainly none with the concept and basic design. But Neutra's sketches of the chapel were indeed novel, a striking contemporary structure with a huge tower. It did not look much like a traditional New England church. Kerstetter, whose taste in architecture leaned toward eighteenth or nineteenth century design, didn't like the Neutra plans, and said so. More importantly, the prospective donors he had in mind adamantly insisted on a traditional church. Further, two more building projects were in the works: the large addition to the women's dormitory and three or four fraternity houses. Who would design these? The controversy simmered for months.

By mid-1960 the dispute was hobbling the College's forward movement. The climax came when the two sides squared off against each other in a special meeting of the whole board of trustees on June 17, 1960. A real breach was avoided when the modernists and traditionalists, after a spirited discussion, agreed to have Neutra design the library and fraternity houses and to find a new—and indeed traditional—architect to design the chapel and women's dormitory addition. Like most such exercises in compromise, the decision made no one completely happy, but at least the College could get on with its building plans.[150] That fall Arland Dirlam, a church architect of Boston, Massachusetts, was selected to draw up plans for the women's dormitory addition, it being understood that the architectural style would duplicate that of the existing structure. Dirlam would also produce sketches for the proposed chapel, after which he would be hired to design the building "if his plans were approved by the chapel donors."[151] When the final dormitory plans were ready in the summer of 1961, Kerstetter judged Dirlam's work to have been done "imaginatively, efficiently and promptly."[152] Bids were received and the contract awarded October 7 to Philip L. Caron of West Des Moines in the amount of $375,675.[153] Attached directly and inconspicuously to the west gable of the original building, the new 117-bed addition stretched toward C Street, right across from the Lambda Chi Alpha house. At the suggestion of Leona Kerstetter, an enclosed garden was constructed south of the building, surrounded by an eight-foot high, solid brick "privacy wall" presumably to protect sun-bathing coeds from prying glances of campus swains.[154]

Apart from some unforeseen serious problems with subsoil conditions—at Simpson there were *always* subsoil problems, lots of underground water and springs—that turned the excavated area into a small lake, construction proceeded smoothly through the academic year and into the fall of 1962.[155] It was first occupied when women moved in right after the Christmas holidays.[156] A few months later, in gratitude for the Kresge Foundation's generosity to Simpson, the entire women's dormitory was named "Kresge Hall."[157]

The naming of Kresge and Barker Halls had been preceded in 1961 by naming the administration building Hillman Hall, in honor of the president whose administration at Simpson had spanned the better part of two decades. Hillman had died July 13, 1957, at the age of ninety-two. Four stone plaques imbedded near the four corners of the east and west sides of the building were appropriately marked "Hillman Hall." At the same time a portrait of Dr. Hillman was commissioned to hang beside that of Bishop Matthew Simpson outside the president's second floor office. The artist for both portraits was Cloy Kent of Iowa City. During the years that followed, any number of her portraits of Simpson greats would grace campus buildings. Thirty years later she was still being referred to as "Simpson's official portraitist."[158]

* * *

With the single exception of the Lambda Chi Alpha house, fraternity housing at Simpson had been wholly inadequate since both Alpha Tau Omega and Kappa Theta Psi had sold their houses during the Second World War. All the fraternity houses, including Lambda Chi and the two ramshackle structures serving ATO and Kappa, together with the old house that had been occupied by the now-defunct Pi Kappa Phis, were owned by the College. Kerstetter believed that it was unconscionable for Simpson to continue to be a Greek-letter slum landlord. The situation looked especially bad by comparison after the opening of the new men's dormitory. In an effort to nudge the fraternities to improve their housing, he therefore ruled, with the concurrence of the board, that the fraternities either buy or vacate the premises they occupied.[159]

Understandably, only the Lambda Chi Alphas wanted to buy their house, and once a price was agreed upon, the building was sold to them for $33,000.[160] Meanwhile a new fraternity, calling itself Phi Alpha, purchased a house at 605 West Ashland.[161] Neither ATO nor KOY, however, wanted to buy an old dwelling, yet neither had the funds to build a first-class fraternity house. The ATOs did have plans drawn up for an attractive thirty-six-man $60,000 brick house to be built at the northwest corner of Franklin and D Streets. But the site was too small—only 71 feet by 140 feet—and local residents, fearful of traffic and congestion, successfully blocked the project before the Indianola Planning and Zoning Commission. Kappa Theta Psi meanwhile did buy an older dwelling at 310 West Ashland Avenue, but considered the move there temporary.

Led by C. Max Miller, the president of the ATO house corporation and ebullient insurance executive from Des Moines, who would later be elected to Simpson's board of trustees, the fraternity alumni made a series of proposals to the College, all of which involved some level of institutional participation in financing, in view of the College's borrowing power. By 1959 they were urging the board of trustees to permit the erection of fraternity houses on a part of the 4.3-acre new land west of E Street. When consulted, architect Richard Neutra found the site ideal.

Now to financing such a project. Board member Roy L. Miller, himself a national officer of Sigma Alpha Epsilon—which fraternity had granted the Phi Alphas a charter—suggested that Simpson take a look at the fraternity house construction at Westminster College in Fulton, Missouri. The buildings, college-financed and owned, were leased to the fraternities on a long-term basis. The College maintained and operated the houses precisely as it did its regular dormitories. On the basis of this model, C. Max Miller went to work with a proposal by three fraternities—Lambda Chi Alpha chose not to participate—to erect three identical houses on the North E Street site, and over the next two years plans for the project were refined.[162] Without Max Miller's commitment and perseverance, it is doubtful the project would ever have been seen through. The board gave its assent on October 16, 1959.[163] Soon thereafter, with only minimal opposition by a single neighborhood resident, the city's zoning commission approved the construction site.[164]

Architect Neutra went to work, producing his first plans in mid-1961, and by late summer the College applied for a thirty-eight-year $395,000 loan at three and three-eights percent interest.[165] Each fraternity would contribute $25,000 in cash. When bids were received on October 30, the winning contractor was Irvinbilt Construction Company of Chillicothe, Missouri. The total cost of the three buildings was estimated at approximately $514,000, requiring an infusion of something less than $50,000 of Simpson money. Work on the project began in early December.[166]

When Richard Neutra asked fraternity representatives what quality they wanted in their new houses, without a second thought their response was "indestructibility," and that is what they got. Built of steel and reinforced concrete, the buildings would be certified as bomb shelters and rated earthquakeproof. Housing forty-two men each, the houses had a large lounge, housemother's suite and three dormitory rooms on the first floor, together with nine student rooms and large bathroom on each of the two upper floors. The basement was given over to a large dining room, kitchen facilities and storage and mechanical space. Students in the houses would pay the College standard charges for room, while each fraternity was authorized to provide dining facilities for its members. Thoroughly modern in design, the three buildings were handsomely located on the site Neutra liked, a commanding eminence overlooking an intramural athletic field and the city's Memorial Park, although their design suggested southern California more than Iowa.

Although there were delays in the construction schedule, the three fraternities occupied their new houses at the beginning of the second semester in 1963.[167] Thus at both ends of the Kerstetter administration the College provided new housing for 249 men and 159 women, a remarkable accomplishment.

* * *

Neutra's plans for the fraternity houses were quite acceptable. His design of the new library was a triumph. That a new library was needed at the College had been evident for many years. The campus Carnegie Library, which had seemed so large to President Shelton when it was built, looked pathetically small a half century later. It was cramped and crowded even with Simpson's meager collection of books and periodicals. Without exception, former presidents of the College found the library the easiest place to cut expenditures whenever finances were tight, and they usually were. During the years immediately preceding Kerstetter's arrival, less than one-half of one percent of the College's budget went for library materials. The book collection was scarcely forty-thousand volumes, and too few of those had been purchased since the Hillman years.[168] As enrollments began to rise after 1953, study facilities in the reading room were overrun. Little could be done, however, until such priorities as student housing and science facilities had been met. As soon as they were, the College could go ahead with a new library.

There was no unanimity on campus about what was most needed in the library. Not surprisingly, the faculty wanted more books; the librarians wanted more staff; the students wanted the library open longer hours; the administration preferred the status-quo, at least until the physical plant became humiliatingly inadequate.[169] Ultimately, everyone agreed that a proper building was their first priority.

As early as 1957 Kerstetter appointed Clayton Lane to head a Library Planning Committee. Taking his duties seriously, Lane visited a number of library experts on the East Coast. If Simpson was to have a new library, it must be a good one. "It is intended," he said to the *Simpsonian* "that the Simpson book collection will be made first class and that library facilities will be made the most adequate available."[170] Neutra was asked in early 1959 to prepare preliminary plans for both the library and the chapel.[171] When it became clear that because of architectural disagreements and the hesitancy of donors the chapel project would be delayed, Kerstetter and the board agreed to go ahead with the library.[172] Neutra went to work in earnest.

On a Simpson scale the building would be huge—180 feet by 90 feet—built on an east-west axis on the site of the old heating plant, which was razed to make way for the new structure. It would seat 630 students at one time, including 103 individual study carrels. The book capacity of the stacks would be approximately 150,000. Special features of the building would include on the ground floor a student lounge, current periodicals room, a fountain in the central stairway area, several seminar and listening rooms, periodicals stacks and library offices and work area. On the second floor were the main book stacks, a separate rare book room, several more seminar rooms and twelve faculty cubicles.

When the plans were submitted to the faculty Library Planning Committee, a number of specific suggestions were made. They would eliminate, for example, eight doorways from the south glass wall of the building leading out into a "garden area," pointing out that any doorways other than the front west entrance would create a security horror for the library staff. And a most felicitous suggestion called for raising the ceiling of the second floor by three or four feet to accommodate a mezzanine office area above the seminar rooms and an additional stack floor that, when finished off, could accommodate 96,000 more volumes, bringing the total capacity to just under 250,000. The committee suggested a revised treatment of the library's south facade. These and a series of other minor proposals were graciously accepted by the architect. The result was a remarkably beautiful and functional building.[173]

Neutra visited the campus frequently, often bringing his wife, checking on this or that detail—soil studies, temperature and humidity checks, aesthetic considerations.[174] He loved long, philosophical conversations, but rarely started a sentence in English he did not finish in German, or vice versa. Kerstetter, whose patience with this eccentricity was probably greater than his taste for contemporary architecture, still found a conversation with Neutra exhausting. More than once he telephoned me, saying "Joe, with your proficiency in German, would you be willing to entertain the Neutras this evening?" I enjoyed hugely these meetings with the architect, even if our conversation sounded like an exercise in Pennsylvania Dutch.

The plans were ready in early 1962, but the financing was not. Kerstetter reported that the New Century Fund stood at something over $1,390,000 in April that year, but of that amount only $658,027 was now available for the library. They were still $291,973 short of their $950,000 goal for the project.[175] However, enough pledges were received during the summer to enable the board to advertise for bids. When bids were opened November 8, Henkel Construction Company of Mason City, Iowa, got the general contract at $616,523.[176] Construction would begin in March.

Then lightning struck. Rex A. Dunn '13, who had already contributed just over $50,000 for the library, increased his pledge to $225,000, the largest single gift toward the project. Now the library was assured.

When ground was broken after chapel on Tuesday morning, March 26, 1963, Kerstetter was joined by Osceola banker Ralph McGee, chairman of the board of trustees, Jack Padgett, chairman of the Library Planning Committee, secretary of the board Luther L. Hill of Des Moines, librarian William Garton, and student body president Phil McEldowney of Jabalpur, India.[177] Although neither Rex nor Norma Dunn could be present for the groundbreaking, the decision was soon taken to name the building the "Dunn Library."[178]

Construction required more than a year. Dedicated on October 31, 1964, the new library took its place as the dominant structure on the campus. "Now," said librarian Bill Garton, "we have a fine building. Let's get a book collection worthy of it."

* * *

Two more minor construction projects completed the "bricks and mortar" part of Dr. Kerstetter's presidency. The first was a new heating plant, constructed because of obsolete equipment in the old one and because the old structure, with its huge, hideous smokestack, occupied the site for the new library. The location of the campus's underground heating lines, all emanating from the existing plant, dictated a location nearby. Sensibly, the decision was taken to raze the old building, smokestack and all, and to locate the new plant underground, adjacent to the new library, hiding the flue inside the library. As Kerstetter put it, "The heating plant was out of sight, swallowed up within the library, merged into a thing of beauty, forever."[179] The new equipment could easily be hooked up to the old heating lines. Built in 1962 at a cost of $143,000, south of Pfeiffer Hall and north of the library site, the sixty-five-by-twenty-eight-foot structure contained two large gas-fired boilers weighing seventeen tons. A temporary smokestack was put up until the new library was built. The general contractor for the plant, built on a cost-plus basis, was Irvinbilt Construction Company of Chillicothe, Missouri. With construction of the heating plant, the College, with city approval, closed Euclid Street, which ran east and west through the campus from North Buxton to North C Street at this location.[180]

Because the College's maintenance department had been housed in part of the old heating plant building, Kerstetter and the board, with the advice of Robert Feyerharm, decided to enclose the area under the bleachers at Neff Field along D Street for the maintenance people. The enclosed area, utilizing the bleachers for a roof, was divided into two large and three smaller rooms. Contractor for the $15,000 project was Godwin Brothers construction Company of Indianola.[181]

Not counting Barker Hall, whose construction was assured before he arrived at Simpson, Kerstetter was responsible for nine new buildings on the campus, if one counts each of the fraternity houses as a separate entity: Pfeiffer Hall, Carver Hall of Science, the large addition to Kresge Hall, the Kappa Theta Psi, Alpha Tau Omega and Sigma Alpha Epsilon fraternity houses, the new heating plant, the new maintenance department and the Dunn Library, for which construction was under way before the president departed. And his doubling of the campus acreage must not be forgotten. By any calculation, Kerstetter was the most prolific builder in the history of the College.

* * *

Simpson students, at least the most able among them, responded enthusiastically to the Vital Center Program, to the Christian Liberal Arts Festivals and to the new emphasis on the liberal arts. Most of them liked the new, attractive undergraduate housing. All of them came to believe that they were a part of a college on the move. Student morale had never been better.

There were, of course, students whose educational plans included as little exposure to the liberal arts as possible, those who in Dr. Kerstetter's view "had not yet caught the vision." Basketball star Bob Tidgren was one of them. "I was just there to play basketball. The only attention paid to the curriculum was to stay eligible," he recalled years later.[182] The *Simpsonian* reminded the student critics, "Before most of you groan in anguish at the mention of liberal arts and Vital Center, stop and take a look at the newspaper. Did you notice how many times Simpson and Simpson people are mentioned?" A few years later another editor declared that "the Vital Center Program has proven to be one of the most important segments of the Simpson College curriculum."[183] And finally one of the editors did catch the vision: "At Simpson the aim is to educate for a better way of living with our fellow-man, not to train for higher incomes in a world of competition."[184] Yet another agreed: "The Vital Center is not course work, but a way of educative life . . . the Simpson way of life."[185] Some did not like the Christian Liberal Arts Festival, although most did, especially after students were permitted to be more involved in the planning process. Students, said sophomore Jim Willis, "should consider it a privilege" to participate in CLAF. "Even more, though, we might consider it an opportunity to prove that the intellectual soil of Iowa is as fertile as the rich soil of the countryside."[186]

However edified by their education at Simpson, a large number of students also participated as actively as ever in the booming extracurriculum. Student government was pleasant, collegial and for the most part noncontroversial. During the "happy days" of the fifties, few public issues could rouse students out of their political torpor. It is noteworthy, however, that for the 1953–54 year, students elected Perry Wilkins president of Student Congress. Wilkins, a good student and excellent athlete—he held the AAU indoor and Simpson long jump records—was the only American black student on the campus. What was gratifying is that he was chosen for his competence and popularity, not because he was a compromise candidate or the object of some sort of political statement about race.[187]

As enrollments swelled and more and more students were being housed on campus, the system of student government, based on one representative for each housing unit, seemed less democratic than heretofore, the Greek houses being overrepresented. Accordingly, a new constitution was proposed and approved overwhelmingly (387–63) by student vote in 1959, creating what would thereafter be called the "Student Senate," with considerably more balanced representation from housing constituencies as well as off-campus students.[188] Subsequently several amendments were adopted, chief among them the fixing of elections earlier in the academic year.[189] By the end of the decade, as national issues began to loom more important on campus, the senate was urged by representatives of the National Student Association to shift its attention markedly. The senate was deeply divided about whether to focus its concern on national affairs or local matters. In any case as time went on, national issues crowded in and occupied more of the senate's agenda.[190]

Meanwhile the seven fraternities and sororities, in 1953 still housing more students than did the College itself in its dormitories, flourished in spite of low enrollments. More than half of Simpson's undergraduates were affiliated with them. And with the upturn in admissions in the next two years, Greek membership grew apace. As it did, Kerstetter urged the fraternities to defer rushing until the freshmen's second semester in order to give them a chance to become familiar with Simpson. In early 1955 the Interfraternity Council agreed, but for quite different reasons. Concerned about the inordinate size of one fraternity, they decided it was best "to give the new rushes a better chance to become acquainted with each fraternity."[191]

Before their deferred rushing plan had its first test, a new player appeared in the person of Charles Gray, a sophomore from Ames who transferred to Simpson in the fall of 1955 from Northwestern University, where he had been pledged to Phi Delta Theta, but not initiated. Eligible to join a Simpson fraternity at once because of his sophomore status, he and a few other transfer and upperclass students were entertained by the three campus groups, but found them less attractive than they had hoped. Led by Gray, six of these transfer and upperclass students decided to organize their own fraternity, with the object of gaining a charter of a strong national fraternity. Although predisposed to go after a charter of Phi Delta Theta, Gray decided for two reasons to seek a charter of Sigma Alpha Epsilon. First, when he learned that SAE had once had a chapter at Simpson (1889–98), he reasoned that it would be easier to revive an inactive chapter than to pioneer with a newcomer. Secondly, one of the best friends of his family in Ames, Dr. Chester D. Lee of the Iowa State faculty, had just concluded his term as national president of SAE, and Lee offered encouragement. Thus the six men founded what they called Phi Alpha, on September 23, and SAE was their goal.[192] Approved unanimously by I.F.C. in less than a week,[193] the group won faculty and board of trustees' approval during the course of the semester.[194] With an enlarged upperclass membership, the new fraternity participated in the College's first formal deferred rushing the following February with great success, pledging twenty freshmen. Selecting as faculty advisers David Mobberley and Joe Walt, the Phi Alphas purchased a house at 605 West Ashland, the historic O. C. Brown house, built in 1868. From that time on, the Phi Alphas took a strong place among the fraternities. After two years in the petitioning process they received a charter from SAE and were installed as the revived Iowa Sigma chapter on October 19, 1957.[195] From its inception the new fraternity compiled an enviable academic record, winning first place in interfraternity scholarship eleven of its first fifteen semesters between 1955 and 1963.

During this period two ATOs won national fraternity recognition, Dick Buxton in 1957 won the Thomas Arkle Clark Award, the highest honor accorded an ATO undergraduate, while Gary Vanderwerff repeated, receiving the same award in 1962, a remarkable record for a single chapter.[196] At the same time Lambda Chi Alpha was the perennial men's winner in All-College Sing, losing to ATO and SAE only once each, while all the groups shared honors in Miniature Orpheum.

Independent students tolerated the fraternities, and not all faculty people were enthusiastic, especially Clifford Meints, who spoke out most emphatically against fraternities in one of his periodic jeremiads published in the *Simpsonian*. Faulting them for excessive conformity, embarrassing behavior, forced participation in activities, interference with study—fraternities "pay lip service to academic achievement"—and "tacit encouragement to cheating," he charged that the I.F.C. merely "talks of high ideals, motives and good conduct, both socially and morally. I submit," he wrote, "that the fraternities act to thwart each and every one of the above goals by their attitude toward study and by their condoning cheating!"[197] This outburst understandably angered the Greeks, while President Kerstetter himself was moved to point out that Simpson had been singled out by the National Interfraternity Conference only that year as one of the nation's campuses where every fraternity ranked academically above the all-men's average. Upon investigation, it was indeed evident that fraternity membership either fostered good scholars, or perhaps the fraternities simply pledged the best scholars in the first place.

The sororities excelled scholastically, their grades consistently higher than those of the men. Either the Pi Phis or the Alpha Chis won the scholarship trophy most of the time. In size, to be sure, the four groups were not evenly matched; Theta Upsilon, though small in numbers, continued active and were delirious with joy when they captured the coveted Tomahawk award at Homecoming in the fall of 1959.

Just two years later the entire twelve-chapter Theta Upsilon national sorority merged with the much larger Delta Zeta, founded at Miami University in 1902. Members were initiated May 7, 1962.[198] Because the ceremony which brought a new sorority to the campus took place without consultation with the College at any point in the process of merger, Kerstetter and the board of trustees required the sorority to maintain a probationary status until a proper study could be completed. The formal installation was thus delayed until the fall of 1963.[199]

The sororities grudgingly accepted deferred rushing, effective in the 1958–59 academic year, but found their first experience with it "not a complete success."[200] Both women and men complained that, whatever the merits of "making an informed decision," the freshman was confronted with either what amounted to a semester-long rush week or, if rush was not permitted, a semester of isolation from sophomores and upperclassmen. The administration relented, but not because of the complaints of the Greeks. When plans for the new fraternity houses were being prepared, it was obvious that freshmen men would have to be permitted to live in them. Therefore because fall pledging became a kind of practical necessity, fall rush was restored for both men and women in the fall of 1961.[201]

*   *   *

Apart from the Greek-letter societies and a struggling Independent Student Association, there were organizations to suit every taste, most of which had survived the years of poor enrollments. The Epsilon Sigma Honor Society continued to elect the College's top scholars, but its campus visibility remained low because nearly all its membership typically graduated the day after their induction. Kerstetter urged the Epsilon Sigma faculty people to work toward a charter of Phi Beta Kappa, especially after he had brought a number of Phi Beta Kappa members into the faculty. It was soon clear, however, that favorable consideration by Phi Beta Kappa of a petition from Simpson was some years away. Other honor societies—Beta Beta Beta in biology, Alpha Psi Omega and Blackfriars in drama, Sigma Tau Delta in English and Pi Kappa Delta in forensics—continued active through the Kerstetter decade, their existence owing as much as anything to the enterprise of their faculty advisers. Looking to the possibility of attracting chapters of leadership societies, Mortar Board for women and Omicron Delta Kappa for men, students and faculty organized in the spring of 1960 two local groups, Gold Key for women and Delta Kappa for men, which selected between them twenty-two students who combined high scholarship with campus leadership.[202]

Meanwhile, education students could join the Future Teachers of America or one of its successor groups, the National Education Association or the Student Educational Association; business students had the Bizad Club, Ethel D. Anderson's proteges the Home Economics Club, the musicians Mu Phi Epsilon and Phi Mu Alpha Sinfonia, the athletes the Women's Recreational Association or the sometimes infamous S Club, and for a couple of years there was even a Sociology Club. A very active International Club was organized during the 1958–59 academic year. The College's chapter of Alpha Phi Omega, very large and active when young men like Art Campney, Mac MacFarland and John Sayre were running it, declined as interest flagged, and the group voted to disband in 1959.[203] Reactivated a year later under the leadership of sophomore Loren Gruber, the Alpha Phi Omega continued with limited success a few years longer, then failed again.[204]

Religious groups abounded, although their aggregate membership, with the exception of the healthy Y.W.C.A., was small. Several, such as the Student Fellowship, the Town and Country Church, the Warren County Group Ministry and Kappa Chi served primarily the preministerial students, whose number declined during the decade. As the student body became more religiously heterogeneous, a Methodist Student Movement group, organized in 1958, sought to unite the large number of students of that faith,[205] while Episcopalian students created an informal organization with the generous help of Robert and Edith Feyerharm. Then, in 1961, a Newman Club was founded for Catholic students. Indeed, Simpson had changed.

But then so had Indianola undergone a social transformation. After many years as a county seat-college town, it was taking on more and more the character of a commuters' suburb as an increasing proportion of its working population was employed in Des Moines. These newcomers brought diversity to the community at the same time the College was beginning to attract more students of varied backgrounds from greater distances.

What had once been believed unthinkable happened. The first Roman Catholic church service in the history of Indianola was held on Sunday, January 6, 1957, at the American Legion Hall.[206] No one was more surprised than the Catholics to discover how many of them there were in Indianola, and within months a parish was created,[207] followed a year later by the erection of a large church on the west end of town.[208]

Most Simpson people were happy with the new religious cosmopolitanism. For his part, Dr. Kerstetter had quite consciously contributed to it. Loyally Christian but never sectarian, he had sought out new faculty and staff for their competence, not for their contribution to religious conformity. He had hired Bob Feyerharm, an active, committed Episcopalian layman; Joe Walt, a Mormon, who had served a mission abroad; Cliff Meints, a dedicated Missouri Synod Lutheran; and Terry Hoy, an Irish South Dakota Catholic. And he defended them and Simpson from those who would demand a Methodist litmus test of the College staff.

Students reflected the new religious diversity, but most of them, Catholic or Protestant or free thinker, were united in their opposition to required chapel. A few students, Christian stalwarts like Don Gibson, Dennis Bergren and Bruce Hann defended chapel as a worthwhile part of a student's education, but as time went on the protests grew more shrill. Charlie Turner, who refused on principle to attend chapel, weighed in with a diatribe in the *Simpsonian* in the last days of 1962. Calling "forced worship" absurd and a "transgression of the students' rights," he cried out for justice. "I do not believe that anyone has the right to force me into believing their ideas," he expostulated, demanding to know who those "powerful people" were who "do not have enough consideration for student rights to try to force their bigoted views on everyone they can."[209] A week later Mike Herzfeld, a talented East Coast import, softened the tone of complaint a bit, asserting that "it is difficult to imagine anyone being indoctrinated in chapel," since most students didn't listen to what was being said anyway.[210] Kerstetter listened patiently, even sympathetically, to their complaints, whereupon he said simply, "Simpson is not required; chapel is."

The College continued to welcome the annual Methodist pastors' school during the week between semesters. Once the men's dormitory was constructed, it was possible to house all of the clergymen in campus housing. Fortunately, the ministers tended to have a good sense of humor. At least one of them did when he moved into one of the first-floor rooms at the men's dorm, where typically the two student occupants had left most of their possessions while home on vacation. When he entered the room, he found on the desk an open Bible, where he could read the words carefully underlined in red ink: "Thou shalt not steal." When the students returned to their room the next Monday, they found the same Bible, opened to a new page, the words underlined in red ink: "Lay not up for yourselves treasures upon earth, where moth and dust doth corrupt, and where thieves break through and steal."

Religious activities and organizations, like other groups and events, were accorded ample space in the *Simpsonian* and *Zenith*. History professor Gerard L. Buckhout, a sophisticated New Yorker not customarily given to offering praise for much of anything in Iowa, did respond warmly to a *Simpsonian* editorial by Wayne Osborn urging an honor system at Simpson. Although the paper, he said, was too often merely a "portable bulletin board," he was delighted to see "the inclusion of an editorial of some depth and acumen and a few columns of critical appraisal."[211] Admissions counselor A. Bruce Schroer likewise wrote a strong letter of commendation to sharp-witted Paul Brown, running the paper almost single-handedly in 1959–60, who was by all odds one of the two or three best *Simpsonian* editors in the College's history.[212] Sometimes, nevertheless, the editors of the paper felt unappreciated, as did Charles Fillman when he lamented that "all efforts to revive the status of this organ in the last three years have met with little enthusiasm on the part of the administration and the faculty."[213]

If the *Simpsonian* imagined itself unloved, the *Zenith* during the decade was indeed an object of criticism. Some editions were really quite good, but a few of the early ones were either frightfully amateurish (1955), or mere picture books with a few—often incorrect—captions (1956). Although the quality of workmanship improved in the early sixties, the *Zenith* had a long way to go. On the other hand, the annual editions of *The Sequel* were generally well gotten up, attractive and thoroughly worthwhile reading.[214]

Their publications recorded events, happy and sad, and some of the fads and fashions of the era. It was an age of sloppy joes and saddle oxfords and Bermuda shorts—and the wondrous debate about how long or how short coeds' shorts could be. It was watching editor David Gater fight a losing battle against jeans— "work clothes," he called them, inappropriate for campus wear—or dorm residents opposed to "dress up" night every Wednesday at Pfeiffer dining hall.[215] It was dozens of young men enthusiastically hailing the advent of black and white television in the men's dormitory. It was complaints about campus recreational facilities at a "suitcase college" where too many went home weekends.[216] It was demands for more places where students could smoke on campus, or where women *would* smoke.[217] Or griping about the new short-lived ban on freshman automobiles and motorcycles,[218] or a new phenomenon called the "parking problem."[219] It was storming the president's house late in the evening, demanding Friday of Homecoming week off—and winning Kerstetter's grudging, somewhat intimidated assent.[220] Or the notoriety accorded Loren Gruber as campus hunkering champ.[221] Or the ominous appearance of the tape man, a nocturnal marauder who scared the daylights out of the coeds.[222] Or the annual fuss about freshman beanies, beloved of the S Club.[223] It was student-body president Jim Vawn fulminating against the principle of *in loco parentis*. He didn't know much Latin, but he knew what he didn't like.[224] On a more somber note, it was fifty SAEs volunteering to serve as pallbearers when their brother Roger Hellman was killed in a motorcycle accident. Or the campus-wide mourning when Paul Lamb died or when two youngsters were killed accidentally, Gerald Noland out in Estes Park, Colorado, and Fred Pease on an icy highway on the way to Des Moines.

* * *

The sports story of Simpson during the 1950s and early 1960s was not a tale of glory, nor had it been since 1949, the year Hap Miller's football team won the conference championship. In neither football nor basketball could the College seem to field a winning team for several years. Kerstetter, who had loved sports in his college years, discussed the matter with the board of trustees in mid-1955, fearing "what a continuous lack of victories did to public relations and student morale." While it was surely Simpson's purpose "to develop the minds and spirits of our students," it would be nice to win some games. Bill Buxton, as loyal a Simpson sports fan as anyone, expressed a heretical notion: "I wonder," he said, "if the sky would fall in if we eliminated one of our major sports, namely football." Kerstetter replied that few colleges could succeed without a sports program. "Even when they abandon sports, they come back to them." A losing football team was preferable to none at all.[225]

Things did improve a little. After five losing seasons, the football team in 1955 went 5–2 in the Conference and 6–2 overall, and very nearly repeated this success in 1956 with a 5–2–1 record. Center Bob Klisares and halfback Chuck Burnett were named all-conference players those years. But in spite of placing three men on the all-conference team in 1957—Al Haughey, Bill Hulen and Marlin Bell—the team managed only a disappointing break-even 4–4 record.[226]

It was not the win-loss record of the football team but rather the coaching style of Hap Miller that led Dr. Kerstetter in early 1958 to ask him to step down from his post. There was more to it than that. Kerstetter was looking for a man with the best educational credentials to whom aging Frank Casey could pass the torch of leadership in Simpson's athletic and physical education program. While all the ingredients of Miller's "coaching style" were not made clear, it was known that his language with players went beyond the colorful. The president's letter informing Miller of his decision, although confidential, was released by Miller himself to the press, its contents published in both the *Simpsonian* and the Indianola paper. In his letter Kerstetter stated that because athletics at Simpson were being "fully revised and revitalized," the president had concluded that "a different conception of leadership and a different educational competence in football coaching is now needed."[227]

Never in recent history had a presidential action caused such controversy. Miller was well liked on campus and in the community, his shameless language and Marine Corps training style notwithstanding. A firestorm of opposition led to a huge, noisy protest meeting at Great Hall, students demanding an explanation from the president. To his credit, Kerstetter braved the hostile crowd and spelled out the reasons for the firing. No sooner had he completed his statement than Coach Miller himself appeared at the rear door of the hall, shouting to the president an expletive-laden "greeting," which had the effect of neutralizing the anger of the crowd. Still, a few weeks later students walked out on campus on a Saturday morning to find two effigies hanging in the trees south of the old library, one dummy representing the president and another—for inscrutable reasons—Dean of Men George Montagno. Apparently erected by Miller supporters, the effigies were accompanied by "numerous rhythmical derogatory signs" scattered around the campus.[228] The following Monday student body president Ken Ross called a special meeting of the Student Congress, where angry students passed 22–2 a stirring resolution condemning the effigy hanging and calling for discipline of the perpetrators.[229] Apparently the effigy-makers expected to be punished, but never were. Don Berry felt sorry for them. "Nothing," he wrote, "is so utterly disheartening as to be all cocked and primed to be a martyr and then have no chance to mart."[230] For his part, Miller wrote that "I will accept the decision of the College, as I have accepted their decision for the past eleven years, to my regret."[231]

True to his promise, Kerstetter found the kind of man he wanted for director of athletics, Physical Education Department head and football coach. He was E. G. Booth, a professor of physical education at Grinnell College, who served there also as backfield football coach and as head track coach. Booth was a Grinnell graduate in the class of 1949, where he was elected to Phi Beta Kappa. He held a Ph.D. in physical education from the University of Iowa. Booth, then, was far more than merely a replacement for Miller in football. In his administrative duties he was taking over for Frank Casey, who continued teaching in the department.[232] For his part, Casey missed Hap Miller, but he was delighted that a strong educator was assuming leadership in Simpson's athletic program.

Booth's handling of his duties as athletic director and department head was admirable, but even though his football players were disciplined and gentlemanly, they didn't win many games.[233] After a tie with Central and two other conference wins in the early fall of 1958, the team compiled a string of thirty-five straight conference losses, a modern record.[234] There was a lone nonconference victory in 1961, when Simpson bested Illinois College 32–15. There is no question but that student morale sagged, even though the College was succeeding in attracting more and better students to its academic programs.

When John Dahl decided to take an early retirement as head of the Department of Education in the spring of 1961, he was succeeded by Orville F. Moore, an experienced educationist from Nebraska.[235] Dr. Moore stayed only one year, however, whereupon Kerstetter took a daring step and assigned E. G. Booth to head the Department of Education. It proved to be one of the best appointments he ever made.[236] Booth, who remained in charge of the entire teacher education program until his retirement in 1988, proved to be a man of quiet competence, one of those few on the faculty who seemed to enjoy committee work and who excelled in it.

Meanwhile Kerstetter had hired Simpson alumnus Les Deaton '47 in 1955 to take over basketball duties from ailing Frank Casey.[237] With E. G. Booth's transfer into the Department of Education, Les Deaton took over as director of athletics and head of the Department of Physical Education. Now what Simpson needed was a football coach, preferably one who could win games.

Kenneth E. Heizer, the outgoing, enthusiastic and somewhat unconventional football coach at Otero Junior College at La Junta, Colorado, was recruited during the spring of 1962 to take over Simpson's coaching duties. Heizer's first year at Simpson was a disaster—nine losses and no wins—although he could enjoy the reported discomfort of the president of Central College about the press coverage of its 40–20 defeat of Simpson that fall: "We defeated Simpson soundly on Saturday and what is the headline in the Des Moines paper on Sunday? Simpson loses No. 32!" Fortunately, during the next three years he coached at the College Heizer's football teams improved markedly.

The Caseys, Frank and Mona, retired, much loved and much honored, in the spring of 1960. Frank's basketball teams and his track aggregations had compiled an enviable record in the Iowa Conference during his twenty-five years at Simpson. One of the organizers of the N.A.I.A., he had been elected to its hall of fame in 1958.[238]

Replacing Frank Casey was Larry Johnson, a 1956 graduate of the University of Omaha who had earned his M.A. in physical education at the University of Iowa in 1960. He coached baseball and wrestling, assisted in just about every sport and handled a regular schedule of classes in physical education. Taking over for Mona Casey was Barbara Stoner, who like Johnson, had received the M.A. from Iowa only that spring.[239]

Any number of young men contributed to Simpson's basketball teams during this decade, but two stood out. Bob Tidgren was top scorer as a senior in the Iowa Conference in 1961 and scored the third highest total number of points in conference history during his four years, with 1,690 points.[240] The other was Tom Hensley, who in 1962 broke Simpson's single-season scoring record and was selected first team all-conference in his freshman year.[241]

Some of Hap Miller's baseball teams were very good, especially the 1958 nine, his last one, that won the conference and went on to the N.A.I.A. playoffs, where it won the consolation title, beating Sul Ross 13–10.[242] The following year business administration professor Mike Sorden coached the team, filling in until Larry Johnson was employed.[243] That was the same year Simpson put up a press box atop the bleachers on the west side of the football field. After all, every self-respecting college should have a press box, although *Simpsonian* editor Paul Brown was not so sure. A press box to Brown meant big-time athletics, and he feared Simpson was treading "this primrose path to our destruction as a guardian of the lamp of knowledge," or to choose another metaphor, permitting "opening of a door to a devil which will devour us all."[244] It was a good thing Brown was no longer at Simpson when some years later they added a second story to the press box.

Of the other sports, track was clearly the most important and popular. Although during this decade the conference championship eluded the team, several star performers did very well. Perry Wilkins set a conference record in long jump—23′ 2½″—in 1954, and Don Cleveland set the record in high jump, 6′ 3½″ in 1959.[245]

The College continued to award athletic grants-in-aid, as did its conference competitors, but in the board of trustees there was a growing disposition to find a way to reduce or eliminate entirely a practice that many board members believed to be inconsistent with amateur athletics.[246]

The Iowa conference reorganized in 1954, reducing its member colleges to nine—St. Ambrose, Loras, Westmar and William Penn were dropped, although William Penn would be readmitted in 1960. Then, in 1963, Parsons College, whose swollen size and aggressive athletic policies in the early days of the "Parsons bubble," thrust it into a different level of competition, was dropped from the I.I.A.C.[247]

* * *

One of the undoubted benefits of Simpson's progress during the fifties was the enriched cultural opportunities for students and faculty alike. Especially noteworthy was the array of speakers who appeared on campus—men and women of national and international stature—bringing, as it were, the world to Simpson. Most of these luminaries came, as we have already observed, during the Christian Liberal Arts Festivals, but others enlivened the school year with their addresses or performances. Some, like Tennessee balladeer Grace Creswell, enchanted their audiences.[248] Others dealt with controversial international topics. Several, for example, discoursed on the volatile Middle East problem, like Zionist Walter Goldstein, an accredited correspondent to the United Nations, or marvelously articulate Dr. Fayez Sayegh, former acting director of the Arab Information Bureau, or Don Soliday, newscaster from Des Moines television station KRNT.[249] Students could hear historian Henry Steele Commager hold forth on American nationalism or author, journalist, and professor Max Lerner on "The Idea of America as a Civilization."[250]

Perhaps symbolic of the immense changes at Simpson were two speakers, one early in Kerstetter's years and the other at the end. In the fall of 1955 students heard seventy-one-year-old missionary E. Stanley Jones, called "the world's greatest living Christian . . . evangelist to the castes of India." His chapel appearance, however well intended, was not well received. Complained the *Simpsonian*, "Some feel Dr. Jones took advantage of [students'] required attendance at chapel. They were unprepared for the closing five minutes of evangelism. They felt the public demonstration was an unprecedented play on emotion." One student was truly sorry for the old man, whose conversion efforts that day were utterly without positive response, "He's thirty years behind the times."[251]

If E. Stanley Jones was behind the times, the Reverend Martin Luther King was ahead of his. Unfortunately, King's several-day appearance at Simpson, with three addresses scheduled for Religious Emphasis week beginning February 26, 1962, was cancelled. The famous civil rights leader, after a nonviolent boycott of busses and stores in the South that refused to employ African-Americans, had to appear on the witness stand in a trial at Albany, Georgia, on February 27. The original announcement of King's coming to Simpson had been greeted on campus with excitement and delight, and most of the churches in Indianola scheduled a Race Relations Sunday for the twenty-fifth.

Not everyone, however, was pleased at the prospect of Dr. King's visit. A pamphlet, "Unmasking Martin Luther King, The Deceiver," published by Billy James Hargis's Christian Crusade, was mailed locally and anonymously to Indianola households on the eve of King's anticipated arrival. Disappointed and exasperated, Joe Walt spoke for the Simpson community when he fired off an angry letter to the *Record-Herald*. Calling the Hargis attack on King "an almost classic example of the technique of 'guilt by association,'" he deplored the "tendentious arguments [and] false logic of Dr. Hargis' literary nonsense," arguing that "those who want to take issue with [Dr. King] should be willing to do so openly and publicly." Worst of all, he said, that the civil rights leader should be attacked in the name of Christianity was "monstrous." Walt concluded that "a Christianity that denies the brotherhood of all mankind—however thinly presented as anti-Communism—appears to me to be alien to everything that Christianity has stood for through the centuries."[252]

* * *

During the 1960–61 academic year Simpson celebrated its centennial with a series of events that did honor to the College's founders. The Christian Liberal Arts Festival in the fall of 1960 adopted the theme "Simpson's History and Higher Education Today," featuring Robert D. Clark, dean of the school of liberal arts at the University of Oregon and biographer of Matthew Simpson; Arthur S. Flemming, secretary of the United States Department of Health, Education and Welfare, whose analysis of the role of higher education—especially the place of independent liberal arts colleges—was outstanding; past president of the College John O. Gross, speaking for the Board of Education of the Methodist Church; long-time faculty member and recently appointed historian of the College Ruth Jackson; and Dr. Kerstetter.

The next spring the College hosted the seventy-third annual meeting of the Iowa Academy of Science. Nearly fifteen hundred participants heard nearly two hundred papers, several of which were delivered by Simpson faculty or alumni, including Harold Heckart and Jack Carter.[253] A week later the Department of Music produced a three-day Centennial Festival of Music, featuring opera commentator Boris Goldovsky of the New England Conservatory of Music, a concert by the eighty-voice Oskaloosa High School Choir under the direction of Simpson alumnus Charles A. Bretsch '38, an afternoon chamber musicale, a student-cast performance of Menotti's *The Medium*, a performance by the Madrigal Singers presenting "Music of the Renaissance," a request program of Sven Lekberg compositions and a violin recital by Samuel Minasian.[254]

During the centennial year faculty member Donald Koontz, a flying enthusiast, put together the first of several annual Aerospace Institutes, inviting a number of distinguished scientists, theologians and writers to examine the role of flight in the contemporary world.[255]

At the centennial commencement in early June 1961, Harold Dudley '17, a public relations consultant in Washington, D.C., loyal Simpson alumnus and member of the College's New Development Council, presented to Dr. Kerstetter a magnificent framed scroll, signed by a number of famous persons, congratulating Simpson College on the hundredth anniversary of its birth. The scroll bore the words of Matthew Simpson, uttered in Indianola in 1882: "The Christian School is our hope. You have founded an institution that in its influence will live forever. . . . You are building for eternity. Great is your work. The day hastens when all power shall be given into the hands of educated Christians; when the kingdoms of earth shall become the kingdoms of our Lord and His Christ."[256] Signers included President Dwight D. Eisenhower, Helen Keller, Marian Anderson, former Simpson presidents Gross and Voigt, the Governor of Iowa Norman Erbe and Presidents Hancher of the University of Iowa, Hilton of Iowa State and Harmon of Drake, Bishops Ensley and G. Bromley Oxnam, together with a host of other major figures in the life of Iowa and the nation.[257]

At this centennial commencement Simpson honored two of its oldest living alumni, Dr. John P. Morley '93 of Los Angeles and the Rev. Willis N. Graves '98 of Logan, Iowa. Both men had been clergymen whose careers embraced many secular activities as well. Rev. Graves was in fact still serving as head of an insurance firm, supervised all the work on his own farm and in his day had been president of three banks. Dr. Morley was well known to Simpson people, for he had come back to Indianola to attend more than sixty commencements— and to visit his cousins Don and Bertha Berry. He had attended the College for six years, two as an Academy pupil and four as an undergraduate. He was the principal founder of the SAE chapter at Simpson. "From my first memory of Simpson on an early morning in September, 1887," wrote Morley to Dr. Kerstetter, "Simpson was my first and is my lasting love." He had served the College as a member of the faculty in philosophy and religion, as a trustee, field agent and vice-president. He subsequently served as the development officer of the University of Southern California. The Special Centennial Citation "for a life of service to community and college" recognized both men whose lives had spanned nearly as many years as had the life of the College.[258]

By the time of the centennial, commencement had been trimmed down to a two-day affair, consisting of an Alumni Day on Saturday, a baccalaureate service on Sunday morning and the commencement ceremony on Sunday afternoon. A feature of each Alumni Day since 1957 had been the presentation of several Alumni Achievement Awards.[259]

* * *

As the time for the centennial drew near in early 1960, President Kerstetter asked Ruth Jackson, a faculty member for twenty-eight years, to write a history of Simpson suitable for publication that next year. It was in a way an impossible demand, for it would require months, probably years, to research and write an acceptable manuscript, but Jackson agreed to undertake the task.[260] She knew that Francis Moats had worked off and on to put together a College history but had given up because of the paucity of documentation for the early years. But she attacked the job with vigor, wrote dozens of letters to alumni, solicited information from people who still remembered the Simpson of yesteryear, collected and identified hundreds of historical photographs and other memorabilia. That summer the alumni were informed that "while it is too early to announce the publication date, pre-publication orders may be reserved now with the alumni office."[261] It is doubtful if many alumni placed orders, and a good thing they did not. Ruth Jackson discovered the same problems that had confronted Dr. Moats: the loss of virtually all of Simpson's archival records in the great fire of 1918. Though discouraged, she persevered doggedly for years to come, continuing her researches after her retirement in 1968. She died a year later.

If the College's history would have to wait for another generation, the institution did get a proper coat-of-arms at the time of its centennial. Like family coats-of-arms, institutional heraldic devices should be adopted *after* an institution's purposes and traditions have had an opportunity to be tested and confirmed. The notion of designing a coat-of-arms was conceived during an afternoon of rambling conversation in the spring of 1960 between Harold Watson and Joe Walt in Watson's old Hillman Hall office, the two men dwarfed by the ceiling-high bookcases that lined every wall. Watson was nostalgic, contemplating his retirement two months hence. He wanted to leave something tangible to Simpson. Walt wanted to know what it was that made Simpson unique. Together they hit upon the idea of designing a coat-of-arms for Simpson, something that could represent the College's ideals and traditions in graphic form. In the weeks that followed, they put some of their ideas in writing and pictorial form. Watson's knowledge of heraldry was invaluable, his suggestions always thoughtful and sometimes hilarious. They agreed that the design should include a council fire to represent the fire of knowledge and the Indian heritage in the name of Indianola, the leaves of the "whispering maples," an open Bible representing the College's Christian commitment and tradition, and the hands breaking the shackles of ignorance as George Washington Carver had broken the shackles of slavery. The crest with its bright sun of knowledge dissipating the clouds of ignorance, the elegant mantling and the scroll beneath the escutcheon completed the heraldic rendering. The motto "Et veritas te liberabit" from holy writ, was of course taken from the text etched into stone in the east entrance of Hillman Hall: "And the truth shall make you free." The final drawing of the coat-of-arms was completed by director of public relations Robert D. Goodloe.[262]

* * *

It was perhaps appropriate that the Oxford exchange program was initiated during Kerstetter's last full semester at Simpson, for it tied together two institutions, one he respected most with one he had come to love. It was a happy union, and the reason was the remarkable appearance of J. Steven Watson, Senior Censor and professor of history at Christ Church, the Oxford College with which the exchange had been arranged.

The forty-six-year-old Watson, tall, husky, with gray stubborn hair, limping because of a leg lost as a boy, was personable, approachable, engaging and a master of English history. Author of the volume on the reign of King George III in the *Oxford History of England* series and other works, he had come to the United States in the early weeks of 1962. He taught for a semester at the University of South Carolina, the summer at Harvard, and came to Simpson for the fall semester of 1962. He was not sure what to expect in Indianola. "Americans were most unkind to Iowa," he recalled, warning him that it was one huge, unrelieved cornfield. "I was immediately struck by the hills and trees . . . by the wonderful feeling of space as I drove up here on a rainy day," he remarked. At Simpson he taught a regular class in eighteenth and nineteenth century English history and conducted Oxford-style tutorials for Philip McBlain of Adel and student body president Philip McEldowney, both history majors who had to grow accustomed to reading six or seven source books a week in preparation for their weekly assigned essay and tutorial session.

With Watson was his wife Heba and, during late summer and Christmas holidays, his sons John Philip, eighteen, and Paul Francis, eleven. While Steven edified and entertained his learners with his erudition and wit, Heba charmed the entire community with her civilized manners and warm personality.

Watson came away from Simpson with positive impressions. "I was hale fellow well met in South Carolina after one week," he recalled: "You in Iowa are rather like Englishmen are supposed to be—reserved, self-contained and well-mannered—South Carolinians are explosive but light-hearted. They like to tell you they speak better English than Englishmen do—in spite of the obvious fact that one is quite unable to understand them. The Midwest accent is really one of the least difficult to understand. Iowans expect you to be unkind to them when they first meet you. If you show appreciation for Iowa they seem to unfold."[263] For her part, Heba expressed her surprise at the freedom of women in America. "Here men listen to what I have to say. At Oxford they look on it as the interruption of a child," she said ruefully. "I'm so spoiled here. I don't know what I shall do when I get back."[264]

In addition to his classes and tutorials, Steven Watson presented three public lectures to packed audiences in Great Hall. He chose his topics deliberately, suggesting an Englishman's view of America and its origins calculated to twit his hearers, discourses delivered with wit and humor: "George III, the Maligned Monarch" (a rehabilitation of the king scorned by American revolutionaries), "America, the Retarded Child" (emphasizing Americans' tardy and sometimes faulty adoption of English liberties), and "On the Virtues of an Aristocratic Society" (questioning American egalitarianism). Most everybody loved Watson's delightful verbal excursions into the Anglo-American past.

* * *

During the Kerstetter decade Simpson mourned the loss of board members, faculty past and present and prominent alumni. Board member and distinguished Warren County leader Raymond Sayre, a man "of good cheer and good judgment," died May 23, 1954. Past board chairman William T. Hamilton collapsed and died at a Simpson basketball game at Hopper Gymnasium in midwinter 1957. A year later Frank P. Henderson, who had retired from the board only in 1954, died at the age of eighty-two. For the first time in 111 years Warren County was without a resident descended from the legendary pioneer Paris P. Henderson. Earle Hale '07, active board member, passed away at Eau Claire, Wisconsin, in early 1961 at the age of seventy-seven. Hale, whose business interests had included a printing enterprise, had some years earlier generously printed the brochure containing the proceedings of the First Christian Liberal Arts Festival. And only months after he had made a handsome gift that made Simpson's new library possible, Rex A. Dunn died in California June 22, 1963.

Among the prominent alumni who were lost to the College were Clifton Beatty '03, September 22, 1954, at Sioux City; Everett "Tip" Olive '00, Simpson's greatest composer of college songs—the "Scalp Song," "Campus Song," and "Hoch der Simpson"—at seventy-four in 1955; the College's oldest alumna, Harriet Stidger Breniman '83, September 10, 1956, whose funeral service was conducted by John P. Morley '93; Loren Talbot '03, long associated with Don Berry at the local newspaper, February 20, 1957; Robert Guy McCutchan '04, former dean of the school of music at DePauw University, May 15, 1958, at the age of eighty; John Horsley '09, former alumni secretary at the College, at Perry, Iowa, on the eve of his fiftieth class reunion; J. Hugh Jackson '12, dean emeritus of the graduate School of Business Administration at Stanford University and brother of Simpson faculty member Ruth Jackson, at Palo Alto, California in January 1962; and Merrill J. Holmes '08, former president of Illinois Wesleyan University (1947-61), at Normal, Illinois, October 27, 1961, at the age of seventy-five.

Closer to home, College people learned of the death of two former presidents, John L. Hillman at Des Moines on July 13, 1957, at ninety-two, and Francis L. Strickland, while vacationing in the Thousand Islands in eastern Canada, August 26, 1959, at the age of eighty-eight. It was learned that Dr. Hillman had made a generous bequest to Simpson in his will.[265] Several former faculty, the ones Harold Watson had called the "old guard," died in a period of only three years—Francis Moats in 1960, J. Allen Baker in 1961, at the age of seventy-eight and Frank Casey in 1962 at his retirement home in Florida. Three former Music teachers, John J. Landsbury (1958), Lester Spring (1958) and Alice Barrows (1959), together with science teacher Bert Gose (1960) and Academy stalwart Grace Beam (1962), were remembered by faculty and students alike.

But by far more immediate were the deaths of three Simpson faculty people while they were still in service. We have already noted the loss of veteran Hiram Doty in 1963. Two years earlier students and faculty were stunned by the sudden and unexpected death of Stuart Peterson, April 18, 1961, at his home at the age of sixty-three. A man of dignity and genuine piety, he was serving as chairman of the Division of Social Sciences, professor of psychology and director of student personnel services at the time of his death. The following fall the campus was thrust into mourning by the passing of redoubtable Ethel D. Anderson, after a several-week illness. She died October 2, 1961, at the age of sixty-seven. At the funeral service at the First United Methodist Church in Indianola, Dr. Kerstetter presented one of the most memorable statements faculty and students had ever heard. Praising her "integrity, her high professional competence," he sought to "get close to the heart and soul of Ethel D." He recalled that

> she seemed always in the highest sense of the term to be "keeping house," keeping a house in order and beauty in the confidence that thereby her students . . . would generate more and more of beauty and of order in their own lives. . . . Throughout her life, and especially in these last days and weeks, with a perfection of which her closest friends were aware and which none of them, I presume, had ever witnessed in another person, she gave meticulous attention to keeping her own life's house in order with such spiritual and intellectual dignity and thoroughness as to prompt the word "beautiful."[266]

* * *

There were those in Indianola who sensed an estrangement between the town and the College. Some were resentful of the wrenching of the control of Simpson from the hands of local people. Some were put off by the formality of an "Eastern" president and wife who they believed disdained Midwestern small-town simplicity. Some feared that Simpson's Methodist purity was being compromised by a sort of cosmopolitan ecumenicity. Yet the ties that had bound College and town were still there, and most Indianolans rejoiced as Simpson grew and prospered. And the issues that demanded attention in the town were equally a matter of concern to the College. Both were growing and both were changing. Simpson doubled in size in a decade, and so did Indianola grow, its population in 1960 passing the 7,000 mark.[267] The town and the College became more accessible with the building of the interstate highways, the north-south Interstate 35 running along the western border of Warren County and Interstate 80, the "nation's main street," stretching east and west from Des Moines. With the highway boom of the Eisenhower years came a concomitant decline of the railroads, including the loss of all but one of the branch lines that served Indianola.[268]

As the town grew it struggled to keep up the services it required to take care of its burgeoning population. Streets were paved as new housing developments sprouted, a fine municipal outdoor swimming pool was built, elementary schools and a handsome high school were erected, a new post office put up. Parks were improved, notably North Park, which in 1957 was re-named "Moats Park" in honor of Francis Moats and his wife, Fannie.[269] The town set aside a large area on the northeast side of town near the Rock Island railroad for industrial development and began a vigorous search for enterprises to fill it. The old canard that the College opposed industry, because ostensibly it would bring "too much blue-collar riff-raff," was laid to rest. Simpson applauded Indianola's economic initiatives.

When the chain stores increased their hold on local commerce—a new Hy-Vee grocery store came in 1956 and Graham's and J. C. Penney's in 1959—local old-time merchants had to scramble for business. The new Hy-Vee store, in a frontal assault on Indianola's blue laws, announced in May 1958 that it would start selling groceries on Sundays, beginning June 1.[270] And that wasn't all. A year later Floyd Spray's Twin Pines grocery store out on Highway 92 started selling package take-out beer (Spray closed on Sunday to avoid problems with the state prohibition on Sunday sales of beer and alcohol), and there was a spirited county-wide discussion on whether to allow cigarette vending machines.[271]

There were obviously customers for these temptations to vice, and they were probably Democrats. Or Catholics. In any case, the town was shocked when, in the 1958 gubernatorial election, Democrat Herschel Loveless carried Warren County 3,507 to 3,137 for Republican candidate, economist Bill Murray from Iowa State University. Even worse, Democrats put four people into office in the Warren County courthouse. It was, said Don Berry, as stunned as anyone, "an election unlike any in recent memory."[272] A year later the news was darker still: Democrats gained control of the Warren County Board of Supervisors for the first time in the history of the county.[273]

Somehow the town and the county survived. But Indianola almost failed to survive the great dog fight of 1957 and 1958, and College people entered the fray with gusto. It was a classic battle between dog lovers and the garden people who were determined to see all dogs confined, preferably in small cages. The townspeople were entertained for weeks as the dog people, led by Helen Carpenter—Luther Hill's redoubtable mother-in-law—fought against the garden people, led by a local physician's wife. When the city council ruled, after a bruising fight, that Indianolans must keep their dogs at home, Don Berry, who didn't own a dog, fairly exploded:

> We get a world of pleasure out of the neighbors' dogs. They usually start their peregrinations across our back yard while we are at breakfast. There are all kinds of dogs, big dogs, little dogs, black dogs, yellow dogs, brown dogs, white dogs. In the social register they range all the way from a little black mongrel with no

collar to Carpenter's modishly barbered French Poodle. And that French Poodle, despite his aristocratic pedigree, his erect Lord Chesterfield carriage and his high knee action, is thoroughly democratic when it comes to trading smells, and romping on the green. The other dogs treat him with a familiar camaraderie that probably could not happen anywhere but in the free atmosphere of the United States of America.

And now that is all to come to an end. What will we do for entertainment at breakfast? What is this country coming to?[274]

Tying up dogs was just one way the modern world crowded in upon Indianola and Simpson. In 1956 one could see color television sets advertised for the first time.[275] Three years later in a victory for modern technology, dial telephones replaced the old telephone switchboard with its friendly operators.[276] Movies were getting expensive. By 1961 it cost sixty cents to go see Elvis Presley gyrate his way through *Wild in the Country* at the Empress. But there were compensations, for only a year or so later they were advertising pizza down at Cloud's Maid-Rite on the highway.

Costs for everything were up, but far from the astronomical heights to which they would ascend in the years to come. In 1959, for example, at J. C. Penney's one could buy ladies' nylons for 50¢ or men's wash and wear shirts for $1.98, or a pair of Levi's at Ce-Doc's for $3.98. Chuck steak was 69¢ a pound at the Super-Valu market and fryers 29¢ a pound at Hy-Vee. The good news was that Peoples' Trust and Savings Bank was paying three percent on savings accounts.

* * *

While Indianola and Simpson were undergoing profound change in the 1950s, there still remained an affection for the venerable Methodist connections of the College. At no time was this better demonstrated than the night the Methodist Church burned. When the alarm was sounded a few minutes before midnight, February 14, 1956, the fire was already out of control. When they heard the siren, students piled out of the dormitories and fraternity houses to join townspeople as firemen fought the blaze. Students helped firemen with their hoses. In twenty minutes, eighty students removed all the possessions of the Reverend Arthur Kindred family from the parsonage when the building was threatened by the hungry flames. The parsonage and the parish hall were saved, though the church was a total loss.[277] The next day Simpson coeds helped the Methodist women clean up the smoke-damaged parsonage while the boys helped move furniture back into the house. And later, as the congregation raised money for a new church building, Simpson people contributed generously to the cause.

Another strong bond was forged between the College and Indianola through the presentation of the annual Community Service Awards. First created in 1952—master teacher Arthur Eady was the first winner—these awards recognized citizens whose generous and effective public service deserved special commendation. When Don Berry was selected in 1956, he was not sure whether to mention it in his newspaper at all, for he saw a conflict between modesty and courtesy. "Modesty," he wrote, "would seem to indicate that one who has received some honor at the hands of his neighbors should keep still about it unless spoken to. But if the recipient of such an honor is accustomed to writing or speaking for public scrutiny, courtesy would seem to demand that he make some decent expression of appreciation." He thanked Indianola. "We would rather live where we are than any place else in the world."[278]

* * *

In a world polarized by two superpowers, students all over the nation were caught between fear of Communism and disgust at the excesses of some of the anti-Communists in the United States. Simpson was no exception. On the one hand Simpson people talked of building bomb shelters—after all, the S.A.C. Air Force base at Omaha was not far away—and on the other listening with horrid fascination to the witch-hunting hearings in Washington conducted by Senator Joseph R. McCarthy of Wisconsin. They expressed delight and satisfaction when the senator was censured and condemned by Senate resolution.[279]

"On the other side of the world," said a *Simpsonian* editorial in 1955, "behind the impregnable iron curtain, an enemy may be smiling at us now only to give itself time to build a larger stockpile of H-bombs."[280] Their fears were intensified when the Russians launched Sputnik I and II in 1957, even though Iowa Congressman Paul T. Cunningham discounted the Soviet achievement: "Why so much fuss about Sputnik? It's not a bomb. . . . "[281] That year America's technological answer to Sputnik was the Edsel, a new Ford car with "dramatic styling, dual headlights and wrap around turn indicators."[282]

Simpson people responded to the civil rights movement with virtual unanimity. When federal troops were dispatched to Little Rock in 1957 to enforce integration of the schools, Simpsonians were "surprised and horrified at the ignorance and brutality of those who are treating their fellow humans so shamefully." The time has come to change "our hypocrisy of the past and to bring an age of racial harmony and true equality of opportunity."[283] Student body president Jerry Willis chided the Methodist Church for its failure in racial integration. The all-black "Central Jurisdiction does give black Methodists influence in church councils," he said, "but it does *not* integrate the church."[284]

Simpson students responded much like most Americans to international developments. They collected money to help student refugees in the Hungarian revolution, trekked to Des Moines in droves to see Soviet leader Nikita Khrushchev when he came to town in 1959, cheered for Fidel Castro in his revolt against the dictator Batista and reacted unfavorably to President Kennedy's exercise in brinkmanship in the Cuban missile crisis. Yet politically they remained relatively conservative. A *Simpsonian* poll in 1956 gave Eisenhower 335 votes to 118 for Adlai Stevenson; a similar poll in 1960, eliciting only limited student interest, counted 217 for Richard Nixon and 88 for John F. Kennedy. Editor Ed Bomberger noted wryly that Simpson students had been on the losing side in six of the eight national elections since 1932.[285]

* * *

The Simpson community was shocked and surprised when it learned, on February 16, 1963, that Dr. Kerstetter had been elected President of DePauw University in Greencastle, Indiana, succeeding Russell J. Humbert, who had died unexpectedly the previous June. DePauw, a 126-year-old institution with a powerful Methodist tradition, enrolled 2,300 students at the time of Kerstetter's election.[286] Simpson people expressed their delight at the recognition of Kerstetter's reputation as an educator; they were at the same time disappointed that he was leaving Simpson. Some of them did note the fact that one of Dr. Kerstetter's predecessors at DePauw, back in the days when it was called Indiana Asbury University, was Matthew Simpson himself.

The board of trustees accepted the president's resignation "with deep regret." His decade on campus has seen "a performance which has reflected great credit on himself and has brought the College to a new peak of excellence."[287] He was invited to deliver the 1963 commencement address and receive an honorary degree. Kerstetter said of his decade at Simpson, "These years have been most meaningful for Mrs. Kerstetter and me, in personal associations and in our work. Simpson will always be close to our hearts. . . . We shall miss it."[288]

Whenever Dr. Kerstetter spoke of his work at Simpson, he never failed to mention the support and assistance of his wife Leona. To be sure, every presidency of the College was in many ways the team effort of a presidential couple. It is also true that the Kerstetter era saw an expansion, an intensification of the role of the president's wife in the life of the College, partly because the times were right and partly because of the striking personality of Leona Kerstetter. In a touching tribute to his wife—for theirs was not only a happy marriage but also a successful, creative merging of two strong wills—Kerstetter recalled that at Simpson Leona was "my chief counselor," the consummate hostess at countless entertainments for visitors great and humble, aesthetic adviser and counselor to faculty and students. "Through these Simpson years," he recalled, "just by her *presence* . . . she was a symbol or 'statement' which said that Simpson was a college of special quality."[289]

Theirs was a crucial decade in the history of Simpson College. That they "had builded better than they knew" would become ever more manifest as time went on. Simpson had indeed been transformed.

EDITORIAL

"The king is dead; long live the king." Modern educational institutions are not so different from old European monarchies in the case of a change in administrative leadership. We hardly pause to reflect on the old, but rather immediately begin our speculation about the new.

This is, perhaps, as it should be. President Kerstetter brought ten years of change to Simpson and, perhaps, it is not trite to use the word, progress. However, he is leaving, with the congratulations of the school, and it is understandable that the immediate question centers around a successor.

This is where both reflection and speculation meet. Boards of Trustees are not noted for asking student opinion in matters such as these; but neither are students (particularly editors) noted for any hesitance or need for invitation in volunteering their services.

The vital center program has been quite popular with students. It was one area in which students felt a very real pride in their school. Last year in Washington, we were quite surprised to find that what all the publicity releases had been telling us was true: the vital center curriculum was nationally recognized. People, who didn't know where Indianola, Iowa was, had heard of V. C.

We think that the worst that could happen is that such a program would fall by the way. The vital center is not course work, but a way of educative life. It is, after ten years, identified as the Simpson way of life.

Perhaps, a column at this time should be devoted to tribute to the outgoing president. Such a column could be filled with glowing comment and purple prose. But it seems more meaningful to say that President Kerstetter initiated at Simpson a way of life, and that it is our hope that this educative life process will not be interrupted.

☆ ☆ ☆ ☆ ☆

The death of almost any man leaves a void in the lives of others. The death of Hiram Doty, however, is beyond the usual. With Dr. Doty goes a tradition, a heritage, and a legend.

Thousands of students in the last forty years have sat under Hiram Doty. He could recall almost instantly the names of almost all of these students and probably all remember him.

We did not know Dr. Doty personally. We would see him walking across campus or down a hall and say hello, and that was the extent of our acquaintance.

Along with many others, though, we will never forget the man. Perhaps in some future year we will remember him most vividly as we saw him this summer: sitting in his car near the campus on a deserted Sunday afternoon. Holding a book, but not reading it, he simply looked over the campus, perhaps remembering or perhaps just watching.

Those close to him have countless stories and anecdotes about the man; those who barely knew him will not forget him. And this makes his passing not quite so sad.

A *Simpsonian* editorial lauded warmly the administration of President William E. Kerstetter when he resigned to take the presidency of DePauw University in 1963. At the same time it mourned the death of longtime faculty stalwart, Hiram Doty.

XVIII

Ralph John and the Democratization of Simpson 1963–68

Dr. Kerstetter's election to the presidency of DePauw University took the Simpson campus by surprise. More disquieting was the pressure put on the president to take up his duties at Greencastle at the earliest possible date, DePauw having been without a president since the previous June. Members of Simpson's board of trustees, aware that it would take months to select a new president, decided to appoint an interim administration. While most of them were inclined at first to rely on a committee of College staff people to take the reins of leadership, they discovered that well-known Simpson alumnus Hurford E. Stone had only recently retired as dean of students at the University of California at Berkeley. Perhaps he might be willing to accept the post of acting president of Simpson. Within a little more than fortnight after they hunted down their quarry at his home in California, they were able to announce that Stone and his wife Mary would come to Indianola April 1, 1963, to serve as interim head of the College.

Hurford Stone was a Monroe County native, his wife a native of Indianola. Born May 7, 1892, he grew up in Indianola and entered Simpson as a matter of course. A good student, he orated in the Everett Literary Society, sang in the glee club, preached in the gospel team and served as Y.M.C.A. president his senior year. But probably his happiest college memories centered around "Old Brick," where he felt at ease in the company of his Kappa Theta Psi brothers, two of whom in his class of 1916, Max Dunn and Clifford Barborka, were destined, as was he, to make names for themselves in higher education. Soon after his graduation from Simpson, he served for two years as an officer in the Navy during the First World War. He married his college sweetheart, Mary Alice Samson, back in Indianola, where he was associated with William Buxton, Jr., in the early days of the Peoples Trust and Savings Bank. From there, by way of a short time selling Buicks—his sales skills were formidable—he served as superintendent of the Hartford Consolidated School in Warren County.

School work attracted Stone, so he went on to Ames, where he earned a master's degree in vocational education at Iowa State while serving as inspector of consolidated schools for the Iowa Department of Public Instruction. Upon completion of the M.S. in 1928 he acted upon an old dream—he was "in love with the golden West," said the 1916 *Zenith*—and accepted a position of assistant dean of undergraduates at the University of California at Los Angeles when the school was still at its Vermont Avenue campus, moving with the institution to its spacious Westwood campus the following year. Some years later (1935) he completed his Ph.D. at the University of Southern California, where he was elected to Phi Beta Kappa. During his last years at U.C.L.A. (1939–40) he served as acting dean of undergraduates, at which time he came to the attention of the administration at Berkeley. He joined the University of California at Berkeley staff in 1940 as dean of students, but was granted a leave of absence the next year to enter naval service. From early 1942 until 1945, during virtually the entirety of World War II, he served as commanding officer of the Naval Training Schools at Treasure Island in San Francisco Bay. The next year (1945–46) he was a commander in the Pacific Naval Transport Service.[1] He returned to the Berkeley campus, where he was dean of students for the remainder of his academic career.[2]

People in Indianola welcomed the bluff, genial, utterly unpretentious veteran back home as one of their own.[3] He and Mary arrived in Indianola on the first of April. Three days later he met for the first time with Dr. Kerstetter and the executive committee of the board of trustees.

Stone surveyed the situation at Simpson, was impressed favorably by the fine new buildings and campus expansion, the curriculum and the faculty, and quickly acquainted himself with as many students as he could find.[4] He looked into everything from the College's finances to its trash collection practices. Three weeks later—only about a week after Kerstetter and his family had departed for Greencastle—he astonished his board executive committee by launching into action, and with the confidence of a banty rooster he ticked off a whole list of "must do" recommendations. There should be student speakers at some of the otherwise too-often boring required student convocations; the College's catalog should be simplified and shortened for clarity and cash savings; the whole chapel project, still dragging on after too many years, should be "re-evaluated" and the size of the proposed building reduced by half; his old friend Max Dunn should be brought in from U.C.L.A. as a consultant to recommend improvement in science facilities and instruction; a new mathematics position should be created for the fall of 1963; Simpson's new development man, Jess Mullin, would, he hoped, do his job well, because "I lack either the experience or aptitude" for fund-raising. He explained further that chapels and convocations had already been moved out of Great Hall, for the fire exits there were inadequate. The Reverend Glen Lamb, he said, had been very cooperative, and on April 15—the day Dr. Kerstetter departed—Stone gave the order to transfer convocations to the First Methodist Church in town. Perhaps later, he said, some "architecturally acceptable" fire escapes could be installed at Pfeiffer Hall.[5] As one of the board members recalled later, "Had [Stone] merely cast anchor and held the ship steady until the arrival of his successor," no one would have been surprised. "But we discovered that such a neutral position was uncharacteristic of him. He moved out, full speed ahead, with a display of vitality and energy that amazed and delighted everyone in the Simpson family.'"[6]

Stone was especially sensitive to student needs and student opinions, setting aside three hours a week for unscheduled "open house" for any undergraduates who wanted to discuss anything at all. Some, like the growing number of Catholic students, objecting to the unmistakable Methodist flavor of chapel held now in a Methodist sanctuary, asked to be excused, and such excuses were granted. He listened patiently to a litany of student complaints about dining hall policies, athletics, student government, codes of conduct, college parietal rules, space needs for activities and organizational racial discrimination.

It was the discrimination issue that got him into trouble with student body president James Vawn. Virtually on the eve of the installation of the new Delta Zeta sorority chapter, press reports circulated about alleged racial discrimination by a Delta Zeta colony at the Defiance College in Ohio. In a letter to Joe Walt, chairman of the faculty committee on organizational discrimination, Vawn, joined by a number of other students, demanded that the Simpson Delta Zeta installation be held up until an investigation of the Ohio incident could be completed. Stone, certain that Simpson people were in no position to examine objectively alleged discriminatory policies in a distant college, stated "unequivocally" that Walt's committee "regard itself as concerned with our College community alone." He went on to say that the College's position, backed by the board of trustees, was clear. It was intended "to ensure the democratic freedom of our student organizations [to select] their own members without dictate from any national organization which might have within its constitution or by-laws any restrictions with reference to race, color, religion or national origin."[7] The Delta Zeta chapter was duly installed on October 20.[8] And lest there be any doubt that Simpson people were concerned about racial justice, more than one thousand people jammed into Great Hall to listen spellbound to John Howard Griffin, author of the controversial book *Black Like Me*, relating his experiences in the South after having his skin darkened to resemble a black.[9]

Stone did not confine his attention to the campus. He found relations between the College and the town to be strained at best, the result of a decade of an administration that was deeply admired, highly respected and little loved, for many townspeople regarded the Kerstetters as outsiders, Eastern Brahmans with whom it was difficult to be comfortable. The judgment was probably unfair, but nonetheless was expressed. The Stones, on the contrary, were the quintessential insiders, solid Indianola folks who had gone forth into the world and had succeeded. Now they were coming home again, to a place they loved, to a community they understood, to friends they had known since childhood. Theirs was an exercise in nostalgia. Nostalgia tempered, to be sure, by forty-six years of experience and a dash of realism.

No sooner had he settled in than Stone marched downtown, calling on the merchants and professionals and courthouse politicians. Each Friday he gathered a few of them together for breakfast to talk about old times and present problems and about the College and Indianola and their interdependence. These intimate get-togethers led to the organization that summer of the Indianola Breakfast Club, with seventy-two charter members, "to foster closer acquaintance, friendship and working relationships" between the College and the town. To no one's surprise, Stone was elected the first president of the club. The Breakfast Club remains a healthy association as this history is being written.[10]

Stone travelled out across southern Iowa, visiting alumni, community leaders and clergymen in towns and villages from which Simpson drew many of its students. He found talking to them a lot easier than discussing the new chapel with the Smiths, the brother and sister alumni whose vision of the edifice they proposed to finance was considerably more grand than was his own. "Further negotiations with the Smiths will be required," he confided to board members, who were happy *they* didn't have to talk with the Smiths.

When the search for the new president extended into the autumn, Dr. and Mrs. Stone agreed to stay on an extra two months. "We promise it won't go beyond November first," the board assured them. It didn't. Everyone was genuinely sorry to bid goodbye to the Stones that gray November day. But they carried with them a framed citation that said something about the impact Dr. Stone had on Simpson during the few months he spent in his hometown: "As he leaves us now to take up his own pursuits once again, we want him to know that he carries with him our thanks, our respect, and our affection. In the years to come, when we speak together of loyalty and unselfish devotion to our college, we shall surely find on our lips, as in our hearts, the name and the spirit of Hurford Stone."[11]

* * *

It has become fashionable of late to deride the comfortable intimacy, the confident assuredness of the "old-boy" network that often comes into play whenever an important executive appointment is the prize. Defenders of what may appear to be an undemocratic procedure, far fewer in number than those who avail themselves of its attractive confidentiality, assert that a known quantity is manifestly better than uncertainty, that trusted confidants are the best sources of recommendations in personnel matters. Ralph Candler John came to the attention of Simpson through what he later called this "old-person" network. Chairman of the presidential search committee, appointed within days after Kerstetter announced his resignation, was Bishop Gerald Ensley. This time the bishop's role in the selection of the new president was anything but decorative.[12] Almost his first act was to write to leading Methodist churchmen and academic figures requesting nominations. It did not occur to him to proceed any other way.

Among those to whom Bishop Ensley wrote was his old friend and former Ohio Wesleyan roommate Hurst R. Anderson, president of The American University. Anderson had brought Bill Kerstetter to Hamline as Ensley had introduced Kerstetter to Simpson a decade earlier. Now Ensley was disposed to take seriously Anderson's nomination of his dean of the College of Arts and Sciences, Ralph Candler John. Ensley remembered John as a bright young student in his classes at the Boston University School of Theology. He wrote to John: Would he like to be considered for the Simpson presidency? John answered quickly and unequivocally, "No, thank you." A few days later Hurst Anderson told John he wanted to see him in the president's office, and in a long, fatherly talk, attempted to persuade him that it would be a good experience to go through the interview process "to see how it is done."

Still uncertain, John let the matter rest. He thoroughly enjoyed his deanship at American University, with its exciting relationships with faculty and enriching concern for academic programming. He tried to put Simpson out of his mind. "But more trouble," he recalled of those early summer days: "In a couple of weeks I got a call from Luther Hill, then secretary of the Simpson board, saying that he was coming to Washington on business. He said that he knew that I had indicated no interest in the Simpson position, but would I meet him for lunch at the Hay-Adams House, where he had a reservation? Common courtesy dictated as much, so the invitation was accepted."[13] Persuaded to become a candidate for the Simpson presidency, he and his wife Dorothy made a trip to Des Moines to talk with the search committee, and he came for a second round of interviews when the candidate list had been trimmed to two or three. In the end, he stood out among his peers and was an easy selection. Bishop Ensley's instincts had been right. The election of Ralph John was accounted by just about everybody as a most felicitous turn of events for Simpson.

* * *

Ralph John was a child of the parsonage. Born at Prince Frederick, a tiny town not far from the Chesapeake Bay in southern Maryland, February 18, 1919, he was the first of four children of a minister in the Methodist Episcopal Church, South, Byron Wilson John and Gladys Bennett, nee Thomas. Prince Frederick was Byron John's first appointment, the first of many.

Ralph John recalls an itinerant youth, not only because of his father's frequent reassignments. When he was but six years old his mother was stricken by an acute staphylococcus infection and died while she was with her husband at the annual conference in Baltimore, where he was being transferred once again, this time to Rockville, Maryland. A widower with three little boys and a girl, Byron John sent them off for a time to live alternately with two sets of farmer grandparents near Roanoke, Virginia. Two years later he married a second cousin, Donella Margaret McCulloch. Ralph John remembers her as the "archetypically wonderful stepmother," a fine musician and trained nurse. She took on the rearing of the four children and had a son of her own. Only twenty when she married, she was but thirteen years older than Ralph, managing a brood of five in a parsonage. Ralph reached the eighth grade in school while his father was minister at Shepherdstown, West Virginia, where the public schools were abysmally poor. Seeking a good high school education for his son, Byron, who had attended Fork Union Military Academy, sent Ralph off to Randolph-Macon Academy in Front Royal, Virginia, also a military school, like so many of the best prep schools in the South. Ralph liked military school. "I was reared in that briar patch," he recalled.

It was taken for granted that when John graduated from the academy he would go on to Randolph-Macon College, but during the Christmas holidays of his senior year he was persuaded to apply to Berea College in Kentucky. Founded in 1855 by abolitionist leaders with a Yale and Oberlin background, the school first offered college-level instruction in 1869. The principal aim of Berea was to provide education for recently emancipated blacks and other students of limited means, primarily from the southern Appalachian region. All students were required to spend at least ten hours a week in gainful employment. It was not difficult for the John family to demonstrate need. A West Virginia minister and wife, with five children to educate, were needy by definition.

At Berea John acquired a first-rate undergraduate education. There he also met Dorothy Corinne Prince from Spartanburg, South Carolina. After his graduation from Berea in 1941 and two years at Duke University Divinity School, they were married on August 17, 1943.[14] At the same time he decided to abandon Duke and transfer to Boston University's School of Theology, "the place that was known for turning out bishops and educators."[15] More importantly, he had become increasingly interested in philosophy and wanted to study with Edgar S. Brightman, *the* Methodist philosopher of his day, the same man who had so impressed William E. Kerstetter a few years earlier. Ralph John entered Boston University that fall, and it was Brightman who directed his master's thesis for the S.T.M. in 1944–45.[16] Having been ordained to the ministry in the Methodist Church in 1941, two years after the momentous merger of the northern, southern and Methodist Protestant branches of the church, John made a modest living as the student pastor of a small church at North Salem, New Hampshire, while doing his graduate work at Boston. "Dot"—no one ever called her Dorothy—contributed to the family exchequer by working in a defense plant at nearby Lawrence, Massachusetts.

Upon completion of his academic work, John accepted a position at Washington, D.C., as associate minister at the Foundry Methodist Church, a powerful old northern Methodist Episcopal church within a stone's throw of the White House, at Sixteenth and P Streets, where Frederick Brown Harris, one of Methodism's great preachers, presided. Dr. Harris was also chaplain of the United States Senate. In the Foundry congregation was Paul F. Douglass, president of The American University, who urged John to complete a Ph.D. in political and social philosophy, and during the next four years the associate minister divided his time between the Church and graduate study. His doctoral dissertation, examining the transition from monarchial to democratic systems in the Western world, from Platonic realism to Aristotelian nominalism, led him into fascinating theoretical concerns and analyses. As soon as his doctoral studies were completed, he accepted Paul Douglass's invitation to take the chairmanship of the Department of Philosophy and serve as university chaplain, a position he held until 1955, except for a military leave (1951–53) for service as an Army chaplain in Korea.

When he returned to The American University in 1953, Hurst Anderson had come from Hamline to take over as president and soon appointed Ralph John American University's first dean of students, a post he held for three years. In 1958 he was appointed dean of the College of Arts and Sciences. Meanwhile his marriage had been blessed with three sons, Douglass, Byron and Randy, and they had settled into "what was to be our lifetime home in Rockville," Maryland, a pleasant Washington suburb.[17] He was quite prepared to make a career of it at The American University. That is, until Luther Hill invited him to lunch.

* * *

"Those who have known him over a period of time are outright jubilant that he has come to Simpson," wrote editor Lewis Kimer in the *Record-Herald* in an editorial welcoming President John and his family to Indianola.[18] Dr. and Mrs. John had most recently visited the campus on the Friday of Simpson's 1963 Homecoming weekend. Elected unanimously by the full board of trustees that same morning, he was pleased to hear his acceptance of the presidency announced at a mid-day barbecue. The presidential couple were then introduced publicly for the first time at the football game the next day as he and Dot watched the Redmen fall to the Peacocks of Upper Iowa by a score of 19 to 0 in sweltering ninety-five degree heat before a huge crowd. Needing something to cheer about, the assemblage accorded the Johns a thunderous ovation. Even Sven Lekberg was there, obliged to attend because he had been elected "Big Chief" by the students, and joined in the cordial welcome.[19]

The Johns took up residence at the president's house at Girard and B Streets, on November 1, 1963, put the three boys in school and began to familiarize themselves with the College and the town. One of the first things Dr. John noticed was the convenience of the five-minute walk—through a lovely park— between their home and his office at Hillman Hall. After the hassles of commuting in Washington, the setting seemed idyllic.

During his first days at the College, as the crisp air presaged the onset of winter, the new president found much at Simpson to admire: "I was struck," he recalled later,

> by the genuineness of trustees, faculty and students. There was commitment and excitement over evidences of a new day for the College. I sensed real energy behind aspirations and dedication to goals. A much improved faculty offered a solid educational program with some impressive wrinkles: the Vital Center core in the general education offering and the Christian Liberal Arts Festival. There was the Oxford exchange program, with little parity in the swap but a great showpiece for a small college in the Heartland. The trustees were enthusiastic and promised support. The alumni were among the most loyal anywhere.[20]

At the same time, he could see obvious deficiencies. The faculty was too thin for the program Simpson was trying to offer, with too many one-person departments in which majors were offered. A beautiful new library was under construction, but the book collection was poor. "A major emphasis had to be put on accessions," he decided. The College's food service was the object of more than the usual student grumbling. For all that Dr. Kerstetter had been able to do, there was still a number of capital projects awaiting funding: a student center, a performing arts center—the old theater in College Hall was a disgrace— and the long-delayed chapel project. The old science building was locked up, unusable. It needed to be renovated or razed. Inflation nationwide meant increasing pressure on faculty salaries and student financial aid. The development function of the College needed an overhaul. And the president needed a new academic dean, for Les Bechter, who it will be recalled had accepted the position on an interim basis, was anxious to return to full-time teaching.

Most of all, it was evident that Simpson required a real breath of freedom. Governed for a decade by a sort of benevolent patriarchy, the College had grown and prospered mightily, but now there was need for "making the Simpson community, student and faculty, a more democratic one." That this was part of the thrust of the times did not make it any the less an imperative. The new drive for democratic governance at Simpson led some faculty members and townspeople to make odious comparisons to the immediate past, to heap compliments upon Ralph John and to disparage the cards-held-close-to-the-chest administration of Kerstetter. "That's not fair," countered Dr. John. "I can do what I do at Simpson because Bill Kerstetter did what he did."[21] He took a sick, almost moribund institution and breathed life back into it. Those days required decisive, bold, and sometimes perhaps authoritarian methods exercised by a determined, skilled leader who was absolutely confident of his own vision of how to make the College prosper.

If the renaissance of Simpson had been Bill Kerstetter's triumph, the democratization of the place, a revolution of collegiality, was Ralph John's ineffaceable achievement.

* * *

Sunday, April 5, 1964, dawned dismally, a lowering sky threatening a spring downpour. The Simpson grounds looked forlorn and almost empty as faculty people, carrying their academic regalia, and visitors, not sure where they were expected to be, skittered across the campus seeking shelter from the drenching rain. The day was indeed dreary, but the event scheduled for it was uncommonly bright and full of promise. Faculty, visitors and students had attended a worship service earlier that day at Indianola's First Methodist Church, and the formal inaugural ceremony was set to begin at 10:45 A.M. at Hopper Gymnasium, the only place on campus large enough to accommodate the anticipated crowd.

From Hillman Hall a great procession marched across the rainswept campus toward the gymnasium, faculty people and some 170 delegates of colleges and universities and representatives of learned and professional societies, all of them clad in their black gowns and colorful hoods. As the long procession, led by a color guard of student flag bearers—Tom Hensley, John Hedges and Phil McBlain—entered the crowded gymnasium to the strains of the "Apotheosis" from the Grand Symphony of Berlioz, played by the College band under the direction of Bruce Degen, everyone forgot the soggy weather outside. In the platform party were Dean of the Chapel Waller Wiser, who delivered the invocation, Ralph K. McGee, chairman of the board of trustees, who joined Bishop F. Gerald Ensley in inducting the new president, Honorary Grand Marshal Sven Lekberg, the Rev. Byron John, the new president's father, who delivered the benediction, and Stanley Kresge, who with his wife Dorothy, was an honored guest at the inaugural ceremony. Following these dignitaries were Dr. Arthur S. Flemming, who delivered one of the two principal addresses, and Dr. John, who delivered the other.

Dr. Flemming felt at home with the Simpson people. A distinguished educator and government servant, he was president of the University of Oregon, a position he had held since his retirement in 1961 as U.S. Secretary of Health, Education and Welfare in the Eisenhower cabinet. Earlier Flemming had served as the president of Ohio Wesleyan University, his alma mater, where he had been a classmate of Bishop Ensley. Flemming, whose career in government, spanning a twenty-five-year period, was matched by his long-time service as a churchman, had been a lay leader at the Foundry Methodist Church in Washington when Ralph John was associate minister there in the late 1940s and had also served for a time as vice-president of the National Council of the Churches of Christ in America. "I know of Dr. John's dedication to the dignity and worth of each individual human being," said Flemming in his address. "I know Simpson College will receive from him the leadership that will make it possible for Simpson to make its contribution in the years ahead to the cause of freedom."

In his inaugural presidential address, Ralph John called upon the Simpson community "to re-dedicate ourselves to the life of the mind." In spite of the lamentable streak of anti-intellectualism in American life, the nation could "not afford to ignore or oppose education and knowledge, even if it wants to," he said. "The growing complexity of the world in which we live demands precision of knowledge and exactness of understanding on ever-higher levels and in ways unanticipated in the early lifetime of most of us here today." He concluded with a plea for the elevation of intellectualism: "Mine is not a voice crying in the wilderness when I affirm my faith in the capacity of the mind, in some measure at least, to see and understand the world of which it is a part."[22]

The twin themes of freedom and intellectualism, set forth that rainy inaugural day, would become together the lodestar of Ralph John's years at Simpson.

* * *

President John started by strengthening the administration. He wanted first of all a strong academic dean to whom he could delegate with confidence the important matters of faculty relationships and curriculum. After a search lasting about three months, Charles N. "Ned" Peterson, Jr., a faculty member at Smith College, was brought in from a leave of absence for post-doctoral research as a "Michigan Fellow in College Administration" at the University of Michigan, whose program in higher education was perhaps the best in the nation. Peterson was a graduate of Lycoming College—magna cum laude in 1950—and held a master's degree from Bucknell University (1951) and a doctorate in higher education from Johns Hopkins University (1960). With his wife, Marjorie, who held a master's degree in library science from Drexel Institute of Technology, and a nine-year-old son, Eric, the new dean of the College took up his duties at Simpson in the fall of 1964.[23] Ralph John found Peterson to be "conservative educationally, religiously and politically, and a solid scholar. In many respects," recalled John, "he was a Brahman with class and integrity."[24]

When Frank Beu, dean of men and director of student personnel services, retired in the spring of 1964, John appointed Waller Wiser, then dean of the chapel and instructor in psychology, Simpson's first dean of students, scuttling the old coordinate pattern of deanships differentiated by student gender.[25] Helen Malone continued for one more year as dean of women, whereupon a new position was created: associate dean of students–dean of women. To this post came Evelyn Morris from the staff of St. Andrew's Presbyterian College in North Carolina. A 1955 graduate of Montreat College in North Carolina, Morris had received her M.A. degree in student personnel administration from Syracuse University in 1957. She had done additional graduate study in psychology at the University of Arkansas.[26] With a soft Southern accent and a measure of charm that could be disarming, she took up her duties with zest. Helen Malone returned to full time teaching in music, happy to leave to another the difficult issues that were increasingly confronting people responsible for student affairs.

Wally Wiser's move into the dean of students' office necessitated the appointment of a new chaplain. Here again the old-boy network was tapped to find a youngster. He was James E. Allen, who had completed his Ph.D. in social ethics at Boston University only that spring of 1964. A graduate of the University of Arizona (1957), Allen had earned the S.T.B. from the Boston University School of Theology in 1960. A member of Phi Beta Kappa, Allen brought with him both academic and ecclesiastical credentials. During his first year at Simpson he taught three sections of Introduction to the Bible for freshmen in addition to his chaplaincy.[27]

Although the College had employed counsel when conducting capital fundraising campaigns, there was really no proper development office. Once again Robert Feyerharm was directing both the financial and development programs, but in view of the increasing complexity of financial management in higher education consequent to both private and public programs, John decided that the responsibilities of the position needed to be divided. Still, it was only in 1966 that action was taken. To handle the development work, John and his close advisers on the board found James A. Robinson, a 1957 graduate of Iowa State University who was in community relations with the Equitable Life Insurance Company of Iowa. A quick study, Robinson adapted to college development work with ease. With Robinson in charge of this important part of the College's management, the president gained an important ally in his campaign to push Simpson forward.

When much-admired Mary Grassfield retired at the conclusion of the 1966 academic year after eight years as registrar, John offered the position to Dr. Louis E. Smith, Jr., principal of the Indianola High School since 1958. Smith held both his B.S. and M.S. degrees from Drake University and had only recently completed the Ed.D. degree at Colorado State College at Greeley (now the University of Northern Colorado). As ambitious as he was competent, Smith subsequently took on increasing administrative responsibilities, earning the title of associate dean of academic affairs.

* * *

Ralph John inherited as good a board of trustees as existed in any college in the Midwest, its excellence a legacy of his predecessors and the recruiting skill of board members themselves. In late 1963 there were thirty regularly elected trustees, plus six ex officio clerical members and the president, together with a growing list of honorary nonvoting life members. Of the thirty regular members, elected in staggered three-year terms, seven were from Indianola and Warren County, twelve from Des Moines, three other Iowans and eight from outside Iowa. Only two of the thirty were clergymen. Nearly all were alumni of Simpson. Only two were women, Amy Robertson of Promise City and Ruth Buxton Sayre of Ackworth, the latter a sister of William Buxton III and past president of the Associated Country Women of the World. Most of the men were bankers, attorneys, journalists, industrialists, a cross-section of middle American leadership. The six ex officio clerics, in accordance with the College's bylaws, included the resident bishop of the Iowa Annual Conference of the United Methodist Church, the four district superintendents in southwest Iowa (Des Moines, Boone, Creston and Council Bluffs) and the minister of the First United Methodist Church in Indianola.[28]

Although the board's membership was admittedly less cosmopolitan than that of some of Simpson's sister institutions, the quality of the people who served was superior, their devotion to Simpson unquestionable and their contributions in time, energy and money extraordinary. Of their number, eleven served on the executive committee, without whose advice and counsel the president was unlikely to take any important action. It was this group, strengthened immensely by Kerstetter and led by Luther Hill, Ken MacDonald and board chairmen Ralph McGee and Jim Wallace, that gave Simpson its edge. It is simply astounding how much time and talent, how much undergirding they provided for Simpson, most of their work unseen and unheralded. Ralph John considered himself a fortunate man indeed to have these remarkable people behind him. They met monthly and were always only a telephone call away. Many years later he was as enthusiastic as ever. "There are those today," said Dr. John in 1991, "who think the collegiate trustee has had his day and should be replaced. I disagree—categorically. In the independent colleges particularly, these are the people who keep the places afloat financially and who—at best with no semblance of internal interference—make other contributions through consultation and encouragement. Most revel in an academic affiliation and in the friendship of academic types."[29]

On campus the president met formally with his Administrative Council—Feyerharm, Peterson, Wiser, Robinson—every Monday morning, but they were as often brought together as a "kitchen cabinet" whenever an issue demanded discussion. John was as likely, indeed, to consult any faculty or staff member or student on a wide variety of questions. It required time and patience to convince Simpson people that the president really wanted to talk with them and that sometimes he might even take their advice.

* * *

While the focus at Simpson for a decade had been on the general education of students, both Hurford Stone and Ralph John saw the need to strengthen the individual academic departments offering majors. "We are seriously understaffed," observed Stone in the early fall of 1963. There was pressing need, he said, in biology (physiology) and French and a number of other fields.[30] Speaking two months later, he noted a "conspicuous need to add faculty depth" in a number of instructional areas.[31] And at the annual board meeting the following May, John lamented that "we are trying to do a major in Sociology with one person who is not a sociologist, Psychology with two administrators with heavy commitments outside the classroom and a major in Russian with two-thirds of one person's time."[32] The College, he argued, must either provide the staff to give some depth to its majors or drop them altogether. Because of low class enrollments, the Russian major was dropped, but other majors were strengthened.

During the next four years no fewer than twenty-three new positions were created and only one (in Russian) discontinued, increasing the size of the faculty from forty-nine in 1963 to seventy-two in 1968, very nearly a forty-seven percent growth. During that same time student enrollment grew thirty-six percent, but the 1968 faculty was large enough to handle more than a thousand students, if a generous faculty-student ratio of one-to-fifteen were to prevail. It was hoped, however, that an even larger student population would make possible a one-to-eighteen faculty-student ratio, allowing a faculty of seventy to serve approximately 1,250 students. The enrollment goal of 1,250 was set as early as the spring of 1964. It was, to be sure, an ambitious plan, perhaps, one should say, a gamble. But Ralph John was convinced that without a substantial growth of faculty the enrollment aim would never be met. He was fond of saying, "You build an excellent program first; then you attract the students to that program." And he had no illusions about how difficult it would be to recruit topflight faculty people, who were much in demand in the rapidly expanding world of higher education in the United States.

In a period of economic inflation and scarcity of qualified faculty, it was inevitable that salaries would increase at a rapid rate. In an attempt to keep Simpson's comparative compensation levels reasonably good, Bob Feyerharm made annual studies of salaries in sixty or seventy private liberal arts colleges in the Midwest, noting each year that Simpson fell about at the mid-point of the institutions surveyed.[33] While salaries rose, staff benefits increased much more rapidly. Group insurance—medical, life and disability—were provided the faculty and staff, with modest cost for dependents. Tuition exemption for qualified faculty and staff children was expanded. The College's contribution to the faculty retirement program was increased incrementally over several years from five percent to eight percent of the participant's gross earnings. Most importantly, the College shifted its retirement program from the Bankers Life Company of Des Moines to the Teachers Insurance Annuity Association, the largest such retirement system for college personnel in the nation, with gratifying results.[34]

In the mid-sixties it was not just a matter of recruiting a faculty, but keeping it. Turnover was a constant problem at Simpson, as it was everywhere. The demand for teachers so outran the supply that many Simpson professors, like their colleagues elsewhere, were receiving several attractive offers a year, some at salaries that precipitated a sort of national academic bidding war for good people.[35] Despite the mobility of teaching staff, Simpson was fortunate to have considerable stability, at least during the first five years of the John administration. Twenty-eight faculty people remained throughout the volatile 1963–68 period. Of these, three had come just in the fall of 1963, Donald R. Dittmer in mathematics, Fred L. Holder in religion, who taught in the Vital Center program, and Edna Bowersox in home economics.[36]

Dittmer was a 1961 graduate of Central Missouri State College, earned his M.A. there the next year and took additional graduate work at the University of Kansas. He earned a curious popularity among Simpson undergraduates, who marveled at some of his eccentric teaching techniques. Fred Holder took over the important non-Western Vital Center course for Richard Hostetler, who had resigned in the spring of 1963. Holder was a Baylor University graduate who had completed the S.T.M. at the University of Dallas and his Ph.D. from the University of Iowa. He came to Simpson from a teaching post at Carthage College in Illinois. Edna Bowersox was an experienced home economist. A graduate of Coe College, she held an M.A. from Illinois Wesleyan University. She had taught previously at the University of Iowa and Albion College.

During the next four years new faculty positions were created in biology, chemistry, mathematics, English (2), German, Spanish (2), French (2), religion, philosophy, American studies, political science, business administration, psychology (2), art (2), theater, music and physical education (2)—a total of twenty-three.

The new biology position went to A. Duane Addleman, who held the B.S. and M.S. in agriculture and was completing the Ph.D. in genetics at Oregon State University. But Addleman stayed only two years, whereupon the College brought back to the campus one of its most able young alumni, Beverly Stockton '63, who had completed the M.A. at the University of Oregon, where she was working on her doctorate.[37] In chemistry came Lee Maria Kleiss, a Grinnell graduate who had earned both her M.A. and Ph.D. at Columbia University and had taught at Wayne State University in Detroit and several years at institutions in

Nigeria, India and Paraguay. Arline J. Bohl was recruited for the new position in mathematics. She had earned her B.A. and M.A. at the University of Iowa and had taught several years in secondary school at New Hampton, Iowa. But she remained at Simpson only a year, replaced in 1965 by James Gehrmann, a graduate of the University of Wisconsin, who completed his M.A. that spring. He, too, resigned at the end of the year, and the position went to Philip O. Berge, whose B.A. was from Lake Forest College and M.A. from Kent State University. He was fairly near to completion of his doctorate at Iowa State University.

The two new English positions were filled by Marjorie J. Crabb and Grace Eckley. Crabb had already been teaching part-time for two years at Simpson when she accepted the English instructorship in 1965. An alumna of Simpson (1945), she subsequently earned a doctorate at Drake University. Eckley, who also joined the Simpson faculty in 1965, was a graduate of Mount Union College, Ohio, and held her M.A. from Western Reserve. The wife of a faculty member at Drake University, she remained three years at Simpson.

With the boom in foreign language teaching at Simpson during the sixties, an outstanding addition to the faculty was Katherine M. Love in German. With a B.A. and M.A. from the State College of Iowa, she had earned her doctorate at Heidelberg University in Germany. A specialist in German immigration in America, Love added real maturity to the faculty and remained at Simpson eight years, until her retirement in 1973. Four other new language positions were created, two in Spanish and two in French. In Spanish there was Bessie W. Stadt, whose B.A. and M.A. came from the University of Rochester and who was a candidate for the doctorate at the University of Arizona, having spent many years in teaching and the export business. She stayed only a year, her place taken in 1966 by VeAnna Christensen Morgan, a Grinnell graduate who had earned her M.A. at the University of Illinois only that spring. The other position in Spanish was given to Miguel Federico Cano, a talented young native of Mexico who had earned both the B.S. and M.A. at St. Louis University (1966). Fluent in French, Italian and Portuguese as well as his native Spanish, he was a strong addition to Foreign Language instruction at Simpson. Faculty and students alike would remember Federico not only for his superb teaching but also for his willingness, on any occasion, to entertain everyone with his guitar.

For one of the two French positions the College recruited Dennis M. Schwank, who joined the faculty in the fall of 1964. A graduate of Augustana College, Illinois, he held an M.A. from Washington State University. When two years later Schwank resigned to continue his education, he was replaced by Evadne P. Ruggeri (later Eve Goodhue), a 1965 graduate of Rosary College, Illinois, who had received her M.A. from the University of California at Berkeley and had studied abroad at the University of Fribourg in Switzerland. She taught at Simpson for five years (1966–71) and then married Simpson alumnus attorney Darrell Goodhue, whose residence was in Carlisle. In later years she did part-time teaching for the College when the need arose. For the second French position Dr. John brought to the College in 1966 Patricia T. Roberts, a native of Northern Ireland who had been in the United States eleven years. She had earned her B.A. at the University of California at Berkeley, the Diplome d'Etudes Francaises at the University of Paris and the M.A. at Columbia University. She came to Simpson from a teaching position at Emory University in Atlanta.

When John found his new chaplain for the College, he created a new position in religion for the new appointee, James Allen. In religion and philosophy, seeking a strong person in non-Western Studies, the College was fortunate in enlisting in 1966 the talents of Paul O. Ingram, a Californian with excellent credentials, whose specialty was Japan and Buddhism. Ingram, a graduate of Chapman College in California, held a M.Th. degree from the Claremont Graduate School, where he was completing the Ph.D. He was brought to Simpson from the University of California at Santa Barbara. He remained at Simpson nine years, becoming one of the most respected members of the faculty.

As a direct consequence of the remarkable success of the College's Summer American Studies Program, the faculty urged the incorporation of that field into the Simpson curriculum. Accordingly, a new position in American studies was created in 1967, and invited to teach in it was John L. Oldani, who was completing his doctoral studies at St. Louis University. Oldani was appointed assistant professor of American civilization, the first step toward an American studies program and, perhaps a major. To assist Terry Hoy, the lone political scientist on the campus, Dean Ned Peterson in 1966 found N. Doran Hunter, an energetic young Mormon from California—he had been student body president at Brigham Young University—who was working on his doctorate at the University of Washington. While Hoy was a political theorist, Hunter brought to the department an interest in practical politics—he had worked in a successful campaign for a U.S. senator—and political behavior. Two new positions in psychology—one in 1964 and the other created two years later—saw the addition to the faculty of Bradley Bremer, who had earned his M.A. at Michigan State, and William E. Greable, who was completing his Ph.D. at Utah State University. Greable was a 1959 graduate of Whitman College, Washington, and earned his M.A. from Fresno State College in 1963. When Bremer left after only two years, Associate Dean of Students Evelyn Morris filled in for a year (1966–67), whereupon the College employed W. Clark Eldridge, who held both a B.A. and a B.S. from Maryville College, Tennessee, an M.A. from Ohio University and the Ph.D. from the University of Delaware. A specialist in social and experimental psychology, he came to Simpson from a post at Idaho State University. Eldridge remained many years on the faculty.

In each of the fine arts fields the faculty was enlarged. The first full-time person in art in many years was Jack Ragland, a talented painter who picked up where Bent Lane had left off four years before. There was much to do, equipment to buy, teaching facilities to find and courses to plan. Ragland was another Westerner, with both a B.A. and M.A. from Arizona State University. He was working on his Ph.D. at U.C.L.A. During the twelve years of his tenure at Simpson he developed an admirable art curriculum, commandeered a building—the old Carnegie Library—and secured additional staff, at first on a part-time basis, later with one full-time colleague plus part-time specialists. The full-time colleague, Gail Gallatin Hoag, was brought into the Art Department in the fall of 1967. A graduate of Smith College and an honor student at the University of Iowa, she complemented the work done by Jack Ragland. Soon art at Simpson became a thoroughly respectable field of study, much the same as theater, under the direction of Richard deLaubenfels. A second theater position was created in 1965, and appointed to take it was Eugene A. Peyroux, Jr., who had both the B.A. and M.A. from Stanford and the doctorate from Carnegie-Mellon University, one of the premier schools of drama in the land. A man of remarkable talent, he produced plays that were truly memorable—his Moliere was superb. Regrettably, he stayed only a year. Two more men came along during the next two years in the theater position: John E. Torrents (1966–67), a doctoral candidate at Indiana University, and David Press (1967–69), like Peyroux a product of Carnegie-Mellon. The rapid turnover in this new position made life hectic for deLaubenfels, confusing for student thespians and unprofitable for the College. The new post in music went to Gregg E. Magnuson in the fall of 1967. He was a band man par excellence, with B.A. and M.A. in music from the University of Michigan. During his three years at Simpson the College band sounded better than it had in years.

The final two positions created during Dr. John's first half-decade were in physical education. In 1966 a part-time position held by Melvie Maigaard was expended to full-time, and Maigaard received a regular faculty appointment. A graduate of Augustana College, she had earned her M.S. at Arizona State University. When she resigned in 1967, Carol Berger was appointed to take her place. Berger held the B.A. and B.S. from Central Missouri State College. Finally there was Richard B. Starr, added to the physical education staff in 1967 as basketball coach and assistant football coach. He had taught ten years in secondary school, most recently in Indianola. A 1957 graduate of Drake University, he had earned his M.S.E. degree there in 1962. Starr, a good coach and an outstanding classroom teacher, was still teaching at Simpson in the 1990s.

Apart from the twenty-six new positions created during Ralph John's first five years at Simpson, there were other significant, sometimes bewildering changes in personnel in several departments of the College. Some of the new people, recruited in an ever more competitive national market, were highly qualified, some less so. The president's job, together with his academic dean, was to persuade the best of these people to stay on at Simpson and to find the means to pay them a good salary. That he was not able to do so is evident in the rapid turnover that marked those years. Of the twenty-one faculty members he appointed in the already-existing positions between 1963 and 1968, only ten remained five years or longer; seven stayed only one or two years.

Among those whose tenure at Simpson was substantial was Loren Gruber, a 1963 Simpson graduate who held the M.A. from Western Reserve (1964) and who was planning on working for the doctorate at Denver University. Gruber, whose serious, scholarly demeanor—he was happiest when reading Old Icelandic sagas in the original tongue—disguised his tender age, joined the English department in 1966 and stayed until 1982, with the exception of the year he took leave to complete the doctorate. Gruber's English position had been held by James Schreiber (1962–64) and James Anderson (1964–66).[38] Then, when Joe Brewer went west in 1967 to become a dean at Stanislaus State College in California, a young, serious scholar, Mitchell A. Kalpakgian, was appointed to an assistant professorship in English. A native of Milford, Massachusetts, he was a recent graduate of Bowdoin College in Maine (1963) and had completed his M.A. in English literature at the University of Kansas, where he was at work on his doctorate. Deliberate, soft-spoken, a medievalist deeply committed to a conservative interpretation of Christianity, he was said to be quite convinced that no one since St. Thomas Aquinas had much to say. He did not seem to be really at home in the twentieth century. At the same time, however, he was a dedicated runner

524   History of Simpson College

who could be seen every morning jogging along the streets of Indianola—he competed for years, and well too, in the Boston Marathon—even on the coldest days of a subzero prairie winter. A Kalpakgian English class was soon known to be well-taught and informative, a place where there was little toleration for laggards, procrastinators or dilettantes.[39]

No department needed bolstering more than sociology, perhaps the College's weakest academic area at the time. Therefore Ralph John recruited an able Simpson graduate, Everett L. Laning '53, who had earned a B.D. at Garrett Theological Seminary, an M.A. at Northwestern University and was in the last throes of writing his doctoral dissertation at Iowa State University. Laning brought strength to the department and remained at Simpson into the 1990s. In education, when Louella Specht retired in 1964, the president appointed Minerva K. Fair to that position given over to the training of students in elementary education. A delightful, mature woman with a splendid record, she had earned the B.S. in home economics in 1938 at Iowa State College and the M.Ed. degree at the University of Maryland in 1959. In her early professional life she taught for two years at the American College for Girls in Istanbul, Turkey. Later she taught four years at Ohio University in the School of Home Economics, worked for a time as a home economist for commercial concerns, and was teaching in a public school when Simpson found her. Her seventeen years at the College—she retired in 1981—were fruitful for the institution and for her as well.

The loss of Jack Padgett in 1965 was especially difficult, for he had been supervisor and mainstay of the Vital Center program. Yet Ralph John, recalling their conversation about his departure, believed that Padgett, "in his profession of Philosophy, could not validate himself in a Vital Center program. If he was to get on in his academic life, he had to leave."[40] To replace Padgett he found Paul S. Bosley, son of the almost legendary minister of the First Methodist Church in Evanston, Illinois. Young Bosley had earned his B.S. degree from Northwestern University in history and geology, held a B.D. from Union Theological Seminary and an M.A. from the University of Chicago, where he was completing his doctoral studies. Bosley stayed five years at Simpson, five years of considerable curricular transformation, as we shall see.

There were no fewer than eight appointments in the Department of Music during the five years between 1963 and 1968. Only one turned out to be for a long term, that of pianist Ray Songayllo. Others included one medium-term appointment in voice and a spate of one- or two-year people whose tenure was too short to exert much influence on the music program at the College. The pianist, Ray Songayllo, was a 1951 graduate of Northwestern University, where he also received the M.M. degree (1952). He was working on the doctorate at Boston University, but did not complete it. He remained on the faculty until his resignation in 1987. Janice Hanson, an experienced teacher of vocal music, was employed in the fall of 1967 and served five years in the department. A 1950 graduate of the University of Minnesota, she gained at Simpson a remarkably good reputation in her work, and the College was sorry to lose her to the University of Iowa in 1972.

Other music appointments were relatively brief. Paul D. Hartley, whose education was at the Eastman School of Music, served three years (1964–67). In voice the turnover was brisk, and disturbing. David Nott, who had been appointed in 1962, left in 1964. Wayne Nelson (B.M. Manhattan School of Music), who took Nott's place, lasted only two years. Nelson's successors managed to stay for only one year each, Stanley J. Norseworthy (M.Mus. at Baylor University, 1966) and Donald N. Gray, a 1965 Simpson graduate who held the M.M. from Northwestern. During the decade 1966–1976 no fewer than seven men held the same voice position, none longer than two years. Such a turnover could hardly make for a sustainable program in voice.[41] On a happier note, when Robert Larsen took a full year off to work on his doctorate at Indiana University, recent Simpson graduate William J. Tuttle was invited to fill in for one year, which he was happy to do. His good work was not forgotten, and several years later he was invited to join the faculty once again.

In physical education two important changes were made. In 1965, when Barbara Stoner resigned, the College employed Barbara A. Zupancic of Pueblo, Colorado, who only that year graduated from Colorado State University. She helped Melvie Maigaard in physical education, and toward the end of her decade of service to Simpson served as chair of the Physical Education Department. Then, when football coach Ken Heizer resigned in mid-1966 to join the staff at Iowa State University as defensive coach, the College recruited the highly successful coach at Iowa Falls High School, John L. Sullivan. A graduate of the State College of Iowa (now University of Northern Iowa), Sullivan was completing the requirements for the M.A. He coached football and track, and as we shall see, brought about a dramatic change in the College's football fortunes.

There are just five more faculty appointments in this five-year span that are to be recorded. Two of them came in 1966. Ed Cell, for seven years a dutiful acolyte in the Vital Center program, resigned. Appointed to take his place was Thomas Charles Slate, who had earned his B.A. at George Washington University, the S.T.B. at Boston University School of Theology, and his M.A. at the University of Southern California, where he was completing the Ph.D. He remained at Simpson only two years. Also in 1966 came Clarence Stennes in economics, replacing Charles Conklin. Stennes was a 1963 graduate of Concordia College in Minnesota and had earned the M.A. in 1966 from the University of Iowa. He taught at Simpson four years.

Three more faculty people were recruited in 1967. One of these was Paul A. Gwinner in chemistry. A 1959 graduate of Drexel Institute of Technology, Philadelphia, he held a doctorate from Pennsylvania State University awarded in 1965. He spent only two years at Simpson. In home economics, President John selected Mary Bitsianes to replace Dolores Gade. Bitsianes, who served as chairman of the department, held degrees from the University of Minnesota and Cornell University. Finally, the College was able to find R. Thomas Douglass to take over the management of the foreign language program, the department having been leaderless since the resignation in 1966 of Jay Gossner, who accepted a position at Rhode Island College in Providence. Douglass was well qualified, holding a B.A. from George Washington University and the Ph.D. from the University of Pennsylvania. Regrettably, he stayed at Simpson only three years before being lured away to teach at the University of Iowa. During his brief tenure, however, he presided over a revolutionary—and, as it turned out, not very successful—change in the way Simpson taught foreign languages.

* * *

While the faculty are central in carrying out the educational mission of the institution, the curriculum is the framework in which they function. In 1963 Simpson had a liberal arts curriculum that was the envy of many colleges. But no curriculum, however praiseworthy, is engraved on stone tablets. It must respond to the needs of the times, and more importantly, to the needs of the particular generation of students being educated.

Simpson's curriculum, anchored in the Vital Center program and bolstered by the vigorous improvement of depth in many departments of instruction, did not need in 1963 the fundamental reorientation it had required in 1953. Nevertheless, in a chapel address at the opening fall convocation in September 1964, President John stated that the administration "hopes to re-evaluate the curriculum."[42] Some adjustments, he suggested, were clearly needed, and a careful study of the academic program should be made by the faculty. But as is so often the case with proposals for reform of almost anything, John's project languished for months. Everyone's attention was distracted by the feverish planning and fundraising preliminaries for several big construction projects. Bricks and mortar, certainly much needed, sapped the corporate energy of much of the College. For a time it was being rumored that the board of trustees suffered from sort of a collective edifice complex.

All those buildings notwithstanding, John revived his curricular reform proposal in the spring of 1966 and asked the faculty Educational Policy and curriculum committee to study the matter, and not to delay. No restrictive guidelines were laid down; no academic sacred cows were declared inviolable; no new ideas were rejected out of hand. During the last months of the school year an agenda was prepared, based on a number of free-for-all discussions about curricular needs. During the 1966–67 school year the committee went to work with extraordinary vigor to hammer out a new, richer academic program. When the new curriculum was finally presented to the full faculty in the fall of 1967, it required a series of marathon sessions to amend, revise and adopt it. It went into effect at the beginning of the 1968–69 year.

One of the more revolutionary changes was the adoption of a new calendar. For more than half a century Simpson had followed the traditional division of the nine-month academic year into two semesters. Apart from the introduction of the quarter system on some campuses, few colleges had yet felt free to tinker with the almost sacrosanct semester calendar. What seemed clear to many academicians was that a weakness of the conventional semester system was the long Christmas holiday followed by a "lame duck" fortnight of classes followed in turn by a week of final examinations in January. Typically, Simpson's fall semester students put off writing term papers and other academic chores until the Christmas holidays. With admirable resolution they carried armloads of books home, laid them on a shelf, thought seriously about studying, did precious little of it, and returned to Simpson in January with little to show for their time at home but a guilty conscience. Thereupon they ran to classes while trying to make up what they had failed to do during the holidays. And suddenly they found themselves in final examinations.

The faculty committee, led by Chairman Joe Walt during the 1966–67 year, considered ways to revise the academic calendar, permitting one term to end at Christmastime and the next to commence immediately following the new year. The quarter system suggested itself as a possibility, but this required postponing the opening of fall classes to early October in order to achieve an even tripartite division of the academic year. They studied a new plan, already adopted by a number of colleges. They could schedule a four-month term beginning in early September and ending with the Christmas holidays, a one-month interim term during January, and then a four-month session ending in late May. The semester-hour value of most courses would increase from three to four credit hours, permitting each four-hour course to meet in four or five sessions per week. The typical student would enroll for four courses in each of the two shortened semesters. During the January interim the student would study one course intensively without the conflicting demands of other academic work. Courses could be offered on or off campus; they could take the form of class work or independent study. Their work could involve internships, career observation and other innovative academic experiences.

As adopted by the faculty in late 1967, the plan for the January interim called for offering a wide range of options for sophomores and upperclassmen. Students could select from among a large number of departmental or interdisciplinary courses. They could engage in independent study or attend another cooperating college. A number of schools had already adopted the 4-1-4 calendar. The short term also afforded unique opportunities for off-campus study, ranging from classroom observation of inner city schools in Chicago or St. Louis to oceanography in La Jolla or Jamaica. Freshmen would remain on campus, enrolling in one of four interdisciplinary courses designed for them. While academic departments were permitted to require their majors to complete one January interim in the department during the sophomore, junior or senior year, the program was designed to encourage students to move outside their field of specialization and experiment in less familiar areas. To this end, all grades for the January interim courses were awarded on a pass or fail basis.

In the new general studies curriculum the Vital Center program was retained and enlarged. Dr. John praised it as a liberal arts core program "which has proven itself through more than a decade, has been recognized nationally as a model of excellence in relation to the purposes held for it." Previously independent courses that were seen to be appropriate to the aims of the Vital Center were absorbed. The Western civilization course was enlarged to an eight credit-hour study of the heritage of Western man, a correlated core program for freshmen combining three hours of history, three of literature and two hours in art, music or drama. Thus students could correlate a study of Greek history with Greek literature and say, Greek art, or Renaissance history, literature and music. In the sophomore year students would complete two four-hour courses in the Vital Center, one called "the Enduring Questions" and the other providing an option to study East or South Asia. In addition, the general studies segment of their curriculum included one course in social science, a two-semester sequence in one of the natural sciences, and one physical education activity class in each of the semesters of the freshman and sophomore years. Instead of an unvarying requirement of English composition, students would be required to demonstrate writing proficiency throughout the curriculum. Students whose writing was judged deficient would be assigned to a writing laboratory for remedial work and would not graduate until acceptable performance was achieved. More radical was the foreign language requirement. Students were required to demonstrate proficiency in one language by passing an examination at the intermediate level, irrespective of the amount of time it required to reach the proficiency level. Finally, students would complete a major ranging from twenty-four to forty hours, as determined by the department. Ralph John called the new curriculum "an exciting academic design."[43]

Meanwhile the faculty adopted stiffer rules governing the repetition of courses, was pleased to note that Air Force R.O.T.C. at Drake University was open to Simpson students, debated whether to drop home economics from the College's offerings, continued sending students into the Washington Semester program and accepted the United Nations Semester program sponsored by Drew University.[44] It approved a faculty exchange program with a number of other colleges and sanctioned Simpson's first summer travel seminar for academic credit, a program conducted by Gail Gallatin Hoag in Europe for twelve art students.[45] It approved a summer remedial program for students who had not met all of Simpson's entrance requirements.[46]

One of the most sensitive faculty issues during these years had to do with the advent of student course evaluations. Most students agreed that some form of course and teaching evaluation was desirable. Predictably, faculty reaction to the idea ranged from supportive to apoplectic. Herb Alberding thought it was "a marvelous idea." Bill Helfrich was convinced that students were "competent to judge" what they were getting from their courses, and their evaluations, he said, "should be distributed to students, for they have a hell of a stake in it!" Hoy agreed, noting that "the problems of courses might as well be aired . . . no matter what all the faculty thinks." Tom Slate was in favor of it. So was Joe Walt, who warned, however, that the evaluations "should omit questions of a personal nature" about the professor. Paul Bosley thought such student response would "encourage our strengths and correct our weaknesses." Cliff Meints wasn't so sure, arguing that there was no need for evaluations "except in the obtaining of a popularity poll." An English professor, who chose to remain anonymous, was livid. "There is no such thing as an objective student," he said confidently, "and for them to have an evaluation of the courses offered here at Simpson would be pure and unadulterated revenge—a blood vendetta of the worst variety."[47] Whatever the faculty response, course evaluations were an idea whose time had come. It remained only for students, with faculty assistance, to devise a proper "instrument" that would ensure a combination of reasonable objectivity with freedom of anecdotal expression. Adopted by the faculty that same year (1966–67), the principle of course evaluations persisted even though the format of the evaluation questionnaires varied, and the results came to be used increasingly by the Faculty Personnel Committee and administrators as a factor in decisions about reappointment, promotion and tenure.[48]

* * *

Two of the programs of which President Kerstetter was justifiably proud did not long survive the change of administration at Simpson. The Oxford exchange program, actually an arrangement with a single Oxford college, Christ Church, might have continued longer than it did, but conditions both at Oxford and Christ Church itself hobbled the exchange.

Yet while it lasted, the Oxford program served Simpson well. In the fall semester 1964, Charles H. Stuart, a specialist in eighteenth century English history who had recently revised Basil Williams's *The Whig Supremacy: 1714–1760* in the *Oxford History of England* series, taught a class, a seminar and individual directed studies in Simpson's History Department. His public lectures, carefully crafted and thoughtfully delivered, revealed the mind of a conscientious scholar whose high Tory predilections led him to eschew much of what passed for wisdom in the modern world. Yet for all his conservative sympathies, he was, in informal situations, a delightful companion and accomplished raconteur whose thoroughly British sense of humor was adjudged by some to be amusing, by others mystifying. He brought his wife, Pamela, and two children with him and enrolled the son and daughter in the Indianola schools for the semester.[49] After Stuart and his family returned to England, he served as a mentor and guide for Simpson graduate Van Davis, who entered Christ Church in the fall of 1965.[50]

In the fall of 1967, Christ Church physicist Carl Collie taught advanced courses in physics, including nuclear physics, at Simpson. His public lectures, dealing variously with radioactivity, the quantum theory and the phenomenon of light, were well received.[51] Townspeople soon became accustomed to seeing Collie and his wife walking around town at an almost furious rate as they sought to keep fit in a determined British way. They truly enjoyed Indianola. "The Midwest," he said, "is much nicer than the people of the East told us it would be."[52]

Not long after the Collies returned home, however, the Dean of Christ Church informed Ralph John that it might be difficult to find additional members of their small faculty who would be able to take a leave from their teaching duties at home to come to Simpson for a semester. Further, he said, it might be almost impossible to set aside a place at Christ Church for a Simpson student—or any other student, for that matter—in view of new restrictions at Oxford limiting the rights of individual colleges to recruit and admit their own students. These new regulations were a part of the recent democratization of British higher education, following the recommendations of the parliamentary Franks Commission, of which J. Steven Watson had been a member. Thus after Van Davis completed his B.A. with honors at Oxford in 1969, the program was regrettably terminated.[53]

The Christian Liberal Arts Festival was another matter. The tenth festival was carried off in the fall of 1964 as planned, but the old enthusiasm was gone. Even though Ralph John had answered student queries about the future of the festival by saying "I expect to build on Dr. Kerstetter's legacy," it was clear to just about everyone that his heart was not in it, for reasons both philosophical and practical.[54] "I do not know what a *Christian* Liberal Arts Festival is," he wrote later, "any more than I can conceive of a Capitalist, Republican or Surrealistic one. That was something at Simpson which I did not know how to approach because of what I felt to be a conceptual flaw or an internal contradiction in the name itself."[55] Thus when the event took place during the early days of October, it was called simply the "Tenth Liberal Arts Festival." John also questioned the advisability of concentrating so much of the College's resources on one major event, with its parade of speakers. Why not spread the richness over the academic year in a more evenly paced concert and lecture series?

When the Tenth Festival days passed "with an uncustomary lack of pomp and circumstance," suggesting to many participants that the event was being played down, Ed Purcell, the bright *Simpsonian* editor who let nothing of importance on campus escape his attention, took issue with the dropping of "Christian" in the festival title. "Have we become too secularized?" he asked. "Or is it perhaps only that they have decided that if an Art is to be liberal it cannot be Christian at the same time! . . . Wherein lies the future of a college that cannot maintain its Christianity?"[56]

The following year Simpson people saw the festival transformed into a fall convocation series which featured addresses on October 4 and 5 by Dr. Raymond Seeger of the National Science Foundation on "Humanism in Science." While he pointed out to a huge audience of 1,200 that "modern civilization has not been built by agnostics and doubters, but by men of faith," his main thesis was that "all subjects can use the humanistic approach and that education must recognize and use this method."[57] And as the humanists took the field at Simpson, few harbored hopes that the Christian Liberal Arts idea could long survive. John was the first to assert that it was a Kerstetter creation that simply ceased to flourish once its creator departed the scene.

The appointment in 1967 of John Oldani to a new faculty position in American studies coincided with the sixth and last summer American studies program sponsored by the College and financed in large part by the Coe Foundation. Actually, the Coe funding had continued much longer than Simpson people had dared hope it would, and the incorporation of American studies in the regular College curriculum was precisely what the Coe people had hoped would happen.[58]

That same summer Simpson offered a summer remedial program for thirty prospective students who had not completed all of their college entrance requirements.[59] It seems to have been "a modest success, and we learned much from the experiment," said the College's academic dean. It was repeated in the summer of 1968 and possessed "great potential for success, especially with disadvantaged youth."[60] The following year Simpson was awarded $36,400 by the U.S. Office of Economic Opportunity as the delegate agency to operate a Head Start program for disadvantaged preschool children in Warren and Marion counties. Professor Don Koontz in sociology was appointed director of the summer program.[61]

Meanwhile the College attempted to initiate a student exchange with a southern black college, but it was difficult to recruit southern black students who wanted to study for a semester or a year at a predominantly white college, and few Simpson students showed much enthusiasm for the project.[62]

* * *

During the first five years of the John administration, enrollments continued to climb substantially, from 724 in the fall of 1963 to 989 in the fall of 1968. (See table 10.) These figures should have been gratifying, but the College's forecasts called for no fewer than 1,250 students by the fall of 1970, and it was clear by 1968 that such an ambitious goal would not be met. We have an "inordinately high" attrition of students, especially at the end of the sophomore year, observed John at the end of his first year at the College.[63] Although he hoped that the growth of faculty, together with the enrichment and expansion of upper division course offerings, would help keep more students on campus to graduation, results were disappointing. There were only eleven more seniors on campus in the spring of 1968 than there had been in the fall of 1963. Surely affecting the College's ability to recruit either the number or quality of the students it wanted were a number of problems: the mounting cost of private education, driving tuition rates inexorably upward; the virtual explosion of two-year com-

Table 10
Fall Enrollment 1963–1973

	Senior	Junior	Soph.	Fresh.	Uncl. Special	FT Total	Part Time	Total
1963–64	153	168	180	223	0	724	26	750
1964–65	145	161	199	266	19	790	22	812
1965–66	132	151	245	345	0	873	36	909
1966–67	122	172	305	300	11	910	19	929
1967–68	142	237	243	312	9	943	24	967
1968–69	201	195	273	309	11	989	24	1013
1969–70	165	189	254	308	10	926	18	944
1970–71	189	198	247	351	16	1001	37	1038
1971–72	176	224	259	284	14	957	41	998
1972–73	172	218	199	264	4	857	62	919
1973–74	205	180	234	281	16	916	66	982

munity colleges, most of which ostensibly provided vocational and technical training but were rapidly expanding into general liberal arts institutions as well; and Simpson's decision in 1965 to require the Scholastic Aptitude Test of the College Entrance Examination Board of all entering students in the fall of 1966 and beyond.[64] "The most devastating thing," recalled Ralph John many years later, "was the emergence [in several states] of non-portable state student aid programs. The number of freshmen from the Chicago area, for example, dropped from 60 or 70 to about 30. The same thing happened in Minneapolis on a smaller scale."[65] There was consequent frustration and anxiety in the area of admissions. At the same time, the student body continued to be quite homogeneous: forty-five percent of the students were Methodist among the twenty-two religious groups represented on campus; seventy percent were from Iowa, twenty-eight percent came from other states and two percent from foreign countries; twelve percent were commuters and six percent were married. Its "Iowa image," John concluded, was hurting the College. "We try to dispel the stereotype of the midwestern church-related college," he said ruefully, although of course that is exactly what Simpson was. "We must nonetheless make a necessary and deliberate change. . . . We want to be more cosmopolitan." Out-of-state enrollment did grow perceptibly until in 1966 it reached nearly forty percent of the undergraduate student body.[66] But the emphasis on numbers inevitably affected deleteriously the academic quality of those whom the College admitted.

* * *

During the 1960s people at Simpson became increasingly aware of the College's long record of "going it alone." Apart from its membership in the Iowa Intercollegiate Athletic Conference since its inception in 1922 and participation in planning the Midland Conference which never really got off the ground, the College had not joined many intercollegiate associations. But by the time Dr. John took the helm at Simpson in 1963, academic consortia were becoming popular everywhere. "Public agencies and foundations," recalled John, "were encouraging homogeneous institutions to league up with each other to share human and program resources, thereby averting unnecessary duplication, and hopefully to save money."[67] Two such consortia, both highly successful, already existed in the Midwest: The Associated Colleges of the Midwest (ACM), of which three Iowa colleges were members (Coe, Cornell and Grinnell), and the Great

Lakes Colleges Association, made up of twelve colleges in Michigan, Indiana and Ohio. Their most successful undertakings were programs—most of them off-campus—which "could not be carried on by one college alone, or for some reason are to be specialized on a single campus."[68]

In January 1965, Simpson and eight other colleges, all church-related, met at St. Louis and organized the Central States College Association (CSCA).[69] The nine charter members included Augustana College (Illinois), Carroll College, Gustavus Adolphus College, Illinois Wesleyan University, Luther College, MacMurray College, Manchester College, Millikin University and Simpson.[70] At the association's first meeting, Ralph John was elected secretary of the board of directors.[71]

With its membership enlarged a few months later to twelve by the addition of Alma College, Mundelein College and St. John's University (Minnesota), CSCA undertook a number of programs.[72] For example, a short-term faculty exchange took several Simpson faculty members for a week at a time to a number of other CSCA colleges, and visiting faculty brought their special expertise to Simpson. Overseas study opportunities were developed for students in cooperation with the Institute for European Studies; "telelectures" were beamed from one campus to another; January charter flights to Europe were offered for students and faculty from the six of the twelve CSCA colleges that had adopted the 4-1-4 calendar; dual enrollment, allowing students to move from one campus to another, was encouraged; cooperative programs in the sciences provided students an opportunity to use research facilities at the Argonne National Laboratory and to participate in field work in marine biology, geography, geology, sociology and psychology. A 1966 promotional brochure stated somewhat extravagantly that "CSCA, in effect, is a university of 15,000 students and 1,112 faculty and staff located on twelve different campuses."[73] A central office was opened in Evanston, Illinois, with Dr. Pressley C. McCoy, who had formerly served with the Danforth Foundation, as president of the association.

Unlike the ACM consortium, CSCA decided against becoming an athletic conference out of consideration for long-standing athletic commitments of the member institutions, uneven levels of participation in the several varsity sports, and the very considerable cost of team travel in a six-state area. It was believed that common commitment to liberal learning and church-relatedness would provide the consortium a real identity without shared athletic activities and that mutual needs would pull them together. Thus with real hope for meaningful cooperation the CSCA colleges embarked on a "noble experiment" in higher education. And for the next few years the consortium seemed to be off to a good start.[74]

* * *

In the early fall of 1966 Ralph John reported to Simpson's board of trustees that he was working on a ten-year plan for the College,[75] and a few weeks later he laid the document before them.[76] While much of the plan had to do with new buildings, enrollment projections and potential curricular changes, John felt it necessary to speak to the College's church relationship, which, "sometimes misunderstood on both sides, is an historic and meaningful fact." He pointed out that "there is a difference between a church and a college. The first is a community of people bound together by a common religious commitment. A college is a community of scholars where there is freedom to explore all intellectual options, religious or otherwise. These frequently seem to be in conflict where a mutual relationship maintains. This is because some expect a church to be a college or, on the other hand, a college a church, when neither can be the other in any significant sense."[77] While this statement, drafted primarily for external consumption, did not allay the fears of some conference clerics that Simpson's growing secularism was leading it to the brink of perdition, it was accepted by the board and the campus constituency as a fair statement of Simpson's church relationship.

When the ten-year plan was explained in the *Simpson Alumnus* in early 1967, it was pointed out that "while the greatest implications of the . . . program are in terms of human aspirations, physical centers of learning must first be established."[78] The rest of the article was devoted to a $7.2 million building program. Included in the plans were the renovation of the old science hall, the building of a new coeducational dormitory, a large, well equipped student center, the long-awaited new chapel and a performing arts center. Beyond these ambitious projects were plans for "two additional dormitories, a new wing on Barker Hall dormitory, a swimming pool addition to Hopper Gymnasium, renovation of Pfeiffer Dining Hall and a new Field House."[79] Altogether this plan projected the most extensive building program in the history of the College. Apart from bricks and mortar, the ten-year plan called for raising $2 million for the College's endowment and $2.6 million for operating expenses.

Some of the capital funds had already been raised before the ten-year plan was announced, and several construction projects were already underway or in an advanced stage of planning. When Ralph John took over the reins of the College in November 1963, the Dunn Library was already under construction. The building was partially enclosed to permit interior work to proceed throughout the winter, allowing it to be completed during the summer of 1964.[80] Soon after the commencement of classes that fall, on a sunny October Saturday, students, faculty, staff and townspeople pitched in to help move 40,000 volumes of books and thousands of bound periodicals from the old Carnegie Library to the new Dunn Library. Some lugged heavy cartons of books; others formed a sort of bucket brigade to pass the thousands of volumes from one building to the other, the library staff showing the workers where to shelve them. Librarian Bill Garton counted 5,889 trips to and fro, not counting the books passed between the buildings. It was hard work. Petite Rosemary deLaubenfels, daughter of the head of the Theater Arts Department, worked eight hours. Even E. G. Booth got tired. It took all day to complete the job, the participants rewarded with coffee and doughnuts for their labors. The *Simpsonian* exulted, "Dunn is Completely Done."[81]

An open-house reception on October 25 introduced the handsome new library to the public. Floral bouquets and potted plants helped provide a festive atmosphere as faculty, students and an estimated 425 townspeople wandered in and out, milling around and admiring the spacious building, with its lovely staircase above the decorative pool near the entrance. Then it happened. A woman marched in through the entrance, looked up, awed by the dimensions of the magnificent structure, and strode directly into the pool. She splashed, spread-eagled, into the water, her hat bobbing in the waves that spilled out over the terrazzo floor and fine new carpet. Joe Walt, who happened to be sitting nearby, was momentarily transfixed. Then he attempted to help the sputtering woman to her feet. Don Koch ran to fetch some towels, as did Comptroller Doyle Woods and Vice-President Bob Feyerharm, who mopped up the floor and patted dry the fine new carpet. The lady took her leave, and has never been known to reappear on the Simpson campus.[82]

After the excitement of the reception, the dedication of Dunn Library on Homecoming day, October 31, seemed something of an anticlimax. And no one was again recorded having fallen into the indoor pool, although it was reported late that fall that "Mr. Garton had the goldfish taken out of the library pool. He plans to replace them with piranha."[83]

Speaking of pools, architect Neutra had been adamant that a large reflecting pool be built outside the southwest corner of the new library.[84] The *Simpsonian* could not resist the observation that the pool "is a good Methodist pool. It is too shallow for immersions."[85]

Scarcely a fortnight after the dedication of the Dunn Library, Robert Feyerharm announced to the board's executive committee that the availability of federal funds might make possible the renovation of the old science building, standing unused because of its deteriorated condition.[86] The building was certainly worth saving. Board member Kenneth Brown sent in members of his Des Moines engineering firm to do a thorough examination of the structure. They concluded that the place was "built like a battleship." Moving ahead cautiously, the board voted in early 1965 to go ahead with the project at a cost not to exceed $388,000.[87] Brown Engineering was asked to draw up plans for the renovation, which would provide adequate facilities for physics, mathematics and geology. Later the plans were modified to bring the cost under $300,000, of which amount they would seek a major portion from the federal government.[88] What they received was generous: a grant of $98,455 and a twenty-five-year loan of $125,000.[89] The college provided the balance of $74,700 in cash.[90] The contract for the reconstruction project was awarded to the W. H. Breiholz Company of Des Moines.

During commencement weekend in 1967 the building was rededicated in a modest ceremony held in front of the handsome entrance, above which was an entablature with rich golden Roman lettering, bearing the inscription "Henry A. Wallace Hall of Science." Dedicated to the memory of the great geneticist and former vice president of the United States whose wife, Simpson alumna Ilo Brown Wallace, participated in the ceremony and whose brother, board of trustees member James Wallace, presented the key to the building to Simpson's science division chairman, Clifford Meints, the building received that day a new lease on life.[91]

A second building project planned during 1965 was the new coeducational residence hall. The concept was considerably less daring than some of Simpson's more conservative alumni feared, their vivid imaginations conjuring up scenes of bacchanalian revelry among cohabitating undergraduates. College officials pointed out patiently that men would reside in one part of a large building, women in another. Quite apart from the design of the structure, it was clear that by 1965 student enrollment was putting a strain on housing. If Simpson was to remain a residential college, new dormitories were essential. Government financing of such revenue-producing facilities was available, so the board of trustees agreed in March 1965 to go ahead with the project.[92] Selected to design the building to house 136 was Charles Herbert Associates of Des Moines. The site chosen was a relatively spacious area on the south side of Franklin Street running east from North E Street. A loan of $600,000 was negotiated with the federal government to meet most of the cost of the $627,690 project.[93]

When bids were received on November 24, 1965, the general contract went to the Henkel Construction Company of Mason City.[94] By February the dormitory was reported to be "going up in spite of unreasonably cold weather."[95] Due to unforeseen delays, however, construction required more than a year. Finally, on April 3, 1967, students were able to move in, sixty of them coming from the all-male Hopper Terrace barracks, those "temporary" units that had served several generations of students over two decades.[96] The new building was provisionally called the Franklin Street Dormitory. A brick "Tudor Modern" structure, it consisted of two connected towers containing thirty-four suites housing four students each. A suite was comprised of a study room, sleeping room, and bath.

Of more interest to students was the new student union, the need for which had been evident for many years. In the spring of 1965 the board of trustees concluded that "as a more heterogeneous student body comes and stays on campus more, the more need there is for a student center." No one was pretending that a downstairs corner of Pfeiffer Hall was even minimally serving the purpose.[97] That summer the Charles Herbert Associates firm was employed to design an appropriate building, while a group of Simpson administrators visited twelve colleges, examining their student center facilities.[98] A whole series of meetings with various undergraduate constituencies sought to elicit student opinion and desires "to insure optimum advantages." Meanwhile the College's trustees "agreed to assume personal responsibility for financing the project."[99] And that they did. To meet the estimated $700,000 cost of the building, the board authorized a private twenty-five-year $400,000 loan at six percent interest and undertook to raise the rest among themselves.

Never before had board members committed themselves to such an ambitious capital project, and for some of them it meant a real financial sacrifice. Among their number they eventually came up with nearly $250,000, but by far the largest single gift was the $100,000 subscribed on behalf of the Brenton Foundation by W. Harold Brenton, president of the large Brenton Bank empire and a member of Simpson's Development Council, an important Simpson support group created during the latter years of Kerstetter's administration. Only $50,000 shy of their goal, the board went ahead with the project, and soon enough the fundraising goal was met.[100] When contracts were let in July 1966, Garmer and Stiles Company of Des Moines was the winner with a general contract bid of $378,181. The total cost of the building was $699,976.[101] Construction began late that summer on a site along the north side of Franklin Avenue between C Street and D Street. Several old residences, including the old president's house built by Fletcher Brown in the 1890s, had been purchased and razed to make room for the sprawling new structure.[102]

The student center, stretching on an east-west axis, was described as "unique architecturally," containing "few interior walls and more glass so that an unusual amount of visual relationship will be possible from one vantage point to another." Of brick and concrete construction, its main interior architectural feature was a large sunken gallery, open to the roof of the building, its ceiling covered with nine transparent sky domes "so as to give the appearance of being open to the sky." All the spaces in the building were related in one way or another to this central gallery. The main floor of the multilevel building consisted of offices, a game room, a large informal lounge on the west end and a large grill and kitchen on the east end. The lower floor included meeting rooms, student government and publications offices, darkrooms and an intimate "president's dining room." On the upper floor level were study lounges, a music lounge, a coffee house and a large formal lounge at the east end, with a fine balcony overlooking a huge seventy by seventy-five foot plaza, with Buxton Park in the background.[103] It was a stunning design that won a major award for the Charles Herbert architectural firm. Scheduled to be completed before the opening of the 1967–68 academic year, the project was stalled by slowed deliveries of materials and a five-day strike during the spring of 1967.

The new Brenton Student Center was formally dedicated at an open house on the evening of February 16, 1968. Ralph John introduced W. Harold Brenton and his wife, Etta Spurgeon Brenton, in recognition of their part in making the student center possible. Dean of students Waller B. Wiser and student body president Sam Martin spoke of the importance of the new building to the campus community, after which board of trustees vice chairman William Buxton III presented the keys to the building to young Martin. With rich carpets that contrasted with the stark concrete interior walls, the center contained rooms named for principal donors: the Fern L. Graves Gallery, the informal Alden C. Smith Lounge, the formal Louise Meek Camp Lounge and the Barborka Senate Room.[104]

Hired as director of the new Brenton Student Center was Lu Jean Cole, who had resided with her husband, Indianola hog buyer Jack Cole and their two children, coincidentally in the old Fletcher Brown house before it was razed to make way for the new building. Mrs. Cole's credentials were modest: she had worked briefly for the local Indianola newspaper as a society columnist, dallied with Republican politics and had essayed a few courses at Drake and Simpson, one of which was in elementary German with Gary Valen, who recalled that her pronunciation of the language was probably the worst he had ever encountered. All of this mattered not at all to Ralph John, who knew her to be intelligent, witty, possessed of remarkable interpersonal skills and a marvelous sense of humor. Moreover, he believed her to be the most fashionable, most striking personality he had met in Indianola. His instincts were right. Lu Jean Cole took the position—the salary was terrible but this was, after all, her first real job—and almost singlehandedly opened the building and created its programs. More than that: she worked creatively with students during days both halcyon and troubled. She talked with them, listened to them, sympathized with their problems, goaded, inspired and thoroughly charmed all those who crossed her path. The students loved her.

The completion of the Smith Memorial Chapel in 1968 was the successful culmination of probably the longest and surely the most exasperating building project in the history of the College. It had all started during the early days of the Kerstetter administration. During his first year at Simpson Dr. Kerstetter included a chapel in the College's long range plans.[105] He later recalled that a "beautiful chapel" was "a special top priority in our minds," that it would be "strategically located on our campus as the ultimate symbol of the highest aims of education, of the fact that Simpson had been founded and supported through all its years by the Methodist Church."[106] Although the First Methodist Church of Indianola was only a few blocks away, it was important, he said, to have a structure that would have "many daily practical academic and religious uses, since it was *our* building and it was *on our* campus."[107]

Soon Kerstetter had found potential donors for the project. They were Miss Alida Smith, a Simpson graduate in the class of 1907, who had been a long time Latin teacher, and her brother, Dr. David O. Smith '08, a physician with the United States Public Health Services, both of them residing in Washington, D.C. Don Berry told Kerstetter that Dr. Voigt had come to know the Smiths back in the 1940s. Berry recommended that they continue to be cultivated, with the understanding that the only project that would interest them was a chapel. Kerstetter took Berry's advice, and he and Leona visited the Smiths regularly. "In our continuing cultivation process," wrote Kerstetter, Leona "was more important than I was." He recalled that "we devoted far more time to them than to any other persons in the Simpson family, calling on them personally, at least once a year, during the ten year period we were at Simpson."[108] Their efforts seemed to have paid off by 1957, when Kerstetter was able to report to the board of trustees that he had an "anonymous" pledge of $150,000 to meet half the estimated cost of the chapel.[109] The building would be a memorial to the Smiths' mother.

Born and reared in Lucas, Iowa, near Chariton, David and Alida were powerfully—some would say slavishly—devoted to their aged mother, who had been widowed when they were children and whom they painstakingly watched after until the day of her death in her eighties.[110] The Smiths knew what they wanted in a building, and it must be good enough for their mother. Kerstetter recalled that they "were absolutely insistent that the chapel be built according to *their* conception of what a chapel should look like."[111]

Enter Richard Neutra, the College's new architect, whose early assignment included plans for both a library and chapel for Simpson.[112] Neutra's design for the library pleased everyone, but his preliminary sketches for the chapel, suggesting a bold, strikingly modern structure, were almost certain to displease the Smiths, whose tolerance of the avant garde in architecture was known to be limited. No one realized just *how* limited until the Smiths saw the Neutra sketches in the spring of 1959 and found them totally unacceptable. What they wanted, they said, was a traditional, white New England church, fronted by at least six columns and crowned by a huge spire. As we have already noted, Kerstetter didn't like the Neutra plans either, but he was caught between the stiff-necked conservatism of the donors and the professional pride of the architect. The removal of Neutra from the chapel project in 1960 and the appointment of Arland Dirlam of Boston to prepare "traditional" plans should have pleased the Smiths, but they continued to make demands that were almost impossible of fulfillment. They liked Dirlam, but their specifications for the size, the structural materials, the facilities and the function of the chapel slowed the project almost to a halt.[113]

The matter was still dragging on when Ralph John arrived on campus late in 1963. He took a careful look at the demands of the Smiths; the sanctuary must seat at least 1,000 (they preferred 1,200); the building could contain only one office—that of the chaplain—and no classrooms, for it must be used strictly for worship; and "they were obsessed with the idea of having six solid marble Doric columns on the front of a colonial structure." Those columns alone, pointed out Dr. John, "probably would have cost most, if not all" of the large contribution they had provisionally promised, a pledge that had grown incrementally as their interest in the chapel project intensified.[114] None of their grand demands could be met, but John hoped that his prior acquaintance with the Smiths—they were members of the Foundry Methodist Church in Washington, where John had been associate minister while finishing his doctorate—would enable him to deal with them comfortably. He was mistaken.

On campus there was growing resistance to the chapel project. Dean of Chapel Jim Allen, recalled Dr. John, "was no classicist and wanted a modernistic chapel, which took the situation even farther from Dirlam's competency." A student poll conducted in the closing weeks of 1963 showed only seven percent favoring a chapel as the top campus construction priority.[115] The attitude of the executive committee of the board of trustees had shifted to a "to hell with the Smiths" mode. Ralph John himself observed that "the feeling on campus was that the chapel was a low priority . . . , particularly in view of the elimination of the old chapel-convocation requirement and the other glaring needs" of Simpson, especially a student center. John tried to persuade the Smiths to use their gift for a "small meditation type chapel" in a new student center, but to no avail. "The Matterhorn," said John, "could not be budged." The Smiths "couldn't understand why we didn't want—or couldn't afford—what they wanted. But I went [to Washington] for my regular flagellations and to renew my frustrations."[116]

Meanwhile the College had discovered another donor for the chapel. He was Robert A. MacBain of Rochester, New York, a Simpson graduate in the class of 1910. Kerstetter had cultivated MacBain and had seen to it that he was awarded an honorary degree in 1954. A man of considerable means, MacBain died April 30, 1965, and in his will left Simpson $100,000 for a scholarship fund, $25,000 for carillon bells as a memorial to his wife for the chapel, and nine-fifteenths of the balance of his estate. The total MacBain legacy amounted to $425,000.[117]

MacBain was hardly a typical Simpson alumnus. It had required eight years for him to work his way through Simpson back in the early days of the century. Determined, stubborn and intelligent, he taught school for a while after graduation in 1910, then joined the National Park Service at Yellowstone as a guide. There he met a park visitor named Martha Matilda Harper, a wealthy eastern woman who took an instant liking to Ranger MacBain and invited him to join her in her business, a highly successful beauty concern which bore her name. He accepted her tempting offer and served as her executive assistant until he entered the Army during the First World War.[118] In the service he reached the rank of captain and was known as Captain MacBain from that time on. He rejoined Harper's firm after the war, and after her surprise proposal, married her, even though she was fifteen years his senior. He lived happily with her until the time of her death, at which time he inherited from her a considerable fortune.

"It is somewhat surprising," said publisher Don Berry in 1966, "that MacBain left so much money to Simpson because of his intense dislike for college fraternities." Berry, who lost no love for the Greek-letter societies himself, had talked a number of times recently with MacBain and perhaps "had convinced him that fraternities were not all bad" and reminded him that "many good men who had become his close friends had been members of fraternities."[119] MacBain had a hard time believing that fraternity men could be good Christians, but conceded that perhaps some of them had been won over to the gospel. In any case, Simpson needed a proper chapel where the gospel could be preached.

The MacBain estate gave Ralph John important leverage with the Smiths. From the captain's legacy, $300,000 could be allocated to chapel construction, topping the Smiths' $250,000. Thus armed, he made one more trip to Washington. The Smiths were still adamant. And Ralph John had reached the end of his patience. "I told them as nicely as I could that we had discussed the matter many times and that I had worked at reconciling differences. Other major things were developing at the College, and I pointed this out. I concluded by saying that I thought that regrettably the chapel project would just have to be dropped and that I did not anticipate returning on that question."[120] Ralph John was not bluffing, and the Smiths knew it. Suddenly, as John remembered the incident, "they melted completely." The plans for the chapel went ahead without incident. To be sure, the structure was a lopsided compromise between the Smiths' dream of a New England church and Jim Allen's desire for a contemporary chapel. Architect Dirlam did his best, produced a fairly modern building that contained a whole lower floor of classrooms and offices, and a really very attractive sanctuary with a seating capacity of 490, a flexible chancel arrangement with no fixed furnishings and movable organ console. A fine Reuter organ was ordered and a striking elevated pulpit planned.

When Dirlam's plans were presented to the executive committee of the board during the first week in January 1966, the architect was instructed to revise them so that the total cost of the building would not exceed $575,000.[121] When contracts were awarded the following November, Dirlam had come close, if one did not count the cost of the organ and the carillon.[122]

Construction of the chapel, which was underway as soon as the frost was out of the ground, required more than a year. At commencement in early June 1967, the cornerstone was laid in a ceremony conducted by board chairman James W. Wallace. Representing the Smiths was their grandniece, Simpson senior Dana Worley, while two grandnephews of Captain MacBain, James and Robert Hoskinson, also participated. In the cornerstone was sealed a time capsule containing symbols of the College and the mid-twentieth century.[123]

The chapel was dedicated on October 20, 1968, during Simpson's Homecoming, in a ceremony remarkable for its ecumenicity. Participating were Bishops Edwin E. Voigt, former president of Simpson, and James S. Thomas of the Iowa Area of the United Methodist Church, Roman Catholic Bishop Maurice J. Dingman of the Diocese of Des Moines and Rabbi Jay B. Goldberg of the Temple B'nai Jeshurun in Des Moines. Grand marshal of the occasion was Jim Allen, who had been the College's chaplain during some of the tortured negotiations incident to the chapel's construction. Allen's successor, the Reverend Gilbert Y. Taverner, who had come to Simpson as chaplain only in the late summer of 1968, generously deferred to those who had brought the long-delayed project to fruition.[124] The chapel was formally presented by board chairman William Buxton III to Bishop Thomas, who in turn appropriately performed the act of dedication. For David O. and Alida Smith the moment was deeply personal. Alida stood before the throng and spoke for both of them. She was, she said, grateful that the job was done and was delighted to be present. Now her voice took on a warmer and softer tone than anyone had heard from her before. As she concluded her brief address, she spoke these words: "I dedicate this Smith Memorial Chapel to the glory of God and to the Christian inspiration of the students of Simpson College—an inspiration 'which shall develop and bloom forever,' [125] and I reverently dedicate this Chapel to the memory of my beloved parents: Mrs. Annie Catherine Smith and Henry Gardener Smith."[126] Also dedicated that day was the Martha Matilda Harper Carillon, containing one hundred fifty-nine precisely tuned symphonic carillon bells. Located in the eighty-foot campanile that adorned the west facade of the chapel, it was played publicly that day for the first time from the organ console by guest carillonneur Roland Pomerat of Rice University. At the top of the tower, above the carillon, was installed the old 1856 Simpson chapel bell, once rung to mark the change of classes and most recently rung to signal the start of the annual Campus Day.

Presented also at the dedicatory ceremony was the handsome inscribed "Oxford Stone" that had been sent by Dean Simpson of Christ Church to Dr. Kerstetter several years earlier. Placed in a prominent niche in the narthex of the chapel, the stone was presented formally by History Department chairman Joe Walt, who had himself participated in the Oxford exchange program.

Those who attended the dedicatory ceremonies could take note of a number of additional features of the building that enhanced both its beauty and its utility. At the left of the main entrance was a pleasant lounge for meetings, receptions or seminars. At the right was a meditation chapel, seating about seventy, containing two colorful art glass windows depicting the Smiths' parents. In the large, open sanctuary with its solid brick and stone walls and great cathedral ceiling were striking faceted stained glass windows, some of which, at Dr. John's suggestion, contained symbols of all the world's great religions. And in keeping with the theme of ecumenicity, the first religious service held in the new chapel was a Catholic mass, celebrated by Father Larry Burns of the local St. Thomas Aquinas parish and held in the small chapel for the College's Catholic students the first Sunday the chapel was open.[127]

By the time the Smith Memorial Chapel was dedicated, yet another major building project was within days of beginning. In sharp contrast to the chapel, the planning for the new fine arts center went relatively quickly and without incident. No one questioned the need for a fine arts complex. Although Barrows Hall was still adequate enough, it was old and had no facilities for Simpson's burgeoning opera program. The College's theater was pathetically inadequate. And the recently revived program in art—Jack Ragland had come in 1964 and Gaile Gallatin joined the department in 1967—had almost no place to call its own. Thus when Ralph John informed the board of trustees that he had a donor in sight who was interested in a fine arts center, everyone took heart.[128]

Soon enough it became clear that it would be impossible to build at one time a facility large enough to accommodate all the fine arts, so the board decided to focus first on a theater. Hence they started talking about a performing arts center. Enamored of the style employed by the Charles Herbert Associates in their design of the Brenton Student Center, the Simpson people asked that firm to draw up plans for the new theater.[129] Once the plans were in hand, the College made application for a Title I construction grant to the United States Office of Education through the Iowa Higher Education Commission. The amount sought was $274,830,[130] and several months later Congressman John Kyl notified the College that the grant had been approved. President John announced that available resources, including funds already raised privately, totaled $707,000 toward the $836,000 estimated cost of the project.[131] As fund-raising continued for another year, it was discovered that the College had to purchase more land to accommodate the large structure.[132] Fortunately the land was available and the purchase completed in time to advertise for bids in August 1968. They would call the building "the Blank Center for the Performing Arts," named for the generous gift of Dr. Abraham H. and Mrs. Theo Blank of Des Moines. A. H. Blank, owner of a large theater corporation, was known for his wide-ranging philanthropic interests, including hospitals, a number of civic enterprises and youth programs.[133]

When bids were received in mid-November, the board was shocked by the effects of inflation on the cost of building, the lowest bids coming in at more than thirty percent above estimates. Contracts totaling $1,157,440 were awarded to the successful bidders, and the board went to work to raise the nearly $300,000 needed.[134]

Ground was broken for the new structure on June 1, 1968, at commencement time, with the participation of Dr. and Mrs. A. H. Blank, Myron N. and Jackie Blank, Dr. John, immediate past board of trustees chairman James W. Wallace and newly elected board chairman William Buxton III, together with other board members and faculty of the Departments of Music and Theatre. In his short address, President John expressed gratitude for the Blank gift. The new building, he said, "will add new dimensions to the life of the College itself and also will provide a center for a larger service to the central Iowa community, of which Indianola and Simpson are a part."[135] His words were more prophetic than he knew, for the Blank Center soon was selected to house the performances of the Des Moines Metro Opera, whose artistic director was Simpson's Robert L. Larsen.

The new theater was a long time abuilding, and perhaps a good thing too, for it gave the College enough time to raise the additional funds needed to meet the structure's inflated cost. A. H. Blank himself gave an additional challenge gift of $25,000, matched by the contributions of others to make up the last $50,000 needed. Completed and equipped in early 1971, the theater formally opened with a production of *Peer Gynt* in March, directed by Joe Graber.[136] The building was formally dedicated April 3, 1971.[137]

The Blank Center for the Performing Arts, a formidable boxlike poured concrete structure, contained a splendid theater, featuring a conventional proscenium stage combined with a hydraulically operated thrust platform, providing a remarkably versatile performing area. Designated the "Pote Theatre" in honor of alumni Dr. and Mrs. Harold F. Pote of La Jolla, California, the playhouse had excellent acoustics. The Potes had made a major commitment to the construction of the new building.[138] A smaller studio theater was located in the basement level of the building, designed for experimental and informal productions. On the south side of the building, providing access to both theaters, was a huge foyer, called the "Barborka Gallery," named for alumni Dr. and Mrs. Clifford Barborka of Chicago. The downstairs greenroom was named in honor of Gertrude B. Schloss and her late husband, Sam M. Schloss, friends of the College. The rest of the building consisted of offices and classrooms for the Department of Theater Arts and Speech, makeup and dressing rooms, equipment storage areas and a production workshop.[139]

Apart from the land purchase required for the Blank Performing Arts Center, the College bought additional parcels of land to fill out the campus boundaries. In 1965 the board decided on the purchase of what was known as the Young property, a small piece just north of the three new fraternity houses. It further authorized the College to purchase any appropriate properties that became available—at a fair market price—in an area bounded by Girard and Boston Avenues on the north and south and C Street and E Street on the east and west.[140] Two years later the College agreed to purchase for a sum "not to exceed $35,000" a 1.8 acre parcel known as the McAninch property, also north of the fraternity houses, just before it was about to be sold to an apartment builder.[141]

Once these improvements, both in handsome buildings and campus acreage, had been undertaken, Ralph John warned the board of trustees that "we must slow down on capital projects," for "we are in general 'tooled' to serve more students than we have."[142] Indeed, during these years capital projects absorbed much of the time and attention of the board, not to speak of most of the externally raised funds that might otherwise have been committed to the academic programs of the College. At the same time, inflation inexorably drove the cost of running the College even higher, especially salaries and wages for ever-scarcer faculty and staff in a strongly labor-intensive enterprise.[143] Employment of new faculty outran the increase in student enrollment, exerting even more pressure on resources.

One answer to the budget crunch was a steady increase in student tuition charges from $970 in the 1963–64 academic year to $1,490 for 1968–69. During that same period the cost of board and room rose only ten percent, from $730 to $800. These increases, together with the thirty-seven percent growth of full-time students—from 724 to 989—did provide increased total income for the College, from $1,384,737 in 1963–64 to a budgeted $2,722,447 in 1968–69, but expenses rose as rapidly.[144] Final reports for nearly all these years show the College's operations in the black, but in more than one of these years it required a transfer of nondesignated endowment money to balance the budget.[145] In 1965 such a transfer changed a $20,000 deficit to a $2,553 surplus; in 1968 an expected $25,000 deficit was trimmed to "only $2,500" by a judicious infusion of endowment reserves.[146] Vice-President Bob Feyerharm stated the obvious: "It is increasingly difficult to maintain a balanced operating budget."[147] Still, on the whole the College's finances were managed responsibly, even creatively, given the volatility of the nation's economy.

One means of supplementing the annual operating income of the College was the Indianola Simpson College Sustaining Fund program initiated in the fall of 1964 by board member William Buxton III. Although its early results were modest—$17,423 contributed the first year by ninety-five donors—subsequent years saw a substantial increase in the number of donors and the amount contributed.[148] Such gifts, pointed out the editor of the *Simpson College Bulletin*, "are used where the need is most urgent; this includes such things as library books for the new Dunn Library, funds for scholarships, and salaries for additional faculty members."[149] More importantly, the Indianola Sustaining Fund represented the best possible evidence that a warm relationship between the College and the town had been restored by Simpson's new president.

As the cost of higher education increased for students all across the nation, federal programs were forthcoming, providing loans at attractive interest rates. Back in 1955, Simpson students had borrowed $10,852, primarily from the College's own loan fund; in 1968 there were 754 students borrowing $930,209 through the National Defense Student Loan Program.[150] Some observers praised the loan program as a timely and much needed federal initiative; others found it an act of profligacy on the part of bleeding-heart liberal Democrats in Washington. Students, without political partisanship, were quite willing to accept the loans, from whatever source.

* * *

President John discovered that administrators could be as mobile as faculty. In the spring of 1967, Ned Peterson, having lost the sight in one eye and contemplating risky surgery to save the sight in the other, felt compelled to resign the academic deanship and take a teaching position at Ohio University.[151] A faculty search committee recommended as Peterson's successor Joe Walt, who declined to accept the position on a permanent basis but agreed to serve for a year, until a new dean could be found.[152] Walt was at the time chairman of the important faculty curriculum committee that was completing its proposal for the new 4-1-4 calendar and revised general studies program, both of which were adopted during his tenure as dean. He enjoyed administrative work. "The job," he said, "is interesting and challenging, but I still see myself as a teacher."[153] A new search committee recommended once again an appointment from within the College's staff, moving Waller Wiser from the student to the academic deanship, the position now to be denominated "Vice President-Dean of Academic Affairs."[154] During the following five years (1968–73) Wiser handled with aplomb a position that came increasingly under fire as student unrest mounted.

Replacing Wiser as dean of students in the fall of 1968 was Bill R. Webster, whose credentials were good and whose promise was excellent.[155] To work with Webster as associate dean of students and dean of women, Ralph John selected Jane Templeton, an outstanding 1966 graduate of Simpson who had earned the M.A. in English at Johns Hopkins University. She replaced Evelyn Morris, who accepted a similar position at Luther College.[156]

In the sensitive area of admissions, in 1968 John appointed Richard Banning, longtime guidance counselor at Mason City, director of admissions, moving Dan Seaton to the post of director of financial aid, an area of increasing importance in a time of ever-higher college costs.[157] In his new position Seaton replaced Edd McKee, an Indianolan and retired dean of the College of Technology at the University of Vermont, who had taken over the office in 1965.[158]

During the early John administration, two young Simpson alumni served as associate directors of development, Charles "Chuck" Kayton (1963–66) and M. L. "Jack" Siefkas (1966–69). Both were young men on their way up. Simpson was fortunate to have each of them for a season.

When Robert Goodloe won a Metropolitan Opera contract in 1964, his successor as director of public relations was Vivian Herrick Jones, a Missourian with impressive experience in journalism. She was a graduate of the University of Missouri's prestigious Mott School of Journalism in the class of 1939.[159] Unfortunately she remained at Simpson only a matter of months, and a permanent replacement was not appointed until 1966, when John employed Charles S. Rock, a graduate of the University of Colorado and the Brooks Institute of Professional Photography, who came to Simpson from Hope College in Michigan, where he had been director of publications.[160] After two years Rock was succeeded by Larry A. Myers, appointed director of publications.[161]

The post of alumni secretary or director of alumni affairs customarily went to a young Simpson graduate who could relate well to the College's scattered alumni. Gary Ogden '55, who joined the Simpson staff in January 1964, was succeeded in 1966 by L. Edward Purcell '66, who served for two years before entering a graduate program in history at the University of Iowa.[162] Upon Purcell's departure, the *Simpson College Bulletin* announced the appointment of Gordon Brown '68 to the "newly created" position of alumni secretary,[163] a curious assertion in view of the decades-long history of the alumni post.

When historians tell the story of their colleges, they often overlook the support staff, the secretaries, the maintenance people, the food service personnel, the library workers, the bookstore employees, in short the men and women whose hard, often unrewarding work helps to create the physical environment in which the administration and faculty and students can flourish. A few of these people—like Peter Ross in the Hopper Gymnasium—became truly memorable. And few would forget motherly Maxine Speed, secretary to the academic dean, clad preferably in a new purple dress and taking home yet one more stray cat. Or redoubtable Anna Jean Breuklander, secretary to more than one Simpson president, before whom faculty quailed and trustees tiptoed, and who stayed around the place long enough to become an institution. Paul Borthwick kept the campus trim and in repair as superintendent of buildings and grounds until his retirement in 1967. He was succeeded by Donald Barnett, a Simpson alumnus of 1961 who had resided in Indianola for several years prior to his appointment.[164] They were helped by the likes of Dwight Hinkle, who could fix anything and whose command of Anglo-Saxon profanity was awe-inspiring, or young Larry "Red" VanPelt, whose skill as a painter was matched only by his irreverence, his disdain for pretentiousness and his rock-solid, if well-disguised, loyalty to the College.

* * *

As had been the case in decades past, student life at Simpson during the mid-sixties balanced Greek and independent living, cultural offerings and social good times, varsity and intramural athletics and an array of traditional events that punctuated each academic year. If any one element of undergraduate life stood out during those years, it surely was varsity athletics. And even though most Simpson teams lost a lot more contests than they won, student loyalty remained true and morale high.

In his second year as Simpson's football coach, Ken Heizer produced in the fall of 1963 a winning team. At least with a 5–4 record it won more games than it lost. The season started off with three conference wins, but in the next game at Upper Iowa Simpson's nationally ranked quarterback, Tony Spencer, was injured and lost for the rest of the season. Disastrous losses to Central (62–0), Parsons and league champion Luther marred an otherwise good season. George Yaniger was named Little All American. He and Al Paone, both of them "imports" who transferred to Simpson to play under Heizer, were named to the N.A.I.A. all-district team, and the two of them, together with fullback Glenn Kuehl, made the all-conference team. The 1964 season was even better, as the team posted a 6–3 record, with Spencer, Jerry Brumit, linebacker Al Paone and center Gary Hargis named to all-conference honors. After the Homecoming victory that year, students demonstrated on campus, demanding the cancellation of Monday's classes. The faculty refused, and responsible students were disgusted with the demonstrators' behavior. Charlie Turner thought the whole thing childish, and said so in the *Simpsonian*: "These rejuvenated infants also threw firecrackers in large quantities, which almost blew up Mother Kester [the housemother in Kresge Hall] and regardless of our feelings toward Mother Kester, blowing her up is to most of us an approach that is to be condemned."[165]

Although the 1965 season, the year they were calling the Redmen "The Crimson Wave," with its 3-6 record, was a disappointment, three Simpson seniors made the all-conference team: Craig Saunders, Gary Hargis and Lyle Loebach. And tackles Loebach and Bob Baier were both drafted by professional football teams, Loebach by the Houston Oilers and Baier by the Detroit Lions.[166]

When the following spring Ken Heizer resigned to accept a defensive coaching position at Iowa State University, Simpson recruited John L. Sullivan of Iowa Falls, head coach of football and track at Ellsworth Junior College.[167] His first season at Simpson the team won three and lost five games. The next year, however, was a different story as Simpson exploded for a 7-1-1 season, losing only to Central 26-14 before a record crowd of 2,500 at Neff Field in late September. When the Redmen defeated Luther that year for the first time since 1949, students mobbed the president's home demanding once again a day off the following Monday, presumably to allow time to recover from the wonder of it all. John turned them down. "Come back when you win the conference championship." He repented to the faculty at its next meeting, the "reckless" promise he had made under pressure. Still, at season's end the president, after conferring with the academic dean, gave students a Monday off for *almost* winning the conference. "Thanks for Mon." read a scrawled sign hung over Dean Walt's door. It was a good year. Freshman quarterback Joe Blake set a Simpson record, passing 1,295 yards for twelve touchdowns. Blake, an Indianola boy, was one of five Redmen named to the 1967 all-conference team; the others included end Jim Henderson from Toronto, Ontario, offensive tackle Don Federwitz from Chilton, Wisconsin, center Jerry Lafferty from Des Moines and guard Gordon Weber from Ackley.

If Simpson's football fortunes were vastly improved, its record in basketball ranged from fair to little short of dismal. Coach Les Deaton's 1963-64 team did quite well, with an 8-8 record—and fourth place—in conference play and 13-10 overall. Junior Tom Hensley made the all-conference team and led Simpson's scoring with 371 points for the season.[168] The following years, however, were disappointing; Simpson made a 7-17 record in 1964-65 and ranked the next year dead last in the conference with only four wins all season. Nor did their play much improve when Dick Starr took over coaching duties from Les Deaton, who continued coaching in other sports. Starr's first year produced an unenviable conference record of 3-11 (6-15 overall), but the team did show new resolve. The *Zenith* put it well: "Under Coach Starr, the Simpson team displayed a new vitality and perseverance."[169] They would all hope for better days.

In other sports, with the single exception of golf, Simpson teams ranged from mediocre to poor. In 1964 the baseball team produced a 4-13 record, in 1968 a 6-17 season, and the years in between were not much better. The 1968 nine saw junior Jack Blake earn all-conference honors.[170] About the best Simpson could do in track was fifth place in conference meets in 1964 and 1966 and second in its own Redman Relays those same years. Although 1965 was generally a poor track year, Tom Hensley did set a new Simpson record of 1.556 in the 880-yard run.[171] The cross-country team shared the woes of track. The 1967 tennis team did well, placing fourth in the conference and playing surprisingly well in the nationals in Florida. In wrestling Simpson men had their best year in 1967, when they went 9-9-1 overall. But it was in golf that Simpson men shone. In 1966 the team scored first place in N.A.I.A. District 15 and second place in N.A.I.A. nationally, with Bill O'Connor the medalist in both events. In 1967 the team won the Iowa Conference and repeated in 1968.

Simpson even tried a bit of intercollegiate soccer in 1964. Under the leadership of senior Musa Qutub from Jordan, an international team was put together and played five games with Drake, Omaha and Parsons, earning a respectable 2-2-1 record.[172] Unfortunately, however, soccer was a sport whose time had not yet come at Simpson. It would be many years before the College would again field a soccer team.

One of the problems with athletics was that it was costly. The cost of facilities, coaching staff, equipment and student grants-in-aid was difficult to justify. Ralph John pointed out to the board of trustees in 1966 that, for example, Iowa Conference grant-in-aid practices were "a real problem." The support of athletics, he said "by any kind of defensible standard . . . is excessive at Simpson." Yet he found it necessary in order "to make even a modest showing in the community of our competition." His remarks were no doubt stimulated by inquiries from the North Central Association, the accrediting agency making its first investigation of Simpson in fourteen years. The N.C.A. asked John, "How do you justify the disproportionate amount of your student aid resources going to athletics?"[173] He conceded that it was indeed difficult to justify the practice. What he might have added, but did not, was that no grants-in-aid whatever went to women athletes. All women's sports were still intramural, still not rating as much as one page in the *Zenith* of those years. But the answer was not to compound the problem by subsidizing female athletes. It would be better somehow to stop giving athletic grants altogether. That, too, was an idea whose time had not yet come at Simpson.

* * *

Aside from intercollegiate or intramural athletics, the eight campus Greek organizations commanded more powerful loyalty among their members than did any other activity, involving a fair proportion of the student body, indeed well over half of the resident undergraduates. Their popularity continued to rest on the opportunities afforded their members for human interaction and personal growth in a corporate living group, their provision of social good times at modest cost, their intramural sports competitions and traditional activities and above all a sense of belonging. By the mid-sixties membership was at an all-time high, and all eight organizations were strong. The chapter of Delta Zeta, installed in the fall of 1963 while Hurford Stone was acting president of the College, was doing well and showing real promise.

It was in the fall of 1963 that the Kappa Theta Psis, having through the years resisted the blandishments of several national fraternities, finally agreed to accept a national charter. They could take their pick, for any national fraternity would be attracted to a local with a strong group of undergraduates, an alumni body of more than six hundred and a fine new house. More than that, the acting president of the college was a Kappa alumnus, as was the chairman of the board of trustees, banker Ralph McGee of Osceola. Their choice of national fraternity, Delta Upsilon, a venerable organization founded at Williams College in 1834, was influenced by the fact that board member Luther Hill was an alumnus of DU's mother chapter and Jim Wallace, who succeeded McGee as board chairman in 1965, was a DU alumnus from the University of Pennsylvania.

Officials of Delta Upsilon visited the campus in the fall of 1963 and conferred with Stone and undergraduate members.[174] Negotiations were continued by McGee and Dr. G. A. Grant '17, the local Kappa alumni leader, and officers of the undergraduate chapter. Upon the approval of the executive committee of Simpson's board of trustees, the Delta Upsilon national organization made its own decision and granted a charter to Kappa Theta Psi.[175] The formal installation took place on Saturday, May 30, 1964.[176] Undergraduates were pleased with the chartering. "Going national will help the whole campus as well as just the house," said undergraduate president Roger Underwood.[177] With some nostalgia a Kappa wrote for the *Zenith*, "We will no longer be an independent organization, but in our hearts we will always live up to the ideals set up in 1902."[178] Many Kappa alumni had misgivings; some agreed that it was best to "go along with the boys," while others not surprisingly opposed the move because it took away the uniqueness of the old Kappa Theta Psi.

Several of the fraternities and sororities at Simpson won honors in their own national organizations. Outstanding was the performance of Lambda Chi Alpha in 1965 when the Simpson chapter ranked first in the nation in scholarship among the fraternity's 137 chapters.[179] Speaking of scholarship, the Lambda Chis and SAEs tended to share top honors in men's scholarship on campus, while Alpha Chi Omega won the women's grade cup more often than not. After 1965, however, the *Simpsonian* declined to print scholarship averages, even though the office of the registrar obligingly compiled them. And in 1967 the student senate voted not to make scholarship awards any more. "It is demeaning to independent housing units and smacks of elitism," was the explanation.[180]

Clearly, there was dissatisfaction with the Greeks on campus. Student dean Wally Wiser reported to the board of trustees: "Some think the [Greek] system is contrary to the goals and objectives inherent in a liberal arts philosophy of education." Some people "don't like the regimentation and ritualistic traditions of the Greeks." His remarks were in part a response to a "practical problem"; a number of national Greek-letter societies had recently made inquiry about establishing chapters at Simpson, and he questioned the wisdom of expanding the Greek system.[181] Dean Wiser's words were mild, however, when compared to the broadside against the Greeks published in the *Simpsonian* by new faculty member Dr. Eugene "Rip" Peyroux, whose enthusiasm for theater was matched by his distaste for what he called the "chicken yard atmosphere" created by the Greeks. Rising to the defense of the Greeks, not unexpectedly, was Joe Walt, who proclaimed the value of worthwhile voluntary associations, and the *Simpsonian* published a letter from Neil Goeppinger, a junior SAE from Boone, questioning Peyroux's judgment.[182] Chaplain Jim Allen's response to Peyroux's outburst was more succinct: "Re Dr. Peyroux's open letter to the editor, HURRAH. Sincerely, James E. Allen."[183] In its turn, Allen's response drew the fire of Lambda Chi sophomore Steve Dasenbrook, who wrote "If [Dr. Jim Allen] is so moved to criticize the Greeks by his "Hurrah" to Dr. Peyroux's letter, why in the name of God doesn't he write one of his own?"[184] The best response, however, came in the form of query: "Dr. Peyroux's next play—a Greek tragedy?"[185] That same year the fraternities and sororities pledged a record 149 freshmen, nearly half of the entering students.[186]

The service and honor societies continued to flourish. Alpha Phi Omega was in the midst of one of its periodic revivals. Pi Kappa Delta was active, hosting a speech tourney in 1966 in which senior Fred Jones was a standout. That same year Simpson hosted a three-day Iowa Inter-Collegiate Forensics Association tournament with eighteen colleges participating. The Simpson team placed fourth, with senior Roger Grant carrying off honors.[187] Beta Beta Beta raised money at the Carver Science Hall by selling coffee for five cents a cup and doughnuts for seven cents each.[188] Sigma Tau Delta, under Ruth Jackson's practiced eye, continued to publish the *Password*, the student directory, and the *Sequel*. The Home Economics Club enrolled forty-seven women and three men. Blackfriars and Alpha Psi Omega included most of the theater majors, while Phi Mu Alpha and Mu Phi Epsilon corralled the music majors. The Student Education Association curiously enrolled only women as members, while the Epsilon Sigma scholarship honorary continued to honor the top seniors and a selected few junior students.

The burgeoning foreign language program stimulated the chartering of a chapter of Alpha Mu Gamma honor society in the spring of 1968 with thirty-three students and several faculty members.[189] And the Bizad club served a fair share of those majoring in business and accounting. The S Club continued its antics, especially the modest hazing of freshmen students, and as late as the fall of 1967 attempted to enforce the wearing of red and gold beanies by new students.[190]

Student government during the mid-sixties was interesting and for the most part competent. When Ralph John arrived in late 1963, student body president James Vawn was trying unsuccessfully to fend off a revolution after three student officers resigned in protest against Vawn's policies, none of which were made very clear. Students decided to take a new look at their system of governance.[191] "A favorite pastime of students is the revision of their constitution," John observed to the board of trustees. This time the burning issue was the creation of a student judiciary, which would appropriately include both administrators and students.[192] Student elections were hotly contested, and voting was enthusiastic, especially in 1965 when 485 voters cast 540 ballots.[193]

For the most part the *Simpsonian* was well edited during these years, especially so under Roger Grant (1965–66) and Gordon Brown (1967–68). Brown had great fun taking issue with Grinnell College's *Scarlet and Black*, which billed itself as "the oldest college newspaper west of the Mississippi." He proved that the *Simpsonian* was one year older than Grinnell's paper, reporting with insufferable righteousness that his investigation of this weighty matter had led the *Scarlet and Black* "off its path of falsehood and misrepresentation."[194] Near the end of the school year Brown editorialized that on the whole "it has been an interesting year. As a crusading newspaper, we've had our ups and downs. The grand design for a campus mail system got lost in the mail, the [much criticized] Religious Life Council is still in business (and still not speaking to me), and Grinnell's 'Scarlet and Black' still claims to be 'The oldest college newspaper west of the Mississippi.' "[195] Although it was not imaginative, the *Zenith* continued to chronicle student life in words and photographs. Some years it was pedestrian, but the 1965 edition, said the *Simpsonian*, "hit an all-time low."[196] A week after its appearance, editor Tom Teague was hanged in effigy.[197]

Religious life on the campus, under the leadership of Chaplain Wally Wiser and his successor, Jim Allen, touched relatively few students. Recognizing the increasing religious heterogeneity of the student population, the Methodist Student Movement in 1963 was incorporated into a new, ecumenical Christian organization.[198] Midweek vespers was a thing of the past. Chapel, still required weekly for all students when Ralph John came to Simpson, had become mostly secularized, but students still didn't like it. Many in the growing contingent of Catholic students were quite convinced that there lurked somewhere a dastardly plot to preach the gospel of John Wesley to them. The opposition from all sides grew so shrill that in the fall of 1964 President John persuaded the staff to require only one convocation or chapel each month.[199]

Still, some students continued to see old-time Methodist values informing Simpson's policies and teaching. Although he allowed that there were a few gifted faculty members—and he named them—senior Phil McBlain wrote that "the college has always substituted, and continues to substitute, piety, the Puritan Ethic, for the promotion of learning. Learning . . . is fraught with dangers, of indecision, of doubt, of despair. Our college . . . tries to discourage us in our search for true knowledge. . . . Instead, they tell us to accept their truths."[200]

Whatever their moral and religious proclivities, Simpson students were expected to observe the Simpson Code, contained in a document setting forth the somewhat liberalized standards of behavior on and off campus. Adopted at the end of 1963, during the early weeks of the John administration, it was approved by the faculty, although an increasing number of them expressed discomfort with their role as arbiters of student conduct, a subject they regarded with growing incomprehension. And predictably student editor John Hedges dismissed the new code as "trivial, stupid and inadequate," although he did not specify why indeed it was.[201] Code or no code, students behaved for the most part reasonably well, although there were egregious exceptions, like the day early in 1968 when a freshman accidentally shot one of his classmates in the throat while playing with the latter's .22 pistol in his Barker Hall dormitory room. As the injured student—who fortunately later recovered—was taken away in an ambulance, Indianola's new police chief, Earl Pace, ordered an inspection of the building, and their search turned up an astonishing number of weapons, mostly hunting rifles, in student rooms, enough guns to equip a small army. College regulations, to be sure, called for storing all firearms in the resident counselor's office in the dormitory, a rule obviously honored in the breach. For several years after that, people could not resist referring to the dormitory as "Fort Barker."[202]

Not all College activities were as exciting as gunplay in the residence halls, but the traditional events scattered through the school year, together with exceptionally good cultural offerings and light entertainments, provided a balanced cocurricular program for those students who chose to participate. Homecoming, with its parade and house decorations, its royalty and Tomahawk award, the big football game followed by an all-campus dance, was still the most popular event in the fall. All-College Sing, omitted in 1963–64 because of a dispute over ground-rules between sponsor Phi Mu Alpha Sinfonia and the participating singing groups, returned harmoniously the next year. Predictably Lambda Chi Alpha regularly won the men's division—their 1968 win was the eleventh in a row—and the SAEs were always second, while the Trideltas were either first or second nearly every year in the women's division. Similarly, the barbershop quartet competition attracted a large number of entrants, most of them from among the Greek societies, with the Lambda Chis, SAEs and Alpha Chis sharing honors. The Miniature Orpheum skit night was revived in the spring of 1964, but died out again after the 1967 performance, not so much because of indelicate language but for lack of interest among contestants.

To compensate for the discontinuance of the Christian Liberal Arts Festival, Ralph John determined to bring a variety of speakers to Simpson, their appearances carefully spaced throughout the academic year, and during the mid-sixties the lineup of speakers and entertainers was impressive. They included poets Paul Engle, James Dickey and Alastair Read; popular sociologist Vance Packard, author of *The Hidden Persuaders*, who was so taken with Brenton Student Center director Lu Jean Cole that he quoted her in his next book; Joseph Fletcher, whose *Situation Ethics* challenged Americans' concepts of right and wrong; and outstanding British historian Arnold Toynbee, whose multivolume *Study of History* represented the most profound synthesis of the development of world civilizations put together in the twentieth century.[203] Another historian of note, liberal William Appleton Williams of the University of Wisconsin spoke on contemporary student protest and the war in Vietnam.[204] A good speaker who was ill received was Sergio Rojas, former Cuban ambassador to the United Kingdom, whose tirade against the Fidel Castro regime drew only twenty-eight mostly hostile listeners. Because the Six-Day War of 1967 brought the Middle East to everyone's attention, several speakers appeared at Simpson in support of either Israel or the Arabs. Remarkably effective was Dr. Abdul Aziz Said from American University, whose reasonableness impressed his listeners. Rabbi Balfour Brickner spoke brilliantly at the spring convocation in 1968. Yet not everyone was persuaded by the oratory of those who held forth on the Arab-Israel issue. Few who were present that day at a convocation at the Indianola Methodist Church would forget feisty Musa Qutub, one of several Jordanian—really Palestinian—students at Simpson, who charged up the aisle of the church, shaking his fist at the pro-Israel speaker, shouting "Lies, all lies!"[205] Equally controversial was Edward Hoffman who advocated resistance to military conscription—he called it the "Selective Slavery System"—and admitted when pressed by the faculty that he rather preferred anarchy to order. And hardly less disputatious was Dr. Alan F. Guttmacher, president of the national Planned Parenthood organization, who called for liberalization of "hypocritical" abortion laws. At different times two members of the British Parliament spoke, and spoke well. Conversely, probably the biggest disappointment was author Erskine Caldwell, whose novels were still widely read but whose appearance at Simpson revealed a burnt-out cinder of a man, consumed by terminal ennui.

Surely the most memorable speaker during these years was Alex Haley, who worked with Malcolm X in writing *The Autobiography of Malcolm X* and who had become perhaps the best-known black writer in America. He was invited to speak at Simpson in May, 1968, on "The Virus of Violence." When he arrived on campus, people were impressed with Haley as a man of great single-mindedness, remarkable discipline and a modest but adamantine self-confidence. At a small supper in the President's Dining Room at the student center just before his evening address, Haley asked the faculty and students present if they really wanted to listen to yet one more speech on "the black problem," or indeed "the white problem," depending on one's point of view. "Would you let me talk about what

I'd like to talk about?" he asked. In accordance with the incontestable theory that a speaker will be more interesting when permitted to choose his subject, the group assured him that he should do as he pleased. "I'm working on a new book," he said. "The working title of it is 'Before This Anger.' I'd like to talk about it."

The book Haley was researching would not be published for eight more years and would be renamed *Roots*, destined to become a best-seller and subject of one of the most popular television series of all time.[206] Haley talked that May evening about his research, captivating his audience with the account of how he traced the story of his family back to its origins in The Gambia in West Africa. He related the history of his maternal forebear, one Kunta Kinte, who was captured, clapped into chains and transported on a slave ship to America, where he was sold to a John Waller at Annapolis, Maryland, in 1767.

When his account of "the African" and his descendants was concluded and the audience was departing, one of his hearers stayed behind to have a word with Haley. He was Wally Wiser, at that time dean of students, who approached the speaker and said simply, "My name is Waller Wiser. I am a direct descendant of John Waller of Annapolis, Maryland. I believe, sir, that it was my great-great-great-great grandfather who bought your great-great-great-great grandfather."

"You're surely joking," replied Haley with a mixture of astonishment and incredulity.

"I've never been more serious in my life," replied Wiser.

That evening was born a friendship that lasted until Haley's untimely death in 1992. They sat down together during the next days and compared genealogies, pushing the line back to the one-time relationship between John Waller, plantation owner, and Kunta Kinte, "the African" among Haley's ancestors. And neither of them could escape the meaning of two centuries of change wrought by blood, time and good will, allowing two men, one black and one white, to meet in a small Iowa town as unquestioned equals, each regarding the other with respect, and in time, growing affection.

* * *

Music continued to enrich the life of the whole Simpson community. Student and faculty recitals, operas produced with local College talent, concerts by the College band or the Simpson-Community Symphony Orchestra under the direction of Sam Minasian and performances by the choir or madrigal singers provided an abundant musical fare for the College and townspeople alike. Under young Robert Larsen's gifted direction, opera was taking its place as a permanent art form at Simpson. It helped in the beginning to have singers like Bob Goodloe, Carol Stuart and David Nott, all of whom appeared in the fall 1963 performance of *The Marriage of Figaro*, followed the next year by a brilliant production of *The Magic Flute*, with a cast of faculty and students. Soon Larsen was essaying contemporary opera with the performance of Menotti's *The Consul* in 1968. So successful were these presentations that Larsen brought Bob Goodloe and Carol Stuart back to sing in the Des Moines Civic Opera Association's production of *La Boheme* in the summer of 1965. The maestro was testing the cultural waters in Des Moines to ascertain whether it would be feasible to inaugurate a proper opera company in the capital city.

Larsen also directed the Simpson madrigal singers, whose Christmas dinner presentation was on its way to becoming a College tradition. A *Simpsonian* writer in 1964 remembered "the glow of candles, the scent of spicy pine, the savory aroma of mutton broth, the blare of golden trumpets" as the singers, clad in Elizabethan finery, regaled the diners with song.

Popular artists, including Dave Brubeck and Count Basie, the pianist Peter Nero, the New Christie Minstrels and the Chad Mitchell Trio provided music for those who found opera or madrigal singing stuffy. One member of the Mitchell Trio was a youngster by the name of John Denver. The students liked him so much that they would invite him back later for a solo appearance in the campus coffee house.

On a more academic note, Don Koontz's Aerospace Institutes met annually in late fall, drawing a large number of air enthusiasts and clergymen, while the summer program in American studies for secondary school faculty featured distinguished scholars through the summer of 1968. And of course commencement in the spring continued to draw huge crowds.

No event on campus, however, attracted a larger attendance than the crowd that thronged to the campus to watch the burning of Hopper Terrace, the last of the postwar barracks. The completion of the new residence hall on Franklin Street made possible the abandonment of Hopper Terrace, which the Indianola Volunteer Fire Department burned, or tried to burn, as a practice exercise. Actually, the audience was disappointed and the fire department embarrassed when they could not get the barracks to burn. In view of the many warnings issued to the College about violations of the fire code in the barracks, the firemen were truly chagrined. Perhaps they had not noticed that the construction was of cinder block and asbestos siding. Later the Simpson maintenance people had to bring in bulldozers to finish the job in a somewhat less colorful way. Few mourned the loss of the superannuated barracks.

* * *

During the mid-sixties Simpson mourned the loss of a number of people who had served the College at one time or another in their lives. Rex Dunn, whose handsome contribution made possible the erection of the new library, died in California June 22, 1963.[207] Board member Harry A. Bullis, retired chairman of General Mills, died September 28, 1963, leaving a generous bequest to the College.

When Dr. John P. Morley died in Los Angeles on January 31, 1964, at the age of 96, Simpson lost its oldest living alumnus and one of its staunchest supporters.[208] He was justifiably proud of his unique record of never having missed a Simpson commencement in the seventy years since he graduated in 1893, recalling that since about 1920 he had stayed with his cousin Don Berry and his wife during his annual visits. Morley had attended the Simpson Academy as a prep student, continued at the College for four years as an undergraduate, taught a number of years in the Department of Philosophy and was vice-president of the College in 1918–19. As an academy student he had founded the Phi Lamda Mu fraternity and led the local group to a charter of Sigma Alpha Epsilon in 1889. His wife, Hattie Berry Morley, who preceded him in death, was the sister of Mary Berry.

Vera Ingram Mott '07 died September 13, 1964, at Columbia, Missouri, followed only weeks later by her Pulitzer Prize winning husband, Frank Luther Mott '07, Simpson alumnus and former faculty member, October 23, 1964.

Henry A. Wallace's death, November 8, 1965, occurred regrettably a year-and-a-half before Simpson's old science building was named in his honor. The former U.S. secretary of agriculture and vice president under Franklin D. Roosevelt, had shown great interest in Simpson during his entire adult life, especially because of the good will of his wife Ilo, a Simpson alumna.

Simpsonians were especially saddened by the death of Hurford Stone, March 2, 1966, at Oakland, California, at the age of seventy-three. Known not only to the alumni of his own undergraduate days, he had brightened the lives of faculty, students and townspeople during his months as interim president before the arrival of Ralph and Dorothy John.

* * *

Anyone old enough to remember the event will recall exactly where he or she was the moment the news was flashed reporting the gunning down of President John F. Kennedy in Dallas. Ralph John would never forget. Together with a number of other Simpson people, he was attending the weekly Rotary meeting that Friday at Shannon's Restaurant down on the square when, just as the meeting was about to be adjourned, someone hurried into the room to announce that the president had been shot. As stunned members stood silently, the Reverend Glen Lamb offered a prayer for the president's recovery. But as they slowly filed out of the restaurant, they learned from Pat Shannon's television set that the president had died.

It was as if the whole nation had been kicked in the stomach. Hardly anyone seemed able to function normally, "shocked beyond anything we have ever seen," wrote Lew Kimer in the Indianola paper. "We are sure," he said, "that Friday, November 22, will go down as one of the blackest days in our memory."[209]

That weekend nearly everything shut down in Indianola, in keeping with the rest of America, as a nation mourned. Monday classes were cancelled out of respect for the president's funeral, and, in view of the upcoming Thanksgiving holiday, Tuesday classes were dismissed as well, classes to be made up on Saturday, December 7.

At the Indianola Breakfast Club on Saturday, the twenty-third, Ralph John spoke "about the heavy responsibilities of the office of President of the United States," recalling the earlier, happier day when he placed the hood of an honorary degree upon Kennedy at American University. Reflecting on the events of the past twenty-four hours, he said "I was shocked at the thought that this could happen in the United States. We know it can happen in nations where governments are unstable, but not in this country where the government *is* stable and where we are considered to have a high level of education and sophistication."[210]

The rest of our mid-sixties era coincided with the presidency of Kennedy's successor, Lyndon Johnson, during whose term-and-a-half of office—he buried Barry Goldwater at the polls in 1964—the nation saw forward-looking domestic legislation like the 1964 Civil Rights Act and at the same time an intensifying of the Cold War internationally. Especially after the Gulf of Tonkin Resolution of 1964, Americans became more deeply involved in Vietnam, leading to the decision to permit U.S. troops to assume a combat role there in mid-1965. The ousting of Nikita Khrushchev by the supporters of hard-liner Leonid Brezhnev in the U.S.S.R. in 1964 and Mao Tse Tung's Great Proletarian Cultural Revolution in China after 1966 seemed to make the world a very dangerous place indeed.

As the U.S. sank deeper into the quagmire of Vietnam, with more than half a million troops there by 1968, protests against the war forced President Johnson to declare that "I shall not seek and I will not accept the nomination of my party as your president." Less than a week later, when a lone gunman shot and killed Martin Luther King at a Memphis motel, America lost its most powerful, effective, eloquent civil rights crusader. Only two months after that, in the midst of the presidential election campaign, Robert F. Kennedy was assassinated at a Los Angeles celebration of his California primary victory.

The mid-sixties witnessed college and university students, at first primarily on the West and East Coasts, becoming aware of and responding to national and international events as they never had before. Soon enough student unrest would reach the heartland of America. And when it did, Simpson would never again be the same.

XIX

The Student Revolt 1968–75

It was inevitable that the winds of Berkeley would blow eastward across the land, a portent of the storm to come in many of the colleges and universities of America. It was understandable, too, that the storm would rage with uneven force—intensely in some places, mildly in others, and scarcely felt at all in those schools either protected by the bulwarks of religious rectitude or numbed by the novocaine of indifference. Compared to Berkeley or Columbia or Kent State, the storm at Simpson was mild; compared to its sister institutions in Iowa, it was strong.

It started innocently enough, not a wind at all, but more nearly a breath of freedom. Most college faculties and administrations were taken by surprise when they discovered that the new generation of students in the late sixties was far more experienced and worldly-wise than those who had come to college a decade or so earlier. That is not to say they were more mature or were capable of better judgment than their predecessors, although there were those who asserted that indeed they were. Reared in an age of instant communication, of increased openness in personal relations, of broken barriers in dress, language and behavior, of changing family relationships, of secularization, students—or most of them—were prepared to challenge the traditions of college life and governance.

One can fairly well date the beginning of the real student revolt at Simpson in the presidential campaign of 1968, which pitted Richard Nixon against Hubert Humphrey. Although President Lyndon Johnson had withdrawn from the race because of the growing opposition to the war in Vietnam, both Nixon and Humphrey were committed to carrying on the war, hoping for an early and successful outcome. The only powerful political voice calling for ending the conflict in Southeast Asia was Senator Eugene McCarthy, whose third-party candidacy captured the imagination of thousands of young people who thronged to join the "Kiddie Crusade."

The McCarthy movement caught on powerfully at Simpson. Student leaders not only assisted in organizing support for the senator at Simpson and in Indianola, but sent teams of eager partisans out across the state. During the spring of 1968 a good share of the McCarthy Iowa campaign was directed by twenty-nine-year-old Don Gibson, a Simpson alumnus (1960) teaching history at the College for a year, filling in for Joe Walt who was serving as dean of academic affairs. Students flocked to the "movement," worked unceasingly with Gibson, who during these months discovered political organizing skills that would eventually take him to Washington. Politicized students were joined by a fair share of the faculty, especially after the riotous Democratic National Convention in Chicago, and shared in both the quixotic McCarthy campaign that fall and the disappointment at the Nixon victory at the polls.

* * *

Often Simpson people who lived through the several-years-long student rebellion are asked, "What in the world did the students want, anyway?" What was so important that it could very nearly bring the work of the College to a halt? These are fair questions and deserve a considered answer. It seems to me that the students wanted several things, all of them understandable if one places their aims into the context of the times.

First, they wanted what they liked to call "participatory democracy." By this they meant the freedom, indeed the right, to participate in making the decisions and formulating the policies that affected their own lives, especially in the College itself. At Simpson this took the form of demands for participation in faculty meetings and voting membership on faculty committees, the creation of an all-student judiciary to handle violations of the rules of the College community, voting membership in the board of trustees, participation in determining academic requirements and the right to evaluate courses and the faculty who taught them.

Secondly, students sought the elimination of institutional restraints on the conduct of their personal lives. They objected mightily to anything that smacked of paternalism, of regulation, of an institution *in loco parentis*, ranging from required chapel or dress codes to residence hall rules governing closing hours and visitation privileges. They knew, if the faculty did not, that the sexual revolution was taking place, and most of them were quite anxious to join it.

Thirdly, they were overwhelmingly in favor of civil rights for minorities. Though most of them, even those from urban areas, had experienced little association with blacks or Indians or Hispanics or Jews, they recognized the compelling merits of the massive civil rights movement. However awkward they might be when confronted with their own inherited attitudes, they were ready to make common cause with minorities in their worthy effort to create an integrated America.

Fourthly, they opposed the Vietnam War and the draft with growing intensity. They wanted to end the war, and they wanted it now. They realized that male college students were in a way a privileged class, deferred from military service so long as they remained in school, showing "normal progress toward a degree," but they sought by ending the war to bring the soldiers in Vietnam home before more of them were sacrificed in what surely was the most unpopular war in America's history.

Finally, they asserted the primacy of individual rights. That meant the right to dress as one pleased, wear one's hair as one pleased, above all to think and act as one pleased, "doing one's own thing." The powerful stress on individualism meant an equally powerful opposition to any institution, whether government or church or school which was seen to inhibit self-expression.

If these were, generally speaking, the aims of the students—and certainly of those faculty and administrative people who supported them—there were some things the movement was *not*.

First and foremost, it was decidedly not a Communist movement, as some of its opponents, ranging from Richard Nixon to the Young Americans for Freedom charged. While surely some Communists were delighted to see American students opposing the policies of their national government, most Simpson students would have found the charge of Communism little short of ludicrous. For one thing, Communists were accustomed to creating tight bands of true believers organized hierarchically, taking orders from above, strictly disciplined, constantly on the lookout for any act of deviation or insubordination. The student protest in America, with its emphasis on individualism, suffered constantly from its failure to organize much of anything beyond the matter of the moment. So opposed were these youngsters to hierarchy that often they were unable or unwilling to allow their leaders to lead. One observer, when describing the militant Students for a Democratic Society at Simpson, called them the "shock troops of nihilism." That may not have been fair, but it was a lot closer than the labeling of such a group as "Communists."

Neither was the student revolution monolithic, either in its aims or its methods. While nearly all of the protesters were sympathetic to the aims of the movement as a whole, large numbers of them pursued one avenue of protest more assiduously than others. Some, for example, focused on the removal of barriers in the way of personal freedom of choice; others—including a good share of the men—directed their energies to the demand that the war and the draft cease; still others—especially the growing corps of black students—fought to change the institutions that prevented minorities from realizing their own potential as free Americans.

Nor was the movement universal. A few students actively opposed some or all of the demands of the protesters, but their numbers were few. Others viewed the revolution negatively, but avoided confrontation, a few preferring to apply themselves to their studies. Still others frankly didn't care, lavishing their time and attention on social events or athletics or off-campus employment. Similarly, there were those who generally favored the aims of the movement, but declined an activist role in it, preferring to stand on the sidelines and watch the protesters parade.

* * *

Simpson, like many other colleges in the land, changed profoundly during the six or seven years of student revolt. But not all would agree about the meaning of that change. Some found it powerfully liberating, healthy, exciting and permanently efficacious. Others found it—or at least aspects of it—frightening, vulgar, given to vapid sloganeering and outrageous posturing, and in the short run destructive. Probably both the supporters and the detractors of the protest movement are at least partly right in their judgment. To arrive at any sort of fair evaluation, we must look at the record of what actually happened at Simpson during those few years.

Driven partly by student demands and partly by their own inclination, faculty and administrators took up seriously the issue of participatory democracy. They agreed to permit students to attend regular faculty meetings and for some of the student officers to have speaking privileges in those meetings.[1] Gradually they accepted student representation in faculty committees, one or more students in each committee, with the single exception of the Faculty Personnel Committee, which dealt with sensitive issues of promotion, tenure and reappointment. And even on that one protected committee, faculty agreed to accept student course evaluations as one of the important elements in personnel actions. All student voting representatives on faculty committees were appointed by the president of the student body with approval by the Student Senate.[2] The consequence was to give the student president far more appointive power in faculty committees than that possessed by the president of the College.[3]

In an honest effort to put more responsibility into the hands of students, the campus judiciary was crafted anew, providing for a student-staffed body which would examine and judge all student violations of the Simpson Code. The Simpson Code itself underwent a liberalization. The point was that student conduct should be more nearly amenable to student control. Still, in matters of serious code violations, the student judiciary made recommendations to the dean of students, who of course answered to the president of the College.[4]

Recognizing the important policy-making role of the College's board of trustees, students demanded voting membership on the board and membership on the board's student affairs committee. While the board was inclined to accede to the student demand, a practical consideration forced a compromise only partially satisfying to the students. Board members were elected for three-year terms, and the board refused to make an exception for the student representative. Therefore, it was agreed that the student body could elect each year a senior student who would serve on the board for three years, at the close of which term the students could choose a successor. And because board membership terms commenced at the annual board meeting at commencement time, the senior elected would serve effectively only as an alumnus or alumna.[5]

In a further move to democratize, President Ralph John made himself more accessible than ever to students. He urged students or student groups to come to see him in his office, and many an evening he trooped over to the Brenton Student Center for a "rap session" with activist students. Some of these discussions were enlightening and productive; others were unfortunately unpleasant, even abusive. However, throughout hours of give and take the president never lost his poise, his confidence, or his temper, even when verbally whiplashed by students whose understanding of civility was markedly deficient. For his willingness to be accessible to students, for not hedging when difficult questions were asked, for his everlasting good humor under fire, John won the praise of all the students, even those who thought his liberal policies weren't liberal enough.[6]

There were those, of course, who thought Ralph John's policies were much too liberal, that he was "letting the students run the College," that the campus was "wide open." Few of these critics, to be sure, were students. And often John said to fellow administrators and faculty alike that it made more sense to meet the desires of the students before their wishes became nonnegotiable demands. It was better to be reasonably and responsibly proactive, he believed, than to capitulate to student demands in a sea of acrimony.

Thus when students raised the question of dormitory closing hours for women, the president helped to convince the faculty—which still had jurisdiction over that sort of thing—that the old ten-o'clock closing time for women's dormitories and sorority houses was an unnecessarily harsh curfew. Hours were extended and ultimately virtually eliminated altogether.[7]

It was much the same with dormitory visitation, that is, permitting male students to visit the sleeping rooms of coeds and vice versa. The hours during which visitation was permitted were extended again and again, until twenty-four hour visitation was the rule in the residence halls, if not in the more conservative sororities, which elected—or were coerced by their national officers or alumnae—to maintain a more decorous approach to the issue. Once such liberties were granted in the dormitories, it would be extremely difficult in later years to reimpose any kind of visitation restrictions, however sensible such limitations might seem.

An increasing number of students, especially those who were twenty-one years old or older, sought to avoid on-campus housing altogether, preferring to live in apartments or other, sometimes more exotic accommodations in town. Here College authorities had to exercise great care. As long as enrollments were high enough to fill all the dormitories without all the twenty-one-year-olds—or all the seniors—the housing policy could be generous and relaxed. But John and others, reminded of the obligations they had undertaken when Simpson received government loans to build new dormitories, could go only so far in meeting student requests to live off campus. Pledged to maintain a residential policy that would guarantee full residence hall occupancy in order to ensure amortization of the loans, the College's housing authorities were forced to be fairly conservative. Some students, of course, thought the College's rules were draconian, even before a downturn in enrollment after 1971 which necessitated more restrictive housing regulation.[8]

A casualty of the more liberal housing policies was the fraternity housemother, a time-honored institution which had long since been in fact mandatory for any student group that occupied either College- or privately-owned accommodations. Although women's groups, especially the four sororities, kept their housemothers or housemother-cooks, the men's housing units abandoned housemothers, one by one. At the SAE house the student need for "participatory democracy" took away the housemother's management of the food service, while their use of coarse language, signaling the abandonment of even the most fundamental principles of civility, drove the well-mannered and competent housemother to conclude that "I have no further role here." She departed, and neither the housing authorities nor the students mourned the loss of her presence in the house. It was perhaps worse at the DU house, where the students' self-destructive behavior would see the loss of their housemother as but one step in the extinction of the chapter itself. The ATOs and Lambda Chis, with housemothers of long standing, hung on a little longer, but soon enough they too retired these long-suffering women and never replaced them.[9]

Similarly, in the independent on-campus residence halls housemothers were replaced by "resident counselors," young and flexible and for the most part exceedingly resilient. Although they never really replaced the housemothers, they did maintain a modicum of restraint in an otherwise uninhibited environment.

Not dissociated from the general liberalization of student housing was the relaxation of the College rule about drinking on campus, especially in campus housing units. To be sure, violations of the College's alcohol policy were frequent, indeed common. Student ingenuity in finding ways to consume strong drink was a skill truly to be marveled at; student inventiveness in finding places to drink, with only minimum risk of detection, had been developed into a fine art. Still, the College, loath to condone drinking among students, held its ground on the principle that student purchase and consumption of alcohol was illegal for minors under local, state and federal law, and eighty percent of Simpson students were minors. When, however, the age of majority was lowered to eighteen, making ninety-eight percent of Simpson students adults by definition, the College's principal defense against alcohol collapsed. Students argued that their on-campus rooms at Barker Hall or at the ATO house were their castles and that if they wanted to have a six-pack of beer in the little refrigerator near their bed, they were clearly entitled to do so.[10] Women's housing units, especially the sororities, influenced by their more conservative national organizations and alumnae, maintained an alcohol policy far more restrictive than that of the College itself, the effect of which was not so much to curb drinking among the women as it was to limit the places where they could do it.

Required chapel was abandoned. The weekly chapel, or convocation, had been under fire for many years. But during the sixties the opponents grew in number and the level of their complaints became more shrill. There were also practical reasons for dropping required chapel. As full-time student enrollment grew it was impossible to shoehorn all the students into any one place on campus or into the sanctuary of Indianola's First United Methodist Church. Indeed, there was something to be said for gathering the whole "Simpson family" together once a week, but this was no longer physically possible. Further, as we have already noted, the growing cosmopolitanism of Simpson inevitably meant an increase of Catholic and other non-Protestant students who objected to what they deemed compulsory religion.

* * *

From the point of view of the faculty, both the democratization of governance and the liberalization of student life were overshadowed by the revolution that took place in the College's curriculum. The rather formidable set of all-college graduation requirements adopted in 1968, which included the Vital Center program along with a sixteen-hour freshman immersion into the history, literature and culture of the Western world, had moved against the stream of American higher education, which was caught up in a powerful, almost unstoppable move to liberalize curricula, to abandon universal requirements for a degree. At the same time, there were legitimate complaints about the way the freshman courses were taught. Classes, said the program's critics, were far too large. In the fall of 1969, for example, enrollment in Western Civilization was 159 and 174 in two lecture classes, and because the small-group discussion sections had been eliminated in the interest of economy, students found their huge classes cold and impersonal, certainly not interactive. The other components of the freshman core were also questioned, as were some of the other requirements. And there was more. Students charged that they were being forced into a "lock step" to a degree, each student submitting to the same set of requirements for graduation. Where was freedom to be an individual, where each student's needs would be determined by his or her educational goals?

The Educational Policy and Curriculum Committee was ready to revise but not abandon the required curriculum. In the spring of 1970 it reported to the faculty that some desirable alterations should be made, more nearly an act of fine-tuning the existing program. At its regular monthly meeting in February 1970, the faculty took up the proposals. Several academic departments, apparently convinced that their disciplines had been somehow slighted, attempted to introduce specific course requirements that would have overloaded the program if other segments had not been reduced as compensation. When yet one more faculty member moved the inclusion of yet another "101" course there was a sort of visible explosion among the faculty. In utter dismay, Joe Walt, after hastily scrawling a proposal on his knee, moved that Simpson abandon all-college requirements. Each student would simply complete a major and a total of thirty-five units (thirty-six in music)—a unit was equivalent to a one-semester course—with a 2.00 grade point average, "students' liberal arts 'requirements' to be determined by their own needs, producing a program worked out by them and their advisers." At least eleven of the thirty-five units had to be taken in areas of study outside the division of the major, hardly a restrictive provision. Thus there would be no "lock step" to a degree. Each student would find his or her own path to graduation, the academic integrity of the path to be determined by the approval of the adviser and the dean of academic affairs.[11] For Simpson, this was a revolution. Ralph John was delighted. "I didn't think we were ready for this," he said. Many faculty, like Walt, dismayed by the unfortunate display of tribalism, were inclined to take a chance on a "liberated" curriculum. After all, Harvard had already done the same thing. And if it was good enough for Harvard.... The matter was referred to the Educational Policy and Curriculum Committee, smoothed out, altered not at all in principle, presented to the whole faculty at its next regular meeting and passed overwhelmingly.[12] Students were ecstatic, and if they were, some faculty people suspected that the students knew something they did not. They would learn soon enough.

* * *

During the College's first century no thought was given to recruiting students from any particular segment of the population. Most Simpson students came from Iowa, where the minority population was small. Simpson was simply not accustomed to enrolling more than an occasional minority student and until the 1960s had experienced no pressure, from inside or outside, to do so.

Led mostly by an attack of conscience, Simpson's administration, faculty and many students determined to make special efforts to recruit qualified minority—especially black—students, not only in Iowa but in those urban areas where blacks were far more numerous. It wasn't easy; other colleges and universities were doing so too. Even with offers of scholarship assistance, qualified black students—defined as being at least above the bottom quarter of their graduating class and with a twenty-fifth percentile score on entrance examinations—a woefully low standard—were hard to find. Too often the director of admissions lamented the loss of a good black prospective student to Dartmouth or U.C.L.A.

In the fall of 1969 Simpson appointed an able and attractive black graduate, Garfield Jackson, as an admissions counselor whose task was primarily to recruit disadvantaged students.[13]

One part of the problem of minority admissions was lack of scholarship funds. It was unrealistic to expect many able black students to come to Indianola without massive assistance. Hence the board of trustees authorized a special fund to provide a number of George Washington Carver Opportunity Grants specifically for African-American students. Four such grants of $2,700 each were awarded for the 1968–69 year.[14] Each subsequent year four more such scholarships were to be awarded, until as many as sixteen minority students would be assisted in their education. Funding for the Carver grants, however, never reached the projected level, and the failure of the College's administration to provide the expected support was a source of keen disappointment and not a little anger among minority students.[15]

Still, there was a commitment to recruit black students, even though the scholarship funding was inadequate for the numbers sought. As expected, some faculty expressed considerable misgiving about admitting black students whose academic preparation often fell considerably short of the College's standard, but the social utility of "giving them a chance" seemed to outweigh all other considerations. Tutoring, special summer classes and a learning skills laboratory would, it was hoped, bring academically disadvantaged students up to speed.

With a generous grant from the Hawley Welfare Foundation of Des Moines, the College opened the Hawley Writing Laboratory—later called the Hawley Learning Skills Center—in the fall of 1968 in the second floor of Sigler Hall. The laboratory's purpose was clearly stated in the grant proposal: "It must offer tutorial, person-to-person guidance" as well as "small-group refresher and re-enforcement training in reading skills, grammatical usage, and compositional techniques to a very high percentage of all our incoming students."[16] It was estimated that at least ten percent of all incoming freshmen, not to speak of deficient sophomores and upperclassmen, needed some form of language remediation.[17]

Driven by a sincere desire to give disadvantaged students, especially blacks, an opportunity to acquire a college education, stung by criticisms of provincialism and racism, and tentatively convinced that they had put into place a satisfactory means of remediation, the College opened its doors to low-ranking high school graduates who would earlier have been rejected. By no means were all the black students poor academic risks. Some were really very good indeed, succeeded academically and graduated with no special academic assistance. Yet many were insufficiently prepared for Simpson's modest rigors. Even the well-intentioned Hawley Lab, together with the requirement that low-ranking students, white or black, had to enter in early summer prior to their freshman year for remedial work, could not make up for years of deprivation. Many failed.

During the next four years black enrollment increased by 150 percent—from twenty-one to fifty-three. By the fall of 1973 nearly 6 percent of the student body was black, hardly an overwhelming presence, but for Simpson it was a new and sometimes bewildering situation. Too many undergraduates, reared in rural, small-town Iowa or in suburbs of larger cities, were unprepared to relate comfortably with urban blacks.

For the black students it was infinitely more difficult to adjust to life in a small Midwestern college town, especially one in which there was no black community. Until Garfield Jackson was employed as an admissions counselor, there was no black faculty or staff member to whom they could turn for support. And with the combination of unexpected academic demands and an overwhelmingly white social climate, it is small wonder many felt alienated.

Moreover, blacks were understandably caught up in the civil rights struggle, galvanized to action by the brutal assassination of Martin Luther King, Jr., in 1968. Ralph John stated the situation at Simpson clearly. "Our black students," he said, "as black people everywhere, have moved for what they consider full emancipation and freedom. They are seeking their identity as a race and want it respected."[18] He was deeply concerned about the powerful thrust of the civil rights struggle since the death of King. "I remember," he later wrote, "the day Martin Luther King was assassinated."

> The event shocked and frightened us, as it did thinking and feeling people everywhere. When the news broke, I wondered where our Black students were and what I should do. I walked out on the campus and found them in the pool room of the Brenton Student Center. All were there, with four [of them] indifferently hitting pool balls on the two tables. The rest were leaning against the walls, sullen, grief-stricken, shocked, silent. When I walked in there was never a glance in my direction or the least recognition of my presence. I had the feeling that they neither wanted to see nor hear anything from a "Honky." So I just took my position, joining them for the vigil for five minutes or so (which seemed like half the time between the Fall of Rome and The Declaration of Independence), simply said "I'm sorry," and left. I cannot describe the moment. It was existential. I will never know whether they appreciated my coming, resented it or wished I had stayed away.[19]

As their numbers increased, blacks on campus at first simply sought acceptance in all areas of college life: fair treatment in the classroom, equal living accommodations and access to all elements of the extracurriculum. The ideal was integration, and considerable integration took place, especially in academics and athletics.[20] Less successful were attempts to integrate the social life of the campus.

Students were becoming increasingly sensitive to the crusade for civil rights for America's minorities, especially among the nation's black population, for many of whom liberation was still a dream. Whether because of genuine conviction or a sense of vicarious guilt, white students were supportive of the worthy efforts of blacks to enter the mainstream of American life. On the whole students had responded well, for example, to the faculty insistence on nondiscrimination in selection of members in all school organizations, especially among the Greek-letter societies, some of which had been burdened in the recent past by all-white membership clauses in their national constitutions. By the time of the outbreak of the student protest movement at Simpson, however, all of the fraternities and sororities could say quite honestly that, on paper at least, they were free to select any student they chose without restriction as to race, creed, color or national origin.

It was easier said than done. The issue of recruitment of black members in the Greek-letter societies was largely a reflection of Simpson's failure to recruit black students in the first place. While some of the sororities at Simpson had broken the ice back in the 1950s, the fraternities did not seek out black members until the mid-1960s. When they did, the SAEs pledged and initiated several black students; DU and ATO followed suit sometime later. In the Lambda Chi chapter there was trouble. Ralph John remembered the matter as one of the most painful of his presidency at Simpson.

Earlier, in the fall of 1966, the Lambda Chi Alpha fraternity had rushed and pledged Stanley Crosswhite of Urbana, Ohio, who had entered Simpson as a freshman in the early summer that year and had lived in the Commons House just next door to the Lambda Chi house.[21] Regrettably, local chapter alumni reaction to Crosswhite's pledging was severe, some of the undergraduates subjected to what one of them called "brutal harassment."[22] Suspecting that the chapter had been pressured to pledge a black by its new faculty adviser, Gary Valen, an instructor in history and Simpson Lambda Chi alumnus, the alumni prevailed upon the fraternity's national office to dismiss Valen as chapter adviser, calling him "a radical liberal, a bohemian and an ardent civil rights worker."[23] Angry alumni reorganized their alumni board, effectively dropping from its membership one alumnus who defended the chapter's pledging a black.[24]

Speaking for the chapter, Robert S. Crandall explained the chapter's action to the Lambda Chi national secretary. "I believe that the active chapter has fully discussed the implications of the move, and decided that although an issue of race was involved, we had to look at Stan as a *person* and decide whether or not we wanted *him* as a pledge of Lambda Chi. It was primarily on this basis, and not from the point of trying to be "civil rightists" or radicals, that we made our commitment."[25]

President Ralph John remembered the incident vividly. One afternoon in September, several Lambda Chi undergraduates came to his office for an "emergency" meeting. "I had never before sat with such a beaten, distressed group of students," led by their president, Bob Crandall, "a very fine young man." It was clear that after pledging young Crosswhite "apparently inquisitorial hell broke loose" on the chapter. "When the students left," recalled John years later, "I immediately called the national executive secretary, who was both unfriendly and evasive. I ended up telling him that if he were not on our campus to settle this problem in a manner satisfactory to us within two days I would suspend the charter of Lambda Chi at Simpson and recommend lifting it to the trustees. He was here the next day."[26] The conversations between secretary Cyril Fladd with John and dean of students Wally Wiser "were cool to say the least." But the pledging, which had become a cause celebre in Lambda Chi Alpha, stood, and the action of the undergraduates was vindicated.[27]

The pledging of Stan Crosswhite broke the ice, and during the next few years a number of minority students joined Simpson's Greek-letter organizations, in every case without incident. But the drive for integration on the part of blacks soon gave way at Simpson, as it did elsewhere, to an understandable ethnocentrism. While it looked to whites as if blacks were engaging in acts of self-segregation, blacks themselves made it abundantly clear that they were seeking to foster pride in their own identity. Integration, which many regarded as a questionable goal, would have to wait.

During the next few years blacks sought, indeed demanded, a number of changes that accorded with their drive for identity and their pursuit of the power to achieve it. As early as 1968 they elected a black Homecoming queen, Norma Bradman, and her court, Velma Clark and Brenda Hall, who reigned alongside their white counterparts.[28] That same year they created the Black Students Organization in order to provide mutual support and a forum for minority concerns. Although membership was open to whites, only blacks could vote, "a restriction . . . necessary to insure that there is a Black voice on campus."[29] White reaction was predictable. The *Simpsonian* editorialized that "the BSO presents to the campus community an image of collective, self-righteous superiority and segregation through activities such as the election by the Black students of a Black Queen at Homecoming and the more recent demand of the Black Students' Organization for a Black Student Center."[30] Blacks were urged not to "emphasize racial pride at the expense of tolerance and love."[31] For their part, black students were unimpressed, noting acidly that they experienced few evidences of tolerance and love at Simpson. Still, the College's administration wanted to be responsive to their needs. President John, enthusiastically backed by student center director Lu Jean Cole, agreed that blacks needed a place to call their own. On March 16, 1969, the Afro-American Cultural Center was opened in a College-owned house at the corner of West Girard Street and D Street. A huge crowd attended the opening day ceremonies, their animated chatter accompanied by African drum music.[32] The center and its successor locations served the students well. It "represents the struggle that Black students have endured and must continue to endure," wrote one of them in 1974.[33] Symbolic of their intent, the Black Students Organization was renamed the Organization for Black Unity in 1972.[34]

Aside from the continuing demand that more blacks be recruited to attend Simpson, the principal concerns of minority students were the appointment of more black staff and faculty together with the creation of a black studies curriculum. Unable to find a full-time faculty person, the College appointed Dr. Henry Parker in the fall of 1972 to teach a course called "The Culture of the Ghetto." Parker, a staff member at the State College of Iowa—later the University of Northern Iowa—presented the course during the first semester, and it proved so successful that it was continued through the second semester and was offered again the next year.[35] In 1974 James H. Rogers was employed full-time as director of a new Afro-American Studies Program and assistant professor of English. He had taught at Portland State University and remained at Simpson four years.[36] That same year Simpson graduate Tom Simmons '72 was hired as an assistant football coach.

Meanwhile the faculty had authorized in 1973 a black studies program, in fact a black studies minor, incorporating five specific courses in Afro-American history, literature, sociology and culture, together with opportunities for independent study. Henry Parker assisted Rogers and other faculty in this new program.[37] Most black students were pleased with the College's response. For Al Gardner, one of their leaders, however, it simply was too little too late. It was, he said, a "semi-quota system."[38]

*   *   *

If the black students were understandably preoccupied with the struggle for civil rights and cultural identity, the rest of the student body, while generally sympathetic to the black cause, at least in the abstract, was primarily concerned, indeed obsessed, by their opposition to the Vietnam War. Never in Simpson's history had a public issue so aroused undergraduates. Few Simpson students could have located Vietnam on a map before, say, 1964. They were perhaps only vaguely aware of the growing involvement of the U.S. in support of the South

Vietnamese against North Vietnam and the Viet Cong, and they were unsure of the effect of the Gulf of Tonkin Resolution passed by Congress in the summer of 1964. That fall a South Vietnamese spoke at Simpson in the first of four lectures on world revolutions. "Few Americans," he said, "know why their sons, husbands and fathers are in Vietnam; many of the men themselves do not know why they are there." It was not enough, he said, to be anti-Communist. One must attempt to build a stable government in Vietnam—the government of President Ngo Dinh Diem had been overthrown and Diem assassinated only a year earlier—and bring the conflict to an end. He challenged his hearers "to re-examine our actions as a nation in Vietnam."[39]

As the American commitment in Vietnam escalated dramatically during 1965, Simpson undergraduates joined other students across the nation protesting the war. The first to speak out editorially was history major Roger Grant, editor of the *Simpsonian*, who inveighed against "America's imperialistic war in South Vietnam," calling upon students to register as conscientious objectors in order to avoid military conscription and to demonstrate "opposition to our sickening Vietnamese policy."[40] Taking issue with Grant, former Simpson student Dick Gerstell at the State College of Iowa pointed out with venom: "It is interesting that you did not choose to attack the draft as long as the dying was limited to the professional soldiers, high school drop-outs, and others not sheltered behind the ivy-covered walls," but "chose to wait until your own little world was threatened" by mounting call-ups.[41] These words stung, for it is true that much of the opposition to the war was based upon student exposure to the draft, and it is likewise true that much of the antiwar movement collapsed as soon as the draft was called off. "The entire movement against the war," wrote Richard Cohen, recalling those years of turmoil, "was white and middle class, comprised in no small part of the kids who would be handed drab, green uniforms when they came off the stage with their diplomas. I don't think we thought it through that way, but our vague notions of self-interest were exactly that. The fact is, the movement was born with the draft."[42]

Others would judge their state of mind less generously. Congressman Bill Scherle, representing the southwest Iowa district in which Warren County was located, who has been described as "loose, quarrelsome," never "bogged down by logic,"[43] and who surely wins a prize as one of the most contentious politicians in Iowa history, put it plainly a generation later: "Cowardice was the trigger that provoked college students [at Simpson, Iowa State and the University of Iowa] to engage in vicious wanton acts such as flag burning, desecration of public buildings, sit-ins, shutting down educational institutions, depriving others of their rights, destroying draft cards and civil disobedience. The 'war' was their feeble, depraved excuse for their shocking conduct."[44]

What Congressman Scherle and many others could not or would not understand was that there was more to the protests than fear of the draft. There was genuine opposition to the war as a matter of public policy, a conviction that it was the wrong war in the wrong place at the wrong time. And as the American involvement in the war escalated, protest demonstrations were held throughout the land. Simpson students and faculty participated in antiwar marches in Des Moines during 1966 and the year following. Toward the end of 1967 a chapter of the Students for a Democratic Society was organized at Simpson.[45] It was probably not as radical in Indianola as it was on many campuses, for the principal reason that its members seemed to be unwilling to submit themselves to any sort of rigid organizational structure, each person going his or her own way. Even Bill Helfrich, their radicalized chief faculty "adviser" and mentor, was dismayed by the inability of the S.D.S. to organize for coherent action. A few of its members did publish an "underground" newspaper in its name, called *The Gadfly*, the irregular emanations of which were always entertaining and sometimes informative.[46]

However well organized the antiwar movement was in some parts of the nation, at Simpson it remained minuscule and not really visible until it found an attractive national standard-bearer around whom to rally and, even more importantly, a local undergraduate leader with the charisma and political savvy to give substance to the students' feelings. The spark that set the movement off was the appearance on the campus one autumn evening in 1967 of David Mixner, "a pudgy fellow in his mid-twenties, bent on signing up an army . . . to follow the anti-war pied piper, Senator Eugene McCarthy" of Minnesota.[47] A number of students responded to Mixner's persuasive allure, especially Richard Cohen, a bright sophomore from West Hartford, Connecticut, who soon emerged as the natural leader of the antiwar forces on campus. While history instructor Don Gibson helped to organize Iowa in the McCarthy campaign for the nation's presidency, Cohen organized Simpson students. "It would later be noted," recalls Cohen, "in *The New Republic*, that the McCarthy campaign in Iowa, which represented such a success nationally, was born on the Simpson campus."[48] The antiwar movement focused on McCarthy's bid for the presidency, and students worked very hard indeed on his behalf. When the McCarthy supporters were overwhelmed in the March 25 Iowa caucuses, some of them refused to give up their crusade. At the caucuses, "the Democratic machine took over," wrote Leonard E. "Ed" Tinker in the *Simpsonian*. Tinker "felt that [at the caucuses] we had been taken for a ride by the 'Establishment.' "[49] The antiwar protesters felt betrayed when Robert Kennedy entered the presidential race in March. Rich Cohen remembers that "some of us later met Kennedy at a Des Moines reception. We defiantly wore our McCarthy buttons to tell him what we thought. I was almost disappointed that he and his wife were so gracious and warm."[50] And they mourned with the rest of the nation when Kennedy was assassinated in June the night he won the California primary.

A few Simpson students that summer attended the Democratic National Convention at Chicago where riots were brutally crushed by an overwrought Chicago police force. Don Gibson was there, and a few Simpson people like Joe Walt managed to appear on the scene just when the melee in the streets was at its worst.[51] Rich Cohen was there too, and found it hard afterwards to return to Indianola. All year he had been "clean for Gene," with his "short haircut, close shave, and return to conventional attire (it killed me)." After the Chicago political disaster, "somehow going from Michigan and Balboa to a food committee meeting in Kresge Hall gave me whiplash."[52] Others experienced much the same feeling. Joe Walt spoke in chapel on September 15; his topic was "Chicago: An Interpretation," in which he deplored the actions of both the police and the convention. A week later he and Cohen conducted a "talk-in" on politics, the first of many such gatherings as the war dragged on.

It required months for "the movement" to get moving again after the stunning defeat of November which put Richard Nixon into the White House. Apart from a *Simpsonian* editorial by senior Jim Noseworthy arguing that "the draft, in any form . . . hinders the creativity of the United States and should be eliminated" and an equivocal piece in the University of Iowa *Spectator* by Simpson graduate Tom Hensley calling America's record in Vietnam "a series of tragic blunders," little was said or written about the war.[53] A few Simpsonians marched in support of Cesar Chavez and the grape strike, but it was a lackluster performance. "If there had been something to do, we might have done it. There was almost a vacuum," recalls Cohen.[54]

Then came the nationwide Vietnam Moratorium in the fall of 1969, and the local troops were galvanized to action. Now once again the focus was no longer a candidate for public office but the war itself. Plans were formalized for a major demonstration on October 15, coordinated with similar events all across the nation. Fortuitously, from the standpoint of the protesters, a Hollywood movie called *Cold Turkey* was being filmed that fall in nearby Greenfield, Iowa. A number of Simpson undergraduates who were hired as extras, became acquainted with director Norman Lear, actors Dick Van Dyke, Pippa Scott and others, and persuaded them to participate on October 8 in a program billed as a premoratorium rally. Attracted by the lineup of celebrities, more than a thousand spectators from Simpson, Des Moines, Grinnell and beyond jammed into Hopper Gymnasium to hear one after another speaker call for an end to the war. In addition to the Hollywood stars were Vance Bourjaily, prominent writer from the University of Iowa, and both Don Gibson and Rich Cohen, all of whom spoke to the foot-stomping, cheering crowd. Gibson, who had organized the event with Cohen, closed the speechmaking "by demanding withdrawal of U.S. troops from Vietnam this year, and an exposure, in facts and figures, of the Nixon Peace Fraud."[55]

A few days later when the College's board of trustees held its fall meeting on campus, the protesters managed to persuade them to support the moratorium and issue a resolution "opposed to the continuation of the war in Vietnam."[56] That, by the way, was the first—and last—time the board of trustees ever spoke out on a political issue. On the fifteenth, student dissidents conducted an all-day moratorium program to which the public was invited. The day started with philosophy professor Norman Thomas, veteran Navy flyer of World War II and the Korean War, speaking on the need to pull out of Vietnam, followed by Far-Eastern specialist Paul Ingram and Joe Walt conducting a discussion on why people had come to oppose the war. In the interest of fairness, the late morning speaker in Great Hall was Nguyen Hoan, political counselor from the South Vietnamese Embassy in Washington, who sought in vain to explain the South Vietnamese war policy. At noontime something less than a hundred persons met at Smith Chapel and participated in a silent march several times around the Indianola square, followed by a "mass rally" where students and faculty spoke.[57] After participating in a march in Des Moines, Simpson people met at eight o'clock in the evening at the Brenton Student Center for a Journalism Institute panel discussion, "The Nature of Freedom," featuring national columnist Sydney Harris, *Des Moines Register* editor Ken MacDonald, *Register* political cartoonist Frank Miller, columnists Donald Kaul and Gordon Gammack. Gammack's daughter Julie, a Simpson sophomore, was one of the more dedicated dissidents.[58] Perhaps more moving, however, than all the speeches that day was the ringing of the College's Chapel bell 39,400 times, once for each American who had given his life in the Vietnam War. The incessant tolling was not well received in the community, nor was it intended to be. Wrote the students: "We are hoping that the noise of the bells will, indeed bother you, and that the reason for their being sounded will bother you, also."[59]

It bothered a lot more than local residents. The morning after the October 8 rally, the Federal Bureau of Investigation sent agent Ellsworth Gustafson to find out who was behind this much-publicized event. The investigator first talked with dean of academic affairs Wally Wiser and dean of students Bill Webster, neither of whom when asked was willing to identify student antiwar leaders responsible for the rally.[60] Undeterred, Gustafson next appeared at Ralph John's office, flashed his badge, and got to the point: "Would you consider the students [at the rally] last night loyal to Hanoi or Peking?" Furious that the agent, having apparently made up his mind, did not include the possibility of loyalty to Washington, Ralph John responded sharply: "Sir, if your question indicates your understanding of the significance of last night's event, I invite you to leave this campus." The man turned and left, and was not seen at Simpson again.[61]

President John reported the incident the next evening—October 10, 1969—to the board of trustees in their fall meeting. He called the FBI probe "political paranoia."[62] He asked board members to keep the matter confidential, and they did.

A few days later John called together his Administrative Council, and for their information told them confidentially about the investigation and "expressed the opinion that the matter was closed."[63] "Two days later," he recalled, "I picked up a just-off-the-press [copy of the] *Des Moines Tribune* as I passed through the airport on my way to Chicago, sticking the paper under my arm." When the plane took off he turned to his paper "for the shock of my life." On page one was splashed the story "Simpson Charges FBI With Harassment."

When he arrived home the next afternoon, "all hell had broken loose." Telephone calls, angry notes and newspaper reporters everywhere. He hastily called together his Administrative Council to discover what had happened. Dean of students Bill Webster "admitted that he had leaked the story" to the press. At that moment Ralph John was not certain whether he was angrier at the FBI for impugning the loyalty of Simpson students or at Bill Webster for his unforgivable breach of confidentiality. He decided on the spot to fire Webster "for the simple reason that I could not have a senior colleague whom I could not trust."[64]

John had to brave a firestorm of criticism. Letters poured in castigating his stand against the FBI when it was merely "doing its duty." Letters to the editor deplored Simpson's stand. "There is lots of evidence that subversive people *are* on campuses. There is lots of evidence also that these people *do* receive direction from Hanoi and Peking," wrote John B. Walters in the *Cedar Rapids Gazette*. Alumni wrote threatening to withdraw financial support from the College, and many of them made good their threat. Editorials appeared in a number of newspapers, all defending the FBI. Calling the Simpson administration "naive," the *Waterloo Daily Courier* concluded that "no loyal American should resent inquiries from the FBI. No loyal American has anything to fear from the FBI."[65]

In the midst of the furor, John hinted to longtime Simpson board member Ken MacDonald, editor of the *Des Moines Register*, that because the press seemed unwilling to let the story go, "it would be helpful if he could cool things down." MacDonald looked at John and asked, "Do you tell your faculty what to teach?

Neither do I tell my reporters what to write." But he comforted John with the observation that "the public memory is short, and in a couple of weeks it would all be forgotten." That, recalled John, "taught me a lesson."[66]

A few people—precious few—commended the president for his action. Louis A. Haselmayer, the grand old man of Iowa Wesleyan College, expressed his "deepest concern" and offered every assistance.[67] George Kramer of Waukee was pleased that John "spoke out against the FBI snooping." A heartwarming letter, dated the evening the story broke in the *Tribune*, from Robert Burlingame, longtime WHO radio personality and loyal Grinnell College alumnus, congratulated John "on your and Simpson's courageous resistance to the frightening gestapo terrorism now abroad in this country."[68]

While Ralph John lay low until his critics tired of scolding him, student dissidents persisted in their condemnation of national policy. As their strongest on-campus opponents, the Simpson Veterans Association, lay a wreath at the base of the College flagpole in honor of "those who served,"[69] Cohen and three other students were on their way to Washington to participate in the "March against Death" on the ellipse in Washington, D.C.[70] The following February 1970, Marine Corps recruiters on campus experienced a signal lack of response.[71] Then, in early March, Rich Cohen announced plans for another Vietnam moratorium, scheduled for April 15. The big feature would be the appearance, on the evening of the fourteenth, of William Kunstler, defense attorney in the conspiracy and contempt trial of the "Chicago Seven." Kunstler was reputed to be the most radical lawyer in the land.[72] If anyone could stir up the locals, he could.

And if Ralph John had been under fire for the FBI incident, he was in far worse straits as soon as word of the impending Kunstler speech was out. Local reaction ranged from apathetic to apoplectic, the flames of opposition fanned by tendentious, alarmist reporting in the Des Moines press. Some Indianolans like Ethel Trueblood, Republican stalwart, genuinely feared that Kunstler's appearance posed a serious risk of violence in the community. Bill Bowles, Iowa Director of Selective Service, an Indianolan too, argued that Kunstler and his ilk would destroy the very constitutional rights that permitted him to speak out: "Simpson does not need Kunstler and his like . . . neither does Indianola."[73] Because of the controversy, Lew Kimer, editor of the local paper, invited Dr. John to write an editorial explaining the College's position on the Kunstler speech. John's piece, entitled "Freedom of the Forum," appeared nearly two weeks before Kunstler came to the campus. He noted that critics were denouncing Simpson's "inept administration which does not step in to cancel" the student government's invitation to Kunstler, asking—and not rhetorically—"Do the students run the College?" But he defended their action and his, arguing for freedom for the likes of Kunstler to speak and the equal right of students to hear him, however radical his ideas. And, in his most reassuring way, he suggested that "it is not likely that Mr. Kunstler, or any one else, not even parents or teachers, will take [students] down the primrose path."[74]

He was right. When he spoke that night to a capacity crowd of a thousand or more in Hopper Gym, Kunstler, while asserting that the United States was on the path to revolution, counseled against violence. Most of his speech simply reviewed the issues and procedures involved in the "Chicago Seven" trial.[75] If any of his hearers had hoped for a call to action, they were sorely disappointed.

Less than a month later the nation was shocked by the news from Kent State

University in Ohio, where four students were killed when inexperienced, nervous National Guard troops fired at some 600 antiwar demonstrators, some of whom had taunted and thrown rocks at the soldiers. Quite apart from the question of why the National Guard was called out to deal with a campus disturbance, the victims of the "Kent State massacre" of May 4 earned instant martyrdom as campuses erupted in fury all over America. "What followed was a national debate," recalls Cohen, "not just about the war, but about what it was doing to us as a society."[76] It was more than a debate, for wrathful students took action. "At Simpson, finally, we had everyone's attention."[77] Dissidents learned that campuses were being closed down at one college after another—eventually more than 400 of them, Grinnell and the University of Iowa among them—so that students could take to the streets, knock on doors, beard the political lions of Washington in their dens, in short, attempt to convince America once and for all that the war must be ended forthwith.

The Simpson campus fairly exploded. Within hours after the Kent State killings, dissident students called for a mighty antiwar rally and boycott of classes, set for Friday, May 9, 1970. To be sure, many students simply packed up and went home, taking advantage of a lengthened Mother's Day weekend, and others slept late. But those who walked out on campus that morning beheld an eerie, dramatic sight. White wooden crosses—700 to 800 of them—were planted all across the central campus, each cross representing an Iowa serviceman killed in Vietnam. Some 350 students attended the peace rally, responding to Kent State and to the recent U.S. invasion of Cambodia, which seemed only to broaden the war.[78] Among other things, students demanded that the College close in order to free students for their antiwar activities. Because the faculty was and is sovereign in such matters, a special meeting of the teaching staff was called for 4:00 P.M. in the large lecture hall of the old Carnegie Library. When the time came, the crowd—including hundreds of students—was so large that the meeting had to be moved to the Great Hall, which was soon packed to capacity and then some. Student leaders made their case for suspending classes for the balance of the semester, allowing students full credit with the grade they had earned up to that time. One young woman had the temerity to oppose the protesters, insisting that classes be held, for after all she had paid tuition for a full semester of instruction. The faculty agreed with her, and the student petition was denied by a lopsided vote. "When the vote was taken," wrote Ralph John later, "the place exploded. The students jumped to their feet angrily, shouted invectives, gestured defiantly and began to shout "burn, burn, burn!" An ashtray with burning cigarette butts was thrown through the glass of the door opening out onto the deck. The hall emptied, and everywhere "whirl was king.""[79]

While Dr. John walked across Buxton Park to his home, he realized he needed to be on the campus, and walked back. Near the Dunn Library he ran into four faculty members—Paul Ingram, Todd Lieber, Bill Helfrich and Joe Walt—earnestly struggling to find a compromise that would meet at least some of the students' demands and at the same time maintain the College's academic integrity. Leaving them to work out a proposal, President John walked over to the chapel where a number of students, including their leaders, were meeting to plot their next move. He decided to try, at least, to engage them in conversation. "Things fell to a dead calm when I appeared," he remembers.

> Don't ask me what I said, because I don't know. When they began to open up, they expressed disappointment in me, because they thought it was in my power to override the faculty, which I had not done. This took us into a little discussion of the ABC's of academic governance. . . . They listened intently and courteously, some later thanking me for explaining how things worked. I also told them of the faculty initiative presently on foot to get reconsideration that evening. The students seemed relieved to see a way out of the situation they had created.[80]

When the second special faculty meeting of the day convened at seven o'clock that evening, the Great Hall was jammed. The Ingram-Lieber-Helfrich-Walt proposal was presented and passed by the faculty to the accompaniment of tumultuous student applause. The compromise agreement stipulated that students who wanted to leave the campus and go out into the peace movement could do so if validated by the so-called Student Coordinating Committee, i.e., the antiwar leaders. They could either take a grade of incomplete in their courses, such courses to be completed within thirty days of the students' next registration, or, if class attendance was "indispensable," could terminate their course work on May 11 and "receive three-fourths the normal course credit."[81] It seemed a fair compromise. Delighted students thanked the faculty. "In fact," recalls John, "the whole thing turned into a kind of love feast."[82] Thereupon, students voted to send a delegation to Washington to express their concerns to the entire Iowa Congressional delegation and invited President John and Terry Hoy to go with them at the students' expense. "That was the greatest and most appreciated compliment I ever received," wrote John. "It was Simpson College at her best with faculty, students and administration struggling creatively together with a megaton problem that could have shattered the place."[83] They did go to Washington, and their entreaties did seem to have some effect. Actually, not very many students opted to leave the campus, and those who did admitted later that they did little that was important with their time. Simpson did not shut down and was the better for it.

What became of all the sound and fury of the antiwar movement? Did it harm the College? More importantly, how did it affect the lives of those students who participated in it? Most importantly, did it shorten the agony in Vietnam? Or prolong it? Rich Cohen, a generation later, remembers it this way:

> Today, what I do is, in some small part, an extension of the values and beliefs of the 1960s. I do not miss the war. I do not miss the death. I do not miss the rage of the ghetto. I do not miss the division, anger and suspicion among citizens.
>
> I do miss the belief that things could be made better, and the willingness to try. Younger friends and colleagues say strange things about that period in our history. They think we ended a war that others think we prolonged. I think neither is correct. We should not mythologize ourselves and what we accomplished in those disturbing years. It was a great adventure to search for the best side of ourselves. . . .[84]

The spring of 1970 marked the climax of the antiwar hysteria at Simpson. To be sure, there were more demonstrations, more calls for an end to the war and to the draft as the nation went through the agonizing process of deescalation of the war and the on-again, off-again peace talks at Paris. But the worst of the furor was over. In early 1971 the *Simpsonian* one more time called for an end to the draft, and students were dismayed when the Selective Service Act was renewed and the draft extended to mid-1973.[85] A two-day seminar on Vietnam was held at the College on May 1 and 2, 1972, followed by a town meeting May 4 on the steps of Smith Chapel.[86] A few days later, following the news that President Nixon had ordered mining Haiphong Harbor, somehow hoping for a knockout punch against North Vietnam, the Student Senate called for a general strike to protest the Nixon policy. Accordingly, on the ninth about 150 students and faculty attended a rally in front of Smith Chapel, but little came of their efforts except to create some unfortunate, short-term hostility in the Indianola community. Yet another meeting two days later on the Indianola courthouse lawn did not satisfy either the protesters or their opponents.[87]

As the American presence in Vietnam declined, opposition to the war softened perceptibly. In August the last U.S. ground combat troops were withdrawn, and three months later Richard Nixon won a second term in a landslide victory over George McGovern, who never attracted students the way Eugene McCarthy had four years earlier. When the draft call-ups ended the following January 17, students were of course relieved. The next day the local *Record-Herald* editor, Lewis Kimer, dismayed by a month of "the most sustained bombing attack in the history of warfare," called for an end to the war. America's recent "annihilation campaign," he wrote, had "brought a wave of moral revulsion" among even the nation's staunchest allies. To get the U.S. out of the "Indochina quagmire," Congress must deny the funds "for continuation of this cancerous and futile war."[88] Kimer's words were from the heart, and he found his sentiments shared by a growing number of Indianolans. At the College, many faculty and students were happy that community sentiment had come around to share their hopes for peace.

* * *

Although the student revolt seemed to dominate the Simpson scene for very nearly seven years after its outbreak in 1968, the College did continue to function, part of the time quite admirably, given the powerful distractions from within and without. The board of trustees, under the able leadership first of William Buxton III (1968–72) and later of Luther Hill, whose seven years at the helm (1972–79) was the longest since the days of William T. Hamilton, proved to be remarkably responsive to the concerns of the students, genuinely sympathetic with their aims and ideals and prepared to break new ground in the way the board related to the several constituencies that made up the Simpson community—the administration, the faculty, students, alumni, Indianola townspeople and the Methodist Church. It need hardly be pointed out that not all these constituencies were agreed on the course Simpson should take. They were not even agreed as to what the problems were. The role of the board of trustees, therefore, was crucial in bringing people together, at least for discussion of the important issues that confronted Simpson and all American institutions of higher education, and it must be said that the board played its role well.

In 1968 the board's membership included thirty-five regular members serving in staggered three-year terms, seven ex officio members and twelve honorary life members.[89] Of the regular trustees, eight were from Warren County, fifteen from Des Moines, two from the rest of Iowa and ten from out of state. Half of them—eighteen—were Simpson alumni. Only one—the Reverend Paul M. Hann, pastor of the First United Methodist Church in Des Moines—was a clergyman. Twenty-one were businessmen. Four were attorneys, and two were journalists.

Only three were women: Ruth Buxton Sayre, past president of the Associated Country Women of the World, Frances Ledlie Dawson, a representative in the Illinois state legislature and Amy Robertson, listed in the College catalog as a "farm manager and industrialist." All three women were Simpson alumnae. All seven ex officio members were ordained Methodist clergymen, including Ralph John, Bishop James S. Thomas, Jr., four district superintendents and the minister of the First United Methodist Church in Indianola, Glen W. Lamb. Six years later (1974–75), the makeup of the board had changed perceptibly. On a board whose membership had increased to forty-two—fourteen in each of three classes—the contingent of women had grown from three to seven; and two blacks had joined the board—John Estes, Jr., a Des Moines funeral director, and student-nominated Bernard W. Franklin of Montclair, New Jersey. At the same time, in accordance with new board procedures, one member of each three-year class was nominated by the Methodist bishop, resulting in the election of two clergymen and one layman. The number of ex officio members had been accordingly reduced from seven to four, including the president of the College, the bishop, the superintendent of the Des Moines district of the church and Robert V. Gildner, who had succeeded Glen Lamb at the Indianola congregation in 1971.

Ralph John remained at Simpson until the end of the 1971–72 academic year. During the last four years of his tenure, a number of changes took place in the College's administration. When Robert Feyerharm retired in 1969 after fifteen years, the president appointed as his new vice-president for financial affairs Dr. Rhae M. Swisher, Jr., director of management services at the University of Kansas. Swisher, a graduate of the law school at Indiana University (1950), had also taught in business administration both at Indiana and Kansas.[90] He remained at Simpson three years. Consequent to Swisher's appointment, Doyle Woods was named comptroller, a post he retained for many years. Jim Robinson remained a most effective vice-president for development, assisted by Jack Siefkas and retired clergyman Robert W. Pinnell in later years. Pinnell proved to be remarkably capable, especially in the field of estates and bequests.

Waller Wiser, former chaplain and dean of students, was appointed vice-president and dean of academic affairs in the fall of 1968.[91] Taking his place as dean of students was Bill R. Webster, who came to Simpson from Wisconsin State University at River Falls.[92] At the same time, when Evelyn Morris resigned her position as associate dean of students and dean of women, her post was filled by recent graduate Jane Templeton.[93]

Two years later, when Templeton resigned to resume graduate studies, Evelyn Morris returned to Simpson as associate dean of students. With the departure of Bill Webster, Morris then took over as dean of students. Louis Smith continued as associate academic dean and registrar until taking over as dean of admissions and records in 1969.

When Chaplain James E. Allen accepted a new assignment at the University of North Carolina, John selected the Reverend Gilbert Y. Taverner, whose ministry had been conducted entirely in New England. A down East Maine native, Taverner had earned his B.A. at Colby College and the S.T.B. at the University of Boston School of Theology in 1952. The first to occupy the chaplain's office in the new Smith Chapel, he possessed the remarkable talent of making his ministry to students meaningful in an era when the religious establishment, like every establishment, was in most places either attacked or, worse, ignored. Known for his clipped New England accent and his infectious sense of humor, Taverner did more than his share of counseling in a time when counseling was much needed and little sought, conducted chapel services more in the spirit of Woodstock than of Aldersgate and introduced changes in the traditional year-end baccalaureate service that Matthew Simpson probably would not have liked but the students loved.

Dan Seaton, who had served as director of admissions for more than a decade was appointed in the fall of 1968 director of financial aid, his place in admissions taken over by Richard Banning, guidance counselor at Mason City High School. Seaton's move, explained John, recognized that "the area of scholarships and student aid is one of the most complex and fast growing in academic administration," especially in private institutions. Banning moved in 1969 to the post of assistant dean of academic affairs, and two years later (1971) became director of cooperative education.[94]

In 1969 Dr. John appointed sociology professor Donald H. Koontz, assistant to the president for special programs, his work ranging from church and special educational programs to the Aerospace Institute, Koontz's favorite.

In publications and public relations Larry A. Myers resigned when he was inducted into military service. He was succeeded by Gordon Brown, a Simpson graduate who had served as alumni secretary the previous year. When Brown left Simpson in early 1971, the president appointed James M. Zahnd to take his place. Zahnd, a 1963 graduate of William Jewell College and the journalism school of the University of Missouri, came to Simpson after three years as director of public relations at the Kansas City College of Osteopathic Medicine.[95]

Replacing Gordon Brown as director of alumni affairs in October 1969 was Thomas R. Ackerman, a Simpson alumnus (1967) and graduate of Seattle University, who took over the position upon completion of his military service. During his four years as Simpson's director of alumni affairs, Ackerman earned a sort of left-handed immortality. At least it was all unintentional. It happened during his first year in the office. One day in mid-1970 Ackerman, who was looking for a big hot air balloon to fly over the campus as a Homecoming special attraction, talked with the people who were staging the hot air balloon national championship event at the Iowa State Fair. He learned that members of the Balloon Federation of America, a relatively small group of ballooning enthusiasts, were looking for a site somewhere near Des Moines where they could hold the preliminary events of the contest before the fair opened. There was no room for them on the fairgrounds.

Ackerman suggested they consider coming to Indianola. They could use the intramural field down in front of the three fraternity houses. They liked the idea. Enlisting the help of the Indianola Chamber of Commerce, Ackerman and Simpson hosted eighteen balloonists and their crews on August 19 and 20, volunteered as ground crews, manned chase vehicles, ran errands and begged rides in what looked ever so much like gigantic lollipops in the sky. People in Indianola were spellbound by the beauty of the balloons as they floated lazily over their homes. The balloon championship, thanks to Ackerman and dozens of volunteers, went exceptionally well. The president of the Balloon Federation said of the event that it was "without a doubt, the most successful race, either regional or national, that we have ever had, and this was in no small measure due to the warm welcome given us by the town of Indianola and Simpson College.[96]

The balloonists returned again and again, and Indianola became the longtime site of the National Balloon Championships. Even when, years later, the championships moved to other cities, each summer, the Indianola Balloon Classic drew thousands of spectators as the skies were filled with hundreds of colorful balloons. And on the road leading to Des Moines from Indianola the National Balloon Museum was built, an enduring monument not only to a popular sport but also to the quick thinking and keen perspicacity of Tom Ackerman.

Only a very few administrative people remained long in the positions to which they were appointed. In the faculty the turnover rate was truly dizzying as people came and went as if through an academic revolving door. During the four years after the fall of 1968 no less than forty-one full-time faculty appointments were made, considerably more than half the number of the total teaching staff. Of these, only nine would make their career at Simpson. Fourteen stayed for periods ranging from five to fifteen years, while eighteen remained less than five years, including seven who taught only one year. It is doubtful that Simpson was more severely affected by rapid turnover than were most colleges and universities, but the recruitment of new faculty in most fields was difficult, in a few disciplines almost impossible.

Part of the new appointments, to be sure, represented a net increase in the size of the faculty in accord with Ralph John's plan to pull together a staff that could serve 1,200 students. New positions were created in English, physics (2), history (2), Russian, sociology, theater arts and education.

Among those who would stay at Simpson many years were nine who became the backbone of the College's faculty. Five of them were among the record seventeen appointments announced in the fall of 1969. Norman L. Thomas came that fall in the Department of Philosophy and Religion from Bakersfield, California. A Nevada native, Thomas was a veteran naval officer from the Second World War and the Korean War and had earned his B.A. and M.A. from the University of California at Berkeley. Within a week after he had taught his first classes at Simpson he was awarded the Ph.D. in philosophy from the Claremont Graduate School. A remarkably versatile man, Thomas was equally at home in the seminar room, where his classes in ethics and morality or in logic or in Aristotle were brilliantly taught, or in the seat of an airplane as a licensed flight instructor. With him in Indianola were his wife Marjorie and four children, all of whom attended Simpson.[97] Thomas remained on the faculty, serving many years as chairman of the Department of Philosophy, until his retirement in 1991.

In religion came M. Bruce Haddox, whose easy-going good humor belied his conservative Southern Baptist upbringing. A 1961 graduate of Stetson University, Haddox earned his B.D. from Southern Baptist Theological Seminary in 1965, his M.A. from Florida State the following year and completed requirements for the Ph.D. in religion from Duke University within three months after he and his wife arrived in Indianola. Soon after Haddox and Thomas joined the faculty, the Department of Philosophy and Religion was divided, as was the Department of History and Political Science.

In the History Department one of the two new positions was filled by Owen L. Duncan, a West Virginia native who had completed his B.A. in 1962 at Marshall University and the M.A. the next year at Ohio State. He would complete the Ph.D. in English history in 1974. If ever there was a fit between a professor and a college, Duncan and Simpson were a splendid match. Dedicated to teaching and to students, he instructed in a broad variety of courses in history, coached the women's tennis team, enlivened conversations in the faculty lounge in Mary Berry Hall, and threw himself unstintingly into faculty committee work, frequently even conveying the impression that he enjoyed it.

When John Oldani resigned in 1969 to accept a position elsewhere, Simpson needed to find a person to coordinate the American studies program and assist in American literature. Don Koch, head of the English Department turned to the most dependable source he knew, his old mentor Lyon Richardson at Western Reserve University. He recommended Todd Lieber, who had completed work for his degree, dissertation and all, in only three years after receiving his B.A. with honors from Duke University, where he had been elected to Phi Beta Kappa. Although some years later the American studies program was dropped, Lieber remained an active and valuable member of the English staff, becoming head of the department in 1989. More perhaps than any other member of the faculty, he came to exemplify the ideal of the teacher-scholar, balancing first-rate teaching with active and productive research and publication. If that did not keep him busy enough, he settled down in the country out near Spring Hill, where he farmed a fine piece of land and kept livestock. Perhaps it was the farming that led to his sartorial unorthodoxy. He pioneered wearing jeans in the classroom at Simpson, though he sometimes compromised by adding a sport jacket, unwilling to offend the sensibilities of his conservative colleagues.

Ronald J. Warnet, who was completing his doctoral dissertation at the University of Nebraska, was appointed to take the place of Paul Gwinner in the Department of Chemistry. Warnet had earned his B.A. at Hope College in Michigan. After completing his doctorate in 1970, he stayed on at Simpson, working well with veteran Clifford Meints in the department and seeking out opportunities to involve students in serious and productive research projects. Like Todd Lieber, Warnet eschewed city—or even small town—life and loved the countryside, where he employed his undoubted talent in science to live in harmony with nature.

In recent years Simpson has only rarely employed its own graduates as members of the teaching corps. One of a few exceptions to this practice, however, was the appointment in 1970 of Fred O. Jones to a new position in the expanding Sociology Department. Reared in nearby Osceola, Jones and his identical twin brother, Floyd, had attended Simpson, where both played football, both joined the same fraternity, and both did superior academic work. Floyd went on to a distinguished career in medicine; Fred went on to complete an M.A. at the University of Iowa and was aiming to complete a Ph.D. in sociology when he joined the Simpson staff. He taught for three years (1970–73), then took a year off to complete the doctorate at Mississippi State University, returning in the fall of 1974 with a promotion in rank. As the years went by, he helped Simpson develop a major in criminal justice, in which he taught some of the key courses. A popular classroom teacher, he continued his interest in athletics and later served as Simpson's faculty representative in the Iowa Intercollegiate Athletic Conference.

Speaking of popularity in the classroom, few could match the record of Alan W. Magruder, who came to Simpson in 1970 and stayed. He had just completed his Ph.D. in educational administration and research at St. Louis University. A graduate of Washington University, where he earned a B.S. in 1961, he had served nearly a decade as a teacher and administrator of schools in the St. Louis area. At Simpson, Magruder taught in the Department of Education, engaged in considerable institutional research for the College and turned out to be a skillful and empathetic counselor. He worked well with E. G. Booth, and together with Minerva Fair and Gladys Moore, the quartet of "educationists" gave Simpson's teacher education programs both rigor and quality, an agreeable contrast to the situation that prevailed in many institutions where teacher training strained the meaning of academic respectability.

When the staff in psychology was expanded in 1971 from two to three full-time positions, President John announced the appointment of Carl R. Halgren to an assistant professorship. A 1966 graduate of Wabash College, one of the nation's few remaining men's colleges, Halgren had earned his Ph.D. at Indiana University in 1970. At Simpson his exceptional teaching skills were soon recognized, vaulting him within seven years into the headship of the department and in 1985 to the chairmanship of the Division of Social Sciences.

The new "no-general-requirements" curriculum, which became operative in the autumn of 1970, had an instant and severely deleterious effect on the program in foreign languages, which had already moved under the leadership of department head Tom Douglass from a two-year requirement to a competency-based program. Now, however, few students could be persuaded to enroll in foreign languages at all, and the staff declined within four years from seven full-time people to three. Tom Douglass, probably seeing the handwriting on the wall, accepted a position at the University of Iowa in 1970, and Federico Cano assumed the leadership of the shrinking department. In 1971, when Jewell Campbell departed after teaching French at Simpson for three years, Robert L. Gieber was appointed to replace her. He was a graduate of Kansas State Teachers College, held an M.A. from the University of Iowa and had just completed his Ph.D. at the University of Nebraska. When Federico Cano resigned at the end of the 1973–74 academic year, Gieber was asked to take over the reins in the Department of Foreign Languages.[98] A thoroughly competent, careful and cautiously optimistic leader, Gieber assisted the growth of foreign language instruction, watched with pleasure as enrollments rose, saw to the restoration of instruction in Russian and finally, many years later helped bring about the return of a foreign language requirement for all Simpson students, necessitating an increase in staff. Gieber also continued to teach a full range of courses in French and occasionally added to that a course in Latin.

Ralph John's appointment, then, of Thomas, Haddox, Duncan, Lieber, Warnet, Jones, Magruder, Halgren and Gieber between 1969 and 1971 brought much needed stability to the faculty. Thomas retired in 1991, Magruder in 1995, but the seven others were still at their posts when this history was being written.

Others whose tenure at Simpson was long enough to permit them to have real influence in the enterprise deserve proper mention. Joining the faculty in 1968 was James C. Head in mathematics. The next year brought Joe V. Graber in theater arts, an able director who served briefly a decade later as the College's acting director of development, William K. Updegraff in physics (to 1975), Jerry K. Beatty in political science (to 1974), Judith Considine in biology (to 1975), Richard Dusenbury in history (to 1975), Fathi Abdel-Aziz Mansour (to 1974), Albert S. Paone in physical education, coaching football as well (to 1975) and Robert L. Burns, who had already served since 1964 in a part-time capacity, in music, teaching organ. In 1970 Loren Gruber returned to the faculty in English—he had been an instructor from 1966 to 1969—and remained until 1982. That same year saw the appointment in music of William Tuttle—he had taught earlier for one year (1965–66)—who remained until 1977; Danning Bloom in physics (to 1972); and Anne M. Cermak—her later married name was Battani—in physical education, where she did exceptional work. She resigned only in 1990, to the disappointment of nearly everybody at Simpson. In economics and business administration Wallace L. Nelson, Jr., served as acting head of the department for several years and stayed at the College for seven years. A number of others joined the faculty, but their tenure was relatively brief.[99]

* * *

During the latter years of the John administration faculty and staff morale was not high, in part because of widespread student enthusiasm for controversial political and social issues and student disinclination to study. And some of the new people were unhappy. Dean Wally Wiser put it bluntly in his report to the board of trustees in 1969. "Unfortunately," he said, "there have been a few of our younger faculty who, while being articulate with regard to the need for change, have been more destructive than constructive in their criticisms, due in large measure to their lack of experience. . . . We have a high concentration of young faculty members, resulting in a lack of professional maturity."[100] While no doubt Dean Wiser's observations were valid, so were some of the complaints of the faculty. There were indeed emerging problems with curriculum and teaching that did need attention.

Within a year or two after its adoption, the 4-1-4 program clearly needed revision. More options were needed for freshmen, heretofore limited to a choice of one of only four courses, resulting in unnecessary crowding in huge classes. Some faculty people worked very hard during January; others coasted.[101] Even more students took it easy during January, perceiving in many on-campus courses a marked lack of academic rigor. Even greater problems emerged after the adoption of the new open curriculum in 1970. Although Ralph John pronounced it a success,[102] it was becoming evident that faculty advisers were often lacking in diligence when counseling students, and the office of the academic dean was finding it difficult to monitor the crucial role of advisers. Moreover, those advisers who encouraged students to enroll in demanding courses too often encountered either impassiveness or rugged resistance, resulting sometimes in a change to a more lenient adviser. Easier to remedy was the clear-cut need for a proper computer center for instruction.[103] Another decidedly positive action was the adoption in 1973 of three new majors: public administration, human services and international relations. Somewhat more controversial, but providing new kinds of academic experience for students, was the addition of a program in cooperative education in early 1971. In 1975, consequent to a generous gift by Dr. Louis Wheelock, a member of the Parsons College faculty before that institution failed in 1973, Simpson was able to provide a scholarship for a student who chose to study for a year in Greece, linking up with the College Year in Athens Program.

* * *

Although enrollment continued to climb during the 1960s—from 724 in Ralph

John's first year, 1963, to an all-time high of 1,001 in the fall of 1970—rising costs tended to nullify the benefits of growth. Total cost per student (tuition, room and board) went from $2,290 in 1968-69 to $2,920 in 1971-72, an increase of almost thirty percent, but the total budget of the College rose from $2,817,659 to $3,688,396 during that same period, something over thirty percent. The consequence was a series of deficits—not large, but certainly annoying—that seemed to be ineradicable: $30,495 in 1967-68, $37,298 in 1968-69; $67,548 in 1969-70, and a published deficit of $451 in 1970-71 accomplished by a judicious raid on "unassigned" endowment funds, amounting to nearly $51,000, and in the 1971-72 report there was no deficit at all, a balancing feat accomplished only by assigning a portion of the bequest received from the Marcia Worth estate—the bequest was $189,000—to the operating budget rather than to the endowment.[104] All this is not to suggest mismanagement, but to emphasize how difficult it was to keep ahead of the inflationary economy of those years. Especially discouraging was a downturn in enrollment in the fall of 1971, when 957 full-time students registered, a loss of 44. Much worse was the enrollment the following fall, down exactly 100 to 857.

Why the enrollment downturn? Part of the problem was in the area of admissions, described as a "most critical problem."[105] Freshman enrollment dropped from a high of 351 in the fall of 1970 to 264 in 1972 while the academic standards of entering freshmen also declined considerably. The fact is that few students who applied were rejected for academic inadequacy. A number of reasons can be adduced for this parlous state of affairs. The rapid growth throughout Iowa of two-year community colleges, where tuition costs were minimal, provided a serious challenge to those independent colleges whose constituency was primarily from the state. The growing disparity of tuition charges between private and state institutions everywhere was making it difficult for the former to compete.

The cost squeeze could have been a lot worse had it not been for the creation of the Iowa Tuition Grant program. Such plans had been adopted elsewhere, and the Illinois program, for example, was already having a negative effect on enrollment of Illinois students in Iowa colleges. The purpose of the grants was to "equalize" the cost of tuition between state and private colleges by making a cash award to students who could demonstrate need. While the amount of the awards would never truly equal private college tuition charges, the criteria of need were usually fairly generous, permitting a large number of students to qualify. The idea of the grants had real merit and made good economic sense. The cost to the state for the student receiving the grant was far less than the cost of educating that same student in one of the state universities. Thus, in a sense, the private colleges, which in Iowa were then enrolling nearly half of the state's college population, were providing the state an invaluable service.

When Simpson's board of trustees met in June 1968, members were pleased to hear that a proposal for tuition grants would come before the Iowa General Assembly at its next session. When the matter was taken up the following January, no one was more instrumental in securing its passage after weeks of debate than was Charles O. Laverty, senator for Warren and Marion counties and stalwart member of the Simpson board of trustees. The first grants were made available in the fall of 1969, and Simpson students received an aggregate $131,000 that first year.[106] So successful was the program that it was continued from that time forward, the amount of individual grants increasing from a maximum of $400 the first year to $2,650 in 1993–94. Simpson was deeply indebted to Senator Laverty and the Iowa legislature for creating the program; it was also grateful to the state board of regents for supporting its continuation.

An important, if unintended, effect of the Iowa Tuition Grant program, indeed of those of other states as well, was to keep students in their own states, because tuition grants were not portable across state boundaries. Simpson's Illinois enrollment, for example, declined precipitously, from 144 in 1965–66 to less than 32 decades later. In that same period, total out-of-state enrollment declined from thirty-seven percent to nine percent, making for an unexpected, and somewhat unwelcome, geographical homogeneity.

While the decline in admissions was uncomfortable, retention of students posed a far more serious problem. Too many students dropped out—some from academic failure, more from financial problems or dissatisfaction with the College—at the end of the freshman year, often as many as a third of those enrolled. Another major loss occurred at the end of the sophomore year, most either quitting school altogether or transferring to state institutions. Those who returned as juniors usually stayed on until graduation.

Unquestionably a major problem for Simpson was the image it was projecting throughout Iowa where it recruited most of its students. The shifts in attitudes and lifestyles among students and Simpson's response to those shifts clearly accounted for a fair share of the enrollment problem. One Chariton parent, a businessman whose daughter was about to enter college, said in mid-1972 that Simpson was reputed to have declining academic standards, a radicalized student body, severe racial tension and few if any behavioral rules or regulations because it kowtowed to the demands of irresponsible students. He would send his daughter to another, more wholesome, college where some kind of standards of scholarship and civility prevailed.

While such a criticism of Simpson was probably extreme, it was fairly representative of the way some people looked at the College. One did not have to go beyond the confines of Indianola to hear the same kind of complaints. Soon Simpson's "image" became a lively topic of discussion among trustees, administrators and faculty, not to speak of alumni, whose letters expressed, sometimes quite colorfully, their unhappiness with their alma mater.[107]

* * *

One answer to spiraling expenses was vigorous fund-raising, some of it among those very people who were less than pleased with Simpson's reputation. By 1970, once the funds for the new Blank Performing Arts Center were assured, the board of trustees was ready to undertake a new capital campaign, something they had been talking about for at least a year.[108] In March, 1970, they contracted with Marts and Lundy, Inc, fund-raising specialists, to help Simpson conduct a drive for $2,500,000 over six months, commencing July 1.[109] Named the "Resource Program," the campaign was announced in early 1972 after several months of an intensive search for "leadership gifts" that had produced $687,000, or twenty-seven percent of their goal. William Buxton III was named national chairman of the fund drive, a campaign unusual in that its centerpiece was not a major building but the acquisition of endowment for professorial chairs, an "academic enrichment fund" to attract visiting scholars or artists and to help faculty complete advanced studies. Capital expenditures would be modest: the renovation of the Pfeiffer dining hall—it needed both expansion and modernization—together with refurbishing of several older campus structures.[110] By June 1972, Luther Hill reported $1,078,000 had been raised, including a gift of $200,000 from the Kresge Foundation.[111] Because of Ralph John's resignation and the search for a new president, Hill referred to the money already raised as "Phase One" of the drive. "Phase Two" would await the arrival of the new president.

* * *

When the board of trustees gathered at the Camp Lounge in the Brenton Student Center for its annual fall meeting on a bright Saturday morning, October 30, 1971, at nine o'clock, members could talk of little else than the stunning news that Ralph John had submitted his resignation, accepting the presidency of Western Maryland College. He would, however, remain at his post at Simpson for the entire 1971–72 academic year, allowing the board ample time to find a new leader for the College.[112] Many years later he recalled the difficult parting with a place he had come to love:

> It frequently is said that a college president should stay no more than ten years in one place, a general guideline which I think is statistically valid. There might be some exceptions. I had been at Simpson for nine years, was fifty-three years old and knew that if I were to make a move it had to be soon. Also I felt that I really had given Simpson what it was in me to give and that it would be a mistake both for the College and for me if I attempted to remain on until retirement. I do not think I could have given leadership in making the next ten years as exciting and productive as the past nine had been. [It was] difficult . . . to explain how you can love a place and leave it.[113]

The board appointed a search committee of trustees, faculty, students and alumni under the leadership of Luther Hill, vice-chairman of the board, to find a new president. Soon nominations and applications poured in. The list of candidates was first reduced to eighteen, then to eleven, then to six and finally to three.[114] After months of careful work and intensive interviews with the leading candidates, the committee recommended the election of Richard Bailey Lancaster, associate dean of academic affairs at Oberlin College, and the board formally elected him the eighteenth president of Simpson on June 22, 1972.[115] Lancaster took up his duties nine days later.

When he came to Simpson with his wife, Reta, and three children, Richard, seventeen, Bradley, sixteen and Susan, twelve, Lancaster was just a few weeks shy of forty-one years old. Born in Tulsa, Oklahoma, August 15, 1931, he grew up in Detroit, Michigan, where he attended a private high school run by the Ford Motor Company. Later he earned a B.A. degree from Wayne State University in the class of 1953 and a year later completed an M.A. in sociology at Florida State University. He married Reta Russell, who had grown up in Des Moines.

For twelve years after completing his academic work, he was a member and later head of the Department of Religious Education of the Reorganized Church of Jesus Christ of Latter Day Saints in that church's world headquarters in Independence, Missouri. Both he and his wife had been reared in the R.L.D.S. church, and he was soon recognized as a leader among the quarter million members of that denomination.

During his years at Independence he became increasingly aware of his lack of formal theological training. Accordingly, he entered the St. Paul School of Theology, a Methodist seminary in Kansas City, graduating in 1965 with "the highest average in its history."[116] He then determined to pursue a doctorate, entering the renowned program in higher education at the University of Michigan, where he studied for two years, completing the Ph.D. in higher education administration in 1969. The director of the program lauded his outstanding performance at Michigan.[117]

From Michigan Lancaster was named assistant dean of academic affairs at Oberlin College, where he was responsible for academic advising, academic standards, off-campus study, study abroad and graduate study, giving him broad experience in academic administration. He was promoted to associate dean in 1970.

Interestingly, Hill felt it necessary to point out that although Lancaster was still nominally an R.L.D.S. member and a layman, he did hold a Bachelor of Divinity degree from a Methodist seminary and attended the Methodist Church. Perhaps that would somehow provide the necessary Methodist credentials expected by many of Simpson's constituents. Hill praised Lancaster as "a man of immense talent . . . of highest character, intelligence and rigor, who is irrevocably dedicated to the concepts of liberal arts education."[118]

Although the new president did not find Simpson as innovative a college as was Oberlin, he came to appreciate its "conserving character." Like others before his time and after, he was impressed with the unwavering commitment of the board of trustees and by the ability and dedication of many among the faculty. The beauty of the campus and its fortunate location near Des Moines he found agreeable. But there were some serious weaknesses that demanded early attention. He recalls that a few members of his administrative staff "were not individually well prepared for their position, or had a problem with alcohol, or had serious personal problems" and were unable to work effectively together.[119] Among the tenured faculty were a few who were "weak or tired." And the faculty was too large for the declining student population. Ralph John had increased the size of the faculty substantially to serve a student population of 1,200 or more. But poor admissions and poorer retention had resulted in an enrollment in the fall of 1972 of 857, down 144 in the last two years. One of the first instructions the new president received from the board of trustees was to reduce the size of the faculty by fifteen positions.

When the Lancasters arrived on campus it was easy to see the serious town-gown tensions. Although the Johns had been personally very popular, student activism had alienated many townspeople and alumni. The situation called for a lot of fence-mending. Dissatisfaction with the College's "way-out liberalism" was hurting fund-raising in the Resource Program. It was difficult enough, reasoned Lancaster, to take over the helm in the middle of a fund drive, and considerably more so to attempt its completion amidst the campus climate of the early seventies.[120] Yet fund-raising was crucial, for the College's exchequer was not in robust health; repeated, if modest, deficits during the past few years had been covered by a certain amount of financial legerdemain. There was plenty to do.

* * *

Simpson learned one thing about its new president very soon: he disliked what he considered excessive formality. "Keep it simple," he advised Joe Walt, who was put in charge of the inauguration ceremony scheduled for February 10, 1973. Walt later recalled that the event "was simple by desire, but with a simplicity that should not be taken for a lack of dignity or a lack of importance."[121] Certainly the procession at three o'clock in the afternoon from Dunn Library to Smith Chapel was formal enough, with faculty, representatives from other colleges and universities and learned societies robed in academic splendor. As the columns filed into the chapel filled with 500 spectators, Simpson's choir, with orchestral accompaniment, sounded a welcoming anthem of praise. Formally installing the new president were Luther Hill, the new chairman of the board of trustees, and Methodist Bishop James S. Thomas. Hill placed the medallion symbolizing the presidency around Dr. Lancaster's neck.

In his inaugural address, the new president called for "more cooperation and less competition" among the nation's colleges and universities and on campus. "Education," he said, "is dominated by competition—much of it extravagant and wasteful; some of it is ridiculous, and other aspects are dehumanizing. Plainly, competition is anachronistic in today's world. The future demands that we learn to cooperate. Calling "access to education . . . a prerequisite for the man of tomorrow," he noted the crucial importance of education in "creative use of leisure time and also [in] the need for many adults to change vocations or retool."[122]

The principal speaker of the day, introduced by Dr. Walt, was United States Senator Dick Clark of Iowa. Noting the serious financial difficulty of small colleges because of spiraling costs, he called for more federal funding of higher education, especially in the private sector. Yet in President Nixon's proposed budget for 1973–74, he said, "the *total* expenditure for education is less than just the *increase* for military spending." This, he declared, was not the direction the nation should take. "The Viet Nam War," he said, "has diverted our resources, distracted our attention and upset our values. With our involvement in this conflict finally ending, we should be moving to restore a balance to our lives."[123] People showed their appreciation for Dick Clark and admiration of their new president at a fine reception held in the gallery of the Brenton Student Center.[124]

During the first three years (1972–75) of his presidency, Lancaster saw his administrative council change considerably. He lost two strong men he would have liked to keep on. Jim Robinson, vice-president for college relations, accepted a position at the University of Miami in the fall of 1973. A few weeks earlier, vice-president and academic dean Wally Wiser was named provost at Capitol University in Columbus, Ohio. To replace Robinson, Lancaster found A. Edward Couch, head of the development program for the Culver Educational Foundation, which operated both the Culver Military Academy and the Culver Academy for Girls in Indiana. An ordained Presbyterian minister, Couch held a B.A. from Yale, a B.A. and M.A. from Oberlin and a M.Div. from Vanderbilt University. He had earlier served as associate director of development at Oberlin and before that as pastor in several churches.[125] In Couch, Lancaster found an eloquent and hard-working associate who fell to the task of fund-raising with vigor.

It was more difficult to find a new academic dean. Because Wally Wiser left on fairly short notice on August 15, 1973, Lancaster had to act fast. He telephoned peripatetic Joe Walt, who was thoroughly enjoying himself in Vienna, Austria, visiting old friends.

"Wally Wiser has resigned," said Lancaster.

"Oh," said Walt.

"Would you consider coming home to take up the deanship?"

"No, not really. Thanks, but. . . . "

"Let me re-word that. Would you come home and take the deanship for one year if I promise to let you go back to teaching the next year?"

"Well, I suppose I could. . . . "

"Fine. Be here no later than September 1."

Even with a year to hunt for a new dean, the search proved difficult.[126] For one thing, the makeup of the selection committee was such that conservatives and liberals, old and young, could not find any candidate acceptable to all of them. After months of committee wrangling, President Lancaster took the matter into his own hands. He telephoned an old friend in Rochester, New York, Dr. R. Melvin Henderson, who weeks before had told Simpson he was not interested in the deanship in Indianola. But Lancaster pulled out all the stops and convinced Henderson that it would not hurt at least to come and look at the position. Fortunately, when he visited the College, he liked it, and to everyone's agreeable surprise, the committee liked him. He took the job.

Henderson, a genial, soft-spoken Alabama native, had earned his B.A. at Samford University in Birmingham, seminary degrees from Southeastern Seminary in Wake Forest, North Carolina, and his Ph.D. in theology and philosophy from Princeton Seminary. The consummate school man, he had served as academic dean at Crozer Seminary and was primarily responsible for effecting the merger of Crozer with Colgate Rochester Divinity School and Bexley Hall, developing a unified academic program for the combined institutions. Just prior to his coming to Simpson, he was professor of New Testament at the seminary and on the faculty of the University of Rochester.

In Henderson, Lancaster had found a man in whom he had the greatest confidence. At forty-three, the new dean was at the height of his powers, kind, compassionate, diplomatic, soon known at Simpson for his almost courtly gentlemanliness. And in spite of his quaint practice of keeping most of his office files in unsteady piles on his desk or agonizingly putting off unimportant decisions until every shred of evidence had been collected—in this he was a true scholar—the faculty loved him.

So did President Lancaster. With Henderson's arrival on campus in mid-1974, it was announced that "a major administrative re-alignment" had now been completed.[127] Other changes in this "re-alignment" included the appointment of Ivan Lyddon, the director of alumni affairs, to the post of director of admissions while Louis Smith concentrated his efforts in the office of the registrar. Replacing Lyddon as director of alumni affairs was Lu Jean Cole.[128] She brought flair and style to the work, and she and Lancaster made a great team at alumni gatherings throughout the land.

For a time there was some volatility in the office of student affairs. When Evelyn Morris resigned in 1973, Robert G. Bradford, an experienced young dean of students from Tennessee whose Ph.D. was from Arizona State University, was named vice president of student affairs and dean of students.[129] His year at Simpson was a controversial one, leading him to seek a position in the West.

His successor for a year (1974–75) was the College's chaplain, Roger Betsworth, who returned to the chaplaincy after his stint in the student dean's office.[130] Betsworth had come to Simpson in 1973 as chaplain when Gilbert Taverner departed after five years at that post.[131] Betsworth, who had only recently completed a doctorate in social ethics at the University of Southern California, was a graduate of the United States Naval Academy (1955) and had earned his masters in divinity from Drew University in 1962. He had served as an engineering officer in the Navy and subsequently as pastor of Methodist churches in both New Jersey and California. His appointment at Simpson included an assistant professorship of religion.[132] Betsworth, who would remain at Simpson for many years, proved to be especially valuable to the College for his solid work in interdisciplinary education. Forthright in what he believed to be best for the College, he came to be admired by all, even those who might at times disagree with him on this or that issue. And no one could gainsay his sense of humor, accompanied by the healthiest laugh on campus, nor the fact that he became one of Simpson's most dedicated tennis enthusiasts.

When Daniel Seaton retired from Simpson after sixteen years with the College, Richard McClintic was assigned the position of director of student aid. And as physical plant manager, George Ewers replaced Don Barnett.

* * *

Simpson's catalog of 1972–73 listed eighty-five persons with faculty rank. Among these were five administrators, three librarians, two in student development and one billed as the director of computer development, together with five part-time lecturers. Four more part-timers were not listed. However one counted it, the faculty was clearly too large for 857 students. Counting only the sixty-nine people who taught full-time, the faculty-student ratio was just over 1:12, far richer than Simpson could possibly afford. When Lancaster took up his duties, five new full-time faculty had already been employed. This group included Marvin Van Wyk, a 1967 graduate of Central College who had just completed his doctorate in mathematics at the University of Iowa in the spring of 1972. During the years that followed, he found himself more and more involved with computer science, helping the College establish a major in that discipline in 1980.[133]

In 1972, driven by stern reality, Lancaster determined to hire henceforth only indispensable replacements, carving down the size of the teaching staff to an affordable optimum number. In the next two years, ten more new people—all replacements of those who departed—joined the faculty, only four of whom would stay longer than three years. One of these, Roger Betsworth, we have already encountered. Others included James H. Rogers (1974–78), who provided yeoman service in English and black studies, as noted earlier in this chapter. Two appointments in music were fortunate, providing welcome continuity in that department. One was Anne Ogan Larson, a local Indianola woman who had graduated from Simpson in 1967. Her work with opera at the College soon became the stuff of legend. She remained at Simpson for many years. The other was Carol Stuart Buechler, who had taught part-time for two years before accepting a full-time appointment in the autumn of 1974. She, too, contributed mightily to the opera program.[134]

Bringing new people into the faculty required carefulness and persistence, but it was a pleasant task. Much more taxing was making judicious cuts without damaging seriously the academic program and morale of the College. At first, it was not too difficult. Two people, Richard Ronan in chemistry and Richard Snyder in mathematics, left Simpson to take other positions, and they were not replaced. Two more, Katherine Love in German and Edna Bowersox in home economics, retired. Glenn Buhr took over all instruction in German. Home economics was dropped from the curriculum, eliminating the part-time position of Janet Lynn. It was probably time to drop home ec. A time-honored part of the Simpson curriculum, it was a victim both of changing times and of federal regulations, which specified, for example, that only those students who attended land-grant universities whose programs were regulated by the Smith-Hughes Act could qualify for federally supported home economics positions, effectively giving Iowa State University a local monopoly in that academic area.

It was one of Simpson's own regulations which cost the position of a few nontenured faculty. It had recently been determined that faculty in those fields in which the doctorate was the terminal degree must complete the degree within seven years of their joining the Simpson staff. In 1973 Richard McClintic in economics ran up against this time limit. Loath to ask him to leave the staff and determined to strengthen the admissions program, Lancaster appointed him, as we have seen, director of student aid.

To make as democratic as possible the "managed decline" in the size of the faculty, Lancaster appointed in the fall of 1973 a Faculty Council, including one member from each of the five academic divisions, to consult on faculty reduction with the president, the dean and the elected Faculty Personnel Committee. Some of the cuts, explained Dean Walt to the board of trustees, will be made "due to lack of student enrollment and decrease in [those majoring] in certain fields of study."[135] After a contentious, agonizing examination of every possibility, during which time faculty morale sank to a new low, several cuts were authorized, two in history and one each in physics, art, physical education, plus one-half a position in music, effective June 1975.[136] Only four of the positions were in fact eliminated, the two in history and one each in physics and physical education. Historian Richard Dusenbury remained until the middle of the 1974–75 school year, for his position would in any case be eliminated at the end of the next semester. Gary Valen was moved from history to the post of dean of students; Les Deaton in physical education resigned to enter private business. In addition, William Updegraff and Don Dittmer resigned in 1974 and were not replaced. The other positions were retained, and neither the administration nor the Faculty Council had much to show for their unpopular labors.[137] Nor had President Lancaster come even close yet to the fifteen cuts mandated by the board.

* * *

During the first three years of Lancaster's presidency, the College saw the modest operating deficits of recent years soar to alarming levels: $107,000 in 1972–73, $316,531 the next year and $499,000 the year after that. The reasons for the trickle of red ink becoming a flood were not hard to find. Simply put, the costs of running the College rose much faster than the income received from tuition and all other sources. Enrollment, in spite of a fairly large freshman class in the fall of 1973, was static from 1972 to 1975.[138] Tuition charges were increased—from $2,060 in 1971–72 to $2,300 in 1974–75—but did not keep pace with the galloping national rate of inflation. Faculty and staff costs, especially in fringe benefits, were up sharply, leading to the necessity of virtually freezing salaries and wages in 1974–75, an act not calculated to improve anyone's morale. In order to keep enrollment steady, more and more funds were allocated to student financial aid, claiming more than twenty percent of tuition income in the 1973–74 and threatening to increase substantially in the years to come.[139] Beyond these major outlays, the cost of nearly everything, from library books to soap to football jerseys, skyrocketed.

Moreover, distant events could exacerbate the College's financial problems. When, for example, the 1973 Yom Kippur War between Arabs and Israelis led to an embargo late that year against the United States and other industrialized nations, causing long lines at gas stations and shutting down factories, Simpson took action. The Christmas holidays were lengthened to a full four weeks, allowing a saving of nearly 73,000 gallons (twenty percent of annual use) of fuel oil.[140] Regrettably, the higher price of oil during the energy crisis wiped out any saving the College made. But without such conservation, the deficit would have been even worse that year. The pressure, then, was on to reduce expenses. In a few areas, cuts could be made without a loud outcry. The library budget was slashed shamelessly, and some of the academic departments saw their already small administrative budgets nearly drain away. Each year the deficits were met by "drawing down" on the endowment, an exceedingly risky practice. Still, unless the College wanted to borrow in the financial markets, there was nowhere else to find the money to make up for the unremitting shortfalls in the College's exchequer.

If anyone was able to put a good face on Simpson's shaky finances, board member James W. Hubbell, Jr., vice-president and director of the huge Equitable of Iowa, could do it. In 1975, after reporting a gargantuan deficit, he observed that "in spite of a heavy draw-down on endowment resources to meet an operating deficit this year, the endowment has increased compared to the previous year." Indeed it had, moving up a half million dollars to a total of just over $7,000,000.[141] Everyone seemed to agree that Simpson's financial health was not good, but the place was not in grave danger either.

* * *

Fund-raising continued apace, only modestly slowed by the change in administration in 1972. By mid-1974 the Resource Program "Phase II" was completed, bringing the total of the fund drive of $2,422,921,[142] just short of its original goal.

Hardly had the old campaign been declared successful, when a new fund drive was put together under the leadership of Simpson's new, energetic vice-president, Ed Couch. He called for a ten-year program called "Commitment 125," to raise $11,000,000 by 1985, the time of the College's 125th anniversary.[143] Among other important needs, including increased endowment, the fund drive would provide for several capital projects: a new physical education center and field house, a new music building and—if feasible—the renovation of College Hall, the oldest structure on the campus.[144] Selected to serve as national chairman of the campaign was board member Richard S. Levitt of Des Moines. Levitt was executive vice-president of the immensely successful Dial Finance Company.[145] To help run the campaign—without external professional counsel—two able young alumni were added to Couch's staff. They were Frank Nowasell '60, sirened away from an idyllic teaching position at Punahou School in Hawaii, and Robert

E. MacKenzie '70, who had been working effectively for more than two years in Simpson's admissions office.[146] And soon enough, the goal of the campaign was raised to $20,000,000.

Almost inevitably, as we have seen repeatedly through our history of Simpson, fund drives have centered upon building projects. That is perhaps only natural. For one thing, buildings are expensive and require an immediate capital outlay. Further, opportunities for donor recognition make them attractive to potential contributors. The Resource Program, which straddled Ralph John's and Richard Lancaster's administrations, had been something of an exception to the focus on buildings, but it did provide funds to renovate Pfeiffer Hall. The food service operation had grown substantially and needed more space for seating and for food preparation and serving. Designed by Brooks, Borg and Skiles of Des Moines, the renovation enlarged the building considerably, permitting an increase in seating from 270 to 450, completely reorganizing the service area, extending the building to the south, permitting a covered colonnade along the entire length of the building, and building a service area upstairs adjacent to Great Hall. It required $397,000 to build it, the cost met primarily by a grant of $200,000 from the Kresge Foundation and part of a $250,000 gift from the Cowles Foundation.[147] It was ready for use at the beginning of the fall semester in 1973.

The first priority in the new Commitment 125 campaign was the physical education center. Hopper Gym was too small; it had only limited seating for spectators, too few lockers, inadequate office space and, to be sure, no swimming pool. The College, said President Lancaster in 1974, "must now consider our special need for an adequate physical education facility."[148] A year later, worrying about enrollments, he was more adamant, declaring that "this facility is an absolutely essential requirement for the College's continued success and progress."[149] While willing to wait until funds for its construction were in hand, he hoped that the project could move ahead quickly.

The question of the proper location for the new building led to a call for a new campus plan to replace the outdated Neutra scheme. The board selected Dober and Associates of Cambridge, Massachusetts, to develop a plan to deal with "pedestrian and vehicular traffic, as well as proper utilization of buildings on campus, for the purpose of achieving a coherent and aesthetic integrity."[150] During the following months Richard Dober and others from his firm visited the campus, familiarized themselves with the College's needs and aims, and developed a comprehensive plan. Its immediate value was in the felicitous siting of the new physical education center adjacent to Hopper Gymnasium.[151]

It was estimated the new physical education center would cost approximately $2,500,000. Ed Couch and his staff went to work on the fund-raising at once. After all, there was a huge contingent of alumni who had participated in athletics, some of whom had been reluctant to contribute to earlier fund-raising drives but had assured former presidents that when Simpson chose to build a fine field house, they would contribute generously. They were just waiting to be asked. "The fields are white, all ready to harvest," said Couch, who was never at a loss for a scriptural reference for almost anything.

The harvest was surprisingly poor. Couch asked, but not very many of the ex-athletes gave. Most of the gifts came from some of the same people who had always contributed. By mid-1974 he could count about $650,000 in cash and pledges, and to that amount could be added a U.S. Higher Education Facilities

Grant of $408,676.[152] But at that point the giving for the building seemed to dry up. The project was put on hold.

Meanwhile, alumni in the famed "Heckert group" of successful alumni businesspeople had contributed very nearly $80,000, to which was added a U.S. Higher Education Facilities Grant of $46,389 to renovate the old Carnegie Library for use by the Department of Economics and Business Administration.[153] When completed, the building was renamed Heckert Hall in a ceremony of rededication, May 24, 1975.[154]

Just before the new fund-raising drive was launched in 1974, eighty-year-old George Carpenter, son-in-law of redoubtable Sara Sigler, offered the College his handsome house on West Ashland, one of Indianola's showplaces, in return for a modest annuity.[155] The house, which had been designed and built in 1907, could be renovated and used as the home of the president of the College. It was a fortuitous offer, for the existing house on North B Street was not adequate for the needs of a college president and family, especially for the extensive entertaining that was expected.[156]

In a way, the Carpenter offer was one Simpson could not turn down. But in a time of skyrocketing deficits, it was difficult to justify the price of the building—a small annuity payment to Carpenter—and the inevitable costs of refurbishing the house. Still, a new president's house was truly needed, and the opportunity, reasoned the board, had to be grasped.[157] Plans for remodeling the Carpenter residence were approved later in 1974, and the project, costing $85,000, was completed the following summer.[158] Selected to handle the work were Godwin Brothers, local Indianola builders. Most of the expense of the restoration was for essentials: a new roof, new plumbing, a new heating system and new wiring.

Whatever the merits of a new house for the president, the project caused much controversy on the campus. In a time when staff people were being let go, when inflation made true faculty raises virtually nonexistent, students and faculty were predictably upset, asking where in the world the College's priorities lay. That the renovation would be paid for by sale of the old president's house on North B and by drawing from restricted endowment funds, not from current operating expenses, may have been true, but it did not do much to assuage the wrath of the critics.

The new president's house was probably one of those things that Simpson had to go through. In more than one college the building of a new president's house, usually asserted by critics to be palatial and surely unneeded, had cost the president his job. To be sure, his successor, the next occupant of the house, however sumptuous the dwelling, suffered no vilification for self-serving extravagance. Thus it was at Simpson. There were those who never forgave the Lancasters for living in "that mansion on West Ashland," but understood that their successors would dwell therein as a matter of course. It was and is a nice house.

* * *

During the early Lancaster years, the College continued its policy of buying land and buildings that lay between C Street and E Street and between Clinton and Girard Streets, filling in the area between the traditional campus and the "new" campus west of E Street. Accordingly, a number of properties were acquired as they became available. When the site for the new physical education center was selected, the College purchased the last two houses on D Street between Girard and Clinton, providing space for the new structure.[159] Yet these acquisitions, important as they were to the development of the College, drew fire from students and even some faculty. In the *Simpsonian*, Jim Vint lamented the College's acquiring nine residential properties and "at least" four rural properties while "disposing of five faculty members over a one year period."[160]

It was in 1973 that Simpson's last elm trees died, the result of a decade of the ravages of the Dutch elm disease.[161] To replace these great campus monarchs, new trees were planted either by the College's own buildings and grounds staff or by organizations or individuals in accordance with a landscaping plan.

* * *

By the time President Lancaster came to Simpson, the student antiwar movement was in a state of decline, collapsing entirely with the end of the draft. There was a thoughtful editorial by student body president Steve Schier in the *Simpsonian* in late 1972, lamenting the intransigence of the Nixon representatives at the Paris peace talks, concluding that "nine years of self-deception are enough."[162] A few months later, senior Tim Shea could hope that "Americans will come to the realization that it is indeed our responsibility to extend economic aid willingly to the peoples of North Vietnam" in rebuilding that war-torn nation.[163]

But if the Vietnam protests were past, the goals of the blacks at Simpson and all over the nation had not yet been realized. To many of Simpson's African-American community it seemed as if their demands had either been drowned out by the chorus of antiwar protesters or ignored, their concerns lost in a sea of apathy. Embolded by the extent of their numbers on campus, strengthened by the appearance of several gifted leaders—people like Bernard Franklin, Royal Corbin and Al Gardner—and enraged at what they perceived to be a campus battlefield littered with hypocrisy and broken promises, black students were ready to declare war on "individual and institutional racism." Their demands became more strident, their tone more shrill. They were ready to take on the world. They started with the president of the College.

Ralph John remembered the confrontation well. It happened in the spring of 1972, during his last months at Simpson. The Organization for Black Unity (O.B.U.) invited John and Dean of Students Evelyn Morris for an evening discussion at the Afro-American Cultural Center. When they arrived, the guests found a much larger crowd than expected, for it included a number of other people, older blacks, presumably from the Des Moines black community. "The mood," recalled John, "was mean from the start."

> All of the things they were demanding were reiterated: more student aid, more Black staff, Black faculty, Black studies courses, and separate accommodations for this, that and the other. We heard all about slavery and what the white man owes the Black community for its role, through slavery, in the building of the nation. They said they never intended to repay any student aid loans, public or private, because this money was theirs in the first place. For an hour and a half things got shriller and shriller, more and more profane, and Evie and I were personally vilified. Each speaker tried to outdo the previous one. The situation was scary because of the tone and emotional intensity. Finally I broke in, told them that we had come there at their invitation and in good faith, that Dean Morris and I did not have to endure their insults and personal attacks, and that

we were leaving. We stood up and started moving for the door, there was booing and two of the number blocked the door. I informed them that if they so much as touched either of us the consequences would be very serious for them. They were uncertain about what to do, as we were, but they let us through. That was an experience to forget.[164]

It was, to be sure, an experience the black students would *not* forget. Their frustrations, the failure of their demands, their sense that racism was everywhere, contributed to an almost complete alienation from the rest of the College community.

A year later, in a much less defiant tone, Bernard Franklin challenged white students to demonstrate their asserted desire for desegregation. "The doors are open," he wrote, "but no one seems to enter the building of understanding. We need to get together."[165] There was no response to his plea. Nor did there seem to be any salutary change in the campus climate. Reflecting the blighted hope of the black community, Franklin spoke out in student senate in early 1974, his senior year, warning that students would "no longer tolerate" faculty dismissals, failure to hire black faculty or to implement black studies programs without student participation in the decision-making process.[166] A week later Al Gardner accused the dean of students of "making remarks that were construed as racial slurs."[167] But these complaints were merely preliminary to the big explosion that came in mid-April during Black Awareness Week.

It began on Friday morning, April 12, 1974. About thirty members of the O.B.U. came to the office of President Lancaster and presented him a three-page document containing a list of nonnegotiable demands, calling for administrative response no later than 1:00 P.M. that same day. Asserting that "no longer can Black people tolerate this system of proven racist attitudes" and charging "incompetence and lack of true commitment on the part of the administration of the College," they demanded $75,000 to hire three black faculty and two black administrators no later than July 1, the funds for this recruitment to be handed to the O.B.U. For 1975 they demanded a dean of black affairs and a total of six black faculty, that number to increase to ten by 1976. The list also called for the College to cease using *"white racist niggerologists* (experts on niggers) to teach misconstrued concepts about Black culture." Further, because of alleged abuse of black athletes who were "ill-treated and disrespected as human beings," they demanded the hiring of both a new football and basketball coach, one of whom had to be black. Their ultimatum threatened that "further action will be taken by the O.B.U." if no reply was received by the stipulated deadline.[168]

Lancaster prepared a reply to the O.B.U. and delivered it to them about 1:30 P.M. He reviewed the steps taken to meet the needs of black students—the Afro-American Cultural Center, a seven-fold increase in the O.B.U. budget, the hiring of a part-time black faculty member and full-time admissions counselor, the purchase of more than $3,700 worth of books in black studies during the past year. He could not, of course, respond to their demands for money or firings, nor would he. Most importantly, he reassured them of his commitment to an integrated campus, for, he said, "no form of racial segregation or separateness is in the long run healthy for blacks or whites at Simpson, and I reaffirm our desire to establish opportunity for all races to a full and free participation in Simpson community life."[169]

Meanwhile, the O.B.U. had alerted the Des Moines media, which then heralded the imminent takeover of a Simpson building by the O.B.U. But after a ninety-minute meeting regarding Lancaster's response to their demands, the organization "indicated no further action would be taken until after the weekend when more meetings could be scheduled."[170] The media interpreted this as a failure of O.B.U.'s efforts, leading to O.B.U.'s decision to go ahead and occupy the Brenton Student Center that evening.

Lancaster refused to negotiate with the building's occupiers so long as other students were denied access to the building. He did, however, call upon Henry Parker, Simpson's part-time black faculty member, to serve as an intermediary. Parker and others worked through the night, and by early Saturday morning the Student Center was reopened and a four-point agreement signed by President Lancaster and Al Gardner, representing O.B.U. The document represented a fair compromise: (1) the College would seek to hire another full-time black faculty member by September; (2) the College would create a position of dean of minority affairs; (3) a meeting would be held, bringing together black athletes and the coaching staff and (4) a committee would be created to carry out the agreement.[171]

The following Monday, the Faculty Council, on behalf of the entire faculty, issued a statement consequent to a full discussion of the weekend's events by a faculty meeting that day. They were not in a good mood when they spoke out to the entire campus community: "Serious and possibly irreparable professional damage has been dealt members of the Simpson College faculty and coaching staff by unsubstantiated charges of racism made last week in a public communique by the Organization for Black Unity. We find this act irresponsible and inconsistent with individual dignity, the concept of academic freedom, and the socially progressive record of Simpson College."[172]

Faculty were not the only people upset by the attack on the administration and faculty. Speaking to the blacks, junior Don Merritt, in a long piece in the *Simpsonian*, warned them, "You won this battle, but beware, the war may be in jeopardy." Calling for rational discourse, he wrote, "Let us debate, not demand. Let us seek our common ground, not perpetuate our antagonisms. I don't want to be your white friend. I want to be your friend."[173]

It was probably a good thing that the racial confrontation came near the end of the academic year, for during the summer tempers cooled and the administration did make an honest effort to redress some of the grievances of the black community. Although he graduated that spring, Bernard Franklin continued two more years as a member of the College's board of trustees.[174]

Racial strife was hardly peculiar to Simpson. Indeed it was but one small part of a national phenomenon. Sometimes painful, often frustrating, rife with misunderstanding, the struggle was one in which all of the players were victims of inherited, ingrained attitudes toward race and ethnicity. Neither the hurt of the blacks nor the prejudices of too many of the whites was easily effaced. At Simpson, too few of those affected, students black or white, faculty or administration, could get past the rhetoric of the conflict. Debate gave way to name-calling, civility to ugliness, understanding to contention. Yet in retrospect one can see what happened at Simpson as a necessary, difficult and for the most part instructive chapter in the advance of black Americans toward equality and racial justice.

* * *

Analyses of student ideals and behavior during the late sixties and early seventies have attempted to find one or more major themes or patterns that will somehow explain everything from antiwar demonstrations to racial tension to drug use. At Simpson, and very likely in other colleges as well, at least one theme can indeed be discerned. Students wanted individual freedom and most of them opposed any individual or institution that limited that freedom to "do their own thing."

One has but to thumb through issues of the *Zenith* for those years. Dress was self-consciously sloppy, wondrously colorful, a powerful contrast to the clothing of parents, or, God forbid, the military. "Wear what you want," cried the *Simpsonian*.[175] And they did. Male hair styles rested on the premise that the more hair one had, the better. Beards were "in." A young man's indispensable appliance was his hair dryer. A close-cropped, neatly dressed, unbearded male was suspect, probably a "narc" and surely a fascist. There was probably nothing particularly individualistic about all this, but students *thought* there was, and dressed accordingly. One female sophomore was especially memorable, walking everywhere barefooted through an entire Iowa winter.[176] Students' appearance shocked their elders, at least most of them, and rubbed off on some of the faculty, whose hair grew shaggy and chins bearded. In all this, students were flouting convention while following youthful fashion.

As we have noted, civility was not the organizing principle of the student rebellion, and during those years manners, language and deportment suffered. This, too, represented not only a drive for individual freedom, but also a conscious effort to test, or put an end to, "outmoded" standards.

Most of all, however, these were the days when it seemed proper to attack all "establishments." These included the government, the military, the church, together with all organizations, whatever their purpose. On campus those institutions targeted included the College itself, organized athletics and the Greek-letter societies, all of which came under fire.

Whenever the College—its administration and faculty—attempted to hold the line on student hours or regulate living arrangements, there was loud outcry in the Student Senate or in the *Simpsonian* or in the recesses of the Brenton Student Center. As we have seen, the students won most of the skirmishes as the administration gave in on hours and visitation privileges, to the dismay of parents and townspeople. Demands for more off-campus living were resisted, primarily for intractable economic reasons.

Far greater freedom was achieved, as we have seen, in the new curriculum after 1970, but by 1975 it was clear that it was not functioning well. "It has not been an unqualified success," said Dr. Lancaster. At the same time, the academic gradepoint averages of students were soaring, reflecting a national trend, for the longtime institution of grading was being challenged as well. Unsure of themselves, many perhaps even intimidated, faculty people eased standards and joined the movement toward higher grades. There was yet another factor, at least in men's grades. Many faculty were loath to give low grades that would expose any young male "not making normal progress toward a degree" to the military draft.[177] But women's grades were much higher, too.

It is fairly easy to track the change at Simpson. In 1967, 47 students made the dean's or president's list. One year later it jumped to 63; in 1969 it was 86, and 104 in the fall of 1973. Grades were rising while admissions standards were falling. The average gradepoint of freshman women in 1968 was 2.29 (4.00 = A); in 1969 it was 2.78. The all-women's average in 1968 was 2.58; in 1969 it soared to 2.81.[178] Men's grades, always somewhat lower, rose nonetheless as fast as did those of women. In 1974 President Lancaster admitted that there were "nagging questions about academic standards, levels of faculty expectation, and student scholastic performance. We see grades go ever upward, but many feel performance frankly is no better than it was a decade ago." In fact, on standardized test scores, students were doing more poorly than they had a generation earlier.[179] Another problem was the constant student demand for "relevance" in their course work. By "relevance" they usually meant "immediacy," which was really a very different thing. And too often that which was immediate was not commonly subjected to the kind of rigorous examination that characterized academic endeavor in traditional courses. Thus the demand for "relevance" threatened to water down the curriculum still more.

If, then, freedom from academic endeavor, coupled with relaxed evaluation, had been achieved by students, then indeed they had succeeded in their assault on the Simpson "establishment."

To most students, the church—and by this they meant the United Methodist Church—inhibited their freedom by its "interference" in their lives, especially when it came to the consumption of strong drink. They also objected to any and all required chapels or convocations, whose hardy persistence at Simpson they ascribed to the influence of the church. Some suggested that it was time for Simpson to abandon altogether its relationship to the United Methodist Church.

The relationship was not abandoned, but it was changed. In the fall of 1969 the College, sensitive to legal challenges to the control by religious bodies of church-related colleges, examined its own relationship to the church. The only "control" the church had ever exercised over Simpson was its constitutional right to approve or disapprove all new members of the College's board of trustees. Never in the life of the College had the church—specifically the conference—ever objected to any trustee selected by Simpson. Yet it seemed important to redefine the status of the College. New articles of incorporation were drawn up which declared the relationship between the College and the Church to be "fraternal," permitting Simpson absolute control over its selection of board members and the governance of the institution. Thus Ralph John reported in his 1969–70 annual report that "there is no longer the kind of constitutional dependence or control which traditionally has maintained in relation to the United Methodist Church. This does not mean, however, that the relationship, now mutually voluntary, is less meaningful."[180]

When Gilbert Taverner took up the chaplaincy of the College in 1968, he found that students were still required to attend six convocations during the academic year.[181] Even though the student could choose to attend only secular programs, Taverner believed that attendance should be entirely voluntary, and Ralph John agreed. Responding to changing student tastes and enthusiasms, Taverner put together some highly unorthodox, thoroughly entertaining, even thought-provoking chapel services, drawing fairly substantial crowds and leaving traditionalists sputtering. There were rock chapels and one he called an "un-chapel chapel." But probably something of a record in unorthodox ecumenicity was reached when he and the Reverend Lawrence Burns, Indianola's Catholic priest, concelebrated a Catholic-Protestant service of holy communion, announcing "The Failure of the Reformation to Keep Us Apart," with a huge mixed congregation. Taverner later described Father Burns as "a splendid, extroverted, happy priest, with a commanding tilt towards ecumenicity."[182] The service was something of a personal triumph for both Taverner and Burns.

Students liked Taverner, but they didn't like the church, primarily because they believed the strong hand of the church prevented their having an on-campus pub where beer could be served. The Student Senate in 1972 passed a resolution calling for serving beer in the Brenton Student Center. Education professor Alan Magruder conducted a poll on the issue. Among 319 students surveyed, 207 voted yes, 45 no and 66 were undecided.[183] But when the matter went before the faculty and administration, it was voted down, not in deference to the church but because of the anticipated difficulty of controlling underage drinking. Still, students continued to campaign for a campus pub, charging President Lancaster with negligence because he had not raised the issue with the Methodist Church.[184] Students were still convinced that if only the church would stand aside, beer would flow at Brenton. There were more obstacles than that, argued Jim Vint in the *Simpsonian*. Owners of taverns down on the Indianola square did not want competition. The Indianola City Council might block issuance of a license to Simpson.[185] Students, he said, would have to drink beer someplace else. And they did. Lots of it.

Of all the institutions on the College campus, none were more suspect during these years than the Greek-letter societies. Although they enrolled a fair proportion of the student population—about forty percent—their members were found only rarely among the student protesters. In 1968 senior Cam Howard, himself an initiate of Zeta Psi and an SAE social affiliate, chided fellow Greeks for their lack of involvement in campus life.[186] A few weeks later, fiercely independent junior Sandra Pharo was a bit more direct: "It is only the distorted morality of the alumni which fortifies the original system against extinction."[187] And that was just a warm-up for editor Frank Hudson's post-rush-week warning to those who "decided to go the route of fraternal bondage" in a system that lacks "relevance to a world it has shut out."[188] John Viner tried to respond to these attacks, but to little avail. Student activist Richard Cohen remembered that the Greeks "seemed to us to create their own realities away from political consciousness." As organizations, "The Greeks were not into political activism."[189]

The reason for their reticence was fairly obvious. Fraternities and sororities represented an "establishment" on the campus, and they perceived that the very fact of their being an organization, committed to group activities, made them suspect in the eyes of those whose commitment was to individual freedom and independent action. Many Greek society members simply closed ranks, damned the radicals and pursued their own, for the most part nonpolitical interests. Some of them even wore short hair.

Two of the fraternities, ATO and SAE, remained healthy through these years, their members for the most part undistinguishable in dress or behavior from their independent counterparts. Lambda Chi Alpha suffered a serious downturn in membership, but managed to survive. Delta Upsilon was not so fortunate. Declining numbers, virtually nonexistent alumni support or advice, excessive drug use, and a pernicious practice of offering "social memberships" to those who wanted to avoid the cost of formal initiation doomed the fraternity. In 1973 DU's numbers were so low that the College had to move them from their fine house at 701 North E Street to Park Hall at the corner of Buxton and Girard, a structure in a state of advanced decay. The house they left behind was translated first into the E Street Dormitory and later to Worth House, in honor of Gorham Worth 1906, longtime treasurer of the College's board of trustees, whose bequest to the College (he had died in 1953) through his widow, Marcia Lutz Worth, merited the honor.[190] The DU chapter continued to decline until only a handful of members remained. For practical purposes, the chapter was almost dead by 1975. Its charter was formally withdrawn by the international fraternity in 1976.

The sororities were relatively healthy, but by 1975 their membership was somewhat smaller than it had been seven years earlier. The Pi Beta Phi sorority, the oldest student organization on the campus with unbroken existence, celebrated its centennial in 1974.

* * *

Another important "establishment" at Simpson was intercollegiate athletics. Not really attacked by the dissident students, the athletic teams were simply ignored. Like the Greeks—and many of the athletes were members of fraternities and sororities—the athletes eschewed political activism, limiting their demonstrations to those of physical prowess on the playing field. And some of their play was very good indeed.

Football was a standout. Under coach John L. Sullivan Simpson's teams compiled an enviable record during the three seasons beginning in the fall of 1968. In those three years the team won twenty games, lost only four and tied two. With a 6–0–2 conference record in 1968—they tied Wartburg and Central—the Redmen lost only to nonconference foe, William Jewell. The next year was "Sully's" greatest: a 6–1–0 record in the conference (8–1–0 overall), the only loss suffered at the hands of arch rival Central, and an outright conference championship, the first since Hap Miller's 1949 season. Outstanding players during these years were Danny Reeves, end Jim Henderson from Toronto, Ontario, Rich Clogg from Oklahoma, who would win an N.C.A.A. athletic scholarship award for graduate study, and the almost legendary Joe Blake, an Indianola boy who was surely one of Simpson's greatest all-time athletes. Joe was good at everything, but a standout in football and baseball. During his senior year Blake topped the conference in offense with 1,293 yards, 1,170 of those from passing. Nobody else was even close. Teammate Jim Swanson led the conference in pass receptions and Gary Johnston topped the list in total scoring. The 1969 season brought Simpson's first post-season bowl bid ever. On November 19, the team—together with hundreds of fans—journeyed to Excelsior Springs, Missouri, to meet St. John's University of Collegeville, Minnesota, in the Mineral Water Bowl. Though the Redmen lost 13–0 to an outstanding team, they honored themselves and Simpson with their excellent play.[191] It was only appropriate that Sullivan was named N.A.I.A. coach of the year.[192]

When Sullivan resigned after the conclusion of the 1970 season, his assistant, Al Paone, a Simpson graduate in the class of 1966, was named his successor. During his three years at the helm, the team earned a 9–14–2 record. The 1971 season was a good one (5–4–0), but the next two years were poor (2–5–1 each year). Yet there were bright spots: Tom Simmons was a top ground gainer in

1971; the next year Dave Summy was named to the all-conference first team; and in the 1973 season a young team was led by all-conference guard Gary Noble and defensive halfback Hugh Lickiss. That was the year the Redmen scored a stunning upset of league-leading William Penn 10-3 on October 6. It was also the year Simpson first joined the National Collegiate Athletic Association, retaining for a time its membership in N.A.I.A. as well.[193] Lickiss was subsequently granted an N.C.A.A. graduate scholarship, like Rich Clogg before him, and was drafted by the Pittsburgh Steelers.

Only a matter of weeks before fall practice, in August 1974, Al Paone resigned his coaching position to accept an appointment as defensive coordinator in football at Colorado State University.[194] It was far too late to begin a search for a new coach, so the College pressed baseball coach Larry Johnson into service for the year. The team went 2-6-1 overall (2-5-0 in conference play). While the team's win-loss record was lackluster, three players made the all-conference first team: Walt Kennedy, a senior interior lineman, Ed Robinson, a linebacker and Joe Coppola, a junior defensive back.

The selection of a new coach went well, and in January the College announced the appointment of Maurice "Maury" Waugh, former football mentor at the University of Dubuque and I.I.A.C. coach of the year in 1972. A graduate of Dubuque, Waugh had earned the M.S. at Indiana University in 1966.[195]

Basketball met with only limited success, breaking even 10-10 in 1970, but posting losing seasons the other years between 1969 and 1975. Top players included Verle McGraw and Ron Ritenour in 1969, Denny Engle and Rick Burton in 1970. That year Burton was the top conference scorer, with a 21.5 point average. In 1972 center Denny Engle made the first team all-conference, followed the next year by Doug Shafer who made the conference's second team. Bruce Wilson was named to the second all-conference team in 1975. Hard-working, popular Dick Starr coached the team all these years.

In other sports Simpson's record was only average. With Les Deaton's coaching, the track team did fairly well most years, posting its best record in the 1970 season when the mile relay team (John Dale, Clark Jensen, Bill Johns and Dennis Cumpston) set a new Simpson record, clocking 3:22.1. That same year Johns set a record in the 440-yard dash, David Strovers in the two- and three-mile and Jymm Oplt in the shot put. In 1972 Phil Kuehl was picked to compete in the 440-yard dash at the N.A.I.A. indoor championship meet at Kansas City, while Jymm Oplt bested his own record with 50'1½" in shot put. After Les Deaton's departure the 1975 team was coached by Larry Johnson.

The wrestling team, coached successively by Al Paone, Rich Clogg and Danning Bloom, had its ups and downs, but a few wrestlers were outstanding, especially Chris Creason, who was named to the All Star College Team of Iowa in 1971 and Jerome Stewart, who placed first in conference action, second in the district and third in the N.A.I.A. national tournament in 1975. In tennis Simpson did poorly, managing a fourth place showing in the 1969 and 1975 seasons, the latter under the able coaching of Owen Duncan. Coach Deaton's cross-country teams did quite well, while the golfers, variously under the tutelage of coaches Sullivan, Paone and Richard Ault, managed to score first place in the N.A.I.A. district meet in 1969 and won first place in the conference the following year.

Baseball saw the excellent pitching of Joe Blake until his graduation in 1971, but the team did not have a winning record. Still, Blake was named the most valuable player in the Iowa Conference during his senior year and had a serious go at professional baseball. The 1975 team, coached by Tom Simmons, beat Iowa State 3–1, placed Rick Lathrum and Chuck Klicker on the all-conference team, but peaked only late in the season, posting a 6–10 record.

If their pictures in the *Zenith* during these years are representative, Simpson athletes could and did dress and coif themselves with the same dedication to dishevelment that characterized their nonathletic fellow students. Simpson women looked a lot better, whether they participated in sports or not. For Simpson women, 1973 was a banner year. After decades of only intramural competition, women fielded teams in both basketball and softball in intercollegiate play. This was but the beginning. Women's athletics, reflecting the powerful nationwide development of women's rights and the demands of women for full participation in areas heretofore closed to them, would see a spectacular growth during the next two decades. At Simpson it all started very modestly. Larry Johnson's basketball team played an abbreviated schedule, the women's play exhibiting a great deal of dedication and very limited success. Things went better with Barbara Overton's softball team, which in its third season—1975—posted a winning record. That was the year people began to notice that they were calling the team the "Redwomen." The name sounded strange and would soon undergo revision.

By 1975 Simpson was preparing to become exclusively a member of the N.C.A.A. in that small-college division which forbade granting athletic scholarships to students. This new status solved a problem that had long plagued the College. The awarding of "activity aid," the euphemism for scholarships to athletes, had grown to alarming proportions. In 1969 Ralph John pointed out that Simpson was awarding the equivalent of forty full-time scholarships, worth $59,600, to athletes. That figure represented a quarter of all financial aid granted from the college's own resources. "We must," he said, "get a handle on athletic aid." It had earlier been attempted many times in the conference, but without success.[196] The transfer, therefore, to N.C.A.A. enabled the College to direct its student financial assistance more equitably. Athletes would indeed still be recruited, and they could receive aid in accordance with their financial need, but the College was out of the business of "buying" male athletes. And a good thing, too.

* * *

It was Friday, November 3, 1972, with national elections only four days away. Congressman Bill Scherle from Iowa's fifth district, in which Indianola lay, spoke in the Camp Lounge at eleven that morning. No sooner had the congressman begun answering questions than his feisty opponent, Democrat Tom Harkin, walked in and confronted Scherle, who had earlier refused to debate the challenger. Harkin, whose home was in Cumming, up in northwest Warren County, was making his first bid for office. He went after Scherle like a ferret in a barn, whereupon the congressman refused to answer further questions. As he departed with a group of his young Republican supporters, Scherle told the annoying Harkin to "get lost."[197] Scherle soon defeated Harkin in the election, benefiting from the immense popularity of Republican governor Robert Ray and the Nixon landslide, but Harkin would come back two years later to defeat Scherle soundly, entering the House for several terms before going on to the U.S. Senate in 1986.

The Harkin-Scherle confrontation was perhaps more exciting than many of the speaking events of those years, but surely not more edifying. Students and others in the Simpson community heard syndicated columnist Sydney Harris, television personality Peter Jennings, the remarkable Canadian who would become anchorman on ABC network evening news broadcasts, popular sociologist Vance Packard, Lu Jean Cole's admirer who made a return visit, CBS news correspondent Eric Sevareid, ex-priest James Cavanaugh, internationally known defense lawyer Melvin Belli, anthropologist Margaret Mead and Sander Vanocur, the veteran broadcast journalist.

Regular conferences on the campus, though important and even interesting, attracted few faculty and fewer students. Don Koontz's Aerospace Institutes continued their successful course, drawing large crowds of churchmen and flight enthusiasts. Methodist pastors continued to meet annually and the balloon championships drew spectators by the thousands to their annual colorful meets with hundreds of contestants and their crews. One conference, organized and choreographed by redoubtable Lu Jean Cole in 1971, turned out to be a blockbuster symposium on the status of women, bringing to the campus the feminist movement's most outspoken personalities, Gloria Steinem and Florynce Kennedy, ably supported by Iowa representative Minnette Doderer and television interviewer Mary Brubaker. They did not fail to please their supporters and anger their detractors.

Not many students attended operas, madrigal dinners or other serious musical presentations which drew otherwise large audiences. Rather they flocked to hear popular music ranging from big bands like those of Stan Kenton or Buddy Rich to lone singers clutching their guitars when they came to the campus. There were individual performers like John Denver, whom the students had liked so much in 1967 that they invited him back in early 1969. Denver spent a full week on the campus, lived in the DU fraternity house—which he acknowledged was an education in itself—and performed nightly in the Bernap Room, Simpson's version of a funky coffee house, all for $500. Of all the events, however, they loved most what came to be called the "V-D Weekend," a scaled-down Woodstock festival held in May of both 1974 and 1975 out in the country, complete with kegs of flowing beer and air redolent with some kind of sweet-smelling weed.[198] Actually, these hillside frolics were kept reasonably under control by the genial, well-informed vigilance of Dean of Students Gary Valen.

A few of the old traditions survived during these years. All-College Sing continued to entertain the campus each fall, but even that venerable institution suffered dissonance. Although the SAEs won the men's division twice and the Lambda Chis once during those seven years, the independent men won the rest of the time. The problem was that most of the independent men were members of the Phi Mu Alpha music fraternity. Protesting that Phi Mu Alpha sponsored the event, then entered and won it, Lambda Chi Alpha withdrew from competition in 1972, asserting that members of the music fraternity should be barred from competition, just as were varsity athletes from that intramural sport in which they engaged in intercollegiate action. There was no doubt merit in the Lambda Chi contention, but Phi Mu Alpha refused to change the rules. Similarly, the female independents won the competition most of the time, sharing honors a couple of times with the Alpha Chis. Many observers deplored the strife about winning a cup, pointing out that what was at stake was the enjoyment of an evening of excellent entertainment by the whole campus community. Somehow

All-College Sing survived, and the music was indeed good. Miniature Orpheum was not so fortunate. Cancelled for lack of interest in both 1970 and 1971, it was not heard from again.[199]

The *Simpsonian* during these years ranged from mediocre to poor. Few students were interested in putting the paper out, and those who were preferred editorializing on whatever bothered them most about the world around them, near or far. The paper did celebrate its centennial in 1970 with an appropriate commemorative review of journalism at Simpson. The *Zenith* attracted even fewer workers, but it did appear each year, the quality of the product ranging from quite good to abysmal.

In a way it is surprising that most of the departmental and campus-wide honor societies managed to survive the onslaught on organizations of all kinds. It has been suggested that they were more than likely kept alive by faculty people who sought to preserve some elements of tradition. This had always been true of Epsilon Sigma, whose members were customarily elected only a few weeks before their graduation.[200] But it did recognize the best scholars at Simpson, and it represented the College's highest academic award. Beta Beta Beta in science, Sigma Tau Delta in English,[201] Alpha Mu Gamma in foreign languages, together with Pi Kappa Delta in speech and departmental groups like the Home Economics Club (whose days were numbered), the Student Education Association (later the Iowa S.E.A.), both of the last-two-named admitting only women, were nurtured primarily by faculty. Coeducational membership prevailed in the Business Club—a latter-day version of the old Bizad Club—and in the Physical Education Majors Club, the latter of which seems to have existed for only two years (1969–71). In the fine arts one could still find several venerable groups like Mu Phi Epsilon and Phi Mu Alpha Sinfonia in music, together with Blackfriars and Alpha Psi Omega in theater. To these was added during the 1970–71 school year the Music Education National Conference. The S Club served male athletes and the Women's Recreational Association (W.R.A.) women in sports. The Alpha Phi Omega (for men) and Alpha Gamma Sigma (for women) were service organizations whose members had customarily come through the Boy Scout or Girl Scout movements. General leadership honor society Gold Key for women continued during these years, but the number elected dwindled.[202] Its male counterpart, Delta Kappa, thought by many students to be hopelessly conventional, died out in 1971, never having achieved its goal of acquiring a charter of Omicron Delta Kappa.[203] International students had their own organization, and there was an International Club as well, and both were healthy. In 1969 a number of veterans of military service, including a few who had served in Vietnam, organized a Veterans Club.[204] Leading the group was correct, ramrod-straight Dan McGowan, an ex-paratrooper who represented the complete antithesis of the long-haired "hippie" activist. He was living proof that Simpson undergraduates were not cut from the same bolt of cloth. Nor were he and the other veterans reticent in expressing their distaste for the dissidents or their dismay with many of the College's faculty and administration for apparently embracing the antiwar movement.

Then there was another group of students, neither protesters nor organizational loyalists nor military patriots, who were given to zanier pastimes, ranging from transcendental meditation, which was all the rage in the early 1970s, to streaking, one of the more unrestrained phenomena of that era. Streaking, lest the reader not recognize the term, refers to a favorite, primarily indoor, activity of uninhibited young men who raced naked through crowded places where they were most likely to shock unprepared observers, the speed of their exposure calculated to lessen the likelihood of identification. For the historical record, the first incident at Simpson was actually an outdoor exercise, involving thirty to fifty young men who raced around the campus the uncommonly warm night of March 6, 1974, concentrating their surprise appearance in the area between Barker and Kresge Halls.[205] Their "carnal carnival" was ended by the lateness of the hour and by the arrival on the scene of the local constabulary. No arrests were made, the police concluding that they couldn't think of any Iowa law that had been broken. The *Simpsonian* reported the event as "one of the most historic moments of Simpson College."[206] Carried away by the vision of setting some sort of streaking record, the *Simpsonian* called for a "mass streak." The editorial writer was ecstatic: "Pause with me for a moment and imagine 916 naked bodies circling the Indianola town square. It could happen! It must happen!"[207] It didn't. Town-gown relations were bad enough already.

It was probably a stroke of great good fortune that the streaking phenomenon was short-lived. But while it flourished at Simpson, student life took on a decided glow.

The end of streaking was as abrupt as it was unintentional. A half-dozen bold-spirited souls, rumored to be hard-core streakers, decided to enliven the proceedings of the annual alumni gathering in 1974 with some unscheduled entertainment. At a dinner in Great Hall, where alumni, board members and their guests were enjoying their evening repast, the streakers flew through the west door, ran like gazelles the length of the hall, aiming for the east door exit. Alas, the door was bolted shut tighter than a prison gate. Utter consternation. There they were, running in little circles, in a state of nature just as God had made them, until they broke and ran back the length of the hall and out the door through which they had entered. Their embarrassment was nearly as complete as was the surprised delight of the onlookers.[208]

* * *

On a more somber note, Simpson during those years suffered the loss of a number of people who had contributed in many ways to the life of the College. Ivan Willis, alumnus and retired board member, died at Tucson, Arizona, March 7, 1974, and was buried in a simple ceremony on a windswept hill not far from his Iowa birthplace. Closer to home, venerable Don Berry 1903, age ninety-four, emeritus board member, the man who surely qualified as the patriarch of Indianola and who for more than half a century had served as the town's conscience as publisher of its newspaper, passed away quietly at home November 11, 1974, bequeathing to Simpson his family papers and his huge file of photographs.

John O. Gross, the College's president from 1938 to 1942, who had visited the campus many times since his departure, died at Nashville, Tennessee, February 4, 1971. That same year, on October 18, Robert Feyerharm, recently retired vice-president of the College, died unexpectedly at Indianola. Former academic dean Oliver H. Bimson died in retirement at Boulder, Colorado, May 31, 1974.

Several former faculty members, including Laura Adele Miller, age eighty-eight, and Helen Bass Baker, age seventy-seven, both of whom had taught home economics at the College, died in 1971. Two years earlier Ethel M. Cain, who had taught mathematics at Simpson (1967–69) passed away in Des Moines. The College was especially saddened by the death on June 21, 1969, of one of the great "old hands" at Simpson, Ruth Jackson. Like that of Don Berry, her passing was a grievous loss, for both of them had been a goldmine of information about the institution and its alumni.

Two of Simpson's recent benefactors, banker Harold Brenton and theater owner A. H. Blank, died, Brenton in October, 1968 and Blank in 1970.

Among a large number of alumni deaths, two were especially memorable. One was Laura Bobenhouse '97, the College's oldest alumna, who died at the age of one hundred in early 1969. Best known in Simpson's alumni community was Fred C. Smith '09, the retired vice-president of the University of Tennessee, who died March 17, 1971, at the age of eighty-eight.

* * *

By the end of the 1974–75 academic year, the worst of the student rebellion was over. In some ways, the College could settle into a more nearly "normal" existence. But normality was denied to Simpson and its leaders. If the years of student unrest had been trying, the next four years would prove to be difficult in very different ways.

The New Simpsonian

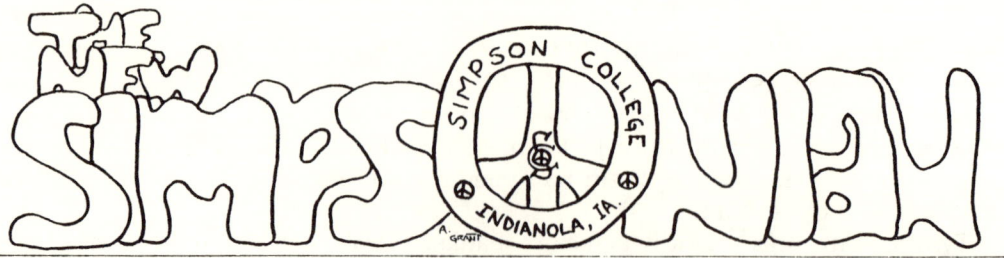

VOL. 100, NO. 16   FRIDAY, FEBRUARY 13, 1970   INDIANOLA, IOWA

R. L. C. To Present Dick Gregory

Sex Symposium Features Author Packard

A symposium in human sexuality featuring social critic and author Vance Packard is planned for February 17-19 at the Brenton Student Center, Simpson College.

The symposium is the third in a series at the Student Center that has included a Journalism Institute in October and a Drug Awareness Symposium in November.

The program begins Tuesday, February 17th with a discussion with Dr. Herbert Roth, clinical psychologist of the Des Moines Child Guidance Center, and the Rev. Gilbert Y. Taverner, Simpson College Chaplain. At 8:00 p. m. Dr. Don O. Newland, Des Moines gynecologist, will speak in the Camp Lounge on abortion.

Wednesday's program includes a session on contraceptives at 8:00 p. m. in the Bernap room conducted by Dr. Robert Kretzschmar of the Department of Obstetrics and Gynecology, University Hospitals, Iowa City, and Dr. L. W. Porter, Indianola physician.

Vance Packard's keynote address "The Bewildered Sexes: Today's Confusion, Tomorrow's Prospects" will be delivered in the Camp Lounge at 7:30 p. m. on Thursday, February 19. Mr. Packard's most recent book "The Sexual Wilderness" is the result in his best selling series of social commentaries and is the result of four years of study and interviews on "Contemporary Upheaval in Male-Female Relationships."

Mr. Packard who also lectured on the Simpson campus in 1968, is the author of such in-depth studies as "The Hidden Persuaders", "The Status Seekers", "The Waste Makers", "The Pryamid Climbers", and "The Naked Society" which have probed such areas as motivational research, planned obsolescence, class stratification and executive status seeking.

All symposium events are open to the public.

Helbe Attends Student ISEA

Donna Helbie, a junior at Simpson College, was the official delegate to the Student Iowa State Education Association Delegate Council in Des Moines, February 6 and 7. As Southwest Region Secretary-Treasurer, she served on the executive planning committee for this meeting which attracted approximately 200 student delegates, observers, and campus advisors from forty-three Iowa schools.

Student ISEA is a 4,100 member organization for college and university students enrolled in teacher training programs. The organization is affiliated with the Iowa State Education Association.

R.L.C. will present comic social critic, Dick Gregory this Sunday.

Martin Speaks At Convocation

Dr. Warren Bryan Martin, a research educator at the Center for Reserve and Development in Higher Education, University of California on Feb. 17 at 1:00 in Hopper Gymnasium.

Dr. Martin, who is also a lecturer in the University's School of Education, joined the Center in February 1966 and, since May 1967, has been the coordinator of a major research program entitled "Liability of Institutional Structures and Functions for the Future of Higher Education." Ten research projects are included in this program including his own on "Institutional Character in the Present Climate of Change."

Because Dr. Martin served for four years prior to his appointment at Berkley as provost of Raymond College, the first "cluster" college to be developed within the structure of the University of the Pacific, Stockton, California, he is well qualified to engage in research and writing on the themes of innovation and experimentation in higher education.

Attendance is mandatory for all students.

Walt Proposes Abolition Of Requirements To Faculty

Last Monday, Feb. 10, a special faculty meeting was called to consider Dr. John's proposal, which concentrated on distributing required courses, Dr. Joe Walt proposed a substitute proposal which would abolish all college requirements and encourage a more personalized education for Simpson students. Dr. Walt's proposal was met with enthusiasm by the faculty, and it was decided to send the proposal to the Faculty Educational Policy and Curriculum Committee.

Chairman of the Curriculum Committee, Mr. Glen Buhr, called an open meeting on the matter for Wednesday, Feb. 11. At that meeting, attended by a considerable number of concerned faculty members and students, the committee made some editorial changes and added a proposal by student committee member Sandy Pharo to institute the program by the Fall Semester of 1970, and voted without opposition to refer the proposal back to the faculty.

The proposal will go before the faculty at the next scheduled Faculty meeting, Thursday, February 19.

The proposal, as presented by Dr. Walt reads:

I move that Simpson College abandon ALL designated course and/or distributive requirements and that the requirement for the B.A. degree be 35 units (with a 2.00 cumulative grade point average), including a major of not more than 12 units; for the B.M. degree 36 units (with a 2.00 cumulative grade point average), including the major of not more than 24 units. The student's total academic program shall be approved in advance by his adviser and the office of the Dean of Academic Affairs, the course distribution to reflect the academic goals of the student in the context of a humanizing liberal arts program.

One of Simpson's outstanding events of the year occurs this Sunday, February 15th, 8:00 P. M. at Hopper Gym, with the visit of Dick Gregory to the campus. His visit is sponsored by the Religious Life Council, Bob Bower, president. He will be hosted on campus by the members of the Afro-American Cultural Center.

Dick Gregory turned his back on a brilliant career as one of the nation's top stand-up comics to devote his time and unique abilities to social justice. Punctuating his sharp social commentary with the penetrating humor born of the Black man's situation, Gregory is spending most of his times these days on college campuses. It is his clear conviction that the muddled problems of racial injustice will find their solution among those of the college generation.

Gregory represents a unique approach to America's racial dilemmas. Deeply concerned for his fellow black citizens and vividly articulating the problems involved, he is likewise aware of the injustices to the American Indian. He asks, for instance, "How do you explain to an Indian child on an Indian reservation that Columbus *discovered* America?" Knowledgeable, angry, hurt, sensible, a brilliant communicator, Dick Gregory is exerting a powerful influence on the college community, as witnessesed by the overflow crowds invariably packing auditoriums for his visits.

Follow Up On Biafran War

The recent ending of the Nigerian Civil War has probably caused some people to wonder what will happen to the funds collected in the recent fast for Biafra. Almost five hundred dollars was raised by the Religious Life Council in December when several students missed their noon meal and contributed their lunch money to the cause. Indianola High School students contributed one fifth of the total amount raised. Other individual members of the Indianola community also contributed. On January 26, RLC Chairman Bob Bower contacted the Biafran Relief Services Foundation in New York. The information as of that date was that Nigeria was not letting any outside countries interfere in the reconstruction and feeding operations. Talks were going on between BRSF and the Nigerian government, but at that time it was not certain if BRSF would be allowed to airlift food into Biafra itself. Over twenty thousand starving children, however, had been airlifted to the Portuguese island of Sao Tome off the coast of Gabon where they are being fed by BRSF. Thus, Simpson students can be assured that the money they raised will help feed the starving Biafran children on the island of Sao Tome, if not in Biafra itself.

In keeping with the campus peace movement, the *Simpsonian* in 1970 adopted a masthead described even by its admirers as "amateurish."

XX
Collegiality and Consternation 1975–79

The end of the student revolt surprised the students as much as it did their bewildered elders. After 1975 there were no more marches round the square in Indianola, no more protest gatherings on campus or down at the courthouse, no more nonnegotiable demands by angry dissidents, no more takeovers of buildings to achieve an agenda of reform. Even black students, clearly that group on campus most entitled to express dissatisfaction with the yet distant accomplishment of their aims, determined to seek racial justice in a less confrontational manner. The time of troubles was over. "Now things can get back to normal," said one College board member.

If "back to normal" meant a return to the halcyon days of the fifties or the relative calm of the early and mid-sixties, the prediction was inaccurate. Indeed as the social and political climate changed, so did the attitudes and behavior of the students, but in no way was there a return to the past. As is true in all times of rapid, disorderly upheaval, neither people nor institutions can ignore events or fail to be shaped by them. After 1975 there was indeed marked change at Simpson and in every other college in America, but it represented something different, something new, drawing upon elements both of earlier days and the more recent turbulence, but in aggregate truly novel.

On campus students had won the right to participate at every level, from the student judiciary to faculty committees to board of trustees representation. And for several years they exercised their new-found influence responsibly and creatively. But as the urgency for reform waned, as students turned their attention away from public issues and on-campus enfranchisement, as their interest was drawn increasingly to career preparation and private satisfactions, student participation in all of their hard-won campus roles declined. On some faculty committees, student members ceased attending altogether. In fairness, it was sometimes difficult to keep students interested in the doings of the library's Learning Resources Committee or the arcane considerations of the Budget and Coordinating Committee, not to speak of faculty meetings which some of them found dreadfully dull. Student-elected board of trustees members served out their terms, but their participation was minimal. Those who attended meetings seemed to be intimidated by their elders, and because they were elected in their senior year for three-year terms, they served at least two years as young alumni. Because few of them could afford the time or expense of returning to Indianola two or three times a year, their representation on the board turned out to be nominal, an empty honor.

If student participation in the governance of the College declined, their hostility to "compulsory religion" did not, and there was no talk of reviving required chapel, although a chaplain's office was maintained. It should be noted, however, that many students enrolled happily in religion courses, and people like Bruce Haddox and Chaplain Roger Betsworth were among the College's most popular instructors.

Students' concern for individual rights, a beacon during the years of protest, continued unabated, but their distaste for campus institutions softened as they recognized the worthwhileness of group activity, the effectiveness of cooperative enterprise. Yet they remained sensitive to any threat of erosion of personal freedom.

The sexual revolution, for example, was here to stay. Although attempts would be made by their mentors to limit the excesses, actual or suspected, consequent to unlimited visitation in the residence halls, most students were extraordinarily nimble in circumventing any and all new rules.[1] And if their male-female relationships had liberalized, so had their political views moved to the left. Of course, conservative political opinions were heard, but a clear majority of the students, for example, supported the Democrats and Jimmy Carter in the election of 1976.

During the most difficult years of the student revolt, one of the excesses in the exercise of individual choice was indulgence in drugs by some students. Never as severe a problem at Simpson as it was in some colleges, drug abuse was nonetheless prevalent among a fair number of undergraduates, some of whom found their academic performance seriously undermined. During the student generation after 1975, drug use declined markedly. If there was a single remaining drug of choice, it was beer, the consumption of which among many students began to border on the heroic.

During this same period the appearance of students began to return to somewhat more conventional standards. Each year—it was especially observable among the men—hair styles changed as flowing locks were shorn and beards shaved. Clothing styles moved away from tie-died dishevelment to clean jeans and logo-laden T-shirts. And while women's dress remained informal, their appearance was seen to be a matter of more fastidious concern than it had been in years.

* * *

Each president of Simpson brings with him a leadership style, different if not better or worse than that of his predecessors or successors. One has but to recall the raw, youthful energy of Sam Vernon or the rigid ministerial rectitude of William Hamilton, whose judgments came down like thunderbolts from on high. Some could remember the fatherly warmth of Charles E. Shelton or the dour countenance of James Campbell. In recent years Simpson had seen the spectacularly successful "reign" of William Kerstetter, who dominated the College with the confidence of a divine-right monarch, followed by the strikingly different leadership of a committed democrat, Ralph John. Conscious of the broad vari-

Professor E. G. Booth, Simpson's football coach and Director of Athletics from 1958 to 1962, went on to head the Department of Education, retiring in 1989.

Clifford L. Meints, Professor of Chemistry who came to Simpson in 1957 was still teaching at the time of this history's publication.

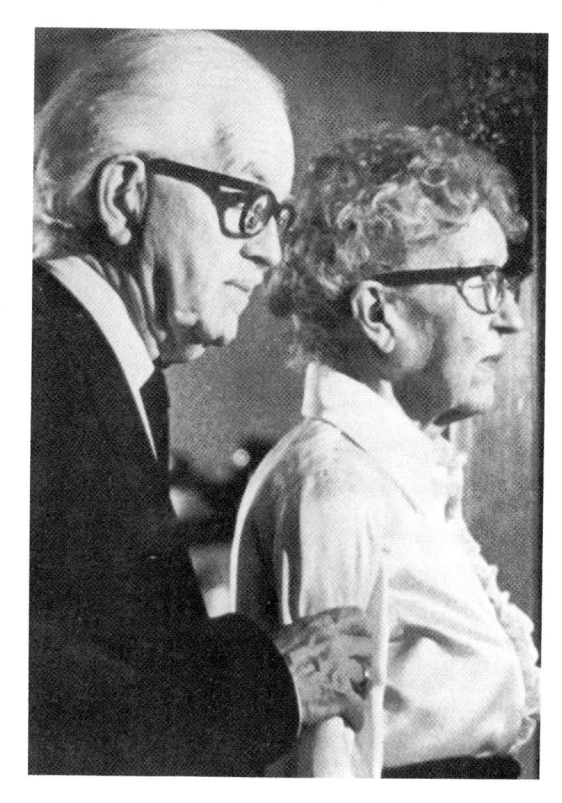

Sven and Mildred Lekberg in 1975. Sven headed the Department of Music from 1940 to 1966. He retired in 1969. Mildred taught Voice during these same years.

Carl R. Halgren, Professor of Psychology (1971–).

Roger G. Betsworth, Professor of Religion (1973–) and sometime Chaplain and Dean of Students.

On a bright summer day balloons crowd the intramural field in front of the fraternity houses.

Herbert Alberding, Professor of Geology (1960–76).

Richard B. Lancaster was Simpson's president from 1972 to 1979.

When hot air ballooning came to Indianola, Simpson got its very own balloon.

Demonstrating students confronted their opponents in their protests against the Vietnam War (1971).

The members of Delta Upsilon were the quintessential representatives of an "alternative lifestyle" at Simpson in 1971.

Frank Colella, Professor of Economics and Management and everyone's favorite M.C. (1977–).

M. Bruce Haddox, Professor of Religion and Acting Dean of Academic Affairs on a fairly regular basis (1969–).

Asian specialist Paul Ingram, Professor of Philosophy and Religion, taught at Simpson from 1966 to 1975.

Owen L. Duncan, Professor of History and women's tennis coach (1969–).

Joe Kay Moody, Professor of Biology (1976–).

Alan Magruder, Professor of Education (1970–95), makes a point to student Alesia Wright.

Commencement, 1970: Dean Waller Wiser "conferred the honorary degree upon a Negro whose ancestor seven generations back had been bought . . . by the Dean's forbear of that time." The recipient was Alex Haley, author of the best-seller, *Roots*.

Honorary degree recipients in 1970 were: Harold A. Bosley, Alex Haley and Clayton Lane, here being greeted by President Ralph John.

Richard Neutra, the architect who designed Simpson's three fraternity houses (Sigma Alpha Epsilon, Alpha Tau Omega and Kappa Theta Psi), called them "indestructible."

In 1975 Simpson's Madrigal Singers performed at Carnegie Recital Hall in New York City.

Sven Lekberg was seldom seen without his pipe.

At the age of 83, Clarence Pickard '16, rode in the first RAGBRAI (*Register's* Annual Great Bike Ride Across Iowa) in the summer of 1973.

Todd Lieber, Professor of English, 1969–.

Robert L. Larsen, head of Simpson's Music Department since 1966, founded and serves as Artistic Director of the Des Moines Metro Opera.

Carol Stuart '56, mainstay of Simpson's opera productions, sang the leading role in "Madame Butterfly" (1979).

The Madrigal Christmas Dinner (left and above) has become a great tradition at Simpson.

The morning after the announcement of the U.S. invasion of Cambodia in 1971, Simpsonians awoke to find the campus covered with hundreds of white crosses, one for each Iowan killed in the Vietnam War up to that time.

African-American student leader Bernard Franklin and President Lancaster take a look at an agreement following tense negotiations between Black students and the College administration.

Garfield Jackson '68, student leader, served after his graduation as an admissions counselor for the College.

Fred O. Jones, Professor of Sociology and Anthropology (1970–).

Everett L. Laning, a Simpson graduate, joined the faculty and has served as Professor of Sociology and Human Services since 1964.

English Department chairman Donald A. Koch presents an honorary degree to Harold F. Watson, thirteen years after Watson's retirement.

Bruce N. Degen, Professor of Music, 1958–.

Norman L. Thomas, Professor of Philosophy (1969–91).

John W. Epperson, Professor of Political Science (1977–).

The completion of the Cowles Center in 1976 gave Simpson a first-class athletic facility. Hopper Gymnasium, right, remained in use.

Plenty of steel went into the construction of the Cowles Center (1975–76).

The Cowles Center boasts an Olympic-size swimming pool.

The aftermath of the Great Hall fire in 1976.

At Homecoming in 1980 there was African-American royalty alongside the general student Homecoming King and Queen. "C.B.S." stood for "Concerned Black Students."

Honorary degree recipients in 1975 were, l. to r.: Franklin D. Scott, Homer H. Woods and J. Steven Watson, pictured here with President Richard Lancaster.

The "Back-forty Bashes" were among the more uninhibited events of the year during the 1970s.

Board of Trustees chairman Fred Weitz confers with President Robert E. McBride in 1980, soon after McBride's arrival on campus.

Excavation for the construction of the Amy Robertson Music Center (1982).

Amy Robertson Music Center.

The oratorio "Elijah" was performed in Smith Chapel as a part of the dedication of the new Music Center (1983).

R. Melvin Henderson, Vice President and Dean of Academic Affairs (1974–87).

The Carver Cultural Center, located on North D Street, was dedicated in November 1982.

Robert E. McBride served as President of Simpson from 1979 to 1987.

James Thorius, Dean of Students (1984–).

Helen M. Malone Mullin, Professor of Music, 1945–74.

Glenn Buhr, Associate Professor of German, 1961–.

Jane Kvetko, Professor of Social Work, 1981–.

Simpson's students took to computers like ducks to water.

Joe Reifert and Dan Doyle model the latest casual evening wear at a student-sponsored fashion show that raised funds for charity (1981).

Simpson's cross-country runners came into their own during the 1980s.

Jim Kutzner '86 was a mainstay of Simpson's tennis team.

Marcia Eubanks '85 belts one into left field (1983).

Terry Hoy, Professor of Political Science (1960–86) helps pulverize "Lake Doyle" on Campus Day.

President McBride appeared properly turned out at the College's Quasquicentennial Founders Day in 1985.

Cheerleaders Tom Petersen and Rozann Hartstack (Beatty) led cheers from a firetruck during the 1984 Homecoming.

Amy Robertson '21 and Robert Larsen break ground for the new Music Center (1981).

Chemistry Professor Ron Warnet (1969–) hopes his student has a good aim.

R. William Helfrich, Professor of History from 1961 to 1988, induced both admiration and terror in his students.

Brenton Student Center.

Lettie McNeill and President McBride outside the McNeill Hall construction site.

John Kellogg, Simpson's extraordinary admissions director—and College Vice President—came to Indianola in 1978.

Janet H. Heinicke, Professor of Art, 1982—.

Robert L. Gieber, Professor of French, 1971—.

William Geiger helped countless students find a way to pay for a Simpson education. Here he talks with Chrissy Rupp '93.

Four presidents of Simpson participated in the College's 125th—Quasquicentennial—commemoration in 1986. L. to r.: Richard B. Lancaster (1972–79), Ralph C. John (1963–72), Robert E. McBride (1979–87) and William E. Kerstetter (1953–63).

Alumni chairperson of the Quasquicentennial, Grace A. Overton '41 (left), serves cake to a statehouse worker at the College's Quasquicentennial.

Alma Robbins White '05 returned to the campus in 1981. At the time she was the oldest Tridelta anywhere in the land.

President Robert E. McBride takes a break from his labors at the 1987 Campus Day.

Football coach Jim Williams came to Simpson in 1986, here seen having a word with Joe Blake, Jr. (1989).

Music Professor Ron Albrecht and Clifford Meints lend a hand with the College's new brick walkway.

Board of Trustees member Dean Prather '32 was Grand Marshall at the 1987 commencement.

The "new" College Hall, long known as "Old Chapel," was restored to its Victorian elegance in 1987.

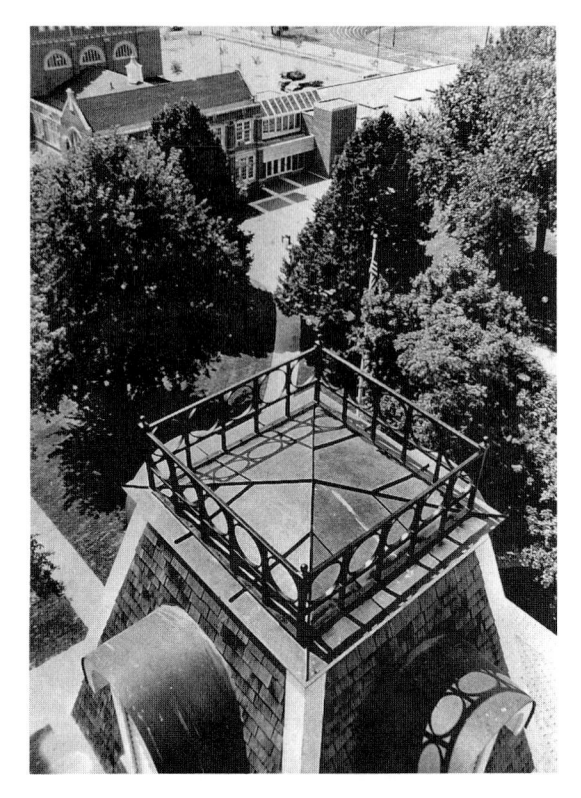

The view from the top of College Hall after the reconstruction of the tower (1987).

The A. H. and Theo Blank Performing Arts Center, dedicated in 1971.

The home of Simpson's president—the old Sigler mansion—was restored and newly occupied by Richard B. Lancaster and his family.

Stephen G. Jennings took up his duties as President of Simpson in 1987.

Nia Kos, Professor of Spanish, 1976–.

Cynthia M. Dyer, Simpson's Director of Library Services, 1978–.

Mitchell Kalpakgian, Professor of English, 1967–.

When American troops engaged Saddam Hussein's Iraqis in Operation Desert Storm in 1991, Marine Cpl. Chris Davidson '94, interrupted his Simpson education to serve four months in Saudi Arabia—from New Year's eve to Easter Sunday. He is shown here with a couple of fairly lethal weapons.

Marvin Van Wyk, Professor of Mathematics and Computer Science, 1972–.

Melvin Wilk, Professor of English, 1981–.

Luther L. Hill, Chairman of the Board of Trustees, 1972 to 1980.

Owen J. Newlin, Chairman of the Board of Trustees, 1985 to 1993.

eties of approaches to academic governance, Richard Lancaster has written of the period during which he was at the helm at Simpson:

> Types of power and the meaning of legitimate social power were being examined. Wise college presidents, as never before, were listening to students, taking faculty meetings seriously, ceasing board of trustees manipulation, bringing alumni back into the life of the college. In my own leadership style I was interested in the reality behind the words such as consultation, consensus and community. . . . As a leader I had a better than average sense of what should be done now, and I was willing to take the risk to say so. Our task was to build consensus, and then support, for this community of memory and hope.[2]

Lancaster, then, sought to conduct his administration of Simpson in an atmosphere of cooperation, of consultation and collegiality. "I did not want to be a conservative, conventional president," he recalled years later. It is tempting to speculate that if the challenges that forced Simpson during the late seventies had not been so threatening or if the personalities with which the president had to deal had been less aggressive, his collegial style might have been successful. He was to discover that Simpson's problems were largely financial, not academic, and they were severe. Its various constituencies were not always in the mood to cooperate and his critics were eager to express their myriad dissatisfactions. There were, for example, difficulties like student recruitment, soaring inflation, mounting deficits, faculty morale in a time of contraction, creating a situation that seemed intractable. Never before had a president of Simpson been more sensitive to the views and concerns of others, but it was this very sensitivity that would, in the course of events, cause severe problems both for him and for the College.

Lancaster could count on a strong board of trustees as he attempted to grapple with Simpson's infirmities. But the very strength of the board became itself a problem, for as the red ink spilled and enrollment sagged, as students and faculty and alumni voiced their discontents, board members, especially its executive committee, felt the urge to manage the College, to go beyond the conventional bounds of policymaking. They interpreted collegiality in the president as weakness, and their response to that perceived failing was to run the College. When, for example, the board authorized a "loan" of $700,000 from the endowment fund in February 1977, it provided instructions—not merely suggestions—as to the precise use of these funds.[3] Or, as we shall see, the board insisted on financing the debt on the new Physical Education Center in a way opposed by the president.[4]

Still, one can understand the temptation of the board to transgress the traditional limits of its authority, for these hardworking people truly cared about the welfare of the College and believed they could help lead the way when the going was rough. No one could gainsay the loyalty and concern of any of them, especially of chairman Luther Hill, who was in almost constant communication with the president or with members of his staff. They did what they thought was best.

The administrative staff underwent significant change during the four years between 1975 and 1979. Able fund raiser Ed Couch resigned in the spring of 1978 to accept a position as chief development officer and associate professor of pastoral theology at Yale University Divinity School. Although it was unfortunate to lose him in the middle of the Commitment 125 fund-raising campaign, which he had designed and launched, Simpson could wish him well as he returned to his alma mater in New Haven.[5] Couch's successor at Simpson was John V. Hartung, academic dean at Dakota Wesleyan University. A Des Moines native, Hartung had earned his B.A. from Grinnell College, his M.A. in zoology from the University of South Dakota and his doctorate from Southern Illinois University. At Dakota Wesleyan he had taught in the Education Department and had coached track and cross-country. An avid sportsman, Hartung was a striking contrast to his scholarly predecessor.[6]

What turned out to be one of the best appointments made by any Simpson president in decades was Lancaster's invitation to John Kellogg to become director of admissions, replacing Ivan Lyddon who resigned to enter private business in December 1977.[7] Kellogg had been working for a year as marketing manager for University Accounting Service on the East Coast, but had a long record of service in the admissions field. A native of Akron, Ohio, he grew up in Cuyahoga Falls, Ohio. In 1958 he entered DePauw University, where he majored in psychology and was a member of Sigma Chi. After college he entered the U.S. Marine Corps, where he served from 1962 to 1966, rising to the rank of captain. In his professional life he had served as assistant director of admissions and financial aid at DePauw and later became director of admissions and financial aid at Dakota Wesleyan University.[8]

Kellogg took up his duties at Simpson on December 27, 1977. Ivan Lyddon stayed on for a few weeks to ease the transition, and during that brief time Kellogg was able to make an analysis of Simpson's admissions operation. He talked with administrators and faculty, became acquainted with the admissions staff and looked at the records of student applicants past and present. More importantly, he went out into the field, met with high school principals and counselors, seeking their opinions and judgments about Simpson.

A few weeks later he had a long talk with President Lancaster. He reported what he had discovered about Simpson admissions and outlined his plans for the future. It was obvious that both the number and academic quality of new students had declined severely during the seventies. The reasons for this were abundantly clear, he said. Iowa school counselors—and Simpson drew more than eighty percent of its students from the Hawkeye state—were saying that Simpson did not rank very high in their estimation because of its supposed willingness to accept just about anyone with a warm body, anyone who was breathing, its reputation for lax behavioral expectations and its tension between white and minority students, and its apparent lack of dedication to the academic enterprise. Lancaster, to be sure, had heard all this before, but he was not prepared for Kellogg's solution. "We need to set a high academic standard for admissions and enforce it. That means that we have to start rejecting poor students. And we must apply the same standard of admission for minorities as we do for all others." The president listened with growing astonishment. "I thought he was about to have a coronary," recalled Kellogg. But as Lancaster listened to Kellogg's ambitious plans for improving admissions, he caught the spirit of confidence with which this new man approached everything he did. "Let's do it," said Lancaster, fighting off the temptation to cross his fingers.[9]

Kellogg made the rounds of Iowa schools again, explaining to counselors that Simpson was turning over a new leaf, that it would no longer accept low-ranking students. Their almost unanimous response was "Yeah, that's what they all say.

Table 11
Fall Enrollment 1974–1986

	Senior	Junior	Soph.	Fresh.	Uncl. Special	FT Total	Part Time	Total
1974–75	157	194	207	236	41	835	66	901
1975–76	178	165	164	310	0	817	120	937
1976–77	90	137	205	318	3	753	107	860
1977–78	85	201	163	292	3	744	95	839
1978–79	125	154	174	300	1	754	56	810
1979–80	116	142	181	328	3	770	60	830
1980–81	108	162	215	263	0	748	85	833
1981–82	128	182	172	289	2	773	227	1000
1982–83	141	136	182	260	1	720	345	1065
1983–84	109	169	187	295	3	763	359	1122
1984–85	123	176	221	292	0	812	412	1224
1985–86	152	169	193	309	2	825	491	1316
1986–87	126	195	223	307	4	855	540	1395

We watch rather what they *do*." Soon enough, however, they discovered that Kellogg was as good as his word. A reasonable standard was indeed adopted and adhered to. Every letter of rejection was brought to the attention of counselors. More importantly, the College sought out and wooed top students, attracting them to the solid academic programs that Simpson offered. Faculty people were cooperative, interviewing students interested in their fields of study. Students in residence halls or fraternity and sorority houses welcomed prospective students when they made campus visits. Kellogg was right when he said that when applicants saw the campus for themselves, the likelihood of their enrolling increased remarkably.

The results of Kellogg's work were stunning. Although he arrived on the scene too late in the academic year to influence the enrollment of new students, fall enrollment in 1978 did inch upward. (See table 11.) The next year 1979–80, with the Kellogg program in full swing, the big turnaround took place. In the spring of 1979 Simpson had counted 205 freshmen; that next fall the number was 325, and total enrollment rose for the first time in five years. But the numbers really didn't tell the story, for what was more impressive was the improved quality of the freshman class.

Years earlier, Ralph John had said that in spite of the many improvements that had been made at Simpson during his nine-year administration, "we never solved the admissions problem." Under Dick Lancaster it was solved, and it was John Kellogg's aggressive enterprise that made the solution possible. Small wonder that years later Lancaster would insist that the appointment of John Kellogg stood beside that of Mel Henderson as the best he ever made anywhere.

While the appointment of John Kellogg and John Hartung's replacement of Ed Couch received the most notice at Simpson, other changes in administrative personnel deserve careful attention. In the fall of 1975 Roger Betsworth, who had served as dean of students for a year, was named chaplain of the College. Rather than look outside for a successor, Lancaster appointed Gary L. Valen to the dean of students post. Valen had been teaching in the Department of History for a number of years, but fell victim to the faculty cuts mandated by the board and necessitated in his case both by declining history enrollments and the "seven-year rule" on acquisition of the doctorate. Neither President Lancaster nor others in the Simpson community wanted to lose Valen, by all odds one of the most popular figures on campus. And because he was known to have excellent relations with undergraduates, the president moved him into the Brenton Student Center and the deanship.[10] It was a wise and fortunate decision. For the next near-decade Gary Valen served with distinction. His appointment brought stability to the office—he was the fourth dean of students in as many years—and exercised insightful direction of student life as the campus quieted down after years of unrest. A year or so later Richard Petersen, Valen's associate dean, left the College and was not replaced.

For a number of years Donald Koontz had been serving variously as director of cooperative education, business manager and finally as assistant to the president for special programs, the last-named position focusing on writing grant proposals. At the end of the 1975–76 academic year, in accordance with the board mandate to cut expenses, Lancaster sought to eliminate Koontz's position, but the formidable sociologist appealed—with counsel present—the president's action before the executive committee of the board and managed to hang on for another year. He formally retired in 1977.[11]

When Jim Zahnd resigned as director of publications in 1976, Lancaster appointed Frank Nowasell, associate director of development, to the post as acting director (in addition to his former job), promising him that it was a "temporary" arrangement.[12] "Temporary" turned out to be two years, until in the fall of 1978 Elinor Beman joined the staff as director of public relations.[13] The assistant director of development, young Simpson alumnus Robert E. MacKenzie, resigned in April 1979, his position filled by Kay Lebeda, a graduate of Marywood College in Scranton, Pennsylvania, who had come to Indianola four years earlier and had worked at Simpson as Lu Jean Cole's assistant in the alumni office. A few months after Cole resigned in early 1980, Lebeda took over the alumni director post and remains in it to this day.[14]

Louis E. Smith resigned in 1978 as associate dean of academic affairs and registrar to accept a position with the Iowa Department of Public Instruction. His position at Simpson was inherited on a part-time basis by two full-time faculty members. Fred Holder, professor of religion, assumed the duties of the associate dean of academic affairs while Alan W. Magruder, associate professor of education, took over as registrar.[15]

William Geiger, associate director of admissions, assumed unheralded the increasingly important position of director of financial assistance in 1977. Whether Lancaster knew it or not, his choice of Geiger was a stroke of genius. In all the complexities of federal, state and private grants, of loans from a growing number of sources, of a bewildering array of application forms and financial statements expected of students, of hopeful recipients of academic largess and their even more hopeful parents, Bill Geiger kept his balance, worked always in the interest of each student, and attained a reputation that fell somewhere between Santa Claus and the Wizard of Oz. A militant, committed activist in the Democratic Party, he was scrupulously fair, even to Republicans. It was and is difficult for anyone to be popular in the role of gatekeeper to the College's vault and dispenser of its bounty, but Bill Geiger managed, with a heart as big as his formidable girth, to bring it off. He remained at his post until the time of his retirement in the mid-nineties, managing an ever-increasing proportion of the College's expenditures.[16]

Meanwhile, two of Simpson's administrators were accorded new titles in 1975,

Mel Henderson named vice president of the College and dean of academic affairs, and Doyle Woods, director of business and finance.

More important, perhaps, than the award of new titles was the addition of Director of Alumni Affairs Lu Jean Cole to the president's cabinet. It was not so much a question of whether Cole's title merited inclusion; rather, she was bright, full of ideas, able to take initiative and willing to do so. She was the first woman ever to serve in the president's inner circle of administrators.

*   *   *

While enrollment remained static, it cost $600,000 a year more to run the College in 1979 than it had cost in 1975. Unable to augment net tuition income substantially, administrators sought to cut costs. And in as labor-intensive an enterprise as higher education is, it was inevitable that a significant proportion of savings had to be sought in either cutting staff or limiting salary increases, or both. Faculty and staff would have to sacrifice for the "common good," reasoned the president.

Reducing the size of the faculty, as we have already seen, was difficult to achieve and caused severe morale problems. But it was achieved, primarily by not replacing some of the people who resigned. And resignations were frequent, mainly because salary increases were minuscule or, in one year, nonexistent. In the five-year period between 1972 and 1977 the size of the full-time faculty declined from 72 to 56, and there was talk of reducing it still more for 1977–78.[17] No across-the-board raises were given at all for the 1977–78 academic year.[18] Accordingly, that year a deputation of faculty members met with a board of trustees committee, pleading for at least a modest salary rise, but to no avail.[19] It was small wonder, then, that eleven teachers—nearly twenty percent of the full-time faculty—resigned in the spring of 1977.[20] To put it another way, of the faculty active in 1975, twenty-seven, or nearly half, were gone four years later.[21] The situation was particularly difficult in the natural and social sciences.

In the four years between 1975 and 1979 forty-two new people joined the faculty, but fifteen of them stayed only a year[22] and eight for but two years.[23] Seven of them, however, would make their careers at Simpson, lending strength and stability to the teaching staff.

When Marjorie Crabb retired in 1975 to go with her husband to Kansas after twelve years at Simpson as a member of the Department of English and, since 1969, as director of the Hawley Learning Skills Center, the president appointed Kay Ellen Fisher to the position which she held until her retirement in 1992. She had earned both a B.S. in Education and a B.A. at Drake University. During her seventeen years at Simpson, Fisher was a remarkably helpful mentor, both of students with writing problems and of those who sought to improve their already adequate skills. Patient, considerate, yet demanding and dedicated to tough standards, she was responsible for ever-increasing usage of the center and won praise for her effectiveness.

Two biologists joined the Simpson staff, Joe Moody in 1976 and William H. Gilbert III in 1978. A native of Hawkins, Texas, Moody was a child of the Southwest. He attended a military academy during high school and junior college years, transferring to Texas Tech to complete his B.A. in 1964. He earned the M.A. in biology at the University of Nebraska in 1969 and the Ph.D. at Montana State University three years later. Before coming to Indianola, Moody taught four years at Houghton College in New York. At Simpson he soon took his place as a popular and highly competent member of the teaching faculty.[24] Apart from classroom teaching and research, Moody worked well with longtime science chair Cliff Meints and was deeply involved with the detailed planning and monitoring of the major renovation and expansion of the Carver Science Hall, completed in 1993. Outside the classroom he won great popularity as an unapologetic supporter of intercollegiate athletics. There was rarely a Simpson team that did not see him helping out in one way or another. And Simpson athletics was better for the enthusiasm of a man whose academic reputation was as solid as was his love for sports. William H. Gilbert III, scholarly, precise, and a dedicated teacher, replaced Maura Ann Gage, who had taught only a year following the departure of longtime biologist Donald DeLisle. A New Jersey native, Gilbert had earned his B.A. at Yale University in 1962 and the Ph.D. in biology at the University of Massachusetts in 1973. Subsequent to the completion of his doctorate he had taught at Colby College in Maine for six years and Ottawa University in Kansas for two. At Simpson he taught courses in ecology and a course called "Interpreting the Environment," as well as introductory biology, and he participated in the development of a curriculum in environmental studies.

If one were to select one new faculty member whose appearance at Simpson would truly make a difference in the quality of the institution's program, it would have to be Frank Colella. Since the retirement of Myron Sorden, the Department of Economics and Business Administration had been in considerable turmoil, its leadership shifting as the president tried in vain to find the right person to head the program. Determined to take action, Lancaster declined to offer a contract to the existing department chairman and instructed Dean Mel Henderson and social science division head Joe Walt to find the best person possible to take over the ailing department. After a nationwide search the choice fell upon Colella, at that time serving as head of the Department of Economics at St. Bonaventure University in New York. He had earned all his degrees at Fordham University, the B.S. in 1964, the M.A. two years later and the Ph.D. in economics in 1973. Much was expected of him when he arrived in Indianola in the fall of 1977. Within three years, Colella put together a strong faculty and an improved program that began to attract an increasing number of students. In the years to come Simpson would have to encourage Colella to fend off offers from other institutions for positions ranging from professorships to presidencies. Meanwhile, he made a mark for himself on the campus as teacher, administrator, emcee at public programs, fraternity adviser and consummate storyteller. The *Simpsonian* was happy to note that he "even plays guitar and tennis."[25]

When Richard Ault resigned in the spring of 1977, Chairman Terry Hoy sought a strong replacement in the Political Science Department. He found one in John Epperson, candidate for the doctorate in political science at the University of Virginia. Epperson had earned the B.A. at Centre College of Kentucky in 1972 and the M.A. at the University of Virginia. His interest in practical politics provided a happy balance for Hoy's specialization in political theory, and for the next decade the two of them provided a strong major program in government. True to his calling, Epperson soon became active in Democratic politics at the local level, where his leadership was gladly accepted.

Carol Soderblom, candidate for the doctorate in music at the University of Iowa, had earned both her B.M. and M.M. at Iowa City. She joined Simpson's music faculty in the fall of 1977. An accomplished pianist, she remained at Simpson many years.[26]

Not unlike the program in economics and business administration, the Theatre and Speech Communication Department suffered from rapid staff turnover and inconsistent management. After the retirement of fatherly, well-liked Richard deLaubenfels in 1973, the department was directed by three persons in five years, each of the last two for one year only, and in the theater tech position between 1975 and 1979, four persons served only one year each. In all, nine different people were employed in three positions during that four-year period. Some of these were truly able people, but they could not be persuaded to stay at Simpson, in spite of the College's possessing one of the most attractive and versatile physical facilities in the state. The one who stood out—and who served for five years (1975–80)—was Douglas W. Larche, whose work in speech communication won praise at every hand. During his tenure at Simpson, work in forensics reached a level of excellence never exceeded before or since. Larche, a 1970 graduate of Graceland College, had earned his M.A. at Wichita State University in 1973 and came to Simpson with the Ph.D. very nearly completed at Indiana University.[27] But Larche's remarkable creativity in speech could not influence positively the unfortunate lack of direction in theater.[28] President Lancaster and Mel Henderson, both of whom were dismayed by what they deemed to be a problem that would not solve itself, decided to make a heroic effort to find the right person to set matters aright in the sagging department. They undertook a careful, nationwide search for a new chairperson, and after months of painstaking effort found a leader in whom they could place real confidence. He was Jack L. Jenkins, then serving as director of theater at George Mason University in Fairfax, Virginia. Earlier he had taught seven years at Elmira College in New York and looked forward to returning to a liberal arts college setting. Jenkins's B.S. and M.A. were from Indiana University (1955 and 1957), and he had earned both an M.F.A. (1967) and Ph.D. (1971) from Case Western Reserve University. What was important was that in Jenkins the College found a mature, seasoned academician with an admirable record.[29] And a bonus in this appointment was the new theater director's wife, Miriam Jenkins, who soon took her place in the Simpson family as registrar and part-time instructor in English.[30] Her contributions to and innovations in registration procedures, one of the liveliest areas of controversy on the campus through the years, came to be appreciated. Another important accomplishment was her development of an exchange program with Hebei Teachers University in Shijiazhuang in People's Republic of China which opened new opportunities for study abroad for Simpson students.

Although their tenure on the Simpson faculty was regrettably short, two other faculty people would be especially memorable among the students whose lives they touched. One was Carol A. Phillips, whose work with early childhood education was outstanding.[31] She served at Simpson for seven remarkably productive years (1977–85). The other was Douglas J. Duncan, an extraordinarily talented musician who helped Robert Larsen make Simpson's program in opera one of the best in the nation. Like Larsen a Simpson graduate (1972), Duncan had earned his Mus.M. at the Philadelphia Musical Academy. Appointed an instructor in music in 1975, he worked on the Simpson faculty for six years, the last year as an assistant professor, until his work with the Des Moines Metro Opera required his relinquishing his Simpson appointment to work full-time with the opera. A gifted teacher and versatile performer, Duncan could sing convincingly just about any tenor role in the operatic repertoire.[32]

* * *

By the mid-1970s Simpson's "open curriculum," lacking any general studies requirements, was clearly not working. Each year fewer students enrolled in courses in the humanities where extensive writing was expected, and not many opted for courses in mathematics or the natural sciences. While expected to work out their academic schedule with their individual advisers, students soon learned that an adviser could indeed advise but not compel. Some advisers, driven by a dedication to high standards and a commitment to the liberal arts, insisted that their charges enroll in liberal arts courses. Too often the result was that the students, opposing the pressure, simply changed advisers, for there were those among the faculty who believed that the students' choices should be absolute and totally free. As enrollments in some departments plummeted, it was only natural that administrators could quite properly justify reduction of staff.

Curiously, too, as enrollments in the various departments became unbalanced, serious students began to complain about Simpson's "flabby" curriculum, precisely the opposite of the old charge of marching students in "lock step" to a degree. And faculty people, even those in the departments with large enrollments, came to admit that the College's curriculum needed a major overhaul.

Change did not come overnight, but it came. As early as 1973 an experimental freshman studies program was launched. It consisted of three existing courses, Owen Duncan's Ideas in Historical Perspective, Todd Lieber's The American Character and Bruce Haddox's Enduring Questions, coordinated by occasional meetings at which presentations brought together the uniting theme of "the quest for identity."[33] After three years, the freshman program was adopted by the faculty as a requirement for all freshmen. The revised program, which commenced in the fall of 1976, consisted of two one-semester interdisciplinary courses and a January term course taught primarily by faculty in the humanities and social sciences in sections of twenty-five to thirty, including lectures, speeches, films and in-class demonstrations on the topic of "the self and the quest for meaning."[34] The program provided at least one common academic experience for first-year students and a modest introduction to the liberal arts. It was ably superintended by Bruce Haddox.[35]

Dean Henderson, delighted by this first step in the resurrection of Simpson's liberal arts component, suggested at the same time the creation of a cultural enrichment program in the form of an all-College colloquium.[36] He realized, as did many others, that the abolition of any chapel or convocation attendance requirement had resulted in embarrassingly poor attendance at lectures, concerts, recitals, plays and operas. Students complained that even concerts by the latest rock 'n roll bands drew disappointing crowds. No one wanted to reinstate required convocations. But how to ensure at least minimal attendance at cultural events?[37] After examining how other liberal arts colleges dealt with the problem, Simpson's faculty adopted what was called the "Simpson Forum." Students were awarded one academic credit-hour for attending as many as fourteen (later twelve) of twenty-plus listed events during a semester. And they could enroll for such credit as many as four semesters. Launched in the fall of 1976, Simpson Forum was an instant success, with 250 enrolled. Although there were problems in validating presence of students at events—no one could underestimate the ingenuity of students in finding ways to short-cut the attendance requirement—the system and the offerings were substantially improved during later years, and Simpson Forum remains a valued part of the College's curriculum.[38]

Several other changes improved the academic enterprise. In 1976 the faculty, encouraged by students and administrators, adopted a new program of student course and faculty evaluation. Although a number of faculty people were still not at all certain students were competent to evaluate course structure or faculty performance, the principle of evaluation was never abandoned and remained an important component in decisions about reappointment, tenure and promotion of all faculty members.

In 1977, in response to student entreaties, grading levels were made more precise by the adoption of plus and minus grades. There was no A+ grade, and indeed failure did not allow qualifying variants. The effect of the new grading system seems not to have caused more grade inflation.[39]

Another response to student agitation was the reduction of the January term from four weeks to three commencing in January 1978.[40] On this matter the faculty was sharply divided, but those who were critical of either the January term concept or the way it operated were happy to make it less objectionable by one quarter. There were indeed problems with the interim term, few of which had to do with its length. Some of the courses were, in students' judgment, "too lax and terminally boring."[41] Too many students found too little intellectual stimulation. There was, observed one faculty member, too much loafing by both students and faculty. In some years, too, there were not enough choices among on-campus courses. On the positive side, internships, career observation experiences and travel programs, especially those that went overseas, were immensely popular and challenging to those who participated. On balance, nearly all students, for whatever reasons, wanted the January term to continue and they were joined by sufficient faculty to keep the program alive.

If January term was popular among students, the faculty decision to alter the date to withdraw from a course was not. Since 1971 students had been permitted to drop any course up to and including the last day of classes during the semester. The faculty, deploring the fact that in just one semester—spring 1977—there had been more than 500 withdrawals from class, believed that students needed more encouragement to make a commitment to a class earlier in the semester. Accordingly, they ruled that after September 1977 a student could drop a course without penalty only up to the end of the ninth week of a semester. Predictably, students opposed the change but learned to live with it.[42]

A year later the faculty, believing that it was important for all students to study in at least one course in which the experience of minorities would be considered, adopted a three-credit hour semester requirement in ethnic and minority studies. Students could select one of a number of courses to meet this requirement. Interestingly this curricular proposal met with almost universal student endorsement.[43] It went into effect in the fall of 1979.

The Educational Policy and Curriculum Committee (E.P.C.C.), chaired in 1978-79 by Joe Walt, took up seriously the readoption of general education requirements for all students, of which the ethnic and minority requirement would be a part. Disappointed that the "open" curriculum had never fulfilled its promise, Simpson academicians, not unlike those in colleges all across America, agreed that a more structured program was called for. As early as the spring of 1977, rumors were flying around the campus that Simpson was going to reinstate required courses, at least for freshmen, beyond the freshman studies program. Because indeed no changes had as yet been considered, Dean Henderson was at pains to deny the rumors. He pointed out that although "Simpson has studied other schools which are moving toward course requirements and other options, he does not foresee this happening in the near future."[44]

The near future came very quickly, for by autumn the E.P.C.C. took up the issue of general studies. Students were kept informed of the proceedings through their committee representatives, whose suggestions and opinions were taken seriously. As the research and discussions became more focused during the next months, faculty and students alike found real enthusiasm for the emerging proposal.[45] There were, of course, several models for general studies programs in the liberal arts from which they could select, but the one which found readiest support was the "distributive studies" plan. The result of their study was a general studies core program that required twenty-one or twenty-two semester hours of work in six areas: (1) the Western tradition, six hours of specified courses in history, English or philosophy; (2) the scientific points-of-view, three or four hours in one of the laboratory sciences or mathematics; (3) the social science perspective, three hours in anthropology, economics, political science, psychology or sociology; (4) the humanities, three hours in American studies, English Literature, philosophy or religion; (5) the arts and languages, three hours in art, creative writing, foreign language, music, speech or theater arts and (6) the American minority perspective, three hours from specified courses in American studies, anthropology, education, history, humanities, religion or sociology. Actually it was a modest proposal, but Simpson was ready for curricular reform, not revolution.

Student body president Amy Schwarz recalled that at first "a number of student leaders opposed the change," but after faculty committee representatives met with the entire student senate, "students decided the plan was good and made a number of recommendations to the committee, many of which were heeded by the faculty." Mel Henderson was not surprised by student response to the faculty proposal. "Students have always wanted structure," he said. In earlier years "they were unhappy with the structure they had. Many institutions made the mistake of removing structure rather than making it work." In the new program, students would find indeed some welcome structure.[46] Acting upon the E.P.C.C. proposal submitted to them on April 4, the faculty adopted the new plan at its regular meeting, May 2, 1978.[47] President Lancaster called the program an excellent one, more than a political compromise between departments.[48]

What Simpson was doing in resurrecting general studies was similar to what was going on all over America as colleges and universities sought to "redefine the fundamentals essential to a college education." Interestingly, unknown at the time in Indianola was the action by the arts and science faculty at Harvard University to introduce a core curriculum, requiring students to take at least six courses in broad, specified academic areas. The decision at Cambridge was taken the very same day the Simpson faculty voted in its new general studies program. Clearly there was a shift in emphasis toward "core curricula" or what people were calling "competency based learning." As the *Christian Science Monitor* put it, "The questioning is an outgrowth of concern in many circles that educational standards at all levels have been slipping. Some college students—even some graduating from the most prestigious educational institutions—make it through four years of classes without ever having read a Shakespeare play, or studied mathematics or learned to write clearly. In short, many seem ill-prepared to assume their expected places in 'the company of educated men and women.'"[49]

The adoption of general studies reaffirmed Simpson's commitment to its liberal arts heritage and restored balance to the education it was providing for a new generation of students.

* * *

Apart from the curricular changes during the latter years of Dr. Lancaster's administration, a number of academic programs—some of them relatively short-term, others more nearly permanent—were undertaken. Three of them were public service programs done in cooperation with and financed by grants from the U.S. Department of Health, Education and Welfare. The first of these was an Upward Bound summer program, the purpose of which was to provide educational opportunity for approximately forty disadvantaged high school students from the Des Moines area.[50] The second was a Special Services program, providing counseling and tutoring to as many as a hundred "economically eligible" Simpson students during the academic year. Both of these programs were under the direction of Valorie Carson, a 1974 Simpson graduate.[51]

A third was the Bridge Project for ten female juveniles whose personal lives were in disarray and who needed institutional assistance without institutionalization. The girls in this program resided in the ground floor of Kresge Hall and attended Indianola High School. Managing the program was Dr. Leon Clodfelder, assistant professor of psychology, and Dennis Rutledge, a 1974 Simpson graduate who served as general counselor and coordinator from his office in the same dormitory which housed the girls. In addition, nine Simpson undergraduate women served as tutor-models, living and working with the delinquent girls as roommates.[52] These three programs functioned on campus between 1974 and 1977.

In 1977 Simpson received an $11,340 grant from the National Science Foundation to conduct a special eight-week summer program in mathematics and political science for thirty gifted high school students. Specifically, students would conduct a mathematical analysis of voting situations, studying methods of apportionment, weighted voting schemes and group decision making.[53] Directing the program was mathematics professor Marvin Van Wyk.

That same summer Simpson offered its first Elderhostel program, a week of tuition-free instruction in college-level courses and an opportunity for stimulating intellectual renewal for people over sixty years of age. Inaugurated in 1975 in New England, the Elderhostel idea was a federally-funded project, and Iowa was the first Midwestern state to offer the program, available in twenty-five colleges and universities throughout the state. Beginning on June 19 and taking advantage of the concurrent season of the Des Moines Metro Opera, performed at Simpson's Blank Performing Arts Center, the entire week cost the thirty participants only sixty-five dollars for board and room in Simpson's residence halls.[54]

In the fall of 1977 Simpson inaugurated the ARCH Program (Academic Resources for Colleges and High Schools). Simpson faculty were to be made available, at no cost to high schools and community colleges, as lecturers and discussion leaders in a broad number of disciplines, each professor making presentations in his or her special area of interest and expertise. Directed by Fred Jones of the Sociology Department, the program was popular in Iowa schools and proved to be for several years an effective device of student recruitment.[55]

Foreign language instruction at the College, the victim during the seventies of the open curriculum, was considerably strengthened when the Department of Foreign Language, under the leadership of Robert Gieber, took over Worth House and transformed it in 1976 into a language house, one floor each dedicated to French, German and Spanish. Three international students were given generous scholarships for serving as native-speaking assistants: Annie Grant in French, Melanie Ott in German and Bertha Armacanqui in Spanish.[56] Students who elected to reside in Worth House agreed that when they were in the building they would speak only the language they were studying. Glenn Buhr, especially solicitous of the well-being of the German students, staged a highly successful Oktoberfest on the weekend before Homecoming. Students were delighted to have an excuse to drink beer as a sort of academic obligation. It should be no surprise that this bock festival became an annual affair.[57] It was the Germans who were most persistent in the language program, and when Worth House, for want of enough foreign language students to fill its forty-four beds, was turned to other uses, Glenn Buhr, whose organizational skills were described by his students as "awesome," organized a Deutsches Haus, using one of the College's houses on North E Street for its Teutonic purposes. By this time—it was 1978—an engaging Bavarian named Tom Streit had entered Simpson, and teacher and student teamed up to provide a living-learning atmosphere for students of German.[58]

In the fall of 1975 the College offered its first course in women's studies. Taught in humanities was a course entitled The Woman in America, instructed by Gaile Gallatin. It included, among other things, "the psychological implications of being a woman in this society, the changing view of women, the changing position of women, and the development of women's liberation as a movement." The course won instant popularity, the class filled with lots of eager young women and a few brave young men.[59]

Providing a powerful contrast to Simpson's growing interest in the women's movement was the arrival on the campus in 1979 of thirty-eight young men from Saudi Arabia, a country where women's rights stood roughly where they had been in the fourteenth century. Sponsored and financed by the Department of Public Security in the Ministry of the Interior of the Kingdom of Saudi Arabia, the students were in a program operated by Systran (Systems for International Training).[60] They would study intensive English at Simpson for eight months in preparation for courses in law enforcement elsewhere in the United States. All of the young men fell into the eighteen to twenty-two age group. And all of them, not to speak of the majority of Simpson students, were in for real culture shock. A group of thirty-eight from anywhere would have been difficult for Simpson and Indianola to handle. These young men, with their lack of language proficiency, their religious sensibilities, their bewilderment with American social relationships, their exotic dress and even more inscrutable dietary and drinking customs and prohibitions, alternately fascinated and mystified their American counterparts.

A number of faculty and staff people were especially cordial, however. Norm and Marjorie Thomas boarded one of the Saudis in their home. Abbie Hade, one of their advisers, counseled, watched after, entertained and mothered most of these young men. Her home on North B Street was open to them day and night. Some American students were friendly and open to learning about a culture very different from their own. But most of the women on campus, put off by what seemed to be immature approaches by the Saudis, tended to ignore them, and a few of the Simpson men were rude and inconsiderate. With probably far more spending money than they needed, some of the young Saudis bought big Transam automobiles and, however inexperienced in the enterprise, started dating high school girls, incurring the jealousy and wrath of "high school boys driving half-ton trucks," spurned suitors who often vented their anger by vandalizing the Trans-ams.

Simpson people were mortified when reports of mistreatment cropped up with increasing frequency. And although the English language program was carried off admirably, the whole experience can be accounted as only conditionally successful. The only people "really sorry to see the program terminated," recalled Simpson's new president Robert E. McBride in his memoirs, "were the local car dealers." In anticipation of the Saudis' departure March 19, 1980, McBride published a letter of apology to the young Arabs for their mistreatment by "a tiny minority" of Simpson students and others. In a difficult world, the Saudis "have provided all of us a wonderful opportunity to gain experience in crossing cultural bridges and cultivating friendships in the neighborhood of nations." He deplored the actions of a few against "a group of young men who . . . came as our guests and found some of us acting like animals." He asked the Simpson community, "Did we do all we could to build bridges instead of trenches in human relationships?" He hoped that the Saudis would not judge all of America and Simpson by "the ill-considered actions of a few," so lamentable because Simpson people had an opportunity "to expand a tragically circumscribed circle of international understanding."[61]

The Saudis were remarkably understanding, responding for the most part warmly. A few of them penned a gracious letter to Dr. McBride and published it in the *Simpsonian*. And interestingly Abbie Hade and Norm Thomas and several others heard from time to time from the Saudis they had befriended, and more than once a few of them visited those in Indianola who had taken the time to be kind to a group of youngsters in a strange land.

* * *

In 1976 Simpson came up for its regular decennial accreditation review by the North Central Association (N.C.A.). As was typical for such examinations, the College's administration and faculty prepared a detailed self-study, reviewing Simpson's development during the past decade and setting forth an account of both its successes and problems. When the investigating team arrived on campus in the early spring, their examination was thorough, constructive and fair. Their report, issued in April, listed what it considered Simpson's strengths: (1) a clear sense of the College's identity among students, faculty and administration; (2) an improving quality of life in the residence halls and fraternity and sorority houses, good student affairs leadership, generally healthy student activities; (3) good progress in minority affairs, taking note of the fact that Simpson had eighty-plus black students but very few from other minorities; (4) "thoughtful and effective" leadership in the College's administration, members of which "understand Simpson's priorities"; (5) faculty dedication to the "liberal arts philosophy of education"; and (6) very good physical facilities. The weaknesses observed were fewer, but they were serious: (1) difficulties encountered in recruiting qualified students, (2) library holdings seriously inadequate for the size and mission of the College and (3) devastating, recurring deficits that were siphoning off funds that could better go into the College's endowment. It was sharply critical of "budget policy and budget control." On balance, the N.C.A. team unanimously recommended that Simpson be reaccredited, its next visit to come ten years hence.[62]

Maybe Simpsonians should not have been surprised by the generally positive N.C.A. report. The association's standards of accreditation were not very stringent. Some of the Simpson people could remember one evening they met with the visiting accreditation team at the president's house. During a frank and open discussion of Simpson's financial woes, one of the team members, a pleasant, fatherly president of a small struggling southern college, asked Lancaster "Do you mean to say you meet your payroll *every* month?" He expressed genuine amazement when Lancaster acknowledged that he did.

* * *

Even if Simpson never missed a payroll, its annual deficits were nonetheless eating into the College's endowment at an alarming rate. Yet it could have been much worse, had it not been for the effective fund-raising done by Ed Couch and his staff during the years he was at Simpson. In 1977, for example, he was able to report that gifts to Simpson for that year exceeded $1,500,000, an all-time high.[63] The annual fund exceeded its $110,000 goal in 1977-78 by $7,476. Alumni fund chairman Joel G. Stewart, pleased that the goal for 1978-79 was increased to $125,000, said confidently, "I'm not concerned about the level of giving at all."[64] Nor should he have been, for the goal was met. Meanwhile the Indianola/Simpson fund drive, the goal of which had been raised from year to year, produced in 1977-78 $24,927, only $73 short of its ambitious $25,000 goal.[65]

Considerably more ambitious was the Commitment 125 goal of $11,000,000— or $20,000,000 according to the dreams of a few of Simpson's more sanguine supporters. In any case, said Chuck Laverty to his fellow board members in 1977, "we are going to have to roll up our sleeves and have some luck to reach the ten-year goal of $11,000,000."[66] A year later the board was talking of completing a "first phase" of $4,500,000, counting $3,200,000 already raised.[67]

Fund-raising for the physical education center, as we have seen, had been extraordinarily slow. Few questioned the need for the building, but the president and some board members were wary about proceeding with construction until the funds were in hand. Their caution, however, met a powerful response from those who argued persuasively in 1975 that the new gymnasium could be a solution to Simpson's student recruitment problem, that the project had taken on a momentum of its own that required their starting construction soon, and that once potential donors saw the building going up, they would be so heartened that they would open their pocketbooks and contribute generously. Timing was everything, they said, and the time was now.

The proponents of action won the day, even though only approximately $1,000,000 of the estimated total cost of $2,500,000 had been raised up to that time, including a U.S. Higher Education Facilities grant of $408,676.[68] Other grant proposals were in the works, and the balance, they assured the doubters, would come in due course.

Plans for the building were prepared by architects Savage and Ver Ploeg of Des Moines. Originally designed to use solar power as its main source of energy, the building would have represented a pioneer demonstration project in such environment-friendly energy use. The estimated $500,000 additional cost of solar panels and accompanying installations could not, however, be justified in view of studies that questioned the effectiveness of the sixteen thousand square feet of solar panels.[69]

Included in the new 56,830-square-foot structure was a huge field house, containing an indoor track, three basketball-volleyball-tennis courts and seating for up to 1,800 spectators. Two ample classrooms and offices occupied the main floor, the long axial hallway lighted by skylights. Alongside the field house on the lower level were equipment rooms, lockers and showers, and a large swimming pool with adjacent sauna. The new complex was connected to Hopper Gymnasium, which would continue to provide a practice basketball court, weight room, possible racquetball courts and additional locker facilities and offices.

When Doyle Woods and some of the faculty looked at the blueprints, they noted with surprise that the swimming pool was twenty-five yards in length. Why not twenty-five meters, since nearly all sports were moving to metric measure? Although it was true that N.C.A.A. swimming meets were still measuring in feet, it was expected that by 1980 they would switch to the metric system, as the A.A.U. had already done. Traditionalists, including a number of students who considered the conversion to metric measure to be as insidious as the threat of Communism, praised the architect's plans as politically and athletically correct. Brad Small, assistant coach and resident counselor at Barker Hall, pointed out that virtually all high school pools were twenty-five yards in length. "If we build a metric pool," he said, "we can still have competitive swimming, but it would be like playing football on a field 95 [sic] yards long."[70] His comments notwithstanding, the metric protagonists fortunately won the argument, and the plans were altered. Doyle Woods, converted to support for metrics, said "in the long run, the school would be glad the pool was in meters."[71]

Selected as construction manager for the building was the Weitz Company, Inc. of Des Moines. A departure from past building contract procedures, the arrangement represented "a relatively new approach to construction which results in efficiency in design, close coordination of construction, and a short construction period."[72] Bids were received October 16, 1975, from many contractors on eighteen specified parts of the project, and further bids were received a few weeks later.[73]

Ground was broken at one o'clock on October 25, a bright, sunny afternoon, just before the kickoff of the Homecoming football game. The first to thrust his shovel into the soil was board chairman Luther Hill. "This occasion," said Lancaster, "will be a milestone in the history of Simpson College. This facility has been needed, planned for, discussed, and even promised for nearly two decades. Now it is becoming reality."[74] And with the College's brass ensemble keeping everyone in tune, the assembled groundbreakers sang the "Red and Gold."

A few days later two houses on North D Street were burned as a practice exercise by the Indianola Fire Department and two other houses were razed to make room for the new physical education center.[75] Construction crews appeared immediately thereafter and started excavation.[76] Eleven months later the construction was reportedly "on schedule," and it was completed in time for the November 17, 1976, basketball game between the women of Simpson and Mount Mercy College. The first men's home game was played December 4 against Grinnell.[77]

Meanwhile, about three months after construction commenced, the Cowles Foundation made a $400,000 contribution to Simpson's Commitment 125 and designated it for the physical education center.[78] Appropriately, recognizing "the many gifts made to the College over the years," the board and administration named the building the "Cowles Center," a tribute to the Cowles Foundation.[79] The formal dedication of the new complex took place February 19, 1977, before an enthusiastic crowd of 1,800, the honored guests including all but one trustee of the Cowles Foundation, board chairman Luther Hill, board member and construction manager Fred Weitz of the Weitz Company, Physical Education Department head Anne Cermak, Indianola mayor Kenneth E. Smith, Methodist conference representative Dr. Edwin C. Boulton and student body president Ken Cunningham.[80] Larry Johnson would be the center's first director.

As soon as the euphoria of the dedication of the handsome new building gave way to reality, Simpson leaders took a square look at the debt on the project. They had negotiated a $2,000,000 line of credit with the Iowa-Des Moines National Bank, "to be repaid as soon as pledges are received."[81] But there were not many pledges. The hoped-for enthusiastic giving that would follow groundbreaking never materialized. Alumni athletes, whose support had been counted on, tried to raise $40,000 for a memorial to Hap Miller, but had great difficulty reaching their goal.[82] Even a $100,000 challenge grant from the Kresge Foundation, and Simpson's meeting the challenge, was far from enough.[83] When all the dust had settled, the College was forced in early 1977 to borrow $1,598,452 at three-fourths percent over the prime rate, and within the next eighteen months the interest rate would soar to thirteen and one-half percent and more.[84] This would mean nearly $200,000 in interest payments alone, not to speak of amortization of the principal. And Doyle Woods had further bad news: it would cost at least $80,000 per year to operate the Cowles Center. Those who contemplated this addition to an already swollen deficit could understand the irony of it all when Dean Henderson informed them that Simpson's application for a Title III grant for "developing" colleges had been turned down because Simpson was "far too strong to qualify."[85]

And the deficits continued to mount—$332,000 in 1976–77, $468,000 in 1977–78, $615,000 in 1978–79.[86] The total of deficits over the six years from 1973 to 1979 was just under $3,000,000, and that fact came to dominate the thinking of the board to the obliteration of almost everything else. In retrospect, the president called the construction of Cowles "a major mistake" without proper funding, and regretted "my inability to persuade the board to fund the debt [on the building] by bonds rather than borrowing from a Des Moines bank at prime. The idea was too new for the finance committee."[87] He tried to put things into perspective in the May meeting of the board in 1979, the last Simpson board meeting he would attend: "It should be emphasized that the deficit is only a financial deficit, sustained by our endowment. It has not been the more severe or irreparable kind—an academic deficit, a deficit of quality vital to life. . . . I'm not really Pollyanna, but I'm not Chicken Little either. . . . We must resist the tendency to measure success by the bottom line alone."[88] It is doubtful if many board members were persuaded by the president's words. The deficit had become a monster.

* * *

Deficit or no deficit, other constructive, positive projects were undertaken which improved the campus considerably. One of these was necessitated by a costly fire.

Discovered at 8:30 A.M. on Sunday, October 18, 1975, flames ravaged the entire interior of Great Hall, its contents destroyed and huge vaulted ceiling and laminated wooden beams charred by smoke and flame. Probably caused by a cigarette accidentally dropped into a sofa at the west end of the hall, the fire broke out after the 5:30 A.M. conclusion of a marathon dance sponsored by the Organization for Black Unity.[89] Although most of the loss was covered by insurance, it required months to make repairs.[90] Plans were approved during February and reconstruction, including replacement of some of the wooden arches, was completed in late spring. The total cost of the project was $146,000.[91] To replace the severely damaged concert grand piano, two other pianos were purchased, both superb instruments in fine used condition. One came from the Metropolitan Opera in New York and was placed in Camp Lounge in the Brenton Student Center. The other, a rare Bösendorfer from Austria, was purchased at a remarkably favorable price from the New York Philharmonic Orchestra and replaced the one damaged in the fire.[92]

On a happier note, the College purchased all of Franklin Avenue between D and E Streets, adjacent to Buxton Hall, for $1,000.[93] And soon Franklin between C and E Streets was closed to vehicular traffic, creating a pedestrian mall.[94] Large urns containing flowers and blocking traffic, were a gift of the Alpha Tau Omega fraternity. Speaking of pedestrian malls, a fine brick walkway was laid, commencing at Dunn Library and running westward between Mary Berry and Kresge Halls and continuing beyond C Street along the north side of Hopper Gymnasium to the east entrance of the Cowles Center. Campus planner Richard Dober had identified the walk as the "center of the campus." On a beautiful Thursday afternoon, October 14, 1976, the whole campus turned out, from President Lancaster to trustees to new freshmen, to lay 36,000 bricks on the concrete base of the walk. They nearly finished it when they ran out of bricks.[95] It was completed—some called it the "yellow brick road"—in time to be admired by Homecoming visitors.

Later that fall students noticed with sadness that the old front gate to the campus was crumbling away, its soft brick attacked by the extremes of Iowa weather. Lest it collapse entirely, its walls were torn away, only the heavy posts remaining, awaiting the day when someone with a sense of history would come along to restore the gate to its original beauty.[96]

The front gate was not the only structure in an advanced state of disintegration. Barrows Hall, almost seventy-five years old and declared not worth renovating, was going to have to come down.[97] What to do with the Music Department? No funds were yet available for a new building, and Barrows could easily collapse before the money could be raised. Meanwhile, could the Music

Department be moved to new accommodations? A serious proposal emerged to transfer it to the Brenton Student Center, moving student activities to a renovated College Hall. After all, had not the Wigwam, the old snack bar and soda fountain, been housed in College Hall? Examination of the Brenton Student Center, however, revealed that it was ill-adapted to a musical incarnation, and the proposal, one of the least rational in Simpson history, was mercifully dropped.[98] They would have to prop up Barrows and wait.

If the suggested move of Music to Brenton was ludicrous, the sale of Park Hall, by any measure the worst structure owned by the College, was a marketing triumph, the ramshackle house sold to an unsuspecting private buyer in 1978.[99] At the same time, the College purchased another house on North D Street, consistent with its policy of buying individual properties in order to enlarge the campus in the area immediately to the east and west.[100] Other projects during this period ranged from repairing—hardly for the last time—the huge flat roof of Dunn Library to redoing the grill in Brenton Student Center or paving the parking lot north of the ATO and SAE house, the last-named accompanied by a chorus of praise from eighty or more young males with muddy cars.[101]

And there was even talk of renovating College Hall, languishing in a state of advanced decay.

* * *

Student life during the late 1970s settled into a somewhat more conventional pattern than had been the case for some years. Enthusiasm for competitive athletics was clearly on the rise. Athletic performance, however, was for the most part poor, although there were a few welcome exceptions to Simpson's otherwise lackluster record.

Maurice "Maury" Waugh, age thirty-four, was employed as the new football coach in January 1975. Named Iowa Conference coach of the year in 1972, he had built a strong program at the University of Dubuque, his alma mater, since 1969.[102] His coming to Simpson, announced President Lancaster, "will signal the rise of Simpson as a power in the Iowa conference."[103] Waugh's tenure at the College unfortunately did not live up to the promise. His four losing seasons were disappointing, marked by some frustrating fourth-quarter defeats and a 21–20 loss to Central in 1978, in spite of what the *Zenith* called "strong and relentless fan support."[104] Even in the 1976 season, the team bolstered by the addition of transfers Doug Evans and Vince Barborka and led by the record-breaking rushing of Darrell Noble—2,151 yards in four years—and the passing of Blake Weber, Simpson could manage only a 4–5 season. To be sure, that year Simpson faced four teams rated in the top ten in the nation in Division III. Waugh called Noble "one of the best running backs ever."[105] The 1978 team matched the 1976 record, but failed to manage a winning season.

The College's basketball record was only marginally better: three losing seasons out of four. The 1975–76 season was very good, with a 16–8 record overall and third place in the Iowa conference. That year's team went to the N.C.A.A. Division III regional tourney at Rock Island, Illinois, and Dick Starr was named I.I.A.C. coach of the year. The next three seasons, however, were frustrating in spite of the superb performance of 6' 5" Dave Keller, who during his four seasons at Simpson scored 1881 points, smashing Bob Tidgren's long-standing 1692 point record. The 1976–77 team ended up in the conference cellar, and the next two years were not much better. Dick Starr, who had travailed with the team through thick and thin, resigned his coaching position at the end of the 1978–79 season to spend full time teaching and heading the College's health education program.[106] Later that spring Roger Thomas, coach at Mt. Mercy College, was selected to take over Simpson's basketball program.[107]

Although the track teams were only average, a few individuals turned in superior performances. Few would forget Terry Marcussen's tying Bob Coy's 9.9 second 100-yard dash record or Rich Van Pelt winning the 400-meter intermediate hurdles in 56.39 or especially the sensational pole vaulting of junior Tom Forsgren who broke his own and Simpson's record with a 15' 6" vault.[108] Forsgren, born in India the son of missionary parents, alumni Bob '54 and Eva Bok-Jensen Forsgren '55, was not only a superb athlete; he was at the top academically and served as student body president.

In other men's sports the record was mixed to poor. Wrestling was up and down, but a standout was 158-pound Jerome Stewart who in 1975–76 compiled a 27–0 record, won an I.I.A.C. title and placed fifth in the national tourney. Rugby did poorly as interest in the sport declined. Baseball was especially disappointing, ending up with a 7–15 record in 1978 and 3–15 in 1979. In cross-country, the Redmen runners, as the *Simpsonian* put it, "did not fair [sic] too well," although Danny Doyle from Carlisle won individual honors in the fall of 1978. Coach Owen Duncan and young Kyle Bottorf kept the tennis team in the running, but golf was not successful, in spite of the fine coaching of Dale Ann Kile, the first female ever to coach a male sport in Simpson's history.

By 1976 Simpson was fielding teams in five women's sports. By all odds the most advanced of these was basketball, coached for a year by Barbara Hibner, who came to Simpson in 1975 as a full-time member of the faculty.[109] During Hibner's first year at Simpson the team did only moderately well, although it defeated the University of Iowa. That was the year they called the team, of all things, the "Redmenettes." Immediately after that season, however, Lancaster appointed Rod Lein, the highly successful women's basketball coach at Grand View College, to the Simpson post—together with an assignment on the admissions staff—promoting Barbara Hibner to the position of acting women's athletic director.[110] Lein would coach both basketball and softball and work in admissions. Explaining his hiring of Lein, whose academic credentials were minimal, Lancaster said that "quality women's athletic programs are being established throughout the nation and it is time—perhaps past time—that we provide them for Simpson's students."[111]

No sooner had Lein, a spirited promoter, arrived on the Simpson campus than rumors started to fly with respect to his unorthodox, and by all reports, overzealous recruiting practices. "It seems," reported the *Simpsonian* in May 1976, "that [Lein] has flown in recruits from distant places," their expenses paid for "by a certain party interested in the well-being of the Simpson women's basketball team."[112] While such practices were probably acceptable in some places, they coincided with the fact that Simpson—and the entire Iowa Conference—formally joined the N.C.A.A. at their fall meeting held at Wartburg College that same spring. In recruiting, for example, whichever rules were the more stringent—N.C.A.A. or I.I.A.C.—would prevail. But women's sports were not yet included, still retaining membership in Association of Intercollegiate Athletics for Women (A.I.A.W.). Simpson was still offering athletic grants-in-aid to women, and Lein took advantage of that fact. Still, he said, he would "not go overboard in making Simpson a national power."[113]

Nevertheless, on the road to "regional greatness," Lein soon discovered that there would be trouble with Barbara Hibner. Although she had been formally appointed women's athletic director, Lein was calling himself the "Coordinator of Women's Athletics," leading to confusion as to who was running the program.[114] Weeks later, Hibner, who never disguised her misgivings about the appropriateness of big-time basketball at Simpson, felt obliged to report that she had discovered three specific violations of A.I.A.W. rules and "numerous ethical violations in recruiting and scholarships."[115] Although it was apparent that some of the violations might have been unwitting, a subsequent investigation by A.I.A.W. resulted in Simpson's women's basketball program being placed on probation for two years "for alleged recruiting and financial aid violations." Rod Lein resigned his position in June 1977, "due to pressing business interests."[116] Unfortunately, Barbara Hibner had already resigned a month or so earlier. Appointed to take her place as director of women's intercollegiate athletics and basketball coach was Barbara A. Quinn of Fort Lauderdale, Florida, most recently an instructor in physical education at the University of Nevada at Las Vegas.[117] She remained at Simpson only a year.

The alleged violations and investigation tended to obscure the fact the women did play basketball and, despite the cloud over their heads, played quite well. In 1977 the predominantly freshman team compiled an impressive 13–8 record and finished second in the state A.I.A.W. small college competition. Named most valuable player was Carla Horstmann. The next year, coached by Barbara Quinn who eschewed the razzle-dazzle recruitment tactics of her predecessor, the team managed only a 6–16 record, but Horstmann that year became the first woman basketball player at Simpson to hit 1,000 points.[118]

The women's basketball imbroglio, together with the I.I.A.C.'s joining the N.C.A.A., underscored the problem of inconsistency in the awarding of athletic grants-in-aid to women. Senior Mark Perrine stated the obvious: "The Simpson administration ought to develop a consistent philosophy on the subject of athletic scholarships for both men and women."[119] In 1979 the College decided to eventually abandon athletic grants-in-aid altogether. "Eventually" turned out to be 1984.

Women's softball, coached by Dan Rourke and after 1978 by Dan Moulton, was respectable. Tennis, played by the women for the first time in 1975, had a poor record, although Melanie Olson from Jackson, Mississippi, was outstanding. Volleyball very nearly scored a winning season in 1978. Women participated in intercollegiate track for the first time in 1977, but suffered from a lack of experience.

Both men and women athletes, once they were deprived of athletic financial aid, asked for academic credit—one credit hour each semester—for participation in sports. It was a proposition that gained virtually no support at all from the faculty, which was sovereign in such matters.

Neither faculty nor students were happy with the state of Simpson's intercollegiate athletics. Some faculty, to be sure, ignored athletics, and a few were openly hostile, believing that too much emphasis on sports had a deleterious effect on academic enterprise. Yet others believed that a healthy balance between athletics and scholarship was an ideal to be sought, that the Hellenic goal of "a sound mind in a sound body" was not empty rhetoric. Put another way, thoughtful faculty, joined by many alumni and most students, believed that whatever Simpson undertook, it should seek to do it well, whether in the classroom or on the playing field. Thus, an editorial in the *Simpsonian* in the spring of 1979 hit home when the writer observed that "Simpson has failed to produce consistent winners in virtually everything in recent years." Hence there was "some disillusionment among the athletes."[120]

Larry Johnson had served loyally as athletic director from 1965 to 1976, and Dick Starr for two years after that. In 1978 the president appointed a new athletic director and head of the Physical Education Department. He was Gordon D. Jeppson of Washington, D.C., program administrator for the National Association for Sport and Physical Education. Educated at Concordia College (Minnesota), where he earned his B.S. in 1960, he taught and coached for three years in Minnesota public schools before completing his M.S. at South Dakota State University in 1964. After teaching-coaching stints at Wartburg College and the College of Wooster he studied for the Ph.D. at Ohio State University, receiving the degree in 1972. Soft-spoken, serious and demanding of himself and others, he assumed his duties at Simpson in midsummer, 1978.[121] At the same time Sharon Holmberg, who had been teaching and coaching at Oklahoma State University, was appointed director of women's intercollegiate athletics and women's basketball coach. She was a graduate of Central State University, where she earned her B.S. in 1962. Her M.S. was from Oklahoma State University (1964) as was her Ed.D. (1978).[122]

Apart from the active, if not universally successful, program in intercollegiate athletics, the College maintained a lively intramural program. Sometimes, failing proper supervision and plagued by less-than-professional officiating, intramural matches took on the character of a free-for-all. Complaints and recriminations filled the air, but the program remained popular, Barker Hall and the SAEs sharing honors as overall winners during the late seventies.

When the excellent facilities of the Cowles Center were opened, Simpson opened its doors to the people of Indianola and Warren County. It organized the Simpson Athletic Club, offering individual annual memberships for $100 or family memberships for $150.[123] Cardholders could use the facilities whenever they were not reserved for class instruction or College team practice or competition. Further, an arrangement was made to permit the Indianola High School to use the swimming pool and other facilities when scheduling permitted it.

* * *

As campus life "returned to normal" after 1975, it was expected that the Greek houses would flourish once again. Some of them did, but others had been damaged or even crippled by student activism that disdained social organization of any sort. Fraternity and sorority pledging was down—in 1976 only sixty-five joined altogether—both because the Greeks were less attractive than heretofore and because, in view of sagging admissions, there were fewer freshmen from which to draw new members.

Two national organizations, one fraternity and one sorority, collapsed entirely. We have already observed the decline of the Delta Upsilon chapter. In the fall of 1975 it pledged only five new men, whose induction into the group provided them what may only be described as an alternative life style. In its first issue of the school year the *Simpsonian* noted—without comment—that the Delta Upsilons were said "to be walking in and out of their house nude."[124] And as their behavior began to border on the bizarre, national Delta Upsilon officials gave up and closed the chapter in the spring of 1976.

But the group refused to stay disbanded, at least for a time. Charterless, they continued under the title of the D.U. Commune, their eccentric conduct and wondrous camaraderie alternately amusing and shocking their undergraduate peers. John Graber published a rather intemperate letter in the *Simpsonian* calling the remaining DUs "crummy fraternity men" and the local organization "a crummy chapter." He observed that "they'd make great independents," which in a sense they already were. The chapter, concluded Graber, "is an absolute failure."[125] Some of Graber's vitriol—he was, after all, an ATO—could be chalked up to interfraternity rivalry, but it had to be admitted that next to the DUs the ATOs looked like a troop of Boy Scouts. The DU response, published in the next issue of the paper, was predictable. "We are not going to answer John Graber," they wrote. "Instead we are going to get stoned and listen to loud music, which is our house project this year."[126]

While the DUs departed the Simpson scene colorfully, the Delta Zeta sorority passed from the scene almost unnoticed.[127] A victim of declining numbers and the financial burden of a large house, the sorority approached the College administration in the spring of 1977, indicating that they had to sell their house and that they hoped the College owned a more modest dwelling they could rent.[128] There really seemed to be nothing available that was appropriate for them, and the discouraged group disbanded at the end of the school year.

The six remaining chapters on campus were sufficiently strong to weather the period of low membership.[129] Then at the beginning of the 1978–79 school year the unexpected happened. Chartered September 5, 1978, the Kappa Gamma chapter of Phi Beta Sigma, a national fraternity whose membership was primarily African-American, appeared on the campus. Founded at Howard University in 1914, Phi Beta Sigma claimed more than three hundred undergraduate chapters and eighty-five thousand initiates nationwide. Earl Wilson, a junior from Chicago, was the Simpson chapter's first president. At the same time the founders organized the Sigma Chapter Silhouettes as its "Women's auxiliary," with twelve charter members. The new fraternity was noted in the *Simpsonian* only in early 1979.[130]

The chartering of a black fraternity reflected a fact of life at Simpson. Racial integration was not happening on the campus, nor was it being sought by most students, either white or black. Simpson leaders were committed to the principle of integration and were loath to give up the belief that it could and would happen soon. True, a handful of black students had joined the older fraternities or sororities, but most remained aloof, seeking identity in separateness. Phi Beta Sigma was a natural consequence of the powerful attractive force of African-American distinctiveness.

Thus the Simpson black community, which reached its greatest number in the late seventies, continued to elect black royalty at Homecoming and found their voice through the Organization for Black Unity, reconstituted in 1976 as the "Concerned Black Students" (C.B.S.). The new organization, said its creators, was not merely an extension of O.B.U. Rather it would speak to the students of the late seventies, "a new breed of black student." Professor James Rogers agreed that the new name was important. C.B.S. president Wanda Brownlee, who possessed outstanding leadership skills, explained that "both organizations worked toward some of the same goals, but in *totally different* ways."[131] Most importantly, "we are focusing on educating black people."[132]

Some blacks still felt alienated from the predominantly white culture, even in those areas, such as athletic teams, where considerable integration had taken place. Blacks in football, said Jack Williams, were "neo-slaves." Moreover, black men were being recruited for their athletic ability, he said, while too few black females were being attracted.[133] But minority affairs director Tom Simmons asserted that "the total minority experience at Simpson is the best in Iowa."[134]

* * *

Several student societies reorganized during the late seventies. The Bizad Club reappeared in 1978. Alpha Phi Omega was revived yet again, and the Young Republicans experienced another of their quadrennial resurrections.[135] The theater honorary Alpha Psi Omega was seen to be active again, but was taken to task for its adolescent hazing of new members.[136]

By far the most successful activity at Simpson during these years was forensics, an activity sponsored by Pi Kappa Delta and coached by Douglas Larche. Ranking first in the state in both 1977 and 1979, the team was the College's pride, hosting the state tournament in 1979.[137]

At the Brenton Student Center people liked the new grill and admired the new Women's Center, located up on the top floor in what had earlier been called "The Niche."[138] Probably most controversial was the subject of salaries for student government officeholders, totaling $2,925 per year in 1978. In a time of financial stringency, it seemed only appropriate that these students take a reduction in their pay. Some critics even ventured to suggest that officers receive no remuneration at all, serving only for the glory of it all. Salaries were reduced slightly.[139]

The *Simpsonian* improved considerably during these years, fortunate to be managed by competent editors and vigilant faculty advisers, people like faithful Mitchell Kalpakgian. One event stood out when the paper's staff invited *Des Moines Register* retired editor Kenneth MacDonald to speak to them. He held forth on a topic about which they needed to hear: being careful to distinguish between a news story and an editorial.

The *Zenith* was at the nadir. In the fall of 1975, it was reported that the yearbook was "practically dead." Indeed it was, and no *Zenith* appeared that year. It required coaxing and promises of help to find competent editorial leadership, but a 1977 *Zenith*, incorporating a "75–76 Supplement" of thirty-three pages, was published by coeditors James D. Lierow and Lynn Marie Thomas.[140] After that, the yearbook continued to be published without any further lapses, but was not always a model of journalistic accomplishment.

The *Sequel*, appearing annually, put out a special commemorative edition in 1977, celebrating its thirtieth year of continuous publication.[141] Meanwhile, Simpson enjoyed at least one issue of another emanation of its "underground" press. This publication, called *Iskra*, was intended to "unite socialists on campus" and "to present unpopular opinions." Above all, it promised "to present Bolsheviks in a better light."[142] Its circulation, effectiveness and duration was probably affected by the limited number of confirmed socialists on campus or in the city of Indianola. If there was a second issue, it does not survive.

If they did not pay much attention to the underground press, Simpson students could enjoy an array of entertainments or be edified by a parade of lecturers. There were musical aggregations like Chick Corea or Harry Chapin. There was the annual "Back Forty Bash," successor to the "V-D Weekend" country frolic. Students could also hear outstanding speakers, people like black New York congresswoman Shirley Chisholm, poet of the "Beat Generation" Allen Ginsberg, English poet Elizabeth Sewell, Iowa Congressman Jim Leach, or black historian John Hope Franklin. They could watch as a time capsule was buried in Buxton Park, honoring the U.S. Bicentennial in 1976.

The most durable competitive event was All-College Sing, but it continued to find critics who urged the members of Phi Mu Alpha not to participate in their own sponsored event. Each year the Barker Hall chorus, made up primarily of Phi Mu Alpha music majors, won the men's competition, except for one year when the SAEs were adjudged to have sung better.[143] In 1979 more complaints poured in. Phi Mu Alpha, replied Steve Stolen, "will not change" and urged contestants to "have fun making music" and not worry about who wins.[144] Responding to Stolen's comments, young SAE freshman Tim Thomas wrote: "We recognize your professionalism; now please recognize our amateurism."[145] Barker Hall and Tridelta, the perennial women's winner, carried off the honors that year.

Other competitions included the revived College Bowl, dominated by Barker Hall and the SAEs. Important, too, was the grade cup awarded each semester. During the late seventies the ATOs and SAEs shared honors for the men, while the Tridelts usually prevailed among the women.

When students were not involved in classes, study, sports, entertainments or competitions, they watched television. Faculty began hearing reports that some students were arranging their academic class schedules so that they would not miss their favorite soap opera at 12:30 or 1:30 in the afternoon. "Students need to kick the TV habit," urged a *Simpsonian* editorial.[146] Few did.

When he took over the dean of students post in 1975, Gary Valen, in a thoughtful report to the board of trustees, reflected on the attitude of students as the era of student unrest seemed to be ending. Students of 1975, he said, were "individual, serious, insecure and unsophisticated . . . the product of television education." Now that the Vietnam War was over, they "show little compassion or interest in the issues that brought on the war or forced it to a conclusion." Students have "grown up with political assassination, racial conflict, a nation divided by war, inflation, and the lack of a clearly defined future." Thus, he said, "there are few goals or beliefs that have a universal appeal to the present college generation." Few of the College's social programs, even the dances, interested even a fraction of Simpson students. They showed little concern for "national issues including ecology, population, race relations, and the energy crisis." Rather they "seek escape from problems" in television or alcohol. Simpson's student personnel staff, he said, "struggles with these realities."[147]

Four years later, things had improved somewhat. Valen saw "more commitment to the College as a whole" and considerably less student apathy.[148] At the same time, efforts to control alcohol abuse were only partially successful. Because it seemed inappropriate, for example, advertisements for Busch beer in the *Simpsonian* were dropped.[149] And serious efforts were made to curb excessive drinking and rowdyism at home football games.[150] Alcohol abuse would remain one of the most obdurate problems Simpson—and nearly every other college in the land—faced in the coming years.

* * *

Plagued by instability and excesses in student life, not to speak of recurring deficits, President Lancaster could only nod in sympathy with Clark Kerr, president of the University of California, who said "I find three major administrative problems on a campus are sex for the students, athletics for the alumni and parking for the faculty."[151] Lancaster would, however, probably have substituted "salaries" for "parking."

Popular in the Des Moines community, the president was appointed to several blue ribbon committees by the governor of Iowa and moved comfortably with Des Moines civic leaders in circles of influence which could be helpful to Simpson. He was elected vice-president of the Central States College Association and attempted to help breathe life into a consortium that was not functioning well.[152] He was also selected by his presidential colleagues to head the Iowa College Presidents Association. These associations were immensely helpful to him and to Simpson, but, he realized only later, "I failed to pay sufficient attention to Indianola, in my efforts to reach Des Moines and the State."[153] And Indianolans, who claimed a kind of proprietary interest in the College, fretted.

On campus, however, in keeping with his dedication to collegiality, he opened his door to students and faculty alike. And on at least one occasion such approachability turned out to be advantageous for the student and for the College. "I remember a student, Patricia "Trish" Frey, coming to see me about a problem with the Business Office," recalled Lancaster years later. She asserted that the business office was insisting she pay a bill she had already paid. "I knew Trish quite well and trusted her," reflected Dr. Lancaster. But Doyle Woods argued that if they credited Frey's account, other students would get wind of it and make similar claims. Nevertheless the president "ordered him to credit her account and suggested [they] wait to see what happened regarding others." Soon enough another student, hearing from Trish Frey that the president would listen, came up with a similar, suspiciously similar, claim, "triggering an investigation which uncovered a serious embezzlement by a trusted, long-time employee" in the business office.[154]

Students complained about more than the business office. The food service was the constant source of disgruntlement. Sometimes it was merely a matter of resistance to institutional food unattractively served, different from mother's cooking back home.[155] But in 1977, after four different managers in one year, the College's old Szabo professional food service was discontinued and a new one installed in its place. It was supposed to be better.[156] It wasn't.

In order to deal more effectively with student concerns, the College employed in the fall of 1977 three new resident counselors. One was Jed Willoughby, a 1975 Simpson graduate who, in a previous incarnation, had been known to engage in most of the mischievousness to which human nature was subject. Now reformed, indeed born-again, he could watch after his charges with the confidence of an expert. He served as director of housing. He was joined by Thomas and Jovanka Westbrook, he a graduate of Tusculum College in Tennessee, she of DePaul University. The two of them turned out to be gratifyingly effective, Tom as director of student activities and Jovanka as counselor and director of the Women's Center.[157]

The effort to improve student life was one facet of a many-sided plan to give Simpson a real sense of direction. To this end, a few months after the North Central Association visit in 1976 the board and president organized what they called the "Goal Setting and Review Program." "Every institution," said Dr. Lancaster, "should take stock now and then to see what it is doing and where it is headed." Led by retired trustee Dean Prather '32, a group consisting of chief administrators, the five academic division heads and representative trustees, met periodically for a year and a half. They found "management by objective" a helpful format, examining academic programs, financial concerns, student affairs and external relations. Probably one of the most productive features of their study was the completion of a self-evaluation of personal effectiveness and goals of each member of the administration and faculty.[158]

* * *

During the four years after 1975 Simpson lost a number of people who had been important to the life of the College. Past president Bishop Edwin E. Voigt, eighty-five years old, died August 31, 1977, at his home in Seattle, Washington.[159] Two emeritus board members, Harold N. Graves of Boca Raton, Florida, and Max Dunn of Los Angeles, retired faculty member and administrator at U.C.L.A., died in 1976. More immediately, two sitting members of the board died, Sears Lehmann, Jr., of Pueblo West, Colorado, December 19, 1978, and Roger E. Dunn of Long Beach, California, January 23, 1979.

The entire campus was thrown into mourning with the death of Mildred Lekberg, January 9, 1977, whose remarkable talent, extraordinary generosity and gentility, had graced Simpson for nearly four decades. A number of prominent alumni whose lives had touched the College in many ways died during this brief period, not the least of whom was Joe Meek, age seventy-two, prominent Chicago public figure and spokesman for Illinois retailers, in Western Springs in January 1976. J. Clare Hendrickson, one of the College's greatest all-time athletes, died at seventy-eight in early 1976, and patron and formidable Washingtonian Alida Smith on New Year's Day, 1977.

But surely the most difficult loss to sustain—for it happened to two young men in the bloom of youth—was the death of Greg Westbrook and J. K. Miggins, two young Simpson undergraduates, in an automobile accident on December 16, 1976, while driving home to the East Coast for Christmas. Everyone at Simpson, especially their closest friends in the Concerned Black Students organization, were struck as if by a body blow.

* * *

After the years of intense political activism on campus, one might have expected that in reaction Simpsonians would isolate themselves from the rest of the world. It is true that in the late 1970s Simpson students were being described as apathetic and uninvolved, yet there were some issues and events it was impossible for them to ignore. The cost of attending Simpson, for one thing, reflected the soaring inflation in the nation's economy. The total cost of tuition, board, room and student activity fee rose from $3,485 in 1975–76 to $4,920 in 1979–80, an increase of more than forty percent. At the same time, interest rates moved sharply upward, creating a paradise for investors and a nightmare for borrowers. And most Simpson students, like the College itself, were in the latter category.

One could not have shut out national politics if one had wanted to. Ever since President Nixon's resignation in mid-1974 and advent of the Ford administration, people watched the political process heat up as the Democrats, lots of them, vied for the presidency. The one who captivated Iowans was Jimmy Carter, whose candidacy brought him to Iowa to campaign for the vote in the first-in-the-nation test in the Iowa caucuses. More than once his campaign swings through Iowa brought Carter to Indianola, the last time on December 5, 1975, when he spoke at the College. And Carter's victory in the Iowa caucuses a few weeks later vaulted him into prominence and led to his nomination for the presidency the following summer. In the 1976 presidential election, although Carter lost Iowa by a scant 13,000 votes, he carried Warren County handsomely, 7,653 to President Ford's 6,098.[160] Most Simpson people said they voted for Carter.

Nor could people at Simpson overlook the whirlwind of controversy that surrounded the ordination of women as priests in the Episcopal Church. To be sure, Methodists had early adopted the practice of ordaining women to the pastorate, but other faiths were slower, and some remained obdurately unmoving. Although it was slow in doing so, the Episcopal Church did move, authorizing ordination of women after January 1, 1977. Less than three months after it became permissible, Kathryn Ann Piccard, age twenty-seven and a 1971 Simpson graduate, was ordained as the first woman priest in the Iowa Episcopal Diocese. She had attended the Episcopal Divinity School in Cambridge, Massachusetts, after her years at Simpson. In her ordination she followed the lead of her remarkable eighty-one-year-old grandmother, Dr. Jeannette Piccard, who resided in Minneapolis. Dr. Piccard had been ordained a priest in January, one of the first eleven in America, within days after the ban on women priests was lifted.[161] It would have been uncharacteristic at Simpson for people to be anything but enthusiastic about this important step in the empowerment of women.

Because author Alex Haley was a good friend of Simpson, people at the College were especially interested in the appearance of *Roots*, the powerful account—partially fictionalized—of the author's search for and discovery of his family's history, tracing his lineage back to the Gambia in Africa. Simpsonians felt they were somehow a part of that search, and they shared the joy of Haley when the book became a bestseller. The next year they enjoyed the miniseries adaptation of the book, the television hit show of 1977.

* * *

During his last years at Simpson, President Lancaster once quoted E. B. White who lamented, "When I arise in the morning, I am torn between the twin desires to reform the world or enjoy the world. This makes it hard to plan the day." Reforming or enjoying Simpson was not easy in the late seventies, let alone dealing with the rest of the world. Nonetheless, when he announced in January 1979 to the board his decision to resign the presidency, Lancaster could point to a number of reforms, or at least important changes, that had taken place during his seven years at the College. He recalled that when he came to Indianola in 1972, he "thought Simpson's image and vitality could be communicated better." And there is no doubt that things did improve, partly because student unrest subsided. Also, in the most recent year Simpson's academic standards for admission had been raised as never before. The board of trustees, with sixteen new members, had been "improved tremendously," and there was little doubt that it was as good as any in Iowa. The faculty had improved, with more than seventy percent of them holding earned doctorates. Fund-raising had broken all records.[162] The College's endowment had more than doubled, in spite of "draw-downs" from it "invested" in current operations. Significantly, new structure had been reintroduced into the curriculum and in student life. The admissions program, invigorated during his penultimate year by new personnel, was succeeding as never before. The Goal Setting and Review Committee had done its work well. As Lancaster put it, "we have developed a three- to five-year plan for the College through the group—something that will continue to benefit Simpson's well being."[163] Above all, he had made a number of exceptionally good appointments: Mel Henderson, his scholarly and fatherly academic dean; Ed Couch, the extraordinarily successful development officer; Roger Betsworth, student dean, chaplain and later classroom teacher who won a deserved place among Simpson's faculty leaders; John Kellogg, the man who made admissions work; and Bill Geiger, the dextrous manager of the burgeoning financial aid program.

These impressive accomplishments were a matter of record. As to whether he "enjoyed the Simpson world," Dr. Lancaster later recalled that the job of being president of Simpson was never "lonely in the sense of being excluded, or with nothing going on socially." On the contrary, speaking for himself and his wife, "We were never so busy and involved and enjoyed it very much."[164] They enjoyed especially the relationships they established in Des Moines. They seemed to have less success in Indianola. "I was never sure Indianola appreciated the College, the faculty and students and what they contributed to the community." Although he made a few close personal friends among the townspeople, he felt "the actions of the College community were subject to critical scrutiny always." Over the years there had developed a real sense of alienation. Despite the fact that he found the mayor to be "always helpful," Lancaster "did not feel the town could be characterized as progressive or that it supported progressive ideas," and he was dismayed to find town politics influenced everything from fundraising to who was selected to receive Simpson's Citizen of the Year award.[165] He remembered that when his wife organized the League of Women Voters in Indianola, some of the conservative elements of the community—especially those redoubtable gentlemen who regretted ever having given women the vote at all—voiced their displeasure readily and openly.[166]

Strained local community relations, however, were a minor problem when compared with the College's unremitting financial deficits piling up year after year. Even the record of solid achievement of the Lancaster administration could not lighten the gloom that settled on the whole enterprise. Like a disease that racks the sufferer's body, the deficit obliterated everything else in the management of Simpson and produced a feeling of resignation as Simpson's leaders confronted each new year with the certainty of yet another shortfall, eating into the growth and long-term strength of the endowment.

Yet they expressed hope, that "this too shall pass." But as they approved yet one more budget with a huge deficit built into it, Lancaster remembered Dean Inge's saying that "Faith is the choice of the nobler hypothesis."[167] Board member Stephen Garst put it less delicately: "Sometimes you have to bet the farm." Others on the board were less kind, a few of them referring to Simpson's leadership as a failed administration. Whether such an assessment was fair or not, it was true that no one had yet found the way to stop the flow of red ink. Few were prepared to suggest that Simpson's economic indisposition had reached a crisis stage, but they could think of little else.

Believing that he had no doubt accomplished all he could at Simpson, President Lancaster announced his resignation early enough in the 1978–79 school year to permit an easy transition to a new administration the following summer.[168] "It seems appropriate," he said, "to make other personal plans and move in a new professional direction."[169]

He would take up a new position at Beloit College in Wisconsin. The president of Beloit, Martha Peterson, had been "very persistent and made me an offer I can't refuse," he said. "Each of us," he added, "has to seek out his own fulfillment in his own way and in his own time." At Beloit he would become vice-president for college relations, coordinating an expanded development, alumni relations and information services program planned by the college.[170]

At the festive commencement on a fine day in May 1979, the College conferred an honorary LL.D. upon Lancaster. It was an appropriate way of expressing thanks to the man who had performed valiantly during a very difficult seven years. For his part, Dr. Lancaster acknowledged that the Simpson experience was one he would remember always. "The College will always be in my heart. I hope to return—and often."

The 1980 *Zenith* picked up the theme of the owl, honoring the tradition of the return each spring of the family of great horned owls whose nest was high up in one of Simpson's huge maples.

XXI

From Strength to Strength 1979–87

No sooner had Richard Lancaster announced his forthcoming departure than board of trustees chairman Fred Weitz appointed a search committee to start looking for a new president. It was a strong committee, including, in addition to Weitz, five trustees: past chairman Luther Hill, Bishop Lance Webb of the Iowa Area of the United Methodist Church, Katie Meredith of Des Moines, Charles O. Laverty, farmer, agribusinessman and former state senator, and Richard Buxton, president of Indianola's Peoples Trust and Savings Bank. Representing the faculty was longtime Education Department chairman E. G. Booth, while the student body president—first Tom Forsgren and then his successor Gary Streaty—acted on behalf of the undergraduates. Assisting in a consultative capacity was a faculty committee of five persons, chaired by Dr. Booth, and a student delegation of eight, chaired by the student president. Staff assistant for the search committee was director of alumni affairs Lu Jean Cole.[1]

After examining some 120 nominations and applications, the search committee came up with a list of ten prospects by mid-April and soon reduced that number to three.[2] One of the "survivors" on the short list was Dr. Robert Edward McBride, vice-president and dean of academic affairs at Albright College in Reading, Pennsylvania. He had been recommended to Simpson by ex officio board member Kenneth E. Metcalf, superintendent of the Des Moines district of the United Methodist Church. Metcalf had met McBride when the latter was an almost-successful candidate for the presidency of Morningside College in Sioux City. Indeed, the Methodist "old boy" network was still alive and well.[3]

Early in May McBride received a telephone call from Chuck Laverty, who informed him of his nomination and inquired if he was interested in pursuing the matter. He was, and only a week later Laverty and Luther Hill showed up in Reading in a balky rented car to talk with the candidate—and his colleagues—about the presidency. McBride remembered the two of them as a most unlikely pair, Laverty a "typical slow-talking Iowa farmer" and Hill an "articulate and witty" urbane lawyer. He noted that although they "represented contrasting styles," they "seemed to enjoy a special camaraderie between themselves." Their conversations went well, and only a few days later Fred Weitz invited McBride to visit Indianola the following week.[4]

They put him up in the guest suite in Kresge Hall and interrogated him thoroughly for two days. When it was all over, he was pleased with the conversations, especially the one with the student group, whose spokesman, he recalled, was "a young black man by the name of Gary Streaty, a member of the football team of imposing physical stature and mental alertness."[5] For its part, the search committee was well impressed with McBride and invited him to return with his wife for a second visit, which also went well.

But soon enough it became evident that the search committee—not to speak of the rest of the board—was split between support for McBride and a rival candidate. McBride's potential weakness, reasoned some of them, was his lack of extensive financial background, and in view of Simpson's financial crisis, that could not be overlooked. McBride reasoned that there might still be other problems. He noticed, for example, that the outgoing president "was ten years younger than I, articulate, and much more handsome than I could claim to be." He sensed that the board was "frankly looking for someone with that happy mixture of charm, vivacity, suavity . . . combined with Platonic-like intelligence and wizardly financial abilities."[6] He was not at all sure he would measure up.

Fred Weitz was refreshingly yet brutally blunt, informing McBride that there was no consensus for any candidate. The search committee was leaning in McBride's direction and the board was really split. What seems to have brought the matter to resolution was the staunch support for McBride in the student committee, especially from its chairman Gary Streaty. Even though there was still a minority in the board, led by one member who "was disappointed that the College had not been able to find a more Ivy League type of president," the job was offered, and McBride, fully aware of the lack of unanimity, accepted. After all, he had "worked with critics in the past and . . . had no doubt that there would be critics in the future."[7]

In mid-June, McBride met with the executive committee of the board, together with Jim Wallace, over lunch at the Brenton Student Center. An hour later, at a brief meeting of the entire board in the Camp Lounge, Robert E. McBride was elected the nineteenth president of Simpson College. Minutes after the vote was taken, he was ushered into the room and introduced to the group by Fred Weitz, whereupon he formally accepted the position and spoke briefly.[8] He then hurried back to Pennsylvania where he and his wife Luella packed their belongings in record time, sold their home, bade farewell to old friends and colleagues and "piled into our Buick LeSabre and headed out once again, this time west—to Iowa."[9]

* * *

At the age of fifty-five, Robert McBride was prepared to make the Simpson presidency the crown of his career. Born May 11, 1924, at Washington, Indiana, the son of Isaac Edward and Edna Louise Gray McBride, he grew up in a solid working-class home in which Christian piety was taken for granted. Educated in the public schools in his hometown, he and his parents and brother Elwood worshiped in the local United Brethren in Christ Church.[10] He entered Indiana Central College in the fall of 1942, but soon dropped out to enter military service. Although as a pretheology student he had a military draft deferment, he thought it proper, as did almost all young men of his day, to do his part in the war. In the Army he rose to the rank of sergeant, serving in the Seventeenth Airborne under General William Miley. Before shipping overseas he married Luella Kathleen Hart, June 4, 1944. She was a Terre Haute native whom he had first met at church and later dated when they both attended Indiana Central. He was twenty, she nineteen.

First sent to England in August 1944, weeks after the Allied invasion, McBride and his fellow glider paratroopers were attached alternately to the British Ninth Army and General George Patton's U.S. Third Army, seeing their most dangerous action in the famous Ardennes campaign when the Germans, in a last-gasp effort to split the Allied forces in the West, launched an ill-fated offensive, the Battle of the Bulge. Moving across the Rhine, Allied troops swept across Germany in the last months of the war in Europe. From August until December 1945, McBride served with the U.S. occupation forces in Berlin.

Mustered out of service, he returned home in January 1946 to Luella and to Indiana Central, where he completed his work in 1948. While still a senior he served as pastor in a four-point circuit at Freetown, Indiana. At the same time he played end on the football team, entering the record books that year as one of the leading scorers in the state.[11] Upon graduation he enrolled at the United Theological Seminary at Dayton, Ohio, completing his Master of Divinity degree in 1951.

Because the end of his seminary education found him still wrestling with philosophical and religious questions, McBride decided to enter graduate school. He enrolled in 1952 at the University of Chicago, completing his course work in philosophy in two years. And four years after that he would be awarded the Ph.D. in philosophy.[12]

McBride returned to his alma mater at Indianapolis, where he instructed philosophy for twelve years. While at Indiana Central he took on the added duties of dean of students (1956–62) through which he learned the rewards of administrative work and discovered that he was good at it. And as he later admitted, administrative work commanded a higher salary than did teaching, and he had three children to educate: a daughter Judith Kay and two sons, Ronald Wesley and Steven Edward. Hence he accepted the position of academic dean at Albright, a liberal arts college founded in 1856 and affiliated with the Evangelical United Brethren Church. Five years later he was promoted to the vice-presidency for academic affairs, the position he held when he accepted Simpson's invitation.

The years at Albright were "challenging and creative." In appraising his role there, he later recalled that "I had served as a top academic administrator during one of the most difficult and contentious periods of American higher education," and moreover had, "in the judgment of many colleagues, been the 'real' president of the college in a period in which its top leadership had been in disarray." He "had been instrumental in holding the college together in a time of crisis."[13] That experience gave him confidence as he approached the formidable task of leading another college in another place.

* * *

When the new president and his wife arrived in Indianola in midsummer 1979, bone tired from their two-day journey, they drove straight to the "new" president's home on West Ashland. As they explored the big, rambling house that was to be their residence for the next eight years, they found on the kitchen table a lovely rose with a note attached from board of trustees member Grace Overton, suggesting they look into the refrigerator for a light meal she had prepared for them. They decided that if this gracious gesture was a sign of Iowa hospitality, they were certainly going to like Indianola and Simpson.

Once he settled in at his office in Hillman Hall, Dr. McBride began to take the measure of Simpson. Marching around the campus on hot summer days, he looked inside every building, checked out the entire physical plant and made mental notes of his impressions. He talked with administrative people, secretaries, maintenance employees and even a few stray faculty members and students. He kept in close touch with Fred Weitz and the members of the executive committee of the board of trustees. And in this rigorous examination of the College, he found some of his earliest impressions of the place confirmed, others modified. Simpson, he discovered as had others before him, was in some ways an enigma. It possessed some undeniable strengths and some debilitating weaknesses.

The strengths were impressive. Simpson's board of trustees, for the most part men and women of power, wealth and ability, was superb, the envy of many of its sister institutions. He soon discovered also a core of dedicated faculty people, teachers and scholars of quality who could have succeeded anywhere and who chose to remain at Simpson. He found some capable, effective people in his administrative staff. He was especially struck by the ability and resourcefulness of John Kellogg in admissions. He had met him earlier at DePauw University, where Kellogg had been McBride's son Ron's freshman football coach. Beyond this, the new president also discovered what others already knew: the College possessed a body of fiercely loyal alumni who valued their Simpson experience as a pearl of great price. On campus, he was happy to find several very attractive and well-designed buildings of all ages and forms, "a mixture of 19th and 20th century styles that made for a pleasant blend."[14] He recognized, too, the manifest advantage of Simpson's central location, certainly the best of the five Methodist-related colleges in Iowa.[15] He learned that the Iowa Methodist Area was the third largest conference in the world and that Methodists represented the largest protestant denomination in the state. At Simpson, he concluded, there was much on which to build.

But an intimidating amount of building was needed, for the College's weaknesses were as indubitable as were its strengths. First and foremost was the staggering deficit. It would have to be attacked—and conquered—as his administration's first order of business. A number of problems were directly related to the recurring deficits. Many buildings were in a poor state of repair, a consequence of maintenance too long deferred. Especially noticeable were some of the residence halls and College-owned fraternity houses, dirty and in a state of advanced neglect. The campus grounds showed want of care, lending an air of shoddiness to the whole enterprise. Worse yet, the financial bind had kept faculty and staff salaries and wages down, with minuscule raises or no raises at all in a time of galloping inflation. This, together with recurring staff reductions, kept morale dangerously low.

The quality of the administrative staff was at best "uneven." There were severe internal strains and high-level bickering, together with obvious and disturbing problems in financial management. Although most faculty were cooperative and productive, still others were extraordinarily "laid back," the best euphemism McBride could think of for "lazy." He was put off by the unkempt appearance of two or three members of the teaching staff, one of whom "had shown up barefooted for a faculty procession on a previous occasion." Faculty standards, he decided, must be raised. Far more disquieting yet was the academic quality, not to speak of the behavior, of the students. While many were "warm and friendly," and some were superior scholars, too many were marginal, "below the academic quality" of students he had known elsewhere. The average American College Testing composite score for entering freshmen had been until recently a dismal 18 or 19, indeed a low standard—except for the remarkably improved freshman class. He was shocked by their slovenly dress, the almost incurable "hickish" habit of young men wearing their baseball caps in the classroom and even in the chapel.[16] "I was not impressed," he recalled later, "with what appeared to be accumulated problems of student control, behavior and conduct . . . not complimentary to the image certainly of a church related college or, in my estimation, to that of a quality college of any relationship. Drinking in the dormitories seemed to be poorly controlled, if at all; visitation privileges between the sexes had led to patterns of overnight 'sleep-ins' that seriously reflected upon the academic quality of life. . . . "[17]

To McBride, then, "the intellectual interests of the students seemed to center essentially on issues relating to drinking privileges or visitation rights." He found the language of some of them imprecise, even barbarous. "I came away from an early meeting with a group of minority students almost in disbelief at the low level of grammatical competence reflected in our discussions."[18]

Clearly, in his judgment, Simpson students, those who were capable of handling it, needed a stronger curriculum than they had. "A great deal of deterioration had occurred since the Vital Center days" of Bill Kerstetter.[19] Although Simpson's new general studies represented a solid step in the right direction, he saw it as "a cafeteria approach to education, a smorgasbordic display" that did not have the integrity, the organic unity of the old Vital Center.

While McBride's pronouncements on student quality and the curriculum were perhaps unduly harsh, his assessment of Simpson's intercollegiate athletics was not.[20] In every sport, whether for men or women, performance was mediocre to poor. Athletics needed "new vigor and better direction." As a former college football player himself, McBride valued athletic endeavor in the pursuit of excellence.

In sum, the new president saw an administration and faculty in need of a sense of direction, a student body in need of an emphasis on both academics and civility. The whole College, he observed, had no cohesive sense of its own identity. McBride loved a challenge, and he found plenty at Simpson that was intensely challenging. In a note to the College's alumni during his first month on campus, he quoted José Ortega y Gasset, who declared that humanity consists of two kinds of people, "those who make great demands on themselves, piling up difficulties and duties; and those who demand nothing special of themselves." For this latter group, declared Ortega, "To live is to be every moment what they already are, without imposing on themselves any effort towards perfection; mere buoys that float on the waves."[21] Dr. McBride assured his readers that "we are not content that Simpson remain simply what we already are."[22]

* * *

The scheduling of the inauguration, in accordance with venerable custom, was timed to take advantage of the coming of spring. A two-day celebration, it permitted the College once again to indulge its taste for ceremony, its yearning for a new beginning. In keeping with the season of the year, Simpson people could look ahead to brighter, more congenial days. On Friday evening, March 28, 1980, a festive faculty feast was held in Great Hall. Speakers included Willard L. Boyd, president of the University of Iowa, whose address "The Liberal Art of Shaping the Human World," reflected some of the concerns addressed by the Governor's Conference on "Iowa in the Year 2000," a grass-roots experiment in future planning which Boyd chaired. Responding to Boyd was President David R. Ruffer of Albright College and, speaking for the faculty, Dr. Bruce Haddox, professor of philosophy and religion.

Earlier that same day a student convocation at the Blank Performing Arts Center opened the inaugural program. Its topic was "The Liberal Arts and the World of Work."

On inaugural day, March 29, the formal procession moved from Dunn Library to the First United Methodist Church a few blocks distant. Leading the entourage were flag bearers Walter Lain, a junior from New Orleans, Louisiana, and Cynthia Martin, a sophomore from Des Moines, followed by honorary flag bearers Kenneth Smith, mayor of Indianola and board member and alumna Grace Overton. Others in the procession included the Simpson choir, delegates from dozens of colleges and universities, representatives of learned societies, Simpson faculty, administration and board of trustees members. Completing the procession were members of the platform party including the honorary grand marshal, William Buxton III, the honorary presidential medallion bearer, Alvin L. Jordan, alumnus and board member from River Forest, Illinois, and other inaugural ceremony participants.

In the packed church at two o'clock in the afternoon, the installation took place. In their turn speakers presented greetings and felicitations to the new president and to Simpson: David Ruffer, representing Albright College, McBride's latest academic association; Dr. Keith Briscoe, president of Buena Vista College, speaking for the Iowa Association of Independent Colleges and Universities; Dr. R. Melvin Henderson, representing Simpson's administration; Dr. Margaret Watson its faculty; student body president Gary Streaty its undergraduates; and John C. McDonald, president of the Simpson Alumni Association, its graduates.

The investiture ceremony was conducted by Fred Weitz, chairman of the board of trustees, and Bishop Lance Webb of the Iowa Area of the United Methodist Church, who placed around the new president's neck the handsome new bronze medallion, the official seal of his office. In McBride's honor the Simpson Choir sang an original composition using Dag Hammarskjöld's "Prayer," created for the event by Sven Lekberg.

In his inaugural address, entitled "Recovery of the Common," Dr. McBride lamented the "intellectual and moral malaise" which overtook education during the sixties and seventies. Too much preoccupied with "spiraling inflation, high energy costs, demographic declines of student pools, rising student consumerism and career preoccupation," colleges had lost sight of the fact that "the real issues are still those dealing with the questions of the human spirit and human destiny. . . . We have lost," he said, "a sense of what it is we are trying to preserve." Hence "the need to recover the common." This meant calling for "a renewal of what education has always been at its best—a search, a pursuit after a structure of knowledge that makes human existence meaningful."[23]

After the colorful recessional brought the participants back to the campus, they all attended a reception at the Dunn Library. And that evening the festivities closed with a performance of Robert Ward's operatic version of *The Crucible*, Arthur Miller's American theater classic.[24]

* * *

President McBride realized that reducing and eventually eliminating the operations deficit took priority over all other tasks at Simpson. Until this financial albatross could be cast aside, not much else was possible. He gave himself three years to erase the deficit entirely.[25] The components of the deficit were easily identified. One was the huge debt on the Cowles Physical Education Center, the interest and principal payments on which amounted to more than a third of the College's total 1978–79 deficit of $649,059.[26] It would make up more than half of the anticipated $388,640 deficit in 1979–80.[27] The other major component was inadequate budget control.[28] The business office "seemed overpowered by the problem."[29]

The new president immersed himself for two or three weeks in a study of the College's internal finances and budgeting. He found any number of areas where expenses could be reduced without violating the academic or fiscal integrity of Simpson. Systematically he took it upon himself to wield the ax, budget by budget. He instituted a set of guidelines that imposed controls on food and travel expense, insisted on presidential approval for attendance at major conferences, and informed certain offending academic departments that budget overruns, a common and hallowed practice, would henceforth under no circumstances be tolerated. He would find means to conserve energy on the campus. During his first year, for example, he extended the Christmas break to a full month, effecting real fuel savings during one of the coldest times of the year.

The Cowles debt was attacked differently. The board of trustees learned in the fall of 1979 that the Iowa General Assembly during its most recent session had passed legislation making it possible to use tax-exempt financing in the form of industrial revenue bonds both for the purposes of refinancing debt and financing new projects. While there was nothing revolutionary about this legislation, for the issuance of bonds had been an option for Simpson for some years, the new law simplified the process.[30] McBride and the board, anxious to refinance the huge Cowles debt that carried an astronomical rate of interest, moved ahead as quickly as possible. The City of Indianola authorized a one million dollar five-year bond issue at an interest rate of nine or ten percent, the bonds guaranteed by Simpson's endowment. The funds realized from the bonds, sold in the spring of 1980, refinanced the Cowles debt and met the cost of several other important and expensive capital projects.[31]

At the end of the fiscal year President McBride had the entire staff make an intensive analysis and audit of expenditures. He recalled that "when I came to my office about a week later, Doyle Woods was waiting for me. . . . [He] could not hide his elation and a smile extended on his face from ear to ear. He grabbed my hand as he announced that we had reduced the operating deficit from $640,000 [in 1978–79] to $80,000 at the close of our first year." Although McBride hid his disappointment—he would have liked to have eliminated the deficit entirely—he said he was delighted. To be sure, the electrifying news of Simpson's coming within even $80,000 of a balanced budget raced through the faculty, staff and Indianola community, and on campus, morale soared.

Reducing expenditures proved to be one important way to restore the College's financial health. The other was to improve income through increased enrollment and more diligent fund-raising. John Kellogg's revitalization of admissions was already showing splendid results, but there was another virtually untapped source of students the College had scarcely considered. As early as 1970 Ralph John had suggested the creation of a part-time evening program for adult learners, but at the time the idea seemed somehow inappropriate for Simpson. There appeared to be little market for such a program which would have to compete with Drake University and the community colleges for a relative handful of students. More importantly, Simpson was a small-town residential college of full-time eighteen- to twenty-two-year-olds, with only a fringe of non-traditional students, their presence more nearly tolerated than sought out. During the Lancaster years the number of part-timers exceeded one hundred only twice, and in McBride's first year, the registrar reported only sixty in the fall semester and fifty-seven in the spring, and most of those were from the traditional age group.

McBride had seen a successful evening program flourish at Albright and was determined to give it a try at Simpson. Carving $40,000 out of a lean 1980–81 budget, he moved Tom Westbrook, "a bright but underused young man" from housing director to the position of director of special programs, his work to be under the direction of John Kellogg, the newly appointed vice-president for institutional advancement.[32] Westbrook went to work with a will, creating not only a program of evening and Saturday classes, but also undergirding these with a number of support services, including seminars, short courses, conferences, on-the-job educational opportunities, faculty counseling and social events. He also managed the summer Elderhostel program and the College's regular two-session summer school program. To lure out-of-town people, especially Des Moines residents, into trying a kind of reverse commuting, Westbrook devised a modest partial tuition rebate scheme to meet the cost of transportation to and from Indianola: "You Take the Class, We'll Pay the Gas."[33] The evening program worked well, the 1980–81 enrollment surging to 85 in the fall semester and 137 in the spring. Each year after that saw a healthy enrollment increase as Simpson's program became better known in central Iowa. By the spring of 1985 it reached 425, far beyond what anyone had hoped for it.

Increasing enrollment helped, especially with the budget for operations. But capital funds for much-needed renovation of old buildings and the construction of new facilities would have to come from energetic fund-raising. Here the president faced a problem, for he had little professional experience in development work, and he soon discovered that "our newly appointed vice president for development, John Hartung, had little more." He knew also that the ambitious fund-raising program of his predecessor never got beyond "phase one," a fact which could make a very brave man cautious. Therefore, he persuaded a reluctant board of trustees to employ an experienced financial consultant. At a cost of $35,000 a year they brought in Robert Nelson from Chicago. Roly-poly, blunt but not abrasive, shrewd and extraordinarily persuasive, Nelson extracted money as well as admiration from the board, studied carefully the College's fund-raising potential and concluded that the College needed a large and effective development council. "Simpson is supported far below its capabilities," he said, "and in comparison with other similar Iowa colleges we are falling drastically behind in alumni percentage of giving and in total annual giving."[34] A major fund-raising drive could wait. Meanwhile, the College should seek financial support for specific, identifiable projects.

It was surely not difficult to identify a number of campus facility needs, but little could be undertaken until the budget was in balance. Meanwhile, in an effort to provide a larger and more attractive facility, the bookstore was moved from the basement of Mary Berry Hall to Brenton Student Center, occupying the space used by the grill. For a number of years the grill, although it was spacious and pleasant, had not attracted enough business to justify its size. A much smaller, more intimate grill would be built in the lower level of the building, opposite the mail room, while the bookstore, no longer crowded into cramped quarters, could arrange its wares more attractively. Its wares, to be sure, included a lot more than books. On display were stationery items, school supplies, a colorful array of "soft goods"—T-shirts, sweatshirts, caps and Simpson memorabilia—sweets and personal care items. This change of location had a profoundly positive effect on undergraduates' use of the Brenton Student Center.[35]

A less felicitous development was two fires during the spring of McBride's initial year. There was a minor one in Brenton, where burning cushions ignited by adjacent floodlights caused nearly $20,000 in smoke damage to the building, and a major one in Center House, serving at the time as an annex for the Music Department and containing two classrooms, three studio rooms for music faculty and storage space. Smoke and water damage was extensive, $27,000 for the building and $18,000 for costumes and props stored there by the Des Moines Metro Opera. The whole thing was a loss, so the building was taken down, and at least part of the $69,000 in replacement insurance was squirreled away as a nest egg for a new music building.[36]

During the summer of 1980, spurred by the Center House fire, an exchange of property was effected between Simpson and Godwin Brothers Investment Corporation, local builders. Simpson deeded three properties on North Buxton, including Center House, to the Godwins in exchange for three parcels of land on North Howard at Detroit, less than one block east of the main campus. This enabled the Godwins to build some apartment housing and the College to move its physical plant from inadequate quarters under the football stadium to a building on the Howard Street property.[37] To realize the funds with which to remodel the structure on North Howard, the College sold a metal building it already owned adjacent to the new properties and supplemented it with part of the Center House insurance.[38] Thus, at minimal cost the College acquired an adequate and well-located physical plant.[39]

The next year the College disposed of several properties, investing the sale price in bonds and equities that produced considerably more endowment income. In addition to the house at 707 West Ashland, next door to the president's home, the College sold the Lorraine Apartments and a duplex at 606 North Buxton to Harold Heisey for $130,000 cash. The Lorraine Apartments had served the College well, but they had not been used for years for student housing, and faculty people who had once occupied them were either buying their own homes or renting more modern apartments in town.[40]

The sale of real estate was only the beginning. Between renewed efforts in fund-raising and some diligent grantsmanship the College was able to improve its income substantially, and a good share of the new money could be allocated to operations. During the 1979–80 academic year, at the urging of Robert Nelson, the board of trustees raised their giving from 1978–79 a total of $63,520 to $113,816, a 79 percent increase. The Indianola/Simpson campaign raised $60,327 under the leadership of local board member Bob Downing, an increase of 118 percent over the previous year's $26,662. The Des Moines/Simpson campaign, chaired by John McDonald, went from $68,713 to a 1979–80 total of $104,144, up 52 percent. The total number of donors to the alumni annual fund advanced from 1,438 to 1,535, raising $162,312, an increase of $35,041, or nearly 22 percent over the previous year.[41]

Apart from two significant bequests totaling $125,000,[42] the College received two important federal grants during the 1979–80 academic year. A $160,000 grant from the National Endowment for the Humanities, requiring over a three-year period a three-for-one match, would support both the College's endowment and operations. A second stimulus was a $545,000 Title III grant for developing institutions—Mel Henderson had convinced authorities that Simpson's serious deficit problem made the College eligible—payable over a three-year period to support efforts in Tom Westbrook's Special Programs, strengthening of the writing and learning skills program in the Hawley Laboratory, assisting the development of a full-fledged career development program under Jed Willoughby's direction, and what they called "foundational research" and development of "management resources."[43] McBride estimated that the Title III grant would provide $100,000 in budget relief during its three-year duration.[44] To superintend the entire Title III program he selected a recent Simpson graduate, Sumner "Sandy" Opstad '74, who saw to the proper allocation of funds and watched carefully to ensure the successful completion of each component in keeping with the intent of the grant.

Four institutions—Simpson, Drake, Central and Grinnell—shared a grant, one of six in the nation, from the Northwest Area Foundation in the amount of $131,000 to fund an Inter-institutional Faculty Renewal program. Over a period of three summers a total of twenty-four seminars was provided, allowing faculty to study and exchange ideas in academic disciplines other than their own. A number of Simpson faculty people participated, either as instructors or seminar participants.[45]

As might be expected, fund-raising was even better in McBride's second year. There was plenty of stimulus for it. In the early fall of 1980, at the suggestion of Robert Nelson, McBride and board member James Kent approached Robert F. Picken, alumnus and board member from Chicago, president of the Peerless Confection Company, manufacturer of candies that were retailed in the nation's most elegant department stores. Picken, open-faced, genial, and a gentleman to his fingertips, was receptive to their request that he consider making a $100,000 challenge gift, contingent upon whatever conditions he chose to impose. What he asked for was reasonable: the College must match his gift with $200,000 of new private contributions, increase the number of alumni donors to 2,500, balance the budget, secure one hundred percent board member participation in gifts and create a ten-year development plan.[46] Typical of Picken's genuine modesty, he wanted the gift to be anonymous, but he discovered soon enough that at Simpson it was difficult to keep a secret.

The Picken challenge was matched and all the conditions met. The most difficult was increasing the number of donors, but an all-out effort, supported by the first annual "phonathon" ever at Simpson, nearly doubled the number of alumni givers from 1,535 to over 2,800, raising a record $274,000, a huge increase over the previous year.[47]

* * *

It was typical of President McBride that he put human resources far ahead of physical facilities. When, at the end of his second year at Simpson, the deficit had been totally eliminated and the College's operations boasted a small surplus, he was prepared to share Simpson's good fortune with the faculty and staff. Conspiring secretly with Suzanne Miller in the business office, he saw to it that on December 1, 1981, a check for $250 went out to every Simpson full-time employee, irrespective of rank or position, accompanied by a letter of gratitude to "everyone for the sacrifices made and their contributions to our ability to turn the situation around."[48] Only one Simpson staff member did not share in the bonus: McBride himself. He promised that future surpluses would be shared with the College's employees and that much-delayed raises would come as early as possible. Accompanying the letter was an invitation to a festive Christmas party and dance to be held in Great Hall.

As the College's financial health improved, President McBride felt emboldened to attack some of the most egregious problems that plagued the College. The first was salaries. Inviting the faculty's Budget and Coordinating Committee to select seven other Iowa colleges of comparable size and quality, he undertook to bring Simpson salaries to at least the average of these schools within five years.[49] In 1979 the annual salary range for faculty at Simpson was between $12,500 and approximately $22,000, with the average just under $18,000. Eight years later, when he retired, the average had moved far beyond the average seven-college levels, with salaries ranging from $22,000 for first-year appointees to $42,000 for veterans, the average about $32,000, an increase of 137 percent.

To achieve not only salary improvement but also other immediate projects—maintenance of good buildings, removal and replacement of poor ones, upgrading academic departmental budgets, rescuing a "floundering athletic program"—the College needed both careful and competent management of its resources, together with improved admissions and aggressive fund-raising. Most of this effort would fall upon the shoulders of the administration.

There were, however, tensions within the administrative staff, the most immediate of which surfaced during McBride's first year. It seemed that alumni director Lu Jean Cole, who had got on famously with her earlier superior, Ed Couch, had difficulties with Couch's successor, John Hartung. It was a clash of principle, of personality and style. And as the year wore on, their mutual hostility grew. From her perspective, Hartung was "incompetent, outlandishly [male] chauvinistic, overly ambitious and overbearing . . . [and] an outright clod." To him, Cole was "a pampered princess whose main interests were in courting and dining an elite group of alumni [and] who . . . misused college funds by taking expensive trips." Each demanded that the other be fired.[50] McBride temporized, and soon Lu Jean Cole decided to seek her fortune elsewhere. She later accepted an important executive position as director of corporate giving and programming for the huge Pioneer Hi-Bred International in Des Moines, where she superintended the distribution of Pioneer's philanthropy, continuing "to assist Simpson in many ways." She may not have liked Hartung, but she loved Simpson and proved it time and time again. Hartung remained at the College several more years, and if he was no model of sophistication, he was, in McBride's considered opinion, "instrumental in Simpson's financial success in my first five years." He resigned in 1984, with McBride's blessing, accepting the post of president of the Iowa Association of Independent Colleges and Universities.

Appointed to take his place was Dennis D. Hunt, who at the time was serving as assistant vice-president and director of development at Nebraska Wesleyan University in Lincoln. Taking up his duties at Simpson September 1, Hunt moved to Indianola with his wife Linda and three children. A graduate of Ohio Northern University, he held an M.A. from Miami University in Ohio, had taught and coached football at an Ohio high school and had seven years of experience in university institutional advancement.[51] At Simpson he took hold of the job quickly, brought to it fresh insights and sound critical judgment, together with a kind of down-home charm. It was difficult to say "no" to Dennis Hunt. Several years later, in the midst of Simpson's most ambitious fund-raising drive ever—a spectacularly successful $35,000,000 effort, a professional fund-raiser called Hunt one of the best development officers in any college in America.

Raising money was of course crucial in an independent college; careful control of operational expenses was critical in *any* college. And McBride was dismayed to discover distressing weaknesses in campus finance and budget control. While prepared to seek new leadership in the business office, he delayed doing so for several years. In the last weeks of 1983, however, he encouraged Doyle Woods to accept a position as a stockbroker in Des Moines and later assisted him in securing a position at another Iowa college and appointed as the new vice-president for business affairs Charles L. Beatty, former chief financial officer at Olivet Nazarene College in Kankakee, Illinois. Beatty had earned his B.S. at Olivet Nazarene College in 1958 and his M.B.A. at the University of Illinois in 1977.[52]

Beatty remained at the helm of Simpson's business affairs, but appointed controller in 1985 was Victoria Payseur, a young woman with impressive credentials both in private business and in teaching at Grand View College and Des Moines Area Community College. She was a graduate of Luther College, where she received her B.A. in English and history in 1973, and had earned two M.A.s, one in business from Drake University (1981) and the other from Washington State University in history (1975). She was given control of the business office activities of the College, systematizing all financial transactions, establishing more thorough internal auditing procedures and, to McBride's everlasting relief, preparing and controlling the annual budget.[53] Tough, unbending, extraordinarily competent, she kept everyone she suspected of spending irresponsibly, or even liberally, on a very short leash. Sometimes faculty and indeed some administrators grumbled, but her exacting standards and vigilant supervision of the exchequer worked. Payseur subsequently inherited the position of her supervisor when Beatty resigned to enter private business. She was later named vice-president for business and finance, the first female in Simpson's history to hold the title of vice-president.

In keeping with McBride's leadership style and in accordance with his predilection for more structured student life, he sought to channel what he judged to be the wondrously uninhibited student lifestyles into somewhat more conventional patterns and urged his student personnel staff to work to that end. While some modest changes were effected in areas like residence hall visitation or alcohol policy, the course of the movement seemed glacial. After five years he reluctantly concluded to bring in new leadership. In a way, he disliked making a change, for he thoroughly liked dean of students Gary Valen, whom he described as "soft-spoken, gentle, intelligent, nondirective in his approach to students and problems in general, likable and supportive." Valen, he believed, after nine years as dean, was more "laid back" than perhaps the situation demanded, someone who saw himself as "a reactor, a problem solver," but who seemed not to have found specific goals for student development.[54] The problem perhaps could be ascribed to Valen's having lived much of his life at Simpson, as student, faculty member and dean. He could probably exercise his undoubted talents better in another place. Accordingly, McBride assisted Valen in finding a new position as dean of students at Hendrix College in Arkansas. For Valen it proved to be a good move, for he met with great success at Hendrix, where for a number of years he supplemented his administrative work with teaching in history.

Replacing Valen in the fall of 1984 was James D. Thorius, who was at the time enrolled in a doctoral program in higher education at Iowa State University. He had earned both the B.S. and M.S. at Iowa State (in 1973 and 1975, respectively) and had recently served as vice-president and dean of students at Westmar College in LeMars, Iowa. Thorius brought to the position a strong professional preparation, together with a successful record at another college. Evenhanded, deliberate, candid, indeed driven, he was resolute in his intention to provide students with greater opportunities for self-realization in an atmosphere that was both nurturing and free, insisting that students and their mentors alike be held responsible for their actions. Thorius never succumbed to the temptation to "become one of the kids," an occupational hazard among student personnel people. Rather he was content to play the role of responsive and responsible adult.

Because there was discontinuity in liaison between the administration and the rest of the College's staff, McBride decided to promote a remarkably able business office employee, Suzanne Miller, to the position of director of personnel, later called the director of human resources. Miller possessed the requisite knowledge of insurance issues, retirement benefits and options as well as the ability to counsel employees with proper discretion and confidentiality. McBride later recalled that she did "a tremendous job by providing creative and concerned leadership in this vital area."[55]

In view of the growing importance of Special Programs and what appeared to be inadequate oversight of this new enterprise in the academic dean's office, Tom Westbrook was brought into the president's cabinet. Some traditionalist faculty were distressed by the elevation of a "fringe area" of the College to cabinet level, but thereafter the work among nontraditional students did proceed more smoothly.

Of all the people President McBride first encountered at Simpson, none would be more knowledgeable or helpful than was Anna Jean Breuklander, the presidential secretary he inherited from his predecessor. "A.J." knew everything, possessed unshakable opinions on all she knew and was happy to share them—all of them—with the president. McBride couldn't help liking her and even appreciating her counsel at times, but as the years went by he "did not take eagerly to the presence of a mother surrogate in the office."[56] She was promoted in 1983 to the post of administrative assistant for information services, whereupon the president "orchestrated the transfer" of quiet, efficient, unflappable Kathy Ohnemus from Dean Mel Henderson's office to his own.[57] For his part, Henderson was too much of a gentleman to suggest that the president's blandishments had lured away his treasured secretary by "pulling rank." Whatever the propriety of his stealthy methods, McBride had chosen well. Kathy Ohnemus was still serving a grateful president of Simpson a decade later.

One member of the administrative team was soon judged by McBride to be indispensable to Simpson's success. John Kellogg was extraordinarily effective, and it was important to keep him at the College, for his accomplishments were soon widely known, leading to tempting offers from other colleges. Usually Simpson met the handsome salary promised by competitors. "Basically," recalled McBride some years later, "I valued him as one of the most valuable members of my staff, and his salary reflected my esteem." The president, whose characterizations of his colleagues were always colorful and usually accurate, described Kellogg as "ambitious, a perfectionist, thin-skinned, astute . . . a Type-A in behavior, cynical and smart," one who "could not abide fools graciously." And he knew admissions, ruled his office with an iron hand and was remarkably skilled in public relations. It was Kellogg's "passion for excellence" that led to increasing enrollments of better and better students.[58] McBride worked hard to keep Kellogg happy and in Indianola.

* * *

Never before in the history of Simpson had the board of trustees held greater power than it did in 1979, having worked for several years with a president in whom its collective confidence had been shaken. It required a period of readjustment before the board—especially its executive committee—was prepared to resist the temptation to make management decisions for the College. McBride found board chairman Fred Weitz to be brilliant, indeed at first somewhat forbidding, "possessed of one of the most penetrating and incisive minds I have ever known." Weitz was "a true German . . . stern in countenance, forthright, honest," and "blunt but persuasive." At the same time McBride noted with relief that the chairman had "a ready sense of humor, an appreciative vision of the possible and an astonishing sensitivity to political and personal relationships."[59] In time the president came to value Weitz's counsel, his ability to persuade the board membership to consent to a course of action the administration thought best to pursue. In short, Fred Weitz was invaluable.

James W. Hubbell, Jr., chairman of the board at Equitable of Iowa and one of Des Moines's most influential and respected business leaders, possessed perhaps the greatest influence of any on board decisions. His conspicuous conservatism led him to husband the resources of the College—primarily the endowment—resisting all suggestions that the College commit its funds to any but the most rock-solid investments. His policies frustrated those more daring, but Simpson's modest resources remained gilt-edged.

Luther Hill, McBride has said, "was and remains one of the creative geniuses on the board." Never reticent with advice for presidents, he was, as McBride put it, "a man of unbridled energy and creativity, with the capacity to enlist others with his enthusiasm and persuasiveness" and "fully dedicated" to the College. At the same time, McBride has pointed out, with a kind of amused tolerance, that "if I had carried out all of the things Luther wanted me to do, the College would have gone broke."[60]

As dedicated a trustee as any was Dean Prather, whose leadership in the College's strategic planning process had given him exceptional insight into Simpson's needs. During the first two years of McBride's administration, Prather took the time and effort to come to Indianola from his home in Chicago, providing what the new president called "the benefit of his experience and wisdom."

Other strong and productive members of the board included volatile, committed, passionate Michael Gartner, a professional journalist whose talent for debate rivalled that of a dedicated college forensics champion. Richard S. Levitt was especially supportive of the College during the early eighties. Strong Indianola people anchored the board in its hometown, especially Charles "Senator Chuck" Laverty, who was always able to convey the views of Indianolans to the board as a whole, or quiet, strong Robert Downing or conservative, sensitive Grace Overton or solid, genial, hard-working Richard Buxton until his tragic death from cancer July 16, 1984.[61]

When Simpson reached its 125th anniversary year in 1985, its board of trustees included forty-three regular and eighteen honorary life members. Of the regular members, nine were from Indianola, eighteen from Des Moines, ten from other locations in Iowa and only six from out of state. Twenty were Simpson alumni. Seven were women. Only three were clergymen, and they, together with those whose membership was a consequence of alumni election, appear to have been less effective than were most others in board business. Of the out-of-state board members, three were gaining experience and influence: Bob Picken, whose $100,000 challenges vaulted him into instant prominence; Lee McGraw, vice-president of finance in Chevron U.S.A., the oil giant in San Francisco; and Dr. John B. Farnham, Phoenix radiologist and mainstay of Simpson's alumni in the Southwest.

* * *

During the years between McBride's assumption of the presidency and 1985–86, the year of the College's 125th anniversary, faculty turnover slowed. Salary improvement encouraged some to stay who might otherwise have moved on to more promising employment. Faculty morale soared during these years, a major part of which was job satisfaction. It is also true that declining enrollments in many colleges and universities meant shrinking faculties, while graduate schools were turning out more Ph.D.s than ever. In the 1960s Simpson sometimes got only a handful of applicants for a full-time position in most academic fields. By 1980 the market had changed dramatically. One opening in the humanities brought more than two hundred qualified applicants from all over America and even a few from abroad. Faculty recruitment had always been conducted in a national arena, and now there was a surfeit in the academic marketplace.

Simpson's growing enrollment—almost all of it in the nontraditional, part-time category—required a slightly larger full-time teaching staff and a considerable growth of part-time people. Between the fall of 1979 and the spring of

1985 full-time student enrollment actually dropped from 770 to 757, but the part-time numbers shot up during the same period from 60 to 425. Full-time faculty grew from sixty during the 1978–79 academic year to sixty-two in 1984–85. During that same period, however, the number of part-time, or adjunct, faculty increased from five to thirteen.

Among the forty-one people who joined the Simpson faculty during the six years after 1979, fifteen were still teaching at Simpson in 1994, providing a fairly high level of academic stability. Four of them were a part of Frank Colella's reconstitution of the Departments of Business Administration and Economics as the Department of Economics, Management and Accounting. In 1979 he brought James R. Carter and his wife D. Kay Carter to Simpson. Both were graduates of Whitman College, he in the class of 1963 and she in 1964. He had completed both his M.A. and Ph.D. in economics at the University of Oregon (in 1968 and 1969, respectively) and also held an M.B.A. from the University of South Dakota (1979). Before coming to Simpson he had taught at the Oregon College of Education and the College of Idaho at Caldwell, and had served two years with the CIA. Kay held a masters degree in public administration from the University of South Dakota (1979) and was a C.P.A. At Simpson he taught primarily economics, she accounting. The next year Margaret Aten, a graduate of Drake University, also joined the staff in accounting. She had earned her B.A. in 1975 at Drake, where she was a member of Phi Beta Kappa, and likewise her M.S. there in 1980. She, too, was a C.P.A. In 1984 Mark C. Green replaced Norman Bezouska, who had instructed in management at the College since 1979. A graduate of Lawrence University in 1973, Green had earned the Ph.D. in Slavic linguistics at Cornell University in 1980, not a conventional preparation for teaching in management. After completing his doctorate, however, he earned an M.B.A. at Syracuse University. He then taught at Eisenhower College until it closed and then for a time in New York City. A gifted teacher, whose classes in management were sought out by students, he conceded that his first love was Russian language, and when a few years later Simpson's language offerings were expanded to restore Russian to the curriculum, Mark Green taught a two-year sequence in the language while continuing his work in management. Because of his remarkable skill as an interpreter, he found himself called upon again and again to exercise his linguistic skills with visiting delegations of Russian visitors in Des Moines and central Iowa.

In music two people joined the staff and remained many years at Simpson. Ron Albrecht, a talented young pianist who was finishing his doctorate in music at the University of Minnesota, was brought by Robert Larsen into the Simpson faculty in the fall of 1979. He was a graduate of Augsburg College in Minneapolis. To help finance his education he had worked as a pianist for formal dining establishments in the Twin Cities area, playing both popular and classical music.[62] At Simpson he became a popular teacher and gifted performer.

In 1980 vocalist Maria di Palma joined her husband Douglas Duncan in the Music Department. She had already worked part-time in music for three years while serving Simpson as an admissions counselor. Although Duncan resigned at the end of the 1980–81 academic year to devote himself full-time to the Des Moines Metro Opera, she continued at Simpson for many years, working creatively with the College's renowned voice program.[63]

In 1981 eight new people joined the faculty, four of whom made Simpson their home for many years. In sociology, or more precisely social work, M. Jane Kvetko came to Simpson from the Hawkeye Institute of Technology in Waterloo, Iowa, where she had been an instructor in behavioral and social science. She had earned her B.A. at Wittenberg University in 1967 and a master's degree in social work at the University of Connecticut two years later. At Simpson Kvetko soon became known as one of the most ardent and effective advocates for women's rights, raising the consciousness of any number of stubborn males among her colleagues. Another strong addition was Mary K. Lose, who was brought to Simpson after four years as a consultant for the Heartland Education Agency. Having earned both her B.S.E. and M.S.E. at Drake University, the latter degree in 1976, she was hard at work on her doctorate, which she completed a few years later. Lose taught elementary education.

Werner S. Kolln taught both chemistry and physics at Simpson. A 1973 graduate of the State University of New York at Albany, he had completed his Ph.D. in chemistry in 1978 at the University of Utah. Tall, blond, one whose appearance confirmed his German ancestry, he came to Simpson from Miami University, where he had coordinated the general chemistry program. The fourth of the 1981 arrivals was Melvin Wilk, appointed an assistant professor of English. He held a B.A. from the University of Montana (1962), two M.A.s, one from Boston University (1966) and another from Brandeis University in contemporary Jewish studies (1969). He completed the Ph.D. in English at the University of Massachusetts in 1978. At Simpson he proved himself to be a happy combination of teacher and scholar, with an impressive list of publications to his credit.[64]

With the resignation of Gaile Gallatin in 1980, the art program at Simpson lapsed for all practical purposes. A succession of part-time people kept the flame of art flickering. Tim Benson, a Ph.D. candidate in art at the University of Iowa, was employed as a visiting instructor of art during the 1980–81 academic year, helping students majoring in art to complete their work. He continued, with the help of John Joyner, to fill in during the fall of 1981 until a new permanent head of the Art Department could be selected. Then in January 1982, art at Simpson was given new life with the arrival of Janet Hart Heinicke, a mature, soft-spoken, proven artist to whom could be entrusted the development of a strong program. With cooperation of Mel Henderson and the backing of the president, she set to work immediately to rejuvenate art instruction, and she did it with a kind of "evangelical spirit."[65] Facilities were very limited until Heckert Hall became available, together with space on the ground floor of Mary Berry, as a result of new construction on the campus. Heinicke was a graduate of Wittenberg University (1952), held an M.S. from the University of Wisconsin, and both an M.F.A. (1977) and an Ed.D (1976) from Northern Illinois University. She came to Simpson from a tenured teaching position and an additional role as administrative assistant to the president of Kankakee Community College in Illinois.

In 1982 Margaret "Peg" Watson retired, full of honor. She was by any count the faculty's veteran, whose tenure at Simpson went back to 1937. One didn't "replace" Peg Watson—no one could. But the appointment of Patricia B. Singer was as close as one could come. A graduate of St. Olaf College in 1976, she had only recently completed the Ph.D. in biology at Kansas State University. She was a geneticist with a strong background in biochemistry.[66]

In the spring of 1983 Simpson's capable librarian, Jim Christopher, who had been a staff member since 1967 and head librarian for nine years, resigned to take a position at the University of Texas at Arlington. Appointed to take his place was Cynthia L. Myers, who had joined the Simpson library staff in 1978. She was a Phi Beta Kappa graduate of the University of Iowa (1977) and had earned the M.A. in library science in 1978. She married Simpson graduate Grant Dyer '77 in 1984, the same year she received the new title of director of library services, reflecting the expanding role of the library in the educational mission of the College. She served also as the College's archivist with extraordinary competence and unfailing good humor, helping student researchers and even a crotchety College historian with their labors. She also displayed remarkable equanimity when promises to improve the library's anemic budget were repeatedly made and broken, each time with a genuine apology. McBride himself recognized the problem: "I would have liked to strengthen the library resources during our tenure," he later wrote.[67]

William C. Dunning in mathematics was one of two long-term appointments in 1984. A graduate of Union College in Schenectady, New York (1965), he completed both his M.A. in 1968 and the Ph.D. in mathematics in 1969 at Duke University. Until Dunning arrived, the Department of Mathematics was in the doldrums, its number of majors minuscule. Within a few years he had revitalized the math program, attracting strong new faculty and a host of majors.[68] Dunning's fame would spread beyond the confines of the Mathematics Department, for soon his rotund figure could be seen, papers in hand, moving stealthily around the campus, wearing a conspiratorial grin as he superintended the faculty-staff sports pool, supremely confident in the assurance that he understood the mathematics of probability better than did most of his colleagues.

In addition to Margaret Watson, three other faculty stalwarts completed their Simpson careers during these years. Don Koch, who had chaired the English Department with distinction for twenty-one years, and Minerva Fair, who had taught seventeen years in elementary education, both retired in 1981.[69] They remained in Indianola as emeritus professors, participating regularly in the life of the College. Don Koontz, whose activities at Simpson were legion, retired in 1980 after twenty-eight years.[70]

Twice during these years the campus was saddened by the death of retired longtime faculty members. Herbert "Doc" Alberding, surely one of the most colorful figures in Simpson's history, died February 5, 1982. He had retired in 1977 and was a resident of Indianola until his death.[71] Two years later Sven Lekberg, whose character and reputation had ensured the excellence of Simpson's music program during the twenty-nine years he led it (1940–69), died January 11, 1984, after a brief illness. A remarkable pianist, he was one of the most published choral composers in America. Beyond that, Sven Lekberg was a universal man. He conversed comfortably and intelligently on everything from French literature to modern architecture, collected a library so large that he had to have his house equipped with steel beams to carry the load, and always took time to be a friend, a loving husband and father. He had continued to teach from the time of his formal retirement until the time of his death. He was as much at home on the streets of New York or Paris as he was in Indianola. "He was the only person I knew," recalled Robert Larsen, "who could walk into a shop on Broadway and cash a check without identification."[72]

* * *

Although it may be an inexact science, the identification and selection of new faculty was and is one of the most important tasks of an administrator, and it was best done in an atmosphere of collegiality. At Simpson the principal responsibility for faculty recruitment lay with the academic dean, who typically relied on department heads and appointed search committees to assist in finding the best person for any position. Dealing with problem faculty—those whose behavior was unacceptable or whose teaching was inadequate—was more difficult. It was not only a matter of careful and impartial evaluation, but also a concern for proper procedures, for due process, for scrupulous fairness.

There were a few "problem" faculty, including one McBride judged to have "risen to his full potential as a role model for rebellious students during the student 'revolution.'"[73] A handful of others were reported to have problems with drugs, alcohol or sexual misconduct. In most cases these were handled quite satisfactorily with personal counseling and clarification of the College's legitimate behavioral expectations. One of the most difficult problems in any faculty in America was the removal of incompetent tenured faculty. However difficult it was to define precisely what one meant by incompetence, it was really not difficult to recognize it. Academic tenure was a hallowed institution, but McBride observed that "the main function of tenure had shifted from protection for academic freedom to that of job security."[74] The hazards encountered in proving incompetence had led one Simpson cynic to observe that "the only way a tenured professor around here can be fired is if he rapes the dean's daughter."

Maybe. Dr. McBride accepted the challenge, determined to replace a few faculty members he judged to be irredeemable, whatever the risks.[75] Conscious of the presence of the College's A.A.U.P. chapter and its vigilant leader, Norm Thomas, the president moved ahead, certain that he could effect his purpose and at the same time avoid confrontation with the defenders of faculty prerogatives.[76] Within three years he was able to eliminate three tenured positions "largely through judicious use of a one-year salary termination procedure," effectively "buying out" a contract. Fortunately, the A.A.U.P. agreed that the three were indeed incompetent and that the president and dean had followed agreed-upon guidelines and procedures, but "some were shocked to discover that a tenured position could be terminated."[77]

Less complicated were the decisions not to rehire nontenured faculty or not to grant tenure or promotion, even if the president's judgment ran counter to the recommendation of the faculty personnel committee. McBride could recall placing conditions on the contract with the exceptionally popular forensics coach which led to a resignation, a subsequent attempt on the part of the coach to withdraw the resignation and the president's refusal to accept the withdrawal. Student reaction was predictably intense.[78] Faculty reaction was not. A decision to put all athletics, men's and women's, under a single director, leading to the nonreappointment of Sharon Holmberg in the spring of 1982, provoked loud student protest. "Does President McBride want to get rid of quality instructors?" asked a *Simpsonian* writer. Another student complained that Simpson would be left with only one Ph.D. and six M.A.s to instruct some seventy-five physical education students. "That isn't exactly the kind of student-instructor ratio Simpson likes to brag about."[79] Actually a one-to-eleven ratio was excellent compared to one-to-thirteen for the rest of the College.

Whatever the faculty-student ratio, most of the people on the faculty were doing well in the classroom, their student and colleague evaluations consistently scoring high. Students, never at a loss when asked to comment on the performance of faculty in the classroom, had a unique way of describing both the merits and the eccentricities of their mentors. They said it well in the 1982 *Zenith*. "We remember," they wrote,

> Professor Bill Helfrich assigning yet one more reading about the wickedness of the White Eyes toward the Native Americans. . . . Nia Kos' easy European charm as she relaxed famously with her Spanish students. . . . Dr. Bruce Haddox's wit and humor which he used along with his soft, smooth Southern accent to intrigue his students with religious thought. . . . Dr. Jim Van Deventer's enjoyable, laughable, yet educational calculus lectures, but let's not forget those comprehensive finals. . . . Dr. Joe Walt and Dr. Owen Duncan and their informative lectures on Western Civilization which inevitably led to the necessity of pulling all-nighters to study for the final. . . . Glenn Buhr's unpredictability which kept his students awake and interested in his German classes (how do you laugh in German?). . . . Jane Kvetko's friendly personality which was shown by her final discussions in sociology over brunch or strawberry shortcake at her house. . . . Dr. Marv Van Wyk's ability to win the Computer Programming class' confidence only to lose that confidence at the end of the period by assigning another unimaginable program (due the next class meeting). . . . Dr. Margaret Watson's love of Biology and her desire to have students learn to love the subject. . . . Dr. Francis Colella's uncensored humor which kept his economics and management students wondering how this humor was to exemplify the topic of his lecture. . . . Dr. Carol Phillips' perfection and positive concerns about the education students.

Although Simpson emphasized and rewarded its faculty for good teaching, it was surprising how many of them were also engaged in important research and writing. In just a five-year period after 1980 at least a third of the faculty published books, articles, book reviews or delivered papers at learned societies. In 1982 Fred Jones was elected president of the Iowa Sociological Association, and a year later Joe Walt was named chairman of the board of trustees of the State Historical Society of Iowa, a post he held for seven years. Norm Thomas served as a member of the Iowa Humanities Board, while Jay VerLinden was elected president of the Mid-America Forensics League in 1983. Librarian Cynthia Dyer served a three-year term on the executive board of the Iowa Library Association, beginning in early 1984. Robert Gieber was president of the Iowa Chapter of the American Association of Teachers of French, and Carol Phillips was elected state vice-president of the Iowa Association of Education of Young Children for a two-year term in 1984.

Although salaries had remained low during the late seventies, faculty benefits were quite good. These included the TIAA retirement program, to which the College continued to contribute eight percent of the employee's salary, good health benefits, term life insurance at no cost, group automobile insurance, a sabbatical leave system, modest support for attendance at professional meetings and tuition remission at Simpson for qualified children and spouses of faculty.[80] In the early eighties these benefits continued, and other substantial forms of assistance were developed, together with attractive awards. In 1980, for example, Simpson joined the National Tuition Exchange Program on a trial basis for three years, enabling faculty and staff children to attend other member institutions tuition-free, offering Simpson tuition to children of their colleagues from other member colleges.[81] Dental benefits were added to the usual health and hospitalization plan for employees and at modest cost for their families.

A handsome gift of $60,000 from Lettie McNeill, an alumna of the College from the class of 1927, was used to underwrite the cost of several programs to assist faculty research and education or for awards. It was called the Lettie McNeill Faculty Development Fund, and within a few years the principal grew to more than $200,000. With a portion of the income the president and Dean Henderson initiated three annual awards of $1,000 each for faculty: one distinguished teaching award for senior-rank faculty, one distinguished teaching award for junior-rank faculty, and one for excellence in research and publication.

* * *

Most faculty were pleased that the new general studies program, adopted during President Lancaster's last year, was in place just as the new president arrived on the scene. A number of academic departments whose enrollments had been devastated by the open curriculum—history, English, foreign languages, physics and other natural sciences, and mathematics—experienced new growth, primarily in the service courses they offered for the general student body. Certainly this reemphasis on the liberal arts was a step in the right direction.

But it was only a step. With President McBride's urging, Dean Melvin Henderson and the Educational Policy and Curriculum Committee (E.P.C.C.), chaired by Joe Walt, undertook a careful study of the general requirements, examining Simpson's history and current needs and looking at the programs of other liberal arts colleges. Their year-long examination led to a proposal for a considerable expansion of required courses from twenty-two to thirty-eight semester hours in the six areas: the Western tradition and the scientific, social science, humanistic, aesthetic and minority perspectives.[82] To be instituted at the same time was a writing competency requirement to be taken by all freshmen and transfer students upon their arrival at Simpson. The faculty also was asked to approve a senior colloquium requirement, an interdisciplinary course—or array of courses—that would be "value oriented and [would] focus on important intellectual and moral issues confronting society."[83]

Students continued to be apprised of the planning process through their representatives in the E.P.C.C. and through frequent reports in the *Simpsonian*. At the formal spring convocation in February 1981, Dean Henderson and Joe Walt reported on the committee's progress.[84] Walt stated "the need to hear all points of view on the proposal," reporting that the committee had already met with the Student Senate, and would hold another public session to which everyone was invited. "Curriculum," he said, must be monitored "closely and constantly," for "the worst thing we could do is have a curriculum in 1981 designed for a very different world, like 1931 or even 1971." At the same time, no one was proposing "change for change's sake." Rather the curriculum must be designed anew "in the best interest of the students."[85]

The refined, completed proposal was submitted to the faculty on April 7 and voted on May 5. Only the Department of Music held out against the plan, extracting some concessions and exceptions for students enrolled in the Bachelor of Music program. The rest of the faculty accepted the new general studies curriculum overwhelmingly.[86] It would go into effect for all students entering in the fall of 1981. The senior colloquium, then, would first be taught in the fall of 1984.

What to call the new program? It certainly was not a reincarnation of the Vital Center, for it followed a different, distributive studies model. It was John Kellogg, the man who would be called upon to "market" the new program, who suggested "Cornerstone Studies in Liberal Arts." Except for a handful of grouches who opposed the whole concept of general studies, everyone liked the name. "Cornerstone Studies" it was. And is.

The faculty gave attention to more than general studies. In 1980 a computer science major was adopted and within a year attracted more than twenty majors.[87] Beyond this, there was discussion of instituting a "computer literacy" requirement.[88] Another major, agriculture resource management, looking to career education for agribusiness persons, was adopted in May 1981, but did not go into effect until the fall of 1982. Employed to teach in that field was Raymond H. Walke, who served two years (1982–84), succeeded by Robert J. Ford. This major attracted only a few students, and after a few years it was discontinued. Art under Jan Heinicke's leadership experienced a resurgence, forcing a scramble for space to accommodate classes and studios. Soon enough rooms were made available in the ground floor of Mary Berry Hall, necessitating a move of the local office of Planned Parenthood of Iowa, which had been lodged since June, 1969, on campus, to less attractive quarters upstairs. There were, to be sure, a number of faculty and staff, not to speak of townspeople, who bitterly opposed the Planned Parenthood organization anywhere and were outraged that it should be headquartered on Simpson's campus.[89]

The faculty also debated the merits of the January term.[90] Science faculty people were especially unhappy, arguing that they wanted to get their students into the field during this concentrated short term, but that in January the fields in Iowa looked too much like the Arctic. Why not a May term at the end of the academic year when the weather was pleasant? While some preferred the "change of pace" afforded by the January term in the middle of the academic year and feared a sort of letdown at the end of the year, the majority soon favored the May term idea. Proposed in 1981, it was adopted only in the fall of 1983 and went into effect in the 1984–85 academic year.[91] The change did affect athletics, music and a number of activities in the extracurriculum.

The College formalized its efforts to expand and promote overseas study by the adoption of the Wider Horizons Program in 1984.[92] Although for many years individual Simpson students had studied abroad, relatively little attention had been given to foreign study until the advent of the January term. For several years after 1970 the Central States College Association had sponsored annual charter flights to Europe in January, for a number of the CSCA institutions operated on the 4-1-4 calendar, and several Simpson overseas programs took advantage of the nominal cost. By the late seventies, however, CSCA disintegrated for a number of reasons, one of which was that most of the colleges overestimated the amount of joint educational enterprises they could initiate and nurture. But when CSCA discontinued operations, the one successful cooperative effort that remained was the charter flights to Europe. Simpson volunteered to take on the task of running the annual flights and did so for a number of years, not uncommonly making arrangements for as many as 450 faculty and students from a dozen colleges to London or Paris or Amsterdam. When the deregulation of airlines under President Jimmy Carter eliminated the price advantage of the charter flights, each of the cooperating colleges could advantageously make its own flight plans. Simpson continued to sponsor groups to Europe and Latin America on its own. The May term, if anything, increased the numbers traveling abroad, for certainly European destinations were more attractive at that time of year.

But the best overseas program by far was the one initiated by Glenn Buhr for students of German. Buhr, whose thorough knowledge of Germany was matched by his formidable organizational skills, put together a model semester-long program, to which was added the May term, in a town called Schorndorf, near Stuttgart in Baden-Württemberg. He took his first group of thirteen students in January 1985, lodged them privately with German families, rented facilities for instruction, hired additional instructional help, arranged daily lunch for all of them in a local inn, superintended weekend travel to nearby important sights and managed a more extensive journey to Berlin during May term. Through it all, the students had little opportunity to speak English and found themselves thoroughly immersed in German culture. Many of the participants remained in Germany the following summer, working in internships at nearby Daimler-Benz or as substitutes for vacationing Germans in shops and factories. Best of all, they came home reasonably fluent in the language and with some familiarity with the culture of the country. Their horizons had indeed been widened.[93]

On campus, several physical improvements were applauded. For example, the old six-lane 440-yard cinder track at Neff Field was replaced with a fine new eight-lane 400-meter track with an all-weather surface. The $127,000 cost, which included fencing and new bleachers to seat five hundred persons, was shared by Simpson ($40,000), the Indianola Community School District ($77,000) and the City of Indianola ($10,000), and all three entities would share in the future maintenance of the track.[94] Thus the track would be used by the high school and junior high school teams, the city's recreation programs and the College's track and field teams, and would be open in nonscheduled times to all residents of the community. In recognition of the joint venture, the stadium was renamed the "Simpson-Indianola Community Field."[95]

Off the field, in the library there were problems. Apart from perennially constricted budgets limiting both staff and book and periodical purchases, the library, according to its head Jim Christopher, suffered from "shrinkage." Stolen books and journals virtually cancelled any gains the library might make in its acquisitions. Christopher pointed to the experience of the 1979–80 academic year during which he added 1,600 books and subscribed to 440 journals. But during that same year 1,000 books and more than 400 individual issues of journals "disappeared." The library, he said in a statement of the obvious, needed a proper detection system. He argued that it would pay for itself in a year. His plea was heard, and by the fall of 1981 a proper security system was in place.[96]

Far more interesting to library patrons was the acquisition of the outstanding Avery Craven library. Some years earlier, despite the importuning of universities like Purdue and the University of Chicago, Dr. Craven decided to bequeath to Simpson his entire library, containing a magnificent collection of works, a few of them unique, on the antebellum South. Representing a lifetime of collecting, these holdings had been lodged in his home in the Indiana Dunes, the historian's fine country house literally built around the library. Craven died January 21, 1980, but it required some time before his widow, Georgia, could arrange to have the collection packed and shipped to Indianola. When the several-thousand item book and periodical collection, together with Dr. Craven's notes and scholarly files, arrived, they were housed in what had served as the Dunn Library's upstairs reception and rare book room. Dedicated as the Avery O. and Georgia Craven Room and Collection on September 29, 1983, in a simple ceremony featuring former Iowa State University professor and Craven student Dr. E. B. Smith, the library was available to scholars and to those students whose research on Craven or the antebellum South required access to it.[97]

* * *

Once the budget was in balance and salaries for faculty and staff were somewhat more respectable, the president and the board could look to a number of much-needed capital projects. The most urgent was the construction of a new music building before old Barrows Hall, still called the Con by the denizens of music who inhabited it, fell down. Already by mid-1980 the new building was in the planning stage and raising funds for it began in earnest. After many months of effort, including dedicated endeavor by Robert Larsen, the board and President and Lue McBride, more than $1,200,000 was raised toward an estimated $2,000,000 required to complete the project. Major gifts were contributed by John and Doris Salsbury of Clear Lake, the Fred Maytag Family Foundation, the Kinney-Lindstrom Foundation and, to the surprise of some and the delight of everyone, an impressive $600,000 by Amy Robertson, a 1921 Simpson graduate in music.

Amy Robertson was already something of a legend at Simpson and in her home territory down in Wayne County. And because of her long-time service on the board of trustees and her record-breaking generosity to the College in the latter years of her life, her story deserves to be told. She was born August 28, 1897, in Promise City, Iowa, a tiny hamlet in Wayne County on the old Mormon Trail, the only child of Greenleaf Lincoln and Iona Sharp Robertson. Amy always called her home town "more promise than city." In Corydon her father had owned a small general store whose principal claim to fame was that it had been robbed by Jesse James back in the late nineteenth century. She grew up in a serious, no-nonsense Methodist household, graduated from Promise City High School and, because she demonstrated real talent in music, entered Simpson College, where she earned the B.M. degree in 1921. She taught music briefly at Allerton in her home county and then for many years at Audubon High School, taking time off to complete work for a master's degree in music in 1930 at DePaul University in Chicago.

A woman of courage, fiercely independent, an earthy pioneer, strong-willed, given to forceful opinions and more entrepreneurial spirit than was characteristic of high school music teachers, she could not be confined to leading choruses or directing bands. In her spare time she whittled beautiful wooden dolls, practicing a skill she had learned from her father. A friend suggested that since she had more than a houseful of these toys, she ought to consider selling them. Thereupon Amy took the train to Chicago, showed her dolls to the huge Marshall Field and Sears Roebuck companies, and came home with a large order for as many as she could make. That same summer she rented an abandoned school building in Promise City, trained some local women in the art, opened a doll factory and did a thriving business for several years. Meanwhile she invested every spare dollar she could find in farmland in Wayne and Appanoose Counties until she finally owned seven farms containing 1,380 acres of land. She also invested in "worthless" land in Texas sold to her by some distant relatives in the Southwest. Although her father advised against it, "I was willing," she recalled, "to take much of this land off their hands." She made sure that she obtained all mineral rights on these properties. For many years the land did indeed seem to be worthless—until oil and gas were discovered, creating a bonanza for Robertson. Board member Luther Hill, who came to know her well during her later years, said "I have thought of her as being one of Iowa's first emancipated women. In the twenties she was far ahead of her time." Indeed, her role as farm manager and entrepreneur was uncommon in those days.

Amy Robertson never married. She explained that she just never thought marrying was worth the trouble. "Men—at least most of them—are not totally useless," she was wont to say, "but they are about as close to it as they can get." She could do without them.

She quit teaching during the middle of the Second World War, returning to Promise City to care for her elderly, ailing parents during their last days. A few years later—it was in 1951—she was invited to join the Simpson board of trustees, the seventh woman ever accorded that honor. She recalled that she was not favorably impressed when she walked into her first board meeting. "I never before saw such a bunch of broken-down preachers." There were far too many clergymen on the board, "most of whom couldn't organize a three-car funeral." She was not easily persuaded that Simpson had much of a future.

Nor did she contribute when the College periodically tried to raise money. In one of the fund drives, President Voigt decided to ask Robertson for one hundred dollars, but as a good churchman he was solicitous of the attitude of the local Methodist minister in Promise City, whose church was located next door to her and who might be trying to raise money himself. The minister replied and wished the College luck. "I haven't been able to get anything out of her all year," he wrote. She did not contribute to the fund drive.

Amy Robertson would give to Simpson in her own time and in her own way. When she began to feel some confidence that she would not die in penury after all, she began helping worthy Wayne County youngsters attend Simpson, and within a few years she was the College's best recruiter in southern Iowa. She could never remember exactly how many students she helped with their tuition and living costs, but the number was impressive.

She spent almost nothing on herself. She continued to live in the house in which she was born and lived an almost Spartan existence, with a single egregious exception. She drove a big Lincoln town car, a luxurious vehicle, and bought a new one every two or three years. And she drove her powerful automobile at breakneck speeds, earning a reputation as one of the daredevil drivers of southern Iowa. She knew all the highway patrolmen by their first names, attempting to bribe each of them with pieces of delicious hard rock candy which she carried along for the purpose. Parents took their children inside whenever Miss Amy backed out of her driveway. Finally, when she was in her late eighties, she was denied a driver's license and had to be driven by others, to the everlasting relief of several counties.

After considerable cultivation by President and Mrs. McBride and Luther and Sara Hill, "Miss Amy" was persuaded in 1980 to pledge $600,000 toward the construction of Simpson's new music building, an amount matched by John and Doris Salsbury. A few weeks later Amy called McBride and said to him, "Now, Robert I want to talk to you about that $600,000 gift."

Alarmed that she might be having second thoughts about her pledge, he asked with some trepidation if there were some problem.

"Yes, there is." His heart sank.

"I'm not going to be able to give you the whole sum at once. I'll have to do it over a three-year period." His heart leapt.

"Amy, you can do it any way you want to," he reassured her.

"Well, you don't think I'm going to take this gift out of my capital, do you?" she said, almost accusingly.

"Of course not," he replied, trying to restrain the urge to shout for joy.

Simpson was not Amy Robertson's only beneficiary. She was generous with the local hospital in Corydon, and her special project was the creation and nurture of the Wayne County Historical Museum in Corydon. With Amy's leadership it became arguably the best county historical museum in the state of Iowa. She saw to it that they collected everything and displayed everything. And because she knew that the great Mormon hymn "Come, Come Ye Saints" had been composed around a pioneer campfire on a cold night in 1846 in rural Wayne County, she managed to persuade Mormon authorities in Salt Lake City to finance the construction of a wing on her historical museum, complete with pioneer images, a Conestoga wagon and a fine recording of the Mormon Tabernacle Choir singing the famed hymn.[98]

In Indianola, fund-raising continued until enough cash and pledges were in hand to go ahead with construction of the music building. A generous gift of $100,000 from the Kresge Foundation ensured finally that the building costs and furnishings would be funded.[99] Ground was broken October 23, 1981, at the time of the fall board meeting, and construction began soon thereafter.[100] Designed by architects Brooks, Borg and Skiles of Des Moines, the building was located just north of Smith Chapel along North Buxton Street. It contained 19,000 square feet, including a 250-seat auditorium designated the Lekberg Recital Hall, an instrumental music center, teaching studios, practice rooms, and a long, bright gallery along the west side of the building with display area for paintings and sculpture. A connection to Smith Chapel by a lower level underground passageway permitted the addition of the basement classrooms and offices in the chapel to the music complex.[101] General contractor for the construction was Betts and Beer of Adel, Iowa. In honor of her gift, the building would be called the Amy Robertson Music Center.[102]

Completed in the spring of 1983, the building was dedicated at 2:30 in the afternoon on Saturday, May 21, under a lowering sky. The outdoor ceremony on the plaza of the new structure climaxed several days of guest and student recitals, together with the premier of a new choral work by Lee Hoiby, and it preceded a grand performance on Saturday evening of Mendelssohn's powerful oratorio *Elijah*.[103] Participating in the afternoon dedication were board chairman Fred Weitz, President McBride, Amy Robertson and Doris Salsbury, together with chaplains Art and Nancy Allen and Frank Nichols, administrative assistant to the Methodist bishop of Iowa. Renowned soprano Kay Griffel of the Cologne opera spoke and also sang an American hymn and a piece by Robert Schumann, and the Simpson choir and symphonic wind ensemble provided appropriate music. Several speakers emphasized the importance of the building and praised its builders. It was Amy Robertson, however, who said it best; for her, as it was for others, the new building was "a dream come true."[104] While Miss Amy and others were speaking, everyone kept a close watch on the threatening weather which, almost as if it was timed to provide a dramatic finale, held off until the last minute, whereupon a great thunderclap, followed by a downpour brought the proceedings to a hasty conclusion.

Not long after the Music Department completed its move into the new building, both Barrows Hall and the Music Annex in the northeast corner of the campus were demolished, making space for a parking lot for Barker Hall.[105] And a year later, on September 29, 1984, a fine metal sculpture, entitled "Orpheus," by Barbara Lekberg of New York City, rising on its pedestal to a height of thirteen feet, was installed outdoors in the "light court" between the Robertson building and the chapel. The sculptor, daughter of Sven and Mildred Lekberg, was present for the dedication.[106]

* * *

Simpson's Music Department continued its record of excellence under the direction of Robert Larsen. President McBride called music Simpson's "spire of excellence" and its chairman "probably the most valuable and indispensable member of our entire staff in terms of public relations, including the president himself."[107] No one at Simpson worked harder than Larsen; no one produced work of higher quality; no one was more gifted professionally. The sheer quantity of the work he accomplished, the powerful impact of his personality on the College, the impressive performances he coaxed out of talented students, led both insiders and outsiders to regard Larsen as an irreplaceable treasure.

A worthy successor to Sven Lekberg, Larsen had guided Simpson's music program toward a level of quality that won for it a regional, even national reputation. Perhaps more importantly, he had founded, with the help of friend and former student Douglas Duncan, and with little fanfare, the Des Moines Metro Opera in 1973. From the day of its birth, the Metro Opera was developed at Simpson and, as soon as the Blank Performing Arts Center was erected, was performed at Simpson. The early seasons were put together with borrowed sets, piano accompaniment and a tiny budget. But the singing was superb, sponsors were found, and the budget fairly exploded. "We are in the [opera] business to create something magical," said Larsen, "to create something as close to a realization of what the composer intended the opera to be as possible."

Within a few years the Metro Opera was truly up and running. In 1979, M. A. Feldman, a tough reviewer for *Opera News*, commented that "to witness seven years of opera in repertory on the fringe of the Iowa cornfields is to observe the rich growth of an unlikely enterprise." However unlikely it was, Larsen himself found it a "miracle." Each summer the company did three operas, usually two standard classical productions and one modern one, in repertory, in a season of a few weeks. And each season seemed to be better than the last—its singers more polished, its sets more professional, its orchestra fuller. By 1981 Ms. Feldman was truly impressed: "No longer a fledgling," she wrote, "Des Moines Metro has taken wing and soared into the stratosphere of regional American opera companies.[108] And Robert Larsen was "the idol of the Des Moines cultural world."[109]

Each summer the Metro Opera brought lead singers, some of them from New York City or other cultural centers, to Indianola, together with fifty or seventy-five or more choral singers and support staff people, all of them housed on the

Simpson campus. Their performances, sold out well in advance, brought to the Pote Theatre people from Des Moines, the state, the Midwest and sometimes from the coasts. Among the local Indianolans in these audiences were Robert and Lue McBride. The president remembered later that "although Lue and I had had little exposure to opera before coming to Iowa, we grew first to tolerate it, then to appreciate it, and slowly developed a minor passion for it."[110]

But it was not only opera that enriched the musical life of Simpson. The Madrigal Singers, senior recitals, jazz concerts, musicals like *Camelot* or *Pippin* or *Kismet*, holiday performances of *The Messiah* or the madrigal dinner, band concerts and faculty recitals contributed to the richness of the College's cultural offerings.

For all this there was, however, a price. Because the Music Department demanded of its students that they be not only acquainted with music but performers of it, the cost of instruction was exceptionally high. Fiercely labor intensive, music was the most expensive thing the College did, even more expensive per participant than athletics, whose time-honored reputation for devouring dollars was a thing of legend.

There was also a tendency for Music to see itself a thing apart. McBride observed that although the old conservatory of music had long since been integrated into the College as a department, "it seemed to many faculty and administrators that it was still a separate academic kingdom."[111] The reason for this exclusiveness was twofold: the program and the king. The academic program for the Bachelor of Music degree, requiring some eighty-one hours for the performance major or eighty-six for music education, was thoroughly professional, not unlike that of conservatories elsewhere. Dr. Larsen recognized a trend in many music programs to emphasize music education at the expense of performance, and insisted that all students perform, and regularly too. At the same time, the monarch of the kingdom, possessing a power base that was the envy of other departmental chairpersons, was able to function independently in ways not open to them. He selected his own faculty, managed a substantial budget that dwarfed that of other departments, recruited students in ways not open to any other program except, of course, athletics. On one occasion, when a faculty position in music was cut by the president because of financial exigency, Larsen simply went outside the College, solicited contributions to the amount of a salary and hired on his own. Soon the position was restored by a new president, and the new person stayed on. Such a procedure would never have been possible in any other department.

As for the College's presidents, Larsen remembered Kerstetter to be "wonderfully supportive" of music, Ralph John "noninterfering" but not very musically inclined, Richard Lancaster to be "very supportive and helpful in bringing prestige to Simpson's program," and Robert McBride to be his "greatest challenge."[112] McBride found the musician to be "talented, creative, energetic, enigmatic, frustrating, likable, paradoxical,"[113] in short, "difficult." He recalled that "while most faculty are near-sighted when viewing college operations, Bob's preoccupation with the needs of his department in the face of other needs was unusual. If any budget was overdrawn, his would be the first and the most," and his relations with most other faculty people were not cordial. He could be depended on in faculty meetings either to oppose outright or demand exceptions to any curricular changes that increased the required liberal arts segment of the undergraduate program. McBride also had to cope with reports that Larsen's driving of students, in his demands for excellence, amounted to intimidation. There were, he said, "gross inadequacies in the area of personal sensitivities."[114] Yet, with all these problems, he regarded the monarch of music as brilliant and so much a part of Simpson that one could not imagine the place without him. Larsen remained "one of the most capable persons, in terms of ability and productivity, I have ever known."[115]

For some years the turnover of faculty in music was exceptionally rapid. Larsen pointed out, however, that the competition nationwide for talented music faculty was keen and that some of the people he appointed did not meet his standards. It is true that by the mid-eighties the faculty was much more stable than it had been.

As Simpson's reputation in music grew, in large part because of the remarkable success of the opera program, it was perhaps inevitable that the number of voice students increased faster than those in other areas of music. By the mid-eighties, out of approximately sixty music majors, thirty-five or so were in voice, ten or fifteen in keyboard and ten or so in instrumental music. The one real weakness was in the area of stringed instruments. In any case, recruitment of new students, made more difficult by intensive recruiting in the Midwest by Eastern conservatories, was improved by the excellent work of Maria di Palma and the College's regular admissions staff. Music weekends, recitals, performances, together with a week-long "Orpheus Festival" for sixty or so high school prospective students, the latter event held after the Des Moines Metro Opera season in July, were all effective recruiting tools.

* * *

Music was, to be sure, in many ways the ancient crown of the liberal arts at Simpson, while computer science signaled the new, uncrowned royalty of the modern technological age. The new computer science major, requiring installation of new and expensive equipment, together with the rapid upswing of instruction in economics, management and accounting and the sophisticated installations needed for those burgeoning programs, put great pressure on Simpson's limited facilities. McBride had been at Simpson less than a year when he recognized that something needed to be done to provide first-class physical resources for this growing part of the curriculum. Somehow he must find the means to put up a proper building for it.

He was in luck. Bob Pinnell, whose yeoman service out among the College's alumni deserves greater recognition than it has ever been accorded, introduced McBride to a remarkable eighty-one year old alumna, Lettie Judkins McNeill, a New Virginia, Iowa, native who graduated in the class of 1927, one of the few women among Professor J. B. Heckert's famed group of business students.[116] She had taught high school business for twenty-seven years, then at the age of fifty-five married Henry Hammond McNeill, a prominent real estate magnate in Chicago. In 1982 she was residing in retirement in Fort Lauderdale, Florida, having been widowed for only a year. Like so many alumni from her era, she was fervently loyal to Simpson and proud of her unusual status in the "Heckert group." Because she was a woman of considerable means, Pinnell and McBride "conspired" to seek a substantial gift from her for a new business and computer science building. When she visited Indianola and the Simpson campus in 1982, the two prepared a "typed proposal of some five or six pages," asking for a gift of $100,000. True, Amy Robertson had given $600,000, but they didn't want to frighten Mrs. McNeill away. With some apprehension the president, who had never asked anyone for more than a thousand dollars before he came to Simpson, met with McNeill for twenty minutes or so, talking about this and that, trying to work up enough courage to mention the gift proposal. As McBride remembered the conversation, he never got to present their written proposition, still hidden in the inner pocket of his jacket.

> Suddenly, as Lettie was talking, she stopped, looked at Bob and me and with a smile on her face said, "Now, Mr. President, I think I know what you gentlemen have on your mind. I will tell you what I have already decided." In the next few minutes she told us of the love which both she and her husband had for Simpson, and her distaste for the government taking so much of her income for taxes. . . . She had decided to turn over some stock to the College. . . . She did not indicate what she considered its total value would be.

Her broker, she said, would call the next week and complete the transfer of the stock.

The following Tuesday McNeill's broker called to report that he was transferring stock that day to Simpson and that Simpson should immediately sell it in what appeared to be a favorable market. Then came the surprise: "At current prices, he estimated the value of the gift to be [almost] $1,150,000! After closing our conversation, I walked on a cloud back to my office, almost hugged my demure and proper secretary and called my friend Bob. I had learned one of the most important lessons in fund raising: never underestimate the potential generosity of a donor and to keep my mouth shut until I knew which way the wind was blowing."[117]

Suddenly enriched, the administration moved ahead rapidly with plans for the new building. Directed to locate the facility "in or near Hillman Hall," four architectural firms prepared conceptual drawings.[118] In order to provide an elevator, and hence handicap access to Hillman Hall, the architects were instructed to attach the new structure to the old building. Three of the firms did so—Brooks, Borg and Skiles, Bussard/Dikis Ltd. and Savage and Ver Ploeg, but Charles Herbert and Associates designed a freestanding building, refusing, as Chick Herbert put it, "to desecrate the integrity of a building that was a gem of collegiate Gothic architecture."[119]

Because the board, and especially buildings and grounds committee chairman Jim Hubbell, were committed to the economy and convenience of making the new facility a wing on Hillman Hall, the Herbert plan was discarded. Savage and Ver Ploeg got the contract, their spokesman insisting that the attachment "would enhance the appearance of both buildings." The cost of the project was estimated at $2,400,000.[120] Savage and Ver Ploeg were instructed to go ahead with detailed plans,[121] which were published in the *Simpson Alumnus* in its spring 1984 issue. According to one writer at the time, "there can be no doubt that the future of business education will rest on greater integration of the computer into the business curriculum," concluding that "the facility will truly be a computer center of the 21st century."[122]

Influenced by the rapid growth of the College's continuing education program, the "business and computer science building," wrote Georgia Voysey, editor of the Indianola *Record-Herald*, "represents a departure from a strict emphasis on liberal arts at Simpson and an effort to meet the changing needs of changing students." McBride himself stated that "if we are going to gain strength, we need to operate in today's environment and for the future."[123] These were interesting, even plausible comments, but a constant at Simpson had always been "operating in today's environment," and the environment of the College throughout had reflected the hard-headed, career-oriented, no-nonsense practicality of the Midwest. Simpson was hardly departing from the liberal arts. Had not the College only recently shored up the liberal arts component of all its students' academic programs? Simpson, in fact, continued to be what it had always been: a College that was not only *in* Iowa but *of* it, one which combined in a happy ecumenicity the powerful tradition of the liberal arts and sciences with vocational preparation.

Once plans for the building were refined, the College advertised for bids in May 1984. Soon thereafter ground was broken, and on June 22 construction began. The successful bidder, Downing Construction of Indianola, started excavation.[124] Construction manager was Vulcan Construction Company, a division of the Weitz Corporation in Des Moines. Built on two levels on an east-west axis running from the northwest of Hillman Hall, the building contained nineteen thousand square feet, housing the central Prime computer system used by Simpson employees, together with classrooms, offices, two spacious computer laboratories and a splendid conference room. Some of the classrooms were tiered, and all of them were equipped with the most modern audiovisual equipment. While the new building was under construction, the old tennis courts along Clinton Avenue were removed and a large paved and landscaped parking lot was laid out, covering the entire southwest corner of the main campus.

There was little doubt about what to call the building. For one thing, in addition to the $910,000 portion of her gift that set in motion the fund-raising for the project, Lettie McNeill gave the College some Chicago properties that sold for $850,000. At her suggestion the building was called the "Henry H. and Thomas H. McNeill Business and Computer Science Center," honoring her husband and his identical twin brother who had passed away in 1979.[125] A luncheon on Thursday, October 24, 1985, opened the dedicatory exercises at Great Hall, at which event James C. Hickman '50, dean of the School of Business at the University of Wisconsin, was the principal speaker. The formal dedication took place at 3:15 the next afternoon. It was a sunny Homecoming weekend. Lettie McNeill participated, along with President McBride, Frank Colella, Dean Mel Henderson and Mayor Irene Richardson of Indianola in a colorful ceremony held on the south outdoor plaza adjoining both the new building and Hillman Hall.[126]

Mary Berry Hall, the aging matriarch of the campus, was still providing offices for a large number of faculty members, having been adapted to that purpose soon after the enlargement of Kresge Hall in 1963. It also contained a few classrooms and the faculty services center, superintended by efficient Helen Strovers, whose diplomatic skills, practical know-how and everlasting patience could never be adequately appreciated. The old, comfortable reception room, breathing the faded elegance of yesteryear, provided a place of refuge for faculty who craved a cup of coffee or a tidbit of gossip. In the fall of 1983 the board of trustees began to examine the possibility of a complete renovation, authorized selection of an architect and set about to raise funds for the project.[127]

Preliminary architectural plans were produced, calling for a modified atrium inside the main entrance, access for handicapped people, including an elevator, creation of a tiered classroom in the west wing, refurbished offices, two seminar rooms, two art galleries, art studios, a foreign language laboratory and refurbished offices, arranged in four suites. The entire building would be air-conditioned.[128] However, the project was delayed during the next two years until full funding could be assured. More importantly, the realization of the renovation of Mary Berry Hall was soon tied to the fate of Old Chapel, or, as many were calling it once again, College Hall. And thereby hangs a tale.

No single issue in two decades so divided the College as did the question of whether or not to renovate College Hall. For lack of proper maintenance the neglected building had deteriorated until it stood in a state of advanced decay. Closed completely in 1980 because classes could no longer be held there comfortably, even safely, its lovely paned windows were boarded up to discourage vandals, its great white front doors barricaded with heavy wooden beams, its once-thronged halls silent and cold. Even its forlorn ghost was left to haunt the empty spaces alone. Its sagging, rusting fire escape had long since been given over to a family of great horned owls that returned each year to perch there, looking accusingly at people who hurried by. Abandoned, the old patriarch of the campus received callers only once a year when young Halloween ghost hunters crept through its dank, creaky halls.

A small part of the faculty, many alumni and, interestingly, nearly all students, whether for sentimental, historical or preservationist reasons, favored the restoration of the building to its former grandeur. It was, they argued, not merely Simpson's oldest collegiate building; it was a visible anchor that tied the College to its past, a constant reminder of their link to the institution's beginnings.

Modernists, shunning sentimentalism and urging common-sense practicality, insisted that the building in its present state was an eyesore, an ugly blot on an otherwise attractive campus.[129] They could find no real use for the building. It was too small to accommodate the whole administration, no longer needed as a theater since the construction of the Blank Performing Arts Center and not required for classroom needs or even for storage.[130] A number of serious studies of the matter had examined the possibility of converting it to a student center or a music building or, before the completion of the McNeill Center, a business administration building. Good judgment suggested that the old building be demolished. The cost of renovation would be between half a million and a million dollars, money that could be used for far more urgent needs, like faculty and staff salaries. "Suffering from lean salary increases in high inflation years," recalled McBride, "the faculty were almost unanimously opposed to diverting funds for such a purpose."[131] Moreover, argued some of the critics, it was unlikely that any alumni would want to contribute to such a restoration project, and it might well threaten fund-raising to remodel Mary Berry Hall. Some people believed also that "the architectural decision to place Dunn Library in its position had been made on the assumption that Old Chapel was to be removed."[132]

The sides were clearly drawn, and the issue simmered during the early years of McBride's presidency. Between 1980 and 1982 students circulated no fewer than five petitions to save the building. They called it "a landmark and a reminder of humble beginnings." Destroying it, they said, would be a "demolition of history." Only one student ever expressed in writing opposition to the overwhelming sentiment of his comrades. Signing himself simply as "Doug," he wrote that the place was a "death trap." What students saw now "is not the original building. Most of it burned down many years ago. The College never saw fit to replace the whole thing."[133] But "Doug's" view was discredited when the supporters pointed out that the building had never burned, although they conceded that its appearance had been altered in the 1921 renovation.

The local Indianola press reported the controversy, weighing in mostly on the side of the preservationists.[134] Alumna Mary Matz '72, writing in the *Record-Herald*, observed that "there is a close relationship between the respect we have for old, obsolete buildings and old, obsolete people." And besides, what would happen to the ghost or to the great horned owls whose habitat was provided by the ancient building and the great spreading maple tree that shaded it?[135] Another alumna, Patrice Beam '78, president of the Iowa Chapter of the Victorian Society in America and professional historical preservationist, spoke of her "shock and dismay" when she learned that Old Chapel might be razed and implored Simpson's leaders "to postpone . . . any demolition plans and to reconsider re-adaptive uses of the building."[136] Mary Shandley, an alumna in the class of 1940 and the College's counselor in basic skills and career development, agreed, noting that Old Chapel was "a symbol of our past and an opportunity for the present student today to feel roots and tradition." More importantly, "other countries maintain and care about their old buildings. They mend, they patch; old objects retain their usefulness. Americans destroy outmoded, dated objects and replace them with the new, the shiny, the efficient. We destroy our heritage as we go," yet "we spend money and time to go see the old, the traditional, the 'ivy-covered' in another country."[137]

One week after Mary Shandley's plea, on October 15, 1982, the students took their case directly to the board of trustees. At its meeting-day luncheon in Great Hall, it was the custom of the board to invite student representatives to report on student life and concerns. Thus the students had an appropriate forum to present their views. Several of them stood before the board members, faculty and administrative officials, and addressed them on any number of issues. But they held back their best speaker until last. Student body president Jane Paulsen announced, "Now I would like to call upon Dan Doyle to say a few words to you about a very important matter which we take most seriously." Doyle, a senior, came to the rostrum. Dressed conservatively in gray slacks and blue blazer, his tie neatly tied and his demeanor equally appropriate, he stood calmly, resolutely, and with a remarkable demonstration of restraint, said simply, "I want to talk to you about an old friend." His old friend had served thousands of students well, but had been somehow forgotten, sickened for lack of care, suffered the indignity of neglect and was even now at risk of being put to death.

When young Doyle was done, there was hardly a dry eye in the hall. His plea for saving Old Chapel was delivered in love, not anger. Nothing more was to be said, and the meeting ended. The response was instantaneous. One board member rushed up to Doyle and said, "You know, I met my wife in that old building. We must save Old Chapel!" And the campaign to save the building began that day in earnest.[138]

The *Simpsonian* called Doyle's presentation "stirring."[139] But for all its eloquence, the student plea met powerful, unyielding and thoroughly rational resistance. Dean Henderson warned that if College Hall were saved, at least one other building would have to be destroyed.[140] A faculty committee selected to study the matter began to see formidable obstacles to saving the building. But the board, led by Luther Hill and Michael Gartner, voted to select an architect "to undertake a schematic design for possible renovation of Old Chapel," the project's cost not to exceed $600,000.[141]

The whole matter was in a state of precarious balance during the spring of 1983. Then, at the May 20 board meeting, the architect, Savage and Ver Ploeg, presented two options for overall campus planning. "Plan A" called for the renovation of College Hall; "Plan B" would "remove" the building. The faculty committee, chaired by Professor Alan Magruder in education, after three years of study "unanimously endorsed Plan B." Immediately thereafter Robert Downing stated that his board committee endorsed Plan B "by majority vote."[142] After a fierce discussion in which trustees Hill and Gartner tried "dramatic pleading" and nearly every possible parliamentary delaying tactic, the board voted twenty-three to seven, with three abstaining, to raze College Hall in the summer of 1983.[143] A bid on the dismantling was submitted, and "the act of final execution had been set," recalled McBride. "With visions of student protests and human chains from the seventies still lingering in my own memories, I had determined that if Old Chapel was to be demolished, it would be done at least when most students were off campus—in the summer."[144]

So volatile was the issue, however, and so determined the opponents of demolition that President McBride delayed taking action during the summer. Luther Hill and Michael Gartner were not going to give up, and organized a "Committee to Save Old Chapel." They asked McBride to delay the implementation of the board's decision until they could find sufficient funds for the project. The building, they insisted, could be used as an admissions center. The president and Fred Weitz had to make an agonizing decision, but did agree, with some misgiving, to delay the demolition, and Fred Weitz informed the board by letter of their decision. Architect "Chick" Herbert looked at the building, concluding that it was "highly impractical to restore [it] to its original brick structure, but suggested a possible blending of its original and remodeled form might be possible." He found the basic structure to be sound. The board now gave the building a reprieve, voting to delay demolition "until further studies are completed."[145]

The "further studies," confirmed that the building could not be restored to its original state, determined that the high cost of renovation made the project a low priority and declared that "we can't find any use for the building if it were to be renovated." But the board, still uncertain, voted in May 1984 to postpone the removal of Old Chapel until the spring of 1986. Board chairman Fred Weitz pointed out what everyone knew: "This is a very emotional issue but one which must be resolved."[146] McBride recalled that "while I and other administrators had stood firmly on both sides of the issue at various times, we had come to a reluctant position favoring its demolition if no defensible use for the structure or funds could be found."[147] Three days later, on May 20, commencement speaker Michael Gartner could not resist bringing the matter up before such a large audience: "I promised some folks that I'd say only a couple of words about Old Chapel. So here are those words: Save it!"[148]

Because they hoped to bring this divisive issue to a conclusion, the board voted in its fall meeting in 1984 to allow College Hall supporters until January 25, 1985, to raise the $600,000 to renovate the building. If funds were not pledged or in hand, demolition would be ordered.[149] Against this ultimatum, Hill, Gartner and a few others went to work. By the deadline they had commitments for $350,000 and expected most of the balance from the Cowles Foundation.[150] And Amy Robertson had decided to come forth with $300,000 when it became clear that the cost of renovation would reach $900,000. On the basis of these prospects the project was permitted to go forward. Tom Baldwin, representing the Des Moines firm Schiffler, Frey and Baldwin, prepared detailed architectural drawings and a committee chaired by Lu Jean Cole planned the interior decoration—it would be lavishly Victorian—of the building's second floor.

At about this time John Kellogg and Bill Geiger agreed that the ground floor of College Hall would be the ideal location for admissions and student financial assistance. The second floor, once restored to its original state as one large hall, could be fitted out as the College's reception room, which they would call the "Matthew Simpson Room." The upper floor could contain meeting rooms and house alumni paraphernalia and publications.

After fund-raising was completed satisfactorily, bids for construction were received June 6, 1985, and the contract awarded to Downing Construction of Indianola.[151] Construction proceeded into the College's quasquicentennial year.

The rededication of College Hall took place at 4:30 P.M. on Saturday, October 25, 1986, right after the conclusion of the Homecoming football game.[152] Included in the brief ceremony was the unveiling of a fine granite wall stretching from floor to ceiling along a part of the north side of the Matthew Simpson Room. Etched into its rich surface were "Names that Live at Simpson," honoring outstanding faculty, alumni and benefactors. In front of the building the old campus gates had also been restored.

Speaking for the alumni at the ceremony, but in a way speaking for everyone, Ruth Prather '34, who had worked with the redecoration, called College Hall "the center of Simpson's tradition," proving the College's respect for its past and pride in its growth and progress. Pleased that the admissions office was located in the building, she said "this will be, for many college students, where their college experience will begin—at the center of Simpson's history."[153] When it was all over, Dr. McBride paid tribute to "that small band of people who persevered." The building was "a monument to the efforts of a few who would not let her die." He thanked those who "kept the faith with 'An Old Friend,' as student Dan Doyle had described her."[154]

* * *

Once College Hall was completed, the delayed renovation of Mary Berry Hall could be undertaken. To raise the funds for the venture, the College created the Historical Anchorage Project, capitalizing on the interest shown in both College Hall and Mary Berry. Cochairpersons for the fund-raising were Leland McGraw '46 and Alice Sayre '42. Honorary cochairs were Al and Erma Shaw Jordan, '26 and '28. Principal donors were the Kresge Foundation—once again—with a gift of $250,000, the Bohen Foundation of Des Moines with $100,000, the Meredith Corporation of Des Moines with $100,000, and $150,000 from an anonymous donor. Hundreds of other gifts helped meet the total construction cost of $776,914. The architects, Schiffler, Frey and Baldwin produced detailed plans, including air conditioning, and the contract for construction was awarded to Downing Construction of Indianola.[155] After faculty and secretarial services moved to Sigler Hall, where they were installed in temporary cubicles, construction started in ninety-six-year-old Mary Berry on July 7, 1986, the same summer workmen were completing the work on College Hall. For the faculty, their year in Sigler was, as one of them put it, "like camping out." Most of them admitted that it was not really bad at all. Completed in the spring of 1987, the "new" Mary Berry was comfortable, commodious and accessible to all. A few faculty members, to be sure, missed the casual, ramshackle atmosphere of the old lounge. The new one, properly color coordinated with predominantly mauve and blue accents, fine furnishings provided by conscientious Marilyn Leek, and a coffee table one dared not put one's feet on, was almost too much. It required months for most of them to adjust to the formality. Some never did. The building was rededicated during alumni weekend in May 1987 in a ceremony held outdoors on the handsome new brick plaza between Mary Berry and Dunn Library.[156]

The new buildings for music and business and computer science, and the restoration of College Hall and Mary Berry composed the four major "brick and mortar" accomplishments of the McBride administration. To these, however, could be added a number of other important campus improvements. Perhaps most noticeable was attractive landscaping of the campus, including new walkways, flower beds and tree planting, made all the more pleasant by meticulous gardening. New lighting, both decorative and serviceable, made for better appearance and safety on the campus at night. Buildings were identified with proper signage. "Lake Doyle," the reflecting pool by Dunn Library, too often filled with leaves, was removed on Campus Day in 1984 as faculty and students vied for honors breaking up great chunks of concrete. Six new tennis courts, replacing the ones removed to make room for parking next to Hillman Hall, were constructed just north of the fraternity house parking area off E Street. Named for the late Richard Buxton, the new courts were dedicated May 27, 1985.[157] They were built by contractor Robert Downing, who also constructed new parking facilities on the campus.[158] In November 1982, the Afro-American Cultural Center was moved from its house on North C Street to a new location at 609 North D Street.[159] Renamed the "Carver Cultural Center," it was dedicated on November 4, the event attended by nearly two hundred students, faculty and townspeople.[160] Two other moves were made: the Hawley Learning Resources Center was transferred from Sigler Hall to the upstairs mezzanine floor in Dunn Library, while most of the work of the Department of Art was moved into Heckert Hall as soon as the McNeill Building was able to accommodate management and economics classes.[161] At the Blank Performing Arts Center the orchestra pit was expanded, at a cost of $100,000, to accommodate sixty players.[162] In this and other projects in the theater, the College cooperated in financing and management with the Des Moines Metro Opera.[163] An expensive but needed project was an entirely new telephone system for the campus. Eliminating the central switchboard installed back in 1970, it permitted direct dialing to and from all offices and individual residence hall rooms. Installed by the Continental Telephone Company, with offices and maintenance facilities in Knoxville, Iowa, the new installation cost $350,000, the total amount financed by private college revenue bonds.[164]

* * *

These many campus improvements were expensive, their realization requiring aggressive fund-raising. Each new building or renovation necessitated a special fund drive, and in each case the new construction was accomplished without incurring new debt. Equally important—and much more difficult—was soliciting bequests and gifts to the College's endowment fund, the income from which helped to subsidize current operations. Some bequests came unannounced, like the valuable farmland willed in the Della M. Doidge Trust, valued at $478,000, split evenly between Simpson and Cottey College.[165] Some gifts established named scholarship funds honoring alumni like Noel "Red" Seney '50, Frances Ledlie Dawson '25, Dr. Floyd S. Doft '21, Lewis S. Kimer '39, Elsie Bingaman Phillips '25, Wilene Holden Woods '59, and Jacie Arnold Pillsbury '73, or retired professors like Hiram Doty or Nina Brown, to name only a few.

A handsome gift from Anna D. Hunt '14 of Pasadena, California established the second fully-funded endowed chair in the Simpson faculty. Although they had resided in California for many years, Anna and her sister Marion had remained close to Simpson, their Tridelta sorority sisters, and relatives in Indianola, including late *Record-Herald* editor and cousin, Don Berry. Neither of the sisters ever married. Anna was the businesswoman of the two, self-possessed, shrewd, careful yet generous, loyal to people and places, given to amused tolerance of everything that went on around her. She had served for years as the private secretary to novelist Lloyd Douglass, who valued both her editorial skills and sound advice. When she provided, through an estate note, the funds for the endowed chair in history, she suggested naming it for her cousin Don Berry, but accepted, with real modesty, the urging from the College that she allow it to be named for herself. Named the first holder of the professorship was Joseph W. Walt.[166]

Occasionally a major gift came out of the blue. One day in 1981 a telephone call to the College was routed to Professor Emeritus Don Koch, who was at that time assisting in the development office. "Does your College accept gifts?" asked an elderly caller. Such a question was something like asking a relapsed alcoholic if he drank. With admirable control Koch acknowledged Simpson's willingness to accept gifts. Pleased with that response, the caller identified himself as John W. Harvey, age eighty-two, of Lowry City, Missouri. The result of this spontaneous conversation was an annuity arrangement with Harvey and the gift of several farms.[167]

That same year the Cowles Foundation made a $1,000,000 challenge grant to Simpson's endowment, conditioned on the College's matching that amount two for one. It was the largest single gift commitment ever made to Simpson by a private foundation, and it was matched by mid-1982.[168] Giving to the College reached an all-time high in the 1981–82 academic year.[169] Not only were the dollar figures high; the number of donors was increased sharply, especially after the inauguration in 1981 of a several-week Student National Alumni Phonathon (S.N.A.P.). Staffed mostly by fraternity and sorority undergraduates whose members competed for everything from free pizza to trophies for their houses, the S.N.A.P. in just two years increased the number of alumni participants in the College's annual fund from 1,555 to 3,409. It was hard to turn the students down, and S.N.A.P. became a permanent institution.[170]

In 1984 McBride and the board decided to mount a major campaign for funds. Called the "Fund for Excellence," it would seek to raise $20,000,000 in a five year period. Some of the funds already collected for new buildings were counted in this drive, but with surprising ease the goal was reached in just three years.

The Historical Anchorage Project, especially designed to pull together funds to renovate Mary Berry Hall, was likewise included in the Fund for Excellence. It was Simpson's most ambitious fund drive up to that time, and its success can be attributed primarily to the renewed confidence in the College on the part of alumni, the public, foundations and other philanthropic organizations.

* * *

If Simpson's fund-raising effort was successful, its minority recruitment was not. And when one mentioned "minority" in those days, one meant black. There was, for better or worse, no pressure whatever to recruit Asians, Hispanics, Jewish or international students. A few of these groups joined the faculty or student body, and they were welcome but not sought out. All of Simpson's flagging minority recruitment program was aimed at black faculty and students, for it was among African-Americans that the inequities had been the most glaring, the need the most urgent.

Prodded by a genuine desire to provide a black presence in the faculty and stung by undergraduate reproach, the College's administration had attempted to attract qualified black faculty in a number of areas. They enjoyed only modest success, bringing four into the faculty in as many years. James H. Rogers in English stayed four years, Linda Walker in psychology three, Keith Guy in sociology two and Glenda Gill in English only one. All four were good people, and Simpson would have been happy to have kept them, but all moved on. It was not easy to keep black faculty in Indianola. As Dr. McBride put it, "We scanned candidates for staff positions every year looking for capable black professionals, but when we did find [them], found we could not hold them long."[171]

At the same time, it was becoming increasingly difficult to staff and teach the requisite courses to make up a viable ethnic and minority studies minor, which required eighteen semester hours of course work. Already such programs were finding diminishing support all over America.

It was much the same for other minorities. Jessie Tsuey-Fang Hu (1982–83) and Warapote Tipayamongkol (1984–87) in computer science and Gatsinzi Basaninyenzi (1982–83) in English came and went. They, too, sought positions in places where greater heterogeneity prevailed than was the case at Simpson. It appears that, in addition to their desire to associate themselves with larger institutions, these minority people were influenced by other factors which drew them away from Simpson. Although close to a city, the College was in a rural setting, and these people had no community in Indianola with which they could identify. They encountered students and some faculty whose experience with other races or ethnic groups was minimal. In short, they felt as if they had entered an alien land, not so much hostile as it was untutored. Some of them agreed with one of the social philosophers of the day who observed that "freshwater colleges" of rural America had no business trying to make a place for urban minorities on their campuses, not because such a well-intentioned effort was wrong in its motivation, rather because they were ill-equipped culturally or demographically to cope with the bruising consequences of their endeavor.

More noticeable than Simpson's inability to retain black or international faculty was the precipitous decline in the number of black undergraduates. The drop from a total of more than eighty in 1976—roughly eleven percent of full-time students—to just over twenty in 1982 was primarily the consequence of creating a single—and higher—standard for admission.[172] The reasons for the change were fairly obvious. For one thing, the compassionate policy of "giving these young people a chance" was not working. Simpson had lowered its standard of admission, but it had not lowered appreciably its expectations of performance for a degree. "Already," recalled McBride, "we were losing sixty percent of our first year blacks at the close of the second semester, and only about ten percent were persisting to graduation despite our efforts."[173] Was it fairer to turn down unqualified applicants or to admit them and submit them to failure?

The new standard of admission adopted in 1978 called for a reasonable graduating class rank from all applicants, but it took into account the fact that average A.C.T. or S.A.T. scores of blacks were thirty-five percent lower than those of others. The tests, it was hotly argued by some, were "culturally biased" in favor of the majority culture. But even allowing for lower test scores, far fewer minority students were meeting even this modest standard, and in spite of criticism, McBride backed John Kellogg's resolve to improve student academic quality. At the same time, admissions efforts to recruit blacks continued, together with "above average scholarship assistance," but they failed to attract more than a few qualified applicants. The results of this new policy were almost immediately apparent. Although the black student population was reduced by over seventy per cent, the number of minority graduates remained very nearly the same as it had been, matching the graduation rate of all other students.

Relations between administrators and faculty with minority students were often strained. "Almost weekly [during his first year at Simpson]," recalled President McBride, "I faced some group of black students in my office, protesting some perceived injustice, usually with Gary Streaty, the black president of the student body, their chief spokesman." McBride was not unconscious of the irony here. Streaty, more than anyone, had supported his candidacy for the presidency of the College, and "eventually carried the day in his opinion."[174]

McBride actually enjoyed his relations with the black students, whether in a relaxed social setting or in head-to-head discussions of problems. "Lue and I," he recalled, "visited minority programs in the Afro-American Center, invited groups of black students into our home, and went out of our way attempting to cultivate communications with these young people and in a few instances, friendships. We came to know many of them quite well and to appreciate better the severe challenges most of them faced economically, socially and academically."[175] Still, it was frustrating neither to be able to attract enough minority faculty or qualified minority students. McBride summed it up in a sentence: "While we were to have many successes on the campus, I never felt that our handling of the minority problems was one of them."[176]

*   *   *

Minority problems may have been frustrating, but surely improving Simpson's athletics was equally vexing. With very few exceptions, the College's intercollegiate teams did poorly. McBride found himself "quietly embarrassed" by poor performance of the athletes, in spite of a "reasonably competent staff and acceptable facilities." He remembered his own days in college. He had, he said, never lost his love for athletics, and he was determined that something had to be done to restore health to an ailing program.

But why the importance of athletics? Was there any real correlation between the success of a college as an academic institution and its athletic performance? Probably not, but in Iowa it seemed to matter. McBride's analysis was probably not much different than that of many other college presidents in the upper Midwest. "Iowa," he said,

> had no professional football or basketball teams and the major focus of young men and women was on college and university programs. Iowa seemed to have more small towns than any state in the nation, and sixty per cent of high school graduates seemed to harbor a desire to participate in sports at the college level. . . . This was one of their major motivations behind coming to small schools like Simpson. One survey we did indicated that about forty per cent of our student body was involved in some level of varsity sports participation. . . . Students, even good academic students, seemed to want to be associated with a "winner," and by any standard, Simpson was not a winner athletically.[177]

However, there were far more pressing problems confronting Simpson in 1979. Consequently McBride held off taking action until the real strength of the College had been restored. Meanwhile, he recalled ruefully, "I found it difficult to sit in the stands and cheer with so little reason for doing so except to interrupt my depression."[178]

There was indeed little to cheer about. In the most visible sports, the record was poor. Football enjoyed only one winning season (5-4) out of six between 1979 and 1984. The 1979 season, coach Maury Waugh's last, scored a disappointing three wins against six losses (2-4 in the conference). Greg Holland, Richard Carroll and Tom Miner won recognition for their play, but the team did relatively poorly. Miner wrote an agonizing piece in the *Simpsonian*, expressing his disillusionment with football and the College.[179] Student body president Gary Streaty wrote "I think having a 90-guy football squad is overemphasizing sports at Simpson, because we don't have the type of program that allows 90 guys to play."[180] Of course, no other college did, either.

Replacing Waugh was Alex Glann, who had been teaching and serving as assistant football coach in the Des Moines public schools. He had earlier coached the North High School team in Des Moines, compiling a 32-28 record. A graduate of Central College (1970), he held an M.A. in public school administration from Northeast Missouri State College (1979).[181] Glann's first year started off brilliantly with four consecutive wins—the best since 1924—but faltered, winning only one more game in a nine-game schedule. During the next four years, 1981 through 1984, the team did not have a single winning season, culminating in a heartbreaking 2-7 record during the final season. Yet in the midst of despair came an unbelievable victory, September 24, 1983, when Simpson beat Central 17-15 on Central's home field. It was the first win against Central in twenty-seven years. McBride was ecstatic. "We cancelled school the following Monday for half a day and invited the entire town to a noon picnic with the students on the town square." That was one of only two Simpson conference wins that year.[182] After that one stunning victory, the football program went downhill. The 1984 season was Glann's last at Simpson.[183] His successor, selected at the end of the year, was Lloyd Krumlauf, whose appointment was announced at a press conference January 9, 1985.[184] He came to Simpson from North Central College in Naperville, Illinois, where he had coached four years, earning a 16-19 record. After graduating from North Central (1973), Krumlauf had gone straight into coaching at his alma mater. "We'll play ball-control offense and run out of the 'I' formation," said the new coach, but "I'm not promising any miracles."[185]

There were no miracles. The 1985 season saw the Redmen post a dismal 2–7 record, and the 1986 season was even worse with only one win—against Upper Iowa—and eight losses.[186] It was small comfort that the one win was Simpson's 300th in all time. It was clearly time for another change.

Meanwhile, once the College's financial and academic well-being was assured, President McBride looked for new direction of the whole athletic program. The better to monitor its development, he moved the responsibility for athletics from the academic dean's office to his own. Then, with the urging of the faculty's personnel committee, he decided to seek new leadership in Simpson's sports. Gordon Jeppson, ever the gentleman, stepped aside.[187] Appointed to take his place was John Sirianni, who had joined the Simpson staff in August 1984 as assistant athletic director, baseball coach, instructor in physical education and admissions counselor.[188] A Des Moines native, Sirianni was a graduate of Iowa State University (1972), where he also earned an M.S. in 1982. He had taught and coached at Dowling and Nevada High Schools before coming to Indianola High School in 1977 as athletic director. After two years at Indianola he was named head baseball coach, meeting with great success. His teams finished in first place in the Central Iowa Conference for three years—1982 to 1984. Elected a member of the board of directors of the Iowa High School Athletic Directors Association, he had demonstrated real leadership ability. As Gordon Jeppson prepared to leave Simpson, Sirianni was named athletic director, assuming his new duties on January 1, 1985.

When it was time to look for a new football coach after the calamitous 1986 season, Sirianni suggested the appointment of Jim Williams, with whom he had coached at Dowling and who was known to be dissatisfied with the football situation at Iowa State, where Williams had been a member of the coaching staff for the better part of twelve years. Williams was already something of a legend in Iowa. He was a graduate of the University of Northern Iowa, where he earned the B.S. degree in social studies and law in 1956. He coached first at East Dubuque, Illinois, then at Audubon High School in Iowa before going to Dowling High School in Des Moines, where his teams compiled an astounding 118–9–3 record, winning twelve Des Moines Metro titles and putting together one string of 64 consecutive wins, the nation's longest. Recognized Iowa coach of the year in 1964, he was named the national coach of the year nine years later at Dowling. After twelve years at Dowling he accepted the position of offensive line coach at Iowa State, later advancing to assistant head coach.

No sooner had he come to Simpson than Williams inspired new confidence in Simpson's football program. He recruited a number of excellent young athletes, learning soon enough that his players had to meet Simpson's ever-higher academic standards for admission. During Williams's first season at Simpson, the team lost its first four games but won three of the last four. After that Simpson became a major contender for the Iowa Conference title.

Basketball, the other most visible sport at Simpson, was an on-again off-again affair. Under coach Roger Thomas the 1980 team had a poor record—3 and 11 in the conference. However, its star player, John Hines, scored 615 points, breaking the season scoring record of Dave Keller, and was named to the all-conference first team. The next two years were better, with the 1982 aggregation ranking first in offense in the conference and finishing with their highest overall conference performance (9–5) in twenty years. Keith Edmonds, the Redmen's lead scorer, was named to the conference first team. When coach Thomas resigned in mid-1982 to take a position in Yuma, Arizona, the College invited Dennis Dearden, a 1974 Simpson graduate, to take the reins.[189] During his three seasons as head coach, Dearden saw the fortunes of his teams decline. The 1983 season was very good with a 13–12 overall record and 9–5 in the conference for a second place finish. Four players were named that year to all-conference teams: Ronnie Lindsey, Brad Bjorkgren, Scott Clark and Bob Goedken. Lindsey repeated as an all-conference selection the next season, but the team posted only a 10–16 record. And in 1985 the results were yet more disappointing, with a record of 8–18 (4–10 in conference play). When Dearden resigned in 1985, the College brought in another Simpson alumnus, Bruce Wilson '76, who made a real place for himself at Simpson. Wilson built the team gradually until the Redmen were able to win the Iowa Conference championship in 1992.

Although Larry Johnson's baseball team posted a good record in 1980, including contests against southwestern powers like the University of Texas, Simpson's performance on the diamond was poor during the years that followed. After Johnson's resignation in 1983, Gordon Jeppson and Jim Donohue shared coaching duties for a year until John Sirianni joined the coaching staff. During his first year—1985—Sirianni coached the Redmen to a 16–20 record. The next year the team won 23 and lost 17, taking 10 of its final 11 games. Bryan Marlay and Brent Clark earned all-conference honors that year. And the 1987 team won its first Iowa Conference title in twenty years with a 26–9 record, with three players selected to the all-conference first team: Jim Valley, Greg Christy and Brent Clark. After that, Simpson's team was always in contention for the conference crown.

Wrestling under a succession of coaches—Jerome Stewart, Mike Thompson, Larry Marfise and John O'Connell—was only modestly successful, twice ranking fourth in the conference for the team's best finish. Men's golf, coached by Gordon Jeppson until the 1982–83 school year, then by Bob Lane and Lloyd Krumlauf, managed for two years to place third in the Iowa Conference, with an outstanding performance by Rick Flesher, a local Indianola boy. In tennis the men managed a winning season only twice.

It was different in track. Hired in 1989 to coach both track and cross-country was young John Curtin, a Drake graduate who was at the time serving as the successful director of the Indianola Parks and Recreation program. Under Curtin, track flourished. During his first season, Simpson's team finished third in the conference, and Curtin was named coach of the year. The next year saw the team repeat its conference performance and rank eighteenth in the N.C.A.A. Division III finals. Curtin's men in 1982 had a great year, with eight wins and fourteen Simpson records broken. When Curtin resigned in 1986 to accept a coaching position at Emory University, Keith Ellingson took his place and maintained Simpson's excellent record in track and field.

In cross-country it was even better. Under Curtin the team hit its stride in 1980, with Danny Doyle and Brad Joens leading the way. Then, in the fall of 1981, a wiry, boyish freshman named Danny Bauer, distance runner and superior student from North English, Iowa, started setting records in what was to be a phenomenal career at Simpson. Backed by a number of other talented runners, Bauer topped his own record time after time. In 1982, his freshman year, he became Simpson's first runner ever to win an I.I.A.C. championship and was the only Iowa athlete to qualify that year for the N.C.A.A. Division III national championships. As a sophomore he earned All-American honors and repeated each of the next two years. Without question, he was one of Simpson College's greatest all-time athletes. But Bauer always knew why he came to college, finishing his academic career with superb grades and an N.C.A.A. scholarship for graduate study.

This period in the history of Simpson athletics was marked by greatly expanded participation in women's athletics. By 1982 the College was fielding teams in seven sports for women, a huge increase in just a few years.

In basketball, especially after Janet Schafer took over as coach in 1981, the teams did very well indeed.[190] Standout players included Annette Christensen, Lori Shelley and Laurie Sankey. The team's best record was in 1985, with eleven wins and only three losses in conference play, earning them a berth in the N.C.A.A. women's regional championship tourney. In volleyball Simpson women were superior in 1980 and 1981, winning the conference championship both years. Thereafter, however, the team faltered, scoring barely a winning season in 1982 and sinking to a dismal 4–36–2 record in 1985. Meanwhile, the "Lady Reds" softball team under coach Janet Schafer had a great 1981 season, with nineteen wins against seven losses, a third place finish in the state tournament and fifth in the A.I.A.W. Division III national tourney in Michigan. In 1982 Annette Christensen was an all-conference selection. Other years saw the team playing well, although after 1983 it was less successful than it had been. Women's track and cross-country were only modestly prosperous, with coaching duties passed from one person to the next. John Curtin coached the first women's cross country team in 1982. Although they did poorly that first season, their performance improved markedly in the years that followed. Women's tennis was not strong, but in golf they played increasingly well, placing second in the Iowa Conference in both the 1982 and 1983 seasons.

Intramural sports, which involved almost as many participants as did varsity athletics, continued to be very popular. Women's competition was keen and their play sporting; the men's program was described variously as "too rough" or "out of hand."[191] Under John Sirianni's direction, however, men's intramurals improved considerably, their success dependent at least in part upon the strength and personality of the individual designated to serve as director of intramural sports.

There were students on campus, actually quite a few of them, whose interest in sports ranged from wearied indifference to outright hostility. Some of these were dedicated scholars, caught up in their studies to the exclusion of everything beyond the walls of the library; some were musicians or thespians who had as little taste for sports as they had time to devote to them.

* * *

Labeled the "me generation," students in the 1980s were said to be apathetic and self-centered, driven only by personal career goals. As is perhaps true with most labels, such a description contains a modest element of truth and a lot of distortion. At Simpson, as Dean of Students Gary Valen put it, students found that they were simply overwhelmed by external pressures. "The problems and issues are so complex, so immense, they don't feel they can make a difference on a personal level," he said, "and so they have turned their energies inward—toward individual goals."[192] Such an indifferent response to the world around them made students appear to be apathetic, apolitical, even asocial. But their record at Simpson during these years suggests that appearances can deceive, that their inner-directedness did not prevent or inhibit their relating creatively to others individually or in groups. True, they found the development of the American economy during the Reagan years, with its emphasis on the well-being of the affluent not to be especially reassuring, for most Simpson students came from the great middle class that benefitted little from supply-side economics. Their anxiety about the future was understandable.

They were far less anxious about the present, and their activities, on and off campus, reflected that fact. In contrast to the Simpson of the early seventies, the students of the eighties recovered their enthusiasm for doing things together in groups. As a consequence, athletic teams, academic societies, musical, theatrical and oratorical groups as well as the Greek-letter fraternities and sororities flourished once again.

The most obvious evidence of a new mood among students was the growth of membership in the Greek societies, a development already under way when McBride came to Simpson. Among the fraternities, ATO and SAE had remained strong, but the Lambda Chis had suffered serious losses, with membership reduced one year in the late seventies to only nine. Fearful that the chapter might close, a group of dedicated Lambda Chi alumni, led by Frank Nowasell '60, the College's associate director of development, went to work and revived the chapter impressively. By the fall of 1980 its membership was up to forty-nine and its future assured. Soon enough, it was evident that if Simpson was to provide the "Greek option" to all the young men who wanted to choose it, a fourth fraternity was needed.

Because of the College's long-standing reputation as a healthy fraternity college and because the school could offer a fine dwelling, Worth House, to a new organization, Simpson was very attractive to a number of excellent national fraternities. A committee of Greek alumni and student representatives that met with Dean Gary Valen to consider the matter decided, however, not to consider a national organization at all. Rather it would invite the alumni of the old, distinguished local fraternity Kappa Theta Psi to reorganize their chapter. The committee's reasoning was simple: there were nearly six hundred living Kappa alumni who would be delighted to see their old fraternity on campus again and who could be of great assistance to the restoration of the chapter. Fortuitously, the alumni of Kappa Theta Psi were holding a reunion in Des Moines and Indianola in the summer of 1979. When more that 150 of them, including a number of wives, gathered for dinner at a Des Moines airport motel, President and Lue McBride, who had just arrived to take up their duties at the College, attended. It was the new presidential couple's first official appearance at a Simpson function. The next day the alumni group drove down to Indianola, toured the campus and enjoyed a festive luncheon at Great Hall. At this luncheon the Simpson committee extended a formal invitation to the Kappas to reestablish the old chapter and promised the College's assistance in the enterprise. The alumni were as delighted as they were surprised. Led by people like Dr. G. A. "Chick" Grant '17 and George Grant '33 of Osage, they vowed support.

Two individuals put the new fraternity together: staff member Tom Westbrook, director of student activities, and an outstanding senior student named Craig Collins, serving that fall as Homecoming chairman. With an initial group of nine undergraduate members, the fraternity was formally initiated on December 1, 1979.[193] In the fall of 1980 the Kappas, already expanded to twenty-four members, occupied Worth House, sharing it with independent students until its membership was large enough to justify exclusive occupancy of the building. At least one Worth House inhabitant objected to sharing the house with the Kappas unless the fraternity would become coeducational. That was a concept for which neither Kappa Theta Psi nor Simpson was quite ready.[194]

There was talk during the early eighties about relocating Lambda Chi Alpha by building a house for its members on "fraternity row" in exchange for the chapter house, which by this time sat majestically in the middle of the campus. The matter was discussed by the board of trustees and an offer made to the Lambda Chis.[195] Reaction of both undergraduates and alumni was unexpectedly fierce. Calling the "offer" of the College "shortsighted . . . dictatorial and ignorant," Lambda Chis rose almost to a man to save the "Chopper" house from demolition. Simpson was attacking their very identity. "This same college that sells uniqueness is now attempting to rob the Lambda Chis of theirs," wrote an irate Lambda Chi undergraduate in the *Simpsonian*. Calling their house a "landmark," he branded the deal "a shabby way to treat the Lambda Chis."[196] McBride and the board, surprised and dismayed by the vitriol of the Lambda Chi response, backed off.

The SAEs got on better with College authorities, especially after Dean Gary Valen helped them recover their treasured coat-of-arms. Years earlier, at the time of the chapter's revival in 1957, the SAE province, or district, in the upper Midwest made a gift of a magnificent, hand-carved fraternity coat-of-arms to the new chapter. It had hung on the wall in the living room of the chapter house for years, but was stolen in the late spring of 1981. The chapter offered a reward for its return, but to no avail. Two years later, convinced that their coat-of-arms was lost forever, the chapter arranged with the Iowa Woodcarvers Society to have a new plaque hand carved—at a very high price. As soon as news of the chapter's plan leaked out, however, Dean Valen received a telephone call. A conspiratorial-sounding, disguised male voice stated that if the five hundred dollar reward was still offered, he could direct the dean to the coat-of-arms. After contacting the SAEs—it was in the fall of 1983—Valen, "alone and unarmed," carrying the reward in cash per instructions, donned his trench coat on a cold, damp morning, walked stealthily into "a back street garage somewhere in Indianola," and quietly exchanged the $500 for the woodcarving. Valen had probably given the money either to the thief or a go-between. But the SAEs were delighted to have their coat-of-arms back, and they praised Valen's cloak-and-dagger operation forever after.[197]

The ATOs celebrated their centennial at Simpson in the spring of 1985. Bob MacKenzie '70 was chairman of the event, held May 10 and 11 on campus and at the Fort Des Moines Hotel in Des Moines. A large number of alumni returned to participate in the activities of the weekend. A highlight of the centennial banquet was the presentation to the College of a twenty-five hundred dollar endowment for a scholarship fund. While the celebration was highly successful, the most impressive contribution to the event was the publication of the chapter's history, entitled *The First Century at Simpson: Iowa Beta Alpha Chapter of Alpha Tau Omega*, by Wendell Tutt '28, whose writing skills were still as sharp as they had been when he edited the *Simpsonian* during his undergraduate days. Three years in the research and writing, Tutt's history was one of the best chapter histories ever produced for any college fraternity, a volume of which all of Simpson could be proud.[198]

That same year the Alpha Chi Omegas celebrated the centennial of their national organization, founded at DePauw University in 1885.[199] The Simpson Alpha Chis, together with their two older rivals, Pi Beta Phi and Tridelta, flourished. Sometimes independent women enjoyed laughing at the sororities, on one occasion mocking the Ph Phi tradition of requiring their pledges to wear huge, preposterous arrows in their hair. Deanna Haunsperger, a loyal Tridelt, infuriated independent women by arguing that members of the Greek societies had a more powerful sense of identity than did those who were unaffiliated.[200]

Whatever their sense of identity, the Greeks, by virtue of their being organized and goal-oriented, continued to dominate campus social life and student government. Their members also continued to perform academically very well, especially the women's groups. Among the fraternities, both Alpha Tau Omega and Sigma Alpha Epsilon received national recognition for outstanding achievement, with Tridelta and Pi Beta Phi receiving similar recognition among the sororities.

Of all organized college activities, probably none was more successful during these years than forensics. The leadership of Douglas Larche and Jay Ver Linden was of course crucial, but the students who competed in state and regional contests handled themselves remarkably well. Simpson publications for several years were full of accounts of the stunning success of the Simpson contestants. In 1979–80 alone the team garnered fifty-nine trophies, and subsequent years saw similar success. The team ranked second in the state in both 1982 and 1984, third in 1983, competing against teams from all other colleges and universities, large and small.

Three new honor societies, all nationally affiliated, appeared at Simpson during the early 1980s. A chapter of Alpha Lambda Delta, a freshman scholastic honor society, was organized in March 1983, its creation owing primarily to the signal efforts of Miriam Jenkins, the College's registrar.[201] Phi Alpha Theta, the huge national honor society in history, was chartered at Simpson in November 1983, its development primarily the work of Owen Duncan.[202] The third group was Phi Beta Lambda, the college subdivision of the Future Business Leaders of America, installed at Simpson February 9, 1984.

Older groups continued to function actively. Beta Beta Beta hosted a regional convention at Simpson in 1981.[203] Sigma Tau Delta sponsored films and poetry readings.[204] Epsilon Sigma, the prestigious scholastic honor society, in 1982 placed a handsome plaque in the library, commemorating its founding in 1924.[205]

Both the *Simpsonian* and the *Zenith* continued without interruption. Generally well edited, the College's newspaper continued to be published with a very limited budget. Proofreading was, however, a perennial problem, even if the news was competently reported. Some features, like Steve Newell's "Principia Scientiae," a series of rambles through modern science, described by students as "weird," were presented uncritically, but others were thoughtful. Alumnus Ben Campney was predictably "shocked and outraged" when the *Simpsonian* published an advertisement for the U.S. Army, but a few years later the U.S. Air Force recruited for a whole day at the Brenton Student Center without a word of editorial protest. Times were changing.

The *Zenith* was well done. A standout was the 1983 edition edited by Rolf Swanson, ably assisted by a staff headed by business manager Rich Patrick. But its budget was as constricted as was that of the *Simpsonian*. The *Sequel* was worse off. Its 1984–85 budget of only $530 would not meet the cost of publication, and its mentors in the English Department had to go begging.[206]

Student government and the College Activities Board were energetic, sometimes controversial and always urging change, from policies regarding alcohol and dormitory visitation—they thought both were too strict—to academic programming. Elections were described variously as "lively" (1980) or "boring and predictable" (1985).[207]

* * *

One of the casualties during the years of student unrest had been Simpson's relationship with the United Methodist Church. Although church-relatedness tended during the 1970s to weaken in colleges all over America, the once-powerful ties that had bound Simpson to the church seemed to loosen more rapidly and more profoundly than elsewhere. It would be easy to ascribe this development to student militance or antiestablishment sentiment and be done with it. But it wasn't that simple; a number of other factors must be taken into account if we are to understand what happened. Contributing to the decline of church influence was the change in the composition of the board of trustees. As we have already seen, the clerical contingent of the board had been reduced through the years in both number and power. Gone were the days when clergymen and laymen on the board voted separately, effectively giving the churchmen a veto on any action. By 1979 only four clergymen sat on the board, three of whom were ex officio, the fourth a designate of the bishop of the Methodist conference.

The position of the president of the College was also significant. Until the end of Edward Voigt's administration in the early fifties, presidents had nearly always played a prominent role in the life of the church and were expected to lead the College in accordance with church teachings and practices. Rarely were non-Methodists appointed to serve either on the faculty or staff. But with the assumption of the presidency by William Kerstetter came a major change. Though a dedicated, loyal Methodist clergyman, Kerstetter selected faculty and staff without respect to their religious affiliation. While he gave everyone to understand that they were indeed teaching in a church-related College, he never applied a Methodist litmus test to anyone. His successor, Ralph John, went much further, presiding over a greater secularization and liberalization of the College than many churchmen found palatable. Faculty were selected for their expertise and ability to teach in their fields, and no one was describing Simpson as a "defender of the faith" institution. In fact, many Simpsonians, faculty and students alike, saw the traditional church relationship as provincial, indeed parochial. Thus by 1972, when Richard Lancaster was selected as Simpson's president, it was no surprise to anyone that he was not a Methodist at all. And while Lancaster was sensitive to the concerns of the church and the College's relationship to it, as a non-Methodist he had no role in its councils.

Meanwhile, in what may have been a bit of overreaction to threats of denial of federal money to "church-controlled" institutions, the board and President Ralph John altered the Simpson charter to remove any trace of formal church control of the College, stating that henceforth the church relationship would be "fraternal." Practically, as we have seen, this meant simply that the conference would no longer be asked to approve the appointment of members of Simpson's board of trustees. This change was more symbolic—some would even say cosmetic—than real.

It is true that students, or most of them, were less interested in religious activities than had been their predecessors, and some of them suspected the sinister hand of the church in even the slightest resistance on the part of the administration or staff to any of their demands, especially for more liberal rules regarding drinking or dormitory visitation.

The College's chaplains, Gil Taverner, Roger Betsworth and later James Noseworthy, together with directors of church relations Art and Nancy Allen, travailed with an often reluctant student body to provide a meaningful and active religious life program.[208] Effective in counseling, they found less success in attracting more than a fraction of the students to an array of church services, study groups and activities. President McBride found religious life "a surprisingly difficult area to cultivate at Simpson." McBride was a Methodist, indeed a clergyman, and sought to enliven the religious dimension of the College and to restore to some degree Simpson's tenuous relationship with the church. In the latter effort he had signal success, but he could not overcome "student apathy," despite "good leadership." To McBride, religious life at the College was "an area of general disappointment."[209]

* * *

In many ways the rhythm of the school year's activities and campus events remained much the same during the eighties as it had been in earlier decades. Although the academic calendar, calling for a May term instead of a January interim, changed the beat, if not the tempo, of the school year after 1985, traditional campus events were little affected, with the possible exception of Campus Day, which was pushed into April in order to keep it within the spring semester.

Each year the first to arrive on campus were the football players and other fall-sport athletes, anxious to prepare for early autumn contests. Housed in dormitories and nourished by indestructible Pfeiffer meals that represented a monumental caloric intake, athletes sweated their way through a fortnight of drills in the typically unforgiving late August heat.

Freshman orientation, managed by the student development staff and assisted by Student, Counselor, Advisor, Friend (S.C.A.F.) undergraduates, introduced new students to Simpson in a flurry of placement tests, auditions, lectures, discussions and recreational events, including a freshman talent show. By the time classes commenced, fraternity and sorority rush was underway, climaxed by pledging ceremonies and a major shift in housing, distributing students among the residence halls and Greek houses that would become their home for the year.

Parents Day in early October and Homecoming a bit later highlighted the fall calendar. Homecoming still usually involved a parade that circled the Indianola square, a skit contest, a "Yell like Hell" pep rally, street-painting in front of the Brenton Student Center, the Greek Olympics, and a succession of open houses and receptions on and off campus, a coronation of Homecoming royalty—after the early eighties minority students, whose numbers had dwindled, discontinued the election of black royalty—and, to be sure, the football game. During the halftime ceremonies the coveted Tomahawk was awarded to that organization that best exemplified the Homecoming spirit. A "faculty representative," no longer designated the "Big Chief" an appellation that sounded both sexist and racist in the eighties, was also honored in the parade and at halftime.[210]

The Simpson Forum brought a parade of speakers to the campus. One was specially selected as the George Washington Carver lecturer, attracting annually an outstanding black scholar or public figure, and another was selected as the Matthew Simpson lecturer, honoring the great bishop. During political campaigns Simpson saw one office seeker after another, especially in presidential election years when virtually every candidate came to the campus as a part of his swing through Iowa prior to the first-in-the-nation party caucuses.

Spring brought Greek Week, Minority Emphasis Week (primarily a celebration of black heritage) and All-College Sing. This durable and controversial contest was still won fairly automatically by Barker Hall, except for 1982, when the Lambda Chis sang better, and variously by the Trideltas, Pi Phi, Alpha Chi and Kresge Hall. During the one-week spring break the dormitories were filled to overflowing with upwards of four hundred souls during the annual pastors' school.[211] And for a few years a spring college bowl, pitting groups of instant-recall campus intellectuals against each other, was entertaining and informative, won nearly every year by the ATOs.[212]

Probably the biggest party of the year was still the Back Forty Bash. It was pointed out, without comment, that "thirty kegs will be tapped at six p.m." for the 1983 edition of this outdoor bockfest, an event that was reportedly "well attended."[213] However, the event which always brought the largest participation was Campus Day, with its happy combination of work and play. "Campus Day was last Wednesday," reported the *Simpsonian* in April 1983. "Everyone was there, laying sod, painting the stadium, washing windows, sweeping sidewalks and raking leaves."[214]

Commencement climaxed the school year. It remained as it had always been, a happy occasion for students whose degrees testified to their having completed the course satisfactorily, sometimes brilliantly, and a bittersweet time for faculty who were proud of their graduates and sad to see them move on.

A few memorable events were unplanned but long remembered. Few could forget the fall of 1979 when Ed and Lorraine Warren, who billed themselves as "demonologist and clairvoyant," respectively, poked around the eerie rooms of College Hall on Halloween, declaring that they had indeed found a ghost in its dark recesses. "Her spirit remains in the building because she is not ready, or willing to die," they assured all who would listen.[215] Many believed; some did not.

* * *

When the McBrides arrived in Indianola in 1979, they were prepared neither to romanticize small-town Iowa nor to disdain its putative charms. At first sight, they found the place not impressive, "a combination of disparate forms of housing, scattered business structures of varying appearance," and a "potentially attractive but generally nondescript square." More troubling were the relationships between the College and the citizenry, which they discovered were "not as positive as they should have been."[216] Both of the McBrides were determined to remove the chill and "change the climate" of indifference or hostility that was evident at every hand. Moreover, they soon learned that appearances can indeed be deceiving. As time went on, the town looked better and better. And both of the occupants of "the Carpenter House," as local residents called the president's home on West Ashland, worked assiduously to foster healthy and productive town-gown ties.

In their endeavor they were extraordinarily successful. Soon they discovered "the warmth and friendliness of the people" and responded easily, naturally to their overtures. "From the very beginning," recalled Dr. McBride, "Lue fell in love with Indianola." She plunged headfirst into community activities, shopped in most of the businesses around the square, joined a sewing club, played bridge with the town's leading women, and joined the P.E.O., a women's adult secret society as influential as it was inscrutable. Soon Dr. McBride was known as "Lue McBride's husband, the one who runs the college." Together they became Simpson's "roving ambassadors," and the relationship between the College and the town was restored to a state of cordiality.[217]

The McBrides' entertaining was simple, comfortable, extensive. There were dinners for faculty and board of trustees people, receptions for students and townspeople, parties at the college, sociables for benefactors upon whose generosity the college depended.

Beyond Indianola, they cultivated friendships in Des Moines and undertook long, sometimes exhausting trips to meet with Simpson alumni groups all over the country. The response to their reaching out to the community, to Des Moines and the alumni was heartwarming.

* * *

During the first three years of McBride's presidency the college lost by death two active and five honorary life members of the board of trustees. The active members were Dr. Thomas R. Viner, '43 who died July 1, 1979, and Lewis S. Kimer '39, editor of the *Record-Herald and Indianola Tribune*, December 17, 1981. The honorary life members included a number of longtime trustees whose services to the College had been generous and much appreciated: Alden Smith '24, retired Price Waterhouse executive at Naples, Florida, September 18, 1979; former board chairman and retired banker Ralph McGee '20, October 10, 1979; women's leader Ruth Buxton Sayre '17, whose biography by Julie McDonald had been published only months before Sayre's death at Des Moines, November 23, 1980; the Reverend Walter M. Scheuermann '28, retired Methodist clergyman whose relationship to Simpson started when he entered the Academy right after the First World War, October 16, 1982; and the only non-alumnus, retired engineering executive Kenneth R. Brown, whose services to Simpson were highlighted by his assistance in several major construction projects, who died at Des Moines December 9, 1980.

A bit later came the worst blow to the active Simpson board and to the Indianola community, the loss of Richard Buxton '58, president of the Peoples Trust and Savings Bank and the representative in the young generation of an honored Buxton dynasty that reached back to Simpson's earliest days. He died on July 16, 1984, at the age of forty-nine.

Among the many alumni whose deaths were mourned at Simpson were Avery Craven '08, whose legacy to Simpson we have already described, and two remarkably durable souls who were probably the college's two oldest alumni during the early eighties. One was Edmund H. Genung '06 of Upland, California, who died September 17, 1983, not long after he visited Simpson to inspect the new Amy Robertson Music Center and the rehearsal room that bore his name. He had sung at the dedication of the Barrows Conservatory building in 1904. When Alma Robbins White '05 died at the age of ninety-eight on January 23, 1984, she was known to be Simpson's oldest alumna and the oldest living member of the entire Tridelta national sorority. Only a few years earlier, at commencement time in 1981, she had been feted at a luncheon in Great Hall. Fragile, strong-willed, wearing a lovely wide-brimmed spring hat over exquisitely coiffed, silver hair, she was brought to the festive meal in a wheelchair. But when she was asked to speak, she stood up straight, walked resolutely to the stand, to the surprise of everyone, grasped the podium and announced: "I may have lost my equilibrium, but I haven't lost my balance," whereupon she entertained her audience with anecdotes of her days at Simpson. She told of coming to the college at the age of sixteen, of meeting a boy who became her "first love," sixteen-year-old freshman Whitford Shelton, son of the college's president, majoring in Latin and then of meeting her future husband, Paul White, who was also a Simpson student and Whit Shelton's Kappa Theta Psi fraternity brother. Although she averred in her speech that her main function any more was only "providing reminiscences," the audience loved her.[218]

Unlike the early days at Simpson, when too many undergraduates died of disease and accident, it was rare in the 1980s for students to have to confront the loss of a classmate. Thus when J. R. McBride, a lively young freshman, a boy "with an unforgettable smile" was killed in an automobile accident November 15, 1980, students, especially his Lambda Chi Alpha brothers, were struck hard, many of them joining faculty and administrators at the funeral at Maxwell, Iowa, McBride's hometown, and at a memorial service two days later in Smith Memorial Chapel.[219]

* * *

In an era of instant communication, the world closed in on the college as never before. The "information age," bringing with it new technology from electronic retrieval in the library to fax machines in Hillman Hall, heightened Simpsonians' awareness of happenings and conditions throughout the world. One could see in the pages of the *Simpsonian* and hear on campus, discussions of national and world events as seldom before. To be sure, the College's sharply higher admissions standards were attracting to Simpson a larger proportion of academically oriented students who could be expected to show an interest in world affairs. They watched the Soviet 1979 invasion of Afghanistan and President Carter's response by pulling the United States out of Moscow Olympic Games the next year, a reaction they called "meaningless."[220] They were even more concerned about the Iranian revolution which overthrew the 2500-year-old monarchy and saw Islamic fundamentalists hold fifty-two Americans hostage in the U.S. embassy in Teheran.[221] After the disastrous attempt to free the hostages in April 1980, the government of the Ayatollah Khomeini released the hostages only after Ronald Reagan was inaugurated president in January, 1980. The *Simpsonian* contrasted the heroes' welcome accorded the returning hostages to the ignoring of Vietnam veterans which had made them "social outcasts."[222]

In other international developments, Simpsonians opposed sharply American policy in El Salvador, fearing the Reagan policy there could lead to "another Vietnam,"[223] and deplored aid to the Contras against the Sandanistas in Nicaragua. On the other hand they cheered the British defense of Falkland Islands in 1982, "Margaret Thatcher's fine nineteenth century war" against what she called a "tin-pot regime" in Argentina, but called the U.S. invasion of Grenada "illegal."[224] While at Simpson there was little pro-Arab sentiment in the long-standing dispute between the Arabs and the Israelis, the *Simpsonian* criticized sharply the landing of U.S. Marines in Lebanon and the subsequent tragic loss of life when their headquarters in Beirut were bombed, in October 1983, resulting in the death of 244 Marine and Navy personnel.[225]

In national affairs students at Simpson spoke out against the draft,[226] the death penalty,[227] the possession of hand guns,[228] the huge military buildup crafted by the Reagan administration,[229] the Reagan effort to "restore prayer to the public schools of America,"[230] and, perhaps above all, the raising of the legal drinking age, first to nineteen in 1978 and to twenty-one in 1984.[231] They were less articulate about what they favored. But they did like the Equal Rights Amendment, an attitude in keeping with Simpson's tradition of support for women's rights; they supported an annual holiday to honor Martin Luther King,[232] and in national and local elections favored Democratic candidates for the most part.[233]

Certainly there were Simpsonians who disagreed with some or all of the above-mentioned stands on public issues. The College was always an open forum for debate.

* * *

During the 1985–86 academic year the college celebrated its quasquicentennial, or 125th anniversary. The name "quasquicentennial" was perhaps not a felicitous choice. For one thing, the word did not fall easily from an untutored tongue; for another, it somehow sounded more like a skin disorder than a celebration. The word didn't even appear in *Webster's Third New International Dictionary*, but a scholarly search for what to call a 125th anniversary turned up the polysyllabic term in some thesaurus, and quasquicentennial it was.

Selected chair of the year-long commemoration was board of trustees member Grace A. Overton of Indianola, a Simpson alumna in the class of 1941. She managed a complex set of events, watching with care every detail of the year's busy schedule. Appointed to serve with her were board members William Buxton III '28 and Richard Gilbert '62; two wives of board members, Sara Hill and Peg S. Mikulanec '71; Dr. McBride, Kay Lebeda and church relations director Nancy S. Allen '69 for the administration; faculty members E. G. Booth and Joe Walt; and student body president Jim Kutzner '86. In his turn, Kutzner headed a student committee of three competent undergraduates: Deanna Haunsperger, Paula Witke and Chris Goodale.[234]

Although the first major event was scheduled for September 1985, a preliminary introduction to the celebration was presented at the spring all-campus convocation, January 17, 1985, when Joe Walt, who couldn't resist an opportunity to talk about Simpson's history to a captive audience, delivered an address entitled "Simpson College: Its Beginnings."[235]

On September 12, the college celebrated Founders Day, an event reminiscent of the old Founders Day commemorations held in the late nineteenth century. Speaking at a mid-day formal convocation, complete with academic procession, Bishop James S. Thomas of the Ohio East Area of the United Methodist Church, recalled the "rising tide of the late nineteenth century," during which Methodists established colleges all over the land. He compared that time with the "rising tide of the 1980s" when Simpson was being called upon to reaffirm its commitment to both quality and "radical diversity." He charged the leaders of the College to take seriously their commitment "to educate whole human beings and to do so unashamedly in a context of values under pressure. . . . For Simpson, this is not a creed to be superimposed, but a life to live."[236]

Earlier in the day students staged a pep rally on the steps of College Hall, the gaunt old building now assured of restoration, and processed to Smith Memorial Chapel. At 12:15 P.M. the chapel bell rang 125 times. In the early evening, students, faculty and members of the Indianola community came together to enjoy a picnic. The fare of the day was selected with care by Dr. E. G. Booth's Founders Day committee, each food item intended to be reminiscent of an 1860 outdoor feast.

Following the picnic, a pageant, written and directed by Dr. Jack Jenkins, recalled the story of Simpson's early days. Presented by a readers' theater group of faculty and students, the performance was light-hearted and well received by a capacity crowd at Pote Theatre. The historical production was followed by a series of skits, songs and historical readings presented by representatives of student publications and organizations in order of their antiquity, from the *Simpsonian* (1870) to the Concerned Minority Students (1964). The event concluded with a rousing chorus of "March on, Simpson."[237]

Less than a fortnight later, on September 24, the Quasquicentennial Matthew Simpson Lecture was delivered at Lekberg Hall by Martin Marty, professor of the history of modern Christianity at the University of Chicago and probably the most outstanding religious historian in America. At an earlier dinner attended by nearly a hundred students, faculty and guests, Dr. Marty provided a preview of his formal lecture which was entitled "The Serious Game of Musical Chairs: Religious Change in America Today."

At the beginning of his lecture, Dr. Marty pointed out goodnaturedly to his audience that he had never before heard the word *quasquicentennial*, had looked it up in a very large dictionary and couldn't find it. Had someone at Simpson made up the term and foisted it upon a gullible public whose innocence of a knowledge of Latin rendered them victims of linguistic charlatanism? Still bothered after he returned to Chicago from Indianola, he checked with a Jesuit classicist and a medievalist colleague, neither of whom had heard of the term. He wrote to Simpson's Bruce Haddox, demanding an explanation. After all, Simpson's motto on its coat-of-arms was "Et Veritas Te Liberabit." He wanted to know the truth. Haddox replied that "no faculty member would own up to having proposed [the term] for the school's 125th." Was this Simpson's Quasquigate?

Haddox turned to librarian Cyd Dyer, who went to work on the puzzle. She wrote to the Library of Congress. If they didn't know, no one would. Their reply came as a relief: in a volume called *9,000 Words: A Supplement to Webster's Third New International Dictionary* was the entry on page 165: "quas-qui-cen-ten-ni-al n. [fr. L *quadrans* quarter, after L *semis* half: E sesquicentennial]: a 125th anniversary." Haddox thereupon sent this information to Dr. Marty, together with a number of photocopies of programs from Iowa towns which had celebrated "quasquicentennials." If the term was widely enough used, it must be right, he reasoned. Then Marty himself found the term in Kenneth Versand's *Polyglot Lexicon: 1943-1966*, with the explanation that it had "entered the vocabulary in 1962, and means 'a 125th anniversary.'" Cyd Dyer was amused; Bruce Haddox was relieved; Simpson was off the hook; and Martin Marty was so delighted with the search that he published a piece about it in *The Christian Century* a few months later. He called it "No Quasquigate, After All."[238]

A little more than a month later, on October 19, Joe Walt presented a historical piece called "Celebration of Simpson Women of the Past" at a meeting of the Simpson Guild, that durable society of women from the faculty and the town. The generosity of this group, providing substantial gifts to the college year after year, deserved more recognition than their quiet assistance was ever accorded.[239]

The following Saturday at Homecoming, the dedication of the Henry H. and Thomas H. McNeill Hall for Business and Computer Science was made part of the Quasquicentennial commemoration, recalling Simpson's long-standing commitment to business education. At the same time, Lettie McNeill's "Heckert group" met on campus with their ninety-two-year-old mentor.[240]

At Christmastime the Department of Music presented *The Messiah* with a chorus, appropriately, of 125 voices including students, faculty, and townspeople, together with an impressive orchestra. Performances, conducted by Robert Larsen, were held December 7 and 8 at Smith Memorial Chapel.

The George Washington Carver Lecture that year featured Dr. J. Herman Blake, president of Tougaloo College in Mississippi. His presentation on February 6 was the highlight of Minority Emphasis Week, which had begun three days earlier. The thoroughly positive note of Blake's lecture contrasted unfortunately with a story in the *Simpsonian* a few days earlier reporting a seventy-five percent decline in minority enrollment at Simpson during the five years after 1980, reflected in the virtual ignoring of the Martin Luther King national holiday.[241]

The most impressive single event of the quasquicentennial year was the one-time revival of the Liberal Arts Festival on April 4, 5 and 6, 1986. The weekend event would address "a major international issue, Simpson history and spiritual enrichment," promised the *Simpsonian* in its March 28 issue. There would be "something for everyone."

On Friday evening a festive dinner honored Simpson's three living past presidents, William E. Kerstetter, Ralph C. John and Richard B. Lancaster, whose administrations spanned most of the prior thirty years. Kerstetter spoke nostalgically of his years at Simpson, recalling the unique contributions he had made in Simpson's renaissance. Ralph John focused on the difficult times of student unrest and of his pride in the way Simpson met the challenges of the time. Dick Lancaster was eloquent in his description of Simpson's hard journey back from chaos to a semblance of normality. Letters from family members of the late John Hillman and Edwin E. Voigt were read to the audience. For many at Simpson and Indianola, the reunion with the past presidents and their wives was the most enriching experience of the quasquicentennial year.

Saturday, April 5, brought a number of celebrities to the campus for an evening of serious discussion of the topic "Nuclear Weapons in a Divided World: Prospects for Peace." At a well-attended dinner prior to the evening's main event,

Dr. Gregory Guroff, Chief of the Soviet and East European Research Office of the United States Information Agency, spoke persuasively about U.S.-Soviet relations. He warned that Americans and Soviets misunderstood each other because "we are tied up in visions we have of each other, tied up, not only in actions that each side makes, but in our evaluation and assessment of the intentions behind the actions." Contact declines as rhetoric increases. Russians, he said, are very different from Americans, "If I suggested to a Soviet that he could live as Americans do—engaging in free speech and political activism—my bet is that he or she would not choose to do so." Neither Guroff nor surely any of his audience that evening could possibly foresee the cataclysmic changes that in only a few years would destroy the Communist empire and witness the collapse of the Soviet Union.

The evening's major address at Pote Theatre was delivered by Jeane Kirkpatrick, former U.S. ambassador to the United Nations, who reminded her listeners that nuclear power was no longer the possession of the two superpowers, arguing that Ronald Reagan's S.D.I. (Strategic Defense Initiative) was "the only way for the United States to defend itself from a nuclear attack." Kirkpatrick's assertions were disputed by Victor Isakov, Minister-Counselor of the embassy of the U.S.S.R., who saw S.D.I. as an offensive system. In light of the departure of Anatoly Dobrynin, the Soviet ambassador to the U.S. only days earlier, Isakov was acting as chief representative of the Soviet Union in the U.S. when he came to Simpson. In a panel discussion moderated by Joe Walt, Guroff, Kirkpatrick and Isakov were joined by Des Moines banker and internationally known trade expert John Chrystal, a man personally acquainted with many in the Soviet leadership. Chrystal seemed to enjoy disagreeing with Dr. Kirkpatrick, took the measure of Guroff and endured Counselor Isakov's barbs. The general question and answer session which followed featured a lively debate between ardent conservatives in the audience and Guroff and Isakov. At one point it appeared that the dispute might come to blows, taken by some of the Simpson people as a sign that the evening was a rousing success.[242]

On Sunday morning, April 7, Dan Clark, Midwest projects coordinator for the Stanley Foundation of Muscatine, spoke at Smith Chapel. "Tell Our Leaders" was the title of his address which provided a Christian perspective of the U.S.S.R., drawing upon the experiences Clark had gained during a visit to the Soviet Union in 1984.[243]

* * *

It was my intention to conclude this account with the quasquicentennial. There is indeed something neat and tidy about rounding out the story of the life of anything in 100s or 125s or 150s. Yet there is also something accidental, almost arbitrary, about such chronological orderliness, and adhering slavishly to it runs the risk of concluding the Simpson story in mid-sentence. It is not hard to find that episode in the life of the college that provides the proper moment to pause, take note of where the institution is and fix one's gaze, Janus-like, both toward the record of the past and the promise of the future.

It was Campus Day, 1987, one of those crystal-clear early April days that seemed to be made for the occasion. With the ringing of the Old Chapel bell a few minutes after eight, students either fled their early classes or piled sleepy-eyed out of residence halls to see what all the excitement was about. This year, by careful prearrangement, there was real work to be done. Old concrete walkways were to be removed, bricks from other walkways taken up and cleaned, campus areas raked and cleaned up—in spite of the fact that improved campus maintenance made some of the cleanup almost superfluous. By sheer coincidence, a team of observers from the Council of Independent Colleges (C.I.C.) was on campus, doing a case study of Simpson for their national organization.

In its examination of the "academic workplace," the C.I.C. had surveyed colleges all across America "in an effort to identify organizational factors that support faculty morale." After tabulating faculty responses to a long list of questions intended to reveal the degree of satisfaction in the academic workplace, the C.I.C. selected ten institutions "where faculty satisfaction and high morale abound," for further study. Simpson was one of the ten institutions chosen for a site visit.[244]

The case study team arrived in Des Moines on the evening of April 6 and were driven to Indianola by acting dean Bruce Haddox and Roger Betsworth. Chosen by the C.I.C. because they were "noted nationally for their work on faculty issues," the two team members, Shirley Clark of the University of Minnesota and Peter Frederick of Wabash College, settled in for a two-day visit. They were as surprised as was most of the Simpson community when the bell signalled the beginning of Campus Day the next morning. They watched as students and faculty and administrators, including Dr. McBride himself, clad like others in work clothes, worked together at their assigned tasks. They talked about Simpson with anyone they could pry away from their labors. Almost without exception they found them decidedly positive. One administrator put it colorfully: "The college was on its butt in 1979," he said. "McBride put the college on its feet." Faculty people reportedly confirmed that sentiment. "The common mission in recent years is to get better," said one. "Here's a good school getting better all the time," said another. "People care about you here," was a frequent student comment. The team watched with growing interest the rest of the day's activities. Campus Day, they later reported, included "a very well-attended noontime picnic with a spontaneous program of students doing imitations of individual faculty members' teaching styles, and faculty/staff members (including the academic dean) then taking turns in front of the crowd doing imitations of some of their students in high camp and with good humor on all sides. Later in the day, many students, faculty, and staff turned out in the bright sunshine to cheer the men's baseball team as they beat arch rival Central College."

They heard people praise the decision to restore College Hall, all of them apparently understanding "the heavily symbolic role now played" by the building "in recovering a sense of historical perspective." Beyond this, the team saw a campus looking prosperous and well kept, a faculty whose morale was even higher than they had anticipated, a community with powerful loyalty to the institution, to each other and to a firm leader. In the modern saga of Simpson, "President McBride emerges as the popular organizational leader-hero."[245]

"You know," one of the team members was overheard the next morning to say to the other, "this is one hell of a place." Small wonder their report about Simpson fairly glowed. They had caught the College in one of those special moments when it was at its best.

But they had seen the real Simpson. In a century and a quarter the College, its faculty, students and leaders had changed; Indianola and Iowa and the larger world had been altered almost beyond recognition. But the qualities treasured by the College's founders were still there: collegiality, caring, dedication to the cultivation of both intellect and character and an almost palpable sense of community in the heart of the vast prairies of mid-America.

Simpson College
Department of Music

presents

Mozart's

Cosi fan Tutte
in English

under the direction of
Steven L. Stolen

Musical Direction by Nancy Hodge
Scenic Design by Kevin Wall

Studio Theater

Blank Performing Center

February 7 & 8, 1986 at 8:00 p.m.
February 9, 1986 at 2:00 p.m.

As opera became increasingly important at Simpson, student productions became a highlight of the College's musical year.

Epilogue

It is perhaps only fair to provide a brief outline of the major developments—or what in 1994 *seem* to have been the major developments—of the eight years that have elapsed since the quasquicentennial commencement of 1986.

Not long after the sunny Campus Day of 1987, President McBride retired at the age of sixty-three. At the 1987 commencement both McBride and his wife Luella were awarded the honorary doctorate, hers the first ever given to a president's wife. And the new baseball diamond on the west campus was named McBride Field. The president had announced his decision to retire a year earlier, allowing the board of trustees adequate time to seek a successor. Their choice fell upon the president of the School of the Ozarks, Stephen G. Jennings, determined by the search committee to be the best of nearly 150 candidates. Unlike most of Simpson's presidents during the twentieth century, Jennings presented credentials that were neither clerical nor strictly academic. He had indeed taught classes at the college level, but his professional experience had been primarily in the field of student development. He had served as dean of students at Furman University and Tulane University. His doctorate in counseling and human development from the University of Georgia was awarded in 1976.

In Steve Jennings, Simpson got a thoroughly competent manager who determined to take a good college and make it better. He came to Indianola with neither a ready-made agenda for dramatic academic reconstruction, as had Bill Kerstetter three decades earlier, nor a mandate for change in order to rescue Simpson from economic crisis, as had Bob McBride, his immediate predecessor. Rather he sought to direct the task of fine-tuning an already smoothly operating educational enterprise and to do so with as little fuss as possible.

By any measure Simpson prospered during the late 1980s and early 1990s. Enrollment continued to grow, until in the fall of 1993 an all time record of 1,718 were registered, including 1,116 full-time undergraduates and 602 part-time students in adult and continuing education. At the same time the quality of entering freshmen and transfer students, measured by high school rank, college preparatory courses taken, and ACT or SAT scores, continued to rise. Published college guides began listing Simpson as "very competitive," a designation reserved for only a handful of Iowa colleges. The college was listed for the first time in *Peterson's Guide*, which confined its listings to America's more prestigious institutions. *U.S. News and World Report* listed Simpson variously as "up and coming" or as one of the leading liberal arts colleges in the Midwest.

In 1990, with the local leadership of Dennis Hunt and excellent professional assistance, a fund-raising drive dubbed "Secure the Promise for Simpson," was undertaken. The most ambitious in Simpson history, the drive sought to raise $35 million during a five-year period, the funds to be used for endowment, a major science facility project, current operating expenses and the library. By 1993 the drive went over the top with $37 million raised. The linchpin of the drive was Amy Robertson's estate, amounting to very nearly $10 million, far and away the largest gift received by Simpson during its long history. Amy Robertson died May 31, 1992, at the age of ninety-four.

The growth of the college, together with the national rate of inflation, the latter far more moderate than it had been only a few years earlier, saw the annual budget soar past $20 million in the fall of 1993. Tuition that fall, having risen considerably faster than the inflation rate, was $10,720 for the year, while board, room, and student activity fee brought the total cost to $14,635. Lest these figures seem frightening, be it noted that ninety-two percent of all Simpson students that year received financial assistance in the form of scholarships, grants-in-aid, state tuition grants, work-study employment and loans. In fact, that year thirty-six percent of all tuition collected by the college was returned to students in one or another form of outright grant.

Supporting the whole enterprise was the College's powerful board of trustees, led by Owen Newlin, vice-president of Pioneer Hi-Bred International, a man of powerful convictions and unstinting devotion to Simpson's interests. In guiding Simpson he was given welcome assistance by other board members, including new young people like Jymm Oplt '72, Tom Schmidt '67, Bob Lester '64 and Karen A. "Kacie" Conner '69. When Newlin retired as chairman in 1992, his place was taken by Charles E. "Chuck" Rohm, vice-president of The Principal Financial Group.

Several new administrators joined the Simpson staff during these years. Soon after Jennings's arrival, a new vice-president and academic dean was selected. He was Jerry Israel, historian and administrator from Illinois Wesleyan University, replacing acting dean Bruce Haddox, who had filled in since the departure of Mel Henderson. Israel gave strong academic leadership until he was sirened away in 1993 to take over the presidency of Morningside College in Sioux City. In the office of development there was remarkable stability until the fall of 1993 when Bob Lane, director of development, was named the new director of development at Cornell College. Replacing him was Simpson's own highly competent associate admissions director, Cole Zimmerman '76, as director of major and planned gifts.

The core of the faculty also remained remarkably stable. A combination of good salaries and benefits at Simpson, combined with a generally dismal outlook for employment in the academic marketplace, meant that Simpson could keep most of the faculty it had and could attract superior people to fill the few places that became available. Especially noteworthy was the rapid growth of part-time adjunct faculty employed to assist with the adult and continuing education program. The College's catalog in the fall of 1993 listed eighty-two of these people in a wide variety of academic disciplines.

Burgeoning enrollments put real pressure on existing student residence facilities. During McBride's administration the college had purchased an apartment building at the corner of D Street and Clinton Avenue across the street to the south from Irving Elementary School. Named Hamilton House in honor of former president William E. Hamilton, it provided for only a fraction of housing needs. Therefore, in 1988 the board decided to erect a new residence hall on the west side of North D Street across from the Cowles Center. Called West Hall, it would accommodate seventy-two students in two attached units. Each unit contained a full basement and a two-story complex with lounge, student rooms and bathing facilities. West Hall was used, after 1992, as a freshman honors housing unit. Then, when the Kappa Kappa Gamma sorority reinstated their chapter at Simpson in 1990—one hundred years almost to the day since they had withdrawn the charter in 1890—the College agreed to finance a new chapter house. Actually it was a renovation of the old Watson residence on E Street just south of the College's intramural field. The handsome new house would accommodate forty women.

By all odds the most important construction project was the enlargement of the George Washington Carver Hall of Science, now designated as the George Washington Carver Science Center. For Simpson the cost was breathtaking—9.2 million dollars—but the results were outstanding. A new section was erected on the south which more than doubled the size of the facility, and between the new part and the old was constructed a huge atrium, separating while joining the two parts of the science complex. As soon as the new section was completed, workmen stripped the old building to its walls and refurbished everything. When the building, carefully shepherded to completion by Clifford Meints and Joe Moody, was dedicated on October 22, 1993, Simpson could boast one of the finest science facilities in the Midwest.

*   *   *

Simpson's students still reflected fairly faithfully the ethnic and racial makeup of Iowa, and nine-tenths of them were Iowans. They were mostly white and descended from English, Irish, German or Scandinavian immigrants. There were only a few students from abroad. Black students were relatively scarce, and there were only a handful of Asian, Jewish or Hispanic students or an occasional Native American. Methodist enrollment held up, while Catholic enrollment continued to increase modestly. Although religion was important to a fair segment of the campus population, denominational preference was no longer very important at all.

To the unsophisticated observer, all students looked more or less alike. Nearly everyone—male and female—wore jeans most of the time. Everyone wore extralarge sweat shirts or T-shirts, insisting that "one size fits all." Some wore shorts even in the wintertime, and most—especially young men still addicted to wearing baseball caps everywhere—would rather miss a meal than dress up to dine. It was not an era of sartorial splendor.

Their clothing represented only a fraction of the possessions they brought to school in the fall of the year. Eschewing the Spartan simplicity of bunk beds in the residence halls, many of them arrived early—usually with a willing father in tow as chief carpenter—to construct elaborate "loft" beds, the better to ensure privacy and room for the other impedimenta deemed essential for the rigors of dorm life. Indispensable were a stereo outfit capable of producing sound sufficient to entertain the entire campus, a refrigerator to contain sufficient snacks and beverages to keep one nourished at a college that provided only three meals a day, a microwave oven—mostly used for warming up leftover pizza, the latter an expensive student addiction—of course a television set, together with scrounged aging overstuffed sofas and a carpet sturdy enough to bear up for nine months without meaningful cleaning. Nearly every student owned an automobile, putting parking space at a premium.

Thus insulated from the rigors of college living, students engaged in as bewildering an array of activities as ever. Contrary to the conviction of a majority of faculty members, they did study. At least most of them did, some, to be sure, a lot more than others.

There were encouraging signs of change from earlier destructive behavior. By 1993 almost no one smoked any more. In 1992 President Jennings declared the entire campus a smoke-free zone, relenting only to permit smoking out-of-doors and in student rooms by prior agreement of roommates. Drug use was virtually nonexistent, condemned by nearly all students. In this, Simpson differed from many other colleges and universities, where drug use remained a vexing problem. Beer drinking, however, remained the favorite indoor student recreation, although valiant efforts by College officials and the national Greek-letter fraternities, driven by skyrocketing liability insurance costs, pressured Simpson's chapters to adopt serious "risk management" practices. Most of the groups responded positively, but excessive drinking continued to be the most important factor in student discipline problems at Simpson, as it had been for decades.

The fraternities and sororities continued to flourish, although membership in the men's groups varied widely. With their quota system, the sororities shared members more evenly. The colonization and installation of the Kappa Kappa Gamma chapter in 1988 and 1989 was very successful. These organizations, probably because of the members they selected or because of the fierce loyalties they engendered, enjoyed the lowest attrition rates of any identifiable campus grouping. A larger percentage of their members persisted to graduation than did nonaffiliated students.

By far the worst attrition rate at the College was in the football team. Because the gridders represented more than one-quarter of all fulltime male undergraduates, their dropout rate was a matter of serious concern. During the three years between 1990 and 1993 an average of forty-two percent of freshmen football players left Simpson by the end of the freshmen year. In other areas of athletics, male or female, the attrition rates were "normal." On the whole, athletics continued, under John Sirianni's leadership, to be as successful as they had ever been at Simpson and remained enormously popular with students.

One of the more difficult problems Jennings faced during the early years of his presidency was the need to change the nickname of Simpson's athletic teams, known since the early thirties as the Redmen. Simpson students and alumni were not anxious to change the name. Yet "Redmen" seemed increasingly to demean the American Indian, however unintentionally. It seemed to be the most sensible course of action to change the name before the request to do so came from outside the College as a nonnegotiable demand. A committee consisting of administrators, faculty, students and alumni considered a bewildering array of potential names before coming up with a recommendation that Simpson's teams be known henceforth as the "Simpson Storm." It was safe, alliterative, descriptive and calculated not to offend anyone except perhaps Zeus up on Mt. Olympus. Jennings accepted the recommendation, and beginning in the fall of 1992 the new name, with appropriate graphic symbolism, was quite smoothly adopted and put into use.

* * *

In an age of instant communication, the world has crowded in on Simpson as it has elsewhere. Among an increasing number of students one could discern a new cosmopolitanism. Few who returned from a May Term in China or six months in Germany would ever be quite the same again. When young men like Alan Sells and Chris Davidson returned to Simpson from "Desert Storm," the Gulf War, where they had served with their Marine reserve units, their view of the world had changed. The reinstatement of a foreign language requirement in the fall of 1992 contributed, too, to the change in atmosphere at the College. While some students remained sturdily resistant to the growing awareness of the world beyond Simpson, most joined willingly in this move toward a better alignment of the academic agenda of the faculty and the personal agendas of their students.

* * *

When, in the spring of 1995, Steve Jennings completed the eighth year of his presidency, he could look back upon a period of exceptional growth and development at Simpson, a healthy enterprise he ably superintended. In 1995 Simpson also found itself better equipped than it had ever been to take advantage of the opportunities afforded it. It had acquired the strength and the self-confidence to be itself, to be authentic, to cherish its past and savor with anticipation its future. And it had the resilience to anticipate and cope creatively with change. For if the history of Simpson could be any guide, no one could know what the morrow might bring.

Bibliography

Documents and Unpublished Manuscripts

Badley, Arthur Jr., diary.
Boss, Stephen C. "The Conservatory of Music under the Administration of Frank Ellis Barrows (1891–1924)." Simpson College, 1982.
Brown, Carl F. "Pigs Went to Chapel, and Some Other Unrecorded Events in the History of Simpson College." Paper presented to Indianola Iowa Quarter Century Club, November 1959.
Bys, Neil D. "A History of Dramatics at Simpson College." Simpson College, 1965.
Caldwell, Gilbert R. "History of Simpson College." Simpson College, 1947.
Calkin, Richard, "Simpson College Buildings." Simpson College, 1941.
Carpenter, Bernadine. "Statement of the Credits of Dr. George W. Carver." Simpson College, Registrar's Office, 1974.
Central States College Association, Board of Directors, Minutes, 1965–75.
Central States College Association Articles of Incorporation, April 1965.
Cohen, Richard M. "The Sixties at Simpson." Simpson College, 1992.
Dahnke, Dawnette M. "The Women's Issue at Simpson College as Seen through the Pages of the First Fifty Years of the *Simpsonian*." Simpson College, 1975.
"Declaration of Causes for Separation." Simpson College, president's file, 1938.
Des Moines Conference Seminary, Articles of Incorporation. Indianola, Iowa, 1864.
Des Moines Conference Seminary, Board of Trustees, Minutes, 1864–67.
Detlie, Edward. "History of the Iowa Sigma Chapter of Sigma Alpha Epsilon, 1889–1898." Simpson College, 1965.
Gamelin, Frank C. "CSCA: Twilight or Dawn?" Bloomington, Illinois, 1971.
Hartstack, Rozann. "Avery Craven's Simpson College Connection." Simpson College, 1986.
Hill, Luther L., Jr. "Simpson College Beginnings and College Hall." Simpson College, 1987.

Hillman, John H. "Memoirs." Simpson College, [1951].
"History of Delta Chapter, Delta Delta Delta: 1889–1989." Indianola: Delta Delta Delta, 1989.
"History of Iowa Beta [of Pi Beta Phi] House Corporation." Simpson College, 1971.
Indianola Male and Female Seminary, Articles of Incorporation. Indianola, Iowa, 1860.
Indianola Male and Female Seminary, Board of Trustees, Minutes, 1860–64.
"Ingram-Lieber-Helfrich-Walt Proposal." Simpson College, May 1970.
Jackson, Ruth. "A History of Simpson College." Simpson College, 1960.
John, Ralph C. "Recollections about Simpson." Berlin, Maryland, 1991.
Kerstetter, William E. "Simpson Memoirs." Sandwich, Massachusetts, 1991.
La Charité, Virginia A. "The History of Omicron Chapter of Kappa Kappa Gamma." Simpson College, February 1990.
Lancaster, Richard B. "Notes about Simpson, 1972–1979." Minneapolis, Minnesota, 1991.
LaVelle, Douglas, "The Survival of Peoples Bank, 1929–1933." Simpson College, 1970.
McBride, Robert E. "Simpson Recollections." Hot Springs Village, Arkansas, 1991.
———. "Memoirs." Hot Springs Village, Arkansas, 1992.
Moats, Francis Ireland. "The Educational Policy of the Methodist Episcopal Church Prior to 1860." Dissertation, University of Iowa, 1926.
Morley, John P. "Memories." Los Angeles, California, 1960.
"A Plan to Save College Hall." Simpson College, June 1983.
Purcell, Edward. "Memorandum to President Ralph John." Simpson College, November 1966.
"Proposal for Writing-Reading Laboratory for Culturally Deprived and Other Students Requiring Special Tutorial Assistance." Paper presented to Trustees of the Hawley Welfare Foundation of Des Moines, Iowa. Simpson College, April 1968.
"Report of President William E. Kerstetter to the Board of Trustees." Simpson College, June 1960.
"Report of a Survey of Simpson College: Under the Auspices of the Commission on Survey of Educational Institutions of the Methodist Episcopal Church," Floyd W. Reeves, Director. Chicago, June 1930.
"Simpson Alumni and Former Students Who Are Listed in *Who's Who in America*, 1946–47." Simpson College, 1948.
Simpson Centenary College, Articles of Incorporation. Indianola, Iowa, Simpson Centenary College, 1867.
Simpson Centenary College, Board of Trustees, Minutes. Simpson College, 1867–85.
Simpson Centenary College, Executive Committee of the Board of Trustees, Minutes. Simpson College, 1867–85.
Simpson College, Articles of Incorporation. Indianola, Iowa, Simpson College, 1885.
Simpson College, Board of Trustees, Minutes. Simpson College, 1885–.
Simpson College, Board of Trustees, Executive Committee, Minutes. Simpson College, 1885–.
Simpson College, Faculty Minutes. Simpson College, 1953–.

Taverner, Gilbert Y. "Years of Challenge: Religious Life at Simpson College—1968–1973." Simpson College, 1992.
Van Syoc, Edna. "Simpson College Library." Simpson College, n.d.
Warren County, Iowa, Warranty Deeds, Book E.
Watson, Harold Francis. "Memoirs of the Hillman Administration, 1919–1936." Simpson College, 1974.
Wright, Thomas. "A Historical Perspective of the Buildings on the Simpson College Campus." Simpson College, 1986.

Simpson College Publications

Alumni News Bulletin
"Annual Report of the President: 1969–1970." *Simpson College Bulletin*. Autumn 1970.
"Annual Report of the President of Simpson College to the Board of Trustees, 1939–1940."
Catalogue of the Des Moines Conference Seminary. Des Moines: Iowa State Register Book and Job Office, 1865.
Catalogue of Simpson Centenary College, 1867–1885.
Catalogue of Simpson College, 1885–.
College in Its Context: Annual Report of the President 1968–1969. Indianola: Simpson College, 1969.
Commencement Daily.
Educator. Simpson College, 1889–98.
First Annual Catalogue of the Officers and Students of the Indianola Male and Female Seminary for the Year 1860–61. Des Moines: Iowa State Register Office. 1861.
Honnold, Dora G., Sara E. Sigler, and Frank P. Henderson. *The Simpson College Songbook*. New York: Hinds, Noble and Eldredge, Publishers. 1910.
Password [Student handbook]. 1940–.
Presidential Papers. January 1986.
Quarterly Bulletin of Simpson College. 12 series. 1911–.
"The Seeking of a President." *Simpson College Bulletin*. Spring 1972.
Simpson Alumnus.
Simpson College Alumni Directory. 1960–.
Simpson College Bulletin.
Simpson Magazine.
Simpson Scene.
Simpsonian. 1870–.
Student's Handbook. Simpson College. 1894–.
Swain, Christie. "History of Simpson College." *Zenith*, 1935.
Tangent. 1889.
Zenith. 1896–.

Iowa Newspapers

Advocate-Tribune (Indianola), 1882–1923.
Atlantic News-Telegraph, 1970.

Burlington Hawkeye, 1879.
Des Moines Register, 1916–.
Des Moines Sunday Register, 1916–.
Des Moines Register and Leader, 1902–16.
Indianola Independent, 1870.
Indianola Herald, 1874–1944.
Indianola Journal, 1868–74.
Indianola People's Advocate, 1879–82.
Indianola Record, 1896–1944.
Indianola Record-Herald, 1944–45.
Indianola Republican, 1855–6.
Indianola Republican, (II) 1879.
Indianola Times, 1892–96.
Indianola Tribune (I), 1875–82.
Indianola Tribune (II), 1923–45.
Indianola Weekly Visitor, 1866–68.
Iowa State Register, 1860–1905.
Mount Pleasant Journal, 1870–78.
The People's Advocate, 1880–81.
Record-Herald and Indianola Tribune, 1946–.
Waterloo Daily Courier.
Warren County Leader, 1870–74.
Warren County News, 1884–89.
Warren County Record, 1893–96.
Warren County Tribune, 1873–75.
Warren (Iowa) Eagle, 1859.
Warren (Iowa) Record, 1874–79.
Weekly Indianola Banner, 1864–66.
Weekly Indianola Visitor, 1864–66.
Weekly (Indianola) Iowa Visitor, 1857–64.

Books and Periodicals

Algona College: A Story of Educational Beginnings. n.p.: n.d.
Armstrong, Florence A. *History of Alpha Chi Omega Fraternity 1885–1921.* 3rd ed. n.p.: Alpha Chi Omega, 1922.
Arrow of Pi Beta Phi.
Aurner, Clarence Ray. *History of Education in Iowa.* 5 vols. Iowa City: State Historical Society of Iowa, 1914–20.
Baird's Manual of American College Fraternities. 20th ed. Indianapolis: Baird's Manual Foundation, Inc., 1991.
Bangs, Carl. *Our Roots of Belief: Biblical Faith and Faithful Theology.* Kansas City: Beacon Hill Press, 1981.
Bangs, Nathan. *A History of the Methodist Episcopal Church.* New York: n.p., 1842.
Beineke, John A. "The Mark of Horace Mann in Iowa Education." *Palimpsest* 66 (May-June 1985), 101–05.
Belding, Robert E. "Academics and Iowa's Frontier Life." *Annals of Iowa* 44 (summer 1978), 335–58.

———. "Iowa's Brave Model for Women's Education." *Annals of Iowa* 43 (summer 1976), 342–48.
Biederman, Paul, ed. *Economic Almanac: 1967–1968 Business Factbook*. New York: The Macmillan Company, 1968.
Boesiger, W., ed. *Richard Neutra, 1961–66: Buildings and Projects*. New York: Frederick A. Praeger, 1966.
Bonomi, Ferne Gater. "Surprising Simpson." *The Iowan* 5 (October-November 1956), 14–17, 49ff.
Brickley, Donald P. *Man of the Morning: The Life and Work of Phineas F. Bresee*. Kansas City: Nazarene Publishing House, 1960.
Bucke, Emory Stevens, general. ed. *The History of American Methodism*. 3 vols. New York: Abingdon Press, 1964.
Bulletin of the American Association of University Professors 26 (December 1940), 613.
Cameron, Richard M. *Methodism and Society in Historical Perspective*. New York: Abingdon Press, 1961.
———. "The New Church Takes Root." In *The History of American Methodism*, Emory Stevens Bucke, ed., vol. 1, 241–90. New York: Abingdon Press, 1964.
Campbell, J. Duncan, and Harry S. Gorgas. *The Centennial History of the Phi Kappa Psi Fraternity: 1852–1952*. 2 vols. (1852–1902). n.p., Phi Kappa Psi Fraternity, 1952.
Cannon, William R. "Education, Publication, Benevolent Work, and Missions." In *The History of American Methodism*, ed. E. S. Bucke and Emory Stevens, vol. 1, 546–600. New York: Abingdon Press, 1964.
Carstensen, Vernon. "The University as Head of the Iowa School System." *Iowa Journal of History* 53 (July 1955), 213–46.
The Christian Century 103 (January 15, 1986), 55.
Christian Education Magazine. (January-February 1942).
Clark, Robert Donald. *The Life of Matthew Simpson*. New York: The Macmillan Company, 1956.
Clarke-Helmick, Elizabeth Allen. *The History of Pi Beta Phi Fraternity*. n.p.: Pi Beta Phi Fraternity, 1915.
Clayton, Benjamin F. "The 'Athens' of Iowa Methodism." *Midland Monthly* 4 (July 1895), 80–87.
Colleges With a Plus. Evanston: Central States College Association, 1966.
College-Related Church: United Methodist Perspectives. Nashville: National Commission on United Methodist Higher Education, 1976.
Country Journal, 9 (September 1982), 120.
Crescent of Delta Tau Delta.
Crooks, George Richard. *The Life of Bishop Matthew Simpson of the Methodist Episcopal Church*. New York: Harper and Brothers, 1890.
Cross & Crescent of Lambda Chi Alpha.
Cummings, A. W. *The Early Schools of Methodism*. New York: Phillips and Hunt, 1886.
Daniel, Dorothy. *Circle 'Round the Square: Pictures from an Iowa Childhood*. New York: Wilfred Funk, Inc., 1959.
Delta Upsilon Quarterly.
The Dial of Theta Upsilon
Diamond of Kappa Theta Psi.

Dodge, Estelle. *Sixty Years in Kappa Alpha Theta: 1870–1929*. Menasha, Wisconsin: Kappa Alpha Theta, 1930.

Duvall, Sylvanus M. *The Methodist Episcopal Church and Education up to 1869*. New York: Bureau of Publications, Teachers College, Columbia University, 1928.

Ensign, Forest C. "The Era of Private Academies." *Palimpsest*, 27 (March 1946), 75–85.

Erickson, Lori, "Simpson College." *The Iowan* 41 (September 1992), 34–41.

Fulton, C. J. "The Beginning of Education in Iowa." *Iowa Journal of History and Politics* 23 (April 1925), 171–91.

Girvin, E. A. *Phineas F. Bresee: A Prince in Israel*. Kansas City: Nazarene Publishing House, 1982.

A Good Place to Work: Sourcebook for the Academic Workplace. Washington, D.C.: Council of Independent Colleges, 1991.

Gross, John O. *The Beginnings of American Methodism*. New York: Abingdon Press, 1961.

―――. "The Field of Education, 1865–1939" In *The History of American Methodism*, E. S. Bucke, ed., vol. 3, 201–49. New York: Abingdon Press, 1964.

Higher Education for American Democracy. Report of the President's Commission on Higher Education, VI. Washington, D.C.: U. S. Government Printing Office, 1947.

Holt, Rackham. *George Washington Carver: An American Biography*. Rev. ed. Garden City: Doubleday, Doran and Company, Inc. 1963.

Jeffrey, Herbert N., ed. *Historical Sketch and Alumni Record of Iowa Wesleyan College*. Mount Pleasant: Mount Pleasant News Journal, 1917.

Johnson, Keach. "The State of Elementary and Secondary Education in Iowa in 1900." *The Annals of Iowa*, 49 (Summer-Fall 1987), 26–57.

Journal of the Thirteenth Annual Session of the Des Moines Conference of the Methodist Episcopal Church. Des Moines: Mills and Co., Printers, 1876.

Kappa Alpha Theta Catalogue. Ann Arbor: Kappa Alpha Theta Fraternity, 1908.

Kappa Alpha Theta.

Kerstetter, William E. "In All . . ., Get Understanding." *Journal of Higher Education*, 28 (December 1957), 489–93.

Kerstetter, William E. and Phillips Moulton. *An Experiment in General Education: Development and Education*. Nashville: Board of Education, the Methodist Church, 1957.

Key of Kappa Kappa Gamma.

Kirby, James E. "Matthew Simpson and the Mission of America." *Church History*, 36 (September 1967), 299–307.

Kuehn, Roy D., ed. *Grand Catalogue of the Phi Kappa Psi Fraternity*. Chicago: Phi Kappa Psi Fraternity, 1910.

The Lamp of Delta Zeta

Leckie, Robert. *The Story of Football*. New York: Random House, Inc., 1965.

Leuchtenburg, William E. *The Perils of Prosperity: 1914–32*. Chicago: University of Chicago Press, 1958.

Levere, William C. *History of the Sigma Alpha Epsilon Fraternity*. 3 vols. Evanston: Sigma Alpha Epsilon Fraternity, 1911.

Lorch, Fred W. "George Washington Carver's Iowa Education." *Iowan*, 13 (fall, 1964), 13–16, 51–52.

Lyre of Alpha Chi Omega.

McConn, Max. "Tired Business Men of the Campus." *North American Review*, 226 (November 1928), 548–49.

McCulloh, Gerald O. "John O. Gross (1894–1971)." In *Something More Than Human*. Nashville: United Methodist Board of Higher Education and Ministry, 1986.

McMurry, Linda O. *George Washington Carver: Scientist and Symbol*. New York: Oxford University Press, 1981.

Martin, W. C. *History of Warren County, Iowa*. Chicago: S. J. Clarke Publishing Co., 1908.

Minutes of the Annual Conferences of the Methodist Episcopal Church for the Year 1858. New York: Carlton and Porter, 1858.

Minutes of the First Session of the Western Iowa Annual Conference of the Methodist Episcopal Church. Des Moines: Mills Brothers, Printers, 1860.

Minutes of the Second Session of the Western Iowa Annual Conference of the Methodist Episcopal Church. Des Moines: F. W. Palmer, State Printer, 1861.

Minutes of the Third Session of the Western Iowa Annual Conference of the Methodist Episcopal Church. Des Moines: Iowa State Register Print., 1862.

Minutes of the Fourth Session of the Western Iowa Annual Conference of the Methodist Episcopal Church. Des Moines: Mills and Company, Printers, 1863.

Minutes of the First Session of the Des Moines Annual Conference of the Methodist Episcopal Church. Des Moines: Iowa State Register Office, 1864.

Minutes of the Second Session of the Des Moines Annual Conference of the Methodist Episcopal Church. Des Moines: n.p., 1865.

Minutes of the Third Session of the Des Moines Annual Conference of the Methodist Episcopal Church. Des Moines: Mills and Co., 1866.

Minutes of the Fourth Session of the Des Moines Annual Conference of the Methodist Episcopal Church. Des Moines: Mills and Co., 1867.

Minutes of the Fifth Annual Session of the Des Moines Conference of the Methodist Episcopal Church. Des Moines: Mills and Co., 1868.

Minutes of the Sixth Annual Session of the Des Moines Conference of the Methodist Episcopal Church. Des Moines: Orwig and Co., 1869.

Minutes of the Seventh Annual Session of the Des Moines Conference of the Methodist Episcopal Church. Omaha: Press of the Omaha Daily Republican, 1870.

Minutes of the Eighth Annual Session of the Des Moines Conference of the Methodist Episcopal Church. Omaha: Tribune and Republican Steam Printing House, 1871.

Minutes of the Eleventh Session of the Des Moines Annual Conference of the Methodist Episcopal Church. Des Moines: Clarkson Brothers, Printers, 1874.

Minutes of the Twenty-Ninth Annual Session of the Des Moines Conference of the Methodist Episcopal Church. Council Bluffs: Pryor's Bee Job Print, 1888.

Minutes of the Forty-Sixth Session of the Des Moines Annual Conference of the Methodist Episcopal Church. Harlan: Republican Office Print, 1905.

Minutes of the Sixteenth Session of the Iowa Annual Conference of the Methodist Episcopal Church. Des Moines: Mills Brothers, Printers, 1859.

Morison, Samuel Eliot. *Three Centuries of Harvard: 1636–1936*. Cambridge: Harvard University Press, Belknap Press, 1963.

Mott, Frank Luther. *A History of American Magazines*. 5 vols. Cambridge: Harvard University Press, 1938–68.

———. *American Journalism, A History: 1690–1960*, 3rd ed. New York: The Macmillan Company, 1962.

Norwood, Frederick A. *The Story of American Methodism.* Nashville: Abingdon Press, 1974.

Official Record of the Journal and Reports of the Twenty-First Session of the Des Moines Annual Conference of the Methodist Episcopal Church. Edited by W. T. Smith. Atlantic: Telegraph Steam Printing House, 1880.

Official Record of the Journal and Reports of the Twenty-Second Session of the Des Moines Annual Conference of the Methodist Episcopal Church. Edited by James Lisle. Des Moines: State Journal Printing House, 1881.

Official Record of the Journal and Reports of the Twenty-Third Session of the Des Moines Annual Conference of the Methodist Episcopal Church. Edited by James Lisle. Des Moines: Capital Publishing Company, Steam Printers, 1882.

Official Record of the Journal and Reports of the Twenty-Fourth Session of the Des Moines Annual Conference of the Methodist Episcopal Church. Edited by James Lisle. Des Moines: State Journal Mammoth Printing House, 1883.

Official Record of the Journal and Reports of the Twenty-Fifth Session of the Des Moines Annual Conference of the Methodist Episcopal Church. Edited by M. D. Collins. Indianola: Taylor and Schooley, Printers, 1884.

Official Record of the Journal and Reports of the Twenty-Sixth Session of the Des Moines Annual Conference of the Methodist Episcopal Church. Edited by M. D. Collins. Des Moines: Daily Capital Book and Job Printing House, 1885.

Official Record of the Journal and Reports of the Twenty-Seventh Session of the Des Moines Annual Conference of the Methodist Episcopal Church. Council Bluffs: Pryor's Bee Job Print, 1886.

Oneal, H. H., ed. *Register of the Ninth Session of the Des Moines Annual Conference.* Council Bluffs: Daily Nonpareil Steam Book and Job Office, 1872.

———. *Register of the Tenth Session of the Des Moines Annual Conference of the Methodist Episcopal Church.* Council Bluffs: Christian Advocate Book Press, 1873.

Ortega y Gasset, José. *The Revolt of the Masses.* New York: Norton, 1957.

Our Martyr President: Abraham Lincoln. New York: Abingdon Press, n.d.

Parish, Arlyn J. *History of Highland Community College.* Troy, Kansas: Trojan Graphics, 1983.

Parker, George F. *The History of Warren County, Iowa.* Des Moines: Union Historical Company, 1879.

Parker, L. F. "Evolution of the Iowa High School." *Annals of Iowa* 33 (April 1956), 289–95.

Petersen, William J. "Public Education in 1854." *Palimpsest* 35 (November 1954), 469–84.

Priddy, Bessie Leach. *A Detailed Record of Delta Delta Delta: 1888–1931.* Menasha, Wisconsin: George Banta Publishing Company, 1932.

Proceedings of the Fifteenth Session of the Des Moines Annual Conference of the Methodist Episcopal Church. Atlantic, Iowa: Telegraph Steam Book and Job Office, 1878.

Proceedings of the Twentieth Session of the Des Moines Annual Conference of the Methodist Episcopal Church. Des Moines: State Leader Job Rooms, 1879.

Purinton, Edward Earl. "Big Ideas from Big Business." *The Independent* 56 (April 1921), 395.

Rainbow of Delta Tau Delta.

Record of Sigma Alpha Epsilon.

Register of the Ninth Session of the Des Moines Annual Conference. Council Bluffs: Daily Nonpareil Steam Book and Job Office, 1872.

Register of the Twelfth Session of the Des Moines Annual Conference of the Methodist Episcopal Church. Des Moines: Mills and Company, Printers, 1875.

Register of the Fourteenth Session of the Des Moines Annual Conference of the Methodist Episcopal Church. Des Moines: State Journal Steam Printing House, 1877.

Ritchey, Charles J. *Drake University through Seventy-Five Years: 1881–1956.* Des Moines: Drake University, 1956.

Rudolph, Frederick. *The American College and University: A History.* New York: Alfred A. Knopf, 1965.

Schultz, Gerard and Don L. Berry. *History of Warren County, Iowa.* Indianola: The Record and Tribune Company, 1953.

Scott, Beth and Michael Norman. *Haunted Heartland.* Madison: Stanton and Lee, Publishers, 1985.

Scudder, M. L. *American Methodism.* Hartford: S. S. Scranton and Company, 1867.

Seventh General Catalog of the Delta Tau Delta Fraternity. New York: Delta Tau Delta Fraternity, 1917.

Simpson, Matthew. *Cyclopaedia of Methodism.* Philadelphia: Everts and Stewart, 1878.

———. *The Methodist.* II. n.p.: n.d.

Spectator 53 (December 1968).

Star and Lamp of Pi Kappa Phi.

Stevens, Abel. *The Centenary of American Methodism.* New York: Carlton and Porter, 1866.

Stone, Arlington J. "The Dawn of a New Science." *The American Mercury* 14 (August 1928), 446.

Swisher, Jacob A. "The Rise of Education." *Palimpsest* 16 (May 1935), 137–66.

———. "Public School Beginnings." *Palimpsest* 20 (September 1939), 281–94.

Tewksbury, Donald G. *The Founding of American Colleges and Universities Before the Civil War.* New York: Bureau of Publications, Teachers College, Columbia University, 1932. Reprint, New York: Arno Press and the New York Times, 1969.

Tridelt of Delta Delta Delta.

Trueblood, Elton. *The Idea of a College.* New York: Harper and Brothers Publishers, 1959.

Turnbull, John E. *The Iowa Conference Story: Forty Years of Intercollegiate Sports, 1922 to 1961.* Iowa City: State Historical Society of Iowa, 1961.

Tutt, Wendell. *Alpha Tau Omega: First Century at Simpson, 1885–1985.* Indianola: Beta Alpha of Alpha Tau Omega, 1985.

The Urn of Beta Sigma Omicron

Van Cleave, Charles L. *The History of the Phi Kappa Psi Fraternity.* Philadelphia: Franklin Printing Company, 1902.

"Vietnam Moratorium Observance." Handout "courtesy of Monad Free Press," October 15, 1969.

Vickers, John. *Thomas Coke, Apostle of Methodism.* Nashville: Abingdon Press, 1969.

Wall, Joseph Frazier. *Iowa: A Bicentennial History.* New York: W. W. Norton and Company, Inc., 1978.

Walt, Joseph W. *The Era of Levere: A History of the Sigma Alpha Epsilon Fraternity, 1910–1930.* Evanston: Sigma Alpha Epsilon Fraternity, 1972.

——— "On What Really Matters . . ." *Simpson Alumnus* (March 1968), 6–9.

Wentworth, Harold, and Stuart Berg Flexner, eds. *Dictionary of American Slang*, 2nd supplemented ed. New York: Thomas Y. Crowell Company, 1975.

Wieck, P. R. "Hard-pressed Democrats in Iowa." *New Republic* 159 (October 1968), 14.

Wilson, Clarence True. *Matthew Simpson: Patriot, Preacher, Prophet.* New York: Methodist Book Concern, 1929.

Notes

Preface

1. As quoted in Jerry W. Knudson, "Late to the Feast: Newspapers as Historical Sources," *Perspectives* (American Historical Association), 31 (October 1993), 11.

Prologue

1. Citizens delayed the incorporation of Indianola, fearing increased taxation. Articles of incorporation were filed in October 1863, and the first city elections were held March 7, 1864. The county courthouse was completed in 1868.
2. George F. Parker, *The History of Warren County, Iowa* (Des Moines: Union Historical Company, 1879), 479.
3. Ibid., 480.
4. John O. Gross, "The Field of Education, 1865–1939," in E. S. Bucke, ed., *The History of American Methodism* (New York: Abingdon Press, 1964), III, 202.
5. *Minutes of Several Conversations Between the Rev. Thomas Coke, LL.D., the Reverend Francis Asbury and Others, at a Conference Begun in Baltimore, in the State of Maryland, on Monday, the 27th of December, in the Year 1784. Composing a Form of Discipline for the Ministers, Preachers and Other Members of the Methodist Episcopal Church in America* (Philadelphia, 1785), 12.
6. M. L. Scudder, *American Methodism* (Hartford: S. S. Scranton & Co., 1867), 395.
7. In 1787 one-third of all Methodists in America were in Maryland.
8. Scudder, *American Methodism*, 393.
9. The Presbyterians were clearly outdistanced by the Methodists, but by 1860 Irish and German immigration into the United States was bringing in large numbers of Catholics and Lutherans.
10. John O. Gross, "The Field of Education," 201.
11. William R. Cannon, "Education, Publication, Benevolent Work, and Missions," in E. S. Bucke, ed., *The History of American Methodism*, I, 550.
12. Sylvanus M. Duvall, *The Methodist Episcopal Church and Education up to 1869* (New York: Bureau of Publications, Teachers College, Columbia University, 1928), 43.
13. Cited in ibid., 47.
14. "We must educate our children to keep them with us," wrote one Methodist cleric, pointing out that education had always been the province of the Christian church. Richard M. Cameron, *Methodism and Society in Historical Perspective* (New York: Abingdon Press, 1961), 231–32. See also Sylvanus M. Duvall, *The Methodist Episcopal Church and Education up to 1869*, 76.

15. McKendree College in Lebanon, Illinois, the first Methodist college in the West, was founded in 1828. It claims to be the oldest permanent Methodist college in America. It was a teacher training academy until 1834 when it was first converted into a college, and it was only in 1841 that the first students were admitted to collegiate-grade academic work. Establishing the founding dates of colleges and universities is an inexact science. See William R. Cannon, "Education, Publication, Benevolent Work, and Missions," 559.

16. John O. Gross, *The Beginnings of American Methodism* (New York: The Abingdon Press, 1961), 117.

17. Upper Iowa College continued its Methodist affiliation until 1928. Since that time it has been under private control, and is now known as Upper Iowa University. See John O. Gross, "The Field of Education," 204.

18. Jacob A. Swisher, "Pioneer Learning," *Palimpsest* 16 (May 1935), 137–39; Jacob A. Swisher, "Public School Beginnings," *Palimpsest* 20 (September 1939), 281–94; Vernon Carstensen, "The University as Head of the Iowa School System," *Iowa Journal of History* 53 (July 1955), 215–16; William J. Petersen, "Public Education in 1854," *Palimpsest* 35 (November 1954), 473–79.

19. "Biennial Message of the Governor of Iowa . . . December 9, 1854," *Iowa Senate Documents, 1854–1855*, 5, as cited in Vernon Carstensen, "The University as Head of the Iowa School System," 218.

20. Vernon Carstensen, "The University at Head of the Iowa School System," 223.

21. The rest included 104 in the preparatory department and 129 in the normal course.

22. The first graded school in Iowa was established at Muscatine in 1851.

23. Iowa reflected what was going on in the rest of the country. It is estimated that more than 6,000 academies were established in the United States, most of which were closed as public secondary education spread.

24. L. F. Parker, "Evolution of the Iowa High School," *Annals of Iowa* 33 (April 1956), 292.

25. Vernon Carstensen, "The University as Head of the Iowa School System," 232, 235. At that same time, sixteen of twenty private colleges in Iowa maintained preparatory departments.

Chapter 1

1. *First Annual Catalogue of the Officers and Students of the Indianola Male and Female Seminary, for the Year 1860–61* (Des Moines: Iowa State Register Office, 1861), 16.

2. This account of the first meeting of the founders is drawn from the *Weekly Indianola Visitor*, August 9, 1860.

3. Both Griffith and his associate, R. W. Manley, had attended Ohio Wesleyan University.

4. Originally constructed by School District No. 3 of Washington Township in 1855, the building was sold to Charles C. Griffith on February 29, 1856, for $1,131, the vendors "authorized to sell and convey the same by vote of the District." Warren County, Iowa, WD, Book E, p. 159.

5. *Indianola Republican*, December 6, 1855.

6. Ibid.

7. An announcement calling attention to the opening of the spring term, 1857, appeared in the *Weekly Iowa Visitor*, April 2, 1857.

8. *Advocate-Tribune*, June 9, 1910.

9. *Weekly Iowa Visitor*, April 2, 1857.

10. No mathematics was offered beyond plane geometry nor were any of the foreign languages, ancient or modern.

11. *Weekly Iowa Visitor*, June 3, 1858.

12. Ibid., December 2, 1858.

13. *Minutes of the Sixteenth Session of the Iowa Annual Conference of the Methodist Episcopal Church*, Muscatine, Ia., Sept. 7–12, 1859 (Des Moines: Published by Order of the Conference, 1859), p 30.

14. Arthur Badley, Jr., Diary, 134.

15. *Weekly Indianola Visitor*, August 16, 1860.

16. *Minutes of the First Session of the Western Iowa Annual Conference of the Methodist Episcopal Church*, Indianola, Iowa, August 22 to 27, 1860 (Des Moines: Published by Order of the Conference, 1860), 9.

17. Ibid., 8. Italics in the original.

18. *Weekly Indianola Visitor*, August 30, 1860.

19. Queensware was relatively inexpensive glazed English earthenware.

20. In a later incarnation this institution was called the First National Bank.

21. George F. Parker, *The History of Warren County, Iowa* (Des Moines: Union Historical Co., 1879), 655. One must, of course, be exceedingly cautious in accepting as factual the laudatory language contained in biographies appended to county histories.

22. That was in 1864. Indianola, ever leery about high property taxes, did not incorporate until October 5, 1863.

23. Winans would be selected principal of the Seminary during its second year, and Badley was the uncle of the College's first graduate, Brenton T. Badley, in 1870.

24. *Weekly Indianola Visitor*, April 26, 1860.

25. Ibid., August 23, 1860.

26. The Warren County vote was 1,152 for Lincoln, 795 for Douglas, 40 for Bell and 2 for Breckenridge. Iowa gave Lincoln 70,118 and Douglas 55,639.

27. *Weekly Indianola Visitor*, October 18, 1860.

Chapter 2

1. September 10, 1860.

2. It will be recalled that Augusta was the first Methodist college organized (1822) after Cokesbury had been destroyed. It survived until 1844, was briefly resuscitated a few years later and then went down for the second time. Gray's M.A. was an unearned degree, awarded a few years after his graduation from college. That was consistent with the practice of the day.

3. Chartered in 1842, the school changed its name to Iowa Wesleyan University in 1854 and in that same year erected a fine new building, 55 by 100 feet and three stories high, at a cost of $22,000.

4. *Weekly Indianola Visitor*, September 13, 1860.

5. *Minutes of the First Session of the Western Iowa Annual Conference of the Methodist Episcopal Church*, August 22–27, 1860 (Des Moines: 1860), 25.

6. *First Annual Catalogue of the Officers and Students of the Indianola Male and Female Seminary, for the Year 1860–61* (Des Moines: Iowa State Register Office, 1861), 9.

7. Ibid., 12.

8. *Weekly Indianola Visitor*, September 13, 1860.

9. The second thirteen-week term commenced December 31, 1860, and the third term, of fourteen weeks duration, opened on April 8, 1861, ending July 12. Of the 184 students, 109 were girls and 75 boys. Only thirteen came from outside Warren County, one of whom was from Illinois.

10. *Weekly Indianola Visitor*, December 27, 1860.

11. Of these streets only North C Street remains, the others closed off as the campus of the College expanded.

12. *Weekly Indianola Visitor*, January 17, 1861.

13. Indianola Male and Female Seminary, Board of Trustees, Minutes, February 6, 1861.

14. Fortunately the contractor was able subsequently to collect the pledges. Ibid., March 29, 1861.

15. *Weekly Indianola Visitor*, April 4, 1861.

16. Ibid., January 17, 1861. It may strike the reader as strange that these teachers would consent to meet all day on Christmas Eve or Christmas Day. For them it was not unusual at all. Christmas was a religious but not a secular holiday, and it was little observed among protestants on the frontier in the nineteenth century. Extensive celebration of Christmas was only indulged in by "Irish papists" and "sentimental Germans."

17. This institute, in addition to lamenting the evils of profanity, tobacco chewing, irregular

attendance and illegible handwriting, resolved that in the matter of teachers' salaries, "like services should receive like compensation, whether rendered by male or female teachers." As recently as 1859, the average weekly salary for male teachers in Warren County had been $13.55, for women teachers $4.49. Ibid.

18. *Advocate-Tribune*, May 26, 1910.

19. *Weekly Indianola Visitor*, March 7, 1861. The "Querist's" questions seem to concede that the teaching in the seminary was superior to that received in the common schools.

20. Ibid., March 21, 1861. Stover also indulged in an attack on the person he wrongly guessed to be the "Querist," calling him a "penurious scavenger," a non-taxpayer who was "sucking the life blood of the public."

21. Ibid., March 28, 1861.

22. Ibid., April 4, 1861. At no time during the controversy did Stover's superior, Wesley M. White (also a Methodist), speak out on Stover's behalf. White, who served as county superintendent of schools from 1859 to 1863, was even suspected for a time to have been the "Querist," a suggestion flatly denied by editor Knox, who was in a position to know.

23. Ibid., July 18, 1861.

24. Indianola Male and Female Seminary, Board of Trustees, Minutes, July 10, 1861.

25. *Historical Sketch and Alumni Record of Iowa Wesleyan College* (Mount Pleasant: Iowa Wesleyan College, 1917), 21. Hereafter cited as *Historical Sketch, I. W. C.*

26. Indianola Male and Female Seminary, Board of Trustees, Minutes, July 10, 1861.

27. Ibid., August 1861.

28. He is listed as Iowa Wesleyan's tenth graduate, one of four in the class of 1858. *Historical Sketch, I. W. C.*, 134.

29. William E. Hamilton penned the recollections of his early years at the College in the *Simpsonian*, February 1894. See also *Simpsonian*, October 15, 1904.

30. Ibid.

31. Ibid.

32. *First Annual Catalog of the Officers and Students of the Indianola Male and Female Seminary, for the Year 1860–61* (Des Moines: Iowa State Register Office, 1861).

33. Ibid.

34. Indianola Male and Female Seminary, Board of Trustees, Minutes, April 2, 1863.

35. Today this position is called district superintendent.

36. During Rev. Winans's second year (1862–63), J. C. Jordan, Rev. A. H. Murphy and Rev. U. P. Golliday left the board of trustees; the Revs. Dugald Thompson and R. S. Robinson (who had served in 1860–61) were elected. Also named was attorney Hugh W. Maxwell, who later would be appointed a district judge. On the bench, it was said, he was "the great enemy of violators of the liquor laws of the State, and his judgments, though warranted by the law, were often thought severe." George F. Parker, *History*, 372.

37. He would later recall with dismay, however, the time the *Weekly Indianola Visitor* reported one of his sabbath evening lectures alongside a display advertisement run by a local pharmacy: "Bininger's Old London Dock Gin—Gin as a Remedial Agent—This Delicious Tonic Stimulant—Especially designed for use of the MEDICAL Profession and the Family. . . ." He realized that his work was cut out for him.

38. George F. Parker, *The History of Warren County, Iowa* (Des Moines: Union Historical Company, 1879), 532.

39. Ibid., 531–32. No sooner had Rev. Arthur Badley come to Indianola (in the fall of 1864) as pastor of the Methodist church than reports reached the town that the war had come closer to home than they imagined. Badley wrote in his diary that "the rebellion is still raging and this evening rumor comes to town that the rebels are making a raid up in Iowa and are within 12 or 14 miles of the town. All is commotion and excitements. The drumbeats, the fife peels [sic] out its clear shrill notes—the men gather at the Court House. Finaly [sic] the meeting is organized. The Mesingers [sic] state what they know, but more of what they have heared [sic]. . . . So they Call for Volenters [sic] to go out." No rebels were found, but the town remained in an uproar for days.

40. *Minutes of the Second Session of the Western Iowa Annual Conference of the Methodist Episcopal Church*, September 4–7, 1861 (Des Moines: F. W. Palmer, State Printer, 1861), 6–7.

41. Orlando H. Baker, Sydney, N. S. W., Australia, letter to J. B. Gifford, Indianola, Ia., August 19, 1903.

42. The writer of an article in the *Atlantic News-Telegraph*, September 26, 1970, identifies the seminary at Brookville as the predecessor of Simpson College, stating that the school at Brookville "was later moved by the Methodist church to Indianola." It was not. Only the coincidence of name ties the two institutions. Others have erred in creating associations with Simpson College that never existed. The *Simpsonian* reported in its November 20, 1945, issue that the Osceola Seminary, founded by John H. L. Scott, father-in-law of Simpson's first graduate, Brenton H. Badley, "was later moved to Indianola and developed into Bluebird Seminary which became Simpson College."

43. *Minutes of the First Session of the Des Moines Annual Conference of the Methodist Episcopal Church*, August 31–September 4, 1864 (Des Moines: Iowa State Register Office, 1864), 14.

44. Orlando H. Baker to J. B. Gifford, August 19, 1903.

45. Ibid.

46. Ibid.

47. Ibid.

48. *Advocate-Tribune*, May 26, 1910.

49. Arthur Badley, Jr., diary, 146.

50. The faculty included Baker and his wife, together with L. Helen Boothby in mathematics, Celeste Scott in the primary department, and the Misses J. Causin Kern and Emma D. Thorpe in music and drawing.

51. The name of the conference was changed from "Western Iowa" to "Des Moines" in 1864.

52. *Minutes of the Second Session of the Des Moines Annual Conference of the Methodist Episcopal Church*, August 30–September 4, 1865 (Des Moines: Iowa State Register Office, 1865), 10.

53. Arthur Badley, Jr., diary, 148, 153.

54. The board did regret Baker's departure and on June 27, 1866, passed a resolution of thanks for his three years of work during which he had "labored unremittingly and successfully" for the school. Des Moines Conference Seminary, Board of Trustees, Minutes, June 27, 1866.

55. Ibid., July 2, 1866.

56. Ibid.

57. Belle Babb had graduated valedictorian of her class at Iowa Wesleyan University in the spring of 1866, and upon her return in 1867 to Mount Pleasant after her sojourn in Indianola, began the study of law in the office of her brother, Washington I. Babb. The next year she married John M. Mansfield, a professor of science at Iowa Wesleyan, but did not interrupt her legal studies. In those days few attorneys were educated in law schools; rather they "read law" in the office of a practicing lawyer until they felt ready to sit for the state bar examination. Miss Babb was ready soon enough, and upon successful completion of the law examination before two Mount Pleasant attorneys, she was admitted to the Iowa bar in the U.S. district court at Mount Pleasant.

58. Arabella Babb Mansfield was not the first to attempt to be admitted to the bar. Earlier that year—1869—one Myra Colby Bradwell was refused a license to practice law in Illinois because of the "disability" of being a wife and mother. See *Simpson College Bulletin*, Summer 1969.

59. Des Moines Conference Seminary, Board of Trustees, Minutes, August 11, 1866.

60. See W. C. Martin, *History of Warren County, Iowa* (Chicago: The S. J. Clarke Publishing Co., 1908), 253.

61. St. Matthew, 6:19.

62. Trustees had probably considered at least one alternative to naming the College for Bishop Ames. In what was apparently a lapse of the pen, the secretary of the board of trustees at one place in his minutes referred to the school as Kingsley College. Calvin Kingsley of Cleveland, Ohio, was another prominent Methodist bishop of that day. Des Moines Conference Seminary, Board of Trustees, Minutes, August 11, 1866.

63. "The citizens take a deep interest in the Seminary, and are now raising a building, and an endowment fund. The subscriptions for the former have reached nearly $20,000, and it is

the intention to lay the foundation of the new building the coming Autumn. . . . The endowment fund has not been fully subscribed. They hope to raise $20,000, and judging from the united effort put forth, it is not improbable that they will succeed." *Weekly Indianola Visitor*, May 23, 1867.

64. Arthur Badley, diary, 154.
65. Ibid.
66. *Minutes of the Fourth Session of the Des Moines Annual Conference of the Methodist Episcopal Church*, September 19–24, 1867 (Des Moines: Mills & Co., 1867), 12.
67. Ibid., passim.
68. Arthur Badley, diary, 154.
69. *Minutes . . . Conference*, 1867, 17.
70. *Weekly Indianola Visitor*, September 5, 1867.

Chapter 3

1. *Simpsonian*, December 1893. As early as 1869 the board of trustees was urging the conference to use the name "Simpson College." Simpson Centenary College, Board of Trustees Minutes, June 9, 1869.
2. Madison College, at Uniontown, Pa., closed in 1832 when the Methodist Church shifted its patronage to Allegheny College at Meadville, Pa. Two detailed biographies of Matthew Simpson exist. The earlier volume is George R. Crooks, *The Life of Bishop Matthew Simpson* (New York: Harper and Brothers, 1891); the more recent one is Robert D. Clark, *The Life of Matthew Simpson* (New York: The Macmillan Company, 1956).
3. Allegheny had already awarded Matthew Simpson an honorary M.A.
4. The college, named in honor of Bishop Francis Asbury, changed its name in 1883 to DePauw University, in recognition of a gift from Washington C. DePauw.
5. James E. Kirby, "Matthew Simpson and the Mission of America," *Church History*, 36 (September 1967), 302.
6. Matthew Simpson, "The Missionary Cause," *The Methodist*, 2 (November 23, 1861), 362, as cited in ibid., 304.
7. Indianola people had met Simpson when he presided at the Des Moines conference at Osceola in 1865, only a few months after he had delivered the funeral oration for Lincoln.
8. The seven carry-over trustees were George E. Griffith, David Hallam, Rev. Simpson Guyer, Jephtha Turner, John Cheshire, J. D. McCleary and Rev. J. F. Goolman. Rev. Guyer was the Methodist minister at Indianola; Rev. Goolman served as presiding elder of the Des Moines district.
9. No copies of the 1866–67 or 1867–68 catalog exist, and it is possible that none was published in any of those years. Hence, enrollment figures for those years can only be guessed. It does appear that, in anticipation of elevating the seminary to collegiate grade, the Rev. Vernon offered some college-level instruction during the 1866–67 academic year, for we know that there was a small sophomore class in 1867–68 and a junior class of six in 1868–69. The seminary, during the seven years it operated independently, offered a four-year program that was a fairly typical classical secondary course of study. When the school was upgraded to a college in 1867, the preparatory course was reduced to two years, suggesting that at least a part of the seminary's work was considered to be at the collegiate level. In fact, the conference seminary catalog for 1864–65 announced a one-year "preparatory" course and a four-year collegiate course of study. "The degree of A.B. is conferred upon students who complete the [Classical Course] of study and B.S. upon those who complete the [Scientific Course]." It is doubtful, however, that much of this instruction was truly of collegiate grade. Further, in 1865–66 the catalog lists by name seven sophomores and eighteen freshmen in this "collegiate" program, together with sixty-three in the preparatory department and thirty-nine in the primary department, not to speak of twenty-five music students. *Catalogue of the Des Moines Conference Seminary* (Des Moines: Iowa State Register Book and Job Office, 1865).
10. In 1866, for example, Northwestern University enrolled 39 in the collegiate course and 94 in its academy, Illinois Wesleyan 53 and 183, Iowa Wesleyan 24 and 100.

11. *Simpsonian*, February 1894. Hamilton was exaggerating a bit. Vernon was scarcely four years his senior.

12. *Indianola Weekly Visitor*, March 19, 1868.

13. *Simpsonian*, February 1894. Hamilton was not one to complain. He said of his chemistry students, "Every one of that class achieved success in life. Some did valiant work on both sides of the sea, but I never claimed that any considerable measure of it was due to the chemistry they learned of me." Ibid.

14. *Iowa Weekly Visitor*, May 14, 1868.

15. *Indianola Journal*, August 27, 1868.

16. Ibid., September 3, 1868.

17. Ibid., October 29, 1868 and December 24, 1868.

18. Gerard Schultz and Don L. Berry, *History of Warren County, Iowa* (Indianola, Ia.: The Record and Tribune Co., 1953), 37.

19. Simpson Centenary College, Board of Trustees, Minutes, June 9, 1869. These minutes contain a fairly complete account of the board's travails with contractor Reichard.

20. *Warren County Leader*, September 15, 1870.

21. *The Quarterly Bulletin of Simpson College*, 12th series, April, 1911.

22. The financial problems consequent to the failures of the contractor continued to plague the College for several years. As late as 1875, for example, one Charles Nichols was still trying to collect on some work he had done on the construction of the building. And in 1880 the College lost in a legal action, a mechanic's lien, brought against the College by some of Reichard's workers.

23. *Iowa Weekly Visitor*, March 19, 1868. After graduation from Drew Theological Seminary in 1869, Vernon had a distinguished career in the ministry in the eastern part of the United States. In 1906 he was elected to the chair of Christian Ethics and Biblical Theology at Temple University. He was the author of several books, one of them on his favorite topic: *Prohibition* (1887). He died May 27, 1920.

24. Simpson Centenary College, Board of Trustees, Minutes, March 2, 1868.

25. *Iowa Weekly Visitor*, March 26, 1868.

26. *Indianola Journal*, June 4, 1868. Editor Knox changed the name of the *Visitor* to the *Indianola Journal* in the spring of 1868.

27. The thermometer had soared to 105 degrees on the twentieth. Burns's wife, who was pregnant, "suffered mightily" from the heat.

28. *Indianola Journal*, January 7, 1869.

29. Ibid., August 13, 1868.

30. Henry F. Douthart married in 1871 and raised a family, and ended up in Kansas, where, in 1896, he successfully pushed through a prohibition amendment to the Kansas constitution and unsuccessfully ran for governor on the prohibition ticket. He died in 1899.

31. It is worthy of note that Miss McKean, whose teaching experience—none—matched that of Douthart, earned less than he. But the discrepancy in women's salaries at Simpson was not nearly as bad as it was in the public schools, where men were earning one-third more than women for the same work.

32. No one based his claim for improved salary on inflation. From the end of the Civil War until after the turn of the century the American economy experienced a prolonged period of deflation. In general, prices declined sharply until they stood, in 1903, where they had been in 1851. See Paul Biederman, ed., *Economic Almanac: 1967–1968 Business Factbook* (New York: The Macmillan Company, 1968), 397.

33. *Minutes of the Fifth Annual Session of the Des Moines Conference of the Methodist Episcopal Church* (Des Moines: Mills and Co., 1868), 21.

34. *Minutes of the Sixth Annual Session of the Des Moines Conference of the Methodist Episcopal Church* (Des Moines: Orwig & Co., 1869), 20.

35. *Indianola Journal*, September 2, 1869. See also *Minutes of the Seventh Annual Session of the Des Moines Conference of the Methodist Episcopal Church* (Omaha: Omaha Daily Republican, 1870), 16.

36. It was not until the 1879–80 year, when the Rev. Thomas S. Berry took over as president of the College, that the scientific course was expanded to four years.

37. During the mid-nineteenth century, literary societies were by all odds the most popular student organizations all over America, their contribution to the life of the colleges being both academic and social.

38. *Catalogue of Simpson Centenary College,* 1870–71 (Indianola: Mills and Co., 1871), 25. This same statement, essentially unaltered, remained in the catalog throughout the decade of the Burns administration.

39. While it was open, Joseph Wachenheimer's saloon was referred to as the "Blue Goose." Lewis Todhunter called that a slander on the goose.

40. Grant carried Warren County 1,946 to 933 for Horatio Seymour, the Democratic candidate. In 1872 Grant outpolled Horace Greeley 2,128 to 791.

41. *Indianola Journal,* January 14, 1869.

42. *Mt. Pleasant Journal,* as quoted in *Indianola Journal,* January 21, 1869.

43. *Indianola Journal,* April 29, 1869.

44. Ibid.

45. Ibid.

46. The fifth district, one of Iowa's seven at that time, was immense, embracing twenty-three counties in the southwestern part of the state including Polk.

47. That commencements were considered to be of major importance is reflected by the coverage this "trial-run" commencement received in the local press, which gave long synopses of all the principal addresses and sermons and extensive reviews of all the exhibitions and examinations, in all more than two full columns. *Indianola Journal,* June 10, 1869.

48. He was widely suspected of being a Democrat.

49. No program of the 1870 commencement is known to have survived. Nor is there any file of the *Indianola Journal* for the months from January to October 1870. The short-lived *Independent* and its successor, the *Warren County Leader,* did not begin publication until July 1870, and the establishment of the *Simpsonian* came only the following October.

50. William A. Burke '09, stated many years later that his mother, Louisa Anderson, was runner-up in scholarship and so should have delivered the salutation, but that she gave way to Emma Cary, because "Miss Cary could write such beautiful Latin."

51. Both the diplomas and the seal had been procured from Mills and Co., engravers, lithographers and printers in Des Moines.

52. Badley's uncle, the Rev. Henry Badley, had been a member of the first board of trustees of the old Indianola Seminary; for several years his father had been a seminary trustee and a conference visitor. His brothers, Ed and Charlie, and his sisters, Mary, Flora and Sophia were seminary and early College students; his wife, Mary Scott, had been a seminary pupil, and their three sons would be Simpson students in the 1890s: Ernest Vernon (named for Simpson's first president), Theodore C. and Brenton T. It was Brenton T. who would become the Methodist bishop of India. Many years later, Bishop Badley presented to the College his father's diploma at chapel exercises on campus November 23, 1945.

53. Both she and Louisa Anderson would be parents of later Simpson students.

54. *Indianola Journal,* November 3, 1870.

55. *Simpsonian,* November 1, 1870.

56. Ibid., January 1893.

57. Grumbling went from Simpson to Iowa Wesleyan in 1882 and taught there until 1898, when he moved for a few years to Washington (Ia.) Academy. The last years of his career were spent at the College of Puget Sound, Tacoma, Wash. He died in 1914.

58. *Warren County Leader,* October 6, 1870.

59. In the fall of 1873 the frequency of publication was reduced to once a month, and the newspaper remained a monthly until early in the twentieth century.

60. The College's archival copy of this first issue belonged to the first editor, who penciled in a notation of Burns's authorship.

61. In all the years it has been published since 1870, it has never been suspended. It is, to be sure, the most enduring of Simpson's student enterprises.

62. Christie Swain, "History of Simpson College," *Zenith,* 1935.

63. *Simpsonian,* October 1, 1870.

64. Ibid., January 20, 1871.

65. No edition of *Baird's Manual of American College Fraternities* contains any mention of the I.I.I.

66. The Cheshire home was located at what is today 200 East First Avenue, where Indianola's First Baptist Church now stands.

67. The history of the Simpson chapter of Delta Delta Delta states that the L.F.V. was founded in March, 1871, but it appears from the record that its establishment was a bit earlier, probably in January. *History of Delta Chapter, Delta Delta Delta: 1889–1989* (Indianola, Iowa: Delta Delta Delta, 1989), 1.

68. *Simpsonian*, February 3, 1871.

69. *The Seventh General Catalog of the Delta Tau Delta Fraternity* (New York: Delta Tau Delta, 1917), 174.

70. Elizabeth Allen Clarke-Helmick, *The History of Pi Beta Phi Fraternity* (n.p.: Pi Beta Phi, 1915), 33–34. In addition to Cheshire and Walter, the charter members included Fannie Andrew, Kate Barker, Ella Todhunter, Marie Morrison, Louise Noble, Emma Patton, Elizabeth Cooke and Elizabeth Guyer.

71. *Simpsonian*, October 1, 1870. When Griffith platted the College Addition, a large section just north of the main part of Indianola, a portion of the new plat was dedicated to the College and became the north part of the campus. When that part of the campus was subsequently in litigation in the federal court because of financial difficulties experienced by Griffith, attorney William H. Berry and board of trustees secretary J. H. Henderson appeared before the court and won the case, which gave perfect title to the College. See *Advocate-Tribune*, May 26, 1910.

72. *Warren County Leader*, October 6, 1870.

73. *Simpsonian*, October 1, 1870. Most Methodist clergymen in the itinerancy were paid even less than college professors.

74. Ibid.

75. Captain Berry was father of William H. Berry and grandfather of Don L. Berry '03, longtime publisher of the Indianola newspaper.

76. *Warren County Leader*, June 15, 1871; *Indianola Journal*, June 15, 1871; *Simpsonian*, June 16, 1871. Of the total of $8,533 raised that day, very nearly half was given by active members of the College's board of trustees.

77. *Minutes of the Eighth Annual Session of the Des Moines Conference of the Methodist Episcopal Church* (Omaha: Tribune and Republican Steam Printing House, 1871), 23. The College would not remain long entirely free of debt, for the great financial crash of 1873 soon devastated the whole country. "Half the pledges became worthless because of the inability of the donors to meet the payments." *Simpsonian*, October 9, 1916.

78. Besides Simpson Centenary, Methodists supported Cornell, Upper Iowa and Iowa Wesleyan.

79. *Warren County Leader*, July 20, 1871.

80. *Indianola Journal*, May 4, 1871.

81. *Warren County Leader*, June 22, 1871.

82. *Simpsonian*, September 25, 1871.

83. *Warren County Leader*, May 16, 1872.

84. Ibid., June 8, 1871.

85. *Iowa State Register*, November 2, 1871.

86. See Simpson Centenary College, Board of Trustees, Minutes, for June 13, 1871 (two sessions), and June 29, 1871.

87. Ibid.

88. *Algona College: A Story of Educational Beginnings* (n.p., 1925), passim. The college was founded in 1872 and continued with modest success until 1884.

89. No copy of the pamphlet survives. We rely on comments about it by its readers.

90. *Register of the Ninth Session of the Des Moines Annual Conference* (Council Bluffs: Daily Nonpareil Steam Book and Job Office, 1872), 37.

91. *Warren County Leader*, August 3, 1871. Nightingale had served three years as principal of Northwestern Female College at Evanston, Illinois, but when that institution merged with Northwestern University he became available. Prior to his stint in Evanston he had taught at

Upper Iowa University for three years. He was a graduate of Wesleyan University, Methodism's premier New England school, where he was valedictorian of his class.

92. Ibid., July 11, 1872.

93. Ibid., October 26, 1871.

94. The best account of this case appears in George F. Parker, *History of Warren County*, 367–72. Miss Cooke, by the way, was re-elected in 1877. Later she taught in public schools and married the Rev. William C. Martin. After she was widowed she served as dean of women at Simpson College from 1912 to 1915.

95. He died in 1885.

96. This was the first contest held under the auspices of the newly organized Oratorical Association of Simpson College. See *Simpsonian*, November 1874.

97. *Warren County Tribune*, October 29, 1874. A later editor of this same newspaper could not resist a political jab in April of 1877: "We attended the meeting of the Smithsonian literary society last Friday evening and heard a young man trying to prove that President Grant retired with more honor than any of his predecessors. He made a good argument, considering the subject he had." Ibid., April 19, 1877.

98. *Simpsonian*, March 11, 1872.

99. There was really no loss of time, argued the editor of the *Simpsonian*, in granting seniors this free time. "For with the approach of the warm weather, comes a certain degree of relaxation and looseness on the part of the students and especially on the part of the seniors who feel that their year of jubilee has come." *Simpsonian*, May 1878.

100. A long account of this commencement week may be found in the *Simpsonian* for June 1878. The *Weekly Indianola Herald* carried only a brief review of the principal events, while the *Warren Record* gave the whole week extensive coverage, as did John Clarey's *Indianola Tribune*, which devoted fully two of its four pages to the festivities. All three of the town newspaper accounts were carried in their June 13 editions.

101. *Indianola Tribune*, June 13, 1878.

102. *Weekly Indianola Herald*, June 13, 1878.

Chapter 4

1. Simpson Centenary College, Executive Committee of the Board of Trustees, Minutes, July 12, 1875.

2. Ibid., July 17, 1875.

3. The library room was twenty-two by forty feet and the lecture hall twenty-two by sixty, in addition to "a convenient and sizable professors' room."

4. Simpson Centenary College, Board of Trustees, Minutes, October 5, 1875.

5. Ibid.

6. *Register of the Twelfth Session of the Des Moines Annual Conference of the Methodist Episcopal Church* (Des Moines: Mills and Co., 1875), 26.

7. *Western Jurist*, August, 1875, as quoted in the *Simpsonian*, October, 1875.

8. Ibid.

9. *Simpsonian*, November, 1875.

10. *Western Jurist*, August 1875, as quoted in the *Simpsonian*, October 1875.

11. Altogether, during its five years of operation, the law department enrolled 132 students, 25 of whom came from out of state.

12. Simpson Centenary College, Board of Trustees, Minutes, June 12, 1877.

13. Ibid.

14. Ibid., June 27, 1877.

15. Ibid., September 23, 1880.

16. See Charles J. Ritchey, *Drake University through Seventy-five Years: 1881–1956* (Des Moines: Drake University, 1956), 32, 36.

17. *Register of the Twelfth Session of the Des Moines Annual Conference of the Methodist Episcopal Church* (Des Moines: Mills and Co., 1875), 26.

18. *Des Moines Register*, August 4, 1875.

19. *Catalog of Simpson Centenary College, 1875–6* (Des Moines: State Register Print, 1876), 35.

20. The *Des Moines Register* scoffed at the pretensions of the College. "The Medical Department of Simpson Centenary College," editorialized the *Register*, "is to be organized at Des Moines this year. Which reminds us of the Dutchman who was called upon by Hans to test his cider. Old Tuetonic [sic] sent down [to the] cellar for a mug of cider, quaffed it, and handing the mug to Hans, said: 'Dot ish good ciderish—smell de mug.' What an anomalism to call it 'Medical Department of Simpson Centenary College'—located at Des Moines." Cited in *Weekly Indianola Herald*, July 20, 1876.

21. *Weekly Indianola Herald*, May 2, 1878.

22. By the end of the decade, forty-four Grange lodges had been organized in Warren County, with a total membership of between 1,800 and 2,000. George Parker, *History*, 428–29.

23. "The suit against Mr. Schooley," wrote a local editor, "brought by the College for interest on an endowment note, was decided in favor of the College. These suits are a bad thing for all parties. . . . They will engender bad blood and ill-feeling toward the College, and work evil, and evil only." *Weekly Indianola Herald*, March 29, 1877.

24. It had been a practice for several years, when the College had no cash to pay its bills, to issue warrants, or promises to pay. These notes bore interest, but frequently the interest was as uncollectible as was the principal amount.

25. Simpson Centenary College, Board of Trustees, Minutes, June 11, 1877.

26. To the modern-day reader, $16,462 may not seem to be a large sum, but one might compare it to the cost of running the College in later years. In 1986–87, for example, the College's budget exceeded $10 million. A debt of $20 million would be comparable to that $16,462, at least in the eyes of those who were responsible for it.

27. Simpson Centenary College, Board of Trustees, Minutes, June 11, 1877.

28. Parker, an Indiana native who grew up in Carlisle, Iowa, is already known to the reader as the author, or compiler, of *The History of Warren County Iowa*, published in 1879. He edited the *Indianola Tribune* from 1873 until he sold it to W. E. Andrew in 1876, whereupon he went to Des Moines, where he edited the *Daily State Leader* for a time. Later, having moved to the East, he worked as an editorial writer and, having earned the political gratitude of President Grover Cleveland, served as consul-general in Birmingham, England (1893–97) and wrote an exhaustive biography of Cleveland (1909). He died in New York May 31, 1928. His two-volume work *Pioneer Foundations* was published posthumously in 1940 by the State Historical Society of Iowa. See Gerard Schultz and Don L. Berry, *History of Warren County Iowa* (Indianola: The Record and Tribune Co., 1953), 243–44.

29. *Indianola Tribune*, June 3, 1875.

30. *Weekly Indianola Herald*, June 3, 1875.

31. *Indianola Tribune*, May 2, 1878.

32. Ibid.

33. Ibid., May 16, 1878.

34. By almost any measure, Des Moines was not a very large city. The 1880 U.S. census listed a population for the city of only 14,005. All of Polk County had 27,857.

35. *Indianola Tribune*, May 2, 1878.

36. Ibid.

37. Ibid., May 9, 1878.

38. Ibid.

39. Ibid.

40. *Weekly Indianola Herald*, June 20, 1878.

41. To Clarey's credit, he published both the Everett and McCoy letters defending Burns. Ibid., July 4, 1878.

42. *Warren Record*, May 16, 1878.

43. *Weekly Indianola Herald*, June 13, 1878.

44. *Indianola Tribune*, July 18, 1878.

45. *The Warren Record*, June 27, 1878.

46. The county gave the Greenback candidate only 146 votes, but the movement had not yet matured in Iowa. That same year, P. Gad Bryan, who had just retired as secretary of the executive committee of Simpson's board of trustees, was called upon in his Des Moines office

by a group of influential Democrats who wished to persuade him to run for Congress. Bryan, who had been Simpson's token Democrat for years, after "rubbing the barefoot part of his cranium, letting his left hand slide gently over his face, and pinching the end of his nose . . . arose from his easy chair, pulled down his vest, and remarked . . . 'No. This will be a bad year for Democrats. It's the "off year,"' The gentlemen left." *Weekly Indianola Herald*, June 15, 1876. The *Simpsonian*, preoccupied with the campaign of Elizabeth Cooke over her "little-minded, half-souled" opponent, did not even mention the national elections.

47. Weaver received only 3.3 percent of the national vote, but he got 22.8 percent in Warren County. In view of the fact that Garfield's total vote was only 1,898 votes greater than his Democratic opponent's nationwide, the Greenback vote in Iowa was significant. To be sure, the electoral vote favored Garfield 214 to 155.

48. *Indianola Tribune*, January 17, 1878. Whether editors Everett and Clarey sang in harmony with each other is not recorded. They were rarely in concord on anything else, and a few months later Everett was damning Clarey as a "hair-brained [sic] idiot," a "bench-legged wart," while Clarey was responding editorially in language equally colorful.

49. *Iowa State Register*, February 6, 1878.

50. *The Warren Record*, July 18, 1878.

51. *Weekly Indianola Herald*, October 25, 1877.

52. *Iowa State Register*, November 27, 1877. Six months later Burns would feel quite differently about the press or at least about some of the obstreperous Indianola editors.

53. *Indianola Tribune*, July 18, 1878. Burns remained at the Wesleyan Female College until the time of his death in 1900. See *Indianola Herald*, June 21, 1900.

54. Simpson Centenary College, Board of Trustees, Minutes, June 11, 1878.

55. Ibid., June 12, 1878.

56. *Zenith*, 1905, 25. Burns was, indeed, a brilliant speaker. Sometimes too brilliant. The editor of the *Herald*, in a review of Burns's 1875 commencement address, complained: "Were it possible for the Doctor to speak with more deliberation and use language in more common use, his discourses would be more highly appreciated by the mass of the community." *Weekly Indianola Herald*, June 10, 1875. Most who heard him, however, were captivated by his eloquence. Even in the midst of the worst of the press attacks in 1878, Clarey of the *Tribune*, who hated the man, reviewed Burns' famous, oft-repeated "Age of Reason" lecture, delivered this time at the Indianola Methodist Church on May 27, as "a master production of a master mind." *Indianola Tribune*, May 30, 1878.

57. *Zenith*, 1905, 25–26.

58. *Simpsonian*, April 1894.

Chapter 5

1. *Weekly Indianola Herald*, July 11, 1878.

2. *Indianola Tribune*, July 18, 1878.

3. *Warren Record*, July 18, 1878.

4. Both Henderson's letter and Rev. Berry's reply were published in the *Weekly Indianola Herald*, August 8, 1878.

5. *Simpsonian*, March 1880.

6. *Warren Record*, September 5, 1878. The weather soon changed, for by the end of September, the local buckwheat crop was ruined by an early frost.

7. Carpenter was granted a leave of absence for the balance of the academic year. Simpson Centenary College, Executive Committee of the Board of Trustees, Minutes, November 4, 1878.

8. When the executive committee of the board of trustees met on November 24, 1878, they found, as usual, that they did not have enough cash resources to pay the faculty for the fall term, so they issued warrants to each employee for one-third of his or her salary. On the basis of these warrants, it appears that President Berry's annual salary was $2,000, Carpenter's $1,250 (less the amount deducted during his leave of absence), Grumbling's $1,000, Burke's $1,000 and Pierce's $625. Janitor S. H. Van Pelt's annual wages amounted to $187.50. Simpson Centenary College, Executive Committee of the Board of Trustees, November 24, 1878.

9. *Zenith*, 1905.
10. *Proceedings of the Fifteenth Session of the Des Moines Annual Conference of the Methodist Episcopal Church*, September 18–23, 1878 (Atlantic, Ia.: Telegraph Steam Book and Job Office, 1878), 13.
11. T. S. Berry himself received a salary of only $1,200 when he was pastor at Indianola (1877–78), and he was one of the highest paid in the conference.
12. This meeting was best reported in the *Weekly Indianola Herald*, October 24, 1878.
13. *Simpsonian*, March 1894.
14. Simpson Centenary College, Board of Trustees, Minutes, June 10, 1879.
15. Ibid.
16. Ibid.
17. Ibid.
18. *Indianola Herald*, October 26, 1916.
19. *Indianola Republican*, June 12, 1879.
20. Simpson Centenary College, Board of Trustees, Minutes, June 10, 1879.
21. Ibid., June 11, 1879. The board borrowed the $2,200 at the bank, against payment of pledges. President Berry was paid $500, Carpenter $600, Grumbling $300, Burke $500 and Pierce $300.
22. Ibid. The president would receive $1,500, the professor of natural sciences $1,000, the chair of Latin and Greek language $800, the chair of mathematics $800, the chair of English literature $600 and the janitor $250. They allocated $90 for insurance, $200 for fuel and $60 for publishing the catalog.
23. Ibid.
24. Ibid. The resolution was proposed by B. C. Berry, E. W. Perry, John Kern, William Buxton and John H. Henderson, the most stalwart of the loyalists.
25. *Indianola Republican*, June 12, 1879. The Chicago, Burlington and Quincy Railroad had opened a line from Chariton to Indianola in February 1879, and another C. B. & Q. line was under construction in the extreme northeastern part of the county. See *Indianola Republican*, February 20, 1879 and March 27, 1879.
26. Ibid., June 19, 1879.
27. *Weekly Indianola Herald*, June 19, 1879. The mid-year issues of the *Indianola Tribune* are missing from the files.
28. *Weekly Indianola Herald*, September 25, 1879.
29. *Simpsonian*, December 1878.
30. Ibid., December 1879.
31. The College won, the north end of the campus being confirmed as indisputably in its legal possession.
32. See the *Des Moines Register*, July 22, 1879.
33. *Weekly Indianola Herald*, October 30, 1879.
34. *Simpsonian*, October 1879.
35. Accounts of President Berry's last days appeared in the *Indianola Tribune*, January 22, 29, February 5, 12, 1880.
36. Simpson Centenary College, Board of Trustees, Minutes, February 12, 1880.
37. *Simpsonian*, March 1880.
38. *Indianola Tribune*, February 19, 1880.

Chapter 6

1. It was February 16, 1880.
2. Parks wrote an account of his presidency in the *Simpsonian*, January 1894.
3. He received the M.A. from Northwestern in 1876 and the honorary D.D. from Garrett in 1887.
4. *Simpsonian*, January 1894; Simpson Centenary College, Board of Trustees, Executive Committee, Minutes, March 1, 1880.
5. *Simpsonian*, January 1894.

6. Parks, wrote John Clarey, "started work yesterday [March 10]. He is a young and modest appearing gentleman" who "seems to have the practical working vim so much needed in the college." *Indianola Tribune*, March 11, 1880.

7. *Simpsonian*, January 1894.

8. Simpson Centenary College, Board of Trustees, Executive Committee, Minutes, March 5, 1880. They gave Ellinwood $10 toward the cost of his move to Indianola.

9. Now West Ashland Avenue.

10. *Burlington Hawkeye*, July 31, 1879.

11. A long obituary appeared in *Proceedings of the Twentieth Session of the Des Moines Conference of the Methodist Episcopal Church*, Aug. 27–Sept. 1, 1879 (Des Moines: State Leader, 1879), 48–49.

12. *Simpsonian*, October 1879. The College received three shares of the Republican Valley Land Assn. at $200 per share and $100 worth of stock in the Equitable Silver Mining Co. Neither was marketable or ever paid a dividend. Simpson Centenary College, Board of Trustees, Executive Committee, Minutes, February 20, 1882.

13. *The People's Advocate*, October 5, 1880.

14. Ibid., September 7, 1880.

15. Simpson Centenary College, Board of Trustees, Minutes, September 23, 1880. Interestingly, Rev. Walters left the Methodist Episcopal church entirely two years later, joining another denomination.

16. *The People's Advocate*, September 7, 1880.

17. Ibid.

18. Of the total debt, $20,000 was bearing interest at seven percent, an intolerable burden.

19. Simpson Centenary College, Board of Trustees, Executive Committee, Minutes, September 27, 1880. She was paid $550 "for the remainder of the collegiate year." See also *People's Advocate*, October 5, 1880.

20. *Simpsonian*, January 1894.

21. Buxton later gave the College $10,000 in a single gift and became, in his day, Simpson's greatest benefactor.

22. *Simpsonian*, January 1894.

23. Ibid. Many years later, at Simpson's "semi-centennial" celebration in 1910, Parks gave Gorham Worth credit for saving Simpson. "By becoming personally responsible for a large balance that was nowhere in sight, and by working enthusiastically, doggedly, and prodigiously, Mr. Worth was able to pay off all that debt." It was, he said, "a heroic deed." *Indianola Herald*, October 26, 1916.

24. Enrollment figures are taken from the *Catalogue of Simpson Centenary College* or the *Catalogue of Simpson College* for the respective years.

25. When Burke resigned, his position was first offered to the Rev. C. F. Bradley, who declined the offer, going instead to Hamline University in Minnesota. Orlando Baker was back in town and applied for the position, as did Charles W. Fisk, who was a graduate of Simpson in the class of '79. Baker, who wanted more salary than the $800 the board was offering, was disappointed, for he would have enjoyed returning to Simpson now that Dr. Burns was gone. A few months later he bought an interest in the *Weekly Indianola Herald* with A. J. Graham. "In Prof. Baker," wrote Don L. Berry, "the press of Warren County probably had the most accomplished scholar it has ever had within its ranks." Gerard Schultz and Don L. Berry, *History of Warren County Iowa* (Indianola: The Record and Tribune Co., 1953), 242.

26. *Indianola Tribune*, August 12, 1880. Mathews earned the A.B. from Syracuse in 1877 and received the A.M. in 1880.

27. Telegraphy had been dropped in 1876, but was reinstated in 1880, along with "railroad dispatching" (!), only to be discontinued again in the spring of 1882.

28. *Simpsonian*, May 19, 1871.

29. Ibid., April 1875.

30. Ibid., May 1875.

31. Ibid., April 1878.

32. George F. Parker, *History*, 360, 363, 366–67, 503, 551, 556, 572–73, 739.

33. His candidacy was supported, for example, by the *Red Oak Daily Record*. See *The People's Advocate*, February 16, 1881.

34. *Indianola Tribune*, October 13, 1881. This was Clarey's parting shot. He sold his interest in his paper to Frank B. Taylor, who had also purchased *The People's Advocate* and consolidated the two in the *Advocate-Tribune*.

35. Simpson Centenary College, Board of Trustees, Executive Committee, Minutes, July 19, 1882.

36. Ibid., August 29, 1882. Had Giles accepted, he would have been the first holder of an earned doctorate on the Simpson faculty. It should be pointed out that in the 1880s few Americans held the doctorate, for graduate education, on the German model, was just beginning to take hold.

37. Grumbling spent the next year writing histories for several Missouri counties. In the fall of 1883 he joined the faculty of Iowa Wesleyan University, where he taught for fifteen years. After 1898 he spent a few years at Washington, Iowa, Academy. The Rev. Phineas F. Bresee, a prominent board member from Council Bluffs who admired Grumbling, visited him in Tacoma at Christmastime in 1904: "We had the pleasure of meeting Professor and Mrs. Grumbling, friends of other years. He has charge of the Department of Science at the University of the Puget Sound, a Methodist institution." Grumbling died in 1914. E. A. Girvin, *Phineas F. Bresee: A Prince in Israel* (Kansas City, Mo.: Nazarene Publishing House, 1982), 250. This book is a reprint of the 1916 edition.

38. Simpson Centenary College, Board of Trustees, Executive Committee, Minutes, August 29, 1883.

39. *Simpsonian*, February 1882. Ida May Pierce Burke later remarried. She died January 16, 1946. See *Simpson College Bulletin*, May 1946.

40. Simpson Centenary College, Board of Trustees, Executive Committee, Minutes, March 8, 1882.

41. *Simpsonian*, October 1882.

42. Her salary was set at the rate of $600 per year.

43. *Simpsonian*, January 1894.

44. *Weekly Indianola Herald*, April 13, 1882.

45. Students "who take delight in gymnastics can climb the center pole for a change," suggested the *Simpsonian*, May 1882. See also the *Advocate-Tribune*, May 25, 1882.

46. In their May issue the editorial corps of the *Simpsonian* promised a June issue, double the usual size, which would give a full account of the commencement week exercises, and if possible they would print in full Bishop Simpson's Sunday sermon and lecture to the societies. Those who wanted extra copies were urged to indicate the number desired. If it was published, no copy of that June 1882 issue exists.

47. *Advocate-Tribune*, June 22, 1882. Taylor's exhaustive account of the 1882 commencement week proceedings filled a page and a half—ten and a half columns—of the paper for that week.

48. Ibid.

49. Ibid. Frank Taylor called his long piece "Simpson at Simpson."

50. It didn't cost them much. The board of trustees authorized the following expenses for commencement: $25 for Bishop Simpson, $26 for E. W. Fortney, who provided the tent, $3 for Richey Brothers, the local furniture dealer who provided chairs. and $1.17 for Eikenberry and Co. for carrying donated lumber on commencement day. Simpson Centenary College, Board of Trustees, Minutes, June 20, 1882.

51. Simpson Centenary College, Board of Trustees, Minutes, June 19, 1882.

52. In those days sororities were not too fussy about accepting preparatory students into their ranks.

53. "Among her many returning students Simpson welcomes Miss Kate Shelley." *Simpsonian*, November 1883.

54. "Miss Kate Shelly [sic] is now delivering lectures throughout various portions of the state. Her most popular theme is the adventure that won for her a life-long renown." *Simpsonian*, April 1889. For reasons that are not entirely clear, Kate Shelley is the only member of her family who spelled her name "Shelly." Her nephew, Jack Shelley, became a celebrity in

his own right, serving for many years as anchor man on the WHO nightly television news in Des Moines. He retired after a distinguished career as a member of the journalism faculty at Iowa State University. His son, Stephen, graduated from Simpson in 1969.

55. Although obituaries published at the time say that she died after an operation for appendicitis, it appears that the actual cause of death was Bright's disease, a kidney disorder.

56. Buxton's wife Betsy died in 1901. The next year he married Frances Cheesman Carpenter, the widow of professor George Carpenter, who had died in 1895.

57. Carl Bangs, "The Making of a Founder: Phineas F. Bresee," *Our Roots of Belief* (Kansas City, Mo.: Beacon Hill Press of Kansas City, 1981), 19.

58. E. A. Girvin, *Phineas F. Bresee: A Prince in Israel* (Kansas City, Mo.: Nazarene Publishing House, 1916), 74–76.

59. Ibid., 77–80. Carl Bangs's account of the mining fiasco differs considerably from that of E. A. Girvin, who ascribes the failure of the enterprise to an explosion that caused flooding of the old Prieta mine at Parral. Bangs bases his account on a written reminiscence, penned in about 1922, of a Bresee intimate of those days, the Rev. Frederick Harris of the Des Moines Conference. Bangs's interpretation is consistent with other accounts of the Parral fraud, while Girvin's may be ascribed to the somewhat natural tendency for biographers to fall in love with their subjects. Girvin's work is more nearly hagiography than biography.

60. It was Rev. William S. Hooker who told Harris that Bresee had paid back the investors. Hooker was a longtime Simpson trustee, serving continuously from 1881 to 1907.

61. *Official Record of the Journal and Reports of the 24th Session of the Des Moines Conference of the Methodist Episcopal Church* (Des Moines: State Journal Mammoth Printing House, 1883), 23.

62. *The People's Advocate*, May 4, 1880, and June 1, 1880.

63. Ibid., April 27, 1881.

64. Simpson Centenary College, Board of Trustees, Minutes, June 7, 1881.

65. *Advocate-Tribune*, June 1, 1882, and September 7, 1882; *Simpsonian*, June 1883.

66. *Advocate-Tribune*, July 12, 1883; *Simpsonian*, December 1883.

67. The board of trustees authorized its construction in 1883. Simpson Centenary College, Board of Trustees, Minutes, June 26, 1883; *Advocate-Tribune*, May 22, 1884.

68. Simpson Centenary College, Board of Trustees, Minutes, June 25, 1884.

69. See *Indianola Weekly Herald*, September 20, 1883.

70. Ibid., July 3, 1884. The Simpson Memorial Hall scheme was dropped when solicitation of funds turned out to be disappointing.

71. *Indianola Weekly Herald*, July 23, 1885.

72. *Catalogue of Simpson Centenary College*, 1879–80, 32. Italics in the original.

73. *Advocate-Tribune*, April 1, 1886.

74. *Catalogue of Simpson College*, 1885–86, 45.

75. Ibid.

76. Three years earlier the *Advocate-Tribune* lamented that "smoking is becoming alarmingly prevalent among a certain class of students [at the College]." May 10, 1883.

77. *Simpsonian*, March 1886. President Parks left no doubt about where he stood, preaching a Sunday sermon on "the injurious phases of the commonly accepted popular amusements in student life." Ibid.

78. Simpson Centenary College, Board of Trustees, Minutes, June 25, 1884.

79. *Des Moines Register and Leader*, December 10, 1911. Thompson later became attorney general of Nebraska and then solicitor for the United States treasury.

80. Ibid.

81. *Indianola Herald*, February 1, 1912.

82. Edmund Holmes, who graduated in 1880, would later serve as president of the College (1889–92).

83. *Indianola Herald*, February 1, 1912.

84. *Simpsonian*, March 1881; April 1882; and May 1884.

85. Some student orations were much too broad, complained the *Simpsonian* editor in 1885. "The Problem of the Universe" or "The Past, Present and Future" did not, he wrote, lend themselves to concise treatment. *Simpsonian*, October 1885.

86. Ibid., March 1878.

87. Ibid., November 1879.

88. Estelle Dodge, *Sixty Years in Kappa Alpha Theta: 1870–1929* (Menasha, Wisconsin: Kappa Alpha Theta, 1930), 131–32.

89. Virginia A. La Charité, "The History of Omicron Chapter of Kappa Kappa Gamma," 1990.

90. *Simpsonian*, June 1880.

91. J. Duncan Campbell, *The Centennial History of the Phi Kappa Psi Fraternity: 1852–1952*, 2 vols. (n.p.: The Phi Kappa Psi Fraternity, 1952), I, 270–73.

92. Ibid., 271–72.

93. Ibid., 272.

94. The charter members, in addition to Buxton, were Henry L. Loft, Isaiah H. Cook, Charles H. Parks and Ormsby M. Mitchell. See Wendell Tutt, *Alpha Tau Omega: First Century at Simpson, 1885–1985* (Indianola, Iowa: Beta Alpha of Alpha Tau Omega, 1985), 3–6.

95. "The L.F.V. has 15 in school—8 in college classes, the rest in preparatory and musical departments. Phi Kappa Psi has 19 men in school." *Simpsonian*, October 1885.

96. Ibid.

97. Ibid., December 1883.

98. No copies of this first yearbook are known to exist.

99. *Indianola Weekly Herald*, June 19, 1884. The board of editors included N. B. Ashby, O. A. Kennedy and E. L. Davis from Delta Tau Delta and G. G. Martin, C. J. Evans and J. H. Newland from Phi Kappa Psi.

100. When the *Simpsonian* announced the non-appearance of the *Tangent* in 1885, it was severely critical: "If those who have claimed the *Tangent* as an inheritance, and of whom the leadership in this enterprise were expected have so betrayed their trust, the inheritance should be given to those who have enough public spirit to make a little sacrifice in its behalf." But of course it was not a matter of public spirit but of inadequate financial support. Needless to say, no one came forward to undertake the task until the Greek societies published the second *Tangent* in 1889.

101. *Indianola Tribune*, August 4, 1881.

102. *People's Advocate*, July 13, 1881.

103. *Advocate-Tribune*, April 26, 1883.

104. *Simpsonian*, April 1885.

105. *Record-Herald and Indianola Tribune*, May 6, 1948. Kelly became a distinguished Methodist minister. He died in 1947.

106. The Alumnal Association's first officers, for 1877–78, were the Rev. T. McKendree Stuart '72, president; Albert S. Jewett '73, secretary; and John A. Everett '72, treasurer.

107. "The [Ladies] College Aid Society . . . will have an ice cream social at the College chapel next Tuesday evening." *Indianola Tribune*, April 22, 1880.

108. Simpson Centenary College, Board of Trustees, Minutes, June 7, 1881.

109. *People's Advocate*, September 28, 1881.

110. *Simpsonian*, April 1882.

111. Simpson Centenary College, Board of Trustees, Minutes, June 23, 1885.

112. *Indianola Weekly Herald*, June 26, 1884.

113. Simpson Centenary College, Board of Trustees, Executive Committee, Minutes, August 29, 1884.

114. Simpson Centenary College, Board of Trustees, Minutes, June 23, 1885.

115. Dr. Neely's letter is quoted verbatim in the board of trustees' minutes for June 29, 1886.

116. Simpson College, Board of Trustees, Minutes, June 29, 1886. This bas-relief is displayed today just outside the Matthew Simpson room of College Hall.

117. Ibid.

118. The March 1886 *Simpsonian* reported that the charge for meals was being increased from $1.90 to $2.05 per week.

119. *State Register*, May 14, 1886.

120. *Advocate-Tribune*, May 20, 1886.

121. Ibid. The reader a century later cannot but marvel that such a furor could have been

caused by allocation of seating for a concert of classical music. Musical tastes among the young have changed considerably in a hundred years.

122. *Simpsonian*, March 1886.

123. Simpson College, Board of Trustees, Minutes, June 30, 1886; *Simpsonian*, February 1886; *Indianola Weekly Herald*, February 11, 1886.

124. *Indianola Weekly Herald*, March 18, 1886.

125. Ibid., April 29, 1886.

126. Both had been members of Phi Kappa Psi as undergraduates. On June 29, 1886, both of them attended a "sociable" at the Simpson Phi Psi hall, which event they "hugely enjoyed."

127. *Simpsonian*, May 1886.

128. These words are extracted from an address by Parks at the Second State Methodist Episcopal Convention in Des Moines in 1881. *Indianola Weekly Herald*, June 9, 1881.

129. Simpson College, Board of Trustees, Minutes, June 29, 1886.

130. Ibid., June 30, 1886.

131. *Indianola Weekly Herald*, July 29, 1886.

132. Simpson College, Board of Trustees, Minutes, April 27, 1887.

133. *Advocate-Tribune*, July 1, 1886.

134. In the 1885–86 Simpson catalog Carpenter was listed, as he had been for several years, as professor of Latin, but he continued to teach some of the science courses as well. Charles Ellinwood held the chair of natural sciences, and if he had any predilection to support the theories of Mr. Darwin, he kept it to himself.

135. *Advocate-Tribune*, July 1, 1886.

Chapter 7

1. He served at Onawa (1868–69), Harlan (1869–71), Tabor (1871–72), Woodbine (1872–75), Fremont City (1875–78), Guthrie Center (1878–80), Adel (1880–82) and once again at Harlan (1882–83).

2. *Simpsonian*, February 1894.

3. Simpson College, Board of Trustees, Minutes, April 27, 1887. As early as June 9, 1886, the board of trustees met to elect a successor to Parks. A leading contender was the Rev. Thomas J. Bassett, principal of the preparatory department at DePauw. But because several ballots resulted in a deadlock between Bassett and others, no election was possible. At one point the exasperated board pleaded with Parks to reconsider his resignation, but their effort was in vain. A few weeks later a notice appeared in the Indianola press that the Rev. H. A. Gobin, D.D., professor of Greek at DePauw, "who has lately been elected President of Simpson College, arrived in the city last evening." If Gobin did indeed arrive, it was surely not to accept the presidency of the College. *Indianola Weekly Herald*, July 29, 1886.

4. Hamilton's mother died in 1905 at the age of 85; his father died the next year at 90.

5. Much of the above is drawn from the biography of Hamilton published in W. C. Martin, *History of Warren County, Iowa* (Chicago: S. J. Clarke Publishing Co., 1908), 971–73.

6. Ibid., 972.

7. *Simpsonian*, February 1894.

8. Ernest Thornbrue (penmanship) was a freshman from Logan; Elmer Evans (shorthand) was a freshman from Linden; J. B. Mather (elocution) was another freshman from Shelley; William Mercer (mathematics), from Indianola, taught in the academy and was listed as a student in "special studies"; Bertha Todd and Fannie Patteson (also called "Patterson" in the 1886–87 catalog) were both students of voice culture in the School of Music. See *Catalogue of Simpson College, 1886–7* (Indianola: Herald Printing House, 1887), passim.

9. Indianola Methodists moved into a fine new church building in 1886. Their pastor, Rev. Hooker, was one of the most able clergymen on Simpson's board of trustees during the nineteenth century. English-born, well educated, he was at fifty-one a mature, thoroughly civilized gentleman whose erudition sometimes intimidated some of his small-town parishioners. In August 1886, he suffered the loss of his wife, Sarah, whom he had married in England in

1862, seven years before they emigrated to America. A strange, inappropriately worded obituary appeared in the conference minutes, describing her as a "symmetrical Christian lady" of whom it could be said "she did what she could." *Official Record of the Journal and Reports of the Twenty-seventh Session of the Des Moines Annual Conference of the Methodist Episcopal Church* (Council Bluffs: Pryor's Bee Job Print, 1886), 47.

10. *Simpsonian*, February 1894.

11. By mid-1887, the accumulated debt stood at $9,945, and two years later, in spite of record income, shortfalls forced the debt up to $15,678. See Simpson College, Board of Trustees, Minutes, June 29, 1886, June 27, 1887 and June 19, 1889.

12. *Simpsonian*, February 1894.

13. Simpson College, Board of Trustees, Minutes, June 27, 1887. Brown's starting salary was $1,000 a year. The board had offered the position to popular Rev. Thomas S. Hooker, who turned them down. Simpson College, Board of Trustees, Executive Committee, Minutes, April 26, 1887.

14. A good biographical sketch of Brown appeared in the first edition of the *Zenith*, the College's new yearbook, in 1896.

15. A classic picture of Brown appeared in the 1899 edition of the *Zenith*, which annual was dedicated to him.

16. Simpson College, Board of Trustees, Minutes, June 26, 1887.

17. He commenced his duties in early October 1887. See *Indianola Weekly Herald*, October 6, 1887.

18. Ibid., June 21, 1888.

19. *Minutes of the Twenty-ninth Annual Session of the Des Moines Conference of the Methodist Episcopal Church* (n. p., 1888), 51.

20. *Advocate-Tribune*, October 27, 1887.

21. Ibid., November 3, 1887. Actually, such a number today would make any development officer shout for joy.

22. Ibid. The *Indianola Weekly Herald*'s announcement of the October 31 meeting was much more positive than that of Schooley's review in the *Advocate-Tribune*, but then the meeting had not yet been held. *Indianola Weekly Herald*, October 27, 1887.

23. Ibid., November 10, 1887.

24. Ibid., December 8, 1887.

25. Simpson College, Board of Trustees, Executive Committee, Minutes, November 9, 1886.

26. Ibid., March 13, 1888. Proudfoot's fee was two percent of the cost of the building.

27. Ibid., November 16, 1886.

28. Ibid.

29. The best description of the plans for Science Hall appeared in the *Advocate-Tribune*, June 21, 1888, probably written by that newspaper's colorful longtime editor, William H. Schooley, who could not resist editorializing in a news column when the temptation to do so was present. He was, for example, certain that the fine new art studio, together "with the advantages of superior instruction, will doubtless supplant the host of indifferent teachers, who are pretending to afford instruction in a branch of the principles of which they are lamentably ignorant." Another well-written description of the new building appeared in the *Indianola Weekly Herald*, June 21, 1888, whose senior editor, Thomas T. Anderson, saw the new building making the hard business of learning more attractive. "The bitter root of knowledge," he wrote, "will not be tasted unless garnished with delicacies. Science Hall is needed as the sugar coating for an acrid but necessary pill" and "will constitute a substantial ornament," making students proud of their alma mater.

30. Simpson College, Board of Trustees, Executive Committee, Minutes, April 19, 1888, May 2, 1888, May 3, 1888 and May 7, 1888.

31. Ibid., August 14, 1888, November 12 and 16, 1888, and June 21, 1889. Later in 1889, they paid Davis and Hamilton an additional $392 to paint the interior of the building. And further "extras" totaled $1,976.55. See Ibid., July 12, 1889.

32. Ibid., December 20, 1888.

33. *Indianola Weekly Herald*, June 27, 1889.

34. Ibid.

35. Ibid., December 27, 1888; *Simpsonian*, January 1889. Born in Japan in 1869, Miyada came to the United States in 1883, worked in San Francisco for a time, then moved to Missouri Valley, Ia., where he was converted to Christianity. He decided to seek an education for the Christian ministry and came to Simpson in the fall of 1887, without friends or money. He worked for his board and lectured on Japan during vacations, earning a few dollars for his efforts. At Simpson he was an unusually good student, was a member of two of the literary societies at one time or another, winning the Buxton prize for oratory in the spring of 1888.

36. Although Ellinwood's resignation was not announced until June 20, his intention must surely have been known earlier to the board, for they elected Tilton that same day, an action not likely taken without weeks of preparation and search.

37. Simpson College, Board of Trustees, Minutes, April 27, 1887; *Advocate-Tribune*, May 5, 1887.

38. *Indianola Weekly Herald*, July 25, 1889. One donor insisted on a five-year lease on one room as a condition of his $250 contribution. Simpson College, Board of Trustees, Executive Committee, Minutes, September 22, 1888. See also *Simpsonian*, February 1889. A brass plaque was put up over the door of each of the sleeping rooms, announcing that Mr. and Mrs. So-and-so had contributed an endowment for the room. One confused young freshman girl looked around the building, saw all those plaques, and prepared to return home, declaring that all the rooms were already occupied by couples.

39. *Simpsonian*, October 1888; *Indianola Weekly Herald*, October 18, 1888. The bricks were delivered in October by Indianola Brick and Tile Co. at a cost of $425. Payment was authorized on November 30. Simpson College, Board of Trustees, Executive Committee, Minutes, November 30, 1888.

40. *Simpsonian*, February 1890. They found a new one.

41. Simpson College, Board of Trustees, Executive Committee, Minutes, April 2, 1889.

42. Ibid., February 19, 1890, March 11, 1890, April 1, 1890 and April 5, 1890.

43. Simpson College, Board of Trustees, Minutes, June 18, 1890.

44. *Zenith*, 1903, 22.

45. *Simpsonian*, May 1889; *Indianola Weekly Herald*, June 21, 1888 and June 20, 1889; Simpson College, Board of Trustees, Executive Committee, Minutes, June 20, 1889.

46. It was the Greek-letter societies that came up with the money: $100 each from Delta Tau Delta, Alpha Tau Omega and Phi Kappa Psi, $50 from L.F.V. and $25 each from Kappa Kappa Gamma and I.C. (Pi Beta Phi).

47. *Advocate-Tribune*, April 12, 1888.

48. *Simpsonian*, May 1889.

49. Ibid., June 1889. Their efforts that first year did not strike the editor of the *Advocate-Tribune* as being unqualifiedly praiseworthy, for by fall he was complaining: "It seems to us that it would be more inviting to students as well as give the college more prestige among visitors if the campus were kept in some kind of presentable condition." *Advocate-Tribune*, September 26, 1889. Nevertheless, each year after that spring of 1889, some such effort was made to remove the detritus of a long winter. In time this event came to be called "Campus Day," and soon enough it was invested with the sanctity of hoary tradition.

50. *Catalog of Simpson College, 1888-9* (Indianola, Ia.: Herald Printing House, 1889), 37–43. The title page of this document explains that the use of the word "catalog" is a consequence of "spelling reform—by agreement of ten Iowa Colleges."

51. Simpson College, Board of Trustees, Executive Committee, Minutes, July 10, 1888 and July 13, 1888.

52. *Indianola Weekly Herald*, November 25, 1886.

53. Ibid., November 28, 1889.

54. *Advocate-Tribune*, January 24, 1889; *Simpsonian*, April 1889.

55. *Simpsonian*, November 1889.

56. Ibid., December 1888.

57. *Advocate-Tribune*, November 15, 1888. The board of trustees had ordered the curfew a few months earlier. Simpson College, Board of Trustees, Minutes, June 20, 1888.

58. *Advocate-Tribune*, April 1, 1886. This was a quick turnaround, for the *Simpsonian* of that month carried a cigarette advertisement.

59. *Simpsonian*, December 1889.

60. Simpson College, Board of Trustees, Minutes, June 19, 1889.

61. Ninety-five women had been initiated into the L.F.V. since its founding in 1871. Eleven of these were initiated into Delta Delta Delta at the May 10, 1889 installation.

62. *Zenith*, 1899.

63. See *Advocate-Tribune*, October 24, 1889.

64. Ibid., November 7, 1889. During these years the Y.M.C.A. and Y.W.C.A. equipped a small gymnasium that functioned with modest success.

65. See *Catalogue of Simpson Centenary College, 1871–72* (Indianola, Ia.: The Republican Printing Co., 1872), 25.

66. *Simpsonian*, April 1889. See also *Catalog of Simpson College, 1889–90* (Indianola, Ia.: Herald Printing House, 1890), 35.

67. *Advocate-Tribune*, October 31, 1889.

68. *Simpsonian*, June 1886.

69. Ibid., June 1889.

70. The first student senate included seniors J. E. Bunting, O. A. Kennedy, Alice A. Evans and Mamie Newell; juniors B. F. Miller, R. E. Shaw and Josie McCleary; sophomores L. W. Haworth and Edith McGee; and freshman C. E. Bentley. *Tangent*, 1889, 40.

71. *Advocate-Tribune*, May 16, 1889.

72. Brenton H. Badley, Lucknow, India, to Mary Scott Badley, Pauri, India, August 4, 1887.

73. Mary Scott Badley, Pauri, India, to Brenton H. Badley, Lucknow, India, August 9, 1887.

74. He was buried in the Paper Mills Cemetery in Lucknow with two of his six sons. Both of the boys had died in infancy.

75. The thirteen member colleges were Iowa State University (University of Iowa), Iowa State Agricultural College, Iowa College (Grinnell), Cornell, Tabor, Iowa Wesleyan, Coe, Parsons, Lenox, Drake, Upper Iowa, Central and Simpson.

76. *Indianola Weekly Herald*, December 8, 1887.

77. *Minutes of the Twenty-ninth Annual Session of the Des Moines Conference of the Methodist Episcopal Church*, Creston, Ia., September 12–17, 1888 (Council Bluffs: Pryor's Bee Job Print, 1888), 17–18. The vote was 80–14.

78. *Indianola Weekly Herald*, December 5, 1889.

79. Ibid.

80. Simpson College, Board of Trustees, Minutes, June 17, 1889. Many years later it was suggested that Hamilton's resignation was a consequence of an ugly disagreement with the board: "In the 1880s a man resigned as acting president of Simpson College because the Board of Trustees would not accept his recommendation to enlarge the size of the campus." Ibid., June 3, 1950. If this was the case, there is no written evidence of it in the earlier minutes of the board of trustees.

81. See biography of Holmes in W. C. Martin, *History of Warren County, Iowa*, 991–93. Holmes's second son, Stephen, was born December 20, 1889, during the first year of his presidency.

82. Many years later Holmes returned to the Simpson faculty after a lapse of nearly three decades in the itinerancy.

83. *Simpsonian*, October 1889.

84. As quoted in the *Advocate-Tribune*, September 5, 1889.

85. During the first year of her tenure at Simpson, Joanna Baker was saddened by the death of her mother, formerly a professor of Latin at the College, February 2, 1890. The *Simpsonian* noted that Mrs. Baker had been a "great friend of the College." *Simpsonian*, February 5, 1890.

Chapter 8

1. John Owen Gross, Interview with George Washington Carver, Tuskegee, Alabama, July 17, 1940. Simpson College has in its archives an indexed collection of more than fifty files on George Washington Carver and his association with the College. These files include correspondence, periodical and newspaper articles, interviews and photographs. Simpson College Archives, File 8/6/1/8.

2. Carver never did know really when he was born, and his biographers disagree, estimating the year of birth from 1861 to 1864. Thus Carver would have been between twenty-five and twenty-nine when he entered Simpson.

3. Jim died in 1883 of smallpox.

4. Because Highland University had grown out of an old frontier Presbyterian Indian mission, it would accept Native Americans as students. But by 1885 it enrolled all, or nearly all, white students. In that year only eighty-eight youngsters registered. Of those, thirty-five were elementary pupils, forty-nine academy pupils and only four were classified as university-level students. In the story of Carver's meeting that fateful day with Dr. Duncan, some of Carver's biographers have improved on the facts of this episode, inventing conversations that could have been known only to Carver and Dr. Duncan. The latter was a Missourian in his first year at Highland, and he did believe that no blacks should enter his university, even if Indians were admitted. His decision was supported by his board of trustees, some members of which are known to have been less than convinced of the correctness of their denial to Carver. The historian of Highland University, now Highland Community College, has lamented that "because of this one act of discrimination, Highland University lost an opportunity to have a truly famous alumnus." See Arlyn J. Parish, *History of Highland Community College* (Troy, Kans.: Trojan Graphics, 1983), 50. Some of Carver's biographers place Highland University in Iowa, and later presidents of Simpson believed that he was rejected by an unnamed Iowa college, a simple error of fact that Carver himself was not at pains to correct. Perhaps Carver did contribute to some of the legends and apocryphal tales about him, but his biographers have often been careless or given to telling a good story in a dramatic way with something less than careful attention to accuracy. By all odds the best biographies are Rackham Holt's *George Washington Carver: An American Biography*, rev. ed. (Garden City, N.Y.: Doubleday, Doran and Company, Inc., 1963, and Linda O. McMurry, *George Washington Carver: Scientist and Symbol* (New York: Oxford University Press, 1981).

5. All of Carver's biographers tell this story, for it is the stuff of which legend is made, and Carver himself recalled the events of his first days at the College in substantially the same way. In a letter to Simpson president Edwin E. Voigt, during the last year of the great scientist's life, Carver wrote "I managed to get to dear old Simpson with ten cents in cash, and every opportunity was given me to pursue my most cherished desire. God only knows what would have happened if I had been refused." George W. Carver, Tuskegee, Ala., to Edwin E. Voigt, Indianola, Ia., June 2, 1942.

6. John P. Morley, "Memories," 41. This manuscript of typewritten memoirs was put down in 1957 when Morley was eighty-nine years old. Morley described Carver's shack: "He had no furniture. We sat on boxes he had picked up behind stores. He must have slept on the floor without any bedding."

7. But he was probably only the second. A black student had enrolled at the College earlier in the 1880s, but had left before Carver arrived on campus.

8. Ibid., 40.

9. *Catalogue of Simpson College, 1889–90* (Indianola, Ia.: Herald Publishing House, 1890), 28.

10. John P. Morley, "Memories," 41. In a letter to Mrs. Milholland in Winterset, Carver wrote, "The people are very kind to me here and the students are wonderfully good. They took it into their heads I was working too hard and had not enough home comforts so they clubbed together and brought me a whole set of furniture—chairs, table, bed, and such things as I needed. I never found out who did it." Quoted in Rackham Holt, 74.

11. As quoted in Rackham Holt, 77.

12. Bernadine Carpenter, Registrar, Simpson College, "Statement of the Credits of Dr. George W. Carver," March 21, 1974.

13. Rackham Holt, 80.

14. *Des Moines Tribune*, July 14, 1953.

15. *Simpsonian*, June 1891.

16. It required the intervention of Mrs. Liston just to have him seated at mealtime with the rest of the students rather than in the basement with the kitchen help.

17. In those days the Iowa State academic year started in the spring and ended in November, permitting the long vacation to fall during the cold winter months.

18. *Simpsonian*, February 1893.

19. *Catalogue of Simpson College, 1892–93* (Indianola: Educator Press, 1893), 57.

20. *Simpsonian*, December 1894.

21. George W. Carver, Tuskegee, Ala., to John L. Hillman, Indianola, Ia., March 16, 1928.

22. George W. Carver, Tuskegee, Ala., to John O. Gross, Indianola, Ia., July 20, 1940.

23. *Christian Education Magazine*, (January-February 1942), 22.

24. *Simpsonian*, May-June 1892.

25. The board of trustees determined on June 19, 1889, to fill the English and history chair, which had been vacant for a year since Minnie Jay's resignation, "at a salary not to exceed $600." Simpson College, Board of Trustees, Minutes, June 19, 1889.

26. *Advocate-Tribune*, August 14, 1890.

27. Holmes regretted Phillips's resignation too: "Under his experienced management the Normal department rose into prominence; but wider fields called for his talents and we could not retain him in the work so well begun." See Holmes's reminiscences in the *Simpsonian*, March 6, 1894.

28. "Prof. C. W. Bricker is making a grand success in teaching Voice, Violin, Coronet [sic] and Chorus. Mrs. Bricker is unexcelled as a Piano teacher. They both come from the foremost Conservatory in the country." *Indianola Weekly Herald*, January 8, 1891. The next year the couple opened a conservatory in Iowa City in connection with the state university. Ibid., August 25, 1892.

29. *Zenith*, 1910 (Indianola, Ia.: Simpson College, 1909), [135].

30. At that time there were four Methodist conferences in Iowa: the Iowa, Upper Iowa, Des Moines and Northwest Iowa. The Iowa Conference sponsored Iowa Wesleyan, the Upper Iowa Conference Cornell and Upper Iowa, the Des Moines Conference Simpson, and the Northwest Iowa Conference Morningside. The church later dropped its relationship with Upper Iowa University in 1928. See Emory Stevens Bucke, general editor, et al., *The History of American Methodism* (New York: Abingdon Press, 1964), III, 204.

31. The clerical contingent of the 1890–91 board of trustees included Fletcher Brown of Indianola, the only College staff member thus honored; T. McK. Stuart of the Broadway Church in Council Bluffs; A. T. Jeffrey of Harlan; W. T. Smith, the presiding elder of the Corning district; W. B. Thompson of Mt. Ayr; W. C. Martin, the presiding elder of the Chariton district; Emory Miller, the pastor at Indianola; Dinsmore Austin of Chariton; W. F. Bartholomew of Sidney; W. S. Hooker, presiding elder of the Council Bluffs district, residing in Shenandoah; and William E. Hamilton, pastor at Corning and former president of Simpson. Among the laymen were longtime board members William Buxton of Carlisle; Indianolans Gorham A. Worth, M. R. Barker, William H. Berry and John H. Henderson; George G. Wright of Des Moines, in his last year on the board after twenty-two years of service. Other lay members included G. S. Allyn of Mt. Ayr, Stephen R. Page of Boone, John Gibson of Creston, E. A. Rea of Corydon, J. B. Romans of Denison and John C. Mitchell of Des Moines, together with a contingent of several lawyers and judges—other than those already mentioned: Benjamin F. Clayton of Macedonia, Albert Head of Jefferson, David S. Sigler of Corning and D. M. Woodfill of Conway.

32. When Charles Eldred Shelton became president of the College in 1899, he renounced the chairmanship of the executive committee and participated in meetings as a member ex officio.

33. "It is a matter of surprise that [the financial panic] has affected college attendance so little. The enrollment at Simpson is as large as at this time last year." *Simpsonian*, October 1893.

34. The board of trustees reported on June 15, 1892, that "the financial affairs of the institution have never been more wisely administered" and that credit for that happy state of affairs "is due almost entirely to Vice President Fletcher Brown." Simpson College, Board of Trustees, Minutes, June 15, 1892.

35. Ibid. Brown's salary was $1,400 per year, and it was not increased during the six years of his presidency.

36. See Simpson College, Board of Trustees, Minutes, for those years; also see *The Educator*, 8 (Jul.-Aug. 1896), 6.

37. Simpson College, Board of Trustees, Minutes, June 15, 1897.

38. *The Educator*, 3 (October 1891), 2–3.

39. Tuition in the Academy or Normal School was less: $30.25 in 1890–91 and $31.00 (including incidental fees) in 1899–1900; in the Commercial or Business School it was more: $38.50 in 1890 and $39.80 a decade later. The highest rates in 1900 were for the "School of Shorthand and Typewriting": $63.35 for the year, reflecting presumably the putative costs of *fin de siecle* high technology.

40. *The Educator*, 5 (Jan.-Feb. 1893), 1–11.

41. *Indianola Times*, February 2, 1893. Or as the editor of the *Herald* put it: "May a kind providence deal gently with and bless every individual person who contributed however small or large the amount to the twelve thousand dollars raised at the Methodist church last Sabbath for Simpson College." *Indianola Weekly Herald*, February 2, 1893.

42. Simpson College, Board of Trustees, Minutes, June 13, 1894. Fletcher Brown gave the details: Dr. Golliday willed the College his library and $150 in cash; Mrs. Southard's gift of $2,184.36 was for "the support of ministerial and missionary students." *The Educator*, 5 (March-April 1894), 8. Mrs. Southard, a former student at Simpson, died of the grippe in 1892 at the age of 36. A notice of her death appeared in ibid., 4 (Sept.-Oct. 1892), 7–8.

43. Rev. Vail's gift was first noted in *The Educator*, 5 (Sept.-Oct. 1893), 6. See also ibid., 6 (March-April 1894), 8, which lists the amount of land as 208 acres, while later that year a printed board of trustees report cited the figure of 206 acres. Ibid., 6 (July-August 1894), 11.

44. Ibid., 7 (March-April 1895), 5. See also Simpson College, Board of Trustees, Minutes, June 12, 1895, acknowledging the receipt of "446 acres from Bro. Vail" valued at $17,840, or $40 an acre.

45. Ibid., 8 (Jan.-Feb. 1896), 3–4.

46. Simpson College, Board of Trustees, Minutes, June 17, 1896.

47. The *Iowa State Register* praised the appointment of Baker, "one of the best educated men in central Iowa, . . . a man of integrity, a citizen esteemed by all, and an educator of more than usual ability." But Baker's tenure in Denmark was brief. The election of 1892 swept Cleveland and the Democrats back into power, and diplomatic and consular appointments were among the spoils of victory. Republican Baker lost his post in late 1893 and returned to Iowa. *Iowa State Register*, October 4, 1892. See also *Indianola Weekly Herald*, October 6, 1892. The *Simpsonian* reported Baker's return from Copenhagen, "the [Cleveland] administration having given his office to a Southern man of the opposite political faith." *Simpsonian*, January 1894.

48. *The Educator*, 10 (July-August 1898), 3.

49. "The main college building," wrote Schooley, "is no more a business college than it is a coal house or an armory or a recitation building or a chapel. . . . This method of quack advertising comes with bad grace from an institution of learning." *Advocate-Tribune*, October 6, 1892.

50. The editor of the *Times* was livid. This "jerk water" print shop, employing a few "incompetent" students at sweatshop wages had won away the contract to print the *Simpsonian* for "one dollar less than the Schooleys" at the *Advocate-Tribune*. "Now if the college itself don't [sic] pay expenses what in thunder is the use of the Methodist Conference having another expense attached to the institution. Throw away the print shop, put the financial agent on a circuit and then let all go to work to redeem our school." *Indianola Times*, August 1, 1896.

51. *Simpsonian*, February 1892. The next year, however, the editor—a different editor, to be sure—acknowledged that *The Educator* "has done much for Simpson." *Simpsonian*, May 1893.

52. Ibid., November 1888.

53. *Advocate-Tribune*, January 4, 11 and 18, 1894; *Indianola Weekly Herald*, June 14, 1894; *Simpsonian*, December 1893. Although the building was very simple, it was instantly popular with students. Professor Tilton signed up 100 young men in four classes of 25 each to work out several times a week.

54. A brief biographical sketch of Sedgwick appeared in the *Simpsonian*, February 1896. President Brown heralded Sedgwick's advent on the campus in *The Educator*, 7 (Sept.-Oct. 1895), 11. See also ibid., 7 (Nov.-Dec. 1895), 3–5 and ibid., 8 (Jan.-Feb. 1896), 1, 3.

55. Sedgwick's proposal was first presented to the board of trustees September 27, 1895. Simpson College, Board of Trustees, September 27, 1895.

56. See *Simpson College [Catalog]: Collegiate Year 1895–96* (Indianola: Simpson College, 1896), 28–31.

57. *Iowa State Register*, quoted in *Indianola Times*, March 5, 1896.

58. *Indianola Weekly Herald*, December 26, 1895.

59. Ibid., March 12, 1896; *Indianola Times*, April 23, 1896.

60. Two of the board's June sessions were consumed with discussion of the Sedgwick contract. Simpson College, Board of Trustees, Minutes, June 16 and 17, 1896.

61. Sedgwick wrote a long letter to the editor of the *Times* explaining his side of the controversy with Simpson. *Indianola Times*, August 29, 1896.

62. Ibid., August 15, 1896.

63. Simpson College, Board of Trustees, Minutes, June 13, 1899.

64. A good, brief biography of O. C. [Oswell Chase] Brown appears in W. C. Martin, *History of Warren County, Iowa*, 398–402.

65. Dorothy Daniel, *Circle 'Round the Square: Pictures from an Iowa Childhood* (New York: Wilfred Funk, Inc., 1959), 161.

66. *Simpsonian*, October 1892. Soon thereafter Budd started teaching art at the Iowa Agricultural College in Ames.

67. Stacy's biography appeared in the *Simpsonian* as part of a series of informative sketches of all faculty members during the 1895–96 academic year. *Simpsonian*, April 1896.

68. Watson learned of his election the day before he delivered his senior oration entitled "American Progress" at commencement. *Indianola Times*, June 15, 1893. See also *Simpsonian*, June 1893.

69. Watson's biography appears in W. C. Martin, *History of Warren County, Iowa*, 874–75.

70. The *Country Journal* printed an 1897 photograph of Waggener and four coeds—Jessie Boyd, Birdie Brown, Roxie Stuart and Laura Johnston—playing golf with primitive equipment. *Country Journal*, 9 (September 1982), 120.

71. A brief biography of Youtz appeared in the *Simpsonian*, December 1895.

72. Carpenter resigned on September 6. A fortnight later the *Herald* reported that he was engaged in "a continuous fight for life." *Indianola Weekly Herald*, September 20, 1894.

73. *Indianola Times*, October 4, 1894.

74. Simpson College, Board of Trustees, Minutes, June 12, 1895.

75. Baker had returned from his consulship in Copenhagen only a few months earlier.

76. *Indianola Weekly Herald*, March 12, 1891.

77. *Advocate-Tribune*, January 19, 1893.

78. Simpson College, Board of Trustees, Minutes, June 13, 1894.

79. *Advocate-Tribune*, January 24, 1895.

80. He was awarded the M.A. degree pro forma by his alma mater in 1893.

81. A brief biography of Jenkins appeared in the *Simpsonian*, February 1896.

82. Ibid., February 1895.

83. During a period of nearly eighty years, Simpson's music program was directed by only three men: Frank Barrows (1891–1924), Herbert A. Harvey (1924–40), and Sven Lekberg (1940–69).

84. His appointments required approval of the executive committee of the board of trustees, approval that was routinely given.

85. *Indianola Weekly Herald*, August 9, 1894; *Indianola Times*, August 2, 1894; *Advocate-Tribune*, August 9, 1894.

86. *The Educator*, 7 (Nov.-Dec. 1895), [12]. See accompanying illustration.

87. *Simpsonian*, December 1893.

88. Barrows's two years in Germany enabled him to work with two of the recognized masters of German music, Karl Klindworth and Ernst Jedlicsky. While in Berlin he taught

counterpoint and for more than a year served as organist at Berlin's American Church. In the spring of 1896 he studied further in Leipzig, returning to Indianola in June of that year.

89. "The campus fence has at last succumbed along the south side. The old wire fences on the other sides should be treated likewise." *Indianola Weekly Herald*, April 28, 1892. See also Simpson College, Board of Trustees, Minutes, June 14, 1892.

90. "The coeducationists," reported W. H. Schooley in the *Advocate-Tribune*, "may now repose under the majestic trees and upon the velvety lawn and there listen to the enchanting notes of the little bird and inhale the intoxicating aroma of the summer zephyr, without having their olfactories disturbed by the pungent odor of the pig pen, for thanks to the senior class the pig pen is no more." *Advocate-Tribune*, May 28, 1891.

91. Simpson College, Board of Trustees, Minutes, June 12, 1895.

92. Ibid., June 13, 1894.

93. Ibid., June 15, 1897. "The chapel looks different with new paint and *electric lights.*" *Simpsonian*, October 1897.

94. "Why not have electric light in the college?" queried the *Herald* in 1890. *Indianola Weekly Herald*, October 9, 1890. "The Everetts and Smithsonians are thinking of putting in electric lights." *Simpsonian*, October 1890. Indianola's municipal electric light plant had just opened that year, after voters had decided 299 to 128 to authorize the city to own and operate it. See W. C. Martin, *History of Warren County, Iowa*, 283.

95. Simpson College, Board of Trustees, Minutes, June 13, 1894.

96. *Simpsonian*, February 1894; *Indianola Weekly Herald*, February 8, 1894.

97. Simpson College, Board of Trustees, Minutes, June 14, 1898.

98. Eight bath rooms were built, two with tubs and six with "sprinklers." Students could use the gymnasium and baths for $2.50 per year or one dollar per term, the charge imposed at least until the $500 cost was recovered. The fee entitled the student "to bathe as many times as he might choose." The student provided his or her own soap and towel. W. H. Schooley could not wait to urge regular use of the baths: the student "should take prolonged tub baths at frequent intervals as the surest means of promoting a godly demeanor and a godly frame of mind in his fellow students." *Advocate-Tribune*, November 17, 1898.

99. *Simpsonian*, March 1899.

100. *Indianola Weekly Herald*, October 9, 1890.

101. Ibid., November 24, 1892.

102. *Zenith*, 1896, [114].

103. *Advocate-Tribune*, October 3, 1895. He also thought the protective equipment looked ridiculous: "A team equipped with these unbecoming arrangements might easily be mistaken for a crew of submarine divers or a band of gnomes escaped from a Christmas pantomime." Ibid.

104. *Indianola Weekly Herald*, November 3, 1898.

105. Ibid., October 13, 1898.

106. *Zenith*, 1896, [118].

107. *Indianola Weekly Herald*, May 3, 1894.

108. *Simpsonian*, April 1898.

109. Ibid., March 1895.

110. Ibid., February 1896.

111. Ibid., March 1897.

112. Ibid., January 1894.

113. See ibid., May 1900.

114. Simpson College, Board of Trustees, Minutes, June 15, 1897.

115. *Advocate-Tribune*, February 26, 1891.

116. Ibid., February 21, 1895. The earlier yell: "Hip! Haec! Tra boom; Que bizzum, yah zoom! Hullabaloo balonia; 'Rah, zoo, Simpsonia!!" *Indianola Weekly Herald*, January 15, 1891. In this *Herald* article the writer reported that on Tuesday afternoon [January 13, 1891] at a meeting of the Oratorical Association "red and gold were adopted as the college colors." This action, if correctly reported, was certainly belated, for the College colors had already been announced in the 1889 edition of the *Tangent*, 97.

117. The 1889 *Tangent* listed the membership of the "Cadet Corps" and described the Simpson uniform in a "War Department History," 89–90.

118. *Simpsonian*, October 1891; *Advocate-Tribune*, June 4, 1891.

119. On July 17, 1891, the secretary of the Simpson board of trustees was authorized to sign bond to the State of Iowa for the rifles and munitions required by the battalion, and in September the board's executive committee approved the construction of gun cases to be placed in the College's museum room under Professor Tilton's control.

120. *Simpsonian*, October 1891. No one was required to buy the uniform, but most did.

121. *Advocate-Tribune*, September 10, 1891.

122. Ibid., November 19, 1891.

123. "The flag was made by the ladies from the best grade of silk in the College colors and is about 42 x 60 inches in size." It was said to have cost nearly eight dollars. *Indianola Weekly Herald*, April 28, 1892.

124. Simpson College, Board of Trustees, Minutes, June 13, 1894.

125. *Advocate-Tribune*, February 24, 1898 and March 3, 1898.

126. *Simpsonian*, April 1898.

127. *Indianola Weekly Herald*, April 28, 1898.

128. The 1899 edition of the *Zenith* published the names of the enlistees in five different regiments: Elton B. Rogers and Ludwig J. Schmidt, the Forty-ninth Iowa; H. M. Havner, Guy J. Winslow and Albert H. Wood, the Fiftieth Iowa; Charles Baker, J. A. Beebe, George E. Fisher, Erwin Huffman, Frank Meredith, Thomas A. Neill, Ellis J. Rogers, J. B. Ross and Robert E. Slocum, Fifty-first Iowa; R. E. Humphrey, Sixth Illinois; and L. E. Conrad, North Dakota. *Zenith*, 1899, [113]. The *Simpsonian* of May 1898, listed three more: W. T. Black, Iowa Second; and D. Gaines and Gilbert Gander, Iowa Third.

129. *Simpsonian*, November 1899.

130. *Indianola Times*, October 17, 1896.

131. Ibid., April 1895, January 1897 and February 1897.

132. Ibid., January 1892.

133. Ibid., October 1894. "A surprisingly small number of students in the college have ever read through the Bible," was the comment about what was obvious. If a student engages in a "critical study of biblical literature treated historically, objectively, and scientifically," the likelihood of the "formation of true Christian character will not be diminished."

134. *Indianola Weekly Herald*, March 3, 1892 and March 10, 1892; *Advocate-Tribune*, January 17, 1895 and March 14, 1895; *Indianola Times*, December 6, 1894.

135. *Indianola Weekly Herald*, February 12, 1891. Two sororities, Pi Beta Phi and Delta Delta Delta, and two fraternities, Delta Tau Delta and SAE, maintained chapters at Simpson in the spring of 1891.

136. Ibid., June 18, 1891. The *Simpsonian* printed in March 1895 its first halftone cut, a photo of B. F. Clayton, who was then serving as president of Simpson's board of trustees and also as president of the Farmers' National Congress, a nonpartisan agricultural reform group.

137. Simpson College, Board of Trustees, Minutes, June 16, 1896 and June 15, 1897.

138. *Advocate-Tribune*, May 22, 1890.

139. *Simpsonian*, January 1898.

140. *Indianola Weekly Herald*, September 6, 1894; *Simpsonian*, April 1897.

141. The *Herald* explained this unthinkable dereliction politically: all of these students were known to be Democrats "and hence for the saloon." *Indianola Weekly Herald*, October 15, 1891. Their "severe discipline" included confinement to their quarters during evening hours and probationary status for the balance of the academic term.

142. *Simpsonian*, April 1892.

143. *Indianola Weekly Herald*, January 28, 1892.

144. Benjamin F. Clayton, "The 'Athens' of Iowa Methodism," *Midland Monthly*, 4 (July, 1985), 86.

145. *Simpsonian*, December 1891.

146. Ibid., December 1892.

147. Ruth Jackson, "A History of Simpson College" [incomplete manuscript], 1960, [141].

148. *Zenith*, 1897.

149. *Advocate-Tribune*, December 3, 1891 and December 10, 1891.

150. *Catalog of Simpson College*, 1890–91 (Indianola: College Print, 1891), 39.

151. The *Advocate-Tribune* announced the reorganization as early as December 17, 1891, but the *Simpsonian* carried the list of Philomathean officers until the end of the 1891–92 academic year.

152. *Simpsonian*, October 1892.

153. Ibid., February 1895.

154. Ibid., November, 1897.

155. According to the *Tangent*, published in the spring of 1889, of ninety-seven regular undergraduates sixty-two, or nearly two-thirds, were members of the eight Greek societies. The largest Greek group numbered twelve and the smallest four, but it must be recalled that some of them included additional preparatory students in their membership.

156. Phi Kappa Psi did not reopen in the fall of 1889; and Alpha Tau Omega, citing the "unnatural intensity of Fraternity life at Simpson" and "hostility and opposition" of nonfraternity students, surrendered its charter with the conviction that "the best interests of Simpson College would be subserved by abandonment of Greek Fraternities." *Simpsonian*, June 1890. Delta Tau Delta continued until 1894, when it withdrew in the face of determined Christian "barb" opposition. The SAEs managed to hang on alone until the end of the 1897–98 school year, when their chapter, too, succumbed. Meanwhile the Kappa Kappa Gamma sorority withdrew its charter in 1890, explaining that it was adopting a policy of confining its chapters to larger universities. The next year Kappa Alpha Theta, apparently for the same reason, closed its Simpson chapter. And throughout the nineties, all of these groups, with the single exception of SAE, lost individual members who almost invariably gave religious reasons for their withdrawal.

157. *Simpsonian*, October 1896.

158. Ibid., March 1895.

159. "Five members of the band have entered the [missionary] field—Ada Lauch and Lizzie Tryon to Cawnpore, India, Lydia Wilkinson in Foochow, China, Kitty Wood in Haidarbad [sic] Deccan, India, Takeshi Ukai in Tokio [sic], Japan." *Zenith*, 1896, [127].

160. *Simpsonian*, May 1891, October 1892 and March 1896.

161. Ibid., April 1897.

162. Ibid., April 1891.

163. Ibid., December 1891.

164. Ibid., January 1892.

165. Ibid., January 1897.

166. Brown was assigned by the Des Moines Conference to the pastorate in Nevada, Ia.

167. *Indianola Weekly Herald*, June 23, 1898. The *Herald* was edited for many years by two brothers, Thomas T. and James M. Anderson, who had lived in Warren County since 1857. James M. was elected to the Iowa legislature in 1899 and 1901. See Gerard Schultz and Don L. Berry, *History of Warren County, Iowa*, 247.

168. Harris served pastorates in Lewis (1883–86), Audubon (1886–89), Denison (1889–94), Prospect Park, Des Moines (1894–95), and Indianola (1895–98). See the Rev. Emory Miller's "memoir" of Harris in the *Minutes of the Forty-sixth Session of the Des Moines Annual Conference of the Methodist Episcopal Church* (Harlan, Ia.: Republican Office Print, 1905), 583–84. Harris married Mary Adella Berry in 1884 and had two children, both of whom graduated from Simpson, Bess in 1906 and Bert in 1909.

169. Harris remained at Denison a year (1899–1900) before being assigned to Boone (1900–05). In his fourth year at Boone he was struck by "an occult and malignant disease . . . [which] invoked the surgeon's knife." He recovered, attended the church's general conference in Los Angeles as a delegate and was reappointed to Boone for a fifth year. Unfortunately, however, "a second development of his former disease more virulent than the first" came upon him, and after two months of intense suffering he died on April 29, 1905, at the age of forty-five. See Emory Miller's memoir in the *Minutes* of 1905, cited above.

Chapter 9

1. See *Advocate-Tribune*, May 11, 1899.
2. See the brief biography of Shelton in *Historical Sketch and Alumni Record of Iowa Wesleyan College* (Mount Pleasant, Ia.: Mount Pleasant News Journal, 1917), 209–10.
3. Simpson College, Board of Trustees, Minutes, June 14, 1899.
4. Alma Robbins White, Interview, Davenport, Ia., October 4, 1981. Many would learn also to call him Dr. Shelton after 1902 when he was awarded an honorary LL.D. by his alma mater, Iowa Wesleyan.
5. Ibid.
6. Those trustees who served the entire eleven years of Shelton's administration were laymen William Buxton, Gorham A. Worth, Benjamin F. Clayton, William H. Berry and John H. Henderson of Indianola; Leroy Mann of Des Moines; E. W. Weeks of Guthrie Center; Joseph A. Brown of Chariton; E. A. Rea of Corydon; and G. S. Allyn of Mount Ayr (except for the last named who seems not to have served in 1900–01). Clergymen serving all eleven years were Fletcher Brown, former Simpson president; William E. Hamilton, faculty member and former president; Emory Miller, pastor in Indianola (1899–1902), Denison (1902–05) and Des Moines (1905–10) and William B. Thompson, pastor in Chariton (1899–1904), Bedford (1904–07), Des Moines (1907–09) and Red Oak (1909–10). Lay members for ten of the eleven years were President Shelton (1900–10) and E. D. Samson of Des Moines for that same decade.
7. *Advocate-Tribune*, May 11, 1899.
8. Ibid.
9. Alma Robbins White, Interview, Davenport, Ia., October 4, 1981. Any number of students would have disagreed sharply with White, for many remembered the old man as an inspiring lecturer.
10. *Simpsonian*, April 29, 1905.
11. Ibid., October 1902.
12. Alma Robbins White, Interview, Davenport, Ia., October 4, 1981.
13. *Simpsonian*, March 14, 1908.
14. "He has raised the standard of his department to an excellence that it has never reached before," and in the religious life of the College "he has been a quiet, yet powerful factor." Ibid., March 26, 1910.
15. First Corinthians, 6:19–20. See *Simpson College Bulletin*, Series 1, no. 1, Collegiate Year 1899–1900, May 1900, 76.
16. *Simpsonian*, September 19, 1908.
17. The bachelor of music degree was approved by the College's board of trustees June 12, 1900. Barrows had anticipated this action, and the first five diplomas were awarded at commencement two days later. See also *Indianola Herald*, June 14, 1900.
18. Landsbury was definitely on the faculty through the 1906–07 year. Whether he returned for the 1907–08 year is not clear. Regrettably the College in 1907 ceased publication of a complete annual catalog, substituting a series of editions of the *Simpson College Bulletin* for each academic program. Some of these publications are missing in the College archives. Landsbury later became head of the music school at the University of Oregon.
19. *Simpson College Bulletin*, Series 24, March 1, 1923, 3. See also Stephen C. Boss, "The Conservatory of Music under the Administration of Frank Ellis Barrows (1891–1924)," 1982. Ms. in Simpson College archives.
20. *Simpson College Bulletin*, Series 24, March 1, 1923, 3.
21. *Advocate-Tribune*, July 17, 1902.
22. In the 1901–04 years art enrollment ranged from 5 to 8, and it was noted with some asperity by Shelton that such small numbers hardly justified the expense of the school. Under Eunora Maxson's leadership the enrollment increased, with 20 studying art in the 1906–07 academic year. In that year, however, music enrollment stood at 333.
23. In his second year he was assisted by Edna Hull, another student. *Simpsonian*, September 19, 1908.

24. *Indianola Herald*, October 3, 1907.

25. A copy of Craven's "Count Tolstoi" is on file in the Avery O. and Georgia Craven Room in the Dunn Library at Simpson College.

26. A good account of Craven's undergraduate years and professional accomplishments in history are contained in Rozann Hartstack, "Avery O. Craven's Simpson Connection," *The Sequel*, Simpson's Magazine of Literature and Art, 1986, [25–34].

27. *Simpson College, Catalog*, 1898–99, publishing the announcement for the 1899–1900 academic year, 19.

28. The required segment of the curriculum for all degrees included mathematics (10 hours), astronomy (5), modern language (15), English Bible (8), natural science (15), English language (9), English literature (6), history (9) and philosophy (15). Candidates for the B.A. were required to earn an additional 45 hours in Greek and 15 hours in Latin; for the B.Ph. 30 hours of Latin, 9 hours of advanced English and 30 hours of philosophy; for the B.Sc. 30 hours of modern language, 9 hours of drawing and 45 hours of natural science.

29. Frederick Rudolph, *The American College and University: A History* (New York: Alfred A. Knopf, 1965), 290.

30. Samuel Eliot Morison, *Three Centuries of Harvard: 1636–1936* (Cambridge: The Belknap Press of Harvard University Press, 1963), 389–90.

31. Rudolph, 296.

32. As quoted in Ibid., 298.

33. In 1908 the first semester opened on September 14, ending on December 23. The second semester commenced January 5 and concluded at the end of May. Commencement week ran from June 1 to June 10. It is perhaps worthy of note that nowhere in the minutes of the board of trustees is any discussion or any action on adopting the semester calendar to be found. The board seems to have been too busy discussing the "three F's": finances, fraternities and football, leaving calendar and curriculum to the faculty. Only in 1900 did the board secretary make note of the fact that "last year the course of study was entirely re-arranged upon the credit system with large numbers of electives so that each course would be more adaptable to the needs of the various students than [in] any former year." Simpson College, Board of Trustees, Minutes, June 12, 1900.

34. The enrollments of Business and Shorthand and Typewriting have been combined. In some cases, especially for the years 1907 to 1910, the College's total enrollment is exaggerated because a fairly substantial number of students were counted twice.

35. In 1907 Barrows limited the number of younger children who could receive instruction in the conservatory.

36. Simpson College, Board of Trustees, Minutes, April 10, 1900.

37. Ibid.

38. Ibid., June 12, 1900. The bid on the conservatory was $7,471 and on the administration building $5,327. Bids were received June 1, but apparently no contracts were signed because the College still did not have sufficient funds on hand to go ahead with both projects at one time. *Indianola Herald*, May 17, 1900. A few weeks later the board agreed to go ahead with the conservatory as soon as three-quarters of the amount of the contractor's bid for both buildings was pledged or in hand. Actually, the administration building would be constructed first, the conservatory having to wait two years longer until funding was available. See also *Indianola Herald*, June 14, 1900.

39. *Advocate-Tribune*, August 30, 1900.

40. Ibid. October 25, 1900.

41. *Indianola Herald*, September 6, 1900; *Zenith*, 1910 (May 1909), no pagination.

42. *Zenith*, 1910.

43. *Simpsonian*, May 31, 1902; Simpson College, Board of Trustees, Minutes, June 10, 1902.

44. *Indianola Herald*, October 16, 1902; *Advocate-Tribune*, November 27, 1902.

45. *Catalog and Bulletin of Simpson College*, series 18, 1917, no. 4, 127.

46. Years later—in the 1920s—a severe storm destroyed two of the five windows in Edgerton Hall, but the remaining windows were saved and later lovingly removed from the building when it was demolished in 1983 and installed in the new Amy Robertson Music Center.

47. *Indianola Herald*, December 18, 1902.
48. *Simpsonian*, October 1902.
49. See Simpson College, Board of Trustees, Minutes, June 18 and June 19, 1901.
50. Ibid., June 10, 1902.
51. The boilers, built by the Des Moines Manufacturing and Supply Company, were each sixteen feet tall and five feet in diameter, with a total of fifty-four flues.
52. *Simpsonian*, November 1901.
53. *Simpsonian*, October 1901. Worse yet, within a week or so after it was first fired up, in a bad case of first-time jitters, the "refractory" plant failed, forcing the dismissal of classes in Science Hall for a day or so. *Simpsonian*, December 1901.
54. *Simpsonian*, October 1901; January 1902.
55. *Advocate-Tribune*, October 2, 1902.
56. The 1901 drawing penned by Prof. Keith of the Simpson Art department, was long on display down on the square at Cole and Connoran's Jewelry Store. *Indianola Herald*, March 28, 1901. Another plan for the building appeared in the 1905 edition of the *Zenith*. It was a considerable improvement on the 1901 version.
57. *Indianola Herald*, March 25, 1909. A long article in this edition of the paper includes a front elevation, floor plans and a detailed description of the facilities that would be contained in the hoped-for building.
58. Ibid. April 8, 1909.
59. Simpson College, Board of Trustees, Minutes, February 15, 1910.
60. *Indianola Herald*, February 10, 1910.
61. *Advocate-Tribune*, November 27, 1902.
62. Ibid., May 2, 1901.
63. Carnegie gave the city $10,000 in early 1903. *Indianola Herald*, January 29, 1903. Books were moved into the completed building in May 1904. *Advocate-Tribune*, May 12, 1904.
64. The population of Indianola in 1900 was 3,261.
65. *Indianola Herald*, February 23, 1905.
66. Ibid.
67. Ibid., May 24, 1906.
68. Ibid., August 23, 1906.
69. Ibid., June 13, 1907.
70. Ibid. The dedication ceremony took place at 2 o'clock in the afternoon of June 8.
71. Simpson College, Board of Trustees, Minutes, June 11, 1907.
72. See Edna VanSyoc, "Simpson College Library," probably written in the early 1930s, [4], and Richard Calkin's, "Simpson College Buildings," written in 1941, 12. These manuscripts are held in the College's archives in Dunn Library.
73. Simpson College, Board of Trustees, Minutes, June 18, 1901, June 19, 1901.
74. Ibid., March 22, 1904.
75. *Simpsonian*, January 1904.
76. *Indianola Herald*, December 28, 1905. See also *Advocate-Tribune*, January 11, 1906.
77. The 1901–02 deficit of $626 worried Shelton, but it was not nearly so great as the $1,711 shortfall in the one-year Harris administration. The first mention of the need of a budget can be found in Simpson College, Board of Trustees, Minutes, June 13, 1906.
78. *Indianola Herald*, September 1, 1904.
79. Ibid., November 16, 1905.
80. Simpson College, Board of Trustees, Minutes, September 15, 1905.
81. *Advocate-Tribune*, April 26, 1906.
82. In addition to Homan, those who pledged $1,000 included William Buxton, Harry Hopper, Mary J. Sandy, Fletcher Brown and family, B. F. Clayton, the Simpson Faculty as a group, the Class of 1906, Carl and Sara Sigler, William E. Hamilton, William Buxton, Jr., H. C. Howser and William H. and Mrs. Berry. *Indianola Herald*, January 17, 1907.
83. *Advocate-Tribune*, January 27, 1910.
84. *Indianola Herald*, January 2, 1902.
85. Ibid., July 3, 1902.

86. Quoted in ibid., February 12, 1903.
87. Keach Johnson, "The State of Elementary and Secondary Education in Iowa in 1900," *The Annals of Iowa*, 49 (Summer-Fall 1987), 32. In 1900 only 1,246 elementary schools were graded; 12,615 were ungraded. Further, nearly 60 percent of all Iowa youngsters lived in districts with no high school at all.
88. *Indianola Herald*, June 18, 1908; *Advocate-Tribune*, September 17, 1908.
89. *Advocate-Tribune*, June 1, 1905.
90. Interestingly, Effie Silliman also taught that year at the Simpson Conservatory.
91. *Indianola Herald*, September 28, 1905.
92. Ibid, January 18, 1906.
93. Ibid., December 14, 1905.
94. *Advocate-Tribune*, April 26, 1906. See also *Indianola Herald*, March 22, 1906. The performances were held on May 1 and 2.
95. *Advocate-Tribune*, for the dates indicated in the text.
96. Ibid., November 22, 1906.
97. *Advocate-Tribune*, January 3, 1907.
98. Ibid., May 9, 1907.
99. Simpson won only one game in the 1904 season. *Indianola Herald*, October 27, 1904.
100. *Simpsonian*, October 1900.
101. Frederick Rudolph, 377.
102. *Des Moines Register and Leader*, December 1, 1905.
103. Quoted in *Indianola Herald*, January 4, 1906.
104. *Indianola Herald*, January 22, 1903.
105. Simpson College, Board of Trustees, Minutes, June 12, 1906; *Indianola Herald*, June 21, 1906. The *Herald*, while admitting that football was "brutal to a certain extent," asserted that Simpson had so neglected athletics during the past few years that "had not football been abolished . . . it would have of itself died out for want of material." The writer went on to blame football's demise on lack of encouragement and "favoritism among players and poor coaches." The article suggested that perhaps now "ping pong, tennis and tiddle-wink [sic]" could "be played in the shade of the old maple trees."
106. Somehow a "practice" game was played with Drake in the fall of 1907. *Advocate-Tribune*, October 3, 1907.
107. Simpson College, Board of Trustees, Minutes, June 11, 1907; *Simpsonian*, March 14, 1908 and May 23, 1908.
108. The Board agreed that "during the season of 1908 [the football team] be allowed to contract for and participate in six inter-collegiate contests." Ibid., June 9, 1908.
109. *Simpsonian*, December 1902.
110. The boys soon discovered that Alpha Phi was already the name of a prominent national sorority.
111. *Simpsonian*, January 1903.
112. The reinstallation took place on May 20, 1905.
113. Simpson College, Board of Trustees, Minutes, June 6, 1905.
114. Ibid., June 9, 1908.
115. Ibid., June 6, 1905.
116. *Indianola Herald*, October 19, 1905.
117. Simpson College, Board of Trustees, Minutes, June 13, 1906. At that same time the office of dean of women was created. Elizabeth Bentley was the first appointee, and for this additional obligation she received one hundred dollars per year.
118. *Simpson College Bulletin: College of Liberal Arts, 1907–08*, Series 8, no. 5, 7.
119. *Advocate-Tribune*, May 12, 1904.
120. *Simpsonian*, February 1901 and February 1902. At the turn of the century the Simpson Y.M.C.A. declared, "For a Methodist school whose influence does not clearly and definitely advance the spiritual experience of Christian students and make almost certain the redemption of the unsaved ones, there is no excuse for its existence." *Simpsonian*, November 1900.
121. *Simpsonian*, October 16, 1909.
122. Ibid., March 1902.

123. Ibid., February 1902.

124. Simpson College, Board of Trustees, Minutes, June 9, 1903 and June 10, 1903. For years thereafter John Tilton kept trying to get his hands on the income money, but the board of trustees found ingenious ways to put him off.

125. *Simpsonian*, November 7, 1908. The *Indianola Herald*'s editor declared that "it is now a real pleasure" to know that the Hall is named for the daughter of Reverend T. S. Berry "of precious memory to all those who knew him in life." *Indianola Herald*, November 19, 1908.

126. *Indianola Herald*, January 9, 1902.

127. *Simpsonian*, March 1903; *Indianola Herald*, March 5, 1903.

128. Their elders set the tone. Dr. Homer C. Stuntz's commencement lecture on missionary work abroad boasted that "the Philippine Islands now enjoy the privileges of free thought and free institutions. . . . Before America entered the Philippines there were no civilizing forces at work." *Indianola Herald*, June 9, 1910.

129. *Zenith*, 1901 (Indianola: Record Printing House, 1901), [no pagination].

130. *Indianola Herald*, February 10, 1910; Simpson College, Board of Trustees, Minutes, February 15, 1910.

131. *Indianola Herald*, February 17, 1910. She was ill enough to be hospitalized a few months later. Ibid., May 26, 1910.

132. Rumors flew around the icy streets of Indianola that winter, speculating about the reasons for Shelton's resignation. The most persistent had it that the Methodists were about to take over ailing Highland Park College in Des Moines and that Shelton would head it. That was nonsense, wrote the editor of the *Advocate-Tribune*, who said that he did not know Shelton's future plans, "but take it for granted that he knows pretty well what he is doing and when he gets ready he will tell the people what he wants them to know." *Advocate-Tribune*, February 17, 1910.

133. *Indianola Herald*, June 23, 1910.

134. Simpson College, Board of Trustees, Minutes, June 3, 1910.

135. *Advocate-Tribune*, June 9, 1910.

136. *Commencement Daily*, June 4, 1910.

137. *Indianola Herald*, June 9, 1910.

138. Ibid., June 9, 1910.

139. That summer Julia Shelton recovered sufficiently that she could accompany her husband on a long European tour. Her health did not hold out, however, and she died in 1917, and was buried in Indianola. Dr. Shelton later remarried, this time to Fannie Roseman of Washington, D.C., on July 18, 1919. See *Indianola Herald*, July 24, 1919. After a number of years of educational work and lecturing in the eastern U.S., including a stint as superintendent of Mountain Lake Park Summer Resort and Assemblies in Maryland, he entered the ministry, but not in the Methodist Church. Rather, in 1913 he became a Congregational clergyman, holding pastorates in Scranton, Pittsburgh and Germantown, Pennsylvania and Portsmouth, Virginia, where the Shelton Memorial Church was named in his honor. After years of devoted service in these churches he retired and moved to be near his son, Dr. Whitford H. Shelton, who was head of the Department of Modern Languages at the University of Pittsburgh, and died at Pittsburgh May 13, 1940. *New York Times*, May 14, 1940. Shelton's funeral was held in Indianola, and he was laid to rest next to his wife Julia in the Indianola cemetery.

Chapter 10

1. It did not, however, offer an irresistible financial inducement. His salary was $3,000 a year during all five years of his tenure at Simpson.

2. They had two daughters, Florence May and Mary Edith.

3. *Indianola Herald*, July 28, 1910.

4. *Christian Advocate*, quoted in *Indianola Herald*, August 4, 1910.

5. *Indianola Herald*, July 28, 1910.

6. He certainly tried to do the best he could, but there was a note of frustration when

in 1914 he wrote an open letter to students regarding some upcoming revival services: "Are you a Christian? Is it . . . not a fitting time to test the gold of our loyalty to Christ? The fire of faith on the altar of your heart may have been burning rather low of late." *Simpsonian*, February 2, 1914.

7. *Zenith*, 1912.

8. Ibid.

9. Ibid.

10. Tilton was royally entertained by his faculty colleagues, honoring his "brand new Ph.D.," at a party with ice cream, cake and cocoa. *Simpsonian*, January 21, 1911.

11. See Simpson College, Board of Trustees, Minutes, June 6, 1911.

12. An extensive account of Hamilton's career at the College is found in the *Simpsonian*, June 3, 1911.

13. Goodwin earned the M.A. degree from Albion in 1913.

14. *Simpsonian*, April 20, 1914.

15. In his three years at Simpson Dodson gained considerable popularity with students, respect from faculty and notoriety in Indianola. His reputation for "fearlessness" was earned when he did a striking series of lectures which related Darwinian evolutionary theory to the process of historical change. Some religious conservatives in town found his utterances offensive, and said so, but most Simpson people, including the president, found his ideas truly thought-provoking.

16. *Simpsonian*, October 6, 1915.

17. See Ibid., September 16, 1911, September 15, 1913, and September 14, 1914.

18. Ibid., September 21, 1914.

19. Salaries for regularly employed faculty members were nearly always recorded in the minutes of the meetings of the board of trustees. For Strickland's comments, see Simpson College, Board of Trustees, Minutes, June 12, 1912.

20. Carl F. Brown, "Pigs Went to Chapel, and Some Other Unrecorded Events in the History of Simpson College," an address presented to the members of Indianola's Quarter Century Club, November 18, 1959, [6]. "For a long time," writes Brown, son of Simpson president Fletcher Brown (1893–98), "my mother kept a letter [Worth] had sent to my father: 'Dear Fletcher, I am sick. If I should die, I would go straight to Hell. Why don't you come to see me?'"

21. In 1914, for some reason, only eight new trustees, all laymen, were elected. See *Catalogue of Simpson College* (Indianola: Published by the College, 1915), an issue of the *Quarterly Bulletin of Simpson College*, series 16, no. 3 (April 1915), 5.

22. Garrett awarded him the Doctor of Divinity degree in 1912.

23. The *Quarterly Bulletin of Simpson College*, series 12, no. 2 (February 1911), 34.

24. The *Catalog of Simpson College*, an issue of the *Quarterly Bulletin of Simpson College*, series 12, no. 4 (May 1911), 26.

25. Ibid., 27–29. More groups would be added subsequently: in 1912 physics and pre-engineering were made separate groups and music was added; and in 1915 home economics was instituted.

26. *Indianola Herald*, October 5, 1911.

27. Ibid., April 18, 1912. A versatile young woman, June Hamilton Rhodes had studied at Columbia University and in Berlin. She had taught in the dramatic school of the Chicago Conservatory of Music and had served as director of physical culture in the Y.W.C.A. at Nashville, Tennessee. See *Simpsonian*, October 6, 1915.

28. Christie Swain, "History of Simpson College," *Zenith*, 1934.

29. Simpson College, Board of Trustees, Minutes, June 9, 1915.

30. Ibid.

31. She had taught at Lenox, Iowa, during the 1914–15 academic year. See *Simpsonian*, September 13, 1915; October 6, 1915.

32. *Simpsonian*, October 6, 1915.

33. Ibid., September 13, 1915. At first only a part of the building was needed, but within three years the program had grown so rapidly that the entire building was used. Christie Swain, "History of Simpson College," *Zenith*, 1934.

34. Ibid., October 6, 1915.
35. *Zenith*, 1912.
36. *Indianola Herald*, October 5, 1911. The board of trustees instructed Dr. Strickland to inform the War Department that "we don't want an officer here on their terms." It is clear that "their terms" would mean increasing the battalion's enrollment above the one hundred-man minimum by making drill compulsory for nearly all men in the College. Simpson College, Board of Trustees, Executive Committee, Minutes, August 11, 1911.
37. *Simpsonian*, March 24, 1913; *Indianola Herald*, April 3, 1913.
38. Academy enrollment was down. Only eleven students entered in 1911 compared to twenty-one in 1910. Such a sharp decrease was probably due to "the new law which grants free tuition to all students in the state at the High School in their county seat." Simpson College, Board of Trustees, Minutes, June 12, 1912.
39. *Indianola Herald*, April 20, 1911. The *Simpsonian* editor doxologized, "Praise God from whom all blessings flow." *Simpsonian*, April 15, 1911.
40. Ibid., June 29, 1911.
41. *Des Moines Register and Leader*, June 29, 1911.
42. *Quarterly Bulletin of Simpson College*, series 13, no. 1 (November 1911), 3. A biography of Hopper appeared in W. C. Martin's 1908 *History of Warren County, Iowa*, 412–16, and a good account of Hopper's stock farm can be found in Gerard Schultz and Don L. Berry, *History of Warren County, Iowa*, 47–50.
43. Ibid, 4. Of course Don Berry, who wrote these words, was as rock-ribbed a Republican as one could find, and he took special pleasure in blaming Democrats for all manner of national woes.
44. A son, Byron, was born to the Hoppers in 1899 and a daughter, Dorothy, five years later.
45. *Indianola Tribune*, October 4, 1944.
46. Ibid.
47. The Hopper swimming pool, alas, was never built.
48. Ibid. See also Carl Brown's account of the incident in "Pigs Went to Chapel," 4.
49. *Indianola Tribune*, October 4, 1944. Dorothy Daniel, whose delightful book *Circle 'Round the Square* recounts her experience growing up in Indianola with her grandparents during the decade after 1910, remembered that the decline of Harry Hopper's empire "involved farm lands and horses. . . . Grandmother said she knew for a fact that the gym had ruined Harry. Grandfather [attorney O.C. Brown] said she didn't know what she was talking about, that Harry had been bailed out of his philanthropic role." Actually they were both wrong. No one came to Hopper's rescue, and he paid for the gymnasium in full. A sacrifice to be sure, but one he could manage. And it is a matter of record that Hopper bought the county fairgrounds that same year (1912) and spent a lot of money rebuilding the race track in order to have a place to run his horses. Seven years later he sold the track back to the county fair board for $25,000. See Dorothy Daniel, *Circle 'Round the Square*, 204–05; Gerard Schultz and Don L. Berry, *History of Warren County, Iowa*, 47.
50. At Hopper's funeral in Pasadena, both Dr. Fletcher Homan, former vice-president of Simpson, and Dr. John P. Morley, his classmate and old friend, read scripture and offered prayer while Dr. Morley's daughter, Alice McAbery, sang, accompanied by Everett "Tip" Olive.
51. Meanwhile Hopper paid the first five years' insurance premiums on the new building. Peter Ross's $750 salary was picked up by the College in 1913. See Simpson College Board of Trustees, Executive Committee, Minutes, September 23, 1913.
52. *Indianola Tribune*, October 4, 1944.
53. In 1913 the Board of Trustees did note that "one benefactor, Mr. Harry Hopper . . . has given at least $125,000, almost as much as all the others combined." Simpson College, Board of Trustees, Minutes, June 11, 1913.
54. See Simpson College, Board of Trustees, Minutes, November 29 and December 13, 1910.
55. In addition to Hopper's $25,000, major gifts included $10,000 from William Buxton, Sr., $7,000 from Carl Sigler, $5,000 from J. A. Brown of Chariton, $2,000 from William Buxton,

Jr., $1,800 from C. A. McCune of Des Moines (Mrs. McCune was Mrs. Sigler's sister) and twenty-one $1,000 contributions. *Quarterly Bulletin of Simpson College,* series 13, no. 2 (January 1912), 20–22; *Simpsonian,* January 13, 1912, January 20, 1912.

56. These books, stated the directive of the state board, must be suited for the College's various academic departments. "Public documents and books having no reference to college work do not count." *Indianola Herald,* November 23, 1911.

57. *Simpsonian,* November 23, 1911; November 30, 1911.

58. Ibid., December 14, 1911.

59. See Simpson College, Board of Trustees, Minutes, June 12, 1912. By 1914 the president could report 9,302 volumes in the library, in 1915 10,450 volumes, including 785 given from Kate Corkhill's library at the time of her death.

60. Ibid. During four of the five years of the Strickland administration the College operated at a deficit: approximately $2,000 in 1910–11 and $5,000 in 1912–13; and exactly $5,339.78 in 1913–14, and $5,579.11 in 1914–15.

61. *Simpsonian,* September 9, 1912. See also Simpson College, Board of Trustees, Minutes, June 11, 1913.

62. *Simpsonian,* April 13, 1912; October 21, 1912.

63. Ibid., November 25, 1912; April 7, 1913; May 5, 1913; September 15, 1913.

64. By the end of the 1914–15 year the College, which already had a bonded indebtedness of $25,000, was forced to issue an additional $20,000 gold bonds bearing six percent interest to cover current shortfalls. Simpson College, Board of Trustees, Minutes, June 9, 1915. It was costing about $44,000 to run the College, and the board could count on not more than $38,700 in income.

65. Simpson College, Board of Trustees, Minutes, June 10, 1914.

66. Ibid., June 9, 1915.

67. Simpson College, Board of Trustees, Minutes, June 11, 1913. The conference raised $2,565 for education that year, eighty percent of which went to Simpson and twenty percent to Methodist institutions in the South.

68. *Simpsonian,* December 6, 1915.

69. *Indianola Herald,* September 30, 1915.

70. Simpson College, Board of Trustees, Minutes, June 7, 1916; *Simpsonian,* September 27, 1915; October 6, 1915; October 18, 1915; November 15, 1915; December 6, 1915; December 13, 1915; and especially January 10, 1916. See also *Indianola Herald,* December 23, 1915.

71. That figure, however, included $38,000 in annuities and unproductive funds of something more than $25,000.

72. Simpson College, Board of Trustees, Minutes, June 9, 1915.

73. Simpson not only met the church's requirements; it had also been a charter member of the North Central Association of Schools and Colleges in 1912. By 1914, the N.C.A. had accredited only nine Iowa colleges and universities. Three of the five Methodist-related institutions were approved: Simpson, Morningside and Cornell. Simpson was also on the New York list of accredited colleges, important for those seeking educational certification or qualifying for medical or bar examinations. See Simpson College, Board of Trustees, Minutes, June 10, 1914.

74. It appears that the Des Moines Conference, meeting at Mount Ayr at that same time, had no prior knowledge of the Parsons proposition.

75. Herbert N. Jeffrey, ed., *Historical Sketch and Alumni Record of Iowa Wesleyan College* (Mount Pleasant, Iowa: Mount Pleasant News Journal, 1917), 52–53.

76. See the report of William E. Hamilton to the Board in Simpson College, Board of Trustees, Minutes, June 7, 1916. See also Dr. Strickland's earlier report to the Board in ibid., June 11, 1913.

77. The president's announcement came on June 4, 1915. See *Zenith,* 1917; Simpson College, Board of Trustees, Minutes, June 9, 1915; *Indianola Herald,* June 10, 1915.

78. *Indianola Herald,* June 17, 1915.

79. Simpson College, Board of Trustees, Minutes, June 9, 1915. His salary commenced on August 15, 1915, and ended nine months later, May 15, 1916, when his successor took over. Thus the interim presidency cost the College only $1,500.

80. Ibid., June 7, 1916.
81. *Indianola Herald*, March 23, 1916; *Simpsonian*, April 17, 1916.
82. Simpson College, Board of Trustees, Minutes, April 26, 1916.
83. There were those "friends of Simpson College" who were disappointed that Harry Hopper was a member of the search committee. "Their regret is founded on the belief that he should be selected president . . . and they assume he will not let his committee name him." *Des Moines Register and Leader*, August 18, 1915.
84. Simpson College, Board of Trustees, Minutes, April 26, 1916.
85. *Simpsonian*, October 9, 1916.
86. The *Advocate-Tribune* announced Campbell's election in its April 26 edition. Campbell at first insisted on $4,000 per annum salary, but compromised when the board assured him that they would try to do better the following year. They did.
87. James W. Campbell, Newtonville, Mass., to J.H. Henderson, Indianola, Iowa, May 4, 1916.
88. *Advocate-Tribune*, May 25, 1916.
89. In addition to the words of Crawford, responses were delivered by Presidents Lemuel Herbert Murlin, Boston University; Alfred E. Craig, Morningside College; and Albert Walter Jessup, State University of Iowa, together with Albert M. Devoe, State Superintendent of Public Instruction; Dr. E. E. Higley, pastor of Des Moines Grace Methodist Church; and, for the alumni, Martha Stahl Beall '88.
90. *Zenith*, 1917.
91. *Zenith*, 1918.
92. *Simpsonian*, May 29, 1916.
93. Ibid., February 5, 1917.
94. Ibid., February 12, 1917.
95. *Advocate-Tribune*, February 8, 1917.
96. Ibid., February 19, 1917.
97. *Zenith*, 1918.
98. *Simpsonian*, April 2, 1917.
99. Ibid., April 16, 1917.
100. *Advocate-Tribune*, April 26, 1917; *Simpsonian*, May 28, 1917. John L. Tilton had sent out a call for volunteers in February. They drilled Monday and Friday evenings until June.
101. *Simpsonian*, September 17, 1917.
102. Ibid., September 24, 1917.
103. Ibid., November 12, 1917.
104. Ibid., May 20, 1918.
105. *Indianola Herald*, May 23, 1918.
106. Simpson College, Board of Trustees, Minutes, June 4, 1918.
107. Ibid.
108. Ibid. The S.A.T.C. would, it was hoped, prevent "indiscriminate volunteering" and the "wasteful depletion of the colleges."
109. *Advocate-Tribune*, October 17, 1918. They paid Dr. Weeks five dollars per week.
110. Simpson College, Board of Trustees, Executive Committee, Minutes, September 1, 1918; September 4, 1918; September 5, 1918; September 7, 1918.
111. *Zenith*, 1920. President Campbell importuned the War Department to continue the S.A.T.C. until January 1, 1919, but to no avail.
112. An earlier influenza outbreak had wreaked havoc with the spring semester of 1918, when the College was required to close down for a time, forcing the extension of the school year to June 5. See *Simpsonian*, February 4, 1918.
113. Students were to meet once a week to receive their classroom assignments, and they might meet in small groups to study. Ibid., November 25, 1918.
114. Ibid., December 2, 1918.
115. Ibid., November 18, 1918.
116. On January 19, 1919, Lieutenants Frey and Pierce departed.
117. When officials of the Pi Kappa Delta forensic fraternity arrived on the campus on De-

cember 8 to install their new Simpson chapter, only the Indianola people showed up for the ceremony.

118. *Simpsonian*, January 6, 1919.

119. Ibid., February 10, 1919. Dr. Rogers's name was omitted in the 1920 *Zenith* listing of Simpsonians who had served during the war.

120. In fact, Morley left on April 4, 1917, and Campbell persuaded William E. Hamilton, who thought he had truly retired, to come back for a few weeks to take care of Morley's classes.

121. Simpson College, Board of Trustees, Minutes, June 4, 1918.

122. *Zenith*, 1919.

123. Simpson College, Board of Trustees, Minutes, June 4, 1918. Maxwell left on April 23.

124. Geauque continued in this position until the spring of 1920, when J. Allen Baker returned to his post.

125. Still, J. Hugh Jackson '12 defended Simpson's program: "The school of business," he wrote in 1916, "has oftentimes received unjust criticism, and it is to be regretted that, in times past, even members of our faculty have desired the abolishment of so important and efficient a part of Simpson College, yet the old school has flourished through it all." *Simpsonian*, January 17, 1916.

126. *Simpsonian*, January 6, 1919.

127. Simpson College, Board of Trustees, Minutes, June 5, 1917; June 4, 1918.

128. Ibid., June 4, 1918.

129. Ibid.

130. *Indianola Herald*, October 26, 1916; Simpson College, Board of Trustees, Minutes, June 5, 1917.

131. Buxton died on March 5, 1918.

132. Clyde Proudfoot served only briefly as treasurer. He resigned late that fall. Simpson College, Board of Trustees, Executive Committee, Minutes, October 28, 1918.

133. Miss Todd was a graduate of Simpson in the class of 1898 and was serving her first year as the College's dean of women.

134. A vivid description of the fire appeared in the *Simpsonian*, February 18, 1918. See also *Indianola Herald*, February 14, 1918.

135. Drake did not score a single basket. All its eight points were on free throws. See *Zenith*, 1919.

136. "The campaign for . . . a new central building . . . has been going very slowly," commented the *Advocate-Tribune*, March 28, 1918.

137. Simpson College, Board of Trustees, Executive Committee Minutes, July 17, 1918; July 19, 1918.

138. Ibid., August 9, 1918.

139. *Simpsonian*, November 25, 1918; January 27, 1919.

140. Simpson College, Board of Trustees, Executive Committee, Minutes, August 9, 1918.

141. Ibid., September 14, 1918.

142. Ibid., January 7, 1919.

143. Ibid., December 30, 1918.

144. Ibid., December 30, 1918; January 17, 1919.

145. *Indianola Herald*, March 20, 1919.

146. Simpson College, Board of Trustees, Executive Committee, Minutes, March 19, 1919.

147. *Simpsonian*, May 26, 1919.

148. The general contract totaled $103,463 and the smaller Carstens contract $16,105. Simpson College, Board of Trustees, Executive Committee, Minutes, May 20, 1919.

149. The Baker house had been sold and removed early in April. Ibid., April 5, 1919; *Simpsonian*, June 16, 1919. The groundbreaking is pictured in the *Zenith*, 1921.

150. *Simpsonian*, June 16, 1919.

151. Simpson College, Board of Trustees, Minutes, June 24, 1919. Years later, in 1972, Indianola editor Don Berry, in an article in the *Simpson Alumnus* recounting the careers of Simpson presidents, wrote that President Campbell "didn't make a hit at all." This assertion triggered a fast response from Campbell's daughter, Ruth E. Campbell, who graduated from

Simpson in the class of 1921 and was in 1972 a professor emeritus at the University of Wyoming. Disappointed at Berry's "unkindness to my father," she pointed out his several accomplishments as president of the College. Conceding that he "may have made some mistakes," she believed he should receive credit for his accomplishments while he was in Indianola. *Simpson College Bulletin*, Autumn, 1972; December, 1972.

152. *Simpsonian*, October 14, 1912.

153. Ibid., November 17, 1913.

154. Ibid., March 6, 1916.

155. See the *Zenith* for 1918, 1919 and 1920 (for the years 1916 to 1919). See also *Simpsonian*, February 23, 1920.

156. The *Simpsonian* in 1912 devoted an entire issue to the history and activities of the College's literary societies. *Simpsonian*, March 16, 1912.

157. Ibid., February 11, 1911; May 20, 1911.

158. Ibid., February 17, 1912. There were reports that literary societies were declining in the large universities, where few participated in their activities.

159. Ibid., April 15, 1918.

160. Ibid., October 13, 1919.

161. *Zenith*, 1915.

162. "Women are barred from intercollegiate athletics," wrote June Hamilton Rhodes in 1914. See *Zenith*, 1914.

163. In the fall of 1912 Iddings, who was seriously ill on his ranch out in Wyoming, was unable to return to the campus. The College hired as his temporary replacement Walter "Stub" Stewart, who coached the team throughout the 1912 season. When Iddings recovered, he returned to the campus in time to coach the 1913 basketball team.

164. Once the *Simpsonian*, lamenting Simpson's undistinguished football record, suggested that the College offer athletic scholarships. John Tilton, whose interest in sports no one could gainsay, opposed that idea vigorously, and Simpson remained, at least for some years, athletically pure. *Simpsonian*, June 12, 1912.

165. *Des Moines Register and Leader*, as quoted in *Zenith*, 1917.

166. See *Indianola Herald*, February 13, 1913. The Des Moines press seemed to side with Simpson in its dispute with Grinnell.

167. *Zenith*, 1918.

168. *Zenith*, 1920.

169. Simpson College, Board of Trustees, Minutes, June 7, 1916.

170. See *Simpsonian*, January 20, 1913.

171. They did take note of the fact that the number of fatalities in football nationwide declined from thirty in 1909 to ten in 1912, the improvement probably due to better equipment and stricter playing rules.

172. *Simpsonian*, October 27, 1913.

173. Ibid., December 17, 1913.

174. Ibid., November 10, 1913.

175. *Zenith*, 1914.

176. The Committee included board members F. Carl Sigler, Harry Hopper and John H. Henderson, together with faculty members John Tilton, Lora Hagler and Mary Hunting. See *Simpsonian*, September 24, 1910.

177. Especially embarrassing was the revelation that the grades of Kappa Theta Psi, lowest of all the Greek societies, were considerably higher than those of the preministerial students.

178. Simpson College, Board of Trustees, Minutes, June 6, 1911.

179. Ibid. The league consisted of several "lady members of the faculty, three resident alumnae, two women from each college class and one each from the academy, the conservatory and the school of business.

180. Ibid., June 12, 1912.

181. "Kappa Theta Psi has moved into the Sprague house." *Simpsonian*, September 9, 1911; "The Kappa Theta Psi alumni have bought the Porter property on East Franklin." Soon the Kappas were calling it "Old Brick." Ibid., May 11, 1912. "Alpha Tau Omega has bought the Porterfield property," a large house the fraternity occupied until the outbreak of the Second

World War. Ibid., September 15, 1912. "Two fraternities," said President Strickland, "have bought houses even though the Board of Trustees has told them they can't." Simpson College, Board of Trustees, Minutes, June 11, 1913.

182. Simpson College, Board of Trustees, Executive Committee, Minutes, March 18, 1917.
183. Simpson College, Board of Trustees, Minutes, June 7, 1916.
184. Ibid., June 4, 1918.
185. *Simpsonian*, May 28, 1917. See also *Zenith*, 1919.
186. Ibid., March 5, 1917.
187. Ibid., November 5, 1917.
188. Stephen C. Boss, "The Conservatory of Music under the Administration of Frank Ellis Barrows (1891–1924)," [1982], 15.
189. Simpson College, Board of Trustees, Minutes, June 11, 1913.
190. *Simpsonian*, April 6, 1914. In 1917 the attendance requirement was reduced from five to four days per week.
191. Ibid., February 4, 1918.
192. Ibid., November 25, 1918; January 20, 1919.
193. Ibid., March 8, 1915; February 16, 1914.
194. Ibid., March 16, 1914.
195. Ibid., April 7, 1911. The *Simpsonian* even carried a picture of Golisch being transported by loyal coolies in a sedan chair to a place of safety. Ibid., November 18, 1911. Later Miss Golisch returned to Simpson to complete her B.A. degree.
196. Ibid., February 2, 1914.
197. The Reverend Dr. E.M. Evans of Des Moines collected $566 for Soelberg in Indianola in 1914. Ibid., October 26, 1914.
198. *Case*: "The act or an instance of being romantically attached to one of the opposite sex; an obsession for one of the opposite sex; a crush." Harold Wentworth and Stuart Berg Flexner, eds., *Dictionary of American Slang*, 2nd Supplemented Ed. (New York: Thomas Y. Crowell Co., 1975), 89–90.
199. Dora G. Honnold, Sara E. Sigler and Frank P. Henderson, *The Simpson College Songbook* (New York: Hinds, Noble and Eldredge, Publishers, 1910), 4.
200. Dorothy Daniels, 41.
201. While frowned on by college authorities, going to see motion pictures was not an offense against the rules, but theater going was absolutely forbidden. It was acceptable to go to the Empress to watch Theda Bara vamp her way through *Salome—Seven Veils Fell from Her and Yet She Danced*,—but not to see *Hamlet* performed on stage. The logic of all this was frequently questioned by students. See *Simpsonian*, November 25, 1911; December 9, 1911; September 27, 1915.
202. Yet some of the boys did smoke. In a 1913 poll of 171 undergraduate men, 58 admitted that they smoked a pipe or cigars or chewed tobacco—few smoked cigarettes, which were thought to be effeminate—but only five of the users said they had become "addicted" after entering Simpson. *Simpsonian*, November 17, 1913.
203. Simpson College, Board of Trustees, Minutes, June 11, 1913. Dancing is "not spiritual, and may and often does have immoral results." Ibid., June 4, 1918.
204. Ibid., June 4, 1918.
205. Ibid.
206. But not everyone. Professor Aubrey Goodenough announced that "I can think of nothing more absurd when viewed in the light of cold reason than going on a picnic." *Simpsonian*, September 29, 1913.
207. Dorothy Daniels, 105.
208. Sixteen students voted for Eugene W. Chafin, the Prohibitionist candidate, and one (suspected to be a faculty member) voted for the Socialist Eugene V. Debs. *Simpsonian*, October 28, 1912.
209. This volume was published in 1910. London died in 1916.
210. *Simpsonian*, March 22, 1915.
211. Ibid., April 12, 1915.
212. It met every other Monday in the philosophy room.

213. *Simpsonian*, January 17, 1916.
214. Ibid. It was rumored in the *Simpsonian* that a Simpson alumnus out in Utah had become a socialist. Utah, of course, was believed to have strange effects on people. Ibid., April 3, 1916.
215. In the period from 1910 to 1919 the *Simpsonian* was printed in the shop of Indianola's *Advocate-Tribune*.
216. *Simpsonian*, April 27, 1914.
217. Ibid.
218. Ibid., April 8, 1911.
219. Irl Marshall, interview by author, Evanston, Illinois, March 12, 1967. Marshall graduated from Drake, went out into the world and became a rich man. He said he enjoyed not giving money to Simpson as an alumnus.
220. Baker died August 6, 1913, aboard the American ship *Thomas* as it lay at anchor in Nagaski Harbor, Japan.

Chapter 11

1. Hillman would receive an LL.D. from the College of Puget Sound in 1928 and the L.H.D. from Simpson upon his retirement in 1936.
2. Their wedding was held on August 27, 1889.
3. He was pastor at West Liberty, Ohio (1889–91); Richwood, Ohio (1891–92); Marion, Ohio (1892–96) where he became acquainted with an ex-school teacher, Warren G. Harding, who had established himself as the editor-publisher of the *Marion Star*; First Church in Columbus, Ohio (1896–99); Franklin Avenue Church, Cleveland, Ohio (1899–1904); Lincoln Avenue Church, Pittsburgh, Pennsylvania (1904–09); and Trinity Church, Youngstown, Ohio (1909–12).
4. Harold Francis Watson, "Memoirs of the Hillman Administration, 1919–1936," unpublished ms., 1974, 6.
5. Growth of undergraduate enrollments is reported as follows: 1900, 146,000; 1910, 345,000 (est.); 1920, 582,000; 1930, 1,053,000. *Higher Education for American Democracy*. Report of the President's Commission on Higher Education, VI (Washington, D.C.: U.S. Government Printing Office, 1947), 20.
6. Max McConn, "Tired Business Men of the Campus," *North American Review* 226 (November 1928), 548–49.
7. *Simpsonian*, March 30, 1925.
8. Some of the classes were held temporarily at the Methodist Church building down the street south of the campus. Ibid., October 11, 1920.
9. Ibid., October 27, 1919; May 3, 1920.
10. Ibid., April 26, 1920.
11. Ibid., May 3, 1920.
12. Of the $37,000, alumni contributed $17,000, $2,000 of which was contributed by the class of 1920. *Simpson College Bulletin*, series 22, no. 7, December 1, 1921. See also *Simpsonian*, September 13, 1920. The work on Old Chapel commenced on June 1, 1920.
13. *Indianola Herald*, January 13, 1921. In his memoirs Dr. Hillman recalled that "after [the renovation of Old Chapel] was completed I received a letter from the Hon. William Berry . . . in which he stated that he had been opposed to the attempt to preserve the building and had refused to contribute, but that since the work was completed he had changed his mind and enclosed his contribution for the repairs. It was a check for $300." John H. Hillman, "Memoirs," [handwritten ms.], [8].
14. *Simpsonian*, September 27, 1920.
15. Ibid., April 12, 1920.
16. Rae Dean was one of Simpson's all-time great athletes and had been named an all-state football player when an undergraduate. He lived at North English, Iowa, from 1903 until he was invited by President Campbell in the spring of 1919 to take over the financial management of the College. Junia Todd had been serving as dean of women and matron of Mary Berry Hall since 1917.

17. Simpson College, Board of Trustees, Minutes, June 24, 1919. Proudfoot resigned on October 28, 1918; on December 4, 1918, Rae Dean was elected business manager and secretary—later treasurer—at a salary of $2,500 beginning May 1, 1919. Simpson College, Board of Trustees, Executive Committee, Minutes, October 28, 1918 and December 4, 1918.

18. Watson, "Memoirs," 22.

19. Frank's sister Inez was married to Clyde Proudfoot.

20. *Zenith*, 1921.

21. Ibid. "I think," says Harold Watson, "it fair to assert that Dr. Holmes was venerated." "Memoirs," 19.

22. *Simpsonian*, September 13, 1920.

23. Moats was born December 1, 1884, at Villisca, Iowa.

24. He died at Indianola on October 24, 1960.

25. Watson, "Memoirs," 20.

26. Later Jones returned to his alma mater, Wake Forest College, to teach English.

27. Watson, "Memoirs," 2. Actually, the graveled road had not yet been laid down by the time Watson arrived in Iowa. It was still a dirt track, and Watson was lucky it wasn't raining the day he first drove over it.

28. Ibid., 2–5.

29. Ibid., 23.

30. Interspersed with her graduate studies were several teaching experiences, including year-long appointments in English at the College of Puget Sound at Tacoma, Washington (1927–28) and Denison University at Granville, Ohio (1930–31). At Chicago she worked with J. M. Manly and Edith Rickert.

31. The next year (1927–28), Helen Scott taught full time in the Department of English.

32. For this and the following few paragraphs, I have relied heavily upon my earlier work entitled *The Era of Levere: A History of the Sigma Alpha Epsilon Fraternity, 1910–1930* (Evanston, Ill.: Sigma Alpha Epsilon Fraternity), 1972.

33. *Indianola Herald*, September 13, 1923.

34. Ibid., May 1, 1924.

35. Ibid., September 13, 1923.

36. *The Record*, October 24, 1923.

37. Leonard Bowman, Interview, November 10, 1979.

38. William E. Leuchtenburg, *The Perils of Prosperity: 1914–32* (Chicago: The University of Chicago Press, 1958), 187–88.

39. Ibid., 187.

40. Edward Earl Purinton, "Big Ideas from Big Business," *The Independent* 56 (April 16, 1921), 395.

41. Arlington J. Stone, "The Dawn of a New Science," *The American Mercury* 14 (August 1928), 446.

42. *Advocate-Tribune*, April 10, 1919; *Indianola Herald*, April 10, 1919; June 5, 1919.

43. *Simpsonian*, March 7, 1921.

44. See typical advertisement in ibid., April 24, 1922.

45. Ibid., May 15, 1922.

46. See *Annual Catalog of Simpson College*, 1924, 64–65; *Simpsonian*, September 24, 1923. See also *Simpson College Bulletin*, series 24, no. 16, December 1, 1923.

47. When Heckert was hired in 1920, his salary was $2,500, even higher than J. Allen Baker, who had joined the faculty in 1908, and much higher than E. L. Miller, who had been around since 1889.

48. Simpson College, Board of Trustees, Executive Committee, Minutes, August 2, 1922 and January 23, 1923.

49. Ibid., August 25, 1925.

50. Today one of the classrooms in McNeill Hall, the College's Business and Computer Science building, is dedicated to Heckert. Upon his death on December 6, 1990, Heckert left the College $1,000,000 in his estate.

51. Payne was a graduate of the University of Utah and held an M.A. from the University

of Chicago and his doctorate from Ohio State University, where he heard about Simpson from Heckert.

52. *Simpsonian*, October 6, 1930.

53. It will be recalled that an endowed chair was created in 1910 by Harry Hopper to honor his father-in-law, the late George Carpenter, in classical languages.

54. William Buxton III replaced Albert M. Jarvis, who left the position after only one year to do research on the Ph.D. at the University of Illinois.

55. He taught at Simpson and retained his position as assistant cashier at his father's Peoples Trust and Savings Bank.

56. *Simpsonian*, May 23, 1930.

57. After her marriage some years later she was Nina V. Goltry. Ibid., April 23, 1928.

58. Ibid., September 17, 1928.

59. See *Simpson College Bulletin*, series 22, no. 2, April 1921. Catalog issue, 141–44; Ibid., series 31, no. 1, April 1930. Catalog issue, 152–58.

60. Watson, "Memoirs," 29–30.

61. "It would seem," said President Hillman as early as 1922, "that the accessibility of high schools all over our state would make it unnecessary for us to continue our Academy." Simpson College, Board of Trustees, Minutes, June 6, 1922.

62. Hillman, "Memoirs," [22].

63. In his memoirs, President Hillman wrote that "I felt compelled to recommend the discontinuance of the academy even though I knew its going would be a grief to many of the friends and alumni of the college." Hillman, "Memoirs," [23]. The Simpson catalog for 1923–24 stated that "the College no longer maintains an academy," but explains that courses would be offered to enable those already enrolled to complete their work. A similar announcement was included the following year. The 1925–26 catalog still listed eighteen holdover people in what they called the "sub-collegiate" category, and that number dropped to three the following year. After 1927 it appears that there were no sub-collegiate students at all, unless one wants to count a few children taking music lessons at the conservatory.

64. *Simpson College Bulletin*, series 25, no. 3, June 1, 1924.

65. As quoted in ibid.

66. Ibid., series 25, no. 7, December 1, 1924.

67. See Simpson College, Board of Trustees, Minutes, June 3, 1924, June 8, 1926, and June 4, 1928.

68. The librarian's salary in 1920 was $1,300; by 1929 it had risen to $1,400. In the four years (1921–24) that they employed an assistant librarian the salary ranged from $550 to $700.

69. Watson, "Memoirs," 22.

70. *New York Times*, October 19, 1924.

71. The wife of Michigan's coach, "Hurry up" Yost, remarked innocently, "Don't you think it would have helped if you'd sent in someone to tackle that red-headed boy?" Robert Leckie, *The Story of Football* (New York: Random House, Inc., 1965), 76.

72. As quoted in ibid., 78.

73. Simpson did build new reasonably sturdy bleachers with seating for 750 in 1923. *Indianola Herald*, October 11, 1923.

74. Had Simpson been able to use its freshmen—Iowa Conference forbade freshman participation in varsity sports—things might have been different, for in four contests that fall the College's freshmen scored 166 points to their opponents' 14. See *Zenith*, 1922.

75. The basketball team had just completed a losing season, but few remembered that in 1920 Simpson had won the conference championship in basketball.

76. The committee was a powerful one, comprised of a number of influential alumni: Carl Pryor '09, a prominent attorney in Council Bluffs; Mark R. Tennant '12, a commercial land agent in Sioux City; Joe O. Watson '93, Indianola attorney; Clyde Proudfoot '02, long associated with the Worth Savings Bank in Indianola; Ernest C. Rea '05, of Des Moines; and John Horsley '09.

77. Simpson College, Board of Trustees, Executive Committee, Minutes, April 17, 1921.

78. See *Indianola Herald*, May 12, 1921; May 19, 1921; May 26, 1921; June 2, 1921.

79. E. D. Samson '76, who was present, declared that in "potential possibilities [sic] [this]

meeting was the most important in the history of Simpson College." *Simpsonian*, April 25, 1921.

80. Ibid., June 16, 1921.

81. *Simpson College Bulletin*, series 22, December 1, 1921.

82. To clinch the argument, proponents cited the example of little Centre College down in Danville, Kentucky. Two years earlier few people had ever heard of Centre College. That fall the "Praying Colonels" played Harvard to a standstill in football and defeated some of the best colleges of the East. Then in the fall of 1921 they defeated Harvard in one of the great upsets of the century. Centre "has gained a reputation as a winning school because she turns out winning athletic teams." A men's college with about 265 students, "already this fall 1,800 applications have been filed for entrance to Centre College." Ibid.

83. He resigned in June 1929, disappointed about the "irregularity and uncertainty of alumni funds." He returned to the *Record* as city editor. Ibid., series 30, no. 6, September 1, 1929. Talbot's successor was John L. Horsley '09.

84. Cushman had played varsity football for the Texas Aggies, and had seven years of coaching experience. His arrival on campus was trumpeted by the *Indianola Herald*, August 11, 1921, and September 15, 1921. Simpson paid $2,500 of his salary, the alumni $500.

85. *Simpsonian*, October 31, 1921; *Indianola Herald*, October 27, 1921.

86. The new Iowa Conference undertook "to purge intercollegiate athletics in the state of Iowa of professionalism." The new rules which came into effect June 15, 1922, stipulated no scholarships, no state championship contests, a limit of four years in any sport for any participant, and approval by faculty of elected managers and captains. *Simpsonian*, May 15, 1922. Although some of the rules have changed during the decades that followed, Simpson has remained a member of the Iowa Conference down to the present day.

87. See John E. "Buck" Turnbull, *The Iowa Conference Story* (Iowa City: The State Historical Society of Iowa, 1961), 15–16.

88. Ibid., February 26, 1923. See also *Indianola Herald*, March 1, 1923; *Advocate-Tribune*, April 26, 1923.

89. "Buck" Turnbull recalls how Mercer got his nickname: "After a rough basketball game at Parsons, in which Mercer was ready to mix it up with the whole Parsons squad, his teammates tagged him with the nickname Moco from a *Des Moines Register* comic strip called 'Battling Moco.'" Turnbull, 21.

90. In the fall of 1927 the two Workmans coached their respective teams as Simpson met Iowa State on the gridiron, the Redmen losing the encounter 26 to 6. In October 1930 Workman took a twenty-one-man squad on the longest football trip up to that time in Simpson history to Delaware, Ohio, to play Ohio Wesleyan University. Simpson played well but lost the game 21–12. Ibid., October 20, 1930. Two years earlier, in September 1928, Simpson played its first night game against Drake in Des Moines, illuminated by "ten giant 2000-watt floodlights mounted on both sides of the field." Ibid., September 17, 1928. The *Indianola Herald*, September 24, 1929, reports a second game under the lights with Drake.

91. The senior class in 1922 assessed each of its members $15 to build a cement tennis court and two dirt courts south of Hopper Gym. Ibid., April 10, 1922.

92. *Simpsonian*, January 7, 1924. This first meet was scheduled for January 30.

93. Ibid., February 11, 1924.

94. Ibid., May 16, 1927.

95. Ibid., February 8, 1926; *Indianola Herald*, February 11, 1926.

96. *Simpsonian*, January 7, 1924.

97. Ibid., November 17, 1930.

98. The Simpson Women's Athletic Association became a chapter of the national organization of the same name in April 1922. Ibid., April 24, 1922.

99. Directors of physical education for women during this period were Katherine K. Frisbee (1917–20), Idell Pyle (1920–21), Ruth Lenore Hutton (1921–22), Irene L. Springer (1922–25), Irene S. Kunze (1925–27), Helen Westfall (1927–29), and Chloe Carson (1929–31).

100. McConn, 550.

101. Ibid.

102. He probably had never been upstairs in the ATO or Kappa houses.

103. Watson, "Memoirs," 66–67.
104. Sigma Delta Chi was founded March 9, 1920.
105. J. Raymond Smith graduated from Simpson in 1923 and the next year joined the faculty in business administration. Ward Rockey was a sophomore at the time they organized Theta Kappa Nu. The chapter was installed on October 10, 1924, at its chapter house at 224 West Ashland. More than 150 persons attended a reception honoring the thirty-two charter members and its seven pledge members. See *Simpsonian*, October 13, 1924.
106. *Simpsonian*, January 9, 1922.
107. The Simpson chapter hosted the first national convention April 10–11, 1925.
108. The idea for Omicron originated with Eva Stahl, long-time member of the Department of English, and members received much cooperation from Dean of Women Edna Stuntz. *Simpsonian*, September 8, 1926.
109. Watson, "Memoirs," 10.
110. *Simpsonian*, March 7, 1927.
111. Ibid., September 20, 1926.
112. Simpson's most glaring deficiency at the time was the College's inadequate library collection.
113. *Simpsonian*, January 10, 1921. It was not for want of faculty support that the health of the literary societies was poor. A statement in the catalog of the College in 1920 was typical of most of the decade: "Each student is advised to connect himself with one of these societies. Their work affords excellent facilities for acquiring self-possession, originality, power of expression, and a knowledge of the topics of the day, as well as important preparation for public life." A decade later the same message was repeated, except for the significant omission of the faculty's advising students to join. See *Annual Catalog of Simpson College*, 1920, 20; and *Simpson College Bulletin: The Catalog*, 1929–30, 25.
114. Ibid., January 16, 1922.
115. Harold Watson recalled that there was gossip that "the editor of one particularly complete and attractive *Zenith* came out with over $1,500, more than some faculty members were paid. Since her family was well-to-do, I heard some comments that it wasn't fair somehow, but no one explained just why." Watson, "Memoirs," 62.
116. Ibid., 61.
117. *Simpsonian*, November 1, 1920.
118. Ibid., April 7, 1924.
119. Ibid., November 14, 1921.
120. Ibid., December 7, 1925; January 4, 1926.
121. Ibid., January 16, 1928; April 2, 1928.
122. Ibid., April 30, 1928.
123. Ibid., February 1, 1927.
124. Ibid., February 16, 1920.
125. *Simpson College Bulletin*, series 25, no. 3, June 1, 1924.
126. Hillman, "Memoirs," [20–21].
127. Ibid., [21].
128. *Simpson College Bulletin*, series 25, no. 7, December 1, 1924. There is little doubt that Hugh Jackson '12 played a decisive role in achieving Simpson's elevation to A.A.U. approval.
129. Hillman, "Memoirs," [18].
130. See Simpson College, Board of Trustees, Minutes, February 16, 1925, and June 6, 1927. Further success was achieved when in 1927 Simpson received word that its graduates in home economics would henceforth be entitled to teach in secondary schools supported by funds under the Smith-Hughes Program. Iowa State College was the only other institution in the state thus recognized.
131. Watson, "Memoirs," 28.
132. Hillman, "Memoirs," [9].
133. Ibid., [10].
134. Ibid., [11].
135. Simpson College, Board of Trustees, Executive Committee, Minutes, May 30, 1923;

Simpson College, Board of Trustees, Minutes, June 5, 1923; *Simpson College Bulletin*, series 24, no. 11, June, 1923.

136. In several broad surveys of international affairs, the bishop, deploring the war between Muslim Turkey and Christian Greece, urged the Christian churches of America to "throw all their force into the effort to meet [the] onsweep of Moslemism, with its degrading ideals of life." He called for an understanding of France as it invaded Germany's Ruhr to collect war reparations. He praised the British in India and assured his audience that Mahatma Gandhi had no future. He lauded the Soviet government's recent "about-face" on the subject of capitalism and religion and "waxed eloquent on the great possibilities for the Methodist Church there in Russia." *Indianola Herald*, January 25, 1923.

137. Ibid.

138. Simpson College, Board of Trustees, Minutes, June 5, 1923; *Simpsonian*, January 22, 1923, and March 26, 1923. For the duration of the drive the campaign offices occupied the South Society Hall and part of the Y.M.C.A. Room. Dr. Perry arrived on campus March 22, 1923.

139. The student pledges were truly impressive when one considers that tuition and fees for the full year were $118, and the average gift per student—even counting the 162 in the conservatory—was nearly $65, considerably more than one-half of the tuition bill. Faculty contributions, totaling nearly $33,000, represented more than half of the entire faculty salary budget for a year. The local press followed the campaign with interest. See *Indianola Herald*, April 19, 1923; May 10, 1923; May 24, 1923; and May 31, 1923. See also *Advocate-Tribune*, March 8, 1923; May 15, 1923; and May 29, 1923.

140. The minute-by-minute account of the last days of the campaign is found in the *Simpson College Bulletin*, series 24, no. 15, September 1, 1923.

141. Simpson College, Board of Trustees, Minutes, June 20, 1923. See also *Indianola Herald*, June 21, 1923, and March 13, 1924; *Simpsonian*, September 17, 1923.

142. Simpson College, Board of Trustees, Minutes, February 26, 1924.

143. Ibid., June 3, 1924.

144. Ibid.

145. *Simpson College Bulletin*, series 30, no. 1, March 1, 1929.

146. Ibid., series 30, no. 8, March 8, 1930.

147. Ibid., series 32, no. 1, March 1, 1931.

148. Simpson College, Board of Trustees, Minutes, June 5, 1923; *Indianola Herald*, February 22, 1923. Rae Dean estimated that it would have cost the College at least $25,000 more to build a new dormitory than it paid for Lorraine Hall.

149. In 1924, for example, Grinnell College's tuition was $215. Drake charged $200, Des Moines University $165, Morningside $155, Cornell $150, Parsons $135 and Upper Iowa $130. By the end of the decade all of these had increased substantially, leaving Simpson far below average.

150. The annual charge for board was $216 throughout the decade, while a room at Mary Berry Hall went from $45 to $56.

151. *The Annual Catalog of Simpson College*, 1924, an issue of *Simpson College Bulletin*, series 25, no. 3, April 1924, 18.

152. Ibid., 26.

153. Watson, "Memoirs," 9.

154. Ibid.

155. *Indianola Herald*, December 8, 1927.

156. *Simpsonian*, November 28, 1927. They had believed W. E. "Pussyfoot" Johnson, a leading prohibitionist speaker, who had told them only that week that "few college students drink."

157. Ibid., February 20, 1928. A student poll that same year at Simpson produced 241 votes for prohibition and 47 against it.

158. Watson, "Memoirs," 11.

159. See *Simpsonian*, October 17, 1921.

160. Watson, "Memoirs," 16.

161. *Simpsonian*, November 6, 1922.

162. Ibid., February 4, 1924.

163. Ibid., December 1, 1924; May 6, 1929.
164. *Simpson College Bulletin*, series 23, no. 9, December 1, 1922.
165. *Simpsonian*, March 9, 1925.
166. Ibid., March 4, 1929.
167. *Simpson College Bulletin*, series 28, no. 7, March 1, 1928.
168. *Simpsonian*, January 26, 1925; Watson, "Memoirs," 57.
169. Daniel, *Circle Round the Square*, 148.
170. *Simpsonian*, April 29, 1929.
171. Daniel, *Circle Round the Square*, 151.
172. Leuchtenburg, *The Perils of Prosperity*, 197.
173. Student slang, lamented President Rufus Von KleinSmid of the University of Southern California, betrayed a poverty of vocabulary. "The word 'swell' alone," he said, "is used to describe 4,792 situations." *Simpsonian*, November 30, 1931.
174. Ibid., September 12, 1921.
175. Ibid., January 18, 1926.
176. Ibid., May 14, 1928.
177. See ibid., January 14, 1929; January 21, 1929; and February 4, 1929.
178. Ibid., February 21, 1927.
179. Ibid., October 25, 1926.
180. The first college homecoming anywhere was held at the University of Illinois in 1910. And under its legendary director, Aus Harding, Illinois produced the nation's first marching band.
181. Watson, "Memoirs," 53.
182. *Simpsonian*, January 12, 1925.
183. Ibid., January 16, 1928.
184. Ibid., December 6, 1929.
185. Dillon's address, "The Menace of the Labor Union," was printed verbatim in the *Simpsonian*, March 26, 1923. Talley, whose 1927 winning oration was entitled "U.S. No. 9653," was the son of Dr. M. Roy Talley, who had won the state contest for Simpson in 1903. See ibid., March 7, 1927.
186. Watson, "Memoirs," 5.

Chapter 12

1. *New York Times*, October 30, 1929.
2. Corn prices in Iowa fell from $1.19 per bushel in 1920 to 41¢ in 1921.
3. Joseph Frazier Wall, *Iowa: A Bicentennial History* (New York: W. W. Norton & Co., Inc., 1978), 174.
4. The *Indianola Record* reported on September 4, 1930 that "Indianola's Warren County State Bank and Worth Savings Bank failed to open Tuesday [September 2]. The two were leading concerns of their kind until a short time ago when a series of unfortunate circumstances started their decline. Deflation and financial depression contributed heavily and the banks suffered losses from creditors who were unable to meet their obligations." For a good study of Indianola's bank crisis. see Douglas LaVelle, "The Survival of Peoples Bank, 1929–1933," [unpublished ms.], Indianola, Iowa, 1970.
5. In the liberal arts college the decline was from 650 to 483. In the conservatory it was catastrophic: 218 in 1929 and 71 in 1933.
6. Simpson College, Board of Trustees, Minutes, February 17, 1932.
7. Ibid., June 7, 1932.
8. Its appropriation, reduced to $11,000 in 1931, declined further to $7,800 in 1932, $3,000 in 1933 and to $2,100 in both 1934 and 1935. Simpson College, Board of Trustees, Executive Committee, August 27, 1931; Simpson College, Board of Trustees, Minutes, February 9, 1938.
9. Simpson College, Board of Trustees, Minutes, February 10, 1931.
10. Ibid., June 7, 1932; *Simpsonian*, September 26, 1932. The *Buffalo Courier* put it well: "Indeed, to bill an otherwise noble spirited alumnus [for alumni dues] is merely to seek a

new way to the Indies, and generally results in the discovery of the waste basket." Quoted in the *Simpson College Bulletin*, March 1, 1931.

11. Simpson College, Board of Trustees, Executive Committee, Minutes, March 8, 1932.

12. Simpson College, Board of Trustees, Minutes, February 15, 1933; June 5, 1933. Cable's salary had been $3,800 in 1931–32. The following year his duties were reduced to one-third time. See ibid., June 7, 1932.

13. *Indianola Record*, June 22, 1933.

14. Simpson College, Board of Trustees, Minutes, February 10, 1931.

15. Ibid., June 7, 1932; Simpson College, Board of Trustees, Executive Committee, Minutes, April 24, 1932; *Simpsonian*, April 18, 1932; May 20, 1932. Horn's salary had been $2,700. Vera Horn's was only a fraction of that amount.

16. "Their plans for next year are not known," was the comment of the *Simpsonian*, May 30, 1932.

17. Cox received a munificent salary increase of $200 for her instructional duties.

18. Simpson College, Board of Trustees, Minutes, June 7, 1932. They called Stewart the "Health Supervisor."

19. Ibid.

20. Instruction in Spanish was dropped from the curriculum altogether.

21. Holmes died on December 28, 1933. He was seventy-four years old.

22. Simpson College, Board of Trustees, Minutes, June 5, 1933.

23. Simpson College, Board of Trustees, Executive Committee, Minutes, May 21, 1931.

24. See *Indianola Herald*, June 11, 1931; June 25, 1931.

25. Ibid., April 21, 1932.

26. In 1934 the examinations were scheduled between May 7 and May 12. *Simpsonian*, April 23, 1934.

27. See ibid., May 4, 1936.

28. Ibid., September 26, 1932. The new grading system was first described in the College's catalog for 1932–33. *Simpson College Bulletin: The Catalog*, 1932–1933, 27.

29. *Simpsonian*, September 24, 1934.

30. Not a word of this "individualization experiment" found its way into the College catalog or its alumni publications. But the story was picked up and published both in the *Simpsonian* and the *Indianola Herald*, March 26, 1931.

31. *Indianola Herald*, September 10, 1931.

32. Simpson College, Board of Trustees, Minutes, February 15, 1933.

33. The Board of Education's full report on Simpson totaled 332 mimeographed pages and an appendix of 95 pages. The *Simpson College Bulletin* noted that "enough criticisms and suggestions are made in this volume to keep us both humble and busy for years to come." The report, a copy of which rests in the Simpson College archives, was widely quoted in the Indianola press. See, for example, the *Indianola Herald*, October 2, 1930.

34. Simpson College, Board of Trustees, Minutes, June 7, 1932.

35. Watson, "Memoirs," 71.

36. Ibid. Not long afterwards President Hillman asked the faculty to elect a committee of five to serve as "advisers." If further difficult decisions were to be made regarding reduction of faculty or salaries or both, the president wanted the faculty to be involved in the process. Soon known as the "Axe Committee," this group functioned throughout the rest of the Hillman years. In some ways it was the predecessor of the faculty council that was created after Hillman's retirement.

37. In 1932 prices in Indianola hit the bottom. Merchants and grocers in town advertised men's overalls at 89¢, women's rayon stockings at 22¢, 100 pounds of potatoes for 90¢, bacon at 10¢ per pound, a 49-pound sack of flour for 79¢, milk at 8¢ a quart and ham at 12¢ a pound. See *Indianola Herald* or the *Record*, 1932, passim.

38. Watson, "Memoirs," 72. "I remember the wave of indignation that swept over us when the City Fathers voted to repave the streets adjoining the campus—possibly to make work for impoverished road-builders, though the repairs had been necessary for some time. The assessment would of course come out of College funds—that is, out of faculty salaries." Ibid.,

75. As it turned out, the College borrowed the $15,000 to pay the assessment. Simpson College, Board of Trustees, Minutes, June 5, 1933.

39. Watson, "Memoirs," 73.

40. Faculty still on hand in 1936 were Fillman, Doty, Gose, Baker, Emmons, Hilmer, Watson, Stahl, Moats, Renich, Whitaker, Payne, Buxton, Carr, Inman, Brown, Burrows, Beam, Goltry (nee Mitchell) and Miller. In the conservatory were Harvey, Weiler, Spring, Ellis and MacGregor. Dean of women Edna Stuntz and librarian Inis Smith also remained during these last years of the Hillman administration.

41. Simpson College, Board of Trustees, Executive Committee, Minutes, December 14, 1934.

42. Ibid., January 24, 1935.

43. Harold Watson, "Journal," October 26, 1934.

44. Simpson College, Board of Trustees, Minutes, February 27, 1935.

45. The entire letter was reproduced verbatim in the *Simpsonian*, March 13, 1933.

46. *Indianola Herald*, March 12, 1931.

47. Simpson College, Board of Trustees, Minutes, February 14, 1934; *Indianola Herald*, August 17, 1933.

48. *Simpsonian*, September 18, 1933.

49. Simpson College, Board of Trustees, Minutes, June 4, 1934; *Indianola Herald*, August 25, 1932.

50. Simpson College, Board of Trustees, Minutes, February 14, 1934; June 4, 1934.

51. *Simpsonian*, February 12, 1934.

52. Although he loved Simpson and favored anything that would keep college students in school, Don Berry of the *Record*, Indianola's most redoubtable Republican, found it galling to give F.D.R. or the Democrats credit for anything, even student aid. The S.R.E. program continued several years, replaced eventually by the National Youth Administration programs. See *Indianola Tribune*, July 18, 1934.

53. *Simpsonian*, January 9, 1933.

54. Ibid., March 2, 1931.

55. Ibid., January 11, 1932.

56. Ibid., January 23, 1933.

57. Ibid., October 24, 1932.

58. Ibid., November 3, 1934.

59. Ibid., February 12, 1934; February 19, 1934.

60. Ibid., October 26, 1931; February 15, 1932.

61. Simpson College, Board of Trustees, Minutes, February 15, 1933. Indianola was ailing too. The First National Bank closed its doors on August 4, 1932. Of Indianola's five banks only one, the Peoples Trust and Savings, remained out of the hands of the receivers. *Indianola Herald*, August 11, 1932.

62. *Indianola Herald*, February 16, 1933.

63. Watson, "Memoirs," 76.

64. Simpson College, Board of Trustees, Minutes, February 14, 1934.

65. *Simpsonian*, September 17, 1934.

66. *Indianola Herald*, November 28, 1935.

67. *Simpsonian*, May 1, 1933.

68. Workman's record was 22–21–3 in football, the team scoring 600 points to their opponents' 465, and 54–43 in basketball. He won a track championship in 1926 and a second-place standing in 1929. See *Indianola Herald*, April 2, 1931.

69. Simpson's athletic board was looking at Ed Wright at William Penn College and Simpson alumnus Harold "Bud" Fisher '26, whose Boone High School basketball team had won the state championship. See ibid., April 16, 1931.

70. Ibid., May 14, 1931.

71. Ibid., July 27, 1933. He had graduated from Simpson in 1932 and was athletic director and coach at Stuart, Iowa, during the 1932–33 school year. See also *Simpson College Bulletin*, October 1933.

72. *Indianola Herald*, January 11, 1934.

73. Ibid., August 3, 1933; August 17, 1933. The lights cost $1,000 plus installation.

74. Because none of the fourteen conference teams played all the others, the Stanley-Dean system tried to reward teams that played the tougher opponents in the league. A valiant effort was made to explain the system to the local public in the *Indianola Herald*, November 23, 1933.

75. Turnbull, 50, 173.

76. *Simpson College Bulletin*, October 1933; *Simpsonian*, May 15, 1933.

77. Simpson College, Board of Trustees, Minutes, February 27, 1935. See also *Indianola Herald*, February 28, 1935; *Simpsonian*, March 4, 1935.

78. *Simpsonian*, February 4, 1935; March 25, 1935; *Indianola Herald*, February 7, 1935.

79. Simpson College, Board of Trustees, Executive Committee, Minutes, March 15, 1930; May 6, 1930; October 29, 1930.

80. Ibid., March 6, 1931. The national Delta Delta Delta sorority lent the chapter $3,000 and the local Tridelts borrowed locally $9,000 on a ten-year mortgage at six percent.

81. Ibid., May 27, 1931.

82. The fraternity would pay the College $125 per month to amortize the loan. Ibid., August 11, 1931.

83. *Simpson College Bulletin*, December 1931.

84. Simpson College, Board of Trustees, Executive Committee, Minutes, December 30, 1932; June 2, 1934; August 24, 1934.

85. Ibid., December 22, 1931; March 3, 1932. The Alpha Chis were providing $5,000 in cash and securing a $5,000 loan from their national organization. The lot was purchased early in 1932. *Indianola Herald*, April 14, 1932.

86. Simpson College, Board of Trustees, Executive Committee, Minutes, March 3, 1932.

87. *Indianola Herald*, June 16, 1932.

88. Simpson College, Board of Trustees, Minutes, June 1, 1931; *Indianola Herald*, July 31, 1930.

89. Early fall pledging during these years was as follows: 1929—149; 1930—118; 1931—123; 1932—79; 1933—101; 1934—66 (only 22 men); and 1935—67. The low 1932 pledging figure is in part accounted for by the very small freshman class of that year, only 165.

90. *Simpsonian*, September 17, 1934.

91. Ibid., May 18, 1936. In the faculty decision was a provision that if students did not meet their financial obligations—tuition, loan payments and the like—they could not be initiated into a Greek-letter society or could be compelled to drop their membership until their bills were paid.

92. *Simpson College Bulletin*, May 1931.

93. Simpson's Pi Kappa Delta chapter in 1930 was ranked thirteenth out of 132 chapters in its oratorical accomplishments. *Simpsonian*, November 17, 1930.

94. *Indianola Herald*, March 17, 1932; *Simpsonian*, March 14, 1932.

95. *Simpsonian*, February 13, 1933. "We do not have the money to publish a larger paper." May 29, 1933.

96. Ibid., January 11, 1932.

97. See *Zenith*, 1935.

98. Simpson College, Board of Trustees, Minutes, February 10, 1931; June 1, 1931.

99. *Indianola Herald*, July 9, 1931; September 10, 1931.

100. Simpson College, Board of Trustees, Minutes, February 27, 1935; *Indianola Herald*, February 28, 1935.

101. *Simpsonian*, April 25, 1932.

102. Ibid., October 5, 1931.

103. Ibid., October 10, 1932.

104. Ibid., October 27, 1933.

105. Ibid., April 29, 1935; *Simpson College Bulletin*, May 1935.

106. Ibid., November 7, 1931.

107. Simpson College, Board of Trustees, Minutes, June 1, 1931.

108. *Simpsonian*, March 2, 1931.

109. *Indianola Herald*, December 17, 1931; See also *Indianola Tribune*, December 15, 1931.

110. Dr. Hillman's speech was reprinted verbatim in the *Indianola Record*, December 24, 1931.

111. *Indianola Herald*, December 17, 1931.

112. *Indianola Record*, December 17, 1931. The presence of police officers at the gymnasium lent credence to his assertion.

113. Ibid., December 24, 1931.

114. See *Simpsonian*, April 18, 1932; April 25, 1932; May 2, 1932; May 9, 1932; May 23, 1932; May 30, 1932.

115. It was later charged that board members misrepresented the vote as having favored retention of the ban. Reverend Shipman did say that it was appropriate to weigh most heavily the votes of "those who had the greatest right to have [their] opinions considered," by which he clearly meant the parents and clergy. See Simpson College, Board of Trustees, Minutes, March 25, 1933.

116. Ibid., June 7, 1932.

117. *Indianola Herald*, March 16, 1933. A large number of students simply adjourned and went to several private homes where they resumed dancing.

118. Simpson College, Board of Trustees, Executive Committee, Minutes, March 22, 1933. It is probably safe now to reveal the names of the lawbreakers: Morris Jones, Ronald Masters, Geraldine Hughes, Yvonne Yager, Marian Guth, Harriet Harlan and Lola Hubbard. These were only 7 of more than 150 students at the dance, not to speak of "alumni and outsiders" urging them on to delinquency. *Indianola Herald*, March 23, 1933.

119. *Indianola Herald*, March 30, 1933.

120. Simpson College, Board of Trustees, Minutes, March 25, 1933.

121. Simpson College, Board of Trustees, Executive Committee, Minutes, March 24, 1933.

122. Simpson College, Board of Trustees, Minutes, March 25, 1933.

123. *Simpsonian*, April 3, 1933. The Watson resolution stated that "It is the sense of the board of trustees now assembled that, if the student body will in good faith observe the rule against dancing until the June meeting of the board, the rule will be revised so as to allow regulated dancing."

124. *Indianola Herald*, June 8, 1933; September 28, 1933. They reprinted widely Sec. 73 of the 1932 Discipline.

125. *Simpsonian*, January 22, 1934.

126. Simpson College, Board of Trustees, Minutes, June 4, 1934.

127. He resigned the presidency of the league January 29, 1932. *Indianola Herald*, February 25, 1932.

128. Simpson College, Board of Trustees, Executive Committee, Minutes, August 24, 1934.

129. H. M. Cooper, Iowa Liquor Control Commission, Des Moines, Iowa, to John L. Hillman, Indianola, Iowa, August 30, 1934.

130. Hamilton passed away on October 16, 1929. Parks died May 25, 1930. Tilton's untimely death occurred November 17, 1930. Holmes's death took place on December 28, 1933.

131. Hedges's accidental death occurred on May 6, 1935. See *Simpson College Bulletin*, October 1935.

132. J. O. Watson, the board hero of the students in the great dancing revolution, was the victim of an automobile accident in early 1936 and died "of a virulent form of pneumonia" while recuperating from his injuries. *Simpsonian*, February 10, 1936. Watson had graduated from Simpson in 1893. About this same time in 1936 Simpson people heard of the death of Joanna Baker, who had served many years on the faculty (1889–1919).

133. Hillman, "Memoirs," [11–17]. See also *Simpsonian*, November 20, 1933; March 16, 1936. Elizabeth Simpson died February 29, 1936, at Philadelphia.

134. Simpson College, Board of Trustees, Minutes, June 4, 1934.

Chapter 13

1. *Simpsonian*, February 17, 1936.

2. The search committee consisted of board president A. V. Proudfoot, the Rev. Levi P. Goodwin, superintendent of the Des Moines district of the church, and William Buxton, Jr.

3. Simpson College, Board of Trustees, Executive Committee, Minutes, December 21, 1935.

The faculty committee, chaired by Francis Moats, included Harold Watson, Charles Hilmer and J. Allen Baker.

4. Simpson College, Board of Trustees, Minutes, January 6, 1936.

5. Earl E. Harper, Evansville, Indiana, to Aaron VanSyoc Proudfoot, Indianola, Iowa, December 27, 1935.

6. Thus in 1935 he was receiving $2333 plus house and automobile.

7. Simpson College, Board of Trustees, Minutes, January 6, 1936.

8. His father and both his grandfathers were Methodist ministers.

9. Nebraska Wesleyan awarded him an honorary doctorate in 1928; Boston University gave him an honorary LL.D. in 1936, the same degree awarded him a year earlier at Central Methodist College, Fayette, Mo.

10. See *Indianola Herald*, April 23, 1936.

11. *Simpsonian*, April 20, 1936.

12. Harper's address was printed verbatim in the *Indianola Herald*, April 23, 1936.

13. Four honorary degrees were awarded: the Educ.D. to Agnes Samuelson; the Educ.D. to Charles Edgar Torbet, dean of the college at Evansville College; the Mus.D. to James Russell Houghton, a graduate of the University of Iowa, a baritone and former football player who had been much involved with Dr. Harper in Methodist musical endeavors; and the Hum.D. to Dr. Hillman. See the account of this event in the *Indianola Herald*, April 23, 1936.

14. Hillman said, "As I lay down the administration work at Simpson I would have you give the same fine support to President Harper that you have given me in order that the college may achieve greater victories in the future." *Simpson College Bulletin*, October 1936.

15. The letter was written to John Fletcher, "a great contemporary preacher, and suggests some of Wesley's plans for the early [Methodist] church." *Simpsonian*, February 3, 1936; *Simpson College Bulletin*, May 1936.

16. Dr. Hilmer, who had been vice-president, would continue to teach full time, preside over the chapel program and "generally lend his strength and support of his gracious personality to the administration as it goes forward with its work." Simpson College, Board of Trustees, Minutes, June 4, 1936.

17. Division I included English language and literature, speech, and the fine arts; in Division II were history and political science, economics and business administration, and sociology; Division III included biology, chemistry, geology, home economics, physics and mathematics; Division IV consisted of philosophy and Bible, education, and psychology; Division V included health and physical education. The conservatory would continue to operate separate from the regular College program. Ibid.; *Indianola Herald*, May 21, 1936. The reorganization had been passed by the faculty on May 16. *Simpsonian*, May 18, 1936.

18. *Simpsonian*, October 19, 1936.

19. This form of college governance lasted only five years, but it seems to have been fairly effective. Perhaps it was too much dependent on the leadership style of Earl Harper. His successor found it less attractive and urged reorganization in 1941.

20. Simpson College, Board of Trustees, Minutes, June 4, 1936.

21. The "ideal" national averages, according to the American Council of Education, for liberal arts colleges in 1936–37 were $4,050, $3,400 and $2,800 in the three ranks mentioned here.

22. Somehow Harper found a distinction between discounting faculty salaries by 15 percent and asking for a 15 percent "contribution." Most faculty failed to see the difference, since the "contribution" would be expected and surely exacted from each.

23. Simpson College, Board of Trustees, Minutes, June 4, 1936.

24. Ibid., February 11, 1937.

25. The College issued bonds, the entire issue taken by the Carleton D. Beh Co. of Des Moines at the effective interest rate of 5.13 percent. See ibid., June 7, 1937.

26. He died June 7, 1936. He would have reached his seventy-fourth birthday on June 13.

27. *Zenith*, 1938. This was the *first* 1938 *Zenith*, chronicling the events of the 1936–37 academic year. A second *Zenith* appeared in 1938, recording the 1937–38 academic year—finally getting the year of issue synchronized with the year reviewed. A few weeks after Senator

Proudfoot's death another trustee, W. P. Wortman, sixty-eight, editor of the *Malvern Leader*, was killed in an automobile crash near Plattsmouth, Nebr. *Indianola Herald*, July 16, 1936.

28. *Simpson College Bulletin*, May 1936; *Simpsonian*, April 20, 1936; *Indianola Herald*, August 6, 1936.

29. Simpson College, Board of Trustees, Executive Committee, Minutes, December 10, 1936. Burrows lectured in Kansas, California, Texas, North Carolina and points in between. See *Simpsonian*, March 1, 1937. John Horsley took over Burrows's duties as dean of men for the year.

30. *Simpson College Bulletin*, October 1936; *Simpsonian*, September 21, 1936.

31. Margaret Liebe Watson, interview by the author, Indianola, Iowa, April 21, 1992.

32. *Indianola Herald*, September 10, 1936; November 11, 1936; December 3, 1936.

33. Ibid., September 17, 1936.

34. *Simpson College Bulletin: The Catalog: 1936–1937*, 27–28. See also Simpson College, Board of Trustees, Minutes, February 11, 1937.

35. Clyde Emmons put it well: "The tendency of instructors to grade benevolently has two effects: it raises the apparent scholarship level and it lowers the real scholarship level." Such a lack of uniformity in standards of grading, he said, was "intolerable." Simpson College, Board of Trustees, Minutes, June 7, 1937.

36. Ibid., February 11, 1937.

37. Toward the end of Harper's first year at Simpson the *Indianola Record* announced that "Dr. Harper will deliver the baccalaureate address at Nebraska State Teachers College on May 23 and Ankeny (May 25), Columbus, Ind. (May 27), Brazil, Ind. (May 28) and at the Thomas Jefferson High School at Council Bluffs (June 3). On June 10 he will address the high school commencement at South Bend, Ind." *Indianola Record*, May 21, 1937.

38. Ibid., February 12, 1937; Simpson College, Board of Trustees, Minutes, February 9, 1938.

39. Simpson College, Board of Trustees, Minutes, February 9, 1938. Of these "talkies" the *Simpsonian* commented, "no action is taken but many and varied views are exchanged." *Simpsonian*, November 6, 1937.

40. These lines are excerpted from a speech delivered by Nolte to members of Epsilon Sigma at their commencement breakfast May 19, 1984, and reprinted in the *Simpson Alumnus*, 10 (Summer 1985), 4. The first proper mid-year commencement at Simpson was held the next year when five graduates were awarded their diplomas.

41. *Indianola Record*, May 28, 1937.

42. *Simpsonian*, May 9, 1938.

43. *Indianola Record*, May 6, 1938.

44. Gilbert R. Caldwell, "History of Simpson College," unpubl. ms., 1947, 10. Caldwell's "History" covers the decade from 1936 to 1946. Well-recorded and interestingly written, this fifty-one-page study was prepared as a seminar paper for Professor Francis I. Moats. The choir was not the only group receiving Harper's attention. In spite of the dismal state of the College's finances, he managed to find enough money to purchase smart, military-style uniforms for the marching band, the first really proper attire ever for that ensemble at Simpson.

45. Ibid.

46. *Simpsonian*, November 16, 1936.

47. Ibid., March 16, 1936.

48. Gilbert R. Caldwell, "History," 11. Both students and faculty, not to speak of board members, grumbled about the commercializing of the College presidency.

49. Simpson College, Board of Trustees, Minutes, February 9, 1938.

50. Ibid., June 6, 1938.

51. Ibid., February 9, 1938.

52. Ibid., February 11, 1937.

53. Ibid., June 7, 1937.

54. Ibid.

55. Simpson College, Board of Trustees, Executive Committee, Minutes, May 13, 1937.

56. Simpson College, Board of Trustees, Minutes, February 9, 1938.

57. Ibid.
58. Ibid.
59. Ibid., June 6, 1938. Simpson paid Tamblyn and Tamblyn only $6,000.
60. Ibid., February 9, 1938.
61. The total deficit for the 1937–38 academic year was expected to be $32,545. *Indianola Record*, February 25, 1938.
62. The College's income on its $1,424,175 endowment was almost exactly three percent during the previous year. Because of the depression, the market value of the endowment in 1938 was estimated to be approximately $1,200,000. See *Indianola Record*, February 25, 1938.
63. Ibid., April 1, 1938.
64. Simpson College, Board of Trustees, Minutes, February 9, 1938.
65. There seems little question but that the overriding reason for discontinuing the deanship was the crushing burden of retrenchment in the face of the depression. Contemporary documents suggest no other motive on the part of the president or the board. Only later did people seem to recall Payne's "dismissal" as dean in 1932 as anything but financial exigency. Yet in 1938 it was remembered that Payne as dean had "irritated other faculty members, had nothing constructive to offer and presented recommendations both visionary and impractical. . . . He proved himself to be a poor administrator, and . . . did not serve any useful purpose as dean." And it seems that "he did not appreciate the consideration shown him by the Advisory Committee on Administration [of the board of trustees] when it temporarily discontinued the office of Dean rather than cause him embarrassment by replacing him." President's File, "Declaration of Causes for Separation," 1938, 2.
According to Gilbert R. Caldwell whose viewpoint was no doubt considerably influenced by the recollections of conservative Francis Moats, Payne's retention "was more or less an act of charity because there was a significant dissatisfaction among the administration and his colleagues with his lack of ability." Gilbert R. Caldwell, "History," 16. It is true that when Harper appointed Francis Moats dean of the faculty in 1936, he deliberately passed over Payne, whom he believed less qualified.
66. John L. Hillman, Eustis, Florida, to the Reverend R. M. Shipman, Des Moines, Iowa, March 21, 1938.
67. Earl E. Harper, Indianola, Iowa, to Raymond M. Shipman, Des Moines, Iowa, Chairman of the Faculty Trustee Committee, March 23, 1938.
68. Earl E. Harper, Indianola, Iowa, to Executive Committee of the Board of Trustees of Simpson College, Indianola, Iowa, March 10, 1938.
69. Ibid.
70. Winfred E. Payne, Indianola, Iowa, to Earl E. Harper, Indianola, Iowa, March 2, 1938.
71. Dr. Seaton's paragraph is printed verbatim in *Bulletin of the American Association of University Professors*, 26 (December 1940), 613.
72. Gilbert R. Caldwell, interview with Harold F. Watson, Indianola, Iowa, November 12, 1946.
73. Gilbert R. Caldwell, "History," 19.
74. Earl E. Harper, Indianola, Iowa, to Members of the Faculty Committee of the Board of Trustees, Indianola, Iowa, April 1, 1938.
75. *Bulletin of the American Association of University Professors*, 26 (December 1940), 609.
76. The reporter was Ethel F. Katz of the Municipal Court in Des Moines.
77. *Bulletin of the American Association of University Professors*, 26 (December 1940), 610–11. One member of the hearing committee, the Rev. Benjamin F. Schwartz, was not so sure that the evidence against Payne was in any way conclusive. He was supported in his views by a number of clergymen in the conference. He wrote, "While serving as a Trustee of Simpson College and Pastor of the Methodist Church at Indianola, Iowa, I was appointed a member of the 'hearing committee' which investigated the matter of Dr. Payne's acceptability as a teacher of Economics. You can understand the delicate situation in which I was placed due to the fact that I was not only a Trustee, but was also pastor and personal friend to Dr. Payne and to the then President of Simpson College, Dr. E. E. Harper. As the investigation developed, I found myself convinced of the fact that Dr. Payne was a leader of outstanding ability, a master of his field, and a thoroughly competent scholar. I felt that our investigation thor-

oughly vindicated Dr. Payne in every particular except one. That was that he had clearly become unacceptable to the administration and for that reason alone the committee felt that he should be given a chance to demonstrate the cooperative spirit along with his undeniable ability as a scholar."

78. Report of the Faculty [Trustee] Committee to the Executive Committee of the Board of Trustees, Simpson College, April 8, 1938. It is clear that by this time a de facto departmental structure of the College was once again in place.

79. *Simpsonian*, May 3, 1938.

80. Simpson College, Board of Trustees, Executive Committee, Minutes, May 3, 1938.

81. *Simpsonian*, May 3, 1938.

82. *Indianola Record*, May 6, 1938.

83. *Simpsonian*, May 3, 1938.

84. *Indianola Record*, May 6, 1938.

85. The committee included two Indianolans, William Buxton, Jr., and Frank P. Henderson; two from Des Moines, the Reverend Levi P. Goodwin and Henry Sampson; and Bishop Oxnam and Hamilton serving ex officio. Simpson College, Board of Trustees, Executive Committee, Minutes, May 3, 1938.

86. Serving with Moats were Clyde Emmons, William Hilmer, Harold Watson and Charles Burrows. See *Indianola Record*, May 6, 1938.

87. The secretary of the Methodist Board of Education was Dr. William J. Davidson. See Simpson College, Board of Trustees, Minutes, August 10, 1938; *Indianola Record*, August 12, 1938.

88. Simpson College, Board of Trustees, Minutes, August 10, 1938.

89. Gerald O. McCulloh, "John O. Gross (1894–1971)," in Charles E. Cole, ed., *Something More Than Human* (Nashville: United Methodist Board of Higher Education and Ministry, 1986), 111.

90. Asbury College, founded in 1890, also produced E. Stanley Jones, one of Methodism's most outstanding missionaries and evangelists. John Gross was helped through college by an old family friend, Christine Dykes.

91. *Indianola Record*, August 12, 1938.

92. Ibid., November 4, 1938.

93. More than ninety percent were from Iowa. Seventy-four percent of Simpson's 1938 students were Methodists. Twenty-six of the students were children of clergymen. Twenty denominations were represented in the student body. Simpson was one of only two Iowa colleges showing a decline in enrollment that year. The reasons for the loss were several: (1) misperception by some that the suspension by A.A.U. represented the loss of North Central accreditation, (2) serious attrition at the junior and senior levels, (3) poor student housing, (4) relatively poor relations with conference clergy, and (5) weakness of the conservatory, where much of the enrollment loss occurred.

94. A further disappointment was the inability of Bishop Brenton T. Badley of India to attend these services.

95. See accounts of the inauguration in the *Indianola Record*, March 10 and April 21, 1939; *Simpsonian*, April 24, 1939.

96. He had been notified on June 16, 1938, that his appointment at Simpson would terminate at the close of the 1938–39 academic year.

97. *Bulletin of the American Association of University Professors*, 26 (December 1940), 616.

98. President's File, "Declaration of Causes for Separation," 1938, 2.

99. *Bulletin of the American Association of University Professors*, 26 (December 1940), 607.

100. Ibid., 615.

101. Ibid., 616.

102. Ibid., 617.

103. Ibid., 618.

104. *Des Moines Register*, January 2, 1940.

105. Ralph E. Himstead, Washington, D.C., to John O. Gross, Indianola, Iowa, January 4, 1940.

106. John O. Gross, Indianola, Iowa, to Ralph E. Himstead, Washington, D.C., January 6, 1940.

107. Eugene R. Melson, Chicago, Illinois, to Earl E. Harper, Indianola, Iowa, n.d., 1938.
108. Margaret Liebe Watson, interview by author, Indianola, Iowa, April 21, 1992.
109. Gilbert Caldwell, "History," 25.
110. Simpson College, Board of Trustees, Minutes, June 5, 1939.
111. During the five years from 1936 to 1941, of an average of 181 freshmen, only 153 returned as sophomores, 88 as juniors and 84 as seniors.
112. "Annual Report of the President of Simpson College to the Board of Trustees, 1939–1940," 7.
113. Simpson College, Board of Trustees, Minutes, September 6, 1940. See also ibid., March 1, 1940 and June 4, 1940.
114. Ibid.
115. Simpson College, Board of Trustees, Minutes, February 23, 1939. In 1939 these were the University of Iowa, Iowa State College, Coe, Cornell, Drake, Grinnell and Loras, seven out of some thirty colleges.
116. Watson, "Memoirs," 77. See also Simpson College, Board of Trustees, Executive Committee, Minutes, July 7, 1939.
117. Of 122 classes (not counting the conservatory), only 30 had an enrollment of more than 30. Sixty-six had fewer than 20, 27 fewer than 10 and 14 fewer than 5.
118. These staff reductions followed very closely the recommendations presented to the board early in 1939. Simpson College, Board of Trustees, Minutes, February 23, 1939.
119. See *Simpsonian*, March 29, 1943.
120. Guyton had earned his B.S. from Mississippi State in 1927 and his M.A. from Northwestern University in 1932. He had taught eight years at Mississippi State before undertaking work on his doctorate at Duke University in 1936. During the 1938–39 year he worked in research at the Brookings Institution in Washington, D.C. Although close to his Ph.D., he did not complete it during the seven years he taught at Simpson. President Gross reinstated the rank of associate professor in 1938.
121. Ibid., June 4, 1940. At the time of the installation of the new stacks, the library contained 29,285 volumes and was receiving 215 periodicals.
122. *Simpson College Bulletin*, March 1940. See also "Annual Report of the President of Simpson College to the Board of Trustees, 1939–1940," 12.
123. Brewer was hired at a salary "not to exceed $1,200 per year." Simpson College, Board of Trustees, Executive Committee, Minutes, October 24, 1938.
124. See Simpson College, Board of Trustees, Minutes, June 6, 1939, June 4, 1940, February 11, 1941; see also Simpson College, Board of Trustees, Executive Committee, Minutes, May 17, 1938, May 12, 1939, June 19, 1939; *Indianola Record*, October 6, 1939. In the late fall of 1940 Dr. Gross launched what he called the "silver dollar campaign." Simpson students, faculty and the College itself would pay for everything they purchased in Indianola with silver dollars (exchanged against paper money at the local bank). This was intended "to make the people of Indianola aware of the financial significance of Simpson College." Some weeks later people heard the story of one prominent Indianola merchant who promised to give his wife each silver dollar they took in at the store. He was upset when the dollars began to roll in from Simpson students and faculty, "but when the college office paid a bill for several hundred dollars in the silver coin, he nearly had apoplexy." His wife made him stick to his bargain. *Simpsonian*, November 9, 1940.
125. See *Indianola Record*, November 22, 1940; *Alumni News Bulletin*, January 1941; *Simpsonian*, November 25, 1940.
126. Simpson College, Board of Trustees, Minutes, February 23, 1939; *Simpsonian*, March 4, 1940.
127. Simpson College, Board of Trustees, Minutes, June 5, 1939.
128. Ibid., June 4, 1940.
129. Ibid., March 1, 1940; *Simpsonian*, March 4, 1940. Remaining for the 1940–41 year permitted Dean Harvey's son, Jack, to complete his senior year at the Indianola High School. Harvey's older son, Addison, was at that time in the United States Aeronautical Service.
130. *Indianola Record*, April 26, 1940.

131. Ibid. Lekberg's initial salary for 1940–41 was $2,400. See Simpson College, Board of Trustees, Executive Committee, Minutes, April 22, 1940.

132. Sven Lekberg, interview by author, Indianola, Iowa, December 8, 1968.

133. *Indianola Record*, May 24, 1940.

134. Only a few months after he arrived in Indianola, Reisman married a fellow Hungarian, Clara Szekely, at Cleveland, Ohio. She held a B.M. degree from the Institute of Music at Cleveland. *Simpsonian*, January 13, 1941. In late 1941 the couple went briefly to Windsor, Ontario, and reentered the U.S. on the Hungarian immigration quota, permitting them to apply for U.S. citizenship. Ibid., November 17, 1941. See also *Indianola Record*, November 14, 1941.

135. They departed from Indianola on July 15. *Indianola Record*, July 12, 1940.

136. George Washington Carver, interview by John Owen Gross, Tuskegee, Alabama, July 17, 1940.

137. At the George Washington Carver National Monument at Diamond, Missouri, is displayed a several-page handwritten autobiographical sketch penned by Dr. Carver late in his life. Nearly a third of that narrative he chose to devote to his time at Simpson.

138. George Washington Carver, interview by John Owen Gross, Tuskegee, Alabama, July 17, 1940. There exists what appears to be a complete typed transcript of the interview.

139. Grant's *Register* story was reprinted in Simpson's *Alumni News Bulletin*, October 1941.

140. Simpson College, Board of Trustees, Executive Committee, Minutes, March 28, 1939; *Indianola Record*, June 9, 1939; *Simpsonian*, September 18, 1939; Simpson College Board of Trustees, Minutes, June 4, 1940. Center House had been used by Theta Upsilon, Park Hall by Beta Sigma Omicron, and Campus Cottage, located on the southeast corner of the campus had been occupied by Omicron. Omicron was noted in the spring of 1940 as having become defunct. Simpson College, Board of Trustees, Minutes, June 4, 1940.

141. Simpson College, Board of Trustees, Minutes, June 4, 1940.

142. Simpson College, Board of Trustees, Executive Committee, Minutes, August 7, 1941.

143. *Simpsonian*, September 8, 1941.

144. Simpson College, Board of Trustees, Executive Committee, Minutes, September 26, 1940, October 14, 1940.

145. Ibid., August 9, 1941.

146. *Simpsonian*, April 13, 1942.

147. The College built a garage for the president's home and was forced to buy new boilers for the heating plant.

148. "The use of invested funds for dormitory purposes may be justified if the proper procedure is followed to liquidate the initial cost and pay along with it a reasonable return on the investment." "Annual Report of the President of Simpson College to the Board of Trustees, 1940–1941," 9.

149. An egregious exception was the *Simpsonian*'s first issue in the fall of 1937, beginning "Volume XXXVIX." Clyde Emmons wrote to the editor, who in his turn apologized for not being a scholar of the classics. See *Simpsonian*, October 4, 1937.

150. Ibid., November 16, 1936.

151. Ibid., January 9, 1939; January 26, 1942; *Indianola Record*, January 13, 1939.

152. The Kappas' average was one one-hundredth of a point ahead of the ATOs, just a hair above a C average. *Simpsonian*, March 13, 1939.

153. *Simpsonian*, November 4, 1939; November 13, 1939; *Simpson College Bulletin*, December 1939.

154. *Alumni News Bulletin*, January 1941.

155. *Indianola Record*, September 15, 1939; *Simpsonian*, September 18, 1939, October 16, 1939.

156. *Simpson College Bulletin*, October 1936; *Zenith*, 1938 (1).

157. *Simpsonian*, October 24, 1938.

158. Ibid., November 9, 1940.

159. *Alumni News Bulletin*, January 1941.

160. *Indianola Tribune*, November 26, 1937.

161. *Simpsonian*, April 22, 1940.

162. *Indianola Record*, July 12, 1940; September 6, 1940.

163. *Simpsonian*, February 16, 1942; March 16, 1942.

164. The St. Ambrose Bees played their two closest games against Simpson (they were 12–0 in the conference), winning at Indianola 39–36 and at Davenport 36–34.

165. Mike Reed was named all-conference guard in 1941.

166. Major set a conference record in the 440 with a time of 50.5 seconds and broke his own record the next year at 50.4 seconds. See J. E. (Buck) Turnbull, *The Iowa Conference Story*, 142–43.

167. *Simpsonian*, December 8, 1941.

168. Simpson College, Board of Trustees, Executive Committee, Minutes, January 26, 1940.

169. The ATOs won the men's division in Miniature Orpheum three of the five years under study. The women's cup was taken by Pi Beta Phi twice, Tridelta once, and for two years no winner was proclaimed.

170. *Simpsonian*, January 16, 1939. In the spring, at the interfraternity or intersorority songfests—later called All-College Sing—the ATOs and Tridelatas usually won.

171. Simpson College, Board of Trustees, Minutes, February 9, 1938.

172. *Simpsonian*, February 3, 1941; February 10, 1941; February 22, 1941; *Simpson College Bulletin*, October 1941.

173. Dr. Moats expounded on the origin of the green caps. The tradition, he explained, went back to about 1480 at Heidelberg University, where new students were called "greenhorns." Such hazing came to America and was common in the days of intense class rivalry. At Simpson, the caps were said to have made their appearance in 1922, when freshmen "on their own initiative" adopted this distinctive headgear. Soon enough the student council took over the administration of cap wearing. Moats was quite sure that "the appearance of the caps is always welcomed by students, faculty and townspeople. It is a splendid tradition and adds much to college spirit." *Simpsonian*, October 4, 1937.

174. Ibid., November 7, 1936.

175. Ibid., March 18, 1940. The girls had timed the boys at dinner and found that the average finished his meal in seven minutes flat.

176. Ibid., October 23, 1939.

177. "Annual Report of the President of Simpson College to the Board of Trustees, 1940–1941," 10; *Simpsonian*, April 21, 1941.

178. Smith's daughter Christine graduated in Simpson's class of 1935.

179. *Indianola Record*, June 11, 1937; December 22, 1939; *Simpson College Bulletin*, October 1937; March 1940.

180. *Indianola Record*, May 5, 1939. Mott had many Indianola connections. His wife, who was Vera Ingram, was a graduate of Simpson. His father, D. C. Mott, lived in Indianola, as did his sister, Mrs. Clarence Pickard.

181. Simpson awarded the elder Smith a D.D. degree in 1921. His grandson, Paul Miller, of Summit, Miss., was a senior at Simpson when the old man died. After Smith's death, his family donated to the College one of his most treasured possessions, bound copies of the first three volumes of the *Simpsonian*.

182. *Simpson College Bulletin*, October 1939.

183. Simpson College, Board of Trustees, Minutes, June 2, 1941. Former trustee Clyde Proudfoot '02 died January 5, 1936. *Simpson College Bulletin*, May 1936.

184. *Indianola Record*, November 4, 1938.

185. Gordon had been charged by one B. F. Sells with having promised Sells a job in exchange for political support in the mayoral election the previous March. Sells was still jobless. The mayor was arrested and much embarrassed by the accusation. See ibid., April 16, 1937.

186. The dedication took place August 24, 1939. Ibid., August 11, 1939.

187. Simpson College, Board of Trustees, Executive Committee, Minutes, April 7, 1937.

188. *Indianola Record*, March 29, 1940; November 8, 1940.

189. *Simpsonian*, April 18, 1938.

190. *Indianola Record*, January 27, 1939.

191. "Annual Report of the President of Simpson College to the Board of Trustees, 1939–1940," 3. Students paid an extra forty dollars tuition for the ground course. The U.S. Gov-

ernment paid the College twenty dollars for each student enrolled and paid the entire cost of the flight training.

192. Simpson College, Board of Trustees, Minutes, June 2, 1941.
193. *Indianola Record*, July 12, 1940.
194. Ibid., July 26, 1940.
195. *Simpsonian*, February 10, 1941.
196. Ibid., May 19, 1941.
197. Ibid., November 10, 1941.
198. Ibid., November 17, 1941.
199. *Indianola Record*, May 9, 1941; *Simpsonian*, May 12, 1941.
200. "Annual Report of the President of Simpson College to the Board of Trustees, 1940–1941," 16.
201. John O. Gross, Indianola, Iowa, to Conference Pastors of the Des Moines Conference, May 27, 1941.

Chapter 14

1. Two days earlier the selection committee had reported to the executive committee of the board that "a careful investigation of all prospects is being made and it takes time. . . . Several promising men are still under consideration. No invitation has yet been extended to anyone." Later asked by a reporter if "it is necessary to get a Methodist preacher for college president," Bishop Magee replied that being a clergyman had nothing to do with it. "However," he stated, "bear this in mind. It seems that we can often get more brains in a minister for the salary we can pay because we are bidding against ministerial salaries rather than against business or professional salaries." *Indianola Record*, August 29, 1941; Simpson College, Board of Trustees, Executive Committee, Minutes, August 27, 1941.
2. Ibid.
3. Ibid., December 15, 1941.
4. *Indianola Tribune*, December 17, 1941; *Simpsonian*, December 15, 1941.
5. Watson, "Memoirs," 5. Dr. Voigt repeated this same thought in 1943: "It has been most unfortunate for Simpson College that the two previous administrations were of such short duration." Simpson College, Board of Trustees, Minutes, June 1, 1943.
6. Wartime enrollments of men and women reflect, of course, the loss of men to the military service: 1941–42—174 men and 252 women; 1942–43—198 men and 215 women; 1943–44—66 men and 203 women; 1944–45—85 men and 240 women.
7. These were Bishop J. Ralph Magee of Des Moines, Levi P. Goodwin of Jefferson, who was back on the board after five years, and R. M. Shipman, minister at Muscatine.
8. Included were Don Berry, publisher of the *Indianola Record* ; Vinton C. Watson, agent for Bankers Life Insurance Company; William Buxton, Jr., and William Buxton III, president and vice-president respectively of the Peoples Trust and Savings Bank; Dr. G. A. "Chick" Grant, dentist; William T. Hamilton, grocery store manager; Frank P. Henderson, attorney; Dr. E. E. Shaw, physician; and Sara Sigler, whom we remember as the godmother of the Simpson home economics program.
9. Jennie Cosson, social leader; Loren Crowe of the Penn Mutual Life Insurance Company; Henry E. Sampson, attorney; N. D. McCombs, superintendent of schools; Agnes Samuelson, secretary of the Iowa State Teachers Association; and attorney Truman S. Stevens.
10. Members included Kenneth Karr, an attorney from Glen Ellyn, Illinois; Robert G. Collins, assistant vice-president of the First National Bank of Chicago and guardian of the College's endowment funds; and Harold W. Flint, an insurance man from Sioux Falls, South Dakota, elected by the alumni. Other members included two from Council Bluffs, banker W. A. Allensworth and principal Ray F. Myers of Thomas Jefferson High School; W. P. Butler, an attorney from Mason City; O. F. Howard, a farmer from Imogene; and two elected by the alumni, Ralph McGee, cashier of the Clarke County State Bank in Osceola and Edmund Blair, superintendent of schools at Winterset.
11. The four conference district superintendents were the Revs. F. C. Edwards of Perry,

George A. Lawton of Des Moines, W. H. Meredith of Council Bluffs and Walter A. Morgan of Creston. And of course there was the minister of Indianola's First Methodist Church, Walter M. Scheuermann.

12. Simpson College, Board of Trustees, Minutes, June 1, 1943.

13. Simpson College, Board of Trustees, Executive Committee, Minutes, April 19, 1943.

14. Simpson College, Board of Trustees, Minutes, June 1, 1943.

15. Dr. Voigt was the fifteenth man to hold the office and the sixteenth if one counts the two Hamilton presidencies separately (1886–89 and 1915–16). Others were acting interim presidents never fully appointed to the office. *Indianola Record*, May 22, 1942.

16. *Zenith*, 1943, 83.

17. Dr. Horace Greeley Smith, president of Garrett Biblical Institute, delivered the baccalaureate sermon at commencement. *Indianola Record*, May 22, 1942.

18. Gilbert R. Caldwell, "History," 39.

19. *Simpsonian*, December 8, 1941.

20. *Indianola Record*, December 19, 1941.

21. Simpson College, Board of Trustees, Minutes, February 26, 1942; May 25, 1942; June 1, 1943.

22. Ibid., February 12, 1943.

23. Ibid., May 26, 1943; *Indianola Record*, March 26, 1943.

24. *Indianola Record*, April 23, 1943; *Alumni News Bulletin*, May 1943. McKeehan did not return to Simpson after his discharge from the Navy, but went instead into graduate study. The College, hoping for his return, carried him on leave-of-absence until the spring of 1949, when it appears hope for his return was abandoned. Listed as a faculty member for seven years, he actually taught at Simpson just over seven months.

25. *Alumni News Bulletin*, May 1943.

26. Ibid., July 1944.

27. *Zenith*, 1944, 9–25.

28. *Simpsonian*, November 4, 1944.

29. The executive committee of the board of trustees approved the physical education major "together with the expense of the necessary increase in personnel that might be involved." Simpson College, Board of Trustees, Executive Committee, Minutes, February 23, 1944.

30. *Simpsonian*, January 25, 1943. The first aid course was first announced in the College's 1943 catalog, "War and Social Welfare" in the 1944 catalog.

31. *Indianola Record*, December 25, 1942.

32. Simpson College, Board of Trustees, Executive Committee, Minutes, July 21, 1941.

33. Simpson College, Board of Trustees, Minutes, June 1, 1943.

34. In 1941–42 the deficit reached $8,882; in 1942–43 "nearly" $3,000; in 1943–44 over $12,000; and 1944–45 nearly $5,000.

35. Simpson College, Board of Trustees, Executive Committee, Minutes, April 20, 1942; June 18, 1942.

36. The components of the million dollar campaign were: $100,000 to pay off the College's debt; $250,000 for women's housing; $100,000 for a new chapel; $150,000 for a new science building; $200,000 for a student union and auditorium; $50,000 each for additions to Hopper Gymnasium and the library; and $100,000 for a scholarship or "war emergency" fund. See *Indianola Record*, November 13, 1942.

37. Simpson College, Board of Trustees, Minutes, February 12, 1943; Simpson College, Board of Trustees, Executive Committee, Minutes, May 11, 1943.

38. *Indianola Record*, November 20, 1942.

39. Ibid., December 4, 1942.

40. For Miller's services the College had to pay $30,665 plus $14,000 for expenses.

41. Simpson College, Board of Trustees, Minutes, June 1, 1943.

42. Ibid.

43. If one was comparing endowment funds, this was true. Simpson ranked fifteenth. But in other categories it did not fare so well. Its total annual income of $196,262 ranked twenty-ninth; its enrollment of 413 thirty-second; its tuition of $200 a year thirty-third; the library

book collection of 29,821 thirty-fourth; its equipment and furnishings ($98,386) thirty-sixth; and the value of buildings and grounds ($477,597) forty-fifth.

44. Simpson College, Board of Trustees, Minutes, June 1, 1943.

45. *Indianola Record*, June 23, 1944. In January 1945, a fund drive was undertaken to raise the $30,000 in matching funds and was completed successfully. Ibid., December 15, 1944.

46. *Alumni News Bulletin*, July 1944.

47. "This song," wrote Lekberg at the bottom of the manuscript, "was written to mark the gift of the Gardner Cowles Foundation for a memorial to George Washington Carver—Simpson alumnus—." See ibid.

48. Simpson College, Board of Trustees, Executive Committee, Minutes, July 31, 1944.

49. *Indianola Record*, August 14, 1942; *Alumni News Bulletin*, October 1942.

50. *Alumni News Bulletin*, July 1944.

51. Simpson College, Board of Trustees, Minutes, June 1, 1943.

52. *Indianola Record*, September 3, 1943.

53. *Simpsonian*, December 20, 1943.

54. Ibid., October 30, 1943.

55. Simpson College, Board of Trustees, Minutes, February 26, 1942. Lamb's committee included Wylie King, Dick Flint and Catherine Wilson.

56. The two rooms housing the Student Union had served economics and typewriting. Economics classes were transferred to the third floor of the building and typewriting classes to the lower floor of the science building.

57. The whole project cost $1,500, and students reimbursed $300 of that.

58. Simpson College, Board of Trustees, Minutes, June 1, 1943.

59. Simpson College, Board of Trustees, Executive Committee, Minutes, November 23, 1943. Poundstone's firm had also done plans for eight Methodist related colleges and was highly recommended by the brethren in Nashville.

60. *Indianola Record*, December 3, 1943.

61. *Alumni News Bulletin*, July 1944.

62. *Indianola Record*, July 21, 1944. See also ibid., October 6, 1944.

63. *Indianola Record-Herald*, January 12, 1945.

64. Ibid., May 25, 1945.

65. Ibid., April 20, 1945.

66. Ibid., March 9, 1945.

67. Ibid., July 6, 1945; February 4, 1947.

68. *Alumni News Bulletin*, July 1944.

69. *Indianola Record*, April 28, 1944; November 3, 1944; *Alumni News Bulletin*, July 1944.

70. Though not a member of the faculty, Dean received from the College a monthly pension of $32.50 per month. Simpson College, Board of Trustees, Executive Committee, Minutes, August 8, 1945; *Alumni News Bulletin*, July 15, 1945.

71. Tutt went to work in the real estate department of the Central Life Assurance Society in Des Moines after earning the M.B.A. at Harvard in 1932. Four years later he joined the Weitz Investment Company in Des Moines, and during his seven years there rose to the position of assistant secretary. In 1943 he moved to the Fox Chemical Company. By the time he came to the Simpson staff, he was married to Mary L. Simpson of Norwalk and had a five-year-old daughter, Wendy, a future Simpson student. See *Indianola Record-Herald*, April 13, 1945; *Simpsonian*, April 25, 1945.

72. See *Indianola Record*, February 6, 1942; Simpson College, Board of Trustees, Minutes, May 25, 1942. The whole College was saddened two years later by the news that Kunkel had died of cancer at Rochester, Minnesota on March 24, 1944. *Indianola Record*, April 21, 1944; *Alumni News Bulletin*, July 1944; *Simpsonian*, April 3, 1944.

73. *Indianola Record*, June 23, 1944.

74. *Simpson College Bulletin*, July 1944.

75. *Indianola Record-Herald*, September 7, 1945.

76. Simpson College, Board of Trustees, Executive Committee, Minutes, March 18, 1942.

77. Simpson College, Board of Trustees, Minutes, May 26, 1945.

78. *Indianola Record*, May 29, 1942.

79. She died February 21, 1943. *Alumni News Bulletin*, October 1943.
80. *Simpsonian*, February 26, 1945; *Zenith*, 1945, 11.
81. *Alumni News Bulletin*, July 1945.
82. He died March 14, 1942. Ibid., July 1944.
83. Only Simpson and Central fielded teams in 1943. The next year those two were joined by Wartburg and Luther.
84. The team scrimmaged early in the season with R. G. "Hap" Miller's strong Indianola High School squad and played fairly well. The "practice" game, however, caused Miller and the Indianola school administration trouble with the state's high school authorities.
85. *Zenith*, 1944, 116–17.
86. *Simpsonian*, October 30, 1943; *Indianola Record*, October 22, 1943.
87. Its conference victory took Simpson to the national playoffs at Kansas City, where Simpson won its first game against the University of Portland 59–43, then lost the second game to Indiana State Teachers, Terre Haute 51–43.
88. *Indianola Record*, May 28, 1943.
89. A short-lived group called the Mary Berry Independents was organized in 1942. *Simpsonian*, October 24, 1942.
90. The ATO house committee included A. V. Proudfoot, Everett Overton and W. C. Stewart. See *Indianola Record*, February 18, 1944.
91. *Simpsonian*, March 19, 1945.
92. In addition to James Hashimoto, there were Stanley Tados Aoyagi of Alameda, California; Sumiko Hashimoto of Amache, Colorado; Marion Konishi of Amache, Colorado; Arthur Tetsu Sugino of Poston, Arizona; and Karen Toda of Heart Mountain, Wyoming.
93. *Zenith*, 1944, 73; *Indianola Record*, August 13, 1943; October 29, 1943.
94. *Zenith*, 1944, 72; *Indianola Record*, February 4, 1944.

Chapter 15

1. Total enrollment the spring semester of 1945 was only 235, the lowest in decades. These figures do not include enrollment in Public School Music.
2. The faculty-student ratio in 1945 was 1:11; in 1946 it was 1:16.
3. Inman would receive a monthly pension of "$21.25 for life," reported the board with an eminent sense of satisfaction. Simpson College, Board of Trustees, Executive Committee, Minutes, October 9, 1946.
4. At the last minute Legg was called out of his California retirement to take over in psychology for the 1946–47 year, after which he returned with his wife to the West Coast.
5. *Record-Herald*, January 10, 1946; Simpson College, Board of Trustees, Minutes, May 4, 1946; *Indianola Tribune*, September 3, 1946. Burrows had talked of going to Trinity as early as 1945, but Dr. Voigt had talked him out of it. Simpson College, Board of Trustees, Executive Committee, Minutes, October 10, 1945.
6. It appears that Percy Guyton, who had been on a leave-of-absence status for several years to serve with the Office of Price Administration, was the last person to occupy the William Buxton, Jr., Professorship of Economics and Business Administration.
7. In addition to White, new instructors that fall included Virginia Wayt Frank in English; Grace van der Heurk in dramatics; Urith Copeland in home economics; Gene Carter in sociology; in physical education Ken Tannatt, who would also coach football; and three in music, Helen Capell (piano), Donald H. Price (voice) and returning Mildred Lekberg. Replacing Dr. Emmons was a Simpson graduate (1941) mathematician named Victor Gunn, and taking the place of twenty-five-year veteran Arthur Blaine Carr in physics was Roy Lester Horn.
8. Ken Tannatt continued as assistant football coach under Miller.
9. Among those appointed in 1947 who stayed at Simpson only one or two years were Kay Sorden in typewriting and Persis George Flint, wife of Simpson's director of public relations and admissions, who served as a "graduate assistant" in shorthand; Edna Caroline Miller, who served as associate professor of education and dean of women during the 1947–48 academic year replacing Ruth Jackson, who returned to full-time teaching in English; Max

E. Thompson, war veteran from Kansas in psychology; Kennon Shank, a 1942 Simpson graduate and veteran of three years of military service with a masters degree from Denver University, replacing Donald H. Ecroyd in speech; Herbert J. Markle replacing Robert Samson, who had resigned to join the Western Auto Supply in Kansas City; Frederick Carl Prussner, a Methodist missionary's son, who had grown up in the Dutch East Indies and was educated in France and Germany before earning his B.D. at Garrett in 1941 and the M.A. from Northwestern University the next year, joining the faculty in Bible and religion replacing Kwang-Won Kim; and Lois E. Clark in dramatic arts, who set something of a modern day record by resigning at Christmastime in her first year "to go into theatrical work," succeeded by Frederick B. Vacha, who lasted just one semester.

10. See *Simpsonian*, May 12, 1947.

11. Virgilia Wade, replacing Kennon Shank in speech and drama, was at Simpson three years, as was Elva M. Bramhall in English and speech, replacing Clark and Vacha; Dean of Women Emily L. Philpott and Elizabeth Stone, who replaced Helen Capell Johnston in piano, stayed two years each; while Laura Miller in English remained only a single year.

12. Edwin E. Voigt, interview by author, Champaign, Illinois, June 13, 1961.

13. *Simpsonian*, April 26, 1948.

14. *Simpson College Bulletin*, November 1946.

15. Tutt had already investigated buying or leasing trailer houses, but, he said, "We believe them to be unsanitary, unhealthful, too costly for the facilities afforded, and the forerunner of a slum neighborhood in the town." *Record-Herald*, January 10, 1946. The board of trustees agreed that it was best to seek government surplus housing "during the present emergency." Simpson College, Board of Trustees, Executive Committee, Minutes, January 15, 1946.

16. *Simpsonian*, January 15, 1946.

17. Ibid., January 29, 1946.

18. Simpson College, Board of Trustees, Executive Committee, Minutes, February 27, 1946. The twenty units were contained four each in five 100-foot-by-20-foot converted Army barracks. Ibid., March 13, 1946.

19. *Simpsonian*, May 22, 1946; October 28, 1946.

20. Simpson College, Board of Trustees, Executive Committee, Minutes, May 8, 1946; August 14, 1946; *Indianola Tribune*, May 28, 1946; July 9, 1946. The government allowed ground rent for the barracks and even paid $600 for utilities installation.

21. "The gas isn't on yet, but it will be soon," reported the *Simpson College Bulletin* on October 8.

22. For these services the College paid $1,449.49 in 1947 and repeated its contribution for several years. Simpson College, Board of Trustees, Executive Committee, Minutes, June 10, 1947; April 13, 1949; *Simpsonian*, March 15, 1948.

23. Net profit for 1946–47 was $2,426.79 and for 1947–48 $2,164.34. Simpson College, Board of Trustees, Executive Committee, Minutes, July 14, 1948.

24. Public Law 796 provided, among other things, for disposition of temporary housing among those institutions already using it. *Record-Herald*, July 15, 1948. Meanwhile the City of Indianola had provided a five-year zoning exemption to this nonconforming housing, expiring July 15, 1951, at which time the College obtained a five-year extension. After that it didn't seem to matter. Some of the barracks were still in use in the mid-sixties. See Simpson College, Board of Trustees, Executive Committee, Minutes, March 14, 1951.

25. *Indianola Tribune*, September 17, 1946.

26. *Record-Herald*, January 10, 1946.

27. Simpson College, Board of Trustees, Executive Committee, Minutes, January 15, 1946. Poundstone's associate was James B. Goodwin.

28. *Simpsonian*, September 22, 1947.

29. Members of the executive committee at the time were William T. Hamilton, William Buxton III, Frank P. Henderson, Dr. G. A. Grant, Wendell Tutt, "Chic" McCoy, Vinton Watson and (ex officio) Dr. Voigt. They received Poundstone's plans January 8, 1947.

30. Simpson College, Board of Trustees, Minutes, February 12, 1947.

31. Ibid., April 29, 1947.

32. Ibid., May 29, 1948.

33. Simpson College, Board of Trustees, Executive Committee, Minutes, April 23, 1948. Yet even at this point Vinton Watson, who led the opposition, contended that the old athletic field should be kept inviolate and urged unsuccessfully that the College retain another firm of architects to come up with a different location.

34. Ibid., August 7, 1948; August 11, 1948. The contract was signed August 21, 1948. See *Indianola Tribune*, August 24, 1948.

35. *Record-Herald*, September 29, 1949.

36. Simpson College, Board of Trustees, Executive Committee, Minutes, July 10, 1946; *Indianola Tribune*, August 27, 1946.

37. Overhead expenses were high; it was difficult to find reliable, competent kitchen employees; and need for the service was declining. Four restaurants in Indianola catered to off-campus men, many of whom preferred the freedom to eat when and what they liked. It was estimated the College could save $2,500 a year by closing the Chieftain. Simpson College, Board of Trustees, Executive Committee, Minutes, December 10, 1947.

38. *Record-Herald*, January 15, 1948.

39. Ibid., February 5, 1948.

40. *Simpsonian*, January 12, 1948.

41. This time it was the Federal Works Agency that made the offer. The several buildings Simpson accepted were cost free. Simpson College, Board of Trustees, Executive Committee, Minutes, June 10, 1947. The buildings were secured from the Sedalia Army Air Base at Knob Noster, Missouri. *Simpsonian*, September 20, 1948.

42. *Record-Herald*, July 15, 1947; *Simpsonian*, September 22, 1947; October 13, 1947; November 24, 1947.

43. Simpson College, Board of Trustees, Executive Committee, Minutes, August 11, 1948.

44. *Indianola Tribune*, January 11, 1949; *Simpsonian*, January 17, 1949; *Simpson College Bulletin*, February 1949. The Rev. Calkins was a graduate of Simpson in the class of 1927.

45. Simpson College, Board of Trustees, Executive Committee, Minutes, November 29, 1948; *Simpsonian*, January 17, 1949.

46. Simpson College, Board of Trustees, Executive Committee, Minutes, January 6, 1949; *Simpsonian*, January 17, 1949.

47. *Indianola Tribune*, January 11, 1949.

48. *Simpsonian*, January 17, 1949; February 21, 1949; February 28, 1949.

49. *Zenith*, 1949, 170. Meanwhile, in Old Chapel the bookstore was considerably enlarged and began for the first time to offer merchandise apart from books and classroom supplies. Simpson College, Board of Trustees, Executive Committee, Minutes, August 7, 1947; August 11, 1947.

50. Simpson College, Board of Trustees, Executive Committee, Minutes, May 31, 1946.

51. Ibid., February 27, 1946.

52. Simpson College, Board of Trustees, Minutes, September 17, 1946.

53. *Simpsonian*, November 6, 1946.

54. Ibid., May 5, 1947.

55. Simpson College, Board of Trustees, Executive Committee, Minutes, October 2, 1947.

56. Ibid., October 19, 1947.

57. Ibid., April 23, 1948.

58. Ibid., July 14, 1948; October 13, 1948.

59. *Simpsonian*, April 17, 1950.

60. *Record-Herald*, October 19, 1950.

61. As late as 1953 the board of trustees was concerned "to determine ways and means of lighting the college field." Simpson College, Board of Trustees, Executive Committee, Minutes, January 14, 1953.

62. College officials urged using durable and attractive metal poles, but wooden telephone poles were cheaper, the unaesthetic results blighting the campus for nearly four decades. Ibid., July 8, 1953.

63. *Record-Herald*, November 16, 1945; *Simpsonian*, November 20, 1945.

64. It will be recalled that Sara Sigler had attended Simpson from 1891 to 1894. She was

born February 2, 1874, at Chariton, the daughter of Daniel and Elizabeth Alexander Eikenberry, whose extensive farm and lumber holdings included property in Indianola. At Simpson she roomed with Agnes Buxton, the daughter of William Buxton, Sr., and both of them were members of Pi Beta Phi. It was also at Simpson that Sara met F. Carl Sigler of Corning, and by the time of their marriage in 1895, he was connected with the old Warren County State Bank. They moved into a home on West Ashland, and when a few years later they built another home in the same block, it became the Indianola showplace, with its magnificent gardens, the creation of Sara Sigler. The house with its gardens now serves as the home of the president of Simpson. Gardening, flower arranging, teaching a girls' class at the Methodist Church, membership on the local park board and participation in countless other civic affairs together with wartime Red Cross work kept her constantly busy. She helped organize the Federated Garden Club of Iowa and was its president for three years. She was one of fifteen who signed the articles of incorporation of the National Council of State Garden Clubs, and in time became recognized as one of the leading authorities on gardening in America, writing for a number of magazines and manuals. She served Pi Beta Phi as local alumnae president, province president and national historian. After the death of her husband, who, as we have seen, had served thirty years on the Simpson Board of Trustees, she was elected to the board and served six years until the time of her death at the age of seventy-three. Nearly all of the information in this note is drawn from Don Berry's eloquent article in the *Record-Herald*, May 22, 1947.

65. Simpson College, Board of Trustees, Executive Committee, Minutes, August 7, 1947.
66. Ibid., June 29, 1950; *Simpsonian*, September 17, 1951.
67. Simpson College, Board of Trustees, Executive Committee, Minutes, December 13, 1950. At Christmastime Ethel D. and her new associate, Virginia E. Bice, who served on the faculty from 1950 to 1952, dramatized the imminent construction of the building by making a model of it from thirty pounds of sugar cubes. It took two and a half weeks to put it together before they showed it off at a reception. *Simpsonian*, December 18, 1950.
68. *Record-Herald*, October 4, 1951. Because Sara Sigler's beneficence did not cover the final total cost of the building, $17,465.48 was taken from the so-called Century Fund to complete the payment to contractor Threlkeld. Simpson College, Board of Trustees, Executive Committee, Minutes, July 15, 1952.
69. *Simpsonian*, October 15, 1951. The total cost of the tennis courts was reported $4,913.34. Simpson College, Board of Trustees, Executive Committee, Minutes, September 10, 1952.
70. This and the following report by President Voigt appear in Simpson College, Board of Trustees, Minutes, May 24, 1946.
71. *Indianola Tribune*, March 5, 1946. "It is due to [Professor Lekberg's] competent leadership of the Simpson division of music that Simpson has been found worthy of admission into this national body." When granted full membership into the 140-member N.A.S.M., Simpson was one of six Iowa member institutions, which included Cornell, Drake, Iowa State Teachers College, Morningside and the University of Iowa. Ibid., January 20, 1948. See also *Simpsonian*, February 26, 1946.
72. Simpson College, Board of Trustees, Minutes, May 24, 1946.
73. *Indianola Tribune*, July 22, 1947. See also Simpson College, Board of Trustees, Minutes, May 24, 1947.
74. Simpson College, Board of Trustees, Minutes, May 29, 1948.
75. Carter also held an M.A. in sociology from Northwestern University.
76. Simpson College, Board of Trustees, Minutes, September 17, 1946.
77. *Time*, 48 (December 23, 1946), 70.
78. *Record-Herald*, January 1, 1948.
79. *Indianola Tribune*, January 21, 1947; *Simpson College Bulletin*, February 1947.
80. *Simpson College Bulletin*, June 1946.
81. Simpson College, Board of Trustees, Minutes, June 4, 1949. Entering scores on A.C.E. (American Council of Education) tests rose from the fortieth percentile in 1942 to the fifty-fifth percentile in 1949.
82. Ibid., May 29, 1948.
83. *Indianola Tribune*, March 15, 1949. Simpson had affiliated with the N.V.G.A. in 1948,

offering testing and guidance services to entering college students. Simpson College, Board of Trustees, Executive Committee, Minutes, May 12, 1948.

84. *Indianola Tribune*, February 7, 1950; *Simpsonian*, February 6, 1950; *Simpson College Bulletin*, March 1950.

85. Simpson College, Board of Trustees, Minutes, June 3, 1950. Two years earlier board charges were actually reduced when the Chieftain was moved into Mary Berry Hall, cutting overhead expense.

86. *Simpsonian*, May 30, 1949.

87. Ibid., February 13, 1950.

88. Summer enrollment for the first summer session in 1947 was over 400. See *Indianola Tribune*, May 20, 1947.

89. Simpson College, Board of Trustees, Minutes, February 18, 1947.

90. Ibid., September 20, 1949; June 3, 1950; Simpson College, Board of Trustees, Executive Committee, Minutes, July 14, 1948; January 26, 1949.

91. Simpson College, Board of Trustees, Minutes, February 18, 1947.

92. Ibid., February 17, 1949.

93. Simpson College, Board of Trustees, Executive Committee, Minutes, April 13, 1949; June 15, 1949; April 12, 1950.

94. In 1946 Cora Munns of Corning, who had earlier made substantial gifts to the College, gave a 240-acre farm valued at $24,000; Grace Spriecher of Denison, a past grand worthy matron of the Eastern Star, gave a 200-acre farm valued at $20,000; and an anonymous Simpson alumna donated $10,000 in cash. In December 1948, Simpson received $10,000 from the estate of Belle Myers; a year later Simpson shared equally with Grinnell and Cornell colleges the Helen Henshaw estate of approximately $30,000; and in 1951 the Bailey estate provided $33,973.47.

95. Simpson College, Board of Trustees, Minutes, June 2, 1951.

96. Ibid., February 5, 1946; Simpson College Board of Trustees, Executive Committee, Minutes, December 11, 1946; February 12, 1947. For the 1947–48 academic year the board adopted a salary scale reflecting increases in all ranks: instructors, $1,800–$2,500; assistant professors, $2,400–$2,800; associate professors, $2,700–$3,300; and full professors; $3,000–$3,600. Simpson College, Board of Trustees, Minutes, February 18, 1947.

97. Simpson College, Board of Trustees, Executive Committee, Minutes, August 7, 1947.

98. Ibid., May 12, 1948.

99. Ibid., April 10, 1946; Simpson College, Board of Trustees, Minutes, September 17, 1946.

100. Simpson College, Board of Trustees, Executive Committee, Minutes, May 8, 1946.

101. Leslie Bechter bought his house for $6,000. When Gerard Schultz offered $5,500 for the Harlan house at 600 West Boston, the College said if he would offer $5,750, he had a deal. Gene Carter gave $7,000 for his house at 1110 North Howard. Ibid., August 3, 1949; October 12, 1949.

102. Simpson College, Board of Trustees, Minutes, February 18, 1947.

103. Simpson College, Board of Trustees, Executive Committee, Minutes, May 12, 1948.

104. Ibid., August 7, 1947; October 2, 1947; October 19, 1947. After 1948 all faculty members were obliged to participate in the annuity plan after one year of service on the faculty and reaching the age of thirty-five.

105. Ibid., February 11, 1948.

106. Simpson College, Board of Trustees, Minutes, May 29, 1948.

107. Ibid.

108. *Simpsonian*, September 23, 1946.

109. *Indianola Tribune*, October 8, 1946.

110. Ibid., May 11, 1948; *Record-Herald*, May 13, 1948.

111. Simpson College, Board of Trustees, Minutes, June 4, 1949.

112. Ibid., May 29, 1948.

113. Ibid., June 4, 1949.

114. *Simpsonian*, March 7, 1949. In 1947–48, the first postwar year the College used the sanctuary of the Methodist Church for chapel services, attendance was optional. Relatively

few students attended. Simpson College, Board of Trustees, Minutes, September 16, 1947. The church charged the College twelve dollars for each chapel service.

115. Hap Miller was a graduate of Iowa State Teachers College where he was a varsity lineman for three years. Before joining the Simpson staff he had coached at Dubuque, Tama, Indianola and Keokuk high schools. He was three years at Keokuk before accepting the Simpson offer. See *Simpsonian*, May 5, 1947.

116. After William Penn was dropped, the remaining twelve schools were divided as follows: Loras, Upper Iowa, Buena Vista, Westmar, Luther and Wartburg in the North Division and St. Ambrose, Parsons, Iowa Wesleyan, Dubuque, Central and Simpson in the South Division.

117. See *Zenith*, 1948.

118. The College's administration ruled that at least eight or ten initiated members must return before a group could be reorganized and reopen its house.

119. *Simpsonian*, October 1, 1945.

120. The ATOs pledged twenty-one, the Lambda Chis sixteen and the KOYs twenty-one.

121. The ATO house was purchased by Clarence Blackburn and his wife from Illinois. They converted it into a restaurant and apartment house. *Simpsonian*, December 18, 1945; *Record-Herald*, October 12, 1945; January 31, 1946.

122. Ibid., October 1, 1945.

123. Simpson College, Board of Trustees, Executive Committee, Minutes, May 8, 1946.

124. Actually only sixteen pledged that fall; seven to ATO, six to Lambda Chi Alpha and three to KOY. *Simpsonian*, September 23, 1946.

125. Ibid., January 27, 1947.

126. *Record-Herald*, March 10, 1949; *Simpson College Bulletin*, June 1949; *Zenith*, 1949, 146. Trevethan actually became editor of the *Simpsonian* in January, 1949, when Dean Newman resigned. *Simpsonian*, January 17, 1949.

127. *Zenith*, 1950, 115.

128. *Simpsonian*, February 13, 1950; *Record-Herald*, February 16, 1950; *Simpson College Bulletin*, April 1950. Unfortunately, in their first appearance as Pi Kappa Phi in the 1950 *Zenith*, the boys noticed that the yearbook editor pictured the badge of Psi Upsilon fraternity instead of that of Pi Kappa Phi.

129. On the following evening thirteen freshmen were formally pledged to Pi Kappa Phi.

130. During the late 1940s the ATOs took fraternity scholarship honors for five semesters and the Lambda Chis for three.

131. *Simpsonian*, December 13, 1948.

132. Ibid., February 26, 1945.

133. Ibid., April 3, 1950; *Record-Herald*, April 6, 1950

134. *Indianola Tribune*, February 19, 1946; *Simpsonian*, November 10, 1947.

135. *Simpsonian*, December 5, 1949; *Record-Herald*, December 15, 1949; *Simpson College Bulletin*, February 1950.

136. *Zenith*, 1947, 76.

137. *Simpsonian*, September 30, 1946.

138. *Indianola Tribune*, October 22, 1946.

139. *Zenith*, 1947, 76. See also *Record-Herald*, April 29, 1948; *Simpson College Bulletin*, June 1949; December 1949; *Indianola Tribune*, May 30, 1950.

140. *Simpsonian*, April 12, 1948; *Zenith*, 1949, 52. Keeton was later business manager of the *Simpsonian*.

141. *Simpsonian*, September 27, 1948; *Indianola Tribune*, September 28, 1948.

142. The six faculty initiated that day were Gerard Schultz, Victor Gunn, Livingston Witten, Grover Hawk, John Cooper and Glaydon D. Robbins. *Simpsonian*, December 20, 1948. Also initiated into Alpha Phi Omega at the installation were Dr. Voigt; A. C. Berkowitz, president of the Tall Corn Council of the Boy Scouts of America; and Harold F. Pote, a Simpson alumnus in the class of 1916, who was personnel director of the national B.S.A. organization. *Simpson College Bulletin*, June 1949.

143. *Simpsonian*, May 1, 1950. Simpson College, Board of Trustees, Minutes, June 3, 1950.

144. *Simpsonian*, May 8, 1950.

145. Ibid., February 21, 1949.

146. *Record-Herald*, February 2, 1948.

147. Ibid., April 21, 1947; *Indianola Tribune*, October 14, 1947. Sigma Tau Delta also got the right in 1948 to print the *Password*, the directory of enrolled students at Simpson. *Simpsonian*, April 26, 1948.

148. *Simpsonian*, May 9, 1949.

149. The 1946 winner was Lambda Chi Alpha; in 1947 it was Tridelta; and in both 1948 and 1949 the award went to Pi Beta Phi. See ibid., October 7, 1946.

150. Ibid., December 11, 1945; November 10, 1946; December 1, 1947.

151. *Record-Herald*, February 5, 1948; *Indianola Tribune*, February 10, 1948; *Simpsonian*, November 1, 1947. The winners in 1948 were Tridelta and Lambda Chi Alpha, in 1949 Alpha Chi Omega and Lambda Chi again, and in 1950 Pi Beta Phi and Alpha Tau Omega.

152. *Simpsonian*, February 23, 1948; February 28, 1949; March 7, 1949. No winner was declared either in 1946, when only women competed, or in 1947. In 1948 Alpha Chi Omega and Lambda Chi Alpha won, in 1949 Pi Beta Phi and Lambda Chi, and in 1950 Pi Phi and Kappa Theta Psi.

153. Ibid., February 17, 1947.

154. Ibid., March 31, 1947.

155. They would be able to meet a victim of Soviet aggression personally when Heino Aalde, a "handsome, blond, blue-eyed" refugee boy from Estonia came to Indianola in 1946 to live with Professors Sven and Mildred Lekberg. *Indianola Tribune*, January 21, 1947; *Simpsonian*, November 13, 1946.

156. See Ibid., December 11 and December 18, 1945. In a poll conducted in 1948 they voted 170 to 142 in favor of a peacetime draft. Ibid., February 16, 1948. See also *Record-Herald*, February 19, 1948.

157. The poll gave Progressive Henry A. Wallace 49 votes and Socialist Norman Thomas 15. *Simpsonian*, November 1, 1948. See also *Record-Herald*, October 28, 1948.

158. *Simpsonian*, November 8, 1948.

159. Ibid., September 22, 1947.

160. *Indianola Tribune*, September 23, 1947.

161. *Record-Herald*, January 8, 1948.

162. *Indianola Tribune*, July 29, 1947.

163. A record 15.26 inches of rain fell during June in Indianola, according to Dr. Moats, who was the town's "official weather observer."

164. *Indianola Tribune*, June 10, 1947; December 30, 1947.

165. Ibid., September 9, 1947.

166. *Simpsonian*, April 24, 1950.

167. *Record-Herald*, December 29, 1949.

168. *Indianola Tribune*, May 23, 1950. The city's population had increased 1,022 in ten years.

169. Jackson was elected international president of the Kiwanis Club at its thirty-fourth annual convention at Atlantic City, New Jersey in 1949. *Simpson College Bulletin*, October 1949.

170. Ibid., February 1949.

171. *Indianola Tribune*, January 20, 1948.

172. *Simpson College Bulletin*, July 1950.

173. The United States had issued a stamp honoring Booker T. Washington in 1940.

174. *Simpson College Bulletin*, October 1948.

175. Ibid., May 1946. Simpson College, Board of Trustees, Executive Committee, Minutes, December 19, 1945.

176. *Simpsonian*, November 14, 1949; *Simpson College Bulletin*, December 1949. Simpson mourned the passing of a number of others who had figured prominently in the history of the College. Lizzie Hillman, wife of former President John Hillman, died at Moline, Illinois, April 28, 1947, and was buried in Indianola. Ervilla Brown '78 alumna and wife of former President Fletcher Brown, died at Indianola December 19, 1947, at the age of 85. She was also the sister of President Edwin M. Holmes. Several former faculty members expired during the early postwar years, including Clyde W. Emmons (December 29, 1945), Ida Pierce Newell (January 16, 1946), Alexander Emslie in Los Angeles in 1948, Estella Trueblood at Whittier,

California (July 13, 1948), and fund-raiser Rev. Willis H. Cable (November 27, 1949). Other prominent Simpsonians were lost, including former vice-president Fletcher Homan '95, a member of the legendary football team of 1893 and former president of Willamette University (1949); Horace M. Havner '96, former attorney general of Iowa, who was remembered for his part in trying to solve the notorious Villisca axe murders in 1912 and for his serving as commander-in-chief of the United Spanish War Veterans (1949); Dora Honnold '75, at the time of her death (October 11, 1949) the oldest living graduate of the College; and Forrester C. Stanley '07, president of William Penn College (November 5, 1949).

177. The *Simpsonian*, reprinted it on October 6, 1947.

Chapter 16

1. Not included are 87 public school music students, none of whom were either full time or, of course, college level. They *were* sometimes included in the 856 figure college officials liked to submit to the newspapers.

2. Simpson College, Board of Trustees, Minutes, June 3, 1950.

3. During the first months of the fall semester 1950, seven young men were forced to drop out of school to enter the armed services. Over Christmas, twenty-six men dropped out to enlist, twenty-two in the Air Corps and four in the Navy. January 1951, nineteen more dropped their classes. See *Simpsonian*, November 13, 1950; January 8, 1951; January 15, 1951.

4. Ibid., January 8, 1951.

5. Ibid. Psychologist Stuart Peterson was a member of the Warren County draft board. David Mobberley, a new member of the Biology Department, had been a lieutenant in the Air Corps during the Second World War.

6. *Indianola Tribune*, February 20, 1951; *Simpsonian*, February 26, 1951. A board of trustees executive committee meeting on February 15, only four days before the inspection team arrived, was still unable to come to a conclusion about seeking an Army Air Force unit, lest a positive vote alienate some of the ministers on the board.

7. Simpson College, Board of Trustees, Executive Committee, Minutes, March 14, 1951; March 18, 1951. Local trustees Vinton Watson and Raymond Sayre strongly supported an A.F.R.O.T.C. unit at Simpson.

8. Ibid., March 14, 1951.

9. Simpson College, Board of Trustees, Minutes, May 31, 1952.

10. Simpson's recruitment program in fact was mostly confined to the Methodist churches in the conference. Its success, concluded the Simpson board of trustees, "depends on religious education in the churches, choirs and deputation teams" from Simpson, "sermons and speakers from the College" and scholarships for church youth. Simpson College, Board of Trustees, Executive Committee, Minutes, October 8, 1952.

11. Ibid., June 2, 1951. At the same time, Dr. Voigt tried to be hopeful. "The first hurried and almost hysterical attempt to get men under arms, and the resulting over-crowding has so slowed up the selective service program that it now appears obvious that very few, if any, 19 year old boys will be called this fall."

12. *Simpson College Bulletin*, March 1951.

13. Simpson College, Board of Trustees, Minutes, May 31, 1952.

14. Ibid., September 16, 1952.

15. Simpson College, Board of Trustees, Executive Committee, Minutes, October 11, 1950; December 13, 1950; January 3, 1951. Within months it was learned that ordained clergymen on the faculty were not entitled to participate in the Social Security system. Ibid., June 13, 1951.

16. Ibid., January 3, 1951; November 14, 1951.

17. *Record-Herald*, November 1, 1951.

18. Simpson College, Board of Trustees, Minutes, September 18, 1951; September 16, 1952; and May 30, 1953. Actually in June 1951, Dr. Voigt reported the 1950–51 deficit to be $32,000.

19. *Record-Herald*, April 5, 1951; *Simpson College Bulletin*, April 1951.

20. The ten conference members were Augustana College (Illinois), Carroll College, Ham-

line University, Jamestown College, Lake Forest College, Macalester College, North Central College, St. Olaf College, Simpson and United College in Winnipeg, Manitoba.

21. Dr. Voigt was unable to attend the March meeting, but he was kept fully apprised of the deliberations and was happy to accept the constitution of the new conference. The first president was Dr. Conrad Bergendoff, president of Augustana College. See *Simpson College Bulletin*, April 1951; *Simpsonian*, April 9, 1951.

22. The *Simpsonian* noted a meeting of the Midland Conference in the early fall of 1952. *Simpsonian*, September 29, 1952. Interestingly, one searches in vain for even a mention of the Midland Conference in the minutes of the board of trustees.

23. Simpson College, Board of Trustees, Executive Committee, Minutes, October 8, 1952.

24. Articles of Incorporation, Indianola Male and Female Seminary, 1860.

25. "The only way we could muster votes for a respectable program was to require co-educational photogenics and principles of drivel also. The result was of course too wide a range of obligatory work and too little opportunity for election. But at least the Simpson student was now assured of a respectable education and the other stuff probably did no harm." Watson, "Memoirs," 81.

26. Simpson College, Board of Trustees, Minutes, September 16, 1952.

27. Simpson College, Board of Trustees, Executive Committee, Minutes, February 15, 1951.

28. Simpson College, Board of Trustess, Minutes, February 14, 1952.

29. *Simpsonian*, March 12, 1951.

30. Ibid., September 24, 1951.

31. Ibid., October 29, 1949. The Pfeiffer gift for the student union and dining hall had been promised "provided the boys' dormitory is erected along with it." The Pfeiffer gift, promised as early as 1946, was contingent on awarding contracts for the two buildings. Although they had extended the deadline again and again, the Pfeiffer trustees grew impatient with Simpson's delay in raising matching funds. Mrs. Pfeiffer's death in 1947 did not affect the grant, but it made more urgent Simpson's response. Still, the matter dragged on for years as the College found it increasingly difficult to meet a financial goal that kept receding as construction costs soared.

32. See *Indianola Tribune*, February 20, 1951.

33. Ibid., April 24, 1951.

34. Simpson College, Board of Trustees, Minutes, June 2, 1951.

35. Simpson College, Board of Trustees, Executive Committee, Minutes, June 13, 1951.

36. Ibid., June 18, 1952; Simpson College, Board of Trustees, Minutes, February 14, 1952. Dr. Fansher was paid $3,600 per year.

37. *Simpsonian*, October 15, 1951; *Simpson College Bulletin*, November 1951.

38. Simpson College, Board of Trustees, Executive Committee, Minutes, May 14, 1952. Later $10,000 of the Kelly estate was used for a "maintenance reserve fund to meet abnormal repair and maintenance costs." Ibid., June 18, 1952. See also *Indianola Tribune*, May 6, 1952.

39. *Simpsonian*, April 7, 1953.

40. Simpson College, Board of Trustees, Executive Committee, Minutes, November 17, 1952; June 17, 1953.

41. Ibid., November 14, 1951. The interest rate on the loan was four and a half percent.

42. Ibid., May 14, 1952.

43. Public Law 475, the Housing Act of 1950, passed by the Eighty-First Congress, authorized loans under Title IV to academic institutions for dormitories through the Housing and Home Financing Agency.

44. Simpson College, Board of Trustees, Executive Committee, Minutes, June 18, 1952.

45. Ibid., July 15, 1952; Simpson College, Board of Trustees, Minutes, September 16, 1952.

46. Simpson College, Board of Trustees, Executive Committee, Minutes, November 12, 1952; November 17, 1952.

47. *Indianola Tribune*, January 13, 1953. Dr. Gross had written on September 8, 1952, that the only justification for extending the deadline was "evidence that the college is actually moving toward the objective we have agreed upon." It was clear from the tone of his communication that Dr. Gross, not to speak of the Pfeiffer trustees, was out of patience with

Simpson's procrastination. See Simpson College, Board of Trustees, Executive Committee, Minutes, September 10, 1952. See also *Indianola Tribune*, September 30, 1952.

48. *Record-Herald*, August 7, 1952.

49. Simpson College, Board of Trustees, Executive Committee, Minutes, April 24, 1953. Time was of the essence; Simpson had to sign before May 1 on which date the interest rate would rise one-fourth percent.

50. Ibid., April 30, 1953.

51. Ibid., December 12, 1951; March 12, 1952.

52. Ibid., March 12, 1952.

53. Ibid., October 8, 1952. That same fall the Indianola schools stated their interest in sharing some of Simpson's athletic facilities. The matter was discussed during that school year. Ibid., January 14, 1953.

54. Ibid., February 26, 1953.

55. See ibid., November 2, 1952; November 12, 1952; February 11, 1953; February 26, 1953; May 13, 1953. Actually, it was only ATO and KOY that were distressed. Lambda Chi Alpha was quite well housed, and Pi Kappa Phi disbanded in the early months of 1953.

56. Ibid., September 22, 1952. See also ibid., September 18, 1950, for the institution of the deferred pledging rule.

57. *Indianola Tribune*, March 3, 1953; *Simpsonian*, March 9, 1953.

58. Actually, the Lambda Chis won almost everything from the scholarship trophy to All-College Sing and Miniature Orpheum. They were also awarded the Tomahawk at Homecoming in 1952.

59. *Simpsonian*, October 25, 1952; *Record-Herald*, October 23, 1952. The Kappa Theta Psi records showed 548 initiates since 1902, of which number 506 were still living, including most of the charter members.

60. *Indianola Tribune*, February 10, 1953. See also Simpson College, Board of Trustees, Executive Committee, Minutes, February 26, 1953; *Simpsonian*, February 2, 1953.

61. *Simpsonian*, December 17, 1951.

62. Ibid., February 2, 1953.

63. *Zenith*, 1951, 1952 and 1953.

64. William Penn's athletic fortunes hit the bottom in 1953 when Iowa Wesleyan humiliated the Statesmen in football by a score of 103–0. On that afternoon William Penn was able to field only sixteen players. See Turnbull, *The Iowa Conference Story*, 63–66. Interestingly, both St. Ambrose and Loras dropped football altogether nine years later.

65. *Simpsonian*, November 19, 1951.

66. Simpson College, Board of Trustees, Minutes, May 31, 1952.

67. Ibid.

68. Ibid., October 15, 1951.

69. "The 1952 *Sequel* is now on sale," announced the *Simpsonian* May 19, 1952.

70. Ibid., April 7, 1952.

71. In the fall of 1950, 279 of 597 students were fraternity or sorority members; in the spring of 1953 the number was 217 of 377.

72. *Record-Herald*, September 20, 1951.

73. *Simpsonian*, February 19, 1951.

74. Ibid., January 12, 1953; February 2, 1953.

75. Gerard Schultz and Don L. Berry, *History of Warren County, Iowa*, 179–80.

76. *Simpsonian*, March 12, 1951.

77. Gerard Schultz and Don L. Berry, *History of Warren County, Iowa*, 180.

78. *Simpson College Bulletin*, January 1951.

79. *Record-Herald*, November 20, 1952.

80. *Simpsonian*, March 27, 1950; February 26, 1951.

81. *Simpson College Bulletin*, March 1951.

82. The survey was conducted by B. W. Kunkel of Lafayette College and D. B. Prentice of the Scientific Research Society of America, and published in the October 20, 1951, issue of *School and Society*. There were 963 colleges and universities represented in the 1950–51 edition of *Who's Who in America*, thirteen of them in Iowa. *Simpson College Bulletin*, February 1952.

83. *Indianola Tribune*, June 5, 1951.
84. *Simpson College Bulletin*, September 1950.
85. *Record-Herald*, November 6, 1952.
86. Ibid.
87. *Indianola Tribune*, February 14, 1950.
88. *Record-Herald*, March 22, 1951; *Simpsonian*, April 2, 1951.
89. *Simpsonian*, February 12, 1952.
90. *Indianola Tribune*, January 29, 1952; *Simpson College Bulletin*, April 1952.
91. *Indianola Tribune*, July 15, 1952. At the same conference one of the new bishops elected was the Rev. Gerald Ensley, who was assigned to the Iowa-Des Moines Conference, succeeding Bishop Charles W. Brashares, who was reassigned to the Chicago area. See *Simpsonian*, September 22, 1952.
92. Simpson College, Board of Trustees, Executive Committee, Minutes, July 15, 1952.
93. Ibid.
94. *Record-Herald*, July 17, 1952. Tutt also announced that Simpson would benefit from a bequest of $300,000 to the College by Mrs. G. C. Guillams of Winterset upon the death of the heirs to her estate. Ibid.
95. Simpson College, Board of Trustees, Executive Committee, Minutes, July 15, 1952; August 6, 1952.
96. Hamilton's resignation created a vacancy in the chairmanship of the board's executive committee. William Buxton III was elected chairman for a one-year term. Ibid., August 6, 1952.
97. Ibid., July 15, 1952.
98. *Simpsonian*, November 10, 1952. The selection of faculty members was apparently not thought to be sufficiently important to be mentioned in either the board's minutes or those of the executive committee.
99. Simpson College, Board of Trustees, Executive Committee, Minutes, August 6, 1952.
100. Edwin E. Voigt, interview by author, Champaign, Illinois, June 13, 1961.

Chapter 17

1. In later years Robert Clayton Kerstetter, accompanied by his wife and three children, became a missionary in Africa with the African Inland Mission in the Belgian Congo, Kenya and Uganda.
2. William E. Kerstetter, interview by author, Sandwich, Massachusetts, June 14, 1991. To be sure, all ethnic and racial groups were not yet represented at Girard in Kerstetter's years there. The school had been founded for "poor male white orphan children." In 1968, in response to a U.S. Supreme Court ruling, it began to admit students without respect to race.
3. During the summer of 1952 Kerstetter taught at the Garrett Biblical Institute in Evanston, Illinois.
4. William E. Kerstetter, "Simpson Memoirs," 49–50.
5. The new president's salary was fixed at $7,200 plus the house and its maintenance, an automobile and the "customary entertainment allowance." Simpson College, Board of Trustees, Executive Committee, Minutes, December 29, 1952.
6. Ibid., December 30, 1952.
7. Local board members included William Buxton III, president of Peoples Trust and Savings Bank, attorneys M. D. Hall and Frank P. Henderson; Don L. Berry, publisher of the *Record-Herald and Indianola Tribune*; Vinton C. Watson, agent for Bankers Life Insurance Co.; dentist G. A. "Chick" Grant; real estate man J. C. Hickman and ex officio members Rev. Arthur J. Kindred, minister of Indianola's First United Methodist Church and Dr. Kerstetter. Raymond Sayre, a prosperous farmer from rural Ackworth, completed the Warren County contingent. From Des Moines were attorneys Paul G. James and Allen Whitfield; Kenneth MacDonald, executive editor of the *Des Moines Register and Tribune*; Eugene H. Sprague, a rental manager; J. J. Van Dreser, president of the Wright Coal Co.; Roy L. Miller, executive

secretary of the Bureau of Municipal Research; A. E. Sargent, president of Sargent & Co.; Kenneth R. Brown, president of Brown Engineering Co.; N. D. McCombs, Des Moines superintendent of schools; Agnes Samuelson; and A. Paul Thompson, vice-president and treasurer of Iowa Power and Light Company. Des Moines clergymen included Bishop F. Gerald Ensley; Methodist Conference Treasurer W. F. Clayburg and C. Clifford Bacon, minister of the First United Methodist Church, together with ex officio member Raoul C. Calkins, superintendent of the Des Moines district of the church. Other Iowa members of the board included Judge W. P. Butler of the twelfth judicial district, from Mason City; Imogene farmer O. F. Howard, who died before the expiration of his term in 1953; Ralph McGee, president of the Clarke County State Bank in Osceola; retired minister Rev. R. M. Shipman from Ames; Rev. W. M. Scheuermann of the Central Methodist Church in Oskaloosa; Amy Robertson of Promise City; George D. Woolson, editor and publisher of the Clarinda *Herald-Journal*; and ex officio clergymen including Methodist District Superintendent Ernest M. Buehler of Boone, O. E. Cooley of Council Bluffs and Walter A. Samp of Creston. The people from beyond Iowa were Kenneth Karr, an attorney with the Crane Company, living in Glen Ellyn, Illinois; Chicagoans Ivan L. Willis, vice-president of the International Harvester Company and Robert G. Collins, vice-president of the First National Bank of Chicago; Harry A. Bullis, chairman of the board of directors of General Mills in Minneapolis; Harold F. Pote, personnel director of the Boy Scouts of America in New York City; and Dr. J. Hugh Jackson, dean of the graduate school of business at Stanford University, California.

    8. A native of Oklahoma, Thompson had excelled at Ohio Wesleyan, where he was an active member of Phi Gamma Delta and was elected to Phi Beta Kappa and Omicron Delta Kappa, graduating cum laude in 1931. His legal training was completed at the Cleveland Law School in 1935, and a decade later he graduated from Rutgers University's Graduate School of Banking. Simpson awarded him the LL.D. in 1954.

    9. In 1952–53 the board's officers included a president, vice-president, secretary and treasurer. In 1953–54 the expanded executive committee included seven positions: president, three vice-presidents, the chairman of the executive committee, a secretary and a treasurer. See Simpson College, Board of Trustees, Minutes, May 30, 1953. See also ibid., June 5, 1954. This action was accomplished by amending the College's articles of incorporation.

    10. William E. Kerstetter, "Simpson Memoirs," 16.

    11. Ibid.

    12. William E. Kerstetter and Phillips Moulton, *An Experiment in General Education: Development and Education* (Nashville: Board of Education, the Methodist Church, 1957), 9.

    13. Ibid., 10–12.

    14. Ibid.

    15. William E. Kerstetter, interview by author, Sandwich, Massachusetts, June 14, 1991.

    16. *Simpsonian*, January 11, 1954. While the name was not original—it was the title of a 1949 book on international politics by American historian Arthur Schlesinger—it was employed in a very different context at Simpson.

    17. Ibid.

    18. Ibid.

    19. *Simpson College Bulletin*, 55 (October 1955), Catalog Issue, 1956–57, 55.

    20. William E. Kerstetter, interview by author, Sandwich, Mass., June 14, 1991. The philosophy and scheme of the Vital Center program were described in detail by Kerstetter in an article entitled "In All . . . , Get Understanding," published in *Journal of Higher Education*, 28 (December 1957), 489–93.

    21. *Record-Herald and Indianola Tribune*, June 10, 1954.

    22. "Although I studied at three different universities after my two years at Simpson," wrote Lane in early 1955, "my sentimental ties are wholly with Simpson. The more I see of other colleges and universities the more regard I have for what I acquired there, though [I was] an indifferently good student or worse because of excessive extra-curricular activities." Clayton Lane, Annapolis, Md., to William E. Kerstetter, Indianola, Iowa, January 24, 1955. A few weeks later, he admitted that "while I had not thought I should ever again wish to live in the Middle West, I do find it pleasant to think of teaching at Simpson. . . . I might overcome my strong inclination to live near salt water." Clayton Lane, Annapolis, Md., to

William E. Kerstetter, Indianola, Ia., February 17, 1955. It surely helped that Lane knew and liked Don Berry and Frank Henderson and the Sayres. Thus two months later: "While my wife is reluctant to consider living in the Middle West—I, too, for that matter—we are chiefly concerned with carrying on our work where there is good prospect for response . . . and [we are] very much interested in what you are doing [at Simpson]. Clayton Lane, Annapolis, Md., to William E. Kerstetter, Indianola, Ia., April 19, 1955.

23. Simpson got two Lanes for the price of one. Because neither desired to teach full-time, they agreed to come to Indianola for a combined salary of $5,000, $3,500 for Clayton and $1,500 for Bent. William E. Kerstetter, Indianola, Iowa, to Mr. and Mrs. Clayton Lane, Annapolis, Maryland, May 16, 1955.

24. May 24, 1955.

25. Faculty participants included Ethel D. Anderson, Hadley Crawford, Ruth Jackson, Mildred and Sven Lekberg, Jane Merkle, David Mobberley, Phillips Moulton, Stuart Peterson, Roberta Riegel, Luella Specht, Kenneth Uglum, Harold Watson, Margaret Watson and Elizabeth White.

26. *Record-Herald and Indianola Tribune*, August 30, 1956; *Simpsonian*, September 23, 1956.

27. William E. Kerstetter and Phillips Moulton, *An Experiment in General Education: Development and Evaluation* (Nashville: Board of Education, the Methodist Church, 1957), 18.

28. Ibid., 51, 54.

29. Kerstetter, "Simpson Memoirs," 51.

30. Ibid.

31. A few years later Trueblood managed to alienate a fair number of faculty members as well when they read for a faculty seminar Trueblood's *Idea of a College*, published in 1959. Some took exception to his assertion that no one should teach in a Christian liberal arts college who was not an active, dedicated, committed Christian scholar. See Elton Trueblood, *The Idea of a College* (New York: Harper & Brothers Publishers, 1959), esp. 18–28.

32. *Record-Herald and Indianola Tribune*, September 15, 1960; October 27, 1960; November 15, 1960.

33. Kerstetter, "Simpson Memoirs," 61.

34. In the fall of 1955 Simpson's enrollment reached 583. A number of other colleges in Iowa boasted considerably higher numbers: Grinnell, 1019; Coe, 1121; Cornell, 713; Luther, 1039; Dubuque, 610; Upper Iowa, 620; Wartburg, 756. A number of others were smaller: Buena Vista, 507; Central, 425; Iowa Wesleyan, 446; William Penn, 197.

35. Admissions counselors included during the Kerstetter years the following: Elmer Johnson (1953–55), Clyde Finke (1955–57), George Hladky (1955–56), Dan Seaton (1956–59), Ralph Rambow (1957–58), A. Bruce Schroer (1958–60), David Schoonover (1958–63 and beyond), Alan Batchelder (1960–62) and William D. LeVere (1961–63). In 1956 alumna Genevieve Hohstadt Vondracek '33 was retained on a part-time basis to handle Simpson's admissions effort in the Chicago area. *Simpsonian*, May 14, 1956.

36. *Record-Herald and Indianola Tribune*, August 26, 1958.

37. The John Hay Whitney Foundation supported one-half of the salary of selected recently retired faculty who still desired to teach.

38. *Simpsonian*, April 12, 1957; *Record-Herald and Indianola Tribune*, April 25, 1957. In 1954 Dr. Bimson had been named vice-president of the College. His duties incorporated the academic deanship together with direction of the office of admissions and the work of the registrar. He was as loyal to Simpson as he was to the organizations to which he committed both time and energy. A Scottish Rite Mason, a militant Rotarian—he was district governor in Iowa during 1951–52—and devoted Methodist, he was never too busy to spend time with a student who sought his advice and counsel. He was a scholar too, having gotten out two books in the field of professional education, *Participation of School Personnel in Administration* (1939) and, as coeditor, *Learning the Ways of Democracy* (1940).

39. *Record-Herald and Indianola Tribune*, June 11, 1957.

40. Ibid., April 2, 1957.

41. Ibid., April 4, 1957.

42. Ibid., April 11, 1957. A few weeks later, Walter B. Nance, a former Methodist missionary to China, who served fifty-three years there—forty-eight of them as a teacher at Soo-

chow University—wrote a lengthy and thoughtful piece in the *Record-Herald* defending the work of missionaries.

43. Kerstetter, "Simpson Memoirs," 39, 59.

44. Simpson College, Board of Trustees, Minutes, May 30, 1958.

45. *Record-Herald and Indianola Tribune*, March 22, 1960.

46. Doty died at home on North Buxton Street on the evening of February 15, 1963. He had never married, "devoting full time to his profession and teaching." Don Berry said of Doty "Here is a man who has had a wide quiet influence. He is not the kind who makes a crowd immediately aware when he enters a room, but when he leaves you may know somebody has been there." Ibid., February 18, 1963. Although Simpson had adopted a standard retirement for all faculty members at age sixty-five, no one ever had the heart to ask Hiram Doty to retire. Shortly after Doty's death, alumni spontaneously started the formation of a Hiram Doty Scholarship Fund, which through the following years grew to a substantial sum.

47. The new language requirement was adopted by the faculty on February 4, 1960.

48. "Report of President William E. Kerstetter to the Board of Trustees," June 3, 1960. See also *Simpson Scene*, Summer 1960, 2.

49. Harold Watson, "Memoirs," 82.

50. Floyd Pace's brother, Earl, later served as chief of police in Indianola.

51. A graduate of Columbia University (1907), Dr. DeBoer held the Ph.D. from Johns Hopkins University (1925). Her salary at Simpson of $7,200 during her first year was reduced to $6,200 the second year because of a less demanding class schedule. She had suffered a serious fall on the ice in January 1962, necessitating a somewhat lighter teaching obligation.

52. Let the names of those people whose tenure was brief at Simpson during the Kerstetter years, a period of real volatility in college faculties everywhere, be recorded. In biology were Dixon Lee Riggs (1952–53), Edward Wright Huffman (1954–55), William T. Battin (1958–59) and Jack L. Carter (1960–63); in chemistry Frederick J. Lotspeich (1954–56), Chester A. Rumble (1956–57), Kenneth L. Uglum (1956–59)—his last year he taught in physics and mathematics—and Robert W. Schmidt (1958–61); in physics and mathematics Lloyd O. Ritland (1952–56), Stella Mizell (1956–59), William F. Herrin (1958–59), Paul Harms (1959–61) and Ivor Rhys Jones (1961–64). In the humanities there were in English David E. Pullman (1952–55) and Daniel Thornburgh (1955–57)—both of whom taught primarily journalism and served also as the College's director of publicity—Lee Ball (1958–60), Wilma Dahl (1959–61), Alan H. Korte (1960–62) and James A. Schreiber (1962–64); in speech and theater Priscilla Bussan (1958–59) and, as mentioned in the text, Marla Del Wright (1959–61) and Emma Sue Phelps (1961–62). In the Division of Social Science there were Donald S. Barnhart (1953–57), who also served as dean of men, Gerard L. Buckhout (1957–60), whose work with foreign students was as exemplary as was his teaching style, and George L. Montagno (1956–60), who served two years also as dean of men and who received during his Simpson years two prestigious foreign teaching assignments, a Fulbright lectureship in Helsinki and an Asia Foundation grant in Pakistan, the latter of which necessitated his leaving Simpson; in economics Everett L. Refior (1952–54), Clinton Lee Warne (1954–56), Albert L. Olson (1956–58), W. E. Gordon (1958–59) and Otis E. Miller (1960–62); in business administration Merle F. Sandy (1958–60); in psychology Frank A. Beu (1961–64) the retired former president of Western Illinois University, who served primarily as dean of men and director of student personnel services; and in sociology RuthAnn Sayre (1960–64). In another division, after the departure of John Dahl, Orville F. Moore took over the headship of the Education Department (1961–62) but remained for only a year, when he was replaced by E. G. Booth, who had been serving four years as football coach at the College. Another in education was Lorena Riebhoff (1954–57); in home economics Mary Bronner (1952–55), E. Ruth M. Iverson, part-time for several years and full-time in 1959–60, Marilyn Houghton Kayton (1960–64) and Ethel J. Horner (1961–62).

53. Although in departing from Simpson Dr. Christie stated as a reason for his move that "in many ways I feel that my vocation is that of teaching," he was named academic dean at Mount Union within a few months. See *Record-Herald and Indianola Tribune*, January 13, 1959, May 19, 1959. Christie later served as dean at his undergraduate alma mater, Hendrix College.

54. Ibid., March 8, 1960.

55. Lambert was appointed dean of the Evening College at Fairleigh Dickinson University in New Jersey. Ibid., June 4, 1962.

56. *Simpsonian*, September 12, 1962. When Howard Greenlee left Simpson in 1955, his position as associate dean of the College was discontinued.

57. Ibid., May 17, 1960; *Record-Herald and Indianola Tribune*, May 12, 1960; Simpson College, Board of Trustees, Minutes, November 11, 1960; Simpson College, Board of Trustees, Executive Committee, Minutes, April 21, 1960.

58. Simpson College, Board of Trustees, Executive Committee, Minutes, November 23, 1953. Ewing had resigned in order to accept a position as controller at American University in Washington, D.C. See also ibid., February 8, 1954.

59. Ibid., March 3, 1956; *Simpsonian*, February 13, 1956; *Record-Herald and Indianola Tribune*, February 16, 1956.

60. *Record-Herald and Indianola Tribune*, June 23, 1959.

61. Ibid., August 23, 1962. Mullin received his B.S. and M.S. degree from the University of Pittsburgh. See also *Simpsonian*, September 12, 1962.

62. *Record-Herald and Indianola Tribune*, February 23, 1961.

63. It did not escape Kerstetter's attention that Goodloe's father was the vice-president of Woolworth International.

64. *Simpsonian*, February 20, 1963.

65. Ibid., September 28, 1959, March 15, 1960; *Record-Herald and Indianola Tribune*, November 15, 1962.

66. Larsen's Mus.M. degree was awarded in 1958.

67. *Record-Herald and Indianola Tribune*, January 16, 1958.

68. Ibid., January 27, 1959; *Simpsonian*, February 9, 1959.

69. The music people did agree in 1962 to give up the Bachelor of Music Education degree.

70. Simpson College, Board of Trustees, Minutes, November 7, 1953; *Simpsonian*, April 7, 1953; *Simpson College Bulletin*, May 1953; *Record-Herald and Indianola Tribune*, January 21, 1954.

71. See report in *Simpsonian*, January 13, 1958. Prior to this time, few guidelines existed for good academic standing except for the requirement of a C average for graduation.

72. Tuesday-Thursday classes typically met at 8:05 and 10:30 a.m., and 1:05, 2:30, and 4:00 p.m.

73. *Record-Herald and Indianola Tribune*, June 2, 1960.

74. See ibid., March 15, 1960.

75. See *Record-Herald and Indianola Tribune*, December 6, 1960, July 13, 1961. Simpson College, Board of Trustees, Executive Committee, Minutes, January 19, 1961.

76. *Simpsonian*, December 5, 1962.

77. Simpson College, Board of Trustees, Executive Committee, Minutes, February 18, 1960, March 17, 1960; see also ibid., May 10, 1961.

78. The Faculty Council—Dean Les Bechter, Jack Padgett, Joe Walt, Cliff Meints and Sven Lekberg—approved the discrimination resolution in January 1963, and the Faculty voted its overwhelming approval in March. See *Simpsonian*, January 9, 1963, March 22, 1963.

79. See Simpson College, Board of Trustees, Executive Committee, Minutes, May 22, 1963.

80. Ibid., January 19, 1961.

81. Ibid., April 20, 1961.

82. Ibid., October 26, 1961.

83. *Simpsonian*, December 5, 1960.

84. Ibid., April 4, 1960.

85. Ibid., April 12, 1960.

86. *Simpson College Bulletin*, December 1957; *Simpsonian*, September 27, 1957.

87. As quoted in *Record-Herald and Indianola Tribune*, February 18, 1963.

88. The general fee included "admission to all athletic home games, artists' series, plays, concerts, debates, recitals, the *Zenith*, college yearbook, the *Simpsonian*, weekly newspaper, campus handbook, laboratory fees (except Chemistry and Music Methods), library service, gymnasium, locker and towel service, intramural games and sports program and equipment, student union facilities, and social life program." *Simpson College Bulletin*, February 1954, Catalog Issue, 97.

89. Only $11,000 in cash had come to the College that same year from all other sources.

90. See Simpson College, Board of Trustees, Executive Committee, Minutes, January 22, 1954; *Simpsonian*, February 15, 1954.

91. See *Record-Herald and Indianola Tribune*, February 26, 1954. The College's board adopted a goal of $100,000 to raise among themselves within three months.

92. The company "woefully failed to deliver what was promised," and eventually the College cancelled its contract. See Simpson College, Board of Trustees, Minutes, November 6, 1954.

93. Simpson College, Board of Trustees, Executive Committee, Minutes, January 22, 1954. Even so, the campaign in Indianola exceeded its $125,000 goal, collecting $127,540 in cash and pledges. *Record-Herald and Indianola Tribune*, December 9, 1954.

94. *Record-Herald and Indianola Tribune*, February 15, 1955.

95. *Simpsonian*, October 15, 1954.

96. *Record-Herald and Indianola Tribune*, February 15, 1955.

97. Simpson College, Board of Trustees, Executive Committee, Minutes, October 20, 1956; *Record-Herald and Indianola Tribune*, May 22, 1956, July 12, 1956; *Simpsonian*, May 28, 1956.

98. *Simpson College Bulletin*, July 1956.

99. *Simpsonian*, October 13, 1958.

100. Ibid., December 19, 1962.

101. Simpson College, Board of Trustees, Minutes, October 16, 1959, June 27, 1960; see also Simpson College, Board of Trustees, Executive Committee, Minutes, June 17, 1960, November 11, 1960.

102. Simpson College, Board of Trustees, Minutes, November 11, 1960; Simpson College, Board of Trustees, Executive Committee, Minutes, September 15, 1960; *Simpsonian*, October 13, 1960.

103. Simpson College, Board of Trustees, Executive Committee, Minutes, July 5, 1960.

104. Ibid., May 19, 1960, August 24, 1960.

105. Ibid., August 24, 1960.

106. Ibid., November 19, 1959.

107. *Record-Herald and Indianola Tribune*, March 16, 1961. The campaign was formally announced in ibid., March 7, 1961, and in the *Simpson College Bulletin*, April 1961.

108. Thirty thousand dollars of Barker's $227,000 estate was designated for the new Sigma Alpha Epsilon fraternity house.

109. See Simpson College, Board of Trustees, Executive Committee, Minutes, May 17, 1962; *Record-Herald and Indianola Tribune*, February 15, 1962, March 22, 1962, May 24, 1962, July 19, 1962, July 26, 1962, March 28, 1963, September 2, 1963; *Simpsonian*, January 3, 1962, March 22, 1963, March 27, 1963.

110. William E. Kerstetter, "Simpson Memoirs," 16.

111. As we have seen, the government loan for the men's dormitory was approved in April 1953, several months after Kerstetter arrived at Simpson.

112. Simpson College, Board of Trustees, Executive Committee, Minutes, September 4, 1953.

113. Ibid., September 15, 1953.

114. *Simpsonian*, September 28, 1953.

115. See *Record-Herald and Indianola Tribune*, June 22, 1954.

116. The dedication was held at Homecoming time in October 1955. See ibid., October 17, 1955; *Simpsonian*, November 7, 1955.

117. Simpson College, Board of Trustees, Executive Committee, Minutes, April 24, 1963; Simpson College, Board of Trustees, Minutes, June 1, 1963; *Simpson College Bulletin*, September 1963. The lounge of the building was named the "Kelly Lounge," honoring the bequest of alumnus Dr. Elmer E. Kelly in 1952.

118. Simpson College, Board of Trustees, Executive Committee, Minutes, October 21, 1953.

119. Simpson College, Board of Trustees, Minutes, February 5, 1954.

120. Of the remaining $170,000, the allocation for the student union—now they were calling it the "dining hall"—was $113,000; the Carver Science Hall, $37,000; maintenance shop and stadium enclosure, $5,500; removal of barracks and relocation of three houses, $6,000; guest room in women's dormitory, $1,000; landscaping, $7,500. See ibid., February 6, 1954, June 5, 1954.

121. Simpson College, Board of Trustees, Executive Committee, August 7, 1954.
122. The contract price was $209,625. The balance of $258,000 included furnishings, equipment and architects' fees.
123. *Record-Herald and Indianola Tribune*, August 12, 1954.
124. Simpson College, Board of Trustees, Executive Committee, December 10, 1955.
125. I ate the first meal ever served in Pfeiffer Hall. It was pretty awful.
126. *Record-Herald and Indianola Tribune*, November 8, 1955.
127. Simpson College, Board of Trustees, Minutes, November 6, 1954; *Record-Herald and Indianola Tribune*, November 9, 1954.
128. The Board of Trustees noted the following autumn that $75,000 was still owing on Carver Hall. Simpson College, Board of Trustees, Executive Committee, Minutes, September 20, 1956.
129. *Record-Herald and Indianola Tribune*, October 9, 1956. It was appropriate that Dr. Kerstetter had delivered an address at the dedication in 1953 of the George Washington Carver National Monument at Carver's birthplace just outside of Diamond, Missouri. *Simpson College Bulletin*, October 1953.
130. *Simpson Scene*, March 1956; *Simpsonian*, March 19, 1956; *Simpson College Bulletin*, May 1956.
131. Simpson College, Board of Trustees, Executive Committee, Minutes, August 7, 1954.
132. Ibid., November 6, 1954, November 11, 1954.
133. *Record-Herald and Indianola Tribune*, January 27, 1955. The city of Indianola bought the rest of the McAninch property for a city park, soon named "Memorial Park." See ibid., December 20, 1956.
134. *Simpsonian*, May 14, 1956. The actual purchase was reported in Simpson College, Board of Trustees, Minutes, June 2, 1956.
135. Simpson College, Board of Trustees, Executive Committee, Minutes, November 14, 1957.
136. Ibid., December 19, 1957. Another parcel owned by Paul Bishop came onto the market in January at the price of $5,000. See ibid., January 23, 1958.
137. *Record-Herald and Indianola Tribune*, January 9, 1958.
138. Ibid., February 6, 1958.
139. Ibid., February 11, 1958.
140. Ibid., February 20, 1958.
141. William E. Kerstetter, "Simpson Memoirs," 65.
142. See, for example, purchases authorized as early as mid-1956. Simpson College, Board of Trustees, Executive Committee, Minutes, July 12, 1956.
143. *Record-Herald and Indianola Tribune*, January 14, 1954.
144. Ibid., June 30, 1953.
145. *Simpsonian*, March 22, 1957.
146. Simpson College, Board of Trustees, Minutes, October 19, 1957, October 16, 1959, June 30, 1960; Simpson College, Board of Trustees, Executive Committee, Minutes, September 19, 1957, June 8, 1959, September 10, 1959.
147. The contractor for the project was the Fane-Vawter Company of Des Moines. See *Simpsonian*, September 21, 1959. Earlier a downstairs room in the dormitory was refurbished at a cost of $1,300 and converted into a guest room for campus visitors. Hotel and motel accommodations in Indianola were poor in the 1950s. Simpson College, Board of Trustees, Executive Committee, Minutes, March 16, 1954.
148. Simpson College, Board of Trustees, Executive Committee, Minutes, November 14, 1957.
149. Simpson College, Board of Trustees, Minutes, May 30, 1958, October 24, 1958. Neutra visited the campus for the first time in April 1958. He explained to the board the location of the two new buildings "in their relationship to the Old Chapel." Many years later it was asserted erroneously that Neutra foresaw the razing of Old Chapel (or College Hall). Quite the contrary, he viewed the old building as the "center of the campus . . . the best designed structure at Simpson." For the contract with Neutra, see Simpson College, Board of Trustees, Executive Committee, Minutes, February 27, 1958, July 7, 1958.

150. Simpson College, Board of Trustees, Minutes, June 27, 1960.

151. Simpson College, Board of Trustees, Executive Committee, Minutes, September 15, 1960. Dirlam was asked to proceed with the dormitory plans only in January 1961. Ibid., January 19, 1961.

152. Ibid., June 22, 1961; Simpson College, Board of Trustees, Minutes, October 7, 1961.

153. *Record-Herald and Indianola Tribune*, October 10, 1961.

154. Alas, when Mary Berry Hall was subsequently given over to faculty offices, reports of male faculty members whose offices graced the second floor announced that the view of the walled garden was splendid.

155. The building was scheduled for completion in 320 days, in time for women to occupy the building in the fall of 1962, but unstable subsoil conditions delayed construction by several months. See Simpson College, Board of Trustees, Executive Committee, April 5, 1962.

156. *Record-Herald and Indianola Tribune*, January 21, 1963. The total cost of the building was $410,000.

157. Simpson College, Board of Trustees, Minutes, June 1, 1963.

158. *Simpsonian*, November 16, 1960; Simpson College, Board of Trustees, Executive Committee, Minutes, February 23, 1961; *Record-Herald and Indianola Tribune*, June 6, 1961.

159. Simpson College, Board of Trustees, Executive Committee, Minutes, August 2, 1954, May 7, 1955. The College also owned the Pi Beta Phi and Theta Upsilon sorority houses, and soon sold them to the sororities. Ibid., January 8, 1955, February 12, 1955, May 9, 1957, February 27, 1958, July 7, 1958.

160. Ibid., January 21, 1956. The $33,000 price was lower than two independent appraisals of the house, one for $35,000, the other for $45,000. Lambda Chi was reluctant to purchase the building, for it had been paying the College a rental of only $214 per month, nine months a year. Their decision to purchase was hastened because the Kappa Theta Psis were bargaining to buy the house too. The College agreed, however, that Lambda Chi had first claim on the building. Ibid., December 10, 1955, June 2, 1956.

161. Ibid., April 27, 1956.

162. Simpson College, Board of Trustees, Minutes, May 31, 1959. A suggestion to put all three fraternities into a single larger structure was rejected by the fraternities and the board of trustees itself. See Simpson College, Board of Trustees, Executive Committee, Minutes, June 8, 1959.

163. Ibid., October 16, 1959.

164. Simpson College, Board of Trustees, Executive Committee, Minutes, February 19, 1959.

165. Ibid., August 17, 1961.

166. Lest there be objections to the use of any College funds for the fraternity project, board member James Wallace pointed out that "not to do so would have endangered the increasingly cordial relations" between fraternity alumni and Simpson, and could have adversely affected New Century Fund gifts. Ibid., November 2, 1961. See also *Record-Herald and Indianola Tribune*, December 11, 1961.

167. Ken Brown explained in January 1962 to fellow board members that there was "a problem involving labor union objections to the use of nonunion labor on the fraternity housing projects." Indeed there was a problem. Union members picketed the construction site for weeks. Simpson College, Board of Trustees, Executive Committee, Minutes, January 11, 1962. The final cost on the entire project was $539,000, or approximately $180,000 for each house, including furnishings. *Simpsonian*, February 27, 1962. ATO and SAE paid their $25,000 in cash at the time of groundbreaking. Kappa Theta Psi sold their Ashland Avenue house, giving the College the proceeds, later paying out the entire $25,000. Simpson College, Board of Trustees, Executive Committee, Minutes, December 14, 1961.

168. The library's problems included the difficulty of retaining able personnel. After the departure of Beryl Hoyt in 1954, the leadership in the library was very poor indeed until the appointment of Simpson graduate William Garton in 1960. Garton was well prepared for the job, having completed his M.S.L.S. at the University of Illinois.

169. *Simpsonian*, November 16, 1960. In a comparative study of library hours at seven Iowa colleges, Simpson ranked the lowest: Grinnell, 98 hours per week, Cornell 90, Coe 83, Iowa Wesleyan 74, Central 71 $^3/_4$, Morningside 66 $^1/_2$ and Simpson 66. Ibid., February 27, 1962.

170. Ibid., January 13, 1958.

171. Simpson College, Board of Trustees, Executive Committee, Minutes, March 19, 1959.

172. The president pointed out, hardly impartially, that the chapel donors "while earlier eager to proceed, are now committed to giving their fund for a beautiful traditional style chapel with a central spire." Putting immediate emphasis on the library "does not mean that the chapel is less important," but it was simply necessary to go ahead with the library while waiting for the chapel. Ibid., April 21, 1960.

173. Ibid., July 27, 1961. When Clayton Lane retired in 1960, Jack Padgett took over as chairman of the Library Planning Committee.

174. Neutra's caution and expertise prevented some serious errors in construction. For example, he discovered through soil bores that the library site was unstable—for that matter, the soil on the whole campus is unstable, to the unending surprise of each new builder—and designed the building so that it "floated" on a whole series of concrete pylons sunk thirty feet deep into the ground.

175. Ibid., April 5, 1962.

176. *Record-Herald and Indianola Tribune*, December 20, 1962. See also Simpson College, Board of Trustees, Executive Committee, Minutes, September 6, 1962, November 15, 1962.

177. *Record-Herald and Indianola Tribune*, March 28, 1963.

178. Simpson College, Board of Trustees, Executive Committee, Minutes, May 22, 1963; Simpson College, Board of Trustees, Minutes, June 1, 1963. An illustrated description of the Dunn Library is contained in W. Boesiger, ed., *Richard Neutra, 1961–66: Buildings and Projects* (New York: Frederick A. Praeger), 138–41.

179. William E. Kerstetter, "Simpson Memoirs," 23.

180. Simpson College, Board of Trustees, Minutes, June 1, 1962, October 12, 1962, June 1, 1963; Simpson College, Board of Trustees, Executive Committee, Minutes, November 21, 1961. To finance the project the College borrowed $100,000 from the Iowa-Des Moines National Bank for three years. Ibid., September 6, 1962; *Record-Herald and Indianola Tribune*, August 30, 1962.

181. Simpson College, Board of Trustees, Minutes, June 1, 1963; *Record-Herald and Indianola Tribune*, August 30, 1962.

182. Bob Tidgren, interview by Chad C. Rodgers, Red Oak, Iowa, September 26, 1993.

183. *Simpsonian*, October 15, 1956; April 4, 1960.

184. Ibid., March 6, 1962.

185. Ibid., February 20, 1963.

186. Ibid., October 7, 1957.

187. *Zenith*, 1954, 45, 62, 128; *Simpson College Bulletin*, October 1953.

188. *Simpsonian*, November 3, 1959, November 10, 1959.

189. Ibid., December 5, 1960, December 12, 1960.

190. Ibid., March 15, 1961, March 24, 1961, April 4, 1962, *Record-Herald and Indianola Tribune*, March 23, 1961.

191. Ibid., February 21, 1955. Lambda Chi Alpha had pledged thirty-nine men in the fall of 1954, ATO twenty-five and KOY eleven. See ibid., October 4, 1954. The sororities adamantly insisted on fall rushing and were permitted to continue that system.

192. Ibid., September 26, 1955.

193. Ibid., October 3, 1955. "We as a group of IFC gave them a vote of confidence and are behind them all the way," said I.F.C. President Doyle Fidler.

194. Ibid., January 16, 1956.

195. Ibid., September 20, 1957, September 28, 1957, October 21, 1957; *Record-Herald and Indianola Tribune*, September 3, 1957, October 17, 1957, October 22, 1957, October 24, 1957.

196. *Record-Herald and Indianola Tribune*, May 28, 1957, May 31, 1962.

197. *Simpsonian*, February 9, 1960. See also ibid., October 27, 1959.

198. Ibid., May 14, 1962; *Record-Herald and Indianola Tribune*, May 24, 1962. With the addition of the 12 Theta Upsilon chapters, Delta Zeta boasted a chapter roll of 145, including 5 in Iowa: Drake, Iowa, Iowa State, Parsons and Morningside.

199. *Record-Herald and Indianola Tribune*, October 24, 1963.

200. *Simpsonian*, May 27, 1958, February 16, 1959.

201. Ibid., April 12, 1961.
202. Ibid., May 17, 1960.
203. Ibid., December, 6, 1954, October 19, 1959.
204. Ibid., December 12, 1960.
205. A religious census of 1953 indicated that sixty-five percent of Simpson's students were Methodists. Fourteen other denominations were represented among Simpson's 385 students, including only 5 Catholics, 8 "Congressional"(!) and 7 with "no affiliation." Ibid., October 5, 1953. A decade later, the student body was fifty-two percent Methodist, while the number of Catholics on campus had increased to 41 (5.47%).
206. *Record-Herald and Indianola Tribune*, January 3, 1957.
207. Ibid., September 5, 1957.
208. Ibid., July 3, 1958. The new church was dedicated December 21, 1958.
209. *Simpsonian*, December 5, 1962.
210. Ibid., December 13, 1962.
211. Ibid., November 24, 1958; January 13, 1959.
212. Brown's later distinguished career in publications at the University of Michigan bore testimony to his remarkable journalistic skills. For Schroer's letter, see ibid., January 12, 1960.
213. Ibid., January 22, 1962.
214. See ibid., March 26, 1956; *Record-Herald and Indianola Tribune*, March 8, 1960.
215. *Simpsonian*, December 5, 1955, April 5, 1957.
216. Ibid., November 12, 1956, February 14, 1962.
217. Ibid., February 15, 1961.
218. Simpson College, Board of Trustees, Executive Committee, Minutes, September 18, 1959; *Record-Herald and Indianola Tribune*, August 27, 1959, September 15, 1959; *Simpsonian*, March 4, 1960.
219. *Simpsonian*, February 22, 1961. As early as 1955, students and faculty were required to affix parking stickers to their windshields. Ibid., October 19, 1955.
220. Ibid., October 17, 1962.
221. Ibid., December 8, 1959.
222. Ibid., April 24, 1963.
223. Ibid., September 28, 1960, October 13, 1960.
224. Ibid., March 13, 1963, April 3, 1963.
225. Simpson College, Board of Trustees, Minutes, June 4, 1955.
226. That year Jack Repplinger was second highest scoring leader in the conference, with forty-three points.
227. *Simpsonian*, March 3, 1958; *Record-Herald and Indianola Tribune*, February 25, 1958.
228. *Record-Herald and Indianola Tribune*, April 1, 1958.
229. Ibid.
230. Ibid., June 12, 1958.
231. Ibid., February 25, 1958.
232. *Simpsonian*, April 21, 1958.
233. Only twenty-six men came out for football during Booth's first year as coach. *Record-Herald and Indianola Tribune*, September 13, 1958.
234. The previous longest losing streak was William Penn's twenty-three games, between 1942 and the time the college was suspended from football competition by the conference in 1949. Turnbull, *The Iowa Conference Story*, 38.
235. Moore, a graduate of the University of Iowa, had earned his Ed.D. in 1945 from Indiana University.
236. *Record-Herald and Indianola Tribune*, January 25, 1962.
237. Deaton had coached basketball two years at Columbus Junction and five years at Belle Plaine. Earlier he had played professional basketball for two years. See *Record-Herald and Indianola Tribune*, April 19, 1955. Casey had actually quit coaching basketball at the end of the 1954 season. His replacement for one year was part-timer Gus Ollrich, a twenty-six-year-old former Drake University basketball star. See ibid., October 12, 1954.
238. Ibid., March 13, 1958.
239. Ibid., May 19, 1960.

240. See Turnbull, *The Iowa Conference Story*, 77; *Record-Herald and Indianola Tribune*, February 23, 1961.
241. *Zenith*, 1962, 130.
242. *Record-Herald and Indianola Tribune*, June 17, 1958.
243. Ibid., February 19, 1959. Sorden, whose contributions to Simpson's athletic program were many, served a number of years as faculty representative to the Iowa Conference and was president of the group in 1961–62. *Simpsonian*, December 5, 1961.
244. *Simpsonian*, October 19, 1959.
245. Turnbull, *The Iowa Conference Story*, 125.
246. Simpson College, Board of Trustees, Executive Committee, Minutes, February 9, 1954, March 12, 1955, December 19, 1960, February 21, 1963.
247. Ibid., April 4, 1963.
248. *Record-Herald and Indianola Tribune*, November 8, 1956; November 22, 1956.
249. Ibid., April 1, 1958, December 10, 1959, February 9, 1960.
250. Ibid., April 27, 1961, May 4, 1961.
251. Ibid., October 13, 1955; *Simpsonian*, October 17, 1955, October 29, 1955. Dr. Jones's chapel address was delivered on October 18.
252. *Record-Herald and Indianola Tribune*, February 8, 1962, February 26, 1962. Walt's letter appeared in ibid., March 1, 1962.
253. Ibid., April 11, 1961.
254. Ibid., April 18, 1961.
255. *Simpsonian*, May 19, 1961.
256. "The Centenary of Simpson College," scroll presented at Indianola, Iowa, June 4, 1961.
257. *Record-Herald and Indianola Tribune*, June 22, 1961.
258. *Simpson Scene*, Summer 1961.
259. *Simpson College Bulletin*, February 1957.
260. *Record-Herald and Indianola Tribune*, April 7, 1960.
261. *Simpson College Bulletin*, Summer 1960.
262. Ibid., September 1962.
263. *Des Moines Sunday Register*, January 20, 1963.
264. *Simpson College Bulletin*, May 1963.
265. The bequest amounted to $7,524. *Record-Herald and Indianola Tribune*, May 27, 1958.
266. *Simpson College Bulletin*, December 1961.
267. According to U.S. census records, the population of Indianola in 1940 was 4,123; in 1950, 5,145; in 1960, 7,062; and in 1970, 8,852.
268. See *Record-Herald and Indianola Tribune*, June 30, 1955, July 7, 1955, March 8, 1956, August 16, 1956, January 22, 1957, February 12, 1957, November 11, 1958. For highways see ibid., October 3, 1957, May 22, 1958 and January 13, 1959.
269. Ibid., July 4, 1957.
270. Ibid., May 29, 1958.
271. Ibid., February 19, 1959, March 5, 1959, April 21, 1959.
272. Ibid., November 6, 1958.
273. Ibid., January 5, 1960.
274. Ibid., April 18, 1957.
275. Ibid., June 7, 1956.
276. Ibid., March 3, 1959.
277. The Methodist Church fire was the second conflagration in twenty-four hours. Tuesday morning, the fourteenth, the huge Honneger and Company grain elevator and feedmill burned. In that blaze, fifteen Simpson students pushed a semitrailer and three boxcars out of the path of the flames. *Simpsonian*, February 20, 1956.
278. *Record-Herald and Indianola Tribune*, February 9, 1956.
279. *Simpsonian*, April 26, 1954.
280. Ibid., September 26, 1955.
281. *Record-Herald and Indianola Tribune*, December 17, 1957.
282. Ibid., August 29, 1957.
283. *Simpsonian*, September 28, 1957.

284. Ibid.
285. *Record-Herald and Indianola Tribune*, October 30, 1956; *Simpsonian*, November 16, 1960.
286. *Record-Herald and Indianola Tribune*, February 18, 1963; *Simpsonian*, February 20, 1963.
287. Simpson College, Board of Trustees, Executive Committee, Minutes, February 21, 1963.
288. *Simpsonian*, February 20, 1963.
289. William E. Kerstetter, "Simpson Memoirs," 7.

Chapter 18

1. He later reached the rank of captain in the U.S. Naval Reserve.
2. He was the author of two books: *Un-adjustment Among Undergraduate Men* (1935) and *The Veteran in College Fraternities* (1946).
3. *Record-Herald and Indianola Tribune*, March 7, 1963. The chairman of the board of trustees announced to his executive committee Stone's acceptance of the interim presidency on March 5.
4. He was formally introduced to the students at a convocation on April 9.
5. Simpson College, Board of Trustees, Executive Committee, Minutes, April 24, 1963.
6. *Simpson College Bulletin*, 63 (December 1963).
7. Hurford Stone, Indianola, Iowa, to Joseph W. Walt, Indianola, Iowa, October 9, 1963.
8. *Simpson College Bulletin*, 63 (December 1963).
9. Ibid.
10. Ibid., 63 (September 1963); Simpson College, Board of Trustees, Executive Committee, Minutes, July 17, 1963.
11. *Record-Herald and Indianola Tribune*, November 4, 1963.
12. The bylaws of the College required that the presidential search committee include the resident bishop of the Methodist Church, the Des Moines district superintendent of the South Iowa Conference, in which Indianola was located, the chairman of the College's board of trustees and others named by the chairman. Often the bishop's appointment was pro forma and his participation minimal.
13. Ralph C. John, "Recollections about Simpson," 2.
14. They might have been married sooner, but John's endowed scholarship at Duke was available only to single students.
15. Ralph C. John, interview by author, Berlin, Maryland, June 16, 1991.
16. John completed his S.T.B. in a year (1943–44).
17. John, "Recollections about Simpson," 1.
18. *Record-Herald and Indianola Tribune*, November 7, 1963.
19. By no means hostile to football, Lekberg rather enjoyed watching the game. "I've been meaning to come to one of these things for years," he said, but pointed out that this was the first football game he had managed to attend since coming to Simpson in 1940. See *Simpson College Bulletin*, 63 (December 1963).
20. John, "Recollections about Simpson," 3.
21. Ralph C. John, interview by author, Berlin, Maryland, June 16, 1991.
22. For announcements of or reviews of Ralph John's inauguration, see Simpson College, Board of Trustees, Executive Committee, Minutes, January 23, 1964; *Simpson College Bulletin*, March 1964 and May 1964; *Record-Herald and Indianola Tribune*, March 30, 1964 and April 6, 1964. The *Simpsonian* editor didn't like the inauguration at all. It was, he said, poorly publicized, ill-attended by students, given to too much ceremonialism and, worst of all, boring with "speeches that were long and dry." Of Dr. Flemming's address he wrote a review, hardly a triumph of journalism, that was not flattering. *Simpsonian*, April 10, 1964.
23. Simpson College, Board of Trustees, Executive Committee, Minutes, February 27, 1964; Simpson College, Board of Trustees, Minutes, May 29, 1964; *Record-Herald and Indianola Tribune*, April 23, 1964.
24. John, "Recollections about Simpson," 7.
25. Simpson College, Board of Trustees, Minutes, May 29, 1964.
26. Ibid., May 29, 1965; *Record-Herald and Indianola Tribune*, May 31, 1965.

27. Simpson College, Board of Trustees, Minutes, May 29, 1964; *Record-Herald and Indianola Tribune*, May 18, 1964.

28. In June, 1969, the four Iowa conferences of the United Methodist Church were consolidated into a single conference known as the Iowa Annual Conference, alternately as the Iowa Area.

29. John, "Recollections about Simpson," 8.

30. Simpson College, Board of Trustees, Executive Committee, Minutes, September 12, 1963.

31. Ibid., November 14, 1963.

32. Simpson College, Board of Trustees, Minutes, May 29, 1964.

33. Minimum annual salaries were set in 1964 at $5,000 for instructors, $6,500 for assistant professors, $8,000 for associate professors and $10,000 for full professors. Two years later they were $5,500, $7,000, $8,500, and $10,000 respectively in the four ranks. Simpson College, Board of Trustees, Executive Committee, Minutes, January 23, 1964; January 27, 1966.

34. The College offered the TIAA-CREF (College Retirement Equities Fund) to faculty and staff beginning July 1, 1966.

35. Simpson College, Board of Trustees, Minutes, May 28, 1966, June 1, 1968; Simpson College, Board of Trustees, Executive Committee, Minutes, May 5, 1966.

36. The other twenty-five included Alberding, DeLisle, Watson, Meints and Curtis in the science division; Koch, Buhr and Bechter in the humanities; Walt, Helfrich, Valen, Hoy, Sorden, McClintic and Koontz in the social sciences; deLaubenfels, Sven Lekberg, Larsen, Degen and Malone (Mullin) in the fine arts; Deaton, Johnson, Booth and Moore in education; and Garton the librarian.

37. She completed the doctorate in 1972.

38. Schreiber was a 1958 graduate of Baldwin-Wallace College—Don Koch had known him there—and had studied at the University of California at Berkeley between 1958 and 1962. Anderson earned his B.A. and M.A. at Southern Illinois University (1958 and 1961).

39. When Ruth Jackson retired in the spring of 1966 after a long and illustrious career at Simpson, the College appointed R. Lowell Mark, a 1964 Simpson graduate who had just earned his M.A. in English at Michigan State University, for one year. The following year the position was vacant.

40. Ralph C. John, interview by author, Berlin, Maryland, June 16, 1991.

41. Yet another person held a voice position at Simpson for only one year. She was Patricia J. Hawkins, a 1964 graduate of St. Olaf College, who earned her M.M. at the University of Illinois. She joined the faculty for the 1966–67 school year.

42. *Simpsonian*, September 18, 1964.

43. Joseph W. Walt, "On What Really Matters . . . ," *Simpson Alumnus* (March 1968), 6–9. I have felt free here to plagiarize with impunity my own prose. See also Simpson College, Board of Trustees, Minutes, May 18, 1966, October 18, 1967, June 1, 1968; Simpson College, Board of Trustees, Executive Committee, Minutes, April 20, 1967; *Simpsonian*, September 25, 1967, September 29, 1967, December 1, 1967; *Record-Herald and Indianola Tribune*, December 11, 1967.

44. *Record-Herald and Indianola Tribune*, May 10, 1965; *Simpsonian*, September 12, 1965, November 5, 1965, October 21, 1966, March 22, 1968.

45. *Simpsonian*, February 17, 1967, March 17, 1967, September 29, 1967, November 3, 1967.

46. *Record-Herald and Indianola Tribune*, April 27, 1967; Simpson college, Board of Trustees, Minutes, June 1, 1968.

47. *Simpsonian*, October 28, 1966.

48. For a number of years the College utilized the "instrument" devised by Northwestern University.

49. *Record-Herald and Indianola Tribune*, February 13, 1964; September 21, 1964; *Simpson College Bulletin*, March 1964. Born in India, Stuart was himself a graduate in 1941 of Christ Church, where he had been a student of Keith Feiling. After the Second World War he worked for a time in the Foreign Office, but preferred teaching. His coming to the United States was exceptional, for he generally disdained travel. "I shall visit Europe again," he said, "if I can do it in comfort." *Simpsonian*, September 24, 1964.

50. *Simpson College Bulletin*, May 1965.
51. Ibid., December 1967; *Simpson Scene*, January 1968.
52. *Simpsonian*, September 29, 1967.
53. *Simpson College Bulletin*, May 1965; Simpson College, Board of Trustees, Minutes, June 1, 1968.
54. *Simpsonian*, January 15, 1964.
55. Ralph C. John, "Recollections about Simpson," 11.
56. *Simpsonian*, October 1, 1964. The 1964 festival, the theme of which was "The Predicament of Man in Contemporary Literature," featured Dr. Stanley Hopper, dean of the graduate school at Drew University, and Dr. Henri Peyre, professor of French literature at Yale University, billed as a "scintillating and vivacious speaker." *Simpson College Bulletin*, September 1964.
57. *Record-Herald and Indianola Tribune*, October 11, 1965. See also ibid., September 30, 1965, which proclaimed that "Seeger Will Address Liberal Arts Festival."
58. Ibid., June 12, 1967; June 15, 1967; Simpson College, Board of Trustees, Minutes, June 3, 1967.
59. *Record-Herald and Indianola Tribune*, April 27, 1967.
60. Simpson College, Board of Trustees, Minutes, June 1, 1968.
61. *Record-Herald and Indianola Tribune*, May 13, 1968; June 10, 1968.
62. *Simpsonian*, January 18, 1965; February 25, 1965.
63. Simpson College, Board of Trustees, Minutes, May 29, 1964.
64. Ibid., May 29, 1965; *Record-Herald and Indianola Tribune*, November 10, 1966. It is also true that some junior colleges that had customarily provided the first two years of liberal arts education expanded offerings in vocational and technical areas as well.
65. Ralph C. John, Berlin, Maryland, to Joseph W. Walt, Indianola, Iowa, January 27, 1993.
66. Simpson College, Board of Trustees, Minutes, May 29, 1965; May 28, 1966.
67. Ralph C. John, "Recollections about Simpson," 12.
68. Statement of purpose of the Associated Colleges of the Midwest, cited in Frank C. Gamelin, "CSCA: Twilight or Dawn?" 1971.
69. Simpson College, Board of Trustees, Executive Committee, Minutes, January 28, 1965; Simpson College, Board of Trustees, Minutes, May 29, 1965. Their organizational session was held at the meeting of the Association of American Colleges.
70. Central States College Association, Articles of Incorporation, April 1, 1965.
71. *Simpson College Bulletin*, February (March) 1965; *Record-Herald and Indianola Tribune*, February 1, 1965, May 3, 1965.
72. The association's board of directors, after rejecting the application of Iowa Wesleyan College, took an early decision to enlarge CSCA membership only by invitation. "We should not put ourselves in the position of accepting and evaluating applications." Central States College Association, Board of Directors, Minutes, March 31, 1965.
73. *Colleges With a Plus* ([Evanston, Illinois]: Central States College Association, 1966), 2.
74. In 1968 Alma College withdrew from CSCA, but within a few months Valparaiso University was added. See Central States College Association, Board of Directors, Minutes, May 8, 1968, January 10, 1969.
75. Simpson College, Board of Trustees, Executive Committee, Minutes, September 22, 1966.
76. Simpson College, Board of Trustees, Minutes, October 15, 1966.
77. Ibid.
78. *Simpson College Bulletin*, March 1967. See also *Record-Herald and Indianola Tribune*, January 19, 1967.
79. *Simpson College Bulletin*, March 1967.
80. More than 2,350 cubic yards of concrete and 158 tons of reinforcing steel were used in its construction.
81. *Record-Herald and Indianola Tribune*, October 15, 1964; *Simpsonian*, October 22, 1964; *Simpson College Bulletin*, December 1964.
82. *Simpsonian*, October 29, 1964; *Record-Herald and Indianola Tribune*, October 29, 1964.
83. Ibid., November 12, 1964.

84. The reflecting pool was finally approved by the board of trustees late in the summer of 1964. Simpson College, Board of Trustees, Executive Committee, Minutes, August 20, 1964.

85. *Simpsonian*, October 15, 1964. The large reflecting pool unfortunately collected leaves and other debris in the autumn, and some years later it was removed. While it was there, however, students referred to it as "Lake Doyle," commemorating the generally futile attempts of College comptroller Doyle Woods to keep the pool tidy. See ibid., October 4, 1968.

86. Ibid., December 16, 1963.

87. Ibid., February 25, 1965.

88. Ibid., September 23, 1965.

89. *Record-Herald and Indianola Tribune*, December 6, 1965. The grant and loan were negotiated under Title I of the Higher Education Facility Act of 1963 with the U. S. Commissioner of Education in the Department of Health, Education and Welfare. See ibid., July 8, 1966. The loan was slow coming through, forcing the College to take out an interim loan with the Peoples Trust and Savings Bank of Indianola in May, 1967. Ibid., May 17, 1967. A portion of the loan was designated for modest renovation of the Carver Hall of Science.

90. Simpson College, Board of Trustees, Minutes, May 28, 1966.

91. *Simpson College Bulletin*, June 1967. The Breiholz base bid was $207,100. A contract for renovation of the exterior walls was awarded to H. D. McRoberts, Inc. in the amount of $4,582. Simpson College, Board of Trustees, Executive Committee, Minutes, September 2, 1966.

92. Simpson College, Board of Trustees, Executive Committee, Minutes, March 18, 1965. The site selected for the new dormitory required the purchase and removal of two older residences.

93. Ibid., September 23, 1965; Simpson College, Board of Trustees, Minutes, May 29, 1965, May 28, 1966; *Record-Herald and Indianola Tribune*, February 7, 1966, April 14, 1966.

94. The Henkel bid was $374,716. The cabinet work contract went to the Alfred Bloom Company of Omaha, Nebraska ($42,800); the plumbing and mechanical contract to Fulton Plumbing and Heating of Leon, Iowa ($88,250); and the electrical contract to Brown Brothers Company of Des Moines ($38,187). The balance of the $627,690 went for site preparation, architect's fees, landscaping and furnishings. Simpson College, Board of Trustees, Executive Committee, Minutes, November 26, 1965; *Simpsonian*, January 7, 1966.

95. Simpson College, Board of Trustees, Executive Committee, Minutes, February 17, 1966.

96. *Simpsonian*, May 26, 1967.

97. Simpson College, Board of Trustees, Minutes, May 29, 1965.

98. *Simpsonian*, September 17, 1965. The visiting team included Ralph John, vice-president Robert Feyerharm, academic dean Ned Peterson, dean of students Wally Wiser and chaplain Jim Allen. See also *Record-Herald and Indianola Tribune*, September 13, 1965.

99. *Simpson College Bulletin*, September 1965.

100. Simpson College, Board of Trustees, Executive Committee, Minutes, July 8, 1966. The $400,000 loan was taken from the United Federal Savings and Loan in Des Moines.

101. The mechanical contract went to Fulton Plumbing and Heating of Leon ($117,600), the electrical contract to Brown Brothers, Inc. of Des Moines ($44,500), while the cost of an underground steam line, equipment and furnishings, architectural fees, landscaping and bank interest during construction totaled $116,195. Land acquisition costs were $43,500. Simpson College, Board of Trustees, Executive Committee, Minutes, July 8, 1966; *Record-Herald and Indianola Tribune*, July 18, 1966.

102. *Simpson College Bulletin*, December 1965; Simpson College, Board of Trustees, Minutes, May 28, 1966.

103. *Record-Herald and Indianola Tribune*, July 18, 1966.

104. *Simpson College Bulletin*, March 1968; *Record-Herald and Indianola Tribune*, February 15, 1968.

105. Simpson College, Board of Trustees, Executive Committee, Minutes, January 22, 1954. At that time the cost of a new chapel was estimated to be approximately $250,000.

106. William E. Kerstetter, "Simpson Memoirs," 24. Perhaps Kerstetter could be forgiven for a slight error. Simpson was founded not by the Methodist Church but by Indianolans, most of whom were Methodists.

107. Ibid. Italics are from the original manuscript.
108. Ibid., 24–25.
109. Simpson College, Board of Trustees, Minutes, October 19, 1957.
110. Ralph John recalled that when their mother died, "They buried her in a windowed mausoleum in Rock Creek Cemetery (D.C.) so that you could go there (and they always wanted to take you) and see her elaborate casket. They built two other crypts, also visible, where they are buried today (without David O's latter-day wife). He did not marry until after his mother died." Ralph C. John, "Recollections about Simpson," 22.
111. William E. Kerstetter, "Simpson Memoirs," 25.
112. Simpson College, Board of Trustees, Executive Committee, Minutes, February 27, 1958; July 7, 1958; Simpson College, Board of Trustees, Minutes, October 24, 1958.
113. William E. Kerstetter, "Simpson Memoirs," 26.
114. Ralph C. John, "Recollections about Simpson," 22.
115. Forty-two per cent favored a new building for the Fine Arts; 27 percent wanted a new gymnasium and 24 percent a student union. Only those four choices were offered in the poll. *Simpsonian*, January 8, 1964.
116. Ralph C. John, "Recollections about Simpson," 22.
117. *Simpsonian*, October 8, 1965; *Simpson College Bulletin*, September 1965.
118. MacBain had been captain of the Simpson College Battalion during his senior year at Simpson.
119. Don L. Berry made extended remarks about the life of Captain MacBain at the annual meeting of Simpson's board. Simpson College, Board of Trustees, Minutes, May 28, 1966. As student editor of the *Simpsonian*, MacBain had stirred up considerable controversy with his diatribes against the Greek-letter organizations and their members.
120. Ralph C. John, "Recollections about Simpson," 23.
121. Simpson College, Board of Trustees, Executive Committee, Minutes, January 6, 1966.
122. The general construction contract went to Henkel Construction Co. of Mason City, Iowa ($373,900), the electrical contract to Brown Brothers, Inc. of Des Moines ($31,339) and the mechanical contract to L. A. Fulton and Sons, Inc. of Des Moines ($60,300). Additional contracts were negotiated for landscaping and walkways ($7,000), for the organ with the Reuter Organ Company of Lawrence, Kansas ($69,360), for fixtures and stained glass with Otto Winterich ($51,350), furnishings for offices and classrooms ($12,000) and the Maas-Rowe carillon ($23,579), together with architect's fees ($39,211) and a contingency fund of $10,000. The grand total was $678,039. Simpson College, Board of Trustees, Executive Committee, Minutes, November 17, 1966.
123. *Simpson College Bulletin*, June 1967.
124. Ibid., Winter 1968. Gil Taverner was a graduate of Colby College in Maine and had earned his S.T.B. at Boston University School of Theology in 1952. He came to Simpson from the Parkway Community United Methodist Church in Milton, Massachusetts.
125. These words were quoted from Matthew Simpson's funeral oration at the grave site of Abraham Lincoln in 1865.
126. The entire text of Alida Smith's dedicatory address was printed in the *Simpson College Bulletin*, winter 1968.
127. Ibid., Fall 1968.
128. Simpson College, Board of Trustees, Executive Committee, Minutes, January 27, 1966.
129. Ibid., November 17, 1966.
130. *Record-Herald and Indianola Tribune*, June 12, 1967.
131. Simpson College, Board of Trustees, Minutes, October 28, 1967. Later a supplemental federal educational facilities grant was received, bringing the total government participation to $349,502.
132. Simpson College, Board of Trustees, Executive Committee, Minutes, June 20, 1968.
133. At its annual spring session in 1969, the board of trustees elected to its membership Myron N. Blank, son of A. H. Blank.
134. The general contract was awarded to Garmer Construction Company of Des Moines ($717,136), the mechanical contract to L. A. Fulton Sons of Leon ($184,700), the electrical con-

tract to Bel Electric of Newton ($96,000). The balance of $159,604 went for architect's fees, landscaping and walkways, equipment and furnishings.

135. *Simpson Scene*, Summer 1968.

136. Simpson College, Board of Trustees, Executive Committee, Minutes, January 14, 1971; *Record-Herald and Indianola Tribune*, March 18, 1971. The last production staged in the old theater in College Hall was Archibald MacLeish's *J. B.*, February 18–20, 1971. Ibid., February 15, 1971.

137. *Record-Herald and Indianola Tribune*, April 1, 1971. The final cost of the Blank Performing Arts Center was $1,246,048. Unfortunately A. H. Blank was unable owing to illness to be present for the dedication.

138. The Potes contributed $90,000 toward the building, the Barborkas $30,000. The other major gift for the project was the Cowles Foundation's $175,000.

139. *Record-Herald and Indianola Tribune*, May 27, 1971. See also *Simpson College Bulletin*, Spring 1971.

140. Simpson College, Board of Trustees, Executive Committee, Minutes, July 15, 1965.

141. Ibid., July 5, 1967.

142. Simpson College, Board of Trustees, Minutes, June 1, 1968.

143. Ralph John observed in 1965 that the "faculty is the most important single element in the collegiate system, and the faculty has never been in a more favorable power position." Ibid., May 29, 1965.

144. Ibid., June 1, 1968.

145. The book value of the College's endowment in 1965 was $2,377,409.

146. Simpson College, Board of Trustees, Minutes, June 1, 1968; October 19, 1968.

147. Ibid., June 3, 1967.

148. Ibid., May 29, 1965.

149. *Simpson College Bulletin*, December 1965.

150. Simpson College, Board of Trustees, Minutes, June 1, 1968.

151. Simpson College, Board of Trustees, Executive Committee, Minutes, April 26, 1967; *Simpsonian*, April 14, 1967; *Record-Herald and Indianola Tribune*, April 17, 1967.

152. Simpson College, Board of Trustees, Executive Committee, Minutes, April 26, 1967; *Simpson College Bulletin*, June 1967; *Record-Herald and Indianola Tribune*, May 1, 1967.

153. *Simpsonian*, September 25, 1967.

154. Simpson College, Board of Trustees, Executive Committee, Minutes, June 20, 1968; *Simpsonian* March 8, 1968; *Record-Herald and Indianola Tribune*, March 11, 1968.

155. Bill Webster earned his B.A. at State Teachers College (now Wayne State College) in Wayne, Nebraska, in 1954. He taught in high school in Nebraska and Iowa while completing the M.Ed. (1958) and Ed.D. (1963) degrees at the University of Nebraska. He had served more recently on the staff of Mankato State College (1962–65) and Wisconsin State University, River Falls (1965–68).

156. *Simpson College Bulletin*, Summer 1968; *Simpsonian*, May 29, 1968.

157. Ibid.; *Simpsonian*, May 29, 1968. For Seaton's appointment see Simpson College, Board of Trustees, Minutes, June 1, 1968.

158. *Record-Herald and Indianola Tribune*, September 20, 1965; *Simpson College Bulletin*, September 1965.

159. *Record-Herald and Indianola Tribune*, July 27, 1964.

160. Simpson College, Board of Trustees, Minutes, May 28, 1966; *Simpsonian*, May 25, 1966; *Simpson College Bulletin*, June 1966.

161. *Record-Herald and Indianola Tribune*, September 12, 1968; *Simpson College Bulletin*, Fall 1968.

162. *Simpson College Bulletin*, March 1964; Summer 1968; *Record-Herald and Indianola Tribune*, January 30, 1964.

163. *Simpson College Bulletin*, Summer 1968. That two of these three young men, Ogden and Purcell, were initiates of Simpson's Lambda Chi Alpha Chapter attested to the continuing excellence of that fraternity on the campus.

164. Ibid., June 1967.

165. *Simpsonian*, November 6, 1964.

166. *Record-Herald and Indianola Tribune*, November 25, 1965. The *Simpson College Bulletin* boasted that these professional contracts were "the first in Simpson history," an assertion that would have surprised Moco Mercer or Elvin "Kink" Richards who had played professional football for some years. The same thing appeared in the *Simpsonian*, April 15, 1966.

167. *Simpson College Bulletin*, June 1966; *Record-Herald and Indianola Tribune*, July 28, 1966.

168. At the end of his senior year Hensley shared the prestigious Barborka trophy with his teammate and fraternity brother Ron Miller. They were pictured on the cover of the *Simpson Alumnus (Simpson College Bulletin)* for May 1965.

169. *Zenith*, 1968, 83.

170. *Record-Herald and Indianola Tribune*, June 6, 1968.

171. *Zenith*, 1965, 77.

172. *Simpson College Bulletin*, September 1964.

173. Simpson College, Board of Trustees, Minutes, May 28, 1966.

174. Simpson College, Board of Trustees, Executive Committee, Minutes, November 17, 1963.

175. Ibid., April 16, 1964.

176. *Simpsonian*, May 14, 1964; *Record-Herald and Indianola Tribune*, June 1, 1964.

177. *Simpsonian*, May 14, 1964.

178. *Zenith*, 1964, 117.

179. *Record-Herald and Indianola Tribune*, April 1, 1965; *Simpson College Bulletin*, May 1965.

180. *Simpsonian*, September 29, 1967.

181. Simpson College, Board of Trustees, Minutes, May 28, 1966.

182. *Simpsonian*, February 18, 1966; February 25, 1966.

183. Ibid., February 25, 1966.

184. Ibid., March 11, 1966.

185. Ibid., February 25, 1966.

186. Ibid., October 1, 1965.

187. Ibid., March 4, 1966; March 11, 1965; March 18, 1965.

188. Ibid., October 15, 1965.

189. Ibid., April 5, 1968.

190. Ibid., September 29, 1967. Earlier S Club president Don Drake deplored the decline of hazing: "When they took away the use of paddles, they took away respect. We do not wish to humiliate the freshmen; we just want respect." Ibid., October 23, 1963.

191. Ibid., February 20, 1964; February 26, 1964.

192. Simpson College, Board of Trustees, Minutes, May 29, 1964.

193. *Simpsonian*, February 19, 1965.

194. Ibid., March 22, 1968.

195. Ibid., May 3, 1968.

196. Ibid., November 12, 1965.

197. Ibid., November 19, 1965.

198. Ibid., October 23, 1963.

199. Ibid., September 18, 1964.

200. Ibid., April 30, 1965. McBlain's father was the minister of the Adel Methodist Church.

201. Ibid., January 8, 1964.

202. *Record-Herald and Indianola Tribune*, January 25, 1968.

203. With the encouragement of fellow Oxonian Charles Stuart, Toynbee assisted in Simpson's senior historiography course during the semester he was in Iowa.

204. Quite appropriately, Williams's lecture was introduced by political scientist Terry Hoy, probably the most gentlemanly radical ever to grace the Simpson campus.

205. Qutub, one of the most engaging, intelligent young men ever to graduate from Simpson, was known both for his pleasant wit and fiery temper. He went on to a distinguished career in college teaching.

206. The research and writing of *Roots* required twelve years. A condensed version of a portion of it first appeared in *Reader's Digest* in 1974.

207. His wife, Norma Alice Dunn, followed him in death four years later, on November 7, 1967. See *Record-Herald and Indianola Tribune*, June 24, 1963; November 16, 1967.

800   History of Simpson College

208. When the Rev. Willis N. Graves '98 died in the early days of 1966, he was ninety-seven years old, only one year John Morley's junior.
209. *Record-Herald and Indianola Tribune*, November 25, 1963.
210. Ibid.

Chapter 19

1. Article V, Section 3 of the Simpson College constitution was revised in late 1968 to provide for unlimited student attendance at all faculty meetings as observers, granting floor privileges to six student representatives, discontinuing confidentiality regarding any actions taken in faculty meetings, and granting to faculty members the privilege of inviting guests to faculty meetings. At the same time, only faculty could vote in their meetings, and faculty could determine by a simple majority vote to meet in executive session. One-half the faculty constituted a quorum. Simpson College, Board of Trustees, Executive Committee, Minutes, December 18, 1969. See also *Simpsonian*, January 29, 1970. Led by uninhibited sophomore Julie Gammack, students had earlier campaigned vigorously for opening faculty meetings to students. See ibid., September 12, 1969. And Louis Fusco, another sophomore already vice-president of student government, elevated the issue to a nonnegotiable demand. Sophomores were uncommonly busy that year. Ibid., November 14, 1969.

2. As early as 1968 students were accorded seats on all faculty committees save one. The Faculty Personnel Committee, which dealt with reappointments, promotion and tenure of the teaching staff, was thought to be too sensitive and its discussions too privileged to permit student representation. Demands for student representation on faculty committees had first surfaced in 1966. See *Simpsonian*, October 28, 1966.

3. When it came to placing people on faculty committees, Ralph John pointed out wistfully in 1968 that student president Ralph Kegel, probably not one of Simpson's more memorable student leaders, possessed more influence on faculty actions than did he. *Simpsonian*, September 20, 1968.

4. "For my part," Ralph John has written, "as long as the College By-laws made me responsible for student life, which always was the case, I reserved commensurate authority. . . . In rare instances student recommendations were not accepted. A few times students had to be protected from students." And for its part, the College's faculty was slow to approve radical changes in the Simpson Code, their standards of appropriate behavior somewhat less extravagant than those of their more unrestrained student charges. See *Simpsonian*, February 10, 1967; May 7, 1971; Simpson College, Board of Trustees, Minutes, May 31, 1969. On a vote in the board of trustees' executive committee which approved a considerable liberalization of the student judiciary, Luther Hill insisted that his "no" vote be recorded. Simpson College, Board of Trustees, Executive Committee, Minutes, June 17, 1971.

5. Ralph John reported in 1972 to the board of trustees that the United States Senate had "incorporated a provision for student membership with vote on college boards of trustees" in its version of the higher education appropriations act. Needless to say, he pointed out, students at Simpson were demanding such representation. Simpson College, Board of Trustees, Executive Committee, Minutes, March 16, 1972; April 20, 1972. Under a student representation plan adopted by the board in early 1973, senior undergraduate Kathleen R. Moore '73, was named a trustee for a standard three-year term. The next year, on nomination by the student body, Bernard W. Franklin was elected, and in 1975 Dawn Dahnke. See Simpson College, Board of Trustees, Executive Committee, Minutes, February 27, 1973; March 29, 1973; May 18, 1973.

6. *Simpsonian*, March 7, 1969; March 28, 1969.

7. Flamboyant Jamal Al-Tunisi, the student body president from Elmira, New York, who had defeated straight-arrow Ed Detlie by nine votes in a campus-wide election that brought out barely thirty-two percent of the potential voters in the spring of 1971, was adamant about visitation: "If people want it, they should be able to have it. . . . If the students are ignored on this issue, the residence hall and college administrators deserve only contempt and possibly more." *Simpsonian*, April 30, 1971. While most students agreed with al-Tunisi—who had

entered Simpson as Henry Miller—on visitation, they threw him out of office by a unanimous vote one cold January day in 1972, charging all manner of corruption in office ranging from absenteeism to huge, improperly charged telephone bills. Ibid., January 21, 1972; January 28, 1972. The visitation policy became in fact a nonpolicy, the faculty for its part determined to extract itself from decisions about student life and the student personnel people hard-pressed by students to accord them ever greater freedom. By 1974 the campus was, by one student's description of it, "wide open."

8. Students, reported Ralph John in 1971, want much to live off campus, weary of the "regimentation and uniformity" of dorm living. "But we must continue to require students to live in our residence halls, for mandatory occupancy is a part of our guarantee on government loans granted for dorm construction." Simpson College, Board of Trustees, Minutes, May 28, 1971.

9. Long tenure as a fraternity housemother must not have been too debilitating. One of these stalwart women, Vada Thompson of the Lambda Chi Alpha house, retired in the late 1960s, but was still in remarkably fine fettle when she celebrated her 100th birthday in 1993, serenaded and congratulated that day by a contingent of another generation of young Simpson Lambda Chis.

10. Several things helped to determine what the College could and could not do. It was influenced by its own traditions and its fraternal relationship with the United Methodist Church, by its sensitivity to the mores and expectations of the Indianola community, by a concern about legal liability for students who consumed alcohol on the campus, and above all by the changes in state laws regarding the legal drinking age. Until 1972 the age of majority for alcohol purchase and consumption was twenty-one. Influenced, however, by the twenty-sixth amendment to the United States Constitution (June 30, 1971) which lowered the age of majority to eighteen, the General Assembly of the state of Iowa enacted legislation which changed the definition of "legal age" to nineteen. In 1973, responding to the logic that one who can vote and go to war at eighteen should be permitted to purchase and consume legal beverages, the legislature lowered the legal age to eighteen. Five years later the age was raised again to nineteen, for the most part to accommodate the state's secondary schools whose senior students were mostly eighteen. In 1986, under the federal threat of loss of massive highway funds if the drinking age was not raised, the General Assembly capitulated, and defined the legal age of majority to be eighteen but the legal drinking age to be twenty-one. As this Simpson history is being written in 1994, twenty-one continues to be the legal drinking age in Iowa.

11. Simpson College, Board of Trustees, Minutes, May 29, 1970; *Record-Herald and Indianola Tribune*, March 26, 1970. Walt's proposal stipulated "that Simpson College abandon ALL designated course and/or distributive requirements and that the requirement for the B.A. degree be 35 units [one unit was equivalent to 3.5 semester hours under the earlier and subsequent method of calculating academic progress toward a degree] (with a 2.00 cumulative grade point average), including a major of not more than 12 units; for the B.M. degree 36 units (with a 2.00 cumulative grade point average), including the major of not more than 24 units. The student's total academic program shall be approved in advance by his adviser and the office of the Dean of Academic Affairs, the course distribution to reflect the academic goals of the student in the context of a humanizing liberal arts program." See *Simpsonian*, February 13, 1970.

12. Simpson College, Faculty, Minutes, March 20, 1970.

13. *Simpson College Bulletin*, Autumn 1969.

14. Simpson College, Board of Trustees, Minutes, October 19, 1968; Simpson College, Board of Trustees, Executive Committee, Minutes, February 20, 1969; *Simpsonian*, October 4, 1968. Tuition charges (including the "general fee") for 1968–69 were $1,490, room $360 and board $440, for a total of $2,290.

15. In a meeting with the executive committee of the board of trustees in March 1974, Albert Gardner and Valorie Carson, representing minority students, asked why the Carver Opportunity Grants had not received funding "up to $12,000, as promised." Simpson College, Board of Trustees, Executive Committee, Minutes, March 19, 1974. In fact, that year $11,400

was awarded to a number of black students, the amount of each award dependent upon the financial need of the recipient. See *Simpsonian*, February 22, 1974.

16. "Proposal for Writing-Reading Laboratory for Culturally Deprived and Other Students Requiring Special Tutorial Assistance," to the Trustees of the Hawley Welfare Foundation of Des Moines, Iowa. Simpson College, April 17, 1968.

17. Ibid.

18. *A College in its Context: Annual Report of the President 1968–1969* (Indianola: Simpson College, 1969), [1].

19. Ralph John, "Recollections about Simpson," 14. Methodist Bishop James Thomas, Iowa's first black bishop, and President John, together with clergy from several Indianola churches, led a memorial service for Martin Luther King in the Great Hall on campus on April 8. *Record-Herald and Indianola Tribune*, April 11, 1968.

20. Seven of forty-five members of the varsity football team in the fall of 1966 were black.

21. An editorial in the *Simpsonian* congratulated the Lambda Chis for their pledging of Crosswhite. *Simpsonian*, September 23, 1966.

22. Edward Purcell, "Memorandum to President Ralph John," November 2, 1966.

23. Ibid.

24. Ibid.

25. Robert S. Crandall, Indianola, Iowa, to Cyril Fladd, Indianopolis, Indiana, September 20, 1966.

26. Ralph C. John, "Recollections about Simpson," 24.

27. In a sense, however, the Lambda Chi chapter had won a battle and very nearly lost the war. Crosswhite did not make grades for initiation and left the College at the end of his sophomore year. The chapter, reacting to the hostility of its local alumni, became defiant and, as Ralph John put it, "went into the doldrums." Ibid., 25.

28. This practice continued for fourteen years. The first black Homecoming royalty were pictured in the 1969 *Zenith*, 87. See also *Record-Herald and Indianola Tribune*, October 24, 1968; *Simpsonian*, November 1, 1968; *Simpson College Bulletin*, Winter 1968.

29. *Simpsonian*, November 1, 1968.

30. Ibid.

31. Ibid.

32. *Record-Herald and Indianola Tribune*, November 25, 1968, announced the forthcoming opening. Five years later (October 20, 1973) the Center was moved to a new location in the old Commons House at the corner of Franklin and C Streets. See *Simpson College Bulletin*, January 1974; *Simpsonian*, October 19, 1973.

33. *Zenith*, 1974, 42.

34. *Simpsonian*, October 2, 1972.

35. Ibid., September 25, 1972. See also the President's Report for 1972–73 in *Simpson College Bulletin*, November 1973.

36. *Record-Herald and Indianola Tribune*, July 15, 1974.

37. See "President's Report 1973–1974," 2; *Simpsonian*, March 1, 1974.

38. *Simpsonian*, March 1, 1974. During the five years between 1968 and 1973 a number of distinguished black speakers appeared at Simpson. Alex Haley in 1968 and 1969, returned to deliver the commencement address in 1970. Georgia legislator Julian Bond, Boston Celtics great Bill Russell and activist Dick Gregory, and several well-attended black symposia sought to bring an awareness of black concerns to Simpson's largely white population.

39. Ibid., November 6, 1964.

40. Ibid., October 22, 1965.

41. Ibid., October 29, 1965.

42. Richard M. Cohen, "The Sixties at Simpson," 1992, 6.

43. These are the words of James Flansburg, "the old reporter" in the *Des Moines Register*, November 2, 1991.

44. Bill Scherle wrote these words in a letter to the editor in the *Des Moines Register*, October 29, 1991. He was explaining his decision to donate his Congressional papers to Creighton University in Omaha rather than to the University of Iowa or Iowa State or Simpson or

Graceland. Creighton students "were patriots who hadn't rioted or destructively demonstrated against the war."

45. *Simpsonian*, October 20, 1967; December 11, 1967.

46. Ibid., March 8, 1968.

47. Richard M. Cohen, "The Sixties at Simpson," 1.

48. P. R. Wieck, "Hard-pressed Democrats in Iowa," *New Republic* 159 (October 19, 1968), 14; Richard M. Cohen, "The Sixties at Simpson," 1. The *New Republic* article pointed out that in the spring Democratic caucuses in Warren County "a strong McCarthy element, built around the college, scored heavily in Indianola and, in fact, lured some prominent Republicans (one was the dean of the college) over to the Democratic Party where they have stayed to fight on." The statement was slightly in error, for the dean had already been won over to the Democrats four years earlier when he supported Lyndon B. Johnson for president.

49. *Simpsonian*, April 26, 1968. Tinker, a sophomore, was a member of the family that figured in the landmark Tinker case, having protested the war while in high school in Des Moines by wearing black armbands, for which they were suspended from school. In 1968 their case was on its way to the U.S. Supreme Court, which the next year would rule in favor of the Tinkers.

50. Richard M. Cohen, "The Sixties at Simpson," 2.

51. Earlier in the day of the worst rioting, Don Gibson had been a guest speaker at the SAE fraternity annual Leadership School out in peaceful, quiet Evanston. Holding forth on the need for political involvement he expected his 500-plus listeners to bristle at his ideas—after all, it was conventional wisdom that fraternity men were unblushingly conservative—and was flabbergasted when he received a standing ovation.

52. Richard M. Cohen, "The Sixties at Simpson," 4.

53. *Simpsonian*, February 21, 1969; *Spectator*, December, 1968. See also *Simpson College Bulletin*, Spring 1969.

54. Richard M. Cohen, "The Sixties at Simpson," 4.

55. *Simpsonian*, October 11, 1969. That same month, the *Simpsonian* redesigned its traditional masthead, incorporating a rather amateurish peace symbol into its design.

56. Simpson College, Board of Trustees, Minutes, October 11, 1969.

57. *Record-Herald and Indianola Tribune*, October 16, 1969.

58. See *Zenith*, 1970, 38–39.

59. "Vietnam Moratorium Observance," dittoed handout, "courtesy of Monad Free Press," October 15, 1969.

60. Wiser recalled at the time that he had been asked by an FBI agent the previous summer to single out students he thought might be "radicals or agitators." He refused to do so.

61. Ralph C. John, "Recollections about Simpson," 18–19; Ralph C. John, Indianola, Iowa, to John B. Walters, Cedar Rapids, Iowa, October 28, 1969; Ralph C. John, Indianola, Iowa, to Mrs. Kingsley Clarke, Adel, Iowa, October 27, 1969.

62. *Des Moines Tribune*, October 17, 1969.

63. Ralph C. John, "Recollections about Simpson," 19.

64. Ibid.

65. *Waterloo Daily Courier*, October 20, 1969.

66. Ralph C. John, "Recollections About Simpson," 19.

67. Louis A. Haselmayer, Mt. Pleasant, Iowa, to Ralph C. John, Indianola, October 20, 1969.

68. Robert Burlingame, Des Moines, Iowa, to Ralph C. John, Indianola, October 17, 1969. Burlingame went on to say that "All the SDS'ers laid end to end (no doubt with their heads split open!) could not pose half the menace to freedom which is building up, like an angry storm cloud, through the malevolent political weather-making of the Clement Haynsworths, John Mitchells and their ilk. . . . " It will be recalled that Haynsworth, a Nixon nominee for the U.S. Supreme Court, was rejected by the Senate November 21, 1969. John Mitchell, Nixon's Attorney General, would later (1975) be sentenced to prison for his part in the infamous Watergate cover-up. Robert Burlingame and Dr. John were well acquainted. Both were members of the Prairie Club in Des Moines, a distinguished old essay society that monthly broke bread together and engaged in a sort of intellectual free-for-all.

69. *Record-Herald and Indianola Tribune*, November 13, 1969.

70. Reported in the *Simpsonian*, November 21, 1969. With Cohen were Janey Gleichenhaus, Charles "Chuck" Beach and Jim Smith.

71. Ibid., February 13, 1970.

72. Ibid., March 13, 1970.

73. *Record-Herald and Indianola Tribune*, April 9, 1970.

74. Ibid., April 2, 1970. The *Des Moines Tribune* editorialized strongly: "We agree and are pleased that President John is so valiantly maintaining the tradition of free thought in Iowa." *Des Moines Tribune*, April 10, 1970.

75. Ibid., April 20, 1970.

76. Richard M. Cohen, "The Sixties at Simpson," 7.

77. Ibid.

78. See *Record-Herald and Indianola Tribune*, May 11, 1970. That Friday morning I talked with a cameraman from one of the Des Moines TV stations on campus photographing the crosses and the rally. I was curious why the TV stations chose to come to Indianola. "Maybe not Grinnell, for that is 50 miles away, but why not Drake right there in Des Moines?" The cameraman answered, "You don't understand, do you? Don't you know that Drake is seething with rest?" That was unfair to the antiwar forces at Drake, but apparently Rich Cohen and his cohorts had done their job well.

79. Ralph C. John, "Recollections about Simpson," 16.

80. Ibid., 16–17.

81. "Ingram-Lieber-Helfrich-Walt Proposal," May 8, 1970.

82. Ralph C. John, "Recollections about Simpson," 17.

83. Ibid.

84. Richard M. Cohen, "The Sixties at Simpson," 8.

85. *Simpsonian*, February 26, 1971; October 15, 1971.

86. Organizers had sought to stage their town meeting on the Indianola courthouse steps but were denied permission by the county board of supervisors. *Record-Herald and Indianola Tribune*, May 4, 1972.

87. Ibid., May 15, 1972.

88. Ibid., January 18, 1973.

89. Honorary life members were welcome to attend and participate in board meetings, but did not vote.

90. *Record-Herald and Indianola Tribune*, March 10, 1969.

91. Ibid., March 11, 1968.

92. Webster had earned his B.A. at State Teachers College, Wayne, Nebraska (1954) and his M.Ed. and Ed.D. from the University of Nebraska (1958 and 1963). *Simpson College Bulletin*, Summer 1968.

93. Ibid.

94. The position of associate dean of academic affairs was discontinued for a time.

95. *Simpson College Bulletin*, Winter 1971; *Record-Herald and Indianola Tribune*, January 25, 1971.

96. *Simpson College Bulletin*, Autumn 1970.

97. Three of the Thomas children graduated from Simpson. The fourth—and youngest—defected to Iowa State after his freshman year. He has since been forgiven.

98. Actually, the chairmanship was offered one fine spring day first to Glenn Buhr, who by virtue of seniority—he had been a staff member since 1961—was entitled to the position. Buhr accepted the appointment at four o'clock in the afternoon, but called the next morning at eight fifteen and resigned the chairmanship. He said he couldn't stand the dignity of it all. Buhr's tenure as a department chairman broke all records for brevity at Simpson.

99. These appointees included Jaroslav J. K. Piskacek in Russian (1968–69), Jewell Rochelle Campbell in French (1968–71), Terry A. Bowers in music (1968–70), Gerald R. Randolph in English (1968–70), Robert H. Hartman in philosophy and religion (1968–69), Harold Brown in philosophy and religion (1968–69), Herbert B. Mosher in English (1968–70), David E. Koos in mathematics (1969–71), Melathathil J. John, a visiting professor in sociology from India (1969–70), Joseph M. Barron in English (1969–70), James R. Norton in Spanish (1969–70), Lu

C. Bro in art (1970–71), Thomas P. Chaney in theater arts (1970–74), Lee R. Mathews in music (1970–71), Richard J. Ronan in chemistry (1970–73), Peter L. Gilman in foreign language (1971–72), Stanley Irwin in music (1971–73) and Janet Linn in home economics (1971–73). Also holding faculty rank was William John Hare, who served as public services librarian and College archivist from 1970 to 1975.

100. Simpson College, Board of Trustees, Minutes, May 31, 1969.
101. Ibid.
102. Ibid., May 28, 1971.
103. Ibid., October 24, 1970.
104. See comparative statistics provided in *President's Report, Simpson College, 1970–71*, published also in *Simpson College Bulletin*, Autumn 1971; Summer 1972.
105. Simpson College, Board of Trustees, Minutes, May 31, 1969.
106. Ibid., June 1, 1968; Simpson College, Board of Trustees, Executive Committee, Minutes, November 19, 1970.
107. Simpson College, Board of Trustees, Executive Committee, Minutes, March 12, 1970. President John discussed with the executive committee "those issues affecting the College's status with the various groups with which it must relate (townspeople, trustees, alumni, etc.). He indicated that, at this time, he was looking for both understanding and guidance." See also Simpson College, Board of Trustees, Minutes, October 14, 1972.
108. Simpson College, Board of Trustees, Executive Committee, Minutes, February 13, 1969; February 19, 1970.
109. Ibid., March 12, 1970. The company actually started work on July 6, 1971. Ibid., June 17, 1971.
110. *Simpson College Bulletin*, Spring 1972.
111. Simpson College, Board of Trustees, Minutes, June 22, 1972.
112. Ibid., October 30, 1971; *Record-Herald and Indianola Tribune*, October 25, 1971; *Simpsonian*, November 12, 1971.
113. Ralph C. John, "Recollections About Simpson," 10.
114. "The Seeking of a President," *Simpson College Bulletin*, Spring 1972.
115. Simpson College, Board of Trustees, Minutes, June 22, 1972.
116. Ibid.
117. Ibid.
118. Ibid.
119. Richard B. Lancaster, "Notes About Simpson, 1972–1979," 1991, 4.
120. Ibid.
121. *Simpson College Bulletin*, April 1973.
122. Ibid.
123. Ibid.
124. *Record-Herald and Indianola Tribune*, February 5, 1973; February 12, 1973.
125. Ibid., May 13, 1974.
126. Earlier they had also had to look for a new secretary for the dean. Maxine Speed, who had served several deans for nineteen years, retired in 1972. She died May 11, 1974. Wally Wiser came back from Ohio to serve as minister at her funeral in Pleasantville.
127. *Simpson College Bulletin*, June-July 1974.
128. *Record-Herald and Indianola Tribune*, October 1, 1973.
129. Ibid., June 11, 1973.
130. During the year Betsworth served as dean of students, the chaplaincy was filled by Carolyn Stahl, a recent graduate of the Claremont School of Theology, where she earned a doctorate in theology and counseling. She was a graduate of U.C.L.A. and an ordained minister in the United Methodist Church.
131. *Record-Herald and Indianola Tribune*, March 12, 1973; May 24, 1973.
132. *Simpson College Bulletin*, September 1973.
133. Simpson College, Minutes of the Faculty, April 1, 1980. The other four new faculty members in 1972 were D. Leon Clodfelder in psychology (1972–76), Gregory Isaacs in music (1972–74), Kenneth L. Anderson in sociology and anthropology (1972–73) and Richard D. Snyder in mathematics (1972–73).

134. Seven more people joined the faculty in 1974: Richard Ault, Jr., in political science (1974–77), Marla Nedelman in theater arts and speech (1974–76), Samuel L. Slick in Spanish (1974–76), Bertil C. Nyman in business administration (1974–75), Wayne Wilms in biology (1974–75), Martha Sue Orrell in music (1974–75) and Hal S. Chase in history (1974–75), who came to Simpson under a foundation grant as director of a faculty development program.

135. Simpson College, Board of Trustees, Minutes, October 19, 1973.

136. Ibid., May 24, 1974. When Donald Dittmer resigned in the spring of 1974, his position was not filled.

137. An additional cut was made in chemistry.

138. Only four of twenty-one reporting Iowa colleges had a larger freshman class in 1973 than the year before (Simpson, Coe, Central and Northwestern). See *Simpson College Bulletin*, January 1974.

139. Simpson College, Board of Trustees, Minutes, May 24, 1974.

140. Simpson College, Board of Trustees, Executive Committee, Minutes, November 20, 1973; see also Simpson College, Board of Trustees, Minutes, May 24, 1974; *Simpson College Bulletin*, January 1974; *Simpsonian*, November 16, 1973.

141. Simpson College, Board of Trustees, Minutes, May 23, 1975. A year earlier, the endowment had doubled when Pioneer Hi-Bred stock went public and was traded openly for the first time. Simpson's holding of Pioneer stock was a 1973 gift of George Wallace, brother of board member James W. Wallace. See ibid., October 19, 1973; May 24, 1974. Still, the College was victim of the worst bear market since the Great Depression. From January 1973 to January 1975 the Dow Jones Industrial average fell nearly 45 percent, from 1181 to 595. The endowment of the College was not immune to the bear market, but because much of it was in farm lands, the impact was masked by the astonishing growth in farm values. "The issue before the administration," recalled President Lancaster, "was how to realize the skyrocketing gains in Iowa farm assets to provide an income stream to support income from tuition and gifts." Richard B. Lancaster, Minneapolis, Minnesota, to Joseph W. Walt, Indianola, Iowa, July 25, 1994.

142. Simpson College, Board of Trustees, Minutes, May 24, 1974.

143. Ibid., October 18, 1974; May 23, 1975.

144. *Record-Herald and Indianola Tribune*, November 14, 1974.

145. Ibid., December 26, 1974.

146. Simpson College, Board of Trustees, Minutes, May 23, 1975; *Simpson College Bulletin*, May 1975.

147. *Simpson College Bulletin*, September 1973; *Record-Herald and Indianola Tribune*, July 10, 1972; *Simpsonian*, October 10, 1972; Simpson College, Board of Trustees, Minutes, October 19, 1973.

148. Simpson College, Board of Trustees, Minutes, May 24, 1974.

149. Ibid., May 23, 1975.

150. Ibid., October 18, 1974.

151. Ibid., May 24, 1974; Simpson College, Board of Trustees, Executive Committee, Minutes, February 26, 1974; May 13, 1974.

152. Simpson College, Board of Trustees, Minutes, May 24, 1974.

153. Ibid.

154. *Record-Herald and Indianola Tribune*, May 29, 1975; Simpson College, Board of Trustees, Minutes, May 23, 1975.

155. Simpson College, Board of Trustees, Executive Committee, Minutes, March 13, 1974.

156. As Luther Hill put it, the president's house has a public function, "a place for the president to present the College to the public, alumni, prospective donors, new students and others." *Record-Herald and Indianola Tribune*, August 14, 1975.

157. Simpson College, Board of Trustees, Minutes, October 18, 1974.

158. Simpson College, Board of Trustees, Executive Committee, Minutes, October 15, 1974.

159. Simpson College, Board of Trustees, Minutes, May 24, 1974.

160. *Simpsonian*, March 8, 1974.

161. *Record-Herald and Indianola Tribune*, October 22, 1973.

162. *Simpsonian*, December 4, 1972.

163. Ibid., March 12, 1973.

164. Ralph C. John, "Recollections about Simpson," 14–15.

165. *Simpsonian*, May 7, 1973. A year earlier Franklin had received 199 votes in his losing bid for the presidency of student government against Steve Schier, who won with 281 votes.

166. Ibid., February 22, 1974. See also Simpson College, Board of Trustees, Executive Committee, Minutes, February 26, 1974.

167. *Simpsonian*, March 1, 1974.

168. Organization for Black Unity, Indianola, Iowa, to Simpson College Administration, Faculty and Student Body, April 12, 1974.

169. R. B. Lancaster, Indianola, Iowa, to Organization for Black Unity, April 12, 1974.

170. *Simpson College Bulletin*, June-July 1974.

171. Organization for Black Unity and Simpson College Administration, Indianola, Iowa, to the Simpson College Community, April 13, 1974.

172. The Faculty, Simpson College, Indianola, Iowa, to the Simpson College Community, April 16, 1974.

173. *Simpsonian*, April 26, 1974.

174. Franklin had been elected to the board on October 19, 1973. Simpson College, Board of Trustees, Minutes, October 19, 1973.

175. *Simpsonian*, October 30, 1972.

176. She survived.

177. See ibid., May 21, 1971.

178. *Simpson College Bulletin*, Autumn 1970.

179. "President's Report, 1973–73," 1974. Five years earlier Ralph John had noted "too wide a spread" in students' academic ability at Simpson. Simpson College, Board of Trustees, Minutes, May 31, 1969.

180. "Annual Report of the President: 1969–1970," published in *Simpson College Bulletin*, Autumn 1970. See also Simpson College, Board of Trustees, Executive Committee, Minutes, September 19, 1968; Simpson College, Board of Trustees, Minutes, October 19, 1968.

181. *Simpsonian*, September 27, 1968.

182. Gilbert Y. Taverner, "Years of Challenge: Religious Life at Simpson College—1968–1973," 1992, 5. Father Larry Burns was always accounted as one of the warmest friends of Simpson. Ralph John recalled that earlier "on the Sunday morning the Chapel was opened, with the dedication perhaps at 11:00 a.m., Larry Burns celebrated an early morning mass. He always reminds me that there was a Catholic mass in the Chapel before there was a Protestant service, which is true."

183. *Simpsonian*, September 25, 1972; October 2, 1972; October 16, 1972.

184. Ibid., September 27, 1973.

185. Ibid., May 3, 1974.

186. Ibid., November 22, 1968.

187. Ibid., January 17, 1969.

188. Ibid., September 12, 1969.

189. Richard Cohen, "The Sixties at Simpson," 3.

190. See *Simpson College Bulletin*, January 1974.

191. *Record-Herald and Indianola Tribune*, November 20, 1969; December 4, 1969.

192. Ibid., December 4, 1969.

193. Simpson did not break its ties with the N.A.I.A. until the spring of 1976. See *Simpsonian*, May 14, 1976.

194. *Record-Herald and Indianola Tribune*, August 26, 1974.

195. Ibid., January 9, 1975; *Simpson College Bulletin*, March 1975.

196. Simpson College, Board of Trustees, Minutes, May 31, 1969.

197. *Simpsonian*, November 13, 1972.

198. See ibid., March 15, 1974; May 10, 1974; May 16, 1975.

199. The last Miniature Orpheum performance, in the spring of 1969, was emceed by Rich Cohen and Craig Wenk. Winning skits were those of Pi Beta Phi and SAE.

200. A few exceptional juniors could be elected, but the extent of their participation in the organization was always minimal.

808   History of Simpson College

201. Sigma Tau Delta seems to have been translated to the "English Club" in 1969, reverting to Sigma Tau Delta in 1971.

202. Some, indeed many, students thought the honor societies were a waste of time, and said so. As Jim Richardson put it, Gold Key and other organizations like it "which have no purpose but transcript decoration," should be permitted "to perish for lack of worth." *Simpsonian*, March 25, 1971. Richardson's sentiments were clear, even if it was true that no organizational memberships ever appeared on a student's transcript of record.

203. Some years later, in 1990, when students were a bit more conventional in behavior, Simpson was granted a charter of Omicron Delta Kappa, and the "circle," as ODK chapters were called, flourished.

204. The Club was founded December 8, 1969.

205. The rumor that three young women also disrobed and joined in the frolic has never been confirmed.

206. *Simpsonian*, March 8, 1974.

207. Ibid.

208. *Simpson College Bulletin*, April-May 1974.

Chapter 20

1. There were, however, limits. While prepared to liberalize the code of sexual behavior between men and women, Simpson remained for many years quite conservative in dealing forthrightly with homosexuality. It was not until the 1992–93 school year that the *Simpsonian* did a feature on the problems encountered by gay and lesbian students on the campus. And at the time this history was being written, there had not as yet emerged on campus an organized gay-lesbian movement, although the College surely had its share of homosexual students.

2. Richard B. Lancaster, "Notes about Simpson, 1972–1979," 23–24.

3. Simpson College, Board of Trustees, Executive Committee, Minutes, February 21, 1977.

4. Richard B. Lancaster, "Notes about Simpson, 1972–1979," 9.

5. Simpson College, Board of Trustees, Minutes, May 12, 1978; *Simpson Alumnus*, May 1978. Couch had informed Simpson of his impending departure as early as February 1978. See Simpson College, Board of Trustees, Executive Committee, Minutes, February 17, 1978.

6. Simpson College, Board of Trustees, Executive Committee, Minutes, September 19, 1978; *Record-Herald and Indianola Tribune*, August 28, 1978; *Simpson Alumnus*, September 1978.

7. Lyddon announced his resignation in early October. Simpson College, Board of Trustees, Minutes, October 7, 1977; May 12, 1978; Simpson College, Board of Trustees, Executive Committee, Minutes, October 4, 1977; November 22, 1977; January 17, 1978.

8. *Simpson Alumnus*, February 1978; *Record-Herald and Indianola Tribune*, December 22, 1977.

9. John A. Kellogg, interview by author, Indianola, Iowa, March 28, 1992.

10. Simpson College, Board of Trustees, Minutes, October 24, 1975; Simpson College, Board of Trustees, Executive Committee, Minutes, August 26, 1975.

11. Simpson College, Board of Trustees, Executive Committee, Minutes, September 1, 1976.

12. *Simpson Alumnus*, November 1976.

13. Beman, a graduate of the University of Nebraska School of Journalism and former reporter and copy editor, was employed as director of the Iowa Senate's Public Information Program at the time she accepted the Simpson appointment. *Record-Herald and Indianola Tribune*, June 22, 1978; *Simpson Alumnus*, September 1978.

14. Simpson College, Board of Trustees, Executive Committee, Minutes, April 17, 1979. For a small college, Simpson had acquired a wondrous hierarchy of administrative titles, including three layers in the Office of Development alone, with a director, an associate and yet an assistant director. Few large universities could match it.

15. *Record-Herald and Indianola Tribune*, September 4, 1978; September 21, 1978; *Simpson Alumnus*, September 1978.

16. Geiger proved himself to be a public-spirited citizen, serving for a time as an elected

member of the city council of Indianola and subsequently as a member of the city's public utilities board of trustees.

17. Simpson College, Board of Trustees, Minutes, May 20, 1977; Simpson College, Board of Trustees, Executive Committee, Minutes, January 18, 1977.

18. Simpson College, Board of Trustees, Executive Committee, Minutes, March 29, 1977; October 4, 1977.

19. Ibid., April 19, 1977.

20. Ibid., June 27, 1977.

21. Of the twenty-seven, three retired (Myron Sorden, Herbert Alberding and Gladys Moore), one was a one-year appointment (Hal Chase) and four were dropped and their positions abolished (Lee Kleiss, Richard Dusenbury, Richard McClintic and Leslie Deaton). The remaining nineteen resigned and moved to other, presumably more remunerative, employment.

22. The fifteen included: (1975–76) Beverly Stockton, Biology; Robert M. Dieffenbach, mathematics; Rosalynne Bradham, sociology; (1976–77) Clifford Kottman, mathematics; Virginia Johnson, theater arts and speech (she had taught part-time in 1975–76); Stephen Brockway, theater arts and speech; Marcella M. Poppen, music; (1977–78) Maura Ann Gage, biology; Douglas Peterson, mathematics; Bennett T. Oberstein, theater arts and speech; D. Martin Bookwalter, theater arts and speech; Donald O. Acrey, music (Acrey had taught part-time in 1974); Barbara A. Quinn, physical education; (1978–79) James P. Beaghan, business administration; and Fred E. Stickle, psychology.

23. These eight included: (1975–77) Bruce G. Meyers, business administration; Barbara Hibner, physical education; (1976–78) W. Keith Leonard, theater arts and speech; Linda Walker, psychology; (1978–80) Regina Blackburn, American studies; Alva Keith Guy, sociology; and Joe and Marilyn Mattys, theater arts.

24. *Simpsonian*, March 29, 1985.

25. Ibid., September 30, 1977. See also Simpson College, Board of Trustees, Executive Committee, Minutes, October 4, 1977; *Record-Herald and Indianola Tribune*, April 21, 1977; *Simpson Alumnus*, August 1977.

26. Simpson College, Board of Trustees, Executive Committee, Minutes, August 16, 1977; *Record-Herald and Indianola Tribune*, September 12, 1977; *Simpsonian*, September 30, 1977.

27. Larche completed the Ph.D. in 1977.

28. While young John Graber, son of the former head of the Theatre and Speech Communications Department, may not have been an unbiased observer, his harsh comments in the *Simpsonian* were echoed by many others: "The department," he wrote, "suffers from inept, irresponsible, misguided, and, to some degree, unconcerned leadership and administration by the faculty in charge of the whole operation." *Simpsonian*, December 2, 1977.

29. Simpson College, Board of Trustees, Minutes, May 12, 1978; *Record-Herald and Indianola Tribune*, June 22, 1978; *Simpsonian*, September 29, 1978; *Simpson Alumnus*, September 1978.

30. Miriam Jenkins (later Miriam Bower Barr) received the B.A. from Ohio University (1952) and the M.A. from Columbia University (1954).

31. Phillips earned her B.S. in education at Drake University (1961), her M.S. at Drake as well (1967) and her Ph.D. at the University of Iowa (1978).

32. Apart from athletic coaches, other faculty appointed during the 1975–79 period were Daniel Rutz in business administration and accounting (1976–79); Alan W. Brush in physics (1977–81); Carl Hogsed, Jr., in business administration and accounting (1972–80); James E. VanDeventer in mathematics (1978–82); Nancy Yeend Stewart in theater arts (1978–84); and David Shaner in music (1978–82).

33. Two years later President Lancaster rather mildly announced to the board of trustees the existence of this (at first) optional program whose purpose, he said, was "to ensure breadth without neglecting the major studies depth." Simpson College, Board of Trustees, Minutes, October 24, 1975. See also *Simpsonian*, November 14, 1975.

34. The faculty adopted the program February 12, 1976. The vote was 34–24. Simpson College, Minutes of Faculty Meeting, February 12, 1976.

35. Haddox soon emerged as the natural faculty leader in interdisciplinary studies.

36. Simpson College, Board of Trustees, Minutes, May 21, 1976; *Simpsonian*, March 12, 1976.

37. I can recall attending one evening a delightful, if exotic, performance of a company of Japanese Kabuki dancers at Smith Lounge in the Brenton Student Center. The audience totaled five persons.

38. Simpson College, Board of Trustees, Minutes, May 20, 1977; *Record-Herald and Indianola Tribune*, August 23, 1976; *Simpsonian*, November 5, 1976.

39. See *Simpsonian*, December 3, 1976; March 11, 1977.

40. Ibid., November 19, 1976; November 11, 1977.

41. Ibid., April 2, 1976.

42. Ibid. April 29, 1977; October 7, 1977.

43. See ibid., November 3, 1978; November 10, 1978; November 17, 1978. The faculty adopted the requirement by a vote of 31–17. Simpson College, Minutes of Faculty Meeting, November 14, 1978.

44. *Simpsonian*, May 6, 1977.

45. See ibid., March 10, 1978.

46. *Simpson Alumnus*, September 1978. Amy Schwarz had been elected vice-president of the student body and president of the Student Senate but was vaulted into the presidency of the student body upon the resignation of Nick Sialmas in February 1978.

47. Simpson College, Minutes of Faculty Meeting, May 2, 1978. The American minority perspective segment of the program was passed two weeks later.

48. Simpson College, Board of Trustees, Minutes, May 12, 1978.

49. *The Christian Science Monitor*, cited in *Record-Herald and Indianola Tribune*, May 4, 1978.

50. Simpson College, Board of Trustees, Minutes, October 24, 1975.

51. *Simpsonian*, September 19, 1975; April 30, 1976.

52. *Record-Herald and Indianola Tribune*, April 10, 1975.

53. *Simpson Alumnus*, May 1977; *Record-Herald and Indianola Tribune*, March 21, 1977.

54. *Simpson Alumnus*, May 1977.

55. Simpson College, Board of Trustees, Minutes, October 7, 1977; *Simpsonian*, December 2, 1977.

56. Simpson College, Board of Trustees, Minutes, October 22, 1976.

57. Soft drinks were available for the young. See *Simpsonian*, October 15, 1976.

58. See ibid., October 13, 1978.

59. *Simpson College Bulletin: General Catalog—1975–77*, 56.

60. Systran also trained Peace Corps volunteers and personnel traveling overseas for American corporations. See *Record-Herald and Indianola Tribune*, May 17, 1979; Simpson College, Board of Trustees, Minutes, May 11, 1979; Simpson College, Board of Trustees, Executive Committee, Minutes, June 19, 1979; *Simpson Alumnus*, July 1979.

61. Robert E. McBride, "Memoirs," ms., 1992, 315; *Simpsonian*, February 29, 1980.

62. "Report of a Visit to Simpson College," April 5–7, 1976; Simpson College, Board of Trustees, Minutes, May 21, 1976; May 20, 1977; *Simpsonian*, April 30, 1976.

63. Simpson College, Board of Trustees, Minutes, May 20, 1977.

64. *Simpson Alumnus*, September 1978.

65. *Record-Herald and Indianola Tribune*, November 13, 1978.

66. Simpson College, Board of Trustees, Minutes, May 20, 1977.

67. Ibid., May 12, 1978.

68. Ibid., October 24, 1975. The U.S. Office of Education had earlier approved the plans for the building, clearing the way for the grant.

69. Simpson College, Board of Trustees, Executive Committee, Minutes, July 22, 1975; August 26, 1975; *Simpsonian*, February 20, 1976.

70. If Small is accurately quoted, he seems to have reckoned the meter shorter than a yard. Twenty-five meters, of course, is 27.35 yards.

71. *Simpsonian*, March 12, 1976. Woods also pointed out that if it was absolutely necessary to run a swim meet in yards, a baffle barrier could be erected in the pool at the appropriate distance.

72. Simpson College, Board of Trustees, Minutes, May 21, 1976.

73. Simpson College, Board of Trustees, Executive Committee, Minutes, October 21, 1975.

74. *Record-Herald and Indianola Tribune*, October 23, 1975; October 27, 1975; Simpson College, Board of Trustees, Minutes, October 24, 1975.

75. *Simpsonian*, November 7, 1975.

76. Simpson College, Board of Trustees, Executive Committee, Minutes, November 18, 1975; *Simpsonian*, November 21, 1975.

77. The women won 80–69, the men by a resounding 104–88.

78. Simpson College, Board of Trustees, Executive Committee, Minutes, February 25, 1976; *Record-Herald and Indianola Tribune*, February 26, 1976; *Simpsonian*, February 27, 1976; *Simpson Alumnus*, May 1976.

79. *Simpsonian*, November 19, 1976; *Record-Herald and Indianola Tribune*, November 22, 1976; Simpson College, Board of Trustees, Executive Committee, Minutes, November 16, 1976.

80. Simpson College, Board of Trustees, Executive Committee, Minutes, February 21, 1977; *Record-Herald and Indianola Tribune*, February 10, 1977; *Simpson Alumnus*, May 1977.

81. Simpson College, Board of Trustees, Minutes, May 21, 1976.

82. *Simpson Alumnus*, May 1976.

83. Simpson needed to raise an additional $100,000 "in new gifts" to meet the challenge. *Record-Herald and Indianola Tribune*, July 26, 1976; *Simpson Alumnus*, November 1976.

84. Simpson College, Board of Trustees, Minutes, May 20, 1977.

85. *Simpsonian*, October 8, 1976.

86. Simpson College, Board of Trustees, Executive Committee, May 17, 1977; Simpson College, Board of Trustees, Minutes, May 12, 1978; May 11, 1979.

87. Richard B. Lancaster, "Notes about Simpson, 1972–1979," 9.

88. Simpson College, Board of Trustees, Minutes, May 11, 1979.

89. *Record-Herald and Indianola Tribune*, October 20, 1975; *Simpsonian*, October 24, 1975.

90. It was estimated that the nine-foot grand piano in the hall would require $6,000 to repair or $13,000 to replace. Robert Larsen wanted to repair the old one. Instead they gave him a new (used) one. Simpson College, Board of Trustees, Executive Committee, Minutes, November 18, 1975.

91. Simpson College, Board of Trustees, Minutes, May 20, 1977.

92. *Record-Herald and Indianola Tribune*, September 9, 1976; *Simpsonian*, September 17, 1976.

93. *Record-Herald and Indianola Tribune*, August 5, 1976; *Simpsonian*, April 9, 1976.

94. *Simpsonian*, March 18, 1977.

95. Ibid., October 15, 1976; *Record-Herald and Indianola Tribune*, October 18, 1976; *Simpson Alumnus*, November 1976.

96. *Simpsonian*, December 3, 1976; March 18, 1977.

97. Simpson College, Board of Trustees, Executive Committee, Minutes, November 18, 1975.

98. Ibid., November 18, 1975; Simpson College, Board of Trustees, Minutes, October 6, 1978; *Simpsonian*, December 1, 1978.

99. Simpson College, Board of Trustees, Executive Committee, Minutes, January 17, 1978; March 28, 1978.

100. Ibid., January 25, 1978.

101. *Simpsonian*, February 10, 1978; February 23, 1979; March 10, 1978; April 28, 1978; Simpson College, Board of Trustees, Executive Committee, Minutes, March 20, 1979; April 17, 1979. The cost of repairing the Library roof was $43,000.

102. He held an M.S. in physical education from Indiana University (1966).

103. *Record-Herald and Indianola Tribune*, January 9, 1975.

104. *Zenith*, 1979, 95.

105. Ibid., 1977, 113.

106. *Simpsonian*, March 30, 1979; *Record-Herald and Indianola Tribune*, March 29, 1979; Simpson College, Board of Trustees, Executive Committee, Minutes, March 20, 1979.

107. *Simpsonian*, May 4, 1979; *Record-Herald and Indianola Tribune*, May 3, 1979; *Simpson Alumnus*, July 1979.

108. *Simpsonian*, April 27, 1979.

109. Hibner earned her B.S. at Pennsylvania State University (1964) and her M.S. at the State University of New York at Cortland in 1970.
110. *Record-Herald and Indianola Tribune*, February 26, 1976.
111. *Simpson Alumnus*, May 1976.
112. *Simpsonian*, May 14, 1976.
113. Ibid., September 17, 1976. Simpson, said Lein, was a member of A.I.A.W., which permits grants-in-aid, and Simpson would continue to do so. In 1976–77 the College granted the equivalent of twelve full scholarships to women, at least half of these in basketball.
114. Ibid., September 24, 1976; October 22, 1976.
115. Ibid., November 12, 1976.
116. *Record-Herald and Indianola Tribune*, August 15, 1977. The A.I.A.W. letter was dated June 27, 1977, and contained three pages of alleged violations by Rod Lein. See also Simpson College, Board of Trustees, Executive Committee, Minutes, October 18, 1977.
117. *Simpsonian*, September 23, 1977. Quinn earned her B.S. at Ursinus College in 1955 and the M.A. at Trenton State College in 1968.
118. *Zenith*, 1977, 118–19; *Zenith*, 1978, 120–23.
119. *Simpsonian*, May 14, 1976.
120. Ibid., April 27, 1979.
121. Ibid., May 18, 1978; Simpson College, Board of Trustees, Minutes, May 12, 1978.
122. *Simpson Alumnus*, September 1978; *Record-Herald and Indianola Tribune*, July 3, 1978.
123. In its first year of operation, the Simpson Athletic Club produced $13,450 toward the maintenance of the building. By early 1979 there was a waiting list to join the Club. *Simpsonian*, February 23, 1979.
124. Ibid., September 19, 1975.
125. Ibid., October 15, 1976.
126. Ibid., October 22, 1976. The letter was signed by Rick Gallagher, Stan Vriezelaar and Jim Lierow of the D.U. Commune, 711 North E Street.
127. Not a word of the Delta Zeta departure from Simpson was noted in any of the College's publications.
128. Simpson College, Board of Trustees, Executive Committee, Minutes, May 17, 1977.
129. During the four years between 1975 and 1979, for example, the fraternities' fall pledging totaled 186: SAE 79, ATO 59, Lambda Chi 43 and DU 5. The poorest year for the Greeks was 1976, when only 65 students pledged to all seven men's and women's chapters.
130. *Simpsonian*, February 16, 1979.
131. Italics in the original.
132. *Simpsonian*, February 20, 1976.
133. Ibid., October 21, 1977.
134. Ibid., October 22, 1976.
135. Ibid., March 3, 1978.
136. Ibid., April 27, 1979.
137. Ibid., February 18, 1977; February 9, 1979; February 23, 1979; *Simpson Alumnus*, May 1977; March 1979.
138. *Simpsonian*, November 19, 1976; February 25, 1977; *Simpson Alumnus*, May 1977.
139. *Simpsonian*, September 29, 1978.
140. They thanked "our advisor, Dr. Joseph W. Walt, who was brave enough to take the responsibility that no one else would." *Zenith*, 1977, 3.
141. *Simpson Alumnus*, November 1977.
142. *Simpsonian*, October 10, 1975.
143. That was in 1977.
144. *Simpsonian*, March 9, 1979.
145. Ibid., March 30, 1979. Interestingly, Tim Thomas later entered upon a successful career in New York as a professional singer.
146. Ibid., April 15, 1977.
147. Simpson College, Board of Trustees, Minutes, October 24, 1975.
148. Ibid., May 11, 1979.

149. For one of the Busch beer ads, see *Simpsonian*, March 31, 1978. See also ibid., April 14, 1978.

150. Ibid., October 8, 1976.

151. Quoted in ibid., December 5, 1975.

152. Ibid., April 30, 1976; *Simpson Alumnus*, May 1976.

153. Richard B. Lancaster, "Notes about Simpson, 1972–1979," 8.

154. Ibid., 25; Simpson College, Board of Trustees, Minutes, May 20, 1977. Ultimately the $30,000 was recovered. See *Record-Herald and Indianola Tribune*, May 9, 1977; August 1, 1977.

155. The word "different" is used here advisedly, not "worse." Some students, when pressed, admitted that mother's cooking had been only marginally edible.

156. Simpson College, Board of Trustees, Minutes, May 20, 1977.

157. *Simpsonian*, September 30, 1977.

158. Simpson College, Board of Trustees, Minutes, May 20, 1977; May 12, 1978; *Simpson Alumnus*, November 1977.

159. *Simpson Alumnus*, November 1977.

160. *Record-Herald and Indianola Tribune*, November 4, 1976.

161. *Des Moines Register*, March 16, 1977. Dr. Piccard was remembered as the one who set the woman's world altitude record in a balloon in 1934. At a social event attended by Piccard in the summer of 1977, I asked the newly-ordained priest how she would prefer to be addressed. With a glint in her eye, she responded, "Oh, just call me Father Piccard."

162. *Simpsonian*, February 9, 1979. "It is easy to forget," wrote Lancaster years later, "that we were much richer as a college in 1979 than we were in 1972." Richard B. Lancaster, "Notes about Simpson, 1972–1979," 20.

163. *Simpson Alumnus*, March 1979.

164. Richard B. Lancaster, "Notes about Simpson, 1972–1979," 19.

165. Ibid., 15.

166. Lancaster remembered that his wife Reta "was not a traditional president's wife," and that "although willing to pour the tea," she wanted "to be a significant person and leader in her own right." Ibid., 27.

167. Ibid., 21.

168. He made the announcement on January 15, 1979. Simpson College, Board of Trustees, Executive Committee, Minutes, January 23, 1979.

169. *Record-Herald and Indianola Tribune*, January 15, 1979.

170. *Simpson Alumnus*, March 1979; *Record-Herald and Indianola Tribune*, April 19, 1979.

Chapter 21

1. Simpson College, Board of Trustees, Minutes, May 11, 1979. See also *Simpsonian*, March 2, 1979. Although the board preferred not to rely overmuch on the services of a professional search organization, it did avail itself of assistance offered by Dr. Frederic Ness and Associates as well as the Association of American Colleges and the Association of Governing Boards.

2. Simpson College, Board of Trustees, Executive Committee, Minutes, April 17, 1979; Simpson College, Board of Trustees, Minutes, June 19, 1979.

3. McBride had been the nominee of Morningside's search committee whose selection had been overridden in favor of a candidate more acceptable to the board of trustees. See *Simpsonian*, April 20, 1979.

4. Robert E. McBride, "Memoirs," unpublished ms., 1992, 308. He entitled the chapter recounting his Simpson presidency "In the Land Where the Tall Corn Grows."

5. Ibid., 309.

6. Ibid.; Robert E. McBride, "Simpson Recollections," 1.

7. Robert E. McBride, "Memoirs," 310.

8. Simpson College, Board of Trustees, Minutes, June 19, 1979.

9. Robert E. McBride, "Memoirs," 311.

10. In 1946 the Church of the United Brethren merged with the Evangelical Church to form the Evangelical United Brethren Church. In its turn, the E.U.B., 750,000 strong, voted

in 1966 to merge with the 10,000,000-member Methodist Church to form the United Methodist Church, the actual union to take place in 1968.

11. Robert E. McBride, Hot Springs Village, Arkansas, telephone interview by author, August 19, 1993.

12. Later Indiana Central University bestowed upon him an honorary Doctor of Letters degree (1976) and Simpson a Doctor of Humanities degree (1987).

13. Robert E. McBride, "Memoirs," 311.

14. Robert E. McBride, "Simpson Recollections," 3.

15. The five were later reduced to four when Westmar College, which had become a Methodist college when the E.U.B. church united with the Methodists in 1968, later came under the control of a Japanese-dominated board with the new name of Teikyo-Westmar. The Methodist Church dropped the institution from its list of affiliated colleges in 1990.

16. If McBride was shocked by the appearance of Simpson students in 1979, he should have seen them six or seven years earlier, when their attire tested the limits of the bizarre.

17. Robert E. McBride, "Memoirs," 313.

18. Robert E. McBride, "Simpson Recollections," 2.

19. Ibid., 1. McBride had met Kerstetter at DePauw when his son was a student there "and had received a generally positive image of Bill, and indirectly of Simpson, through him."

20. McBride did concede that he "was later to discover qualities . . . that mitigated against the severity of some of my negative impressions." Ibid., 2.

21. José Ortega y Gasset, *The Revolt of the Masses* (New York: Norton, 1957), a later edition of the work published in 1930, quoted in *Simpson Alumnus*, July 1979.

22. *Simpson Alumnus*, July 1979.

23. *Record-Herald and Indianola Tribune*, March 31, 1980. He concluded his address by relating an incident that had taken place only weeks before during a trip to California. A Simpson alumnus asked him why he would take a college presidency in the 1980s, given the intimidating problems faced by today's colleges. "Well," answered McBride, "in addition to the fact that I like to jog and missed this turn in Pennsylvania and ended up in Iowa before I realized it, and the fact that I did have an urging to see the Hot Air Balloon Championships in Indianola, I do happen to believe in what small colleges like Simpson are trying to do." Ibid.

24. Ibid., March 24, 1980. See also Simpson College, Board of Trustees, Minutes, November 2, 1979; *Simpson Alumnus*, July 1980.

25. Simpson College, Board of Trustees, Minutes, November 2, 1979.

26. Of the total deficit of $649,059, $615,000 had been met by "drawing down" from "quasi-endowment" funds. The balance of $34,059 had to be met by similar means during McBride's first year at the College. See Simpson College, Board of Trustees, Executive Committee, Minutes, September 18, 1979; February 12, 1980.

27. Ibid., October 23, 1979. The interest payment alone on the $620,000 remaining debt was over $120,000 in 1979–80.

28. It will be recalled that inadequate budget control was the one most serious deficiency at Simpson, according to the report of the North Central Association on its accreditation visit in 1976. At that time Simpson people, including board of trustees members, thought the judgment was wrong. It wasn't.

29. Robert E. McBride, "Memoirs," 315. He went on to say that "While the previous president [Dr. Lancaster] had borne most of the criticism for the financial problems, he had not been served well, in my opinion, by a business officer who should have been more in control himself."

30. Simpson College, Board of Trustees, Executive Committee, Minutes, October 23, 1979.

31. The additional expenditure of $380,000 included necessary fire safety compliance measures ($80,000), energy conservation projects ($63,000), computer and word processing equipment ($170,000), together with $28,000 bond insurance costs and a $39,000 contingency fund. Ibid., February 12, 1980.

32. Actually it required carving only $10,000 out of the regular budget. The remaining $30,000 "seed money" came from a specified portion of a Title III federal grant. In addition to his new responsibilities, Kellogg remained director of admissions.

33. See *Simpson Alumnus*, Summer 1981.
34. Simpson College, Board of Trustees, Minutes, May 23, 1980.
35. Simpson College, Board of Trustees, Executive Committee, Minutes, May 29, 1980.
36. *Record-Herald and Indianola Tribune*, March 20, 1980; May 5, 1980; *Simpson Alumnus*, July 1980.
37. In order to make the deal, the College purchased the Veatch house at 508 North Buxton for $39,000, which it then deeded to the Godwins along with the Hagins house at 510 and Center House at 512. See *Record-Herald and Indianola Tribune*, September 22, 1980.
38. The cost of the remodeling project was approximately $50,000.
39. For details of the property trade see Simpson College, Board of Trustees, Minutes, October 31, 1980. The original decision to move the maintenance operation was taken in August 1980. Simpson College, Board of Trustees, Executive Committee, Minutes, August 26, 1980. An open house invited the public to see the new physical plant on May 8, 1981. *Record-Herald and Indianola Tribune*, May 14, 1981.
40. Simpson College, Board of Trustees, Executive Committee, Minutes, April 9, 1981.
41. *Simpson Alumnus*, September 1980.
42. Most unexpected was $75,000 from the estate of Marian Thomas, a California resident, formerly of Coon Rapids, who had attended Simpson only one semester in 1939. In the spring of 1980 the College learned that it was beneficiary under the estate of former board chairman Ralph McGee in the amount of $50,000.
43. The N.E.H. grant was one of only two granted over a three year period in Iowa. Simpson College, Board of Trustees, Executive Committee, Minutes, December 18, 1979; *Record-Herald and Indianola Tribune*, December 24, 1979; *Simpson Alumnus*, March 1980. For the Title III Strengthening Developing Institutions Program grant, see Simpson College, Board of Trustees, Minutes, May 23, 1980; Simpson College, Board of Trustees, Executive Committee, Minutes, April 30, 1980; *Simpson Alumnus*, July 1980; September 1980.
44. Simpson College, Board of Trustees, Executive Committee, Minutes, April 30, 1980.
45. Ibid.
46. Simpson College, Board of Trustees, Minutes, October 31, 1980. See also *Record-Herald and Indianola Tribune*, October 13, 1980.
47. *Simpson Alumnus*, March 1981; summer 1981; fall 1981; *Record-Herald and Indianola Tribune*, July 16, 1981.
48. Robert E. McBride, "Memoirs," 317.
49. Bruce Haddox visited his office during McBride's first year at Simpson and pointed out that "as a tenured professor at Simpson he was, by government guidelines, listed as eligible for welfare." Ibid., 316.
50. Robert E. McBride, "Simpson Recollections," 7.
51. *Record-Herald and Indianola Tribune*, August 23, 1984.
52. See Simpson College, Board of Trustees, Minutes, January 20, 1984; May 17, 1984; Simpson College, Board of Trustees, Executive Committee, Minutes, February 22, 1984; *Record-Herald and Indianola Tribune*, May 21, 1984. During the six-month interim between Woods's resignation and the arrival of Beatty on July 1, 1984, the College was well served by comptroller Robert L'Heureux and administrative assistant Marilyn Leek.
53. *Simpson Alumnus*, summer 1985.
54. Robert E. McBride, "Simpson Recollections," 7.
55. Ibid., 8.
56. Robert E. McBride, "Memoirs," 312.
57. *Simpson Alumnus*, winter 1983; Robert E. McBride, "Memoirs," 312.
58. Robert E. McBride, "Simpson Recollections," 7–8.
59. Ibid., 6, 16.
60. Ibid. "With all due respect to Luther, I felt he was partially responsible for some of the financial problems the College had when I arrived. He became so enthused about a project that it overrode all other considerations, even the necessity of paying for it." Ibid., 6.
61. Because no church in Indianola could accommodate the huge crowd of mourners, Dick Buxton's funeral was held in the field house at the Cowles Physical Education Center. As much as Buxton loved athletics, he must surely have approved of the site.

62. *Record-Herald and Indianola Tribune,* August 30, 1979; September 20, 1979; Simpson College, Board of Trustees, Executive Committee, Minutes, September 18, 1979. Others who were employed in 1979 included Rose deLaubenfels, a Simpson alumna, filling in for Glenn Buhr, who served for two years (1979–81) as the director of the Iowa Development Commission's European office in Frankfurt am Main, Germany. DeLaubenfels taught German, and very well indeed. The other new faculty member was Fredric W. Moses, a baritone who, like so many others, served only a year in the Department of Music.

63. In 1980 only two people joined the teaching faculty: in music there was Carroll M. Proctor (1980–83), who had completed his Ph.D. at the University of Iowa a year earlier, and J. Frederick Vesper in theater (1980–84).

64. The other four new faculty who came that year included Glenda E. Gill, a remarkably able black woman who had only that year completed her Ph.D. in English at the University of Iowa; Karin E. Niemeyer, who served as assistant in the Hawley Resources Center and as instructor in English; C. Lanette Poteete, a graduate of Southwest Missouri State College (M.A., 1979), in mathematics; and Kristin M. Evenson, a Coe graduate with an M.A. from the University of Iowa, in the College library. Gill served at Simpson only one year (1981–82), Niemeyer and Evenson two (1981–83) and Poteete three (1981–84). See *Simpson Alumnus*, Fall 1981. One of Wilk's poems, for example, selected from among thousands submitted annually to the *New Yorker*, was published in that magazine's November 11, 1990 edition.

65. *Record-Herald and Indianola Tribune,* November 3, 1983.

66. Others who joined the faculty in 1982 were Kenley J. Hinrichs, instructor in mathematics, who taught at Simpson three semesters (1982–December 1983); Donald W. Perrilles, an extraordinarily good bandsman and specialist in percussion, in instrumental music (1982–89); Dr. Raymond H. Walke, who came to Simpson as head of its new agricultural resources management program (1982–84); Jessie Tsuey-Fang Hu (1982–83) in computer science; and Gatsinzi Basaninyenzi, a candidate for the Ph.D. at the University of Iowa and a native of Zaire (1982–83) in English. See *Simpson Alumnus*, fall 1982.

67. Robert E. McBride, "Simpson Recollections," 5. Also joining the faculty in 1983 was Dr. David Mather in mathematics and computer science. He remained at Simpson only a year.

68. Other appointments in the fall of 1984 included Steven D. Vincent, who during his seven-year tenure as instructor (1984–91) in theater was in part responsible for the growing success of Simpson dramatic productions; in theater tech, Jonathan H. Darling (1984–86), who had experience at St. Benedict College in Minnesota and Baldwin-Wallace College at Berea, Ohio; James B. Davis in mathematics, who taught at Simpson only a year (1984–85); Robert J. Ford, who took Ray Walke's place in the agricultural resources management program (1984–89); Warapote Tipayamongkol in computer science (1984–87); and media services librarian Connie Marker (1984–87).

69. Simpson College, Board of Trustees, Minutes, May 22, 1981.

70. *Simpsonian*, May 25, 1980.

71. *Simpson Alumnus*, winter 1982; *Simpsonian*, February 19, 1982.

72. Ibid., spring 1984; *Record-Herald and Indianola Tribune*, January 16, 1984.

73. Robert E. McBride, "Memoirs," 323.

74. Ibid., 9.

75. Actually, he put it less delicately: "I determined that I would find a way within the system to rid Simpson of some of its worst teachers." Ibid.

76. On behalf of A.A.U.P., Dr. Thomas questioned the "faculty personnel policies" of the president and the board of trustees out of a concern for the sanctity of tenure. Simpson College, Board of Trustees, Minutes, May 20, 1983.

77. Robert E. McBride, "Memoirs," 324.

78. Ibid.; *Simpsonian*, April 11, 1980; April 18, 1980; May 9, 1980.

79. *Simpsonian*, March 5, 1982; March 12, 1982.

80. A 1985 ruling of the U. S. Internal Revenue Service ordered that if tuition remission was offered, it must be made available to the children and spouses of all employees, not just faculty. See Simpson College, Board of Trustees, Minutes, May 17, 1985.

81. Simpson College, Board of Trustees, Executive Committee, Minutes, April 30, 1980.

So successful was the program that after the three-year trial, Simpson's membership was made permanent.

82. The year-long study of an expanded general studies curriculum started as early as February 1980, during Dr. McBride's first year. See *Simpsonian*, February 29, 1980.

83. See *Simpson Alumnus*, fall 1981.

84. Their performance was a bit rough, for they learned only shortly before the convocation that invited guest Kathryn Koob, an Iowan who was one of the American hostages only recently freed by the Iranians, was unable to appear.

85. *Simpsonian*, February 20, 1981.

86. Simpson College, Faculty, Minutes, April 7, 1981; May 5, 1981. See also *Simpsonian*, April 24, 1981; May 8, 1981.

87. *Simpsonian*, April 11, 1980.

88. Ibid., March 2, 1984; March 9, 1984; March 16, 1984.

89. Ibid., October 26, 1979.

90. A student poll in early 1980 strongly supported the idea of the shorter January term, 212 to 18. Ibid., February 29, 1980.

91. Ibid., October 9, 1981; Simpson College, Board of Trustees, Minutes, October 21, 1983.

92. *Simpsonian*, November 2, 1984; Simpson College, Board of Trustees, Minutes, January 25, 1985.

93. Ibid., January 25, 1985; October 21, 1983.

94. More than half of Simpson's contribution consisted of two gifts to the College, one for $25,000 from the People's Trust and Savings Bank and a second from Elizabeth and William Buxton in the amount of $15,000. The contractor for the new track was the Hillis Company of Des Moines. The architectural firm of Crose-Gardner Associates designed the improvements.

95. *Record-Herald and Indianola Tribune*, August 6, 1979; September 10, 1979. Indianola High School football games continued to be played on the field as well. See also *Simpsonian*, September 12, 1979.

96. Its total cost was $10,668. See *Simpsonian*, October 2, 1981.

97. *Simpsonian*, October 7, 1983. Librarian Cynthia Myers (Dyer) found it necessary to explain that the Craven collection focused on the antebellum South, not the Civil War, lest the place be overrun by peripatetic Civil War buffs. Ibid., October 14, 1983.

98. For Amy Robertson's story, I am indebted to several interviews with Amy Robertson, together with Robert E. McBride, "Memoirs," 318–19; *Simpson Magazine*, summer 1992.

99. Simpson College, Board of Trustees, Executive Committee, Minutes, July 22, 1982; *Simpsonian*, October 1, 1982.

100. *Simpsonian*, October 23, 1981.

101. Simpson College, Board of Trustees, Executive Committee, Minutes, July 22, 1982; *Simpsonian*, September 24, 1982; *Record-Herald and Indianola Tribune*, October 26, 1981.

102. *Record-Herald and Indianola Tribune*, October 18, 1982.

103. At the time of the dedication, it could be announced that the project was fully funded. The Kresge $100,000 challenge grant specified that $2,000,000 must be raised for the building and a $200,000 endowment fund for its maintenance by May 15, 1983. The challenge was met. See *Simpson Alumnus*, winter 1983.

104. Ibid., fall 1983. See also *Record-Herald and Indianola Tribune*, May 16, 1983.

105. Simpson College, Board of Trustees, Executive Committee, Minutes, October 12, 1983.

106. *Simpson Alumnus*, winter 1984; *Simpsonian*, October 5, 1984.

107. Robert E. McBride, "Memoirs," 325.

108. For the foregoing paragraphs, the author is indebted to Amy Duncan, managing editor of the *Record-Herald and Indianola Tribune* and daughter of history Professor Owen Duncan and his wife, Karen, a longtime staff member at the College. Amy Duncan's excellent review of the history of the Des Moines Metro Opera appeared at the time of its twentieth anniversary. *Record-Herald and Indianola Tribune*, June 10, 1992.

109. Robert E. McBride, "Simpson Recollections," 8.

110. Robert E. McBride, "Memoirs," 325.

111. Ibid., 324.

818   History of Simpson College

112. Robert L. Larsen, interview by author, Indianola, Iowa, September 16, 1993.
113. Robert E. McBride, "Simpson Recollections," 8.
114. Ibid., 9.
115. Ibid.
116. She was born February 11, 1901, to Estes N. and Prudence McIntosh Judkins of New Virginia. Her family moved to northern Minnesota and then to South Dakota, but Lettie returned to Warren County to enter Simpson, where she earned a B.S. in business administration, minoring in mathematics. She took graduate courses at the University of Illinois, Northwestern and the University of Chicago. She married Henry McNeill on June 25, 1956, whereupon the couple moved to Florida to enjoy their retirement. Henry died on October 3, 1981. In mid-1993 Lettie, though ailing, was still residing in Delray Beach, Florida, at the age of ninety-two.
117. Robert E. McBride, "Memoirs," 320–21. Actually, the McNeill gift netted $910,000, of which $850,000 was used toward the building and the balance for a faculty development endowment fund.
118. Simpson College, Board of Trustees, Executive Committee, Minutes, April 5, 1983.
119. Charles Herbert, interview by author, July 27, 1993; Simpson College, Board of Trustees, Executive Committee, Minutes, October 12, 1983.
120. Simpson College, Board of Trustees, Minutes, October 21, 1983.
121. Simpson College, Board of Trustees, Executive Committee, Minutes, December 28, 1983.
122. *Simpson Alumnus*, Spring 1984. Unfortunately it would not quite reach the twenty-first century. Computer science moved to a much-enlarged Carver Science Hall in 1993. See also *Simpsonian*, March 16, 1984.
123. *Record-Herald and Indianola Tribune*, March 1, 1984.
124. Simpson College, Board of Trustees, Minutes, May 17, 1984; *Record-Herald and Indianola Tribune*, June 25, 1984.
125. Henry H. McNeill was a graduate of the University of Illinois (1914) and a member of the Illinois bar. He and his brother managed the McNeill Building in Chicago. He died at the age of ninety-one on October 3, 1981. His twin brother Thomas H. McNeill was a graduate of Trinity College in Hartford, Connecticut, and, like Henry, served in the U.S. Army during World War I. He married Frances Shepherd in 1956. She preceded him in death in 1962. He died December 5, 1979. Both brothers were thirty-second degree Masons.
126. *Simpson Alumnus*, winter 1985.
127. Simpson College, Board of Trustees, Minutes, October 21, 1983.
128. *Simpson Alumnus*, winter 1985.
129. George Ewers, superintendent of buildings and grounds, who knew at first hand the problems of maintaining the building, observed that "there are people around who want Old Chapel saved for sentimental reasons. But they dwindle each year." *Simpsonian*, November 14, 1980.
130. Since the building was closed in 1980, there had been "no academic program demand for space that the building could have provided," and prior even to that time "the building had been under-utilized for a number of years." *Simpson Alumnus*, summer 1982. The building had 13,044 square feet of floor space.
131. *Simpson Alumnus*, winter 1986.
132. Ibid. Actually, the Dunn architect, Dr. Neutra, declared Old Chapel to be "the best building on the campus," and designed the portico of the library to pick up the lines of its roof.
133. Ibid., October 1, 1982.
134. *Record-Herald and Indianola Tribune*, September 16, 1982.
135. Ibid.
136. Ibid., September 23, 1982.
137. *Simpsonian*, October 15, 1982.
138. "Old Chapel Will Be Saved," *The Diamond* [of the Kappa Theta Psi Fraternity], 49 (August 1985), 13–15. Later that same day, after Doyle's address, Dr. McBride stated that both College Hall and Mary Berry represented "a historical connection to Simpson's past which will be severed irrevocably with their passing." He knew that "a number fear that the de-

struction of our '19th century charm' would constitute a significant loss for current and future students." At the same time, he knew that saving these buildings carried a very expensive price tag, one the College might not be willing to pay. Simpson College, Board of Trustees, Minutes, October 15, 1982.

139. *Simpsonian*, October 22, 1982.

140. *Record-Herald and Indianola Tribune*, October 21, 1982.

141. Simpson College, Board of Trustees, Minutes, January 21, 1983. See also *Record-Herald and Indianola Tribune*, January 20, 1983.

142. "Trustee Hill asked that it be recorded that he had cast a dissenting vote on the committee's recommendation." Student body president Jackie Niels "also spoke in opposition to Plan B." Simpson College, Board of Trustees, Minutes, May 20, 1983.

143. Ibid.

144. *Simpson Alumnus*, winter 1986.

145. Ibid., October 21, 1983.

146. Ibid., May 17–18, 1984.

147. *Simpson Alumnus*, winter 1986.

148. *Record-Herald and Indianola Tribune*, May 21, 1984.

149. Simpson College, Board of Trustees, Minutes, October 19, 1984. See also *Record-Herald and Indianola Tribune*. October 29, 1984.

150. The Cowles gift was $200,000. Simpson College, Board of Trustees, Executive Committee, April 23, 1985. The board's decision to go ahead was taken on January 25, 1985, and they voted unanimously to proceed with restoration work on April 23. Others who contributed generously were, of course, Hill and Gartner, together with Morley Ballantine and Bob Picken.

151. Ibid., June 11, 1985.

152. Simpson lost the game 17 to 7.

153. *Simpson Alumnus*, winter 1986.

154. Ibid. For a review of the history of the building and its importance to the College, see L. L. Hill, Jr., "Simpson College Beginnings and College Hall," an address delivered at the College February 26, 1987.

155. *Simpson Alumnus*, summer 1986.

156. Ibid., summer 1987.

157. Simpson College, Board of Trustees, Minutes, October 19, 1984; May 16, 1985; *Record-Herald and Indianola Tribune*, May 20, 1985; *Simpson Alumnus*, summer 1985.

158. The contract for these projects amounted to $221,000. Simpson College, Board of Trustees, Executive Committee, Minutes, November 12, 1984. Downing also constructed the parking lots adjacent to Barker Hall and Dunn Library on the east side of the campus along North Buxton Street. The cost was just over $80,000. Ibid., October 12, 1983.

159. The old house, next to the Lambda Chi Alpha fraternity house, was razed and removed at a cost of $1,500. The new dwelling was refurbished at a cost of $7,500. Ibid., July 22, 1982.

160. *Simpsonian*, November 12, 1982.

161. Ibid., March 29, 1985; Simpson College, Board of Trustees, Minutes, January 25, 1985.

162. Simpson College, Board of Trustees, Executive Committee, Minutes, April 23, 1985.

163. See Simpson College, Board of Trustees, Minutes, January 20, 1984.

164. The Series 1983 bonds bore an interest rate of 9.25 percent. Simpson College, Board of Trustees, Executive Committee, Minutes, April 5, 1983; July 7, 1983; *Record-Herald and Indianola Tribune*, May 23, 1983. Additionally the board on January 25, 1985, approved four projects: a parking lot at Detroit and North D Street ($58,000), the Buxton Hall parking lot ($27,000), athletic field improvements ($47,000), and air conditioning Buxton Hall ($30,000).

165. Simpson College, Board of Trustees, Executive Committee, Minutes, April 5, 1983; December 28, 1983.

166. See *Simpson Alumnus*, winter 1983. It will be recalled that the first fully-funded endowed professorship was the George Washington Carver Chair in Science, held for many years by science division chairman Clifford Meints.

167. Simpson College, Board of Trustees, Executive Committee, Minutes, July 24, 1981.
168. *Record-Herald and Indianola Tribune*, December 21, 1981; *Simpson Alumnus*, Spring 1982; *Simpsonian*, February 26, 1982; Simpson College, Board of Trustees, Minutes, May 21, 1982.
169. *Simpson Alumnus*, summer 1982.
170. Ibid., winter 1983.
171. Robert E. McBride, "Memoirs," 314.
172. *Simpsonian*, October 22, 1982.
173. Robert E. McBride, "Memoirs," 313.
174. Ibid., 314; Robert E. McBride, "Simpson Recollections," 12. "Gary and I, however, considered ourselves friends, and he always came to visit me in my office when he returned to campus in later years."
175. Robert E. McBride, "Memoirs," 314.
176. Ibid.
177. Ibid., 326.
178. Ibid.
179. *Simpsonian*, November 30, 1979.
180. If he thought ninety players excessive, he should have seen teams a decade or so later of 140 men or more. Ibid., December 7, 1979.
181. Simpson College, Board of Trustees, Executive Committee, Minutes, December 18, 1979; *Simpson Alumnus*, March 1980; *Record-Herald and Indianola Tribune*, November 12, 1979; December 24, 1979.
182. Robert E. McBride, "Memoirs," 327; *Record-Herald and Indianola Tribune*, September 26, 1983. The victory pleased athletic director Gordon Jeppson too. In a classic statement he recalled that "when I arrived [at Simpson], they [the Central team] were kind of an Albatross around our necks, so it was good to get that kind of monkey off our backs." The metaphors may have been mixed, but the sentiment was pure. See ibid., January 2, 1985.
183. Ibid., October 28, 1984.
184. Simpson College, Board of Trustees, Minutes, January 25, 1985.
185. Krumlauf coached men's golf during his first semester at Simpson in the spring of 1985.
186. Free safety Larry Allen was named to the first team in the I.I.A.C. in 1985.
187. *Record-Herald and Indianola Tribune*, July 26, 1984; *Simpsonian*, October 26, 1984.
188. *Simpson Alumnus*, winter 1984.
189. Simpson College, Board of Trustees, Executive Committee, Minutes, July 22, 1982; *Record-Herald and Indianola Tribune*, May 31, 1982; July 15, 1982; *Simpsonian*, September 24, 1982; *Simpson Alumnus*, summer 1982.
190. Regrettably, Schafer resigned at the close of the 1985 season. See *Record-Herald and Indianola Tribune*, March 27, 1985.
191. *Simpsonian*, October 23, 1981; November 6, 1981; May 13, 1983.
192. *Simpson Alumnus*, winter 1982.
193. *The Diamond of Kappa Theta Psi*, 44 (August, 1980); *Simpson Alumnus*, December 1979. For reasons that are not clear, the *Simpsonian* did not note the revival of Kappa Theta Psi until March 7, 1980.
194. *Simpsonian*, May 2, 1980.
195. Simpson College, Board of Trustees, Minutes, January 20, 1984.
196. *Simpsonian*, March 1, 1985.
197. Ibid., February 18, 1983.
198. *Simpson Alumnus*, spring 1985. See also *Simpsonian*, February 8, 1985; Simpson College, Board of Trustees, Minutes, May 17, 1985.
199. *Simpsonian*, February 22, 1985.
200. Ibid., February 15, 1985.
201. *Simpson Alumnus*, fall 1983; *Simpsonian*, March 11, 1983.
202. *Simpson Alumnus*, winter 1983; *Simpsonian*, November 4, 1983.
203. *Simpsonian*, April 3, 1981.
204. Ibid., March 11, 1983.
205. Ibid., October 15, 1982.

206. Ibid., February 22, 1985.
207. Ibid., April 25, 1980; March 29, 1985.
208. Arthur L. Allen was a Simpson graduate in the class of 1970, his wife Nancy Shepherd Allen in the class of 1969. Both had earned theological degrees. In order to strengthen Simpson's relationship with the church, Dr. McBride in 1980 created a new position—in the case of the Allens, new positions—of Director of Church Relations.
209. Robert E. McBride, "Simpson Recollections," 14.
210. Frank Colella could remember the year he was accorded the faculty honor but was not informed of his election until a few days after Homecoming. *Simpsonian*, October 23, 1981.
211. See *Simpsonian*, April 3, 1981; March 25, 1983.
212. Ibid., April 27, 1984.
213. Ibid., April 29, 1983; May 6, 1983.
214. Ibid., April 29, 1983.
215. Ibid., November 9, 1979.
216. Robert E. McBride, "Simpsonian Recollections," 10.
217. Ibid., 10–11; Robert E. McBride, "Memoirs," 328–29. One gesture of friendship to the community was the offer of free tuition for all courses at the college for people over sixty-five years of age, together with free admission to all Simpson events. *Record-Herald and Indianola Tribune*, September 17, 1981.
218. See *Simpson Alumnus*, summer 1981; spring 1984.
219. *Simpsonian*, November 21, 1980.
220. Ibid., April 18, 1980.
221. Ibid., November 16, 1979.
222. Ibid., February 27, 1980. See also *Record-Herald and Indianola Tribune*, January 22, 1981. Later Dunn Library received a set of U.S. State Department papers chronicling the Iranian hostage crisis. These papers were the gift of Vivian Homeyer, the sister of Kathryn Koob, an Iowan among the hostages. *Record-Herald and Indianola Tribune*, July 13, 1981.
223. *Simpsonian*, March 6, 1981; March 5, 1982.
224. Ibid., May 7, 1982; November 4, 1983. Later two letters to the editor took R. Scott Boots to task for his anti-Grenada editorial. Ibid., November 11, 1983.
225. Ibid., October 28, 1983. A well-informed and thoughtful piece on the Arab-Israeli imbroglio by longtime foreign relations expert Alice E. Sayre '42, entitled "A View From Both Sides of the Jordan," was published in the *Simpson Alumnus*, summer 1982.
226. *Simpsonian*, February 22, 1980; March 19, 1982.
227. Ibid., April 3, 1981
228. Ibid., April 10, 1981
229. Ibid., April 10, 1981; April 9, 1982.
230. Ibid., April 27, 1984.
231. Ibid., On July 17, 1984, President Reagan signed a bill giving states until October 1, 1986, to raise the drinking age to twenty-one or face a five percent cut in federal highway funds. All states complied. See ibid, March 11, 1983, anticipating the twenty-one year old rule.
232. Ibid., October 28, 1983.
233. They did support Ronald Reagan and Senator Charles Grassley in 1980. There was strong support otherwise for Democratic candidates.
234. Simpson College, Board of Trustees, Minutes, January 20, 1984; *Simpson Alumnus*, Summer 1984.
235. *Simpsonian*, January 25, 1985.
236. Simpson College, *Presidential Papers*, January 1986.
237. *Simpsonian*, September 20, 1985.
238. *The Christian Century*, 103 (January 15, 1986), 55.
239. For example, Simpson Guild provided during the 1984–85 academic year three $600 scholarships, a "women's athletic scale" for $260 and a contribution of $1,240 to the Hawley Learning Center.
240. *Des Moines Register* writer Chuck Offenburger related the story of Heckert and his "group" in his "Iowa Boy" column, October 27, 1985.

241. *Simpsonian*, January 31, 1986.

242. Ibid., March 28, 1986; April 11, 1986; *Record-Herald and Indianola Tribune*, April 9, 1986; *Simpson Alumnus*, summer 1986.

243. *Record-Herald and Indianola Tribune*, April 9, 1986.

244. *A Good Place to Work: Sourcebook for the Academic Workplace* (Washington, D.C.: Council of Independent Colleges, 1991), 9. Five of the ten colleges selected by the C.I.C. were in the Midwest: College of Saint Scholastica, Duluth, Minnesota; Greenville College, Greenville, Illinois; Nebraska Wesleyan University at Lincoln; and William Jewell College, Liberty, Missouri.

245. Ibid., 124–26.

autobiography, 767; career at Tuskegee Institute, 150; baccalaureate address, 150, 357; courses, 147, 149; death, 386; homesteader, 146; honorary doctorate, 150, 356; in Winterset, 146–47; laundry business, 147; remembrance of Simpson, 150; science hall named for, 482; student at Iowa State, 149–50; visit from President Gross, 356–57; youth, 146, 732
Carver Cultural Center, 672. *See also* Afro-American Cultural Center
Carver Hall of Science, 398; construction, 481–82; dedication, 482; expansion, 697; proposed, 381
Carver Opportunity Grants, 562, 801
Cary, Emma M., 48, 56, 61, 79, 718
Cary, Leonard B., 48
Casey, Frank, 362, 387–88, 395, 404, 412, 434–35, 464, 497, 791; appointed athletic director, 314; assigned to teaching, 496; death, 503; honored, 388; retirement, 497
Casey, Mona, 388, 464, 497
Catholicism: prejudice against, 177–78
Catlin, Edward H., 219
Cavanaugh, James, 600
C.B.S. *See* Concerned Black Students
Cell, Edward C., 462
Centennial activities, 499–500
Centennial Exposition (U.S.), 84
Centennial Festival of Music, 499
Centennial Fulfillment Program, 478
Center House, 645, 815
Central Building, 224, 227, 237, 254; completion, 254; construction, 239, 748; location, 238. *See also* Administration Building (second); Hillman Hall
Central States College Association, 532, 658
Centre College, 754
Century Fund, 430
Cermak, Anne M., 579, 622
Chad Mitchell Trio, 552
Chaffee, Carlton, 464, 471
Chaney, Thomas P., 805
Chapel (activity): in 1910s, 244; in 1920s, 290; in 1930s, 320; attendance, 115, 137, 171, 244–45, 290, 364, 411, 493–94, 560, 595–96, 606, 750, 776–77
Chapel (building): design controversy, 484–85. *See also* Smith Memorial Chapel
Chapin, Harry, 630
Charles Herbert Associates, 536, 540, 670
Chase, Hal S., 806, 809
Chavez, Cesar, 568
Cheney, Charles B., 167
Cheshire, Hattie, 50
Cheshire, Ida, 53
Cheshire, John, 50, 56, 716
Cheshire, Wesley, 56

Chew, John L., 232
Chieftain, 400, 774
Chisholm, Shirley, 630
Chisman, Frank, 358
Christ Church memorial stone, 459–60, 540
Christensen, Annette, 679
Christian, James L., 455, 461
Christian Liberal Arts Festival, 457–59, 490, 499, 529–30, 690
Christie, M. Francis, 461–62, 469, 785
Christmas: observance on frontier, 713
Christopher, Jim, 653–54, 659
Christy, Greg, 678
Chrystal, John, 691
Church of the Nazarene, 113
Church-College relations, 683–84, 821
C.I.C. *See* Council of Independent Colleges
Civil War, 714; Methodist response, 23; Warren County response, 22–23
CLAF. *See* Christian Liberal Arts Festival
Clammer, George, 175
Clarey, John E., 84, 722; attack on Burns, 81–82; College move controversy, 81; sale of newspaper, 725; quoted, 69, 89, 97, 105
Clark, Brent, 678
Clark, D. W., 28
Clark, Dan, 691
Clark, Dick, 584
Clark, J. C., 27
Clark, Lois E., 773
Clark, Olive Pearl, 480
Clark, Robert D., 499
Clark, Scott, 678
Clark, Shirley, 692
Clark, Velma, 564
Clarke, G. W., 231
Clarke, Marvel "Marty," 388
Clarke, Morrill, 232
Clary, D. B., 34
Class competition, 204
Clayburg, W. F., 783
Clayton, Benjamin F., 112, 173, 206, 207, 733, 739, 741; personal information, 182–83
Cleveland, Don, 498
Cleven, Roger, 434
Cline, Clarence "Cowboy," 362
Clionian Society, 282, 317–18
Clodfelder, D. Leon, 805
Clogg, Rich, 597, 598
Coat-of-arms (College), 500–501
Coat-of-arms (Sigma Alpha Epsilon), 681
Coe, Cassius C., 118
Coeducation, 63
Cohen, Richard, 566, 567, 568, 570, 571, 572, 596, 807
Coke, Thomas, xiii
Cokesbury College, xiv
Cola, 177

Colburn, Jay, 438
Cole, C. C., 72, 73, 74, 75, 101
Cole, Hugh A. 227
Cole, Lu Jean, 536, 550, 585, 600, 611, 637, 647–48, 671
Colella, Frank, 612, 656, 667, 821
College Activities Board, 683
College Bowl, 630, 685
College calendar. *See* calendar, College
College colors, 140
College Council, 204, 239
College Hall: bankruptcy of contractor, 36–37, 717; completion, 37; construction contract, 36; construction, 36; dedication, 37; "hog chute," 114, 254; illustration of, 38; mechanics liens, 79, 97; refurbished, 135, 166. *See also* Old Chapel
College histories. *See* histories of Simpson College
College Ladies Aid Society, 120
College name. *See* name (College)
College of Liberal Arts, 164, 190
College Womens League, 243, 749
College yell, 168, 736
Collegiate Council, 240
Collie, Carl, 529
Collins, Craig, 681
Collins, Ira, 241
Collins, Mahlon D., 65, 93, 111
Collins, Robert G., 769, 783
Colors, College 140, 736
Colton, Winfred M., 187, 199
Columbus Seminary, 4, 24
Commager, Henry Steele, 498
Commencement: in 1869, 46; in 1870, 48; in 1878, 62, 66–70; in 1882, 106–110; in 1886, 124–25; in early 1900s, 208; in 1910, 208–9; in 1920s, 296; in 1930s, 363, 763; in 1940s, 390; in 1961, 499–500
Commercial Course. *See* business administration
Commercial Department. *See* business administration
Commercial School. *See* business administration
Commitment 125, 588, 620
Commons Club, 280
Communism, 417
Community Service Award, 439, 505
Comprehensive examinations. *See* examinations: comprehensive
Concerned Black Students, 628–29. *See also* Black Student Organization; Organization for Black Unity
Condit, Mary, 161
Conklin, Charles, 525
Conner, Karen A. "Kacie," 696
Conrad, J. M., 65

Conrad, John F., 115–17
Conrad, L. E., 737
Conser, E. C., 152, 164
Conservatory of Music. *See* music
Conservatory of Music Building: bids for, 740; construction, 193; dedication, 193; renamed, 272. *See also* Barrows Hall
Considine, Judith, 578
Cook, Isaiah H., 727
Cooke, Elizabeth S., 63–64, 66, 70, 719, 720
Cooledge, Ethel, 164
Cooley, O. E., 783
Coolidge, Calvin, 265
Co-op ed, 303
Cooper, John H., 394, 411, 424, 777
Copeland, Urith, 772
Coppola, Joe, 598
Corbin, Royal, 591
Corea, Chick, 630
Corkhill, Emma Kate, 163, 171, 184, 213, 249
Cornell College, xvi, xvii
Cornerstone Studies in Liberal Arts, 657–58
Cosmopolitan Club, 281
Cosson, Jennie, 769
Cost of attendance: in 1910s, 228; in 1930s, 310; in early 1950s, 427; in 1953–63, 477; in 1968–75, 580; in 1975–79, 632; in 1993, 696. *See also* tuition
Cotton, Mary, 101
Couch, A. Edward, 584, 588, 607, 620
Council of Independent Colleges, 692–93
Course evaluation, 528, 615
Courthouse, 366
Cowles, Gardner, 256, 381, 429, 458, 482
Cowles, Hulda C., 15, 18, 22
Cowles Center, 589–90, 620–23; construction, 621–22; dedication, 622; design, 621; financing difficulties, 622
Cowles Foundation, 381, 479, 589, 622, 671, 673
Cox, Florence H., 302, 336, 356
Coy, Bob, 625
Crabb, Helen Rohrer, 438
Crabb, Marjorie J., 521, 611
Craig, Alfred E., 747
Craig, Loris, 419
Crandall, Robert S., 564
Craven, Avery, 419, 438, 474; commencement speaker, 390; death, 687; library donation, 659–60; professional career, 188; Simpson student and instructor, 188
Craven Room and Collection, 659–60
Crawford, Edward I., 385
Crawford, Hadley, 417, 464, 472, 784
Crawford, William H., 231
Creason, Chris, 598
Creationism, 476
Creek, Ellen, 273

Crescent Society, 240, 282, 317–18
Creswell, Grace, 498
Criswell, Myron, 378
Cromer, Catherine, 128, 151, 171
Cross-country running: in 1963–68, 546; in 1968–75, 598; in 1975–79, 625; in 1979–87, 678–79
Crosswait, Belva, 433
Crosswhite, Stanley, 564, 802
Crowe, Loren, 769
Crozier, Benjamin F. W., 111
CSCA. *See* Central States College Association
Cumming, Charles A., 188
Cummins, Robert A., 235
Cumpston, Dennis, 598
Cunningham, Ken, 622
Curfew. *See* hours
Curriculum: in late 1860s, 42–43; in 1879, 96; in late 1880s, 135, 136–37; in mid 1890s, 164; in 1900s, 189–91, 740; in 1910s, 216–19, 744; in 1920s, 269–70; in early 1930s, 303–304, 335–36; in 1940s, 378–79; post WWII, 396; post WWII strengths, 403–4; in early 1950s, 427–29, 447; in mid 1950s, 451–53; in 1963–68, 525–28; in 1968–75, 560–61, 801; in 1975–79, 614, 615–17; in 1979–87, 657–58. *See also* Conerstone Studies in Liberal Arts; Vital Center; *and names of specific disciplines*
Curtin, John, 678–79
Curtis, Waldo, 468
Cushman, Cecil A., 275, 754
Cuykendall, Eudelmer Fitch, 105

Dahl, John E., 394, 464, 496
Dahl, Wilma, 785
Dahnke, Dawn, 800
Dale, John, 598
Dancing, 43; in late 1880s, 115; in 1900s, 205; in 1910s, 244, 246; in 1920s, 291; in 1930s, 320–23, 363, 761; post WWII, 410
Daniel, Dorothy, 160, 246–47
Darling, Jonathan H., 816
Darrow, Lew E., 111
Darwin, Charles, 120, 162
Darwinism, 124–25, 476, 744
Dasenbrook, Steve, 547
Davidson, Chris, 699
Davidson, William J., 765
Davis, Charles W., 8, 23, 46, 85
Davis, James B., 816
Davis, Van, 529
Dawson, Frances Ledlie, 574, 673
Day, Robert, 387
Dean, Cora, 383
Dean, Lloyd C. "Judd," 313, 314
Dean, Rae L., 305, 327, 346, 371, 373, 752, 771; appointed business manager, 255–56, 751; retirement, 384–85; Stanley-Dean System, 314

Dearden, Dennis, 678
Deaton, Leslie, 497, 545, 587, 598, 809
DeBoer, Josephine, 467–68, 785
Debt: in late 1870s, 79, 86, 94, 95; in early 1880s, 102, 103, 110; in late 1880s, 129–30, 729; in 1890s, 154–55; in 1900s, 198; in 1910s, 237, 746; in 1920s, 286, 288; in 1930s, 302, 333. *See also* financial problems
Deferred rushing, 490, 492
Degen, Bruce N., 472, 516
Degrees offered: in late 1860s, 43; in 1879, 96; in late 1880s, 136; in mid 1890s, 164; in early 1900s, 217; in early 1910s; in 1930s, 335–36; Bachelor of Music, 271; Bachelor of Music Education, 786; B.S.B.A., 267, 474; B.S. in Education, 269; B.S. in Home Economics, 269, 302, 336
deLaubenfels, Richard, 468, 522, 613
deLaubenfels, Rosemary, 533, 816
DeLisle, Donald, 468, 612
DeLong, Ira M., 66, 70, 75; commencement oration, 69
Delta Delta Delta, 175, 203, 389, 682, 731; academic performance, 359, 414; chapter founded, 138; housing, 315–16, 760. *See also* L.F.V. Sorosis
Delta Epsilon, 281
Delta Kappa, 492, 601
Delta Tau Delta, 118, 175; chapter founded, 53; disbanded, 738
Delta Upsilon: chartered Kappa Theta Psi, 546–47; charter withdrawn, 596–97, 627–28; D.U. Commune, 628. *See also* Kappa Theta Psi
Delta Zeta, 511, 546; chartered, 511; demise, 628, 812; merger, 492, 790
Demaree, Cornelius, 56
Demaree, Ireaneus, 56
Dennis, Wilbur C., 263, 292
Denver, John, 552, 600
Departments (academic), 331
DePauw University, 716
Depression. *See* Great Depression
Des Moines Conference (Methodist): financial support of College, 92, 95, 156, 226, 301, 380, 746; merger, 301; named, 715
Des Moines Conference Seminary. *See* Indianola Male and Female Seminary
Des Moines Metro Opera, 663–64, 672
Detlie, Ed, 800
Deutsches Haus, 618
Devoe, Albert M., 747
Dewey, Thomas E., 417
Dickey, James, 550
Dickinson College, xv
Dieffenbach, Robert M., 809
Dillon, Chester C., 241
Dillon, Walter, 296

Dingman, Maurice J., 539
Dining facilities, 400, 481
di Palma, Maria, 652
Dirlam, Arland, 485, 537
Discipline: in late 1860s–early 1870s, 43; in 1886, 114–15; in late 1880s, 137–38; in 1890s, 173; in 1900s, 204; in 1930s, 364; in early 1950s, 437; in 1963–68, 549; in 1968–75, 558, 594. *See also* alcohol; card-playing; chapel: attendance; dancing; hours; sex; Simpson Code; smoking; theater-going
Dittmer, Donald R., 520, 587
Divisions (academic), 331, 356
Dixon, Le Roi, 470
Doby, A. A., 27
Dodds, J. S., 402
Doderer, Minnette, 600
Dodge, Eleanor Hemstead, 372
Dodson, Samuel H., 214, 744
Doft, Floyd S., 673
Doidge, Della M., 673
Dolliver, Jonathan P., 195
Donohue, Jim, 678
Dormitories, 534–35; federal financing, 431–32; mens, 480; need for, 358, 377, 396, 484; post WWII construction, 398–99; womens, 485. *See also* Barker Hall; Kresge Hall; Ladies Hall; Lorraine Hall; Mary Berry Hall; West Hall
Dornbos, Ervan S., 394, 424
Dotts, Harold W., 450
Doty, Hiram S., 374, 394, 395, 433, 463, 465, 759; appointed to faculty, 258; death, 466, 503, 785; honorary doctorate, 477
Douglas, Lloyd, 363
Douglass, R. Thomas, 525, 578
Douthart, Henry F., 40, 46, 47, 717
Downing, Robert, 651, 670
Doyle, Dan, 625, 669, 671, 678
Drake, D., 799
Drake, Francis M., 76, 159
Drake University, 76
Dress. *See* fashion
Drinking age, 801, 821
Drugs, 698
Drury, Don, 401
DuBois, W. E. B., 324
D.U. Commune, 628
Dudley, Harold, 499
Dudley, William M., 216, 225, 287, 744
Duncan, Amy, 817
Duncan, Douglas J., 613, 652, 663
Duncan, Ella Dowler, 437–38
Duncan, Owen L., 576–77, 598, 655, 682
Dunham, C. A., 28, 36
Dunn, Max, 365, 419, 509, 510, 632
Dunn, Norma, 488, 799
Dunn, Rex, 241, 480, 502, 552; library donation, 488

Dunn, Roger E., 632
Dunn Library: completion and opening, 533–34; construction, 488–89, 790; design, 487–88, 790, 818; financing, 488
Dunning, William C., 654
Durant, Will, 363
Dusenbury, Richard, 578, 809
DuVal, Alan, 367
Dyer, Cynthia "Cyd," 689–90
Dyer, Grant, 654
Dykes, Christine, 765
Dykstra, Robert, 388

Eady, Arthur, 439
Earl, Marjorie, 283
Eason, Clair "Skip," 434
Eckles, J. G., 65
Eckley, Grace, 521
Economic conditions: in 1860, 10–11; in late 1870s, 77–78; in 1890s, 154; in 1920s, 265, 300; in 1930s, 301, 306, 310–11, 312, 337, 758
Ecroyd, Donald H., 773
Edgerton Hall, 193, 740
Edmonds, Keith, 678
Educational Policy and Curriculum Committee, 526, 615–17, 657–58
Education in Iowa: early history, xvi–xvii; in early 1900s, 198–99, 742
Educator, The, 157
Edwards, F. C., 769
Edwards, Gus, 294
Eikenberry, Daniel, 775
Eikenberry, Elizabeth Alexander, 775
Eisenhower, Dwight D., 438
Elderhostel, 617
Eldridge, W. Clark, 522
Elections: of 1860, 10; of 1868, 44, 45; of 1876, 84, 713
Electives, 189–90
Electricity, 736
Eliot, Charles W., 189
Ellingson, Keith, 678
Ellinwood, Charles M., 101, 104, 128, 133
Elliot Seminary, 4
Elliott, Charles, 32, 44
Elliott, G. N., 20
Emerson, Ralph Waldo, 7
Emmons, Clyde, 211, 214, 219, 258, 281, 308, 346, 360, 371, 375, 759, 763, 765; appointed registrar, 256; death, 778; I.I.A.C. president, 275; retirement, 384; supporter of athletics, 242
Empress Theater, 246, 292, 366
Emslie, Alexander, 187, 199; appointed to faculty, 186; death, 778; later career, 201; resignation, 200; rivalry with Barrows, 200–201
Endowed professorships: Anna D. Hunt Chair

in History, 673; George C. Carpenter Chair in Latin, 209; George Washington Carver Chair in Science, 478, 819; William Buxton Chair of Economics and Business Administration, 268; William Buxton Chair of Moral Sciences, 183
Endowed scholarships. *See* scholarships: endowed
Endowment: in late 1860s–early 1870s, 41–42, 53–56, 719; in 1877, 79; in 1895, 156; in early 1900s, 197–98; in 1910s, 224–25, 227, 745–46; in 1920s, 285–89; in 1930s, 301–302, 353, 764; post WWII, 407–8, 776; in early 1950s, 447; in 1965, 798; in 1968–75, 588, 806
Engelking, Doris, 302
Engineering, 158–60
Engineering building: constructed, 158; converted to gymnasium, 166
Engle, Denny, 598
Engle, Paul, 550
English proficiency examination, 474
Enos, Charles, 223
Enrollment: in 1867, 35; in 1868–1880, 41; in 1878–79, 91; in 1879–80, 96; in 1880–1890, 104; in 1882, 110; in 1886–87, 122; in 1890–1900, 153–54; in 1900–1910, 191; in 1910–1920, 220; in 1920s, 252; 1920–1936, 253; in 1930s, 301, 312, 335, 338, 757, 765; in 1936–41, 350; in 1940s, 373, 377, 768; in 1941–53, 373; post WWII, 391–92, 772; in 1950s, 421, 423–24, 460–61, 779; 1953–62, 461; 1963–68, 530–31; 1963–73, 531; in early 1970s, 580; in 1975–79, 609; in 1974–86, 609; in 1987–93, 695; attrition, 349, 765; black, 562
Ensley, F. Gerald, 440, 443, 446, 458, 482, 512, 516, 782, 783
E.P.C.C. *See* Educational Policy and Curriculum Committee
Epperson, John, 612
Epsilon Sigma, 415, 492, 548, 601, 682; founded, 281
"Epworth Auditorium," 194
Erickson, Grace, 206
Estes, John, Jr., 574
Eta Pi, 117
Evaluation. *See* course evaluation
Evans, Alice A., 731
Evans, Chuck, 362
Evans, Doug, 624
Evans, E. M., 286
Evans, Elmer E., 128, 728
Evening program. *See* night classes
Evenson, Kristin M., 816
Everett, John A., 56, 84, 89, 722, 727; defense of Burns, 82; Greenback supporter, 83
Everett Society, 46, 48, 67, 173, 176, 240; chartered by Kappa Phi Sigma, 282; conflict with Burns, 82; founded, 44; merger, 175

Evolution. *See* Darwinism
Ewers, George, 586, 818
E. W. Fortney and Son, 132, 134
Ewing, Merrill, 426, 470
Examinations: comprehensive, 303, 396; final, 137; for seniors, 67. *See also* honor system
Experiment in General Education: Development and Evaluation, 457

Faculty: in 1867, 35; in 1868, 40; in 1870s, 61–63; in 1878, 91; in early 1880s, 101, 104; in 1886, 128–29; in early 1890s, 151–53; in mid 1890s, 161–64; in 1900s, 183–88; in 1910s, 213–15, 235–36; in 1920s, 255, 257–63, 271, 272; in 1930s, 302–3, 307–8, 759, 333–34, 355; in 1940s, 374–75, 385; post WWII, 392–95; in early 1950s, 424–26, 447; in 1953–63, 454–56, 461–69, 471–73; in 1963–68, 519–25; in 1968–75, 576–79, 586–87; in 1975–79, 611–14, 809; in 1979–87, 651–57, 816; in 1987–93, 696; black, 565, 674; cutbacks, 302–303, 587, 611, 809; housing, 408, 426; minority, 565, 674; morale, 579; part-time, 128–29, 696; rank, 331–32; religious diversity, 493; research, 656; travels, 199; WWII service, 377
Faculty Council, 385–86, 758
Faculty evaluation. *See* course evaluation
Faculty salaries. *See* salaries, faculty
Fair, Minerva K., 524, 654
Fansher, Guy, 430
Farb, Robert C., 394, 454, 464
Farley, Gerald "Skip," 470
Farmers' Union, 311
Farnham, Byer, 382, 387
Farnham, John B., 651
Faser, Christian, 121
Fashions: in 1880s, 119–20; in 1920s, 291; post WWII, 417–18; in 1950s, 494; in 1968–75, 594; in 1975–79, 606; in 1987–93, 697
Faucett, R. I., 426
Faulkner, William J., 390
FBI, 569–70, 803
Federwitz, Don, 545
Felton, Ruth Schooler, 383
Fete des Fous, 246
Feyerharm, Edith, 493
Feyerharm, Robert, 470, 478, 493, 518, 533, 574, 602
Fidler, Doyle, 790
Field, A. D., 165
Fields of concentration, 331, 335
Fillman, Charles, 494
Fillman, Louise, 259, 759
Financial aid, 350. *See also* grants-in-aid; scholarships
Financial problems: in late 1870s, 78–79, 86, 91, 94; in 1890s, 154–55; in 1910s, 226–27, 746; in 1920s, 289; in 1930s, 300–303, 304–5,

338–39; in 1940s, 380; in early 1950s, 427, 431, 779; in 1972–75, 587–88; in late 1970s–early 1980s, 622–23, 643–44. *See also* debt
Fink, V. P., 20
Finke, Clyde, 784
First Methodist Church of Indianola, 382; fire, 505; founding, 9; new building, 728–29
Fisher, George E., 737
Fisher, Harold "Bud," 759
Fisher, Kay Ellen, 611
Fisk, Charles W., 66, 91, 106, 724
Fisk, Hezekiah, 1, 2, 9, 20, 23
Fisk, John B., 63, 91
Fladd, Cyril, 564
Fleming, Archie, 171
Fleming, Eli M. H., 1–2, 5, 7, 13; personal background, 10
Flemming, Arthur S., 459, 499, 516
Flesher, Rick, 678
Fletcher, Joseph, 550
Flint, Charles W., 231
Flint, Dick, 771
Flint, Harold W., 769
Flint, Persis George, 772
Flunk Day. *See* Campus Day
Fluoride, 405
Flying saucer, 418
Foot, Hugh, 459
Football: in 1880s, 120, 139; in 1890s, 166–67; in 1900s, 201–2; in 1910s, 241; in 1920s, 273–76, 753, 754; in 1930s, 313–14, 360–61; in 1940s, 361, 387–88; post WWII, 411; in early 1950s, 434; in 1953–63, 495–96; in 1963–68, 544–45; in 1968–75, 597–98; in 1975–79, 624; in 1979–87, 676–77; abolished, 202; alumni dissatisfaction, 274–75; attrition, 698; Hap Miller firing, 495–96; lighted field, 314; press box, 497; protective gear, 736; restored, 202; Stanley-Dean System, 314, 760
Ford, Robert J., 658, 816
Foreman, Albert G., 66, 70
Forensics, 629, 682. *See also* oratory
Forsgren, Bob, 625
Forsgren, Tom, 625, 637
Forward Movement campaign, 407–8, 430. *See also* Century Fund
Forward Simpson campaign, 380–81, 770
Fossum, Julie, 334
Founders and Benefactors Day, 207, 688–89
Frank, Virginia Wayt, 394, 772
Franklin, Bernard W., 574, 591, 592, 800
Franklin, John Hope, 630
Fraternities (social): first chapters established, 50–53; in 1880s, 118–19; in 1890s, 175–76, 738; in 1900s, 203–4; in 1910s, 243–44; in 1920s, 279–80; in 1930s, 315, 359–60; in 1940s, 389; post WWII, 412–14; in early 1950s, 432–33; in 1953–63, 491; in 1963–68, 546–47; in 1968–75, 596–97; in 1975–79, 627–28. 812; in 1979–87, 680–82; deferred rushing, 490; housemother, 559; housing, 432, 485–87, 781; integration, 414; reputation, 138. *See also* Greeks; *and names of individual fraternities and sororities*
Frazier, Leo, 483
Frazier, Pearl, 483
Frederick, Peter, 692
Freshman caps, 364, 495, 548, 768
Freshman studies program, 614
Freshman Week, 295
Frey, Burt, 362
Frey, Gerald, 233
Frey, Patricia "Trish," 631
Frick, Willard B., 424
Friley, Charles E., 376
Frisbee, Katherine K., 754
Fund for Excellence, 673–74
Fund-raising: in late 1860s–early 1870s, 41–42, 53–56, 719; in 1878–79, 92–93, 94–95; in early 1880s, 102–3; in late 1880s, 130–31; in 1890s, 155–56; in early 1900s, 197–98; in 1910s, 224–25, 226–27; in 1920s, 285–89; in 1930s, 339–41, 353; in 1940s, 380–81; post WWII, 407–8, 776; in early 1950s, 429–31; in 1953–63, 477–80; in 1968–75, 581–82, 588–89; in 1975–79, 620–21; in 1979–87, 646–47, 672–74; in 1987–93, 695–96
Furst, Henry M., 394
Fusco, Louis, 800
Fussner, Ruth E., 362–63
Future Business Leaders of America, 682
Future Teachers of America, 415, 492

Gade, Dolores, 468, 525
Gadfly, 567
Gage, Maura Ann, 612, 809
Gaines, D., 737
Gaines, Richard J., 140
Gallagher, Rick, 812
Gamma Kappa Delta: chartered by Alpha Delta Alpha, 280; founded, 280. *See also* Alpha Delta Alpha
Gamma Sigma Rho. *See* Pi Kappa Phi
Gammack, Gordon, 568
Gammack, Julie, 568, 800
Gander, Gilbert, 737
Gardner, Albert, 565, 591, 592, 593, 801
Gardner, Harry, 233
Gardner Cowles Foundation. *See* Cowles Foundation
Garfield, James A., 120
Gartner, Michael, 651, 670, 819
Garton, William, 488, 789
Gate, campus, 226, 238
Gater, David, 494
Geauque, Harry A., 235, 748

Gehrmann, James, 521
Geiger, William, 610, 671, 808–9
General Education Board: endowment challenge, 285–89
General studies, 615–17, 657–58
Genung, Edmund H., 687
George, Marilyn, 378
George Washington Carver Chair in Science, 478, 819
George Washington Carver Hall of Science. *See* Carver Hall of Science
George Washington Carver Lecturer, 685
George Washington Carver Opportunity Grants, 562
German: WWI suspension of instruction, 233
Gerstell, Dick, 566
GI Bill, 391
GI enrollment, 391–92, 421
Gibson, Don, 493, 556, 567, 568, 803
Gibson, John, 733
Giddens, Paul, 419, 438
Gieber, Robert L., 578, 618
Gifford, Dora, 66
Gilbert, Richard, 688
Gilbert, William H., III, 612
Gildner, Robert V., 574
Giles, Arthur H., 105, 725
Gill, Dorothy E., 394, 424
Gill, Glenda E., 674, 816
Gilman, Peter L., 805
Gilmore, Eugene A., 329, 345
Ginsberg, Allen, 630
Girard College, 444–45, 782
Girard, George A., 68
Glann, Alex, 676
Glascock, Fred, 483
Gobin, H. A., 124, 728
Goedken, Bob, 678
Goeppinger, Neil, 547
Goldberg, Jay B., 539
Golden Jubilee, 207, 208–9
Golden Jubilee Campaign, 197–98
Gold Key, 492, 601
Goldovsky, Boris, 499
Goldstein, Walter, 498
Golf, 161, 735; in 1920s, 277; in 1930s, 362; in 1963–68, 546; in 1968–75, 598; in 1975–79, 625; in 1979–87, 678
Golisch, Lulu, 245, 750
Golliday, Uri P., 21, 28, 156, 714, 734
Goltry, Nina V., 262, 269, 424, 753, 759
Goodale, Christopher, 688
Goodenough, Aubrey W., 184, 214, 235, 237, 248, 750
Good Housekeeping, 406
Goodhue, Darrell, 521
Goodhue, Eve, 521
Goodloe, Robert D., 471, 501, 543, 551

Goodwin, J. G., 185
Goodwin, James B., 773
Goodwin, Levi P., 213, 744, 761, 765
Goolman, J. F., 28, 55, 716
Gordon, N. D., 366, 768
Gordon, W. E., 785
Gose, Bert, 426, 503, 759
Gossner, Jay W., 468, 525
Graber, Joe V., 541, 578
Graber, John, 628, 809
Gradatim Society, 175
Grading: in 1910s, 219; in 1930s, 335, 763; inflation, 594–95; letter system adopted, 303; plus-minus adopted, 615
Graham, A. J., 82, 724
Graham, R. J., 66
Graham, S. J., 82
Grahl, Charles H., 376
Grange, Red, 273
Grant, Annie, 618
Grant, G. Arthur "Chick," 242, 547, 680, 769, 773, 782
Grant, Genelle, 414
Grant, George, 680
Grant, Roger, 566
Grant, Ulysses S. 44, 45
Grants-in-aid, 407, 434–35, 498, 546
Grassfield, Mary, 469–70, 518
Graves, Fern L., 536
Graves, Harold N., 450, 632
Graves, Lucinda, 378
Graves, Nile "Soup," 241, 274, 276
Graves, Willis N., 500, 799
Gray, Charles, 491
Gray, Donald N., 524
Gray, Elias W.: appointed seminary principal, 7; disappearance from Indianola, 18–19; early career, 13; later life, 19; leadership, 16–17; "Querist" controversy, 17–18; term as seminary principal, 13–18
Gray, J. H., 20
Greable, William E., 522
Great Depression, 301, 306, 310–11, 312, 327
Great Hall, 481, 623
Greeks: in 1880s, 117, 138; in 1890s, 175–76, 738; in 1900s, 202–4; in 1910s, 243–44; in 1920s, 279–80; in 1930s, 315–17, 359–60, 760; in 1940s, 389, 412–14; in early 1950s, 432–34; in 1953–63, 490–492; in 1963–68, 546–48; in 1968–75, 596–97; in 1975–79, 627–28, 812; in 1979–87, 680–82; in 1987–93, 698; academic performance, 317, 359, 767; concerns about, 243, 547–48; dancing, 244; discrimination, 475, 511, 563–64; first chapters established, 53; Greek-"barbarian" rivalry, 119, 175, 248–49; housing, 243, 315–17, 749–50; opposition to, 203–4; popularity, 138, 436, 490, 546, 781; publish *Tangent*, 119, 140. *See also* fraternities

836   Index

(social); sororities (social); *and names of individual fraternities and sororities*
Green, Mark C., 652
Greenback Party, 83–84, 721–22
Greenfield, Leroy B., 235
Greenlee, Howard S., 424, 429, 440, 454, 463–64
Gregory, Dick, 802
Gregory, Lou, 101, 104
Griffel, Kay, 662
Griffin, John H., 511
Griffith, Charles C., 3
Griffith, Dudley D., 214, 244
Griffith, George E., 28, 35, 42, 56, 716; bankruptcy, 65; college agent, 53, 55; death, 120; land donation, 28, 53, 719; personal information, 9; whispering maples donation, 47–48
Grimes, James W., xvi
Grinnell College, xvii, 424; oldest newspaper controversy, 548; tornado, 108–10
Groomes, Gwen, 464
Gross, George, 371
Gross, John O., 371, 376, 430, 458, 499; appointed president, 345–46; death, 602; fund-raising, 353; inauguration, 346–47; "Payne Case," 347–49; presidency, 347–369; resignation, 368; visit to George Washington Carver, 356–57; youth and pre-Simpson career, 346
Group Ministry. *See* Warren County Group Ministry
Group System, 217, 269
Groves, John T., 417
Gruber, Loren, 493, 495, 523, 579
Grumbling, Christian M., 48–49, 61, 79, 91, 104; appointed professor, 48; death, 249; fired, 105; Kern controversy, 104–5; later career, 718, 725
Guillams, Mrs. G. C., 782
Gunn, R. J., 352
Gunn, Victor, 394, 772, 777
Guroff, Gregory, 691
Gutafson, Ellsworth, 569
Guth, Marian, 761
Guttmacher, Alan F., 550
Guy, Alva K., 809
Guy, Keith, 674
Guyer, Elizabeth, 66, 70, 719
Guyer, Simpson, 716
Guyton, Percy L., 351, 360, 377, 382, 766, 772
Gwinner, Paul A., 525
Gymnasium, 226, 731, 736; engineering building conversion to, 166; need for new, 194–95, 218, 220–21; original building, 157–58, 484. *See also* Cowles Center; Hopper Gymnasium

Haddox, M. Bruce, 576, 606, 642, 655, 689, 696, 815
Hade, Abbie, 619
Hagler, Lora, 749
Haines, Sanford, 10
Hale, Earle, 502
Haley, Alex, 550–51, 633, 802
Halgren, Carl R., 578
Hall, Brenda, 564
Hall, Edward, 92, 112, 129
Hall, Harold, 395, 418
Hall, M. D., 782
Hallam, David, 28, 48, 716
Hallam, Imogene, 48, 718
Hallam, Mrs. Thomas, 56
Hamilton, J. M., 66
Hamilton, Mary "Mate," 66, 70
Hamilton, William "Obie," 241
Hamilton, William E., 120, 183, 208, 211, 255, 307–8, 606, 696–97, 733, 748; acting president (1868), 38, (1886–87), 123, (1905–06), 199, (1915–16), 228, 231, 746; anti-Greeks attitude, 138, 203–4; antitheater attitude, 139; appointed president, 127; appointed to faculty, (1867), 35, (1883), 105, (1892), 153, 161; board member, 183, 256; construction program, 131–35; death, 324; emeritus retirement, 213; illness, 206; move to Des Moines controversy, 141–42; presidency, 127–43; opposition to athletics, 168, 242; resignation as president, 142, 731; resignation from faculty (1868), 40; youth and pre-Simpson career, 127–28
Hamilton, William T., 433, 449, 769, 773; board president, 345, 347, 371, 373, 401, 440; death, 502
Hamilton House, 696–97
Hancher, John W., 286
Hancher, Virgil M., 372, 375
Hanford, S. A., 15, 18
Hann, Bruce, 493
Hann, Paul M., 573
Hanson, Janice, 524
Hardin, Wilma, 336
Hare, William J., 805
Hargis, Billy James, 499
Hargis, Gary, 544, 545
Harkin, 599
Harlan, Harriet, 761
Harms, Paul, 785
Harnard, M. R., 177
Harned, W. F., 93
Harper, Earl E., 367, 372; appointed president, 327–28; educational philosophy, 330; honorary degrees, 762; inauguration, 329–30; on international affairs, 337–38; "Payne Case," 341–44, 764–65; presidency, 327–45; public relations, 329, 336–38, 763;

reorganization, 331–32, 762; resignation, 344–45; youth and pre-Simpson career, 328–29
Harper, Martha, 538
Harris, Frederick, 726
Harris, Joseph B., 104; appointment as president, 183; later career, 738; presidency, 179–80; youth and pre-Simpson career, 179, 738
Harris, Nell, 244
Harris, Sydney, 568, 600
Harrison, Roland G., 403
Hartley, Paul D., 524
Hartman, Robert H., 804
Hartung, John V., 608, 644, 647–48
Harvey, Herbert A., 244, 354; appointed music head, 262, 272; appointed to faculty, 214; resignation, 354
Harvey, John W., 673
Harvey, Margaret E., 425, 464, 471
Haselmayer, Louis A., 570
Hashimoto, James, 387, 390
Hashimoto, Sumiko, 772
Hatfield, Ed, 177–78
Haughey, Al, 495
Haunsperger, Deanna, 682, 688
Haven, E. O., 37
Haven, Gilbert, 80
Havner, Horace M., 737, 779
Hawk, Grover, 393, 424, 777
Hawkins, Patricia J., 794
Hawley Learning Resources Center, 562, 672
Hawley Learning Skills Center, 562, 646
Hawley Welfare Foundation, 562
Hawley Writing Laboratory, 562
Haworth, Lester W., 140, 731
Haywood, Lucy M., 164
Hazing, 174, 295, 364, 413, 548, 629, 768, 799
Heacock, Henry B., 24
Head, Albert, 733
Head, James C., 578
Heating plant, 193–94, 489
Heaton, Persis, 244, 271
Hebei Teachers University, 613
Heckart, Harold A., 465, 499
Heckert, Josiah B., 266–68, 690; background, 266; death and estate gift, 752; departure from Simpson, 267; "Heckert Group," 267–68; role of women, 266–67; years at Simpson, 266–67
"Heckert Group," 267–68, 590, 690
Heckert Hall, 590
Hedges, John, 516, 549
Hedges, Mildred, 324–25
Heinicke, Janet Hart, 653, 658
Heizer, Kenneth E., 497, 525, 544, 545
Helfrich, R. William, 468, 474, 528, 567, 571, 656

Hellman, Roger, 495
Hemmes, Luike J., 461
Henderson, Daisy, 383
Henderson, Frank P., 194, 256, 345, 371, 373, 380, 432, 440, 449, 502, 765, 769, 773, 782
Henderson, Harriet, 365, 366
Henderson, Jim, 545, 597
Henderson, John H., 25, 85, 90, 96, 169, 365, 366, 733, 739; board secretary, 111, 129, 153, 183, 230, 237, 256; Golden Jubilee recognition, 208
Henderson, John M., 186
Henderson, Paris P., 1, 4, 23, 56, 111, 502
Henderson, R. Melvin, 585, 611, 616, 642, 657, 667, 696
Hendrickson, J. Clare, 242, 632
Henry Wallace Hall of Science. See Wallace Hall of Science
Henshaw, Helen, 776
Hensley, Tom, 497, 516, 545, 568, 799
Herrin, William F., 785
Herring, Clyde L., 329
Herzfeld, Mike, 494
Hibner, Barbara, 625–26, 809
Hickman, James C., 667, 782
Hidlebaugh, Everett, 434
Hier, Florence, 214
Highland University, 146, 732
Higley, E. E., 747
Hill, Luther L., Jr., 484, 547, 819; trustee, 450, 488, 518, 573, 584, 607, 622, 637, 650–51, 670, 800; youth and early career, 450
Hill, Sara, 688
Hillis, Dick, 378
Hillman, John L., 331, 690; attitude toward dancing, 291; death, 503; described, 251–52; fund-raising, 285–89; honorary degrees, 751, 762; political views, 283; portrait of, 485; presidency, 251–326; president emeritus, 328; resignation, 325, 328; retirement recognition, 329; temperance views, 323–24; youth and pre-Simpson career, 251, 751
Hillman, Lizzie Howes, 251, 778
Hillman Hall: named, 485
Hilmer, William C., 258, 374, 759, 762, 762, 765; vice-president, 302, 330; retirement, 352
Himstead, Ralph E., 348
Hines, John, 677
Hinkle, Dwight, 544
Hinrichs, Kenley J., 816
Hiram Doty Scholarship Fund, 785
Historic Anchorage Project, 671–72, 674
Histories of Simpson College, vii–viii, 318–19, 500, 763
Hladky, George, 470, 784
Hoag, Gail Gallatin, 522, 528, 540, 618, 653
Hoan, Nguyen, 568
Hobbs, Dick, 378

Hoffman, Edward, 550
Hogsed, Carl, Jr., 809
Hoiby, Lee, 662
Holder, Fred L., 520, 610
Holladay, Leslie, 276
Holladay, Samuel M., 170, 256
Holland, Greg, 676
Holmberg, Sharon, 627, 655
Holmes, C. J., 185
Holmes, Edmund M., 117, 128, 207, 208, 209, 229, 357; appointed president, 142; appointed to faculty, 106, 258; death, 324; presidency, 151–54; resignation, 154; retirement from faculty, 303, 308; youth and pre-Simpson career, 142–43
Holmes, Ervilla, 67, 70, 130
Holmes, Merrill J., 365, 419, 503
Holt, Ivan L., 459
Homan, Fletcher, 196, 745; College field secretary, 197–98; commencement speaker, 390; death, 779; football captain, 167
Homecoming, 295–96, 300, 363, 389–90, 416; black royalty, 564, 802; Tomahawk award, 359–60, 416
Home economics, 755; B.S. degree eliminated, 302, 336; B.S. degree introduced, 269; building, 358, 484; program eliminated, 587; program established, 218–19; Sigler Home Economics Center, 398, 402–3
Home Economics Club, 415, 493, 548, 601
Homeyer, Vivian, 821
Homiletics Club, 281
Homosexual students, 808
Honnold, Dora Gifford, 69, 70, 779
Honor system, 294–95, 319
Hooker, William S., 93, 111, 129, 133, 249, 726, 728–29, 733
Hopper, Harry E., 741, 747; board member, 195, 229, 256; Carpenter Professorship donation, 209; gymnasium donation, 221; illness and financial ruin, 223; land donation, 221, 238; youth and career, 221–22
Hopper, Stanley, 795
Hopper Gymnasium: cost, 223, 224, 745; dedication, 223–24; design and construction, 223
Hopper Terrace, 397, 552
Horn, Byron E., 302
Horn, Roland, 398, 414
Horn, Roy L., 394, 772
Horn, Vera E., 302
Hornaday, Lochie, 400
Horner, Ethel J., 468, 785
Horsley, John, 208, 302, 322, 336, 345, 365, 384, 408, 502, 753, 763
Horstmann, Carla, 626
Hoskinson, James, 539
Hoskinson, Robert, 539

Hostetler, Richard W., 520
Houghton, James R., 762
Houghton, Marilyn, 470
Hours, 115, 246, 437, 559, 730
Housemother, 559
Housing: post WWII, 396–400; in 1987–93, 696–97; faculty, 408, 426, 776; married student, 397–98, 773; requirement, 559. *See also* dormitories; fraternities: housing; Greeks: housing
Howard, Cam, 596
Howard, O. F., 769, 783
Howlett, Jerry, 435
Howser, H. C., 741
Hoy, Terry, 466, 528, 572
Hoyman, Jim, 387
Hoyt, Beryl E., 385, 396, 426, 464, 789
Hu, Jessie Tsuey-Fang, 674, 816
Hubbard, Lola, 761
Hubbell, James W., Jr., 588, 650, 666
Hudson, C. G., 61
Hudson, Frank, 596
Huff, Howard A., 64
Huffman, Edward W., 785
Huffman, Erwin, 737
Hughes, Geraldine, 761
Hulen, Bill, 495
Humphrey, R. E., 737
Hunt, Anna D., 673
Hunt, Dennis D., 648, 695–96
Hunt, Marion, 673
Hunter, N. Doran, 522
Hunting, Mary O., 184, 199, 214, 215, 237, 386
Hurst, John F., 105
Hutchins, Robert M., 459
Hutton, Ruth Lenore, 754

I.C. Sorosis, 117, 437; chapter founded, 53; founding members, 719. *See* Pi Beta Phi.
Iddings, Harold J., 241, 749
I.F.C. *See* Interfraternity Council
I.I.A.C. *See* Iowa Intercollegiate Athletic Conference
I.I.I., 50, 54, 719
Illness: in 1880s, 117; in 1890s, 170–71; in 1900s, 206
Independent Conservatory of Music
Independents: in 1920s, 280; in 1940s, 359, 389, 772; post WWII, 414–15. *See also* "barbs"/"barbarians"; Greeks: Greek-"barbarian" rivalry
Independent Student Association, 492
Independent Women's Organization, 389, 414
Indiana Asbury University, 32, 716
Indianola: in 1860, xii; in 1920s, 261; in 1950s, 503–5; bank failures, 301, 757; centennial, 418; cultural importance of College, 65–66; demographic change, 493; electrification, 736;

financial support of College, 92, 94–95, 130–31, 155–56, 197–98, 225, 341, 380, 430, 542, 787; founding, xii; incorporation, 711; Ku Klux Klan, 264–65; plat of in 1872, 55; politics of, 44, 83–84, 366, 438; population, xi, 504, 792; railroad, 58, 723; temperance views, 44, 323–24. *See also* town-gown relations
Indianola First Methodist Church. *See* First Methodist Church of Indianola
Indianola Male and Female High School, 2–3
Indianola Male and Female Seminary, 13–29; campus (*see* campus); collegiate status, 27, 28–29; curriculum, 15, 21–22; designated "Des Moines Conference Seminary," 26; disappearance of Principal Gray, 18–19; enrollment, 15, 19, 22, 24, 25, 26, 27, 713; faculty, 15, 715; founding meeting, 1–2; fund-raising, 28, 715–16; incorporation, 13; level of instruction, 716; Methodist sponsorship, 4–5, 20, 24, 26; new seminary building (*see* Old Bluebird); normal department, 22; "old" seminary building, 7; opening, 13, 14; "Querist" controversy, 17–18; principals (*see* Gray, Elias W.; Winans, Ephraim H.; Baker, Orlando H.; Vernon, Samuel M.); purpose, 2; role of religion in, 22; trustees, 7–10, 13, 20–21; tuition, 13, 24–25; wartime difficulties, 24
Indianola Seminary, 4
Indianola Women's Club, 219, 225
Influenza epidemic, 234–35, 747
Ingham, Harvey, 195, 255, 381
Ingram, Paul O., 522, 568, 571
Ingram, Vera, 768
Ingvolstad, Fred, 247
"Inhumanities," 269
Inman, Ethel G., 302
Inman, James H., 262, 375, 377, 392, 759, 772
Interfraternity Council, 295
Interfraternity Council Sing. *See* All-College Sing
Interim term. *See* calendar: 4-1-4 system
International Club, 493, 601
International Relations Club, 415
International Harvester, 480
Intramural sports, 388, 627, 679
Iowa: population, 11. *See also* education in Iowa
Iowa Academy of Science, 499
Iowa Annual Conference, 794
Iowa Area, 794
Iowa College. *See* Grinnell College
Iowa College Foundation, 427
Iowa College of Law. *See* Law Department
Iowa Collegiate Association, 141, 731
Iowa Conference (athletic). *See* Iowa Intercollegiate Athletic Conference

Iowa Conference (Methodist): merger, 301, 794; schools sponsored, 4; split, 4
Iowa-Des Moines Conference: financial support of College, 430–31
Iowa High School Athletic Association, 277
Iowa Intercollegiate Athletic Conference, 242, 625; divisions, 411, 777; grants-in-aid policy, 435; reconstituted, 275, 498; reforms, 754; Stanley-Dean System, 314, 760
Iowa Pastors School, 436–37, 494
Iowa Power, 480
Iowa Tuition Grant Program, 580–81
Iowa Wesleyan, xvi, xvii, 4, 407, 713; financial weakness, 5; merger proposal, 227–28
Irwin, Stanley, 805
Isaacs, Gregory, 805
Isakov, Victor, 691
Isinger, Flora, 124
Iskra, 629
Israel, Jerry, 696
Iverson, E. Ruth, 785
Iwasaki, Yasu, 419

Jackson, Garfield, 562
Jackson, J. Hugh, 236, 265, 284, 329, 339, 347, 419, 420, 458, 480, 503, 748, 755, 778, 783
Jackson, Russell, 232
Jackson, Ruth, 281, 375, 395, 396, 429, 454, 463, 499, 772, 784; appointed to faculty, 263, 334; death, 603; history of College, vii, 500; pre-Simpson career, 752; retirement, 794; quoted, 174
Jacobs, Elwyn, 387, 388
Jacoby, Lillie, 118, 151
James, Paul G., 782
Janes, Edmund S., 5
January term. *See* calendar: 4-1-4 system
Japanese-American students, 390
Jarvis, Albert M., 753
Jay, Minnie, 128, 733
Jeffrey, A. T., 733
Jend, Hildegarde, 185, 214, 233
Jenkins, Jack L., 613, 689
Jenkins, Miriam, 613, 682
Jenkins, Perry W., 163, 167
Jenner, Edwin A., 214, 226
Jennings, Peter, 600
Jennings, Stephen G.: appointed president, 695; presidency, 695–99
Jensen, Clark, 598
Jeppson, Gordon D., 627, 677, 678, 120
Jessup, Albert W., 747
Jewett, Albert S., 727
Joens, Brad, 678
John, Byron, 516
John, Dorothy "Dot," 514
John, Melathathil J., 804
John, Ralph C., 606, 690; appointed president,

512–13; assessment of College, 515–16; FBI controversy, 569–70; inauguration, 516–17; Kent State, 571–72; O.B.U. protest, 591–92; presidency, 514–82; resignation, 582; ten-year plan, 532–33; William Kunstler controversy, 570; youth and pre-Simpson career, 513–14
Johns, Bill, 598
Johnson, Carl W., 361
Johnson, Elmer, 784
Johnson, H. L., 277
Johnson, Larry, 497, 598, 599, 625, 678
Johnson, Lyndon, 553–54
Johnson, Virginia, 809
Johnson, W. E. "Pussyfoot," 756
Johnston, Gary, 597
Johnston, Helen Capell, 773
Johnston, Laura, 735
Jones, Adam L., 284
Jones, E. Stanley, 53, 296, 364, 498, 765
Jones, Felicia C., 63, 91
Jones, Floyd, 577
Jones, Fred O., 548, 577, 618
Jones, George W., 8, 13, 15, 56, 65
Jones, Henry B., 261, 752
Jones, Ivor Rhys, 785
Jones, Morris, 761
Jones, Vivian Herrick, 543
Jordan, Alvin L., 642, 671
Jordan, Erma Shaw, 671
Jordan, J. C., 20, 65, 714
Jordan, William H., 104
Joshua, the, 278
Joshua Club, 242–43, 278
Joyner, John, 653
Jubilee Campaign, 197–98
Justice, Howard, 434

Kalpakgian, Mitchell A., 523–24, 629
Kappa Alpha Theta, 106, 175; chartered, 118; disbanded, 738. See also Theta Gamma Chi
Kappa Chi, 359, 493
Kappa Kappa Gamma, 175; chapter founded, 118; disbanded, 738; housing, 697; reinstated, 697, 698
Kappa Phi Sigma, 282, 317–18
Kappa Theta Psi, 279, 315, 374, 781; academic performance, 317, 359, 433, 767; chartered by Delta Upsilon, 546–47; chapter founded, 203; housing, 315, 389, 396, 413, 486–88, 749; reestablished, 680–81
Karr, Kenneth, 276, 415, 769, 783
Kauffman, Benjamin F., 111
Kaul, Donald, 568
Kayton, Charles H., 470, 543
Kayton, Marilyn Houghton, 785
Kearney, Leland, 464
Keeton, Jack, 415–16

Keith, Fred N., 188
Keller, Dave, 624, 677
Kellogg, John, 608–9, 640, 644, 650, 671
Kellogg Foundation, 480
Kelly, Elmer E., 431, 780, 787
Kelly, Gladys, 234
Kelly, Winfield S., 120, 727
Kennedy, Clarence K., 53, 58
Kennedy, Florynce, 600
Kennedy, John F., 553
Kennedy, Louella, 66, 70
Kennedy, Olin A., 117, 731
Kennedy, Robert F., 554, 567
Kennedy, Walt, 598
Kent, Cloy, 485
Kent, James, 646
Kenton, Stan, 600
Kent State, 571–72
Kern, Byron, 378
Kern, Charles W., 394, 424
Kern, J. Causin, 715
Kern, John, 104–5
Kerr, Chuck, 412, 434
Kerstetter, Leona Bateman, 445, 451, 507
Kerstetter, Robert C., 782
Kerstetter, William E., 606, 690; appointed president, 448; board revitalization, 449–50; campus expansion, 482–83; construction program, 480–489; curriculum reform, 451–53; education philosophy, 450–51; fund-raising, 477–80; Hap Miller firing, 495–96; language requirement, 467; leadership style, 475; Oxford Exchange Program, 459–60, 501; presidency, 449–507; resignation, 506; town-gown relations, 503; youth and pre-Simpson career, 444–46
Keyhoe, Katherine, 424, 464
Kies, Joe, 167
Kile, Dale Ann, 625
Kim, Kwang-Won, 393, 773
Kimer, Lewis S., 514, 553, 570, 573, 673, 686
Kimer, Maxine Keyes, 384
Kindred, Arthur J., 505, 782
King, Martin Luther, 802; assassination, 553, 563; scheduled appearance, 498–99
King, William A., 61
King, Wylie, 771
Kingsley, Calvin, 715
Kirk, Archie "Bunt," 241
Kirk, Carroll N. "Chick," 241
Kirkpatrick, Jeane, 691
Kirkwood, Samuel J., 11
Kleiss, Lee Maria, 520, 809
Klicker, Chuck, 599
Klinger, A. Conn, 214
Klisares, Bob, 495
Knox, James H., 3, 15, 19, 39, 89
Koch, Donald A., 466, 474, 533, 577, 654, 673

Kolln, Werner S., 653
Konishi, Marion, 772
Koob, Kathryn, 817, 821
Koontz, Donald, 425, 463, 499, 530, 552, 575, 600, 610, 654
Koos, David E., 804
Korean War: effect on enrollment, 421–22, 779
Korte, Alan H., 785
Kos, Nia, 656
Kottman, Clifford, 809
KOY. *See* Kappa Theta Psi
Kramer, George, 570
Krebs, Adin C., 185
Kresge, Dorothy, 516
Kresge, Stanley S., 458, 516
Kresge Foundation, 478, 479, 480, 582, 589, 622, 671
Kresge Hall, 485
Kruidenier, David, 484
Krumlauf, Lloyd, 676–77, 678, 820
Kuchan, Chuck, 388, 412
Kuehl, Glenn, 544
Kuehl, Phil, 598
Ku Klux Klan, 264–65
Kunkel, Casey W., 351, 385, 771
Kunstler, William, 570
Kunze, Harry, 268
Kunze, Irene S., 754
Kurtz, Nelda C., 352, 377
Kutzner, Jim, 688
Kvetko, M. Jane, 653, 656

Ladies' Drill Corps, 169
Ladies' Hall: construction, 133–35; need for, 114; opening, 134; remodeled and renamed, 206. *See also* Mary Berry Hall
Lafferty, Jerry, 545
Lafollette, O. N., 432
LaFollette, Walter, 387
Lain, Walter, 642
Lake Ahquabi, 366
"Lake Doyle," 796
Lamb, Glen, 376, 382, 436, 510, 553, 574
Lamb, Paul, 495
Lambda Chi Alpha, 432–33, 596, 680, 798; academic performance, 547; housing, 389, 396, 413, 486, 681, 789; merger, 360; racial discrimination, 563–64
Lambert, Byron C., 469
Lancaster, Richard B., 690; appointed president, 582; inauguration, 584; leadership strategy, 606–7; O.B.U. protest, 592–94; presidency, 582–635; resignation, 633, 635; review of presidency, 633–34; town relationship, 631, 634; youth and pre-Simpson career, 582–83
Landon, Alfred M., 363
Landsbury, John J., 187, 503, 739

Lane, Bent, 455, 784
Lane, Bob, 678, 696
Lane, Clayton, 233, 419, 455–56, 462, 476, 484, 487, 783–84; background, 455; missionary controversy, 462–63
Lane, Leota, 292–94, 363
Lane, Lola, 292–94
Langdon, L. C., 400
Language house, 618
Laning, Everett L., 523
Larche, Douglas W., 613, 629, 682
Larsen, Robert, 464, 663–64; appointed to faculty, 471; opera, 472, 551–52; Simpson student, 433
Larson, Anne Ogan, 586
Lathrum, Rick, 599
Lauch, Ada, 738
Lautenbach, Ruth, 362
Lavengood, L. Gene, 394, 424
Laverty, Charles O., 580–81, 620, 637, 651
Laverty, James, 21
Law Department, 72–76; commencement of 1878, 68; defended, 74; discontinued, 76, 101; enrollment, 720; facilities, 73; faculty, 72–73, 75; graduates, 74; management problems, 75–76; method of instruction, 74; opening, 73; opposition to, 73–74; organized, 72–73; revival as unit of Drake U.,76; tuition, 75
Law school. *See* Law Department
Lawton, George A., 770
Layman, James W., 351
Leach, Jim, 630
Leach, Joseph W., 186, 199, 200–201
League for Industrial Democracy, 311
Leake, Howard D., 414
Lear, Norman, 568
Lebeda, Kay, 610, 688
Lecis, Viola, 467
Lee, Chester D., 491
Leek, Marilyn, 672, 815
Leeper, Ross, 433
Leete, Frederick D., 330
Legg, Howard F., 333–34, 375, 392, 408, 772
Lehmann, Sears, Jr., 632
Leicht, William F., 258–59
Lein, Rod, 625–26
Lekberg, Barbara, 653
Lekberg, Mildred, 355, 383, 463, 632, 778, 784
Lekberg, Sven V., 375, 381, 440, 463, 499, 515, 516, 771, 778, 784, 793; appointed music head, 354; death, 654; honorary doctorate, 476–77; smoking, 355; youth and pre-Simpson career, 354–55
Leonard, W. Keith, 809
Lerner, Max, 498
Lester, Bob, 696
Leuchtenburg, William, 265

LeVere, William D., 784
Levitt, Richard S., 588, 651
L.F.V. Sorosis, 54, 117, 727, 731; chartered by Delta Delta Delta, 138; founded, 50–53, 719. See also Delta Delta Delta
L'Heureux, Robert, 815
Library: in 1920s, 272–73; in 1930s, 333, 339; in 1950s, 487, 789–90; budget, 272, 588; collection, 195, 225, 273, 381, 746, 766; Craven Room and Collection, 659–60; security system, 659; staff, 272–73, 753; state minimums, 225, 746. See also Carnegie Library; Dunn Library
Library Planning Committee, 487, 488
Lickiss, Hugh, 598
Liebe, Margaret "Peg." See Watson, Margaret Liebe
Lieber, Clara F., 329
Lieber, Todd, 571, 577
Lierow, James D., 629, 812
Liggett, Jo Hunter, 410
Lincoln, Abraham: elected president, 10; funeral, 33
Lindsey, Ronnie, 678
Link, Arthur, 474
Linn, Janet, 805
Liston, Mrs. Arthur, 148, 184, 357, 732
Literary magazine. See *Rectangle*; *Sequel*; *Simpson Literary Quarterly*
Literary societies, 53, 67; in 1880s, 117; in 1890s, 174–75; in 1910s, 240; in 1920s, 281–82, 755; in 1930s, 317–18; in 1940s, 359. See also Alpian Society; Autokallonian Literary Society; Clionian Society; Crescent Society; Everett Society; Gradatim Society; Kappa Phi Sigma; Lowell Lyceum; Philomathean Society; Pierian Society; Sigma Gamma Rho; Smithsonian Society; Smith-Everett Society; X.Y.Z. Society; Zetalethean Society
Little Chapel, 382
Litzenberg, Clarence C., 426
Loebach, Lyle, 545
Loehr, C. H. G. F., 3
Loft, Henry L., 727
London, Jack, 247
Long, Dean, 328
Loring, V. C., 432
Lorraine Hall: apartments, 357, 408; purchase, 289, 756; sale, 645–46
Lose, Mary K., 653
Lotspeich, Frederick J., 785
Lott, Clifford, 394, 454, 463
Lounsbury, William, 362
Love, Katherine M., 521, 587
Love, Malcolm, 419
Loveless, Herschel, 438
Lowell Lyceum, 175, 240
Lowell Pierean Society, 282

Loyalty oaths, 474–75
Lucas, Robert, xvi
Ludwig, Emil, 363
Lugn, Alvin L., Jr., 394, 425
Lugn, M. Rae, 424
Lutz, Marcia B., 185
Lyddon, Ivan, 585, 608
Lynch, William A., 47, 50, 163
Lynn, Janet, 587

Mabee, C. C., 25, 28, 61
MacBain, Robert A., 538
MacDonald, Kenneth, 449, 518, 568, 629, 782
MacFarland, Mac, 493
MacKenzie, Robert E., 588–89, 610, 681–82
MacLaggan, Katherine, 214, 244
Madison College, 32, 716
Madrigal Singers, 472, 551, 552
Magee, J. Ralph, 371, 374, 380, 382, 769
Magnuson, Gregg E., 523
Magruder, Alan W., 577–78, 596, 610, 670
Maigaard, Melvie, 523
Main, John, 426
Maintenance facility, 489, 645
Major, Al, 768
Majors, 331, 335
Malik, Charles, 457–58
Mallonee, L. Dee, 438
Malone, Helen, 463, 470
Manley, R. W., 3
Mann, Herrold, 402
Mann, Leroy, 739
Manning, Theo, 128
Mansfield, Arabella Babb. See Babb, Arabella
Mansour, Fathi Abdel-Aziz, 578
Marching band, 763
Marcussen, Terry, 625
Marfise, Larry, 678
Mark, R. Lowell, 794
Marker, Connie, 816
Markham, Edwin, 324
Markle, Herbert J., 394, 773
Marlay, Bryan, 678
Marquis, Mary, 457
Marsh, Charles A., 185
Marsh, Daniel L., 347
Marshall, Irl, 249
Martha Matilda Harper Carillon, 540
Martin, A. N., 185
Martin, Claude, 247
Martin, Cynthia, 642
Martin, Elizabeth Cooke. See Cooke, Elizabeth S.
Martin, John D., 185, 213
Martin, Sam, 536
Martin, Stanley, 382
Martin, William C., 103, 112, 733
Marty, Edmund J., 355

Marty, Martin, 689
Mary Berry Hall, 384, 296; dining facilities, 400, 481; named, 206; renovation, 667–68, 671–72. *See also* Ladies' Hall
Masters, Ronald, 761
Mather, David, 816
Mather, J. B., 128, 728
Mathew, Jim, 434
Mathews, Byron C., 104
Mathews, Lee R., 805
Mathias, Ronald, 459
Matthew Simpson Lecturer, 685
Matthew Simpson Room, 671
Mattys, Joe, 809
Mattys, Marilyn, 809
Matz, Mary, 669
Maurois, Andre, 390
Maxson, Eunora, 188
Maxwell, Harold L., 235
Maxwell, Hugh W., 46, 64, 714
May Day, 417
May term. *See* calendar: May term
May, Bill, 233
May, Carroll H., 258
Maynard, Bob, 378
Maynard, Gilbert, 334
Maytag, 480
McAbery, Alice, 745
McAninch, R. E., 482
McBain, Robert A., 381, 797
McBlain, Philip, 501, 516, 549
McBride, J. R., 687
McBride, Luella Hart, 639, 695
McBride, Robert E., 619; appointed president, 637–38; athletics, 675–76; financial controls, 643–44; honorary degrees, 695, 814; inauguration, 642–43; initial assessment of College, 640–41; minority relations, 675; presidency, 639–93; resignation, 695; town-gown relations, 685–86, 821; youth and pre-Simpson career, 638–39
McBride Field, 695
McCarthy, Berthemia, 263, 302
McCarthy, Eugene, 555–56, 567
McCleary, J. D., 46, 716
McCleary, Josie, 731
McClintic, Richard D., 468, 586, 587, 809
McClure, John T., 68–69
McClure, Royal A., 152
McCombs, N. D., 440, 769, 783
McCosh, James, 190
McCoy, A. G., 82
McCoy, Barney, 276
McCoy, Charles "Chic," 276, 773
McCoy, Ivyl, 238
McCoy, Pressley, 532
McCune, C. A., 746
McCutchan, Robert G., 328, 502

McCutcheon, James M., 462, 468, 474
McDonald, John C., 642, 646
McEldowney, James, 438
McEldowney, Philip, 488, 501
McEwan, Eula, 258
McFadden, Barrett, 419, 420
McFarland, John T., 124
McFerrin, Elvin, 167
McGee, Edith, 731
McGee, Ralph, 478, 488, 516, 547, 686, 769, 783
McGowan, Dan, 601
McGraw, Leland, 378, 651, 671
McGraw, Marilyn Scheib, 389
McGraw, Verle, 598
McKean, M. J., 35, 40, 61
McKee, Delber, 394, 424
McKee, Edd, 543
McKee, Edwin R., 470
McKeehan, Morris S., 377, 770
McKendree College, 711–12
McMillen, Edwin L., 139
McMullin, Dick, 417
McNair, H. F., 368
McNeill, Henry H., 818
McNeill, Lettie Judkins, 656–66, 667, 690, 818
McNeill, Thomas H., 818
McNeill Business and Computer Science Center, 665–67; design, construction, and dedication, 666–67; Lettie McNeill donation, 665–66
McPherrin, Fannie H., 128
Mead, Margaret, 600
Means, Bob, 378
Meccawees, 243
Mechanical and Electrical Engineering Building: constructed, 158; conversion to gymnasium, 166
Medical school proposal, 77
Meek, Joe, 276, 415, 632
Meek, Kate, 124
Meints, Clifford L., 528; antifraternity views, 491; appointed Carver Professor, 478; appointed to faculty, 465; creationist views, 476; NSF grant, 478
Melson, Eugene R., 349
Mercer, Kenneth "Moco," 276, 434, 754
Mercer, William, 128, 728
Meredith, E. T., 256
Meredith, Frank, 737
Meredith, Katie, 637
Meredith, W. H., 770
Meredith Corporation, 671
Merger proposal, 227–28
Merkle, Jane M., 424, 464, 784
Merkle, Paul A., 394, 463
Merritt, Don, 593

Metcalf, Kenneth E., 637
Methodist Board of Education, 301, 302, 331, 457, 757; Forward Movement challenge, 430
Methodist Book Concern, 309
Methodist Church: merger, 813; temperance views, 44
Methodist conferences in Iowa: colleges sponsored, 733; conferences merger, 794; merger proposal, 227–28. *See also* Des Moines Conference; Iowa Annual Conference; Iowa Area; Iowa-Des Moines Conference; Western Iowa Conference
Methodist higher education: early history in America, xiii–xvi
Methodist Student Movement, 493, 549
Meyers, Bruce G., 809
Michener, Elizabeth, 164, 187
Mick, Bernard, 378
Middleton, Arthur, 187
Midland Conference, 427, 779–80
Miggins, J. K., 632
Mikulanec, Peg S., 688
Milholland, Dr. and Mrs., 146–47, 149
Military Academy, 191
Military training: established, 139–40; in 1890s, 168–70; in 1900s, 204–5; in 1910s, 219, 231–32, 745; during WWI, 232, 233–34, 747; WWII proposal, 376–77; Korean War proposals, 422–23
Miller, B. F., 731
Miller, Bob, 411
Miller, C. Max, 486
Miller, Earl, 419
Miller, Edna Dean, 384, 395–96, 772
Miller, Edward L., 152, 161, 184, 214, 258, 265, 303–304, 308, 334, 386
Miller, Emory, 141, 733, 739
Miller, Frank, 121
Miller, Henry. *See* al-Tunisi, Jamal
Miller, Herbert E., 334
Miller, J. Wesley, 380
Miller, Laura, 602, 773
Miller, Otis E., 785
Miller, Paul, 768
Miller, R. G. "Hap," 393–94, 411, 412, 434, 464, 622, 777
Miller, Ron, 798
Miller, Roy L., 486, 782
Miller, Suzanne, 647, 649
Miller, Taylor C., 268
Miller, Virginia J., 334
Miller, William E., 68, 73, 75, 76, 101
Mills, John, 411
Minasian, Mary J., 473
Minasian, Samuel, 472, 499, 551
Miner, Tom, 676
Mineral Water Bowl, 597
Miniature Orpheum, 296, 363, 390, 417, 437, 550, 601, 768, 778, 807

Minority Emphasis Week, 685, 690
Minority students: recruitment, 561–62, 674–75. *See also* black students
Miss White's School for Young Ladies, 3
Mission Band, the, 177
Mitchell, Bennett, 34
Mitchell, John C., 75, 101, 112, 733
Mitchell, Nina V. *See* Goltry, Nina V.
Mitchell, Ormsby M., 727
Mixner, David, 567
Miyada, Santaro, 133, 730
Mizell, Stella, 785
Moats, Bob, 362
Moats, Francis I., 259–60, 281, 292, 311, 336, 345, 347, 351, 375, 395, 404, 415, 426, 429, 464, 759, 769; appointed dean, 331; appointed to faculty, 259; death, 503; history of College, vii, 500; pre-Simpson career, 259
Moats Park, 504
Mobberley, David, 394, 422, 424, 425, 429, 437, 454, 463, 476, 779, 784
Mock chapel, 296, 437
Montagno, George L., 496, 785
Moody, Joe, 611–12
Moore, Bob, 434
Moore, Gladys M., 465, 809
Moore, Kathleen R., 800
Moore, N. B., 56, 65
Moore, Orville F., 496, 785
Morain, Claude, 414
Morehouse, D. W., 329, 347
Morgan, Chester, 393, 415, 424, 425
Morgan, H. C., 155
Morgan, VeAnna, 521
Morgan, Walter A., 770
Morison, Samuel Eliot, 189
Morley, Hattie Berry, 206, 552
Morley, John P., 224, 226, 235, 502, 745, 748; appointed to faculty, 213; board member, 206; death, 552; financial secretary, 255; recollections of Carver, 147–48; save Old Chapel drive, 254–55; as Simpson student, 138–39, 175, 244; Special Centennial Citation, 500
Morris, Evelyn, 517, 543, 574, 585, 591
Morrison, Bertha C., 118
Morrison, Marie, 719
Morrison, Susan F., 67, 70
Mortar Board, 492
Moses, Fredric W., 816
Mosher, Herbert B., 804
Mott, D. C., 768
Mott, Frank Luther, 365, 376; appointed to faculty, 260–61; death, 553; literary magazine sponsor, 284
Mott, Vera Ingram, 552
Moulton, Phillips, 137, 454, 457, 461, 476, 784
Move to Des Moines: 1877–78 controversy, 80–

81; 1879 controversy, 93, 95–96; late 1880s controversy, 141–42
Movies, 292
Moy, Sing Bo, 386
Mukoyama, Helen Takehara, 382
Mukoyama, Kazuo Wesley, 382
Mullican, Cora B., 292
Mullican, Len, 292
Mullican, Leota. *See* Lane, Leota
Mullican, Lola. *See* Lane, Lola
Mullin, Helen Malone, 463, 470
Mullin, Jess S., 470, 510
Mundt, Karl, 417
Munns, Cora, 776
Mu Phi Epsilon, 244, 280, 401, 415, 492, 601
Murlin, Lemuel H., 747
Murphy, A. H., 21, 714
Music: in 1880s, 136–37; in 1900s, 186–87; in 1920s, 270–72; in 1940s, 404; in 1950s, 473; in 1963–68, 551–52; in 1979–87, 663–65; administration of, 186, 199–200, 270–71, 272; Bachelor of Music, 271; Bachelor of Music Education, 786; Barrows-Emslie rivalry, 200–201; curriculum, 271; degree requirements, 473; department established, 136–37; first degrees awarded, 739; merger of Conservatory, 353–54, 355; performance, 271; program leadership, 735; quarters in early 1900s, 192–93. *See also* Barrows, Frank E.; Harvey, Herbert A.; Larsen, Robert; Lekberg, Sven V.; Madrigal Singers; opera
Music Annex, 400–401
Music building. *See* Amy Robertson Music Center; Barrows Hall; Conservatory of Music Building; Music Annex
Music Education National Conference, 601
Myers, Belle, 776
Myers, Cloice, 323
Myers, Cynthia L., 654, 817
Myers, Howard, 378
Myers, Larry A., 543, 575
Myers, Ray F., 769

N.A.I.A., 435, 497, 598, 807
Name (College): "Ames College," 27; shortened, 120; "Simpson Centenary College," 29, 31, 120, 716
Nance, Walter B., 784–85
Nash, Arnold, 458
National Air Mail Week, 337
National Association of Intercollegiate Athletics. *See* N.A.I.A.
National Association of Schools of Music, 404, 775
National Collegiate Athletic Association. *See* N.C.A.A.
National Defense Student Loan Program, 542–43

National Education Association, 492
National Endowment for the Humanities, 646
National Vocational Guidance Association, 406
Naylor, Douglas, 249
N.C.A.A., 167, 435, 598, 625–26
Neades, Harriet, 336
Nedelman, Marla, 806
Neely, T. B., 120
Neff, LeRoy N., 399, 402
Neff Field, 401–2, 659, 774
Neill, Thomas A., 170, 737
Nelson, Donald W., 472
Nelson, Robert, 645, 646
Nelson, Wallace L., Jr., 579
Nelson, Wayne, 524
Nero, Peter, 552
Neutra, Richard, 488, 788; appointed campus architect, 484; fraternity house design, 486–87; library design, 487–88, 790, 818
New Century Fund, 479–80
New Christie Minstrels, 552
Newell, Ida Pierce. *See* Pierce, Ida
Newell, Mamie, 731
Newell, Steve, 682
Newland, Lillian A., 164, 167
Newlin, Owen, 696
Newman, Dean, 778
Newman, Jennie W., 185
Newman Club, 493
Newspaper, student. *See Simpsonian*
Newton, E. S., 426
Nicholls, James N., 2
Nichols, Frank, 662
Niels, Jackie, 819
Niemeyer, Karin E., 816
Night classes, 137, 644
Nightingale, Augustus F., 61, 719
Ninde, W. X., 103, 122
Niseis, 390
Nixon, Richard, 567, 573, 633
Noble, B. S., 8, 13, 15, 112
Noble, Darrell, 624
Noble, Gary, 598
Noble, Howard, 236, 265, 365, 419, 420
Noble, Louise, 719
Noble, Mattie T., 112
Nolan, R. M., 205, 219
Noland, Gerald, 495
Nolte, M. Chester, 336–37
Nordstrum, Mary M., 218–19, 744
Normal School, 164. *See also* normal training; teacher training
Normal training: at Indianola Male and Female Seminary, 22; school established, 137. *See also* teacher training
Norseworthy, Stanley J., 525
North Central Association, 284, 619–20, 746; athletic scholarships, 435, 546. *See also* accreditation

Northwest Area Foundation, 646
Norton, James R., 804
Noseworthy, Jim, 568, 684
Noss, William T., 151, 162–63
Nott, David, 472, 551
Nowasell, Frank, 588, 610, 680
Nurses training, 429
Nyman, Bertil C., 806

O'Connell, John, 678
O'Flyng, Mamie, 164
O.B.U. *See* Organization for Black Unity
Oberstein, Bennett T., 809
Off-Campus Coeds, 359, 389, 414
Officer, Walter, 276
Ogden, Gary, 544
Ohnemus, Kathy, 650
Oktoberfest, 618
Oldani, John L., 522, 530, 577
Old Bluebird: completion, 25; construction, 21; construction proposed, 15; contract for, 16; destroyed by storm, 57–58; fund-raising for, 16; name origin, 21; opening, 21; plans for, 16
Old Brick, 315, 389, 397, 749
Old Chapel: bookstore, 358, 774; ghost of, 325, 685; Little Chapel built, 382; reconstruction (first), 254–55, 751; reconstruction (second), 668–71; student union, 382–83; theater, 401. *See also* College Hall
Olive, Everett "Tip," 199, 244, 246, 745; appointed to faculty, 186; College songs composer, 186; death, 502; resignation, 271
Olive, John A., 34, 101
Ollrich, Gus, 791
Olson, Albert L., 785
Omicron: demise, 357, 359, 767; founded, 280, 755
Omicron Delta Kappa, 492, 601, 808
Oneal, H. H., 65
Opera: performance established, 472; in 1963–68, 551–52; in 1973–87, 663–64
Oplt, Jymm, 598, 696
Opstad, Sumner "Sandy," 646
Oratory: in 1860s, 43; in 1890s, 175; in early 1900s, 185; in 1930s, 318; role in College, 65–66; state contest won, 207. *See also* forensics
Organization for Black Unity, 565; protest actions, 591–94; reconstituted, 628. *See also* Black Students Organization; Concerned Black Students
Orpheus Festival, 665
Orr, Marcelyn Taggart, 336
Orrell, Martha S., 806
Ortega y Gasset, José, 641
Osborn, Wayne, 494
Osceola Seminary, 5, 24, 715
Oskaloosa College, 76

Ott, Melanie, 618
"Outlaws," 280
Overseas study, 658–59
Overton, Barbara, 599
Overton, Everett, 772
Overton, Grace, 640, 642, 651, 688
Owen, Ruth Bryan, 363
Oxford Club, 281
Oxford Exchange Program, 459–60, 501, 528–29
Oxford Stone, 459–60, 540
Oxnam, G. Bromley, 340, 345, 347, 364, 765
Oysters, 174

Pace, Earl, 549
Pace, Floyd, 467
Packard, Vance, 550, 600
Padgett, Jack, 462, 488, 524, 790
Page, Carrie Merrill, 143
Page, Rachel, 386
Page, Stephen R., 111, 733
Panamanian students, 390
Panhellenic Council, 295
Paone, Albert S., 544, 578, 597, 598
Park Hall, 396
Parker, George F., 23, 65, 80, 721
Parker, Henry, 565, 593
Parker, L. F., xvii
Parks, Charles H., 727
Parks, Edward L., 99, 208; appointed President, 100; death, 123, 324; fund-raising, 102–3, 122; later career, 123; presidency, 100–25; principles, 123; resignation, 122–23; youth and pre-Simpson career, 100–4
Parks, Isabella Webb, 103, 110
Parmelee, John D., xi
Parrott, R. B., 95
Parsons, 227
Parsons, Galusha, 73, 75
Parsons, Ruth Greenwalt, 383
Password, 358, 548, 778
Patrick, Rich, 683
Patterson, Fannie, 128, 728
Patton, Emma, 66, 70, 719
Payne, Edith M., 230
Payne, Winfred E., 302, 303, 330, 752–53, 759; appointed to faculty, 268; dean, 304; later career, 349; reappointment controversy, 341–44, 347–49, 764–65; socialist views, 311–12; termination, 765
"Payne Case," 341–44, 347–49, 764–65
Payseur, Victoria, 648
Pease, Fred, 495
Pelter, A. Ivan, 408, 430
Pension fund (Methodist Church), 308, 409
Pension plan: proposed, 229, 308; post WWII, 408–9, 776; in 1963–68, 520, 794; in 1979–87, 656

People's Trust and Savings Bank, 817
Perkins, Judson, 450, 479
Perkins, Lester, 65, 76
"Perpetual scholarships," 197, 228, 309–10
Perrilles, Donald W., 816
Perrin, Naoma, 382
Perrine, Mark, 626
Perry, Albertus, 286
Perry, Elias W., 94, 111
Peters, Bill, 471
Petersen, Richard, 609
Peterson, Charles N. "Ned," 517, 543
Peterson, Douglas, 809
Peterson, Stuart, 393, 422, 464, 503, 779, 784
Peyre, Henri, 795
Peyroux, Eugene A., Jr., 522, 547
Pfeiffer, Annie Merner, 429, 780
Pfeiffer Hall, 788; construction, 481; renovation, 589
Pharo, Sandra, 596
Phelps, Emma Sue, 469, 785
Phi Alpha, 491. *See also* Sigma Alpha Epsilon
Phi Alpha Theta, 682
Phi Beta Kappa, 281, 492
Phi Beta Lambda, 682
Phi Beta Sigma, 628
Phi Delta Kappa, 203
Phi Kappa Psi, 175, 727; chapter founded, 118–19; disbanded, 738
Phi Lambda Mu. *See* Sigma Alpha Epsilon
Phillips, Carol A., 613, 656
Phillips, Elsie Bingaman, 673
Phillips, Milton E., 128, 151
Phillips, William, 65, 72, 111
Philomathean Society, 174, 175
Philpott, Emily, 396, 426, 773
Phi Mu Alpha Sinfonia, 244, 280, 324, 415, 417, 493, 548, 601
Phi Mu Gamma, 281
Phonathon, 227, 647, 673
Physical culture, 185
Physical education, 404; major established, 379; requirement, 217–18
Physical education center. *See* Cowles Center
Physical Education Majors Club, 601
Pi Beta Phi, 175, 203, 389, 437–38, 682; academic performance, 359, 414; centennial, 597; housing, 315. *See also* I.C. Sorosis
Piccard, Kathryn Ann, 633, 813
Pickard, Mrs. Clarence, 768
Picken, Robert F., 646–47, 651, 819
Picnics, 246–47
Pierce, Carleton B., 233
Pierce, Ida M., 63, 91, 101, 104, 105, 116, 778
Pierce, J. N., 105
Pierian Society, 240
Piffer, John, 290
Piffer, Robert, 387

Pi Gamma Mu, 281, 415
Pi Kappa Delta, 280, 318, 359, 415, 492, 548, 601, 629, 747–48, 760
Pi Kappa Phi, 778; academic performance, 433; chapter established, 413–14; demise, 433, 781
Pillsbury, Jacie Arnold, 673
Pinnell, Robert W., 574, 665
Piskacek, J. K., 804
Place, B. A., 185
Planned Parenthood of Iowa, 658
Pohle, Helen L., 263
Pomerat, Roland, 540
Poppen, Marcella M., 809
Posegate, Martha, 48
Postel, Paula, 272
Pote, Harold F., 249, 419, 541, 777, 783, 798
Pote Theatre, 541
Poteete, C. Lanette, 816
Potter, John D., 394, 424, 464
Poundstone, Odis C., 383, 398–400, 402
Powell, W. F., 96
Pranks, 173
Prather, Dean, 419, 632, 651
Prather, Ruth, 671
Pratt, Ira, 271
Prayer meetings, 177, 290
Preministerial education, 403
Preparatory department. *See* academy
President's house, 358, 590
Presidents of College. *See* Vernon, Samuel M.; Burns, Alexander; Berry, Thomas S.; Parks, Edward L.; Hamilton, William E.; Holmes, Edmund M.; Brown, Fletcher; Harris, Joseph B.; Shelton, Charles E.; Strickland, Francis L.; Campbell, James W.; Hillman, John L.; Harper, Earl E.; Gross, John O.; Voigt, Edwin E.; Kerstetter, William E.; John, Ralph C.; Lancaster, Richard B.; McBride, Robert E.; Jennings, Stephen G.
Press, David, 523
Pressley, John T., 3
Price, Donald H., 772
Price, Uberto, 394, 424
Princess, 360
Proctor, Carroll M., 816
Prohibition. *See* temperance
Proudfoot, A. V., 159, 761, 772; board president, 236, 256, 286, 308, 309; dancing controversy, 322–23; death, 333, 762
Proudfoot, Clyde, 236, 256, 748, 752, 753
Proudfoot, Elias, 114, 132, 193
Proudfoot, Inez, 752
Proudfoot, Willis: Administration Building architect, 192; Carnegie Library architect, 195; Central Building architect, 238; Conservatory of Music Building architect, 192; heating plant architect, 193; Hopper Gymnasium architect, 222–23; Ladies' Hall

architect, 133–34; Science Hall architect, 131–32
Prussner, Frederick C., 773
Pryor, Carl, 753
Pub, 596
Publications, student, 282–84. *See also* Password; Rectangle; Sequel; Simpson Literary Quarterly; Simpsonian; songbook; Tangent; Zenith
Publications board, 282, 436
Pullman, David E., 426, 463, 470–71, 785
Purcell, L. Edward, 529, 544
Purinton, Edward, 265
Pyle, Idell, 754

Quarterback Club, 361
Quasquicentennial, 688–91
Quinn, Barbara A., 626, 809
Qutub, Musa, 546, 550, 799

Rabuck, Andy, 362
Radio, 292
Ragland, Jack, 522, 540
Railroad, 58, 723
Railroad dispatching courses, 724
Rambow, Ralph, 784
Randolph, Albert, 8
Randolph, Gerald R., 804
Randolph-Macon College, xv
Rea, Earnest A., 733, 739, 753
Read, Alastair, 550
Read, J. C., 10, 13, 16, 23, 34
Read, William B., 184, 206, 249
Reagan, Ronald, 363
Recreation: in late 1860s, 44; in 1880s, 119–20; in 1890s, 173–74; in 1900s, 206–7, 245–46; in 1930s, 324; in 1940s, 389–90; in early 1950s, 437
Recruitment, 407, 423, 460, 561–62, 608–9, 779
Rectangle, 284
"Red and Gold," 161
Redmen: name adopted, 278; name changed, 698
Red Scare, 263–64
Redwomen (name), 599
Reed, Mike, 362, 388, 768
Reeves, Danny, 597
Refior, Everett, 425, 464, 785
Reichard, Jacob, 36–37
Reid, Andrew G., 276
Reisman, Paul, 355, 385, 767
Religious activities: in 1900s, 205; in 1910s, 245; in early 1950s, 436–37; in 1954–63, 493; in 1963–68, 549; in 1970s & 1980s, 684. *See also* revivalism
Religious callings, 245
Religious diversity, 245, 493, 791. *See also* student body demographics

Religious Emphasis Week, 436
Religious Life Council, 382
Remediation, 562, 572, 646
Renich, Katharine, 302, 351, 759
Reno, Milo, 311
Repplinger, Jack, 791
Residence halls. *See* dormitories; *and individual building names*
Resource Program, 581–82, 588
retention. *See* attrition; student retention
Retirement age, 409
Retirement benefit, faculty. *See* pension plan
Revivalism: in 1880s, 106; in 1890s, 176; in 1900s, 203, 205; in 1910s, 245. *See also* religious activities
Rho Alpha, 119. *See also* Alpha Tau Omega
Rhodes, Ellis, 244
Rhodes, June Hamilton, 218, 241, 244, 744
Rice, Grantland, 273
Rich, Buddy, 600
Richards, Elvin "Kink," 313–14, 759
Richards, M., 22
Richardson, Irene, 667
Richardson, Jim, 808
Riebhoff, Lorena, 785
Riegel, Roberta, 352, 375, 395, 463, 467, 784
Riggs, Dixon L., 425–26, 463, 785
Riggs, Edith, 188
Riggs, Martha K., 329
Riker, Stanton A., 431
Ritenour, Ron, 598
Ritland, Lloyd O., 425, 463, 785
Robbins, Glaydon, 392, 394, 777
Roberts, Patricia T., 521
Roberts, Thomas L., 264
Robertson, Amy, 671; biography, 660–61; charitable support, 661–62; death, 696; estate gift, 696; trustee, 449, 518, 574, 661, 783
Robertson, David A., 284
Robinson, Bert, 378
Robinson, Daniel, 205
Robinson, Ed, 598
Robinson, James A., 518, 574, 584
Robinson, Jessie S., 236
Robinson, John S., 266
Robinson, R. S., 10, 714
Rock, Charles S., 543
Rockefeller Foundation. *See* General Education Board
Rockey, Ward H., 280, 755
Rockne, Knute, 273
Roe, Blanche A., 214
Rogers, E. B., 235
Rogers, Ellis J., 737
Rogers, Elton B., 737
Rogers, James H., 565, 586, 629, 674
Rohm, Charles E. "Chuck," 696
Rojas, Sergio, 550

Romans, J. B., 733
Ronan, Richard J., 587, 805
Room. *See* cost of attendance
Roose, Alice E., 362
Roosevelt, Franklin D., 384, 391
Roosevelt, Theodore, 202
Roseman, Fannie, 743
Ross, Earle, 237
Ross, J. B., 737
Ross, Ken, 496
Ross, Peter, 256, 426, 544, 745; appointed Hopper janitor, 224; death, 429; honored, 412; introducer of soccer, 242; literary recitation, 429
R.O.T.C., 422–23, 476, 528
Rowan, Carl T., 459
Rudolph, Frederick, 189
Ruffer, David R., 642
Rugby, 625
Ruggeri, Evadne P., 521
Ruggles, Allen M., 213
Rumble, Chester A., 785
Runnells, J. S., 72, 75
Russell, Bill, 802
Russell, Howard, 75
Rutz, Daniel, 809

SAE. *See* Sigma Alpha Epsilon
Safley, Myra, 424, 425
Sager, Donald "Red," 387
Said, Abdul Aziz, 550
Salaries, faculty: in 1868, 40; in 1878–79, 722; in 1879–80, 723; in 1910s, 215, 228–29, 236; in 1930s, 304–6,332–33, 338, 339, 350–51, 762; in 1940s, 385; post WWII, 408, 776; in 1953–63, 464, 475–76; in 1963–68, 520, 794; in 1968–75, 587–88; in 1975–79, 611; 1979–87, 647, 656; arrears, 79, 94, 95, 721, 722, 723; men's vs. women's, 717. *See also* pension plan
Saleno, Cornelia, 128, 152
Salsbury, Doris, 662
Samp, Walter A., 783
Sampson, Henry E., 765, 769
Samson, E. D., 366, 739, 753–54
Samson, George W., 67, 69, 70, 75
Samson, J. F., 224
Samson, Robert J., 351, 392–93, 404, 415, 773
Samuelson, Agnes, 329, 440, 449, 762, 769, 783
Sanchez, Ramon F., 433
Sandburg, Carl, 296
Sandy, Mary J., 741
Sandy, Merle F., 785
Sankey, Laurie, 679
Sargent, A. E., 783
S.A.T.C. *See* Students Army Training Corps
Saturday classes, 473–74
Saudi Arabs, 618

Saunders, Craig, 545
Sawyer, John, 413
Sayegh, Fayez, 498
Sayre, Alice, 419, 671, 821
Sayre, John, 493
Sayre, Raymond, 502, 782
Sayre, Ruth Buxton, 419, 518, 574, 686, 785
"Scalp Song," 292, 363–64
Schafer, Janet, 679, 820
Scheib, Marilyn, 389
Scherle, Bill, 566, 599
Scheuermann, Walter M., 449, 686, 770, 783
Schier, Steve, 591, 807
Schlick, Dot, 387
Schloss, Gertrude B., 541
Schloss, Sam M., 541
Schmidt, Ludwig J., 737
Schmidt, Robert W., 785
Schmidt, Tom, 696
Scholarships, 696; for children of clergy, 338–39; costs, 407; endowed ("perpetual"), 197, 228, 309–10; for minorities, 562. *See also* athletics: scholarships; financial aid; grants-in-aid
Schooley, Helen, 402
Schooley, W. H., 157, 170, 174
School of Art, 136, 161, 164, 188, 191
School of Business, 136, 164, 190, 265–66, 748; merger, 303–304. *See also* business administration
School of Education and Special Courses, 190
School of Music, 136. *See also* music
School of Oratory and Physical Culture, 164, 185, 190
School of Shorthand and Typewriting, 164, 190
Schoonover, David, 784
Schorndorf, 659
Schreiber, James A., 523, 785
Schroer, A. Bruce, 494, 784
Schultz, Gerard, 393, 424, 776, 777
Schwank, Dennis M., 521
Schwartz, Benjamin F., 764–65
Schwarz, Amy, 616, 810
Science Hall: construction, 131–33; dedication, 133; design, 131–32; renamed, 534; renovation, 534–35
Scientific and Normal Hall. *See* Science Hall
S Club, 320, 361, 493, 548, 601
Scott, Benjamin D., 235
Scott, Celeste, 715
Scott, D. R., 348
Scott, Franklin D., 263, 281
Scott, Helen Giddings, 263, 752
Scott, Howard, 311
Scott, John H. L., 715
Scott, Levi, 33
Scott, Mary, 718
Scott, Pippa, 568

Scott, Robert H., 424
Scouting, 415–16
Scudder, M. L., xiv
Seaton, Daniel G., 280, 462, 543, 575, 586, 784
Seaton, John L., 340, 342–43, 354
Secure the Promise for Simpson, 694–96
Sedgwick, Hiram G., 158–60; death, 249; early career, 158; later career, 160; Simpson engineering program, 158–60
Seeger, Raymond, 530
Seevers, George W., 64, 85
Seley, Daryl, 412
Sells, Alan, 699
Sells, Arthur, 241
Sells, B. F., 768
Seminary. *See* Indianola Male and Female Seminary
Seney, Noel "Red," 673
Sequel, 416, 494, 548, 629
Sevareid, Eric, 600
Sewell, Elizabeth, 630
Sex, 44, 291, 606, 808
Shafer, Doug, 598
Shandley, Mary, 669
Shaner, David, 809
Shank, Kennon, 773
Shannon, Pat, 553
Sharp, Wick, 383
Shaw, E. E., 769
Shaw, Ethel, 254
Shaw, Leslie M., 74, 170, 324
Shaw, Oscar, 124
Shaw, R. E., 229, 731
Shea, Tim, 591
Shelley, Jack, 390, 725–26
Shelley, Lori, 679
Shelley, Stephen, 726
Shelly, Kate, 110–11, 249, 725, 726
Shelton, Charles E., 606, 733; appointed president, 182; construction program, 192–96; education critic, 198–99; farewell address, 209; honorary degree, 739; later career, 743; presidency, 181–209; reputation, 198; resignation, 207, 743; travels, 199; youth and pre-Simpson career, 181–82
Shelton, Julia, 206, 743
Shelton, Whitford, 203, 687
Shenton, Seth, 323
Shepherd, Rebecca C., 185
Shipman, Ray M., 318, 783
Shultz, John, 276
Sialmas, Nick, 810
Siefkas, M. L. "Jack," 543, 574
Sigler, David S., 103, 733
Sigler, F. Carl, 256, 366, 741, 745, 775
Sigler, Henry C., 28, 34; board member, 65, 195, 211; financial support of College, 42, 56, 103; personal background, 34–35

Sigler, Sara, 315, 382, 741, 769; death, 402; home economics sponsor, 218–19; Sigler Home Economics Center, 398, 402–3; youth and career, 774–75
Sigler Home Economics Center, 398, 402–3
Sigma Alpha Epsilon, 175, 596, 680; academic performance, 547; chapter founded, 138–39; coat-of-arms caper, 681; disbanded, 738; housing, 486–88; rechartered, 486, 491
Sigma Chapter Silhouettes, 628
Sigma Delta Chi: chartered by Theta Kappa Nu, 279–80; founded, 279. *See also* Theta Kappa Nu, Lambda Chi Alpha
Sigma Gamma Rho: founded, 318; demise, 359
Sigma Tau Delta, 281, 284, 415, 416, 492, 548, 682
Silcott, Lewis, 10
Silliman, Effie, 200, 244, 742
Silliman, Lucy, 195
Silver dollar campaign, 766
Simmons, Tom, 565, 597, 599, 629
Simpkins, Warren, 378
Simpson, Ida, 325
Simpson, Cuthbert A., 459
Simpson, Mary L., 771
Simpson, Matthew, 84, 325; bas-relief, 120–21, 727; belief in progress, 33–34, 107–8; biographies, 716; commencement address, 107–8; death, 114, 120; elected bishop, 33; Lincoln funeral oration, 33; on church democracy, 34; political influence, 32, 33; portrait of, 485; preaching and oratorical skill, 32, 33; professor and college administrator, 32; reputation, 31–32, 33, 34; visit to College, 106–8; youth and education, 32
Simpson, Sarah E., 325, 331
Simpson Athletic Club, 627, 812
Simpson Centenary College (name), 29, 31, 120, 716
Simpson Code, 549, 558
Simpson College (name). *See* name (College)
Simpson College Battalion. *See* military training
Simpson College Bulletin, 275, 302, 358–59. *See also Alumni News Bulletin*
Simpson College Independent Men's Organization, 415
Simpson College Songbook. *See* songbook
Simpson College Sustaining Fund, 542
Simpson-Community Symphony Orchestra, 551
Simpson Dames, 415
Simpson Development Council, 478
Simpson Extension Association, 229
Simpson Forum, 614–15, 685
Simpson Guild, 690, 821; founded, 383–84
Simpsonian: founding and first issue, 49–50, 51; in 1880s, 117; in 1890s, 172; in 1910s, 248–49;

in 1920s, 283; in 1930s, 318, 358; post WWII, 416; in early 1950s, 435; in 1953–63, 494; in 1963–68, 548; in 1968–75, 601, 803; in 1975–79, 629; in 1979–87, 682–83; continuous publication, 718
Simpson-Indianola Community Field, 659
Simpson-Indianola Symphony, 472
Simpson Literary Quarterly, 284
Simpson Memorial Hall, 114, 726
Simpson Ministerial Association, 176
Simpson Seminary (Brookville, Adams County), 24, 715
Simpson Storm (name), 698
Simpson Veterans Association, 570
Simpson-Wesley Development Campaign, 286–89, 756
Singer, Patricia B., 653
Sirianni, John, 677, 698
S.I.S. Club, 389, 414
Sjeklocha, Evo, 362, 388
Skinner, Cornelia Otis, 390
Slang, 294, 757
Slate, Thomas C., 525, 528
Slick, Samuel L., 806
Sloan, Frank, 187
Slocum, Robert E., 737
Slothower, A. E., 171–72
Small, Brad, 621, 810
Smith, Alden C., 536, 686
Smith, Alida, 479, 537–40, 632, 797
Smith, Claude, 470
Smith, David N., 28, 101–2, 174, 724
Smith, David O., 479, 537–40, 797
Smith, E. B., 660
Smith, Fern, 245
Smith, Fred C., 365, 603
Smith, H. Lester, 347
Smith, Horace G., 770
Smith, Inis, 273, 385, 759
Smith, J. Raymond, 267, 280, 755
Smith, Kenneth E., 622, 642
Smith, Louis E., Jr., 518, 574, 610
Smith, Mary, 302
Smith, O. E., 254
Smith, R. M., 65
Smith, W. T., 733
Smith, William C., 49, 50, 112, 365–66
Smith-Everett Society, 175
Smith Memorial Chapel, 536–40; dedication, 539–40; design controversy, 537–38; design, 539; donors, 537, 538
Smithsonian Society, 67, 174, 175
Smoking, 355; in 1880s, 115, 116, 137, 726; in 1890s, 177; in 1910s, 750; in 1920s, 290; post WWII, 410; in 1950s, 495; in 1987–93, 698
S.N.A.P., 673
Snyder, Richard D., 587, 805
Soccer, 242, 546

Socialism on campus: in 1910s, 247–48; in 1920s, 264; in 1930s, 311–12; in 1970s, 629. *See also* Payne, Winfred E.
Social Security, 426
Sociology, 260
Sociology Club, 493
Sockman, Ralph, 337
Soddy, Frederick, 311
Soderblom, Carol, 612
Soelberg, Chris, 245
Softball, 599, 626, 679
Soliday, Don, 498
Song, College, 161
Songayllo, Ray, 524
Songbook: *Carmina Simpsonii Collegii*, 58; second edition, 172–73; 1910 edition, 208; 1924 edition, 284; 1939 edition, 359
Sorden, Kay, 772
Sorden, Mike, 463, 497, 792, 809
Sorden, Myron L., 393
Sororities (social): first chapters established, 50–53; in 1880s, 117–19; in 1890s, 175–76, 738; in 1900s, 203; in 1910s 244; in 1920s, 280–81; in 1930s, 315, 359–60; in 1940s, 389; post WWII, 414; in early 1950s, 433–34; in 1953–63, 492; in 1968–75, 597; in 1975–79, 628; in 1979–87, 682; deferred rushing, 492. *See also* Greeks; *and names of individual fraternities and sororities*
Southard, Carrie, 156, 734
South Iowa Conference (Methodist), 479
Spanish, 758
Spanish-American War, 170, 737
Specht, Luella, 424, 463, 524, 784
Special Programs, 644, 646
Special Services, 617
Speed, Maxine, 544, 805
Spence, Dorothy, 360
Spencer, Tony, 544
Spiller, Robert, 474
Sports. *See* athletics; intramural sports; *and names of individual sport*
Sprague, Eugene H., 782
Sprague, Thelma Talbot, 316
Spray, Nancy, 111
Spriecher, Grace, 776
Spring, Lester E., 272, 336, 360, 503, 759
Springer, Irene L., 754
St. John, Robert, 417
Stacy, Bertha S., 161
Stadt, Bessie W., 521
Stagg, Amos Alonzo, 202
Stahl, Carolyn, 805
Stahl, Eva F., 259, 282, 302, 351, 755, 759
Stahl, Martha. *See* Beall, Martha Stahl
Stanley, E. G., 314
Stanley, Forrester C., 779
Stanley-Dean System, 314, 760

Index

Stark, Eleanor M., 151, 161
Starr, Richard B., 523, 545, 598, 624–25, 627
Steinem, Gloria, 600
Stennes, Clarence, 525
Stevens, Samuel N., 376
Stevens, Truman S., 769
Stevenson, Adlai, 438
Stewart, Elizabeth A., 302
Stewart, Jerome, 598, 678
Stewart, Joel G., 620
Stewart, Nancy Yeend, 809
Stewart, W. C., 772
Stewart, Walter "Stub," 749
Steyer, Ida B., 185,199, 206
Stickle, Fred E., 809
Stimson, Pauline, 363, 377, 379, 388
Stock market crash, 299–300
Stockton, Beverly, 520, 809
Stolen, Steve, 630
Stone, Elizabeth, 424, 773
Stone, Hurford, 233, 365, 419; acting presidency, 509–12; appointed acting president, 509; death, 553; town-gown relations, 511–12; youth and career, 509–10
Stone, Mary Samson, 509
Stone, S. R., 34
Stoner, Barbara, 497, 525
Storey, John A., 256
Stout, Gilbert G., 426, 439
Stover, George R., 17–18, 20
Strauss, S., 94
Streaking, 601–2
Streaty, Gary, 637, 638, 642, 675, 676
Streit, Tom, 618
Strickland, Francis L., 208; appointed president, 208; death, 503; presidency, 211–28; resignation, 228, 746; youth and pre-Simpson career, 211–12
Strohm, John, 417
Strom, Herman, 387
Strovers, David, 598
Strovers, Helen, 667
Stuart, Carol, 551
Stuart, Charles H., 528–29, 794
Stuart, Roxie, 735
Stuart, T. McKendree, 111, 727, 733
Student body demographics: in 1910, 191–92; in 1910–20, 220; in 1920s, 253; in 1938, 765; in 1960s, 531; in 1968–75, 581; in 1987–93, 697. *See also* religious diversity
Student Congress, 364
Student Council, 240
Student Educational Association, 492, 548, 601
Student employment, 310
Student evaluation. *See* course evaluation
Student-Faculty Federation, 332, 762
Student Fellowship, 493
Student government: organized, 140, 731; in 1910s, 239–40; in 1920s, 294; in 1930s, 319; in 1940s, 364; in 1950s, 490; in 1963–68, 548; in 1975–79, 629; in 1979–87, 683. *See also* College Council; Collegiate Council; Interfraternity Council; Panhellenic Council; Student Congress; Student Council; Student Senate
Student National Alumni Phonathon, 673
Student pilot training program, 367, 768–69
Student Relief Employment Program, 310, 317, 759
Student retention, 581, 698
Student revolt: characterized, 55–56
Students Army Training Corps, 233–34
Student Senate, 490
Students for a Democratic Society, 566–67
Student's Hand Book 173
Student union, 401, 787; in Old Chapel, 382–83. *See also* Brenton Student Center; Pfeiffer Hall
Study abroad, 658–59
Stuntz, Edna, 303, 323, 334, 759
Stuntz, Homer C., 255, 286, 756
Sturm, Philip, 387
Suffrage, 63, 207, 247
Sugino, Arthur Tetsu, 772
Sullivan, John L., 525, 545, 597, 598
Summer Music School, 136
Summer school, 406, 776
Summy, Dave, 598
Sundt, Alice M., 303
Swain, Christie, 50, 318–19
Swan, A. H., 122
Swanson, Jim, 597
Swanson, Rolf, 683
Swisher, John, 320
Swisher, Rhae M., Jr., 574
Systran, 618, 810

Taber, Abbie M., 302
Takehara, Kenneth, 378
Talbot, Loren C., 256, 275, 502, 754
Talley, Ambrose E., 173
Talley, Horton, 296
Talley, Melvin R., 207
Tangent, 727; in 1884, 119; in 1889, 140; demise, 172
Tannatt, Ken, 361, 411, 772
Tannatt, Kermit, 411
Taverner, Gilbert Y., 539, 574–75, 586, 595–96, 684, 797
Taylor, Frank B., 106, 108, 725
Taylor, William, 56
Teacher training: in 1920s, 269; in 1940s, 403; B.S. in Education introduced, 269; two-year program introduced, 269. *See also* normal training
Teague, Tom, 548

Technocracy, 311
Telegraphy courses, 724
Telephones, 84–85, 672
Temperance, 15, 291, 756; prohibition, 247; views of seminary founders, 9; views of Indianolans, 44, 323–24. *See also* alcohol
Temperance alliance, 177
Templeton, Jane, 543, 574
Tennant, Mark R., 257, 274, 753
Tennis: in 1890s, 167; in 1920s, 277, 754; in 1930s, 362; in 1963–68, 546; in 1968–75, 598; in 1975–79, 626; in 1979–87, 678, 679; new courts, 403, 672
Tenure, 409
Term hours, 189
Theater (facility): in Old Chapel, 401. *See also* Blank Center for the Performing Arts
Theater-going, 115, 121, 750
Theta Gamma Chi: founded, 117–18. *See also* Kappa Alpha Theta
Theta Kappa Nu, 315; academic performance, 359; chapter chartered, 280, 755; housing, 316, 760; merger, 360. *See also* Lambda Chi Alpha; Sigma Delta Chi
Theta Lambda Rho, 244
Theta Upsilon, 359, 389, 414, 433–34; chapter chartered, 280; housing, 317, 767; merger, 357, 492. *See also* Beta Xi; Delta Zeta
Thomas, James S., Jr., 539, 574, 584, 689, 802
Thomas, Lynn Marie, 629
Thomas, Marian, 815
Thomas, Norman, 296, 778
Thomas, Norman L., 568, 576, 578, 618–19, 655
Thomas, Roger, 625, 677
Thomas, Tim, 630, 812
Thompson, A. Paul, 449, 783, 783
Thompson, Dugald, 714
Thompson, Max E., 772
Thompson, Mike, 678
Thompson, Thomas, 8
Thompson, Vada, 800
Thompson, William B., 733, 739
Thompson, William T., 115
Thorius, James D., 649
Thornbrue, Ernest H., 128, 140, 728
Thornburgh, Daniel, 471, 785
Thorpe, Emma D., 715
Threlkeld, Harold, 403
Throckmorton, Tom, 213
TIAA-CREF, 656, 794
Tidgren, Bob, 490, 497, 624
Tiffin, James B. 225
Tilton, John L., 151, 161, 162, 165, 184, 211, 214, 743, 744; appointed to faculty, 133; death, 324; military training sponsor, 139–40, 168–70, 204–5, 219, 232; resignation, 258; supporter of athletics, 140, 202, 242

Tilton Court, 397
Tinker, Leonard E. "Ed," 567, 803
Tipayamongkol, Warapote, 674, 816
Title III, 646
Tittle, Ernest, 390
Tobacco. *See* smoking
Toda, Karen, 772
Todd, Bertha, 128, 151, 728
Todd, Edward H., 438
Todd, Florence Moore, 438
Todd, J. W., 28
Todd, Junia, 236, 255, 748, 751
Todhunter, Ella, 719
Todhunter, Lewis, 4, 16, 23, 131; personal background, 9
Tolstoy, Alexandra, 324
Tomahawk award, 359–60, 778
Torbet, Charles E., 762
Torrents, John E., 523
Town and Country Church, 425, 493. *See also* Warren County Group Ministry
town-gown relations, 366, 438–39, 503, 511–12, 583, 634, 685–86, 821; concert ticket controversy, 121–22
Toynbee, Arnold, 550
track and field: in 1890s, 168; in 1910s, 242; in 1920s, 277; in 1930s, 314, 362; in 1940s, 388; post WWII, 412; in early 1950s, 434; in 1953–63, 497–98; in 1963–68, 545–46; in 1968–75, 598; in 1975–79, 625, 626; in 1979–87, 678, 679. *See also* Neff Field; Simpson-Indianola Community Field
Trevethan, Robert "Deac," 413, 414, 778
Tridelta. *See* Delta Delta Delta
Trigg, Joe, 202
Trueblood, Elton, 458, 784
Trueblood, Estella, 152, 161, 184, 778
Trueblood, Ethel, 570
Truman, Harry S., 417, 421
Trustees. *See* board of trustees
Tryon, Lizzie, 738
Tuition: in late 1860s, 42; in 1890s, 155, 734; in 1900s, 198; in 1910s, 228; in 1920s, 289; in 1930s, 301, 310, 350; in 1940s, 380; post WWII, 406; in early 1950s, 427; in 1953–63, 477; in 1963–68, 542; in 1972–75, 587–88; in 1993, 696. *See also* cost of attendance
Tunnicliff, Barbara, 469
Turnbull, "Buck," 314, 754
Turner, Charlie, 493, 545
Turner, Jephtha, 716
Tuskegee Institute, 150
Tutt, Wendell, 281, 283, 290, 385, 396, 397, 401, 426, 431–32, 439, 449, 478, 682, 771, 773
Tutt, Wendy, 771
Tuttle, William J., 525, 579
Twentieth Century Fund, 197
Twyman, Robert W., 393

Uglum, Kenneth, 784, 785
Ukai, Takeshi, 419, 738
Underwood, Roger, 547
United Methodist Church: relation with College, 595, 683–84, 821
United Nations Semester, 528
University of Iowa, xvi–xvii
Updegraff, William K., 578, 587
Upper Iowa (University), xvi, 712
Upward Bound, 617
Urban prejudice, 205–6
U.S. Steel, 480

V-D Weekend, 600, 630
Vacha, Frederick B., 773
Vail, Edward P., 156, 734
Vail, Louise A., 185
Valen, Gary, 564, 600, 679–80; appointed to faculty, 468; coat-of-arms caper, 681; dean of students, 587, 609–10, 630; resignation, 649
Valley, Jim, 678
van der Heurk, Grace, 772
Vandervelde, Benjamin, 393, 464, 472
Vanderwerff, Gary, 491
VanDeventer, James E., 656, 809
Van Dreser, J. J., 782
Van Dyke, Dick, 568
Van Gilder, Carrie, 214
Van Liew, Silas, 165
Vanocur, Sander, 600
Van Pelt, Daniel, 56
VanPelt, Larry "Red," 544
Van Pelt, Rich, 625
Van Wyk, Marvin, 586, 617, 656
Vawn, James, 495, 511, 548
Veblen, Thorstein, 311
Ver Linden, Jay, 682
Vernon, Samuel Milton, 31, 35, 120, 208, 606; appointed college president, 37–38; appointed seminary principal, 26; early career, 26; later career, 717; resignation, 38; term as seminary principal, 26–29
Ver Steeg, Clarence L., 474
Vesper, J. Frederick, 816
Veterans Club, 601
Vietnam Moratorium, 568
Vietnam War protest, 565–73
Vincent, J. H., 124
Vincent, Steven D., 816
Viner, John, 596
Viner, Thomas R., 686
Vinson, Felix W., 91, 94, 111
Vint, Jim, 591
Visitation, dormitory, 559, 800–801
Vital Center, 452–53, 490, 527–28
Vlassic, James, 378
Voigt, Edwin E., 539, 690; appointed president, 371–72; death, 632; described, 376;
elected bishop, 439; inauguration, 375–76; presidency, 372–441; religious concerns, 436–37; resignation, 439; self-evaluation, 440–41; youth and pre-Simpson career, 372
Voigt, Eleanor, 383
Volleyball, 626, 679
Vondracek, Genevieve Hohstadt, 784
von Schuschnigg, Kurt, 417
Voysey, Georgia, 666
Vriezelaar, Stan, 812

Wachenheimer, Joseph, 44, 718
Wade, Virgilla, 424, 773
Waggener, Lucien, 161
Waldorf, Robert J., 361–62
Walke, Raymond H., 658, 816
Walker, J. Robert, 471
Walker, Jessie, 482
Walker, Linda, 674, 809
Wall, Joseph F., 300
Wallace, C. A., 82
Wallace, George, 806
Wallace, Henry A., 458, 482, 534, 553, 778
Wallace, Ilo, 458, 553
Wallace, James W., 450, 518, 539, 541, 547, 638, 789, 806
Wallace Hall of Science, 534
Walt, Joseph, 263, 467, 474, 480, 488, 499, 511, 526, 528, 533, 540, 547, 561, 567, 568, 571, 584, 615, 656, 657, 688, 690, 812; admissions office, 461; academic dean, 543, 585; assistant to president, 470; appointed to faculty, 465; Anna D. Hunt Professor, 673; coat-of-arms, 500–501; history of College, vii; politics of, 803
Walter, Estella E., 53, 66
Walters, L. M., 99, 102, 724
Waring, Fred, 363–64
Warne, Clinton L., 785
Warnet, Ronald J., 577
Warren County: financial support of College, 95; Grange lodges, 721; politics of, 83–84, 504; population, xi, 11; schools established, xii–xiii; settlement and organization, xi–xii; weather, 327, 418, 778
Warren County Group Center, 439
Warren County Group Ministry, 404–5, 425, 493. *See also* Town and Country Church
Washington, Booker T., 150, 778
Washington Semester, 473, 528
Watson, Harold, 303, 308, 395, 404, 416, 429, 454, 463, 759, 762, 765, 784; appointed to faculty, 261–62; arrival, 261; coat-of-arms, 500–501; retirement, 466; as teacher, 374–75; quoted, 252, 256, 269, 270, 279, 281, 283, 285, 297, 305, 306, 373, 379, 406, 428, 451, 467
Watson, Heba, 459, 501

Watson, Joseph C., 161
Watson, Joseph O., 161, 322–23, 753
Watson, Margaret Liebe, 349, 383, 653, 656, 784; appointed to faculty, 334; NSF grant, 478; return to teaching, 465
Watson, Steven J., 459, 501–2, 529
Watson, Vinton C., 334, 361, 769, 773, 782
Waugh, Maurice "Maury," 598, 624, 676
Wayte, Joseph, 224
Weather, 327, 418, 778
Webb, Lance, 637, 642
Weber, Blake, 624
Weber, Gordon, 545
Webster, William R., 543, 569, 574, 798
Weeks, Dale, 234
Weeks, E. W., 739
Weeks, Ed, 434
Weiler, George, 272, 759
Weinman, Jim, 387
Weir, Samuel, 213, 235, 248
Weitz, Fred, 622, 637, 638, 640, 650, 662, 670
Weld, Hiram, 311
Wellwood, Louise, 214
Wenk, Craig, 807
Wesley, John: Christ Church memorial stone, 459–60, 540; letter, 331
Wesleyan College, xvi
Wesleyan University, xv
West, Emory S., 205
Westbrook, Greg, 632
Westbrook, Jovanka, 631
Westbrook, Thomas, 631, 644, 649, 681
Western Iowa Conference (Methodist): 1860 minutes cover (illustration), 6; created, 4; name changed, 715; seminary sponsorship secured, 4–5. *See also* Des Moines Conference
Westfall, Helen, 279, 754
West Hall, 697
Wheeler, Alice L., 284
Wheelock, Louis, 579
Whipple, Ralph E., 384, 426
Whispering maples: planted, 48; fully grown, 145, 226; in decline, 255; 1953 storm damage, 483;
Whitaker, Edith B., 260, 263, 352, 759
White, Alma Robbins, 182, 184, 687
White, Elizabeth, 393, 396, 426, 463, 784
White, Paul, 687
White, Wesley M., 714
Whitfield, Allen, 422, 782
Who's Who, 438
Wickersham, L. B., 193
Wicks, Platt, 111
Wider Horizons Program, 658
Wiggins, Thomas E., 237
Wigwam, 383
Wilk, Melvin, 653

Wilkins, Perry, 490, 497
Wilkinson, Lydia A., 245, 738
Wilkinson, Marvin, 426
Willard, Carrie L., 164
Willard, Frances, 106, 110
William Buxton Chair of Moral Sciences, 183
William Buxton, Jr., Chair of Economics and Business Administration, 268, 772
William Robertson Coe Foundation, 474
Williams, A. C., 46, 61
Williams, Bob, 388
Williams, Casey, 361
Williams, Elizabeth M., 431
Williams, J. M., 431
Williams, Jack, 629
Williams, Jim, 677
Williams, Luther, 337
Williams, W. W., 34
Williams, William A., 550
Williamson, James, 23
Willis, Fred N., 256
Willis, Ivan L., 419, 449, 464, 478, 602, 783
Willis, Jerry, 505
Willis, Jim, 490
Willoughby, Jed, 631, 646
Wilmot, Woodrow B., 422
Wilms, Wayne, 806
Wilson, Agnes J., 164
Wilson, Anna Belle, 302
Wilson, Bruce, 598, 678
Wilson, Catherine, 771
Wilson, Earl, 628
Wilson, George A., 347, 376
Win, U, 459
Winans, Ephraim H., 10; appointed seminary principal, 19; personal background, 19–20; resignation as principal, 22; term as seminary principal, 19–22
Windle, Isaac, 15, 77
Winkley, Florence, 40
Winslow, Guy J., 737
Wiser, Waller B., 584, 805; academic dean, 543, 574; Alex Haley meeting, 551; appointed to faculty, 469; chaplain, 516, 549; dean of students, 517, 536
Withdrawal from courses, 615
Witke, Paula, 688
Witten, Livingston N., 392, 425, 463, 777
WOI radio, 336
Women's Athletic Association, 278, 362, 754
Women's Center, 629
Women's Recreational Association, 362, 388, 601
Women's Society for Christian Service, 382
Women's studies, 618
Womer, Matilda, 426
Wood, Albert H., 737
Wood, Enoch, 10, 22

Wood, Kitty, 738
Woodfill, D. M., 733
Woods, Doyle, 470, 574, 611, 621, 631, 796
Woods, Wilene Holden, 673
Woodward, Julia, 181
Woolson, George D., 783
Workman, C. Noel "Dopey," 275–76, 277, 279
Workman, Harry "Hoge," 276, 313, 759
World War I: anti-German sentiment, 233; armistice, 234; Simpson patriotism, 232; Simpson veterans, 235
World War II: end, 390; faculty service, 377; rationing, 389; student service, 377–78
Worley, Dana, 539
Worth, Gorham A., 130, 724, 733, 739; board treasurer, 96, 100, 111, 129, 153, 183; death, 236; gifts to College, 155; profanity, 215–16, 744; quoted, 94
Worth, Marcia, 580
Worth House, 618, 680
Wortman, W. P., 763
Wrestling: in 1920s, 277; in 1930s, 362; in 1963–68, 546; in 1968–75, 598; in 1975–79, 625; in 1979–87, 678
Wright, Carroll C., 68, 75
Wright, George G., 46, 56, 64, 68, 70, 98, 99, 112, 733; Law Department, 72–76, 101; financial support of College, 103
Wright, Jennie, 68
Wright, Jim, 411

Wright, Marla Del, 469, 785

X.Y.Z. Society: founded, 48, 50; demise, 53

Y.M.C.A./Y.W.C.A., 149, 493, 731; established at College, 139; prominence in 1890s, 176; in 1920s, 280; post WWII, 416; Bible study, 171–72; proposed building, 166
Yager, Yvonne, 761
Yaniger, George, 544
Yearbook. See *Tangent*; *Zenith*
Yell, College, 168, 736
Young, Emerson K., 112
Young Republicans, 629
Youtz, H. A., 140
Youtz, Lewis A., 162

Zahnd, James M., 575, 610
Zaring, Elbert R., 231
Zenith: first volume, 172; in late 1890s, 172; in 1910s, 248–49; in 1920s, 282–83; in 1930s, 318, 358, 762–63; post WWII, 416; in 1950s, 435, 494; in 1963–68, 548; in 1968–75, 601; in 1975–79, 629; in 1979–87, 683
Zetalethean, 46, 48, 56, 67, 173, 174, 240, 317; demise, 359; exhibition program (illustration), 59; founded, 43
Zimmerman, Cole, 696
Zupancic, Barbara A., 525
Zuppke, Bob, 273